A HISTORY
OF ENGLISH LAW

BY
SIR WILLIAM HOLDSWORTH

O.M., K.C., D.C.L., Hon.LL.D.

LATE VINERIAN PROFESSOR OF ENGLISH LAW IN THE UNIVERSITY OF OXFORD ; FELLOW
OF ALL SOULS COLLEGE, OXFORD ; HON. FELLOW OF ST. JOHN'S COLLEGE,
OXFORD ; FOREIGN ASSOCIATE OF THE ROYAL BELGIAN ACADEMY ;
FELLOW OF THE BRITISH ACADEMY ; BENCHER OF LINCOLN'S INN

VOLUME I

EDITED BY
A. L. GOODHART

K.B.E., Q.C., D.C.L., LL.D.

AND
H. G. HANBURY

D.C.L.

WITH AN INTRODUCTORY ESSAY AND ADDITIONS BY
S. B. CHRIMES

*To say truth, although it is not necessary for counsel to know what the
history of a point is, but to know how it now stands resolved, yet it is a
wonderful accomplishment, and, without it, a lawyer cannot be accounted
learned in the law.*   ROGER NORTH

LONDON
METHUEN & CO LTD
SWEET AND MAXWELL

Published by Methuen & Co Ltd
and Sweet & Maxwell Ltd
11 New Fetter Lane, London EC4

First Published 1903
Second Edition 1914
Third Edition, Rewritten 1922
Fourth Edition, Revised 1927
Fifth Edition 1931
Sixth Edition, Revised 1938
Seventh Edition, Revised 1956
Reprinted 1966

Printed in Germany by
Nationales Druckhaus Berlin

TO

THE RIGHT HONOURABLE FREDERICK EDWIN

EARL OF BIRKENHEAD

SOMETIME LORD HIGH CHANCELLOR OF GREAT BRITAIN

THIS WORK

IS

BY HIS LORDSHIP'S PERMISSION

RESPECTFULLY DEDICATED

PREFACE

THE form which my "History of English Law" has now taken requires a word of explanation. The first volume was begun in 1901, and the second and third volumes were finished in 1909. From 1909 to 1921 I have been writing the history of the law from 1485 onwards. I have, therefore, been engaged upon this History of English Law for twenty years; and necessarily both the material available for the study of the subject and my own knowledge have, in the course of that time, increased considerably. For both these reasons it has become clear to me that the first volume in its original form is quite inadequate, and that the second and third volumes need revision to bring them up to date. It has also become clear to me, as the work on the later volumes progressed that the earlier volumes need revision in order that the whole work may form a complete and co-ordinated whole. Therefore, simultaneously with my work on the later volumes, I have been engaged on the work of the revision and co-ordination of the earlier volumes. The first volume is a new book; and the second and third have been considerably added to and altered. The result is a continuous History of English Law as a whole down to 1700, and, in respect to some parts of the subject, down to modern times. The mode of treatment appears from the Plan of the History which will be printed at the beginning of each of the volumes.

Since Pollock and Maitland's classic volumes only carry the history of English Law down to the reign of Edward I., and, since Reeves' volumes go no further than the reign of Elizabeth, this is the first volume of the first continuous History of English Law which has ever been written ; and I hope that the succeeding volumes (which are all written) will be published without undue delay.   In an age which has devoted so much attention to historical research it is surprising that it should be possible to make such a statement about the history of so important a subject as English law.   But, nevertheless, it is the fact that, from the period when Pollock and Maitland's history ends, the wealth of variegated material for the history of English law has never been gathered into an ordered whole. On that account the later volumes of this history are somewhat in the nature of a pioneer treatise.   I can only hope that the result of the book will be to demonstrate, firstly, the essential incompleteness of English histories in which no account is taken of the legal point of view, and secondly, the impossibility of gaining a complete grasp of the principles of English law without a study of their history.   These two truths are still, to a large extent, unrecognized ; and the plea for the further recognition of the study of legal history which I wrote twelve years ago is almost as necessary now as then.   I can, however, say "almost as necessary," and not "quite as necessary," since the Law Society has recently recognized the importance of Legal History by including it in its Honours Examination.

It is well known that publishing conditions are at present difficult.   My publishers have not unnaturally limited the number of pages which each volume is to contain.   But it has not been possible in this volume, and it will not be possible in many of the succeeding volumes, to compress the history of the topic dealt with within these limits.   It is due to the liberality of the President and Fellows of St. John's College, Oxford, and of the Warden and Fellows of All Souls College, Oxford, that I have been able to include in this volume the necessary extra pages, and thus to present a complete treatment of the subject · with which it deals.   That subject—the History of the Judicial System—seems to me to afford a good general introduction to the far more complex subject of the history of the law itself.

The general statement which I made in the preface to the first edition of Volumes II. and III. of this History as to my obligations to the late Professor Maitland and to others who assisted me applies equally to this work. With respect to this volume I have to thank Dr. Hazel, Fellow of Jesus College, Oxford, and Reader in Constitutional Law and Legal History in the Inns of Court, for giving me the benefit of his valuable criticism and for help in correcting the proof sheets ; and Mr. Costin, Lecturer in History at St. John's College, and one of the ablest of the youngest generation of Oxford historians, for help in correcting the proof sheets and for making the list of statutes. Also, I must not forget to put upon record my appreciation of the accuracy and intelligence with which Miss Sunderland of the University Typewriting Office, Lloyds Bank Chambers, Oxford, has typed the difficult MS. of this and the succeeding volumes.

St. John's College, Oxford
November, 1921

NOTE TO FOURTH EDITION

In this edition I have made a few corrections and additions in the text and notes. Others, which I could not incorporate in the text and notes, I have inserted in a list of Addenda et Corrigenda. In the references to the later volumes I have inserted the number of the volume and the page.

All Souls College
February, 1927

NOTE TO SIXTH EDITION

In this edition a few further corrections have been made in the text, and the large amount of new information contained in the Selden Society's volumes and other books has made it necessary to compile a long list of addenda and corrigenda. The list contained in the former edition has been amalgamated with this list.

ALL SOULS COLLEGE
August 1938

NOTE TO SEVENTH REVISED EDITION

THE first volume of this work differs from its successors in that it has always been in common use as a students' text-book. The history of our judicial system is a subject which forms part of the syllabus of the first examination in several Universities, and though shorter works on it have been published, Holdsworth's detailed account has remained unsurpassed as a consultant of final resort. But the work requires correction and supplementation. (*a*) Changes in the law since Holdsworth's death have rendered some of his statements inaccurate. (*b*) Discoveries made during this intervening period must be incorporated in order to bring the volume up to date. The corrections have been supplied by the general editors, but the far more important labour of supplementation has been performed by S. B. Chrimes, Professor of History in University College, Cardiff, as special editor. It takes the form of an introductory essay, in which are set out all recent additions to our knowledge of this vital part of legal history.

A. L. G.
H. G. H.

May, 1955

PLAN OF THE HISTORY

CONTENTS

BOOK I

THE JUDICIAL SYSTEM

CHAPTER I

ORIGINS

CONTENTS

CHAPTER II

THE DECLINE OF THE OLD LOCAL COURTS AND THE RISE OF THE NEW COUNTY COURTS

CONTENTS

CONTENTS

CONTENTS xvii

CHAPTER III

THE SYSTEM OF COMMON LAW JURISDICTION

CONTENTS

CONTENTS

CHAPTER IV

THE HOUSE OF LORDS

CONTENTS xxiii

CHAPTER V

THE COURT OF CHANCERY

CHAPTER VI

The Council

CHAPTER VII

COURTS OF A SPECIAL JURISDICTION

CONTENTS xxxi

CHAPTER VIII

THE RECONSTRUCTION OF THE JUDICIAL SYSTEM

APPENDIX

VOL. I.—c

LIST OF ABBREVIATIONS

Abbrev. Plac.	Placitorum Abbreviatio, Record Commission.
Bl. Comm.	Blackstone's Commentaries, first edition.
Cal.	Calendars of the Proceedings in Chancery, Record Commission.
C.S.	Camden Society.
Co. Litt.	Coke upon Littleton.
D.N.B.	Dictionary of National Biography.
D.B.	Domesday Book.
Dasent	Acts of the Privy Council, edited by John Roche Dasent.
Digby, R.P.	Digby's History of the Law of Real Property, fourth edition.
Dugdale, Orig. Jurid.	Dugdale's Origines Juridiciales.
E.H.R.	English Historical Review.
F.N.B.	Fitzherbert, Natura Brevium, seventh edition.
Hale, P.C.	Hale's Pleas of the Crown, Emlyn's edition.
Hallam, C.H.	Hallam's Constitutional History, ninth edition.
Hil.	Hilary Term.
Hist. MSS. Com.	Historical Manuscripts Commission.
L.Q.R.	Law Quarterly Review.
Leg. Henr.	Leges Henrici Primi.
Mich.	Michaelmas Term.
Lives of the Norths	Edited by Jessopp.
Nicolas	Proceedings and Ordinances of the Privy Council, edited by Sir Harris Nicolas.
Pasch.	Easter Term.
P.Q.W.	Placita de Quo Warranto, Record Commission.
P. and M.	Pollock and Maitland's History of English Law, first edition.
R.C.	Record Commission.
Reeves, H.E.L.	Reeves' History of English Law, Finlason's edition.
R.H.S. Tr.	Royal Historical Society's Transactions.
Rot. Cur. Reg.	Rotuli Curiæ Regis, Record Commission.
R.H.	Rotuli Hundredorum, Record Commission.
R.P.	Rotuli Parliamentorum.
R.S.	Rolls Series.
R.S.C.	Rules of the Supreme Court.
S.S.	Selden Society.
S.T.	State Trials.
Stephen, H.C.L.	Stephen's History of Criminal Law.
Stubbs, Sel. Ch.	Stubbs' Select Charters, sixth edition.
Stubbs, C.H.	Stubbs' Constitutional History, library edition.
Surt. Soc.	Surtees Society.
Trin.	Trinity Term.
Y.B.	Year Book.

LIST OF CASES

LIST OF STATUTES

LIST OF STATUTES

ADDENDA ET CORRIGENDA
TO THE SEVENTH EDITION

P. 37, n. 7, add : see also Holland in Cambridge Law J. (1945) 17.

P. 83, n. 9, add : These franchise coronerships were abolished by the Coroners (Amendment) Act, 1926, s. 4. (16 and 17 Geo. 5, c. 59).

P. 86, n. 7, add : See the learned treatise by Sir George Hill, Treasure Trove in Law and Practice.

P. 123, n. 7, add : This act was repealed by the Welsh Courts Act, 1942 (5, 6, and 7 Geo. 6, c. 40), which authorizes the use of the Welsh language in any court sitting in Wales. See Hanbury, English Courts of Law, 159.

P. 148, lines 11-18 from bottom, delete sentence: 'and in 1863 . . . 25,000 inhabitants', and substitute : and by the Justices of the Peace Act, 1949 (12, 13, and 14 Geo. 6, c. 101, s. 29), a barrister or solicitor of seven years' standing can be appointed as a stipendiary magistrate for any borough having a separate commission of the peace.

P. 158, n. 9, for: 'at p. 36' read : (1842), 4 Y. and C. Ex 538; add: The equitable jurisdiction was not, in the actual case, available, because the action was simply for ejectment from a mine, which fell within the proper jurisdiction of a court of law.

P. 213, lines 6, 7, for: 'Such . . . importance' substitute: The criminal jurisdiction of the King's Bench is reduced almost to vanishing point by the Administration of Justice (Miscellaneous Provisions) Act, 1938 (1 and 2 Geo. 5, c. 63, s. 11).

P. 216, n. 11, insert : These cases were confined to misdemeanours tried in the Queen's Bench Division.

P. 218, line 10 : The Solicitor-General may act for the Attorney-General under the Law Officers Act, 1944.

P. 222, n. 8, add : As to the limits of the power of the King's Bench to correct its own errors, see Y. B. Pasch. 7 Hen. VI, pp. 28-30, and the epitomes in Bacon. Abr. Errors, 68; Rolle Abr. Error (I) ; Vin. Abr. Error (I).

P. 231, line 15, insert : Under the Administration of Justice Act, 1938, the writs of certiorari, prohibition, and mandamus are replaced by orders of certiorari, prohibition, and mandamus respectively, and information in the nature of a quo warranto by injunction.

P. 253, n. 7 : The title of Chief Justice of England was given to the Chief Justice of the King's Bench (Jacob Law Dict.).

P. 255, lines 6, 7, add : Their salaries were fixed at £5000 by the Supreme Court of Judicature Act, 1925 (15 and 16 Geo. 6, c. 49, s. 13). Judicial salaries were increased by an Act of 1954 (2 and 3 Elizabeth II. c. 27), by £2000 per annum in the case of the Lord Chancellor and Lord Chief Justice, and by £3000 in the case of the Master of the Rolls, President of the Probate, Divorce and Admiralty Division, Lords Justices, and Puisne Judges.

P. 292, n. 3, add : see an article by L. E. Stephens in Local Government and Administration, ed. Lord Macmillan, 147-154 ; Hanbury, English Courts of Law, 146.

P. 293, lines 16-20, delete and substitute : During the eighteenth century the custom developed of sending to the assizes all capital cases, which in those days were numerous.[3]

—— line 25, insert : The Chairman of Quarter Sessions in a county may be a layman. But, under the Administration of Justice (Miscellaneous Provisions) Act, 1938 (1 and 2 Geo. 6, c. 63) any court of Quarter Sessions for a county may apply to the Lord Chancellor for the appointment of a person who has not less than ten years' standing as a barrister or solicitor.

—— lines 24-25, delete ' it possesses . . . by statute ', and substitute : It can hear appeals against conviction by the petty sessions, except that, where a defendant has pleaded guilty or admitted the truth of the information, an appeal will lie only against the sentence (Criminal Justice Act, 1948, s. 36 ; Harris and Wilshere, Criminal Law (17th ed.), 655).

P. 322, line 3 from bottom to p. 323, line 7, delete and substitute : Between 1914 and 1948, grand juries had a chequered career. They were suspended during the war of 1914-1918. In 1933 all grand juries were abolished by the Administration of Justice (Miscellaneous Provisions) Act, 1933, with the exception, for the purpose of certain trials, of grand juries of the County of London and County of Middlesex. But even these were swept away by the Criminal Justice Act, 1948 (Above, 213 n.; see Kenny, Outlines of Criminal Law, 16th ed. 488).

P. 350, add : It must be remembered that modern developments have rendered inapplicable certain of the author's comments. Special juries no longer exist. It can scarcely be said that juries are now susceptible to intimidation in Ireland, certainly not in the Republic of Ireland ; in Northern Ireland the emphasis should rather be laid on the importance of the power of challenging jurymen, a power of which little is heard in England. The general remark should also be made that though juries are indispensable in criminal cases before Quarter Sessions and Assizes, in cases where the accused pleads not guilty, but in civil cases they are probably becoming less common, except in defamation and fraud, and in divorce suits in which a charge of adultery is defended.

P. 372, line 8, add : Since the partition of Ireland, the House of Lords is, of course, a final court of appeal in civil cases from the courts of Northern Ireland only.

P. 373, n. 4 : see above as to the present restriction of the appellate jurisdiction to appeals from Northern Ireland. Even before Southern Ireland ceased to be part of the United Kingdom (Ireland Act, 1949) its legislature had taken advantage of the powers conferred by the Statute of Westminster, 1931 (see below p. 525) to abolish appeal to the Judicial Committee of the Privy Council, and the abolition was held to be valid in Moore v. A.-G. for Irish Free State (1935) A.C. 484.

P. 385 (ii) Trial by Peers. This paragraph should now be transferred to p. 379 under the heading ' Obsolete Jurisdiction.' See p. 53* below.

P. 390, second line from the bottom, add : as at p. 218, line 10 above.

P. 393, lines 15-20, delete : ' It is a subject . . . clear rule ', and substitute : Erskine May underlines the difficulty of the subject, in his statement " on the one hand, the House of Commons, while admitting that it could not create new privilege, claimed to be the sole and exclusive judge of its own privilege. On the other hand, the courts maintained that privilege was part of the law of the land, and that they were bound to decide questions coming before them in any case within their jurisdiction, even if privilege were involved ". No formal reconciliation of these conflicting doctrines is possible, but in the course of applying them to a series of cases a considerable measure of agreement has been reached (see Parliamentary Practice, 15th ed., 151 ; cf. Hanbury, 68 L.Q.R., 173, 190).

P. 397, n. 2, add : As to Bentham's views on the necessary reforms of the court, see below, vol. xii, 99, 100, 574.

P. 398, n. 4, delete and substitute : For a discussion of the various theories of the development of actions on the case, see Fifoot, History and Sources of the Common Law, 66 seqq.

P. 405, n. 7, add : see Winder in 57 L.Q.R., 245.

P. 406, n. 2 : see Kildare (earl of) v. Eustace (1686) (1 Vern. 437, 439)

P. 444, line 19, insert : In 1832 certain sinecure offices were abolished, and an annuity of £5000 was provided for the Lord Chancellor on retirement from office (2 and 3 William IV c. 111).

P. 445, line 7, add : But Fifoot maintains that the rule circumscribing covenant by the necessity for a seal was not earlier than 1346 (History and Sources of the Common Law, 258).

P. 449, line 7 from bottom, add : There is a growing tendency to regard the Acts as having, in effect, fused law and equity. See Hanbury, Modern Equity, 6th ed., vii, 20-27, 44).

P. 455, line 19 from bottom : this was of course only a *façon de parler*, not the actual position in Jane Tyrrel's case, but it is perhaps too well-established to be disturbed. The true account of the case is given below, vol. iv, 470-471.

P. 624, line 10 and n. 1, add : The Act was modified by the Supreme Court of Judicature Act, 1925 (15 and 16 Geo. 6, c. 49) and the Matrimonial Causes Act, 1937 (1 Edw. 8, and 1 Geo. 6, c. 57), and is now entirely replaced by the Matrimonial Causes Act, 1950 (14 and 15 Geo. 6, c. 25).

P. 636, line 3 from bottom, after : ' Common Law Procedure Act of 1854 ' add : and the Chancery Amendment Act (Lord Cairns's Act, 21 and 22 Vict. c. 27). For ' that Act ' read ' those Acts '.

p. 640, n. 7, add : Under the Administration of Justices (Appeals) Act, 1934, appeals from the county courts go to the court of Appeal instead of, as formerly (see below p. 641), to a Divisional Court.

—— n. 8, add : But the equity jurisdiction of the Exchequer, which was transferred to the court of Chancery in 1842 (below 242), is now exercised by the Queen's Bench Division.

P. 644, line 14, insert : The crown was empowered by sect. 14 of the same Act to appoint a third and fourth Lord of Appeal ; the number was increased to six, seven, and nine by the Appellate Jusisdiction Acts of 1913, 1929, 1947 respectively.

—— last line, add : An appeal cannot, under the Administration of Justice (Appeals) Act, 1934 (24 and 25 Geo. 5, s. (1)) be brought to the House of Lords from the court of Appeal without the leave either of that court or of the House of Lords.

CONTENTS

INTRODUCTORY ESSAY

BY

S. B. CHRIMES

I. LOCAL JURISDICTIONS

(1) *The County Courts.*[1]

THE early history of the county courts has been treated by Sir Frank Stenton in relation to the general context of Anglo-Saxon history in what is now the classic exposition of that period of English History,[2] and in relation to constitutional development by Mr. J. E. A. Jolliffe.[3] Professor W. A. Morris has brought together and expanded considerably his earlier work on the subject, providing a detailed account of the county courts, especially in the thirteenth and fourteenth centuries.[4] The discovery and publication of certain records of pleas in a few county courts have not only added materially to knowledge of some aspects of county court work, but have also given rise to controversy over the nature of those records and of the county courts themselves.[5]

Both before and for long after the Norman Conquest, the county court was the most important court of general jurisdiction, " the great channel through which flowed the stream of folk-right descending from the past."[6] For the thirteenth and fourteenth centuries surviving material is sufficient to give a comprehensive picture of the practical working of county courts in the age preceding the period of decline.

At that time county courts met normally every four weeks for one day,[7] the same day of the week (differing in neighbouring

---

[1] Cf. below 6-11, 69-81, 187-193.

[2] F. M. Stenton, Anglo-Saxon England (1943, 2nd Ed. 1947).

[3] The Constitutional History of Medieval England (1937, 3rd Ed. 1954).

[4] The Early English County Court (1926). Cf. C. T. Flower, Introduction to the Curia Regis Rolls, 1199-1230 (S.S. lxii, 1944) 61-82. and J. J. Alexander, The Dates of County Days, in B.I.H.R. iii (1925-1926), 89-95.

[5] For references, see below 4*.

[6] Morris, op. cit. 143. The dates of origin of the shires of course varied ; in Wessex they existed before the end of the eighth century, but in English and Danish Mercia not before the eleventh century. Cf. Stenton, op. cit. 289 seqq.

[7] Morris, op. cit. 90 seqq.

counties), usually in the designated "county" town, the same place as in the time of Edward the Confessor unless royal authority varied it, not, by Bracton's time as in the old days, out of doors, but usually in the castle, or sometimes in the "shire hall." Special sessions might be held by royal order, especially to meet the itinerant justices, and on such occasions as well as at normal sessions, some business might be carried over until the next day (the *retrocomitatus*) ; any session might be regarded as *plenus comitatus*, but twice a year the requirement of a wider attendance constituted the *magnus comitatus*.

Normally, however, attendance in practice was a good deal narrower than it was in theory, or at least than it was in the theory of a later age. Many exemptions had been sought and obtained from the king by this time ; withdrawals without licence occurred ; attempts to enforce were sometimes contested as exactions of new suits, and the Provisions of Westminster of 1259 established the rule that heirs of land to which suit was appurtenant should not render more suit than was originally due. In every county, however, some persons by name were required to render suit, and some units, such as the vills, were required to be represented, at least on some occasions, and a mixed body of knights, freeholders, and villeins was provided to make up, together with the sheriff, the personnel of the court. In some counties at least, a small group of the more influential suitors, the *buzones*, or *buzones iudiciorum*, " upon whose nod is said to depend the decision of others," largely determined the judgments of the court as a whole.[1]

The jurisdiction of county courts in this period remained varied and extensive, though inevitably much modified in consequence of the development of the system of eyres and itinerant justices[2] since the time of Henry II. onwards. Minor offences against " the sheriff's peace," involving only pecuniary penalties, continued to be in the jurisdiction of the court, such as thefts, affrays, infliction of stripes and wounds, and similar matters arising through failure of the manorial courts to do justice, where breach of the king's peace or felony was not alleged.[3] But in the pleas of the crown, the proceedings of the county courts had become confined to preliminaries. The making of presentments, the receipt of confessions, the taking into custody of suspected persons, might occur before the sheriff in the county court, but the only cases of felony normally taken through all

---

[1] Morris, op. cit. 100 seqq, 107 seqq. Cf. G. T. Lapsley, Buzones, in E.H.R. xlii (1932) 177-193, 545-567 (reprinted in Crown, Community and Parliament in the Later Middle Ages (1951) 63-110.
[2] Below 42*-47*.   [3] Morris, op. cit. 112-113.

stages in the county court were those arising from private appeal.[1]
Very rarely a royal writ authorized a sheriff to hear a criminal
case with a jury in the county court, and a few instances occur of
a sheriff's holding a plea of the crown without authority and
despite the prohibition of such a practice in Magna Carta.[2] The
manifest thief might be adjudged to death summarily in the
county court as elsewhere, and the pronouncement or pardon of
outlawry continued to be possible only in the county court. But
jurisdiction in the pleas of the crown had, from the late twelfth
century at least, passed to the royal justices itinerant.[3]

The civil jurisdiction[4] of the county courts remained not
inconsiderable in at least the early fourteenth century. It had
become limited, apparently by interpretation of the king's
courts, in personal causes to cases in which the amount involved
was 40s. or less, but this was still a significant sum ; the Justices
of the Peace of the fourteenth century had no civil jurisdiction,
and the popularity of the county in small personal actions of
trespass, debt, replevin, de namio vetito, was maintained. The
jurisdiction of the county court in land litigation, though much
declined as a result of Henry II.'s reforms and innovations, was
not as yet by any means superseded. Many such cases were, it
is true, initiated in the county court only that they might be
transferred to the king's court, but some, in which neither party
sought procedure by Grand Assize, were disposed of by the court
with trial by duel, and the court might award seisin. In addition
to these survivals of the ancient jurisdiction of the county courts,
a fairly extensive variety of minor causes might be determined
before the sheriff, but only by royal writ, whether de cursu,
justicies, de fresca forcia, or the like. The sheriff himself might,
by writ, act ut justitiarius, without the assistance of the suitors of
the court, but this occasional jurisdiction appertained to the
sheriff as royal officer, not to the court as such.[5]

The procedure of the county courts remained basically as it
had been in the past, before the time when royal writs transferred
cases to the royal courts or instructed the sheriff. Proceedings
were normally instituted, whether civil or criminal, by oral plaint,
in a formula including certain words, and with the complainant's
being required to produce two suitors for the prosecution of the
case. The old procedures for setting a day, for essoins, the
foreoath, formulation of charge, for the secta, oath-helping, and
the like, continued without, of course, the proof by ordeal of fire

---

[1] Morris, op. cit. 114. Appeals of felony continued to be so treated until the
Stuart period.
[2] Ibid 116.
[3] Below 42*-47*.
[4] Morris, op. cit. 117 seqq.
[5] Ibid 121-122.

or water after 1215, but with some tendency to reduce formalism from the later thirteenth century, and with an increase in the use of attornies to represent the parties in the fourteenth century. The collection of amercements and fines enforced as penalties for offences and defaults of all kinds constituted a major part of the sheriff's duties and an important element in royal finance. Much business, however, was initiated in the county court only to be transferred to the royal courts, whether by placing upon the Grand Assize and the writ of peace, by petition of the plaintiff, by writ of *pone, de falso iudicio, certiorari, venire facias*, or otherwise, and so passed out of the jurisdiction of the county courts.[1]

The most important contributions to the history of the mediæval county courts made in the last quarter of a century take the form of the discovery and publication of a few rolls recording pleas held in several different counties at different dates.[2] The fresh information that these few known rolls provide, recording the actual working of the courts concerned, has given rise to considerable discussion and some controversy.[3]

These records comprise a unique roll of writs to a sheriff and his returns,[4] several rolls recording pleas held in county courts, and some miscellaneous writings from sheriff's offices. The roll of writs and returns for Bedfordshire and Buckinghamshire, 1333-1334, gives a valuable insight into the working of a sheriff's office at that date, showing as it does in the three columns the bailiwick concerned, the substance of each writ, and a note of the return made. The amount of work involved in the execution of these writs emanating from each of the central courts in great variety was very considerable, and points to what must have been a substantial clerical staff in the sheriff's office, and a developed organization in each hundred.[5]

---

[1] Below 42*-47*.

[2] Morris, op. cit. App. B, 181-196, printed some Extracts from the Rolls of the County Court of Cornwall, 1333; in addition see R. Stewart-Brown, Calendar of County Court. City Court, and Eyre Rolls of Chester, 1259-1297 (Chetham Soc. (n.s.) 84, 1925); G. H. Fowler, Rolls from the Office of the Sheriff of Bedfordshire and Buckinghamshire, 1332-1334 (Quarto Memoirs of the Bedfordshire Hist. Rec. Soc., iii (1929).

[3] H. Jenkinson, Plea Rolls of the Mediæval County Courts, in Camb. H. J. i (1923-1925) 103-107 (including fragments of plea rolls for Oxfordshire and Berkshire, 1 Richard II.); H. Jenkinson and M. Mills, Rolls from a Sheriff's Office of the Fourteenth Century, in E.H.R. xliii (1928) 21-32; T. F. T. Plucknett, New Light on the Old County Court, in Harv. Law Rev. xlii (1928-1929) 639-675; G. E. Woodbine, County Court Rolls and County Court Records, ibid xliii (1929-1930) 1083-1110; T. F. T. Plucknett, A Note on County Court Rolls, ibid 1111-1118; G. T. Lapsley, The Court, Record, and Roll of the County in the Thirteenth Century, in L.Q.R. 51 (1935) 299-325; S. E. Thorne, Courts of Record and Sir Edward Coke, in Toronto Law Journal, ii (1937-1938) 24-29.

[4] Fowler, op. cit. 8-31, 32-46, dated May, 1333 to November, 1334.

[5] Cf. Jenkinson and Mills, op. cit. The total number of entries on the roll is 636.

The plea rolls throw light on parts at least of the civil jurisdiction of the county courts at the dates in question. So far as practice in Bedfordshire and Buckinghamshire is concerned, it seems that felonies were presented in the hundred courts and passed directly to the justices.[1] Even so, the judicial business of the county court remained considerable, with an average number of 35 cases at the seven courts here recorded ; the delays in completing business, however, are strikingly revealed by the fact that the 330 entries on the roll relate to only 74 separate pleas.[2]

Professor Woodbine is no doubt justified in pointing out that these plea rolls are discoveries not of what was believed not to exist, but of what was known to exist.[3] Several well-known references in other sources, from the time of Bracton at least, disclose that a record of pleas in county courts was assumed to exist.[4] The extreme rarity of this type of record, however, has given a special interest to these specimens, and has aroused some discussion as to their character. For the county court clearly was never considered to be a " court of record " (except in the process of outlawry), and there is no evidence that these rolls of pleas, and the doubtless many others that existed or may still exist awaiting discovery, were regarded as authoritative in the king's courts, or indeed anywhere outside the county court concerned. The " record of the county " continued to be a matter of oral or written report conveyed by knights of the shire. The fact is that these plea rolls were maintained by the sheriffs themselves, and were often retained by them among their private papers, and appear never to have been lodged officially with any of the central departments or courts, which is the reason why so few have come to light. Professor Woodbine accordingly had difficulty in regarding such records as records of the county court at all,[5] for as he rightly observed they were not kept by the suitors of the court, and he was unwilling to accept them as *rotuli comitatus*. But the fact that the county court was not a court of record, and that the suitors were not responsible for these rolls, does not invalidate their claim to be considered court rolls. There is no evidence that the suitors ever gave judgment without the sheriff, nor, in " common pleas ", the sheriff without the suitors, and the rolls are a record kept by the sheriff, as

---

[1] Fowler, op. cit. 50.

[2] Ibid. Of these 74 cases, 7 were crown pleas ; of the remaining 67, 38 were debt, 13 trespass, 10 illegal restraint, 3 covenant, 2 detinue, 1 concerning an order for repairing of a bridge.   [3] Op. cit. 1093.

[4] Ibid 1085 seqq. Cf. Fleta ii c. 43. Cf. W. C. Bolland, Article 13 of the Articles of the Barons, in L.Q.R. 36 (1920) 58-60.

[5] Woodbine, loc. cit.

presiding officer, of things done in the county court. They may properly be described as county rolls because they are evidence of what took place in the county court or by its authority and could not have taken place anywhere else or by any other authority except that of the king.[1] The *plenus comitatus* was a public body and the memoranda of its proceedings were kept by its presiding officer.[2]

A number of miscellaneous points of importance emerge from these records. The large number of persons, suitors, parties, jurors, officials and others concerned in a meeting of a county court is a striking feature, and it seems clear that an extensive use of attornies for the transaction of business must have been made, including for the purpose of procuring writs from the central courts on behalf of clients; possibly the sheriff's office acted in some way as an intermediary in that connexion.[3] It is apparent that the old jurisdiction of the county courts still remained capable of expansion, especially in the field of trespass; in certain respects it remained active through the seventeenth, eighteenth, and nineteenth centuries until 1835.[4] Not all suitors acted as doomsmen, and a sufficient attendance of these was probably ensured by a rota system;[5] it is possible that the rôle of the doomsmen has received too little recognition. " Probably the doomsmen of the thirteenth century played as great, or even a greater, part than the bench of judges in building up the customary law of the land as opposed to law laid down by 'provisions' or 'statutes'."[6] Certainly examples exist of "county legislation" by county courts, in some instances anticipating by several years the rules imposed by statute, or receiving the approbation of justices in eyre.[7] The rules applied in the litigation brought into the county court by the bulk of the lesser men of the shires, however, were not necessarily identical with those applied in the Curia Regis, and the full history of the law applied

---

[1] Lapsley, op. cit. 324.

[2] Cf. Thorne, op. cit. 32, " The county plea roll was neither a wholly public or wholly private document in much the same way as the contemporary plea roll of a king's justice was neither, though the fact that they were never called into the treasury, the final test of an official document, led them rapidly into a completely private status."

[3] Fowler, op. cit. 11 seqq, 77 seqq.

[4] Plucknett, op. cit. xlii 646 seqq.

[5] Stewart-Brown, op. cit. xxxiii seqq. It must be remembered that special circumstances arose in Chester because of the palatinate rights of the earl, and Chester documents cannot necessarily be treated as evidence for the normal English county court. The abbot of Chester was responsible for providing the gospels upon which jurors in the county court were sworn. See Stewart-Brown, The Jury Book of the County Court of Chester, in E.H.R. xlviii (1933) 268-269.

[6] Stewart-Brown, Calendar, xxxvii.

[7] Plucknett, op. cit. 653 seqq.

in the county courts, and its relation to the law of the king's
courts remains to be written, if indeed it can ever be written.[1]

(2) *The Hundred Courts.*[2]

By the beginning of the eleventh century, all England south
of the Tees was divided into shires, and except where Danish
influences prevailed, each shire was divided into smaller units
known as hundreds, for the purposes of adjustment of taxation,
the maintenance of peace and order and the settlement of local
pleas,[3] purposes which were carried out in the assembly or court
of each hundred.   The hundred was both a territorial division
and a court, and in a sense a police organization.

The problem of the origins of this local unit and court has
received further discussion,[4] but it remains, and is likely to
remain, very difficult to solve.   There is no reasonable doubt
that the origins were in fact a good deal earlier than the earliest
direct evidence available on the subject, and very little doubt
that the origins in fact were not simple but complex, the result,
not of a single line of development, but of several lines which at
one time were distinct and unconnected with each other.

It seems clear that the origins of the hundred are to be found
in Wessex, and that whatever pre-existing arrangements were
adapted and moulded into the shape of the eventual territorial
unit and court, the institution was the result of West Saxon
government policy, and that the ultimate extension of the system into the later shires of other regions was a consequence of
the expansion of West Saxon influence and the absorption of the
other Anglo-Saxon kingdoms into the one general administrative
system centred on Wessex.

But the earliest known reference to the hundred in Wessex,
in the laws of Edmund (939-946), is only of comparatively late

---

[1] The movement behind the reform of the local courts in the early nineteenth
century has received some detailed consideration by A. L. Cross, Old English
Local Courts and the Movement for their Reform, in Michigan Law Rev. xxx
(1931-32) 369-385.
[2] Cf. below 11-13, 72-87.
[3] Stenton, op. cit. 289.   The term " wapentake," derived from Scandinavian
origins, used in the counties of Lincoln, Nottingham, Derby, Leicester, and the
North and West Ridings of Yorkshire, came to be practically synonymous with
" hundred " used elsewhere.
[4] Ibid 289-298 ; Jolliffe, op. cit. 116 seqq. and The Origin of the Hundred in
Kent, in Historical Essays in Honour of James Tait (1933) 155-168 ; H. M. Cam,
Suitors and Scabini, in Speculum (1935) ; Manerium cum Hundredo, in E.H.R.
(1932) ; Early Groups of Hundreds, in Essays to Tait ; The Hundred outside the
North Gate of Oxford, in Oxoniensia, i (1936), all reprinted in Liberties and
Communities in Medieval England (1944), 49-63, 64-90, 91-105, 107-123 respectively.
Some incidental discussion appears in J. Goebel, Felony and Misdemeanour (1937).
Cf. Flower, op. cit. 83-91.

date, and merely assumes its existence as an established institution.[1] With no specific reference to the hundred earlier than
the reign of Edmund, discussion of its origins is likely to remain
mostly a matter of conjecture, and of arguing back from the
fuller information contained in Edgar's Ordinance of the Hundred
(959-975)[2] and later sources.

It seems probable that the three principal functions of the
hundred in the late Anglo-Saxon period, the adjustment of
taxation, judicature, and " police organization " were derived
from diverse earlier arrangements to meet similar needs, and that
the process of amalgamation, no doubt under royal stimulation,
was a process which will remain very obscure for want of any
contemporary written evidence. The weight of argument, however, points to the fiscal usefulness of the hundred—a territorial
division of the shire—as being the basic and primary factor in
the origin of the institution. The very wide disparity in the size
and number of hundreds within the shire of Wessex, and in the
number of hides, which each shire was reputed to contain, does
not, as Sir Frank Stenton observes, " disprove the theory that
in origin the hundred was a district assessed to public burdens
at a round hundred hides," [3] and the later hundreds of the
midlands were probably the result of deliberate remodelling of
administrative areas in the tenth century. That the term
" hundred " originated to denote a notional or actual group of
one hundred hides for the assessment of contributions to public
burdens seems to be the soundest interpretation that can be put
upon it, and there are certain pieces of later evidence which tend
to confirm this view.[4]

This primary administrative purpose might no doubt have
been achieved, and perhaps for a time was achieved, without the
concomitant of a court of general jurisdiction in each shire.
Gemots for the application of customary law to the affairs of
localities of workable size there had to be, and were in existence

---

[1] III. Edmund, 2 ; see A. J. Robertson, The Laws of the Kings of England from
Edmund to Henry I. (1925) 13. The reference in II. Edward 8 (899-935), see
F. L. Attenborough, The Laws of the Earliest English Kings (1922) 120, to meetings
to be held every four weeks by the reeves for judicial purposes cannot be assumed to
be a reference to a hundred court ; there is nothing to show that this was any more
than a pre-hundred *gemot*.

[2] I. Edgar, see Robertson, op. cit. 16-19.

[3] Op. cit. 295.

[4] For example, in the eleventh century a large number of hundreds were attached
financially to ancient royal manors at which the king's *feorm* must once have been
paid ; in all areas many hundreds continued to bear the names of royal manors.
See Cam, Liberties and Communities, 64-90. In numerous instances a single royal
manor received the profits from a whole group of hundreds, ibid 91-105, E. B.
Demarest, The Hundred-Pennies, in E.H.R. xxxiii (1918) 62-72, and cf. Stenton,
op. cit. 297.

before there was a hundredal system, but there is no direct evidence to connect the hundred courts of the tenth century with the folkmoots mentioned in King Alfred's laws.

Nevertheless, as Sir Frank Stenton remarks, " the need for such an institution (as the hundred court) must have been felt in every part of England. . . . For a long time, perhaps for a century, after the first occupation of a tract of country, the men of each *regio* may have been able to deal with their own affairs in assemblies at which all were present. But as the law of their country became more elaborate, and as the original arrangements by which they maintained their king were complicated by the taking of new land into cultivation, there must have arisen an urgent necessity for some form of assembly intermediate between the meeting of the whole folk and the meeting of a village community."[1]

Somehow or other, the transition from local *gemot* to a court for each hundredal territorial division was made, and the hundred courts of the early eleventh century came into existence. When visible in the light of documentary evidence, these courts showed many of the features of ancient popular assemblies, meeting in the open air at regular intervals of four weeks, their judgments those of peasant suitors guided perhaps but not controlled by their presiding officer, the king's reeve, capable of receiving a collective fine from persons who broke its " dooms," particularly from those who failed to obey its orders in the matter of the pursuit of thieves.[2]

The police functions of the hundred court, the activities of " the tithing men " and hundred, developing later into the system of frankpledge associated with the hundred, may have had their origins in the earlier voluntary associations or frithguilds formed, in parts at least of Wessex, for mutual protection against theft.[3] At any rate, the thief-catching organization had by the time of Edgar's Ordinance become associated with a district and a moot, the hundred. By then, the hundred unit of territory and the hundred court had clearly come into existence, and were to continue to play a great part in local administration, judicature, and police organization, for several hundred years.

A great deal of fresh light has been thrown on the actual working of the hundred court in the first two centuries after the Norman Conquest by Professor Helen Cam,[4] whereby the relations

---

[1] Cf. Stenton, op. cit. 296.
[2] Ibid.
[3] The theory propounded by Mr. Jolliffe, Constitutional History, 116 seqq., that the origin of the hundred itself is to be found in these voluntary peace-guilds, cannot be accepted. See H. M. Cam, in E.H.R. liv (1934) 483-489.
[4] The Hundred and the Hundred Rolls (1930).

of the hundred with the shire and sheriff, and its activities in local government generally can be seen in considerable detail, at least from the time of Henry II. onwards. The most important disclosure from the jurisdictional point of view is the extent to which hundred courts came to be in private hands by the end of the thirteenth century. Professor Cam is able to estimate that at the accession of Edward I. there were about 628 hundreds in England, and of these 270 were royal, and 358 in private hands.[1] It is probable that some hundreds were never at any time in royal hands, and at least a hundred of them were in private hands at the time of the Norman Conquest. Not only had the total number of hundreds been substantially increased since then, but also a great many had been specifically granted by royal charter to private recipients.[2]

The exact implications of the grant of a hundred court into private hands, however, varied a great deal, and it must not be supposed that any such grant removed the court altogether outside the scope of the king's government.[3] The implications of grants depended on the terms of the charter. If the king granted " whatever the sheriff has in the king's hundreds," or if he granted " return of writs," the sheriff, it is true, would not normally enter that hundred. But a great many grantees of hundreds received more restricted rights. In a few instances, the officials of a private hundred dealt direct with the Exchequer, but for administration and legal purposes the sheriff remained the indispensable channel of communication between the central Government and the private hundred in all save the most privileged ; he was constantly required to report what had been done with regard to residents in private hundreds, to account for money due from them, and to ensure that the king's commands were duly carried out within the private hundreds. The conditions upon which a lord held a hundred varied greatly ; they might be free alms, by knight service along with a manor, by lease for a term of years or for life or during pleasure, or, most commonly, by fee-farm and a fixed annual rent. Failure to observe the conditions might involve forfeiture ; hundreds might, of course, change hands, be inherited, or be partitioned and the profits divided.

But whatever arrangements of that sort might be made, " the framework of administration, the routine of government, was the same within liberties and without." The writs served were the king's writs and the bailiffs, even though often appointed on

---

[1] The Hundred and the Hundred Rolls (1930), 137.
[2] Ibid 138.   Henry II. made at least 52 such grants, King John 55, and Henry III. 108.   [3] Ibid 140 seqq.

terms by the lord, were yet the king's bailiffs and answerable to the sheriff for the due discharge of all that appertained to the king's business. The hundred, therefore, whether royal or private, was an integral part of the royal system of administration controlled by the sheriff.

In practice, the bailiff was responsible for arranging the work of the hundred court.[1] Formal summons of suitors was probably not needed for the ordinary sessions of the court, but parties had to be summoned, and summonses for all were issued to the two annual " great or general hundreds." In the tenth century ordinary sessions had been once every four weeks, but by the time of Edward I., a meeting once every three weeks had become normal in many parts of the country, in accordance with a decree of 1234 which lengthened what at that time had often become a fortnightly interval. Custom had prescribed the place of meeting, departure from which was apt to arouse vehement protest ; meetings were still often in the open air, even if cover was sometimes provided for the officials and the clerks who kept records. The obligation to attend and render suit at the court had mostly become appurtenant to specific holdings of land ; attendance for ordinary sessions seems to have been kept down to a minimum, possibly of twelve, to make up a sufficiency of doomsmen, and the duty was performed by a rota system. Suitors with litigants and officials might amount on the average to forty or fifty persons at any ordinary session ; a far larger attendance was required when the sheriff appeared to hold his tourn and view of frankpledge at the six-monthly " law hundred," or great or general hundred, with a full turn-out of suitors by tenurial obligation and by the representation of each vill in the persons of the reeve and four men, who usually would be villeins.

The judical importance of the hundred was doubtless on the wane by the end of the thirteenth century, but it still had a considerable amount of business. It might administer summary justice upon the red-handed thief ; or assist in recording an appeal of murder which the sheriff and coroners would transfer to another court ; incidental processes in lawsuits concerning land, such as the holding of inquests and the viewing of boundaries, might be dealt with, but when it came to litigation over freehold nothing by now could be done in the hundred court without a royal writ of right ; claims for tenurial services might be heard there, and enfeoffments made ; pleas of battery and brawls not amounting to felony, of the wounding and maiming of beasts, and of debts that could be collected without a royal writ ;

[1] The Hundred and the Hundred Rolls (1930), 167 seqq.

trespass here as elsewhere was a widening field for litigation ; detenue and covenant in small cases, and defamation, enquiries and presentments arising from the assizes of bread and ale and measures, might figure among the business, as well as a variety of miscellaneous transactions.[1]

" Proceedings " at an ordinary session " begin with the calling of suitors' names and the presentation of essoins or excuses for absentees. Then comes the regular business : appeals, pleadings, wagers of law, recognitions of debts, reports that a case has been settled out of court, requests for leave to make such a settlement. The clerk is steadily noting down judgments and commands ; this man is to be distrained to appear at the next court, this one is amerced ; an inquest is to be summoned ; so much is to be paid for having the aid of the court. Two or three members of the court are selected to assess or ' affeer ' the amount to be paid by all who have been amerced, so that the rule in Magna Carta about reasonable amercements may be observed."[2]

The hundred court may have been on the wane by the end of the thirteenth century, but its decline was to be very gradual and prolonged.

(3) *The Sheriffs*[3] *and the Coroners.*[4]

Recent work on the history of the office of sheriff has mostly taken the form of detailed amplification of information previously known in little more than outline. Professor W. A. Morris's extended research[5] has provided a broad survey of the many-sided activity of the mediæval sheriffs, and other scholars have added materially to knowledge of the subject.[6]

There is no evidence of the holding of a shire court by a shire reeve earlier than 964-988, and the rise of the office of sheriff appears to coincide with the rise of the police and judicial functions of the hundred, but few materials survive for the history of the office before the time of Edward the Confessor, by which time the office had clearly assumed the shape and part of the scope which it was to possess for several centuries.[7]

---

[1] For a list of hundred courts from before 1307. see The Hundred and the Hundred Rolls (1930), App. V.

[2] Ibid 185.   [3] Below 6-7, 65 seqq.   [4] Below 82-87.

[5] The Mediæval English Sheriff to 1300 (1927), and The Sheriff, in the English Government at Work, 1327-1336, ed. Morris and Strayer, ii (1947) 41-108.

[6] Most of the works cited in the footnotes to section I (1) and (2) above contribute something to the history of the sheriffs ; in particular Cam, The Hundred and the Hundred Rolls has a good deal to say on the sheriffs' duties in the late thirteenth century.

[7] Morris, The Mediæval English Sheriff, 17 seqq.

We are not here concerned with the importance of the sheriff in local administrative, fiscal, police[1] and military work ; his functions in the absence of the earl as presiding officer of the shire court, his responsibilities in connexion with the hundred courts, his duties at the tourn and view of frankpledge, and his importance in judicial administration in the shire, have been touched upon above,[2] and are dealt with below.[3] A matter of importance, however, which remains very obscure in existing literature, needs to be mentioned, although it cannot be pursued here ; namely, the question of how far the sheriff himself acted as *iustitiarus*, and exercised an independent judicial power.

There is very little evidence that the sheriff himself acted as a judge in the Anglo-Saxon period ; judgments of the shire court and hundred court were judgments of the suitors, and although the duties of the sheriff as presiding officer, as executive officer and collector of the profits, and as the king's agent were manifold, these did not constitute him a judge in himself, and it is doubtful whether he became solely responsible for sessions of the shire and hundred courts until after the Norman Conquest.[4]

It may be doubted whether at any time the sheriffs exercised a personal jurisdiction, apart from the disposal of petty offences dealt with in their tourns to the hundreds, except by virtue of royal commission or writ, and there appears to be no evidence of the issue of such authorization until after the Norman Conquest. Thereafter, for a time, it seems that it was a question whether the sheriffs would not develop into at least principal royal justices in the localities, and become primarily judicial officers, as the sheriffs in Scotland were destined to become.   But it soon became a more usual practice to appoint local justiciars with standing commissions to try all pleas of the crown and all actions which might have come before the Curia Regis, who in turn were destined to be displaced by itinerant justices.[5] Sheriffs might, indeed, be appointed justices, itinerant or otherwise, but the ordinance of Richard I. of 1194 forbade sheriffs to be appointed justices in their own counties or in any county in which they had been sheriffs since the king's accession,[6] and Magna Carta of 1215 (cl. 24) and subsequent issues specifically forbade the holding of pleas of the crown by sheriffs or other local officers.[7]

The activities of the sheriff as judge by commission or writ by no means ended with his exclusion from holding pleas of the

---

[1] For the important duties of the serjeants of the peace in the areas where the tithing system was not operative, Cheshire, Wales, and the northern counties, see R. Stewart-Brown, The Serjeants of the Peace (1936).

[2] I (1) and (2).   [3] 6-7, 65 seqq.   [4] Morris, op. cit. 54.

[5] This subject is treated more fully below 42*-43*.

[6] Below 50.   [7] Below 72.

crown. Bracton held that when the sheriff exercised jurisdiction on the authority of a royal writ, he acted as justice. Fleta regarded the jurisdiction of the county as two-sided; that of the court itself wherein the judges were the suitors, and that of the sheriff as justice by delegation from the king by writ.[1]

A comprehensive account of the sheriff's functions in the late thirteenth century is now available,[2] and also a detailed analysis of those functions in the early fourteenth century.[3] The latter is particularly useful as an examination of the shrievalty at a time when the office had entered on its long and slow period of decline.[4]

Some recent work on the history of the coroners has brought this office into a clearer light at certain periods.[5] There is no evidence that the coroners ever held pleas,[6] but their essential function of keeping a record of crown pleas[7] was being performed, before the coroner proper appeared, by other royal officials, some of whom performed judicial functions also, such as local justiciars, sheriffs, and others. The earliest extant eyre rolls (1194) assume the existence of the office of coroner, which probably developed as a distinctive office after an interval subsequent to the Assize of Clarendon, as a deliberate check upon the sheriffs, a check inspired in part at least by the result of the Inquest of Sheriffs.[8]

The coroners were unique in being elected in the county court, in theory for life, and there is little evidence that the sheriffs could interfere in any drastic way with such elections, for the county court had the last word as to the fitness of coroners.[9] There appear in the time of Edward III. to have been more than one coroner for each county, and a recognized district for each coroner, at least for the holding of inquests.[10] One or more coroners sat with the sheriff in every county court and tourn, and above all they had to keep the counter roll of

[1] Cf. Morris, op. cit. 198 seqq., and The Early English County Court 121-122. The whole point is greatly in need of more precise treatment.
[2] Cam, The Hundred and Hundred Rolls, 59-132.
[3] Morris, in The English Government at Work, ii 41-108.
[4] Fresh information on the appointment of sheriffs is contained in J. S. Wilson, Sheriffs' Rolls of the sixteenth and seventeenth centuries, in E.H.R. xlvii (1932) 31-45.
[5] I. G. Langbein, The Jury of Presentment and the Coroner, in Columbia Law Rev. xxxiii (1933) 1329-1365; H. M. Cam, Shire Officials: Coroners, Constables, and Bailiffs, in the English Government at Work, 1327-1336, ed. Willard, Morris, and Dunham, iii (1950) 143-183.
[6] Langbein, op. cit. 1342.
[7] For a short survey of the present state of the history of crown pleas see T. F. T. Plucknett, A Concise History of the Common Law, 4th Ed. (1948) 400 seqq.
[8] Langbein, op. cit. 1363.
[9] Cam, op. cit. 151.   [10] Ibid 157 seqq.

crown pleas in county and hundred.   They had to make record
before the justices in eyre of all such pleas that had arisen since
the last eyre (which might be several decades previously ; the
justices of gaol delivery tried those indicted by a jury before a
coroner, or appealed by approvers before him, or anyone who
adjured the realm before him and returned unpardoned.   The
relations of coroners and sheriffs were close, but the coroner was
first and foremost a recorder, and the sheriff an administrator.
Each coroner was *custos placitorum corone*, and each coroner was
expected to have his own set of rolls : a roll of inquisitions into
sudden deaths, and of treasure trove ; a roll of presentations,
which was a legal record of indictments ; a record of appeals,
outlawries and adjurations brought in the county court was also
kept.   Among miscellaneous duties of the coroners were included
those of acting as a substitute for the sheriff or of restraining the
sheriff or his subordinates in certain circumstances.   Whenever,
in fact, it was necessary to put in action local machinery on
behalf of the crown, independently of the sheriff, the coroners
were the proper agents to employ.[1]

(4) *Private or Franchisal Jurisdiction before and after the
Norman Conquest:*[2] *Feudal and Manorial Courts:*[3] *Royal
Forests:*[4] *Palatinates:*[5] *Borough Courts:*[6] *Courts of the
Universities.*[7]

(i) Few scholars to-day would accept the implication below [8]
that the land-holding and private jurisdictional arrangements of
the late Anglo-Saxon period can properly be called feudal, or at
any rate feudal in the sense in which the word is commonly
applied to conditions prevailing during the century after the
Norman Conquest.   The better opinion is that the essential
features of feudalism, the concept of the *feudum* and the tenurial
obligation of military service, and their concomitants, were not
present before the Norman Conquest, and that therefore the use
of the term ' feudalism ' to describe Anglo-Saxon conditions is
best avoided.   Such rights of private jurisdiction as existed
before the Norman Conquest were not tenurial in character, but
the consequence of express royal grant or of prescriptive right,
and were thus franchisal not feudal in nature.   There is no
evidence that Anglo-Saxon methods of land-holding, not even
laenland with riding-service, would have developed into a tenurial
system at all comparable with the post-Conquest arrangements,

---

[1] Cam. op. cit. 164.
[2] Below 17-32.
[3] Below 176-187.
[4] Below 94-108.
[5] Below 109-132.
[6] Below 30-32, 138-151.
[7] Below 165-176.
[8] Below 17-24.

and bocland might well be described as inimical to tenurial ties of any kind.[1]

The question of the nature of Anglo-Saxon private franchisal jurisdiction has been much debated,[2] a great deal of fresh information and illustration has been provided ; and two opposed schools of thought have emerged.

Private jurisdiction in the form of rights in a hundred court is a matter which is less obscure,[3] and certainly much later in origin than private jurisdiction in the form of rights conveyed by the terms, often far from clear terms, of a charter or writ. The earliest known example of the use of the term " with sacu and socn " in a royal grant comes from 956,[4] but it is possible that a grant of some form of jurisdiction is implied by charters of the pre-Alfredian era which convey an exemption of the land granted from all public burdens except the *trimoda necessitas*. It is clear that in certain instances the lord of a privileged estate received the profits of justice from some cases in which an inhabitant of the estate was involved, but less clear whether the justice was administered in a folkmoot or in the lord's court. But that private courts in respect at least of hand-having thieves existed even in this earlier period seems almost certain. There are other grounds for the belief that " the idea of private jurisdiction was at least in the background of men's minds before the age of Alfred."[5]

The use in grants from the mid-tenth century of terms of jurisdictional import certainly constitutes conclusive evidence of the existence of private rights of some kind in judicature. The difficulty still remains, however, of giving a precise interpretation of the meaning of these terms, whether collectively or individually. Opinions differ on the fundamental question of whether grants in these terms conveyed a right of actual court-keeping, or merely right to receive or share in the profits of species of jurisdiction exercised elsewhere than in a private court. Dogmatism on this point is unwise, but the better opinion appears to be that not only the profits of jurisdiction but also the right of court-keeping where appropriate were in fact conveyed by grants in such terms.[6]

---

[1] A useful summary of discussion of this general point is to be found in Jolliffe, Alod and Fee, in Camb. H. J., v (1935-1937) 225-234. For more detailed study, see Stenton, op. cit. 671 seqq. and The First Century of English Feudalism (1932).

[2] Stenton, Anglo-Saxon England 485-495 ; F. C. Harmer, Anglo-Saxon Writs (1952) 73-82 ; J. Goebel, Felony and Misdemeanour, i 339 seqq ; N. Hurnard, The Anglo-Norman Franchises, in E.H.R. lxiv (1949), 289-327, 433-460.

[3] Above I. (2).   [4] Stenton, op. cit. 487.   [5] Ibid 487.

[6] The principal exponent of the rights-of-profits only theory is J. Goebel, op. cit. 339 seqq, which must be read in conjunction with critical reviews by H. Cam in E.H.R. xliii (1937-1938) 583-587, and T. F. T. Plucknett in L.Q.R. liv (1938)

The terms themselves are numerous, and not always easy to define.[1] (1) *Sacu and socn*, is both the commonest and vaguest ; separately the words appear to mean " cause " and " suit ", and together " jurisdiction," and the formula probably stands[2] for the right to hold a court to deal with offences by people to whom the grant relates, certainly for the profits thereof. (2) *Toll and team* ; " toll " means the right to take toll on the sale of cattle and other goods within an estate, but there is no Anglo-Saxon evidence to show whether or not the right extended to goods in transit ; " team " means the right to take profits, and perhaps to hold the procedure for a separate vouching to warranty. (3) *Infangenetheof* implied the right to try a thief taken on the property and to at least a share in the profits (arising from the forfeitures of chattels after hanging).

The grant of one or more of these rights occurs frequently and the threefold formula began to appear in the time of Edward the Confessor.   More rarely grants to specifically favoured subjects were made of one or more of the king's dues (*gerihte* or *forisfactura*) normally reserved to him alone, and there is no satisfactory evidence for any grant of these earlier than 1020.[3]   There seems no reasonable doubt that the rights in these were financial not jurisdictional, and need not therefore be pursued here.[4]

The continuation of grants, after the Conquest, with the conveyance of them in the same or similar vernacular terms as before, has received a good deal of further study.[5]   It is possible that in time these formulæ came to mean little in practice, but for some time after the Conquest they were certainly not meaningless, for none of the rights went as a matter of course with the

---

295-298.   The theory is not held by Stenton, op. cit., and is specifically rejected by Miss Harmer, op. cit. 73 seqq, who conveniently lists the principal discussions of the subject (73-74 notes), and also by Miss Hurnard, op. cit. 292 seqq.

[1] Harmer, op. cit. 74 seqq.   For varying views and interpretations see footnotes ibid.

[2] As Sir Frank Stenton observes (op. cit. 487-488) some of the contexts in which this formula appears seem unequivocal evidence that court-keeping as well as profit was implied.   [3] Harmer, op. cit. 79 seqq.

[4] These were the monetary penalties for (1) *hamsocn* (forcible entry or assault on a person in a house) ; (2) *grithbryce* (breach of the king's special peace or protection given to a particular person) ; (3) *mundbryce* (*mund* may have had a wider scope than *grith*, but no clear difference is discernible between *mundbryce* and *grithbryce*, which never stand together in Anglo-Saxon writs) ; (4) *foresteal* (probably meant several offences of obstructive character) ; (5) *fihtwite* (the fine imposed for fighting) ; (6) *fyrdwite* (the fine for neglecting military service) ; (7) *fymenafyrmth* (the harbouring of fugitives).   Certain other *gerihta* appear in more dubious contexts, and their occurrence may be anachronistic, such as (8) *miskenning* (fines for mistakes in pleading) ; (9) *sceawing* (toll for display of goods for sale) ; (10) *blodwite* (the fine for shedding blood) ; (11) *weardwite* (fine for neglecting guard duty) ; (12) the *murdrum* fine, definitely post Norman Conquest in date.

[5] Goebel, op. cit. 379-398, and Hurnard, op. cit.

land.[1] Interest has centred mainly on the question of what scope is to be attributed to the powers of criminal justice conveyed, or exercised in Anglo-Norman franchisal jurisdiction. There is no reasonable doubt that the grant of sac and soc conveyed only a very limited jurisdiction over minor offences not including the " bootless " crimes ; it is not contested that *infangenetheof* conveyed jurisdiction over the hand-having thief, and that *toll* and *team* was not of criminal significance.   It has been shown that *frithbryce, forestal, hamsocn,* did not comprise anything like the *haute justice* that was once supposed ; these grants were in any case comparatively rare, and it is still very doubtful whether these conveyed anything but the profits of jurisdiction, except no doubt in the few great franchises, which originated differently.[2]

The actual working of private or franchisal jurisdiction during the first two or three hundred years after the Conquest has received a good deal of additional illustration,[3] and the policies and practices of Edward I. in the Quo Warranto proceedings have been thoroughly investigated.[4]

The history of Quo Warranto enquiries belongs essentially to the history of the Articles of the Eyre, which is a matter to be considered below ;[5] enquiries into claims to hold ' liberties ' dates back to 1255 at least, and the writ of Quo Warranto had been in use earlier still.   The doctrine that every liberty is royal and belongs to the crown or to him who has sufficient warrant, either by charter or from time immemorial was adhered to both before and after the Statute of Gloucester of 1278.   That statute was precise in providing for Quo Warranto enquiries by justices

[1] Goebel, op. cit. 391.

[2] Hurnard, op. cit. Miss Hurnard justly adopts the view that *sac* and *soc, toll* and *team,* and *infangenetheof* probably conveyed rights of court-keeping as well as profits, but assumes the much more dcubtful proposition that grants of the *gerihta* or *forisfacturæ* did also.   She rightly argues, however, that the views on this point as a whole held by Maitland, in P. and M. i 576 seqq. cannot now be maintained.

[3] W. O. Ault. Private Jurisdiction in England (1923) 333 seqq, and Court Rolls of the Abbey of Ramsey and of the Honour of Clare (1938), which need to be studied with Miss Cam's review in E.H.R. xliv (1929) 648 seqq ; A. E. Levett, The Court and Court Rolls of St. Albans Abbey in R.H.S. Tr. (4th ser.) vii (1924) 52-76, and Studies in Manorial History (1938) ; N. Denholm-Young, Seignorial Administration in England (1937), some of whose conclusions require correction in the light of Miss Cam's review in E.H.R. lv (1940) 652-654 ; Flower, op. cit. 92-98.

[4] Notably by Miss Cam, The Quo Warranto Proceedings under Edward I. in History (1926), reprinted in Liberties and Communities, 173-182 ; Studies in the Hundred Rolls, in Oxford Studies in Social and Legal History, ed. Vinogradoff, VI., xi (1921), and The Hundred and Hundred Rolls (1930) ; G. T. Lapsley, John de Warrenne and the Quo Warranto Proceedings in 1279, in Camb. H. J. ii (1927) reprinted in Crown, Community and Parliament 35-62 ; T. F. T. Plucknett, The Legislation of Edward I. (1949) 21-50.

[5] 43*-44*.

in eyre, and the Statute of 1290 which bound the king to accept
and confirm to their holders all liberties which a jury should find
had been enjoyed from 1190, which was defined as the criterion
of time immemorial, did not constitute a departure from the
doctrine, but only a definition of part of it.   Forfeiture of a
liberty as a result of enquiries was most unusual, and clearly
there was no intention or desire to confiscate liberties on any
considerable scale.   The objects of the proceedings were rather
to prevent future usurpation and to fix responsibilities for the
due performance of public duties.[1]

(ii) Recent work in the field of feudal jurisdiction whether of
the baronial or honorial or manorial or franchisal variety, has
taken mainly the form of the investigation and discussion of
such jurisdiction in examples of its actual practice,[2] rather than
that of consideration of it from the theoretical or general stand-
point.   One general discussion[3] of first-rate importance of
Anglo-Norman feudalism includes some account of jurisdictional
matters.   The effect of such studies has been to enhance the
realism of our knowledge of feudal courts, and to complicate and
diversify considerably the picture of feudal jurisdiction as it
actually was in certain places and periods.

Sir Frank Stenton has brought out clearly that the evolution
of anything like a " feudal system " in England was very slow and
neither uniform nor universal.   There was no coherent body of
feudal custom common to all the invaders of the 1066 era :
Breton elements in Anglo-Norman feudalism remained important,
and to the evolution of a body of custom, courts held by individual magnates for their tenants contributed much, though
necessarily diversely.[4]   The part played in feudal courts by the
" honorial baronage," or later by " baronial councils,"[5] has
received more attention than it used to do, and there is no doubt
that profitable lines for further investigation have been opened
up in this direction.

Even so, " the courts of even the greatest tenants-in-chief is
the obscurest institution in Anglo-Norman history.   We know
very little of the composition, procedure or business of a lord's
court."[6]

[1] Cam, The Hundred and Hundred Rolls, 232-239.
[2] Ault, op. cit.; Levett, op. cit.; S. Painter, Studies in the History of the English
Feudal Barony (1943) ;   D. C. Douglas, The Social Structure of Medieval East
Anglia, in Oxford Studies, ed. Vinogradoff, ix (1927), and (ed.) Feudal Documents
from the Abbey of Bury St. Edmunds (1932) ;   Denholm-Young, op. cit.
[3] F. M. Stenton, The First Century of English Feudalism (1932).
[4] Ibid 12.
[5] Levett, Baronial Councils and their Relation to Manorial Courts, reprinted in
Studies in Manorial History 21 seqq.
[6] Stenton, op. cit. 41.

In theory every lord of an honour might hold a court of the barons of the honour, but in fact few erected these and fewer maintained such in the thirteenth century ; many maintained no separate court for their barons or military tenants. Theoretically distinct strands of feudal jurisdiction did not necessarily give rise to separate courts. It might be, and apparently was, not uncommonly convenient for a lord to exercise jurisdictions essentially different in origins and nature, in one court, or in courts fewer than jurisdictions, even though the suitors and the parties would necessarily vary according to the business in hand on any given occasion, whether " baronial," franchisal or manorial.[1] The assumption that a feudal lord of standing necessarily maintained a series of courts for the exercise of the different types of jurisdiction vested in him is one that can no longer be maintained.

(iii) In the matter of the royal forests, the most important contributions have shown that the older doctrine that these large areas were in some way outside the scope and organization of the common law courts cannot be maintained. By the thirteenth century, possibly about one quarter of the area of the realm was designated " forest," and although in this area an elaborate forest jurisdiction with its own courts, officers, justices, wardens, verderers, and foresters was in full swing, it was directed to the enforcement of the forest laws and punishment of offences against them, not to civil and criminal business arising in the forest areas, which was disposed of by the usual common law procedures and courts. Some overlapping occurred ; for example, in some regions the verderers, not coroners or local juries presented pleas of the crown ; the ordinary system of frankpledge did not obtain in the covert, but part of it at least was organized in townships which had to answer for fugitives.[2]

A detailed study of the working of the forest organization in the early fourteenth century is now available.[3] The plea rolls of the forest at this time contain no case not connected with forest offences, and even forest cases involving great offenders or matters of importance might be taken to the common law courts, whilst forest offences coming before common law courts might be relegated to forest courts, and a serious attempt was

[1] Ault, Private Jurisdiction 323 seqq.; Leyett, Studies 117 seqq.; Denholm-Young, op. cit. 95 ; Douglas, Social Structure 144 seqq.

[2] E. C. Wright, Common Law in the Thirteenth Century English Royal Forest, in Speculum, iii (1928) 166-191 ; M. L. Bazeley, The Extent of the English Forest in the Thirteenth Century, in R.H.S. Tr. 4th ser. iv (1921) 140-172 discusses the question of areas.

[3] N. Neilson, The Forests, in The English Government at Work, 1327-1336, ed. Willard and Morris, i (1940) 394-467.

made to ensure that coroners, not forest officials, should duly perform the duties of the coroners' office within the forest.

(iv) Recent work connected with the history of the palatinates relates principally to the palatinate or duchy of Lancaster.[1] On the jurisdictional side several misconceptions have been cleared up. The court that came to be known as the Court of Duchy Chamber has to be clearly distinguished from the Court of Chancery of Lancaster. The Court of Chancery of Lancaster was the result of the palatinate rights granted by Edward III. to the fourth earl of Lancaster in 1350-1357, and it developed an equity jurisdiction similar to that of the royal chancery ; its jurisdiction was and always continued to be limited to Lancashire. But the origins, functions and scope of the Court of Duchy Chamber were quite different.

The origins of this court are to be found in the council of the duchy of Lancaster, which can be traced back to the time of the fourth earl and first duke, and probably did not differ materially in nature from the councils of other great magnates, with functions that were primarily administrative in character. The vast estates comprised in the duchy, the grandeur of the dukes and other circumstances tended, however, to magnify the judicial potentiality of the council and to promote its development into the Court of Duchy Chamber. The presentation to it of oral or written petitions, if calling for more than administrative action, naturally encouraged judicial developments at least within the limits of duchy management. Such a council was a well established feature before the annexation of the Lancaster estates to the crown in 1399,[2] and had nothing in itself to do with the palatinate rights confined to Lancashire. But Henry IV.'s accession did not make any considerable difference to the system, for his charter of 1399 expressly provided for the continuance of the existing administration. For long primarily administrative in its functions, by the early sixteenth century, the council, now commonly called the Court of Duchy Chamber, had become mainly a court of equity jurisdiction, extending over all the possessions of the duchy, with procedure by bill and answer in

[1] J. F. Baldwin, The Chancery of the Duchy of Lancaster, in B.I.H.R. iv (1926-1927) 129-143 ; J. Parker, Plea Rolls of the County Palatine of Lancaster, Chetham Soc. (n.s.) 87 (1928); R. S. Somerville, The Duchy of Lancaster Council and Court of Duchy Chamber, in R.H.S. Tr. (4th ser.) xxiii (1941) 159-177, and The Duchy of Lancaster Records, ibid. xxix (1947) 1-17. For a general survey see also Somerville, The Duchy and County Palatine of Lancaster, in Trans. Hist. Soc. of Lancashire and Cheshire ciii (1951). The full history of the duchy is being published in the same author's History of the Duchy of Lancaster, i (1953) and subsequent volumes.

[2] Two further volumes of John of Gaunt's Register, 1379-1383 have appeared, ed. E. C. Lodge and R. S. Somerville, Camden Soc. (3rd. ser.) lvi, lvii (1937).

English. As such it met commonly in the exchequer of receipt in Westminster, adjudicated upon questions of title, breaches of the peace, bills and petitions, and served as a model for the Court of Wards of Henry VIII.'s creation.[1]

The early history of the county palatine of Chester has been subjected to a good deal of revision[2] in recent years, and the views of historians based upon the observations of Sir Edward Coke can no longer be accepted. The use of the term " palatinate " in connexion with the earldom of Chester is not justified before 1237. The strength and importance of the great independent earls of Chester between 1071 and 1237 did not rest upon palatinate rights or special status, but upon the very extensive lands of the honour of Chester, spreading into numerous counties, and the political influence and wealth that these gave to them. On the contrary, the name and attributes of a palatinate did not apply to Chester until after the earldom became permanently annexed to the crown in 1237, and administered directly by the crown from 1377.

The policy of the crown saved the great earldom from disintegration in the thirteenth and fourteenth centuries, and maintained it as a convenient administrative and judicial entity. As such it became a useful source of supply of men and money to the crown in the late fourteenth century, being raised to a principality by Richard II. for a short time. The principality did not survive the revolution of 1399 but its identity as a palatinate remained unchanged until its absorption into the national administrative and parliamentary framework under the Tudors. The palatinate courts remained down to 1830, but even in this sphere continuity became formal rather than substantial. The justiciar of Chester became in effect the head of a Welsh circuit from 1543, while within Chester the existence of the palatine courts no longer meant immunity from, but simply an alternative form of, application of the common law.[3]

(v) The early history of the English borough and of the borough court has been largely re-written, and has been the subject of much discussion and illustration in the last few decades. Many problems remain, but the work[4] of the late Professor

[1] Below 60*-62*.

[2] R. Stewart-Brown, The End of the Norman Earldom of Chester, in E.H.R. xxxv (1920) 26-54 ; G. Barraclough, The Earldom and County Palatine of Chester (1953), reprinted from Trans. of the Hist. Soc. of Lancashire and Cheshire, ciii (1951), and references therein.

[3] Barraclough, op. cit. 27.

[4] The Mediæval English Borough (1936), which incorporates much earlier work by the same author, and discusses the views held by C. Stephenson in The Origin of the English Town, in A.H.R. xxxii (1926-1927), The Anglo-Saxon Borough in E.H.R. (1930), and Borough and Town (1933).

James Tait has put the whole subject on fresh and firm foundations, and the conception of the early history of the borough court
has become[1] clearer than, and different from, that which formerly
held the field.

It is no longer possible to hold that a specially created urban
court formed a universal legal criterion of the early borough.[2]
The only universal features of the pre-Norman Conquest boroughs
were a market and a free burgess tenement of urban type held
at a low rent and transferable within certain limits. A purely
urban court was a less general feature at that time. Courts
of justice existed in urban centres from a time before the Danish
invasions, but these were not purely urban. There is reason to
believe that at that time the counties were divided for judicial
purposes into districts each of which had a *villa regis* as its centre.[3]
It seems clear that many of the mediæval borough courts
developed from hundred courts, not from any purely urban
tribunal, and it is very difficult to establish a purely urban
character for the *burghgemot* of the tenth century or to link it up
with the post-Conquest borough courts. It cannot be said that
a separate court of justice marked off the typical borough from
the ordinary vill within the Anglo-Saxon period, though there is
evidence that a *burhriht* or borough custom distinct from county
custom, applicable to traders, had developed.[4]

The evidence of Domesday Book,[5] confirmed by the later
title of certain borough courts, suggests that the burghal court
of the mediæval period was very generally in origin a hundred
court. The larger boroughs were treated as hundreds or half-
hundreds in themselves, and London as a group of hundreds,
whilst small boroughs continued to be fitted in to the organization of rural hundreds ; urban hundred courts could and did
develop their own character and the body of *burhriht* and other
customs applied therein. Courts of this kind, once embarked on
their course, provided a centre and instrument for the furtherance
of wider ambitions in the direction of a greater measure of self-
government, which, aided by the growth of merchant guilds, and
often influenced by the London Husting, ultimately secured for
them the attributes of a *communitas*. It is probable, however,
that the mediæval town councils as the administrative centres of
municipal government did not evolve out of the older borough

---

[1] M. Weinbaum, The Incorporation of Boroughs (1937), and (ed.) British
Borough Charters, 1307-1660 (1943); N. M. Trenholme, The English Monastic
Boroughs (1927) ; B. Wilkinson, The Mediæval Council of Exeter (1931) ; M. N.
Lobel, The Borough of Bury St. Edmunds (1935) ; E. T. Meyer, Boroughs, in the
English Government at Work, ed. Willard, Morris, and Dunham, iii (1950) 105-141.

[2] Tait, op. cit. 130 seqq.   [3] Ibid 14.

[4] Ibid 42.   [5] Ibid 43 seqq.

courts, but rather in consequence of their decay. The town councillors of the late thirteenth century and their functions were by no means the same as the doomsmen of the old courts, nor were their judicial functions of the same kind.[1]

The peculiar history of London, and of its judicial organization, has received important fresh study and illustration.[2] The general history of the government of the city after the Norman Conquest has been re-investigated,[3] and the actual working of and the relations between the Mayor's court, the Court of Husting, and the sheriff's courts can now be studied in detail.[4]

(vi) The jurisdiction of the chancellors of the Universities of Oxford and Cambridge has not received much specialized study, but various aspects of it have been incidentally treated in several new or revised publications.[5]

(5) The Justices of the Peace.[6]

The mediæval history of the justices of the peace has been largely written for the first time, or re-written, during the last thirty years, and some account of the new learning must be taken here. Inquests held before *custodes pacis* have been discovered dating from as early as 1277, and there is evidence that inquests were held before special guardians from 1263.[7] The development of the keepers of the peace into justices of the peace in the fourteenth and fifteenth centuries has been explored in great detail and with a wealth of illustration in a number of works by Professor B. H. Putnam.[8]

[1] Tait, op. cit. 289 seqq.

[2] M. Weinbaum, Verfassungsgeschichte Londons, 1066-1268 (Beihefte zur Viertaljahrschrift für Sozial-und Wirtschaftsgeschichte XV., 1929), and London unter Eduard II. (ibid xxviii, 1933); A. H. Thomas (ed.) Calendar of Early Mayors' Court Rolls of the City of London, 1298-1307 (1924), and Calendar of Plea and Memoranda Rolls of the City of London, 1323-1412, 3 vols. (1925-1932).

[3] Weinbaum, ut supra.

[4] Thomas, op. cit. especially the Introduction to Calendar of Early Mayors' Court Rolls.

[5] See especially, H. Rashdall, The Universities of Europe in the Middle Ages, new edition by F. M. Powicke and A. B. Emden, 3 vols. (1936), particularly iii, App. IX; H. E. Salter, The Mediæval University of Oxford, in History, xiv (1929-1930) 57-61; Registrum Cancellarii Oxoniensis, 1434-1469 (Oxford Hist. Soc. xciii, xciv (1932)), and Mediæval Oxford, ibid C (1936).

[6] Below 285-298.

[7] H. M. Cam, Some early inquests before " Custodes Pacis," in E.H.R. xl (1925) reprinted in Liberties and Communities 163-172.

[8] Most of her important conclusions have been brought together in Proceedings before the Justices of the Peace in the Fourteenth and Fifteenth Centuries, Edward III. to Richard III. (Ames Foundation, 1938). Cf. the same writer's The Transformation of the Keepers of the Peace into the Justices of the Peace, 1327-1380, in R.H.S. Tr. 4th ser.) xii (1929) 19-48; Shire Officials : Keepers of the Peace and Justices of the Peace, in the English Government at Work, ed. Willard, Morris and

The transformation of keepers of the peace into justices of the peace in the course of the fourteenth century was a slow and irregular process, and a process inspired not so much by the central government as by the Commons in Parliament, who showed a marked preference for justices chosen from among the county gentry, to be elected, they hoped, in the county court, rather than for magnates or royal justices appointed from above, as the best means for enforcing law and order in the localities. The early growth of the judicial powers of the keepers or justices of the peace was for long hampered by the existence of many competitors, most of whom were favoured in preference to them by the central government ; nevertheless the transformation was well-nigh complete, so far as criminal justice was concerned, a good deal earlier than has been commonly recognized—about two decades before the end of the fourteenth century.

Keepers of the peace for the holding of inquests existed in the later years of Henry III., and that name soon came to be applied to the knights assigned to administer the Statute of Winchester, 1285, although the statute itself did not mention keepers, as was commonly believed by 1347.[1] Power to arrest was given to the keepers from 1314, and to enquire into felonies and trespasses from 1316. In the time of Edward II., petitions of the Commons sought to procure the extension of keepers' powers to include power to punish, but the Act of 1327[2] merely gave statutory recognition to the existing officers, and did not extend their powers, and was not in any sense the origin of the justices of the peace. Commissions of the peace issued in May 1329, February 1332, and 1338, included authority to determine felonies and trespasses ; soon the phrase " justices de la pees " appears, but it was by no means certain as yet that the keepers would become justices permanently. Complaints of the conduct of the keepers had previously induced the government to appoint supervisors from among the magnates or royal justices, and this policy continued at least until 1338. The commissions issued did not include power to determine in 1327-1328, 1330, or March 1332, and it is evident that the government at this time regarded the conferment of judicial powers upon the keepers as at best a

Dunham, iii (1950) 185-217 ;   Kent Keepers of the Peace, 1316-1317 (Kent Archæo-logical Soc. Records Branch (1933)) ;   Records of the Keepers of the Peace and their Supervisors, 1307-1327, in E.H.R. xlv (1930) 435-444.   See also E. G. Kimball, Rolls of the Warwickshire and Coventry Sessions of the Peace, 1377-1397 (Dugdale Soc. xvi, 1939) ;   R. Sillem, Commissions of the Peace, 1380-1485, in B.I.H.R. x (1932-1933 81-104, and (ed.) Records of some Sessions of the Peace in Lincolnshire, 1360-1375 (Lincolnshire Recs. Soc. xxx, 1937).

[1] Putnam, The Transformation of the Keepers, loc. cit. 23-24.
[2] 1 Edward III. st. 2.

doubtful experiment.[1] It preferred to appoint lawyers or magnates to deal with the problem of enforcing law and order, either by commissions with extraordinary powers, or to deal with special cases or classes of offence. No doubt such commissions resulted in greater financial profit to the crown, and were accordingly all the more unpopular in the county. The growth of the judicial powers of the keepers was dogged by the competition of justices in eyre, of trailbaston, of oyer and terminer, of goal delivery, and of assize. No statute authorized powers of oyer et terminer for the justices until 1344 (18 Edward III., St. 2 c. 2), which provided that for such purposes they were to be enforced by *autres sages et apris de la ley*, and so gave origins to the quorum. The power was normally included in commissions from 1350. The act of 1361 (35 Edward III., cc. 1, 5, 6, 9, 10, 11) may be said to have given statutory recognition to the transformation of the keepers into justices, but the Council notwithstanding that Act and the wishes of the Commons, curtailed the commissions in 1364-1368 by excluding the determination of felonies, and the administration of labour laws. The act of 1368 (42 Edward III., c. 6), however, restored both these powers, and henceforth the keepers were always justices with powers including the determination of felonies, with a quorum.[2] Even after the regular issue of judicial commissions of the peace, the activities of the justices were hampered by the frequent migrations of the court of King's Bench in the reigns of Edward III. and Richard II., for the presence of the King's Bench in a county superseded the justices of the peace for most judicial purposes, and it was not until the early fifteenth century that the fixation of King's Bench at Westminster removed this threat to the justices of the peace.[3]

Other circumstances tended to hamper the development of the justices of the peace, even after the inclusion of large judicial powers in their commissions had become regular. Some years of experiment passed before the position of the justices in economic regulation was stabilized. They were not at first the chosen instruments for the enforcement of the Ordinance of Labourers of June 1349, and although authority to enforce that ordinance was included in the commissions of the peace in February 1350, soon thereafter this authority was transferred to *ad hoc* justices of labourers over a period of seven years. Often, however, the justices of the peace and the justices of labourers were the same

---

[1] Putnam, Proceedings, xxxvi-xli.

[2] Ibid xlv seqq ; The Transformation 42 seqq.

[3] Putnam, Proceedings lvii seqq. There is no evidence of migration of King's Bench after 9 Henry V. For table showing its migrations 1327-1422, see ibid 29-33.

persons.[1] Nor did the government rely on the justices in the crisis of 1381 ; special commissions were preferred to deal with the troubles, and the same method was to be adopted after Jack Cade's rebellion in 1450. Special commissions of oyer and terminer continued to be used for dealing with abnormal disorders.

The evident reluctance of the government to develop and consolidate the judical powers of the justices is revealed in the curious illogicality, even obscurity, with which their authority was allowed to grow. The commissions issued often included specific powers which had no statutory basis ; on the other hand often very long delays occurred before statutory powers were included, and some of these were permanently omitted. Moreover, the charges to jurors which they were authorized to make, might imply powers wider in scope than the commissions themselves stated.[2] It must indeed have been difficult for the justices themselves to understand just what their powers were ; and by the early fifteenth century there is evidence of copies of statutes, formula books, and collections of writs being made for them, leading on to the substantial treatises compiled for their benefit in the sixteenth century.[3]

The commissions themselves were never simple documents, and although in substance they remained constant in the period 1380-1485, and were invariably issued from 1438, in one of two forms differing slightly, they were composite in character, and never provided a complete statement of authority, for some (and as time passed a growing number of) statutes conferring powers upon the justices failed to receive mention in the commissions at all.

The normal commission in this period comprised seven main clauses. (1) The peace clause, authorizing the enforcement of the peace, with power to punish offenders and to take security, specifically mentioning the Statutes of Winchester (1285), Northampton (1328) and Westminster (1365) regularly, and others regularly from certain dates, (2) the enquiry clause, requiring sworn inquests into certain offences to be held, (3) the oyer and terminer clause, empowering the justices to hear and determine those offences, with a quorum, including felonies, trespasses, forestalling, regrating, extortion, riding armed in conventicles, ambush to mayhem or kill, livery, maintenance and others, (4) the proviso clause giving instructions about difficult cases of extortion, (5) a clause about inquests to be held on certain fixed days, (6) a clause empowering justices to fix days

---

[1] Putnam, Proceedings, xlv. About three-quarters of the justices of labourers were also justices of the peace.

[2] Putnam, ibid xxx seqq.   [3] Below 28*-29*.

and places for the return of juries, and (7) an instruction to one of the justices to keep writs and records (without as yet specifically mentioning the office of *custos rotulorum*).[1]

A number of statutes conferring powers on the justices were never mentioned in the commissions, others were sometimes brought in or omitted for no apparent reason.[2]

By 1485, the justices had in theory all the powers as criminal judges that they had had in 1380, with some notable additions, but in practice the justices of assize were encroaching upon some of their highest judicial powers. But in local government as crown-appointed and crown-controlled officials and administrators of a great body of legislation, much of it economic, they were superseding the old institutions, both communal and feudal.[3] By then the justices of the peace, although still acting in some degree in competition with other judicial commissions and controlled by writs of mandamus, error, certiorari from King's Bench, or more rarely of terminari from Chancery, and by the council, had made good their position. The Commons had been successful in pressing for the extension of the judicial powers of the justices, but had failed in trying to get them elected in the county courts. The development of Quarter Sessions helped to undermine the criminal jurisdiction of the county courts and the sheriff's tourn and courts of private jurisdiction, even though it was the judges of trailbaston, whose descendants were the justices of oyer and terminer of the fifteenth century, who " stole the thunder " of the justices in eyre.[4]

A considerable literature grew up to assist justices of the peace in the discharge of their duties in the fifteenth and sixteenth centuries. A number of manuscript collections of statutes, and of summaries of statutes were made, apparently for their use in the early and middle fifteenth century, and a Worcestershire Manual of guidance was compiled as early as about 1422.[5] Thomas Marowe gave his comprehensive reading on *De Pace Terre* in 1503.[6] The printed *Boke of Justyces of Peas* (1506) ran

---

[1] This had been usual from 1368, but the term " custos rotulorum " did not come into even official use until the mid-fifteenth century ; there is evidence of the appointment of clerks of the peace from 1351-1352.

[2] See the clear analysis by R. Sillem, Commissions of the Peace, loc. cit., where the texts of the commissions of 1380, 1424, and 1430 may be found.

[3] Putnam, Proceedings lvi.

[4] Putnam, The Transformation, 47-48. For an analysis of the relative numbers of cases of felonies, trespasses, and economic offences dealt with by the justices, 1338-1471, see Putnam, Proceedings cxiii, and for a valuable commentary on the indictments by T. F. T. Plucknett, see ibid cxxxiii-xlxi.

[5] See Putnam, Early Treatises on the Practice of the Justices of the Peace in the Fifteenth and Sixteenth Centuries, in Oxford Studies ed. Vinogradoff, vii (1924) 94 seqq, text printed 237-286.

[6] Ibid 115-162, text printed 286-414.

to thirty-two editions, but is evidence of the justices' practice in
the early and middle fifteenth century rather than in the early
sixteenth century.[1] The well-known work of Fitzherbert on
L'office et auctoryte de Justyces des Peas published, first in
French and then in English, in 1538, went through twelve editions,
and four more as revised by Crompton in 1583, and Lombard's
Eirenarcha, first published in 1531 saw nine editions.[2] The
circumstance that these works were published and popular in
the sixteenth century has tended to obscure the fact that many
of their sources were of fifteenth century origin, and that the
judicial powers of the justices were firmly established and in
operation before the end of the fourteenth century, very extensive
in the fifteenth century, and that the Tudors did little but add to
the tasks of the justices' further duties which were mostly administrative rather than judicial.[3]

The activities of the justices of the peace in the seventeenth
century have received a good deal of fresh illustration,[4] and their
functions in local government in Middlesex from 1660 to 1760 have
been very fully discussed.[5]

II. CENTRAL JURISDICTIONS

(1) *The Curia Regis:*[6] *Court of Common Pleas:*[7] *Court of
King's Bench.*[8]

The judicial activities of the undifferentiated Curia Regis have
received a good deal of fresh discussion and illustration,[9] and the

---

[1] See Putnam, Early Treatises on the Practice of the Justices of the Peace in the
Fifteenth and Sixteenth Centuries, in Oxford Studies ed. Vinogradoff, ii (1924),
7, 94-107.   [2] Ibid 8 seqq., 108 seqq.
[3] For enrolment of commissions of the peace 1558-1688, see Putnam, in B.I.H.R.
(1926-1927) 144-156.   For the introduction of the justices of the peace into Cheshire
and Wales in 1536, see R. Stewart-Brown The Serjeants of the Peace (1936), Apps.
I and II 105-128.

[4] See Quarter Sessions Records of the County of Northampton, 1630, 1657-1658,
ed. J. Wake, with Introduction by S. A. Peyton (Northants. Rec. Soc. i, 1924);
Minutes of Proceedings in Quarter Sessions held for the parts of Kesteven in the
County of Lincoln 1674-1695, ed. S. A. Peyton, 2 vols. (Lincs. Rec. Soc. xxv, xxvi,
1931); Surrey Quarter Sessions Records, 1659-1668, ed. H. Jenkinson and D. L.
Powell, 4 vols. (Surrey Rec. Soc. xiii, xiv, xvi, 1934-1938, and Surrey Quarter
Sessions Records, ix, 1951).   The Guide to Archives ed. by D. L. Powell, with an
introduction by H. Jenkinson (Surrey Red. Soc. xxxii, 1931) provides a valuable
guide to the history of the whole subject.

[5] E. G. Dowdell, A Hundred Years of Quarter Sessions : The Government of
Middlesex from 1660 to 1760, with an Introduction by Sir William Holdsworth.
and a General Preface by H. D. Hazeltine (1932).

[6] Below 32-54.   [7] Below 195-203, 246-264.   [8] Below, 204-221, 246-264.

[9] Notably C. T. Flower, Introduction to the Curia Regis Rolls, 1199-1230
(S. S. lxii, 1944); D. M. Stenton, Pleas before the King or his Justices, 1198-1202,
vol. ii (S.S. lxviii, 1949), vol. i containing discussion is now published.   The Public
Record Office has published editions of the Curia Regis Rolls from Richard I. to

origins and early history of the courts of Common Pleas and of King's Bench have been largely re-written since the text below was composed. In certain respects older views on these subjects can no longer be maintained.

The theme of principal importance in the early history of the central court is the process of differentiation which gave rise to the distinct courts of Common Pleas and King's Bench. Sir Cyril Flower observes that it is very difficult to divide the Curia Regis Rolls into Coram Rege Rolls and De Banco Rolls before the end of Henry III.'s reign,[1] but there is no doubt that the process of differentiation in organization had gone far before that time. By the end of the reign of Henry III., King's Bench and Common Bench were distinct courts each with its own judges, officers and records, even though at the beginning of the reign such clear distinctions are not apparent, and two sets of judges or rolls cannot be discovered at that time. A single court seems to have transacted all the business of the two Benches. But in the reign of John there were, during the first ten years of his reign, normally two Benches, as is shown by the heading of the rolls; some are headed " Placita apud Westmonasterium "; others " Placita coram rege." There is, however, only one series of rolls for the remainder of John's reign and the early years of Henry III. until the eighteenth year, when a new separation into two sets appears. For some time the two Benches look like separate divisions of a single court.[2]

As Mr. Turner remarks, " from the time of the Conqueror there must always have been a *curia coram rege* of some sort. We cannot imagine a time when cases were not reserved to the king and judicial advisers at his side, cases which concerned the king himself and his peace; nor can we imagine a time when other cases were not referred to him for special consideration. Such reservation and reference were part of the burden of kingship. But for ordinary civil litigation and for many of the pleas of the crown, there was no real necessity for a central court moving with the king, sitting day by day and accessible to all men. In ordinary matters, whether civil or criminal, ample justice could have been done in the local courts; and even the courts of itinerant justices were not a necessity for the due administration of the law, except perhaps the criminal law."[3]

5 and 6 Henry III., ten vols. (1922-1949). G. B. Adams, Councils and Courts Anglo-Norman England (1926), posthumously published but largely based upon the author's previously published articles, is useful for certain points, but has to a considerable extent been superseded by later work.

[1] Op. cit. 18.
[2] G. J. Turner, Brevia Placitata (S.S. lxvi. 1951) xxxix-xl.
[3] Ibid.

Views of the origin of the Bench, or later court of Common Pleas have undergone considerable revision in recent years.[1] It is no longer possible to attribute its origins solely or even primarily to the arrangements made in 1178, when five members of the royal household were to hear the complaints of all men in the land and to administer justice, without departing from the king's court, and were to refer problems too complicated for them to the king and the *sapientiores*. It is evident that this arrangement was not unique, nor in any sense decisive.[2]

Three years earlier a group of justices had attended the king as he travelled through the country north of the Thames and heard pleas in Curia Regis, and these do not appear to have been justices in eyre. In 1179 a group of six justices were appointed to act as itinerant justices in the northern counties, and these are described by the chronicles in terms similar to those used for the justices of 1178.[3] It is probable then that the arrangement of 1178 was only one in a series of experiments in judicial organization, and the problem is still to find the origins of the differentiation from the Curia Regis which eventually produced the distinct court of Common Pleas. There is still no altogether satisfactory solution to this problem, which is all the more difficult in view of the fact that the jurisdiction of the later courts of Common Pleas and King's Bench were by no means so sharply distinct as used to be supposed, as we shall see later.[4]

What is required is an explanation of the circumstances in which a permanent court derived from the perambulatory king's court came to be established at Westminster regularly hearing pleas which were mainly civil pleas. Professor Sayles is probably right in suggesting that this phenomenon " was not unconnected perhaps with the fact that Henry II. was abroad for most of his last years and that Richard I. was an absentee king."[5] For judicial business which could be disposed of without reference to the king himself—and most civil pleas between subject and subject would fall in that category—could best be disposed of at a fixed place, if they were to be dealt with at the centre. For civil pleas of this kind to follow the king wherever he might be was obviously an arrangement that could not long survive the multiplication of business and the elaboration of remedies. In such circumstances

[1] G. O. Sayles, Select Cases in the Court of King's Bench under Edward I., 3 vols (S.S. lv (1936), lvii (1938), lviii (1939), further volumes forthcoming. Cf. H. G. Richardson, The Memoranda Roll for the Michaelmas Term of 1 John, Introduction (Pipe Roll Soc. (n.s.) xxi, 1943) ; H. G. Richardson and G. O. Sayles, Select Cases of Procedure without Writ under Henry III. (S.S. lx, 1941).
[2] Sayles, op. cit. I. xx-xxi.
[3] " Isti sex sunt justitiae in curia regis constituti ad audiendum clamores populi " (Gesta Regis Henrici Secundi, i, 239) ; Sayles, op. cit. xxi.
[4] Below 34*-36*.   [5] Op. cit. xxi-xxii.

gravitation of a judicial section of the Curia Regis towards Westminster was doubtless inevitable ; for in so far as the government had a centre at all, it was Westminster, where a branch of the king's court was already well established—the *curia regis in scaccario*, or Exchequer.

Professor Sayles notes the intimate association of this embryonic court of Common Pleas with the Exchequer,[1] whilst Mr. H. G. Richardson goes so far as to identify the Bench with the Exchequer, and apparently draws no distinction between the two in Henry II.'s time.[2] Gradually, he writes, " it became more convenient to speak of the legal side as the Bench, while the financial side retained the name of the Exchequer, but that Bench and Exchequer were identical admits of no doubt." So categorical a statement as this, however, has not won universal acceptance, and moreover does not take account of the fundamental difficulty of the ambiguity of the word ' scaccarium ', which, apart from its primary sense meaning the ' chequered board ', might mean either the Exchequer as a department of finances or the Exchequer as a building or office in which much business of the Curia Regis might, as a matter of convenience, be conducted. This locative sense (comparable with the modern use of " in Whitehall " to mean " in the appropriate government department " tends to vitiate any hard and fast conclusions drawn from the use of such expressions as *in curia regis ad scaccarium*, and should induce caution in accepting any close identification of a tribunal the primary reason for the existence of which was financial and only incidentally judicial, with a group of justices whose only raison d'etre as a group was judicial. It was not, perhaps, a case of the identity of Exchequer and Bench, but rather the case that both Exchequer and Bench were distinct aspects of the Curia Regis, and that the fixed location of the former provided a location for the latter when the time came for the latter to feel the need for a definite location. It is true that the significance of the phrase in the Incipit to Glanville's law book telling us that it contains the law and customs observed " in curia regis ad scaccarium et coram justitiis ubicumque fuerint " ought not to be garbled by the insertion of commas after " regis " and "scaccarium," but neither should the first half of the phrase be emphasized at the expense of the second half. The pleas referred to might be in the king's court *at* the exchequer (not be it noted *in* the exchequer) or before the justices wherever they might be.

It seems clear[3] from the plea rolls that survive after 1194 that the whole system of justice was revolving and had revolved around

---

[1] Sayles, op. cit. I, xxii, n. 1.   [2] Op. cit. xiii-xiv.
[3] Sayles, op. cit. xxvii-xxx. Cf. Lady Stenton in S.S. lxvii (1953).

the person of the justiciar. It was the privilege of the justiciars to issue writs in their own name, and it is evident that in the late twelfth and early thirteenth centuries the justiciars took the chief part in the organization of the judicial work of the Curia Regis. Hubert Walter frequently gave instructions to the justices of the bench, and since many of these were conveyed by writs rather than orally, his presence among the justices of the bench themselves is not probable, or at any rate was not regular. Matters concerning the king and his interests appear to have occupied the justiciar's chief attention, and it is possible that at one time the justiciars held a court of their own distinct from the Bench. The evidence for Geoffrey Fitzpeter's control of judicial administration is still more detailed, not only in respect of the central courts, but also of the eyres, and a great deal of legal business passed through his hands. The full history of the office of justiciar, however, still awaits adequate investigation.

The term " Bench " in the reign of John was used only for the court which later became the Common Bench ; there is no evidence of its use to mean the court *coram rege* before Edward I.'s time. It is not altogether certain that the term was used in the early period to mean the actual tribunal of justices at all, and the terms *curia* and *bancus* may not have meant the same thing. What the judges themselves decided was done *consideracione curie*, and judgment was always *judicium curie* ; a good deal of formal business, however, was transacted outside the judge's presence or even cognizance, and it was in connexion with this kind of activity that the word " bancus " was commonly used. " It is not unreasonable to infer that the judges constituted the curia and that the Bench was the place where the clerks in court arranged its business and dealt with all matters which were not ripe for pleading or, like the appointment of attornies, were merely routine."[1] The judges concerned soon became called " justices *in banco*," and before long " justices of the Bench," and by a transference of ideas, we must assume, the term "the Bench" came to signify the court as a whole. Other terms were sometimes used in John's reign to distinguish this group of justices from others, such as justices of " London," of " Westminster."

The use of such distinguishing terminology was all the more natural because already before 1200 another set of justices with a different identity was in existence. This other court was intimately connected with the person of the king, accompanying him on his travels through the country, hearing pleas both civil and criminal, sometimes in the royal presence, sometimes under directions sent by him or in his name, sometimes refusing to

[1] Flower, op. cit. 31.

continue hearing a plea until the king himself or his representative had been consulted.[1] This, the court *coram rege*, or the later King's Bench, was not in essence a new development; it sprang directly from the judicial discretion inherent in the king and his court, and the evolution of what appears to us to be an off-shoot from the general Curia Regis was due no doubt primarily to a certain intensification of specialized functions on the part of a few members of the Curia, and the multiplication of business. The apparently sudden emergence of a distinctive court *coram rege* in 1200 is explained by the circumstance that for the first time for many years there was a king in England around whose person a regular court could form; such a formation was not, of course, possible during the long absences of Richard I. and Henry II. before him, and as we shall see, the court *coram rege* disappeared temporarily whenever the king was absent or in minority, until such time as the legal fiction of the king's personal presence made sufficient headway to provide the court with a continuous existence.[2] The vicissitudes of the king's movements, and the minority of Henry III. affected not only the fortunes of the court *coram rege*, but also those of the Bench. During the king's absences some of the business that would have been dealt with *coram rege* was diverted to the Bench, and during the minority of Henry III. there could be no court *coram rege*; on the other hand, circumstances might result in the diversion of business away from the justices at Westminster to the justices *coram rege*. Business in the Bench dwindled greatly 1207-1209, and was apparently suspended altogether for several years from Easter 1209 by order of the king, and no doubt " it is no accident that the waning of the business of the bench at Westminster and its suppression coincide with the Interdict, and that when at last the king is reconciled to the Church, the justices once more begin sitting term by term at Westminster."[3] Equally without doubt " the memory of the years when litigants had to seek the king in far-off districts and pay him large bribes to obtain his justice or be subjected to interminable delays must have been in great measure responsible for the clauses in Magna Carta whereby justice was to be neither denied nor sold and common pleas were to be held in some fixed place." [4]

The ease with which business could be transferred from the one court to the other confirms what is evident from other facts, that in the early thirteenth century there was no sharp distinction between the two as regards spheres of jurisdiction. Both heard civil and criminal pleas, and cases were frequently transferred from one to the other either at the suit of one of the parties or

---

[1] Sayles, op. cit. xxii.   [2] Ibid.   [3] Ibid xxiv.   [4] Ibid.

by official command ; it was even possible for a plaintiff to sue in a plea of land in both courts simultaneously.[1] Both no doubt were for a time conceived of as two facets of the omnicompetent Curia Regis ; but a differentiation in their records and different titles for their judges appeared, and the writs of summons were differently worded.[2] The thirteenth century saw the process of differentiation carried further.

During the course of Henry III.'s reign, after Trinity 1234 at any rate, the court *coram rege* began to stand more clearly apart from the king and the council, and its jurisdiction became in some respects more clearly distinct from that of the Bench. It has sometimes been thought that no clear distinction between the court and the council existed until late in the fourteenth century, but Professor Sayles has shown decisively that this view cannot be maintained. Before the end of John's reign the plea rolls show references such as " loquendum cum consilio," or " sit coram consilio," indicating that the court was conscious of its own identity and could take steps to refer difficult points to a group outside itself, namely the council. Similar references came from the Bench, and when, during the minority of Henry III. and his subsequent absences, matters of doubt and difficulty which were not or could not be resolved in the Bench were habitually referred to the council. In certain circumstances, particularly during times of rebellion or public troubles when royal interests were frequently at issue, it was common practice for the council to afforce the court *coram rege*, and the same might occur in the Bench. But the courts did not thereby lose their identity.[3] By the time Henry III. went abroad in 1242-1243 and 1253-1254, although it was still not possible to call the court *coram rege* with the king absent, it was no longer practicable to divert its large business to the Bench. It therefore continued in existence, but its pleas were said to be *coram consilio* or before some specified person or persons acting for the king.[4]

The differentiation of business as between *coram rege* and the Bench was a slow process, and one that remains, and is likely to remain, far from clear. In John's reign their jurisdictions were very similar (both being at first no more than facets of the Curia Regis ; each heard both civil and criminal pleas indifferently, and " whatever distinction there might have been lay not in the type of case but in its importance in the royal eyes."[5] It is noteworthy that cl. 17 of Magna Carta marked not a distinction between courts

---

[1] Sayles, op. cit. xxiii.
[2] Ibid. A litigant might be summoned either coram iusticiariis nostris apud Westmonasterium, or coram rege ubicumque fuerit in Anglia.
[3] Ibid xxxvi.   [4] Ibid xxxvii.   [5] Ibid xxxviii.

but between cases, and reveals a distinction between pleas concerning the individuals and those concerning the king. The desire to ensure that common pleas should be held in a fixed place does not seem to have been satisfied, however, for some time. The point was met during the minority of Henry III. because all the judicial business was transacted before the Bench in the absence of a court *coram rege*. But as soon as the court *coram rege* reappeared it heard both civil and criminal pleas and spent most of its time on the former.[1] It is possible that the development of the action of trespass and its association with pleas of the crown tended to enlarge the scope of *coram rege* business, and that the troubles of the Barons' Wars expedited differentiation in the activities of the two courts, which, however, was not complete for many years. " In point of fact, the King's Bench never ceased to entertain civil pleas and the Bench only gradually ceased to try criminal pleas, but by the opening years of Edward I.'s reign the broad line of demarcation had been already drawn.[2] It seems clear that the line was essentially not one between civil and criminal pleas, but between cases concerning individual subjects only, and cases concerning the king and other persons, which might, of course, be civil pleas. King's Bench became especially the court for all kinds of cases in which the king had an interest.

The jurisdiction of King's Bench in the time of Edward I. has been very fully discussed and illustrated.[3] Its jurisdiction in criminal offences was rarely of first instance. Appeals of murder do not appear to have been made there directly, but were often transferred there by writ from county courts. As yet serious crimes were normally alleged, presented, and adjudged before the justices in eyre or of gaol delivery ; King's Bench did not as yet regularly have before it indictments made in the counties through which it passed, and indictments were only very rarely withdrawn from another court or transmitted on account of difficulty into King's Bench.[4]

In civil jurisdiction there was still no sharp distinction between the courts of King's Bench and Common Pleas. King's Bench probably did not come into the main stream of criminal and cognate jurisdiction until after the eyre system was abandoned in the middle of the fourteenth century,[5] and consequently until then the bulk of its business was civil in character, especially civil business in which the king had a direct interest. To some extent the courts of King's Bench and Common Pleas continued to exercise a parallel jurisdiction, with as yet no more than some traces of a conscious differentiation between the two. The great majority

[1] Sayles, op. cit. xxxviii-xxxix.
[2] Ibid xl.
[3] Ibid II. xxxiv-lxxii.
[4] Ibid xxxvi.
[5] Ibid xxxvii.

of the pleas, however, on the rolls of King's Bench at this time, from two-thirds to three-quarters of this total, originated in a writ of trespass in which *vi et armis* and *contra pacem regis* were alleged, and the extensive growth of this action at the end of the thirteenth century and early fourteenth century doubtless tended to consolidate and perhaps to differentiate the jurisdiction of the court.[1]

The assizes of novel disseisin and mort d'ancestor came before the court in any county in which it happened to be, and this work might at times be heavy ; it was, however, the rule that these assizes must be heard within the county of origin, and the hearing would be relegated to the justices of assize if not terminated before the court moved on to another county.[2]

Another sphere in which the jurisdiction of King's Bench was to stand out, jurisdiction in error, was already prominent.[3]   Its authority to correct the mistakes and supervise the legal processes of other courts inevitably made it superior and them inferior. Pleas were sometimes sent in to the court on the initiative of other courts, from common pleas and justices in eyre and of assize, particularly where the royal rights and interests were involved ; but more often they were evoked by writ on grounds of error or false judgment, from not only the royal courts (other than the non-common law side of the Exchequer), but from the county, hundred' and borough courts, and private courts.   A general supervision over judicial administration was also exercised over a wider range.[4]

The court of Common Pleas in the later mediæval period has received further investigation.[5]   Miss Neilson's analysis of cases on the plea roll of Hilary Term, 1332, gives some idea of the nature of the court's business in the early years of Edward III.,[6] whilst Miss Hastings provides a clear and illuminating picture of the court at work in the fifteenth century.

---

[1] Sayles, op. cit. xlii-xliii.   [2] Ibid xliii-xliv.   [3] Ibid xliv-l.

[4] Ibid l-li.   A great deal of valuable information on other aspects of the King's Bench, the judges (also those of Common Pleas), staffing, attornies, plea rolls, process of pleading, is contained ibid passim.   Further information is to be found in M. Blatcher, The working of the Court of King's Bench in the Fifteenth Century, in B.I.H.R. xiv (1936-1937), 196-199 (Summaries of Theses no. cxlix).

[5] N. Neilson, The Court of Common Pleas, in The English Government at Work, iii, ed. Willard, Morris and Dunham (1950) 259-285 ; M. Hastings, The Court of Common Pleas in Fifteenth Century England (1947).   Cf. P. Vinogradoff, Ralph of Hengham as Chief Justice of the Common Pleas, in Essays to T. F. Tout (1925), 198-196, and Radulphi Hengham Summae, ed. W. H. Dunham (1932).

[6] Op. cit. 271-278.   Of the nearly 6,000 cases on the roll, about 1,550 relate to actions of account, 1,000 debt, 500 detenue, 500 trespass, 400 land as right or on writ of entry, 250 dower, 160 replevin, 140 vouching to warranty, 100 covenant, 90 arrears of rent, 85 waste, 40 mesne, 40 wardship, 30 cessavit per biennium, 20 quod permittat, 20 possessory assizes, 6 neifty, 4 customs and services.

It is evident that there was no falling off in the business of the court in consequence of the political troubles of the fifteenth century ; there were some adjournments on that account, but the continuity of the personnel of the court was remarkably maintained.[1] The enormous delays that occurred in the court were due to "natural causes," and especially to the great difficulty of getting the parties into court at the right time.[2] Common pleas was a great deal busier at this time than King's Bench, which had not yet, through the development of the action of trespass on the case and the use of the bill of Middlesex, attracted to itself the major portion of the civil business of the two central courts.[3] As yet there are about three times as many entries on the plea rolls of Common Pleas as there are on those of King's Bench.

The jurisdiction of the two courts, although further differentiated since the time of Edward I., was still in certain respects parallel. That of Common Pleas[4] was of three main kinds. The most important kind was its common law jurisdiction over pleas between person and person begun by original writ out of chancery; this jurisdiction (no doubt except where the king was a party) appears to have become exclusive in real actions, in the older personal actions of debt, detinue, account and covenant, and in mixed actions such as ejectment. But jurisdiction was shared with King's Bench in maintenance, conspiracy, other breaches of statute, trespass, trespass on the case, and their derivatives.[5]

Two sorts of jurisdiction by privilege brought some cases to the court regularly. The justices of the bench continued to exercise a criminal jurisdiction where the cause arose from within the court or its records ; and they adjudicated also in suits brought by or against officers or ministers of the court.[6] In the third category, of supervisory jurisdiction over the older local courts and the justices of assize, little trace is left by this time,[7] and this work was no doubt largely monopolized by King's Bench. Rivalry between the two courts, however, was not as yet very acute, and the struggles of the seventeenth century in this respect were but faintly foreshadowed.[8]

[1] Hastings, op. cit. 8-12.
[2] About 5,000 of the 6,000 entries on the rolls for Michaelmas, 22 Edward IV. were respites, ibid 8.   [3] Ibid 16. Cf. Blatcher, op. cit.
[4] This title was not yet in general use ; the heading of the plea rolls was still "Placita apud Westmonasterium . . . coram iusticiariis domini Regis de banco . . . ." Hastings, op. cit. 20.   [5] Ibid 16.
[6] Ibid 17 ; for discussion of these, see ibid 59-156 and appendices.
[7] Ibid 19.
[8] Much additional information relating to the working and procedure of the court, its judges, officers, and records is provided ibid passim. For studies of the lives of two chief justices of the King's Bench, see B. H. Putnam, The Place in Legal History of Sir William Shareshull, 1350-1361 (1950), and Sir John Fortescue, De Laudibus Legum Anglie, ed. S. B. Chrimes (1942, rep. 1949).

(2) *The Exchequer of Pleas*.[1]

A thorough investigation[2] has thrown much new light on the Exchequer of Pleas. As a court of law the Exchequer of Pleas was well-known in the sixteenth century, but in the twelfth century it seems to have been quite unknown as an institution. The *placita* which took place at that time at the Exchequer were ordinary cases which happened to come on when the Curia was in session *ad scaccarium*.[3] There must, however, have occurred something resembling a judicial hearing for disputes which actually arose during audit at the upper Exchequer, such as the contradictory claims of the accountants, disputes arising out of revenue questions, and the like.[4] Probably such proceedings were not at first regarded as extending the activities of the Exchequer, which of course itself was only an aspect of the Curia Regis. There are traces of such pleas on the earliest surviving *Memoranda Roll*[5] from the reign of John, and more prominently in the early years of Henry III.

The earliest surviving roll of pleas heard before the barons of the Exchequer separate from the memoranda rolls, however, comes from 20, 21 Henry III., and this date coincides with a well-known period of Exchequer reform.[6] By then it is evident that a number of pleas were being adjudicated upon, cases between the king and accountants, and cases between subject and subject relating to the incidence of taxation, scutage, relief, and money alleged to have been paid but not cleared at the Exchequer. The separation between the two classes of rolls did not, however, become complete. By 43, 44 Henry III. about two-thirds of the writs of process were still being entered on the memoranda rolls, while the substance of the pleas went on the plea rolls; by 27, 28 Edward I. complaints which affected the king only and his revenue were not recorded on the plea roll, but on the memoranda rolls. Cases in which a private person was not involved on both sides to the dispute were recorded on the latter but not on the former rolls.[7]

The basic jurisdiction of the Exchequer of Pleas continued to be cases touching the king's revenue, but the possibilities of extension from this basis were great, especially in view of the fact that it was probably easier to get an original writ from the Exchequer than it was from chancery, to which a plaintiff in

---

[1] Below, 231-242.
[2] H. Jenkinson and B. E. R. Fermoy (ed.), Select Cases in the Exchequer of Pleas (S.S. xlviii, 1932).
[3] Ibid xxviii; cf. above 32*.   [4] Ibid xxviii.
[5] Ibid xxix seqq.; cf. H. G. Richardson, Memoranda Roll of 1 John.
[6] Jenkinson and Fermoy, xxxix seqq.   [7] Ibid lxxi.

Common Pleas or King's Bench had to resort for such a writ. Personal application by a complainant to the barons because of a demand made upon him for payment of moneys[1] would procure a writ, and the circumstances might be favourable to a wide interpretation of the relevance of the case to the king's revenue ; questions of debt, detinue, failure to acquit, and the like, inevitably encroached on the ground of common pleas ; the privilege of hearing actions in which officials of the court were concerned, as usual, widened the jurisdiction,[2] and allegations of malpractices in exactions by local officials made by them on behalf of the Exchequer brought further scope.[3]

This expansion of jurisdiction and consequential encroachment into the sphere of common pleas produced a reaction in the later thirteenth and early fourteenth centuries. The treasurer and barons themselves found the work of adjudication absorbing time which was needed for the hearing of accounts, and sought in 52 Henry III. to curtail the number of days on which they would hear pleas other than those relating to the king's debts and the pleas of Exchequer officials.[4] In the fifty-fourth year the king ordered the remission to the justices of the Bench of all pleas concerning debts pending in the Exchequer except those touching the officials.[5] Possibly this provision was not intended to be permanent, or was not wholly successful, and several further efforts at restricting the jurisdiction were made under Edward I, both by writ and by statute.[6] These attempts, however, were inspired at first by consideration for the avoiding of interference with the accounting work of the Exchequer, and only secondarily by the notion that the hearing of common pleas was contrary to Magna Carta.[7] It is probable, however, that the actual number of pleas heard at this time in the Exchequer which were not genuinely connected with the revenue was not large. There is no trace as yet of the writ *quominus*, whereby jurisdiction was extended. But by 1299 or earlier a new formula was used—" in partem solucionis debitorum que idem debet domino Regi—which had considerable possibilities for extension, and certainly brought in a good deal of executor business. It remained for the court to cease the habit of investigating the genuineness of the alleged debt to the king, and the fictional use of the allegation could make headway. A good deal of extension is evident also in the jurisdiction relating to local officials, to include local officials as injured parties, former officials and officials of very low status.[8] The advantages of Exchequer

[1] Jenkinson and Fermoy, liv.
[2] Ibid xci seqq.
[3] Ibid xciii seqq.
[4] Ibid xciv.
[5] Ibid xcv.
[6] Ibid xcv-xcvi.
[7] Ibid xcvi.
[8] Ibid cii seqq.

procedure might also be granted in special cases, sometimes as a particular favour by the king himself, particularly to foreign merchants.[1] The consolidation of the Exchequer of Pleas as " a court made by lawyers for lawyers " was the work of the later fourteenth century.[2]

(3) The Justices in Exchequer Chamber.[3]

The meetings of all the justices in the Exchequer Chamber have been the subject of careful investigation.[4] This court (if indeed it can properly be called a court at all) was not, of course, the court set up by 31 Edward III. st. 1. c. 12 for the correction of errors in the Exchequer of Pleas, nor the court for errors in King's Bench set up by 27 Elizabeth c. 8, nor the court of equity for the Exchequer. The meetings of all the justices which usually took place in Exchequer Chamber, but sometimes elsewhere according to convenience,[5] had nothing to do with the Exchequer as a department, and as the functions of the justices on these occasions were essentially advisory, their meetings were hardly courts in the normal sense of the word, and effect to the decisions reached therein was necessarily given elsewhere.

The origins of these meetings were informal.[6] It was a common practice for justices of each Bench to consult with each other or with the other Bench, in the fourteenth century. The statute 14 Edward II. st. 1. c. 5, in setting up a commission of magnates to hear petitions in Parliament relating to delays and grievances arising from litigation, may have reflected on the justices and encouraged consultation among the justices themselves, to whose opinion cases were sometimes referred by the Council. The majority of early cases referred to all the justices in Exchequer Chamber came from the Council or Parliament, or Chancery, and the arrangement became more formal in the fifteenth century. Considerable impetus to the procedure was given by the chancellors in the reign of Henry IV., some of whom were not adequately equipped to deal with the difficulties of the growing complexity of jurisdiction. The reference of cases from the common law courts materially added to the prestige of the judgments of all the justices. The number of such references from

---

[1] Jenkinson and Fermoy, cviii seqq.

[2] Ibid xcv. Much information on other aspects of the court in the early fourteenth century is to be found ibid passim.

[3] Below 242-246.

[4] H. Hemmant (ed.), Select Cases in the Exchequer Chamber before all the Justices of England, 1377-1509, 2 vols. (S.S. li (1933), lxiv, (1948)).

[5] Exchequer Chamber was the usual meeting place in the fifteenth century; other meeting places, such as Serjeants' Inn, the Whitefriars, and others, were not infrequent in the following century. " Chequer case " came to mean the function rather than the location. Ibid I. xxiii.   [6] Ibid xl seqq.

all sources was never very large, and so far as Year Book evidence goes, the total was about two-hundred between 9 Henry IV. and 19 Henry VIII., varying from none to seventeen in any one year.[1]

The matters referred, however, were very varied, and usually involved questions of major legal importance. Problems of rival jurisdiction, the legal consequences of changes in the royal dynasty, the rights of foreigners, the prerogative rights of the king, technicalities of procedure and of the land law, and many others, were considered by all the justices, who from 1579 included the barons of the Exchequer. The decisions of the justices appear to have been accepted without question, even if individuals among them dissented, and this custom became in effect a rule by the sixteenth century, and may have done a good deal to develop the principles of judicial decision.[2]

The reference of cases by king and council to all the justices tended to decline from the late fifteenth century onwards, and from the late Tudor period references were almost wholly confined to the courts of common law and chancery.[3] The practice seems to have lapsed altogether under the Commonwealth and Protectorate, and never to have been fully revived thereafter. The last known instance of such references was in 11 George II. It is probable, however, that the old practice was not without influence in the establishment of the Court of Crown Cases Reserved in 1848,[4] the sittings of which were to be held in Exchequer Chamber or other convenient place.

(4) *The Justices in Eyre*[5] *and other Itinerant Justices.*[6]

It is clear that from the time of William Rufus at least the policy of the crown was to appoint local resident justiciars to administer royal justice in the localities. These resident justiciars were the supreme judicial authorities in the shires, above the sheriff and other ministers ; they held in effect a standing commission to try all pleas of the crown and all actions which might have come before the Curia Regis. Such justiciars were in existence everywhere in the time of Henry I., and gained rather than lost importance under Stephen ; the great men of the shires, earls and bishops, were anxious to procure appointments to the office.[7] But within a few years of Henry II.'s accession the

---

[1] H. Hemmant (ed.) Select Cases in the Exchequer Chamber before all the Justices of England, 1377-1509, 2 vols. (S.S. li (1933), lxiv. (1948)), xxxi-xxxiii.
[2] Ibid xxv seqq.   [3] Ibid lix seqq.
[4] Ibid lxiii. This court was abolished in 1907.
[5] Below 264-273.   [6] Below 274-285.
[7] H. W. C. Davis, Regesta Regum Anglo-Normannorum (1913) I. xxx seqq; England under the Normans and Angevins, 6th ed. (1919) 517-523 ; Morris, The Mediæval English Sheriff 56 ; Sayles, Select Cases, I, xix-xx.

local resident justiciars gradually disappear from the records.
" For the reign of Henry II. is definitely a new age in judicial
organization.   The field having been cleared of resident royal
justiciars whose interests were local when they were not personal,
it was possible to create a new instrument of justice.   This
could not be done all at once : but over two or three decades
there were gradually laid the foundations of the system which
endured, modified but substantially unchanged, until the fourteenth century."[1]

The new organization in its central aspect, which was
ultimately to give rise to the courts of Common Pleas and King's
Bench, has been noted above.[2]   Its local aspect, in the form of
the justices in eyre and other itinerant justices, needs further
consideration here, for a good deal has been contributed to our
knowledge of their origins in recent years.

Miss Cam has traced in detail the origins and evolution of the
Articles of the Eyres,[3] and other scholars have illustrated the
practice of the justices in eyre.[4]   Miss Cam brings out the close
relationship of the Articles to the series of special inquisitions
which were held from the time of the Inquest of Sheriffs, 1170,
onwards.   The purpose of these early inquests and general
eyres, although often including enquiries into felonies, was
primarily administrative rather than judicial, and included
enquiries into the proprietary rights of the crown, the assumption
or abuse of franchises, and the official misconduct of sheriffs
and other royal officers.   The eyres were probably initiated as
early as the reign of Henry I., and the inquisitorial procedure
was firmly entrenched in Henry II.'s Assizes of Clarendon 1166
and of Northampton 1176.[5]   In the *vetera capitula* of the eyre,
proprietary rights predominated in the matters for enquiry, with
a strong emphasis on financial interests of the crown, and the
impetus for this side of the eyre may well have come from the
Exchequer.   The importance of the eyre as an instrument for
the enforcement of legislation became marked in the course of
the thirteenth century,[6] with a consequential multiplication of
the Articles themselves, which increased from five to seventy
between 1176 and 1276.[7]   A firm list of general eyres from 1194 to

---

[1] Sayles, op. cit. xx.   [2] 30*-38*.
[3] H. M. Cam, Studies in the Hundred Rolls (1921).
[4] W. C. Bolland, The General Eyre (1922) ; D. M. Stenton, The Earliest
Lincolnshire Assize Rolls, 1202-1209 (Lincoln Record Soc. 22 (1926), The Earliest
Northamptonshire Assize Rolls, 1202 and 1203 (Northamptonshire Record Soc.
v, 1930). Rolls of the Justices in Eyre for Lincolnshire, 1218-1219, and for Worcestershire, 1221 (S.S. liii, 1934), for Yorkshire, 1218-1219 (ibid lvi, 1937), for Gloucestershire, Warwickshire, and Staffordshire, 1221-1222 (ibid lix, 1940). Cf. Cam, The
General Eyres of 1329-1330, in E.H.R. xxxix (1924), 241-252.
[5] Cam, Studies 17.   [6] Ibid 19 seqq.   [7] Ibid 29.

1341 can be compiled,[1] but there is no clear evidence that it was ever the intention to hold a general eyre every seven years as used to be supposed.[2]

The precedent for the additional *nova capitula* of the eyre was set by the extensive special inquest of 1224, and these came to be included in every subsequent general eyre.[3] The emphasis in these upon financial exactions rather than judicial considerations enhanced the unpopularity of the eyres, which may have induced resort to the special inquest of 1274-1275 as an alternative.[4]

This inquest was very comprehensive, influenced as it was by the Provisions of Westminster and the Statute of Marlborough, and its results affected the content of the legislation of the following years, particularly the Statute of Westminster I. (1275) and the Statute of Gloucester (1278), and probably the *Statutum de iustitiis assignatis, quod vocatur Rageman* of uncertain date, whereby justices were to be assigned to hear and determine complaints against the king's officials and others for offences committed over the previous twenty-five years.[5]

The great inquest of 1274-1275 made an impression upon the eyres which was to last for the remainder of the eyres' history. The next general eyre, of 1278, marks something like an epoch in the development of the eyre procedure. The *nova capitula*, based upon the articles of the inquest of 1274, and the articles derived from the legislation of 1275, were administered to the jurors at the eyre, and the writ of the eyre for the first time instructed justices to hear and determine plaints, in the form that endured as long as the eyres themselves—" ad querelas omnium conquerentium seu conqueri volentium audiendas." It is probable that authority for this hearing of plaints or writs was derived from the Statute of Rageman, but in any case the hearing of *querele* had been a prominent feature of the Inquest of 1274-1275, possibly of earlier inquests, and there is no reasonable doubt that the immediate origins of the bills in eyre are to be found in these precedents.[6]

The decline and disappearance of the general eyres in the early fourteenth century is one of the most striking features in the jurisdictional history of the period. The change in government policy manifested in this decline was comparatively sudden

[1] Cam, Studies, App. III, 103-113.
[2] Ibid 83-87.   [3] Ibid 15 seqq., 29 seqq.
[4] This inquest is fully analysed, ibid 114-189.
[5] Ibid 35 seqq.   For explanation of the term " Rageman," see ibid 51-52.
[6] Ibid 136.   The whole subject of procedure by plaint has a longer history than Dr. Bolland supposed in his Select Bills in Eyre, 1292-1333 (S.S. xxx, 1914), and this history has been explored by H. G. Richardson and G. O. Sayles in Select Cases of Procedure without Writ (S.S. lx, 1941).

and rapid. Not more than eight, perhaps only six eyres were held under Edward II., and although there was some revival in the early years of Edward III., no eyre was completed after 1337 ; an eyre was proclaimed in 1341 but not carried out, and although the threat of holding a general eyre continued to be a useful and not unprofitable expedient until 1397, the eyre as a form of jurisdiction had ceased to exist.

It may well be that with the development of non-feudal forms of taxation by this time the fiscal value of the general eyre to the government declined, and the development of new and probably more regular and effective machinery for the enforcement of local order and correction of official misconduct no doubt reduced the judicial value of the old procedure. " The conservators and justices of the peace stole the thunder not only of the sheriffs, but also of the justices *ad omnia placita.*"[1] The commissions of trailbaston from 1364, of oyer and terminer, and of the peace and other judicial commissions all had their share in the super-session of the general eyre, though it may well be the case that these expedients did not succeed in filling the breach left by the disappearance of the eyre, to which, among other factors, " we may attribute the necessity for the jurisdiction of Star Chamber."[2]

Few of the other species of itinerant justices have as yet received much fresh investigation, but the justices of assize in the early fourteenth century have been studied in some detail.[3] The continuance of the system of general eyres until the early years of Edward III., and the migratory character of Common Pleas and King's Bench at that time impeded the development of the justices of assize. Their jurisdiction was still primarily in connexion with the possessory assizes, but was gradually increasing in the thirteenth and early fourteenth centuries. Novel disseisin itself had come to be extended from land to cover servitudes, rights of pasture, cropping, estovers, corrodies, tolls and commodities. Moreover, the powers of the justices were extended by statute several times, and these powers were not necessarily included in their commissions.[4] Thus the statute of Westminster II (1285) gave them power to enquire into failure by sheriffs to return writs ; they were intended to enforce the Statute of Winchester (1285) and the Statute of Northampton (1328) specifically gave them power to enquire into and to punish

[1] Cam, op. cit. 72 seqq. Cf. above.   [2] Cam, ibid 83.
[3] M. M. Taylor, Justices of Assize, in The English Government at Work, iii. ed. Willard, Morris, and Dunham (1950) 219-257. Cf. W. S. Thomson, A Lincolnshire Assize Roll for 1298 (Lincolnshire Record Soc. xxxvi, 1944), and the texts mentioned in n. 70 above.
[4] Taylor, op. cit. 220.

defaults in observance of the former statute. The Statute De finibus (1299) authorized them, when delivering gaols, to enquire whether sheriffs or others had wrongfully released prisoners by replevin, or had offended in any way contrary to the statute of Westminster I, and to punish those found guilty.

But it seems that these and other statutory extensions of the functions of the justices of assize were rarely exercised in the first ten years of Edward III.'s reign.[1] As yet there is little indication of any wide criminal jurisdiction by these justices, nor was there likely to be much scope for it whilst the eyres continued and the King's Bench migrated frequently. Most of the work of the justices of assize continued as yet to be based upon the possessory assizes.

The commission issued to justices of assize might be special or general.[2] The former appointed two or three justices to take only a single action or assize ; it was issued on the complaint of the plaintiff upon payment of a fine, and it was for the plaintiff to give the commission to the justices appointed as their warrant for hearing his action. Notwithstanding the fact that usually the justices so appointed had already received a general commission for the hearing of the assizes in the county, the need for a special commission continued to be upheld, mainly, no doubt, because of the resulting financial profit to the crown.

The general commissions normally authorized the justices to take all the assizes in one, two, or a group of counties. The form of these general commissions never varied at this time, in spite of the various additional powers conferred by statutes. They were, however, issued at irregular intervals, usually at least once a year ; the frequency with which sessions were actually held seems to have depended more upon the discretion of the justices themselves rather than upon the various statutory provisions that had been made on the point at different times. Great distances were often covered by the justices in the discharge of their duties ; usually one or sometimes two days were spent in session at the different places visited, but it is not possible to ascertain how many days in the year were taken up in this way.[3]

During the years 1327-1336, fifty-seven justices of assize were assigned.[4] Of these, thirty-seven were closely connected in one capacity or another with the central courts at Westminster, and the remaining twenty were local gentry commonly employed on governmental work of various kinds in their counties. Magnates were not assigned, but as yet there were no restrictions upon the employment of local residents as justices of assize.

[1] Taylor, op. cit. 221.   [2] Ibid 225 seqq.
[3] Ibid 229, 235-236.   [4] Ibid 231-233.

It is clear that the justices of assize were at first not intended to hold pleas *nisi prius*, and when they did so it was
as justices of the bench before which pleas had originally been
brought.   But to remedy delays the Statute 14 Edward III.
c. 16 provided that issues might be tried at *nisi prius* before
justices of either bench, or the chief baron of the exchequer
if a lawyer, or if none of these came into the county, before
a justice of assize if he were a justice of either bench or a
king's serjeant.[1]

The convenience of employing the justices on circuit for
judicial purposes other than the assizes was obvious.   The
additional powers conferred upon them by statute were as yet
seldom invoked.   But statutes of 1328 and 1330 provided that
justices of gaol delivery were to be the same persons as the
justices of assize, and although these statutes also were more
honoured in the breach than in the observance for some time, the
way was open for the multiplication of the duties of the justices
of assize—by granting more than one kind of commission to the
same persons.   To commissions of assize could be added commissions of gaol delivery, as well as commissions of oyer and
terminer, and sometimes special commissions also.[2]   The advantages to the crown of relying upon the circuit of trained
personnel, and the convenience of the circuits to litigants, alike
assured their permanence.   Moreover, the justices "made their
circuits not to replenish the Exchequer, but to execute a purely
judicial function."[3]

(5) *Magna Carta and the Judicial System.*[4]

Fresh light has been thrown on two principal points regarding
Magna Carta and the judicial system.   The first of these, concerning the provision of clause 17, that common pleas should
be held in a fixed place, has been touched upon above.[5]   The
second point concerns the interpretation to be put upon clause 34,
which asserted that the writ *praecipe* should not in future be
issued so that a free man might lose his court.[6]

This clause has usually been interpreted as a baronial attack
upon an important piece of Henry II.'s procedure for curtailing
feudal jurisdictions, and many assumptions and inferences
have been based upon this interpretation.   But it has become,
to say the least, extremely doubtful whether any such interpretation can be maintained.   The whole subject has been

---

[1] Taylor, op. cit. 240-241.   [2] Ibid 237-240, 241-243.
[3] Ibid 247.   [4] Below 54-63, esp. 56, 58-59.   [5] Above 34*.
[6] "Breve quod vocatur Praecipe de cetero non fiat alicui de aliquo tenemento
unde liber homo amittere possit curiam suam."

re-examined in detail, and important different conclusions have been drawn.[1]

Miss Hurnard points out that a good deal of misconception lay at the root of the hitherto accepted interpretation of the clause. There is no evidence to show that a feudal court was ever competent to deal with all land actions other than those between tenants-in-chief of the lord of the court.   In the time of Henry I. actions between parties holding of different lords commonly went to the county courts, and the incompetence of a lord's court to take such cases must have been a very substantial limitation upon the scope of a court's jurisdiction.   Furthermore, pleas of false judgment, default of justice, and probably certain other classes of action, such as dower *unde nihil habit*, and actions for advowsons, normally were dealt with in a royal not a feudal court.   Feudal courts, in short, did not enjoy exclusive competence in proprietary actions, and there was no reason why the many actions which could be determined only in the public courts should not be brought by the writ *praecipe* into the king's court.   There is no evidence that the writ *praecipe* was intended to be or was normally a weapon to deprive feudal courts of jurisdiction which properly belonged to them, although indirectly it may have had that effect in a few individual instances.   Nor is it likely that the writ would have been effective for such a purpose, for the lord whose court was competent to deal with an action could still claim the action, and the claim might succeed, even though a *praecipe* had been issued.

The business of claiming court, however, must often have been a nuisance, and if claim were not made by the due time, jurisdiction would be lost.   The barons in clause 34 sought, it is argued, to avoid such nuisance as far as possible, and the possibility of such loss, not to restore a competence of which they had not been deprived.   It cannot escape notice that the number of praecipes issued in 1213 had been far larger than usual, and as so often the case, the barons were aiming in clause 34 at the remedy of a specific abuse ;   they sought to save themselves unnecessary trouble in making their claims, with the attendant risk of occasional failures, so that they should not needlessly lose their Curia, i.e. their cognizance of individual cases.   Clause 34, therefore, may have saved the lords inconvenience and some occasional losses, but its effect upon the value of business determined in the feudal courts appears to have been negligible.[2]

[1] N. D. Hurnard, Magna Carta, clause 34, in Studies in Medieval History presented to F. M. Powicke (1948), 157-179.

[2] It should be noted that a valuable account of Magna Carta in litigation and of its later history is to be found in F. Thompson, Magna Carta : Its rôle in the

(6) The Juries.[1]

Little new work specifically upon the jury system has been done, although many points of interest are incidentally brought out in the various editions of plea rolls and select cases to which reference is made above and below. One particular matter, the origins and early history of the jury of presentment, has, however, been the subject of detailed re-examination.[2]

Miss Hurnard has argued that Henry II.'s Assize of Clarendon, 1166, cannot be assumed to have embodied important changes in procedure, that the juries of presentment regulated in the assize are not likely to have been innovatory, and that reliance until that date upon private appeal alone as the means of accusing criminals is improbable. Miss Hurnard points to the well-known text of Ethelred III., 3, 1,[3] which refers to the duty of the twelve leading thegns in making accusations, and argues from this and certain other items of evidence, that a jury of presentment procedure had been common usage in the later Anglo-Saxon period, had been taken over by William I., and remained the basis of criminal justice under his successors. On this argument the importance of the Assize of Clarendon consists mainly in its insistence upon the ordeal for every presented person, its severity for those of notorious ill-fame, and its claim of forfeitures for the king, even though it may have introduced the jury of presentment into the sheriff's tourn and placed greater reliance upon the jury's view. Henry II.'s object, on this interpretation, was to retain in his own hands the machinery of presentment and its profits, at least on the occasion for which the assize was issued ; the extension seems at first to have been temporary, but the stricter procedure laid down became part of the normal machinery, and by the time of the Assize of Northampton, 1176, seems to have become permanent.

Miss Hurnard's argument undoubtedly contains a certain amount of probability, but in the absence of sufficient evidence to support it, can hardly be regarded as convincing. There is some evidence of the use of criminal accusation before the time of Henry II., in addition to the evidence of the Laws of Ethelred for the Danelagh ; there are traces of the imposition of collective fines for concealing crimes in Henry I.'s time ; it is possible that the

making of the English Constitution, 1300-1629 (1948), and that a convenient summary of recent interpretations and the literature relating to the charter in general is provided in T. F. T. Plucknett's revised 10th edition of T. P. Taswell-Langmead's English Constitutional History (1946) 74-104.
[1] Below 298-350, esp. 321-322.
[2] N. D. Hurnard, The Jury of Presentment and the Assize of Clarendon, in E.H.R. lvi (1941) 374-410.
[3] Below 12 n. 10.

making of criminal accusations was part of the functions of the reeve, priest and four men of each vill who were expected to be present at the hundred and shire courts in the absence of the lord or his steward ; criminal accusation in the case of murder may be assumed in the *Leges Henrici Primi*. But none of these things are the same as the jury of presentment envisaged in the Assize of Clarendon, and if, as Miss Hurnard believes, a form of the jury of presentment was in common and continuous use from late Anglo-Saxon times, it is certainly remarkable that so little, if any, direct evidence of it survives. Miss Hurnard's argument therefore must be deemed non-proven at present, and although due weight must be attached to it, it is not strong enough in itself to undermine the view held by Maitland and most other scholars on the subject.[1]

(7) *The House of Lords.*[2]

Whilst a great deal of fresh work has been done in the last thirty years on the early history of Parliament in general, especially on the House of Commons, little that is new has been added to the history of the House of Lords as a court of judicature. The history of Parliament in general is too large a theme to be dealt with here,[3] but reference must be made to certain work that has been done on the jurisdiction of the House of Lords, and on the origins of impeachment.

Professor A. S. Turberville's several works [4] on the House of Lords in the early modern period included some account of its activities as a court of judicature. So far as matters of judicature are concerned, fresh illustration rather than new substance is to be found in these contributions. In appears that the Lords did not assume under Charles II. any judicial powers that they had not exercised under James I. and Charles I., but the dispute with the Commons arising out of their action in *Skinner* v. *The East India Co.*, put an end to the House of Lords as a court of first instance in civil suits. Its function as a court of appeal, however, continued and flourished in the eighteenth century,

---

[1] Below 12 n. 10, and 312-313. E. Toms has shown in another connexion that there is some evidence in the time of Edward II. and Edward III. that jurors were not necessarily local men. See Mediaeval Juries, in E.H.R. li (1936) 268-270.

[2] Below 357-384.

[3] A useful summary of such work, with references to literature, is to be found in Taswell-Langmead, English Constitutional History, 10th Ed. 143-240 ; T. F. T. Plucknett's chapter on Parliament in The English Government at Work, i, ed. Willard and Morris (1940) 82-128, is among the most valuable contributions to the early history of Parliament.

[4] The House of Lords in the Eighteenth Century (1927) (cf. Holdsworth, The House of Lords, 1689-1783, in L.Q.R. xlv (1929) 307-342, 432-458) ; The House of Lords under Charles II., in E.H.R. xliv (1929) 400-417, xlv (1930) 58-77 ; The House of Lords as a Court of Law, 1784-1837, in L.Q.R. lii (1936) 189-219.

with increases resulting from the Unions with Scotland in 1707 and with Ireland in 1801. The business resulting on appeals from chancery and courts of equity, and on error from Common Pleas, King's Bench, Exchequer, and courts in Scotland and Ireland grew steadily, and by the early nineteenth century brought about a state of serious congestion and arrears. By the late eighteenth century few lay lords took part in the work of judicature, and the task was often performed by the Lord Chancellor and one other law lord, assisted by two " mute lay lords." A Select Committee reported in 1811 that 296 appeals and 42 writs of error were pending. Attempts to overcome arrears were not markedly successful, even after the appointment of a Vice-Chancellor in 1813 (which tended merely to add another rank to the appellate hierarchy), and the rule of 1823 which prescribed a rota of four lords to serve each day from 10 o'clock to 4 o'clock. The remedies for the situation were not found until a later date.[1]

The origins and early history of impeachment is a subject which has undergone radical revision in recent years.[2] Professor Plucknett's studies in this field[3] largely supersede previous views on the subject. There is, as Professor Plucknett observes,[4] no evidence whatsoever for the traditional view of the origin of impeachment as an indictment by the Commons. Appeal or indictment were far from being the only means of initiating criminal process in the ordinary course of the common law ; process by bills, *querelae*, informations, and conviction by " record," " notoriety," or " clamour of the people " were also well known usages, and the latter procedures were those which offered analogies upon which " impeachment " was based. The immediate precedents for the " state trials " in the Parliament of 1376, were condemnations based upon " the king's record " and the notoriety of the facts, as in the case of Thomas of Lancaster and Roger Damory, the Mortimers, and Andrew Harcla, earl of Carlisle, in 1322-1323.[5] The subsequent reversal of some of these proceedings, and dislike for convictions without trial of any kind brought a change in the procedure in the early years of Edward III., in as much as the king demanded judgment of the

---

[1] Below 643-645. [2] Below 379-385.
[3] The Origin of Impeachment, in R.H.S. Tr. (4th ser.) xxiv (1942) 47-71. The Impeachments of 1376, ibid (5th ser.) i (1951) 153-164 ; Impeachment and Attainder, ibid iii (1953) 145-158. Cf. also State Trials under Richard II., ibid ii (1952) 159-171. Professor Plucknett's researches appear to supersede or modify the views of M. V. Clarke in Fourteenth Century Studies (1937) 242-271, and of B. Wilkinson, Studies in the Constitutional History of the Thirteenth and Fourteenth Centuries (1937) 82-107. But cf. Wilkinson, Constitutional History of Medieval England, 1216-1399, ii (1952) 204-214.
[4] R.H.S. Tr. (4th ser.) xxiv 50. [5] Ibid 57.

peers on the basis of facts which he invited them to consider as notorious. Conviction by notoriety alone, however, was likewise deemed unsatisfactory, though it sufficed to bring Willoughby, C. J. to a common law trial in 1341, in which it was asserted that the king was not informed in the case by indictment nor by suit of a party, but " by the clamour of the people."[1]

When the time came for the Commons to seek means of "impeaching" Lord Latimer and Richard Lyons in the Good Parliament of 1376, it is clear that after spending about a month feeling their way, the analogy they had in mind was procedure " by clamour of the people,"[2] and it looks as though the Commons at first thought that this was sufficient in itself to procure immediate convictions, but it was a circumstance of great importance for the future of impeachment that Latimer managed to secure what was in effect a trial. His demand for an accuser was met by the Commons' decision to maintain the accusations " in common," and to " prosecute on behalf of the king." A similar procedure was followed in the several other impeachments in this Parliament.

The Good Parliament, considers Professor Plucknett "made considerable progress in settling the forms of impeachment upon legal and modern lines. The roving commission assumed by the Commons to search for scandals in its early weeks, soon turns into preparing material for a trial. Their early assumption that clamour and notoriety were equivalent to a conviction was soon destroyed as a result of the sturdy stand by Latimer. The absence of written charges is conspicuous at first, but the later cases show an unmistakable preference for written bills. Further, the principle of clamour was not even allowed to be an exception to the common law rules of procedure ; Latimer again scored a point for posterity by demanding an accuser, and so the Commons were compelled to manage the prosecution (although protesting all the time that they did so on behalf of the king). Consequently the proceedings took the familiar form of a contest between a prosecutor and an accused, with a steadily increasing legal atmosphere."[3]

It seems that the precedents for impeachment set in the Good Parliament gave disquiet to the government and there is reason to suppose that during the ten years intervening between 1376 and the impeachment of the Earl of Suffolk in 1386, " determined efforts had been made by successive governments to capture the

[1] R.H.S. Tr. (4th ser.) xxiv 65-66.
[2] Ibid 69-70 and (5th ser.) i 153-164. The heading of the record reads " William lord Latimer was impeached and accused by the clamour of the people."
[3] Ibid 164.

impeachment procedure and make it a strictly crown proceeding."[1] How far they succeeded in this endeavour is shown by the answer of the judges to Richard II.'s specific question put to them, *inter alia* in 1387. They were asked whether or not Lords and Commons, without the will of the king, can impeach in Parliament the king's officers and justices for their delicts ; and they unanimously replied that they could not.[2]

" That decision was a heavy blow to the baronial factions. No longer could they put ministers on trial without the concurrence of the crown, simply by inciting the Commons to ' clamour ' and to ' impeach.' " Other expedients had to be sought, and were found by the Lords Appellant by recourse to the criminal appeal, a procedure over which the crown had no control. There was, however, no precedent for the hearing of an appeal of treason in Parliament, and the eventual transference of these appeals to Parliament was probably due to the decision of the king himself, who thus not only gained time for political manœuvre but also got a share in this procedure as well. " The appellants tried to put things right again by their curious declaration exonerating the king from the whole affair. If they succeeded in establishing a criminal procedure independent of the crown it was only by the barest margin."[3]

The jurisdiction of the House of Lords (or rather the Court of the Lord High Steward)[4] has been curtailed by the abolition of the ancient privilege of peers to be tried by their fellow peers in treason and felony, under the Criminal Justice Act, 1948.[5]

(8) *The Court of Chancery* [6] *and the Court of Requests.*[7]

Recent work on the history of Chancery has been devoted to its growth and functions as a department of administration rather than to its origins as a court of judicature, but some important contributions have nonetheless been made to the early history of the chancellor's equitable jurisdiction.[8] It is perhaps not too much to say that this early history has not yet been written in anything like the detail with which it could and may in the future be written, but enough has already been done to show that the standard accounts need to undergo some revision.

---

[1] R.H.S. Tr. (5th ser.) ii 167. [2] Ibid. [3] Ibid 169-170.
[4] Below 388-391. [5] 11 and 12 George VI. ch. 58, § 30.
[6] Below 395-476, esp. 395-409, 454-459. [7] Below 412-416.
[8] L. Ehrlich, Proceedings against the Crown, 1216-1377, in Oxford Studies, ed. Vinogradoff, vi (1921) ; W. Barbour, Some Legal Aspects of Fifteenth Century Chancery, in Harv. Law. Rev. xxxi (1917-1918) 834-859 ; B. Wilkinson, The Chancery under Edward III. (1929) ; Studies in Constitutional History, ch. vii, and The Chancery, in The English Government at Work, I, ed. Willard and Morris (1940) 162-205 ; W. H. D. Winder, Equity in the Courts of Great Sessions, in L.Q.R. lv (1939) 106-121.

The general effect of recent work is to suggest that the exercise of some form of equitable jurisdiction by the chancellor was a good deal earlier in date than the existence of Chancery as a court of equity in the sense commonly recognized by legal antiquarians, and indeed that a recognizable court of Chancery existed a good deal earlier than has often been supposed. As so often in legal and institutional history, judicial activities were being carried on by chancellors and their assistants long before any clear distinctions were drawn between equity and common law in the modern sense, before any rigid distinctions were made between the various parts and off-shoots of the Curia Regis. The diverse and manifold activities of the king's officials in mediæval times seldom fit into the neat categories and classifications of more modern jurists, whose tendency to apply modern terminology retrospectively has often wrought havoc among historical realities.

The heading on the records of pleas heard in Chancery varied for long, but were finally superseded in 36 Edward III. by the phrase " placita coram rege in cancellaria," but long before this date effect was being given to the principle frequently reiterated " let every one who feels aggrieved come to the chancery and right will be done to him." [1] Professor Wilkinson is no doubt justified in suggesting that the executive and judicial functions of Chancery (and of Exchequer) were older than those of the Council itself,[2] if by the term " Council " is meant an organized body of councillors in the sense of the late thirteenth and fourteenth centuries. The seat of judicial discretion was of course originally the king himself, acting usually with the " counsel " of such of his entourage, whether identifiable as councillors or ministers, or of persons not normally part of his Household, as might seem fitting at any given time. By whomsoever wrongs not remediable in the course of common law were remedied, whether by councillors or council or chancellor or other official, it could only be done on the authority of the king, by the tacit or express delegation of his authority. The formal body of legal rules which became the equity administered by Chancery in the modern period did not begin as a body of legal rules, but sprang from several centuries' previous practice in the informal exercise of judicial discretion on behalf of the king by councillors and officials including the chancellor; " 'equity' resided wherever there was a representative of the king." [3]

The indispensable prelude to the growth of an independent court of Chancery exercising an equitable jurisdiction in a modern sense was a high degree of separation of Chancery from

[1] Ehrlich, op. cit. 168-170.   [2] Studies, 196.   [3] Ibid 198.

the Household and the reaching of judicial decisions by the chancellor on matters submitted to him, independently of his colleagues in the Council. The difficulty still is to determine a date by which these processes had gone far enough to make it legitimate to say that such a court had really come into existence. When such a result was brought about, the subsequent development of a more or less regular system of equity might well be described as inevitable, and perhaps also in time the formulation of theoretical explanations of the origin and nature of equitable jurisdiction.

Professor Wilkinson is justified in pointing out that a good many circumstances tended in the long run to single out the chancellor as the special channel for the exercise of the king's grace, even before the days when the " council " as a body possessed any particular executive or judicial functions of its own.[1] The chancellor, although at this time in no sense " the keeper of the king's conscience," was certainly the keeper of the king's seal, and since the use of the seal would almost inevitably be required to give effect to any decisions remedying wrongs, naturally the chancellor was the obvious vehicle for the king's grace ; and since the king could not personally find an answer to every petition that might be put in, naturally also the chancellor and his officials would have to use their wits and exercise discretion, with such advice as they might be able to get, according to circumstances. The growth of departmentalism and the growth of sharper distinctions among the various aspects of the Curia Regis alone could produce greater formality and formalism in the methods adopted and in the procedures and rules followed.

But it is not easy to determine a date at which Chancery had become sufficiently distinct from the Household as to make possible the identification of a " court of chancery " as something different from the " curia in cancellaria." Some of the evidence [2] adduced to show that a " court of chancery " existed independently as early as the reign of Edward I. seems to be open to possible objection on this score. Chancery was hardly distinct from the Household before the early fourteenth century,[3] and caution needs to be exercised in attributing the existence of an independent court of Chancery at too early a date, even if, as has been clearly shown, a more or less formal judicial function outside the course of the common law was being carried on in Chancery at least as early as the reign of Edward I.[4]

---

[1] Studies, 197.   [2] Ibid 200-201.
[3] For a summary of the subject, see S. B. Chrimes, An Introduction to the Administrative History of Mediæval England (1952), esp. 111, 113, 138, 159, 167, and references therein cited.   [4] Wilkinson, Studies 199-202.

The other necessary prelude to the growth of an independent court of chancery—the exercise of a jurisdiction by the chancellor and his own officials in Chancery apart from " the council " —is also difficult to trace. Relations between Chancery and Council continued to be very close in the first half of the fourteenth century. Professor Wilkinson is no doubt justified in saying that there might nonetheless be a court of Chancery in existence, even though on occasions it might be so " afforced " by councillors as to become for the moment indistinguishable from the Council.[1] But we can scarcely speak of an independent court of Chancery exercising an equitable jurisdiction of its own until such time as the chancellor could dispense with such afforcements in all but the most exceptional cases, and apply the " lex cancellariae " without the participation of his conciliar colleagues. It is probable, therefore, that the accepted view which does not put the existence of an independent court of Chancery exercising an equitable jurisdiction much before the fifteenth century is still the sound view. Moreover, it must be borne in mind that a substantial body of equity could scarcely arise until such time as a sustained juristic need for systematic supplementation of the common law became apparent ; and this was in the main the result of the growing formalism of the common law and the rise of new legal requirements in the fifteenth and later centuries.[2]

Although Professor Wilkinson's conclusions may not be accepted in their entirety, his work in this field is important in showing that the antecedents of equitable jurisdiction in Chancery must be looked for at least as early as the reign of Edward I., if not indeed earlier still. As he says, in discharging the judicial tasks put upon him, the chancellor " would not follow common law, but the rules and regulations of his office. This was not equity, for the conception of equity as distinct from common law had not been fully worked out in the Chancery of 1327-1337 ; nor was it, so far as we know, envisaged as a legal as distinct from an administrative code. But it was that from which equity was later to develop ; it essentially involved the exercise, though inevitably the limited exercise, of the king's grace."[3] He is also right to say that " it seems impossible any longer to imagine the Chancery as developing its equitable jurisdiction as a result of delegation from the council,"[4] if by this it is intended to deny that Chancery *derived* its jurisdiction from delegation by the council. The evidence which Professor Wilkinson adduces and which has been referred to in the paragraphs above certainly militates

---

[1] Wilkinson, Studies 206-207.
[2] The English Government at Work, i 191.
[3] Below 453-459.
[4] Studies 197.

against any such theory of *origins*. But—and this is not taken sufficiently into account by Professor Wilkinson—Chancery's judicial activities can scarcely fail to have been widened in scope and increased in quantity in consequence of the relegation to the Chancery of many petitions addressed to the council or king and council in the mid-fourteenth century, and the expansion of business doubtless had its effect upon this consolidation of Chancery's jurisdiction. Such relegation was an important part of the processes contributing to the eventual emergence of a distinct court of Chancery with its own distinctive jurisdiction.

The history of the court of Requests has not been materially added to since the pages below[1] were written, but it should be noted that there is some evidence to show that its origins are to be looked for in the Yorkist rather than in the Tudor period,[2] and it is possible that Richard Fox's long tenure of the Privy Seal (1487-1516) may have helped to establish the close connexion between the Privy Seal and the court of Requests, a connexion which survived Wolsey's apparent attempt to absorb the courts' jurisdiction into Star Chamber.[3] The history of local courts of Requests in the seventeenth century until their abolition by the County Courts Act 1846[4] has been sketched.[5]

(9) *The Council Learned and the Court of the Star Chamber*.[6]

Whilst a good deal of new work has been done on the mediæval council,[7] little that is fresh has been done on its judicial side before the Tudor and Stuart periods.

Some interesting light has been thrown on the judicial activities in the time of Henry VII. of what was apparently a committee of the council which was neither the statutory committee of 1487,[8] nor Star Chamber, but which was referred to as the " king's council learned in the law " sitting at Westminster.[9] The procedure and jurisdiction of this body, of which there are ample records, 1500-1509, were those of the council, but its functions were wholly judicial and its personnel consisted mostly

[1] Below 412-416.
[2] A. F. Pollard, The Growth of the Court of Requests, in E.H.R. lvi (1941) 300-303.
[3] Pollard, Wolsey (1929) 83-84.   [4] 9 and 10 Victoria c. 93.
[5] Winder in L.Q.R. lii (1936) 369-394.   [6] Below 477-525.
[7] For summaries and references, see J. E. A. Jolliffe, Constitutional History of Medieval England (1937) ; Taswell-Langmead, Constitutional History, 10th Ed. (1946) ; S. B. Chrimes, An Introduction to the Administrative History of Mediæval England (1952) ; J. F. Baldwin, The King's Council, in the English Government at Work, i (1940) 129-161.   [8] Below 58*.
[9] R. Somerville, Henry VII's " Council learned in the Law," in E.H.R. liv (1939) 427-442.

of lawyers, including the attorney general and the solicitor. Its jurisdiction was of an equitable nature, and its proceedings often by English Bill. It used the privy seal for warrants of subpoena, and sometimes ordered sheriffs to attach. The change was not usually stated in the privy seals, but on appearance the charge was made known, a copy of the bill supplied, and pleading was by way of answer, rejoinder and replication ; parties and witnesses were heard on oath and evidence taken. Sometimes the court would remit by commission for enquiry into facts and sometimes also to take decision. The orders made are not often recorded, but the imposition of fines, committal to the Fleet, and dismissal from office are among recorded penalties. Some matters dealt with might have gone to the common law courts, such as property disputes between parties. A good deal of the business seems to have related to matters of financial advantage to the crown, such as feudal rights, distraint of knighthood, crown debts. In short, the " council learned in the law " was one of Henry VIII.'s expedients for enhancing the crown's profits from judicature, and seemingly it did not long survive his reign. Part of this work was to be carried on by the Court of Wards and Liveries.[1]

Some important work has been done on the court of Star Chamber.[2] The irrelevance of the " pro camera stellata " Act of 1487 to the history of the Star Chamber has been further exposed, and the actual content of that Act been rehearsed.[3] This topic, and the origins of Star Chamber are sufficiently treated below,[4] but some additional information on the later history of Star Chamber can be given. On the whole, the evidence goes to show that the court of Star Chamber exercised a flourishing and mainly beneficial jurisdiction in the late Tudor and early Stuart period. Under Elizabeth I. its jurisdiction increased materially and widened in scope, especially in the direction of libel, fraud, forgery, and conspiracies. Corruption by officials, particularly local officials, figured largely among the business dealt with.

---

[1] See below 60*-62*.

[2] A. F. Pollard, Council, Star Chamber, and Privy Council under the Tudors, in E.H.R. xxxvii (1922) 337-360, 516-539, xxxviii (1923) 42-60 ; E. Skelton, The Court of Star Chamber in the reign of Elizabeth, in B.I.H.R. ix (1931-1932) 120-123 (Summaries of theses, no. lxxvii) ; H. E. I. Phillips, The Court of Star Chamber, 1603-1641, in ibid xviii (1940-1941) 35-37 (Summaries of theses no. clxxxii), and The Last Years of the Court of Star Chamber, 1630-1641, in R.H.S. Tr. (4th ser.) xxi (1939) 103-131.

[3] C. H. Williams, The So-Called Star Chamber Act, in History, xv (1930-1931) 129-135. Cf. below, iv, 60-61. A facsimile of part of the Act showing the "pro camera stellata" marginal interpolation is given in B.I.H.R. iii (1925) 114. Holdsworth was justified (see below 493-495 and iv, 60 n. 4) in rejecting Pollard's suggestion (loc. cit. xxxvii, 525-557) that the Act of 1487 was designed to deal especially with offences by members of the Household, a suggestion for which no evidence was adduced. [4] 493-495, iv, 60 seqq.

The court at this time largely served the interests of private sub-jects, rather than those of the crown, and all classes of society benefited from its vigorous efforts.[1] The valuable services of the court continued in the Stuart period, and it did something, though little, to merit the attack made upon it in the Long Parliament resulting in its abolition. A curious and still somewhat mysterious feature of its activities in this period (and probably of the later Tudor period also) is the very small proportion of the cases initiated in the court which ever got to the stage of a hearing. Thus, for example, in the period from Hilary Term 1626/7 to the end of Michaelmas vacation 1627/8, out of 775 cases initiated, only 90 (11½ per cent.) reached the stage of calling witnesses, and only 27 (3½ per cent.) reached the book of hearings. On an average, two years elapsed between the issue of a writ *subpœna ad comparendum* and a writ *ad audiendum judicium*, though often a year sufficed. But it does not appear that any considerable arrears were accumulated, and it seems than an extraordinary number of cases initiated were allowed to lapse. Some of these were doubtless vexatious suits, and others were settled without a hearing by the court itself, at any rate there was no falling off in recourse to the facilities of Star Chamber. What does appear—and this may explain a good deal—is a great increase in the proportion of public or crown cases actually heard by the court, particularly cases of breach of proclamation, conspiracies and assaults of individuals.[2]

The penalties imposed, however, were not as a rule savage; the infliction of corporal punishment was rare; the total fines imposed were not very large, and the severity of these was often mitigated by respites, by the acceptance of instalments spread sometimes over many years, and by reductions made at regular reviews held twice a year, or by pardons of arrears. The tendency in financial penalties was in many, but not all, cases in the direction of leniency. In general, the court was flourishing in its last years and on the face of it showed little grounds for abolition, and it is probable that reform rather than abolition was at first intended in the Long Parliament. The widening jurisdiction of the court had attracted the jealousy of the common lawyers and courts, its activities tended to attack the " opposi-tion " to the crown, and its actions in a certain class of case brought it into serious public odium. The corporal punishments it inflicted were mostly for libels against men in high places, especially in the hierarchy of the Church,[3] and the court now commonly included three bishops instead of the one bishop

[1] Skelton, op. cit. passim.   [2] Phillips, B.I.H.R. xviii 35-37.
[3] Phillips, R.H.S. Tr. (4th ser.) xxi 120-123.

normal in Elizabeth I.'s reign. The antagonism to the court which brought about its downfall was primarily a part of the violent anti-episcopal, even specifically the anti-Laudian, feelings of the opposition. The precipitate actions which transformed an intention to reform the court into a determination to abolish it were thus inspired more by considerations of ecclesiastical antagonism than of legal reformation. Nor was the gap in judicature easily filled. . The subsequent comment of Justice Hales is interesting: "since the pulling down of that court," he said, " there had bin in few years more perjuries and frauds unpunished than there had bin in a hundred years before."[1]

(10) *The Court of Wards and Liveries.*[2]

Although the Court of Wards and Liveries was primarily a financial court, it possessed also substantial judicial powers, and the recent appearance of a valuable study of its history and operations gives occasion for noticing here its principal features.[3] The court became established by statutes of Henry VIII.'s reign,[4] but its functions were being carried on by officials well before that date, and the need for the organization sprang primarily from Henry VII.'s deliberate policy of increasing to the utmost the profits from feudal incidents. Every effort was made by the first Tudor to exploit to the full the feudal prerogatives of the crown, especially with regard to rights of wardships, marriages and reliefs in the case of his tenants-in-chief. The number of tenants-in-chief was increased; writs of *inquisitio post mortem* were issued whenever there was the slightest possibility of financial advantage to the king; sustained efforts were made to reveal descents and the succession of minors; alleged concealments were rigorously investigated.[5] The need for keeping track of tenants-in-chief and the large amount of administrative and financial business arising, including the profitable sale of wardships, led to the elaboration of organization, central and local, to cope with it. For some time the business arising from wardships and liveries was not differentiated from other business connected with the king's prerogative rights, but by 1503 the oversight, management and sale of wardships was committed to

---

[1] Philips, R.H.S. Tr. (4th ser.) xxi 131.
[2] Below iv, 271, 466, 469, 470, 472.
[3] H. E. Bell, An Introduction to the History and Records of the Court of Wards and Liveries (1953). Cf. J. Hurstfield, Lord Burghley as Master of the Court of Wards, 1561-1598, in R.H.S. Tr. (4th ser.) xxxi (1949), 95-114.
[4] 32 Henry VIII. c. 46, 33 Henry VIII. c. 22.
[5] Bell, op. cit. 1-6. The best account of Henry VII.'s efforts in this field is to be found in Prerogativa Regis, ed. S. E. Thorne (1949), Introduction, passim. Cf. J. Hurstfield, The Revival of Feudalism in Early Tudor England, in History (n.s.) xxxvii (1952) 131-145.

a single officer, from whose organization was to spring the later court of Wards.[1]   Until the statutory establishment of the court in 1540-1542, much of the judicial business arising was referred to the Council Learned in the Law, which disposed of this class of litigation in the later years of Henry VII. and early years of Henry VIII.[2]   This practice seems to have been abandoned in 1528,[3] from which date the masters of the Wards sat regularly for judicial purposes and employed the forms of a court of law. The statute of 1540-1541 establishing the court of Wards, and of 1541-1542 adding Liveries, did little, therefore, but give a statutory basis for arrangements already in existence.   The occasion for this statutory recognition seems to have been largely the consequences of the Statute of Uses,[4] and to some extent the statute establishing the court of Augmentations.[5]   The growing practice of making feoffments to uses had for long tended to deprive the king of his rights in the lands concerned, and part of the Statute of Uses[6] was designed to prevent settlements which would have that effect.   The act for the court of Augmentations provided that in granting out abbeys and their lands the court should reserve a tenure-in-chief by knight service, and thus increase the number of holdings *in capite*.   The growth of business resulting from these causes inspired the establishment of a court of Wards and Liveries on a statutory basis.[7]   The court was established as a court of record with its seal in the custody of the master ; the king's wards and lands were placed under its survey ; accounts of such were to be made to it and not to the Exchequer, and no process was to issue from the Exchequer for matters under cognizance of the court now established.   It was further provided that upon a ward reaching full age, his livery was not to be passed without reference to the court.   As a consequence liveries were united with wardships in the court in 1541-1542, and the office of master of the liveries merged into it.

The jurisdiction of the court was wholly concerned, directly or indirectly, with revenue matters arising out of wardship and livery ; matters touching the levy or discharge of debts due to the crown, concealment of tenures, refusal of marriage and levy of consequential fines, imperfections in inquisitions post mortem, interpretations of uses and wills, problems of land law, and the like, whether in the interests of the crown, the wards, or tenants.

---

[1] Bell, op. cit. 6.   Cf. W. C. Richardson, The Surveyor of the King's Prerogative, in E.H.R. lvi (1941) 52-75.

[2] Bell, op. cit. 4-5 ; Thorne, op. cit. vi ; cf. above 57*-58*.   Professor Thorne points out that as many as eight Readings on the Prerogativa were given in the Inns of Court in the reign of Henry VII., but none earlier so far as can be ascertained.   [3] Bell, op. cit. 12.   [4] 27 Henry VIII., c. 10.

[5] 27 Henry VIII., c. 27.   [6] Below iv, 450-453.   [7] Bell, op. cit. 13-15.

The legal issues might be settled by master and " the council " of the court or by an official on their own initiative with the advice of the attorney of the court predominant ; or, if the point was difficult, then consultation might be sought with the law officers of the crown, serjeants, or common law judges. Decisions were not always in the crown's favour, but decisions reached resulted in decrees, which were regarded as precedents. Penal powers for enforcement of decrees were used, whether committal to the custody of the usher of the court, to the Fleet or Counter, or the imposition of fines, with the rigours of Star Chamber in the background for heavier sanction if necessary.[1]

Procedure was in general similar to that in use in Chancery, Star Chamber, and court of Requests, and was at first modelled upon that of the Duchy Chamber of Lancaster. Pleadings were all in English, initiated by bill or information. Writs of privy seal were used to procure the appearance of defendants and to enforce penalties. Procedure went by way of sworn answer, demurer if any, rebuttal, interrogations if needed, replication, rejoinder. Commissions to hear witnesses locally might be appointed, or to examine deeds and muniments ; injunctions pending settlement might be issued. Completion of pleadings was followed by publication in court of the depositions of witnesses and the appointment of a day for hearing.[2]

The varying fortunes of the courts' administration of revenues cannot be followed here, nor the curious details of the last years of the court,[3] when, during the years 1643-1645, the king maintained it at Oxford, and Parliament maintained it also at Westminster, to the confusion of litigants and officials but to the profit of both king and Parliament, pending its abolition by ordinance of Parliament in 1645-1646.[4] It was not revived at the Restoration, and the conversion of tenures by knight service into socage and the abolition of feudal incidents[5] of tenure soon after put an end to the reason for the court's existence.

III. COURTS OF A SPECIAL JURISDICTION

(1) *Courts administering the Law Merchant.*[6]

The administration of the law merchant in the central courts has received further illustration and comment, with considerable advantage to the early history of the rules and procedure under the law merchant.[7] Changes in the mercantile jurisdiction in

---

[1] Bell, op. cit. 87-111.   [2] Ibid.   [3] Ibid 150-166.
[4] Acts and Ordinances of the Interregnum, i 833.
[5] 12 Charles II., c. 24.   [6] Below 526-573.
[7] Select Cases concerning the Law Merchant, ed. H. Hall (S.S. xlvi, 1239-1633 (1929), xlix, 1251-1779 (1932)). Much valuable information on the early history of

the seventeenth and eighteenth centuries have been the subject of some illuminating discussion.[1]

The rather rigid lines usually drawn between mercantile courts and the common law courts in the mediæval period have become somewhat loosened as a result. " To the mediæval lawyer the jurisdiction of the merchant courts was little more than a limited devolution of authority made in the interest of speed and simplicity. The common law courts did not hesitate to try cases involving merchants if occasion arose. It was generally recognized, as in the Ordinances of the Staple, that the parties had their choice of pleading in the merchant or common law courts, though the king's council and the Chancery proved the most convenient non-mercantile medieval courts to deal with difficult cases.[2] "

Miss Sutherland calls attention to the curious decay of mercantile courts in England at a time when elsewhere they were being strengthened. This phenomenon is attributed partly to the growth of Admiralty courts in the sixteenth century onwards, courts which took in the administration of maritime laws, with a consequential share in the private international law of Europe ; partly to the sharp distinctions drawn in the sixteenth century between traders and merchants. The merchants were primarily exporters, and as such tended to develop new customs relating to credit instruments and negotiable securities, as well as exchange and marine insurance which were not adequately covered in the law merchant itself.[3] The jurisdiction in this sphere occasionally exercised by the king's council in the sixteenth century did not survive the activities of the Long Parliament, with the result that the common lawyers in the seventeenth century set out to absorb mercantile law in general into the common law system, a process leading in effect to a " reception " in the course of the eighteenth century, a process assisted partly by statutes and partly by the deliberate actions of eminent judges of the common law courts. The well-known achievements of Holt and Mansfield in this sphere had their background in earlier generations.[4]

mercantile law in London is to be found in the Calendar of Early Mayors' Court Rolls, ed. A. H. Thomas. For the earliest recorded case tried before Warden or Mayor according to law merchant, see H. G. Richardson, Law Merchant in London in 1292, in E.H.R. xxxvii (1922) 242-249.

[1] L. Stuart Sutherland, The Law Merchant in England in the seventeenth and eighteenth centuries, in R.H.S. Tr. (4th ser.) xvii (1934) 144-176.

[2] Ibid. 153-153.

[3] The influence of Dutch legal literature upon the publication of treatises on merchant law is marked in this period. Ibid 157.

[4] Cf. v 102-154, vi 519-522, xii 524-542. A valuable study of Mansfield has appeared in C.H.S. Fifoot, Lord Mansfield (1932).

(2) *The Cinque Ports.*[1]

A valuable study of the peculiar courts of the Cinque Ports has appeared.[2] The king's court of Shepway,[3] regularly meeting from 1150, and well-developed in the thirteenth century, was primarily concerned with the royal interests, and resembled a shire court in some respects and a hundred court in others. By the fourteenth century the Portsmen had acquired exemption from all external courts except Shepway, and the Warden had become the only royal officer authorized to summon and preside over this court. It became also a court of appeal from the courts of the ports, and developed an extensive equitable jurisdiction. The Warden having become the sole judge in the court, its sessions tended in the seventeenth century to be transferred to Dover, of the Castle of which the Warden was Constable, and to be barely distinguishable from the court of Castle Gate, which exercised a jurisdiction in civil cases, mostly debt and trespass, over tenants of the Castle.[4] The court of St. James's Church,[5] flourishing from the mid-fourteenth century, with an extensive jurisdiction over the Portsmen in trespasses and cognate spheres, became the most important and active of the Warden's courts, with a permanent trained staff and, to avoid reference to Chancery, with an equitable jurisdiction in the sixteenth century.

The Warden of the Cinque Ports in the fifteenth century onwards was well established with the powers of an Admiral,[6] and developed an admiralty jurisdiction within the Ports; his admiralty courts continued to be held locally in the ports in which cases arose, but those held at Dover tended to be confused with the equitable jurisdiction of the court of St. James's Church, which alone seems to have possessed a machinery for regular jurisdiction.

The general assembly of the Cinque Ports, the court of Brodhull, derived probably from an ancient popular court, which became combined in the fourteenth century with the Guestling, of quite different origin, was primarily concerned with the defence of the privileges of the Ports, and scarcely ranks as a court of jurisdiction.[7]

(3) *Courts of Admiralty and Prize Jurisdiction.*[8]

No fresh work on the Court of Admiralty and Prize Courts of major importance has appeared, but certain items of interest need to be mentioned.[9]

[1] Below 532-533.
[2] K. M. E. Murray, The Constitutional History of the Cinque Ports (1935).
[3] Ibid 60-101.   [4] Ibid 102-104.   [5] Ibid 105-119.
[6] Ibid 120-133.   [7] Ibid 139-190.   [8] Below 544-568.
[9] W. Senior, The First Admiralty Judges, in L.Q.R. xxxv (1919) 73-83, and

Work on the earliest records of the High Court of Admiralty has confirmed that it probably existed as a separate court in the time of Edward III., soon after the Battle of Sluys.[1] Originally intended to deal mainly with piracy and spoil, it acquired a jurisdiction over all cases affecting piracy, privateering, ships, and merchandise on the high seas or overseas. A good deal of this wider jurisdiction continued to be dealt with in Chancery in the fifteenth century, but a great expansion of the High Court's activities came in the early years of Henry VIII., in consequence of his wide patent granted in 1525, well before the statute of 1540. Much business relating to mercantile disputes formerly dealt with in Chancery, now passed to the High Court of Admiralty, records of which begin in 1515.[2]

(4) The Ecclesiastical Courts.[3]

(i) Relations between Church and State.[4]

Recent literature on the subject of relations of Church and State in the mediæval period, on the canon law in England, and on the ecclesiastical courts and their jurisdiction, is very extensive, and from many points of view the history of ecclesiastical jurisdiction in England is being largely rewritten, or written for the first time. It is not possible to do more here than to refer to the more important items in this large and growing literature and to allude to the significance of some of it.

The fundamental theme of the relations of Church and State in the early mediæval period has received a fresh orientation from the researches of the late Professor Z. N. Brooke.[5] We are now able to trace the consequences of the Norman Conquest upon the Church in England with particular reference to the reception and diffusion of the continental collections of canon law of the eleventh century, and the discovery and assessment of Lanfranc's own collection of decrees and canons, with Lanfranc's own marked passages, has provided a new starting point for the history of canon law in England.[6] The introduction and widespread use of the later collections of the twelfth century,

Admiralty Matters in the Fifteenth Century, ibid 290-299; E. S. Roscoe, History of the English Prize Court (1924), and Studies in the History of the Admiralty and Prize Courts (1932); D. O. Skilton and R. Holsworthy, High Court of Admiralty Examinations, 1637-1638 (1932); G. F. James and J. J. Sutherland Shaw, Admiralty Administration and Personnel, 1619-1714, in B.I.H.R. xiv (1936-1937) 10-24. 166-183; A. A. Ruddock, The Earliest Records of the High Court of Admiralty, 1515-1558, in ibid xxii (1949) 139 151. For Admiralty courts in the early colonies, see H. J. Crump, Colonial Admiralty Jurisdiction in the Seventeenth Century (1931).   [1] Ruddock, op. cit. 140.
    [2] Ibid 141.   [3] Below 580-632.   [4] Below 580-598.
    [5] The English Church and the Papacy (1931).   [6] Ibid 57-83.

including Gratian, stressing papal authority as they did, and the absence of any special English collection, has demonstrated beyond question that the law of the Church in England was the same as elsewhere.[1] The Church in England has been fully revealed as simply a part of the Church Universal in matters of papal authority, canon law, and ecclesiastical jurisdiction. With this background, the controversy over investitures, the difficulties between Henry I. and Anselm,[2] the nature of the Constitutions of Clarendon, and the relations between Henry II. and Becket,[3] have been studied afresh, and put into their proper perspective, as well as the meaning of the aspirations of the papalist party in the English Church under Stephen,[4] and King John.[5] The history of the canon law in England,[6] and of the legislation of the English Church itself,[7] has received and is receiving detailed study.

Some of the topics of conflict between Church and State have received further attention. The history of the use by the royal courts of the writ of prohibition to restrain the jurisdiction of Church courts has been examined with a wealth of detail, and a significant fresh light has been thrown on the whole subject by the evident frequency with which the writ was sued out by clerics themselves or by third parties in order to shield clerics from the wrath of their superiors. The whole procedure adopted in con-nexion with this writ from its first use in the early 1180's to the end of the thirteenth century has now been revealed.[8]

The antagonism of the Church authorities to the issue of the writ of prohibition in what they considered improper cases, leading up to Edward I.'s attempt at compromise in the writ *circumspecte agatis* has been re-examined. The decrees of the Council of Reading of 1279, including provision for the pronounce-ment of excommunication upon those who maliciously deprived the Church of her rights by suing out writs of prohibition, were

---

[1] The English Church and the Papacy (1931) 84-154.   [2] Ibid 164-175.

[3] Ibid 191 seqq. The whole subject is fully but not always cogently discussed in R. Foreville, L'Église et la Royauté en Angleterre sous Henri II. Plantagenet (1942).   [4] Brook, op. cit. 188-190.   [5] Ibid 215 seqq.

[6] For a summary, see S. E. Thorne, Le Droit Canonique en Angleterre, in Rev. Historique de Droit Français et Étranger (4th ser.) (1934) 499-513, and for the subject generally P. Fournier and G. Le Bras, Histoire des Collections Canoniques en Occident depius les Fausses Décretales jusqu'au Décrit de Gratian, 2 vols. (1931-1932).

[7] See especially C. R. Cheney, The Legislation of the Mediaeval English Church, in E.H.R. l (1935) 193-224, 385-417, and English Synodalia of the Thirteenth Century (1941).

[8] N. Adams, The Writ of Prohibition of Court Christian, in Minnesota Law Rev. xx (1935-1936) 272-293, and especially G. B. Flahiff, The Use of Prohibitions by Clerics against Ecclesiastical Courts in England, in Mediæval Studies, Pontifical Institute of Toronto, iii (1941) 101-116, and The Writ of Prohibition to Courts Christian in the Thirteenth Century, ibid vi (1944) 261-313, vii (1945) 229-290.

not, as has been thought, withdrawn in the face of Edward I.'s wrath, but substantially conformed by the Council of Lambeth of 1281,[1] and it was the resolute attitude of the Church that induced the issue of the writ *circumspecte agatis* in June or July 1286.[2]

The Statutes of Præmunire have been subjected to fresh interpretations which both reduce their general significance and put them into a better perspective.   The Statute of Præmunire of 1353 has largely been shorn of its political significance,[3] and reduced to a measure to improve process against those who drew another outside the realm in a plea cognizance of which appertained to the king, or who sought to nullify a judgment of a royal court by an appeal to another court.   No new claims against the papacy were made in the statute ; the appeals aimed at therein had been attacked for half a century before.   Over one hundred prohibited appeals to Rome in the period 1307-1353 are known, mostly relating to disputes over patronage.   The statute substituted process by writ of arrest followed by the exigent for the older procedure by distress in the case of defaulters, especially fugitives from justice, but did not declare penalties for those convicted ; the penalties of forfeiture and imprisonment were not declared in the statute, but were agreed upon in Parliament.

The so-called " Great Statute of Præmunire " of 1393 had a very limited purpose in original intention.[4]   Its prohibition upon such bulls and instruments as were against ₊the king, crown, regality, and the realm, seems to have been designed primarily to protect ecclesiastics from punishment for executing the judgment of secular courts and to prevent arbitrary translations of bishops. The threat of it was sufficient to induce Boniface IX to refrain from using translations as a political weapon, and for many years neither Parliament nor courts appear to have taken any notice of the statute, which did not evoke any protest from Rome. After securing its original purpose, the statute fell into obscurity for nearly forty years.   Its re-discovery in the fifteenth century led to its being used to the detriment of the spiritual courts, notably in the Duke of Gloucester's attack upon Cardinal Beaufort in 1426-1431, and paved the way for the wider interpretations and application in the time of Henry VIII.

[1] H. Johnstone, Archbishop Pecham and the Council of Lambeth of 1281, in Essays to T. F. Tout (1925) 171-188.

[2] For discussion and text of the writ, see E. B. Graves, Circumspecte Agatis, in E.H.R. xliii (1928) 1-20.

[3] E. B. Graves, The Legal Significance of the Statute of Praemunire of 1353, in Anniversary Essays by students of C. H. Haskins (1929) 57-80.

[4] W. T. Waugh, The Great Statute of Praemunire, in E.H.R. xxxvii (1922) 173-205.

Nothing fundamentally new regarding the legal aspects of the Tudor supremacy over the Church has come to light, but the whole subject has been re-surveyed,[1] and important new evidence of the decisive intervention by Elizabeth I. in the establishment of the Elizabethan Church Settlement has been brought forward.[2]

(ii) *The Courts Christian.*[3]

The actual working of the ecclesiastical courts, more especially in the mediæval period, is a subject which has only recently been examined and revealed in detail, and the task is one still continuing. .A number of valuable contributions [4] have been made to this large and important subject, and a general picture of the operations of the courts, at any rate in the province and diocese of Canterbury, can be drawn.

Metropolitical Jurisdiction of the Archbishop of Canterbury

The court of Canterbury[5] existed as a metropolitical court of appeal from the Province, with separate records and officials from at least the middle of the thirteenth century, and although the suffragan bishops of the Province viewed the development of the distinct court with some jealousy, it was clearly recognized by 1282 that the archbishop could delegate and had delegated part of his metropolitical jurisdiction to the court of Canterbury. The nomenclature used to identify this court was often varied, and from the end of the thirteenth century the court normally sat in the Church of St. Máry de Arcubus (Bow Church) in the city of London—hence the more modern term " the court of the Arches." In the absence of the Official of the court of Canterbury, it was often presided over by his commissary-general, the Dean of the Arches, or often the ·two offices were combined. Nevertheless, the court of Canterbury from the late thirteenth century onwards had an organization, staff, and substantial appellate jurisdiction from courts in the Province, and a small jurisdiction of first instance arising from the causes

---

[1] Notably by J. D. Mackie in The Early Tudors (1952), J. B. Black, The Reign of Elizabeth (1936), and T. M. Parker, The English Reformation to 1558 (1950).
[2] See J. E. Neale, The Elizabethan Acts of Supremacy and Uniformity, in E.H.R. lxv (1950) 309-332, and in a wider setting in Elizabeth I. and her Parliaments (1953). [3] Below 598-614.
[4] M. M. Morgan, Early Canterbury Jurisdiction, in E.H.R. lx (1945) 392-399; I. J. Churchill, Canterbury Administration, 2 vols. (1933); B. L. Woodcock, Medieval Ecclesiastical Courts in the Diocese of Canterbury (1952); E. F. Jacob, The Register of Henry Chichele, Archbishop of Canterbury, 1414-1443, i (1943), and A. Hamilton Thompson, The English Clergy and their Organization in the Later Middle Ages (1947) both contain information on jurisdictional matters. F. Barlow, Durham Jurisdictional Peculiars (1950) is valuable for its subject.
[5] Churchill, op. cit. i 425-469.

concerning officials and members of the archbishop's household, all of whom were subject to the jurisdiction of the Official of the court. Its appellate jurisdiction comprised mainly appeals from the sentence of provincial courts, by defect of justice, or " tuitorial " appeals for the protection of the " status quo."

The Official of the court of Canterbury usually had someone associated with him as his commissary-general, normally the Dean of the Arches, until in the late fifteenth century the same man was commonly appointed to both offices. An Examiner-general was appointed to hold interrogatories, and he might preside over the court in the absence of the Official and commissary-general. The court had also its accredited advocates and proctors, its registrar and apparitor.

Appeals in the court of Canterbury might in some instances be called into a tribunal closer to the archbishop himself—the court of Audience.[1] The archbishop could not in practice delegate all aspects of his archiepiscopal authority, still less his legatine authority, but the growth of business by direct appeal by complaint or otherwise coming to the Audience led to the forma- tion of a distinct court of Audience. The archbishop claimed to hear all complaints and appeals made by his suffragans' subjects, and heard some of them in person, but delegated more to the hearing of others appointed for the purpose, whether commissaries especially appointed, or auditors or commissaries acting under a general commission. The growth of business led, in the thirteenth century, to a consolidation of what had been a loose and flexible organization and the formation of a court of Audience analogous to the court of Canterbury, whose staff were frequently called upon to act in Audience.

The archbishops claimed that probate, the appointment of executors, and accounts in all cases testate and intestate in which the deceased had goods in more than one diocese of the Province belonged to the archbishop by prerogative of the Church of Canterbury. This claim led by the usual process of delegation to the formation of another court with its commissary or keeper, registrars and apparitors—the Prerogative court.[2] The com- missions were usually to the Official of the court of Canterbury, or the Dean of the Arches, or to the Chancellor, and although its jurisdiction was not exercised without protest from the suffragan bishops of the Province, the Prerogative court con- tinued on its way.

These three courts by no means exhausted the jurisdictional functions of the archbishop even in his metropolitical capacity. He might himself be the recipient of delegated authority by the

[1] Churchill, op. cit. i 470-499.   [2] Ibid 380-424.

papacy. He might be appointed Judge Delegate and Conservator by papal authority, and perhaps himself sub-delegate such authority or part of such authority in certain cases.[1] He was granted spiritual jurisdiction by Urban V. in 1379 in Calais and the neighbouring parts, a jurisdiction delegated to a commissary and continuously exercised until the final loss of Calais in 1577, except for a break of about twenty years from 1421.[2]

Diocesan Jurisdictions of Canterbury.

The higher degree of differentiation and consolidation manifested in the courts of a metropolitan jurisdiction in the late thirteenth century inevitably induced a similar process in the principal court of the diocese at much the same period—the Consistory court. The judge of this court was " the commissary-general " of Canterbury. There is no satisfactory evidence for the separate existence of this judicial office before 1278, and probably such a distinct office was not needed until the Official came to be permanently occupied with the business of the court of Canterbury meeting in London.[3] Probably before that date, or thereabouts, the provincial and diocesan business of the archbishop's court was undifferentiated, but from the late thirteenth century the provincial business went to the court of Canterbury meeting in London, whilst the diocesan business continued to be dealt with at Canterbury in a court which continued to be called the " Consistory Court," in matters of first instance. This court remained, however, in some degree subordinate, for appeals lay from it to the court of Canterbury,[4] or to the court of Audience, whilst appeals from the court of the Archdeacon of Canterbury also lay to those courts, not to the Consistory court.

The Consistory court normally met, at any rate in the fourteenth century, for three days at three-weekly intervals within the Cathedral, probably under the north-west tower of the nave, sometimes outside the Cathedral itself.[5] From the late fifteenth century the court also went on circuit in the diocese a number of times a year.[6]

Awkward problems inevitably arose regarding the carrying on of the jurisdiction of the Consistory court during what might be a prolonged vacancy in the archbishopric, as, for example, during the years 1240-1245, 1270-1273, 1278-1279, and 1292-1294. In the absence of an archbishop, his court could not, of course, be carried on in the ordinary way, but the need for a continuing jurisdiction gave rise, not without complicated conflicting claims,

---

[1] Churchill, op. cit. i 500-507. [2] Ibid 508-519. [3] Woodcock, op. cit. 6-8.
[4] Ibid 12-13. [5] Ibid 31-33. [6] Ibid 33-34.

to a recognized Sede Vacante Jurisdiction.[1]   In the thirteenth
century the three rival claimants for the exercise of Canterbury
jurisdiction on the death or resignation of the archbishop were
the bishop of the province, the prior and chapter of Christchurch,
and the Archdeacon of Canterbury.   A compromise seems to
have been reached as between the bishop and the prior and
chapter in 1278, whereby it was agreed that the Bishop of London
should choose the Official of Canterbury from two persons
nominated by the prior and chapter, and the Official should
then be formally appointed by the prior and chapter.   But
the rival claims of the prior and chapter and the archdeacon
in the sphere of provincial jurisdiction appear never to have
been finally resolved, and remained a matter for fierce dispute,
varying according to circumstances.   On the whole, however, the
prior and chapter were successful in maintaining a commissary-
general of their own nomination for carrying on the jurisdiction
of the Consistory court, and would go to great lengths to enforce
recognition of their nominee upon the archdeacons.

The jurisdiction of the archdeaconry of Canterbury probably
dates at least from the date of Lanfranc's committal to his
archdeacon of all jurisdiction in the city and diocese of Canterbury
excepting churches in the archbishop's patronage (the exempt
parishes) and the hearing of matrimonial causes.[2]   A deputy or
vice-archdeacon, or later the official of the archdeacon, appears
by the end of the twelfth century as the effective head of the
archdeacon's court.   In the fourteenth century especially, the
archdeacons were mostly absentees and their officials tended to
be submissive to the archbishops and their commissaries-general,
to whom they inevitably looked for preferment.   In the late
mediæval period, the court held sessions in Canterbury usually
once a fortnight ; went on circuit through the rural deaneries of
the western part of the diocese fourteen times a year, and about
ten times a year to the deanery of Sandwich.

The existence of a number of " exempt parishes "[3]—exempt
that is from the jurisdiction of the archdeacon—further complicated the jurisdictional organization of the diocese.   The early
history of these exempt parishes remains obscure ; most of them
contained archiepiscopal manors or possessed revenues which provided incomes for offices in the archbishop's administration ; all
were in the archbishop's collation.   In some the rectors had
been granted or had acquired powers which virtually made them

[1] Woodcock, op. cit. 15-19 ; Churchill, op. cit. i 551-570.
[2] Woodcock, op. cit. 19-21.
[3] There was 25 such in the early fourteenth century but the number varied.
See Woodcock, ibid 21-25 ; Churchill, op. cit. 83-94. Cf. Barlow, op. cit. for
Durham.

" petty archdeacons." Much conflict over jurisdiction inevitably arose in consequence of claims to autonomy by such rectors, whose jurisdictional independence, however, tended to lapse, and became virtually extinct by the end of the fourteenth century. The archbishop's commissary-general alone exercised jurisdiction over the exempt parishes as a whole.

The relations between these various jurisdictions within the diocese were necessarily complex and fraught with occasions for disputes, and the surviving records are such as to make impracticable any general account for a period earlier than the late fourteenth century.[1] The commissary-general of the archbishop exercised the sole ordinary jurisdiction in the exempt parishes in matters of correction and probate, whilst the archdeacon had no jurisdiction at all in the exempt parishes. But outside the exempt parishes, the jurisdictions of the commissary-general and the archdeacon were concurrent, except in matrimonial causes, probate, and visitations. Matrimonial causes were reserved for the commissary-general ; in the exempt parishes he also proved wills and granted letters of administration, and exercised the archbishop's prerogative jurisdiction in probate in cases where the deceased left goods in two or more dioceses including that of Canterbury. Routine visitations of the deaneries were carried out normally by the archdeacon's official, whilst the commissary-general " visited " the non-exempt parishes only by specific delegation from the archbishop, usually in connexion with archiepiscopal visitations. In the remaining spheres of Instance and Ex-Officio business (roughly " civil " and " criminal " jurisdiction in the ecclesiastical sense),[2] the commissary-general and the archdeacons' powers were identical, and persons living in non-exempt parishes might be cited to appear in either court in those connexions, according to circumstances and convenience. Neither the consistory court nor the archdeacons' court possessed exclusive jurisdiction. Although the bulk of ordinary litigation was disposed of in one or other of these courts, cases of first instance might be heard by the court of Audience in the course of its travels from one archiepiscopal manor to another, especially when the plaintiffs were persons of consequence, or the cause was one of importance, such as heresy, disobedience, or the purgation of a criminous clerk.

(iii) *The Jurisdiction of the Courts.*[3]

The actual exercise of jurisdiction by the courts christian has received much more concrete and detailed study in recent years [4]

---

[1] Woodcock, op. cit. 26-29
[3] Below 614-632.
[2] See below.
[4] Particularly Woodcock, op. cit.

and some of the conclusions reached can be briefly mentioned here.

The Canterbury courts transacted three main types of business, (1) Instance, the hearing of cases between party and party, (2) Ex-Officio, the correction of faults by the judge by virtue of his office, (3) Probate.

Cases of Instance comprised matrimonial causes, including causes described as *devortii, reclamationis bannorum,* and *restitutionis conjugalium* ; testamentary cases, the majority of which were claims by executors for debts, but including cases described as *impedimenti ultime voluntatis* and *temerarie administrationis bonorum defuncti* ; disputes as to title ; suits relating to ecclesiastical dues, usury, defamation, perjury and other miscellaneous causes.[1]

The jurisdiction Ex-Officio[2] covered a very wide range of offences. In 1474, for example, a total of 158 charges was brought in the Consistory court ; of these 110 for sexual offences, 11 for not attending church, 11 for illicit Sunday trading, 3 for obstructing ecclesiastical jurisdiction, 2 for perjury. The great bulk of cases Ex-Officio arose out of a continuous process of " inquisition " rather than from the periodical visitations of the deaneries, and mainly from the activities of the apparitors, until the late sixteenth century, when the main source of information came to be presentment by church wardens at regular and frequent visitations.[3]

The three sanctions employed by the courts to enforce obedience were suspension *ab ingressu ecclesiae,* excommunication, or " aggravated " excommunication. Suspension was generally used as the first sanction against defendants who failed to appear in court at the due time ; excommunication was resorted to sometimes as a first sanction, but usually only in cases where the culprit's offence was " manifest," and generally only as a reserve penalty for continued obstinacy. The greater or " aggravated " excommunication remained as the severest penalty available in the church courts, which not only cut the excommunicate off from the sacraments of the church and deprived him of the prospect of christian burial, but also cut him off from the society of the faithful—at least in theory. Finally it was possible for the archbishop, his official, or *sede vacante* the prior and chapter of Christchurch, to address a signification to Chancery for a writ of *de excommunicato capiendo* in cases where excommunicates remained contumacious for forty days or longer. Absolution could, of course, be granted to suspended or excommunicated

---

[1] Particularly Woodcock, op. cit. 82-92.
[2] Ibid 79-82. [3] Ibid 68-71.

persons, and the case proceed from the point at which it had been interrupted, whilst penances of various degrees were awarded for the purgation of offences open to correction by the court.[1]

Mr. Woodcock reached the conclusion that the increased professionalism of the ecclesiastical lawyers by the end of the fifteenth century had brought a high degree of efficiency to the jurisdiction of the courts. " Generally," he wrote,[2] " the second half of the fifteenth century appears to have been the apogee of the medieval ecclesiastical court, both as regards efficiency and volume of business. Instance business, largely owing to the increase in the handling of petty debt, increased to such an extent that extra proctors were brought in to handle it. The reasons for this volume of litigation are obscure at the moment, but civil disorder and the expensive or inefficient character of secular courts may have contributed towards it. There can be no doubt that the ecclesiastical courts, in so far as Instance business was concerned, were very popular with many different elements of the population.

There is little evidence that the political disturbances of either the fourteenth or the fifteenth centuries disturbed the business of the courts to any substantial degree, at any rate in Canterbury province. But the sixteenth century was to see the weakening of their jurisdiction. By 1500 a serious decline in Instance business, including much of the litigation for the recovery of petty debt. The reasons for the decline can as yet only be surmised. Possibly the growing efficiency of the secular courts, especially urban courts, and the development of new " courts of conscience " may have tended to divert some of this class of litigation away from the ecclesiastical courts."[3] Their jurisdiction ex-officio, however, continued and flourished for long after the Tudor Reformation.[4]

Several matters of importance in connexion with the jurisdiction of the courts christian and its relations with the secular power have been the subjects of particular study in recent years. The antecedents to the statutory imposition of the death penalty for heresy have been scrutinised.[5] It has been shown that the implications of the Constitutions of Clarendon, clause I, confining jurisdiction in advowsons to the royal courts

---

[1] For details, see Woodcock, op. cit. 93-102. For valuable information on the personnel and practice of the courts, see ibid 37-78.

[2] Ibid 104.   [3] Ibid 109-110.

[4] For a convenient list of ecclesiastical court records in print, see Handlist of Record Publications, ed. R. Somerville (British Records Association Pamphlet no. 3 1951) 109.

[5] H. G. Richardson, Heresy and the Lay Power under Richard II., in E.H.R. (1936) 1-28.

were not finally settled even in the time of Bracton.[1] The conflict between the jurisdictions over tithes—a matter " neither very spiritual nor very temporal " has been examined in detail, and the conclusion drawn that in the thirteenth and fourteenth centuries the common law courts were steadily appropriating an area of jurisdiction long claimed by the church courts.[2] The thorny judicial problems of frankalmoin tenure and the origins of the assize *utrum* have been further elucidated.[3] The attack of the common lawyers on the oath *ex-officio* as used in church courts, and its fruitful results in establishing the principle that no one is bound to accuse himself, has been investigated.[4]

Extensive consideration[5] has been given to the subject of benefit of clergy, and the history of this theme has undergone substantial revision.

In the period from the Norman Conquest to the death of Archbishop Becket, the secular courts were dominant in the matter of the treatment of criminous clerks ; thereafter until about the middle of the reign of Henry III., the position was reversed in favour of the ecclesiastical powers ; but from then onwards the lay power gradually reasserted itself and by slow stages whittled down the privilege of clergy. This latter process is one which has been insufficiently realized, and which requires some attention here.

From the later years of Henry III. onwards to the end of the fifteenth century changes were introduced which modified existing practice and gradually built up the common law doctrine of benefit of clergy.[6] Among these changes was the development of the practice of the lay court in inquiring into charges made, the delivery of a clerk to the ecclesiastical court only after a jury verdict, and the introduction of literacy as a test for benefit of clergy, at first merely as a supplement to older methods of proof, later as competent proof.

In this period, preliminary hearings in the lay court can be

---

[1] J. W. Gray, The Ius Præsentandi in England from the Constitutions of Clarendon to Bracton, in E.H.R. lxvii (1952) 481-509. Cf. below 630.

[2] N. Adams, The Judicial Conflict over Tithes, in E.H.R. lii (1937) 1-22.

[3] E. G. Kimball, The Judicial Aspects of Frank Almoign Tenure, in E.H.R. xlvii (1932) 1-11 ; S. E. Thorne, The Assize Utrum and the Canon Law in England, in Columbia Law Rev. xxxiii (1933) 426-436. Cf. below 630.

[4] M. H. Maguire, The Attack of the Common Lawyers on the Oath Ex-Officio as administered in the Ecclesiastical Courts in England, in Essays in Honor of C. H. McIlwain (1936) 199-229.

[5] C. B. Firth, Benefit of Clergy in the time of Edward IV., in E.H.R. xxxii (1917) 175-191 ; L. C. Gabel, Benefit of Clergy in the later Middle Ages (1929) ; A. Lane Poole, Outlawry as a punishment for Criminous Clerks, in Historical Essays in Honour of James Tait (1933) 239-246 ; C. R. Cheney, The Punishment of Felonious Clerks, in E.H.R. li (1936) 215-236. Cf. below 615-616.

[6] Gabel, op. cit. passim.

classified in three categories, (a) those in which the accused confined himself to claiming benefit of clergy, (b) those in which the accused denied the charge and put himself upon the verdict of a jury, and if found guilty claimed his clergy, and (c) those in which the accused likewise put himself upon the verdict of a jury, but *salvo sibi privilegio clericali*. Even in category (a), however, the usual practice of the lay court, notwithstanding Bracton's account of the matter,[1] was to put the charge to a jury, and then to deliver the accused to the ordinary as a *clericus convictus* or *quietus*.[2] This procedure was in effect one of trial without judgment, for the ultimate fate of the accused was governed by the decision of the church court, and his chattels temporarily forfeited by the lay court might be restored if the church found in his favour.

Procedure in category (b) was not common until the end of Edward II.'s reign, when its frequency increased until it became the established procedure in the fifteenth century.[3] Possibly the accused thought they had a better chance of acquittal under this procedure, for although there were no acquittals in category (a) after the statute *Pro Clero*, 25 Edward III. st. b. c. 4, the percentage of acquittals in category (b) remained high.[4]

Cases falling in category (c) belong mostly to the reign of Edward I. and to Middlesex ; the procedure seems not to have commended itself to the lay court, and 56 convictions out of 150 such cases are recorded.[5]

On delivery to the ecclesiastical court,[6] the accused was normally committed to prison until he was willing to purge his innocence by oath-helpers ; inquest as to life and fame might be decisive without purgation ; the secular court developed restrictions on purgation, delivering sometimes *absque purgatione* ; or imposed abjuration or outlawry[7] (often in the case of fugitives). If found of good fame, or purged—an overwhelming proportion of successful purgations is recorded[8]—the accused's chattels were restored. But conviction by confession, inquest, proof of the accuser, or failure to purge innocence, led to degradation or penance (which might often take the form of imprisonment for life in the bishop's prison) and forfeiture of chattels to the lay court.[9]

---

[1] Bracton, c. xviii, p. 136b.
[2] Gabel, op. cit. 31-40. This was done in 1227 cases out of 1999 between 1 Edward I. and 39 Henry VI. Cf. Staunton J., " You must say that he was delivered after having been found guilty by this court. otherwise he would never have been delivered " (6-7 Ed. II., S.S. xxvii (1912) 106).
[3] Gabel, op. cit. 41-43.   [4] Ibid 43-47.   [5] Ibid 48 seqq.
[6] Ibid 92-115.   [7] Cf. A. Lane Poole, op. cit.
[8] Gabel, op. cit. 98.   [9] Cheney, op. cit.

The frequency of purgation in the canonical court, no doubt among other circumstances, did much to encourage the secular power to seek to reduce the number of clergyable crimes.[1] Treason had never been clergyable; lesser treasons went out in the late thirteenth century; civil actions other than for recovery of money debts were excluded, and 25 Edward III. st. 6. c. 4 better defined the clergyable offences.

On the other hand, although restrictions of this kind tended to delimit the exercise of the privilege, a growing broadening of the interpretation of the term " clericus " accepted by the lay courts greatly extended its scope.[2] In the earlier mediæval period " clericus " meant simply a clerk in holy orders, down to sub-deacons. In Henry III.'s time the first tonsure was regarded as indispensable but not conclusive; garb, certification, literacy were taken into account as well. By a curious and not altogether explicable process, the latter test—literacy, came to take precedence and to supplant other proofs altogether, becoming a sufficient proof by the middle of the fourteenth century. This development was not very significant until literacy among laymen became common, which it did by the late fourteenth century, with the result that numerous laymen, of very diverse occupations, could and did obtain the " benefit of clergy." Literacy became a kind of " insurance against the gallows,"[3] until as a test it was almost abolished by 4 Henry VII., c. 13. That statute allowed the privilege once on grounds of literacy, but imposed branding upon those guilty who were not in fact in holy orders, and confined the privilege to clergy proper after the first offence. Purgation was abolished by 18 Elizabeth I. c. 7, but literacy as a test was not finally abolished until 5 Anne c. 6. Long before then benefit of clergy had become " a kind of statute pardon " in first offences of certain kinds.[4]

[1] Gabel, op. cit. 58-60.
[2] Ibid 62-88. [3] Ibid 86. [4] Ibid 125.

BOOK I

THE JUDICIAL SYSTEM

INTRODUCTION

THE rules which govern the jurisdiction and the procedure of the courts are the substantive part of early bodies of law. As these courts increase in power and enlarge their jurisdictions, the law which they apply gradually becomes more important than the courts which administer it and the procedure by which it is administered. The law becomes the substantive part of the system ; the procedure becomes merely adjective. But a body of law which has thus grown up bears upon it many marks of its origins. Its leading divisions, and the contents of many of its most characteristic doctrines, can often be explained only by a reference to events in the history of the courts and their procedure.

The historian of any legal system must begin his tale in the days before the law courts have made much law. Legal history therefore must always begin with the history of the courts. But the English legal system has, throughout its history, maintained its connection with the courts more closely than any other. This is due mainly to two causes. In the first place, the different component parts of the English legal system have been developed at different periods in many different sets of courts. Courts of Common Law, Courts of Equity, the Court of Admiralty, Ecclesiastical Courts, the Council and the Star Chamber, and many others, have all contributed something to the general body of English law ; and the nature and extent of their contributions cannot be appreciated without some knowledge of the history of these different courts, and of the principles upon which they have acted. In the second place the main body of English legal doctrine has been and is still being made by means of the decisions of the courts. "The English jurisprudence," said Burke, "hath not any other sure foundation, nor consequently the lives and property of the subject any sure hold, but in the maxims, rules, and principles, and judicial traditionary line of decisions contained in the notes taken, and from time to time published, called Reports. To give judgment privately is to put an end to Reports ; and to put an end to Reports is to put an end to the law of England." The solution of modern legal problems often depends upon the correct interpretation of the reports of very old cases ; and, if these reports are to be interpreted aright, English lawyers must know something of the nature of the courts in which these cases were decided, and something of their procedure and jurisdiction. Much more is this knowledge necessary to an understanding of the history of English law. Indeed, without it, no profitable study of English legal history is possible. For the English judicial system is, so to speak, the skeleton round which the rules of English law have grown up ; and the gradual evolution of the form of this skeleton has determined the large outstanding characteristics of the ever-growing body of English law.

The history of the judicial system contained in this Book will thus be a general introduction to the history of the law. It will indicate the main epochs in English legal history, and the origins both of some of the most characteristic features of English legal institutions, and of some of the most important divisions of the English legal system.

CHAPTER I

ORIGINS

A T the time of the Norman Conquest there was no central court which regularly administered a law common to the whole country. English law was, for the most part, administered in many different local courts; and the law thus administered was the customary law of the district. From the books of the beginning of the twelfth century which describe this law,[1] we can see that it consisted of three main bodies of custom, which corresponded to the three main political divisions of the country at the time of the Conquest. There was the Mercian law, the Dane law, and the West Saxon law.[2] They all varied in their contents—indeed, if their provisions were the same on any given point such agreement was thought worthy of note;[3] and within these three districts the customs of different localities varied.[4] These variations were also accentuated by another cause. At the time of the Conquest what we may call the national system of local courts—the system of communal courts[5]—which ad-

---

[1] These books are the *Leges Henrici Primi* composed about 1118; the *Quadripartitus* (1113-1118), of which the third and fourth books are missing; the *Bilingual Laws of William I.;* the *Leges Edwardi Confessoris*, probably composed in Henry I.'s reign; for an account of these books see vol. ii 151-154.

[2] "Legis eciam Anglice trina est partitio . . . Alia enim Westsexie, Alia Mircena, alia Denelaga est," Leg. Henr. vi 2; ibid ix 9; cf. for illustrations of differences between these laws Leges Edwardi Confessoris xii and xxxiii; Bilingual Laws of William I. ii and viii.

[3] "Hoc generale est in Merchenalahe et Danelahe et Westsaxenelahe," Bilingual Laws of William I. xxi.

[4] See e.g. Leg. Henr. lxiv 1, where a custom of Hampshire is mentioned; and these local customs continued to exist for some time after the Curia Regis had begun to establish a common law. Thus Glanvil in his Prologue speaks of the "confused multitude of these customs," and xiv 8, he speaks of pleas heard by the sheriff which, "secundum diversas diversorum comitatuum consuetudines tractari habent et terminari;" and Bracton, f. 1 a, says, "Habent enim Anglici plurima ex consuetudine quae non habent ex lege; sicut in diversis comitatibus, civitatibus, burgis, et villis, ubi semper inquirendum erit quae sit illius loci consuetudo, et qualiter utantur consuetudine qui consuetudines allegant."

[5] Below 5-15.

ministered this customary law, was overshadowed by the existence, all over the country, of various franchise and other private jurisdictions belonging to the larger landowners, both lay and ecclesiastical.[1] The result was that, at the time of the Conquest, England was covered with a network of competing courts and conflicting jurisdictions which had "their roots in various principles, in various rights, the rights of the king, of the church, of feudal lords, of ancient communities."[2] The political dissension which enabled the Normans to conquer the country was reflected in the diversity of the laws and the courts by which it was governed.

The immediate effect of the Norman Conquest was to increase rather than to diminish this confused mass of local customs. The twelfth century law books [3] show that to them had been added an admixture of Norman laws and customs, and some fragments of the canon and Roman law.[4] Nor was there any change in the various local courts which administered these customs. But the Norman Conquest did give England what she most wanted—a strong ruler with the power and the will to make his influence felt throughout the country; and this strong ruler governed through a royal court staffed by the ablest men of the day.[5] Already at the beginning of the twelfth century this royal court was making its influence felt upon the law of the country. The most important of these twelfth century law books—the *Leges Henrici Primi*—recognized the law of this court as a fourth species of law, superior to the tribal customs of the West Saxons, the Mercians, and the Danes in its universality, its stability, and its power.[6] Under Henry I. this strong central court was beginning to get some definite organization;[7] but as yet much depended on the personality of the king. Under a weak king, like Stephen, the nascent central government disappeared. But under Henry II. it was so revived and strengthened that we can see the beginnings of distinct departments of government; and, what is most important from the point of view of legal history, its jurisdiction was so strengthened and extended that we can see the beginnings of a centralized judicial system which administered a law common to the whole country.[8] It is this centralized judicial system which will gradually reduce the local courts to insignificance, and substitute one common law for that confused

---

[1] Below 17-24.   [2] P. and M. i 513.
[3] Above 3 n. 1.   [4] Vol. ii 152-153.
[5] Below 32, 33-41.
[6] " Legis eciam Anglice trina est partitio . . . preter tremendum regie majestatis titislamus (sc) imperium," Leg. Henr. vi 1 ; " Legis eciam trina est partitio; et ad eandem distanciam supersunt regis placita curiae, quae usus et consuetudines suas una semper immobilitate servat ubique," ibid ix 9.
[7] Below 43, 49.   [8] Below 47-53.

mass of local customs of which the law of England had formerly consisted.

The beginnings of this centralized judicial system and this common law were due to the power of the crown. But the abuse of the large powers of the crown by John produced a national uprising which resulted in the granting of Magna Carta. Naturally some of the clauses of Magna Carta dealt with the new centralized judicial system which had just begun to make its influence felt. A few of these clauses represented the views of the great nobility who disliked a system which was the most efficient curb on feudal disorder. But, for the most part, the new central organization was regulated, not destroyed. Its continued existence was taken for granted ; and thus the future of a centralized judicial system and a common law was assured.[1]

This summary of the chief events in the history of the judicial system down to the granting of Magna Carta indicates the main divisions of the subject. I shall deal firstly with the history of the local jurisdictions ; secondly with the Curia Regis and the beginnings of a centralized judicial system ; and thirdly with the clauses of Magna Carta relating to this judicial system.

I. THE LOCAL JURISDICTIONS

The local jurisdictions of the country were either courts of the different communities into which the country was divided, or they were courts which were held by the large landowners lay or ecclesiastical. The first set of courts—the communal courts —represent a national system of jurisdiction and government. The second—the private or franchise courts—represent the encroachment of feudal ideas. I shall deal with the local jurisdictions under these two heads.

The Communal Courts

From the last half of the tenth century the country was divided into shires (which after the Norman Conquest were called counties), hundreds, wapentakes or wards, and vills or townships. The county and the hundred were jurisdictional units—each had its court. The vills or townships were responsible for various public duties ; and in particular the vill, or a sub-division of its population known as the tithing, was responsible for the working of that system of mutual responsibility for the production of criminals known as the Friborh or Frankpledge. We must therefore consider the communal courts

[1] Below 54-63.

under these three heads: (1) The County Court; (2) The Hundred Court; and (3) The Frankpledge System.

(1) *The County Court.*

At the time of the Norman Conquest all England was divided into shires or counties. This division was probably the result of different causes in different places. " The constitutional machinery of the shire," says Stubbs,[1] "represents either the national organization of the several divisions created by West Saxon Conquest; or that of the early settlements which united in the Mercian kingdom as it advanced westwards; or the re-arrangement by the West Saxon dynasty of the whole of England on the principles already at work in its own shires."

In the tenth century the officials of the shire were the earldor-man, the bishop, and the sheriff. The earldormen were origin-ally the chief officials of the shire; but in the last century of the Saxon period they diminished in numbers and became the rulers of provinces.[2] They disappeared after the Norman Conquest; the term earl became a mere title;[3] and the memory of his old connection with the shire was only recalled by the fact that he was endowed with the third penny of the profits of the jurisdic-tion of the county court.[4] The severance, after the Conquest, of the spheres of lay and ecclesiastical jurisdiction[5] tended to remove the bishop from official participation in the business of the shire. He appeared at the shire court simply in his capacity of landowner. Thus, after the Conquest, the sheriff became the chief official of the shire. He derived his powers from two main sources. As a royal gerefa or reeve he was responsible for the enforcement of the king's fiscal rights.[6] As deputy of the earldor-man he was responsible for fulfilling his military police and judicial duties in connection with the shire.[7] By the reign of

[1] C.H. i 130.

[2] W. A. Morris, The Office of Sheriff in the Anglo-Saxon Period, E.H.R. xxxi 27-28; Stubbs, C.H. i 138.   [3] Ibid 407-413.

[4] " Comes autem est qui tertiam portionem eorum quae de placitis proveniunt in quolibet comitatu percipit . . . qui ideo sic dici dicitur, quia fisco socius est et comes in percipiendis," Dialogus de Scaccario I. xvii (Sel. Ch. 171); he also had a third of the receipts from certain boroughs, Ballard, Domesday Boroughs 41-43; in some cases in the twelfth and early thirteenth centuries the earldom carried with it an hereditary right to the office of sheriff, Stubbs, C.H. i 411.

[5] Sel. Ch. 85.   [6] E.H.R. xxxi 23, 31.

[7] Ibid 25-26—" With the person who in the reign of Ethelred, if not earlier, appears in the alderman's absence as the leading lay official in the shire mote, begins the recorded history of the sheriff, as differentiated from that of the king's reeve. About the last decade of the tenth century this official is termed a *gerefa* and also a *scirman*. The shireman is mentioned in Kent, and the natural assump-tion that he is a reeve in charge of the shire in the alderman's absence seems to be confirmed by the identity of *scirman* and *scirgerefa* as established by Kentish documents dating from the reign of Canute; " for his police and military duties see ibid 28-30.

Edward the Confessor the whole government of the shire had fallen into his hands.[1] He was an officer of the king, the earldorman, and the nation.[2] The weakness of the kingship and the increase in the power of the great earldormen had given him this position in the days before the Conquest. That position was strengthened, and consolidated in the century after the Conquest.[3] He became the chief official of the Norman and Angevin kings,[4] and combined the powers and functions of the English sheriff and the Norman vicomte. But, as Mr. Morris points out, the greatest change which the Conquest produced was not in the nature of his office, but in " the new power behind it." [5] As the chief local official of the king he was the executive officer of the county, directly responsible to the crown for its government. He was the leader of the military forces of the shire and its boroughs.[6] He must account for all money due from the county to the king;[7] and sometimes he compounded for the amount due by the payment of a fixed sum—the county was let to the sheriff at a rent or farm and-he made what he could of it.[8] He must execute all royal writs or orders addressed to him.[9] As agent and representative of the central government he remained the most important of all the local officials, till the growth of the system of sending delegates of the Curia Regis round the country, and the rise of a centralized judicial system, began to sap his power.[10]

His court—the county court—[11] was the governing body of the county. In it administrative, military, and financial business was carried on. Charters made by private persons were often read before it;[12] royal commands and enactments of the king and Witan were there proclaimed;[13] and long after it had ceased to be in any sense the governing body of the county, we can see

[1] E.H.R. xxxi 36.　　　　　　　　　[2] Ibid 38.

[3] " Weak kingship seems before the Conquest to be gaining for the sheriff what strong kingship will strengthen after the Conquest," ibid 40.

[4] On his position after the Conquest see W. A. Morris, the Office of Sheriff in the Early Norman Period, E.H.R. xxxiii 145 seqq.

[5] Ibid 146.　　　　　　　　　[6] Ibid 161-162.

[7] Ibid xxxi 31-32; xxxiii 165-166.

[8] Stubbs, C.H. i 430-431; see ibid 431-434 for other items for which the Norman sheriff must account; E.H.R. xxxi 31-32; xxxiii 166-168.

[9] Stubbs, C.H. i 216 n. 2, 446; this part of his duty tended to increase as the strength of the central governments increased after the Conquest; Stubbs says, C.H. i 446, " The custom of the interference of the crown by writ, though not unprecedented, is as a custom, new; " E.H.R. xxxiii 163-164.

[10] Below 49-53.

[11] Its style as finally fixed is, " Buckinghamshire. Curia Comitatus E.C. militis Vicecomitis Comitatus prædicti tenta apud B," Coke, Fourth Instit. c. 55.

[12] Bracton f. 38, advocates this practice—" Utilius et melius si in locis publicis sicut in comitatu et hundredo, ut facilius probari possit."

[13] E.H.R. xxxi 36.

a reminiscence of its old position· in the fact that proclamations
and Acts of Parliament were published there by the sheriff.[1]
But, from the point of view of legal history, it is its judicial work
that is most interesting.

The court had a general jurisdiction over all kinds of cases.
Thus in the Norman period it entertained all manner of criminal
cases and pleas of the crown ;[2] suits for lands arising between
the tenants of different lords ;[3] actions for various wrongs, and
actions for debt.   In the last resort it could outlaw a defendant
who refused to appear ; and this power it retained to the end,
to the exclusion even of the royal courts.[4]   It is for these
reasons that it was, before the rise of the central courts, the most
important agent for the making and declaring of English law.
Most of the law of this period, says Professor Vinogradoff, " was
shaped by the pronouncements and decisions of the County
Courts." [5]

Just as the Norman Conquest strengthened and consolidated
the power of the sheriff, so it added to the power and authority
of the county court.   Before the growth of regular judicial circuits conducted by members of the Curia Regis, the king sometimes sent a deputy, commissioned by royal writ, to try a particular
case in the county court,[6] or in a court drawn from several
counties.[7]   If we look at the composition of the court summoned
to meet the royal deputy we see a meeting of the county court.[8]
But if we look at the royal judge commissioned by royal writ,[9]
and at the occasional use of the royal method of sworn inquest,[10]
we see rather a trial before the Curia Regis.[11]   The connection
between the county court and the courts held by the King's itinerant judges lasted long.[12]   But gradually the courts held by
these itinerant judges became regular tribunals quite distinct,

----

[1] Stephen, H.C.L. i 81.   [2] Leg. Henr. vii 3.
[3] " Et si amodo exsurgat placitum de divisione terrarum, si est inter barones
meos dominicos, tractetur placitum in curia mea; et si est inter vavassoras duorum
dominorum tractetur in comitatu," Writ of Henry I. for holding the shire and hundred courts, Sel. Ch. 103, 104.
[4] P. and M. i 541, 542; L.Q.R. xviii 297.
[5] " The fact is, that before the common law of England was worked out in the
Royal Courts of the feudal age the main body of English law flowed in the channels
of provincial customs,·and the shire moots were the chief institutions concerned with
the definite laying down of it," English Society in the Eleventh Century 91 ; cf.
E.H.R. xxxiii 159.
[6] For a detailed account of some of these cases see G. B. Adams, The Local
King's Court in the reign of William I., Yale Law Journal April 1914.
[7] Ibid 9, 10, 11 ; E.H.R. xxxiii 160-161.   [8] Ibid.
[9] Yale Law Journal loc. cit. 1-3.   [10] Ibid 12, 13.
[11] Ibid 20, 21.   We may note that in a charter of the last half of the twelfth
century cited by G. B. Adams, Am. Hist. Rev. xxi 91-92, a court of this kind is referred to in one place as a county court, and in another as Curia Domini Regis.
[12] Below 71, 267.

both in their procedure and their jurisdiction, from the county court.[1] They became affiliated to the central courts of common law, and therefore quite distinct from the local county courts. We shall see that the growth of this separation was as fatal to the position of the county court as the growth of the importance of the king's judges was to the judicial, and to some of the administrative powers of the sheriff.[2]

That a local court should thus be a court of general jurisdiction is not in accordance with modern ideas. In modern systems of law it is, as a rule, only courts with a jurisdiction over a large area that have a general jurisdiction. Local courts try the less important cases, and there may or may not be an appeal from them to the superior courts. This idea was quite unknown to the Anglo-Saxons. At this period not only the county court but also the hundred court were courts of a general jurisdiction. It was only if a person could not get justice in the hundred court that he sued in the county court; and it was only if he could not get justice in the county court that he brought his case before the king and Witan.[3] Hence it happened that the greater courts were courts for the greater men, and the smaller courts for the smaller men. The difference between them was in the kind of suitors who attended them, not in the extent of jurisdiction which they exercised. And so we find that while the regular attendants at the county courts were "a group of thanes which might be likened to the county families of later days,"[4] or to the "busones" of Bracton's day with whom the justices in Eyre were advised to confer,[5] the regular attendants at the hundred court were the smaller landowners and tenants.[6]

But though in practice the regular attendants at the county court were the more important men, in theory it was composed of a very heterogeneous body of persons. "Let there be present," say the *Leges Henrici*, "the bishops, earls, vicedomini, vicarii, hundredors (centenarii), aldermen, prefects, prepositi, barons, vavassors, reeves, and other landowners."[7] The barons and other

---

[1] Below 267, 276-283.   [2] Below 71-75.
[3] Laws of Cnut (Secular) 17, 19; Stubbs, C.H. i 135, 446.
[4] Vinogradoff, English Society 97.
[5] Below 268.   [6] Vinogradoff, English Society 97.
[7] "Intersint autem episcopi, comites, vicedomini, vicarii, centenarii, aldermanni, prefecti, prepositi, barones, vavasores, tungrevii, et ceteri terrarum domini," vii 2; for conjectures as to the meaning of some of these terms see P. and M. i 532, n. 2, 3; as Maitland says, "the words are vague; they point to no one clearly established rule, but rather to a struggle between various principles," ibid i 533; and a full meeting of the court continued to be a somewhat heterogeneous crowd; Bracton, f. 109 b tells us that there were summoned to meet the justices in Eyre, "Omnes archiepiscopos, abbates, priores, comites, barones, milites et liberos tenentes de tota balliva tua, et de qualibet villa quatuor legales homines et proepositum, et de quolibet burgo duodecim legales homines burgenses . . . et omnes illos qui coram justitiariis itinerantibus venire solent et debent."

landowners represented their estates, and there were representatives from the hundreds and from the townships.[1]　Attendance at the court was a burdensome duty; and in the thirteenth century this duty—*secta* or suit of court—could be performed by attorney.[2]　Moreover there was in the thirteenth century a tendency to treat this burden like the burden of military service, and to impose it on certain pieces of land, the holders of which were, by the terms of their tenure, obliged to discharge this suit of court.[3]　Suit of court tended to become an obligation attached to land rather than an obligation attached to the person—to become rather real than personal.　This tendency had not gone far in the eleventh century.　Suit was then as much personal as real.[4]　But, from the thirteenth century onwards, the "real" principle got the upper hand.　Suit was generally attached to certain pieces of land; and it could be claimed from the tenant like any other service.　If part of the land was sold the purchaser owed a corresponding part of the suit, so that a tenant might owe the half or a third of a suit.[5]　The suitors of a court thus became a defined class,[6] who were clearly distinguished from other persons who, on great occasions, such as the eyre of the king's justices, might be obliged to be present at the court.[7]

The suitors were the judges of the court; the sheriff was simply its president.[8]　But, according to the *Leges Henrici*, only those suitors were qualified to be judges who were "the barons of the county who have freeholds therein."[9]　On principle a person should be judged by his peers who were resident in the same locality as himself;[10] and in some places the parties were allowed to choose their judges.[11]　If there was a difference of opinion it is said by the *Leges Henrici* in one passage that the

[1] "Si quis baronum regis vel aliorum comitatui, secundum legem, interfuerit totam terram, quam illic in dominio suo habet, acquietare poterit. . . . Si uterque necessario desit, prepositus et sacerdos et quatuor de melioribus ville assint pro omnibus qui nominatim non erunt ad placitum submoniti," Leg. Henr. vii 7.

[2] 20 Henry III. c. 10 (Statute of Merton)—the statute applied also to the hundred and the feudal courts.

[3] E.H.R. iii 417 seqq.　　　　　　　　　　[4] P. and M. i 533.

[5] Ibid 526-531 ; cf. E.H.R. iii 418-419.

[6] Thus 7 Henry IV. c. 15, provides that all present at the court must attend at the election of knights of the shire, "as well suitors duly summoned for the same cause as others."

[7] P. and M. i 531.　　　　　　　　　　[8] Ibid i 535-537.

[9] "Regis judices sunt barones comitatus, qui liberas in eis terras habent, per quos debent cause singulorum alterna prosecucione tractari ; villani vero, vel cotseti, vel ferdingi, vel qui sunt viles vel inopes persone, non sunt inter legum judices numerandi," Leg. Henr. xxix 1.

[10] "Unusquisque per pares suos judicandus est, et ejusdem provincie," Leg. Henr. xxxi 7.

[11] "In quibusdam locis utrumque eligitur judicium, medietas ab eis quorum est negocium," ibid xxxi 8.

view of the majority,[1] in another that the view of the better part
should prevail.[2] The suitors continued to the end to be the
judges of the court. Thus it is the county and not the sheriff
which is in later days amerced by the royal judges for false judgment and irregularities in procedure ;[3] and in Blackstone's time,
when a writ of false judgment was brought to reverse a judgment
of the county court, the record of the judgment must be carried
to Westminster by four legal knights who had taken part in the
proceedings.[4]

We are told in the *Leges Henrici* that the court was held
twice a year.[5] But, if it had much business to do, it is difficult
to suppose that it sat so seldom.[6] Possibly in early days the
hundred court did some of the work afterwards done by the
county court; and possibly, as Maitland has conjectured, the
court held less solemn sessions more frequently in which a
good deal of business was done.[7] It certainly held such sessions
in Edward I.'s reign.[8] In fact, before that date, it had come to
sit generally once a month, and, in some places, once every six
weeks.[9]

(2) *The Hundred Court.*

The county was divided into hundreds, wapentakes, or wards.
The name "hundred" first appears in the laws of Edgar, king of
Wessex. Beyond Wessex, to the North and East, the size and
regularity of these divisions increased ; and the name "hundred"
gave place to the name "wapentake" and "ward". These facts
perhaps warrant the conclusion that the hundred was a West
Saxon institution ; and that similar divisions of the county
gradually spread over the country with the growth of the
supremacy of Wessex.[10]

After the Conquest the hundred was liable for the murder
fine,[11] until this liability was abolished in Edward III.'s reign ;[12]

---

[1] "Quod si in judicio inter partes oriatur dissensio, de quibus certamen emerserit,
vincat sententia plurimorum," Leg. Henr. v 6—a very early statement of the
majority principle, see vol. ii Bk. iii c. 5.

[2] "Vincat sentencia meliorum," Leg. Henr. xxxi 2.

[3] Hengham, Magna c. 4.   [4] Bl. Comm. iii 34 ; and App. IX for the writ.

[5] vii 4 ; li 2.   [6] P. and M. i 525.   [7] Ibid i 526.

[8] As is pointed out, ibid, the Hundred Rolls show two classes of suitors—one is
bound to go to the "great" or "general" counties twice a year, and the other to
attend from month to month ; in 1433 there is a reference, in the Acts of the Privy
Council (Nicolas IV. 163), to "pleyne counties"—"Item that if within the laste
lay of Juyn. . . . The knyghts of the shires may not be chosen in pleyne counties
hat the Chancellor have power to sette a longer day withynne whiche the pleine
counties may be holden."

[9] Magna Carta (1217) c. 42 ; 2, 3 Edward VI. c. 25 ; Stubbs, C.H. i 679.

[10] Ibid 109-114 ; P. and M. i 543-544.

[11] Leg. Henr. xcii 1, 8, 9. If a person was found dead, and could not be proved
to be English, he was presumed to be Norman, and the hundred was liable to this fine.

[12] 14 Edward III. St. 1 c. 4 ; but there are cases of presentments occurring after
the statute, Select Coroners Rolls, (S.S.) xliii. Even after this statute the vill was

and, in later days, when the government became more centralized, the hundred, like the county, could be made liable for false judgment, and for the breach of various duties statutory or otherwise.[1] Whether it could be thus made liable in the Anglo-Saxon period there is no evidence to show.

The official of the hundred was a reeve, sometimes styled hundredor, hundred-man, or hundred-reeve.[2] But even in Saxon times the sheriff sometimes presided;[3] and in later days the hundredor was always a bailiff or deputy of his sheriff who farmed the hundred, as the sheriff farmed the shire.[4] He held the hundred court which, according to the *Leges Henrici*, met twelve times a year.[5] In Henry II.'s reign, however, the sessions were fortnightly, till, in 1234, it was provided that they should be once every three weeks.[6] As with the county, so with the hundred, the suitors gave the judgment of the court. They were a set of persons very similar to those who composed the county court,[7] but they were drawn from a somewhat humbler class;[8] and, as in the case of the county, the duty of attending the hundred court came to be incumbent on the holders of certain pieces of land.[9] According to a law of Ethelred the twelve senior thegns were to act as a sort of judicial committee of the court for purposes of accusation;[10] but there is no evidence to

---

still liable to amercement for neglect of its police duties if a person was slain and the murderer escaped; if the vill could not pay, the hundred was in some cases liable, and in default the county, 3 Henry VII. c. 1 § 6; Coke, 3rd Instit. 53; Hale, P.C. i 448.

[1] Stat. of Winchester (1285) § 2; cf. Madox Exchequer i 543-549, 557-568 for a list of varied offences of which vills and hundreds were capable.

[2] W. A. Morris, E.H.R. xxxi 28-29; Stubbs, C.H. i 122.

[3] E.H.R. xxxi 28-29.

[4] P. and M. i 544; this practice led to abuses; sheriffs let hundreds and wapentakes at so high a farm that the amount could not be levied without extortion, and so it was provided by 4 Edward III. c. 15 that they were to be let at the old farm; 4 Henry IV. c. 5 and 23 Henry VI. c. 9 prohibited sheriffs from letting them to farm.

[5] xcii 1, 9.   [6] P. and M. i. 544.

[7] Leg. Henr. vii 8.   [8] Above 9 n. 6.

[9] P. and M. i 528 and references to the Hundred Rolls there cited: E.H.R. iii 419-420.

[10] " And that a gemot be held in every wapentake; and the xii senior thanes go out, and the reeve with them, and swear on the relic that is given to them in hand, that they will accuse no innocent man, nor conceal any guilty one," Thorpe i 295; Stubbs, C.H. i 121-122, 448, seems to think that we can identify these xii senior thanes with the twelve legal men of the hundred on whom the duty of presenting criminals for trial was imposed by the assize of Clarendon; but the jury of presentment was certainly not of Saxon origin, below 312-313; and these xii thanes were not, like the jury, called together by the king; probably Maitland is quite right in refusing to see any connection between the law of Ethelred and the Assize of Clarendon, Select Pleas in Manorial Courts (S.S.) xxxvi, xxxvii; the duties of these xii senior thanes may be accounted for without supposing that they were summoned to present the offences committed by individuals—a matter in Anglo-Saxon times left to the injured party; we know that the hundred had its special peace (Stubbs, C.H. i 122), that it could accuse a person " Quod murdrum fecerit " (Leg. Henr. xcii 16), that it might wish to prove that a murdered man was not French " xii melioribus hominibus " (ibid

show whether or not they acted in other cases in which the court could declare folk-right. The jurisdiction of the court was general, like that of the county court ;[1] but in later days, with the growth of the system of Frankpledge, the sessions of the hundred court which dealt with criminal business tended to fall apart from the sessions which dealt with civil business ; and the sessions which dealt with civil business ceased to hold pleas of land.[2]

To the growth of this system of frankpledge, which ultimately vested the criminal jurisdiction of the hundred in what was in effect a separate court, we must now turn.

(3) *The Frankpledge System.*

The system of fri-borg[3] or frankpledge has been defined as " a system of compulsory collective bail fixed for individuals, not after their arrest for crime, but as a safeguard in anticipation of it."[4] Over the greater part of England[5] all persons, unless excused by reason of their rank or the amount of their property or other cause,[6] must be enrolled in a tithing—a group of ten men presided over by a tithing man ; and if one of the tithing committed an offence the other nine must produce him for trial. If they could not produce him they must make good the damage caused by the defaulter and pay a fine.[7] Twice a year, at a specially full meeting of the hundred court held by the sheriff, enquiry was made whether all who ought to be enrolled in a tithing were so enrolled.[8] These tithings seem sometimes to

xcii 11) ; thus the xii senior thanes may have acted on behalf of the hundred when the hundred was interested ; we shall see that in the later court leet and sheriff's tourn there are reminiscences of a similar body quite distinct from the jury of presentment, below 76-78.

[1] Stubbs, C.H. i 122.   [2] P. and M. i 544.

[3] W. A. Morris, The Frankpledge System 2, shows that its proper name is fri-borg = free security, not frith-borg = peace security.

[4] Ibid 1, 2 ; as the author there points out the *Leges Edwardi Confessoris* cxx give a very good definition of the institution ; the essential parts of it run as follows : " Alia pax maxima est, per quam omnes firmiori statu sustentantur : scilicit fidejussionis stabilitate quam Angli vocant frith borgas. . . . Et hoc est quod de omnibus villis tocius regini sub decennali fidejussione debeant omnes esse, ita quod si unus ex decem forisfecerit, novem eum haberent ad rectum."

[5] As to the northern and western parts of England in which the system was not in operation, see W. A. Morris, The Frankpledge System, chap. ii.

[6] For the various classes of persons exempt see ibid chap. iii ; for the general rule see Leg. Henr. viii 2 ; for the rule that the lord must be responsible for those under his jurisdiction see ibid viii 3.

[7] Leges Edwardi c. xx—" Quod si facere non poterit (the tithing man) restauraret dampnum quod ipse fecerat de proprio forisfactoris quantum duraverit, et de suo ; et erga justiciam emendent secundum quod legaliter judicatum fuerit eis."

[8] Leg. Henr. viii 1—" Speciali tamen plenitudine, si opus est, bis in anno conveniant in hundretum suum quicunque liberi . . . ad dinoscendum, scilicit inter cetera, si decanie plene sint, vel qui, quo modo, qua racione, recesserint, vel superaccreverint. Presit autem singulis hominum novenis decimus."

have been literally a group of ten men, sometimes to have been a territorial unit identical with the township.[1]

We cannot see this precise system in working order before the Conquest; but we can see the roots from which it sprang. In the first place, the laws of Edgar, Edward, and Cnut imposed certain police duties upon the hundred and its subdivision the tithing. Thus the laws of Edgar provided that if a theft has taken place notice must be given to the hundred-man, and he must inform the tithing-men, and they must all go and search for the thief.[2] To ensure the efficient performance of these duties the laws of Cnut provided that all must be brought into a hundred and tithing.[3] In the second place, the Anglo-Saxon laws provided that persons must find a borh or security that they will appear to answer any charge preferred against them.[4] An accused man who could not find a borh could be arrested, and sent to the ordeal.[5] But there is no clear evidence that in the Anglo-Saxon period these two ideas had been combined to form the frankpledge system. Police duties were placed on the tithing. All men must be enrolled in a tithing. All men must if required find borh to appear before a court. But there is no clear evidence that the members of these tithing groups were a compulsory borh for one another.[6]

We do get this development shortly after the Conquest; and we may perhaps see its germ in § 8 of the laws which William I. made after the Conquest. This section provided that, "Every man who wishes to be accounted as free shall be in pledge, so that the pledge hold him and produce him before the court if he offend. And if anyone of such people escape, let the pledges see that they pay the sum claimed by the plaintiff, and prove that they were privy to no fraud committed by him that has escaped."[7] Whether or not it was this law which effected the change, we do get this development shortly after the Conquest; so that it is probably due to a direct change made by the Con-

[1] W. A. Morris, The Frankpledge System 12-14; Stubbs, C.H. i 97-99; Select Pleas in Manorial Courts (S.S.) xxx.

[2] Laws of Edgar, Thorpe i 258-259, Ordinance of the Hundred c. 2.

[3] Laws of Cnut, Thorpe i 387, Secular Ordinance c. 20.

[4] Laws of Edward, Thorpe i 253, c. vii provide that "Omnes infamati et accusationibus ingravati sub pledgio redigantur;" Laws of Ethelred, Thorpe i 281, provide "that every freeman have a true borh, that the borh may present him to justice, if he should be accused;" Laws of Cnut, Thorpe i 387-389, "And that every one be brought into a hundred and in 'borh'; and let the borh hold him and lead him to every plea."

[5] Laws of Cnut, Thorpe i 391, Secular Ordinance c. 25.

[6] W. A. Morris, The Frankpledge System 27.

[7] "Omnis homo qui voluerit se teneri pro libero sit in plegio, et plegius teneat et habeat illum ad justitiam si quid offenderit. Et si quis-quam talium evaserit, videant pledgii ut simpliciter solvant quod caluminatum est, et purgent se quia in evaso nullam fraudem noverint," Sel. Ch. 84.

queror.[1] It is probable that he introduced the idea of communal responsibility for crime under the pressure of the need to protect his Norman followers.[2] If a man were murdered, and he could not be proved to be English, he was presumed to be Norman; the hundred was liable to pay a murder fine;[3] and to this fine the township or tithing must contribute its quota.[4] Already all persons could be compelled to find borh to appear in court if their presence was required.[5] It was a logical development to make each member of a tithing responsible as a compulsory borh for the others; for it emphasized that idea of communal responsibility for the non-production of criminals which the murder fine had introduced. The result is that the special session of the hundred court, in which the sheriff enquired into the proper maintenance of the tithing system, assumed a new importance. It was regarded by the writer of the *Laws of Edward the Confessor* as the main security for the keeping of the peace.[6] We shall see that, in the reign of Henry II., further changes made by the Assize of Clarendon gave to these special sessions of the hundred court an added importance, and new functions, which caused them to split off definitely from the ordinary sessions of the hundred court, and to be known by the new name of the sheriff's tourn.[7]

The greatest part of the judicial and administrative work of government in the Anglo-Saxon period was done in these local courts. The king had, it is true, certain rights and powers over the whole kingdom.[8] He and his Witan—the assembly of the leading men of the nation—from time to time exercised wide legislative, judicial and executive powers; and the Witan on occasion both elected and deposed the king.[9] The later Saxon kings possessed also a body of trained clerks who did the clerical work done by the Chancery of the Norman kings.[10] The

---

[1] " Between the voluntary pledging of a man by his neighbours in 1030, and the duty in 1115 of every man in a tithing to serve as a surety for every other man in the tithing, without right of refusal or withdrawal, no matter what the character of the associates, is a break that can be explained only by governmental action of a deliberate and rigorous nature, prompted by the imminent danger to which the public peace was exposed from the ordinary freeman of the realm," W. A. Morris, The Frankpledge System 29, 30.

[2] Ibid 36.   [3] Above 11.
[4] P. and M. i 552.   [5] Above 14.
[6] Above 13 n. 4.   [7] Below 72, 76-81.
[8] Vol. ii 16, 23.

[9] For a full account of its position see F. Liebermann, The National Assembly in the Anglo-Saxon Period.

[10] W. H. Stevenson, E.H.R. xi 731 seqq.; ibid xxvii 3, 4, where Mr. Stevenson points out that Cnut's Charter of Liberties (Liebermann, Gesetze i 273) is, "In substance and in form the direct lineal ancestor of the Anglo-Norman charters of liberties and, in consequence, of Magna Carta;" vol. ii 209.

influence of these institutions was no doubt felt after the Conquest. William I. and his successors never forgot that they
were English kings—the successors of Edward the Confessor.
Though the principle of tenure from the king, which determined
the composition of the Curia Regis, was very different from the
vaguer principle which determined the composition of the Witan,[1]
we may remember firstly that it was always possible for the king,
because he was king, to summon a person who was not his
tenant;[2] secondly that the great tenants-in-chief who were the
regular attendants on the Curia Regis were the same kind of
persons who attended the Witan; and thirdly that it is possible
that some reminiscences of the powers of the Witan may have
helped to strengthen the opposition to the king which from time
to time appeared in the feudal Curia Regis.[3] It is certain, too,
that the clerical department of the Anglo-Saxon kings influenced
the diplomatic forms of charters and writs which issued from the
Norman Chancery.[4] But, though it may be admitted that a few
influences of this kind made themselves felt after the Conquest,
we shall see that under these kings the power of the king and
the activity of the Curia Regis were so increased, and the
organization of the secretarial department of the state was so
strengthened, that we get in substance a new system of central
government.[5] The institutions of central government which
existed in the Anglo-Saxon period had never succeeded in
developing into an organized system.[6] The strong all-pervading
system of central government, which, as we shall see, began to
develop after the Conquest, must consequently be regarded as
a new departure in English history.

The failure of the institutions of the Anglo-Saxon monarchy
to develop a system of central government allowed the old
disruptive tribal influences to get the upper hand, and left the
country powerless to stem the tide both of the Danish and the
Norman invasions. The result of these disruptive influences we
shall better appreciate when we have examined the extent to

---

[1] Below 32, 33.
[2] G. B. Adams, Origin of the English Constitution 61-63.
[3] Liebermann, National Assembly 88, 90.
[4] Above 15 n. 10.   [5] Below 33, 34-41.
[6] Thus Liebermann says of the failure of the Witan, "If we are to look out for
institutional causes explaining why Norman tyranny could for a time push the
assembly into the background, we should point out that the germs, which seemed
fruitful enough in the seventh century, failed to develop in four centuries into a
constitutional factor able to assist and control monarchy from a broad national
point of view, because the gemot omitted to organize itself as an independent
institution, to determine rules as to who should be summoned and how, or when
and where a meeting should take place, to fix its competence, proceeding, recording,
and executive force, and lastly to limit its sphere over against the rival powers of
king, court council, and ecclesiastical synod," National Assembly 89.

which the growth of private jurisdiction had sapped the national organization of the communal courts.

The Private or Franchise Courts

In the later Anglo-Saxon Laws and in the law books of the twelfth century, the fact that much jurisdiction is in the hands of the larger landowners is assumed.   To this state of things the vague and compendious word "feudalism" is generally applied. But, as Maitland says,[1] "The impossible task that has been set before the word 'feudalism' is that of making a single idea represent a very large piece of the world's history, represent the France, Italy, Germany, England, of every century from the eighth or ninth to the fourteenth or fifteenth.   Shall we say that French feudalism reached its zenith under Louis d'Outre-Mer or under Saint Louis, that William of Normandy introduced feudalism into England or saved England from feudalism, that Bracton is the greatest of English feudalists or that he never misses an opportunity of showing a strong anti-feudal bias?   It would be possible to maintain all or any of these opinions, so vague is our use of the term in question."   In fact a statement that the government of a mediæval state is feudal tells us about as much and as little as a statement that a modern state has a system of representative government.   Both statements give us a very general idea, but nothing more.   In general terms we can say that feudalism comprises two things—a system of land tenure and a system of government.   Land is held by tenants of lords ; the relationship of lord and tenant gives the lord a certain jurisdiction over the tenant, and imposes upon the tenant the duty of attendance upon the lord's court and taking part in its business ; and thus the powers and duties involved in government are split up among the land holders of the country.   We may therefore regard feudalism as an institution partly of private and partly of public law.   So far as it regulates the holding of land it is an institution of private law ; so far as it gives jurisdictional rights it is an institution of public law.   In its former aspect I shall deal with it later.[2]   Here we must consider it in its latter aspect.

This tendency to split up the powers of government among the land holders of the country is the natural result of the absence of efficient central government.   The state was unable to exercise control over the dominions within which it exercised nominal authority.   The more powerful assumed such control, or obtained a grant from the state of the powers which the state

---

[1] P. and M. i 44.   [2] Vol. ii 168-169, 199-201, 260, 348, 576-578 ; vol. iii 34-73.

claimed but could not exercise. The less powerful were glad to submit to the authority of the more powerful, in order to obtain that protection which the state could not give to them. Thus we get a state of things called feudal at many different periods historically unconnected.[1] Before the Barbarian conquests the decadence of the Roman Empire produced a state of things in which many of the conditions precedent to a type of feudalism can be traced.[2] The feeble government of Henry VI. recreated in the fifteenth century similar phenomena.[3] In Europe, in the ninth and tenth centuries, the collapse of all efficient government after the death of Charlemagne caused the almost universal prevalence of feudal conditions. The nominal rulers called themselves by high-sounding titles and arrogated to themselves, partly under ecclesiastical influences, the powers and position of the emperor. They could not fill this position. They could not govern the territories over which they claimed to rule. The powers of the state were in practice exercised by those who had some actual control over some small part of the territory of the state. Thus the authority of the state was divided among those who had rights in the soil of the state. And when the state was able to reassert its claims, it did not easily lose all traces of that connection between the powers of government and the ownership of the soil which is the peculiar mark of feudalism in Europe.

During the ninth and tenth centuries England was affected by somewhat the same causes as those which were affecting the other peoples of Western Europe, and was therefore developing a type of feudalism. But at the time of the Norman Conquest this Anglo-Saxon feudalism had not attained to the clearness and precision of the feudal system of the continent, because the Anglo-Saxons had not completely grasped the theory of tenure which gave to continental feudalism its background of principle. It was, however, so like the feudalism with which the Normans were familiar that the Norman kings and lawyers found no great difficulty in fitting their terminology and conceptions to the English facts. Naturally the English facts were considerably modified by this process; and conversely they helped to modify the system with which the Normans were familiar. If, therefore, we would understand the effects of the Norman Conquest on the private or franchise jurisdictions existing in England we must

---

[1] Esmein, Histoire du droit Francais (11th ed.) 193 says of feudalism, " C'est, d'ailleurs un type, qui s'est réproduit dans d'autres pays et a d'autres époques. Il a existé une féodalité musulmane, originale et puissante. Une féodalité tres developpé a vécu au Japon pendant des siècles; son abolition, aujourd'hui complète, n'a commencé qu'apres 1867."

[2] Fustel de Coulanges, Les Origines de système Féodale 206 seqq.; Esmein op. cit. (11th ed.) 31-32.

[3] Below 483-485, 490; vol. ii 414-416.

consider (1) Anglo-Saxon feudalism; and (2) the effects of the Norman Conquest.

(1) Anglo-Saxon feudalism.

In Anglo-Saxon times such legally distinct things as property, jurisdiction, the profits of jurisdiction, and the produce of taxation seem blended together in a common mass. " The word dominium," says Maitland, "has to cover both proprietary rights and many kinds of political power." [1] The king had land; the earldormen had land. But no distinction was drawn between private property and official property. [2] The king also had certain rights of jurisdiction over land which brought him in certain profits. He granted either the jurisdiction itself or the profits; and little distinction was probably drawn between the two forms of grant. [3] New taxes, for instance the Danegeld, were imposed. This gave another new right or immunity to be granted or sold. [4] The idea that governmental rights and offices and privileges are property to be dealt in was perpetuated in a modified form by the feudalism of later days; and it has died hard. [5] That it was possible to distinguish them seems hardly to have occurred to the Anglo-Saxon mind. It is true that in these grants of governmental rights certain duties like military service and the repair of bridges and fortresses, which are usually compendiously described by the phrase *trinoda necessitas*, were always implicitly and sometimes expressly reserved; but there is one clear case in which exemption even from them was granted. [6] The laws of Cnut reserved certain pleas of the crown, "unless he (the king) will more amply honour anyone, and concede to him this worship." [7] In the laws

[1] Domesday Book and Beyond 344.

[2] Ibid 168; " A vast amount of land is or has recently been held by office holders, by the holders of the kingship, the earlships, or the earldormanships. We seem to see their proprietary rights arising in the sphere of public law, growing out of governmental rights, which however themselves are conceived as being in some sort proprietary," ibid 169.

[3] Ibid 102.

[4] " Every increase in the needs of the state . . . gives the king new rights in the land. . . . If a fleet be formed to resist the Danes the king has . . . a new immunity for sale. If a geld be levied to buy off the Danes the king can sell a freedom from this tax, or he can tell the monks of St. Edmundsbury that they may levy the tax from their men, and keep it for their own use," ibid 240.

[5] For its survival in the common law courts and the Chancery see below 246-248, 259-260, 424-426.

[6] The phrase " trinoda necessitas " is nowhere used in the Anglo-Saxon laws; it owes its currency to Blackstone and the law dictionaries, see W. H. Stevenson, E.H.R. xxix 690; the term " trimoda necessitas " occurs once in a charter of the latter part of the tenth century of doubtful authenticity, ibid 691-692, 696; but there is no doubt that the duties described by the phrase existed, ibid 689 n. 3; for a clear case of exemption from these duties in a charter of 930 see ibid 702; for other possible cases see Domesday Book and Beyond 273-274.

[7] Laws of Cnut (Secular) 12, Thorpe i 383. These rights were in terms granted to the Archbishop of Canterbury, Domesday Book and Beyond 261; Bigelow, Placita Anglo-Normanica 4-9.

of Henry I. it was said that a certain jurisdiction belongs to the crown ; but the qualification was repeated.[1]

The most usual words by which these grants of jurisdiction were conferred were sac and soc, toll and team, infangthef and utfangthef, frithsoken. Little that is certain can be said as to their meaning as, owing to the rise of new remedies and a new legal language, they were already almost obsolete in the thirteenth century. Sac[2] seems to mean a cause or matter before a court—that which in later law Latin is termed placitum. Soc[3] has a similar meaning. It is apparently derived from a word which means seeking. It means either that a man may seek, investigate or enquire into certain causes ; or that certain litigants must seek or make suit to a certain court. Toll[4] is defined as the right to take tallage of one's villeins. Team[5] is variously interpreted. The most probable meaning seems to be that it is the right to hold a court in which a stranger can be vouched as a warrantor. Infangthef[6] means the right to hang a thief under one's own jurisdiction caught " hand-having or back-bearing " on one's own land. Utfangthef[7] means the right to hang such a thief similarly caught, but whether or not the capture is made on one's own land.[8]

The extent to which these grants of mixed proprietary, justiciary, and fiscal rights had gone receive their most striking exemplification in the grants of the Anglo-Saxon kings to the church. It was probably in such grants to St. Cuthbert of Durham that the foundation of the county Palatine of later law was laid.[9] Thus King Oswald endowed Aidan of Lindisfarne. His grants were added to by Ecgfrith and Ceolwulf. Guthred

---

[1] Leg. Henr. xx 3.

[2] Domesday Book and Beyond 84, 259 ; Select Pleas in Manorial Courts (S.S.) xxii, xxiii ; P. and M. i 567.

[3] Ibid.

[4] Select Pleas in Manorial Courts xxii ; P. and M. i 566.

[5] Select Pleas in Manorial Courts xxiii ; P. and M. i 568.

[6] Ibid 564 ; but the meaning was doubtful in the thirteenth century, see ibid n. 2 ; in the Eyre of Kent (S.S.) iii 194 infangthef is said to mean that the lord may " erect gallows and deal with thieves taken within his franchise, but not with those taken without it."

[7] P. and M. i 564 ; in the Eyre of Kent (S.S.) iii 194 it is said that Utfangthef " is merely the right to execute judgment upon a resident within your manor that has been convicted before justices of felony outside your manor."

[8] For a longer list of these franchises see Domesday Book and Beyond 266 ; Red Book of the Exchequer (R.S.) iii 1032-1039. The franchises named in the text are the most common ; they are the franchises explained by Bracton, f. 154 b and in the laws of Edward the Confessor c. 22 (Sel. Ch. 78) ; another, not very common franchise called Frithsoken perhaps gave the right to take the view of frankpledge, P. and M. i 567 n. 4. Offences usually reserved to the crown's jurisdiction were *Hamsocne*, forcible attack on a homestead ; *Forsteal*, a treacherous attack on one's enemy while on a journey ; *Flymena-fyrm*, the harbouring of outlaws. But they were sometimes granted to private persons.

[9] Registrum Dunelmense (R.S.) i, lxiii.

granted all the land between the Tyne and the Wear "cum jure
regali." Alfred granted all the land between the Tyne and the
Tees "cum regalitate," confirmed Guthred's grant, and provided
that all land afterwards purchased should be held as freely.
Athelstan made further grants when St. Cuthbert's body was
transferred to Durham. Cnut granted that no person except
those who served the saint should interfere within these territories.[1] This is but one example out of many such grants to
churches.[2] And these grants were not confined to the churches—
thus we read that Godwin had a manor in Hampshire to which
belonged the third penny of six hundreds.[3] But grants to
churches were the most common. Laymen generally acquired
their rights from other causes with which I shall deal immediately.

What the king did other landowners imitated. Bishop
Oswald leased land to a knight free from all secular service save
the trinoda necessitas.[4] The Bishop of Durham in 1228 granted
land and the most extensive immunities to the Prior and Con-
vent of Durham.[5] It was probably a comparatively new principle which Glanvil stated when he laid it down as a rule of the
king's court that those commissioned by the king to administer
justice could not delegate to others the powers which had been
vested in them.[6]

These grants of land and privileges illustrate the want of
distinction existing between rights of property and powers of
government. What was granted was in many cases not merely
the rights of a landlord, but the rights of the state. If we used
modern terms we should call them, as Maitland has pointed out,
rather cessions than conveyances. It is clear that they directly
fostered the growth of private jurisdiction. But there were also
two other sets of causes resting on different principles, but working toward the same result.

The first set of these causes operated from below.

It was convenient in many ways to the small freeman to
"commend" himself to a powerful landowner. The small man
was more fully protected both from lawlessness and from litigation. The lord got another retainer.[7] He did not however

---

[1] Registrum Dunelmense (R.S.) xv, xx, xxiii, xxix, lx-lxiv.

[2] Domesday Book and Beyond 228, 229. Cp. Ethelweard's charter to Evesham
Abbey (ibid 235) which freed the land from taxes, purveyance, military service, and
royal works " ab omni publico vectigali, a victu, ab expeditione, ab opere regio."

[3] Ibid 170. [4] Ibid 289.

[5] Registrum Dunelmense (R.S.) i, lxxii-lxxvi.

[6] Glanvil xii 19, " Non est consuetudo quod ex quo aliquod negotium pertinens
ad justicias meas aliquibus injungetur tractandum, quod ipsi id in alios transferant
de re aliqua quæ ad justiciam meam pertinet ; " Bracton f. 333 b, " justitiarius
justitiarium substituere non potest."

[7] Domesday Book and Beyond 69-71 ; Leg. Henr. lxxxii 6, " Et in quibusdam
potest dominus homini suo warantus esse, si precepto suo verberaverit, vel alio

necessarily get any rights over the man's land. We read of men who could go with their land to what lord they pleased.[1] But, as we might expect, the lord's rights were regarded as a property which could descend to his heirs.[2] It was easy for this personal commendation to become a servitude of a much more oppressive kind. In bad seasons money or stock must be borrowed. Hostile raids and the Danegeld must have had similar effects; for the weight of the Danegeld was such that "it was fully capable of transmuting a whole nation."[3] The pecuniary fines for injury to life and limb—the bot, wer, and wite, were very heavy.[4] For all these causes the lord was able to tighten his hand on the man. In addition we have those extensive grants of jurisdiction which have already been mentioned. The small freeholder may be at once the man, the debtor, and the subject of his lord. That the lord has jurisdiction seems to be laid down almost as a general rule in the *Leges Henrici*.[5] At the same time we can as yet lay down no general principle upon which this jurisdiction is based. It is not as yet entirely the jurisdiction of a lord over his tenants. It is still regarded as somewhat of a personal matter. "Nec sequitur socna regis data maneria, sed magis ex personis."[6] A man may be commended to one lord and be under the soke of another.[7]

The second set of these causes operated from above.

The state for many reasons found it convenient to connect landownership with jurisdiction. In the first place the state needed a military force which could be mobilized. A responsible landowner who owned five hides had something to forfeit if he made default. A person who had this amount of land was qualified to be independent—to be a Thegn. For this reason the land was divided into "five hide units" the owners of which were made responsible for the due performance of this service.

modo contiistaverit aliquem. . . . In quibusdam vero non poterit;" ibid lxxxii 3, "Et unicuique licet domino suo sine wita subvenire, si quis assaliet eum, et in omnibus legitimis obedire, preterquam in prodicione, furto, murdro, et deinceps similibus."

[1] Domesday Book and Beyond 72. [2] Ibid 74.

[3] Ibid 7, 8. Cp. Maine, Early History of Institutions, Lecture VI.; the effect of a chief, according to the Irish laws, giving or lending stock is there described as producing all the effects of commendation.

[4] Domesday Book and Beyond 44, "The sons of a villanus who had but two oxen must have been under some temptation to wish that their father would get himself killed by a solvent thegn."

[5] xx 2, "Archiepiscopi, episcopi, comites, et aliæ potestates in terris propriis potestatis suae sacam et socnam habent, tol et theam et infongentheaf; in ceteris vero, per empcionem, vel cambicionem, vel quoquo modo perquisitis, socam et sacam habent, in causis omnibus et hallemotis pertinentibus, super suos et in suo et aliquando super alterius homines."

[6] Leg. Henr. xix.

[7] Ibid xx 2; Domesday Book and Beyond 100.

It was a system which wanted little but a change of names to turn it into a system of knights' fees and military tenure.[1] In the second place " the lordless men of whom no law can be got "[2] are always a difficulty to the state. The lord was made responsible for his dependents. He must produce them in court if they were wanted. This did not mean that he had the power to hold a court for them. That right, in theory at least, depended upon express grant.[3] In the third place an inexpensive method of collecting the taxes is a want constantly felt by the state. We have seen how heavy a tax was the Danegeld. It was an advantage at once to the state and to the small taxpayer to get the great lord to do the work of collection. "The small folk will gladly accept any scheme that will keep the tax collector from their doors even though they purchase their relief by onerous promises of rents and services. The great men again may find advantage in such bargains. They want periodical rents and services and in order to obtain them will accept a certain responsibility for occasional taxes."[4] There is some authority for saying that according to the laws of Cnut only four days of grace were given for payment.[5] After these had passed the man who paid the tax could take the land. We have here a cause which clearly tends to make the lord a landlord.

It is to a combination of these causes that we must ascribe the origins of the manor.[6] The compilers of Domesday Book[7] supposed that manors existed all over England in the days of Edward the Confessor. But we shall see that probably their precise terminology and neat classifications, and above all their underlying theory that all relationships connected with the land and with jurisdiction could be translated into terms of tenure, gave a sharper edge, and in some cases an erroneous interpretation, to very various relationships which had grown up gradually from many various causes.[8] As Professor Vinogradoff has pointed out many various causes went to form the incipient manorial system which we find in Anglo-Saxon society. There is the economic dependency of a man on his lord ; the relationship of the grantor of book-land to the inhabitants of the land so

[1] Domesday Book and Beyond 157-160 ; Stubbs, Sel. Ch. 65.

[2] Laws of Athelstan (Sel. Ch. 66).

[3] Domesday Book and Beyond 285, 286.

[4] Ibid 122 ; possibly if the lord will assume this responsibility the geld charged on his land will be released, ibid 121.

[5] Ibid 55, 56.

[6] Maitland, Domesday Book and Beyond 120-128, thought that the manerium of this period meant a house or an estate against which geld was charged ; but this theory has been disproved by Tait, E.H.R. xii 770-772 ; and Tait's conclusions are accepted by Professor Vinogradoff, Growth of the Manor 300.

[7] For the Domesday Inquest see vol. ii 155-165.

[8] Below 25 ; English Society in the Eleventh Century 339, 340.

granted; the relationship created by the tie of commendation; the relationship created by grants of soke and other jurisdictional privileges.[1] All these factors contributed to the formation of very various groups to which the Norman lawyers gave the compendious term "manor." No doubt the terms "manerium," "mansio" or "halla" originally meant a house or a building; and they are sometimes used in this their original sense.[2] But at the end of the Anglo-Saxon period, the term "manor" was coming to mean an estate in the land, or a group of persons cultivating such an estate, which could be looked at as an economic whole, and yet possessed in different places a diversity of external features,[3] which corresponded to and can be accounted for by the diversity of its origins.

All these causes combined to reduce to hopeless confusion the local jurisdictions of the Anglo-Saxon state. The question what court had jurisdiction in any given case must often have been an insoluble problem without the ready aid of physical force. It was the work of the Norman and the Angevin kings first to classify, and then to subdue this conflict of local jurisdictions.

(2) The effect of the Norman Conquest.

England as the result of the Conquest gained a strong line of capable kings with a genius for organization.[4] This is the most important of the immediate effects of the Conquest. The reign of Stephen shows us how much depended upon the personality of the king. It was not until the central power was permanently organized by the creation of administrative and judicial bodies that the personality of the king ceased to have this paramount importance. In the first instance it directed and modified all the other effects which flowed from the Conquest.

Of these other effects the most important from our present point of view is the fact that the Norman lawyers introduced a clear notion of tenure and of some of the consequences of tenure.

[1] " If we look to the antecedents of the Manor in A.S. times we do not find a single institution corresponding to the Conquest manor, but we do find several institutions working each by itself but combining in practice to produce the inchoate manorial system which Domesday supposes everywhere. These institutions are the *ham* or *cotlif*, the estate centre; the *bocland*, privileged land tenure; the soke, jurisdictional franchise; and the *land-rica's* or land *hlaford's* patronage, the element of lordship," English Society in the Eleventh Century 340.

[2] Domesday Book and Beyond 108, 109; cf. L.Q.R. v 114-115 for later instances of the use of the term "manerium" in this sense; a fourteenth century record there cited talks of the time, " quando Dominus Episcopus faciet domum de novo *vel reparari* faciet manerium suum de Stoketon."

[3] Maneria were of all sizes; thus the manor of Taunton was worth £154 1s. and we read of another manor only worth 15 pence, see Domesday Book and Beyond 110-119.

[4] Haskins, Norman Institutions 6.

The Normans had attained a feudal system by the road of personal commendation, by grants of benefices by the king to his dependents, and by grants of immunities.[1] The resulting condition of affairs in Normandy was in many cases similar to the condition of affairs in England. Often it must have seemed to the Normans that names only required to be changed. But undoubtedly they had attained a clearer conception of tenure, and their feudal system was more entirely based upon it. Land is. conceived of as held not merely *sub*, under a lord, but *de*, of a lord. "*Sub* lays stress on the lord's power which may well be of a personal or justiciary rather than of a proprietary kind, while *de* imparts a theory about the origin of the tenure ; it makes the tenant's rights look like derivative rights :—it is supposed that he gets his land from his lord."[2] It was from this new point of view that English society was looked at by the compilers of Domesday Book ; and naturally it was productive of large changes in social relationships. A large number of the older indeterminate forms of dependency, a large number of the older forms of land ownership, tended to disappear in the light of this new theory. Thus, as Professor Vinogradoff has pointed out, "a number of people who could go with their land where they pleased disappear," and, "a number of others who owned to confusing forms of dependency on personal lords and lords of soke, were forced under one or other of the convenient headings supplied by feudal terminology."[3] Moreover it had a large effect upon the relation of the people to the units of local jurisdiction to which they were subject. It tended to emphasize their subjection to the lord of whom they held their land, and to weaken their relations to the older associations of township, hundred, and shire.[4] This will be clear if we look at one of the most important consequences of tenure.

The lord, because he is a lord, has a right to hold a court for his tenants. This theory was well recognized in Normandy,[5] and it is explicitly stated in the *Leges Henrici*. "Every lord may summon his man that he stand to right in his court ; and if he is resident at a distant manor of the honour of which he holds, he must go to the plea if his lord summon him."[6] The

---

[1] Stubbs, C.H. i 286-292.   [2] Domesday Book and Beyond 154.
[3] The Growth of the Manor 295-296.
[4] "People had now to look, not so much to their time-honoured associations in township, hundred, and shire, as to their relations of personal and territorial dependence," ibid 296.
[5] Haskins, Norman Institutions 24.
[6] "Omni domino licet submonire hominem suum, ut ei sit ad rectum in curia sua ; et si residens est ad remotius manerium ejusdem honoris unde tenet, ibit ad placitum, si dominus suus submoneat eum," Leg. Henr. lv 1.

lord's court for his tenants is frequently mentioned by Glanvil;[1] and the refusal of an abbot of Peterborough and a prior of Dunstable to allow their freeholders to hold a court for their tenants was said to be contrary to law.[2] It is obvious that this theory might have led to a growth of feudal courts one above the other, and, ultimately, to the growth of compact feudal provinces. Thus the Bishop of Ely held a court for his manor at Littleport, but difficult cases and complaints of insufficient justice were heard in his council.[3] Many lords held a central court to which their more important tenants owed suit.[4] But compact feudal provinces were not formed in England; and this is due in part to the circumstances of the Conquest; but chiefly to the energy and foresight of the Norman and Angevin kings. Successive rebellions of the English led to successive confiscations. The dominions of the Norman barons were therefore scattered.[5] Except in the cases of the earldom of Chester and the bishopric of Durham no great provinces were created.[6] The Norman and Angevin kings made good use of their position as the successors of Edward the Confessor. They used the organization of the communal courts, as they used Anglo-Saxon soldiers, to keep under their disorderly barons. Thus, although the distinctly feudal conception of jurisdiction dependent on tenure was introduced, it operated under such limitations that it never attained great proportions.

What is true of jurisdiction dependent on tenure is true also of the special grants conferring various franchises. Such franchise jurisdictions were also well known in Normandy.[7] Grants which had been made by the Anglo-Saxon kings were in many cases recognized and confirmed by the Norman and Angevin kings. But it is chiefly in the Palatine counties that the franchises attained large dimensions.[8] To take our old instance of Durham.

[1] ii 8; ix 1 and 11; xii 2-7.
[2] Select Pleas in Manorial Courts (S.S.) xlv.
[3] The Court Baron (S.S.) 111.
[4] E.g. The abbots of Ramsey, Gloucester, St. Albans, St. Edmunds. Select Pleas in Manorial Courts (S.S.) xlv, xlvi; Madox, Exchequer i 107-112; the abbot of St. Augustine of Canterbury could hear complaints of failure of justice in the hundred court of Fordwich, see a fine of 1182 cited Ballard, Borough Charters 149.
[5] Stubbs, C.H. i 310, 311.
[6] Ibid i 307-309; Kent was for a few years a county Palatine under William's brother Odo; Shropshire also under the earls of Montgomery was a palatinate till it was confiscated by Henry I. after the rebellion of Robert of Belesme.
[7] Haskins, Norman Institutions 25-30.
[8] We do sometimes meet with very extensive franchises, Rot. Cur. Reg. (Rec. Com.) i, xxxi, xxxii, 426—in 1199 William de Braosa says that neither king, sheriff, nor justice have any right to enter his liberty, and in 1302 William de Braosa lord of Gower said that he had his chancellor and Chancery and his seal, judgment of life and death, cognisance of all pleas, whether of the crown or not, arising within the liberty; ibid ii 6, 10—the Bishop of Ely deduced the title to his franchise from

" If any other argument were required to prove that William the Conqueror considered the Palatinate of Durham as a dominion entirely separate from those of the crown, it is the fact that in his great territorial survey he entirely omitted all notice of the Palatinate." [1]   We have charters of Henry I.'s and Stephen's reigns confirming its privileges; and even Henry II., when he sent his justices into the Palatinate, admitted that he did so only by the licence of the bishop, and that this special occasion formed no precedent. [2]   The Earl of Chester had similar rights— " he was in fact a feudal sovereign of Cheshire as the king was in Normandy." [3]   That these were exceptional cases is evident from the list compiled by Madox of the fines paid for franchises during this period. [4]   Some of them take the form of a confirmation of existing franchises, or are grants in the old Saxon words. [5] These words no doubt once conferred a wide jurisdiction, but they were soon destined to become meaningless.   In other cases in which franchises were granted in newer technical terms, they were usually of the humbler class.   The most usual was the view of frankpledge.   There are also grants of freedom from suit to the hundred and shire courts and from all payments to the sheriff. [6]   Sometimes a man was allowed to tallage his manor as the king tallaged his demesnes. [7]   In fact, just as considerations of space and distance limited the purely feudal jurisdiction, so it limited the jurisdiction exercised by virtue of these special grants. The average baron had the opportunity to exercise only the humbler class of franchises.   It was franchises of this kind which were least able to maintain themselves against the growing jurisdiction of the king's court.

Edgar, through Charters of Edward the Confessor, William I., and Henry I.; Select Pleas of the Crown (S.S.) case 98.

[1] Registrum Dunelmense (R.S.) i, lxvi, lxvii; it is recorded moreover that neither king nor earl had any rights over the lands of St Cuthbert in Yorkshire, Domesday Book i 298 b.

[2] Registrum Dunelmense (R.S.) i, lxvii, " Sciatis quod consilio Baronum meorum, et Episcopi Dunelmensis licencia, mitto hac vice in terram Sancti Cuthberti justiciam meam, quæ videat ut fiat justicia, secundum assisam meam, de latronibus et murdratoribus, et roboratoribus; non quia velim ut trahatur in consuetudinem tempore meo, vel hæredum meorum, sed ad tempus hoc facio, pro prædicta necessitate;" four other charters of the same king confirm the bishop's franchises, Lapsley, County Palatine of Durham 126.

[3] Stubbs, C.H. i 411.

[4] Exchequer i 397-424.   For grants of freedom from taxation see Dialogus de Scaccario (Sel. Ch.) 222.

[5] A grant to the Prior and monks of Worcester that they have within their four manors " Socam et Sacam et Tol et Team et Infangenethief cum judiciis Aquæ et Ignis et Furcarum et Ferii et cum quietantiis aliarum Libertatum sicut continetur in Cartis Regum quas inde habent," cited Madox i 408.

[6] Grant to the abbot of Ramsey, " quod ipse et dominica sua quieta sint de sectis Schirarum et hundredorum, et de auxiliis Vicecomitum, et pro habendo franco pledgio in Curia sua," cited Madox i 404.

[7] Ibid 418, 419.

Thus, as a result of the Conquest, we can, at the end of the twelfth century, begin to distinguish two species of private jurisdiction. There is firstly a jurisdiction dependent upon tenure—a purely feudal jurisdiction ; and secondly a jurisdiction dependent upon royal grant or confirmation—a franchise jurisdiction. We shall see that, from the thirteenth century onwards, the most common variety of the purely feudal jurisdiction was the manorial jurisdiction ;[1] and that the most permanently important of the franchise jurisdictions was that vested in a borough.[2] During this period the manor as such has not yet become a jurisdictional unit ; and the privileges granted by the king or other lords to boroughs do not entitle the borough courts to rank among the most important of the franchise jurisdictions. But, in certain developments which were taking place in the twelfth century, we can see some of the causes which will give both to the manor and to the borough their positions in later law. Of these developments, therefore, I shall say a few words.

(i) *The Manor.*—We have seen that economic units of very varied kinds, in which we can see the germ of the later manor, were for very various causes springing up all over England in the latter part of the Saxon period.[3] As a result of the Norman Conquest these units got the name "manor ; "[4] and the term "manor" tended to acquire a more definite meaning. It would seem that "at the time of the Domesday Inquest the expression 'manor' was currently used to designate estates organized under aristocratic administration—under knights, or the ecclesiastical corporations which may be substituted for them."[5] But as yet there were many manors which did not answer to this description. There were, in fact, several distinct types or varieties of manor which represented the various conditions under which the manorial system had arisen in the Anglo-Saxon period, and the various causes for the growth of these conditions. Of these types Professor Vinogradoff has distinguished five main classes :[6] There are manors which are capitalistic organizations—which form an economic centre surrounded by the peasant holdings which support them ; there are manors which are administrative centres of scattered or more or less independent settlements ; there are manors which are "sokes," that is jurisdictional units ;

---

[1] Below 179-187.　　　[2] Below 138-151.　　　[3] Above 23, 24.
[4] " Neither the term *manor* nor any corresponding and equally comprehensive designation occurs in Saxon times ; " but, " we find that the summarizing terminology and the unifying legal treatment adopted by the Survey were the results of facts which had actually existed before, though in a rather straggling condition, with many gaps or irregularities," Vinogradoff, English Society in the Eleventh Century 340.
[5] Ibid 311.　　　[6] Ibid.

there are royal manors ; and there are manors which are small estates exploited directly either by their masters or by rustics.

During the twelfth century these different types of manor tended to disappear, and the term manor consequently tended more and more to become "an estate organized under aristocratic administration". This was due partly to the direct results of the Conquest, partly to the universal application of the principle of tenure to all forms of land holding, and partly to the growth of a common law which was beginning to lay down general legal principles applicable to land holding. Let us glance briefly at the influence of these three sets of circumstances.

Firstly, the Conquest was disastrous in its results to the poorer classes.[1] Their new lords were able to exact from them pretty much what they pleased. In Henry II.'s reign, it is true, the humblest freeholder was protected by the king's court.[2] But the poorer classes were generally not freeholders. They were villeins who held merely at the will of the lord.[3] The lord was the person responsible to the central government for military service and feudal dues. Hence "the principal element of an eleventh century manor is the lord, the representative of feudal aristocracy in the place."[4] It was not long before the lord came to be regarded as the owner of the soil of the manor.[5] Secondly, the lord is more than an official responsible for the collection of certain dues, and he is more than a landowner. He is the lord of the inhabitants of the manor who hold their land of him. Thus he is "a man in authority over a district connected with his estate, and this authority he wields in consequence of a contract of feudal service."[6] Thirdly, the growth of general

---

[1] Dialogus de Scaccario i, x ; and this tradition lasted on into the thirteenth century ; thus Bracton, f. 7, says, " Fuerunt etiam in conquestu liberi homines, qui libere tenuerunt tenementa sua per libera servitia, vel per liberas consuetudines, et cum per potentiores ejecti essent, postmodum reversi receperunt eadem tenementa sua tenenda in villenagio, faciendo inde opera servilia."

[2] Below 47 ; vol. ii 201, 260 ; vol. iii 30.

[3] Vol. iii 198-213.   [4] Vinogradoff, English Society 472.

[5] India offers a curious parallel. When a new province was settled the question arose who was to be made responsible for the land revenue. In determining this, the political and social constitution of the province was determined. " Do you on entering on the settlement of a province find that a peasant proprietary has been displaced by an oligarchy of usurpers, and do you think it expedient to take the government dues from the once oppressed yeomen ? The result is the immediate decline . . . of the class above them. . . . Do you, reversing this policy, arrange that the superior holder shall be answerable to the government ? You find that you have created a landed aristocracy which has no parallel in wealth or power except the proprietors of English soil." There is no assumption that new proprietary powers are conferred. " But in the vague and floating order of primitive societies the mere definition of a right immensely increases its strength. . . . All agrarian rights, whether superior or subordinate to those of the person held responsible to Government, have a steady tendency to decay," Maine, Village Communities 149-151.

[6] English Society 472.

rules relating to tenure, and to the rights, and duties and interests of tenants,[1] tended to make manors conform more and more to a uniform type.

As the result of all these causes the very small "maneriola" of Domesday Book which were cultivated by groups of villeins, or of socmen, or thanes, or royal serjeants,[2] tend to disappear by a process of absorption into larger units. "They presented," as Professor Vinogradoff has said,[3] "a kind of compromise between the original independent cultivation and ownership of small households, and the forces of patronage and exploitation embodied in the great lordships." As the latter forces gained in strength the typical manor becomes a unit in which there is a lord with lands of his own in demesne, and free and villein tenants, who have, in addition to their holdings, rights of common in the lord's waste. By the process of borrowing certain ideas from the feudal principle that a lord of tenants has a right to hold a court for them, the lord will get, as the necessary part of his manorial rights, the power to hold a court or courts. The manor will come to connote both proprietary and jurisdictional rights. But it was not until the feudal principle had been reduced to a humbler place than it occupied in the reigns of the Norman and Angevin kings that this result was reached.[4]

(ii) *The Boroughs.*[5]—It is clear from Domesday Book and from the Anglo-Saxon Laws that certain areas were recognized as boroughs, and that certain persons, sometimes resident within these areas and sometimes not, were recognized as burgesses. We shall see that these areas were sometimes fortified places, and sometimes places where a market was held.[6] On that account they were differently organized from the country at large. They had a special court, special customs, special privileges, and, what was most important to the compilers of Domesday Book, they were answerable for special sources of revenue.[7] But they were subject to the control of the sheriff,[8] and in many cases the earl was entitled to the third penny of their receipts.[9] Though they were specially treated by the Domesday commissioners, though they were specially regulated in the Anglo-Saxon laws, it is difficult to see exactly wherein

---

[1] Vol. ii 199-201, 375-381. [2] English Society 332-337.
[3] Ibid 338. [4] Below 176-179.
[5] See Maitland, Domesday Book and Beyond 172-219; Ballard, the Domesday Boroughs; and, British Borough Charters 1042-1216.
[6] Below 138, 139.
[7] Ballard, Domesday Boroughs chap. iv.
[8] Maitland, op. cit. 209; Ballard, Domesday Boroughs 44-46.
[9] Ibid 41-43.

they differed from other areas in the country at large. Most of
the privileges which they possessed were sometimes also possessed
by areas which were not boroughs;[1] and so far were they from
being a unit which was more definite and more capable of acting
for itself than other communities, that it would seem that they
were, in at least one respect, less capable of thus acting than the
counties or the hundreds. Mr. Ballard tells us[2] that "the
Domesday scribes make an important distinction between the
borough and the other areas; the shire, the riding, the wapentake,
and the hundred were represented as being able to give evidence
for or against claims to land; but the borough, and in this
respect it resembles the manor and the vill, is never represented
as giving evidence."

It was after the Conquest that the gift of certain privileges
to certain areas by charters granted by the king or other lords
gradually separated the borough more clearly from other jurisdictional or governmental units.[3] Certain privileges began to
be regarded as distinctly burghal privileges. The boroughs
themselves began to develop bodies of customary law which
were often codified in their custumals.[4] As the institutions of
the central government grew more elaborate, as the working of
these institutions produced a body of law common to the whole
country, the position which these borough areas took in relation
to these institutions and this law, became different from the
position of other areas in the country at large. We shall see
that in consequence the borough became a variety of franchise
which, though it resembled some of the other franchises in certain
respects, yet had certain peculiar characteristics which put it in a
class by itself.[5]

Thus both the manor and the borough owe their final form
to the growth of a strong centralized government and a common
law. This government and this law moulded and adapted certain
institutions existing in the eleventh and twelfth centuries, and
developed certain tendencies which were beginning to appear in
those centuries, in such a way that they produced the manors and
the boroughs of our modern law. At the same time these same
agencies by classifying, defining, and controlling the powers and
duties of the other units and officials which exercised local jurisdiction throughout the country, were influencing them in a
similar manner. Consequently they too began to assume their
modern shape and their modern position in the English judicial

---

[1] Ballard, British Borough Charters lxxxviii-lxxxix; cf. Maitland, Domesday
Book and Beyond 216-217.
[2] British Borough Charters xcv.
[3] For the importance of the Charter see ibid xiii, xiv.
[4] For these custumals see vol. ii 373-375.   [5] Below 140, 141.

and administrative system. But, before the history of these developments can be traced, the origins of those central institutions and that common law to which they were due must first be examined.

II. THE CURIA REGIS AND THE BEGINNINGS OF A CENTRALIZED JUDICIAL SYSTEM

The term "Curia Regis" is used in two senses. It means (i) the place where the king resided attended by the chief officials of his court and household; and (ii) the supreme central court where the business of government in all its branches was transacted.[1] It is the latter meaning which is of interest to the legal and constitutional historian; and it is the meaning which is here attached to the term.

Both England and Normandy possessed a central court, composed of the most important men in the nation,[2] in which all the business of government was transacted. In England there was the Witan[3] which became after the Conquest the Curia Regis, and in Normandy the Curia Ducis.[4] There were many points of similarity between these three bodies.[5] In the case both of the Witan and of the Curia Regis three stated meetings were held at the period of the three church festivals of Christmas, Easter, and Pentecost;[6] and their constitution was so similar that the Anglo-Saxon chronicler has no difficulty in calling the assemblies of the Curia Regis Witans. Nevertheless, though there was this general similarity between the two bodies, they were fundamentally different. Just as Norman feudalism differed from the incipient feudalism of the Anglo-Saxon period in the fact that Norman feudalism was grounded upon a logical theory of tenure from which all the rights and duties of lords and tenants flowed,[7] so the Curia Regis differed from the Anglo-Saxon Witan by the rigid application of this same theory of tenure to the composition of this assembly. It was, like the Curia Ducis of Normandy,[8] composed in theory, if not of all the king's tenants

---

[1] Madox, Exchequer i 81-82.

[2] P. and M. i 50, 51; Madox, Exchequer i 25; Haskins, Norman Institutions 55-58.

[3] Above 15, 16.

[4] P. and M. i 50, 51: cf. Madox, Exchequer i 25; Haskins, Norman Institutions 54-58.

[5] Adams, The Origin of the English Constitution 12.

[6] In Normandy there was only one regular assembly at Easter, Haskins, Norman Institutions 55; Adams, Origin of the English Constitution 65.

[7] Above 24, 25.

[8] " He (the Duke of Normandy) holds a court; we dare hardly as yet call it a court of his tenants in chief; but it is an assembly of the great men and the great men are his vassals," P. and M. i 50.

in chief, at least of all who held *per baroniam.*[1] Among these tenants in chief were comprised all the officials of the government ;[2] and in addition any other persons whom the king chose to summon.[3] It was thus a court which resembled much more closely the feudal Curia Ducis than the Anglo-Saxon Witan. It was Norman not only in its composition, but also in its procedure, and in the terminology used to describe both its constituent members and its activities.[4] We can see therefore a general resemblance, but no institutional continuity between the Witan and the Curia Regis. The institutional continuity which does exist between the Saxon and Norman period must be looked for elsewhere. As we shall now see, some of the indirect effects of the continuity, which undoubtedly exists in the case of other institutions of government, have had important effects upon the development of the Curia Regis during the twelfth century.

We have seen that a certain amount of institutional continuity can be traced in the organs of local government. The powers of the sheriff were retained and even strengthened. The organization of the communal courts was continued.[5] We shall see too that, as William I. and Henry I. promised, the Anglo-Saxon laws —the laws of Edward the Confessor—were the basis of the law administered in those courts ; and that it was for that reason that so many compilations of those laws were made during the reigns of the Norman kings.[6] What is perhaps even more important we can also trace this same institutional continuity in the office of the king. The Norman kings always regarded themselves as the successors of Edward the Confessor. They were lawful kings of the English ; and, as such, they were entitled to exercise those powers of government which men believed were put into their hands for the preservation of peace, the protection of the weak, and the maintenance of justice.[7] Because they were kings they had powers which transcended the powers of a mere feudal suzerain. No doubt these powers were vague. But, because

---

[1] As Adams, op. cit. 57, points out, " One of the clearest statements of the institutional principle of the court is to be found in c. xi of the Constitutions of Clarendon ; that clause runs as follows : ' Archiepiscopi, episcopi, et universæ personæ regni, qui de rege tenent in capite, habent possessiones suas de domino rege sicut baroniam, et inde respondent Justitiis et ministris regis, et sequuntur et faciunt omnes rectitutines et consuetudines regias, et sicut barones ceteri, debent interesse judiciis curiæ domini regis cum baronibus '."

[2] Below 35-38.

[3] " The feudal law provided in no way for the attendance of the non-vassal. Yet it seems clear that the king had the right to make persons whom we cannot show to have been his vassals full members of the court," Adams, op. cit. 61.

[4] Madox, Exchequer i 180. [5] Above 7-15.

[6] Vol. ii 151-154 ; see above 3 n. 1.

[7] Vol. ii 10, 15-16, 23 ; cf. Adams, op. cit. 58-59.

they were vague, they were of the greatest value to kings who were in a position to exploit them to the uttermost, firstly because they were in effect conquerors, and secondly because they were men of exceptional ability and force of character. It was by the help of these prerogative powers, which were regarded as inherent in the office of king, and as belonging to them as the successors to Edward the Confessor, that the Norman and Angevin kings so developed the powers of the feudal Curia Regis that they made it the most efficient organ of centralized government that existed in Western Europe. Thus it can, I think, be said that what continuity there is between the institutions of central government in the Anglo-Saxon and the Anglo-Norman state must be traced through the monarchy, and not through the Witan and the Curia Regis. We shall see this more clearly if we look, firstly, at the constitution and work of the Curia Regis as a whole, and secondly, at the beginnings of the process of disintegration into separate courts and departments of state, which we can discern at the close of Henry II.'s reign.

The Constitution and Work of the Curia Regis as a Whole

The Curia Regis was the king's court; and of it the king was both an essential and an active member. It was therefore an itinerant court which followed the king in his progresses over England, and in his journeyings over his continental dominions. Richard of Anesty has left us a graphic description of his journeys to Normandy and Gascony, between the years 1158 and 1163, to get from the king and his Curia the necessary writs for the conduct of his law suit.[1] Often the king heard suitors in person;[2] and there is no doubt that Henry II.'s ceaseless activity kept the men who staffed his court up to their work. Mapes tells us that, having complimented Glanvil on the justice of the decisions of the Curia Regis and the swiftness with which they were enforced, Glanvil replied that there was no doubt that they decided cases much more quickly in that court "than your bishops decide them in their courts;" "to which," says Mapes, "I retorted, 'that is true; but if your king was as far from you as

---

[1] See Bigelow, Placita Anglo-Normanica 311; P. and M. i 137-138; for other instances see Madox, Exchequer i 87-88.

[2] Bigelow 212, 214; in the case of Abbot Odo (ibid 221), the abbot got from the king's court the renewal of an old charter; the king suppressed one clause and inserted another of his own making "nec dedignatus est inclitus princeps super praedicta clausula reddere rationem;" in the case of the Archbishop of Canterbury and the Abbot of St. Edmunds (ibid 239) the conflicting charters produced were too much for the king, "rex . . . indignans surrexit et recedendo dixit; qui potest capere capiat; et sic res capit dilacionem."

the pope is from the bishops I think you would go equally slowly'." To this retort Glanvil could only give a smiling assent.[1]

We have seen that the court itself was in theory composed of the king's tenants in chief, the royal officials, and anyone else whom the king chose to summon. In practice we can discern two chief types of assembly. On important occasions it was a large assembly composed of all the leading landowners and officials of the country. It was such an assembly as this which enquired into the law as to the boundaries of the lay and ecclesiastical jurisdiction in order to draw up the Constitutions of Clarendon.[2] But probably the ordinary work of government was done by a small body of officials.[3] Of such a kind was probably the assembly which passed wakeful nights in drawing up the assize of novel disseisin.[4] But as yet there is no formal distinction between the two types of assembly. Both were alike Curiæ Regis.[5] Both therefore had the same undefined powers of government. Indeed it would seem that any court held by an itinerant justice commissioned by the king was equally Curia Regis.[6] At first we can discern only a *de facto* distinction between these two types of assembly; but, as we shall see, the fact that it is possible to draw this distinction, and the fact that it grows more marked and more important in Henry I.'s and Henry II.'s reigns, tells us something of the increasing activities and powers of the Curia Regis. It is these increasing activities and powers which are the direct cause of the growth of a centralized judicial system and a common law.

The principal officials of the king's court and household who took the chief part in the government of the country were the justiciar, the chancellor, the treasurer, the chamberlain, the constable, the marshall, and the king's justices.[7] It is the justiciar, the chancellor, and the justices who are the most important in the history of the English judicial system; and therefore of them I must say something.

---

[1] " Certe nos hic longe velocius causas decidimus quam in ecclesiis episcopi vestri. Tum ego, Verum est; sed si rex noster tam remotus esset a vobis, quam ab episcopis est papa, vos aeque lente crederem. Ipse vero risit," Mapes, De Nugis Curialium (C.S.) 241.

[2] " Facta est ista recognitio coram archiepiscopis et episcopis et clero et comitibus et baronibus et proceribus regni," Sel. Ch. 137.

[3] Adams, op. cit. 62-63; Baldwin, The King's Council 10-15.

[4] " De beneficio principis succurritur ei per recognitionem assisæ novæ disseisinæ, multis vigiliis excogitatam et inventam," Bracton, f. 164 b.

[5] P. and M. i 132.

[6] Thus, as Maitland points out, "a fine levied before the itinerant justices always purports to be finalis concordia in curia dominî Regis," P. and M. i 134 n. 1; cf. Poole, The Exchequer in the Twelfth Century 175.

[7] See Madox, Exchequer i chap. ii; Stubbs, C.H. i 389-403.

The justiciar was originally the lieutenant or viceroy of the king during his absences from England. "In this capacity William Fitz-Osbern, the steward of Normandy, and Odo of Bayeux acted during the Conqueror's visit to the Continent in 1067; they were left . . . the former to govern the north of England, and the latter to hold rule in Kent in the king's stead."[1] One chronicler calls them "custodes Angliæ;" and another calls their office a "Præfectura."[2] Other holders of the office were Lanfranc, Gosfrid of Coutances, and Robert of Mortain.[3] It does not seem at this time to have been a p rmanent office, as it ceased to exist as soon as the king returned.[4] It was under William II. that the office became permanent. Its duties "included the direction of the whole judicial and financial arrangements of the kingdom;"[5] but, even after the office had become permanent, the powers of the justiciar seem to have been from time to time "restrained or superseded if the king thought fit," by writs *de ultra mare*, which gave directions as to the course to be pursued in particular matters.[6] Thus the justiciar became the first minister of the kingdom. Probably this development was largely due to Ranulf Flambard. Up to the time of his appointment the office had been held by some one of the great nobles. But the treason of Odo of Bayeux and the Bishop of Durham, both of whom had held the office earlier in the reign, showed that it was dangerous to entrust so important an office to such persons.[7] Flambard was a royal official who had made his name as a financier;[8] and, after him, the office was filled by a succession of royal officials who had similarly made their careers in the king's service. Under Henry I. the most famous was Roger, Bishop of Salisbury. He remodelled the administrative system of the country; and his achievements in organizing the Exchequer were chronicled by his great-nephew Richard, Bishop of London and Treasurer, in his Dialogus de Scaccario.[9] For the first twenty-five years of Henry II.'s reign the office was held by Richard de Lucy;[10] but the most famous of his justiciars was Lucy's successor Glanvil.[11] The book which passes under his name is the earliest book on the common law of England. It describes the judicial achievements of the Norman and Angevin kings, as the Dialogus had described their financial achievements. Hubert Walter,[12] Glanvil's nephew

---

[1] Stubbs, C.H. i 392.   [2] Ibid.   [3] Ibid 393.
[4] Ibid.   [5] Ibid.   [6] Madox, Exchequer i 84-85.
[7] Stubbs, C.H. i 393-394.   [8] Ibid 394.
[9] Ibid 395-396; Stubbs tells us that he started life as a poor priest of Caen, and that "he had attracted Henry's notice long before he came to the throne by his expeditious way of celebrating divine service."
[10] Ibid 548.
[11] For an account of him and his book see vol. ii 188-192.
[12] Stubbs, C.H. 564-565, 567.

and perhaps the writer of the treatise that goes under Glanvil's name,[1] was Richard's ablest justiciar. We can trace his organizing hand in the institution of a regular system of enrolment of the pleas of the Curia Regis,[2] in the separation of the Chancery from the Exchequer,[3] in the institution of the rolls of the Chancery,[4] and perhaps in the institution of the Exchequer of the Jews.[5] He was succeeded by Geoffrey Fitz-Peter who had been trained under Glanvil and Walter.[6] Both Walter and Fitz-Peter exercised a restraining influence upon John; and it was not till after Fitz-Peter's death that the permanent breach between king and nation came. All these men played a large part in working out and securing the success of the reforms of Henry I. and II. They are among the founders of the common law.

The name Chancellor is derived from the *cancelli* or screen behind which the secretarial work of the royal household was carried on.[7] The Carolingian kings had a cancellarius who was a royal notary, and an archi-cancellarius who kept the king's seal. Edward the Confessor, the first English king to have a seal, was also the first king to have a Chancellor to keep it. He was always an ecclesiastic, the chief of the royal chaplains, and charged with the administration of the royal revenue from vacant benefices. But his chief duty was secretarial. He was "the secretary of state for all departments;" and as part of this duty he drew and sealed the royal writs.[8] He was a prominent member of the Exchequer department of the Curia Regis;[9] and he assisted in the judicial business both of the Exchequer and the Curia Regis, and acted as itinerant justice.[10] The increase of the business of the Curia Regis increased the dignity of the Chancellor, and necessitated the employment of a staff of clerks.[11] The Chancellor thus became the head of a department—the Chancery. In 1199 the departments of the Exchequer and the Chancery were separated, and a separate set of rolls—the Chancery Rolls—began.[12] As we have seen,[13] it is probable that

---

[1] Vol. ii 189-190.   [2] Poole, The Exchequer in the Twelfth Century 187.
[3] Ibid 187-188.   [4] Ibid 188.
[5] Ibid 187 n. 4; for this institution see below 45-46; for the rolls of the Curia Regis, the Exchequer, and the Chancery see vol. ii 180-182.
[6] Stubbs, C.H. i 574-575, 588.
[7] Ibid i 398; and for an account of the office at this period see Madox, Exchequer i 60-76.
[8] Stubbs, C.H. i 398-399.
[9] Poole, op. cit. 104; in the Dialogus i 5 it is said, " Cancellarius in ordine illo primus est; et sicut in curia sic ad scaccarium magnus est; adeo ut sine ipsius consensu vel consilio nil magnum fiat, vel fieri debeat."
[10] Madox, Exchequer i 61.   [11] Ibid 75-76.
[12] Poole, op. cit. 187-188; cf. Madox i 196 for another view; see also Select Pleas of the Crown (S.S.) viii; Close Rolls (Rec. Com.) vii, viii.
[13] Above n. 3.

this separation, and the establishment of a new set of rolls, on the model of the rolls of the Exchequer and the Curia Regis, was due to Hubert Walter, who held the office from 1199 till his death in 1205. We shall see that to the end the functions of the Chancellor have been miscellaneous. He is not and will not be for some time the head of a court.[1] Even when he attains this position he does not cease to be an important member of the executive government.

Certain persons "associated in judicature" with the justiciar were styled "justitiæ" in Curia Regis.[2] The term "justices" is a general term for the official class who staffed the Exchequer and the Curia Regis. They were therefore much more than judges, since they took part in all the miscellaneous functions of government which, as we shall see, were performed by the Curia Regis. Naturally they became prominent when the work of the Curia expanded in the reign of Henry II. They acted either in the Curia Regis, at the Exchequer, or as itinerant commissioners. Often they were recruited from the staff of the Exchequer ; and, as their training there gave experience of and facilities for dealing with judicial business, they were especially useful in conducting both the judicial work of the Curia and the business of those judicial tribunals which were beginning, at the end of Henry II.'s reign, to disengage themselves from the Curia.[3]

Let us now turn to the work of the Curia Regis. We shall see that just as we can distinguish the large meetings of the Curia attended by the most important tenants in chief from smaller meetings attended chiefly by officials, so we can begin to distinguish the work done at these larger meetings from the work done at the smaller. The larger meetings partook of the nature of feudal councils, and the work done was that which similar feudal councils in other parts of Europe usually did. The smaller meetings were rather of the nature of legislative and administrative boards, and central courts of law. But the fact that these smaller gatherings were as much meetings of the Curia Regis as the larger gave them all the large indefinite powers of king and Curia ; and we shall see that the fact that they had these powers played no small part in the rapid formation of a centralized system of government and a common law.

---

[1] Below 396-397, 400-409.

[2] Madox, Exchequer i 93-95 ; Stubbs, C.H. i 439-440.

[3] Poole, op. cit. 176-177 ; we find therefore that they were sometimes called "justitiarii," sometimes "Barones," Madox, Exchequer i 141 ; the Domesday Commissioners in the inquest for Ely were styled Barones, Sel. Ch. 86 ; as the Domesday inquest was made for fiscal purposes, this indicates that the title "Barones" is given them when they were doing fiscal business, the title "justitiarii" when they were otherwise employed

It contributed to the idea that a professional judge, who presided in a royal court held by him, was the court itself, and could act with all its powers.[1] If we look firstly at the work done by these larger assemblies, and secondly at the work done by the smaller, we shall see the manner in which, by a skilful combination of the powers of a feudal council and of the powers inherent in the royal office, Henry I. and II. put the law and government of England upon an entirely new basis.

(1) Like other feudal Councils the Curia Regis was a legislative, an administrative, and a judicial body.

With its counsel and consent William I. made new laws and amended the laws of Edward the Confessor;[2] and the same counsel and consent is mentioned by Henry I. in his charter.[3] It was a party to the Constitutions of Clarendon,[4] the Assize of Clarendon,[5] and the Ordinance of the Saladin tithe.[6] It must not be supposed, however, that it had very much power to oppose permanently the king's will.[7] It is true that there is an instance of successful opposition to a proposed tax in 1198;[8] but, until the series of events which led to the granting of Magna Carta, this instance is unique. The king could carry what measures he pleased.[9] But he was sensible that the counsel and consent of the Curia added weight to any measure of permanent importance, and, that its approval of a measure showed that it was possible to enforce it without undue friction.

The fact that its counsel and consent were valuable can be seen in the varied administrative measures to which it was a party. Naturally it exercised supervision over the working of the feudal system—over disputes as to the performance of services and the incidents of tenure.[10] It was consulted by Henry I. as to the appointment and dismissal of bishops;[11] and the fact that it was not consulted in the case of the marriage of Henry I.'s daughter, the empress Matilda, to Geoffry of Anjou, was made a matter of complaint.[12] In 1137, at a council held at Oxford, Stephen caused the outbreak of civil war by the arrest of Roger, Bishop of Salisbury, Alexander, Bishop of Lincoln, and

---

[1] Vinogradoff, Magna Carta Commemoration Essays (R.H.S.) 88 89.
[2] Select Charters, 83, 85.   [3] Ibid 100.   [4] Ibid 137.
[5] Ibid 143.   [6] Madox, Exchequer i 20, 21, below n. 9.
[7] See Baldwin, The King's Council 10.   [8] Sel. Ch. 255-256.
[9] For instance the Ordinance of the Saladin tithe was, according to Hovenden, presented to the Curia as a measure already determined upon—" Dominus vero Rex magnum congregavit Concilium Episcoporum, Abbatum, Comitum, et Baronum, et aliorum multorum tam Clericorum quam Laicorum, apud Gaintington ; ubi in publica audientia recitari fecit omnia supradicta capitula quæ constituerat de Cruce capienda," cited Madox, Exchequer i 21 n. q.
[10] Adams, op. cit. 69, 70.   [11] Madox, Exchequer i 10.
[12] Adams op. cit. 68-69.

his nephew, Roger the Chancellor.[1] In Henry II.'s reign it discussed the coronation of the king's son, the marriage of his daughter, and questions of peace and war, all questions in short, relative to the state of the kingdom.[2]

As a feudal court it exercised jurisdiction over the great tenants in chief of the crown. In this capacity it was a judicial court for great men and great causes civil or criminal. In 1072 William I. heard the dispute between the Archbishops of Canterbury and York touching the primacy.[3] In 1088 the Bishop of Durham was tried by the Curia for treason.[4] In 1165 Henry II. called upon Thomas à Becket to answer before him for a wrong done to John his Marshal, and the barons of the Curia adjudged the archbishop to be in the king's mercy.[5] In 1177 the Curia had before them the kings of Navarre and Castile, who had submitted their disputes to Henry II. ;[6] and, says Hovenden, "The Counts and Barons of the Curia Regis of England adjudged that full restitution be made to both parties."[7] The procedure of the court in such cases as these was the old procedure[8] that we have seen in use in the communal courts ;[9] but, as Professor Adams has shown "there was much informality and much of the freedom of discussion of a deliberative body." As in the communal courts the members of the court were the judges. They, not the king, gave the decision ;[10] and the decision when given was announced by the king or other president of the court.[11]

(2) It is in the smaller meetings of the Curia Regis, attended chiefly by officials, that we can see the beginnings of a centralized administrative and judicial system. It was at them that the finance of the kingdom was regulated. It was at them that those measures were carried out which made the Curia a court to which all manner of cases could be brought. Firstly the financial and then the judicial business done by the Curia was regularly recorded on rolls; and, as we have seen, special treatises were written in Henry II.'s reign upon these two sides of its work. It is clear both from the rolls and from these books that this

---

[1] Madox, Exchequer i 14. [2] Ibid 17, 18; Stubbs, C.H. i 640-641.
[3] Madox, Exchequer i 6.
[4] Stubbs, C.H. i 420, 498-499; for other cases see Bigelow, op. cit. 2, 4, 11, 12, 69, 291.
[5] Ibid op. cit. 212. [6] Madox, Exchequer i 18, 19.
[7] " Henricus Rex Angliæ, prolatis coram omni populo Sanctis Evangeliis, fecit prænominatos Nuntios jurare ante Sententiam prolatam, quod Domini eorum, etc. His itaque peractis, Comites et Barones Regalis Curia Angliæ adjudicaverunt plenariam utrique parti supradictorum quæ in jure petita fuerant, fieri restitutionem," cited ibid i 19 n. 1.
[8] Adams, Procedure in the Feudal Curia Regis, Col. Law Rev. April 1913.
[9] Above 10, 11; below 74.
[10] Thus Hovenden iii 240 (cited Sel. Ch. 253) tells us that in 1194 Richard " petit sibi fieri judicium de comite Johanne fratre suo."
[11] Adams, Origin of the English Constitution 64 n.

financial and judicial business was tending to become specialized. The mass of work was becoming too great for one undifferentiated tribunal. It is for this reason that we can perceive in the course of the twelfth century, the beginnings of a disintegration of the Curia which will eventually lead to the creation of separate departments of state, and separate courts of law. We shall get the best idea of the extent and nature of the work done by these small official assemblies by looking at the beginnings of this process of disintegration.

The Process of Disintegration

It might perhaps be thought that the first signs of disintegration in the Curia Regis would be between the large assemblies of the nobility and the smaller assemblies of officials. But it is not so. Though we can see a difference in the size and character of different assemblies both are, as I have said, Curia Regis, and can exercise the same powers. Right down to the events which led to the grant of Magna Carta we can see no signs that the difference in the size and nature of the assembly will give rise to different organs of government. And the reason is fairly obvious. Until the tyranny of John caused a national rising against him, the royal power was by far the strongest force in the kingdom. It could dominate the Curia Regis, whether the Curia consisted of a large assembly of nobles or a small assembly of officials. But it is clear that, if and when the nobility get the power to oppose the king successfully, we may expect to see a rift between the two kinds of assembly. The larger assembly will then tend to become a body which criticizes or opposes the Government, while the smaller will remain a body of officials who are the king's servants. We shall see that from the time of Magna Carta onwards such a rift appears, and gives rise to important changes in the judicial system.[1]

Before this period the process of disintegration had appeared in these smaller assemblies of officials, because they had succeeded in getting into their hands an ever-increasing control over the administration of the Government. As I have said, this increased control was shown in two chief departments of government—in the department of finance, and in that of judicature. Sound finance, as the Norman and Angevin kings knew very well,[2] is always the first essential of strong government; and a firm control over the judicial business of the state was the

---

[1] Below 351-352, 356-357, 480-481.
[2] This characteristic appears as clearly in Normandy as in England, Haskins, Norman Institutions 191.

best security against internal disorder. I shall therefore deal with this topic under the two heads of finance and judicature. We cannot, as we shall see, draw a hard and fast line between them. The Exchequer, the main business of which was finance, was then and long afterwards much concerned with judicature ;[1] the royal judges were as often as not officials of the Exchequer ;[2] and all the great officials of the kingdom were as much members of the Exchequer as of the Curia Regis.[3] We can, however, see a line of disintegration which makes this division a convenient starting point.

(1) *Finance*.

The Treasury of the Norman kings was kept at Winchester. "It was," says Dr. Poole, "the very centre of the administration of the Court. There was kept Domesday Book to be referred to as evidence of tenure, and there early in Henry I.'s reign we find the whole court sitting to decide a dispute as to the dues of the Abbot of Abingdon and deciding it by reference to Domesday Book."[4] Early in the twelfth century we have reference to the enrolment of payments,[5] and shortly after, in 1118, the word "Scaccarium," or "Exchequer" emerges.[6] "The word," says Dr. Poole, "indicates a revolution in the method of auditing the accounts ; it means the introduction of a precise system of calculation worked out by counters on a chequered table and recorded on rolls."[7] The name "Scaccarium," then, was derived from the chequered cloth, figured with squares like a chess board, with which the table in the Exchequer was covered,[8] in order to work the method of calculation with the abacus which was there used.[9] A chequered cloth, Madox tells us, still covered this table in his day.[10] This suggested to the writer of the Dialogus de Scaccario the analogy between the proceedings at the Exchequer and a game of chess. Both, he says, had their fixed laws ; and "as in a game of chess the battle is joined between the kings, so here the battle is joined and the main contest is between the treasurer and the sheriff who is accounting, in the presence of the other judges who are there to see and judge."[11]

---

[1] Below 231 seqq.   [2] Above 38.   [3] Above 35-38.
[4] The Exchequer in the Twelfth Century 36.   [5] Ibid 37-39.
[6] Ibid 39.   [7] Ibid 40, 41.   [8] Madox, Exchequer i 160.
[9] For this see Poole, op. cit. 42 seqq. ; he thinks that it came to England from Laon in Henry I.'s reign ; Haskins, Norman Institutions 175-176, is inclined to an earlier introduction, and to connect it "with the abacists of Lorraine in the preceding century."
[10] Exchequer i 160 ; the prefatory epistle to his work is dated 1708.
[11] "Sicut in lusili, pugna committitur inter reges : sic in hoc inter duos principaliter conflictus est et pugna committitur, thesaurarium scilicet et vicecomitem qui assidet ad compotum ; residentibus aliis tanquam judicibus ut videant et judicent," Dialogus i 1 ; for this work see vol. ii 186-188.

The Dialogus tells us that there were some who thought that the Exchequer in England could be traced back to Anglo-Saxon times.[1] It is clear that this view is erroneous. As Dr. Poole says, " The Exchequer first came into existence when the chequered table was arranged for working the accounts about the middle of the reign of Henry I." [2] Nor is it true that the English Exchequer was imported from Normandy. On the contrary the English Exchequer, organized by Roger, Bishop of Salisbury, was introduced into Normandy.[3] Naturally the organization of the Norman and English Exchequers were so similar that " The Treasury of Caen could lend an abbot to the Exchequer of Westminster, or the Exchequer of Westminster could lend a baron to revise the accounts of Caen." [4]

There were two divisions in the Exchequer. In the lower division, or Exchequer of receipt, the money was received, weighed, or otherwise tested. In the upper division accounts were settled between the crown and its debtors, or accountants —the chief of whom was the sheriff; and legal disputes as to payments were decided.[5] It is this upper division of the Exchequer which is of importance in legal history. Twice a year, at Easter and Michaelmas, the sheriff and other persons who had received money on behalf of the crown appeared before the board.[6] The central government thus got a general view of the working of the machinery of local government throughout the country, and could exercise over it an intelligent supervision.

All the great officials of the state took their places at the Exchequer. The Justiciar presided—the Treasurer did not take this position till the Justiciar ceased to be a regular attendant.[7] From the first the Treasurer kept a roll which was a duplicate of that kept by the Chancellor.[8] The Chancellor performed part of his duties at the Exchequer, since the great seal was kept in the Treasury.[9] Charters, the original writs of Liberate, Allocate, Computate, and Perdono, and writs of summons against the king's debtors issued from the Chancery in the Exchequer.[10] But we have seen that, when Hubert Walter was Chancellor,

[1] Dialogus i 4.

[2] Op. cit. 66; for fiscal arrangements before the Conquest see ibid 21 seqq.

[3] Poole, op. cit. 57-59, has settled this controverted question; cf. Haskins, op. cit. 176. For the Norman Exchequer see Madox, Exchequer i 162-177; for certain subordinate " receipts or treasuries " sometimes called Exchequers, see ibid ii 3-5.

[4] Stubbs, C.H. i 497; cf. Haskins, op. cit. 192-193.

[5] Stubbs, C.H. i 429; Dialogus i 2.   [6] Stubbs, C.H. i 429.

[7] Dialogus i 4; Poole, op. cit. 103-104.

[8] Ibid 112; Dialogus i 5.   [9] Ibid.

[10] Madox, Exchequer i 214; ii 254. The writ of *Liberate* authorized the issue of money, and the writ of *Allocate* or *Computate* certain allowances or discounts to certain accountants; the writ of *Perdono* released the king's claim to certain payments.

the Chancery became a department distinct from the Exchequer
with a separate set of rolls.[1]   The withdrawal of the Chancellor
led to many changes in the Exchequer.   The Chancellor's clerk
became an important Exchequer official, and eventually gained
the title of Chancellor of the Exchequer; and, when the
Treasurer ceased to busy himself in financial matters, he became
the head of the department.[2]   The higher officials of the Exchequer were the Barones Scaccarii.   As the Exchequer became
more and more a distinct department of state, and as the knowledge required for its proper working became more and more
esoteric, the functions of these Barones became differentiated, and
so we get the rise of a new class of official Barons.[3]   The Dialogus, which was written before 1179, shows us that even then
matters were fast tending in this direction.[4]

There is little sign as yet of a division between the financial
and the judicial sides of the Exchequer.   The Exchequer was
as yet both the Treasury and the law court of later days.   It
both collected the revenue and tried cases.   But we may perhaps see the possibility of the future separation of these two
functions in the fact that the Barons of the Exchequer were
often called upon to decide knotty points in the upper Exchequer,
and that for this purpose they sometimes sat apart from the place
where the general business was done.[5]   Moreover, as we have
seen, these Barons, at the Exchequer and elsewhere, were often
employed on judicial business other than that arising out of the
revenue.[6]   It is clear that, if this increase in the judicial duties
of the Barons continues, it will naturally lead to a separation of
the judicial from the financial side of the Exchequer.   But it
was not till after the lapse of more than a century that this
separation took place;[7] and we shall see that, when it took
place, the distinct origin of the court of Exchequer caused it to
differ markedly from the other two common law courts.[8]

[1] Above 37, 38.
[2] Poole, op. cit. 115, 189; he had got the title of Chancellor of the Exchequer
certainly as early as 1248, Madox, Exchequer ii 51-52.
[3] Below 232.
[4] "The general impression which we derive from the description given of the
board of Exchequer is that, while it retained its character as a meeting of the great
officers of the king's court, yet this theory was already breaking down under the
stress of a more fully organized system of administration. . . . Insensibly the
theory of a royal Court was changed into the reality of a committee of skilled
officials." Poole, op. cit. 126.
[5] Dialogus i 7 (Sel. Ch. 195, 196), "Ad hunc (the upper Exchequer) accedunt
barones, cum proponitur eis verbum ambiguum ad scaccarium, de quo malunt
seorsum tractare quam in auribus omnium; maxime autem propter hoc in partem
secedunt, ne compoti, qui ad scaccarium fiunt, impediantur; quibus moram facientibus in consiliis consuetus cursus compotorum agitur.   Si quid vero natum fuerit
quæstionis, referetur ad eos."
[6] Above 38.   [7] Below 232.   [8] Below 236.

From the end of Richard I.'s reign up till the latter part of Edward I.'s reign there was in existence a separate branch of the Exchequer known as the Exchequer of the Jews.[1]

The Jew was an alien both to church and state. He was regarded as a species of res nullius. But he was valuable for his acquisitive capacity; and for that reason the crown took him under its protection. "As they fleeced the subjects of the realm so the king fleeced them."[2] Jewish communities were allowed to settle in the more important towns; and under Henry II., Richard and John they acquired a certain freedom of trade and a certain measure of autonomy. They were allowed to choose their Chief Rabbi; and their synagogues were not prohibited.[3]

Though they were thus protected by the crown they were hated by all classes of the community. The superstition of the populace combined with the indebtedness of the higher classes to produce this result. In 1189 attacks were made on most of the Jewries in England, and their bonds were destroyed. But the crown suffered much from this diminution in the wealth of its chattels.[4] It was for this reason that measures were taken which resulted in the establishment of the Exchequer of the Jews. The Jews were better protected against violence. But they, and to some extent, therefore, their debtors,[5] were left more completely at the mercy of the crown.

In London, Lincoln, Oxford, and other towns in which there were important settlements of Jews, Archæ, or registries for the Jewish bonds or chirographs were established. They were put under the charge of four Chirographers (two Christians, and two Jews) assisted by clerks. It was provided that all contracts of loan should be in a certain form, and that a copy should be deposited in the Archa. All acquittances or assignments (Starra) must be also enrolled there. The Archa could only be opened in the presence of a majority of the Chirographers at stated times, or by order of the Exchequer.[6] It was this system of registration which seems to have given rise to the Exchequer of the Jews. In 1198 "Custodes Judæorum" were appointed, who were "associated with the Barons of the Exchequer, and

---

[1] Madox, Exchequer, chap. vii; Select Pleas, etc., of the Jewish Exchequer (S.S.).

[2] Madox, Exchequer i 221; Laws of Edward the Confessor c. xxv.

[3] Select Pleas, etc., xi, xii, xiii, 1-3; Madox, Exchequer 244-249, 260, 261. Some towns as Newcastle and Derby paid a fine to the crown in order that no Jews might be allowed to come there.

[4] Select Pleas, etc., xvii, xviii.

[5] This is illustrated by § 10 of Magna Carta, "Si quis mutuo ceperit aliquid a Judæis, plus vel minus, et moriatur antequam debitum illum solvatur, debitum non usuret quamdiu hæres fuerit infra aetatem, de quocumque teneat; et si debitum illud inciderit in manus nostras, nos non capiemus nisi catallum contentum in carta."

[6] Select Pleas, etc., xviii-xx; Madox, Exchequer i 238-240, 246.

were, in fact, Barons in all but name."[1] They were usually
appointed by the king, but sometimes, if the king so directed,
by the Treasurer and Barons ;[2] and they "exercised jurisdiction
in the affairs of the Judaism ; namely, in the accounts of that
revenue, in pleas upon contracts made with the Jews, in causes
or questions touching their lands or chattels, their tallages, fines,
forfeitures or the like."[3] They were under the control of the
Barons of the Exchequer who could annul their judgments or
punish their misdemeanours,[4] "and with whom in cases of exceptional difficulty they were accustomed to confer.[5] The jurisdiction
of these Custodes was not, however, exclusive. Cases in which
Jews were accused of crimes are found among the Crown Pleas.
Various regulations as to different branches of the jurisdiction
exercised by the Jewish Exchequer were in fact made at different
times.[6]

Though this system gave some protection to the Jews it
increased their unpopularity because, as Maitland has said, it
made them the "engines of royal indigence."[7] A clause relating
to usury upon debts owed to the Jews naturally found a place in
Magna Carta ;[8] and, though it was omitted in 1216, because it
impaired the value of the Jew as a source of revenue,[9] the popular
feeling against them grew too strong to be resisted. A severe
ordinance was issued against them in 1253.[10] In 1271 they were
submitted to still further restrictions.[11] In 1275 usury was for-
bidden, and they were required to wear a badge.[12] In 1290
Edward I. gained popularity, supplies, and many escheats by
banishing them.[13] It was not until the Protectorate of Oliver
Cromwell that they attempted to get permission to return. This
permission was refused ; but, after the Restoration, they began
again to settle in England under the protection of the prærogative
powers of the king ;[14] and this exercise of the prærogative was
not called in question after the Revolution.[15]

---

[1] Select Pleas, etc., xx. [2] Madox, Exchequer i 233, 234. [3] Ibid 234, 235.
[4] Ibid 252-255. [5] Select Pleas, etc., xxiii. [6] Ibid xxi-xxiii.
[7] P. and M. i 453-454, "Despised and disliked the once chosen people would
always have been in society of mediæval Christians . . . but they would not have
been so persistently hated as they were, had they not been made the engines of
royal indigence."
[8] Above 45 n 5. [9] McKechnie, Magna Carta 228.
[10] Select Pleas, etc., xxviii, xxix. [11] Ibid xxxviii.
[12] 3 Edward I, Statutes (Rec. Com.) i 221 ; Select Pleas, etc., xxxviii.
[13] Select Pleas, etc., xl.
[14] They were protected by an Order in Council of 1674 which was confirmed in
1685, " and the sole legal basis for their religious freedom rested on the above Orders
in Council till the legislation of the reign of Queen Victoria gave them such freedom
by statute," L.Q.R. xxxvi 426-427.
[15] Lindo v. Belisario (1795) 1 Hagg. Consist. 217 n. ; ibid App. 1 and 2 ; De
Wilton v. Montifiore [1900] 2 Ch. 489; and see on the whole subject H. S. Q. Hen-
riques, The Return of the Jews to England.

(2) *Judicature.*

The legislation of Henry II. added enormously to the jurisdiction of the Curia Regis. Of the details and effects of that
legislation I shall speak more fully in succeeding volumes. Here
it will be sufficient to say that, as its result, the king's court
acquired a wide criminal and civil jurisdiction, and wide powers
of supervision over the conduct of all the local courts and officials.
In the Assizes of Clarendon[1] and Northampton[2] Henry II.
asserted its exclusive jurisdiction over all serious crimes. In the
ordinance of the Grand Assize[3] and the legislation establishing
the petty assizes[4] he asserted its jurisdiction over most disputes
relating to land held by free tenure; and even if a dispute relating to such land, or the services upon which such land was held,
was taken to a lord's court, the lord could not exercise jurisdiction without the king's writ.[5] Under the feudal system, which
made landholding the basis of so many relations between man
and man, this large jurisdiction over this class of cases meant
the absorption by the king's court of jurisdiction over all the
most important civil pleas. By means of the procedure of the
Exchequer he maintained a tight financial control over the
sheriffs and other accountants to the crown;[6] and we shall see
that by means of commissions issued to the itinerant justices he
exercised a constant supervision over the whole conduct of local
government.[7]

All this jurisdiction was exercised through the machinery of
royal writs. But the fact that it was thus exercised did not as
yet hinder its capacity for expansion. "As yet," says Maitland,
"the king is no mere vendor, he is a manufacturer and can
make goods to order; the day has not yet come when the in-
vention of new writs will be hampered by the claims of a parliament; but still in Glanvil's day the *officina justitiæ* has already
a considerable store of ready-made wares and English law is
already taking the form of a commentary upon writs."[8] Thus,
as a result of the increase of jurisdiction of the Curia Regis and
of the methods by which this jurisdiction is exercised, that
formulary writ procedure, which is perhaps the most salient
feature of the full grown common law, is already taking shape.
We shall see that the existence of this procedure will exercise a

[1] Sel. Ch. 143. [2] Ibid 150.
[3] Below 275, 327-329. [4] Below 275-276, 329.
[5] " Preterea sciendum quod secundum consuetudines regni nemo teneatur respondere in curia domini sui de aliquo libero tenemento suo sine precepto domini
regis vel ejus capitalis justiciarii," Glanvil xii 25.
[6] Above 43. [7] Below 49-51.
[8] P. and M. i 130; for the Register of Writs and its history see vol. ii 512-
520.

profound influence not only upon the subject matter of the law,[1] but also upon the evolution of the English judicial system.[2]

As the result of this expansion of jurisdiction the Curia Regis in Henry II.'s reign no longer confined its attention to great men and great causes. It was a tribunal where all classes of causes were tried. The king or his justices ordered cases to be heard there.[3] The privilege of being sued only in the Curia Regis was occasionally granted to certain persons.[4] The popularity of the court is attested by the fact that suitors paid money to the king to have their cases tried there, and by the number of fines which litigants paid for writs, for pleas, for trials, for judgment, for expedition, or for delay.[5] The Court itself began to keep plea rolls. The oldest rolls which we possess come from Richard I.'s reign;[6] but these rolls appear to refer to still older rolls of Henry II.'s reign.[7] We can see from these rolls that the most usual cases were cases concerning the ownership or possession of land. Personal actions were rare.[8] But we can see also that often the matter in dispute is small, and that the quantity of business done is great.[9]

It is not hard to see the reasons for the popularity of the Curia Regis. In the first place, it could both compel the appearance of the defendant and enforce its judgments with all the strength of the central government. In the second place, its methods of procedure both in civil and in criminal cases were superior to those of the older courts. The facts at issue, in the trial of questions of ownership by the Grand Assize, or in the trial of questions of possession by the possessory assizes, were determined, not by battle, but by a species of jury;[10] and in criminal cases the presentment of a jury was found to be a much better method for the discovery and punishment of crime than any hitherto used.[11] In the third place, the fact that litigants could get from it writs ordering sheriffs or lords to hear cases was at any rate some security that the cases would be heard;[12] and, if they were not heard fairly, the litigant was always at

---

[1] Vol. ii 171-172, 192-194, 245, 512.   [2] Below 53.
[3] Bigelow, Placita 176.
[4] Ibid op. cit. 156, a writ of Stephen to the abbot of Abingdon; Madox i 116-119; Bracton f. 411 b, the Templars and Hospitallers and " plures alii."
[5] Bigelow, op. cit. 268, 269, 276, 277; Madox, Exchequer, chap. xii; the number of these payments, as Madox points out, explains cap. 40 of Magna Carta, " Nulli vendemus, nulli negabimus aut differemus, rectum aut justiciam; " as to this clause see below 57-58.
[6] Select Pleas of the Crown (S.S.) vii, viii; for these Rolls see vol. ii Bk. iii c. 2.
[7] Ibid xxvi, xxvii, note A; The entry may refer to the 17th or the 27th year of Henry II.
[8] Select Civil Pleas (S.S.) xiii, xiv.
[9] Rot. Cur. Reg. (Rec. Com.) i, vi.
[11] Below 321-323.
[10] Below 327-330.
[12] P. and M. i 137-138.

liberty to apply for further writs, or even to take the case before the Curia itself. In the fourth place, litigants secured a tribunal which was staffed by the ablest lawyers of the day.[1]

It is clear that the numerous sessions of the court at which these cases were heard will tend to be composed entirely of official members of the Curia Regis. The knowledge needed for the proper working of the new methods of procedure, and the growing number of writs by which that procedure was set and kept in motion, will tend more and more to become the monopoly of the official ; and, as this formulary system of writs grows more complicated, the sessions of the Curia Regis at which ordinary litigation is disposed of will tend to fall apart from those larger meetings of the Curia at which questions of policy and important political cases are heard. But we have seen that the causes which will lead to a division of the Curia on these lines are not yet in being.[2] In the twelfth century the need for differentiation, which this large access of business was causing was met in the sphere of judicature as in the sphere of finance, by a new grouping of the official members of the Curia which foreshadows the development of distinct departments of government. As in the sphere of finance we get the growth of the Exchequer, so in the sphere of judicature we get firstly the growth of the practice of sending members of the Curia Regis round the country to deal with certain specified business, and secondly the institution of a special branch of the Curia Regis to deal with Common Pleas. These two departures are, as we shall now see, the beginnings of important developments in the English judicial system.

(i) The Itinerant Justices.

The practice of sending royal commissioners through the country on royal business began soon after the Norman Conquest. In earlier times the king himself journeyed over the country administering justice. He did not cease to do so after the Conquest. But it is after the Conquest that we first meet with these delegates of the Curia Regis. William I. sent them round the country to collect the evidence from which Domesday Book was compiled. We know from the Pipe roll of the Exchequer that Henry I. sent them round the country on fiscal business.[3] Even in Stephen's reign justices travelled over the country to hear the civil and criminal pleas of the crown.[4] It is probable that before Henry II.'s reign these commissions were not issued either

---

[1] Vol. ii 146, 174-176.   [2] Above 41.

[3] Stubbs, C.H. i 443; in 1096, William II. sent Wakelin, Bishop of Winchester, Randulph the royal chaplain, and two others to Devonshire, Cornwall, and Exeter, " ad investiganda regalia placita," Bigelow, op. cit. 69.

[4] Madox, Exchequer i 146.

frequently or regularly.   Other expedients were adopted for
bringing the local into touch with the central government.   The
king might direct a noble or the sheriff to try a case in the
county court, or before the courts of several counties.[1] Sometimes the sheriffs themselves were royal justices in several
counties.[2] But the former expedient became insufficient to deal
with the large mass of cases regularly heard in the Curia Regis ;
and the latter was liable to abuse.   It led to usurpations of jurisdiction ; and in 1194 Richard I. forbade sheriffs to be justices in
their own counties, or in any county of which they had been
sheriffs since his accession to the throne.[3] What was required
was the suprintendence of professional justices free from local
bias acting as members of the Curia Regis.   This requirement
seems to have been fulfilled by issuing commissions to a number
of persons, some of whom were members of the Curia Regis—a
practice which, as we shall see, was continued for many centuries.[4]

It is from the reign of Henry II. that these justices regularly
travelled round the country.   The assizes of Clarendon (1166)
and Northampton (1176) were enforced by them.   They were in
fact instructions to the itinerant justices.   In 1176 eighteen
justices were assigned to six circuits.   In 1179, twenty-one
justices were assigned to four circuits.   From 1176 onwards some
part of the country was regularly visited by the itinerant justices.[5]
We can see that in Glanvil's day the distinction between the
Curia Regis and the itinerant justices is already well marked.[6]

The commissions under which the itinerant justices acted
were very various.   Under the assizes of Clarendon and Northampton they heard criminal and civil pleas of the crown, and had
in addition other duties which were administrative in character.[7]
They sometimes assisted in the fiscal business of the Exchequer
by assessing the taxpayer.[8]   In 1194 we have a set of "capitula
placitorum Coronæ Regis."   The justices were directed to hear
all pleas pending before the Curia Regis.   They were to enquire
into escheats, and churches in the gift of the king ; into wardships, marriages, criminals, aids, usurers, wine sold contrary to
the assize, and the property of deceased crusaders.   They were

---

[1] Bigelow, op. cit. 4, 17, 33, 71, 200.   [2] Stubbs, C.H. i 144.

[3] "Et nullus vicecomes sit justitiarius in vicecomitatu suo, nec in comitatu
quem tenuerit post primam coronationem domini regis," Sel. Ch. 260; John had
used the sheriffs as the instruments of his tyranny, McKechnie, op. cit. 28, 308, 310;
hence § 24 of Magna Carta, below 57.

[4] P. and M. i 135; below 280.

[5] Madox, Exchequer chap. iii § 10; Gesta Henrici (R.S.) ii, lxiii-lxxiii.

[6] Glanvil, viii 5, "distinguendum est utrum concordia illa facta fuerit in capitali
curia domini regis, an coram justitiis itinerantibus ;" Select Pleas of the Crown
(S.S.) xix-xxi.

[7] Sel. Ch. 143, 150.   [8] Stubbs, C.H. i 656.

to hold the Grand Assize if the property was of the value of £5 or under. They were to tallage the towns and the demesnes of the king. They were to enquire into the value of lands belonging to the king as wardships or escheats.[1] In the justices who acted under these extensive commissions we can see the future justices in Eyre.[2] Sometimes they were commissioned only to hear the possessory assizes; but generally, it would seem, their chief business was to hear both the pleas of the crown and the possessory assizes.[3] In the justices whose chief or only function was judicial work we can see the future judges of assize.[4]

It would seem that the frequency with which these commissions were issued was not altogether popular. In 1178, Benedictus Abbas tells us, Henry II. learnt that the people were grieved by the number of justices.[5] In fact it might be inconvenient for a landowner who had land in many counties to be summoned before several groups of justices; and it is possible that these groups of justices, who were not all members of the Curia Regis, may have taken advantage of the fact that the king and his court were at a distance. At any rate the measure which Henry took to remedy the complaints which he heard was a measure of centralization. In this measure we can discern the germ of the future court of Common Pleas.

(ii) The Court of Common Pleas.

The following is the account which Benedictus Abbas gives us of the remedy which Henry "by the counsel of the wise men of his realm" applied to the complaints which he had heard of the number of the justices: "He selected five men only, two clerks and three laymen, who were all of his own household. And he ordained that those five should hear all the suits of the realm, and adjudicate upon them, and that they should not depart from the Curia Regis, but should remain there to hear men's suits; provided that if any question arose among them which they could not solve, it should be reserved for the king's hearing, and should be settled as it should seem good to him and the wiser men of the realm."[6] Henry did not intend to abolish the

---

[1] Sel. Ch. 258-263.   [2] Below 265-272.
[3] P. and M. i 135; Select Pleas of the Crown (S.S.) xx, xxi.
[4] Below 275-276.
[5] "Itaque dominus rex moram faciens in Anglia quæsivit de justitiis quos in Anglia constituerat, si bene et modeste tractaverunt homines regni; et cum didicisset quod terra et homines terræ nimis gravati essent ex tanta Justitiarum multitudine, quia octo decim erant numero," he devised the remedy described below n. 6, Benedictus Abbas (R.S.) i 207.
[6] "Per consilium sapientium regni sui quinque tantum elegit, duos scilicet clericos et tres laicos, et erant omnes de privata familia sua. Et statuit quod illi quinque audirent omnes clamores regni et rectum facerent, et quod a curia regis non recederent sed ibi ad audiendum clamores hominum remanerent; ita ut si aliqua

practice of sending justices on circuit—as we have seen in the following year twenty-one judges were travelling round four circuits.[1] Probably what he meant to do was to relieve the pressure of business in the Curia Regis which the hearing of the Common Pleas was causing, and to give those of his subjects who brought their cases there a more speedy trial.

We have here indications of a tendency to a division in the Curia Regis to which we can probably trace the court of Common Bench or Common Pleas. Shortly after 1178, Glanvil's book mentions justices " in banco residentes." [2] Cases were removed to the court coram rege from the justices of the Bench.[3] Fines were levied sometimes coram rege, sometimes before the justices of the Bench. Writs of summons were issued by the Bench and amerciaments inflicted by it. But as yet there is no clear division into distinct tribunals. In the reigns of Richard and John, when the king was absent, most of the judicial business seems to be done by the Bench. But when the king was present it is difficult to distinguish the Bench from the court held coram rege. Both were in fact Curia Regis—divisions of the king's court. Whether the court will be the Bench or the court held coram rege would almost seem to depend on the accident of the king's presence.[4]

The rolls of the Curia Regis tell us the same thing. There are not yet two sets of rolls—" coram rege " and " de banco "

quæstio inter eos veniret, quæ per eos ad finem duci non posset, auditui regio præsentaretur, et sicut ei et sapientoribus regni placeret terminaretur," Benedictus Abbas (R.S.) i 207-208 ; I think that Professor Adams, Origin of the English Constitution 136-143, exaggerates the extent to which this court was regarded as a court quite distinct from the Curia Regis at its foundation ; no doubt it became quite separate, and was practically a separate court in Bracton's day, certainly when Fleta and Britton wrote, below 196 ; no doubt its competence was limited, and this helped it to become a distinct court at an early period ; but at first its competence was very vaguely limited ; thus Maitland points out that it certainly heard crown pleas in 1225, and probably also when Bracton wrote, Select Pleas of the Crown (S.S.) xix and n. 3 ; and he points out that, during Henry's minority, " the justices of the bench seem to be the only permanent professional justices that there are," ibid xviii ; and see below 53 n. 4.

[1] Above 50.

[2] Glanvil ii 6 ; viii 1 ; xi 1. The official title of the judges of the court of Common Pleas was " the justices of our Lord the King of the Bench ; " the official title of the judges of the court of King's Bench was " the justices of our Lord the King assigned to hold pleas before the king himself.

[3] In 1207 a fine was paid for removing an assize which was coram justitiariis in banco, coram rege, Madox, Exchequer i 790-791.

[4] In 1202 a plea to the jurisdiction of the Bench of a person privileged to be sued only before the king was overruled on the ground that the Bench was the king's court, Abbrev. Placit. 32. Possibly the case of Gilbert de Plumpton (1184) shows that the king was not always present in the court held coram rege, Bigelow, op. cit. 233, 234 ; Pike, House of Lords 35 ; perhaps the capacity of the king to be present, owing to his being in the vicinity, was coming to be the test, rather than his actual presence, Select Pleas of the Crown (S.S.) xiv, xv ; Madox, Exchequer i 788-795.

rolls. But it is possible to classify the cases on the rolls according as they were heard before the Bench or the king himself. The expression coram rege is used in the latter case; the expressions coram justiciariis de banco or apud Westmonasterium in the former.[1] But the rolls show us that the Bench entertained all classes of pleas—pleas of the crown as well as common pleas.[2] The judges sat now in one division of the Curia Regis now in another.[3] Cases could be moved to one division from another at the pleasure of the king or of the justices.[4]

In the institution of the itinerant justices, and of a separate bench of judges which did not sit coram rege, we can see signs of a coming split in the Curia Regis. As Maitland puts it " The king's court of John's reign shows no cleft, though it does show a well-marked line of cleavage." [5] We must not exaggerate the amount of division which has actually taken place; but, on the other hand, we must not minimize the importance of this line of cleavage. Looking at it in the light of subsequent history we can see that it is significant for three main reasons. In the first place, we can see it in the germ of tribunals with a limited jurisdiction as contrasted with a tribunal with large undifferentiated powers of government; and we can see that the tribunals with this limited jurisdiction were mainly, though not solely, occupied with judicial work.[6] In the second place, because these tribunals are mainly occupied with judicial work begun by writs, they will soon begin to develop a technical procedure; [7] and, as their work develops, they will develop not only procedural rules but rules of law which will be common law because, like their jurisdiction, they will extend over the whole country. In the third place the existence of tribunals occupied with judicial business, and conducting this business in accordance with technical procedural rules, will be bound sooner or later to exercise a powerful attractive influence upon the as yet undifferentiated Curia Regis. There will be a tendency for those sessions of the court which deal with ordinary judicial cases to approximate to these judicial tribunals, and to diverge from those sessions of the court which deal with matters of administration and state policy.[8]

---

[1] Madox, Exchequer i 788, 789; Select Pleas of the Crown (S.S.) xvi, xvii.

[2] Madox, Exchequer i 793.

[3] In a case against the Prior of Christchurch in 1188 there were present not only the justices but the justiciar, an earl, and various barons, Pike, House of Lords 39.

[4] " We may doubt whether a litigant had any reason to expect that an action begun before one division of the court would always continue to be before that division; on the contrary there are entries which seem to show that the Justices of the Bench might give the parties a day before the king, and that the king might give them a day before the Justices," Select Pleas of the Crown (S.S.) xvii.

[5] Select Pleas of the Crown (S.S.) xvii.

[6] Baldwin, The King's Council 47-50.

[7] Ibid. [8] Below 205.

At the end of the twelfth century all these developments were as yet in the future ; and, before they could take effect, the peaceful and regular development of the Curia Regis was interrupted by the national uprising against the tyrannous abuse by John of those large powers of the crown which his predecessors had used to construct a centralized system of government and a common law. The fruit of this national uprising was the Great Charter, which attempted to define the conditions upon which the king must conduct his government. Some of its clauses naturally contained regulations which affected the centralized system of judicature which had been so rapidly expanding during the preceding half century. With the effect of these clauses I shall now deal.

III. MAGNA CARTA AND THE JUDICIAL SYSTEM

We shall see that the gaining of Magna Carta closes one period in the history of English law, and begins another. It closes the period during which the law is developed by the power of the crown alone, and it begins the period which will end in the establishment of a Parliament, with power to take some share in the making and development of the law. Of the significance of the Charter in the legal history of the thirteenth and later centuries, and of the effect of some of its clauses upon the development of the branches of law to which they relate, I shall speak in the next two volumes.[1] Here I shall deal only with its effects upon the growth of those centralized judicial institutions which I have just been describing, and upon the relations of those institutions to the local courts.

We shall see that all classes united to secure the Charter—the official nobility who had made their careers in the king's service no less than the older territorial magnates, the smaller as well as the larger landowners, the churchmen, and the merchants. It is because this union of classes was necessary to coerce the king that the Charter is by no means confined to voicing the aspirations of a reactionary feudalism. The great feudal nobility were the natural leaders of the nation ; and their grievances take a large place in the Charter. But the clauses which aimed at restoring feudal jurisdiction and fettering the activities of the new centralized machinery of justice are much fewer in number than the clauses which recognize and regulate this new machinery. I shall give some account firstly of the clauses of the Charter which recognize and regulate the new machinery of justice, and

[1] For Magna Carta generally and its place in our legal history see vol. ii 207-216.

secondly of the clauses which attempted to fetter it in the interests
of feudalism.

(1) The clauses regulating the new machinery of justice.

The principal clauses relating to this topic are the fourteenth,
the seventeenth, the eighteenth, the twenty-fourth, the thirty-sixth,
and the fortieth.

The fourteenth clause [1] provides that for the purpose of assessing an aid, other than the three regular aids, or scutage, the
archbishops, bishops, abbots, earls, and greater barons must be
summoned by writ individually, and the other tenants in chief
must be summoned through the sheriff. This clause is really
an appendage to clause twelve, which provided that such
aids and scutage were not to be imposed "nisi per commune
consilium regni," and was designed to define the persons who
must be present if the king wished to obtain this "commune
consilium regni." [2]   The clause was dropped in subsequent
reissues of the Charter ; and it may, at first sight, seem to have
little to do with the judicial system. But I think it is the first
official recognition of the fact that the smaller official gatherings
of the Curia Regis were something different from the larger
gatherings which gave the king the "consilium regni"—the advice
of the kingdom on questions of policy. [3]   At any rate it is clear
that this distinction gradually gains in prominence in Henry III.'s
reign. [4]   It is a distinction which will tend to differentiate the
larger body which controls the work of legislation and administration, from the body of officials which actually does the administrative and judicial work of the state. With the growth of

---

[1] "Et ad habendum commune consilium regni, de auxilio assidendo aliter quam
in tribus casibus praedictis, vel de scutagio assidendo, summoneri faciemus archiepiscopos, episcopos, abbates, comites, et majores barones, sigillatim per literas nostras;
et praeterea faciemus summoneri in generali, per viceomites et ballivos nostros, omnes
illos qui de nobis tenent in capite." Note that the tenants in chief summoned
through the sheriff according to this clause might include persons classed as barons
and assessed to the relief of a baron under § 2, Round, Barons and Knights in the
Great Charter, Magna Carta Commemoration Essays 46 seqq.

[2] McKechnie, Magna Carta 130, 248.

[3] Adams, Origin of the English Constitution 202, points out that in the twelfth
century the chroniclers use the terms "magnum" or "generale" if they wish to
denote a large meeting of the Curia.

[4] Adams points out, loc. cit., that in the reign of Henry III. the references to
these large assemblies are much more numerous ; for a meeting of 1242, in which
the Council refused the king's demands for an aid on the ground that some of them
had not been summoned "according to the tenor of Magna Carta," see McKechnie,
op. cit. 255; and it is clear that Bracton distinguishes the competence of the ordinary professional judges to apply the law, from the work of larger assemblies which
could settle wholly unprecedented cases—"Si autem aliqua nova et inconsueta
emerserint, et quae prius usitata non fuerint in regno, si tamen similia evenerint, per
simile judicentur, cum bona sit occasio a similibus procedere ad similia. Si autem
talia nunquam prius evenerint, et obscurum, et difficile sit eorum judicium, tunc
ponantur judicia in respectum usque ad magnam curiam, ut ibi per consilium
curiae terminentur," f. 1 b.

an opposition to the king and with the gradual development of this larger body into a Parliament, it will, at the end of the thirteenth century, fall apart from the smaller official Curia Regis of royal advisers.[1] But we shall see that it will be some time before this smaller official Curia separates into a Council and a Court of King's Bench.[2]

The seventeenth clause provides that "Common Pleas shall not follow our court, but shall be held in some certain place.[3] We have seen that a division of the Curia Regis had, during Richard I.'s and John's reigns, become distinct from the court held coram rege.[4] It is clear that this division was largely, though not solely, occupied with the hearing of common pleas, and that it did not follow the king—in fact it was generally stationary at Westminster.[5] This clause of the charter made it legally necessary that it should be a stationary court. The fact that it did not follow the king in his progresses emphasized its character as a purely judicial court; and we shall see that the existence of this purely judicial court, acting in accordance with fixed rules of procedure, will exercise some influence in separating the purely judicial from the administrative sides of the Curia Regis which is still held coram rege.[6] This clause had thus emphasized the need for a stationary central court for common pleas: the eighteenth emphasized the need for the local administration of justice by delegates from the Curia Regis in the case of certain of these common pleas. It provided that the three possessory assizes of novel dissesin, mort d'ancestor, and darrein presentment should be tried in the counties where the cases arose; and that they should be taken in each county four times a year by two justices, assisted by four knights of the county appointed by the county.[7] It is clear that this clause is the strongest possible testimony to the success of Henry II.'s reforms. No doubt these assizes took business from the feudal courts; but so far were the barons from wishing to see them abolished that they demanded their frequent session. With the subsequent history of these Justices of Assize I shall deal in a later chapter.[8]

---

[1] Below 351-352, 356-360.   [2] Below 209-211.

[3] "Communia placita non sequantur curiam nostram sed teneantur in aliquo certo loco."

[4] Above 52, 53.   [5] Above 53.   [6] Below 205.

[7] "Recogniciones de nova disseisina, de morte antecessoris, et de ultima presentacione, non capiantur nisi in suis comitatibus et hoc modo; nos, vel si extra regnum fuerimus, capitalis justiciarius noster, mittemus duos just⸱ ⸱arios per unumquemque comitatum per quatuor vices in anno, qui, cum quatuor militibus cujuslibet comitatus electis per comitatum, capiant in comitatu et in die et loco comitatus assisas predictas; " for these possessory assizes see below 275-276, 329.

[8] Below 275-283.

The twenty-fourth and the thirty-sixth clauses show that Henry II.'s reforms in the sphere of crown pleas had been as successful as his reforms in the sphere of civil pleas.

The twenty-fourth clause provides that "no sheriff, constable, coroners, or others of our bailiffs shall hold pleas of our Crown."[1] In the past the practice of allowing sheriffs to hold, i.e. to try, pleas of the crown had been found to lead to great abuses. Under Henry II. this power had generally been confined to the king's justices; but John had reverted to the older practice. This clause of the Charter fixed the law for the future. Henceforth the sheriff's criminal jurisdiction was confined to the trial of petty criminal offences in the tourn,[2] and to securing the appearance before the itinerant justices of those accused of more serious crimes.[3] The thirty-sixth clause provides that "nothing shall for the future be given or taken for the writ of enquiry concerning life or limb, but it shall be given without payment and not denied."[4] The bearing of this clause upon Henry's reforms in the criminal law requires a few words of explanation. We shall see that in 1215 there were two methods of beginning a criminal proceeding. There was the older method of appeal, which was brought by a private accuser, and was generally tried by battle; and there was the newer method of indictment which was brought by the king upon the presentment of a jury.[5] The appeal was open to grave abuses, the chief of which was that it was often brought simply to gratify revenge. To remedy this Henry II. had invented a writ "de odio et atia." By means of this writ a person thus appealed could submit the question whether he had been appealed "from hatred and malice" to the verdict of recognitors. If they found that he had been appealed from these motives the appeal was quashed. It thus gave a defendant a chance of avoiding trial by battle if accused of a criminal offence, just as the Grand Assize gave him a chance of avoiding trial by battle if sued by a writ of right.[6] This writ came to be a means by which a person accused either at the suit of the king or at the suit of a private accuser could get release on bail.[7] Because it thus protected liberty it may be regarded as one of the precursors of the famous writ of Habeas Corpus.[8]

The fortieth clause provides that right and justice shall not

---

[1] "Nullus vicecomes, constabularius, coronatores, vel talii ballivi nostri, teneant placita coronæ nostræ."

[2] Below 76-81.

[3] Assize of Clarendon §§ 6, 17, 18; cf. McKechnie, op. cit. 309; below 77.

[4] "Nichil detur vel capiatur de cetero pro brevi inquisicionis de vita vel membris, sed gratis concedatur et non negetur."

[5] Vol. ii 197-198, 256-257, 360-364.   [6] Below 328.

[7] Vol. ix 107-108.   [8] Ibid.

be sold or denied or delayed.[1]   This clause again illustrates the
fact that royal justice was popular.   The complaint is that it is
too dear or that it is not forthcoming.   The clause did not
wholly stop the evils of which it complained, as later Parliamentary petitions show.[2]   But probably it did something to
cheapen justice, and to stop the abuses which were rampant in
John's reign.   Madox says,[3] " Though fines for writs and process of law in many cases were always a part of the crown
revenue, and were constantly paid. . . . Yet, if my observation
does not fail me, the fines which were paid for writs and process
of law, were more moderate . . . than they used to be before;
and, I think, the actual denial of right, and the stopping or
delaying of it, which before, upon paying of money or fines used
to be practised, were . . . quite taken away, or by degrees
brought into disuse."

(2) The clauses which attempted to fetter the new machinery
of Justice.

The only two clauses in which we can see such an attempt
are the thirty-fourth and the thirty-ninth.

The thirty-fourth clause provides that "the writ which is
called Præcipe shall not for the future be issued to anyone concerning any tenement whereby a free man may lose his court."[4]
We have seen that the Barons did not object to the assumption
by the Curia Regis of jurisdiction over questions of possession.[5]
They did object to this assumption of jurisdiction in cases where
the ownership of land was in dispute.   By means of the writ
Præcipe[6] addressed to the sheriff the king ignored the feudal
court of the lord, and brought these cases before his court.   The
Barons demanded that this practice should cease, and that such
cases should be tried by writ of right in the lord's court.[7]   This
form of writ Præcipe therefore ceased to be issued, and tenants
were obliged to bring writs of right in the courts of their lords.[8]
But seigniorial justice was so obviously inferior to royal justice
that as early as 1258 the nation "no longer demanded protection
for seigniorial courts."   It asked rather that "the royal court
should be endowed with yet new and anti-feudal powers."[9]
Under these circumstances it is not surprising to find that, though

---

[1] " Nulli vendemus, nulli negabimus, aut differemus rectum aut justiciam."
[2] Stubbs, C.H. ii 636-637 ; cf. McKechnie, op. cit. 397-398.
[3] Exchequer i 455.
[4] " Breve quod vocatur *Precipe* de cetero non fiat alicui de aliquo tenemento
unde liber homo amittere possit curiam suam."
[5] Above 56.
[6] For this writ see App. V ; and for an account of these writs see vol. iii 5-6.
[7] Maitland, Forms of Action 317-318.
[8] Vol. iii 6.   [9] P. and M. i 182, n. 2.

the full effect was given to this clause,[1] before a century had elapsed [2] means were found to evade its operation. Of the technical methods by which this result was secured I shall speak more at length in a subsequent volume.[3]

The thirty-ninth clause is perhaps the most famous clause of the Charter. It provides that, "No freeman shall be taken or/ and imprisoned, or disseised, or exiled, or in any way destroyed, nor will we go upon him nor will we send upon him, except by the lawful judgment of his peers or/and by the law of the land." [4] Of the important constitutional doctrines that have been read into this clause, and of the large effects which this manner of interpreting it have had on English constitutional history, I shall speak later.[5] Here I shall only deal with it in relation to the judicial system, and attempt to ascertain the meaning which its framers attached to it.

Upon some points all the commentators are agreed. It is quite clear that the words "ibimus" and "mittemus" do not, as Coke supposed,[6] refer to legal process. As Mr. McKechnie says, they were aimed at the use of brute force.[7] It is also clear that the words "judicium parium" do not refer to trial by jury. A trial by a royal judge and a body of recognitors who found the facts was exactly what the barons did not want. What they did want was firstly a tribunal of the old type in which all the suitors were judges both of law and fact,[8] and secondly a tribunal in which they would not be judged by their inferiors.[9] Some of

---

[1] See the Eyre of Kent (S.S.) ii 86-87 for a case in which it was applied.

[2] Hengham, a judge of Edward I.'s reign (vol. ii c. 4) says in his tract called Magna c. 3, "Parvum seu nullum dominis curiarum in hujismodi placitis tenendis proficuum ascribitur."

[3] Vol iii 7-8, 13-14.

[4] "Nullus liber homo capiatur vel imprisonetur, aut disseisiatur aut utlagetur, aut exuletur, aut aliquo modo destruatur, nec super eum ibimus nec super eum mittemus, nisi per legale judicium parium vel per legum terræ."

[5] Vol. ii 214-215.

[6] "No man shall be condemned at the king's suit, either before the king in his bench, where the pleas are *coram rege* (and so are the words, *nec super eum ibimus*, to be understood) nor before any other commissioner or judge whatsoever, and so are the words, *nec super eum mittemus* to be understood," Second Instit. 46.

[7] Op. cit. 385-386; cf. the uses of these words collected by Harcourt, His Grace the Steward and Trial of Peers 243-244.

[8] P. and M. i 152 n. 2; Pike, House of Lords 169-170; McKechnie op. cit. 377-379; Harcourt, op. cit. chap. vii; Adams, Origin of the English Constitution 268-269; Select pleas in Manorial Courts (S.S.) lxv-lxvii; for the procedure in these courts see above 10, 11.

[9] McKechnie, op. cit. 377-379; Harcourt, op. cit. 205, 225-228; as Harcourt says, ibid at p. 225, "The term peer was at this period a very common word used to describe many different things; it was by no means a technical word. . . . It was still primarily used to designate co-vassalship pure and simple without restriction as to rank or condition. Even the villein who purchased land was said by one writer to have for his peers the other tenants of the lord of his fee." Professor Pollard, Evolution of Parliament 91-92, apparently makes the "judicium parium" mean the doom or judgment of the peers—i.e. it refers not to a mode of trial, but to the

them did not consider that the royal judges,[1] none of them would have considered that a body of recognitors, were their peers.[2] It is in this respect that the clause is reactionary. But, like the thirty-fourth clause, it has only had a very limited and partial effect. We shall see that, when the term " peer " had acquired its modern technical meaning, it secured to " peers " accused of treason or felony the right, when Parliament is sitting, to be tried by the whole House of Lords, and the right when Parliament is not sitting to be tried by a jury of peers in the court of the Lord High Steward.[3] But we shall see also that even the trial before the whole House of Lords is not quite the same thing as the " judicium " which the framers of the Charter intended,[4] and that the trial in the court of the Lord High Steward is wholly different.[5]

The two chief points upon which the commentators are not agreed are firstly the meaning of the phrase " per legem terræ," and secondly the meaning of " vel " in the phrase " per judicium parium *vel* per legem terræ." To some extent these two points are connected, so that they can conveniently be considered together.

According to one view " lex terræ" refers, not to the law of the land, but to a trial by battle, ordeal, or compurgation.[6] The " lex " means the test by which the contentions of the parties were tried ; and there is no doubt that the word is often used in this sense.[7] According to this view the barons ask for.a trial before their peers who will adjudicate upon the " lex " to be adopted to decide the case. If we adopt this interpretation it is quite clear that the word " vel " must mean " and ". The

resolution of the peers ; but it is not likely that the framers of the Charter should have used this semi-technical phrase in this wholly new way.

[1] Adams, op. cit. 269-272 ; cf. the famous passage in the chronicle of Matthew Paris (R.S.) iii 251 where he relates that, in 1233, in answer to complaints that persons had been condemned without judgment of peers, " Petrus Wintoniensis episcopus dixit, quod non sunt pares in Anglia sicut in regno Francorum ; unde licet regi Anglorum per justitiarios, quos constituerit quos libet de regno reos proscribere et mediante judicio condemnare ; " this shows that the distinction between royal judges and peers was beginning to be perceived, Harcourt, op. cit. 277-278 ; it would certainly have been difficult to disprove the statement that the royal justices were entitled to judge—their courts had been regarded in the past as curiæ regis, above 35 ; and for a long time the amercements of peers which, by § 21 of Magna Carta must be assessed by peers, were, in accordance with this clause, assessed by the barons of the Exchequer, Bracton f. 116 b ; Pike, House of Lords 254-258 ; McKechnie, op. cit. 297-298 ; for a similar controversy in France see Harcourt, op. cit. 272-274.

[2] P. and M. i 152 n. 2. [3] Below 385-390.

[4] Pike, House of Lords, 174 ; below 389. [5] Below 389-390.

[6] Selden, Notes on Fortescue De Laudibus c. 26 ; Bigelow, History of Procedure 155, n. 3 ; McKechnie, op. cit. 379 ; for a good summary of the discussion see McIlwain, Due Process of Law in Magna Carta Col. Law Rev. xiv 44-51.

[7] Adams, Origin of the English Constitutions 268 ; cf. instances Harcourt, op. cit. 232, n. 1 and 2 ; McIlwain, op. cit. 45.

"judicium" and the "lex" are not alternatives : they are complementary to one another. It is quite clear also that the clause is wholly reactionary, and has no sort of constitutional significance.

According to the other view the term "lex terræ" means simply the law of the land; [1] and, here again, there is no doubt that the word "lex" often bears this meaning.[2] If this interpretation is correct, the barons are asking for a trial by peers, and that no violence be done to themselves or their possessions except, as Coke phrases it, "by due process of law; " and in that case, it would seem that the word "vel" may equally well be translated "and" or "or." The word is, as Maitland suggests, in much the same position as the $\frac{\text{"}and\text{"}}{or}$ of our mercantile documents.[3] It is also clear that this interpretation deprives the clause of some of its reactionary effect, and restores to it some of its constitutional significance. It is in substance a demand that no violence be offered to person or property without legal warrant.

It cannot be said that either view has been proved to be correct. In fact both interpretations are possible. On the whole I incline to the latter for the two following reasons.[4]

In the first place I think that it makes better sense. It would seem to be clear that there might be circumstances in which a man might lawfully be "taken or imprisoned or disseised or exiled" otherwise than by a judicium parium. As Mr. McIlwain has pointed out, he might be disseised as the result of a verdict in an assize of novel disseisin. Clearly that would be a disseisin lawfully effected but it would not be effected by a judicium parium.[5] Therefore unless we give to the phrase "per legem terræ" the meaning of "due process of law," we make

---

[1] Coke, Second Instit. 50, 51; Harcourt, op. cit. 228-233; Adams, op. cit. 262 seqq.; McIlwain, Col. Law. Rev. xiv 44-51.

[2] For a good collection of instances see Harcourt, op. cit. 229-231; a good instance of the use of the term "lex" in the two different senses in the same sentence is to be found in Glanvil xiv 2, "Non solet juxta legem terræ aliquis per legem apparentem se purgare," cited McIlwain, op. cit. xiv 46-47.

[3] P. and M. i 152 n. 2; I think that Harcourt is right when he says, "The Charter treats judgment of peers and the law of the land as to a great extent convertible terms. A large area was covered by both but their boundaries were by no means quite conterminous," op. cit. 223.

[4] This view is taken both by Professor Vinogradoff, Magna Carta Commemoration Essays, 83-85; and by Professor Powicke, ibid 98-107, whose reasons seem to me to be conclusive.

[5] Col. Law. Rev. xiv 48; as Professor Powicke says, Magna Carta Commemoration Essays 102, a contemporary change in Norman procedure illustrates clearly enough this distinction between judicium parium and lex terræ. Phillip Augustus took the trial of ducal pleas from the justices, and gave it to local men, i.e. he instituted a judicium parium; but "The procedure of the court and the law enforced by the court were not affected by the change; the lex terræ was observed both before and after; but henceforward a trial according to law would in Normandy involve a judicium parium. In England this was not necessarily the case."

the barons assert the illegality of a procedure which in clause eighteen they had recognized as legal. And other similar instances can be given—thus the lex terræ might necessitate a trial by battle; or if a person were appealed or indicted, and proper proceedings were taken in the county court, justify an outlawry with all its consequences.[1] As Harcourt says, "There is not the smallest doubt that prior to the Charter (and subsequently) judgment was not a condition precedent to the arrest and imprisonment of a felon caught flagrante delicto; on the contrary, the law of the land, no less than the most elementary principles of justice required that such persons should be instantly captured and secured.[2] Coke too points out that, "if a nobleman be indicted, and cannot be found, process of outlawry shall be awarded against him *per legem terræ*, and he shall be outlawed *per judicium Coronatorum*, but he shall be tried *per judicium parium suorum*, when he appears and pleads to issue."[3] No doubt, as a rule, infringements of personal liberty and rights of property must be preceded by a judicium parium, and that judicium will make the acts done under it acts done by due process of law. But it is conceivable that such acts might be lawful though not done per judicium parium. I think that the barons had these facts in their mind; and that that is why they used the word "vel" which according to the circumstances may be construed either as "and" or as "or."

Secondly, I think that the weight of contemporary exposition is in favour of this view. In May 1215 John made a proposal to the barons in which he promised that he would not take or disseise them or their men, and that he would not go upon them by force or arms, "nisi per legem regni nostri, vel per judicium parium suorum in curia nostra."[4] Here the phrase "per legem regni" can only mean due process of law. Moreover it would appear from the Bull in which the Pope absolved John from his oath to observe the Charter, and from his letter to the barons of the same date, that he understood the clause in this sense.[5] In that letter the phrase "per legem terræ" is expanded into "secundum consuetudines et leges regni."[6]

---

[1] Powicke, op. cit. 106-107.

[2] Op. cit. 223-224; also he points out, ibid 220, that § 9 of the Charter "fully recognizes the right of the king or his bailiffs to disseize a debtor of his lands when his chattels are insufficient."

[3] Second Instit. 49.

[4] "Quod nec eos nec homines suos capiemus nec disseisiemus nec super eos per vim vel per arma ibimus nisi per legem regni nostri vel per judicium parium suorum in curia nostra," Rymer (Ed. 1816) i 128, cited McIlwain, Col. Law. Rev. xiv 39.

[5] Adams, Origin of the English Constitution 267.

[6] "Præsertim cum in causa ipsa vos judices et executores feceritis; eodem Rege parato, in curia sua, vobis, per pares vestros secundum consuetudines et leges regni, justitiæ plenitudinem exhibere," Rymer i 136, cited Adams loc. cit.

For these reasons, then, I think that this famous clause is only in part reactionary, and only in part refers specially to the judicial system. It has, I think, a very considerable constitutional significance because it does lay down the principle that liberty and property are not to be interfered with without " due process of law." We shall see that the fact that it was interpreted in this way in the fourteenth century gave it a very considerable bearing upon the evolution of the judicial system at a later stage in its history. Parliament and the common lawyers interpreted it as meaning " due process of the common law ; " and they used it with some effect against the rival jurisdictions of the council and the Chancery.[1]

All this is as yet in the future. If we return to the beginning of the thirteenth century, and take our stand in 1215, we can see that the Great Charter has made it clear that the future of English law is with royal justice, and that therefore there will be a law common to the whole of England. But before I describe the development and organization of the courts which administered this royal justice, I must first trace the history of the decay of those local courts which this royal justice superseded, and of the rise, in the nineteenth century, of a wholly new system of local courts.

---

[1] Below 464, 487; Professor Powicke, Magna Carta Commemoration Essays 110 seqq. clearly brings out the constitutional significance of the clause both for the men of 1215 and for the law of the future.

CHAPTER II

THE DECLINE OF THE OLD LOCAL COURTS AND THE RISE OF THE NEW COUNTY COURTS

DURING the thirteenth century the central courts were beginning to analyse and distinguish the different principles upon which the local courts exercised their jurisdiction. The distinctions drawn by these central courts will become clearer as the principles of the common law become more settled ; but, by the end of Edward's I.'s reign, they are sufficiently clearly drawn to enable us to distinguish four main groups of local courts. Firstly there are the communal courts. They are the courts of the Anglo-Saxon communities—the courts of the shire and the hundred ; but the officials who hold these courts are royal officials. We shall see, therefore, that in respect of some parts of their jurisdiction they act as the representatives of these old communities, and that in respect of other parts of their jurisdiction they act as direct agents of the king.[1] We shall see also that the distinction drawn between the two capacities in which these courts act is one of the roots of the technical division into courts of record and courts not of record.[2] Secondly there are the courts held by private persons by virtue of some franchise granted by the crown. We shall see that the Quo Warranto enquiries of Edward I.'s reign resulted in laying down the principle that these franchises can exist only by virtue of royal grant or by prescription.[3] Thirdly there are the feudal courts. They depend upon the principle that the lord of tenants can hold a court for his tenants merely because they are his tenants. A lord of tenants will also often have a franchise or franchises by virtue of which he exercises a wider jurisdiction ; but because his purely feudal jurisdiction does not depend upon a special grant from the crown it is, in theory at any rate, clearly distinguishable from the jurisdiction which he exercises as the lord of a franchise. Fourthly there are the manorial courts. We shall see that the term manor gradually acquires a new technical meaning ; and that, while it continues to denote certain pro-

[1] Below 71-72, 78-79.   [2] Vol. v 157-160.   [3] Below 88-89.

prietary rights over land,[1] it gradually comes to connote also certain jurisdictional rights over the tenants of that land.[2]

We have seen that, in the past, many of these courts were, like the Curia Regis, very much more than law courts. They were courts in which administrative as well as judicial work was done.[3] Many of them continued to be courts of this character long after the purely judicial courts of common law had split off from the Curia Regis. For many centuries some of them will continue to play an important part in the local government of the country; and we shall meet them again in this capacity in later Books of this history.[4] Here I shall deal with them chiefly from the point of view of their judicial functions, and of their place in the judicial system. I shall describe them from this point of view under the following three heads: the Communal Courts; the Franchise Courts; and the Feudal and Manorial Courts.

We shall see that, though many of these courts have had a long life, and though some still exist to-day, yet their history has been in the main a history of ·decline and decadence. By the end of the mediæval period all the litigation of the country large and small was being attracted to the central courts of law and equity; and, before the end of the eighteenth century, the want of efficient local courts in which small cases could be quickly and cheaply tried was keenly felt. But it was not till the middle of the nineteenth century that this want was supplied by the creation of the New County Courts. Having traced the history of the decline of the older local courts in the first three sections of this chapter, I shall say something of the rise of these new local tribunals in a fourth and last section.

I. THE COMMUNAL COURTS

This group of courts falls into two main divisions (1) the Sheriff and his courts, and (2) the Coroner and his court.

(1) *The Sheriff and his Courts.*

(i) The Sheriff.

The immediate result of the large jurisdiction assumed by the Curia Regis was an increase in the power of the sheriff. As a royal delegate in close touch with the central government, sometimes a holder of one of the important offices in the king's court, and often a great tenant in chief,[5] he grew in importance

---

[1] Above 23-24, 28-30. [2] Below 180-181. [3] Above 7, 8.
[4] Vol. iv 122-134. [5] E.H.R. xxxiii 150-153.

with the growth of royal power, until he became the ruler of the county. He was responsible for its revenue, for its military force, for its police, for its gaols, for its courts, for the due execution of writs and other orders addressed to him by all the central courts and by the quarter sessions. But most of these powers have gradually been taken away from him. Though he long continued to be "the first man in the county, and superior in rank to any nobleman therein during his office,"[1] though to his office there still clings much of the prestige that belonged to it in days in which he ruled the county as the chief representative of the king, it now gives him very little substantial authority. "The whole history of English justice and police,"[2] Maitland has truly said, "might be brought under this rubric, 'The Decline and Fall of the Sheriff.'"

But for the control exercised by the Norman kings, the office of sheriff might have become hereditary;[3] and, if that had happened, the sheriff, instead of becoming a useful official, would have degenerated into a dangerous potentate.[4] Sheriffdoms in fee are contemplated as existing in a statute of 1300;[5] and in the case of the county of Westmorland the office was hereditary till 1850.[6] But hereditary sheriffdoms were never numerous; and, by Stephen's reign, life tenure of the office was uncommon.[7] Another danger had been surmounted by the beginning of the fourteenth century. In 1300 it had been provided that the sheriff should be elected by the county.[8] If this statute had remained unrepealed the office would have been of much less value to the king, and would probably have fallen a prey to the larger landowners who would have exploited it in their own interests. Fortunately a perception of these consequences caused its speedy repeal. In 1315, in consequence of a complaint that these elected sheriffs were "insufficient," it was enacted by the statute of Lincoln that sheriffs should be appointed by the

---

[1] Bl. Comm. i 332; this statement is repeated in the 1914 Ed. of Stephen's Comm. ii 721, but it is noted that since 1904 the lord-lieutenant takes precedence of the sheriff.

[2] Justice and Police 69.

[3] After the Conquest the duration of the tenure of the office is uncertain; but a number of sheriffs held office for life, E.H.R. xxxiii 149, 150; and a few were hereditary, ibid 154-155.

[4] So efficient was the control of the Norman kings that Mr. Morris says with some truth that, "By the early years of the twelfth century the long process of reducing the sheriff's power was already under weigh," E.H.R. xxxiii 174.

[5] 28 Edward I. c. 8, "The king hath granted unto his people that they shall have the election of their sheriff in every shire (*where the shrivalty is not of fee*) if they list."

[6] Webb, Local Government, the Parish and the County 288 n. 1; cf. P. and M. i 519; for other instances of hereditary or quasi-hereditary sheriffs in Edward II.'s reign see Tout, Edward II. 101 n. 2.

[7] E.H.R. xxxiii 154-155. [8] 28 Edward I. c. 8.

Chancellor, Treasurer, Barons of the Exchequer, and the justices; that they should have land within the shire; and that stewards or bailiffs of great lords should be ineligible.[1] It was provided in 1340 that the office should only be held for one year,[2] and in 1377 that three years must elapse before the same person was reappointed.[3] The Sheriffs Act of 1887 in substance reinacted the provisions of these mediæval statutes, with only such modifications as were rendered necessary by the changes in courts and officials made by such statutes as the Judicature Acts.[4] Thus, at the present day, the sheriff is appointed by the advice of substantially the same officials as are specified in the statute of 1315;[5] but it appears that in practice the list of three names presented by these officials to the king on the morrow of St. Martin's[6] is made up by the judges on their summer circuits.[7] As with other mediæval offices the person nominated was and is compelled to serve, and to serve without payment.[8] When appointed he was responsible for the appointment of an under-sheriff, of bailiffs of the hundreds, and of other officials necessary for the government of the county.[9] For their misdeeds he could be made personally liable;[10] and it was for this reason that he was required to be a landowner. A man of substance was required who could "answer" both the king and the subject.[11]

Between the thirteenth and the nineteenth centuries the large powers which the sheriff once exercised have gradually been taken away from him. In Henry II.'s reign The Dialogus shows that he was the principal accountant of the crown.[12] At Easter and Michaelmas he must appear and answer for the revenue of the shire. But, as time went on, new taxes and rates were imposed with which he had nothing to do;[13] the revenue for which he was answerable gradually became inconsiderable; and his attendance at the Exchequer was no longer required. His control over the military force of the shire ceased with the appointment of lord-lieutenants in Mary's reign.[14] But, as keeper of the king's peace, he still had powers of arrest and committal in order to maintain it,[15] till the rise of a new system of county

---

[1] 9 Edward II. St. 2; L.Q.R. xxxiii 78; see also 14 Edward III. St. 1 c. 7; 23 Henry VI. c. 7; for dispensations with these statutes see L.Q.R. xlii 216-218.

[2] 14 Edward III. St. 1 c. 7.   [3] 1 Richard II. c. 11.

[4] 50, 51 Victoria c. 55 §§ 3-6.   [5] Ibid § 6.   [6] Bl. Comm. i 329.

[7] Webb. op. cit. The Parish and the County 484 n. 1; the list of three names is as old as the fifteenth century, see Fortescue, De Laudibus c. 24.

[8] R. v. Larwood (1695) 1 Ld. Raym. at p. 33.   [9] Bl. Comm. i 334.

[10] "The sheriff being answerable for the misdemeanours of these bailiffs, they are usually bound in a bond for the due execution of their office, and thence are called bound-bailiffs; which the common people have corrupted into a much more homely appellation," ibid 334.

[11] 9 Edward II. St. 2.   [12] Above 43.   [13] Stubbs, C.H. ii 225.

[14] Vol. iv 76-77.   [15] Bl. Comm. i 332.

police deprived him of the opportunity to exercise these powers.[1] All that remains of his once extensive powers over the military and police forces of the shire is his power to call out the posse comitatus; and, says the Sheriffs Act of 1887, "every person in a county shall be ready and apparelled at the command of the sheriff and at the cry of the country to arrest a felon within a franchise or without."[2]   Abuses arising out of the manner in which the sheriff exercised his control over prisoners in his custody was the subject of much legislation in the Middle Ages;[3] and the condition of the gaols for which he was responsible aroused considerable public feeling even in the eighteenth century.[4] He is now only responsible for prisoners condemned to death,[5] and he has nothing to do with the gaols.[6]

The one duty which he still retains is the duty of executing the writs addressed to him by the central courts, the courts held by the itinerant justices, and the courts of quarter sessions.   He must summon the necessary jurors for the assizes or quarter sessions; and he must personally attend upon the judge of assize, and make provision for his lodging and escort.[7]   It is his position as the executor of royal writs which gives him control over Parliamentary elections for the county.   Like other writs, the writ to elect knights of the shire is addressed to him.[8]   But these surviving functions have long been performed by deputy.   At the end of the seventeenth century, "the sheriff always appointed for his year of office a professional under-sheriff, almost invariably the same person as had served his predecessor, in whom was merged the ancient post of county clerk, and who performed all but the ceremonial duties of the sheriff."[9]   The wide powers of the annually appointed sheriff

---

[1] 10 George IV. c. 44; 2, 3 Victoria c. 95; 22, 23 Victoria c. 32 § 18.

[2] 50, 51 Victoria c. 55 § 8.

[3] 3 Edward I. c. 15; 14 Edward III. St. 1 c. 10; 19 Henry VII. c. 10.

[4] Webb, op. cit. The Parish and the County 485-487.

[5] 28, 29 Victoria c. 126; 40, 41 Victoria c. 21 § 32; 50, 51 Victoria c. 55 § 13.

[6] Webb, op. cit. The Parish and the County 486-487.

[7] These were beginning to be his chief duties in the fifteenth century; Fortescue, De Laudibus c. 24, describing the office of sheriff, says, "Moreover in every county there is one certain officer called the king's sheriff, which among other duties belonging to his office, putteth in execution all the commandments and judgments of the king's courts that are to be executed within his counties;" 23 Henry VI. c. 9 § 10 required them to have deputies in the common law courts and the Chancery "to receive all manner of writs and warrants directed to them"—a provision substantially repeated by the Sheriff's Act 1888, § 24; naturally the statutes relating to this part of his duties are very numerous, see e.g. 13 Edward I. St. 1 c. 39; 2 Edward III. c. 5; 29 Elizabeth c. 4; 3 George I. c. 15; 50, 51 Victoria c. 55 §§ 10, 11, 14-16, 20.   He has nothing to do with the new county courts, below 191-193; their process is executed by a High Bailiff, see L.Q.R. iii 9.

[8] Bl. Comm. i 332.

[9] Webb, op. cit. The Parish and the County 289; as Blackstone says, Comm. i 333, 42 Edward III. c. 9 and 23 Henry VI. c. 7 prevent any under-sheriff holding

passed to the permanent body of justices of the peace for the county assembled in quarter sessions ;[1] and the sheriff, while he held office, was prevented by a statute of 1553[2] from acting as a member of this new governing body of the county.

(ii) The Sheriff's Courts.

We have seen that the courts held by the sheriff were the county and hundred courts ;[3] and that, just as the sheriff was an administrative even more than a judicial officer, so these courts through whom he acted were governing bodies quite as much as courts of law.

In the thirteenth century a full session of the county court contained the archbishops, bishops, abbots, priors, earls, barons, knights and freeholders, the reeve and four men from each township, and twelve burghers from each borough.[4] It thus, as Stubbs has said, " contained all the elements of a local parliament—all the members of the body politic in as full a representation as the three estates afterwards enjoyed in the general parliament."[5] It is not therefore surprising to find that, besides its judicial work, it did all sorts of governmental work. It was responsible for putting in execution the laws for the preservation of the peace.[6] The military orders directed to the sheriff from the central government were published in the county court.[7] Very various administrative measures were carried out through it.[8] Demands for taxation were laid before it ;[9] and knights chosen by it took part in the work of assessment and collection.[10] Also it is not surprising to find that the county, through its court, had some of the qualities of a juristic person. As in earlier days, it could negotiate with the crown for the purchase of privileges,[11] and compound for offences ;[12] and the county of Devon had a

office for more than a year; but as 1 Richard II. c. 11, above 67 n. 3, did not apply to the under-sheriff, the same man could be reappointed each year.

[1] Below 292-293 ; vol. iv 142-144.
[2] 1 Mary St. 1 c. 8 ; 50, 51 Victoria c. 55 § 17.
[3] Above 6-13.
[4] Stubbs, C.H. i 681 ; ii 223-224.
[5] Ibid ii 224.
[6] Ibid ii 228.
[7] Ibid ii 230-231.
[8] Ibid ii 227, 231-232.
[9] Ibid ii 232-235 ; " We must not," says Maitland, " endow this assembly with a power of making rates," P. and M. i 542 ; but it appears from Y.B. 11, 12 Ed. III. (R.S.) 636 that on one occasion the county of Kent granted 50 marks to the king; however an abbot who declined to pay rested his refusal on the fact that he had not consented, and that the grant had not been made in Parliament ; it would seem that these county assemblies retained some of the old ideas which demanded the individual assent of its members to a measure and did not recognize a majority vote, see vol. ii 431 ; vol. iv 168 ; it is no wonder that the king found that he could do business more easily through a national Parliament which was not hampered by these ideas.
[10] Stubbs, C.H. ii 232-235.
[11] P. and M. i 520 ; Stubbs, C.H. ii 235.
[12] Y.B. 30, 31 Ed. I. (R.S.) 240—the county of Cornwall compounded with the justices in Eyre.

common seal.[1] It was constantly made liable for very various misdeeds.[2] The communal personality of the community was thus very distinctly realized. It came to be gradually less distinctly realized as the county court, like the sheriff, gradually ceased to be the chief organ of local government. This change was due to two main causes. In the first place the rise of Parliament tended to vest in the assembled representatives of the counties and boroughs and in the House of Lords the powers formerly exercised by these local assemblies. In the second place, just as the rise of the justices of the peace tended to sap the authority of the sheriff,[3] so their court—the court of quarter sessions—tended to sap the authority of the county court.[4] Thus, just as the sheriff came to be chiefly concerned with the execution of writs, so the county court came to be a court used chiefly for judicial or semi-judicial business. At the present day it can, if called on, assess damages and make enquiries under a writ of elegit ;[5] and it would still be the only court in which a person could be outlawed, if outlawry had not been practically abolished.[6]

The county court was tending to descend to this position at the close of the mediæval period ; and naturally its decline affected its constitution. From the first there was a marked difference between the large county assemblies and the smaller courts which met once every four weeks. These smaller courts generally consisted of suitors bound by the tenure of their lands to attend ; and, as the powers of the county court decayed, it tended to become on almost all occasions a small court of this kind. But, till the introduction of the ballot, the assembly in which the knights of the shire were elected recalled some of the features of the large county assemblies of the thirteenth century ; and, "the statute book authorizes the modern county voter to believe if he can, that when in strictest secrecy he is dropping his voting paper into the ballot box, he is attending a county court of the old type held by the sheriff."[8]

The hundred court,[9] like the county court, was an organ of local government. But it was of very minor importance. It was responsible for the murder fine ;[10] and the Statute of Winchester (1285) made it liable for robberies committed within

---

[1] P. and M. i 520.
[2] Below 269-271.
[3] Below 81, 286-287.
[4] Below 292-293.
[5] 50, 51 Victoria c. 55 § 18, (1), (2) ; cf. Halsbury, Laws of England xxv 808-809.
[6] P. and M. i 541-542.
[7] Above 10 ; P. and M. i 526-531. This was also the case with the franchise courts, and apparently the duty to pay such service could be released by the lord, Y.B. 6, 7 Ed. II. (S.S.) 110-118.
[8] Maitland, Justice and Police 22-23.
[9] P. and M. i 545-546.
[10] Above 11, 15.

its boundaries if the robbers were not produced.[1] We shall see that this liability was closely connected with the police duties enforceable in the special meeting of the court which came to be known as the sheriff's tourn.[2]

It is with the judicial duties of these courts that we are here concerned. We shall see that the importance of these duties declined during the Middle Ages as rapidly as the importance of their governmental duties ; and that, though the county court still in name survives for certain administrative purposes,[3] both county and hundred courts have ceased to exist[4] as judicial courts for the conduct of litigation.

In the twelfth century, when sheriffs sometimes acted as itinerant justices,[5] and in the thirteenth century, when the itinerant justices sat in the county court,[6] the county court was one of the most important of courts. Thus, as in the case of the sheriff, so in the case of the county court, the first effect of the growth of royal justice had been to increase its importance. But, as the system of royal justice grew in elaboration, and as those of the itinerant justices who were judges of the common law courts came to be in practice the sole judges of the courts held before them, their courts came to be more closely allied to the central courts of common law, and less closely allied to the county courts.[7] The county court ceased to be a court which administered royal justice, and for that reason was never a court of record. It remained simply a communal court of the old type, which tended to grow more and more ineffective ; and thus it sank to the position which the hundred court had always occupied. We shall see that, in consequence, the greater part of the civil jurisdiction of the county court was, by the end of the thirteenth century, rapidly passing to the itinerant justices and the courts of common law. The decay of its criminal jurisdiction was even more rapid. The Assize of Clarendon had reserved to the royal justices jurisdiction over the robber, the murderer, and the thief ;[8] the Assize of Northampton had added the crimes of forgery, treason, and arson to this reserved list ;[9]

---

[1] 13 Edward I. St. 2, c. 2 ; repealed by 7, 8 George IV. c. 27 ; but 7, 8 George IV. c. 31 made it liable for damage caused by rioters, see Stephen, H.C.L. i 188 n. 1 ; the latter statute was repealed by 49, 50 Victoria, c. 38 § 10 which charged such claims on the police rate of the district in which the riot occurred ; see Eyre of Kent (S.S.) i 80, 129-130 for cases where the liability of the hundred was enforced.

[2] Below 76-81.　　　　[3] Above 70.　　　　[4] Below 74-75.

[5] Above 50.　　　　[6] Below 267.

[7] Below 281-282 ; in Normandy also the growth of the powers of the itinerant justices reduced the powers of the vicomte, Haskins, Norman Institutions 186 ; and even under the Norman kings, " when the king's justice convened a local court within the shire, the sheriff took a lower place," E.H.R. xxxiii 173.

[8] Assize of Clarendon § 4 (Sel. Ch. 143).

[9] Assize of Northampton § 1 (Sel. Ch. 150-151).

Magna Carta in 1215 had prohibited the sheriff from holding pleas of the crown;[1] and Bracton tells us that the sheriff could try no case that involved a breach of the king's peace.[2] Thus, by the beginning of the thirteenth century, the county court had, as a general rule,[3] ceased to have a criminal jurisdiction. It is true that the sheriff could try smaller offences ; but this jurisdiction he exercised in the special session of the hundred court which he held when " he took his tourn," i.e. made his perambulation, through the hundreds to see that the frankpledge machinery was in working order.[4]   Hence this court—the court of the sheriff's tourn—fell apart from the hundred court, which henceforward is, like the county court, a court with only a civil jurisdiction. Thus the courts held by the sheriff have in the thirteenth century fallen into two groups, the county and hundred courts exercising a civil jurisdiction, and the sheriff's tourn exercising criminal jurisdiction.

(a) The County and Hundred Courts.

By the end of Edward I.'s reign the jurisdiction of the county court had been so restricted that, even at that early date, the court was taking a subordinate position in the English scheme of jurisdiction.   This will be apparent if we look at its jurisdiction in the twelfth century, and at the manner in which that jurisdiction had been in some cases diminished, and in others wholly taken away.   Its jurisdiction can be divided into the following four categories: (1) Actions of debt, detinue, and covenant; and actions of trespass, unless the trespass were committed vi et armis, or unless brought for taking away the title-deeds to freehold property.[5]   But the interpretation put upon the Statute of Gloucester deprived the county court of this jurisdiction if the amount at stake exceeded 40s. in value.[6]   This

---

[1] § 24 ; above 57; cf. 50, 51 Victoria c. 55 § 18 (3).

[2] " Cognoscere quidem potest de medletis, plagis, verberibus, et consimilibus pro defectu dominorum, nisi querens adjiciat de pace domini regis infracta, vel feloniam apponat, extunc enim se viceomes non debet intromittere, cum hoc tangat personam ipsius domini regis et coronam suam," f. 154 b.

[3] In Y.B. 17, 18 Ed. III. (R.S.) 217-219, it was alleged that presentments for bloodshed in Furness were made, not to the tourn, but to the county court by the bailiff of the hundred ; Maitland has noted, Select Pleas in Manorial Courts (S.S.) xxxiii, that tourns were a late introduction into Lancashire, and that even in Edward I.'s day there was no tourn in Northumberland; probably in these places the county court exercised the criminal jurisdiction of the tourn, and this Y.B. case represents a survival of a criminal jurisdiction which was rapidly passing from the county court ; it may be noted that Britton i 135, writing in Edward I.'s reign, says that besides the county court which exercised a civil jurisdiction, there was a coroner's court for the pleas of the crown ; but it would seem from the rolls that it was chiefly concerned with appeals of felony ; cf. Camb. Hist. Journal i 105.

[4] Above 13 ; below 76.

[5] Coke, Second Instit. 311, 312; Fourth Instit. 266; Bl. Comm. iii 35-37.

[6] 6 Edward I. c. 8 ; Britton i 155; P. and M. i 540, 541.

was a large sum when the statute was passed ; but it was a fixed sum ; and the decrease in the value of money inevitably decreased the importance of the jurisdiction of the county court.   Moreover by writ of *Pone*[1] any of these cases could be removed into the king's court.   (2) The court held jurisdiction to any amount, and even in cases of trespass vi et armis, by virtue of a writ of Justices[2] directed to the sheriff.   By other writs which, as Coke says, "are in the nature of a commission," the court had jurisdiction in cases of admeasurement of pasture or dower, and in many others.[3]   This jurisdiction depended simply on the issue of the necessary writ ; and such writs gradually ceased to be issued.   (3) From Henry II.'s time cases concerning the possession of freehold land fell under the jurisdiction of the king's court : cases concerning the ownership of freehold land were at first divided between the king's court and the court of the lord of whom the land was held.[4]   The sheriff could, it is true, remove cases from the lord's court by virtue of his precept called *Tolt.*[5] But this power became in practice obsolete, since, as we shall see, such cases came to be always begun in the court of common pleas.[6]   (4) In Henry III.'s reign the county court was prevented from ever becoming a court of appeal from the other courts of the county.   By the Statute of Marlborough (1268) pleas of false judgment were reserved for the king's court.[7]

These limitations upon the jurisdiction of the county court

---

[1] App. VII.

[2] Bracton f. 154 b, " Item habet ex speciali mandato regis, non ex officio vice-comitis, ubi mandatum habet quod justitiet aliquem ; " for the writ see App. VI.

[3] Second Instit. 311, 312; e.g. cases of replevin,(52 Henry III. c. 21) and re-disseisin (20 Henry III. c. 3) ; P. and M. ii 44, 575.

[4] Above 58.

[5] Called Tolt " quia tollit atque eximit causam ; " for the form of the precept see App. VIII.   By this precept cases could also be removed from the hundred court, Bracton ff. 105, 105 b.

[6] Above 58-59; below 198.

[7] 52 Henry III. c. 19; for the form of the writ see App. IX.; a writ of false judgment from the county court was called *recordari facias*, from the hundred court *accedas ad hundredum*, from the court baron *accedas ad curiam ;* the writ lay when the proceedings were in a court which was not a court of record, and the writ of error when they were in a court of record.   On receipt of such a writ the suitors came to testify as to the proceedings of the court, and it would seem that they sometimes put their record into writing, Bracton's N.B. case 243 ; and sometimes brought an oral report which was written out by a clerk of the court, Y.B. 32-33 Ed. I. (R.S.) 364-366; under the old law they might be obliged to defend their judgment by battle, Glanvil viii 8, and cf. P. and M. ii 664; but they were not obliged to defend the correctness of the record in this way, Glanvil, loc. cit. ; the correctness of the record could however in the twelfth century be denied " tertia manu cum sacramento," ibid ; but in 1310 it was held that no averment was permissible against the record, Y.B. 3, 4 Ed. II. (S.S.) 12, 13 ; apparently all the suitors ordered to bring up the record must bring it, Y.BB. 33-35 Ed. I. (R.S.) 116, and 12 Rich. II. 24-26, though it was not necessary that all the suitors who gave the judgment should appear, Y.B. 3 Ed. II. (S.S.) 13.

could be enforced by means of writs of false judgment [1] or prohibition.[2]   But there was little need for them.   It is but rarely
that we hear of any attempt by litigants to bring actions in a
county court which ought to have been brought in the courts
of common law.[3]   " Of his own free will the small freeholder passed by his lord's court and the county court on his
way to the great hall ; " [4] and the reasons are obvious.   The older
methods of procedure prevailed in the county court.   The suitors
were the judges.   Compurgation might still be employed.
Sheriffs were sometimes partial or worse.   A statute of Henry
VII.'s reign would seem to show that they were in the habit of
entering fictitious plaints in the county courts merely for purposes
of extortion.[5]   It is not surprising therefore that litigants preferred to take their cases to the courts of common law.   In 1601
the congestion of business thus caused in those courts attracted
the attention of the legislature, and an Act was passed to "avoid
trifling or frivolous suits in Her Majesty's courts at Westminster." [6]
It provided that the judges should have power to deprive a
plaintiff of full costs if less than 40s. were recovered in the action ;
and that if the action were originally brought for less than 40s.
those who had issued the process should be liable in addition to
a fine of £10.   The Act does not seem to have had much effect, as
litigants seem to have found no difficulty in evading it, and the
judges perhaps connived at their evasions.[7]   The space which
Coke gives to the county court in his Fourth Institute is but
small ; and Blackstone laments its disuse.[8]   But, as at the end of
the eighteenth century it could be denounced as an engine of
nefarious oppression,[9] it is not surprising to find that even
statutory recommendation was powerless to revive it.[10]   In 1887

---

[1] See Y.B. 32-33 Ed. I. (R.S.) 360-366 for an instance of the manner in which
cases of oppression could be dealt with by such a writ.

[2] Below 228-229 ; for the writ see App. XII.

[3] There is a solitary or almost a solitary case in Y.B. 20 Ed. III. (R.S.) ii 146 in
which a debt was divided, and two actions brought in respect of it, to evade the
Statute of Gloucester.

[4] P. and M. i 181, 182.

[5] 11 Henry VII. c. 15.   The "trading justices " of the eighteenth century made
money in much the same way, below 146.

[6] 43 Elizabeth c. 6.

[7] In S.P. Dom. 1639-1640, 599-600, ccccxlix no. 35 some notes of things to be
amended by Parliament contain an allegation that, " this law is by every punny
attorney . . . made void . . . either by laying the debt above 40s. though it be not
10s. or by making it an action on the case, and so they may trouble a man for
5s. . . . yea or even 12d. by which means the charges of the first writ oftentimes
amount to twice the value of the debt.   This is thought to be through the conniv-
ance of the judges."

[8] Bl. Comm. iii 82.

[9] An address to the county gentlemen of England and Wales by James Bland
Burges (1789) cited Webb, Local Government, the Parish and the County 291 n.

[10] 3, 4 William IV. c. 42, § 17; for other fruitless interventions of the legislature
in favour of the county and other inferior courts see 21 James I. c. 23 ; 12 George I.
c. 29 § 3 ; and cf. Bl. Comm. iii 82 ; below 188-191.

it was enacted that the sheriff need not hold a county court unless the court was required for an election, for the execution of some writ, or for any other specific purpose.[1]

The new county courts are the creatures of modern statute. They are given the style of county court, but the statute has merely affixed an old name to a new creation.[2]   Thus " of the two county courts, the old and the new, we may say that the one, if it exist at all is not a law court, while the other, though an active law court, has nothing to do with the county." [3]

The hundred court was held by a deputy of the sheriff ; and originally had a jurisdiction similar to that of the county court.[4] Like the county court it was no court of record, and the suitors were its judges.[5]   Till 1268 its decisions could be reviewed by the county court ; [6] and its suitors could be made liable at the general eyre if they acted without jurisdiction.[7]   It appears from a clause in the Statute of Westminster II. that its process was used by lords and others to oppress their inferiors; [8] but it is only occasionally that we hear of its activities in later law.[9]   The same causes which produced the decay of the county court operated even more rapidly in the case of the hundred court.   Coke mentions it in his Fourth Institute ; but says nothing whatever about its jurisdiction.   We shall see, however, that the life of those hundred courts which were in private hands was considerably longer ; [10] and that there were instances of hundred courts which, because they were situated in urban districts, became important and busy courts.[11]   But hundred courts, whether in private hands or not, are now obsolete, since it was provided by the County Courts Amendment Act, 1867 that no action which could be brought in one of the new county courts should be brought in a hundred court.[12]

---

[1] 50, 51 Victoria c. 55 § 18, 1.   [2] Below 191.
[3] Maitland, Justice and Police 23.   [4] Above 12, 13.
[5] Coke, Fourth Instit. 267 ; P. and M. i 544-545.
[6] 52 Henry III. c. 19.
[7] Eyre of Kent (S.S.) i 64 ; for the general eyre see below 265-272.
[8] 13 Edward I. St. 1 c. 36.
[9] The hundred or wapentake courts in Yorkshire are described as still sitting in 1641, Best, Rural Economy in Yorkshire (Surt. Soc.) xxxiii 91 ; but it would seem that they were as much sheriff's tourns as hundred courts—" The baily of every weapontacke is to keep a courte, which is called the weapontacke courte, three weeke courte, or sheriffes turne ; wheare any public cause or small trespass may bee heard and ended once within three weekes ; " the hundred court of Wirral, because it included the town of Birkenhead, survived till the middle of the nineteenth century, Webb, The Manor and the Borough 61.
[10] Below 134-138.   [11] Below 134.
[12] 30, 31 Victoria c. 142 § 28 ; for the hundred court of Salford which is regulated by special statutes see below 151 n. 11.

(b) The Sheriff's Tourn.

The place of the sheriff's tourn in the judicial system, and its jurisdiction, were, in effect, fixed by the clause of Magna Carta which forbade the sheriff to hold pleas of the crown.[1] As Professor Hearnshaw has pointed out, this clause of the Magna Carta divided it from the king's courts which exercised jurisdiction over greater crimes ; while § 42 of the Charter of 1217, which provided that the sheriff should not make his tourn oftener than twice in a year, divided it from the hundred court which met from three weeks to three weeks, and exercised only a civil jurisdiction.[2]   The tourn, which had thus emerged as a distinct court in the thirteenth century, was a combination of two institutions.   It combined the old jurisdiction to supervise the view of frankpledge,[3] and the new machinery of the jury of presentment introduced by the Assize of Clarendon.[4]   These two institutions were quite distinct.   We have seen that some of the elements of the frankpledge system can be traced back beyond the Norman Conquest.   But we shall see that the jury of presentment was a new and a royal piece of judicial machinery, which was not introduced into England till after the Norman Conquest ; and that it was not generally applied to criminal procedure till the Assize of Clarendon.   That the two institutions were distinct and separable can be seen from the fact that the Statute of Wales (1284) could introduce into Wales the court of the sheriff's tourn, with the machinery of the jury of presentment, and a jurisdiction similar to that of the tourn in England, without introducing the frankpledge system or the machinery for its supervision.[5] Therefore to understand the nature of the sheriff's tourn in its final form we must glance briefly at the manner in which these two institutions were combined in it.[6]

We have seen that after the Conquest we get a combination of the rule that every man must be enrolled in a tithing, with the rule that each member of the tithing is a " borh " or security for the good behaviour of the other members of the tithing.[7] We have seen too that the enforcement of these rules was entrusted to the sheriff who, at a special session of the hundred court, saw that the grouping of the people into tithings was properly carried out.[8]   As yet, however, the members of these tithings were only obliged to produce one of their number if he

---

[1] Above 57 n. 1. [2] Leet Jurisdiction in England 340.
[3] Above 14, 15. [4] Below 321-322.
[5] 12 Edward I. ; Hearnshaw, op. cit. 23-24.
[6] On the whole subject see Maitland, Select Pleas in Manorial Courts (S.S.) xxvii-xxxvii.
[7] Above 14, 15. [8] Above 13.

was wanted by the authorities. They do not seem to have been obliged to take the initiative, and inform the sheriff or the king's judges of occurrences which might lead them to want one of their members. But this further obligation was imposed upon them by the Assize of Clarendon. It was provided by the first clause of that assize that, "for the preservation of the peace and the maintenance of justice enquiries be made throughout each county and hundred by twelve legal men of the hundred and four legal men from each township, under oath to tell the truth ; if in their hundred or their township there be any man who is accused or generally suspected of being a robber or murderer or thief, or any man who is a receiver of robbers, murderers or thieves since our lord the king was king." [1] The manner in which this provision of the Assize of Clarendon was worked in combination with the frankpledge system is described both by Fleta [2] and Britton. [3] The tithings appeared by their chief pledges ; the township by the reeve and four men—sometimes the right to be thus represented was purchased by a money payment called capitagium or chevagium. [4] According to Britton certain enquiries known as the articles of the tourn were addressed to them. In the first place they were to enquire whether the frankpledge system was in good working order ; and then they were required to make presentments of persons suspected of many miscellaneous offences, and as to other matters affecting the maintenance of the order and good government of their district. [5] These presentments were made to a jury of twelve free men of the hundred, who either accepted or rejected them. If they accepted them they passed on the presentments to the sheriff. He sent those accused of more serious crimes to the itinerant justices, or, if they were not in custody, directed their arrest. The lesser crimes he punished by amercement, the amount of which were assessed by two suitors of the court. [6]

[1] " In primus statuit prædictus rex Henricus de consilio omnium baronum suorum, pro pace servanda et justitia tenenda quod per singulos comitatus inquiratur, et per singulos hundredos, per xii legaliores homines de hundredo, et per iv legaliores homines de qualibet villata, per sacramentum quod illi verum dicent : si in hundredo suo vel villata sua sit aliquis homo qui sit rettatus vel publicatus, quod ipse sit robator vel murdrator vel latro vel aliquis qui sit receptor robatorum vel murdratorum vel latronum, postquam dominus rex fuit rex," Sel. Ch. 143.

[2] II. 52. [3] Vol. i 177-185.

[4] Select Pleas in Manorial Courts (S.S.) xxx, xxxi.

[5] Britton i 177-185 ; " a distinction but rarely discernible in the modern treatises stands out bulky though blurred, in the writings of the mediæval lawyers ; I mean the distinction between view of frankpledge and sheriff's tourn. Fleta mentions the distinction ; Britton emphasizes it . . . ; the *Mirror* actually treats the two in different chapters," Hearnshaw, op. cit. 66.

[6] P. and M. i 546-547 ; an amercement was always assessed by the suitors of the court, while a fine was assessed by the judge, 8 Co. Rep. 39 a ; Lambard, Eirenarcha iv c. 16 explains that a person who was amerced was said to be " in misericordia," " because he is therein mercifully to be dealt with."

It is clear that we have here a combination of two very different institutions; and that they are different is brought out in some of the lists of articles of the tourn which separate those which concern the working of the frankpledge system from those which concern the maintenance of peace and order, and in the descriptions of the procedure which accompany them.[1]   But it is clear that the really important business of the tourn is the presentments of the jurors of the hundred to the sheriff.   The information of the chief pledges or the men of the township is really little more than evidence upon which the jurors acted; and they could act if they liked upon their own initiative.[2]

Naturally, as the frankpledge system gradually decayed, the business of the tourn came more and more to centre round these presentments of the jurors to the sheriff.   That system seems to have been obsolete at the close of the fifteenth century,[3] though in some cases, where the right to hold the tourn was in private hands, the connection with the frank pledge system was maintained by the fact that the jurors who presented were themselves the chief pledges.[4]   But whether the tourn was held by the sheriff, or whether, under the name of a court leet,[5] it was in private hands, it was the system of presentment by a jury that became its most important function.   It thus became a court which had been strengthened and improved by the introduction of that most important of all the royal reforms in the administration of justice—the jury.   It was a court, too, which was specially concerned with the maintenance of the peace; and that was a matter which, by the end of the thirteenth century, was recognized as specially belonging to the king.[6]   Therefore, unlike the county and hundred courts, it became a royal court[7] and a court of record.[8]   It was held by the sheriff as a royal deputy,

---

[1] Hearnshaw, op. cit. 49-62.   [2] Ibid 66-69.

[3] For two late references to its working from 1432 and 1470 see Webb, Manor and Borough 22 n. 1.

[4] Select Pleas in Manorial Courts (S.S.) xxxiv-xxxv; Hearnshaw, op. cit. 70, 71; Professor Hearnshaw suggests, loc. cit., that, even after the chief pledges had developed into jurors, we can see in some cases survivals of the time when they were more than jurors, e.g.: "when the jurors, like those of the still existent Savoy leet, do not lay down their offices at the close of the court day, but keep them for a year; secondly when the jurors, like those of Southampton, do not merely receive and make presentments, but go round beating bounds, examining weights and measures, surveying highways, inspecting nuisances and (above all) forcibly resisting encroachments and redressing wrongs; thirdly, where presentments on matters other than felonies are, as at Leicester, made from time to time by less than twelve presenters."

[5] For the court leet see below 135-136.   [6] Above 72 n. 2.

[7] The style of the court is " Curia Visus Francipledgii *Domini Regis* tenta apud B. coram Vicecomite in Turno Suo," Coke, Second Instit. 71, Fourth Instit. 259, 260; for its style when it was in private hands and held as a court leet see below 135 n. 1.

[8] Coke, Fourth Instit. 259.

and he, and not the suitors, was its judge.[1]   And, because it was
a court of this character, all subjects were in theory obliged to
attend in person the tourn of the place where they were resident.[2]
In practice, however, we have seen that the chief pledge represented his tithing, and the reeve and four men his township;[3]
and a large exception to the old rule was made by the Statute of
Marlborough which provided that archbishops, bishops, priors,
abbots, earls, barons, persons in orders, and women need not
attend unless their presence was specially required.[4]   This
statute did much to fix its character as a court which was concerned with petty offences, and with the smaller details of local
government.

The procedure of the tourn thus came to centre round the
articles of the tourn and the presentments made in answer to
those articles.   Many sets of these articles survive, and all these
sets vary in detail.[5]   Perhaps, as Maitland has said, "the sheriffs
were allowed a free hand in settling the articles under the guidance of the general idea that whatever was against the king's
peace was presentable at the tourn."[6]   We may take as an example the list given in the apocryphal statute De Visu Frank-
pledgii.[7]   According to that document the sheriff wishes among
other things to be informed as to purprestures, stoppage of ways,
house breakers, thieves, affrays, escapes, forgers, treasure trove,
breakers of the assize of bread and ale, false weights and
measures, and of "such as sleep by day and watch by night, and
eat and drink well and have nothing."   Clearly the object is to
bring before the sheriff twice a year all that is going on in the
different hundreds which make up the county.   It was in fact a
court of the same pattern as that which was held by the justices
in eyre.[8]   It applied to the punishment of minor offences and to
the supervision of the humbler units of local government the same
machinery as the justices in eyre applied to the punishment of
graver crimes and to the supervision of the whole of the local
government.

---

[1] P. and M. i 547.

[2] Hearnshaw, op. cit. 84 ; 52 Henry III. c. 10.

[3] Above 77.

[4] 52 Henry III. c. 10, "De turnis Vicecomitum provisum est, ut necesse non
habeant ibi venire Archiepiscopi, Episcopi, Abbates, Priores, Comites, Barones, nec
aliqui viri religiosi, nec mulieres, nisi eorum presentia ob aliquam causam specialiter
exigatur ; " for a case turning on the exemption of viri religiosi see Y.B. 20, 21 Ed. I.
(R.S.) 297, where it was held to extend to a clerk studying at Cambridge ; this rule
applied also to the leet, Hearnshaw, op. cit. 85.

[5] Select Pleas in Manorial Courts (S.S.) xxxii ; Hearnshaw, op. cit. 43-63.

[6] Select Pleas in Manorial Courts (S.S.) xxxii-xxxiii.

[7] Statutes of uncertain date, Statutes of the Realm (Rec. Com.) i 246 ; for these
so-called statutes see vol. ii 222-223.

[8] Below 265-272.

During the Middle Ages several statutes regulated the procedure at the tourn. In 1285 [1] it was enacted that the inquests should be taken by twelve lawful men at least who were to set their seals to the indictment—an enactment which Maitland thinks [2] had a good deal to do with fixing the form of the jury in tourn and leet. Other statutes attempted to prevent abuses of the court's procedure. Two of them were directed against the misconduct of the sheriff. Thus, to prevent the embezzlement and suppression of the presentments of the jury, it was enacted, in 1327,[3] that the indictments should be taken by roll indented whereof the one part was to remain with the indictors, and the other part with the person who took the inquest, " so that one of the inquest may show the one part of the indenture to the justices when they come to make deliverance." But this statute does not seem to have been effectual, and the court grew more and more unpopular. In 1344 the commons petitioned that no new articles should be added to the list of matters which could be enquired into at the tourn or the leet; [4] and the rule was laid down by the central courts that these courts could not enquire into any new statutory offence unless special permission was given by the statute.[5] The continued unpopularity and ineffectiveness of the court caused the enactment, in 1461,[6] of the second of these statutes. It provided that sheriffs should no longer have the power to arrest persons, or. to levy any fines or amercements inflicted; but that they should, for the future, transmit the indictments to the justices of the peace, who were to take action upon them. Another statute was directed to securing an improvement of the quality of the jurors. It was enacted in 1483 [7] that, to be qualified to serve as a juror, a person must have freehold of the annual value of 20s., or copyhold of the annual value of 28s. 6d.

---

[1] 13 Edward I. St. 1 c. 13.

[2] Select Pleas in Manorial Courts (S.S.) xxxv; Professor Hearnshaw, op. cit. 87 thinks that, after the passing of this statute, " no great offender could be so much as brought to trial on an accusation vouched for by less than twelve lawful men . . .; but that minor offenders could still be, and constantly were presented by individual chief pledges or constables;" and that, while presentments by twelve jurors were verdicts, presentments by less than twelve were not; but, " it became the universal custom in manorial courts (and probably in the tourn) for chief pledges and constables to make their presentments to twelve or more jurors who, by accepting them and re-presenting them, turned them, in the case of grave offences into valid indictments; in the case of petty offences into binding verdicts; " see vol. iv 124, 144-145.

[3] 1 Edward III. c. 17; cp. Select Cases before the Council (S.S.) lxxxv.

[4] R.P. ii 148, 149, 155, cited Hearnshaw, op. cit. 120.

[5] Y.B. 22 Ed. IV. Mich. pl. 2; Brooke, Ab. *Lete* pl. 26; cf. Hale, Pleas of the Crown ii 69.

[6] 1 Edward IV. c. 2; see Select Cases before the Council (S.S.) lxxxvi-lxxxvii.

[7] 1 Richard III. c. 4.

In fact the statute of 1461 marks the end of the activity of the tourn.[1] It is true that it was given by Henry IV. power to enforce the Statute of Labourers,[2] and that it was given new powers by one or two of the Tudor statutes,[3] and even by a statute of 1624.[4] But long before 1624 cognizance of smaller offences had been absorbed by the justices of the peace;[5] the more serious crimes which it once presented were inquired into by the same officials, and presented by the grand jury of the county;[6] and the duties which it once performed in relation to the local government of the county had also passed to the justices.[7] We shall see that where the tourn was in private hands, or was vested in a borough, under the name of the court leet, it remained an active court for a longer period[8]—just as some of the hundred courts in private hands or vested in boroughs had a longer life than those hundred courts which were held by a deputy of the sheriff.[9] But it is clear that, when Coke was writing his Institutes at the beginning of the seventeenth century, the tourn was obsolete. "The true institution of that court," he says, "has vanished, and it still remains as a mere ghost of its former self."[10] The ghost was not laid till 1887.[11]

But, though by the Tudor period, the old duties were performed by new officials, though the old communities of township, tithing and hundred had been superseded by a new organization, these new officials and this new organization absorbed much of the spirit of the older order through the forms which they inherited from it.[12] It was by the machinery of presentment and indictment, inherited from the procedure of the tourn, that the justices of the peace in quarter sessions punished offenders and governed the county till well on into the eighteenth century;[13] and we shall see that in many rural manors, urban districts, and boroughs the same machinery was used for the same purposes. It is necessary therefore to study the form and the working of the older courts which governed the county and the hundred, if

---

[1] Hearnshaw, op. cit. 96. [2] Ibid 120 citing R.P. iii 602.
[3] 24 Henry VII. c. 13 ; 7 Edward VI. c. 5; 13 Elizabeth c. 19.
[4] 21 James I. c. 21. [5] Below 287-288.
[6] Below 321-323. [7] Vol. iv Bk. iv Pt. I. c. 1.
[8] Below 135-137; vol. iv Bk. iv Pt. I. c. 1 ; Hale, notes, Pleas of the Crown ii 71, that the statute of 1461 did not apply to leets.
[9] Below 135-136, 143.
[10] " Vera institutio istius curiæ evanuit, et velut umbra ejusdem ad huc remanet," Second Instit. 72; Bullen's Case (1608) 6 Co. Rep. at f. 78 a ; Coke applies these words both to the leet and the tourn; but they were, when he wrote, more true of the tourn than the leet, below 137; vol. iv 129-130; in his Fourth Instit. Coke allots five pages to the leet (pp. 261-265) and only just over one to the tourn (pp. 259-260).
[11] 50, 51 Victoria c. 55 § 18 (4). [12] Vol. iv 142-143, 164.
[13] Below 293 ; vol. iv 144-145.

we would understand the form and working either of the newer institutions which superseded them, or of these old institutions themselves in the numerous cases in which, as franchises, they survived almost to modern times.

(2) *The Coroner and his Court.*

We have seen that the powers of the sheriff in the twelfth century were very great;[1] and it is clear from the Inquest of Sheriffs (1170) that the crown was already viewing them with some suspicion.[2]   To put an official by the side of the sheriff to check his powers, and to safeguard the interests of the crown, was an obvious expedient.   It is probable that this was the reason for the institution of the coroner who had, by the end of the twelfth century, become a definitely recognized official.

The first distinct reference to coroners comes from 1194. One of the articles of the eyre in that year provided that there should be chosen in each county "three knights and one clerk as the keepers (*custodes*) of the pleas of the crown."[3]   It is probable, however, that this article did not create a wholly new office, but rather that it gave a greater definition to a pre-existing institution.   There are three reasons for taking this view.   In the first place, certain borough charters of an earlier date seem to recognize an official of this kind.   Thus in Henry I.'s charter to London there is mention of a "justice to keep the pleas of my crown and to plead them ;" and in Richard I.'s charter to Colchester in 1189 a similar officer is mentioned.[4]   Moreover from an early period there are indications of local "justices" placed by the side of the sheriffs, who may have performed somewhat the same functions as the justice mentioned in Henry I.'s charter.[5] In the second place, Mr. Bolland has shown [6] that the Pipe Rolls of 1181, 1188, and 1189 mention officials known as *servientes hundredi* or *servientes regis*, who evidently exercised a supervision over the crown's interests in relation to the pleas of the crown, very similar to that exercised in later days by the coroners ; and Gross has pointed out that in the rolls of the Curia Regis for 1194 mention is made of "knights keeping the pleas of the crown," who gave evidence as to the proceedings in the county court.[7]   In the third place, as Mr. Bolland points out,[8] if the articles of the eyre of 1194 were creating a wholly new office,

---

[1] Above 65-66.   [2] Sel. Ch. 148.
[3] " Praeterea in quolibet comitatu eligantur tres milites et unus clericus custodes placitorum coronæ " § 20 ; for these articles see Sel. Ch. 259-262.
[4] Select Coroners' Rolls (S.S.) xv.
[5] Morris, Office of Sheriff, E.H.R. xxxiii 159 n. 111, 160-161, n. 128.
[6] The Eyre of Kent (S.S.) i liv, lv.
[7] Select Coroners' Rolls (S.S.) xvii.   [8] The Eyre of Kent (S.S.) i lvi.

we should expect a much fuller explanation of the duties which the new officer was to fulfil. The article seems to assume that a direction to elect coroners is, without more, intelligible. For these reasons then, and in spite of Maitland's doubts,[1] it is probable that persons who performed the functions of coroners were known before 1194. Probably Mr. Bolland is right in thinking that it is possible that " long before 1194 the duties of the coroners that were to be were vested in the hundreds and wapentakes and towns that ranked as such; that before 27 Henry II. (1181) this system was superseded by the appointment of special officers[2] in each hundred or wapentake who were made personally responsible for keeping the pleas of the crown, such officers being known as *servientes hundredi* or *servientes regis;* . . . and that in 1194 this system of separate officers for each separate hundred was superseded by the appointment of officers of greater dignity and fewer in number whose duty it was to keep the pleas of the crown for the whole county."[3] As we have seen Magna Carta prevented them (equally with the sheriffs) from trying the pleas of the crown.[4]

In later law there were coroners of many different sorts. The judges of the court of king's bench were coroners *virtute officii;*[5] and, as a result of the Judicature Act, all the judges of the High Court have succeeded to this position.[6] There is a coroner for the king's household,[7] and since 1674 (and perhaps before) a coroner for the Admiralty.[8] London and other towns, the University of Oxford, and certain individuals, had the franchise of appointing a coroner.[9] There was a king's coroner and attorney who had certain duties to perform in the King's Bench in relation to criminal procedure.[10] Here I am dealing only with the ordinary type of county coroner.

Throughout the thirteenth and fourteenth centuries there were usually four coroners for each county,[11] who must be resident

---

[1] E.H.R. viii 758.

[2] It may be noted that a coroner appears to have been known in Normandy as early as 1171, Haskins, Norman Institutions 188.

[3] The Eyre of Kent (S.S.) i lv.

[4] § 24, above 57 n. 1; but it would seem that even after 1215 they sometimes held pleas of the crown, and that, in particular, they held such pleas of the crown as were still tried in the county court, Select Coroners' Rolls (S.S.) xxv, xxvi; Britton i 135 there cited.

[5] Sadler's Case (1587) 4 Co. Rep. at f. 57 b; Fourth Instit. 73; Hale, Pleas of the Crown ii 53.

[6] 36, 37 Victoria c. 66 § 12.

[7] Halsbury, Laws of England viii *Coroners* § 530.   [8] Ibid § 535.

[9] Ibid §§ 539, 540: see Britton i 4; Hale, Pleas of the Crown ii ...; Select Coroners' Rolls (S.S.) xxii, xxiii, xxix; 50, 51 Victoria c. 71 ...

[10] Halsbury's Laws of England viii *Coroners* § 529.

[11] Select Coroners' Rolls (S.S.) xx; Bl. Comm. i 335 ... there were fewer, Select Coroners' Rolls (S.S.) xx; Hale, ...

and have sufficient land in their county to answer the king
and people.[1]   They were elected in the county court;[2] and, like
other mediæval officials, they were obliged to serve without remuneration, till, in Henry VII.'s reign, a fee of 13s. 4d. for every
inquest of death was established.[3]   Hence it is not surprising to
find that persons got royal grants of exemption from liability
to undertake the office.[4]   Modern statutes have put the office on
quite a different basis.   In 1844 the counties were divided into
coroner's districts;[5] in 1860 a fixed salary was provided;[6] and
in 1888 their appointment and the fixing of their salary was
transferred to the county councils.[7]

The duties of the coroner were originally wide.   The office
was established for the purpose of safeguarding the pecuniary
interests of the crown, and more especially its pecuniary interests
arising from the administration of the criminal law.[8]   He must
keep a roll which was of great value to the justices in eyre, because it enabled them to check the verdicts of the juries of the
hundreds, and to provide for the king a plentiful crop of amercements.[9]   He must execute process in the sheriff's stead "when
there is just exception taken to the sheriff"—on the ground, for
instance, that he was party to the case.[10]   He had many various
duties to perform in relation to the criminal law.   Thus he must
receive and enter the appeals or criminal accusations of those
who wished to accuse another of felony; he must receive the
declarations of approvers; he must keep a record of outlawries;
he must receive the confession and abjuration of criminals who
had taken sanctuary.[11]   His services were useful in securing the
appearance of suspected persons.   He could cause such persons
to be arrested;[12] and, in 1554, he was required to put into
writing the effect of any material evidence given at an inquest

[1] Select Coroners' Rolls (S.S.) xx; if they made default the county was liable,
Eyre of Kent (S.S.) i 14, 54, 92; in the thirteenth century they must be knights,
ibid; Coke, Second Instit. 174; 50, 51 Victoria c. 71 § 12.

[2] Select Coroners' Rolls (S.S.) xx; for the writ ordering election see App. XXXI.

[3] 3 Henry VII. c. 1 § 24; 1 Henry VIII. c. 7; it would seem that in the Middle
Ages he sometimes extorted fees, Select Coroners' Rolls (S.S.) xxi.

[4] Ibid.   [5] 7, 8 Victoria c. 92.

[6] 23, 24 Victoria c. 116.   [7] 51, 52 Victoria c. 41 § 5.

[8] Bracton f. 121 b; Britton i 8 seqq.; Fleta i cc. 18, 20, 25; "the apocryphal
statute *De officio coronatoris* ascribed to 4 Edward I. seems to be an extract from
Bracton's treatise f. 121 slightly altered; it is very possible however that Bracton
made use of some ordinance or set of official instructions," P. and M. ii 641 n. 2;
and Gross agrees with this view, Select Coroners' Rolls (S.S.) xxv n. 8.

[9] Ibid xxvii, xxix.

[10] The Eyre of Kent (S.S.) ii 98 note from the record; Coke, Fourth Instit. 271.

[11] Select Coroners' Rolls (S.S.) xxv; for appeals of felony see vol. ii Bk. iii c. 4;
for approvers, i.e. accused persons who to get a pardon offered to accuse their
accomplices see ibid; for abjuration and sanctuary see vol. iii c. 2 § 3.

[12] Britton i 8-11.

held by him, and was empowered to bind over witnesses to
appear at the trial.[1]

The duty which was imposed upon the coroner to hold an
inquest followed from the fact that he was especially bound to
safeguard the rights of the crown. In order to safeguard these
rights he was obliged, in many cases to impanel a jury and hold
a court, which was a court of record, to enquire into their existence. Thus he must hold inquests as to wreck, as to royal fish,[2]
as to the finding of treasure trove,[3] and as to unexplained death,[4]
because in all these matters the crown was pecuniarily interested.
By its prerogative it was entitled to wreck, royal fish, and
treasure trove; and the death of a man might bring the crown
revenue in many ways. The hundred was liable to a fine if
Englishry could not be proved;[5] the thing which caused the
death was forfeit to the crown as a deodand;[6] the chattels of
the man, if a suicide[7] or convicted of felony, were likewise
forfeited.[8]

The jury which the coroner must impanel in order to make
these enquiries consisted, in the thirteenth and fourteenth centuries, of persons taken from the four or more neighbouring
townships together with twelve men of the hundred.[9] It is
clear that the neighbouring townships were more likely to
know the facts of any occurrence than a body of persons
chosen at large from the hundred; and, as a body likely to
know these facts, they appear in the Anglo-Saxon and Norman
period.[10] Thus, according to the laws of Edward the Confessor,[11]
the finder of a chattel should show it to the reeve and the
men of the township; and the reeve should give notice to the
four neighbouring townships. The coroners' rolls show that
duties of a very miscellaneous character were imposed on the four
neighbouring townships;[12] and we shall see that they played

---

[1] 1, 2 Philip and Mary c. 13 § 5, superseded by 7 George IV. c. 64 § 4 containing similar provisions; below 296.

[2] For royal fish see Constable's case (1601) 5 Co. Rep. at f. 108 b; Forsyth,
Cases and Opinions on Constitutional Law 178-179.

[3] Below 86-87.   [4] Below 86.

[5] Above 11.

[6] Vol. ii Bk. ii Pt. II. § 2; cf. Holmes, Common Law 24-26.

[7] Eyre of Kent (S.S.) i 111.   [8] Vol. iii c. 1 § 3.

[9] "The four vills and the twelve men seem often to be regarded as two distinct
bodies; their verdicts may be given separately. Then again each vill may make
its own statement; or the vills may find a verdict collectively and severally. The
number of persons from each villata seems to have been indeterminate . . . as
many were summoned as were deemed sufficient for the inquest," Select Coroners'
Rolls (S.S.) xxx, xxxi.

[10] Ibid xxxviii citing Ethelred's Laws iii 15.

[11] c. 24; for these laws, which probably come from Henry I.'s reign, see vol. ii
Bk. iii c. 2; for the liability of finders who did not give up the goods found, see
Eyre of Kent (S.S.) i 81, 146.

[12] Select Coroners' Rolls (S.S.) xxxvii-xl.

some part in the development of the petty jury.[1]   In later law the coroner's jury came to be chosen, like the other juries employed by the courts of common law,[2] from the body of the county.[3]   It is a jury which is interesting historically because it is the most important modern survival of the many juries which were once employed to answer questions which related rather to the administrative than to the judicial work of government.[4]

Changes in the judicial system and changes in substantive law rendered obsolete many of the duties of the coroner.   When the general eyre ceased,[5] his rolls ceased to be of such great importance to the itinerant justices ; and the abolition of criminal appeals, approvers, sanctuary, and abjuration, and the practical abolition of outlawry took away many of his duties.   The Coroner's Act of 1887[6] expressly abolished others.   Thus section 44, after repeating the old prohibition against holding the pleas of the crown, goes on to provide that he shall not " hold inquests of royal fish or of wreck, nor of felonies, except felonies on inquisitions of death ; and he shall not enquire of the goods of such as by the inquest are found guilty of murder or manslaughter, nor cause them to be valued and delivered to the township."   His chief surviving duty is to act for the sheriff in executing process in cases where the sheriff has an interest in the proceedings ; and the chief functions performed at his court are to hold inquests in cases of unexplained death, and as to the concealment of treasure trove.   The holding of the former kind of inquest is by far his most important function ; and it is a curious illustration of how a procedure, invented for one purpose, has come, in a changed order of society, to be used for another. Such inquests are now held, not to safeguard the pecuniary interests of the crown, but to aid the administration of justice by careful enquiry into the circumstances of any suspicious death. The holding of inquests into the concealment of treasure trove [7]

---

[1] Below 323.   [2] Below 332.   [3] Hale, P.C. ii 167.

[4] Below 313-314; under juries of this sort may be classed the inquest of office— an enquiry held by some official or by special commissioners by means of a jury of uncertain number, concerning any matter which entitles the king to any property real or personal, Bl. Comm. iii 258-260.

[5] Below 272.   [6] 50, 51 Victoria c. 71.

[7] " Treasure trove, is where any gold or silver in coin, plate, or bullion, is found concealed in a house or in the earth, or other private place, the owner thereof being unknown, in which case the treasure belongs to the king or his grantee, having the franchise of treasure trove ; but if he that laid it be known or discovered afterwards, the owner and not the king is entitled to it ; this prerogative right only applying in the absence of an owner to claim the property.   If the owner, instead of hiding the treasure, casually lost it, or purposely parted with it, in such a manner that it is evident he intended to abandon the property altogether . . . the first finder is entitled to the property . . . and the king's prerogative does not in this respect obtain.   So that it is the hiding, and not the abandonment of the property that entitles the king to it," Chitty, Prerogative, 152.

is a much less important duty   And it should be noted that the coroner has power only " to enquire of treasure that is found, who were the finders, and who is suspected thereof." He cannot enquire into the title of the crown, as that does not depend upon the finding of the jury.[1]

II. The Franchise Courts

We have seen that in the Norman and Angevin period there was already a tendency to distinguish the franchise jurisdiction which rested upon royal grant from the purely feudal jurisdiction which rested upon tenure.[2] The growth of the jurisdiction of the Curia Regis intensified this tendency. Bracton, as we might expect, states in a form which was exaggerated for his time the theory that all jurisdiction flows from the crown. "Pax et justitia," he says, belong to the crown. Like a res sacra or a free man they cannot be bought or given. It is true that we see sac and soc, visus francpledgii, judicium latronum, in the hands of private persons. But these persons hold them as royal justices. These things are, so to speak, res quasi sacræ, which can be alienated only to royal justices.[3] In all cases those who claim to exercise these rights must show an express grant. Length of user, without such grant, so far from giving a title, aggravates the offence.[4] "Nullum tempus occurrit regi."[5] Bracton's theory was in his day prophetic rather than true.[6] The reign of Henry III. was a troublous time. The older franchises were exploited to the uttermost. It is true that their meaning was becoming obscure owing to the growth of the newer legal terms and ideas which the lawyers of the Curia Regis were spreading over the country.[7] But we get the rise of newer franchises in the newer legal phraseology. Amerciamenta hominum, catalla felonum, returnus brevium were granted or assumed.[8] Feudal ideas formed the political atmosphere of the Middle Ages, and feudal ideas meant, as we have seen, the distribution of political power among the larger landowners. The larger landowners either assumed or procured the grant to themselves of the new processes and powers

---

[1] Attorney-General v. Moore [1893] 1 Ch. 676; cf. Attorney-General v. Trustees of the British Museum [1903] 2 Ch. 598.

[2] Above 28.   [3] Ff. 14 a; 55 b.

[4] Ff. 55 b; 14 a, " diuturnitas enim temporis in hoc casu injuriam non minuit sed auget."

[5] There is a statement of this principle in the case of the Bishop of Sabina v. Bedewynde (1307) Select Pleas before the Council (S.S.) 25.

[6] P. and M. i 559.

[7] Ibid i 560, 561, 574; Select Pleas in Manorial Courts xxii, xxiii.

[8] P. and M. i 570, 571. Their hindrance to the administration of the criminal law is well illustrated by the state of things in the parts of Northumberland which bordered on the Palatinate of Durham, Northumberland Assize Rolls (Surt. Soc.) xix.

of the Curia Regis; so that under weak kings like Henry III. or Henry VI. even the anti-feudal organization of the central government could easily be turned to feudal uses.

Thus when Edward I. came to the throne he found that this assumption of private jurisdiction had gone to considerable lengths. In 1274 he sent out commissioners to enquire into these usurpations of the royal rights.[1] The results of these enquiries are embodied in the Hundred Rolls. They give us information respecting the franchise jurisdictions of the thirteenth century similar to the information given to us by Domesday respecting the fiscal system of the eleventh century. Upon the information so obtained Edward I. founded his Quo Warranto enquiries.[2] He sent out commissioners, furnished with copies of the Hundred Rolls, to enquire by what warrant different landowners were exercising their jura regalia.[3] The king's pleaders adopted Bracton's theory to its fullest extent. If no charter could be produced they at once claimed judgment for the crown. If charters were produced they minimized the effects of all those which were not expressed in the proper technical terms.[4]

For many of the older franchises no charters could be shown, as charters were not common in Anglo-Saxon times; and, as we have seen, the Norman lords had been tacitly allowed to assume the private jurisdiction of their predecessors.[5] Consequently the proceedings of the royal commissioners aroused so much resentment amongst the barons and other landowners that in the end the king was obliged to consent to a compromise. In 1290 the two Statutes of Gloucester[6] allowed that possession without interruption from the beginning of Richard I.'s reign should confer a good title; that old charters should be adjudged according to their form and tenor; and that those who had lost

[1] Rotuli Hundredorum (Rec. Com.) Introd.; Stephen, H.C.L. i 126-133; App. XIX. A and B.

[2] Writs were issued against the persons where the juries had found them in possession of franchises, etc., and "nesciunt quo warranto;" or they came in under the general proclamation directed by the Statute of Gloucester of 1278; in Gloucester and Lincoln the results of the Quo Warranto proceedings are entered in another hand on the Hundred Rolls; for illustrations see App. XIX. C.

[3] Placita de Quo Warranto (Rec. Com.). The cases were sometimes adjourned "coram rege" or "coram rege in Parliamento."

[4] P. and M. i 559-561; Select Pleas in Manorial Courts xxii-xxiv.

[5] Ibid xxiii-xxvii; P. and M. i 567; the more serious franchises were usually prescribed for; thus "The Bishop of Durham spoke of Egfrith, the Archbishop of York received his gallows from Æthelstan, prescribed to coin money, and could not or would not show anything beyond long seisin in support of many of the famous privileges of Ripon and Beverley;" Coke, Second Instit. 281, distinguishes franchises which can be claimed by usage and those which require a charter to warrant them—the second are the more modern class e.g. felons' or outlaws' goods.

[6] 18 Edward I. Stats. 2 and 3.

their franchises since the preceding Easter "according to the course of pleading in the same writ heretofore used" should have restitution.

Both the king and the owners of franchises gained something.

The theory of the king and his lawyers, that no franchise could exist except by virtue of a royal grant, became the law for the future. And the law was rigidly enforced in litigation before the ordinary courts,[1] and more especially at the general eyre. The control of the general eyre over franchise holders was very strict; and it was exercised in several different ways. Firstly, the enquiries as to franchises contained in the Hundred Rolls were made part of the articles of the eyre.[2] Secondly, at the eyre all franchise holders must appear and make their claims.[3] If they did not so appear and claim,[4] or if they appeared and claimed too much,[5] they ran serious risks of losing their franchises altogether, either then, or if at any future time their franchises were called in question by a writ of Quo Warranto. Thirdly, their franchises could be forfeited if either mal-user[6] or non-user[7] could be proved. Fourthly, it was laid down that a franchise, other than a franchise appurtenant to land, was not assignable by the grantee.[8] Fifthly, it had been settled in Edward I.'s reign that a franchise would not be allowed if, in the opinion of the court, it could not lawfully be granted by the crown.[9] Sixthly, the extent of the jurisdiction conferred by the franchise was always determinable by the common law courts.[10] It is clear that control of this kind rendered the silent usurpation of franchises on a large scale impossible.

---

[1] The mediæval learning on this point is summed up by Coke in the case of the Abbot of Strata Marcella (1592) 10 Co. Rep. 24 a; see ff. 28 a, b.

[2] Eyre of Kent (S.S.) i xl ; see e.g. Art. 72, ibid i 35, which corresponds to Art. 8 in the Hundred Rolls, App. XIX.; for the general eyre and the articles of the eyre see below 265 seqq. 269.

[3] Eyre of Kent (S.S.) i xxxi; and see the writ of general summons, ibid i 3.

[4] Ibid iii 174—the claimant made default with the result that the franchise was taken into the king's hand, and Staunton, J., said, "if he replevy not these franchises within this eyre he will lose them for ever;" ibid iii 183—counsel, in answer to a plea of prescription, said that the franchises in question were not claimed at the last eyre ; Y.B. 4 Ed. II. (S.S.) 94 per Passeley arg.

[5] "If a man claims to have a more extensive franchise in a city than he has warrant for, and it be shown by independent testimony or by his own charter that he has not the franchise after such fashion, he shall be deprived of it, and the franchise shall be seized into the king's hand," Eyre of Kent (S.S.) iii 193.

[6] Y.B. 30, 31 Ed. I. (R.S.) 500—excessive user of franchise of infangthef; Eyre of Kent (S.S.) i 128-129; cf. ibid iii 172 per Hartlepool arg.

[7] Eyre of Kent (S.S.) iii 178 per Hartlepool arg.

[8] Y.B. 30, 31 Ed. I. (R.S.) 220-222 per Mutford arg.; Eyre of Kent (S.S.) iii 180 per Spigurnel, J.; ibid 181, 183.

[9] Y.B. 21, 22 Ed. I. (R.S.) 55-56 per Gislingham, J.

[10] See e.g. Y.B. 5 Ed. II. (S.S.) 164, 206-207; for the control exercised by means of the prerogative writs see below 226-231.

On the other hand the title of franchise holders who could show a good title was secured. Such title could be shown firstly by charter; and this was the easiest method of proving a title, and the most favourably regarded by the court.[1] Secondly by prescription under the statutes of 1290.[2] Thirdly by proof that the grantee had paid a rent for it to the Exchequer.[3] Many persons were able to show a good title to franchises of many varied kinds—and some of them were extensive. Thus in 1313-1314 the Abbot of Battle made good his claim that a special eyre should be held for his liberty at Wye;[4] and at the same eyre the city of Canterbury made good its claims to many franchises.[5] In later Year Books we often come across cases where the existence of a franchise is admitted or allowed;[6] and new franchises were not infrequently granted.[7] For these reasons the number and variety of the franchise jurisdictions which existed in England during the Middle Ages, and survived right down to modern times, is very large. Some of them have played, and a few still play, an important part in our judicial system; others have always been nothing but humble additions to it; and others have long been merely picturesque features in the legal landscape. What then is the reason for the existence and the long life of so many of these franchise jurisdictions?

The mechanism of the central government in a mediæval state was not elaborate, and the force at its command was limited. In England, it is true, the central government possessed a more elaborate mechanism and had a greater force at its command than any other state in Western Europe; but it had attained neither the elaborate mechanism nor the unlimited force of a modern state. Hence the state still found it necessary to delegate to persons or to communities many governmental powers.

[1] " You are now claiming these franchises by prescription, wherefore we hold that you cannot now amend your claim as you might have done if you had been claiming them by a charter, which would have been evidence for the consideration of the Court," Eyre of Kent (S.S.) iii 187 *per* Spigurnel, J. If a claim was made by charter the claimant was estopped from relying on any other title, ibid i 131.

[2] Above 88.

[3] " I think that such a service (payment of half a mark yearly) is as good a specialty for you as the king's charter would be," Eyre of Kent (S.S.) iii 182 *per* Spigurnel, J.

[4] Ibid i lxii 9, 28.

[5] Ibid i lxiii 130-131. In this case Staunton, J., said that a community claiming by prescription was in a different position from an individual claiming in this way, ' *Quia communa non est capax libertatis*, and a city cannot be a city unless it was originally constituted by grant of the king; " I take it that this means that a mere community, not created a city by royal grant, cannot own a franchise; that therefore, if it had been created a city, it could only own franchises as from the date of its creation; and that consequently it was difficult for it to show a prescriptive title.

[6] See e.g. Y.B. 14, 15 Ed. III. (R.S.) 140.   [7] Below 132.

It is true that it resumed many of these powers at a later date. But this method of exercising state control, which was originally imposed upon the state by its own weakness,[1] gradually came to be considered so obvious and natural a method that it continued to be used by the state, even after the state had begun to acquire something like its modern machinery and strength ; and, owing to the uninterrupted development of the English state, the franchises thus created have had perhaps a longer life in England than in any other country in Europe. Thus franchise jurisdictions of different kinds have been created at many different periods in English legal history. Some of them still exist ; and others, though no longer existing, survive in analogous institutions which are their modern representatives.

A work which set out to enumerate and to describe in detail all these franchises would occupy many volumes ; and even an attempt to summarize such a work would be out of place in a history of English law. All that can be here attempted is a classification of the principles which underlie the leading classes of these franchises, and a short description of some of the more important specimens. From the point of view of the principles which underlie these various franchise jurisdictions it is possible to divide them into the following five groups :—

(1) " In early history," says Maitland,[2] " the king appears as first of all franchise holders, the first in point of greatness and the first, it may well be, in point of time." Indeed, from the mediæval point of view, the prerogative itself was a species of liberty or peculiar royal law, which placed the king outside the ordinary law,[3] just as the land over which a franchise exists is outside the ordinary law. This idea can be plainly seen in the incidents of tenure in ancient demesne, which got and kept its peculiar character because the land so held had belonged to the king on the day in which Edward the Confessor was alive and died.[4] It can be seen also in certain minor jurisdictions such as those exercised by the clerk of the market of the king's palace,[5] by his escheators,[6] by the court of the Marshalsea,[7] and by certain officials empowered by statute to take cognizance of crimes committed in the king's palaces or places where he was residing.[8] But in the realm of jurisdiction this idea did not bear much fruit. The king's courts at an early date became in truth courts of common law ; and therefore the king's privileges and franchises were

---

[1] Above 17, 18.
[2] Vol. iii 460.
[5] Coke, Fourth Instit. c. 61.
[7] Ibid c. 18 ; below 208.
[2] P. and M. i 367.
[4] Ibid c. 1 § 13.
[6] Ibid c. 43.
[8] Coke, Fourth Instit. cc. 20, 21 ; 3 Henry VII. c. 14 ; 33 Henry VIII. c. 12.

guarded and applied by them as a part of the common law. There is, however, one notable exception.   The king did assume and exercise an important franchise jurisdiction, separate from the common law, over the royal forests ;[1] and the causes for the assumption and permanence of this jurisdiction are not far to seek.   The Norman and Angevin kings were mighty hunters ; and their successors have usually been sportsmen.   Their powers over the forests both secured their free enjoyment of the pleasures of the chase, and gave them valuable financial and jurisdictional rights.

(2) The second and, in the Middle Ages, by far the most important group of franchise jurisdictions are those which belonged to the landowners.   They were in truth the natural concomitants of a feudal state ; and, as the political ideas of feudalism were shared by king and landowner alike, such franchises naturally sprang up.   But the early centralization of the English government, the precocity of the development of the common law, and the scattered domains of the larger landowners, prevented the growth of numerous compact principalities such as we see abroad.   There are indeed instances of such principalities. There are the Palatinates of Durham, Lancaster, and Chester, and the extensive franchises of the Lords Marchers of Wales ; and, closely connected with Chester and the Lords Marchers, is the principality of Wales, which, from the reign of Edward I., has usually been the appanage of the king's eldest son.[2]   There were also the large liberties of Ely,[3] Pembroke,[4] and Hexham,[5] and the jurisdictions of the Wardens of the Marches between England and Scotland,[6] which may be compared to the counties Palatine.   But, for the most part, the franchises enjoyed by the landowners were of a much humbler kind, and were enjoyed in conjunction with such feudal and manorial jurisdiction as was left to them by the royal courts.[7]

[1] Below 94-107.   [2] Below 118.

[3] Coke, Fourth Instit. c. 39 ; Webb, Local Government, the Parish and the County 314, 316, 317 ; it is sometimes called a county Palatine, e.g. in 5 Elizabeth c. 23 § 11 ; its judicial organization was assimilated to that of the rest of the county by 7 William IV. and 1 Victoria c. 53.

[4] It dates from 1138 when Gilbert Clare was made earl by Stephen, Tout, The Welsh Shires, Y. Cymmrodor ix 205 ; Coke, Fourth Instit. c. 40 ; Webb, op. cit. 313 n. 2 ; it was assimilated to an ordinary county by 27 Henry VIII. c. 26 § 14 ; Tout, op. cit. 205, 208-210 points out that Glamorgan occupied a similar position, though never called a county Palatine.

[5] Coke, Fourth Instit. c. 31 ; Webb, op. cit. 313 n. 2 ; it is called a county Palatine in several statutes ; but, as Webb says, " as such it proved an obstacle to the effective administration of the county of Northumberland after the Northern Rebellion.   For this reason the reputed Palatinate was abolished by 14 Elizabeth c. 13, and was reduced to the position of a private franchise of the crown within the county of Northumberland."

[6] Coke, Fourth Instit. c. 67 ; they disappeared on the accession of James I., see 4 James I. c. 1.

[7] Below 132-138, 176-187.

(3) The third group of franchise jurisdictions are the boroughs. We shall see that there are boroughs of all sorts and kinds, from the small borough which is hardly distinguishable from the rural manor to the great commercial centre which becomes a county in itself, and comprises many varied franchises both governmental and jurisdictional.[1]

(4) The fourth group of franchises are called into existence by the needs of commerce and industry. The most important class of these comprise the franchises by means of which the Law Merchant of the Middle Ages was administered. They include the many and varied powers given both to guilds of merchants and craftsmen, and to special maritime and commercial courts. With them I shall deal in a later chapter.[2] A second class of these franchises are those enjoyed by the mining industry both in the Stannary districts of Devon and Cornwall and in other parts of England.[3] A third class comprises powers given to commissioners to superintend certain matters closely related to commerce and industry. Thus various mediæval statutes created and gave jurisdiction to commissioners of sewers;[4] and under Henry VIII. we can see the beginnings of a law of bankruptcy in powers given to commissioners of bankrupts.[5] The special jurisdictions or franchises so created really represent the transition stage between the mediæval franchise, and its modern counterpart—the grant to a special body of commissioners of the right to exercise jurisdiction over a particular subject matter which demands special treatment.[6] Our modern legislature tends to be as prodigal in the creation of grants of this kind as mediæval kings were in the creation of semi-feudal franchises in favour of landowners; and the modern official tends to be as anxious as any mediæval landowner to increase his power by their acquisition and exploitation.

(5) The last group of franchises I shall, for want of a better word, call professional. Churchmen in the Middle Ages were, as we shall see,[7] governed by a separate law and separate courts which depended not on the king, but on the Pope; and, even after the king had deposed the Pope and asserted his own supremacy, the ecclesiastical courts and ecclesiastical law continued to be and still are very separate from the secular law and secular

---

[1] Below 138-151. [2] Below 530-543. [3] Below 151-165.
[4] For these statutes see vol. ii 467 n. 1; and cf. Coke, Fourth Instit. c. 62, which consists mainly of a comment on 23 Henry VIII. c. 5 which in his day was the principal statute on this subject, and is still in force, see Halsbury, Laws of England ix pp. 220-222.
[5] Below 470-473.
[6] Modern instances are, The Railway and Canal Commission, The Income Tax Commissioners, The Board of Agriculture and Fisheries.
[7] Below 582-583, 599-603.

placed officials generally termed Wardens. They were the executive officers of the crown, to whom the royal writs relating
to the forest business were addressed, and necessary attendants
upon the forest courts.   In fact, their position with regard to the
forests seems to have been somewhat analogous to the position of
the sheriff with regard to the shire.[1]

In all the forests there were a varying number of officers
(usually four) elected in the county court, and styled Verderers.
Manwood says that they should be " gentlemen of good account,
ability, and living, and well learned in the laws of the forest."
Their chief duty was to attend the forest courts ; they served
gratuitously ; and they were immediately responsible to the
crown. Possibly they were regarded as a check upon the
Warden, as the coroner was upon the sheriff.[2]

Under the Wardens there were a varying number of officials
styled Foresters. They did the work of a modern gamekeeper.
In theory they should have been paid by the Wardens.   In fact
they often paid the Wardens to allow them to exercise an office
which gave abundant opportunities for the oppression of the inhabitants of the forest.[3]

In each forest there were usually four Agisters, whose duty
it was to collect the money due for the agistment and pannage of
cattle and pigs in the king's demesne forests.[4]

The king was not the absolute owner of all the lands in the
forests. The owners of such lands could use them as they pleased,
subject to the condition that they could do nothing which would
interfere with the beasts of the forest. " In precise language,
they could not make essart, purpresture, or waste without the
king's licence." [5]   The owners of such lands appointed persons
called Woodwards, whose duty it was to protect the property of
their masters, and also to protect the king's venison.   Their ap-

[1] Select Pleas of the Forest (S.S.) xvi-xix.   They were either appointed by letters
patent and held office during the king's pleasure, or they were hereditary wardens ;
they were sometimes called stewards, bailiffs, or chief foresters.

[2] Manwood 403-407 ; Coke, Fourth Instit. 292, 293 ; Select Pleas xix, xx ;
F.N.B. 164 c.

[3] Manwood 428-439 ; Coke, Fourth Instit. 293 ; Select Pleas xx-xxiv. There
were several varieties ; Manwood at p. 428 says, " Some such foresters are foresters
in fee and have the same office to them and to their heirs, paying unto the king a
certain fee farm or rent for the same . . . and there are some other foresters of the
king that have their office but for term of their life only : and again there are some
foresters of the king that have their office by letters patent from the king . . .
durante bene placito only."

[4] Fourth Instit. 293 ; Select Pleas xxv.

[5] Ibid xxiv.   An *essart* was the destruction of the forest and the reduction
of it to a state of cultivation, Dialogus de Scaccario i xiii (Sel. Ch. 206); Manwood at p. 154 says that it was "the greatest offence and trespass of all other."
A *purpresture* means an encroachment on the forest, Dialogus ii x (Sel. Ch. 225);
Dyer pl. 45 p. 240 b. *Waste* is when any tenants within the forest abused any
rights they had, e.g. the right of lopping wood, Select Pleas lxxxiii.

pointment must always have the sanction of the justice of the forest.[1]

Certain land once forming part of the forest, but disafforested in consequence of a perambulation to ascertain the boundaries of the forest, was under the control of officials called Rangers. We do not hear of them till the end of the fourteenth century.[2] Their duties were limited to these districts, outside the forest, known technically as purlieus. They were officials " of the forest, but not within the forest." Their office " doth chiefly consist in ranging and walking of the pourallées, and in safe conducting of the wild beasts, that they shall there find, into the forest again, and also in presenting of all offenders and unlawful hunters, and of their trespasses and offences, which they have done within the pourallées." [3]

These were the chief officials of the forest. Their powers and jurisdiction were exercised in peculiar courts, the arrangement and procedure of which present certain features of resemblance both to the communal courts, and to the courts of the justices in eyre, as they existed in the thirteenth century.

(1) The court of Swanimote. The word Swanimote has been applied to different courts at different periods in the history of the forest law. Originally it meant a court which, according to the Charter of the Forest, met three times a year, for the purpose of business connected with agistment, pannage, and fawning.[4] It would appear that Manwood confused this court, held at these times, with the inquisitions, held to enquire into trespasses to vert and venison, to which the term Swanimote was often applied.[5]

(2) The court of Attachment.[6] This was a court which was held every forty days by the verderers to view the attachments by the foresters for offences against the vert and the venison. The jurisdiction of the court was small. It could only take cognizance of small trespasses to the vert. Larger trespasses were enrolled and heard by the justices in eyre. In such cases the

---

[1] Select Pleas xxiv, xxv.   [2] Ibid xxv.   [3] Manwood 396-398.
[4] § 8 (Sel. Ch. 349); Select Pleas xxvii seqq.
[5] The term was so applied by the Ordinatio Forestæ 34 Edward I. St. 5 c. 1; see also Manwood c. 23; at pp. 478-485 he gives a list of forty-five aiticles to be enquired into by the court ; these clearly belong to the general inquisition, not to the Swanimote as defined by § 8 of the charter of 1217; the term also seems to be used in this sense in S.P.D. 1635 82, cclxxxix 32—a precept addressed to the beadle of the forests of Essex to cause a Swanimote to be held at Chelmsford at which the forest officers and the reeve and four men from each vill in the forest were to appear; and the beadle was to bring the names of persons summoned, and the names of all prisoners in his custody.
[6] Forest Charter (1217) (Sel. Ch. 349, 350) § 8; Manwood 401, 402, 443-450; Coke, Fourth Instit. 289; Select Pleas xxx seqq. The ubiquitous word Swanimote is sometimes applied to this court, ibid xxxvi.

offender, if an inhabitant of the forest, found pledges to appear at the eyre ; if not an inhabitant he was imprisoned till the eyre, or till released by the Chief Justice of the forest. But, according to statutes of Edward III. and Richard II.'s reigns, such imprisonment could only take place if a person had been duly presented by officers of the forest and other lawful men, or if he had been taken with the mainour.[1]

(3) *Special and General Inquisitions.*[2] According to the *consuetudines et assisa de foresta*,[3] it was the duty of the foresters and verderers, with the assistance of the four neighbouring townships, to hold an enquiry into all offences committed in the forest. A special inquisition was held whenever the commission of an offence was discovered ; for instance, if a deer were found dead in the forest, or if greyhounds were found straying about the forest. The persons whom the townships presented as guilty were attached to appear before the justices in eyre. If the townships did not appear, or appeared and knew nothing of the facts, they were amerced at the eyre. In the reign of Edward I. these special inquisitions, held to enquire into particular offences, gave place to general inquisitions, held for the purpose of enquiring into any offences which had been committed over a certain district within a certain time. In a statute of 1306 [4] they were called Swanimotes, and the method of taking the inquisition was defined. They were always held before a deputy of the justice of the forest, most of the forest officials, and a jury. All offences against the forest law, or misdoings of officials could be presented at these inquisitions.[5]

(4) *The Regard.*[6] The Regard was an enquiry held, once every three years, by twelve knights chosen for the purpose. The subject matter of their enquiry was fixed in Henry III.'s reign. The most important articles of their enquiry related to essarts, purprestures, and waste. Persons who had newly essarted land, or who were guilty of making purprestures or waste, were dealt with by the justices in eyre. Other articles dealt with hawks and falcons, mines, harbours in the forest suitable for the export of timber, honey, underwood, the possessors of arrows, greyhounds, or other things likely to harm the deer.

(5) *The Eyre.*[7] Just as the whole administration of the

---

[1] 1 Edward III. St. 1 c. 8 ; 7 Richard II. c. 4.   [2] Select Pleas xxxvii-l.

[3] Printed at the end of Edward II.'s reign among the Statuta incerti Temporis.

[4] 34 Edward I. St. 5 c. 1.

[5] For an example of a general inquisition, see that of 1369, Select Pleas xlix ; as to the articles of enquiry in the sixteenth century, see Manwood 478-485.

[6] Select Pleas lxxv-lxxxvii ; Coke, Fourth Instit. 292, gives the articles ; Manwood 408, 409 ; cp. Fleta II. 41 " De veteris capitulis Forestæ ; " the first eleven are the chapters of the Regard.

[7] Select Pleas l-lxix.

county was reviewed by the justices in eyre,[1] so the justices in eyre of the forest reviewed the whole administration of the forests. Their court is sometimes called the court of Justice Seat.[2] The justices in eyre were appointed by the crown to hear the pleas of the forest over a certain defined county or collection of counties. Among them the justices of the forest were usually included. The sheriffs of each county were directed to summon by a fixed date all those holding land within the forest, the reeve and four men from each township within the forest, the foresters, verderers, regarders and agisters, with their attachments, regards and agistments. At the eyre all persons presented as guilty of breaches of the forest laws were amerced. The proceedings of the special and general inquisitions, and of the regard, all led up to the final amercement of the offender at the eyre. " By the laws of the Forest all the proceedings of those courts for the greatest offences done in the forest are as nothing until such time as they are presented to the Lord Justice in Eire of the Forest at the Justice Seat."[3] The Dialogus de Scaccario tells us that revenue from these sources was the most valuable part of the revenue from the forests.[4] Like the general eyre,[5] " it was almost as much a financial assembly as a court of law. The records of its proceedings are memoranda of sums of money owing to the king rather than registers of process and judgments."[6] The searching nature of this enquiry into the forest administration is illustrated by the articles of the eyre, given by Fleta.[7] Probably the forest eyre was held, like the general eyre for the county, about once in seven years.[8] Coke[9] and Manwood,[10] however, state that, like the regard, it was sometimes held once in three years. However, it is certain that even in Edward I.'s reign they were held much more irregularly. In the fourteenth century and later, they tended to become more and more infrequent.

These peculiar courts administered the forest law, which was, in the thirteenth century, regarded as a body of law distinct from the common law.[11] Questions which fell within the scope

---

[1] Below 265-271. [2] Fourth Instit. 291, 292 ; Manwood 491-525.

[3] Ibid 505 ; cp. p. 402, "Unto which court (the Justice Seat) the courts of Attachments and Swanimotes are but as it were two hands to deliver matters unto it, to receive judgments thereof from thence ; " Coke, Fourth Instit. 290.

[4] II. xi (Sel. Ch. 232), Quod enim de forestis solvitur pene totum vel ejus maxima pars ex placitis et exactionibus provenit.

[5] Below 271. [6] Select Pleas lx.

[7] Fleta II. 41 caps. 12-51 ; Manwood 509-525 ; in his time they were 84 in number.

[8] Select Pleas lvi, lvii. [9] Fourth Instit. 291. [10] Manwood 411.

[6] Dialogus de Scaccario I. xi (Sel. Ch. 205, 206), Sane forestarum ratio, pœna quoque vel absolutio delinquentium in eas, sive pecuniaria fuerit sive corporalis, seorsum ab aliis regni judiciis secernitur, et solius regis arbitrio vel cujuslibet familiaris ad hoc specialiter deputati subjicitur. Legibus quidem propriis substitit ; quas non communi regni jure, sed voluntaria principum institutione subnixas dicunt.

of that law would not be discussed by the courts of common law.[1]   The jurisdiction of the forest courts could be pleaded in bar to proceedings at common law.[2]   Several particulars are mentioned by Coke and Manwood in which the rules of the forest law were different from those of the common law.[3]

It is common in the Middle Ages to find the various kinds of jurisdiction known to the law in private hands.   Even the highly prized forest law was no exception to this rule.   In two exceptional cases in the thirteenth century grants of the whole forest jurisdiction were made.   In 1266-1267, Henry III. granted these privileges to the Earl of Derby, and in 1285 Edward I. made a similar grant to his brother Edmund.[4]   As a general rule, however, the effect of the grant of a forest was not to vest forest jurisdiction in the grantee, but to give him a "chase."[5] If any jurisdiction was intended to be conveyed by such a grant it must be expressed in it.   It followed that the forest organization and most of the forest law ceased to apply to the land so granted.   The grantee had the right of arresting trespassers, if caught with the mainour, as the beasts were his by the law of the forest; and he could exercise any other jurisdiction specially granted to him.[6]   In some places, for instance, the lords of chases held courts termed Swanimotes.[7]

The right to make a park was possessed by all owners of the soil;[8] but a licence of the crown was required if the proposed park was in a forest, or so near a forest as to be a nuisance to it, by attracting away the beasts of the forest.   The forest law did not apply to a park.   The owner of a park could preserve the beasts therein, not because they were his, but because it was a trespass to enter his park.[9]   Such trespasses were specially penalized by the legislature;[10] and usually the common

---

[1] Keilway 150 b, pl. 43 (citing a case of Edward III.'s reign).

[2] Manwood 490, 491 (citing two cases of Henry VII.'s reign).

[3] Fourth Instit. 315, 317; Manwood 486.

[4] Select Pleas cxi, cxii; Fourth Instit. 314.   In 1615 these grants were discussed in the King v. Briggs, 2 Buls. 295 (also reported 1 Rolle 112, 194); Dodderidge, J., said in that case (at p. 296) that James I. had made a similar grant to Prince Henry; cp. Manwood 72-91.

[5] Y.B. 20, 21 Ed. I. 426 *per* Spigurnel *arg.*; in the King v. Briggs Coke said at p. 295, "It is a chase and not a forest being in the hands of a subject; a Swanimote court a subject may have, but no subject may have a forest, because none can make a justice in eyre but the king;" but in Jennings v. Rocke (1595) Palmer 93, 94, Popham had said that a subject might have a forest by special words of grant; at an earlier stage in the former case Bacon, the Atty.-General, had confessed judgment; Coke was evidently not sorry to have a chance of scoring off him; Manwood, 75, seems to take Popham's view.

[6] Select Pleas cxxii.   [7] Ibid cxiv.

[8] "Any lord may have a park on his own land, if it is not prejudicial to the rights of other people," Eyre of Kent (S.S.) i 188 *per* Spigurnel, J.

[9] Select Pleas cxv, cxvi, cxxii; Cro. Jac. 155 (1608) Case of Leicester Forest.

[10] Below 108.

law courts took cognizance of them ; but possibly in some cases
they were dealt with in the manorial courts.[1]

The right to a free warren was a right granted by the crown
to take certain beasts and birds of warren [2] (other than beasts
of the forest) on the demesne lands of the grantee, provided the
lands were not within the bounds of a forest. The right of
warren belonged to the grantee and his heirs. It did not pass
with his land upon an assignment ; [3] and therefore it might
happen that the right to take these birds or animals might " be
claimed on the land of another, to the exclusion of the owner of
the land." [4] In many cases the lord had a court in which
trespasses upon this right were tried.[5]

The grants of these smaller franchises were no doubt either
caused or suggested by the king's large control over the forests.
We shall now see that the subsequent history of the forest law
and of the protection given to the sporting rights of the landowners by these smaller franchises is somewhat similar. The
forest law decayed, and the sporting rights of the landowners
ceased to be protected by these smaller franchises. The landowners came to regard their sporting rights as rights incident to
their ownership of the soil, and, as we shall see,[6] they secured
protection for them by the Game Laws.[7]

The decay of the forest organization.

When Manwood wrote his treatise on the forest laws in 1598
the forest organization was already in a state of decay. " The

---

[1] The Court Baron (S.S.) 34.

[2] As to these see Select Pleas cxxviii-cxxxii ; it was decided in Duke of Devonshire v. Lodge (1827) 7 B. and C. 36 that grouse were not birds of warren; cf.
Fitzhardinge v. Purcell [1908] 2 Ch. at pp. 163-164.

[3] Select Pleas cxxiv—apparently on such assignment the lands were liable to
be diswarrened.

[4] Duke of Devonshire v. Lodge (1827) 7 B. and C. at p. 39 *per* Lord Tenterden,
C.J.; this rule is as old as the Y.BB., see Y.B. 34 Hy. VI. Mich. pl. 9 ; cp. Bl.
Comm. ii 39.

[5] Select Pleas cxxiii, cxxvii, cxxxix; but apparently he could not compound
with those who trespassed in his warren if he had not such a court, see Eyre of
Kent (S.S.) iii 192 *per* Spigurnel, J.

[6] Below 108.

[7] For the effect of this change upon the law as to the acquisition of possession
and ownership of animals feræ naturæ see vol. vii 493-494. It will be observed
that the account here given of the history of these sporting rights does not wholly
agree with the view which Blackstone takes, Comm. ii 415-419, that no person was
justified in taking beasts of the chase or warren, "or indeed in thorough strictness
of common law in hunting or sporting at all," ibid at p. 417. No doubt hunting or
sporting was prohibited within these franchises, and special penalties were provided
for those who infringed these franchises by sporting therein ; and that was why
they were valued ; for, as Mr. Turner says, "the object of charters of warren would
be inexplicable if the public had not the right of hunting on unenclosed lands outside forests, chases, and warrens," Select Pleas of the Forest (S.S.) cxxiii, citing
P.Q.W. 601; and a fortiori the owners of land not parcels of a forest chase or
warren could hunt the game thereon.

the decay of the forest administration which could put an end to abuses which were inherent in it.

(2) We shall see that in other branches of the law the common law courts tended to encroach upon the jurisdiction of rival courts. They had from early times exercised a sort of superintendence over the court of Justice Seat; and the justices in eyre could always adjourn a point for the consideration of the court of King's Bench.[1] Thus in 1565 it was resolved by the Queen's counsel and by the judges, in the presence of the Justice of the Forests, that the building of a new house on the several soil or waste of any man within a forest is a purpresture and finable.[2] The court of King's Bench might, it is true, decline to hear a case that ought properly to be decided by the forest law.[3] But we can see from Coke's Fourth Institute that the tendency to emphasize the control of the common law courts was growing. Coke laid it down, generally, that the forest law is "allowed and bounded by the common laws of this realm."[4] Thus, if a man was unlawfully imprisoned by a forest officer, he could get his release by habeas corpus from the King's Bench.[5] If injustice was done at the Justice Seat, the case could be removed by certiorari into the King's Bench.[6] If the Justice Seat declined to allow a just claim, the King's Bench might direct that court to hear and allow the claim.[7] If the decision of the Justice Seat was wrong in law a writ of error would lie to the King's Bench.[8]

(3) We have seen that the ordinary forest courts could do very little except present criminals at the eyre. It was at the eyre that they were punished; so that it may be said that the whole execution of the forest law depended upon the regular holding of the eyre. But by the end of the sixteenth century eyres were seldom held, and, if held, seldom completed. Manwood describes the state of things existing at his day, and points to the desuetude of the eyre as one of the main causes of the decay of the forest law.[9] The desuetude of the eyre meant, in fact, the collapse of the whole system.

[1] See case of 1339 cited, Select Pleas xi, in which the King's Bench decided that the roe was not a beast of the Forest.
[2] Dyer, 240 b.
[3] Keil, 150 b, pl. 43; cp. Duke of Norfolk v. Duke of Newcastle (1666) 1 Sid. 296.
[4] Fourth Instit. 290; Manwood, 410, 526.   [5] Fourth Instit. 290.
[6] Ibid 294.   [7] Ibid 297; F.N.B. 230.   [8] Fourth Instit. 297.
[9] 161, 162, "But now of late within these hundred years there have been very seldom any Justice Seats at all kept for Forests. And when that there is any kept, the same is so slenderly performed, that there is very little or no good at all done thereby . . . for the records of the proceedings of the Forest matters are not orderly kept, nor returned into His Majesty's Court of Exchequer . . . whereby the rents growing due unto His Majesty . . . with the fines that are assessed and not paid, and all bonds that are forfeited unto the king for any matter concerning the Forest, might, in due course of law, be levied and gathered to the King's use: for, nowadays,

But though, at the end of the sixteenth century, the forest laws were rapidly becoming obsolete, the financial embarrassments of Charles I. caused an attempt to revive them in the earlier part of the seventeenth century. The Parliamentary opposition to the Stuarts rested their case upon old precedents. The supporters of the prerogative were not slow to follow the lead thus given to them. From 1632 to 1637 Justice Seats were held by Lord Holland, Chief Justice in Eyre.[1] Juries were threatened and intimidated,[2] so that it is not surprising to find that the crown procured a large number of fines and amercements for then almost forgotten offences, and the afforestment of large tracts of country which had long been free from the forest law. In Rockingham forest, for instance, the bounds of the forest were enlarged from six to sixty miles, and the Earl of Salisbury was fined £20,000, the Earl of Westmorland £19,000, Sir Christopher Hatton £12,000.[3] These proceedings were the occasion of an Act of the Long Parliament which finally fixed the boundaries of the forests.[4] The boundaries of the forests were to be the boundaries which were existing in the twentieth year of James I.'s reign. No place at which a forest court had not been held for sixty years preceding the first year of Charles I.'s reign was to be accounted forest. Provision was made for the issue of commissions to ascertain boundaries. No place disafforested since the twentieth year of James I.'s reign was, by reason of the Act, to be afforested.

After the Restoration little more is heard of the forest laws. In a statute of 1667-1668 relating to the Forest of Dean the forest laws were declared to be beneficial;[5] and in a statute of

if it do chance that a Justice Seat be kept for any one forest, the same is seldom or never finished . . . and some few fines, and perhaps none at all, for any offence paid. And then, when the Justice in Eyre of the Forest doth chance to die, the records of the Forest remaining in some private man's hands, and not returned into the court of Exchequer, by some means or other they are smothered, so that they do never come to light. . . . But if that Justices of the Forest would duly hold their Justice Seats, and cause perfect records thereof to be kept ; or else if they would cause the records of their proceedings to be returned into His Majesty's Court of Exchequer, whereby there might be execution of their proceedings . . . then the laws of the Forest would be better known, and also more regarded than they are now at this day."

[1] Gardiner, History of England, vii 363 ; viii 77, 86, 282 ; see also Sir W. Jones' Reports for the Eyre in Berkshire in 1632 at pp. 266-298.

[2] See S.P.D. 1634-1635 xxxiii-xxxvi for a description by the Earl of Warwick of the outrageous conduct of Attorney-General Finch at a forest court for Waltham Forest ; cp. S.P.D. 1638-1639, 140, ccciv 3 ; and see E.H.R. xxi 449 for their proceedings in the Forest of Dean.

[3] As was usual the fines levied were considerably less than those set, below 505-506 ; cp. S.P.D. 1638-1639 109, ccccii 18 for an instance of such reduction.

[4] 16 Charles I. c. 16 ; see Commissioners of Sewers v. Glasse (1874) L.R. 19 Eq. at p. 157.

[5] 19, 20 Charles II. c. 8, § 5

was passed to punish deer stealing in parks; and in 1275[1] the punishment for trespassing and the stealing of tame animals in parks was made more severe. In 1389[2] the series of statutes which limited the right to take game to the landed gentry began. A statute of that year recited that "artificers, labourers, and servants" go hunting in parks and warrens, and prohibited the taking of "gentlemen's game" by any one who had not got land to the value of 40s. As the landed gentry grew in power during the course of the seventeenth and eighteenth centuries the statutes relating to game grew both more detailed and more stringent.[3] Their general effect was to prohibit almost all persons from killing game unless they had a freehold to the value of £100—a property qualification which, as Blackstone points out, was fifty times the amount required to enable a man to vote for a knight of the shire.[4] And so, as Stephen has said,[5] the right to kill game became "the privilege of a class at once artificial and ill-defined." Thus, as the royal monopoly of the chase disappeared with the decay of the forest laws, this new monopoly of the landed gentry was being created by the legislature; and this similarity in the result aimed at and achieved by these two very different sets of regulations justifies Blackstone[6] in calling the Game Laws "a bastard slip" of the forest law.

The Franchises of the Landowners

We have seen that these franchises fell into two fairly well-marked groups. There were the palatine jurisdictions of Durham, Lancaster, Chester, the Lords Marchers on the borders of England and Wales, and Wales; and there were the smaller franchises which were exercised by the landowners in conjunction with their feudal and manorial jurisdiction. Certain extensive liberties may perhaps be regarded as connecting links between these two groups;[7] but, as their history is of local rather than general importance in the development of the judicial system, I do not therefore propose to relate it. I shall therefore deal with this subject under the two heads of the Palatinates, and the Lesser Franchises.

---

[1] Select Pleas of the Forest, cxx-cxxi; for the statute of Rageman of 1276 which provided a new machinery to try these cases, see ibid cxxi, cxxii.

[2] 13 Richard II. St. 1 c. 13.

[3] For these statutes, see Stephen, H.C.L. iii 277-282; for Blackstone's severe strictures on the statute of 5 Anne c. 14, see Bl. Comm. iv 175.

[4] Ibid 175; see ibid for certain other qualifications for the privilege of killing game.

[5] H.C.L. iii 281.   [6] Comm. iv 409.

[7] Above 92 nn. 3, 4, 5.

(1) The Palatinates.

England is governed by a law common to the whole country But there is no rule without an exception; and to this rule the palatinates were the exception. They were independent principalities of the continental type within which the king's writ did not run—small models, as Bacon said, of the great government of kingdoms.[1] Their environment, however, was not favourable to independent development. Their judicial system copied that of the common law. Acts of the English Parliament bound them. The rules of the common law were applied in their courts. When they disappeared their inhabitants were conscious of no revolution.

English law had no term to describe these great franchises. It adopted, therefore, a word of foreign origin.[2] When the word had been adopted it became possible to generalize concerning the entity so described. "The power and authority," says Coke,[3] "of those that had counties palatine was king-like, for they might pardon treasons, murders, felonies, and outlawries thereupon. They might also make justices of eyre, justices of assize, of gaol delivery, and of the peace. And all original and judicial writs, and all manner of indictment of treasons and felony, and the process thereupon was made in the name of the persons having such county palatine. And in every writ and indictment within any county palatine it was supposed to be contra pacem of him that had the county palatine."

The history of the different counties palatine is a history in little of the common law. Their gradual subordination to, and merger in the judicial scheme of the rest of England is a long episode in the advance of royal justice.

Durham.

The history of the Palatinate of Durham falls into two periods: (i) The period of growth up to 1536; and (ii) the period of decline after 1536.

(i) The period of growth up to 1536.

We have seen that the grants of large territories and jurisdiction made to the See of Durham by the Anglo-Saxon kings were confirmed by grants of the Norman and Angevin kings.[4]

---

[1] Works (Ed. Spedding) vii 602.

[2] "Since the distinguishing traits of these franchises lay in the exercise of local sovereignty, in a kind of limited royalty, scholars borrowed from the Continent the convenient adjective palatinus, which was known in theory to imply something peculiarly royal, and in practice (on the Rhine and in Champagne) to denote very much the same sort of local independence that they were seeking to describe," Lapsley, The County Palatine of Durham 11; ibid 3-11; Bracton in one place, f. 122 b, mentions "Comites Paleys."

[3] Fourth Instit. 205.

[4] Above 20, 21, 26, 27.

It is clear from Henry II. s charters that the jurisdiction of the bishop was wide and exclusive.[1] In Henry II.'s reign Bishop Pudsey was appointed to the See, and held it for forty-two years. He had been one of Henry's justices in eyre; and at the beginning of Richard I.'s reign he was justiciar for the northern half of the kingdom. He began to organize his great franchise, and to introduce some of the improved legal ideas of the Curia Regis.[2] His successors continued his work. Over the rest of England the new legal ideas and procedure of the Curia Regis sapped the franchise jurisdiction. In Durham the palatinate jurisdiction became more definite and exclusive by borrowing the new ideas and procedure. It came to be a jurisdiction which differed not merely in degree but also in kind from the jurisdiction possessed by the ordinary holders of franchises.

The case of Geoffry FitzGeoffry, which was before the king's justices in Northumberland between 1205 and 1208, illustrates the beginning of the process.[3] He had been sued for his freehold in the bishop's court and had tried to put himself upon the Grand Assize. But he was told that the Grand Assize did not apply to Durham. He was therefore forced to try his case by battle; and proceedings were taken before the king's justices to settle the question whether he ought to have been compelled to plead in the bishop's court. The result we do not know; but it is clear that the men of Durham desired the procedural advantages of their neighbours. In 1208 and 1217 they paid the king to get the right to use the assizes; and the grant was made " saving the liberties of the bishop." This, as Mr. Lapsley points out, is the psychological moment.[4] Will the bishop leave the new processes to the royal courts and continue to be merely the lord of a franchise, or will he reorganize his judicial system and become the lord of a palatinate?

The latter alternative was chosen. It is clear from a document of 1229 that there was then a central court at Durham. The judges of this court held eyres at the same times as the royal justices. They dealt with pleas of the crown and cases concerning land begun by the bishop's writ. Below this court there were the old county courts. These extensive privileges were recognized when the Quo Warranto enquiries were held. "We have," as Mr. Lapsley puts it, "left behind us the great franchise and are face to face with the county palatine."[5]

---

[1] Above 27.

[2] Lapsley 163-165; for a list of the jura regalia see Registrum Dunelmense (R.S.) I. lv.

[3] Lapsley 166, 313-316.

[4] Ibid 167, 168; for the grand assize and the possessory assizes see below 327-329.

[5] Ibid 169-173. In 1293 Bishop Bek declined to comply with the Statute of Gloucester, and Hugh de Cressingham and his fellow justices in eyre seized the

The judicial system of the palatinate copied closely the judicial system of the rest of England; it developed in a similar way; and the law which was administered by that system was kept in close touch with the rules of English law.

There was a central court of pleas, and a body of justices who sat by virtue of commissions of assize, oyer and terminer, and gaol delivery.[1] The bishop also had a Council and a Chancery. His council corrected the errors of the court of pleas and of the justices, and it had also an original jurisdiction;[2] but in the last resort the King's Bench and House of Lords in England could correct the errors of the bishop's council.[3] His chancery, in the fourteenth century, was getting a concurrent jurisdiction over matters which were brought before the council; and questions concerning the bishop's revenue were long determined by the chancery sitting as a court of Exchequer.[4] But, as was the case with the royal chancery,[5] it did not get a distinct equitable jurisdiction much before the beginning of the sixteenth century. Wolsey was Bishop of Durham in 1523, and seems to have reorganized the episcopal chancery, and developed its equitable jurisdiction in much the same way as he developed the equitable jurisdiction of the royal chancery.[6] In 1596 a book of rules regulating its practice was issued by the authority of the crown;[7] and in the latter half of the seventeenth century appeals from it were heard by the House of Lords.[8] In the sixteenth century also Henry VIII.'s reorganization of the court of Admiralty[9] was imitated, and the bishop acquired a court with a similar jurisdiction.[10] The development of the local courts in the palatinate also followed closely the development of the local courts in the kingdom. As in the kingdom, the county court was superseded by the justices of the peace in quarter sessions.[11] Similarly the law

bishop's franchise; he appealed to Parliament and it was admitted that the seizure was illegal, Registrum Dunelmense (R.S.) I. xl, xli; III. xv-xvii; P.Q.W. 604, 605. At the beginning of the thirteenth century the supremacy of the crown was admitted by the practice of craving court in a civil action before the royal justices, and of petitioning for the pleas of the crown; these marks of dependence had been dropped at the end of the thirteenth century, Lapsley 172, 173; but if a man was outlawed in another county, it was held, in 1346, that a writ could issue to the bishop to take him and to answer to the king for his chattels; and that if the bishop had a right to the chattels of those outlawed outside his franchise he must claim it, Y.B. 20 Ed. III. (R.S.) ii 314.

[1] Lapsley, 174.   [2] Ibid 181-182.

[3] Ibid 212; Coke, Fourth Instit. 218; but this was denied by Fineux, C.J., in Y.B. 21 Hy. VII. Mich pl. 32; possibly also the court of Common Pleas had this power, below 202.

[4] Lapsley, 186-191.   [5] Below 409.
[6] Lapsley, 189.   [7] Ibid 198.

[8] Hist. MSS. Com. 9th Rep. App. Pt. II. no. 15—an appeal from the palatine chancery in 1670-1671.

[9] Below 546-547.   [10] Lapsley, 194.
[11] Ibid 178, 179, 195.

Common Law Procedure Acts.[1]   But the establishment of the new county courts in 1846[2] had removed the former objections to its abolition, and it was therefore possible to merge it, in 1873, in the High Court of Justice created by the Judicature Act.[3]   The same Act also provided that, as respects the issue of commissions of assize and other like commissions, the counties of Durham and Lancaster should cease to be counties palatine.[4] The Court of Chancery still survives.   Its practice was regulated in 1889; and it was provided that appeals from it should lie to the Court of Appeal, and from thence to the House of Lords.[5]

Lancaster.

In 1351 Edward III. made the county of Lancaster a county palatine, and conferred it upon his cousin Henry, Duke of Lancaster for his life.[6]   Henry died in 1361, and the palatinate therefore became extinct.   In 1377,[7] with the consent of Parliament, it was revived in favour of Edward III.'s son, John of Gaunt, who had married Henry, Duke of Lancaster's daughter, and had been created Duke of Lancaster in 1362.[8]   This grant of the palatinate was for the life of John of Gaunt; but in 1390 the dukedom and the palatinate were granted to him and his heirs male.[9]   By these charters John of Gaunt was given the right to have his chancellor and his writs under the seal of his chancery, to have his judges to hold pleas of the crown and any other pleas whatsoever, and all other liberties and royal rights pertaining to a county palatine, as fully and freely as the Earl of Chester enjoyed them within his county palatine.[10]   The king reserved to himself only the tenths and fifteenths granted by Parliament and Convocation, the power to pardon, and the power to correct the errors of the palatine courts.[11]   Under the powers thus given the judicial system of the palatinate was organized on much the same plan as the Durham palatinate.[12]   There was a court of pleas, justices of assize, oyer and terminer, and gaol delivery, and justices of the peace.[13]   There was also a Court of Chancery which administered equity.[14]

---

[1] 17, 18 Victoria c. 125 § 101; 18, 19 Victoria c. 67 § 8; 23, 24 Victoria c. 126 § 40.

[2] Below 191.   [3] 36, 37 Victoria c. 66 § 16; below 639.

[4] 36, 37 Victoria c. 66 § 99.   [5] 52, 53 Victoria c. 47.

[6] W. Hardy, The Charters of the Duchy of Lancaster 9-11.

[7] Ibid 32-34.   [8] Ibid 17, 18.   [9] Ibid 65-70.

[10] Ibid 32-33; in 1390 he was also given the power to have his Exchequer and to appoint justices of the forest, ibid 68.

[11] Ibid 33.   [12] Coke, Fourth Instit. 205.

[13] Thirtieth Rep. of the Deputy Keeper vii.

[14] The Chancery of the Palatinate seems to have been created by letters patent Feb. 28th 51 Ed. III., ibid viii n.

But the county palatine of Lancaster, though it long retained its separate judicial organization, has, from 1399 onwards,
been much more closely connected with the crown than the
county palatine of Durham. John of Gaunt's son, Henry of
Lancaster, succeeded to the throne of England on Richard II.'s
deposition in 1399. He kept his family estates, including the
county palatine, separate from the crown estates;[1] and though
the Duchy of Lancaster, and the county palatine as parcel of the
duchy, were united to the crown by Edward IV.,[2] they were
restored to their original position by Henry VII.,[3] and have so
remained ever since. Thus the county palatine has remained a
separate franchise, but, since 1399, it has always been in the
hands of the crown. Hence, although the Act of 1536 [4] applied
to Lancaster, it did not have the effect upon its judicial independence which it had in the case of Durham. It made a change
in form only. In most cases [5] it meant only that, for the future,
the king exercised as king the same powers that he had formerly
exercised as Duke of Lancaster.

The county palatine of Lancaster was only a part of the
estates of the Duke of Lancaster.[6] He had many other estates
scattered all over England ; and these were increased by the
addition to them of the estates which Henry V. inherited from
his mother,[7] and by other additions made by Henry VIII.
and Mary.[8] "Nearly every county in England and Wales ac-
knowledges to a greater or less extent the jurisdiction and swells
the territories of the Duchy of Lancaster." [9] The separation
which Henry IV. maintained between his family estates and the
royal estates made the former a separate entity. Henceforward
they were all parts of the Duchy of Lancaster. "Henry IV.," as
Mr. Armitage-Smith has said,[10] "gave a unity to his father's
lands which did not exist in his father's lifetime ; lands in Sussex
or Yorkshire which would now be spoken of as 'parcel of the
Duchy of Lancaster' would in the life of John of Gaunt have
been referred to as 'parcel of the Honor of Eagle,' or 'parcel
of the Honor of Tickhill or of Knaresborough,' held by the
Duke of Lancaster in chief." All these territories, including the

---

[1] See the Charter of 1399, Hardy, op. cit. 138-139. [2] Ibid 282-283.
[3] Ibid 346-347 ; cf. Coke, Fourth Instit. 205 ; Lambard, Archeion 223 ; the
effect of these limitations was exhaustively discussed in the case of the Duchy of
Lancaster (1562) Plowden 212 ; and cf. Coke, Fourth Instit. 209-210.
[4] 27 Henry VIII. c. 24 ; Coke, Fourth Instit. 205.
[5] 27 Henry VIII. c. 24 § 4 provided that appointments to judicial offices should
be under the seal of the duchy.
[6] For a description of these estates in the time of John of Gaunt see Armitage-
Smith, John of Gaunt chap. x, and the map at p. 218.
[7] Hardy, op. cit. 163. [8] Coke, Fourth Instit. 210.
[9] Thirtieth Report of the Deputy Keeper iv.
[10] Armitage-Smith, op. cit. 204.

palatinate, were parcels of a greater regality—the Duchy of Lancaster.[1]

From Henry IV.'s reign the Duchy of Lancaster was managed as a whole by a Chancellor and Council, and a staff of duchy officials.[2]   The main business of the Chancellor was to superintend the management by the duchy officials of all the estates, franchises, and privileges comprised in the duchy.   But the existence of a Chancellor came to be thought to imply the existence of some sort of equitable jurisdiction;[3] and, thus we find that, from the beginning of Henry VII.'s reign,[4] the Chancellor of the Duchy is holding a court known as the court of Duchy Chamber, which exercised an equitable jurisdiction in cases concerning lands which were parcel of the duchy,[5] whether situated within the county palatine or not.[6]   This jurisdiction did not exclude the equitable jurisdiction of the king's chancery and the court of Exchequer, but was concurrent with it.[7]   This court has never been abolished; but it has not sat since 1835.[8]

This court of Duchy Chamber was quite distinct from the palatine court of Chancery.   But the Chancellor of the Duchy seems to have got the power to hear appeals from the palatine court of Chancery.[9]   A new Court of Appeal was created by an Act of 1850,[10] which enacted that appeals should be heard by the Chancellor of the Duchy assisted by two judges of assize, for whom, in 1854,[11] two lords justices of appeal in chancery were substituted.

The Judicature Act of 1873 merged the Lancaster Court of Pleas in the High Court, and stopped the issue of commissions

---

[1] Thirtieth Report of the Deputy Keeper vii.

[2] Ibid vi; in the Act of 1461, by which Edward IV. annexed the duchy to the crown, the existence of separate seals and chanceries for the palatinate and the duchy is recognized, Hardy, op. cit. 283.

[3] In Fisher v. Patten (1673) 2 Lev. 24 Hale pointed out that the " constituting of a chancellor does not of itself constitute a court of equity," and he illustrated this by referring to the chancellor of the Order of the Garter; how this court of equity began, he said, did not plainly appear; but he held that the precedents for its existence were conclusive.

[4] Some of the earlier proceedings of the Court (1485-1558) have been edited and printed for the Lancashire and Cheshire Record Society by H. Fishwick.

[5] Coke, Fourth Instit. 206; Bl. Comm. iii 78.

[6] In Fisher v. Patten (1673) 2 Lev. 24 it was held that that court had jurisdiction over land parcel of the duchy, though situated in the county palatine.

[7] Levington v. Woton (1631) 1 Ch. Rep. 52; Fleetwood v. Pool (1660) Hardres 171.

[8] Halsbury, Laws of England ix 120.

[9] This does not appear from Coke, Fourth Instit. c. 36, or from Bl. Comm. iii 78; but the existence of this power seems to be assumed by the Judicature Act of 1873, 36, 37 Victoria c. 66 § 18 (2); below 643; and is so stated in Thirtieth Report of the Deputy Keeper viii n.

[10] 13, 14 Victoria c. 43.   [11] 17, 18 Victoria c. 82.

of assize and other like commissions.[1] But, as in the case of Durham, the palatine court of Chancery survived the Judicature Acts. In 1890[2] that court was brought into closer connection with the judicial system of the country, and fresh arrangements were made for hearing appeals. The palatine court of Chancery was given substantially the same jurisdiction as the Chancery Division of the High Court ; and appeals from it were henceforward to go to the Court of Appeal and the House of Lords. Thus, since the court of Duchy Chamber has ceased to sit, and since the Chancellor of the Duchy has been deprived of his jurisdiction to hear appeals from the palatine Chancery, the Chancellor of the Duchy has ceased to be a judicial officer.[3]

Chester, the Lords Marchers, and Wales.

The county palatine of Chester, the franchises of the Lords Marchers, and the principality of Wales are geographically contiguous ; and the history of the judicial system of all these districts is so interwoven that it must be treated together. That history falls into four well marked periods. Firstly the period before the Statute of Wales of 1284 ; secondly from 1284 to the reforms of Henry VIII. ; thirdly from Henry VIII.'s reforms to 1689 ; and fourthly from 1689 to modern times.

(i) The period before the Statute of Wales of 1284.[4]

During the period which stretches from the Norman Conquest to 1284 the English were constantly encroaching upon the Welsh. At two of the gateways into Wales William I. had created the two counties palatine of Chester and Shrewsbury. Chester he had entrusted to his nephew Hugh, and Shrewsbury to Roger of Montgomery. The gateway into Wales by way of Hereford he had entrusted to William Fitz-Osbern ; and Gloucester was in Norman hands in 1068. The palatine county of Shrewsbury ceased to exist after the expulsion of Robert of Belesme by Henry I. ; and, owing partly to geographical causes, and partly to the control kept by the crown over the barons of this district after Belesme's rebellion, not much real progress was made in the conquest of North Wales. All the country round Snowdon continued to be Welsh. But in South Wales considerable progress was made by the Norman barons. From Hereford and Gloucester they gradually conquered the country,

---

[1] 36, 37 Victoria c. 66 §§ 16 and 99 ; below 639 ; the Act does not put an end to the separate commissions of the peace, so that the justices of the peace for the county palatine are still appointed by the Chancellor of the Duchy.

[2] 53, 54 Victoria c. 23.

[3] For his modern position see Anson, The Crown (2nd Ed.) Pt. I. 206-207.

[4] For this period see generally Skeel, The Council in the Marches of Wales Introd. ; Rhys and Brynmor Jones, The Welsh People, chap. vii.

and in return got almost royal powers of jurisdiction over the land they conquered. Pembroke came to be reckoned as a county palatine,[1] and the other Lords Marchers had almost equally extensive jura regalia.[2] Thus, " between the days of William Rufus and those of Edward I. grew up, slowly indeed, but all the more surely, the famous ' custom of the March.' The position of the Lords Marchers was thoroughly anomalous as compared with that of the ordinary English baron. Their analogies must be sought, not in England, but in France, or, better still, in Germany, where the margraves held somewhat the same position against the Slavs as they did against the Welsh." [3]

The palatinate of Chester had reverted to the crown in 1237 ; and in 1254 Henry III. made his son Edward, Earl of Chester, and handed over to him all his lands in Wales.[4] These lands comprised the present Flintshire and Denbighshire, and a large part of Carmarthenshire and Cardiganshire.[5] These areas Edward began to organize on the model of the English shires.[6] His proceedings naturally aroused the indignation of the Welsh. They turned to Llewelyn for assistance, and a war broke out in 1256 which did not end till 1267. The result of the treaty made in that year was to leave Edward only Chester and Carmarthen ; [7] but the war was renewed in 1276; and this time Edward was victorious. The treaty of Conway " reduced Llewelyn to the rank of a petty baron." [8] Edward again set to work to organize his newly won territory on the English model.[9] This led to a renewal of hostilities in 1282. This time Edward completely subdued Wales. Llewelyn was killed, and his brother David, who was captured, was executed as a traitor. This opened the way to the settlement of Wales which was effected by the so-called Statute of Wales in 1284.[10]

(ii) From 1284 to the reforms of Henry VIII.

The Statute of Wales, after reciting that Wales was now annexed to the English crown, proceeded to enact that it should be divided into six counties, organized on the English model,

---

[1] Above 92.   [2] Below 120-121.   [3] Skeel, op. cit. 6.
[4] Rhys and Brynmor Jones 326-327.   [5] Ibid 327 n.
[6] T. F. Tout, Y. Cymmrodor ix 211-213.
[7] Rhys and Brynmor Jones 328-332.
[8] Ibid 335.   [9] Ibid 337.

[10] 12 Edward I. St. 1; in form this so-called statute is an ordinance of the king with the advice of his nobles; but it has always been accepted as a statute; it should be noted also that the king took power (as Henry VIII. took power, below 124) to vary it—" Ita tamen quod quociens-cumque, et quandocumque, et ubicumque nobis placuerit possimus prædicta statuta, et eorum partes singulas declarare, interpretari, addere, sive diminuere, pro nostro libito voluntate, et prout securitati nostræ et terræ nostræ predictæ viderimus expedire."

and equipped with sheriffs, coroners, and bailiffs. These six counties were Anglesea, Carnarvon, Merioneth, Flint, Carmarthen, and Cardigan. The first three were placed under the justice of Snowdon, Flint was placed under the justice of Chester,[1] and the last two were later placed under a justice of South Wales.[2] These justices were to administer justice for the most part in accordance with the rules of English law;[3] and to enable them to do so English writs and procedure were introduced by the statute.

After the passing of this statute, therefore, the principality of Wales was administered by the justices of Chester, Snowdon, and South Wales; while the rest of Wales, except the county palatine of Pembroke, was governed by the Lords Marchers. We must therefore glance rapidly at the courts and jurisdiction of Chester, the justices of Wales, and the Lords Marchers.

Chester, as Coke said, was the most ancient of the counties palatine.[4] As we have seen, it had this status before the time of legal memory, so that it could claim to be a county palatine by prescription.[5] It was created a principality by Richard II. and settled upon the king's eldest son.[6] The justice of Chester held a court for pleas of the crown and common pleas;[7] and the chamberlain of Chester, assisted by a vice-chamberlain, exercised the equitable and common law jurisdiction of the Chancery, and the jurisdiction of the court of Exchequer.[8] These *jura regalia* were ascertained and certified by a resolution of the judges in 1568, on the occasion of a controversy between the chamberlain of Chester and the President and Council of Wales and the Marches.[9] As in the case of the other counties palatine, a writ of error lay from the justice of Chester, or the chamberlain exercising Exchequer jurisdiction, to the King's

---

[1] Flint had from the first been dependent on Chester, see T. F. Tout, Y. Cymmrodor ix 218.

[2] No provision was made for a justice of South Wales in the Statute of Wales; but Edward I. had appointed a justice of S. Wales in 1280, T. F. Tout, Y. Cymmrodor ix 212; and in Edward II.'s reign regular appointments were made, T. F. Tout, Edward II. 374-381; but sometimes the justices of N. and S. Wales were united in one hand, ibid 377.

[3] The Statute of Wales recites that Edward had considered the laws of Wales, and, "Quibus diligenter auditis aut plenius intellectis quasdem ipsarum de consilio procerum predictorum delevimus, quasdam permisimus, et quasdam correximus; et etiam quasdam alias adjiciendum et statuendum decrevimus; et eas de cetero in terris nostris in partibus illis perpetua firmitate teneri et observari volumus in forma subscripta;" in § 14 there is a proviso that, though in trials of land the jury was to be introduced, in trials of things moveable "as of contracts, debts, sureties, covenants, trespasses, chattels," Welsh law was to be used.

[4] Fourth Instit. 211.   [5] Ibid; above 117.
[6] 21 Richard II. c. 9.   [7] Fourth Instit. 211, 212.
[8] Ibid; Egerton was at one time the chamberlain of Chester, and we have a reference to his equitable jurisdiction in Egerton Papers (C.S.) 207.
[9] Fourth Instit. 212-213.

Bench;[1] but in the case of Chester there were some peculiar and somewhat archaic rules applicable to this procedure in error.[2] The courts of Chester could also be controlled by the writ of certiorari and other prerogative writs.[3] An Act of 1536 provided that in Chester, and the shires of Wales annexed to Chester, justices of the peace and gaol delivery should be appointed by the Lord Chancellor or Lord Keeper;[4] and, like the other counties palatine, it was affected by the other Act of the same session for recontinuing liberties in the crown.[5] We shall see that the position of the justice of Chester was materially altered by the Act of 1543 which constituted the courts of Great Sessions for Wales.[6]

Chester was a county palatine which, like the other counties palatine, had once been part of the realm of England. Wales on the other hand had never formed part of the realm of England. From this the lawyers drew the conclusion that, while error lay from the courts of the other counties palatine to the King's Bench, error did not lie from the courts of the justices of Wales to the King's Bench,[7] but only to Parliament;[8] and that, while the King's Bench could send issues to be tried in the courts of the counties palatine, it could not send such issues for trial to the justices of Wales, because they were courts of a co-ordinate jurisdiction.[9] Thus all through the Middle Ages, and till Henry VIII.'s reforms, the courts of Wales were completely independent of the jurisdiction of the courts of common law. " Breve domini regis non currit in Walliam."

The Lords Marchers possessed an almost equally independent jurisdiction. Their large powers appear from *Cornewall's Case*, the pleadings of which are given in Coke's Entries,[10] and from the provisions of the statutes of Henry VIII.'s reign for reorganizing the judicial system of Wales and the Marches.[11] They may be

---

[1] Fourth Instit. 213-214.

[2] The writ of error was to be read to the justices of Chester and they could reverse their decision; but if they affirmed their decision, and it was afterwards reversed by the King's Bench they forfeited £100, ibid 214; it is only gradually that a complaint of an erroneous decision is differentiated from a complaint against the conduct of the judge who gave the decision, below 213-214; for another illustration of this old idea see below 521.

[3] See a case of Hil. 29 Eliza., cited Coke, Fourth Instit. 214; below 226 231.

[4] 27 Henry VIII. c. 5.   [5] Ibid c. 24.   [6] Below 124.

[7] Y.BB. 32 Hy. VI. Hil. pl. 13 *per* Fortescue; 36 Hy. VI. pl. 34 p. 33 *per* Fortescue; Coke, Fourth Instit. 223; Harg. Law Tracts, A Discourse against the jurisdiction of the King's Bench over Wales by process of Latitat, 393-405; the author states that he was moved to write the tract by hearing, in 1745, the arguments in the case of Lampley v. Thomas (1747) 1 Wils. 193, below 131.

[8] Y.B. 19 Hy. VI. Mich. pl. 31.

[9] Y.BB. 32 Hy. VI. Hil. pl. 13; 36 Hy. VI. pl. 34 pp. 33-34; Vaughan's Report 412; Harg. Law Tracts 404.

[10] At p. 549; cf. Stephen, H.C.L. i 140-142.   [11] Below 122-124.

summarized as follows : [1] (1) The king's writ did not run in the Marches. All writs within the seignory were in the name of the lord, and offences were said to be committed contra pacem of the lord. Consequently each lord had his Chancery for the issue of original writs. (2) They had judgment of life and limb in all capital cases, the forfeitures of all the lands and chattels of felons, and the power to pardon. Consequently they had the power to appoint justices of oyer and terminer and other justices necessary to administer their criminal jurisdiction. (3) They had the right to try all actions real and personal and mixed. (4) Among other prerogative rights they had the right to create boroughs.[2] The only two cases in which the king's court had jurisdiction were, firstly the case in which a Lord Marcher was a party to the action,[3] and secondly in certain cases of mixed ecclesiastical and civil jurisdiction in which it was necessary to get a certificate from a bishop, such as proceedings on a writ of *Quare Impedit* and proceedings to determine legitimacy or the existence of a marriage.[4] In the first case the Lord Marcher could not be a judge in his own case, and therefore the king's court assumed or was given jurisdiction [5]—the necessary writs in the action being sent to the sheriff of the adjoining county.[6] In the second case jurisdiction was given or assumed because the bishop refused to obey an order to give a certificate sent by a Lord Marcher. He would only obey a royal order; and therefore the proceedings necessarily must take place in the king's court.[7]

Thus the Lords Marchers were practically independent potentates of a kind very unusual in England. From this two consequences flowed. In the first place there grew up in their jurisdictions a mixture of Welsh custom and English law known as the custom of the Marches.[8] In the second place, although they held of the king, their allegiance sat so lightly upon them that it was necessary to declare in 1354 [9] that "all the Lords of the Marches of Wales shall be perpetually attending and annexed to the crown of England, and not to the principality of Wales, in whose hands so ever the same principality be." It is

---

[1] Harg. Law Tracts 388-389 ; Rhys and Brynmor-Jones, op. cit. 356-360.

[2] It was provided in 1543 that the king should within seven years have power to dissolve such boroughs in order that he might make other places " more convenient and apt " into boroughs, 34, 35 Henry VIII. c. 26 § 27.

[3] Harg. Law Tracts 390.

[4] Ibid 389 ; Vaughan, Report 409, 410.

[5] Possibly it was by Legislative Act, see Vaughan, Report 403, citing Fitz-Herbert Ab, *Assise* pl. 382—a case of 18 Edward II. ; Harg. Law Tracts 390.

[6] Vaughan, Report 404.

[7] Harg. Law Tracts 399, 403, citing Y.B. 19 Hy. VI. Mich. pl. 31 ; Vaughan, Report 410.

[8] See H. Owen, Y. Cymmrodor xiv Pt. II. 17.

[9] 28 Edward III. c. 2.

their position in relation to the crown which, as we shall now
see, gives them their importance in English history.

Edward I. had attempted to suppress private war in the
Marches, and to bring the Lords Marchers into some sort of subordination by his writs of *Quo Warranto*.[1] Though he had some
measure of success, he paid for it by the loss of their active support. " In the fierce struggle over the confirmation of the
charters the proudest of the baronage were raised against him.
To the very end of his reign he was hampered in his attempt to
conquer Scotland by baronial opposition dating from the Welsh
wars."[2] The task which Edward I. had found difficult Edward II.
found impossible. In all semi-revolutionary, semi-constitutional
struggles of the reign the Lords Marchers played a decisive
part ;[3] and during the Wars of the Roses both the claimants
drew much of their support from the Marches. " From the
great Mortimer estates, whose centre was Ludlow, the Duke of
York drew his armies, while the west of Wales, from Pembroke
to Anglesea, was strongly Lancastrian."[4] It was one of the
happiest results of these wars that they made the elimination of
these centres of disorder possible. The Lancastrian inheritance
in the Marches was added to the crown estates when Henry IV.
became king in 1399, and the Yorkist when Edward IV. became
king [5] in 1461. The fact that these lordships were now part of
the crown demesnes enabled Edward IV. to establish a President
and Council in the Marches.[6] The fact that Henry VII. was of
Welsh descent and bore a Welsh name, and that he had got possession of the Marcher Lordships held by Richard III. as Earl of
March,[7] enabled his successor to put the judicial system of Wales
upon a wholly new basis.

(iii) From Henry VIII.'s reforms to 1689.

The series of Acts relating to Wales begins in 1535.[8] In that
year two Acts were passed dealing with the perjury of jurors in
Wales, and with robbers escaping into South Wales.[9] Another
Act provided a better machinery for the punishment, by the
Council of Wales and the Marches or by the king's justices in the
adjoining English counties, of crimes committed in the Marches ; [10]

---

[1] Skeel, op. cit. 8, 9 ; T. F. Tout, Edward II. 137.
[2] Skeel, op. cit. 9. [3] T. F. Tout, Edward II. 137-143.
[4] Skeel, op. cit. 11. [5] T. F. Tout, Edward II. 156.
[6] Skeel, op. cit. chap. i ; below 502.
[7] Ibid 17 ; and App. IV.
[8] For a very clear summary of these Acts see Skeel, op. cit. 38-46.
[9] 26 Henry VIII. cc. 4 and 5.
[10] Ibid c. 6—murders, other felonies, and certain other crimes committed
in Wales and the Marches were to be tried at special courts to be kept in
Wales (§ 1), and offences by the officers of Lords Marchers were to be tried by the
Council of Wales (§ 2) ; felonies and other crimes in the Marches could be tried in

and two other Acts provided for the punishment of assaults by Welshmen upon the inhabitants of the border counties of Hereford, Gloucester, and Shropshire, and for the conditions under which benefit of clergy was to be allowed to Welsh clerks.[1] In 1536 certain abuses in the administration of the forest law in Wales were remedied ;[2] and in the same year came the Act of union between England and Wales.[3] Wales and England were united, and Welshmen and Englishmen were to be subject to the same laws and have the same privileges.[4] Five new counties were formed—Monmouth, Brecknock, Radnor, Montgomery, and Denbigh ;[5] and 137 Marcher Lordships enumerated in the Act were annexed, some to these new counties, some to the old Welsh counties, and some to the English border counties.[6] Courts were to be kept in the English tongue,[7] and Wales was to be represented in Parliament.[8] There was a saving of certain of the pecuniary profits, and certain of the franchises enjoyed by the Lords Marchers.[9] The king was given power within three years from the end of Parliament to repeal or suspend the Act, and for a period of five years to establish courts in Wales.[10] It was also provided that commissioners should be appointed to divide Wales into shires.[11]

The carrying into effect of the provisions of this Act naturally took some time.[12] When it was accomplished in 1543, a comprehensive Act was passed to provide for the local government and judicial organization of Wales.[13] The country was to be divided into twelve counties—the six counties enumerated in the Statute of Wales, two new counties of Pembroke and Glamorgan, and the counties created by the Act of 1536, with the exception

the adjoining shires (§ 6), and for that purpose process could be issued into the Marches (§ 8), provided the criminal was indicted within two years of the crime (§ 11) ; there was also a provision for bringing to justice fugitive criminals from the Marcher jurisdictions (§ 13).

[1] 26 Henry VIII. cc. 11 and 12.

[2] 27 Henry VIII. c. 7.   [3] Ibid c. 26.

[4] "That the said country and dominion of Wales shall be, stand and continue for ever from henceforth incorporated, united, and annexed to and with this his realm of England ; and that all and singular person and persons, born and to be born in the said principality, Country, or Dominion of Wales, shall have, enjoy, and inherit all and singular freedoms, liberties, rights, privileges, and laws within this his realm, and other the King's Dominions, as other the king's subjects naturally born within the same have, enjoy, and inherit."

[5] § 3.   [6] §§ 3-19 ; Stephen, H.C.L. i 140 n. 2.

[7] 27 Henry VIII. c. 26 § 20.   [8] § 29.

[9] §§ 25, 30 ; it is to be noted that all the jurisdiction reserved in the latter section was the right to hold courts baron, courts leet, and law days ; the other privileges therein enumerated, below 124 n. 14 really only amounted to certain pecuniary rights.

[10] §§ 36, 37.   [11] § 26.

[12] Skeel, op. cit. 43.   [13] 34, 35 Henry VIII c. 26.

of Monmouth which was to be an English county.[1]   For judicial
purposes these counties were to be divided into groups of three,
and a court of Great Sessions was to be held twice a year in
each group—each court lasting six days.   The judge of one
group was to be the justice of Chester, of another the justice of
North Wales, and of the other two two persons to be nominated
by the crown.[2]   In each county there were established sheriffs,[3]
county courts,[4] tourns,[5] and hundred courts,[6] coroners,[7] justices
of the peace, and quarter sessions.[8]   The existence of the President and Council of Wales and the Marches was recognized,
and its jurisdiction was defined.[9]   The king was given power to
alter the Act, and also to make laws for Wales[10]—a power which
was taken away by an Act of 1624.[11]

This statute, together with the legislation which preceded it,
seems to have had the same effect upon the franchises of the
Lords Marchers as the rise of the common law courts had upon
the franchises of the English lords in the thirteenth century.[12]
Their rights to hold courts baron and courts leet,[13] and certain
pecuniary rights arising from their ancient franchises[14] had been
saved in 1536 ;[15] and those so saved, and those alone, were saved
in 1543.[16]   But there was a complaint in 1554 that there was a
doubt whether this saving operated in favour of their heirs or
successors in title ; and a statute was passed in that year to
secure to them these rights.[17]   But it is clear from the statute

---

[1] § 2 ; Glamorgan had been to all intents and purposes organized as a county,
though only called a Marcher Lordship, see Tout, Y. Cymmrodor ix 205, 208-210.

[2] 34, 35 Henry VIII. c. 26 §§ 5-9, 14 ; 18 Elizabeth c. 8 gave the crown power to
increase the number of judges.

[3] 34, 35 Henry VIII c. 26 §§ 61-64.   [4] § 73.   [5] § 75.

[6] § 73.   [7] § 68.   [8] §§ 53-57.

[9] " That there shall be and remain a President and Council in the said Dominion
and Principality of Wales and the Marches of the same . . . in manner and form
as hath been heretofore used and accustomed ; which President and Council shall
have power and authority to hear and determine, by their wisdoms and discretions,
such causes and matters as be or hereafter shall be assigned to them by the King's
Majesty, as heretofore hath been accustomed and used," § 4.

[10] § 119 ; we have seen that the Statute of Wales, 1284, was in substance an
ordinance made by the king, and that he took power in it to vary the laws to be observed in Wales, above 118 n. 10 ; in fact Wales was in much the same position as
a colony acquired by conquest or cession, subject both to the legislative power of
Parliament, and to laws made for it by the king ; this power of the king would, as a
result of the Act, have disappeared if this section had not preserved it.

[11] 21 James I. c. 10 § 4.

[12] Above 87-89 ; below 132-133 ; as Owen says, Y. Cymmrodor xiv Pt. II. 22,
it " practically reduced them to the position of Lords of Manors."

[13] Above 123 n. 9.

[14] 27 Henry VIII. c. 26 § 30 enumerates, " Lawdays, Waife, Straife, Infanthef,
Outfanthef, Treasure-trove, Deodands, Goods and Chattels of Felons, and of persons
condemned or outlawed of Felony or Murther, or put in Exigent for felony or
Murther, and also Wreck de mer, Wharfage and Customs of Strangers."

[15] 27 Henry VIII. c. 26 §§ 25, 30.   [16] 34, 35 Henry VIII. c. 26 § 101.

[17] 1, 2 Philip and Mary c. 15.

that their once wide jurisdiction was now confined to the right to certain payments, and to franchises of the dead or decadent type. The judicial system of Wales now centred round the courts of Great Sessions, and the President and Council of Wales and the Marches.

To the Great Sessions was given a power to exercise within their territorial limits all the jurisdiction exercisable by the courts of King's Bench and Common Pleas.[1] Errors in real and mixed actions were to be redressed by the court of King's Bench ;[2] and in personal actions by the Council of Wales.[3] The Great Sessions also acquired or assumed, before the beginning of the seventeenth century, an equitable jurisdiction, which, after some dispute, was finally upheld by the English courts in Charles II.'s reign.[4] Exactly how they acquired it is not clear. But it is probable that their assumption of it is connected with the fact that, by the Act of 1536, there had been established in Wales separate chanceries for the issue of original writs,[5] and with the fact that, by the Act of 1543, each court of Great Sessions had its seal for the sealing of original writs.[6] As in the counties palatine,[7] the possession of these chanceries was probably considered in the sixteenth century a sufficient warrant[1] for the exercise of a jurisdiction similar to that exercised by the English Chancery ; and since the chancellors or chamberlains appointed to keep the seals of the courts of Great Session were prohibited from exercising this jurisdiction,[8] it was assumed by the judges of these courts. However that may be, it is clear that the Great Sessions were exercising this jurisdiction in the early years of the seventeenth century. But it is probable that they were not often called upon to exercise it while the Council of Wales was at the height of its power.[9]

---

[1] 34, 35 Henry VIII. c. 26 §§ 12, 13.   [2] § 113.   [3] § 113.
[4] It seems to have been assumed in 1661 that the North Wales Sessions had a court of equity, 1 Sid. 52; but the question was raised whether South Wales had a similar court—" Mes le councel cite deux cases estre adjuge in poynt sur solemn debate que South Wales poit erect un court de Equity . . . et les cases fueront " *Bagnall's case* 3 Car. 1, et de pluis darrein temps *Penelope Owen's Case* ; cf. (1648), Style 150, in which the question was put down for argument ; and James v. Procer (1661) 1 Keble 168, in which a prohibition was granted ; in Pulfath v. Griffith (1669) 2 Keble 259, the jurisdiction was finally upheld.
[5] 27 Henry VIII. c. 26 § 9.   [6] 34, 35 Henry VIII. c. 26 §§ 16-22.
[7] Above 111, 116; Bacon in his argument on the jurisdiction of the Council of Wales (Works, Ed. Spedding, vii 602) seems to assume that the possession of a Chancery by the counties palatine carried with it an equitable jurisdiction.
[8] 34, 35 Henry VIII. c. 26 § 21.
[9] It is clear that the Council exercised a considerable equitable jurisdiction, see Skeel, op. cit. 154-155; and cf. the instructions to the Council of 1617 § 15, Prothero Documents, 383-384—the Council is to " examine, hear and determine" all manner of complaints, " for any cause or matter arising within the said dominion and principality as well concerning lands, tenements, or hereditaments . . . as goods and chattels for which there shall upon due proof appear clear matter for the

The Council of Wales, like the English Privy Council and Star Chamber, was both a court of law and an instrument of government; and I shall say something more of it when I deal with the judicial and political work of those bodies.[1] Here it will be sufficient to say that it exercised a criminal jurisdiction similar to that exercised by the court of Star Chamber, and a civil and an equitable jurisdiction co-ordinate with that of the courts of Great Sessions. It also took cognizance of some cases which fell within the jurisdiction of the ecclesiastical courts, such as suits for legacies, and prosecutions for sexual offences.[2] Among the councillors were generally included the Justices of Chester and North Wales; but, as the courts of Great Sessions and the Council exercised jurisdictions which were to a great extent co-ordinate, it is not surprising that friction sometimes arose. Lord Zouche who was President of the Council from 1602-1607, is said to have deliberately slighted the Justice of Chester;[3] and the Earl of Northampton managed to get rid of James Whitelocke, who then held the office of Justice of Chester, because he would not give way to his wishes.[4]

We shall see that at the beginning of the seventeenth century the Council became involved in a long dispute as to its right to exercise jurisdiction over certain English counties bordering on Wales;[5] and that the legality of some parts of its jurisdiction was beginning to be questioned by the courts of common law.[6] It is clear from these disputes that it was beginning to share the unpopularity which attached to the Court of Star Chamber and the other branches of the Council.[7] In so far therefore as it exercised a jurisdiction similar to that exercised by the court of

plaintiff to be relieved in equity and good conscience and that he is without ordinary remedy by common law."

[1] Below 502-503, 507; vol. iv Bk. iv Pt. I. c. 1.

[2] Skeel, op. cit. 154-155; the right to hear these cases was questioned in Evers and Owens Case (1628) Godbolt 431; in that case Whitelocke, J., said, " five bishops, one after the other, were Presidents of the Marches there; and they drew into the Marches spiritual business, but originally it was not so; " in the case before the court the King's Bench refused to prohibit the Council from hearing a suit for a legacy, as " there was much matter of equity concerning the legacy; " the dispute again arose between the Council and the Prerogative Court of Canterbury in 1637, Skeel, op. cit. 157; a prohibition to the Council in a suit for a legacy was awarded in 1670, Win v. Ellis 2 Kebl. 685.

[3] Skeel, op. cit. 130, citing Manningham's Diary (C.S.) 58.

[4] Whitelocke himself says, Liber Famelicus (C.S.) 95, " The erl of Northampton, lord president of the counsell in the marches of Wales, was verye desirous to be quit of me at the counsell; his reason was, I did not give way unto him and his servants, nether in the court nor in the king's house, in bothe whiche I conceaved things to be caryed contrarye to the king's instructions and myne othe. Therefore he made meanes, by the duke of Buckingham . . . to remove me into the King's Benche."

[5] Below 510, 511.

[6] Below 511.

[7] Skeel, op. cit. 139-141; below 513-514.

Star Chamber it was abolished in 1641.[1] But it still continued
to exercise, under ever-increasing difficulties, its civil and equitable
jurisdiction till the outbreak of the civil war.[2] On the outbreak
of the civil war it fell into abeyance ; but at the Restoration it was
re-established in the same position as that which it had occupied
between 1641 and the outbreak of the civil war.[3] Its re-establishment gave the king a considerable amount of patronage ;[4] and a
certain number of persons welcomed it because it gave them the
advantage of having a court in their midst.[5] But the court as
thus re-established was not a success. This was due mainly to
two causes. In the first place the amount of business done did
not justify the expense of maintaining it. The cases brought before it were small in number and often petty in character, while
the costs were often high.[6] The expense of maintaining the
court was large on account of the large number of the officials of
the court who, having little else to do, spent their time disputing
among themselves.[7] In the second place it was never forgotten
that it was the last survivor of those Conciliar courts which, in
the earlier half of the century, had been the most efficient
instruments of prerogative rule.[8] Therefore it was naturally
viewed with dislike and suspicion by those who considered that
all jurisdiction exercised by a branch of the Council was uncon-
stitutional. An attempt to abolish it in 1680 failed ;[9] but at the
Revolution these two causes for its unpopularity were fatal to it.
The preamble to the Act of 1689,[10] which abolished it, dwelt
upon both, and more especially upon the second.[11] Having
abolished it, the Act went on to give its power to nominate persons to be chosen as sheriffs to the judges of the Great Sessions

[1] 16 Charles I. c. 10 § 4; for the history of the progress of this Act see Skeel
op. cit. 157-161 ; the Act only takes away the Star Chamber jurisdiction; in the
same way it took away the Star Chamber jurisdiction exercised by the Council of the
North, the court of the Duchy of Lancaster, and the court of the Exchequer of the
county palatine of Chester ; cp. R. R. Reid, King's Council in the North, 454.

[2] Skeel, op. cit. 161-165.   [3] Ibid 165, 166.
[4] Ibid 169-171.   [5] Ibid 166-168.
[6] Ibid 174 ; and see the evidence given to the House of Lords in 1689, Hist.
MSS. Comm. 12th Rep. App. Pt. VI. no. 80 pp. 105-109.
[7] Skeel, op. cit. 174 says, "references to the court at this, the closing period of
its existence, are for the most part mere records of offices granted and disputes
between their holders."
[8] Below 514.
[9] Hist. MSS. Com. 11th Rep. App. Pt. II. no. 354 p. 261—the bill passed the
Commons, but was dropped in the Lords after a first reading.
[10] 1 William and Mary c. 27.
[11] "Forasmuch as the proceedings and decrees of that court have by experience
been found to be an intolerable Burthen to the subject within the said Principality,
contrary to the Great Charter, the known laws of the land, and the birthright of the
subject, and the means to introduce an arbitrary power and government;" see Hist.
MSS. Com. 12th Rep. App. Pt. VI. 109 for a petition signed by nearly 18,000 persons for the abolition of the court.

and its jurisdiction to redress the errors of the Great Sessions in personal actions to the court of King's Bench.[1]

(iv) From 1689 to modern times.

During the sixteenth and the earlier part of the seventeenth centuries the activity of the Council of Wales, and the rivalry between the courts of common law and all branches of the Council, had prevented any acute controversy between the courts at Westminster and the Great Sessions as to the limits of their respective jurisdictions. But the inactivity of the Council of Wales in the latter part of the seventeenth century, and its abolition in 1689, brought this question of the relation of the Great Sessions to the courts at Westminster to the front.

The problem can be stated in this form : To what extent have the courts at Westminster jurisdiction over Wales?

In certain cases there could be no controversy because statutes had given the English courts jurisdiction. Thus we have seen that the statute of 1543 provided that writs of error should lie from the Great Sessions to the King's Bench ;[2] and it further provided that for "urgent and weighty causes" process might "as heretofore hath been used" be directed into Wales by the special command of the Lord Chancellor or any of the king's Council.[3] A statute of 1547 provided that process of outlawry might be directed into Wales.[4] Certain crimes committed in Wales or the Marches could be tried in the next adjoining counties under a statute of 1534.[5] It seems also to have been admitted that certain prerogative writs could issue into all parts of the king's dominions, and therefore into Wales ;[6] but, till 1670, it was a controverted question whether or not a writ of certiorari could be issued into Wales to remove a criminal case from the cognizance of the Welsh courts ;[7] and it would seem

---

[1] §§ 3, 4.   [2] Above 125.
[3] 34, 35 Henry VIII. c. 26 § 115.   [4] 1 Edward VI. c. 10.
[5] 26 Henry VIII. c. 6 § 6; 34, 35 Henry VIII. c. 26 § 85; Plowden's Rep. 97 seqq.

[6] Vaughan says, "To all dominions of acquisition to the crown of England some writs out of the king's chancery have constantly run . . ." such are "writs that concern not the particular rights or properties of the subjects, but the government and superintendency of the king, nequid Respublica capiat detrimenti, such are writs for safe conduct, and protection, writs for apprehension of persons in his dominions of England . . . of like nature are the writs of ne exeat Regnum," Vaughan's Rep. 401-402; also we might add writs of prohibition, see 12 Co. Rep. 50 for a discussion of writs of prohibition issued to the councils of Wales and the North.

[7] In Soutley v. Price (1630) Cro. Car. 247 it was held that an appeal of murder in Wales could not be tried in the adjoining English counties under 26 Henry VIII. c. 6; but the reporter says in a note at p. 248 that "certioraries have been granted to remove indictments out of the grand sessions ; " in Chedley's case (1634) ibid 331-332 a precedent of 32 Eliza. was cited in which such a writ had been issued, and the court awarded the writ, but afterwards stayed it for further argument, though in 1618 such a writ had been granted, Popham 141; Anon (1670) 1 Vent. 93 a certiorari was awarded; S.C. 1 Mod. 68 sub. nom. the King v. Morris, 2 Kebl. 689, 697-698.

that by 1688 the better opinion in the English courts was that such a writ could be issued to question orders made by the justices of the peace.[1] It was admitted also that both the court of Chancery[2] and the court of Exchequer[3] could exercise their jurisdiction over matters arising in Wales. The great controversy arose over the claim of the King's Bench to execute its process, either final or mesne, in Wales.

Before the end of the seventeenth century it had been decided in the English courts that any of the courts of common law could issue final process into Wales; that is, they could issue writs of fieri facias or elegit to execute a judgment recovered in these courts.[4] But the decision to that effect in *Whitrong* v. *Blaney*[5] had been dissented from by Vaughan, C.J., who has left us an elaborate argument explaining the grounds of his dissent.[6] It would seem from his argument that, in James I.'s reign, the King's Bench had maintained, and the Common Pleas had denied the right of the English courts to issue these writs into Wales;[7] but that in 1613 all the judges and barons of the Exchequer had decided in favour of the view that they could not be thus issued.[8] Vaughan justifies this view by historical considerations based upon the position of the Welsh courts in the Middle Ages. It was clear that in the Middle Ages the Principality of Wales was different from the palatine counties because, as we have seen, it had never formed part of England, whereas the palatine counties had once formed part of England.[9] It was for this reason that the king's writs never ran there, any more than they ran in the Channel Islands, or in any of the subsequently acquired possessions of

---

[1] In Rex v. Inhabitants of Glamorganshire (1701) 1 Ld. Raym. 580 an order of the justices for a levy of money for the repair of Cardiff bridge was removed by certiorari; "Holt, C.J., said, that this matter ought not to be disputed, it being the constant practice to grant certioraris into Wales, as also into the Counties Palatine of Durham and Lancaster, which yet had original jurisdiction. . . . And if the law were otherwise, the Great Sessions were held so seldom, that a man might be ruined before a Great Sessions met;" S.C. 1 Salk. 146.

[2] Tothill 117 (Chester); Harg. Law Tracts 421.

[3] Harg. Law Tracts 421; Stradling v. Morgan (1560) Plowden 199 is an early precedent for the exercise of the Exchequer jurisdiction; see pp. 206-207 where Saunders C.B. held that the words of 34, 35 Henry VIII. c. 26 giving jurisdiction to the Great Sessions did not exclude that of other courts.

[4] Draper v. Blaney (1672) 2 Wms. Saunders 193, S.C. T. Raym. 206; Whitrong v. Blaney (1677) 2 Mod. 10; cf. Needham v. Benet (1668) T. Raym. 171—a fieri facias issued to the sheriff of Chester.

[5] 2 Mod. at p. 13. [6] Vaughan's Rep. 395 seqq.

[7] Ibid 395-397; cf. Hall v. Rotherom (1613) 2 Buls. 54; Sir John Carew's Case (1619) Cro. Jac. 484.

[8] Vaughan Rep. 398—"By this resolution a judgment given in Wales shall not be executed in England, out of their jurisdiction in Wales, and a pari, a judgment given in England ought not to be executed in Wales, which is not of the jurisdiction of the English courts."

[9] Above 120; Vaughan Rep. 412, 418.

England over the seas.[1] It is true that the lands of the Lords
Marchers did form part of England, and that in certain cases
the king's writ ran there;[2] but they had been swept away.[3]
It is true also that Wales and England had been united by Henry
VIII.'s legislation;[4] but that legislation had, he considered,
simply put the whole of Wales into the same independent position as that occupied by the Principality in the Middle Ages,[5]
except in so far as the legislature had provided for the exercise
of control by the English courts in certain particular cases.[6] The
answer given to this reasoning was based on a different interpretation of Henry VIII.'s legislation. It was said that, as by that
legislation Wales was now united to England, there was no
reason why such process should not be sent into Wales, just as it
could be sent into a county palatine.[7] The old maxim " breve
domini regis non currit in Walliam " now only applied, it was said,
to original writs.[8]

The question whether the King's Bench could issue mesne
process (that is, process to compel appearance) into Wales was
not decided till 1779.[9] The question arose upon the claim of
the King's Bench to send their writs of latitat into Wales.[10] We
shall see that these writs of latitat were writs which enabled
common pleas, i.e. actions between subject and subject, to be
tried in the King's Bench.[11] The power to issue these writs into

---

[1] Vaughan, Rep. 400—after the Statute of Wales, " though Wales became of
the dominion of England from that time, yet the courts of England had nothing to
do with the administration of justice there, in other manners than now they have
with the Western Islands, Barbadoes, St. Christophers, Mevis, New England."

[2] Ibid 403-412; above 121; " bringing actions in England, and trying them
in counties adjoining to Wales without knowing the true reason of it, also bringing quare impedits in like manner of churches in Wales, without distinguishing
they were for lands of lordships marchers held by the king, and for churches within
such lordships marchers, has occasioned that great diversity and contrariety of
opinions in our book; and at length that common error, that matters in Wales of
what nature soever, are impleadable in England, and to be tried in the next adjoining county," Vaughan, Rep. 413; but the Y.BB. did not always clearly distinguish
between the Marches and the Principality, see Y.B. 36 Hy. VI. p. 33; cf. Harg.
Law Tracts 404.

[3] Above 124-125.   [4] Above 123.

[5] " So as since this statute the Courts of Westminster have less jurisdiction in
Wales than before; for before they had some in all their lordships marchers, which
were in no county, as by this Act and since, they being all reduced into counties,
either of England or Wales, their jurisdiction is absolute over such of them as are
annexed to English counties, but none over the rest," Vaughan, Rep. 417.

[6] Above 125.

[7] See the successful argument in Stradling v. Morgan (1560) Plowden at p. 207;
Bedo v. Piper (1614) 2 Buls. 156; against which the writer in Harg. Law Tracts
409-411 argues.

[8] Whitrong v. Blaney (1677) 2 Mod. at p. 13.

[9] Penry v. Jones (1779) 1 Dougl. 213, following Lloyd v. Jones (1769) ibid
n. 10.

[10] The argument in Harg. Law Tracts 377-423 is upon this particular point.

[11] Below 219-220.

Wales meant in substance that any person in Wales could elect to sue in the King's Bench instead of in the court of Great Sessions. Much the same reasons were urged against this practice as were urged against the issue of final process into Wales ; and in 1747, in the case of *Lampley* v. *Thomas*,[1] these arguments prevailed. But in *Penry* v. *Jones*[2] in 1779 that decision was reversed; and that reversal was probably justified by a statute of 1773,[3] in which the rights of all the courts of common law to hold pleas and issue mesne process against residents in Wales was assumed to exist.

Thus in almost all actions the courts of Westminster had established a right to exercise a jurisdiction concurrent with that of the courts of Great Sessions. This made the position of the courts of Great Sessions somewhat anomalous. In theory they could exercise the full jurisdiction of the courts of common law and the Chancery : in practice they were in effect local courts for Wales.[4] And both their procedure and the quality of the men by which they were staffed left a good deal to be desired.[5] It is not surprising that, towards the end of the eighteenth and at the beginning of the nineteenth centuries, suggestions were made for their reform or abolition.[6] The beginning of the end came after the attack made by Brougham on the abuses of the judicial system in 1828.[7] As a result of that attack a commission was appointed to enquire into the practice and procedure of the common law courts. Select committees had already reported on the Welsh courts ;[8] and a considerable part of the first report of the common law commissioners was devoted to the same subject.[9] As a result of their report an Act was passed in 1830[10] which abolished the palatine courts of Chester and the courts of Great Sessions in Wales, added an additional judge to the three courts of common law, extended the English

[1] 1 Wils. 193 ; it may be noted that it had been held in Chapman v. Mattison (1738) Andrews 191 that a writ of latitat could issue into Durham ; for some strictures on this decision see Harg. Law Tracts 417-419.

[2] 1 Dougl. 213.

[3] 13 George III. c. 15 § 2—" In all transitory actions which shall be brought in any of His Majesty's courts of record out of Wales, if it shall appear that the defendant was resident in Wales at the time of the service of any writ, or other mesne process served on him, etc."

[4] Between 1825 and 1829 Welsh actions in the court of Exchequer numbered 891, in the King's Bench 2956, in the Common Pleas 383, Parlt. Papers 1830 xx pp. 147, 155; between 1829 and 1839 in all the Welsh courts there were only 355 bills in Equity filed, and only 93 decrees, ibid 99-141, 149-154.

[5] First Report of the Common Law Commissioners, Parlt. Papers 1829 ix 35, 38 ; cf. Rhys and Brynmor Jones, op. cit. 391.

[6] In 1780 Burke had made a proposal substantially similar to that carried into effect in 1830, Rhys and Brynmor Jones 387.

[7] Ibid.   [8] Ibid.

[9] Parlt. Papers 1829 ix 35-52.   [10] 11 George IV. 1, William IV. c. 70.

circuit system to Chester and Wales, and transferred the equitable
jurisdiction of the Welsh courts to the court of Chancery or the
court of Exchequer.

In the long run the assimilation of the English and Welsh
judicial systems has probably been beneficial. But the separate
Welsh system, though it had its defects, had two merits—it gave
to Welshmen a system of local courts, and probably a cheaper
justice than could then be had at Westminster.[1] It was not till
the establishment of the new county courts in 1846,[2] and the
reforms effected during the nineteenth century in the machinery
of the superior courts of law and equity,[3] that the disadvantages
attendant upon the reform of 1830 disappeared.

(2) The Lesser Franchises.

The *Quo Warranto* enquiries resulted, as we have seen, in
confirming the title of the holders of franchises if they could
show that they had enjoyed them from the first year of Richard
I.'s reign.[4] There were many varieties of such franchises. Some
were granted by the old Saxon terms sac and soc, toll and team,
infangthef and utfangthef;[5] and others in the new technical
language of the common law. Instances of the latter are
returnus brevium, amerciamenta hominum, catalla felonum, the
right to hold fairs, the right to appoint coroners, the right to
hold the hundred court, and, most common of all, the view of
frankpledge, to which there is usually attached the right to hold
the assize of bread and beer.[6]

But these lesser franchises tended to become of gradually
less importance. This was due chiefly to two causes. (i) Though
the verdicts of the juries would lead us to suppose that they
were on the whole popular in the time of Edward I., they gradually lost their popularity.[7] Further grants were made the subject
of protests in Parliament. Their creation was a grievance of the
same character as the letting to ferm of hundreds at excessive
rates. We have, for instance, in Edward III.'s reign a complaint
that the king has granted to the Count of Arundel and Surrey
the two sheriff's tourns in the rapes of Chichester and Arundel.
The count has set up within them a new court, held from three
weeks to three weeks, which he calls a shire court. Pleas which

---

[1] On this point the common law commissioners found that the evidence was
conflicting, Parlt. Papers 1829 ix 37.
[2] Below 191.   [3] Below chap. viii.   [4] Above 88-89.
[5] See the Eyre of Kent (S.S.) i 104-105, 130, 133, 147.
[6] P. and M. i. 567-571; for the right to hold fairs see below 535-537; in the
Eyre of Kent (S.S.) iii 193 the right to the goods of felons was limited to the right
to goods of felons who held an estate of freehold from the lord.
[7] Select Pleas in Manorial Courts lxxvii n. C.

ought to be pleaded in the county courts are there pleaded; and the annual profit is £30. Besides the king has granted the count a certain rent which they' assert belongs to the county, and yet the county pays the same ferm as before.[1] The franchise jurisdiction was therefore attacked from two sides. It was obnoxious to the crown and it was disliked by Parliament. (ii) The new processes of the courts of common law, the new jurisdiction of the judges of assize and the justices of the peace, worked more smoothly. The procedure of the old courts was archaic, and so they declined for much the same reasons as the county and hundred courts declined.[2] They did, however, survive, just as the hundred and county courts survived; but they tended more and more to become merely interesting relics of antiquity, such as the Halifax gibbet law,[3]—said by Palgrave to be the last vestige of the law of infangthef—which recall the old customs of the days before the common law.

They survived mainly because it has never been the practice of English statesmen to abolish institutions merely because they are decaying, provided that they do not constitute a crying grievance. And these franchise jurisdictions were, from the thirteenth and fourteenth centuries onwards, so controlled by the courts of common law that they never became very crying grievances. The control thus exercised in the Middle Ages paved the way for the statements and theories of the law books of the sixteenth and seventeenth centuries, which classified the various franchise, feudal, and manorial courts, and definitely fixed their place in the English judicial system.[4] Hence, throughout the course of English history, right down to the eighteenth and nineteenth centuries, these jurisdictions are in evidence. They give rise to reported cases, are mentioned in statutes, and supply material for text-books. Thus, in the middle of the fourteenth century, the franchise of amerciamenta hominum was held to entitle its owners to the penalties imposed by the Statutes of Labourers;[5] in 1674, on the petition

---

[1] Rot. Parl. ii 348 no. 147; with respect to the leet jurisdiction (below 135-137) Parliament in the fourteenth and fifteenth centuries was not altogether consistent; it sometimes asked that no more grants of such jurisdiction be made, sometimes that fresh powers be conferred on leets, see Hearnshaw, Leet Jurisdiction in England 151-152; we have seen that the machinery of the eyre was used to control these jurisdictions, above 89, 90; and the fact that in Edward III.'s reign the crown continued to make frequent use of the procedure of Quo Warranto can be seen from Keilway's reports, Reeves, H.E.L. ii 429 n. a.

[2] Above 89.　　　　　　　　　[3] Stephen, H.C.L. i 265-270.

[4] For these books see vol. iv 120-121, 130-131.

[5] Putnam, The Enforcement of the Statutes of Labourers 138-149; for these statutes see vol. ii 459-463; it would appear that the ordinance of labourers of 1349, as distinct from the Statutes was enforceable in the courts of lords and in the old local courts, Putnam, op. cit. 161, and that these courts occasionally, but not

of Lady Wentworth, the privilege of returnus brevium, annexed to the manor of Stepney, was admitted to exist by the law officers of the crown, and confirmed by the king;[1] in a statute of 1849 it is assumed that there are lords of liberties who have gaols of their own;[2] and we shall see that a thin stream of cases from the Year Books of Edward I.'s reign down to the nineteenth century is concerned with various points connected with the leet jurisdiction.[3]

The most common of these franchises are the right to hold a hundred court and the right to hold a court leet. We have seen that the hundred court and the sheriff's tourn were closely related institutions.[4] Hence it is not surprising to find that the right to hold a hundred court and the right to hold a court leet, that is to exercise the jurisdictions exercised by the sheriff in his tourn, are frequently found in the hands of the same persons. Of these hundred courts and courts leet, therefore, I must say a few words.

There were a large number of cases in the Middle Ages in which the right to hold the hundred court existed, and in a few cases it lasted right down to the nineteenth century.[5] But in the course of the eighteenth century these courts had come to be, for the most part, simply courts for the collection of petty debts.[6] One or two, it is true, in places which developed into densely populated urban districts, continued to be active courts. A striking instance is the court of the hundred of Salford,[7] which, in the nineteenth century, got new statutory powers, attained the status of a court of record, and still exists.[8] In Cheshire also the court for the hundred of Wirral, because it included Birkenhead, continued to be an active court till the middle of the nineteenth century.[9] But it is clear from the description of fifty-six hundred courts, made in a return to the House of Commons in 1839,[10] that in the years 1835, 1836, and 1837, many sat only one or two days in the year, and did little or no work; and even those which sat at more frequent intervals had very little business.

frequently enforced the Statute of 1351, ibid 163-165; this would have been impossible after the rule had been settled that such courts could not enforce statutes unless the statute itself gave it the jurisdiction, see below 136 for the evolution of this principle in the case of the leet.

[1] S.P. Dom. 1673-1675, 240-241, 323.　　　　[2] 12, 13 Victoria c. 101 § 4.
[3] Below 137.　　　　　　　　　　　　　　　[4] Above 72, 76.
[5] See Webb, Local Government, the Manor and Borough 50-63.
[6] Ibid 51.　　　　　　　　　　　　　　　　[7] Ibid 52-57.
[8] In 1846 its jurisdiction was enlarged, 9, 10 Victoria c. 126; in 1866 it was amalgamated with the court of Record held by the Manchester Corporation, and was given the title of the Salford Hundred Court of Record, 31, 32 Victoria c. 130, ibid 57 n. 3; the latest Act dealing with the Court is 1, 2 George V. c. clxxii.
[9] Webb, op. cit. 61.
[10] Return of Hundred Courts, Parlt. Papers 1839 xliii 265.

The term court leet was applied to a court which exercised the jurisdiction of the sheriff's tourn;[1] and to this jurisdiction was usually joined the right to hold the assize of bread and beer.[2] The word "leet" is an East Anglian word.[3] Originally the leet seems to have meant a geographical division of the hundred; but, in the Hundred Rolls and the Placita Quo Warranto, it is used in East Anglia to signify a jurisdictional area. The term did not, however, then denote a definite kind of jurisdiction. Generally the claim to hold a leet was accompanied by a long explanation of the kind of jurisdiction claimed. "It would appear," says Professor Hearnshaw,[4] "that, at the end of the thirteenth century, and in East Anglia, to possess a 'leet' was to have a court which . . . had within a defined geographical area and at specified times certain . . . rights of petty criminal jurisdiction and police control . . . among which the view of frankpledge was the chief." Its use in the Hundred Rolls seems to have popularized the word. In the course of the fourteenth century it spread over England. It was used to express the jurisdiction exercisable in the tourn; and the court which exercised it was, in the sixteenth century, distinguished by the lawyers from the feudal or manorial courts, in which its jurisdiction was exercised, and from which in practice it was seldom distinguished or distinguishable.[5]

This leet jurisdiction was frequently exercised both by lords of manors and by boroughs; and in both cases it was a court of the mediæval type which did governmental as well as judicial work. The franchise was valued by the lords of manors because it gave the lord a better hold over his tenants; it facilitated the work of managing his manor through his manorial courts; and it prevented the sheriff from interfering with his tenants.[6] It was used by many of the boroughs in the Middle Ages as the chief instrument for the government of the borough.[7] At Norwich, for instance,[8] in the precinct of the Savoy,[9] and at Southampton, it was used in this way;[10] and Professor Hearnshaw

---

[1] The style of the court is, "Curia visus franciplegii tenta apud B. coram A.B. senescallo."

[2] Select Pleas in Manorial Courts (S.S.) xxvii-xxxviii; P. and M. i 567-570; in the Eyre of Kent (S.S.) iii 182, 208 it is said that this franchise is included in the view of frankpledge, though these may be claimed separately, ibid 193; there are also some stray dicta to the effect that it might include the rights to wreck and waif, ibid xxxv-xxxvi, and warren ibid 168-169.

[3] For the history of the evolution of the word leet and its derivation see Hearnshaw, Leet Jurisdiction in England 11-17; cf. Select Pleas in Manorial Courts (S.S.) lxxiii n. A.

[4] Op. cit. 13.

[5] Hearnshaw, op. cit. 19; Webb, op. cit. 64-75; below 182.

[6] P. and M. i 568; below 185.   [7] Vol. ii 390; vol. iv 132.

[8] Leet Jurisdiction in Norwich (S.S.).   [9] Webb, op. cit. 96-98.

[10] Hearnshaw, op. cit. Pt. II. section 2.

has collected many other instances in which a court with leet jurisdiction was among the franchises of a borough.[1] In one instance at Manchester the court actually developed with the development of the town, and became its governing authority.[2] But this was an exceptional case due largely to the failure of Manchester to obtain recognition as a true borough.[3] Generally courts leet, whether held by lords of manors or by boroughs, tended to decline in power and importance from the sixteenth century onwards, because they were superseded by the newer and more effective machinery of the justices of the peace both in boroughs and in the country at large.[4] Professor Hearnshaw says of the court leet of Southampton that its records from 1550-1750 show a court which was already " clearly deep sunk in decay and continuously sinking deeper ; "[5] a court, the independent jurisdiction of which was a thing of the past.   The leet jury had become " the mere agent of a higher local authority, viz. the municipal corporation," and particularly of the magistrates—" The nine leading burgesses who, under the charter of Henry IV. had been endowed with the prerogatives of justices of the peace."[6] What happened at Southampton happened at many other towns and places; nor are the causes of this decay far to seek.

In the first place, the fact that it worked by means of the presentment of a jury made it gradually more and more ineffective to deal with the growing number and complexity of the problems of local government.[7] In the second place, even if presentments were made, it could do little to coerce offenders. It could only command the services of unpaid officials,[8] and it could only fine or amerce—it could not imprison.[9] In the third place it could generally only meet twice a year.[10] In the fourth place, it was rigidly limited to its common law powers.   It could only take cognizance of the newer statutory offences if it had been given power to do so by the statute which created the offence.[11]

---

[1] Hearnshaw, op. cit. Pt. II. section 3 chap. xxxiv.

[2] Webb, op. cit. 99-113 ; Hearnshaw, op. cit. 285-288.

[3] Ibid 287-288.   [4] Below 143, 285, 287-288 ; vol. iv 133.

[5] Op. cit. 225.   [6] Ibid 226.

[7] Ibid 356-357; Webb, op. cit. 122-125.   [8] Ibid 125.

[9] Godfrey's Case (1614) 11 Co. Rep. 43 ; Professor Hearnshaw, op. cit. 134, thinks that Coke was the first to lay it down definitely that the leet could not imprison ; and he points out that this opinion was vigorously combated by Ritson, Jurisdiction of the Court Leet xvii.

[10] § 35 of Magna Carta of 1225, which fixed Easter and Michaelmas as the times for holding the tourn, was taken to apply to the leet, Hearnshaw, op. cit. 79-80; but by prescription it could be held more frequently, R. v. Jennings (1711) 11 Mod. at p. 228 *per* Holt, C.J.

[11] Y.B. 4 Ed. IV. Mich. pl. 12; Brook, Ab. *Lete* pl. 25.

But, though it was clearly decadent in the sixteenth century, the process of decay was slow—far slower than in the case of the sheriff's tourn. Duties were still conferred upon it, in conjunction with the justices of the peace, by statutes of the sixteenth and seventeenth centuries [1]—indeed a statute of 1605 [2] would seem to show that Stewards were making considerable profits out of the jurisdiction they exercised in the leet. In 1631 the Council issued a set of Orders and Directions to Stewards who kept their lords' leets as to matters into which they ought to enquire; [3] its doings were supervised by the court of Star Chamber; [4] in 1662 its power to appoint Constables was assumed; [5] and its existence was recognized by statutes of the eighteenth century. [6] Cases of the seventeenth, eighteenth, and nineteenth centuries enforced the performance of the duties which the leet jurisdiction entailed, and recognized the powers still possessed by the court. [7]

The long life of these two franchises which we have just been considering is attested by quite modern statutes, the County Court Acts 1846-1868 recognize the vested interests of lords of hundreds. [8] The Sheriffs Act of 1887, though it abolished the tourn, [9] recognized the existence of the leet; [10] and it is obliged to contemplate, just as the Assize of Clarendon was obliged to contemplate, the liberty into which the sheriff has no right to enter. [11] That they had so long a life is due in large measure to the fact that they belonged, either to lords who exercised them together with their feudal or manorial jurisdiction, or to boroughs

[1] See e.g. 14, 15 Henry VIII. c. 10; 33 Henry VIII. c. 9; 7 Edward VI. c. 5 § 6; 2, 3 Philip and Mary c. 8; 31 Elizabeth c. 7; 21 James I. c. 21; and cf. the list of statutes given by Hearnshaw, op. cit. App. II.

[2] 2 James I. c. 5.

[3] See the Orders cited Webb, op. cit. 117 n. 3.

[4] Abbot of Peterborough v. Power and others (1518) Select Cases in the Star Chamber (S.S.) ii 123-142; cf. Knight v. Gunter and others (1534) ibid. ii 216-217 for a case turning on the manner in which the town of Andover enforced the assize of bread and beer.

[5] 14 Charles II. c. 12 § 15.

[6] E.g. 11 George I. c. 4 § 3; 1 George II. St. 2 c. 19; 35 George III. c. 102.

[7] Cook v. Stubbs (1621) Cro. Jac. 583—case of an inferior within a superior leet; R. v. Jennings (1711) 11 Mod. 215—indictment for refusing to serve as high constable; Colebrook v. Elliot (1766) 3 Burr. 1859—debt for an amercement set and affeered in the leet of the manor of Stepney; Davidson v. Moscrop (1801) 2 East 56 —custom of a leet held bad; R. v. Adlard (1825) 4 B. and C. 772—liability to serve as constable; Willock v. Windsor (1832) 3 B. and Ad. 43—right to examine measures; R. v. Lord of the Hundred of Milverton (1835) 3 Ad. and Ell. 284— Mandamus to compel the lord of a hundred to hold a court leet.

[8] 9, 10 Victoria c. 95 §§ 11, 13, 14; 51, 52 Victoria c. 43 § 6.

[9] Above 81.

[10] " Notwithstanding the repeal of any enactment by this Act every court leet, court baron, law day, view of frankpledge, or other like court, which is held at the passing of this Act shall continue to be held on the days and in the places heretofore accustomed," 50, 51 Victoria c. 55, § 40 (1).

[11] 50, 51 Victoria c. 55, §§ 10 (2), 34, 35.

which exercised them together with the other franchises granted to them by their charter of incorporation. But this we shall see more clearly when we have examined these two sorts of jurisdiction. With the feudal and manorial jurisdiction I shall deal when I have completed my survey of the franchise jurisdictions. The jurisdiction of the borough courts I shall now describe.

The Boroughs

We have seen that, even before the Norman Conquest, the borough community had begun to develop features which distinguished it from the communities of township, hundred, and shire; and that these boroughs often had a distinct organization, a peculiar customary law, special privileges and fiscal responsibilities, and special courts. But we have seen that, though they thus differed from the rural communities, they were organized and governed in a manner very similar to these rural communities; and that they were, for some time after the Conquest, less definitely personified than such rural communities as the hundred and the shire.[1] Of the manner in which the borough community gradually acquired a distinct corporate personality, and thus gradually separated itself from the communities of township, manor, hundred, and shire, I shall say something more in later volumes of this History.[2] Here I shall speak only of the separate franchise jurisdictions exercised by the boroughs, the existence of which was not the least important of the causes which made the boroughs a separate and a corporate entity in the governmental, social, and economic life of the nation. But in order to understand the origin and history of these franchise jurisdictions a few introductory words are necessary as to the genesis of the very many different kinds of borough community which have flourished in England from the thirteenth century onwards.

Many causes, in no two cases quite alike, went to make up the peculiar community which the thirteenth century recognized as a borough; and, on the surface of our older boroughs, we may see memorials of many of those features which formed the differentiæ of this species of community. If we look at the walls and the castles of some of the boroughs; if, with the eye of the military strategist, we look at their geographical position, we may think of the Saxon burh—the more strictly organized form of township—the walls of which were repaired and defended by burgesses who were retainers of the great men of the

---

[1] Above 30-31.   [2] Vol. ii 392-395; vol. iii 474-475.

shire.[1] If we look at the boroughs which are the capitals of their counties we may think of them as fortified and readily defensible places which were the governmental centres of their counties.[2] If we look at the market-places of the boroughs we shall think of them as the centres of the trade of the county, and perhaps of a larger district;[3] and if, knowing something of the institutions of some particular borough and of the history of these institutions, we remember that the borough has or had a gild or gilds, we shall think of the boroughs not merely as a place where at intervals a market is held, but as a place which carries on a permanent trade and perhaps is the seat of some manufacturing industry.[4] We shall think of them as communities of traders, not necessarily resident within the borough,[5] exercising sometimes a greater, sometimes a lesser influence upon the borough government, and making and administering the rules which regulated the conditions of their trade.[6] If we look at the borough courts as they exist at the present day, we shall probably see efficient institutions of statutory origin;[7] but we may perhaps in some boroughs see a court which can deduce its title from a franchise granted by royal charter;[8] and we shall remember that a court—communal or franchise—was always characteristic of a borough.[9] In some of the boroughs we may see that the borough territory comprises many acres, and that the inhabitants of some boroughs have, even at the present day, rights of common.[10] We may remember that in the beginning the burh was simply a more organized township, and that it was only by degrees that it first transformed and finally put off its landowning—its agricultural—characteristics, as the urban and the commercial elements gradually became predominant.[11] These last characteristics

[1] For this " garrison theory " see Maitland, Domesday Book and Beyond 172-219; E.H.R. xii 768; Maitland, Township and Borough 209-211; Ballard, Domesday Boroughs.

[2] Maitland, Township and Borough, 36-40, 51, 52.

[3] Ibid 40; Domesday Book and Beyond 192-195, and references there cited to the Anglo-Saxon laws forbidding purchases except in a burh or port before the official witnesses; as Maitland notes, the coinage of money is limited by many of these laws to certain burhs.

[4] Below 540-541.

[5] Gross, Gild Merchant i 66-68; ii 14; Domesday of Ipswich 171, 173; Green, Town Life i 192.

[6] P. and M. i 651, 652; Gross, Gild Merchant ii 3-12; Records of Leicester (Bateson) i, xxvii 86-114; Green, Town Life ii 202-217 for the gilds at Coventry.

[7] Below 150-151.   [8] Below 151; L.Q.R. xviii 376-387.

[9] Domesday Book and Beyond 210-212; P. and M. i 627-629.

[10] Maitland, Township and Borough 1-11, and Municipal Corporations Report (1835) iii 1849 there cited; Gross, Gild Merchant i 4; Leicester Records ix; Tait, Manchester, 102-104; Green, Town Life ii 234, 238, 239, 314, 317, 335-336; Vinogradoff, English Society 398-401.

[11] We may perhaps see some signs of this transformation in the unsuccessful argument used by Herle in 1312-1313 that, " by common law land cannot be appendant to burgage, for burgage is nothing but a messuage in a vill or borough, and

unite the borough to the land, and should remind us that the
borough community, though a different variety, is not a different
genus from that of the other communities with which England
of the early Middle Ages is peopled.[1]   It is a district, then as
now, more closely peopled.   Then as now, its inhabitants are
occupied with more varied pursuits—commerce and handicrafts,
as well as war and agriculture.   Then as now, its life is more
intense.   But, in its origin and in its history, in its organization
and in its customs, it has experienced similar fortunes and maintained some family likeness to the county at large.

The boroughs felt the influences which made for the growth
of dependency in the latter part of the Anglo-Saxon period.
Some fell under the sway of mesne lords.[2]   Some, again, in the
period just before and just after the Norman Conquest, when the
greater lords were very free to usurp the powers of government,
were created by these lords and were allowed to spring up upon
their estates for reasons of defence or for reasons of trade similar
to those which in past times had made the county boroughs
a distinct yet homogeneous unit in the county organization.[3]
When the jurisdiction of the king's court began to control
effectively the exercise of all franchise jurisdictions, and to reduce them to some order and to definite categories, the boroughs
were treated in the same manner as the other franchise holders
of the county.   We begin to expect to see certain types of
franchise in a borough charter.   One borough will get a charter
in which its privileges are defined by reference to those of another
chartered borough.[4]   Certain types of charters become favourites.
For this reason the term "borough" begins to take upon itself a
more definite meaning ; and when lords allow boroughs to be
set up upon their demesnes, these boroughs will tend to conform
to the type which the law is gradually creating.   One borough
will borrow the customs, just as it borrowed the form of the
charter, of another.   Some will perhaps take their customs from

---

if a common were appendant, how would the admeasurement be made ? "   Y.B.
6 Ed. II. (S.S.) 113.

[1] The case with which a mere vill might become a borough is illustrated by a
statement of Toudeby *arg* in Y.B. 6, 7 Ed. II. (S.S.) 222—" It is all one vill, though
they have established a market at one end of the vill, and they now call that the
vill of Burgh."

[2] Domesday Book and Beyond 212-214, 218.

[3] E.H.R. xvi 343 ; Tait, Manchester 43 seqq. ; R.P. i 26-29 for the founding of
South Shields and Tynemouth ; for the founding of Wearmouth see R.H. ii 20 ;
Parlt. Roll 1305 (R.S.) No. 124 we see the lord petitioning for privileges for the
borough and himself.   It would appear that the king could not grant franchises to
another's tenant over the head of the lord, Y.B. 20 Ed. III. (R.S.) i 158.

[4] Below 529 ; there will also be consultation as to interpretation of the common
customs, see Calendar of Wills in the Court of Hustings i, vi, vii for two cases in
Edward III.'s reign in which Oxford thus consulted London.

a foreign source.[1]   But we shall see that no borough could escape the influence of the common law administered in the king's central courts and by his justices in eyre.   They might exclude the sheriff, just as many other holders of franchises might exclude him.[2]   They might have their courts and their gilds and their special customs.   They could not exclude the royal judges nor escape the influence of a common law which kept a watchful eye upon the reasonableness of the subject matter and upon the efficiency of the administration of their customs.[3]   Thus controlled by the common law, and thus connected in many ways by their history, their organization, and their interests with the counties of which they were an integral part, they naturally took their places in a national Parliament beside the representatives of the counties, as a different section, but, for all that, a section of the same estate of the realm.[4]   And the fact that they thus formed a part of the House of Commons in a national Parliament may remind us that the growth of the power of the House of Commons was the cause for the creation of many boroughs in the sixteenth century merely because they were insignificant. They were from the first under the control of the king or wealthy landowners ; and for that reason they retained their position as constituencies till 1832, and as boroughs for an even longer period.

The diversity of causes which went to the creation of boroughs in the Middle Ages and later explains the diversity between the various specimens of borough community.   In fact, as Webb has pointed out,[5] the series of borough communities displays an almost infinite series of gradations from a community, the organization of which is closely akin to that of the rural manor, to great municipal corporations like London or Bristol.   But, in spite of the diversity of borough institutions thus produced, the control both of Parliament and the common law tended to preserve the likeness between the borough institutions and those of the country at large ; thus it happens that the franchise jurisdictions of the boroughs both in their origin and history display

---

[1] See E.H.R. xv 72, 302, 496, 754, and xvi 92, 322 for the influence of the laws of Breteuil ; below 529 ; vol. ii 399 and n. 8.

[2] Above 137.   [3] Vol. ii 400.   [4] Ibid. 306.

[5] Webb, Local Government, the Manor and Borough, classifies the heterogeneous specimens as follows : (1) Manorial boroughs ; this includes (a) places which had a lordless court, and practically no municipal structure, (b) the lord's borough where there was a municipal structure which centred round the lord's court, and (c) the enfranchised manorial borough (at p. 148).   (2) Municipal corporations, i.e. those boroughs which had a separate commission of the peace (at pp. 266, 267) ; and the extent to which the boroughs in this group were freed from the jurisdiction of the county officials varied considerably (at pp. 281, 282, 382).

many fundamental similarities to the other franchise jurisdictions.

" The immigrant from a rural Manor or a Manorial Borough,"
says Webb,[1] " would take for granted the existence of Courts, at
which his obligations as a ' resiant ' or a Burgess, as a neighbour
or a ' foreignor ' would be enforced.   In some of the smaller and
more archaic Municipal Corporations he would find Courts bearing exactly the same names, and wielding exactly the same powers
as those of rural manors.   In a few instances he would even find
one or other of the courts in the Borough still continuing to be
held by the Lord's Steward, in the name and for the profit of an
individual Lord of the Manor.   But if our rural immigrant
entered the jurisdiction of one of the more powerful of the
Municipal Corporations, he would be surprised at the number
and variety of the Courts held by the Mayor or one or other of
the Chief Officers, at their strange titles, at their multifarious
officials, and above all, at the extent of the authority that they
exercised over his conduct and his property."   In spite, however,
of the variety of these courts it is possible to classify them according to the jurisdiction which they exercised.   They were
courts which exercised either a criminal, a civil, or a special
jurisdiction.   With the last class of courts, the most important
of which were courts exercising either a commercial or an
Admiralty jurisdiction, I shall deal in a later chapter.[2]   Here I
shall deal (i) with the courts exercising a criminal jurisdiction,
and (ii) with those exercising a civil jurisdiction.

(i) Courts exercising a criminal jurisdiction.

We have seen that, before the end of the thirteenth century,
the crown had got exclusive jurisdiction over treason and felony,[3]
and that the court which exercised jurisdiction in petty criminal
cases was the sheriff's tourn or the court leet.[4]   Hence, if a
borough had the right to exercise criminal jurisdiction within its
limits, it necessarily had the right to hold a court leet.   In a
few cases, indeed, the lord of the manor in which the borough
was situated retained the right to hold this court ;[5] but in all

[1] Local Government, the Manor and Borough 337.
[2] Below 535-543; we find also other courts with a special jurisdiction ; thus at
Boston (Halsbury, Laws of England ix 146), High Wycombe (ibid 154), Faversham
(ibid 162), Guildford (ibid 165), Helston (ibid 167), Hertford (ibid 168), Northampton
(ibid 185), St. Albans (ibid 196), Winchester (ibid 212), Windsor (ibid 212), York
(ibid 214), there were courts of the clerks of the market ; there were bailiff's courts
at Chichester and Ipswich (ibid 153, 169) ; at Lynn there was a court of Tolbooth
for determining civil pleas if the cause of action arose on the water (ibid 180) ; at
Newcastle-upon-Tyne and York there were courts of conservancy (ibid 184, 214).
[3] Above 71-72.   [4] Above 76-81, 135-137.
[5] Thus at Macclesfield the Earl of Derby held a court leet in the town, Halsbury,
Laws of England ix 180 ; Webb, op. cit. 344.

but the most rudimentary borough communities this right had generally been acquired by the borough before the end of the seventeenth century.[1] We have seen that the court leet was, like many other mediæval courts, a governmental body as well as a law court.[2] Therefore in some cases the court leet developed into the governing body of the borough.[3] But in most boroughs the court leet gradually disappeared during the course of the seventeenth and eighteenth centuries ;[4] and it disappeared for the same reason as it disappeared in the country at large—the effective rivalry of the justices of the peace.[5]

From about the middle of the sixteenth century it became common for borough charters to make the mayor, some of the other corporate officials, and some of the aldermen, justices of the peace.[6] Some of these charters gave the right to hold a court of quarter sessions with a varying jurisdiction : others only conferred the right to hold a court of petty sessions.[7] Thus it happened that, from this time onwards, the position of the borough, in relation to the administration of criminal justice, depended on the question whether or not it had a separate commission of the peace ; and, if it had, upon the powers conferred upon the justices appointed under that commission.

In the boroughs which had the right to hold a court of quarter sessions the court leet was either gradually superseded by, or amalgamated with, the court of quarter sessions.[8] This amalgamation was the more easy to effect because the procedure of the quarter sessions was originally modelled on that of the leet. For the purpose of both of these courts a jury was summoned ; at both the jury were given a charge as to the matters which they must present ; and at both the business of the court centered round these presentments.[9] Thus in many places the transition from one tribunal to the other was very gradual, and was almost unnoticed.[10] It did not follow, however, that because a borough had the right to hold a separate court of quarter sessions that the jurisdiction of the county quarter sessions was excluded. The jurisdiction of the county quarter sessions was only excluded

---

[1] " In nearly all the Municipalities the Corporation had acquired the right to hold its own Court Leet, in a few cases by specific grant from the king, embodied in a Charter," Webb, op. cit. 344.

[2] Above 135. [3] Above 135-136. [4] Webb, op. cit. 345-349.

[5] Ibid 349-350 ; for the Justices of the Peace see below 285-288.

[6] Ibid 349.

[7] Ibid 280-281—in one case—Chester—the justices could even deal with treason.

[8] " What is peculiar to the process in the boroughs is the curious intermingling of the structures of the two courts—almost simulating an evolutionary process—that we see taking place," ibid 350.

[9] Vol. iv 132, 133. [10] Webb, op. cit. 352-353.

in cases where the borough quarter sessions had the same wide jurisdiction over all misdemeanours and felonies as that possessed by the county quarter sessions, and where the jurisdiction of the county quarter sessions was expressly excluded by a " non-intro-mittant " clause in the charter of the borough ;[1] and this is still the law ;[2] so that, as Maitland has said, the question whether the county justices are excluded depends " rather on past good fortune than on present importance."[3] Before the passing of the Municipal Corporations Acts of 1835 and 1883,[4] the results of this rule were much more anomalous than now, because wide powers of this kind were sometimes conferred upon quite insignificant boroughs, while other much more populous boroughs did not possess them.[5] In the boroughs which had the right to hold only courts of petty sessions these courts, together with the county quarter sessions, tended to absorb the work formerly done by the leet ;[6] and in those boroughs which had no separate commission of the peace this work fell to the county justices.

In those boroughs which had a separate court of quarter sessions it was usual to put upon the commission the chief officials of the borough. Thus says Webb,[7] " The Bench came to be usually occupied by the same three or four persons, and the fact that among them was, in the more important boroughs, the salaried Recorder—nearly always a trained professional lawyer—necessarily made this tribunal much more like a modern court of justice than the amateur shifting bench at the Quarter Sessions of the County." We have seen that many boroughs had either no court of quarter sessions, or no separate commission of the peace. They were therefore necessarily subject to the exclusive jurisdiction of the county quarter sessions. But some of these boroughs had, in consequence of the industrial revolution at the end of the eighteenth century, become very populous places ; and other populous places, such as Birmingham and Manchester, had never been incorporated. In these populous places the number of cases to be dealt with was more than an unpaid body of justices could manage. It was for this reason

---

[1] Webb, op. cit. 282 ; Maitland, Justice and Police 97.

[2] 5, 6 William IV. c. 76 § 107 ; cf. 45, 46 Victoria c. 50 § 154 (2) ; Stephen, H.C.L. i 120.

[3] Justice and Police 97 n. 1.

[4] 5, 6 William IV. c. 76 ; 46, 47 Victoria c. 18.

[5] Webb, op. cit. 281 n. 6 ; for the provisions of the Municipal Corporation Acts of 1835 and 1883 which have diminished this anomaly see below 145; but as Stephen points out H.C.L. i 119 n. 1 a large criminal jurisdiction was still left (in theory) to many small places who were not enumerated in the schedule to the Act of 1835; but many such places have now ceased to be boroughs under the Act of 1883, see Maitland, Justice and Police 94-95.

[6] Webb, op. cit. 357-358.   [7] Ibid 356.

that, in 1835, the Municipal Corporations Act provided a scheme under which the more important boroughs could do what some had done before, and get a court presided over by a paid professional lawyer.

According to that Act certain boroughs specified in the schedules to the Act were allowed to apply to the crown for a separate court of quarter sessions.[1] This court, if granted, was to be presided over by a recorder who was to be paid by the borough. He was to be appointed by the crown from amongst barristers of five years' standing, and was to be the sole judge of the court.[2] All boroughs which had not thus acquired a separate court of quarter sessions were to lose all the criminal jurisdiction which they had heretofore enjoyed, whether by virtue of charter or statute.[3] Since 1835 many new towns—such as Manchester and Birmingham—have acquired separate courts of quarter sessions;[4] and in 1882 a new Municipal Corporations Act consolidated the existing law on this subject.[5]

London does not fall under the provisions of these Acts. It is by charter a county. The Mayor, the recorder, and the aldermen hold a court of quarter sessions both for the City of London and the borough of Southwark;[6] but, as the Central Criminal Court has concurrent jurisdiction in the case of offences occurring in the City, such offences are usually tried there.[7] Since London spreads over a large part of Middlesex it was necessary to make special provisions for the holding of quarter sessions in that county. In 1844 it was provided that quarter or general sessions should be held for Middlesex twice a month, and that they should be presided over by a paid assistant judge.[8]

The causes which led to the creation in the more important boroughs of separate courts of quarter sessions, staffed by professional judges, operated quite as strongly in the case of the summary jurisdiction of the justices exercised in petty sessions. The mass of petty offences arising in a large town was clearly beyond the capacity of amateur justices; and in such towns it was not likely that the persons fit to exercise this jurisdiction would have the leisure to undertake it. The evils of attempting to exercise it by unpaid justices were seen in London at an earlier period than in any other town ; and the remedy devised for London has been applied to other large towns.

As early as the seventeenth century we hear of justices who

[1] 5, 6 William IV. c. 76 § 103.　　　[2] §§ 103, 105.
[3] § 107.　　　[4] Stephen, H.C.L. i 117, 118.
[5] 45, 46 Victoria c. 50 Pt. VIII.　　　[6] Stephen, H.C.L. i 118.
[7] Halsbury, Laws of England ix 177, 178; for the Central Criminal Court see below 285.
[8] 7, 8 Victoria c. 71 ; see also 22, 23 Victoria c. 4.

set out to make a trade of administering justice;[1] and at the beginning of the eighteenth century the "trading justice" was sufficiently common to be the object of Swift's satire,[2] and a stock character in plays and novels.[3]　Webb says[4] that, "Laconic *dossiers* of particular Justices prepared for the Lord Chancellor, and soberly worded summaries laid before the Prime Minister, help to convince us that the worst of the trading justices of Middlesex and Westminster were quite as bad as the contemporary novelists and dramatists have pictured them."　One of the means which they used to make money out of their powers over the administration of the law was clearly explained by a Bow Street runner who gave evidence before a committee of the House of Commons in 1816.[5]　He said, "It was a trading business there was Justice This, and Justice That.　Justice Welch in Litchfield Street was a great man in those days, and old Justice Hyde, and Justice Girdler, and Justice Blackborough, a trading justice at Clerkenwell Green and an old ironmonger.　The plan used to be to issue out warrants and take up all the poor devils in the street, and then there was the bailing of them 2/4 which the magistrates had. . . . They sent none to gaol, the bailing of them was so much better."

In the course of the eighteenth century it became clear that for the performance of government business, justices of a different type must be employed.　The government must have at least one justice to whom it could send confidential communications, and on whom it could rely.[6]　Even in the sixteenth and seventeenth centuries particular magistrates of this type were known in London;[7] and in the course of the eighteenth century there was generally at least one such magistrate who was paid out of the secret service money.　Sir Thomas de Veil held this post

---

[1] James I. in his speech in the Star Chamber in 1616 complained that among the Justices there were "some busy bodies who did so much, embracing many businesses for the enlargement of their private gain and profit," cited Webb, Local Government, the Parish and the County 327; for the small statutory fees of the justices see below 289.

[2] A Project for the Advancement of Religion and the Reformation of Manners, cited Webb, op. cit. 328.

[3] Ibid 328-329.　　　　　　　　　　　　[4] Ibid 329.

[5] Cited Stephen, H.C.L. i 231; Henry Fielding, Journal of a Voyage to Lisbon Introd., Works (Ed. 1775) xii 230, cited Stephen, H.C.L. i 230, says, "A predecessor of mine used to boast that he made £1000 a year in his office, but how he did this (if indeed he did it) is to me a secret.　His clerk, now mine, told me I had more business than he had ever known there; I am sure I had as much as any man could do.　The truth is, the fees are so very low when any are due, and so much is done for nothing, that, if a single justice of peace had business enough to employ twenty clerks, neither he nor they would get much for their labour.　The public will not therefore think I betray a secret when I inform them that I received from the government a yearly pension out of the public service money."

[6] Webb, The Parish and the County 337.

[7] Ibid 338.

from 1729-1747. He finally fixed his office at Bow Street;[1] and he was succeeded by the great novelist Henry Fielding.[2] After his death the Bow Street office was filled by a succession of similarly paid magistrates. This office thus "developed into a central bureau of information as to crime and criminals all over the country;" and to assist this work it "published an early form of police gazette."[3]

In 1780 the Lord George Gordon riots called pointed attention to the inadequacy both of the police system which the justices controlled, and of the justices themselves. Consequently in 1785 a bill was introduced by the solicitor-general to constitute a paid board of police commissioners, which was to control a paid force of police, and nine "public offices" in charge of paid magistrates;[4] but, the bill succumbed to the violent opposition it aroused—though a similar plan was adopted by the Irish Parliament in 1786.[5] In 1792, however, the government managed to carry out their plan of establishing "public offices" and paid justices, who have come to be known as stipendiary magistrates. By the Act of this year, in addition to the Bow Street office, seven other offices were established. To each of these offices three magistrates were assigned, who were paid a salary of £400 a year each. All fees were to be paid to a receiver, and the magistrates were given power to appoint a certain number of constables.[6] A ninth public office of a similar kind was established in 1800;[7] and in 1829,[8] when a new police force was established for London by Sir Robert Peel, it was put under the control of a tenth public office, presided over by two additional stipendiary magistrates.[9] But in 1839[10] the control of the police was turned over to Commissioners; and thus, as Maitland has said, "the judicial and executive duties comprised in the old conservation of the peace fell apart, and we are left with learned magistrates and gallant commissioners."[11]

But these magistrates were not all "learned" until some time after 1792. Gradually, however, their salary was raised and their status was improved; and it became customary to appoint

---

[1] Webb, The Parish and the County 339. [2] Ibid 340.
[3] Ibid 574. [4] Ibid 575. [5] Ibid 576-577.
[6] 32 George III. c. 53; the seven offices were fixed in the Parishes of St. Margaret's, Westminster; St. James, Westminster; St. James, Clerkenwell; St. Leonard, Shoreditch; St. Mary, Whitechapel; St. Paul, Shadwell; St. Margaret's Hill, Southwark; the Act was temporary, but was renewed from time to time, Webb, op. cit. 578 n. 1.
[7] 39, 40 George III. c. 87; Maitland, Justice and Police 100 n. 1, tells us that Bentham drew this Act and that he said that "without the change of a word it became law."
[8] 10 George IV. c. 44. [9] Maitland, Justice and Police 100
[10] 2, 3 Victoria c. 47 § 4. [11] Maitland op. cit. 100.

only barristers.[1] At the present day the crown may create thirteen public offices or police courts with any number of stipendiary magistrates up to twenty-seven; and these magistrates must be barristers of not less than seven years' standing.[2] Under these powers eleven such courts have been established. The magistrates who preside over them are in the commission of the peace for Middlesex, Kent, Surrey, Essex and Hertfordshire; and the chief magistrate at Bow Street is also in the commission of the peace for Berkshire.[3]

Manchester followed the example of London, and established a stipendiary magistrate in 1813;[4] but no reform was made in the arrangements for holding the petty sessions in the other boroughs till the passing of the Municipal Corporations Act 1835.[5] We have seen that that Act provided that all boroughs which did not acquire a court of quarter sessions under that Act lost all their criminal jurisdiction.[6] The Act also provided that the Mayors of those corporations which fell within the Act should be ex officio justices of the peace; and that the crown should have power to nominate as justices any persons it pleased, provided that they were resident within seven miles of the borough.[7] To provide for the need of populous places the crown was given power to appoint a stipendiary magistrate for a borough, if the borough passed a byelaw for that purpose approved by the Secretary of State;[8] and in 1863, by the Stipendiary Magistrates Act, it was given a further power to appoint such magistrates on the application of the Local Board of any place which contained more than 25,000 inhabitants.[9] Thus in boroughs and other populous urban districts petty criminal jurisdiction is exercised sometimes by stipendiary magistrates, but more often by unpaid justices of the peace. The fact that the number of places in which a stipendiary magistrate is employed is comparatively small is the best of testimonials to the efficiency of the amateur justice of the present day.[10]

(ii) Courts exercising a civil jurisdiction.

It was a feature common to all boroughs that they had a court which exercised civil jurisdiction.[11] In boroughs created by mesne lords this court was very like the court baron of a manor

---

[1] Maitland, op. cit. 100; Webb, op. cit. 578-580.
[2] 2, 3 Victoria c. 71; 11, 12 Victoria c. 42; Stephen, H.C.L. i 231-232.
[3] Ibid.
[4] 53 George III. c. 72; Webb, The Parish and the County 580 n. 3.
[5] 5, 6 William IV. c. 76.   [6] Above 145.
[7] 5, 6 William IV. c. 76 §§ 57, 98.
[8] Ibid § 99.   [9] 26, 27 Victoria c. 97.
[10] Maitland, Justice and Police 102.
[11] Borough Customs (S.S.) ii cxlv-cxlviii; Webb, op. cit. The Manor and the Borough 339-343.

without a lord;[1] and in some cases the lord, while granting to the borough the right to hold this court, reserved to himself the right to hold the court leet.[2]   When the boroughs began to get charters from the crown or from their lords, the right to hold this court was specially conferred by the charter; and the character and jurisdiction of the court was defined by it.   It was generally provided that it should be a court of record, and the extent of its jurisdiction was prescribed.   One limitation indeed upon its jurisdiction was fixed by law—it could never hear cases unless they had arisen within the territorial limits of the borough.[3] But, subject to this limitation, the extent of the jurisdiction of these courts was most various.   Sometimes petty suits under 40s. were excluded; but more often a very varying pecuniary limit was fixed above which it had no jurisdiction.   Sometimes its jurisdiction was limited to personal actions, sometimes to personal and mixed actions, and sometimes it extended to all actions—real, personal and mixed.[4]   The titles given to the court were also most various;[5] and in the larger corporations it split into several courts called by different names, and dealing with different causes of action.   "Thus some municipal corporations had, besides a petty debt court, a court of equity for cases involving real estate; a bailiff's court or other tribunal at which minors could execute valid conveyances; and even a separate court, sometimes called Portmanmote or court of Hustings, at which fines and recoveries could be levied, wills proved, and conveyances of real estate executed by married women."[6]   Sometimes the courts for actions against freemen were distinct from the court for actions against non-freemen;[7] and sometimes there seem to have been rival courts in the same borough which exercised the same or a similar jurisdiction in competition with one

---

[1] Webb, op. cit. 340; for a few exceptional cases in which this court continued to be held by a lord see ibid 339 n. 1.

[2] Ibid; above 142.

[3] See e.g. Munimenta Gildhallæ (R.S.), Liber Albus i 183, 209, 210, 405, 466; cf. Domesday of Ipswich, Black Book of the Admiralty (R.S.) ii 37, 39.

[4] This will be made quite clear from a glance at the descriptions of the 165 borough courts of record contained in Halsbury's Laws of England ix 138-214.

[5] Webb, the Manor and the Borough 340-341; some of these names were Three Weeks Court, Court of Pleas, Mayor's Court, Bailiff's Court, Provost's Court, Town Court, Gildhall Court, Court of Burgess and Foreign, Court of Passage, Tolsey Court, Portmote.

[6] Ibid 342; it appears from a law suit in Trinity term 6 Richard II. in which Cambridge was involved, that it had a court which sat five days in the year to hear actions about land; a court which sat to hear personal actions ordinarily once a week, but from day to day if a stranger were involved; a court of Gild merchant which heard cases in which merchants were concerned from hour to hour, as well as two courts leet in the spring and autumn, Bateson, Cambridge Charters xxix, xxx 79-95.

[7] Webb, op. cit. 342; instances were Colchester, Halsbury Laws of England ix 155, Great Grimsby, ibid 163, Lincoln, ibid 172.

another.[1] The right to exercise the office of the clerk of the market of the king's household, which was often granted to boroughs, necessitated the appointment of clerks of the market, and the holding by them of a court which "inquireth of weights and measures whether they be according to the king's standard or no."[2]

In early days, when the borough court was hardly differentiated from the court baron and the hundred court, all the suitors may have been the judges;[3] but from the thirteenth century onwards the judges were generally a group of aldermen or jurats.[4] When the constitution of the borough had been fixed by charter, the mayor or other head of the corporation, and the leading officials and aldermen were the judges.[5] But it would seem from the wording of § 118 of the Municipal Corporations Act 1835 [6] that in some cases the recorder was the presiding judge, and that in others a barrister was appointed by the corporation.

By the end of the eighteenth century these courts were, in the majority of boroughs, in a decadent condition. In 1839 a return was made to the House of Commons of the number of cases heard in 92 of these borough courts. It appears from that return that some were wholly disused, that others had almost no business, and that it was only a very few which were really active.[7] Nor are the causes of this decay far to seek. The presiding judges were often mere amateurs. Their jurisdiction was always bounded by the limits of the borough, and often in respect to the amount recoverable. Their fees were often high, and their procedure antiquated. The common law courts were very ready to hamper the exercise of their jurisdiction by writs of prohibition or certiorari.[8] We shall see, too, that in many places efficient Courts of Request had been established by local Acts.[9]

Some reform of these courts was attempted by the Municipal Corporations Act of 1835. If they were not regulated by any local Act, and if their judge was a barrister of five years' standing, their jurisdiction was extended to a £20 limit; and power was given to the judge to make rules for the procedure of his court.[10] Later Acts have given the crown power to alter the district

---

[1] Webb, op. cit. 342 n. 4; instances are there given at Ipswich, Chester, and Bristol.

[2] Coke, Fourth Instit. 273; Crompton, Courts 220 b says that "Le Clarke de market est auncient officier, et convient voire que touts weights et measures soient accordant al estandard la Roy que demur in leschequer al Westminster;" as Coke points out, loc. cit., he derived his name from that fact that he was originally an officer who supervised the market kept at the gate of the hospitium regis; and that he had retained his name though his duties were then different.

[3] Above 148-149.　　　　　　　　　　[4] Borough Customs (S.S.) ii cxlvii-cxlviii.
[5] Webb, op. cit. 341.　　　　　　　　　[6] 5, 6 William IV. c. 76.
[7] Parlt. Papers 1839 xliii 301.　　　　[8] Webb, op. cit. 343.
[9] Below 190-191.　　　　　　　　　　[10] 5, 6 William IV. c. 76 § 118.

within which the court exercises jurisdiction,[1] and to give it a
jurisdiction in equity and Admiralty similar to that possessed by
the new county courts.[2] Facilities have also been provided for
the alteration of their rules of procedure;[3] and power to remove
their judge for misbehaviour or incapacity has been given to the
Lord Chancellor.[4]

It cannot be said that these statutory powers have been
successful in reviving these old borough courts of record. Forty-
two were abolished in 1883;[5] and of the 165 enumerated in
Lord Halsbury's Laws of England[6] the majority are disused.
It is only in more populous places, and where the courts have
been reformed by local Acts, that they are still active. Conspicuous instances of such courts are the London Mayor's Court[7]
and City of London Court,[8] the Bristol Tolsey Court,[9] the
Liverpool Court of Passage,[10] the court of the Salford Hundred.[11]
In many cases it would seem that the institution of the new
county courts has been fatal to these borough courts of record.
In fact these new county courts have had an effect upon the
courts exercising civil jurisdiction within the borough similar to
the effect which the institution of the justices of the peace had
upon the old court leet in which the criminal jurisdiction of the
borough was once exercised.[12]

Thus, except in those few cases in which a borough has an
active court of record, the courts of the boroughs, whether they
are courts of criminal or civil jurisdiction, have been assimilated
to the local courts of the rest of the county.

The Stannaries [13]

Throughout mediæval Europe miners and the mining industry
had franchises of various kinds, which put them into a position
different from that of other members of the community, and from
that of other industries. In the thirteenth century the idea had
grown up that the crown had certain royal rights over mines and
minerals. Not much warrant for this view can be found in the
texts of the classical Roman law; but there are one or two
passages from which the existence of these rights could be

[1] 8, 9 Victoria c. 127 § 9.
[2] 36, 37 Victoria c. 66 § 88.
[3] Halsbury, Laws of England ix 132-133.
[4] 8, 9 Victoria c. 127 § 10.
[5] 46, 47 Victoria c. 18.
[6] Vol. ix 138-214.
[7] Halsbury, Laws of England viii 42.
[8] Ibid xx 284 seqq.
[9] Ibid ix 147-148.
[10] Ibid ix 173-176.
[11] Ibid ix 197-199.
[12] Above 143.
[13] On the Stannaries generally see G. R. Lewis, The Stannaries, Harvard
Economic Studies vol. iii; E. Smirke's report of Vice v. Thomas; G. Harrison,
Report on the Laws and Jurisdiction of the Stannaries in Cornwall; T. Pearce, The
Laws and Customs of the Stannaries.

deduced ;[1] and they were made the most of by mediæval commentators.[2] Emperors, kings, and other territorial magnates
acted on these ideas and granted both the right to work mines,
and protection and privileges to the miners, in consideration for
the working of the mine and a share in its produce.[3] We can
see these developments both in France and Germany ;[4] and,
"with the conception of mining as an occupation under the immediate supervision of the state, comes the development of the
miners into a specially privileged class of labourers."[5]

England felt the influence of some of these ideas. There is
no evidence, indeed, in the Anglo-Saxon laws or in Domesday
Book that the English kings claimed any regalian rights over
mines ;[6] but, in the thirteenth century, under the influence
probably of these mediæval interpretations of Roman law,[7] they
asserted similar rights.[8] But they never succeeded in making
good their claims over all mines to the same extent as the continental kings. As Dr. Lewis has pointed out,[9] the English mines
fall, from this point of view, into three classes. Firstly mines
of gold and silver over which the regalian rights have always
been recognized.[10] Secondly, mines of coal or of baser metals
such as iron, which belonged exclusively to the owners of the
soil.[11] Thirdly, the mines of special districts, which were specially
privileged by the king in return for the payment of certain dues.
It should be noted, however, that, unless these mines were on the
royal demesnes, the king did not succeed in enforcing his claims
to a right to the produce in competition with the owners of the
land.[12] It is true that to these miners were granted jurisdictional
and other privileges analogous to those enjoyed by miners on the
Continent ;[13] but it would seem that their privileges, unlike those
enjoyed by continental miners, were rather old established customs recognized by the crown than new grants conferred by it.[14]

---

[1] "While, in its general tenor, Roman law is distinguished by an absence of
regalian rights in mines, nevertheless one or two passages in the codes, quite special
and exceptional in character, might be construed as a general assumption of regalian
rights," Lewis, op. cit. 67.
    [2] Ibid.   [3] Ibid 68-71.   [4] Ibid 68, 71-72.
    [5] Ibid 72-73 ; as Dr. Lewis points out, ibid 73-74, in some places in Germany
free mine cities arose.
    [6] Ibid 75.
    [7] For the influence of Roman upon English law in the twelfth and thirteenth
centuries see vol. ii 202-206, 267-286.
    [8] Lewis, op. cit. 75 ; it would seem from the extracts of the Close and Patent
Rolls cited by Smirke in his report of Vice v. Thomas at pp. 115-123 that up to the
reign of Edward III. the king claimed regalian rights in mines of lead and tin.
    [9] Op. cit. 76.
    [10] Plowden, The Case of Mines 310 (1568) ; Lewis, op. cit. 76.
    [11] Ibid 78.   [12] Ibid 78-83.   [13] Below 155-156.
    [14] "There is nothing in England to correspond to the long and detailed codes of
mineral law which the German rulers bestowed upon their miners. . . . The great

And this difference causes a great divergence between England and the Continent in the subsequent history of these mines. "Instead of developing (as on the Continent) into enterprises under state subsidy and control, the mines remained from first to last in the fullest sense private property."[1] Here, as in other branches of English law, the doctrines of the mediæval civilians had a comparatively small and transitory influence upon subsequent legal developments. The older mining communities, with the assistance of privileges granted by the crown, developed their customary mining law on their own lines.

These old mining communities, thus privileged by the crown, developed into franchise jurisdictions of a peculiar kind. The chief districts in which they existed were the Forest of Dean,[2] Alston Moor in Cumberland,[3] the lead mines in the Mendip Hills,[4] the mines in Derbyshire,[5] and the Stannaries of Devon and Cornwall. In all these communities we find the existence of special customs regulating mining, special privileges enjoyed by the miners, and special courts at which these customs and privileges were enforced and protected. To the mediæval statesman and lawyer this was a natural and obvious arrangement. The miners, as Dr. Lewis says,[6] were "merely one of a number of classes which possessed similar rights, though possibly not to so great an extent. . . . The reason is to be found not only in the technical difficulties, abounding in mining law suits, which could not well be solved in an ordinary court, but also in a desire on the part of the King to prevent interruptions of the miners' work by secular courts. The mining classes were under mining law and courts, much as the soldier is subject to military law and courts martial."

Of this group of franchise jurisdictions I have selected for description the Stannaries of Devon and Cornwall. The organization of their courts was more elaborate than that of the other mining communities ; and the extent of the powers exercised by them, and the manner in which they developed, present some points of similarity to the powers and extent of the Palatine jurisdictions.

The Stannaries [7] were districts in Devon and Cornwall where

---

mass of English mining law in the Middle Ages represents usage pure and simple, not legislation or grant," Lewis, op. cit. 82.

[1] Ibid 78-79.   [2] Ibid ; Vice v. Thomas 128-132.

[3] Lewis, op. cit. 79-80 : Halsbury, op. cit. ix 138-139 ; Vice v. Thomas 125-126.

[4] Lewis, op. cit. 80 ; Vice v. Thomas 127-128.

[5] Lewis, op. cit. 80-81 ; Halsbury, op. cit. ix 140-141 ; Vice v. Thomas 123-124 ; 14, 15 Victoria c. 94 ; 15, 16 Victoria c. clxiii.

[6] Op. cit. 87-88.

[7] The word is derived from *stannum*, the Latin word for tin.

tin mining was carried on.   Their exact extent was never accurately ascertained.   They can only be described as districts where
the mines were situate, and over which the jurisdiction of the
Stannary courts extended.[1]

The tin mines in these districts have been worked from the
remotest antiquity ;[2] and, even in the Anglo-Saxon period, the
industry was carried on.[3]   But probably it was not carried on
very actively ; and it is a remarkable fact that there is no reference to the Stannaries in Domesday Book.[4]   The taxes payable
by their owners are, however, referred to in the Pipe Rolls ;[5] and,
from a letter written to Hubert Walter the Justiciar by De
Wrotham the warden of the Stannaries and others, in 1198,[6] it
would seem that certain of their peculiar customs and privileges
were recognized.[7]   It appears also, from this letter that, though
as yet there was no separate organization of Stannary courts, yet
that, in order to improve the royal revenue from the tin mines,
the Stannaries had been placed under a Warden ; and that he
issued regulations for the conduct of the mines and for the sale
of the tin.   Three years later John gave the Stannaries their first
charter.[8]   It confirmed their ancient privileges, released them,
while working at the mines, from suits of court due from villeins,[9]
and for the first time established a special Stannary jurisdiction.
" We have granted," runs the charter, " that the Lord Warden of
the Stannaries and his bailiffs have through him full power over
the tin miners to do justice to them and to hold them to right,
and that they be kept by them in our prisons if it chance that
any of the aforesaid tin miners ought to be seized or imprisoned
for any misdeed ; and if it chance that any of them be a fugitive
or an outlaw, that their chattels be given up to us by the hands
of the Warden of our Stannaries because the tin miners are our
lessees and always under our immediate lordship."

With this charter begins the history of the Stannary courts.
It would seem that in John's reign some of the greater landowners had complained that the privileges granted to the miners

---

[1] Vice v. Thomas 96 ; MacSwinney, Mines (Ed. 1897) 486 n. ; below 159-162.
[2] Lewis, op. cit. 33.   [3] Ibid.
[4] Ibid 34 ; this may be due to the fact that the Stannaries were royal property,
and so it was not thought necessary to include them in a survey which was to be the
basis of taxation; or it may be due to the fact that the ravages of Godwin and
Edmund the sons of Harold in 1068 had caused the miners to cease work, ibid.
[5] Ibid 34.   [6] Ibid and App. A.
[7] " Omnes foditores et nigri stagni emptores et de stagno primi fusores et de
stagno primæ funturæ mercatores habent justas et antiquas consuetudines et
libertatis in Devonia et Cornubia constitutas," ibid and App. A, p. 235.
[8] Lewis, op. cit. App. B, p. 238.
[9] " Sint liberi de placitis nativorum dum operantur ad commodum firmæ nostræ vel commodum marcarum novi redditus nostri."

by this charter impaired their rights over their villeins.[1] But, though John had promised that they should not suffer loss for this reason,[2] Henry III. in 1252 confirmed the charter of 1201.[3] From 1225 to 1300 the Stannaries were in the hands of Richard and his son Edmund, Earls of Cornwall; but, in 1300, they came again into the hands of the crown;[4] and the crown, in 1305, granted two new charters, one to the miners of Devon and the other to the miners of Cornwall.[5] These charters confirmed the existing privileges of the miners, and defined with somewhat greater precision the organization and jurisdiction of the Stannary courts. In effect they gave them jurisdiction over all causes (except those affecting land, life, or limb) arising in the Stannaries,[6] and even in causes in which one of the parties was a foreigner.[7] In Edward II.'s reign the Stannaries were granted to Piers Gaveston.[8] After his death they came again into the hands of the crown, till, in 1338, Edward III. settled the Duchy of Cornwall and the Stannary jurisdiction on the eldest son of the king.[9] In 1508 Henry VII., in return for a fine of £1000, confirmed the privileges of the miners, and gave the Stannary parliaments of Cornwall the right to veto any ordinance made by the king or Duke of Cornwall which should be to the prejudice of any tin miner or dealer in tin.[10] The Stannary parliaments of Devon seem also to have assumed a similar power.[11]

Such in outline is the history of the manner in which the Stannary courts grew up. We must now examine the manner in which they were organized, and their history. But in order to understand that history it will be necessary to say a few introductory words as to the special privileges which these charters conferred upon the tin miners.

The crown, as Dr. Lewis says, showed special favour to the

---

[1] Lewis, op. cit. 37.
[2] See John's Charter disforesting Cornwall printed by Lewis, op. cit. App. C.
[3] Ibid App. B.   [4] Ibid 38.
[5] Ibid; and App. D; this charter was many times confirmed; see Pearce, Laws of the Stannaries 185-186 for confirmations of the Devonshire charter.
[6] " Quod omnes stannatores . . . operantes in stannariis illis quæ sunt dominica nostra dum operantur in iisdem stannariis sint liberi et quieti de placitis nativorum et de omnibus placitis et querelis curiam nostram et heredum nostrorum quoque modo tangentibus; ita quod non respondeant coram aliquibus justiciariis vel ministris nostris seu heredum nostrorum de aliquo placito seu querela infra prædictas stannarias emergenti, nisi coram custode nostro stannariarum nostrarum prædictarum qui pro tempore fuerit, exceptis placitis terræ et vitæ et membrorum ; " cp. Coke, Fourth Instit. 233 ; Pearce, Laws of the Stannaries 186-188.
[7] " Quod custos noster prædictus vel ejus locumtenens teneat omnia placita inter stannatores prædictos emergentia, et etiam inter ipsos et alios forinsecos de omnibus transgressionibus, querelis, et contractibus factis in locis in quibus operantur infra stannarias prædictas similiter emergentia."
[8] Vice v. Thomas 17.   [9] Ibid.
[10] Lewis, op. cit. 126.   [11] Ibid.

mining classes;[1] and the tin miners of Devon and Cornwall were not the least favoured. Among the most remarkable and the most important of their privileges was that of "bounding". This was the right to mark out an area, and to dig for tin on any land within that area (unless the land was used for pasture or tillage) paying a certain toll to the owner. Supplementary to this right, were the rights to water for washing the ore and to wood or turf for smelting it. Further, they were exempt from taxation, and from tolls and market dues.[2] For military service they were separately mustered under the Lord Warden.[3] But it was the existence of their courts which was the most important of their privileges, because these courts guaranteed the enforcement of these privileges, and secured the observance both of the customary rules and of the enactments of the Stannary parliaments which regulated the working of the mines, and of the dealings of the miners with each other and with outsiders. I shall deal with these Stannary courts under the following heads: (1) the Stannary courts; (2) the Stannary parliaments; (3) Controversies as to the jurisdiction of the Stannary courts; (4) the later history of the Stannary courts.

(1) *The Stannary courts.*

The chief Stannary official was the Lord Warden, who was appointed by the Duke of Cornwall. The Lord Warden appointed a Vice-Warden and Stewards.[4] The courts of first instance were held by the Stewards. From them appeals could be carried to the court of the Vice-Warden; and, in exceptional cases, appeals lay to Lord Warden, and from him to the Council of the Duchy.[5] It was settled in 1562 that the ordinary courts of law had no jurisdiction in error,[6] but they could otherwise control the Stannary courts by means of the prerogative writs.[7]

The most important of these courts were (i) the courts of the Stewards, and (ii) the court of the Vice-Warden.

(i) The courts of the Stewards.

In Devonshire there were four districts in which these courts were held—Chagford, Ashburton, Plympton, and Tavistock.[8]

---

[1] Op. cit. 157; and on the privileges of the miners see generally ibid chap. vi.

[2] For these privileges see the Charter of 1305, and Lewis, op. cit. 158-166; it may be noted that by the legislation of the Cornish parliaments the tin thus bound was a chattel real, but that under the legislation of the Devonshire parliaments it was real property, Lewis, op. cit. 161-162.

[3] Ibid 167.   [4] Vice v. Thomas 97; Lewis, op. cit. 87.

[5] Coke, Fourth Instit. 230.   [6] Ibid 229.

[7] Adams v. Lord Warden of the Stannaries (1634) Cro. Car. 333—a writ of prohibition against the Stannaries granted.

[8] Pearce, op. cit. 189-190.

In Cornwall these courts were held at Truro (for the district of Tynwarhayle), at Lostwithiel (for the district of Blackmoor), at Launceston (for the district of Ferrymoor), and at Helston (for the districts of Penwith and Kerrier).[1] Like other mediæval courts, they were administrative bodies as well as judicial tribunals. At two great courts, held in the spring and autumn, a leet jurisdiction was exercised ; and, like other courts leet,[2] they not only tried criminal cases, but also appointed officials and performed other administrative functions.[3] Special juries could also be summoned to declare the customs of the district, and special courts to settle rights to tin works.[4] The ordinary courts were held from three weeks to three weeks. At them all legal proceedings (except those relating to land, life or limb) could be heard.[5] The two great courts were chiefly occupied with criminal, and the three-weekly courts with civil business ; but at any of these courts both criminal and civil business could be taken.[6] Generally the cases were tried by a jury of six, and the Steward always gave the judgment of the court.[7] Besides these courts there were also special customary courts held, "on the morrow after certain fairs within each Stannary, for the benefit of such as do attend the fairs and courts ; "[8] and, by the legislation of the Stannary parliaments, the stewards and the Vice-Warden had a summary jurisdiction over persons accused of infringing certain of the enactments of these parliaments.[9] The executive officers of these and the other Stannary courts were bailiffs appointed by the Duke.[10]

(ii) The court of the Vice-Warden.

In addition to the magisterial and executive powers possessed by the Vice-Warden,[11] he had power to hold a court which had an appellate jurisdiction from the courts of the Stewards, and an original jurisdiction in equity. The origin of the latter

---

[1] Vice v. Thomas 96. [2] Above 135.

[3] Lewis, op. cit. 121-124 ; for the charge of the Steward at the leet see Pearce, op. cit. 152.

[4] Lewis, op. cit. 118.

[5] Ibid 116-117, 119, 120. The early records of these courts were destroyed in 1844, Pearce, op. cit. xxiv. It was said in 1824 Harrison, Report, etc. 124, that there were no records prior to 1754, but Pearce, who wrote in 1725, had access to earlier records than this.

[6] Lewis, op. cit. 118, 120.

[7] Ibid 116, 119 ; a decision in 1632, Cro. Car. 259 that a jury of six was illegal was disregarded ; 6, 7 William IV. c. 106 § 34 provided for a jury of twelve ; but 11, 12 Victoria c. 83 § 7 provided that there should be a jury of five (as in the new county courts, below 192) in actions for the recovery of small debts.

[8] Lewis, op. cit. 118.   [9] Ibid 109, 117.   [10] Vice v. Thomas 97.

[11] " The Vice-Warden's powers were magisterial for the granting of injunctions, the issue of warrants, and the subpœnas of the peace, replevins, and other writs of similar nature, the prevention by summary process of offences against stannary law, and their summary punishment if perpetrated," Lewis, op. cit. 109, citing Harl. MSS. 6380 ff. 43, 51, 70, and Convoc. Cornw. 22 James I. c. 6, 12, 13.

jurisdiction is obscure.[1]   It is clear that he was exercising it at
the end of the sixteenth century;[2] and it' is recognized in the
legislation of the Stannary parliaments in the seventeenth century.[3]   It is equally clear that it was not conferred by the
Stannary charters.   But the Stannary courts, like the courts of
the counties palatine, showed a capacity for imitating the developments of the central courts; and it is therefore probable that
the Stannaries, like the counties palatine and Wales,[4] assumed
a power to exercise an equitable jurisdiction of the same pattern
as that exercised by the royal court of Chancery.   And it is
probable that it originated in much the same way as the equitable jurisdiction of the Chancery.   We shall see that the equitable
jurisdiction of the Chancery originated from the practice of
petitioning the King's Council for relief.[5]   It is probable that the
equitable jurisdiction of the Vice-Warden arose from applications
for relief made to the Duke's Council.[6]   Though the legality of
the jurisdiction was occasionally doubted in the seventeenth [7] and
early eighteenth centuries,[8] it was constantly exercised and, in
1842, was finally adjudged to be legal in the case of *Vice* v.
Thomas.[9]

(2) *The Stannary parliaments.*

In addition to these courts, the Stannaries had, certainly
from the beginning of the sixteenth century, parliaments elected
from the members of the four Stannary towns in each county.
The Devonshire Stannary Parliament met on Crockentor;[10] and
the Cornish parliament met at different towns in the county.[11]
We have no documentary evidence as to the origins of these
assemblies.   Probably, as Dr. Lewis says,[12] they were "an expansion of, and an off-shoot from, the grand juries or special
courts in the Stannary judiciary, which were called upon occasionally to declare the customs of the mines, and which often
prefixed to their presentments of criminals a confirmation of
existing Stannary law."

---

[1] Lewis, op. cit. 109-112; see the arguments in Vice v. Thomas at pp. 15-24 of
the report; Carew, Survey of Cornwall 17.
[2] Vice v. Thomas 45, citing Glanville v. Courtney (1593); Lewis, op. cit. 110.
[3] Ibid.   [4] Above 111, 116, 125.   [5] Below 401-402.
[6] Lewis, op. cit. 110; cp. for instances of these applications, Vice v. Thomas
24, 27.
[7] Pearce, op. cit. 147-151; Harrison, Report, etc. 152-153.
[8] Trelawny v. Williams (1704) 2 Vern. 483.   [9] At p. 36.
[10] Parliaments were held 2, 24, and 25 Henry VIII., 6 Edward VI. and 16 Elizabeth, Pearce, op. cit. 189-240.
[11] Ibid 21-86.
[12] Op. cit. 125; the records of the Devonshire parliaments go back to 1510,
those of the Cornish parliaments refer back to 1588.

The charter of 1508, which gave new powers to the Cornish parliament,[1] defined its constitution.   It consisted of twenty-four members nominated by the mayors and councils of the four Stannary towns.[2]   The members were generally chosen from the leading families in Cornwall; and they represented rather the large mine owners and dealers in tin than the working miners.[3] An attempt was made to change the method of election in 1677; but a bill sent down by the House of Lords for this purpose was laid aside in the Commons.[4]   In Devonshire, on the other hand, each of the four towns elected twenty-four representatives at a special court, at which all classes connected with tin mining had a vote.[5]   We know very little of these Devonshire assemblies.[6] But the Cornish assemblies seemed to have modelled their procedure on that of the House of Commons.   There was a speech from the Lord Warden, a speaker was elected and approved by the Lord Warden, and then the House proceeded to the business of legislation.[7]   The enactments must originally have been signed by the whole twenty-four members, the Warden or Vice-Warden, and the Duke.[8]   The last session of the Cornish parliament was held in 1752; but neither the Devonshire nor the Cornish parliaments have been formally abolished.[9]

(3) *Controversies as to the jurisdiction of the Stannary courts*

The extent of the jurisdiction conferred on the Stannary courts by Edward I.'s charter was by no means clearly defined. Hence we find that, right down to the seventeenth century, there were constant controversies as to its limits.   These controversies turned chiefly on two questions: What persons were entitled to the privileges conferred by the charters? and, What places were within the jurisdiction of the Stannary courts?   In the Middle Ages they were chiefly carried on with the local courts of county, hundred, and manor; and, in the sixteenth and seventeenth centuries, with the central courts of common law, the Star Chamber, and the Chancery.

In the earlier part of the fourteenth century there were many complaints of trespasses committed by the tinners, and of the manner in which they either prevented persons not tinners from attending the ordinary courts, or compelled cases arising outside the Stannaries to be brought into their courts.[10]   The controversy

---

[1] Above 155.   [2] Lewis, op. cit. 126.   [3] Ibid 128, 129.
[4] Hist. MSS. Comm. 9th Rep. App. Pt. II. 93-94 no. 409.
[5] Lewis, op. cit. 126-127.   [6] Ibid 127.   [7] Ibid.
[8] Ibid; this would seem to take us back to the primitive assemblies which did not recognize the power of the majority to bind the minority, see as to this vol. ii Bk. iii c. 5.
[9] Ibid 130.   [10] Ibid 92-95.

was brought to a head in 1376 by two petitions to Parliament from the inhabitants of Devon and Cornwall, which specifically raised these controverted questions as to the definition of a tin miner, and as to the local limits of the Stannary courts.[1]   It was contended by the petitioners that the only tin miners entitled to the privileges conferred by the charters were working tinners on the royal demesnes, and that the jurisdiction of the Stannary courts only extended to places where the workmen were actually at work.   A commission was appointed to enquire into the complaints made and the contentions raised by these petitions;[2] but it does not appear to have reported the results of its enquiries.   The king, however, conceded that "tinners" should include only working tinners, and only for so long as they were working; and that pleas between tinners and foreigners, arising other than in places where mining was actually being carried on, should not be taken to the Stannary courts.[3]

The controversy was re-opened in the sixteenth and seventeenth centuries.   Both in respect of the definition of a tinner, and in respect of the competency of the Stannary courts the tinners attempted to secure a more liberal interpretation of these charters.   The charter of 1507, by which Henry VII. pardoned the tinners for their disobedience to the ordinances of Prince Arthur, included among the tinners not only working tinners, but owners of mines and dealers in tin;[4] and this larger interpretation seems to have been adopted by the Stannary parliaments and acted upon by the Stannary courts during the sixteenth century.[5]   Similarly it was found impossible to restrict the jurisdiction of the Stannary courts to pleas arising in places where mining was being actually carried on—for instance contracts made for the sale of tin in any of the Stannary towns were always taken to be within the jurisdiction of the Stannary courts.[6]   But we shall see that the latter years of the sixteenth

---

[1] Lewis, op. cit. 97, 106; and see the text of the Devonshire petition R.P. ii 343-344, printed ibid App. F.

[2] Coke, Fourth Instit. 236; Lewis, op. cit. 97.

[3] R.P. ii 343-344; it is there stated that the words working tinners were to be understood, " De operariis laborantibus dumtaxat in Stannariis illis sine fraude et dolo et non de aliis nec alibi laborantibus; " and that the jurisdiction was only to be exercised, " In locis ubi iidem operarii operantur, et memye aillours, ne en autre manere; " cp. Lewis, op. cit. 97-98.

[4] " The persons expressly named in the pardon, and styled without exception ' stannatores,' were gentlemen bounders, owners of tin works, possessors of blowing houses, and buyers of black or white tin—thus indicating a return to a more liberal interpretation of the charters than that of 1376," ibid 98; in fact changed economic conditions made a wider definition necessary; the Cornish tinners pointed out in 1606 that the working tinners were " in number and degree the least and meanest part of us, and for the most part are foreigners, and hired to work in our tin works for day wages," Pearce, 148.

[5] Ibid 98-99.   [6] Ibid 106.

century and the first half of the seventeenth century were marked by many quarrels about jurisdiction. The Star Chamber, the Chancery, and the common law courts were all endeavouring to enlarge their respective jurisdiction at the expense either of one another, or of other local or franchise courts.[1] The Star Chamber asserted a right to hear appeals from the Stannary courts, the Chancery interfered in cases brought before them, and the common law courts heard actions properly triable there.[2] Such loud complaints were made by the tin miners[3] that in 1608 the question of Stannary jurisdiction was referred to Fleming and Coke, C.J J.[4] They ruled that persons within the privilege of the Stannaries included " as well blowers as all other labourers and workers in or about the Stannaries of Cornwall and Devon ; " and that " all matters and things concerning the Stannaries or depending upon the same are to be heard and determined in those courts." All transitory actions of any kind between tinner and tinner, or worker and worker, even though the cause of action arose out of the Stannaries, were to be sued in those courts or at common law, at the option of the plaintiff, if the defendant was within the jurisdiction of the Stannary courts ; but, if one party to such an action was not a tinner or a worker, and the cause of action arose out of the limits of the Stannaries, the defendant could plead to the jurisdiction. If he did not so plead, and it was apparent from the plaintiff's own statement that the cause of action arose out of the jurisdiction of the Stannary courts, all proceedings before those courts were *coram non judice.*[5] These resolutions were further explained in 1627.[6] But in 1632 the Privy Council resolved[7] that the privileges of the Stannaries extended to other than working tinners,[8] and again left at large the question of the local limits of the Stannary courts—intimating however an opinion that in Cornwall they extended over the whole county.[9]

[1] Below 459-465, 508-515.
[2] Lewis, op. cit. 99, 100 ; for a dispute between the King's Bench and the Stannaries, in which the king took the side of the King's Bench, see Documents relating to Prynne (C.S.) 81-82.
[3] Pearce, op. cit. 147-151.
[4] For their report see Lewis, op. cit. App. G ; Coke, Fourth Instit. 231.
[5] Therefore an action for false imprisonment would lie if the party against whom the judgment was given was arrested ; but it was otherwise if the want of jurisdiction was not thus apparent, see ibid App. G, p. 245.
[6] Ibid App. H.   [7] Ibid App. I.
[8] Besides the actual workers, " There are other Tynners that doe noe handworke as are the owners of the Soyle, owners of the Bounds, owners of the Bloweing houses, and theire partners, buyers and sellers of Black Tynne, or Whyte Tynne before the deliverence, theise may sue on an other, or working Tynners, or any other man, for any matter concerning Tynne, or Tynne works, in the Stannarie Courte "
[9] " We cannot yet discerne but that the Stannaries doe extend over the whole County of Cornwall."

These controversies were thus still unsettled when the Long Parliament met; and that Parliament made another attempt to settle them by statute.[1] The chief provisions of the statute upon these points were as follows: The replies given by Edward III. in answer to the Commons' petition of 1376 were accepted as the basis of the settlement;[2] but it enacted that the expression "in the place where mining was carried on" was to mean the "vill, tithing, and hamlet where some tin work is or shall be in working."[3] In order to secure that only working tinners should sue, and that the cause of action should both arise within the Stannaries and be within the jurisdiction of the Stannary courts, a defendant was empowered to make the plaintiff swear that he was a working tinner, and that the cause of his suit arose within the Stannaries or concerned tin or tin works.[4] If the plaintiff would not swear, his action was to be dismissed;[5] and if he did so swear, and the action was not triable in the Stannary courts, the defendant was given an action for damages against him.[6] Tinners, if they wished to do so, were to be allowed to sue at common law;[7] and the general law as to costs was applied to proceedings in the Stannary courts.[8]

This statute seems to allow that proceedings "concerning tin or tin works" were within the jurisdiction of the courts. It therefore transcends the narrow definition of 1376, which seems to require that the cause of action must have arisen within the jurisdiction.[9] On the other hand it confines the privilege to working tinners so long as they are working. It seems, however, from a law of the Cornish Stannary parliament of 1687 that the Stannary parliaments and courts continued to give a wider definition to the term "working tinner." They included in it such persons as "lords of the soil and bounders, also adventurers in tin mines, owners of blowing houses, and buyers and sellers of black and white tin;"[10] and they assumed that jurisdiction existed over all dealings with the mines or in tin. The legislature acquiesced in this larger interpretation, when, by the Act of 1836, it extended the jurisdiction to metals other than tin, and "to or over all transactions connected therewith within the county of Cornwall."[11]

(4) *The later history of the Stannary courts.*

In the course of the eighteenth century Devonshire mining and the Devonshire Stannary courts decayed; and in the nine-

---

[1] 16 Charles I. c. 15.   [2] Preamble.   [3] § iv (1).
[4] § iv (2).   [5] Ibid.   [6] § iv (3).   [7] § vi.
[8] § v.   [9] Above 160.   [10] Lewis, op. cit. 103.
[11] 6, 7 William IV. c. 106 § 1; cp. 18, 19 Victoria c. 32 § 32.

teenth century the existence of the Devonshire courts seems to have been forgotten.[1] We shall see that it was not till 1856 that a statutory power was given to reconstitute them if necessary.[2] The Cornish Stannary courts on the other hand have had a continuous history. From the various laws passed by the Stannary parliaments in the sixteenth and seventeenth centuries we can gather that the abuses often attendant on small courts were present. We hear complaints of maintenance and champerty, and of covinous compacts between bailiffs and defendants. We hear of demands that only duly licensed counsel should be employed, that Stewards should not be of counsel with the parties.[3] Things did not grow better in the eighteenth century. The procedure of the courts remained archaic. It was said at the beginning of the nineteenth century that from eighteen to twenty-one weeks was the shortest period within which a simple debt could be recovered ; and that if the case was doubtful the period was still longer.[4] In addition many complaints were heard of the negligence of the Stewards.[5] It was in fact easier to recover a debt through the medium of the ordinary common law courts. Wherever possible this course was pursued. But if the debt was under 40s., or if the case fell within the exclusive jurisdiction of the Stannary courts, this expedient was not available. In consequence a custom had sprung up in the eighteenth century of beginning a common law action in the court of the Vice-Warden.[6] There was also another reason for this practice. We have seen that the court of the Vice-Warden exercised an equitable as well as a common law jurisdiction.[7] Under the system of " adventuring " in vogue in the eighteenth and nineteenth centuries the purser of the adventurers, who was usually one of the adventurers, was directly liable to the creditors ; but he had of course the right to be indemnified by his co-adventurers for payments made by him to the creditors. Instead of suing the purser at law in the Stewards' courts, and leaving him to take equitable proceedings in the Vice-Warden's court to get indemnity from his co-adventurers, it was more convenient for the creditors to sue at once in the Vice-Warden's court in which the rights of the various parties could be adjusted.[8]

For these two reasons, therefore—the defects of the Stewards' courts, and the convenience of suing in a court which exercised both an equitable and a common law jurisdiction—the Stewards'

---

[1] See re South Lady Bertha Mining Company (1862) 2 J. and H. 380-381.
[2] Below 164.
[3] Articles 23, 25, 32 of the Parliament of 1588 ; Vice v. Thomas 53-55; Act 25 of the Parliament of 1685, Pearce 58.
[4] Harrison, Report, etc. 92. [5] Ibid 106, 107.
[6] Ibid 93. [7] Above 157-158. [8] Lewis, op. cit. 113-115.

courts were left with so little business that in the course of the eighteenth century they were all consolidated into one.[1] But it is fairly clear that the exercise of original common law jurisdiction by the Vice-Warden's court was without legal justification. In the sixteenth century both the court of Star Chamber,[2] and an enactment of the Stannary parliament,[3] had declared that causes should be begun in the Stewards' courts. But the legality of the exercise of this jurisdiction was not called into question till 1824. In that year, in the case of *Hall* v. *Vivian*,[4] it was decided by the court of King's Bench that the court of the Vice-Warden had no original common law jurisdiction; and that the Vice-Warden was liable in damages for having exercised it. The result was that all the Stannary courts ceased to sit till the question of the extent of their jurisdiction should be settled.[5] This led to so many inconveniences that in 1836[6] Parliament placed the jurisdiction of the Stannary courts upon a new and improved basis.

The effect of the Act of 1836 and subsequent legislation was to abolish the courts of the Stewards, and to unite the jurisdiction of the courts of the Stewards to the Vice-Warden's court;[7] to give to the Vice-Warden's court a concurrent original jurisdiction both legal and equitable;[8] to extend the jurisdiction of his court over metals other than tin,[9] and over the Devonshire Stannaries;[10] and, as we have seen, to give legislative sanction to the manner in which the Cornish Stannary parliaments and courts had defined the persons subject to the jurisdiction of the Stannary courts, and the places in which this jurisdiction was exercisable.[11] From the Vice-Warden's court appeals lay to the court of the Lord Warden, assisted by three or more members of the judicial committee of the Privy Council; and from him to the House of Lords.[12] The manner in which appeals could be made was assimilated to the ordinary law on this point. Appeals from the equity side of the court were decided by a rehearing of the case.[13] Appeals from the common law side of the court were brought

---

[1] Harrison, Report 160, 161.

[2] See Trewynnard v. Roskarrock, Coke, Fourth Instit. 230; cp. Lewis, op. cit. 113.

[3] In 1588 it had been declared that " every cause that the court will hear should commence in the Stewards' court and have its due trial there, and that for default of justice there, the party grieved might appeal," cited Lewis, op. cit. 113.

[4] Vice v. Thomas 37-38; cp. Harrison, Report, etc. 15, 16.

[5] Vice v. Thomas, 38.

[6] 6, 7 William IV. c. 106; Harrison, Report 112-113.

[7] 6, 7 William IV. c. 106 § 6.   [8] § 2.   [9] §§ 1 and 7.

[10] 18, 19 Victoria c. 32 §§ 32-38.   [11] Above 162.

[12] 6, 7 William IV. c 106 § 7, repealed and reinacted with modifications by 18, 19 Victoria c. 32 § 26.

[13] Ibid.

before the Lord Warden by a writ of error for errors on the record;[1] but, as at common law, the parties could, instead of bringing a writ of error, apply to the Vice-Warden for a new trial.[2]

The court of the Lord Warden was merged in the Court of Appeal created by the Judicature Act of 1873.[3] The Court of the Vice-Warden survived the Judicature Act; but it was abolished in 1896, and its jurisdiction was transferred to such of the new county courts as the Lord Chancellor might direct.[4]

The Courts of the Universities [5]

During the Dark Ages education was the monopoly of the Church. In northern Europe "the clergy were almost the only class which possessed or desired to possess even the rudiments of knowledge;" and "the intimate connection between the Church and the School was stereotyped by the legislation of Charles the Great." [6] He enacted that to every cathedral and monastery there should be attached a school.[7] But, after the death of Charles the Great and the break-up of his empire, Europe retrogressed.[8] It was not till the eleventh century that, with the restoration of a more settled order, a revival of learning and a revival of interest in education began. This revival centred round the monastic and cathedral schools;[9] and it was from the latter that the universities were developed. Therefore both the universities themselves and their system of education were wholly ecclesiastical in character.[10] But, as the state grew more civilized, and as it began to feel the need for educated men to guide it, it began to take as great an interest as the church in the universities. Thus the universities were encouraged both by church and state; and the privileges which they acquired were the gifts not only of popes, but also of emperors and kings. Because they were places which the rival lay and ecclesiastical powers had thus combined to endow, their franchises were unique; for they united powers peculiar both to the ecclesiastical and the secular jurisdictions. Thus, if we look at our two mediæval universities—Oxford and Cambridge—we find that they were

---

[1] 6, 7 William IV. c 106 § 7, repealed and reinacted with modifications by 18, 19 Victoria c. 32 § 26.

[2] 6, 7 William IV. c. 106 § 8; for proceedings in error at common law see below 213-215.

[3] 36, 37 Victoria c. 66 § 18.   [4] 59, 60 Victoria c. 45.

[5] H. Rashdall, Universities of Europe in the Middle Ages; J. Williams, Law of the Universities; L. L. Shadwell, Enactments in Parliament concerning the Universities (Oxford Hist. Soc.); Registrum Privilegiorum Almæ Universitatis Oxoniensis (1770); Munimenta Academica Oxon. (R.S.); G. Dyer, Privileges of the University of Cambridge.

[6] Rashdall, Universities i 27-28.   [7] Ibid i 28 n. 2.   [8] Ibid i 30.

[9] Ibid i 29, 30; below 166 n. 4.   [10] Ibid i 33; and cp. below 166-167.

governed by an episcopal chancellor; and that papal grants helped the chancellor and the university to become independent of the bishop and even of the archbishop.[1] But we see too that these universities, like many other societies of mediæval men, assumed powers of self-government. They legislated for themselves, and they enforced obedience to this legislation; and in this work they were helped by the king, who conferred franchises upon them analogous to those conferred upon other societies.[2] From these various sources the courts of these two universities thus acquired their peculiar powers, some of which, though often in an altered form, have survived to the present day.

In dealing with the courts of the two universities I shall speak first and at greater length of Oxford. Oxford is the older of the two universities, and her privileges are more extensive. In the Middle Ages Cambridge followed and imitated Oxford—she did not come into her own till the Renaissance of the sixteenth century. If, therefore, the history of the development of the university courts at Oxford is first described, the parallel developments at Cambridge can be sketched more briefly.

Oxford.

It is probable that the foundation at Oxford of a *Studium Generale*[3] was due to a migration from Paris in 1167;[4] and that this migration was due to an order, issued by Henry II., in the course of his contest with Becket, to the effect that no clerk should go from England to the Continent or vice versa without royal licence, and that all clerks having revenues in England should return.[5] A dispute between the city authorities and the clerks at Oxford in 1209, in which John took the side of the citizens, led first to a dispersal of the clerks; and afterwards, when John had made his peace with the church in 1214, to the humiliation of the citizens.[6] A clerk arrested by the citizens was to be surrendered at once "on the demand of the Bishop of Lincoln or the archdeacon of the place or his Official or the Chancellor or whomsoever the Bishop of Lincoln shall depute to this office."[7] Oxford was then in the diocese of Lincoln; and it

---

[1] Below 167, 174. [2] Below 167 169, 174.
[3] For this term see Rashdall i 8-10.
[4] Ibid ii Pt. II. 328-329, 345; as Dr. Rashdall at p. 328 points out, "In northern Europe the universities which originated by spontaneous development are always found in connexion with a cathedral or a great collegiate church, never in connexion with a monastery: and Oxford possessed neither cathedral nor collegiate church to account for the growth of its schools."
[5] Ibid 330-331. [6] Ibid 348-351; Mun. Acad i 1-9.
[7] "Si vero contingat amodo clericum capi a vobis, statim, cum fueritis super eo requisiti ab Episcopo Lincolniæ seu Archidiacono loci vel ejus officiali vel a Cancellario seu ab eo quem Episcopus Lincolniæ huic officio deputaverit, captum ei reddatis," Mun. Acad. i 2.

was assumed that the university would therefore be under his jurisdiction. It was not, however, till some years later that the bishop regularly appointed a chancellor;[1] and at first he was "an officer not of the university but of the bishop."[2] "He derived his jurisdiction over scholars from the fact that they were ecclesiastics, not from the fact that they were members of a university; his jurisdiction extended to laymen only so far as laymen were subject to the authority of the ordinary ecclesiastical courts."[3]

But the chancellor was usually appointed from among the teachers in the university; he took his place at its head; and both chancellor and university tended to become more and more independent of a distant bishop.[4] Through its chancellor the university appropriated the ecclesiastical jurisdiction which the chancellor exercised as delegate of the bishop; and a papal bull of 1368,[5] sanctioning an already existing practice, declared that episcopal confirmation of the election of a chancellor was not needed.[6] The chancellor thus became independent of the Bishop of Lincoln; but he was still subject to the metropolitan jurisdiction of the Archbishop of Canterbury, till, in 1395, he was exempted by a bull of Boniface IX.[7] But a majority of the university sympathized with Wycliffe; and the measures taken by the archbishop to suppress heresy were resisted.[8] The result was the revocation of Boniface's bull by John XXII. in 1411.[9] It was not till 1479 that Sixtus IV. again exempted the university from archiepiscopal authority.[10]

Thus the chancellor, and through the chancellor the university, gained an independent jurisdiction over all matters of ecclesiastical cognizance. This, as we shall see, included a wide jurisdiction over morals, and a probate jurisdiction.[11] At the same time, as chancellor, he enforced the statutes made by the university; and in exercising his jurisdiction over all these matters he naturally used the forms and procedure of the canon law. We shall now see that the acquisition by the chancellor and the university of their independence from external ecclesiastical interference in the exercise of their jurisdiction was materially helped by the large additions to it made by royal grant.[12]

In 1244 the Chancellor got jurisdiction over actions of debt and actions affecting moveable property in which one party was

[1] Rashdall, ii Pt. II. 355.
[2] Ibid 357; cp. Y.B. 5 Ed II. (S.S.) 119.
[3] Rashdall, ii Pt. II. 357; for the jurisdiction of the ecclesiastical courts see below 614-632.
[4] Ibid 358-359.   [5] Ibid 427.   [6] Ibid 422-427.
[7] Ibid 430.   [8] Ibid 431-434.   [9] Ibid.
[10] Ibid 437.   [11] Below 169.
[12] Rashdall, ii Pt. II. 393 seqq.

a clerk.[1]   In 1248 the university was allowed to assist in the enforcement of the assize of bread and beer;[2] and in 1255 the Chancellor was given jurisdiction over laymen in the case of breach of the peace.[3]   In 1275 a royal writ gave him jurisdiction over all personal actions in which either of the parties was a member of the university.[4]   In 1290 disputes between the members of the university and the town had led to proceedings before the king and Parliament.   The result of these proceedings was to extend the criminal jurisdiction of the chancellor over all crimes where one of the parties was a member of the university, except in cases of homicide and mayhem; and over all contracts made in Oxford if one party was a scholar.[5]   Further privileges were gained as the result of the fight between the university and the town on St. Scholastica's day in 1354.[6]   The university got the right to hold the assize of bread and ale, and weights and measures, and to punish both laymen and clerks who carried arms.[7]   All these privileges were confirmed with some additions by Richard II.[8]   Henry IV. gave the Steward of the university jurisdiction over treasons, felonies, and mayhems committed by members of the university within the counties of Oxford or Berkshire.[9]   The privileges thus gained at different periods were confirmed by a charter granted by Edward IV. in 1461.[10]   They were again confirmed and added to by the Great Charter of the University which was granted by Henry VIII. in 1523;[11] and all these privileges were given legislative sanction in 1571.[12]   The need for this statute was caused by the fact that the university, having been allowed to exercise its jurisdiction according to the customs of the university,[13] exercised it in accordance with the procedure of the civil law.   The use of this procedure, the com-

---

[1] "In causis clericorum ex mutuis datis aut receptis aut taxacionibus seu locacionibus domorum aut equis conductis venditis seu commodatis, seu pannis et victualibus ortum habentibus seu aliis quibuslibet rerum mobilium contractibus in municipio aut suburbio Oxon. factis, nostra prohibicio non currat sed hujusmodi causæ coram Cancellario Universitatis Oxon. non obstante prohibicione nostra decidantur," Reg. Privil. 4; the form of this grant and the allusion to the writ of prohibition (below 228-229) shows that the Chancellor's jurisdiction was regarded as essentially ecclesiastical.

[2] Mun. Acad. ii 777-779.

[3] Reg. Privil. 5-6—"Si laicus inferat clerico gravem vel enormem lesionem statim capiatur et si magna sit lesio incarceretur in Castro Oxon. et ibi detineatur quousque clerico satisfaciat et hoc arbitrio Cancellarii et Universitatis Oxon."

[4] Rashdall ii Pt. II. 398 n. 4, citing Rot. Pat. 3 Ed. I. m. 6.

[5] Mun. Acad. i. 46-56; Rashdall ii Pt. II. 401-402.

[6] Ibid 403-408.   [7] See Reg. Privil. 23-29.

[8] Ibid 39-42.   [9] Ibid 47-49.   [10] Ibid 3-52.

[11] Ibid 53-75.   [12] 13 Elizabeth c. 29.

[13] The jurisdiction was to be exercised, "secundum eorum statuta et consuetudines vel secundum legem regni nostri Angliæ ad voluntatem predictorum Cancellarii Commissarii sive ejus deputati et successorum suorum," Reg. Privil. 73.

mon lawyers held, was not warranted by the charter without the help of an Act of Parliament.[1]

The university had thus acquired a large and miscellaneous assortment of jurisdictions. It exercised them in a number of different courts.

By far the most important of these courts was that held by the chancellor or his deputy. Its jurisdiction was unique in its width and variety.[2] Firstly, it had the wide jurisdiction exercised by other ecclesiastical courts over ecclesiastics, over the morals of both laymen and ecclesiastics, and over testamentary causes.[3] Secondly, it had a criminal jurisdiction of three distinct kinds. It had jurisdiction over all offences under the degree of felony and mayhem where a member of the university was a party to the proceedings;[4] it had a leet jurisdiction;[5] and, by virtue of Henry VIII.'s charter, the chancellor and his deputy exercised the jurisdiction of justices of the peace.[6] Thirdly, it had exclusive civil jurisdiction in all actions, except those relating to freehold,[7] to which a member of the university was a party; and this jurisdiction was exercisable not only if the cause of action arose within the territorial limits of the university, but if it arose anywhere in England.[8] The wide extent of this jurisdiction makes it unique among franchise jurisdictions. In other cases the rule was that the cause of action must have arisen within the territorial limits of the franchise.[9]

---

[1] "Although King Henry VIII. 14 A.R. *sui* granted to the university a liberal charter, to proceed according to the use of the university; viz. by a course much conformed to the civil law; yet that charter had not been sufficient to have warranted such proceedings without the help of an Act of Parliament," Hale Hist. Com. Law (6th Ed.) 30; in support of this Hale cites Mich. 8 H. 4 Rot. 72 Coram Rege, where the King's Bench reversed a judgment of the Chancellor in an action of debt because he had proceeded "per legem civilem ubi quilibet ligeus domini regis regni sui Angliæ in quibuscunque placitis et querelis infra hoc regnum factis et emergentibus de jure tractari debet per communem legem Angliæ;" Bl. Comm. iii 84.

[2] For some account of the activities of the court in the Middle Ages see Acts of the Court, Mun. Acad. ii 505-527; Rashdall ii Pt. II. 412-416; advocates were admitted to practice before it, below 174 n. 11; and at the present day the vice-chancellor admits solicitors to practice before it as proctors, J. Williams, Law of the Universities 95.

[3] Below 614-632.   [4] Henry VIII.'s charter § 35, Reg. Privil. 73.

[5] Henry VIII.'s charter § 21, Reg. Privil. 65.

[6] Henry VIII.'s charter §§ 2, 3, Reg. Privil. 54-55—the chancellor and his commessary were to exercise this jurisdiction "infra villam nostram Oxon. in comitatu nostro Oxon. et suburbia ejusdem et quattuor hundreda eidem villæ et suburbiis proxime adjacencia nec non infra Comitatus nostros Oxon. et Berks."

[7] This exception was extensively construed to apply whenever the freehold might be affected, thus in Halley's Case (1628) Cro. Car. 87 it was held that the university could not claim conusance of an action of ejectment to recover possession of a term, because the plaintiff, by recovering possession, might put the freeholder out of possession; and cf. Stephen v. Berry (1683) 1 Vern. 212 and note thereto.

[8] Henry VIII.'s charter § 35 Reg. Privil. 73.

[9] The limits of the university franchise were defined by a charter of Henry IV. as, "ab orientali parte ejusdem villæ usque ad hospitale sancti Bartholomei juxta

The anomalous character of the chancellor's court was reflected not only in the variety and extent of jurisdictions which
it exercised, but also in its procedure and constitution. As it
was originally the ecclesiastical court of a bishop's chancellor [1]
it used the procedure of the canon, and, after the Reformation,
of the civil law ; [2] and, by virtue of the Act of 1571, it was able
to use this procedure when exercising its added secular jurisdiction criminal and civil. [3] On the other hand, from the sixteenth century onwards, the chancellors, in whom this wide
ecclesiastical jurisdiction was vested, were generally laymen. It
is true that their deputy was usually in orders ; but this was an
accident ; and from him appeals lay to bodies which tended to
become more and more secular. [4] From the chancellor's court
appeals could be taken in the first instance to the Regent
Masters, i.e. to the Congregation of the university, and from
them to the Convocation of the whole university. [5] If all these
courts agreed the decision was final ; if they differed an appeal
lay to delegates appointed by the crown in Chancery. [6] Thus,
as Dr. Rashdall has pointed out, [7] "it happened that the decision
of the most spiritual causes . . . belonged to a co-opting popular
assembly, many of whose members, though not in the mediæval
sense laymen, were not in orders at all." The chancellor's
court was thus unique among the many franchise courts which
flourished both in state and church in the Middle Ages, not only
by reason of the extent of its jurisdiction, but also by reason of
the manner of its exercise.

The charter of Henry IV. had added to the chancellor's court
a court held by the Steward of the university for the trial of
treasons, felonies, and mayhems committed by members of the
university in the counties of Oxfordshire and Berkshire. He
tried such cases by a jury, half of which was drawn from the
neighbourhood of the place where the crime was committed,
and half from members of the university. His court also exercised a leet jurisdiction similar to that exercised by the chancellor's court. [8]

Oxon., et ab occidentali parte usque ad villam de Boteley, et a parte boreali
ejusdem villæ usque ad pontem vocatum Godstowe Brygge, et ab australi parte
ejusdem villæ usque ad quendam boscum vocatum Bageley," Reg. Privil. 45.
    [1] Above 167.
    [2] Below 592, 594-595 ; " In hiis omnibus Cancellarius utriusque Academiæ causas
dijudicat per jus civile et consuetudines Academiæ. . . . Ideo in libellis, production-
ibus testium, sententiis aliisque omnibus causarum terminis, proceditur secundum
juris civilis formam," Duck, De usu et authoritate Juris Civilis ii 8, 3, 30.
    [3] Above 168-169.   [4] Rashdall, ii Pt. II. 438.   [5] Ibid 437-438.
    [6] Duck, op. cit. ii 8, 3, 30 ; Bl. Comm. iii 85.
    [7] Rashdall, ii Pt. II. 438.
    [8] Reg. Privil. 47-48 ; Charter of Henry VIII. § 4, ibid 55-56.

Two other courts held by the university—the court of the coroner and the court of the clerks of the market—originated in the wide privileges which the university charters had granted to the university. These charters do not give the university the right to appoint a coroner. But they do confer upon it a large collection of royal privileges of the fiscal variety.[1] If these had not been granted to the university a royal coroner would have held an inquisition in order to assert them on behalf of the crown. As they were granted to the university it was necessary for the university to appoint a coroner to enquire into and assert them. Thus the university acquired the right to have a coroner of its own, not by express grant, but by necessary implication. Similarly the charters had given the university the right to enforce the assizes of bread and beer, and of weights and measures, to punish forestallers and regrators, to supervise victuals, and to exclude the royal clerks of the market.[2] To exercise this jurisdiction supervisors were appointed by the university who developed (as in other towns)[3] into the clerks of the market.[4]

Let us now turn to the later history of these various university courts.

The ecclesiastical jurisdiction of the chancellor's court is practically obsolete. It has been held that the Clergy Discipline Act of 1840[5] has taken away its jurisdiction over ecclesiastics accused of ecclesiastical offences.[6] Like other ecclesiastical courts, it has lost its jurisdiction over the morals of laymen[7]— unless it can be said that the disciplinary jurisdiction which the vice-chancellor and proctors exercise over the morals of those *in statu pupillari* is a survival of this jurisdiction in another form. Its testamentary jurisdiction was taken away in 1858 when this jurisdiction was taken over by the state.[8]

The exact position of the criminal jurisdiction of the court is somewhat doubtful. According to one view the effect of the Summary Jurisdiction Act 1879[9] has taken away the criminal jurisdiction formerly vested in the chancellor's court, and left to him only the jurisdiction vested in him as a justice of the peace.[10] But in all probability this Act does not touch the criminal jurisdiction vested in him by charter, and only affects the jurisdiction which he possesses *qua* justice of the peace   I think that Dr.

[1] Charter of Henry VIII. § 12, Reg. Privil. 59, 60.   [2] Ibid 25-26.
[3] Above 150.   [4] Rashdall, ii Pt. II. 409.
[5] 3, 4 Victoria c. 86 ; below 612.
[6] Rashdall, ii Pt. II. 786, citing the decision in Pusey and others v. Jowett.
[7] Below 621.
[8] 20, 21 Victoria c. 77 § 3 ; cf. 23, 24 Victoria c. 91 § 2.
[9] 42, 43 Victoria c. 49.   [10] Rashdall ii Pt. II. 786-787.

Rashdall's reasons in favour of this view are conclusive;[1] and to them may be added the consideration that in Henry VIII.'s charter the jurisdiction exercisable by the chancellor as justice of the peace (to which alone the Summary Jurisdiction Act of 1879 applies) is quite separate from the other criminal jurisdiction conferred on him by the charter.[2]   The leet jurisdiction of the court has of course decayed, just as this jurisdiction has decayed all over the country.[3]   In 1825 an addition was made to the criminal jurisdiction of the court by giving the Chancellor or his deputy power to arrest "common prostitutes and night walkers" found wandering within the precincts of the university,[4] and to deal with them under the Vagrancy Act of 1824.[5]

The civil jurisdiction of the court still exists.   In 1886 in the case of *Ginnett* v. *Whittingham*[6] a claim by the chancellor to withdraw an action for libels published in London by a member of the university was allowed, though the court considered the privilege was inconvenient and oppressive.[7]   And this seems to have been the view of the superior courts since the eighteenth century.   As Lord Coleridge, C.J., explained, the courts have for this reason placed "certain no doubt expedient, but at the same time somewhat arbitrary limitations upon it."[8]   Thus it is probable that the wide words of the charter, though they might be construed to give an equitable jurisdiction, though other franchise courts acquired this jurisdiction, and though the assumption of such jurisdiction has occasionally been allowed, would not be construed to give this jurisdiction at the present day.[9]

---

[1] Rashdall ii Pt. II. 787-789.
[2] §§ 2, 3 of the charter, Reg. Privil. 54-55.   [3] Above 137.
[4] 6 George IV. c. 97 § 3.   [5] 5 George IV. c. 83.
[6] 16 Q.B.D. 761.   [7] At p. 770.   [8] Ibid.

[9] The decisions as to the power of the court to administer an equitable jurisdiction are somewhat conflicting, but on the whole adverse to the claim of the chancellor's court to assume (as the courts of counties Palatine, above 111, 116, 125, and the Stannaries, above 157-158, assumed) a jurisdiction in equity; the only case in which the claim seems clearly to be admitted is Alderidge v. Stratford (1714) Viner Ab. xxii 11 pl. 13; and it would seem from the Chancellor of Oxford v. Taylor (1841) 1 Q.B. at pp. 964-965 that in this case an injunction to the university court was first granted, and that the case was afterwards remitted by the Lord Chancellor to the university court—possibly because, on further consideration the Lord Chancellor considered that the university court could do complete justice; it was not allowed in Prat v. Taylor (1674) 1 Ch. Cas. 237; Draper v. Crowther (1683) 2 Ventr. 362; Stephen v. Berry (1683) 1 Vern. 212; the reason for refusing to allow the claim seems to have been that the court of the university had no power to give effective equitable relief; but, as Lord Coleridge, C.J., pointed out in Ginnett v. Whittingham (1886) 16 Q.B.D. at p. 770, the words of the non-intromittent clause of the university charter, which, "after speaking of the common law judges, go on to say, 'seu alii justiciarii vel judices quicumque,'" prima facie exclude the equitable jurisdiction of the court of Chancery; and, as we have seen, the analogies of the counties Palatine and the Stannaries are in favour of the university; but dicta in Ginnett v. Whittingham makes it almost certain that the courts would now follow the cases cited which deny the university an equitable jurisdiction.

Similarly it has been held that the privilege only applies to residents in the university, and to members of the university who are defendants[1]—"a bold stretch of judicial authority in the face of the words of the charter that the university shall have conusance when any of its members shall be one of the parties."[2]

Modern statutes have altered both the procedure of the court and the arrangements for hearing appeals from it. In 1854 the procedure of the common law was substituted for that of the civil law;[3] and in 1862 the vice-chancellor, with the approval of three of the judges, was empowered to make rules of procedure.[4] By the Judicature Act of 1884,[5] for the assent of the three judges, the assent of the Rule Committee of the Supreme Court is substituted; and in 1892 and 1907 new rules of procedure were made.[6] The system of appeals to Congregation, and from Congregation to Convocation, was exercised in practice by Delegates appointed from both Houses.[7] The last appeal so heard was in 1844; and the entering of an appeal in 1894 was the signal for the abolition of the old system.[8] By Order in Council of that year, issued by virtue of the Judicature Act of 1874-1875[9] and the Statute Law Revision Act 1883,[10] an appeal was given instead to a Divisional Court. As Dr. Rashdall points out, it is perhaps doubtful whether this new right of appeal applies either to the criminal or to the spiritual jurisdiction of the court.[11] But the latter jurisdiction is obsolete; and to the former, if it exists, the provisions of the Criminal Appeal Act of 1907 would presumably apply.[12]

The later history of the other courts held by the university can be briefly related. The court of the Steward still exists. It was apparently an active court in Elizabeth's reign; but only two indictments were heard in it in James I.'s and two in Charles I.'s reigns. Thus, when Blackstone wrote, it had not been used for more than a century, and it has never been used since.[13] The court of the university coroner still exists,[14] and there are two university coroners who hold inquisitions on unexplained deaths of members of the university. Two clerks of the market are still appointed, but they hold practically honorary offices.[15]

[1] Hayes v. Long (1766) 2 Wils, 310.
[2] Ginnett v. Whittingham (1886) 16 Q.B.D. at p. 771 *per* Lord Coleridge, C.J.
[3] 17, 18 Victoria c. 81 § 45.   [4] 25, 26 Victoria c. 26 § 12.
[5] 47, 48 Victoria c. 61 § 24.   [6] J. Williams, Law of the Universities 94.
[7] Rashdall, ii Pt. II. 437.   [8] Ibid 789.
[9] 38, 39 Victoria c. 77 § 15.   [10] 46, 47 Victoria c. 49.
[11] Rashdall ii Pt. II. 790.   [12] 7 Edward VII. c. 23.
[13] Bl. Comm. iv 276.   [14] J. Williams, op. cit. 96.
[15] Ibid 95 n. *y*.

Cambridge.

Just as the foundation at Oxford of a *Studium Generale* in 1167 was probably due to a migration from the university of Paris, so the foundation of a *Studium Generale* at Cambridge was probably due to the migration from Oxford in 1209.[1] The development of the two universities was, as Dr. Rashdall has pointed out, very similar ;[2] and the manner of the development of their franchise jurisdictions was almost identical—though, as we shall see, the Cambridge were less extensive than the Oxford franchises. At Cambridge as at Oxford kings and popes combined to favour the university. From the thirteenth century onwards kings granted many privileges, jurisdictional and otherwise, to its members ;[3] collisions with the town increased these privileges ;[4] and charters of Richard II.'s,[5] and Henry IV., V., and VI.'s[6] reigns confirmed and extended them. Finally a comprehensive charter was granted to the university by Elizabeth in 1561 ;[7] and it and all preceding grants were confirmed by the same statute of 1571 as that by which the privileges of Oxford were confirmed.[8] Similarly in 1432 the chancellor of Cambridge got, not without the help of a forged bull, the same exemption from episcopal and archiepiscopal control as Oxford had previously acquired.[9]

The chancellor's court at Cambridge had a jurisdiction similar to that which the chancellor's court at Oxford enjoyed. It could hear all personal actions, and could try all criminal cases, felony, and mayhem excepted, if one of the parties was a member of the university. But, unlike the Oxford court, its jurisdiction was limited to cases arising in the town and suburbs of Cambridge.[10] Though its procedure was that of the canon, and, after the Reformation, of the civil law, it was the rule that cases should be tried as informally as possible ; and advocates were not allowed.[11]

---

[1] Above 166; Rashdall ii Pt. II. 545-547.   [2] Ibid 547.

[3] A printed collection will be found in G. Dyer, Privileges of the University of Cambridge ; for a short summary see Rashdall ii Pt. II. 547-550.

[4] R.P. iii 106-109, 5 Richard II. nos. 45-60.

[5] Dyer, i 82-84 (5 Richard II.) ; ibid 86-88 (7 Richard II.).

[6] The charter of 9 Henry VI., printed R.P. v 425-433 comprises a charter of Henry IV. which confirms previous charters, and also charters of Henry V.'s reigns; see Shadwell, Enactments in Parliament i 26.

[7] Dyer, i 113-131.   [8] 13 Elizabeth c. 29.

[9] Rashdall, ii Pt. II. 550—" A bull was forged, purporting to emanate from Pope Honorius I. in the year 624. In this audacious document the Pope is made to assert that he had himself studied at Cambridge, and to confer upon the university the privilege of exemption from all episcopal and archiepiscopal authority."

[10] Charter of Elizabeth, Dyer, i 117.

[11] J. Williams, Law of the Universities 96-97 ; perhaps a wise rule as the canonist William of Drogheda (below 582) explains how a " cautus advocatus potest formare tres acciones ex una injuria sicut ego feci in causa scolaris mei in causa versus maiorem Oxoniæ coram universitate Oxonie," Maitland, E.H.R. xii 652-653.

There are therefore no special proctors licensed to plead before the court as at Oxford.[1] Arrangements for the hearing of cases and for appeals were also different. If one of the litigants was not *in statu pupillari* the judges of the court were the chancellor or the vice-chancellor : if both the litigants were *in statu pupillari* the chancellor, vice-chancellor or the chancellor's commissary were the judges. Appeals lay from the commissary to the chancellor or vice-chancellor, and from the chancellor or vice-chancellor to the Senate. There was no further appeal.[2]

The other courts belonging to the university were firstly the court of the Steward,[3] secondly the court of the clerk of the market, and thirdly a court for Stourbridge fair. Firstly, Elizabeth's charter of 1561, had given to the Steward of Cambridge University a jurisdiction over treasons and felonies committed by members of the university similar to that possessed by Oxford University ;[4] but I can find no evidence that such a court was ever held. Secondly, since the university had the right to enforce the assizes of bread and ale, and of weights and measures it necessarily had the power to appoint officials to act as clerks of the market.[5] Thirdly, the right to hold a court for Stourbridge fair was (amongst other rights) confirmed in the most ample terms by a charter of 1589.[6]

The later history of the Cambridge courts has been different from the later history of the Oxford courts.

In the middle of the last century serious disputes broke out between the university and the town as to the legal warrant for some of their privileges, as to their mode of exercise, and as to the expediency of their continuance.[7] Attempts to arrive at a settlement failed ;[8] and eventually the dispute was submitted to the arbitration of Mr. Justice Paterson.[9] After a lengthy hearing,[10] he published an award[11] which very considerably restricted the jurisdictional privileges of the university ; and statutory force was given to it by the Cambridge Award Act 1856.[12] The university abandoned firstly its rights to claim conusance in civil and criminal proceedings in all cases in which a non-member of the

[1] Above 169 n. 2.
[2] Halsbury, Laws of England ix 150 ; J. Williams, op. cit. 97.
[3] Cambridge had possessed a Steward from about 1418, C. H. Cooper, the Earlier High Stewards of the University of Cambridge, Camb. Ant. Soc. Publications i 273.
[4] Dyer, i 126-127.
[5] Ibid 122-124 ; cf. Shadwell, Enactments in Parliament iii 227 n. 3.
[6] C. H. Cooper, Annals of Cambridge ii 468-475.
[7] Ibid v 43-63.   [8] Ibid 148-156.   [9] Ibid 182-183.
[10] Ibid 185-191.   [11] Ibid 192-201.
[12] 19, 20 Victoria c. xvii, printed with a commentary in Enactments in Parliament iii 221-241.

university was a party to the proceedings ;[1] secondly, the powers
which it claimed in respect of the licensing of ale houses, which
were perhaps regarded as incident to the right to enforce the
assize of beer ;[2] thirdly, its powers with respect to weights and
measures, except the right to appoint an inspector ;[3] and fourthly
its powers in respect to fairs and markets.[4] As a result of the
Act the chancellor's court has fallen into abeyance.[5] The
Act did not take away from the university the power to search
for, and to imprison or banish from the town "women bawds,
vagabonds and other suspected persons," which had been conferred upon it by the charter and statute of Elizabeth's reign.[6]
But, in consequence of the proceedings taken against the vice-
chancellor for the imprisonment of Daisy Hopkins,[7] it was
thought desirable to repeal this clause of the charter, and, in lieu
thereof, to give to the university the same powers of dealing with
such persons as those which the Act of 1825 conferred upon
Oxford.[8] The effect is to make it necessary for the chancellor
or vice-chancellor to exercise this jurisdiction in accordance with
the ordinary rules of procedure ; and to make it impossible for
him to proceed as he might have done before, on unsworn evidence not given in open court.

III. The Feudal and Manorial Courts

We have seen that in the twelfth century a lord *qua* lord had
the right to hold a court for his tenants.[9] In spite of the attempt
made in Magna Carta to preserve some part of the jurisdiction
of these courts,[10] they became in the course of the thirteenth
century of gradually less importance. This was due chiefly to
three causes.

(i) The feudal principle would have led to a series of courts
one above the other ; and the higher courts would have been the
courts of provinces. This happened on the Continent ; and we
can see from the Petition of the Barons (1258) that in England a
series of these courts one above the other was common.[11] We
can see also that large landowners sometimes held one court for

---

[1] § 18; for some account of the law relating to claims of conusance see
J. Williams, op. cit. 97-100.
   [2] § 8 and note thereto.   [3] §§ 13, 14.   [4] § 15.
   [5] Halsbury, Laws of England ix 150.   [6] Dyer, i 124-125.
   [7] R. v. Vice-Chancellor of Cambridge (1891) 8 T.L.R. 151 ; and cf. R. v. Elsdon,
cited J. Williams, op cit. 135.
   [8] 57, 58 Victoria c. lx, printed in Enactments in Parliament iv 194-196.
   [9] Above 25-26.   [10] Above 58-59.
   [11] Stubbs, Sel. Ch. 386, 387 (§ 29) ; the complaint is that when the "capitalis
dominus" has made default, the "superior capitalis dominus" craves his court and
has it ; and if he makes default the "alter superior dominus" craves his court and
has it—"et sic de singulis capitalibus dominis quotquot fuerint superiores."

their extended possessions. The Abbot of Ramsey kept a court for his larger freehold tenants at Broughton;[1] and the suitors came from Lincolnshire, Norfolk, Suffolk, Bedfordshire, Hertfordshire, and Northamptonshire. The Abbot of Gloucester adopted a similar system.[2] The Bishop of Ely had a council for which, as we have seen, cases of difficulty were reserved.[3] But the dominions of the greater landowners were scattered. Great feudal courts for a large dominion were made infrequent, and in the long run impossible by considerations of time and space.[4] The same causes which made the lesser franchises the most common, operated to make the feudal courts the courts of small districts. At the same time to the men of that age feudal jurisdiction was the natural jurisdiction. " It is not very rare," says Maitland, "to find the lord of a manor owing suit to a court many miles away."[5] But it is clear that under these circumstances suit of court was a serious burden. We are not, therefore, surprised to find that, in the thirteenth century liability to suit was a pressing question. There seems to have been two views held upon the matter. According to the first, which is supported by Bracton, suit could not be claimed in the absence of express stipulation, unless the business of the court in some way concerned the king. According to the second, all tenants, because they were tenants, owed suit to their lord's court.[6] The first theory was that adopted by the provisions of Westminster[7] and the Statute of Marlborough (1267).[8] The tenant must be specially bound to do suit, or his ancestors must have done the suit within the last thirty-nine years; otherwise the suit could not be claimed. On a division of the property the liability to suit was not increased; and if part of the land held by service of the suit came to the lord the liability disappeared.[9] The statute thus made it definitely impossible to create great feudal courts;

---

[1] Select Pleas in Manorial Courts (S.S.) xlv.   [2] Ibid xlv, xlvi.
[3] The Court Baron (S.S.) 111 ; above 26.
[4] For instances of very numerous courts held by one lord for his domains see Webb, The Manor and the Borough 34-47; it would seem that though one lord might hold many courts, they were disparate and independent; they can hardly be called, as Webb calls them, a "hierarchy."
[5] Select Pleas in Manorial Courts (S.S.) xliv.
[6] Ibid xlviii-l; Bracton, ff. 35, 35 b : " Sunt enim servitia et consuetudines quæ pertinent ad dominum fœdi, et consuetudines et servitia, quæ pertinent ad regem, sicut sectæ ad justiciam faciendam per breve de recto, et ad pacem, sicut de latrone judicando, et pro aforciamento curiæ in prædictis. . . . Item sunt quædam servitia quæ pertinent ad dominum capitalem . . . et de quibus oportet quod fiat mentio in scriptura et alioquin peti non poterunt ut si dicatur faciendo sectam ad curiam domini sui."
[7] Stubbs, Sel. Ch. 401 (§ 1).
[8] 52 Henry III. c. 9; Coke, Second Instit. 116; appropriate writs " contra forman feoffamenti," and, on a division of the property, " de contributione facienda " were provided.
[9] Y.B. 11, 12 Ed. III. (R.S.) 194 per Scharshulle, J.

and because it had this effect it was deservedly popular. "For twenty years past," said Bereford, C.J.,[1] in 1310, "There has not come to England so good a law for poor people ;" and the reason for this view is obvious. It put a stop to a form of oppression which, if the other solution had been adopted, lords would have been tempted to exert ; for, as Bereford points out in the same case, but for the statute, " a bad rascal of a bailiff or hayward by duress might cause a poor man to do suit, and thereby he would remain charged for all time through this false possession." [2]

(ii) Such courts were not in fact needed. The growth of the jurisdiction of the king's court had the same effect upon the feudal courts as it had upon the communal courts. The king's court had assumed jurisdiction over all the more serious crimes, over all disturbances of seisin, over ownership of freehold land if the tenant put himself upon the Grand Assize. Magna Carta might ordain "that the writ præcipe shall not issue so that a man shall lose his court ; " [3] but the growth of writs of entry furnished new remedies which fell exclusively within the jurisdiction of the king's court.[4] In later times the tenant by writs of *accedas ad curiam* or *recordari facias*, and the demandant by writs of *tolt* and *pone* could bring the matter before the same tribunal ; [5] and even the mere insertion of the words " quia dominus remisit curiam," whether or not such waiver had been made, would enable the action to be begun directly in the king's court.[6] By the end of the thirteenth century these feudal courts had become unprofitable.[7] In fact they were so useless that lords were often obliged to make use of the procedure of the king's court to force their tenants to perform their services. This was due partly to the efficiency and power of the royal courts, partly to direct legislation. The statute of Marlborough protected freeholders from being distrained to answer for their services without the king's writ.[8] It also protected them from

---

[1] Y.B. 3, 4 Ed. II. (S.S.) 162 ; and cf. Introd. xxx, xxxi.

[2] Ibid 161 ; and cf. Art. 135 of the Articles of the Eyre of Kent of 1313-1314 directed against illegal distress to compel persons to appear before the courts of lords, Eyre of Kent (S.S.) i. 45 ; Y.B. 8 Ed. II. (S.S.) 20.

[3] § 34 ; above 58.

[4] Writs of entry " in the post," and writs of cosinage, vol. iii 11-14.

[5] For these writs see App. VII., VIII., IX. ; the writs of *accedas ad curiam* and *recordari facias* were writs of false judgment, above 73 n. 7; below 200-201 ; the writ of *tolt* directed the case to be transferred from the court Baron to the county court, and the writ of *pone* directed it to be transferred to the court of Common Pleas ; in real actions the defendant is generally called the tenant, and the plaintiff the demandant.

[6] F.N.B. 3; App. V. c.   [7] Above 58-59.

[8] 52 Henry III. c. 22 ; later attempts by " Lords and Ladies " to compel persons to answer for their freeholds before their councils were put down by statute, 15 Richard II. c. 12 ; 16 Richard II. c. 2.

being compelled to serve as jurors against their wills;[1] and therefore the lord could only use the older methods of proof—compurgation or battle—unless both parties consented to a trial by jury. It also prevented the lord from making his court a court of error by asserting that jurisdiction in error was a matter exclusively for the king's court.[2] The Statute of Gloucester in course of time restricted the feudal courts, as it restricted the communal courts, to be courts for very small matters.[3]

(iii) Feudalism has, as I have said, its two sides—its property side and its jurisdictional side. To use modern terms, it has affinities both with the law of real property and with constitutional law. But the king's court had, on the one hand, drawn from the lord the greater part of his jurisdiction; and, on the other hand, this same court, administering law common to the whole country, had spread over the whole country feudal conceptions of property in land. The English state is therefore less feudal, but the English land law is more feudal than that of any other country in Europe. Hence we find that all the incidents of feudalism were regarded in a commercial spirit—they were looked upon as property. The military duties involved in tenure by knight service became obsolete.[4] The tenure was valued for the profitable incidents of wardship and marriage. The right of free alienation given by the statute of Quia Emptores, the earliest legislation as to mortmain, the law of succession to real property, all point to this conclusion.[5] Under these circumstances the jurisdiction involved in feudalism gradually declined. It became merely appendant to land owning—a survival from the days when feudalism was more than merely an element in our real property law.[6] It is this development which has given rise to the manorial jurisdiction of later law.

We have seen that in the twelfth century the manor meant a tract of land cultivated as an agricultural whole, and " organized under aristocratic administration." We have seen that manors at first varied infinitely in size; but that the typical manor tended to become a unit consisting of demesne lands, and of lands let to free and to villein tenants who had certain rights of common in the waste [7] When Bracton wrote, the term " manor " was still

---

[1] 52 Henry III. c. 22 ; Kitchen, Courts (Ed. 1653) 178, 225 ; P. and M. i 581.

[2] 52 Henry III. c. 19 ; Coke, Second Instit. 138 ; cf. Petition of the Barons (Sel. Ch. 386-387) § 29.

[3] 6 Edward I. c. 8 ; above 72-73.

[4] Vol. iii c. 1 § 3 ; cp. P. and M. i 256.

[5] Vol. ii 348-349.

[6] See on this subject " The decay of feudal property in France and England. Maine, Early Law and Custom, chap. x.

[7] Above 28-30.

an elastic term which signified many different kinds of holding;[1] but, in the course of the thirteenth and fourteenth centuries, it came to mean more than this. It came not only to denote a certain tract of land held in a certain way but also to connote jurisdiction. It is probable that the manor gained this connotation by borrowing from the feudal principle. This is the theory suggested by Maitland. He says that the "feudal principle was the rule of law, but that it had to work under such and so many limitations, some of law and some of fact, that the actual result was not very different from that which would have been produced by the manorial principle; so much so that in the course of time it became possible to regard a private court (when not created by real or supposed grant from the crown) as never existing save as part of a manor."[2]

The process by which the term manor came to connote jurisdiction was exceedingly gradual. It would appear that even in Coke's day a manor was regarded as primarily a tract of land. He tells us that in the thirty-first year of Edward I.'s reign the king brought a Quo Warranto against the Lady of S. to know by what warrant she claimed to hold the manor of C., and that this was the first Quo Warranto that was brought for lands.[3] In later law no doubt a Quo Warranto only lay to recover some usurped jurisdiction or franchise. But the law on that point was hardly settled in this way in Edward I.'s reign[4]—though it was coming to be so settled in Edward II.'s reign;[5] and in fact it was

---

[1] "Et sciendum quod manerium poterit esse per se ex pluribus ædificiis coadjuvatum, sive villis et hamlettis adjacentibus. Poterit etiam esse manerium et per se et cum pluribus villis et cum pluribus hamlettis adjacentibus, quorum nullum dici poterit manerium per se, sed villæ sivi hameletta; poterit etiam esse per se manerium capitale, et plura continere sub se maneria non capitalia, et plures villas et plures hamlettas, quasi sub uno capite et dominio uno," Bracton f. 212; it is clear, however, from the Eyre of Kent (S.S.) iii 31-32 that the judges had then begun to distinguish between a demand for certain acres of land and a demand for a manor; and the reason for drawing the distinction is given by Bereford, C.J., in Y.B. 4 Ed. II, (S.S.) 120, "I believe," he said, "that they say that they hold by the third part of a manor, so that if there was waste or other profit they might enjoy their share of the profit; for if they hold by bovates they will not have this advantage."

[2] Select pleas in Manorial Courts xli; L.Q.R. v. 127-130; to the last writs were directed to the lord *qua* lord of the land held by the tenant, not *qua* lord of the manor, and the manor is not mentioned in such writs; and for many centuries the lands were described by reference, not to the manor, but to the vill in which they are situate, Y.BB. 6 Ed. II. (S.S.) 169 *per* Hedon *arg.*; 8 Ed. II. 3, 5, 7; Stork v. Fox (1605) Cro. Jac. 120; cp. General Estates Co. v. Beaver [1914] 3 K.B. at p. 936 *per* Phillimore, L.J.

[3] Second Instit. 495; cf. Hill v. Grange (1556) Plowden at p. 168—"a manor is compounded of several things and may contain land, meadow, pasture, wood, and rent, and divers other things, all of which are contained in the gross name."

[4] Bracton says a Quo Warranto lies to enable the heir to recover land retained in spite of a verdict in novel disseisin against his ancestor: the writ, he says, "in parte capit naturam mortis antecessoris et in parte novæ disseysinæ," ff. 284 b, 285; below 181 n. 1.

[5] Eyre of Kent (S.S.) iii 173 *per* Staunton, J., who considered that a Quo Warranto was the proper writ to assert a claim to a franchise, and an assize to assert a claim to freehold.

very far from being the first Quo Warranto ever brought for lands.[1] Coke's statement, however, and other cases of the seventeenth century on the question whether a Quo Warranto lay of a court Baron, or a manor, show that even then the law was not quite clear how far a manor was merely property, how far it cannoted jurisdiction.[2] But that it was coming to connote something more than land in the early years of the fourteenth century is clear from a Year Book of Edward II.'s reign. In 1314 it was said that the tenure of a mere tract of land gave a right to the land and nothing more, while the tenure of a manor gave rise also to "the profits of lordship and other appendancies."[3] It was inevitable that in that age jurisdiction should be regarded as perhaps the most natural of all these appendancies.

In the earliest records of manorial courts we find one court—the court Baron—which freeholders and villeins alike attend.[4] But the differences between the freehold and villein tenants grew with time ; and those differences survived when the villein of the thirteenth and fourteenth centuries became the copyholder of the later fifteenth and sixteenth centuries. The freeholder could easily get his case tried in the king's court. He could not be made to serve on a jury in the manorial court. He need not submit his case to the decision of a manorial jury.[5] He sometimes refused to be bound by bye-laws made by the court.[6] All the suitors of the court were his judges, whereas the lord's steward was the judge of the copyhold tenants.[7] All these causes tended

---

[1] Bracton's Note Book, cases 241, 268, 422, 750, 840, 862, 930, 1066, 1111, 1119, 1224, 1274, 1275, 1288, begun by the crown; cases 35, 95, 219, 501, 1013, 1014, 1108, 1136, 1141, 1175 1181, 1296, 1358, 1390, 1512, 1846, begun by a subject.

[2] The King v. Stanton (1607) 2 Cro. 259, 260, " It was moved whether a Quo Warranto did lie of a court Baron; for it is incident to the manor, and is not any liberty which the king can have distinct from the manor; and being of common right, the king cannot have a Quo Warranto thereof; and of that opinion was Fleming, C.J. Fenner doubted thereof: but Yelverton, Williams, and Coke held that a Quo Warranto well lies; for it is a matter of right to hold courts and to administer justice ;" the contrary opinion was intimated in the King v. Hulston (1725) 1 Stra. 621; there was a similar disagreement as to whether a mandamus lay against the steward of a court Baron, see the King v. Churchwardens of Kingsclere (1671) 2 Lev. 18; Stamp's Case (1667) 1 Sid. 40; the King v. Street (1723) 8 Mod. 98.

[3] Y.B. 8 Ed. II. (S.S.) 121 per Bereford, C.J.; above 180 n. 1.

[4] P. and M. i 581 ; cp. Durham Halmote Rolls (Surt. Soc.) i xx, xxi; Webb, The Manor and the Borough 12, 13 ; the style of the court is " Curia Baronis E.C. Militis manerii sui prædicti tenta tali die etc. coram A.B. Seneschallo ibidem."

[5] Thus it is said in the Doctor and Student, f. 14, that, though as a rule in courts of record the trial is by jury, " In other courts that be not of record, as in the county, court baron, hundred, and such other like, they shall be tried by the oath of the parties, and not otherwise, unless the parties assent that it shall be tried by the homage."

[6] P. and M. i 612-617.

[7] Coke, Fourth Instit. 268 ; First Instit. 58 a; cp. Armyn v. Appletoft (1621) Cro. Jac. 582.

to make the court of the freeholder look different from the court of the copyholder.   Littleton, however, does not state that there are two courts in a manor.   But in the sixteenth century the lawyers were beginning to analyse the conception of a manor and the nature of its courts;[1] and so Coke in his commentary on Littleton[2] says that the manor court is "of two natures; the first is by the common law, and is called a court Baron, as some have said, for that it is the freeholders' or freemen's court . . . and of that court the freeholders being suitors be judges. . . . The second is a customary court, and that doth concern copyholders, and therein the Lord or his Steward is the judge." From the statement that the court is of "two natures" it is an easy step to take to say that there are two courts in a manor—a court Baron and a court customary.[3]   But in the books which deal with the holding of the manorial court the distinction is by no means clearly drawn.   Blackstone, though he says that they are "in their nature distinct," admits that they "are frequently confounded together."[4]   And in the world of fact, as distinct from the world of legal theory, not only were the court Baron and the court customary "frequently confounded together," but even such disparate courts as these manorial courts and the franchise courts of the hundred and the leet.[5]

We can thus see how the notion sprung up that there are two courts in a manor.   It is more difficult to understand how the rule sprang up that there can be no manor unless there are at least two freeholders.[6]   If we admit that any freeholders are necessary to constitute a manor we can see why the number two is fixed upon.   The suitors are the judges; and no man can be judge in his own case.[7]   The difficult question to determine is why any freeholders were needed; for, in the thirteenth century there were manors consisting only of villein tenements.[8]   It is indeed admitted that a lord may have only copyhold tenants, and

---

[1] Vol. iv 130.

[2] First Instit. 58 a; Use of the Law (a tract erroneously attributed to Bacon, but probably of Bacon's time) mentions only one court, Bacon's Works vii 485.

[3] Coke so states it in Melwich v. Luter 4 Co. Rep. 26 b.

[4] Comm. iii 33.

[5] "In the model roll . . . the leet entries appear under the general heading 'Entres del Courte Baron,' the only thing which marks them off from the other entries being that they are collected together at the end, and are preceded by an inconspicuous sub-heading 'xii pro rege,' together with twelve sets of initials and the abbreviation 'Jur.,'" Hearnshaw, Leet Jurisdiction in England 35; see also Y.B. 3, 4 Ed. II. (S.S.) xxxii; The Eyre of Kent (S.S.) i 107.

[6] Cases cited from Broke's Abridgement in Select Pleas in Manorial Courts lxi; in Bradshaw v. Lawson (1791) 4 T.R. 443 it was said that the rule as to two free suitors was so well settled that no cases need be cited to support it.

[7] Y.B. 11, 12 Ed. III. (R.S.) 302 *per* Trewith *arg.*; Kitchen Courts 7.

[8] See Select Pleas in Manorial Courts lxii-lxiv for a clear statement of the difficulty; P. and M. i 582.

that he may hold a court for them. But then he has, not a manor, but a customary manor.[1] How then did the notion arise that there is no true manor without freehold tenants?

Possibly a reason may be found in the fact that in the manor the law of property and the law of jurisdiction meet. A dictum, unintelligible if we take either of these branches of law separately, may be the intelligible though illogical result of both taken together.

Looking at the matter from the side of jurisdiction it appears that the manor contains within itself two kinds of jurisdiction— a jurisdiction over freeholders and a jurisdiction over copyholders. It might well be thought that jurisdiction over the freeholder was a kind of "liberty," which must exist by prescription in the absence of express grant;[2] while jurisdiction over copyholders was merely an incident to the property absolutely necessary to its management. It would follow that a manor having as incident to it a jurisdiction over freeholders could not be created by a private person. Looking at the matter from the side of property a similar conclusion is reached. The freeholder's interest must have been created before Quia Emptores. That statute put an end to subinfeudation whenever an estate in fee simple was created. If a man alienates freehold after that statute for an estate in fee simple he does not get tenants. His alienees hold, not of him, but of his lord. It is clear therefore that a man cannot create by his own act a manor which contains both freehold and copyhold tenants of the manor.[3]

But the freeholders were as the suitors of the court Baron the most important class of the manor. If it comes to be said that a man cannot create a manor with such a court, either because he cannot create jurisdiction over freehold tenants, or because he cannot create freehold tenants holding of himself, it will not be long before it is said that a manor is not a manor without freehold

---

[1] 4 Co. Rep. 26 b, "Although the lord by his own act cannot make of one and the same manor at the common law sundry manors consisting upon demesnes and freeholds, yet he may by his own act . . . make a customary manor consisting upon copyholders only, as to the purposes aforesaid. When the lord grants over the inheritance of his copyholds to another, the grantee may hold such court for the copyhold tenants only, as his grantor might;" cp. Sir Henry Nevil's Case (1613) 11 Co. Rep. 17 a; Lemon v. Blackwell (1680), Skin. 191.

[2] The King v. Stanton, above 181 n. 2.

[3] Melwich v. Luter (1588) 4 Co. Rep. 26 b; Sir Moyle Finch's Case (1607) 6 Co. Rep. at p. 64 a; as Kenyon, C.J., said in Glover v. Lane (1789) 3 T.R. 445, "to constitute a manor it is necessary not only that there should be two freeholders within the manor, but two freeholders holding of the manor *subject to escheats.*" It is pointed out in Sir Moyle Finch's case at f. 64 a, that if there be a partition of the manor by act of law, e g. where two parceners inherit, each may have a manor; cp. Marshe and Smith's case (1585) 1 Leo. 26; and Scriven, Copyholds (Ed. 1846) 7; Y.B. 8 Ed. II. (S.S.) xxviii-xxx.

tenants. Their presence thus becomes in later times the test of the existence of the manor. The lord may, it is true, aliene the seigniory of the copyholds; but then he will create merely a customary manor. The same convenient term will easily be applied to the case where all the freeholds have escheated. The lawyers begin to speculate as to the nature of the manor. It must be "constituted by continuance of time."[1] It can neither be created nor divided at the present day.[2]

There is in fact a substantial justification for the conclusion so reached. It is the presence of the freeholder—placed above mere manorial custom by the common law—which has sharply divided the inhabitants of the manor into two classes. The most important of these classes cannot be created by a private person. When in the sixteenth century the lawyers began to analyse the nature of the manor and its courts,[3] they naturally began to doubt whether a manor could be considered to be a manor without its most important members. The common law has in fact created the peculiar status of the freeholder with reference both to property and to jurisdiction. In creating that status it has made a general feudal jurisdiction impossible. But it has created manorial jurisdiction. It has tied down feudal jurisdiction to the tract of land called a manor. It may then be said that, historically, the freeholder is the essence, because he is the cause of the peculiar manorial jurisdiction of later law. The result may seem illogical; but a body of law, formed at the meeting place of the law of jurisdiction and the law of property, is likely to seem illogical if it is approached from one only of these points of view.

The business of the manorial court was petty but varied, more especially when, to the ordinary business of the court Baron and court customary, there was added the business of a hundred court and a court leet. In the court Baron all kinds of personal actions (where the cause of action did not exceed 40s. in value) could be tried. On the court rolls we find actions for breach of contract, trespass, libel, slander, assault; and, on the thirteenth and fourteenth century rolls, actions for wrongs for which the king's court had not yet provided a remedy.[4] If the lord possessed the right to hold a hundred court its jurisdiction was very similar.[5] But in two respects there was a difference. (i) In theory it was only in the court Baron that cases begun

---

[1] Hill v. Grange (1557) Plowden at p. 169.
[2] Morris and Smith v. Paget (1585) 1 Cro. 38; Lemon v. Blackwell (1680) Skin. 191.
[3] Vol. iv 130.
[4] Vol. ii 382-384; and see the court Baron (S.S.) 116-118; L.Q.R. xviii 264-267.
[5] Above 134; cf. Bl. Comm. iii 34-35.

by writ of right for the recovery of freehold land held of the lord of the manor could be tried.[1] But we have seen that in practice these actions were usually begun in the royal courts ; and, if begun in the court Baron, they could easily be removed to those courts.[2] (ii) Till the end of the fifteenth century, all actions connected with copyhold tenements could only be heard by the court customary.[3] Even after the courts of common law and the court of Chancery, and, in the sixteenth and early seventeenth centuries the courts of Requests and Star Chamber, had begun to protect the copyholder,[4] the court still continued to do a certain amount of litigious business connected with copyhold ;[5] and all conveyances of such copyholds must be made by surrender and admittance in the customary court. In the court leet, as we have seen,[6] a considerable amount of petty criminal business was done. And the court, whether sitting as a manorial court or as a court leet, long continued to be an administrative as well as a judicial tribunal. It could make byelaws' both for the good government of the community, and for the regulation of the common field system of agriculture—a system which was common in the seventeenth and earlier part of the eighteenth centuries, and survived till the nineteenth century.[7]

A session of the manorial court, or franchise hundred court where such a franchise existed, was generally held once in three weeks. The court leet was held, as we have seen,[8] once in six months. Over all these courts the lord's Steward presided. From the end of the thirteenth century he was generally a professional lawyer ; and it is clear from the very technical books which were written to instruct these Stewards in their duties that a professional lawyer was needed.[9] In fact in the sixteenth and seventeenth centuries, and probably earlier, court keeping was a useful, and a not wholly unremunerative employment for the youthful barrister. Sir James Whitelocke,[10] the future chief justice of Chester and judge of the King's Bench, began his legal practice by acting as the Steward of the manors of St. John's

---

[1] Above 58; vol. iii 6, 7.   [2] Above 59.
[3] Vol. ii 379-381 ; vol. iii 206-209.
[4] Ibid, 211.
[5] See Pepys Diary (Ed. Wheatley) ii 360-361, and iii 280-281 for an account of a litigation in a manor court in 1662-1663 as to some copyholds in which Pepys was interested.
[6] Above 135-137.
[7] Above 135, 137; and for fuller details see vol. ii 364; vol. iv 369-370; for the common field system see vol. ii 56-61.
[8] Above 136.
[9] P. and M. i 580; a case is there cited in which the post was offered to Sir J. Stonore who had been a royal justice.
[10] For some account of Whitelocke see vol. v 343, 345, 350.

College, Oxford, of which he was a member.[1] Sir Francis
North, the future chief justice of the Common Pleas and Lord
Keeper, began his legal practice by acting as the Steward of the
manors of his grandfather.[2] His brother, Roger North,[3] has
explained why court keeping was so useful to young practitioners
as an introduction to practice. Besides accustoming a man to
transact business and to deal with different kinds of men, it
gives, he says,[4] an excellent training in the actual working of
many different branches of the law. "All the business of court
keeping depends on the fundamental institution of our laws.
As the crown law holds in the court leet, which is a sort of eyre,
and as that eyre is a view of a small vill, so the ancient eyre was
a view of a larger extent, as of a whole country or forest.[5] The
nature and distinction of the court, and suitors, which was the
original of trials by jury[6]—the county being drawn into small
inquests, who in the ancient eyres attended in a body, and
answered for all facts in the country. So in the franchise of the
leet the court is informed by the suitors . . . and then the
court judges and inflicts the penalties according to law.[7] Then
the nature of inquests and offices, the tenderness in capital cases,
in which the suitors and court are but an inquest to certify but
not try. And this small and despised, or rather antiquated,
jurisdiction of the leet gives any student a handle to inform
himself of the ancient constitution and nature of the English
government and jurisdictions. The Copyhold Court, which is
called the court Baron, instructs him in titles, and the way of
examining them, through all the mutations, and to see if they
cohere, and to spy out defects and cure them. And also to accommodate the business for poor men, who are governed by
Mr. Steward. He will have the mortgaging and discharging
mortgages; entailing and barring entails; settling jointures, and
examining feme-coverts who join to convey, all which is working in the porch of the law, in order to be fit to enter the sacred
temple of it. . . . The court Baron, in the genuine sense,[8] is the
court of lord's jurisdiction in his manor, and holds plea of all
land held of the manor, and in debt under 40s., and may be
held from three weeks to three weeks, wherein the process is
after the model of the ancient common law, and the knowledge

---

[1] " At Michaelmas 1601 the colledge of St. John in Oxon. bestowed on me the
stewardship of thear lands," Whitelocke, Liber Famelicus (C.S.) 15.

[2] Lives of the Norths i 29-30.

[3] For an account of Roger North see vol. vi 619-624.

[4] Lives of the Norths iii 107-108.

[5] For the general eyre see below 265-272; for the forest eyre see above 98, 99.

[6] For the jury see below 312.   [7] See above 78, 79.

[8] Notice that North, who got his knowledge from practice, hardly recognizes
the distinction between court Baron and court Customary.

how to conduct such a court fits a man to be a practiser even at
the Common Pleas Bar.   For all which reasons, and more, it is
most advisable to put a young man destined for the law upon
court keeping, and fill him with this sort of business as much as
may be."

Roger North's description seems to tell us that in the latter
half of the seventeenth century the manorial court, though decadent, was still a living institution.[1]   But in the eighteenth
century it rapidly decayed.   Personal actions, if begun there,
were generally transferred to the courts of common law ; and so
it declined in the same way and for the same reasons as the
communal courts.[2]   The leet jurisdiction, as we have seen, became gradually obsolete.[3]   The litigious business connected with
copyholds was generally taken to the royal courts.   All that
was left to the court was copyhold conveyancing business, because it was only in the court customary that the necessary
formalities of surrender and admittance could take place.[4]   The
manor, so says the law, cannot exist without freeholders ; but
copyhold conveyancing business is all that is left to its court—
a court which can be held by the steward or deputy-steward
out of the manor, and with no single tenant present.[5]   Such a
court is truly the vanishing point both of feudal and of manorial
jurisdiction.

IV. The New County Courts

By the end of the fifteenth century the central courts of
common law had definitely established their superiority over
the local courts—communal, franchise, feudal, and manorial.
Some of these local courts then had many centuries of active
life before them ; but, from the fifteenth century onwards, they
tended to grow weaker, and the forces making for a centralized
judicial system tended to grow stronger.   The new courts which
arose in the sixteenth century, such as the Council,[6] the Star
Chamber,[7] the court of Chancery [8] and the court of Requests,[9]
were all centralized courts.   It is true that the needs of poor
suitors, upon whom this centralized judicial system pressed

[1] For some details of the courts which he held see Lives of the Norths iii 108-
109.
[2] Bl. Comm. iii 33-35 ; for some exceptional cases in which the court continued
to act as a court for the collection of petty debts see Webb, The Manor and the
Borough 119 n.
[3] Above 136-137.
[4] P. and M. i 578-579 ; it was no doubt for this reason that the notion of a
customary manor, above 183, was evolved.
[5] 57, 58 Victoria c. 46 §§ 82-85.   [6] Below 492-496, 502.
[7] Below 496-502.   [8] Below 409-412.   [9] Below 412-416.

hardly, were supposed to be met by the establishment at the beginning of the sixteenth century of the court of Requests;[1] that Wales had its separate judicial system;[2] and that the Councils of Wales and the North[3] provided local judicatures. But the court of Requests disappeared after the Great Rebellion;[4] the Council of the North was abolished in 1641,[5] and the Council of Wales in 1688;[6] and the separate judicial system of Wales disappeared in 1830.[7]   At the beginning of the nineteenth century the English judicial system was probably more completely centralized than any in Europe.   With the exception of the petty criminal business entrusted to the justices of the peace,[8] practically all the judicial work of the country was done by the judges of the common law courts, the Lord Chancellor or the Master of the Rolls, and the judge of the court of Admiralty.

The evils of this excessive centralization were obvious.   To the poor man it was almost a denial of justice, since it made the recovery of a small debt a piece of extravagance which only the very rich or the very litigious could think of incurring.   And so we find, from the end of the fifteenth century onwards, that complaints were made of the absence of efficient local courts, and that measures were proposed and sometimes carried to create them.

At the end of the fifteenth century the Venetian ambassador considered that the great prevalence of crime in England was due to the excessive centralization of criminal justice.[9]   In the sixteenth century London had by an act of the common council, established a small debt court, which was placed upon a legal basis by a statute of 1606.[10]   At the beginning of the seventeenth century the legislature had, as we have seen, tried in vain to prevent the bringing of petty actions in the common law courts.[11] In the county of Chester, it would seem, the county court was still efficient because writs of *Justicies*[12] enabled the sheriff to hear actions when the amount at issue was over 40s. in value.

---

[1] Below 412.   [2] Above 118-128.   [3] Below 502-503.
[4] Below 416.   [5] Below 515.   [6] Above 127.
[7] Above 131-132.   [8] Below 285-298.

[9] " Perhaps this great prevalence of crime might have been better prevented, had not former kings condensed the criminal jurisdiction under one head, called the Chief Justice, who has the supreme power over punishment by death.   This officer either goes himself, or sends his lieutenants or commissioners at least twice a year all over the kingdom, but still more frequently to London, to put the unfortunate criminals to death; and it is scarcely possible that one person should suffice for so great an extent of country, though the arrangements are as good as possible," Italian Relation of England (C.S.) 36; the description is not very accurate, but it shows that the centralization of justice in England had already impressed an intelligent foreign observer.

[10] 3 James I. c. 15; its constitution was amended by 14 George II. c. 10.
[11] Above 74.
[12] For this writ see above 73, and App. VI.

There were loud complaints when difficulties were put in the way of the issue of these writs, and the county in 1639-1640 petitioned the king for the restoration of the old custom.[1] Under the Commonwealth, among the drafts of Acts prepared by the Committee appointed in 1653 for the reform of the law, was a draft in which it was proposed to establish in each county, courts to hear civil actions (other than actions in which the title to land came into question, or actions for conspiracy or slander, or certain actions against executors) in which the amount in issue did not exceed £4. The court was to consist of five persons chosen by the justices of the peace out of a list of ten presented by the grand jury; and the persons selected were to be compellable to serve. No professional lawyer was to be retained in any case.[2] Similar suggestions were made by writers of this period;[3] and these or similar proposals, unlike most of the other proposals for legislative reforms brought forward in the Commonwealth period,[4] were not dropped at the Restoration.

At the beginning of Charles II.'s reign numerously signed petitions asked for the re-establishment of the Councils of Wales and the North in order that these distant parts of the kingdom might get the benefit of a local judicature.[5] In 1664-1665 the crown created a court of Record for Stepney and Hackney to try cases where the amount in issue did not exceed £5.[6] But the power of the crown to erect courts of Record by its prerogative was doubtful; and, after the Revolution, places which wanted to obtain such a court applied to Parliament for special Acts. In 1689,[7] 1690,[8] and 1691-1692[9] bills for this purpose passed the House of Commons, but were rejected by the House of Lords. Why the House of Lords rejected them is not very clear; but

---

[1] S.P. Dom. 1639-1640, 249, ccccxxxix 1.

[2] Somers' Tracts vi 184-186.

[3] See Cary, Present State of England Harl. Miscel. iii 559; Shepherd, England's Balm 63.

[4] Below 428-434; vol. vi 416-422

[5] S.P. Dom. 1660-1661 16, i 151—petition by the grand juries of the Northern counties for the re-establishment of the court at York on the ground that " subjects have to travel 250 miles to obtain their rights on a trivial matter;" ibid 1661-1662 36, xxxix 40-47—petitions to re-establish the Council of Wales and the Marches; in 1661 and 1661-1662 bills to establish a court at York were before the House of Lords, but they failed to pass, Hist. MSS. Com. Seventh Rep. Pt. I. 150, 154; Reid, op. cit. 454-457.

[6] S.P. Dom. 1664-1665 14, cii 92; in 1661-1662 (S.P. Dom. 1661-1662 171, xlv 20) there was a petition by Sir J. Robinson, the lieutenant of the Tower, for the establishment in the London suburbs of courts on the model of that established by the Act of 1606; but the petition was not wholly disinterested as he wanted to get the right to nominate the officers of these courts " to gratify loyal sufferers therewith."

[7] Hist. MSS. Com. Twelfth Rep. Pt. V. 388 no. 195—Norwich; a similar bill passed in 1701, 12, 13 William III. c. 7.

[8] Ibid Thirteenth Rep. Pt. V. 218 no. 363—Southwark.

[9] Ibid Fourteenth Rep. Pt. VI. 8 no. 516—Westminster.

possibly it was influenced by the same sort of arguments as those which were used in a petition addressed to the House of Commons in 1675-1676 against a bill for the erection of a court of conscience at Westminster.[1]   In this petition these courts were criticised on the grounds that they interfered with existing local courts such as the court Baron, that trial by jury was not allowed in them, that they were staffed by unlearned men, that there was no appeal from their decisions, that, as the parties were allowed to give evidence, perjury would be encouraged, that it was derogatory to persons of quality to be brought before a court presided over by shopkeepers.   These criticisms were obviously of the most flimsy sort ; but they were the kind of criticisms that would have met with a good deal of favour from the House of Lords of that period.

In the eighteenth century the need for these courts was so obvious that the opposition of the House of Lords was overcome.[2] Courts of Conscience or courts of Request as they were sometimes called, framed on the model of the London court, were established in many large towns.[3]   Their jurisdiction was limited to actions for debt where the amount at issue did not exceed 40s. ; and the judges proceeded in a summary way by means of the examination of the parties as well as of witnesses.   They were successful courts.   It was said at the end of the eighteenth century by a judge of fifteen years' experience in the Birmingham court that 130 cases a week were decided there.[4]   Blackstone admitted the need for them ;[5] but he did not altogether approve of the courts already established because they did not try cases by jury, and in other respects departed from the procedure of the common law.[6]   In spite, however, of Blackstone's disapproval it is clear from a return made to the House of Commons in 1839 that, of

---

[1] S.P. Dom. 1675-1676 86.

[2] The reasons for erecting these courts were forcibly stated in a petition of the inhabitants of Southwark to the House of Lords in 1690—" A Court of Conscience within the City of London being found by above 120 years' experience of great use and advantage to all the inhabitants of the said city; and to have prevented many thousand families from ruin; and the borough of Southwark . . . being grown highly populous and the multitudes of seamen, watermen, handicraft and labouring men, with other poor inhabiting therein, who for want of the like good establishment are daily undone by suits in law for small debts, and their persons thrown into prison to the ruin of them and their families, the great decay of trade and a vast expense to petitioners and the other inhabitants for their support and maintenance," Hist. MSS. Com. Thirteenth Rep. Pt. V. 222 no. 364.

[3] Bl. Comm. iii 81-83, 82 n. k; the name "court of Request" is evidently derived from the court which dealt out equity to poor suitors, below 412; and cf. Select Cases in the Court of Request (S.S.) liii, liv.

[4] Hutton, Courts of Request 11 (Ed. 1787).

[5] " The anxious desire that has been shown to obtain these several Acts proves clearly that the nation in general is truly sensible of the great inconvenience arising from the disuse of the ancient hundred and county courts," Comm. iii 82.

[6] Ibid.

all the existing local courts, these courts of Request were the most effective.[1] There were many local courts in England at that date, as a return made to the House of Commons in 1840 shows.[2] But, with the exception of these courts of Request, they were for the most part merely the debris of past centuries; and many of them had hardly more than a nominal existence.

Although these courts of Request did useful work they were not the direct lineal ancestors of the new county courts. Their direct lineal ancestors are the new county courts for Middlesex, which were established by a statute of 1750.[3] They were courts held in every hundred of Middlesex by the county clerk. The cases were tried by the county clerk and a jury of twelve freeholders in a summary way. The amount at issue in the cause was not to exceed 40s. This was the plan which Blackstone considered to be "entirely agreeable to the constitution and genius of the nation," and wished to see introduced throughout England. But it was not till 1846, more than seventy years after Blackstone wrote, that this suggestion was carried into effect. The Act of 1846[4] solved the problem which had troubled the legislature for three centuries by creating an entirely new set of courts; and, "agreeable to the constitution and genius of the nation," it provided for these courts a name and style of great antiquity. "Whereas," runs the Act, "the county court is a court of ancient jurisdiction, having cognizance of all pleas of personal actions to any amount by virtue of a writ of justices issued in that behalf; and whereas the proceedings in the county court are dilatory and expensive, and it is expedient to alter and regulate the manner of proceeding in the courts for the recovery of small debts and demands (i.e. the courts of Request) and that the courts established under the recited Acts of Parliament . . . should be holden after the passing of this Act as branches of the county court," it is enacted that certain county courts of a new model be established.

With the manufacture of history we touch the limits of even a sovereign legislature. These new tribunals have the name alone of the ancient county court. Their powers, their jurisdiction, their procedure are as modern as the courts themselves. But, even in the modern statutes which create them, we can see traces of the period when there were many local courts of various

---

[1] Parlt. Papers 1839 xlii 159, which gives the statistics of cases heard in those courts in the years 1835, 1836, and 1837; cf. ibid 225, 265, 301 for corresponding statistics of cases heard in the county, hundred, and borough courts.

[2] Ibid 1840 xli 556-557; see the list of these courts taken from this return in App. XXVIII.

[3] 23 George II. c. 33; Bl. Comm. iii 82-83.

[4] 9, 10 Victoria c. 95.

kinds. If the name of these new courts, and the preamble to the statute, takes us back to the old communal courts, the saving to the lords of certain manors, hundreds, and liberties of the right to make the first appointment to the post of county court judge, and the proviso that such lords may surrender their jurisdiction, take us back to the days when private jurisdiction was a competitor to royal justice.[1]

Under this Act England and Wales are divided into 500 districts. These districts are divided into fifty-nine circuits. As a general rule each circuit has a judge, and each district has a court held at least once a month. The judges are appointed by the Lord Chancellor, and must be barristers of at least seven years' standing.[1a] The judge may determine all questions of law and fact. But if the amount at issue is over £5 either party may require a jury of five ; if the amount is under that sum the judge may in his discretion allow a jury on the application of either party.[2]

The chief object of the Act of 1846 was to create courts for the more easy recovery of small debts. Their jurisdiction was limited to cases where the debt or damage claimed did not exceed £20. Certain classes of action they were altogether prevented from entertaining. But the courts succeeded so well that successive Acts have added successive powers, until it has become possible to describe the county court judge as a " judicial beast of burden," and the county court as the " devil " of the High Court.[3] Under the consolidating Act of 1888, and later acts of 1903 and 1934[4], [4a] the county courts can entertain any common law action with the consent of both parties ; any action founded on contract (except breach of promise of marriage) or any action founded on tort (except libel, slander or seduction) up to the limit of £100 ; and any question as to the title to lands, tenements or hereditaments if the annual value of the property does not exceed £100. They have Equity jurisdiction if the cause of action does not exceed £500 ; Probate jurisdiction if the estate in question does not exceed £200 personalty and £300 realty. They have jurisdiction in replevin and bankruptcy to any amount. In actions on contract, transferred from the High Court, they have jurisdiction up to £100 ; in actions on tort, similarly transferred, they have jurisdiction to any amount. They can wind up all companies whose capital does not exceed £10,000.[5] Some county[6] courts have Admiralty jurisdiction in certain cases

---

[1] 9, 10 Victoria c. 95 §§ 11, 13, 14 ; 51, 52 Victoria c. 43 § 6.
[1a] County Courts Act, 1934, s. 5 (1). 43 § 0.
[2] L.Q.R. iii 1-13. [3] Ibid vii 346-348, 350.
[4] 51, 52 Victoria c. 43 ; 3 Edward VII. c. 42 ; cp. L.Q.R. v 3 ; vii 346-348.
[4a] 24 and 25 Geo. 5. c. 53.
[5] 8 Edward VII. c. 69 § 131 (3)
[6] 31, 32 Victoria c. 71 ; 57, 58 Victoria c. 60 § 547.

—generally if the amount at issue does not exceed £300. In addition to this other Acts have given them duties of a very heterogeneous kind.[1] Statistical tables and diagrams show that by far the larger number of cases decided in this country are settled in the new county courts.[2]

Such has been their success that schemes of reorganization and reform have been proposed. A reorganization of jurisdiction involving a further division between petty and important cases, and a rearrangement of the circuits according to the latest census tables and Bradshaw have been advocated.[3] But over schemes which belong to the future the historian has no jurisdiction.

[1] See the list of fifty-five Acts in Lord Halsbury's Laws of England viii 403-515.
[2] *Nineteenth Century* (October 1897) 574, 575.
[3] L.Q.R. iii 3; v 6-10; vii 350-353; ix 321-330; xxii 127 (1906); *Edinburgh Review* ccxxv 319, an article on Economy in Law.

CHAPTER III

THE SYSTEM OF COMMON LAW JURISDICTION

I N this chapter some account will be given of the courts, central and local, which administered the common law after the older local courts had decayed ; and of the great distinctive feature of the system of common law jurisdiction—the jury. This subject will be dealt with under the following heads : the Common Law Courts ; the Itinerant Justices ; the Justices of the Peace ; the Jury.

I. THE COMMON LAW COURTS

The common law courts were royal courts and the judges of these courts were royal justices.   From these facts three consequences followed : (1) The king had a large control over the business before the court.   We have seen that in early days the king actually decided cases; and there are instances of this practice in Henry III., Edward I., and Edward II.'s reigns.[1] But, when Fortescue wrote at the end of the fifteenth century, it had ceased to be usual ;[2] and Coke merely stated the existing practice in answer to James l.'s claim to decide cases for himself.[3] But, though the king could no longer take an active part in the proceedings of courts of law, he had many privileges and prerogatives in relation to such proceedings.   It was claimed for him in James I.'s reign that he could peremptorily interfere to stop proceedings in any common law court by the writ *Rege Inconsulto.*[4] It was clear that he could sue in what court he pleased ; and in addition he had other smaller procedural advantages.[5]   The right of the Attorney or Solicitor-General to reply in a criminal case, though the prisoner has called no witnesses, is one of the best-

---

[1] Above 34; Madox i 100; ii 10, 11; Palgrave, Commonwealth i 292.

[2] De Laudibus c. viii ; Gardiner, History of England ii 39; below 207.

[3] Case of Prohibitions (1608) 12 Co. Rep. 63, 64; see the passage cited below 207 n. 7; cf. 3 S.T. 942.

[4] Brownlow v. Michil (1615) 3 Buls. 32 ; Bacon's Works vii 683-725.

[5] Ibid 693, 694, 700-702.

known illustrations of that "garland of prerogatives"[1] which the
older law gave to him. (2) The judges held their offices as a
rule during the royal pleasure.[2] The manipulation of the bench
by the Stuarts led to the clause in the Act of Settlement which
provided that the judges should hold office "quamdiu se bene
gesserint;" but that it should be lawful for the crown to remove
them on an address by the two Houses of Parliament.[3] (3) Until the beginning of the eighteenth century they vacated their
offices on the demise of the crown. But an Act of Anne provided that the judges, with other officers of the crown, should
continue to hold their offices for a space of six months after the
demise of the crown;[4] and an Act of George III.'s reign[5] provided that the judges' tenure of office should be unaffected by
the demise of the crown.

In this section I shall trace the history of the three common
law courts—Common Pleas, King's Bench, and Exchequer; of
the Court of Exchequer Chamber; and of the official staffs of
these courts.

The Court of Common Pleas

We have seen that, at the end of John's reign, there was a
clear separation between the court which was fixed at a certain
place to hear common pleas, and the court which followed the
king, with jurisdiction over both common pleas and pleas of the
crown.[6] But the two courts were not then completely distinct.
There were not as yet two distinct bodies of judges with distinct
duties. The distinction would seem almost to depend upon the
accident of there being a king to follow. During the minority
of Henry III. there could not be a court held coram rege; and
so, as the king's presence was not as yet a legal fiction, one court
tried all cases. When Henry attained his majority in 1224, the
distinction between the two divisions of the Curia Regis again
appeared. We find a further and more distinctive mark of the

[1] " In the pleadings and proceedings themselves of the king's suits, what a garland of prerogatives does the law put upon them," Bacon's Works vii 693; see
Bk. iv Pt. II. c. 6 § 1.
[2] The commissions, however, of the Chief Baron and other Barons of the Exchequer were always " quamdiu se bene gesserint," Coke, Fourth Instit. 117; this
was made the rule for all the judges in 1648, Acts and Ordinances of the Commonwealth i 1226-1227; and after the Restoration some of the judges were, for a short
time, appointed on similar terms, Foss, Judges vii 4.
[3] 12, 13 William III. c. 2 § 3; for a Bill of 1691-1692, containing similar provisions, which failed to secure the royal assent see Hist. MSS. Com. Fourteenth Rep.
Pt. VI. 76 no. 565.
[4] 6 Anne c. 7 § 8.
[5] 1 George III. c. 23. Before the statute 1 Edward VI. c. 7 all actions were
discontinued by the demise of the crown, and it was necessary to begin them afresh.
[6] Above 52-53.

separation of the two courts in the fact that, shortly after this date, they recorded their proceedings on separate rolls. For the court held before the king himself there are the "Coram Rege," and for the court of Common Pleas there are the "De Banco" rolls.[1] A reported case of 1237[2] shows that the distinction between the two courts was then well recognized. G. Marescallus was summoned to warrant the title to certain manors which the king was claiming against John Marescallus. He pleaded that this was a common plea, and could not therefore be heard "coram rege" in the court which followed the king. The court held that this was not a common plea because it touched the person of the king and crown.[3] Bracton says that the king has several courts;[4] and Britton[5] and Fleta[6] mention the Bench as a separate court. In 1272 a separate chief justice of the Common Pleas was appointed.[7] From that date the separation was complete. It is true that even in Edward I.'s reign it is not always possible to distinguish the court to which the different judges belonged.[8] It is true also that the jurisdiction of the court was not then in all points the same as that which it afterwards possessed—"the special competence of each court is only vaguely defined."[9] But it is a court which has a separate set of rolls; it has a separate chief justice; it is inferior to the court which follows the king, since error lies from it to this court.[10]

Magna Carta provided, as we have seen, that the court should sit at some fixed place. That place was usually Westminster; but it occasionally sat elsewhere. In 1337 and 1392 it was at

---

[1] Select Pleas of the Crown (S.S.) xvi-xix; Bracton's Note Book i 56-59; P. and M. i 177; Foss ii 178; Madox i 793; vol. ii Bk. iii c. 2.

[2] Plac. Abbrev. 105 a; S.C. Bracton's Note Book, case 1220; and cf. ibid case 1213; and a case of 1302, noted in Plac. Abbrev. 244 a, where "Petrus de Corbet dicit quod placitum de dote est commune placitum et communia placita non debent placitari in banco illo."

[3] It may perhaps be regarded as an early application of the rule that the king may sue in what court he likes.

[4] Ff. 105 b, 108 a; these passages are cited below 204 n. 5.

[5] "There be justices remaining constantly at Westminster, or at such other place as we shall be pleased to ordain, to determine Common Pleas according as we shall authorise them by our writs; and these justices shall have record of the proceedings held before them by virtue of our writs," i 5.

[6] ii. 2-7; 34.

[7] Gilbert de Preston, Dugdale, Orig. Jurid. 39; Foss, Judges iii 20.

[8] Ibid 16, 17.   [9] Bracton's Note Book i 56.

[10] Ibid case 1166 (1235), "Et quia fuit ostensum Dom. Reg. ex parte abbatis quod ipsi justitiarii ita mala processerunt vocati fuerunt coram Dom. Reg. et ibi cognoverunt quod ita processerunt;" case 1189 (1236-1237), the Abbot of Osney gave the king a palfrey to have a case before the Justices at Westminster brought before the king and his council; the justices of either Bench might, however, assist one another by their advice even during the course of a case, Y.B. 13, 14 Ed. III. (R.S.) xli.

York,[1] in 1544 it was at St. Albans,[2] and in 1581 it was at Hertford.[3] Indeed Edward III., when complaint was made that the Bench "est errant de Countee en Countee per tout le Roialme," distinctly declined to deprive himself of the power to order the Bench to sit where he pleased;[4] and this power is clearly assumed to exist in a statute of 1328.[5]

The judges of the court in the twelfth and earlier part of the thirteenth century were royal clerks; but, in the latter part of the thirteenth century and in the earlier part of the fourteenth century, these royal clerks were being replaced by men who had made their career at the bar. Of the nineteen judges who staffed the court in the reign of Edward II. eight or nine were clerks, and the rest were practising barristers; and that the latter were rapidly ousting the former is shown by the fact that, with the exception of Hervey of Staunton who became chief justice in 1326, no clerical judge was appointed after 1316.[6] We shall see that by 1316 the order of serjeants at law had been formed. This order consisted of the leading practitioners who were promoted to be members of the order by the crown;[7] and, when the judges ceased to be chosen from the royal clerks, they naturally came to be chosen from this order of serjeants, and soon came to be chosen solely from its members.[8] Probably this rule began with the court of Common Pleas. In the course of the fourteenth century, it was extended to the King's Bench; but it was not till the latter part of the sixteenth century that the same rule was applied to the court of Exchequer.[9] By that time, however, the rule that only a serjeant could be made a judge had become somewhat of a form. From the middle of the sixteenth century onwards it became the custom to make any lawyer, whom it was desired to raise to the bench, a serjeant at law, merely that he might be made a judge.[10] But the rule that no one could be made a judge unless he was a serjeant was not altered till the Judicature Act of 1873.[11]

The jurisdiction of the court can be grouped under the following heads :—

---

[1] Y.B. 11, 12 Ed. III. (R.S.) xxviii; 12, 13 Ed. III. (R.S.) xxxiii-xxxv; Foss, Judges iv 13.

[2] Wriothesley's Chronicle (C.S.) i 146.   [3] 1 Co. Rep. 58 a.

[4] 2 R.P. 286 no. iv (38 Ed. III.); ibid 311 no. 7 (46 Ed. III.); Reeves, H.E.L. ii 298.

[5] 2 Edward III. c. 11.

[6] Tout, Place of Edward II. in English History 368. For the number of the judges at different periods see Bolland, Manuel of Y.B. Studies, 11-12.

[7] Vol. ii 314, 485-492.

[8] Pulling, Order of the Coif 94; serjeants also had an exclusive right to audience in this court till 1847, 9, 10 Victoria c. 54; vol. ii 485-486, 490, 492; vol. vi 477-478.

[9] Below 236.   [10] Vol. v 340-341.

[11] 36, 37 Victoria c. 66 § 8.

(1) The first and most important branch of its jurisdiction was that exercised over common pleas—that is over actions between subject and subject. "This court," says Coke,[1] "is the lock and key of the common law in common pleas, for herein are real actions, whereupon fines and recoveries (the common assurances of the realm) do pass, and all other real actions by original writs are to be determined, and also of all common pleas mixt and personal." The court was the only one of the courts of common law in which real actions and the older personal actions of debt detinue, account, and covenant could be begun;[2] and its jurisdiction over them could only be ousted by express words of exclusion in a charter or other instrument granting this jurisdiction to another court.[3] Its monopoly in this respect lasted till the abolition of these actions by statutes passed from 1833-1873.[4] But, we shall see that, long before their formal abolition, most of these older forms of action real and personal had become obsolete;[5] that new actions which could be brought in the King's Bench had taken their place;[6] and that by means of legal fictions both the King's Bench and the Exchequer had encroached both upon the exclusive and upon the concurrent jurisdiction of the court over mixed and personal actions.[7] It was not, however, till the middle of the sixteenth century that the rivalry of the King's Bench and Exchequer began to affect seriously the business of the court. During the whole of the mediæval period the forms of action were living realities; and, among these forms of action, the real actions, in the trial of which the court had an absolute monopoly, were the most lucrative and the most important.[8] Then, too, the court, because it had become stationary before the other courts of common law,[9] attracted a large and able bar;[10] and this tended to increase its business. In fact, in 1309, it was so full of business that Edward

---

[1] Fourth Instit. 99.

[2] Hale, A Discourse concerning the courts of King's Bench and Common Pleas, Harg. Law Tracts 360, 362; for the few exceptional cases in which a real action could be begun in the King's Bench see below 219 n. 1.

[3] "Your charter purports that if the moneyers be impleaded, or themselves implead others, they shall stand to right before the Warden of the Mint, but the charter does not say ' not anywhere else,' so that the charter does not take away the jurisdiction of this court, because they can stand to right there and here also. And the men of Durham claimed a like franchise, and, because the charter did not say ' not anywhere else ' their charter was not allowed, and so also in this case," Y.B. 20 Ed. III. ii (R.S.) 562 per Sharshulle, J.

[4] 3, 4 William IV. c. 27 § 36; 23, 24 Victoria c. 126 § 26 (real actions); 38, 39 Victoria c. 77 Sched. i (all forms of action).

[5] Bk. iv Pt. II c. 1 § 1; Bk. iv Pt. II c. 2 § 1.

[6] For the actions that could be brought in the King's Bench see below 219.

[7] Below 219-221, 240.   [8] Vol. iii 29.

[9] Above 56, 196; below 199.

[10] Y.B. 3, 4 Ed. II. (S.S.) xxii-xxiii.

II. ordered that it should sit in two divisions.[1]   That, during the Middle Ages, it maintained both its popularity, and its reputation as a court in which decisions of the greatest legal interest were given,[2] can be seen from the fact that by far the larger number of cases reported in the Year Books were cases heard in this court.   Owing to causes which I shall now relate all this had changed in the seventeenth century.   When Hale wrote it was the King's Bench which was "the nursery of young professors," while the Common Pleas was merely "the place of practice of serjeants."[3]

During the sixteenth century, the older forms of action were ceasing to be living realities.   The real actions were so technical, and admitted of so many delays, that, by the end of the century,[4] they had been, in the vast majority of cases, superseded by the action of ejectment.   This was a form of the actions of trespass ; and because it was a form of trespass it could be begun equally well in the King's Bench.[5]   The older personal actions also suffered from similar defects ; and they too were being rapidly superseded by varieties of actions of trespass on the case,[6] which also could be begun in the King's Bench.[7]   At the same time both the King's Bench and the Exchequer were perfecting fictions which enabled them to offer better remedies than those offered by the Common Pleas.[8]   The process invented by the King's Bench was cheaper[9] than the process by way of original writ as used in the Common Pleas.   It was also more efficacious; both because the plaintiff was not so liable to be defeated by the choice of a wrong writ, or by variances between his writ, process

---

[1] Y.B. 3, 4 Ed. II. (S.S.) xxiv-xxv ; Mr. Turner, ibid xxv-xxix shows that probably the second division of the court tried issues joined before the judges of the first division ; in later times such issues would have been tried at nisi prius, below 278-279 ; but the judges did not at this date go on circuit regularly, and try these issues in this way ; cf. Y.B. 4 Fd. II. (S.S.) lvii-lviii.

[2] Mr. Turner speaking of the reign of Edward II. says "Qualitatively, the matters at issue (in the King's Bench) were more often points of fact than of law, and the whole body of business transacted there was relatively small.   It would be no exaggeration to say that for each term of the reign of Edward II. there were twice as many rolls of the Common Bench as of the King's Bench, and in some terms the proportion was considerably greater in favour of the former court," ibid xxi ; in Edward II.'s reign also the younger apprentices would prefer a stationary court because it was more expensive to follow an ambulatory court like the court of King's Bench, ibid.

[3] Harg. Law Tracts 371.   [4] Vol. vii 4-10.

[5] Hale, Discourse, etc., Harg. Law Tracts 360, 362 ; below 219.

[6] Vol. iii 429 seqq. ; vol. vii 402.

[7] Hale, Discourse, etc., Harg. Law Tracts 360, 362 ; below 219.

[8] Below 219-221, 240.

[9] Harg. Law Tracts 366 ; this was still the case at the beginning of the nineteenth century.   The Common Law Procedure Commissioners reported in 1829 that the cost of taking out an original writ was £3 5s., while the cost of proceeding by latitat was £1 5s. 8d., Parlt. Papers 1829 ix 81 ; vol. ix 249-251.

on his writ, and his pleading;[1] and because it enabled him to secure the presence of the defendant by arresting him.[2] It is not therefore surprising to find that, during the seventeenth century, the business of the court was seriously curtailed by the successful competition of the King's Bench. The Common Pleas endeavoured to meet this competition by inventing a new process modelled on that which the King's Bench had so successfully used; but it was not very successful; and so the help of the legislature was invoked. An Act passed in 1661 considerably diminished the efficiency of the process used by the King's Bench,[3] and therefore as Hale points out, restored to the Common Pleas a considerable amount of the business which properly belonged to it.[4] But we shall see that the King's Bench soon evaded the Act by a new fiction.[5] Consequently the business of the court again declined, till Chief Justice North in some measure retrieved the situation by inventing a fiction analogous to that invented by the King's Bench.[6]

Obviously this episode in the history of the jurisdiction of the court cannot be fully told till the fictitious processes used by the King's Bench have been examined. Here it will be sufficient to say that, though the fiction invented by North regained for the court much of its proper business, the King's Bench still continued to offer greater advantages;[7] and, at the beginning of the nineteenth century, still continued to absorb the lion's share.[8]

(2) The court had jurisdiction to supervise or to correct the errors of the older local courts. By the writ of *Pone*[9] it could order a case to be transferred to itself from the county court, the hundred court, or the court Baron; and by various writs of

---

[1] Report of Common Law Procedure Commissioners, Parlt. Papers 1829 ix 81; Hale, Harg. Law Tracts 366, says, " The plaintiff hath the advantage of time to form his suit, as his case requires; and is not bound to any concordance with any original writ or process. Variance hurts not."

[2] Below 220.

[3] 13 Charles II. St. 2 c. 2; Harg. Law Tracts 367; Hale there says, " Still the practice going where the plaintiffs found most advantage, and the King's Bench carrying the practice from the Common Pleas, a second expedient was found;" North also, Lives of the Norths i 129, represents the Act as a deliberate attempt to help the Common Pleas—" They (the Common Pleas) thought to exclude the King's Bench by getting an Act of Parliament that none should be held to bail unless the cause of action was expressed in the writ;" this would seem to show that Blackstone's statement, Comm. iii 287, that the makers did not intend the Act to have this result is unfounded; for the provisions of the Act see below 221.

[4] " By this means the Common Pleas relieved themselves in a great measure against the excess of practice in the King's Bench," Harg. Law Tracts 368; " There the Common Pleas thought they had nicked them," Lives of the Norths i 129.

[5] Below 221.   [6] Below 221-222.

[7] Harg. Law Tracts, 369, 370.

[8] Between the years 1823 and 1827 there were begun in the King's Bench 281,109 actions, in the Common Pleas 80,158, and in the Exchequer 27,197, Report of Common Law Procedure Commissioners, Parlt. Papers 1829 ix 11.

[9] App. VII.

False Judgment—recordari facias, accedas ad hundredum, or accedas ad curiam—the errors of these courts could be corrected.[1] This was an important part of its jurisdiction in the thirteenth and fourteenth centuries ; but it tended to become of gradually less importance as these local courts declined.   We shall see that their place was taken by the Justices of the Peace, and that these Justices were controlled by the court of King's Bench.[2] Whether the Common Pleas had jurisdiction to correct the errors of the local courts of record by writ of *Error*[3] was long a subject of controversy, because there was little opportunity to settle the question.   Parties generally preferred to bring such writs of error in the King's Bench because, if such writs were brought into the Common Pleas, the decision of the Common Pleas might be brought by writ of error into the King's Bench.   "No man," said Vaughan, C.J.,[4] "will advise his client to bring it here (i.e. the Common Pleas) but rather into the King's Bench where it is final."   Fitzherbert,[5] Vaughan, C.J.,[6] Comyn,[7] and Bacon[8] asserted the jurisdiction of the Common Pleas.   But dicta in a Year Book of Edward III.'s reign,[9] and in the case of *Roe* v. *Hartley*,[10] Hale,[11] and later text writers,[12] denied it.   Hale and the later writers relied partly upon the dictum in *Roe* v. *Hartley*, partly upon a statement in Finch's Discourse on law.[13]   But Finch's statement was based partly upon a Year Book case which was not in point,[14] and partly upon a case in Dyer which decided that error would not lie to the Common Pleas from the decision of a judge of assize, because such a judge was substantially in the position of a judge of one of the superior courts of common law.[15]   This was really no authority for the proposition that error would not lie

[1] F.N.B. 18-20 ; App. IX. ; above 73 and n. 7.   [2] Below 297.
[3] App. X. ; for the nature of the writ of error, and proceedings in error generally see below 213-215, 222-224.
[4] " A writ of error out of an inferior court, lyes as properly here as in the King's Bench.   But generally, writs of error for many years have not been brought here ; the reason is matter of conveniency, because if you bring a writ of error here, and the judgment is affirmed, yet it may be brought into the King's Bench, and be there reversed ; though, indeed, if a writ of error be brought here, we must proceed upon it.   But no man will advise his client to bring it here, but rather into the King's Bench, where it is final " (1671) Carter 222.
[5] F.N.B. 20 D.   [6] Above n 4.
[7] Digest, *Pleader*, 3 B 2.   [8] Abridgment, *Error*, I 5.
[9] Y.B. 14, 15 Ed. III. (R.S.) 144 *per* Hillary, J.
[10] (1584) Cro. Eliza. 26.
[11] Harg. Law Tracts 361 ; he says that though anciently the opinion was that the Common Pleas and King's Bench had a concurrent jurisdiction, " yet now the law and practice is settled for the King's Bench."
[12] Bl. Comm. iii. 410-411 ; 2 Wms. Saunders 100 n. ; Tidd, Practice (8th Ed.) 1192.
[13] At p. 480 of Pickering's Ed. (1759) ; for an account of this book see vol. v 399-401.
[14] Bruce v. Wait (1840) 1 Man. and Gr. 2 n. a.
[15] Ap. Richarde v. Jones (1566) Dyer 250.

to the Common Pleas from an inferior court of record; and, in fact, a dictum in this case in Dyer somewhat hesitatingly favoured its jurisdiction in such cases.[1] The controversy was settled in 1841 by the case of *Bruce* v. *Wait*,[2] in which the court exercised this jurisdiction; and this view of the law was accepted as correct in 1902 in the case of *Darlow* v. *Shuttleworth*.[3]

(3) In the seventeenth century the court acquired a general jurisdiction to issue two of the prerogative writs[4]—the writ of Prohibition and the writ of Habeas Corpus. It is probable that in both cases this general jurisdiction was an extension of a much more limited jurisdiction.

(i) It would seem that in the fifteenth century the court had the power to issue a writ of Prohibition, either if proceedings were taken in some other court about some matter which was the subject of an action depending before it, or if an application was made to it to issue a writ of attachment to arrest a person for proceeding in a court which had no jurisdiction.[5] In 1610, however, the judges of the King's Bench and Exchequer, confirming previous decisions of the Common Pleas, resolved that the Common Pleas had the power to issue the writ " without any writ of attachment or plea depending." [6] (ii) It probably issued some forms of the writ of Habeas Corpus from the time when the writ was invented. We shall see that the writ originally was, and that some forms of the writ have continued to be, merely a part of the process of the court to secure the presence of persons—parties, witnesses or jurors—needed for the trial of an action.[7] Thus the court had jurisdiction to issue the writ when it wished to bring before itself a prisoner who was a party to an action in the court, or who was privileged only to be sued in the court;[8] but it had no jurisdiction to bring before itself any other prisoner; and if such a prisoner was under arrest for

---

[1] " If erroneous judgment be given before the justices of the Bishop of Durham within the county palatine, the party grieved shall have a writ of error there before the bishop himself. And if he give erroneous judgment the writ of error may be sued in C.B. or B.R., but see well this case of 14 (Edward III.) and *quære*," Ap. Richarde v. Jones (1566) Dyer 250; this case would seem to be Y.B. 14, 15 Ed. III (R.S.) 142-144, which was also a case of error from Durham.

[2] (1840) 1 Man. and Gr. 1; all the cases are collected at p. 2 n. a of the report.

[3] [1902] 1 K.B. at p. 725.

[4] For the prerogative writs see below 226-231.

[5] Y.B. 38 Hy. VI. Mich. pl. 13; cf. Reeves, H.E.L. iii 108.

[6] Fourth Instit. 99, 100.   [7] Below 227.

[8] By the form *Habeas Corpus ad respondendum* which lay, " When a man hath a cause of action against one who is confined by the process of some inferior court," or the form of *Habeas Corpus ad faciendum et recipiendum* which lay " When a person is sued in some inferior jurisdiction, and is desirous to remove the action into the superior court," Bl. Comm. iii 129-130; for the persons privileged only to be sued in the court see below 203.

felony it could do nothing but remand him.[1]   Both Coke[2] and
Hale[3] state the law in this way; but, when Hale wrote, the
court was beginning to put forward a claim to issue the writ
at the suit of any prisoner, whether or no he was a party to an
action in the court or a privileged person, and to deal with him
as it saw fit.   The court perhaps desired to attract popularity
by extending its jurisdiction in so good a cause as the protection
of the liberty of the subject;[4] and it was not difficult to invent
a technical justification for this extension of jurisdiction.   The
Act of 1641, which abolished the jurisdiction of the Council and
its branches in England, had given the court power to issue the
writ on the application of a prisoner committed by the Council;[5]
and, in other cases, where this Act was not applicable, it was
always easy to allege that the prisoner, on whose behalf the writ
was sought, was a party to an action in the court or a privileged
person.[6]   In *Bushell's Case*[7] the court (contrary to the opinion
of Vaughan, C.J.) decided that it had this general jurisdiction
to issue the writ; and this precedent, in spite of Vaughan's continued dissent, was followed.[8]   The controversy was ended by
the famous Habeas Corpus Amendment Act of 1679 which gave
this jurisdiction to all three of the common law courts.[9]

(4) The court, like the other courts of common law, had
exclusive jurisdiction over its own officials or other persons
privileged to sue and be sued before it.[10]   If the official or other
privileged person was the plaintiff, the action was begun by
attachment of privilege; if he was defendant by bill.[11]

---

[1] Hale, 2 P.C. 144; Anon (1671) Carter 222; Bushell's Case (1670) Vaughan
at p. 156.

[2] "He may have an Habeas Corpus out of the King's Bench or Chancery,
though there be no privilege, etc., or in the court of Common Pleas or Exchequer
for any officer or privileged person there," Second Instit. 55.

[3] "If a person is sued in the Common Pleas, or is supposed to be so sued, and
is arrested for a presupposed misdemeanour, yea or for felony, an Habeas Corpus
lies in the Common Pleas or Exchequer," 2 P.C. 144.

[4] See Bushell's Case (1670) Vaughan at p. 156.

[5] 16 Charles I. c. 10 § 8.

[6] See Hale, 2 P.C. 144 cited above n. 3.

[7] (1670) T. Jones at p. 13.

[8] Anon. (1671) Carter 221; but it would seem that in Bushell's Case a majority
of all the judges (8-4) took Vaughan's view that the Common Pleas had no jurisdiction to issue the writ in a criminal case, S.P. Dom. 1671 xxiv 385-386.

[9] 31 Charles II. c. 2 § 3; a good account of this question will be found in
Wood's Case (1771) 2 W. Bl. 745; and Crowley's Case (1818) 2 Swanst. at pp.
53-56, 65-68.   For the history of the Writ of Habeas Corpus see vol. ix 108-125.

[10] "All privilege is either for officers, clerks or attorneys of the court not to be
sued elsewhere; or for persons impleading or impleaded, having priority of suit in
the Common Pleas, arrested or sued in other jurisdictions; or for the menial
servants of such officers," Vaughan at p. 155; cf. Coke, Fourth Instit. 99.

[11] Report of Common Law Procedure Commissioners, Parlt. Papers 1829 ix
72-73; Harg. Law Tracts 365.

The Court of King's Bench

It was not till upwards of a century after the court of Common Pleas had become a distinct court, with a distinct body of judges and distinct records, that the court of King's Bench attained this position. It was never fixed like the court of Common Pleas in a certain place, because, being held literally coram rege, it followed the king in his peregrinations about the country. We have seen that this idea was so literally adhered to that, when Henry III. was a minor who could not hold a court, the distinction between the court held coram rege and that held before the justices at Westminster almost disappeared.[1] The kind of cases which, later in the reign, were heard by the court held coram rege, were said to be heard "coram consilio nostro," "coram H de Burgo justiciario," "coram nobis et consilio nostro."[2] The court held coram rege revived when Henry III. attained his majority ; and, as we have seen, there are henceforth two sets of rolls—the coram rege and de banco rolls.[3] But, as Professor Baldwin points out, at later periods in the reign when the king was absent from the kingdom, cases were again heard, not coram rege, but coram consilio.[4] This shows us that the court held coram rege was not as yet a court of King's Bench, but simply a continuation of that undifferentiated Curia Regis, which was still performing executive and legislative as well as judicial functions.

That this was the position of the court held coram rege in Henry III.'s reign is shown clearly enough by Bracton's treatise and by the records of the court. Bracton knows three distinct sets of justices. On the one hand there are the justices of the Common Bench with a limited jurisdiction, and the itinerant justices acting under various commissions. On the other hand, there are the king's chief justices who sit in his hall and hear cases which concern the king, or cases affecting great persons privileged only to be brought to justice before the king himself ; who can correct the errors of all other justices.[5] The records of

---

[1] Above 195.   [2] Baldwin, The King's Council 52.
[3] Above 195-196.
[4] "Comparatively late in the reign, as in 1242 and again in 1253, when the king was absent from the kingdom, instead of *coram rege* there were pleas held *coram consilio, coram W. Eboraci episcopo et consilio domini Regis*, and *coram domina Regina et consilio domini Regis apud Westmonasterium*," The King's Council 52.
[5] "Habet enim plures curias, in quibus diversæ actiones terminantur, et illarum curiarum habet unam propriam, sicut aulam regiam, et justitiarios capitales qui proprias causas regis terminant, et aliorum omnium propter querelam vel propter privilegium sive libertatem: ut si sit aliquis qui implacitari non debeat nisi coram ipso domino rege. Habet etiam curiam et justitiarios in banco residentes, qui cognoscunt de omnibus placitis, de quibus auctoritatem habent cognoscendi et sine warranto jurisdictionem non habent, nec coertionem. Habet etiam justitiarios

the court show us that (as in the preceding period) it is a court
of first instance for great men and great causes ;[1] that it not
only corrects the errors of other courts, but also supervises these
other courts,[2] and, as a judge of Edward III.'s reign put it,
" amends and completes their work ".[3]   The records show, too,
that, as in the preceding period, it was sometimes a court held
before a small number of justices, sometimes a large meeting of
the council " attended by an indefinite number of magnates."[·4]

But, towards the end of Henry III.'s reign, there are signs of
a division in this court held coram rege.   This was mainly due
to three causes.   In the first place, the procedure of the common
law was becoming more fixed and more technical.[5]   If cases
came before the court by writs of error or false judgment, or if
it intervened in cases being tried in the Common Pleas or other
lower court, it necessarily used this procedure.[6]   Naturally the
cases heard in accordance with this procedure, and the sessions
of the court at which they were heard, tended to fall apart from
the cases to which this procedure was not applicable, and from
the sessions of the court at which the non-legal element predominated.   In the second place, after the close of the civil
wars of Henry III.'s reign, the writ of trespass came somewhat
suddenly into common use.[7]   The court was much occupied with
the trial of criminal or quasi-criminal cases begun by this writ ;
and, when trying these cases, it naturally used the common law
procedure.[8]   Thus the sessions of the court, at which the professional element predominated, tended to be occupied mainly
with the correction of the errors of inferior courts, and with the
trial of criminal or quasi-criminal cases.   In the third place, after
1234, the office of justiciar was never again permanently filled.[9]
In 1268, when Robert de Brus was appointed capitalis justiciarius,
he was appointed " ad placita coram rege tenenda."   This meant
that the professional court which tried cases coram rege had got
a special chief of its own.[10]

During Edward I.'s reign the differentiation of this court

itinerantes de comitatu in comitatum, quandoque ad omnia placita, quandoque ad
quædam specialia," f. 105 b ; " Item justitiariorum quidam sunt capitales, generales,
perpetui, et majores, a latere regis residentes, qui omnium aliorum corrigere tenentur
injurias et errores," f. 108 a.

[1] See Baldwin, The King's Council 54-56 for some illustrations.

[2] Ibid 56-57.   [3] Y.B. 18, 19 Ed. III. (R.S) 208 *per* Willoughby, J.

[4] Baldwin, op. cit. 53.

[5] Vol. ii 250-251, 334 ; vol. iii 617-618, 623-627.

[6] " It is not long after Bracton's day that a line of cleavage begins to appear,
which in the end serves to set off the King's Bench as a court distinct from the
council.   This is found in the tendency of the court to hear cases in accordance with
the formulaic procedure already observed in connection with the common bench,"
Baldwin, op. cit. 62.

[7] Vol. ii 364-365.   [8] Baldwin, op. cit. 63.

[9] Vol. ii 226.   [10] Dugdale, Orig. Jurid. 38 ; Reeves, H.E.L. i 533.

grew more marked.   Britton limits its competence to the amendment of false judgments and to criminal cases ; [1] and reserves an
overriding power to the king himself. [2]   Fleta's book makes it clear
that the king could exercise this overriding power either in his
council, or in his council in Parliament [3]—as we shall see, the two
bodies were only just beginning to split off from each other. [4]
Both books make it clear also that, though the court held coram
rege still followed the king, though it was therefore held in
theory coram rege, the king was not necessarily present at its
sessions. [5]   It is significant that in 1300 it was necessary to enact
specially that "the justices of this bench shall follow him," [6] and
probably there is a good deal to be said for Coke's view that,
notwithstanding the statute, the court only attended the king if
summoned, and that it was "a settled court during the several
terms of the year." [7]   We must not, however, exaggerate the
extent to which the King's Bench had become a separate court
in Edward I.'s reign.   It was still ambulatory whenever the king
willed that it should be so.   It still drew much of its authority
from the fact that it was held in the presence of the king ; [8] and,
as we have seen, its two distinctive pieces of jurisdiction—its
jurisdiction in error and its jurisdiction over criminal cases—
originated in its close connection with the person of the king.
Its rolls still record, not only the judicial business done by it,
but also the miscellaneous governmental business done by the
Council. [9]   In fact, the court of King's Bench only gradually

[1] " With respect to the justices assigned to follow us and hold our place wheresoever we shall be in England we will that they have cognizance of amending false
judgments, and of determining appeals and other pleas of trespass committed against
our peace, and that their jurisdiction and record shall extend so far as we shall
authorise by our writs," Britton (Ed. Nichols) i 3-4.

[2] " We will that our jurisdiction be superior to all jurisdictions in our realm ; so
that in all kinds of felonies, trespasses and contracts, and in all manner of other
actions personal or real, we have power to give, or cause to be given, such judgments as the case requires without any other process," ibid i 3.

[3] " Habet enim Rex curiam suam in concilio suo, in Parliamentis suis, præsentibus prelatis, comitibus baronibus, proceribus, et aliis viris peritis, ubi terminatæ
sunt dubitationes judiciorum, et novis injuriis emersis nova constituuntur remedia,
et unicuique justitia, prout meruit retribuetur ibidem," Fleta ii 2, 1.

[4] Below 352-355.

[5] " Habet etiam curiam suam et justitiarios suos tam milites quam clericos locum
suum tenentes in Anglia, *coram quibus et non alibi, nisi coram semetipso et concilio
suo* vel auditoribus specialalibus, falsa judicia et errores justiciorum revertuntur et
corriguntur," Fleta ii 2, 5; the words in italics show that Fleta knows that the
court is not always held "coram rege."

[6] 28 Edward I. St. 3 c. 5.

[7] Fourth Instit. 72-73 ; cf. Dugdale, Orig. Jurid. 38.

[8] " He in whose court this inquest was taken is more than a chief lord ; he is
chief lord and king.   And consider whether the king in his court before himself
cannot serve instead of a writ," Y.B. 3, 4 Ed. II. (S.S.) 120 *per* Bereford, C.J.

[9] " Throughout the reign of Edward I. and beyond . . . there was still upon the
rolls a mingling of conciliar cases and cases *coram rege* without any apparent
distinction as to character or procedure," Baldwin, op. cit. 64.

became a separate court of common law as it lost, in the course of the fourteenth century, its former close connection (i) with the king himself, and (ii) with the King's Council.

(i) To the end cases heard before the King's Bench, like cases heard before the Council,[1] were said to be heard before the king himself.[2] But, before the close of the mediæval period, the king had, as a general rule, ceased to be present in the court. Coke does not say that the king was never present in his court,[3] but he cites cases of Henry IV.'s and Henry VI.'s reigns to show that, as the king had entrusted his judicial power to his judges, he could not himself pronounce judgment.[4] I have not found in the Year Books any statement quite so precise as this; but it is not improbable that this view was held in the latter part of the fourteenth and in the fifteenth centuries. In the first place it was quite contrary to the mediæval idea of the supremacy of the law—an idea strongly held by the judges of the common law courts—that the king should be able to interfere with its rules by the exercise of his own personal discretion.[5] In the second place we have seen that in the old Curia Regis it was not the king but the court which gave judgment;[6] and it was obvious that in these specialized courts of common law the judges formed the court. When Coke gave it as his opinion that James I. could not give judgments in his court of King's Bench,[7] he obviously found it difficult to cite a decision to that effect precisely in point. But there is no doubt both of the legal and political expediency of his opinion; and the statutes and other authorities which he cites show that it represented the spirit of much mediæval authority.

The separation of the court of King's Bench from the person of the king was helped by the fact that the king had another

[1] Select Cases before the Council (S.S.) 32.

[2] P. and M. i 177-178; Stephen, H.C.L. i 93.

[3] Fourth Instit. 71; Second Instit. 186; the records make it clear that Edward IV. was occasionally present, L.Q.R., xl 356-357.

[4] Y.B. 8 Hy. IV. Hil. pl. 3 (p. 19)—which is not very conclusive; Y.B. 8 Hy. VI. Hil. pl. 6—a case turning on the franchises of the University of Oxford in which the rule that a man cannot be a judge in his own case was elaborately discussed; in the printed Y.B. there is no very clear statement as to the power of the king to give judgment; but in Fitzherbert Ab. *Graunt* pl. 5 there is a statement that "le roye mesme nest son juge demesne mes par mesme come par ces juges."

[5] Vol. ii 252-255, 435, 441.

[6] Above 40.

[7] (1608) 12 Co. Rep. 65, "the king said," Coke relates, "that he thought the law was founded upon reason, and that he and others had reason as well as the judges; to which it was answered by me, that true it was that God had endowed His Majesty with excellent science and great endowments of nature; but His Majesty was not learned in the laws of his realm of England, and causes which concern the life or inheritance or goods or fortunes of his subjects, are not to be decided by natural reason but by the artificial reason and judgment of the law, which law is an act which requires long study and experience, before that a man can attain to the cognizance of it. . . . With which the king was greatly offended"; see vol. v 430.

court which took cognizance of cases which nearly affected him. This was the court of the Steward and the Marshal. It took cognizance of cases which arose within the verge, that is within a space of twelve miles round the court, or place where the king was actually residing.[1] At common law its jurisdiction fell under two heads : (1) The Steward and the Marshal had general jurisdiction within the verge as deputies of the Lord Chief Justice.[2] Being only deputies of the Lord Chief Justice, when he was present, their general authority ceased. We have seen that by the Act of 1300[3] the King's Bench was ordered to follow the court. The result seems to have been that the general jurisdiction of the Steward and the Marshal practically ceased about this time ; though they sometimes tried cases under a special commission of oyer and terminer issued in Vacation.[4] (2) As judges of the Court of the Marshalsea they had a "very particular and limited jurisdiction." It was confined as to causes ; they could only hear pleas of the crown, and the three common pleas of debt, covenant, and trespass vi et armis. It was confined as to persons ; in debt or covenant both parties must be of the king's household, though in trespass it was enough if one party was of the king's household. It was confined as to place, being limited to the verge. Statutes of Edward I., Richard II., and Henry VI. enforced these limitations upon its authority.[5] Coke points out that all the Acts passed concerning this court restrained, or explained, but never added to its jurisdiction. He decided, in the *Case of the Marshalsea*, that it could not try the newer forms of action such as assumpsit and trover.[6] Its once general jurisdiction had passed to the court of King's Bench, and the attitude of that court to the more limited court of the Marshalsea made the court of the Marshalsea almost useless. There were complaints in the seventeenth century of the conduct of its officials ;[7] and, as it was obliged to follow the king in his progresses, it was a court extremely inconvenient to use.[8] So uncertain was its jurisdiction and so inconvenient that James I.

---

[1] Britton, i 3, 170-173 ; Fleta ii 3-5, 61 ; Michelborn's Case (1596) 6 Co. Rep. 20 ; the case of the Marshalsea (1613) 10 Co. Rep. 68 b.

[2] Fleta, ii 3. 4 calls the Steward the delegate of the chief justice; and Britton, i 3 says that the Steward holds pleas of the crown "taking our place within the verge; " cf. Reeves, H.E.L. ii 297-298.

[3] 28 Edward I. St. 3, c. 5.   [4] 10 Co. Rep. 73 b.

[5] 28 Edward I. St. 3 c. 3 ; 13 Richard II. St. 1 c. 3 ; 15 Henry VI. c. 1 ; 10 Co. Rep. 72 a ; cf. 33 Henry VIII. c. 12 for minute regulations as to the trial and punishment of certain offences committed in the king's house.

[6] 10 Co. Rep. 76 a.

[7] See Hist. MSS. Com. Fourth Rep. App. Pt. I. 118 for the draft of a bill proposed in 1606 to reform some of these abuses ; and cf. S.P. Dom. 1639, 427, ccccxxvi 84—a case of an attorney who had made scandalous speeches against the court.

[8] Bl. Comm. iii 76 ; Reeves, H.E.L. ii 604.

created a Curia Palatii, to be held before the Steward and Marshal, having jurisdiction over all personal actions arising within twelve miles of Whitehall.[1] Though this court was said in a Parliamentary Paper of 1840 to be a "useful and effectual court,"[2] Blackstone had noted many years earlier that, if a case of any importance was begun in it, it was usually removed at once to the King's Bench or Common Pleas;[3] and, as Maitland reminded me in a review of the first edition of this book, the melancholy tale of "Jacob Homnium's Hoss," as related by Policeman X., would seem to show that its effectiveness was confined to the manner in which it could pile up costs.[4]

We shall see that this court is important in the history of the court of King's Bench, not only because it made the separation of the court from the person of the king easier, but also because it is probable that a hint taken from the practice of this court helped the King's Bench to enlarge its jurisdiction at the expense of the court of Common Pleas.[5]

(ii) The connection of the court of King's Bench with the Council lasted till nearly the end of the fourteenth century. Parties were habitually summoned to appear, not simply " coram rege " but "coram rege et consilio;"[6] and errors were redressed not only by the justices of the King's Bench but also by the Council.[7] Thus, in 1315, a case in which the Despencers were concerned relating to a finalis concordia was brought by writ of error from the Common Pleas to the King's Bench. Not only the ordinary judges of the court, but also the judges of the Common Pleas, the Barons of the Exchequer, the Chancellor, the Treasurer, "and other magnates of the King's Council" took part in the judgment.[8] In fact "the proceedings of the courts below, in all their stages were within the cognizance of the Council."[9] The fact is also illustrated by the case of Boddenho. That case was decided by the court of Common Pleas, after frequent interferences by the Council; and, after all, a writ of error

---

[1] Spedding, Letters and Life of Bacon iv 262-264.
[2] Parlt. Papers 1840 xli 10.   [3] Comm. iii 76-77.
[4] Thackeray's Ballads; this is corroborated by a Tract entitled " An Expose of the Practice of the Palace or Marshalsea Court," evidently published about the same date, where it is said that the costs on a debt of £5 amounted to £8. On the whole subject see Juridical Review xxxi 139 seqq.
[5] Below 219.
[6] Bracton's Note Book case 1189; ibid vol. i 57-59; Hale, Jurisdiction of the House of Lords, c. vii, says, " The consilium regis in ancient times did so often sit in the court of King's Bench, and were so often mingled in and with that court and the transactions thereof, that the style of that court many times was ' placita coram consilio regis,' and sometimes ' coram rege et consilio.' "
[7] Y.B. 3, 4 Ed. II. (S.S.) 38, 39, *per* Herle and Toudeby *arg.*
[8] Pike, History of the House of Lords 44, 45; cp. R. v. Rouceby (1354) Select Cases before the Council (S.S.) 38.
[9] Y.B. 12, 13 Ed. III. (R.S.) xciv.

was brought in the King's Bench.[1]   The case of the Stauntons shows that the proceedings of both the court of Common Pleas and of the King's Bench were liable to be interfered with not only by the Council, but also by Parliament.[2]   In 1346 a case was adjourned into the King's Bench and was decided "in the Council before all the justices."[3]   As Hale points out, the cases in which this close connection between the King's Bench and the Council is apparent, can be referred to three categories.   It appears (1) in difficult cases by way of advice and direction; (2) where issue was joined before the Council, and the records were sent into the King's Bench and judgment thereon was given by that court; and (3) in important cases in which the Council sat with the court of King's Bench.[4]

Towards the end of the fourteenth century the growing definition and consequent separation of the organs of government gradually put an end to the connection between the King's Bench and the Council.   The Council was tending to become more especially the organ of the executive side of the government, and Parliament of the legislative side;[5] while the court of King's Bench was tending to become simply a court of common law, which was concerned with the judicial side of government.   It is true that the men of that period were hardly conscious that a separation was taking place on these lines— indeed the functions of government are not perfectly separated on these lines even at the present day.   Both the Council and Parliament were regarded as courts, the powers of which were, to a large extent, undifferentiated.   In particular, both possessed large judicial powers which were destined to play a large part in the history both of the constitution and of the judicial system;[6] and no very clear distinction was drawn between their judicial and their other powers.   But the fact that the organs of government were in fact beginning to separate on these lines was helping to cause a friction between the Council and Parliament which tended to make the separation more marked.[7]   It was inevitable that the common law courts should be affected by this growing separation; and it was not doubtful to which of these two organs of government they would be attracted.   Parliament they recognized as the body whose consent was necessary to the making of the laws which they applied;[8] while the Council

[1] Y.B. 12, 13 Ed. III. (R.S.) xciv-c (1336-1341).

[2] Y.B. 13, 14 Ed. III. (R.S.) xxxvi-xlii (1340-1345).

[3] Y.B. 20 Ed. III. ii (R.S.) 126.

[4] Jurisdiction of the House of Lords c. vii; cp. Baldwin, Select Cases before the Council (S.S.) xxi-xxii.

[5] Below 360-361, 486-487.

[6] Below 365-394, 485-508.

[7] Below 360-361, 486-487.

[8] Vol. ii 441-442.

sometimes did or attempted to do things which in their opinion
went beyond both the statute and the common law.[1]   Common
lawyers were an important element in the House of Commons;[2]
and the judges of the King's Bench and the Common Pleas were
common lawyers similarly educated,[3] similarly employed, often
changing from one bench to the other.[4]   They were tending to
fall apart from that large body of royal clerks who acted in
the various departments of government controlled by king and
council.   It is not surprising, therefore, that the common
lawyers came to think that errors in the King's Bench ought to
be corrected in Parliament, and not by the Council.   As we
shall see, they made good this contention;[5] and so the King's
Bench ceased, not only to be connected with, but even to be
directly controlled by the Council.[6]

Thus the court of King's Bench became simply a common
law court.   But, while thus becoming simply a common law
court, it preserved both in its style and its jurisdiction traces of
the days when it was a court of a very different kind.   In its
wide powers of control over other courts and officials, and in its
wide criminal jurisdiction, it retained powers of a quasi-political
nature which came to it from the days when the court held coram
rege was both King's Bench and Council.   In the future, the
possession of these powers by a common law court which was
allied to Parliament was destined to be a factor of no mean importance in determining the position of the common law in the
state, and in settling the shape of the English constitution.   All
this we shall see more clearly later in this history.   At this point
we must confine ourselves to a description of the various branches
of a jurisdiction which was destined to have so large an historical
effect.

---

[1] Below 487; vol. ii 430, 561-564.   [2] Ibid 430-431.   [3] Ibid 492.

[4] Thus in 1311 Roubury, a judge of the King's Bench, was hearing cases in
the Common Pleas, Y.B. 4 Ed. II. (S.S.) 158 n. 1; in Y.B. 12, 13 Ed. III. (R.S.)
366 the common opinion of the Council and all the Justices is cited; in Y.B. 20
Ed. III. ii (R.S.) 528 Thorpe, C.J., of the King's Bench came into the Common Pleas
and gave an opinion; for the movements of the judges from one court to another
see Foss's Tables of the Judges of these courts, iii 25-26, 201-202, 353-355.

[5] Below 361.

[6] Pike's view, History of the House of Lords 46, that, as no separate proceedings of the Council are known of a date earlier than 1387, the King's Bench was not
completely separated from the Council much before that date, must be modified in
the light of Professor Baldwin's account of the records of the Council, The King's
Council chap. xiv; he shows that " the traditional view that these records first
appeared in the reign of Richard II. has arisen out of a mere accident of collection
which in itself has no historical basis; " he inclines to the view that the two courts
were practically separate by the reign of Edward III. ibid 64; and thus he agrees
with Coke who points out, 10 Co. Rep. 73 b, that, from the passing of the statute
28 Edward I. St. 3 c. 5 to 4 Edward III. c. 3, the justices following the king had
their purveyance, and that its cessation at the latter date shows that by then the
King's Bench had become a settled court.

The jurisdiction of the court of King's Bench was general and universal. The judges of the court "are called *capitales* in respect of their supreme jurisdiction, and *generales* in respect of their general jurisdiction throughout England." [1] Coke sums up the jurisdiction of the court under several heads. [2] (1) It holds cognizance of all pleas of the crown ; (2) It has jurisdiction "to examine and correct all and all manner of errors in fact and in law of all the judges and justices of the realm in their judgments, process, and proceedings in courts of record, and not only in pleas of the crown, but in all pleas, real, personal, and mixt, the court of Exchequer excepted as hereafter shall appear." (3) "This court hath not only jurisdiction to correct errors in judicial proceedings, but other errors and misdemeanours extra-judicial tending to the breach of the peace, or oppression of the subject . . . or any other manner of misgovernment." (4) It has jurisdiction over all trespasses done vi et armis. (5) "This court hath power to hold plea by Bill for debt, detinue, covenant, promise, and all other personal actions . . . against any that is in custodia Mareschalli, or any officer, minister or clerk of the court." (6) The judges of this court are the sovereign justices of oyer and terminer, gaol delivery, coroners, and conservators of the peace in the realm. The authority of justices in eyre, of oyer and terminer, and gaol delivery ceases when the King's Bench comes into the county.

From Coke's summary it appears that the court of King's Bench had, (1) a criminal jurisdiction ; (2) a civil jurisdiction ; and (3) a general superintendence over the due observance of the law by officials and others.

(1) *Criminal jurisdiction.*

This jurisdiction comprises (i) ordinary jurisdiction, (ii) transferred jurisdiction, (iii) jurisdiction in cases where the correctness of the decision of an inferior court is questioned.

(i) *Ordinary jurisdiction.*

It was not common even in John and Henry III.'s reigns to try ordinary criminal cases before the court of King's Bench. [3] Such cases only came before it if they were transferred, unless the court happened to be taking all the crown business for the county in which it was sitting. Probably it was at no period

---

[1] Coke, Fourth Instit. 75.   [2] Ibid 71-73.

[3] Select Pleas of the Crown (S.S.) xxiii ; the court might hear all offences committed in Middlesex, or any other county in which the court was sitting ; in later times misdemeanours committed in any county might be so tried on information filed by the Attorney-General, Reeves, H.E.L. iii 158.

very common for ordinary criminal cases to be tried before it.[1]
But, till 1872, the grand jury of Middlesex was regularly summoned whether or no there were any indictments to be preferred
before them.   In 1872[2] it was enacted that they need not be
summoned unless there was an indictment to be preferred.
Such indictments are preferred only in cases of public importance.[3]   Grand juries were abolished by the Criminal Justice
Act, 1948.

(ii) *Transferred jurisdiction.*

Indictments and other proceedings from inferior courts may
be removed into the court of King's Bench by writ of certiorari.[4]
This will be done when a fair trial cannot be had before such inferior court, or where some difficult question of law is likely to
arise.   In the fifteenth and sixteenth centuries the number of
criminal cases of all kinds so transferred was considerable.[5]   Such
trials when held in term time are called trials *at bar*, i.e. they are
held at the bar of the court before the judges of the court sitting
in banc.   But the court has power, instead of trying these cases
itself, to send them for trial into the counties where the crimes
were committed, or to order them to be heard by the itinerant
justices sitting at nisi prius.[6]

(iii) *Jurisdiction in cases where the correctness of the decision of
an inferior court is questioned.*

Before dealing with the history of the procedure by which the
correctness of the decision of an inferior court could be questioned,
it will be necessary to say a few very general words about the
ideas entertained by primitive legal systems as to the nature of
these proceedings.   In modern law the ideas, firstly that it is
possible to appeal against an erroneous decision, and secondly
that the appellate tribunal should try these appeals by a rehearing
of the case, seem so natural and necessary, that it is difficult to
realize that both were quite unrecognized at an earlier stage in
our legal history.

"The idea," says Maitland,[7] "of a complaint against a judgment which is not an accusation against a judge is not easily

---

[1] Stephen, H.C.L. i 95, 96, says, "It is a curious question, though perhaps the
solution would not be worth the trouble necessary to arrive at it, how far, at different
periods of its history, the court of King's Bench was in practice as well as in theory
a court for the trial of common criminal cases."   [2] 35, 36 Victoria c. 52.

[3] Ordinary cases arising in Middlesex are tried either at the Central Criminal
Court or at the Quarter Sessions, below 285, 292-293.

[4] Below 228; App. XIII.

[5] Stephen, H.C.L. i 96; at the present day they are "almost always misdemeanours partaking more or less of the character of private wrongs as indictments for
libel, conspiracy to defraud, or the like," ibid.

[6] Coke, Fourth Instit. 73, 74; below 279.

[7] P. and M. ii 665; for a similar idea in early French law see ibid n. 9.

formed." We shall see that a complaint against the verdict of a jury took the form of an accusation of perjury ;[1] and, just in the same way, there is plenty of evidence that in the thirteenth century complaints against the judgments of the justices of assize, and even against the justices in eyre, took the form of semi-criminal proceedings.[2] It is not till the following century that complaints against a judgment were differentiated from charges against the judge ; and the older conception had a very permanent influence upon the procedure by means of which these complaints were formulated. Two consequences followed logically from the older conception. Firstly the proceedings were new proceedings. The case must have been settled by final judgment; and therefore the proceedings taken to upset that judgment must be new proceedings.[3] Secondly, the matter of complaint against the judgment must, like any other complaint, be distinctly formulated. But the only manner in which such a complaint could be distinctly formulated was to look at the formal record of the case, and indicate clearly some error or errors appearing thereon.[4] It followed therefore that a complainant could only succeed if he could point out an error on the record ; but any error however trivial was sufficient. It was from these two ideas that the rules of procedure upon a writ of error naturally flowed. The first step was the removal of the record into the higher court. Then came the assignment of errors by the plaintiff in error, the summoning of the defendant in error by writ of Scire Facias to hear the errors assigned, and the joinder of issue on the question whether the errors so assigned were really errors.[5]

Thus the common law knew nothing of an appeal by a rehearing of the case. It only knew a procedure in error in which only errors which appeared on the record could be alleged. It was as we shall see, a most inadequate procedure ; and it was very imperfectly mitigated partly by judicial ingenuity, and partly by small legislative improvements. The idea of an appeal

---

[1] Below 337-342; cp. above 120 n. 2; and P. and M. ii 663-664 for the similar ideas that underlay the writ of false judgment; in Y.B. 5 Ed. II. (S.S.) 229 there is a case in which the suitors of the court Baron were amerced by the Common Bench for false judgment ; and in 1581 it was said that if the Lord Warden of the Cinque Ports reversed a judgment of the court of Shepway " the mayor and jurats who gave the judgment shall be fined and the mayor put out of his office." Dyer, 376 a.

[2] P. and M. ii 665 and references there cited; Baldwin, The King's Council 57-58 ; Thayer, Evidence 144-145. We may see an interesting survival of this old conception in the rule that if a judge died before sealing a bill of exceptions (below 223-224) no proceedings upon it could be had, Newton v. Boodle (1847) 3 C.B. 795 ; and cf. Cole, Ejectment (Ed. 1857) 315.

[3] " One shall not have a writ of error before the original writ between the parties be determined, and they be without day," Y.B. 17 Ed. III. (R.S.) 244 *per* Pole *arg.;* this was the law till the passing of the Common Law Procedure Acts of 1852, below 245-246.

[4] Bl. Comm. iii 405.   [5] F.N.B. 20 E, F, G.

by means of a rehearing of the case came into English law from the Chancery;[1] and it was not till the Judicature Acts that the common law procedure in error in civil cases was swept away, and the Chancery procedure substituted for it.[2]

Having now explained the ideas upon which the common law procedure in error, whether in criminal or in civil cases, was based, let us turn to the history of the manner in which the decision of the court in criminal cases might be questioned. I shall describe firstly the writ of error, secondly, the manner in which the defects of the writ of error were partially remedied by the judges and the legislature, and thirdly, the Criminal Appeal Act of 1907 which has at last provided a rational system of appeal in criminal cases.

(*a*) The writ of error.

Until 1705 the grant of a writ of error was a matter entirely within the discretion of the crown.[3] The crown for any reason, or for no reason, might order the Attorney-General to grant his fiat for the issue of such a writ; and without such fiat the writ could not be issued.[4] If the writ was issued the court was satisfied with the Attorney-General's confession of error. In 1705 in *Paty's Case*[5] ten out of the twelve judges held that the crown could not deny the writ, and that it was grantable *ex debito justitiæ* in cases of misdemeanour where the error was probable. Consequently the court assumed the power, if it could see that there was such probable error, to order the Attorney-General to grant his fiat. But, the issue of the writ having thus become a matter of right, it was laid down that there must really be an error—the mere admission of the Attorney-General was no longer to suffice. The old practice, however, continued in cases of treason and felony. But the Attorney-General never refused his fiat if there was a probable error alleged; and the question whether or no there was error was judicially determined.[6] The writ of error was, however, little used because the procedure upon it was cumbersome, and gave no useful result. The formal history of the case was stated at large on the record—the arraignment, the plea, the issue, and the verdict. But, as the record took no account of some of the most material parts of the trial, where error was most likely to occur—the evidence and the

---

[1] Below 438.   [2] Below 643.
[3] The Rioters' Case (1683) 1 Vern. 175; it was sometimes used to reverse a conviction on political grounds, see e.g. House of Lords MSS. 1693-1695 no. 864—a reversal of the conviction of two persons for treason for taking part in Monmouth's rebellion; and cf. the Writ of Error in Holles' Case (1668) 3 S.T. 331.
[4] Crawle v. Crawle (1683) 1 Eq. Cas. Ab. 414.
[5] 1 Salk. 504.
[6] Wilkes' Case (1770) 4 Burr. 2550-2551; Stephen, H.C.L. i 309, 310.

direction of the judge to the jury[1] the writ could do nothing to remedy the only errors that were really substantial. It was for these reasons that it was abolished in 1907.[2]

(*b*) The manner in which the defects of the writ of error were partially remedied by the judges and the legislature.

(*a*) Motions for a new trial. We shall see that in civil cases both the Common Pleas and the King's Bench granted new trials as early as the fourteenth century.[3] But in criminal cases there do not appear to be any mediæval precedents for such a practice. It is not till the latter half of the seventeenth century that the conditions under which a new trial could be had in criminal cases were settled.[4] In the first place we must distinguish between trials which have resulted in an acquittal and those which have resulted in a conviction. It was settled in the seventeenth century that after an acquittal there could be no new trial,[5] after some doubts whether such new trial might not be had if the case was not capital.[6] In *Reg.* v. *Duncan*[7] in 1881 Lord Coleridge, C.J., said, " The practice of the courts has been settled for centuries, and is that in all cases of a criminal kind where a prisoner or defendant is in danger of imprisonment, no new trial will be granted, if the prisoner or defendant, having stood in that danger, has been acquitted." If the trial resulted in a conviction the rule, in 1671, was, in accordance with previous cases,[8] held to be the same;[9] but the court was equally divided. In 1673,[10] however, a new trial was granted after a conviction for perjury. This precedent was followed; and the rule was settled that in cases of misdemeanour a new trial might be granted on the ground of misreception of evidence, misdirection of the judge, or because the verdict was against the weight of evidence.[11] In the second place we must distinguish between misdemeanour and felony. There is only one precedent for the grant of a new trial in cases of felony.[12] This has not been followed by the Privy

---

[1] Stephen, H.C.L. i 309, " In Orton's trial the question was whether cumulative punishment could be given for two offences charged in different counts of the same indictment. The record was a parchment roll of monstrous size, setting forth, together with much other wholly unimportant matter, every order made by the court for the adjournment of the trial to the next sitting; " the writs of error in R. v. Bradlaugh (1878) and R. v. Orton (1881) are the only ones in modern times in which recourse has been had to this writ; for an explanation of these omissions in the record see below 317.

[2] Below 218.   [3] Below 225.

[4] On the whole subject see Thayer, Evidence 175-179.

[5] (1660) 1 Lev. 9; Rex v. Bowden (1661) 1 Keb. 124; Rex v. Fenwicke and Holt (1663) 1 Keb. 546; Rex v. Jones (1724) 8 Mod. 201, 208.

[6] 1 Lev. 9, *per* Wyndham, J.   [7] 7 Q.B.D. 198.

[8] E.g. Rex v. Lewin (1668) 2 Keb. 396.

[9] Rex v. Hannis (1671) 2 Keb. 765.

[10] Rex v. Lathan and Collins 3 Keb. 143; cp. Rex v. Cornelius 3 Keb. 525.

[11] Stephen, H.C.L. i 310, 311.   [12] Reg. v. Scaife (1851) 17 Q.B. 238.

Council,[1] and has been disapproved by the Queen's Bench Division.[2]

(β) The jury may find a special verdict, i.e. they may find the facts and leave it for the court to say whether, on those facts, the prisoner is guilty or not.[3]

(γ) It was an old practice for the judge, in case of a conviction, if he felt a doubt as to the law, to respite judgment or sentence, and discuss the matter informally with the other judges. If they thought that the prisoner had been improperly convicted, he was pardoned.[4] Statutory authority was given to this practice in 1848 by the establishment of the court for Crown Cases Reserved.[5] All the judges were members of this court ; and five, of whom the Lord Chief Justice must be one, formed a quorum. If the five differed, any one might require the matter to be referred to all the judges. Any judge or chairman of Quarter Sessions might reserve a point for discussion by this court, where a prisoner had been convicted ; but the question whether or no he would reserve the point was within his absolute discretion. The court could only determine questions of law arising at the trial.

The result was that there was no possibility of questioning the ruling of the judge on a point of law except with his leave ; and, except by motion for a new trial (which was only granted in the case of misdemeanours), there was practically no way of questioning the verdict of the jury on the facts. All that could be done, if new facts came to light, was to pardon the man on the ground of his innocence.

(c) The Criminal Appeal Act of 1907.[6]

A bill for the reform of the law, which was before the House of Lords in 1690, attempted to give a remedy for this anomalous state of affairs, by extending both the writ of attaint and the bill of exceptions to criminal cases.[7] But the bill was dropped ;[8] and nothing was done, till the beginning of the present century.

The lamentable case of Adolf Beck who, unfortunately for himself, had a double who was addicted to breaking the criminal law, at length aroused the attention of the legislature to this anomalous state of the law. The Act establishes a court of criminal appeal. Its judges are the Chief Justice of England,

---

[1] Reg. v. Bertrand (1867) L.R. 1 P.C. 520; cp. Reg. v. Eduljee Bryamjee (1846) 5 Moo. P.C.C. 276.

[2] Reg. v. Duncan (1881) 7 Q.B.D. 198, 201.

[3] 13 Edward I. St. 1 c. 30; Coke, Second Instit. 425.

[4] Stephen, H.C.L. i 311.

[5] 11, 12 Victoria c. 78.   [6] 7 Edward VII. c. 23.

[7] Hist. MSS. Comm. Thirteenth Rep. App. Pt. V. no. 244 p. 21 ; for the writ of attaint see below 337-342 ; and for the bill of exceptions see below 223-224.

[8] Ibid at p. 23.

and eight judges of the King's Bench Division of the High
Court.   Three are a quorum, and the number of judges sitting
must always be an uneven number.[1]   It can hear appeals upon
any question of law; and, under certain conditions, upon any
question of fact, and against the sentence passed.[2]   It has full
powers to affirm or quash the conviction, or to alter the sentence
in any way it sees fit.   It cannot grant a new trial;[3] but, since
it has inherited all the powers of the court for Crown Cases Reserved,[4] it can order a *venire de novo* in the case of a mis-trial.[5]
Its decision is final, unless the certificate of the Attorney-General
is obtained that the case "involves a point of law of exceptional
public importance and that it is desirable in the public interest
that a further appeal should be brought;" in which case a further
appeal can be taken to the House of Lords.[6]   The court for
Crown Cases Reserved and writs of error in criminal cases are
abolished.[7]   Nothing in the Act is to affect the crown's prerogative of mercy; but the Secretary of State, when a petition for
mercy is presented to him, may either refer the whole case to the
court, or get its opinion on any point connected with it.[8]

"The number of cases," says Mr. Alexander,[9] "in which convictions have been quashed or sentences reduced since this Act
came into operation has raised a very uncomfortable feeling in
the minds of all thinking men as to what took place before the
Act was passed.   During the nine months of 1908 that the Act
was in operation there were 29 appeals and 326 applications for
leave to appeal, of which 79 were granted.   In 18 cases the
conviction was quashed, and in 14 the sentence was reduced—a
quite sufficient justification for the establishment of this tribunal."

(2) *Civil jurisdiction.*

The civil jurisdiction of the court falls under three heads:
(i) Original jurisdiction; (ii) Jurisdiction in error; and (iii) The
methods, other than the writ of error, by which judicial proceedings might be questioned.

(i) *Original jurisdiction.*

We have seen that original jurisdiction over civil actions belonged properly to the court of Common Pleas.[10]   It alone had

---

[1] § 1.
[2] § 3; all convicted persons have a right to appeal on a question of pure law;
for an appeal on a question of fact or mixed law and fact, or on any other ground,
the leave of the court of Criminal Appeal or the certificate of the trial judge is
needed; for an appeal against the sentence the leave of the court of Criminal
Appeal is necessary.
[3] §§ 4, 20 (1).   [4] § 20 (4).
[5] Crane v. Public Prosecutor [1921] 2 A.C. 299.
[6] § 1 (6); below 390-391.   [7] §§ 20 (1), (4), 22.   [8] § 19.
[9] The Administration of Justice in Criminal Matters 124.   [10] Above 198.

original jurisdiction over most of the real actions and over the older forms of personal action. But the King's Bench had always exercised jurisdiction in cases where a personal wrong or force was alleged.[1] This gave it a jurisdiction over trespass and its off-shoots, which it exercised concurrently with the court of Common Pleas ; and, as in the sixteenth century one or other of the actions of trespass on the case were more than covering the ground occupied by the older real and personal actions,[2] the monopoly of the court of Common Pleas was becoming a thing of the past. But, before this time, the court of King's Bench had invented a process which gave it a concurrent jurisdiction with that exercised by the court of Common Pleas over all personal or mixed actions ; and this process was so much more effective, and so much cheaper than the process of the court of Common Pleas, that, by the beginning of the seventeenth century, it was attracting to itself the greater part of this litigation.[3]

This process was based on the fact or the fiction that the defendant was in the custody of the Marshal of the Marshalsea of the king—the functionary who kept the prison of the court.[4] If a person was in the custody of the Marshal the court had general jurisdiction over him. It was therefore possible to bring any sort of action against him, except real actions. It is possible that this device was borrowed by the court of King's Bench from an analogous device used by the Steward and Marshal's court in Edward I.'s reign.[5] However that may be, it was applied by the court of King's Bench on a far wider scale than was possible in the case of a court with a jurisdiction so limited as that of the Steward and the Marshal.[6]

The first step in this process was to get the defendant either actually or constructively into the custody of the Marshal. In one case in Henry VI.'s reign it was held that actual custody was necessary to found the jurisdiction, so that it could not be exercised against a person who was released on bail. This decision was reversed later in the reign ; and it was ultimately held that the mere record on the rolls of court that the defendant

---

[1] Hale, Discourse, etc., Harg. Law Tracts 360; Coke, Fourth Instit. 72 maintained that it could hear an assize of novel disseisin ; but cf. Hale, loc. cit. ; Hale, loc. cit. says it could hear cases begun by writ of quare impedit, quare non admisit ejectio custodiæ, and ejectio firmæ ; for these writs see vol. iii 17 n. 1, 25, 214 ; also on the same principle cases of replevin, see vol. iii 283-285.

[2] Vol. ii 455-456; vol. iii 350-351, 429 seqq. ; vol. vii 4-10, 402.

[3] Above 199-200.

[4] "And it is to be observed, that he who is a prisoner to the King's Bench is *in custodia Mareschalli Mareschalciæ Domini Regis* and he who is a prisoner to the Marshalsea of the Household is *in custodia Maresc. Mareschalciæ hospitii dom' Regis*," 10 Co. Rep. 71 b, 72 a.

[5] This is the by no means improbable suggestion of Reeves, H.E.L. ii 604.

[6] Above 208.

had given bail would be sufficient evidence of actual custody.[1]
To get this evidence on record what was called a bill of Middlesex [2] was filed by the plaintiff against the defendant, stating that
he was guilty of trespass vi et armis—an offence falling properly
within the jurisdiction of the court.   The plaintiff gave pledges for
the prosecution, which pledges, even in Coke's day, were the fictitious John Doe and Richard Roe.[3]   The sheriff of Middlesex was
then directed to produce the defendant before the court to answer
the plaintiff concerning this plea of trespass.   If the sheriff returned
to the bill " non est inventus," a writ of latitat was issued to the
sheriff of an adjoining county.   The writ recited the bill of
Middlesex and the proceedings thereon, stated that the defendant
" latitat et discurrit " in the county, and ordered the sheriff to
catch him.   The trespass and the proceedings thereon were
fictions invented to give the court jurisdiction.   Thus when the
defendant did not live in Middlesex it was clearly a waste of time
to start with a real bill of Middlesex.   Such a bill was supposed,
and the issue of a latitat was the first step taken in the action.[4]
A real bill was only needed if the defendant actually lived in
Middlesex.   But the bill actual or supposed was the foundation
of the subsequent proceedings against the defendant.

If the defendant appeared and gave sureties for his future
appearance he was sufficiently in the custody of the Marshal to
give jurisdiction to the court.   If he did not appear to the bill
or the latitat he was liable to be arrested for contempt of court
in not appearing.   But as all the proceedings were fictitious, the
contempt would seem to share the fictitious character.   To arrest
a man for a merely fictitious contempt was clearly a hardship.[5]
Therefore, in the event of non-appearance, the plaintiff was
allowed to enter an appearance for him, and to give as sureties
for his appearance his friends John Doe and Richard Roe.   This
was called giving " common bail." [6]   In some cases, however, it
was desirable that the defendant should put in substantial bail

---

[1] Reeves, H.E.L. ii. 602, 603; iii 752, 753; on the whole subject see Bl. Comm.
iii 284-288; for forms see App. XX.

[2] So called because the court sits in that county; if it sat in Kent it would be a
bill of Kent, Bl. Comm. iii 285.

[3] Fourth Instit. 72, " And it is observable, that then putting in bail at one man's
suit, he was in custodia Mareschalli to answer all others which would sue him by
bill, and this continueth to this day.   If any person be in custodia Mareschalli, etc.,
be it by commitment, or by Latitat, bill of Middlesex or other process of law, it is
sufficient to give the court jurisdiction; and the rather for that the court of Common
Pleas is not able to dispatch all the subjects causes, if the said actions should be
confined only to that court."

[4] Reeves, H.E.L. iii 755 n. a.

[5] Many statutes were passed to free defendants sued by this process from this
liability to arrest, 12 George I. c. 29; 5 George II. c. 27; 21 George II. c. 3;
43 George III. c. 46; 7, 8 George IV. c. 71.

[6] Coke, Fourth Instit. 72; Bl. Comm. iii 287.

for his appearance. This was called "special bail." The
question when special bail could be required was a question depending upon the practice of the court. It was usually required
if the plaintiff swore that the cause of action was worth £10
or upwards. In 1661 [1] it was enacted that unless the true cause
of action was set forth in the writ or other process, no special
bail could be required, and no person could be arrested by such
process. It is clear that the process by way of bill of Middlesex
and latitat did not set forth the true cause of action. It was
founded on a fictitious trespass, which was a mere cover for the
real cause of action. Therefore the statute seriously affected the
efficacy of this process; and, as we have seen, [2] it restored, as
its framers intended, some part of its ancient jurisdiction to the
court of Common Pleas. But the court of King's Bench soon
circumvented this statute by the simple device of adding to the
bill complaining of the trespass an " ac etiam " clause, in which
the cause of action was truly stated. The supposed trespass
gave jurisdiction to the court; and the real cause of action, set
out in the " ac etiam " clause, satisfied the statute and authorized
arrest in default of special bail.

The device was successful, and great was the wrath of the
court of Common Pleas. [3] A committee of the House of Lords
in 1670-1671 was inclined to take the view of the judges of the
court of Common Pleas that it was an evasion of the Act of
1661. [4] But the report of the committee was sent back to it; [5]
and, though it adhered to its report, [6] nothing came of it. [7] It
was under these circumstances that North, C.J., set himself to
compete with the King's Bench by the help of a similar device. [8]
The Common Pleas had already made use of the writ of trespass
"quare clausum fregit" in much the same way as the King's
Bench used the bill of Middlesex. The defendant against whom

[1] 13 Charles II. St. 2 c. 2.   [2] Above 200 and n. 3.
[3] " The late Chief Justice Sir Orlando Bridgman and his officers of the Common
Pleas gave this way of proceeding by the King's Bench very ill language, calling it
an arbitrary alteration of the form of the legal process and utterly against law. But
the losers might speak; they got nothing else; and the *triccum in lege* carried it
for the King's Bench; which court ran away with all the business," Lives of the
Norths i 129.
[4] Hist. MSS. Com. Ninth Rep. App. Pt. II. 5 no. 27; Vaughan, C.J., said, ibid
p. 6, " If this course continue a little while longer there will be no causes in the
Common Pleas."
[5] Ibid at p. 5.
[6] Ibid at p. 6; the committee reported, among other things, " that *ac etiam* is
an innovation and an elusion of the Statute," and, "that it is assuming to themselves
a power which they have not;" cf. Lords Journals xii, 469.
[7] The report was ordered to be debated, Lords Journals xii 469, 474, and
counsel were to be heard, ibid 509—but nothing came of it except an order to the
Lord Keeper to issue writs of supersedeas to stop " ac etiams " if asked to do so by
litigants.
[8] Lives of the Norths i 129.

such a writ was brought could be arrested ; and, when he was arrested, the plaintiff was able to bring any action he wished against him. North added an "ac etiam" clause to the writ, and so managed to compete on somewhat more equal terms with the King's Bench.[1] From his time a capias, based upon a supposed writ of quare clausum fregit, became the usual method of beginning an action in the Common Pleas, just as a latitat, based on a supposed bill of Middlesex, was the usual method of beginning an action in the King's Bench.[2]

In 1829 the common law procedure commissioners justly condemned the procedure by bill of Middlesex;[3] and in 1832 the Uniformity of Process Act[4] abolished not only this procedure, but also the other equally fictitious processes used by the Common Pleas and the Exchequer. These courts were left in possession of the jurisdiction which they exercised; but, for the future, all actions were to be begun by a writ in the form prescribed by the Act, and all subsequent process was to be according to the rules and forms therein also prescribed.

(ii) *Jurisdiction in error.*

In the thirteenth and early fourteenth centuries jurisdiction in error belonged almost exclusively to the court of King's Bench ; but we shall see that, at the end of the thirteenth century, a still higher court was emerging—the King's Council in Parliament—which could correct the errors of the King's Bench.[5] At that date, however, neither the constitution nor the powers of this court were fixed. The King's Bench, which was as yet often held coram rege, which was not yet very distinguishable from the Council,[6] was still pre-eminently the court which corrected the errors of other courts, including, till 1830,[7] the court of Common Pleas, and till 1783[8] the court of King's Bench in Ireland.[9]

I have already explained in general terms the nature of a

---

[1] Lives of the Norths i 130-131; North says, at p. 131, "After this process came into common use it is scarce to be conceived how the court revived and flourished; being instead of vacation in term rather term in vacation;" but, as we have seen, above 200 n. 8, the King's Bench still kept the largest part of this business.

[2] Brown v. Babbington (1703) 2 Ld. Raym. at p. 882 *per* Holt, C.J.; House of Lords MSS. (1699-1702) 478 no. 1733 *per* Powell, J.; First Report of the Common Law Procedure Commissioners, Parlt. Papers, 1829 ix 73.

[3] "The instruments taken altogether are worded in a manner so strangely foreign to their purposes, that the party sued can scarcely be expected to understand them without the assistance of his attorney," Parlt. Papers 1829 ix 82.

[4] 2 William IV. c. 39.   [5] Below 352.   [6] Above 207, 209-211.

[7] Below 245.   [8] 23 George III. c. 28 § 2.

[9] Y.B. 5 Ed. II. (S.S.) 152; Baldwin, The King's Council 58, citing a case of 1223 in which directions were given to the Irish courts; Registrum Brevium (Ed. 1687) 132 a note in the margin.

writ of error and the character of the proceedings thereon.[1] That
its defects were more apparent when it was applied to the
correction of errors in civil cases than when it was applied to the
correction of errors in criminal cases can be seen from the fact
that the legislature, from an early date, tried to supply a remedy
for some of them. The writ of error in civil cases did not remain,
as the writ of error in criminal cases remained, entirely unreformed. We have seen that the writ was defective in that it
was both too wide and too narrow. Firstly, it was too wide
because any error on the record, however trifling, was ground for
a writ; and, as records were regarded as very sacred things, the
judges did not dare to make the smallest verbal amendment. A
tradition sprang up that this attitude of the judges was due to
the severity with which Edward I. had punished his judges who
had been guilty of fraudulent alteration of the records and other
mal-practices.[2] But the records of this episode hardly bear this
out.[3] Their attitude was really the result of the extreme technicality and formalism which is always the mark of a primitive
system of law. The result was that writs of error were brought,
and judgments reversed, on account of merely verbal errors on
the record. "Justice," as Blackstone said,[4] "was perpetually
entangled in a net of mere technical jargon." Several statutes
—called statutes of Jeofails—were passed to remedy this defect.[5]
Secondly, the writ was too narrow, because it lay only for errors
on the record. It might happen that the parties alleged matters
upon which the judge pronounced a decision without entering
that decision on the record. Because they were not entered on
the record they could not, though both material and erroneous,
be assigned as errors. To remedy this a clause in the Statute of
Westminster II (1285)[6] enacted that if one of the parties to an
action alleged an exception which the judge refused to allow,
such party might write it down and require the judge to seal it.
The ruling upon such an exception could then be assigned as an

---

[1] Above 213-214.
[2] Coke, Fourth Instit. 255; Bl. Comm. iii 408-410; for an account of this
episode see vol. ii 294-299.
[3] State Trials of the reign of Edward I (C.S.) xxxix-xliii where the cases are
summarized; it is pointed out at p. xlii that the number of cases in which records
were altered was small. On the other hand Mr. Bolland has recently pointed out
(Y.B. 8 Ed. II. xxi-xxiii) that the tale that Hengham, C.J., was fined for remitting a
fine and making an alteration of a record to that effect can be traced back to a statement by Scrope, C.J., in 1329.
[4] Comm. iii 410.
[5] So called because, if a pleader saw and acknowledged the error (Jeo faille), he
was allowed to amend, ibid iii 406; for instances see Y.B. 13, 14 Ed. III. (R.S.)
lxxv, lxxvi.
[6] 13 Edward I. St. 1 c. 31.

error, though it was not upon the record.[1]   This writing was called a Bill of Exceptions.   But this remedy was not very adequate.   The statute did not apply to cases to which the crown was a party, and therefore it did not apply to the revenue side of the court of Exchequer.[2]   Moreover, the proceedings on such a Bill left the court of error as little discretion as the proceedings on a writ of error.   If the ruling excepted against was adjudged to be incorrect the exception must be allowed, even if the court thought the verdict arrived at by the jury was correct.[3]

(iii) *Methods, other than the writ of error, by which judicial proceedings might be questioned.*

(*a*) Certain errors in the process of the court, committed by the defaults of the clerks, or as to matters of fact, could be remedied by the court itself.   The writ issued for this purpose was called a writ of error "coram vobis" if the error was in the Common Pleas; "coram nobis" if it was in the King's Bench.[4]

(*b*) We shall see that in the thirteenth century the common law courts used to administer both law and equity; but that, later, the equitable ideas and rules which then mitigated the rigour of the law tended to disappear.[5]   An illustration of this earlier phase in the history of the common law is to be seen in the writ *Audita Querela* by which "a defendant against whom judgment is recovered . . . may be relieved upon good matter of discharge which has happened since the judgment."[6]   The writ might be directed either to the Common Pleas or King's Bench.   After stating that the complaint has been heard, it directed the court to hear both parties and to do justice to them.   Stonore, C.J., in Edward III.'s reign[7] and Blackstone[8] both recognize its essentially equitable character.   But it gradually became obsolete.   Parties seeking such relief either applied to

" The mischief before this statute was that when the plaintiff or the defendant did offer to allege an exception (as in those days they did ore tenus at the bar) praying the justices to allow it, and the justices overruling it so as it was never entered of record, this the party could not assign for error," Coke, Second Instit. 426-427; Reeves, H.E.L. ii 97-100; for cases illustrating this procedure see Y.BB. 33-35 Ed. I (R.S.) 138, where Hengham refused to sign such a bill; 4 Hy. VI. Hil. pl. 14.

[2] Attorney-General v. Sillem (1863) 2 H. and C. at p. 605; but it would seem that in criminal cases the judge might seal such a bill if he liked, see the Rioters' Case (1683) 1 Vern. 175.

[3] Household Coal and Iron Co. v. Neilson (1843) 9 Cl. and Fin. at p. 804.

[4] Tidd, Practice (8th Ed.) 1191; cf. Debenham v. Bateman (1561) Dyer 195; the difference in form results from the theory of the actual presence of the king in the King's Bench.

[5] Below 446-449; vol. ii 246-249, 334-347.

[6] Bl. Comm. iii 404; see F.N.B. 103 H-105 F.

[7] "I tell you plainly that Audita Querela is given rather by Equity than by Common law," Y.B. 17 Ed. III. (R.S.) 370; cf. Y.B. 20 Ed. III. ii (R.S.) 56 where the fact that the applicant was a poor man was unsuccessfully urged.

[8] Comm. iii 404-405.

the court of Chancery for an injunction,[1] or by motion to the court in which the action had been heard.[2]

(c) By far the most important method by which the decision by the court could be questioned was by motion for a new trial. It would seem that from an early period the court had assumed the power to grant a new trial. In 1345-1346 the Common Pleas clearly considered that it had a power to order a new trial where the finding of a jury at nisi prius was unsatisfactory;[3] and there are other cases in the Year Books in which new trials were awarded because of irregularities in the conduct of the jury.[4] Though precedents of cases in which the court ordered a new trial are not frequent in the earlier reports, it is clear that the court had this power;[5] and in 1648 *Slade's Case*[6] shows that the court regarded itself as possessing the right to grant a new trial as part of its usual powers. In that case Rolle, J., though he refused to stay judgment, advised a new trial. In 1655 Glyn, C.J., in granting a new trial on account of excessive damages stated that "it is frequent in our books for the court to take notice of miscarriages of jurors, and to grant new trials upon them."[7] During the early part of the seventeenth century the court of Common Pleas was accustomed to grant new trials upon the certificate of the judge that the verdict was contrary to his opinion. The court of King's Bench required some matter appearing on the record to justify such a grant.[8] But in Charles II.'s reign they adopted the practice of granting a new trial on the affidavit of the party. This was necessary, partly because parties would otherwise have appealed to equity to be relieved from judgments founded upon unreasonable verdicts; and partly because, after the fall of the court of Star Chamber and the decision in *Bushell's Case*[9] there was no other check upon juries.[10] As Lord Mansfield said, "It is absolutely necessary to justice

---

[1] Below 458.
[2] Wicket v. Cremer (1699) 1 Ld. Raym. 439.
[3] Y.B. 20 Ed. III. i (R.S.) 74-76.
[4] Y.BB. 24 Ed. III. Hil. pl. 10; 11 Hy. IV. Mich. pl. 41; 14 Henry VII. Mich. pl. 3; for a summary and a comment on these cases see Yale Law Journal xxvi 54, n. 12—but note that the references there cited are not correct. In Witham v. Lewis (1744) 1 Wils. at pp. 55-56 Willes, C.J., took a distinction between a *venire facias de novo* and the grant of a new trial; it is possible that the case in Y.B. 20 Ed. III. i (R.S.) 74-76 may have been simply a case of a *venire facias de novo*; but the later cases seem to be genuine cases of new trials, as they were not granted in respect of matters appearing on the record, but on the ground of some misconduct in the jury.
[5] Lord Mansfield in Bright v. Eynon (1757) 1 Burr. 390 accounted for the paucity of authority by saying "that the old report books do not give any accounts of determinations made by the court upon motions."
[6] Style 138.   [7] Wood v. Gunston, Style 466.
[8] Bl. Comm. iii 388; Martyn v. Jackson (1674), 3 Keb. 398.
[9] (1670) Vaughan 135; below 345-347.
[10] Bl. Comm. iii 388; Thayer, Evidence 172 n. 4.

that there should upon many occasions be opportunities of re-considering the cause by a new trial." [1]   If it appears to be necessary they will be granted after a trial at bar as well as after a trial at nisi prius.

Motions for a new trial, a writ of error on the record, or a Bill of Exceptions were therefore the available methods of questioning a decision of the court.   But they could not all be used at once.   If a new trial were applied for, the party waived his right to question the result of the first trial by a writ of error or a Bill of Exceptions.   The result was that if the application for a new trial failed, the party lost all right to question the decision.   If it succeeded he might proceed by writ of error or Bill of Exceptions in case he thought there had been any errors in the proceedings on such new trial. [2]   We shall see that the Common Law Procedure Acts made considerable alterations in these rules; [3] but these alterations cannot be explained until the jurisdiction in error of the court of Exchequer Chamber has been described.

(3) *Superintendence over the due observance of the law by officials and others.*

When the court of King's Bench was indistinguishable from the Council it naturally shared with the Council this work of superintendence.   One branch of this work developed into the procedure in error which has just been described.   Another branch developed into a jurisdiction to amend " misdemeanours extra judicial," partly by its process of contempt, [4] but chiefly by means of the prerogative writs.   Thus the writ of error and these prerogative writs have a common root; and they have a common characteristic.   Unlike ordinary writs by which actions between private persons are begun, [5] they can, with certain limitations, [6] issue to any part of the king's dominions, except Scotland. [7]

---

[1] Bright v. Eynon (1757), 1 Burr. 390, 393.

[2] Attorney-General v. Sillem (1864) 10 H.L.C. at pp. 730, 731, 734.

[3] Below 245-246.   [4] For this process see vol. iii 391-394.

[5] Calvin's Case (1609) 7 Co. Rep. 20 a; cf. Craw v. Ramsey (1670) Vaughan at p. 290; it is otherwise if the suit is "immediately for the king," because, as he can sue in any court, the necessary writs can issue to any part of his dominions, Hale, Hist. Com. Law 268.

[6] The writ of error would not run into a country not governed by the common law, Hale, Hist. Com. Law 269; 25, 26 Victoria c. 20 provides that a writ of Habeas Corpus shall not issue out of England into any colony or foreign dominion of the crown where there is a court established which has authority to issue the writ, for the cases which gave rise to this statute see Forsyth, Leading Cases 452.

[7] Rex v. Cowle (1759) 2 Burr. at pp. 855-856 (the prerogative writs); as to the writ of error, Vaughan, C.J., in his Reports at p. 402, says that it is the only writ, "which concerns right and property between subjects" that can be issued out of England; "the reasons are, first for that without such writ, the law appointed or permitted to such inferior dominion, might be insensibly changed within itself,

Some of these writs were issued from the Chancery, others were issued either from the Chancery or the King's Bench, others were issued either from the Chancery or any of the three common law courts. To appreciate the extent and importance of the jurisdiction thus exercised by the King's Bench it is necessary to glance briefly at these writs.

Habeas Corpus. This writ has a great place in the history of our constitutional law because it has come to be the most efficient protection ever invented for the liberty of the subject. I shall deal with its history in detail in a later volume, when I am considering the history of the liberty of the subject.[1] Here it will be sufficient to indicate very briefly the stages by which it attained to the position which it holds in our modern constitutional law. Originally, as we have seen,[2] it was a writ by which a court could bring before itself persons whose presence was necessary for some legal proceeding pending before it; and some forms of the writ never ceased to be merely procedural.[3] But a writ by which a court can bring persons before it can be used for many different purposes. From the end of the fifteenth century onwards it was used by the King's Bench and Common Pleas to assert their jurisdiction against rival courts, such as the Chancery,[4] the Council,[5] the Admiralty,[6] or the court of High Commission.[7] They could, by means of this writ, bring before themselves and release persons who had been imprisoned by one of these rival courts, if, in their opinion, the court had acted in excess of its jurisdiction. Thus it came to be a writ by which a person unlawfully imprisoned could get released. But, in the great constitutional controversies of the seventeenth century, the Parliamentary opposition always asserted that they were maintaining, and the king was breaking, the law. If members of this opposition or others were imprisoned by the king they naturally had recourse to this writ to get release. Thus it became famous in constitutional law.[8] Its position as the most efficient

---

without the assent of the Dominion Superiour. Secondly, judgments might be then given to the disadvantage or lessening of the superiority, which cannot be reasonable; or to make the superiority to be only of the king, not of the crown of England (as King James once would have it in the case of Ireland *ex relatione J. Selden mihi*, whom King James consulted in this question)."

[1] Vol. ix 108-125.　　　　[2] Above 202.

[3] E.g. Habeas Corpus ad prosequendum, ad testificandum, ad deliberandum, and Habeas Corpora Juratorum, Bl. Comm. iii 130.

[4] Y.B. 22 Ed. IV. Mich. pl. 21.

[5] Glanvil's Case (1615) Moore 838, and the precedents there cited.

[6] Select Cases in Admiralty (S.S.) ii xlvi, xlvii; Prynne Animadversions 99.

[7] Fourth Instit. 333-334.

[8] Selden in his argument at the conference between the Lords and Commons in 1628 calls it, " the highest remedy in law for any man that is imprisoned," 3 S.T. 95.

protector of the liberty of the subject was unquestioned after the Great Rebellion ;[1] and men began to assign as its direct ancestor some of the clauses of Magna Carta, the literal meaning of which had been forgotten.   But, though there is no direct descent there is an indirect connection between the writ of Habeas Corpus and Magna Carta.   The writ helped to realize the Great Charter's ideal of a supreme law which could check the caprice of arbitrary power.[2]   And because the constitutional statesman of the seventeenth century saw that it was the most efficient instrument to effect this object, they wisely concentrated their energies upon making it more efficient.   As the result of statutes of 1641,[3] 1679,[4] and 1816[5] it could be issued by the Chancellor and by any of the judges of the three common law courts in vacation or in term time ; and abundant securities were provided against a refusal to issue it, and for speedy obedience to it when issued.

Certiorari.[6]   This is an original writ which can be issued either out of the Chancery or the King's Bench when the king desires to be certified of any record made by any court of record, or by certain officials, e.g. the sheriff or the coroners.   Thus, as we have seen, indictments can be removed from the itinerant justices by this writ to the King's Bench.[7]   It is demandable in criminal cases as of right only by the crown.

Prohibition.[8]   " A prohibition is a writ issuing properly only out of the court of King's Bench, being the king's prerogative writ ; but, for the futherance of justice, it may now also be had in some cases out of the court of Chancery, Common Pleas, or Exchequer ; directed to the judge and parties of a suit in any inferior court, commanding them to cease from the prosecution thereof, upon a suggestion that either the cause originally, or some collateral matter arising therein, does not belong to that jurisdiction." [9]   Fitzherbert [10] gives many instances of such writs. Thus a prohibition might be directed to the sheriff that he do not hold plea in a writ of right, because the tenant had put

---

[1] " The writ of Habeas Corpus is now the most usual remedy by which a man is restored again to his liberty, if he have been against the law deprived of it," Bushell's Case (1670) Vaughan at p. 136 ; cf. Hale, P.C. ii 143.

[2] Above 61, 63 ; vol. ii 215, 216.

[3] 16 Charles I. c. 10 § 8—dealing with commitments to prison by the Council.

[4] 31 Charles II. c. 2.   [5] 56 George III. c. 100.

[6] App. XIII. ; Holt, C.J. (1 Salk. 263), said that when a new jurisdiction is created by Parliament to act according to the course of the common law a writ of error can be brought from its decision : when they are to act in a summary way, or in a new course different from the common law, a writ of certiorari lies.

[7] Above 213.   [8] App. XII. A.   [9] Bl. Comm. iii 112.

[10] F.N.B. 39 H-47 B ; in some cases it was granted when wrong was done to the party by proceeding in the other jurisdiction, e.g. the case of a lease offered to be proved in the ecclesiastical court by one witness and refused, because by that law two witnesses were required, Home v. Earl Camden (1795) 2 Hy. Bl. at p. 536.

himself upon the Grand Assize; or a prohibition might be directed to the ecclesiastical court if it held plea of lay fee. We shall see that it was by means of this writ that the courts of common law asserted their superiority over the court of Admiralty and the ecclesiastical courts.[1] The ecclesiastical courts tried in vain to restrict its issue at different periods.[2] They succeeded, however, in establishing their right to an appeal in case of the issue of the writ. A statute was made in 1296 which provided that, when a prohibition had been directed to the ecclesiastical judges, the chancellor or chief justice should, if they thought that the matter should be determined in the ecclesiastical court, order that court to proceed notwithstanding the prohibition. This process of appeal was known as the grant of a writ of Consultation.[3] In no other cases was there any appeal directly provided by law against the issue of the writ.[4]

Mandamus.[5] This is "a command issuing in the king's name from the court of King's Bench, and directed to any person, corporation, or inferior court of judicature, within the king's dominions; requiring them to do some particular thing therein specified, which appertains to their office and duty."[6] It lies, for instance, to compel the admission or restoration of any person to a public office, or to compel the holding of a court. As Lord Mansfield put it, "When there is no specific remedy the court will grant a mandamus that justice may be done."[7] But if there is a more convenient remedy it will not be granted.[8]

Quo Warranto.[9] This is a writ "In the nature of a writ of right for the king against persons who claimed or usurped any office, franchise, liberty, or privilege belonging to the crown, to enquire by what authority they maintained their claim, in order

---

[1] Below 553-558, 594-595.

[2] 51 Henry III.; Articuli Cleri 9 Edward II.; Articles exhibited by Bancroft, Archbishop of Canterbury in 1605, Coke, Second Instit. 599-618.

[3] 24 Edward I.; App. XII., B.

[4] 1 Ld. Raym. 545; 5 B. and C. 765; but indirectly an appeal was made possible; Eyre, C.B., in Home v. Earl Camden (2 Hy. Bl. 533) giving his opinion to the House of Lords said, " In modern times when prohibitions are applied for . . . and the parties applying suggest grounds either of fact or law . . . which appear to the court so doubtful as to be fit to be put in a course of trial, the party applying is directed to declare in prohibition, that is, to institute a feigned action . . . in which action, in the shape of a question whether such a prohibition ought *to have been* granted, the real question, whether such a prohibition ought *to be* granted is considered; " this question could be taken to the House of Lords, as in form it was an action for damages for proceeding after a prohibition had been obtained.

[5] App. XV.

[6] Bl. Comm. iii 110; there was a similar writ of procedendo ad judicium issuing out of the Chancery and ordering the judges of any court to proceed to judgment, ibid 109; F.N.B. 153 B.

[7] R. v. Bank of England (1780) 2 Dougl. 506.

[8] Re Nathan (1884) 12 Q.B.D. 461.   [9] App. XIV.

to have the right determined."[1]   We have already seen what an important part the writ played in Edward I.'s reign.[2]   It gradually went out of use; and as early as the sixteenth century[3] its place was taken by an information in the nature of a Quo Warranto filed by the Attorney-General.[4]   The most famous instance of this proceding was the information filed against the corporation of London 1681-1683.[5]   In modern times it has come to be available not only to the crown, when a franchise or office has been usurped, but also to a private person aggrieved by such usurpation.[6]

Ne Exeat Regno.   By the common law the king could forbid his subjects from going outside the realm, "because that every man is bound to defend the king and the realm."[7]   It was issued by the Chancellor for reasons of state on the application, in the sixteenth and seventeenth centuries, of a secretary of state.[8]   But, at the beginning of the eighteenth century, it came to be issued by tne Chancellor on the application of a private person in order to prevent the evasion of legal or equitable liabilities.[9]   Probaby the fact that the Chancellor was both a great official of the state and the head of the court of the Chancery helped to introduce this extension of the use of the writ.

All these writs, except the writs of *Quo Warranto* and *Ne Exeat Regno*, could be issued by the court of King's Bench; and the proceedings taken upon them were, except in the case of the writ *Ne Exeat Regno*, under its control, as, with this exception, all these writs were returnable there.   Thus the court of King's Bench, and, through the court of King's Bench, the common law, gained a large power to prevent the commission of illegal acts by the persons and bodies entrusted with the conduct of both the

---

[1] Selwyn Nisi Prius (Ed. 1842) 1143.   [2] Above 88.

[3] Tindal, C.J., in Darley v. Reg. (1845-1846) 12 Cl. and Fin. at p. 537 pointed out that there are many precedents of informations in Coke's Entries.

[4] The process upon this was different; and it was not, as the writ itself was, conclusive for the future against the crown as well as the subject, the King v. Trinity House (1662) 1 Sid. 86; 12 Mod. 225.

[5] 8 S.T. 1039; for a modern case see Rex v. Speyer [1916] 1 K.B. 595; [1916] 2 K.B. 858.

[6] Darley v. Reg. (1845-1846) 12 Cl. and Fin. at p. 545; R. v. Speyer [1916] 1 K.B. at p. 609.

[7] " By the common law every man may go out of the realm to merchandize, or on pilgrimage, or for what other cause he pleaseth, without the king's leave; and he shall not be punished for so doing; but because that every man is of right for to defend the king and his realm, therefore the king at his pleasure by his writ may command a man that he go not beyond the seas or out of the realm without licence," F.N.B. 85 A.

[8] Forsyth, Leading Cases 181.

[9] It was said by Wilmot, C.J., Opinions and Judgments 97-98, cited Forsyth, op. cit. 180, that the legality of using the writ in this way was settled in the reign of Charles II. " upon an usage first begun in the time of James I."

local and the central government. A court which exercised a jurisdiction of this kind was usual enough in the mediæval state, in which the work of government was done through courts exercising both administrative and judicial functions ; but the survival of such a court in a modern state was by no means usual. The fact that the court of King's Bench has always exercised this jurisdiction was not the least of the causes which ensured the supremacy of the common law in the state, by making the growth of a system of administrative law both less essential and more difficult. The fact that its successor—the King's Bench Division —still exercises these administrative functions is one of the most striking illustrations of the manner in which the continuity of the development of the English state has preserved the mediæval character of English legal institutions, and adapted them to modern uses.

The Court of Exchequer

We have seen that the Exchequer had got a separate organization in the course of the twelfth century, and that it was thus the earliest department of state to get this sepa ate organization.[1] During the greater part of the thirteenth century there was no separation between the financial and judicial sides of this department ;[2] and its relations with the main body of the Curia Regis were constant and close.[3] We must now trace the process by which the judicial side of this department fell apart from its financial side and became a distinct court. We shall see that this court gradually became assimilated to the other two courts of common law ; that this process of assimilation took a long time to accomplish ; and that, to the end, the court preserved many traces of its old connection with the financial side of the Exchequer, which differentiated it from the other two courts.

Bracton does not recognize the Exchequer as a court of law of a kind similar to the two benches and the itinerant justices.[4] But it is clear from both Britton [5] and Fleta [6] that, at the end of

---

[1] Above 42-44.

[2] Thus Maitland, Equity 2, speaking of Edward I.'s reign, says that from the modern point of view, the Exchequer "is not only a court of law, but a government office, an administrative or executive bureau ; " cf. Tout, Edward II. 45.

[3] Below 233-234.   [4] Above 204 n. 5.

[5] " Also our will is, that at our Exchequer at Westminster and elsewhere our Treasurers and our Barons there have jurisdiction and record of things which concern their office, and to hear and determine all causes relating to our debts and seignories and things incident thereto, without which such matters could not be tried ; and that they have cognizance of debts owing to our debtors, by means whereof we may the more speedily recover our own," i 5.

[6] " Habet etiam Rex Curiam suam et justiciarios suos in Scaccario apud Westmonasterium residentes cujus loci capitalis est Thesaurarius, non tamen justiciarius

the thirteenth century, the judicial side of the department was beginning to be more definitely separated from the administrative side ; and there are other indications that this judicial side was beginning to present characteristics resembling those of the other two courts of law. Thus, firstly, the plea rolls of the Exchequer begin in 1236-1237, and are practically continuous after 1267-1268.[1] Secondly, the term "Baron of the Exchequer" ceased to denote any of the high officials of the Exchequer ;[2] and, from 1234, came to be appropriated to a special set of officials with distinct duties of a mixed judicial and administrative kind.[3] And the growing importance of their judicial duties at the beginning of the fourteenth century can be seen from the fact that they were recruited both from amongst the Exchequer clerks and from among the eminent practitioners in the common law courts.[4] Thirdly, just as the other two common law courts had their chief justices so, in Edward I.'s reign, William Carlton, the most senior of the Barons, is described as "capitalis baro."[5] It is probable, however, from Fleta's words[6] that the title merely expressed the fact that he was the senior Baron ; but, in 1312, the position of "capitalis baro" ceased to be merely the title of the most senior of the Barons, and came to be a definite office which gave the holder the right of presiding over the other Barons.[7] Fourthly, the disuse of the office of justiciar in 1234,[8] and the growing separation of the other two courts of common law, were not without their influence on the judicial department of the Exchequer. By the beginning of the fourteenth century therefore, the court of Exchequer had come to be a separate department presided over by official Barons, some of whom were professional lawyers. But the rolls of this department were kept, like the other rolls of the Exchequer, by the Treasurer ; and so,

---

ut in pronunciationibus judiciorum placitorum inter extraneas personas habitorum, sed in hiis quæ commodum Regis respiciant, et tam in rebus forinsecis quam intrin-secis. . . . Justiciarii ibidem commorantes Barones esse dicimus," Fleta ii 25. 26 ; cf. ibid i 48. 1 ; ii 2. 6.

[1] Tout, Edward II. 55 n. 2 ; Poole, The Exchequer in the Twelfth Century 183 n. 5.

[2] Above 44.   [3] Tout, op. cit. 333 seqq.

[4] "Other barons like Thrickingham, Staunton, and Friskney, this latter a lay-man, had been regular justices of one or both of the two benches ; while others had had judicial experience in eyres and similar temporary commissions. . . . Three of the lay barons, Scotter, Friskney, and Passelewe, had been advocates in large prac-tices in the common law courts," ibid 336 ; cf. Y.B. 3, 4, Ed. II. (S.S.) xxii.

[5] Tout, op. cit. 338.   [6] Above 231 n. 6.

[7] Tout, op. cit. 338-339 ; Professor Tout thinks that Norwich's appointment was one of the changes brought about by the ordinances of 1311, and he tells us that a special stipend was assigned to him as deputy Treasurer ; he was probably appointed deputy Treasurer in order to give him the right, *qua* Chief Baron, to preside over the other barons ; this office gave him the place formerly occupied by the Treasurer who, Fleta tells us, above 231 n. 6 had been the president of the court.

[8] Above 205.

when this judicial department became a separate court, it is said to be a court held by the Treasurer and the Barons.[1]

It became a separate court very gradually ; and the process by which this result was attained may be summarized as follows : (i) It lost its close connection with the king and Council. (ii) Its jurisdiction, during the fourteenth, fifteenth, and first half of the sixteenth centuries, was limited almost entirely to the hearing of revenue cases. (iii) The Barons came to be recruited entirely from the lawyers, and the court began to exercise a jurisdiction over cases other than revenue cases. Let us examine the effects of these three developments.

(i) The close connection of the Exchequer with the main body of the Curia Regis was maintained all through the thirteenth century. The king himself sometimes presided there ;[2] and, though the Exchequer was usually stationed at Westminster, it sometimes followed the king in his peregrinations over the country. Thus it was at Shrewsbury in 1280,[3] at York in 1298,[4] 1327,[5] and 1392.[6] Similarly it is clear that during the reigns of Edward I. and II., " the Exchequer did not lose its character as a court of general assemblage. . . . To a considerable extent its sessions were still the sessions of the Council." [7] To some extent, no doubt, the instances which Madox gives [8] of the Council sitting at the Exchequer, can be explained by the probable conjecture that these meetings of the Council were simply held in a room at the Exchequer buildings.[9] It is clear too that in this room judges and officials both of the Exchequer and the Chancery, sometimes met to discuss legal difficulties ; and no doubt other meetings of the Council were there held.[10] But, though the connection of the Exchequer with the Council was necessarily as close and as constant as the connection of

[1] Coke, Fourth Instit. 105, says " Albeit the Barons, as hath been said, are the sole judges, yet the Treasurer of the Exchequer is joined with them in keeping of the records ; " and that " the Lord Treasurer is also Treasurer of the Exchequer ; " cf. Britton i 97 ; Madox, ii 54-55 ; Manning, Exchequer of Pleas 480 n.

[2] Madox, ii 10, 11, 102.   [3] Foss, Judges iii 22.

[4] Ibid iii 23.   [5] Ibid iii 337.   [6] Ibid iv 15.

[7] Baldwin, The King's Council 211 ; Select Cases before the Council (S.S.) xxii.

[8] Madox, ii 29, 32, 102.

[9] Tout, op. cit. 56 says, " I am inclined to suggest that we may find at least a partial explanation of many of the extra-financial acts often described as done ' in the exchequer,' and sometimes imagined to be done by the exchequer, by the circumstances that departments, less well off than the exchequer in the matter of housing, found it convenient to do this work on exchequer premises, lent to them for the purpose. Thus when the chancery holds upon occasion a sitting in the exchequer, we are not to imagine that there is some subtle inter-relation between the two departments. We have simply an instance of the officials of an office with no home of its own meeting in the office of another department better provided with house room. We can explain in the same fashion the instances given by Madox of the king's council sitting in the exchequer."

[10] Ibid 57.

the other Barons were lawyers, they were not all lawyers; and many, as Foss says,[1] "were raised to the Bench from their practical knowledge of the revenue acquired in minor offences connected with it." It is not therefore surprising to find that the judges of the court held a position inferior to that of the judges of the other two courts of common law. They do not appear among the judges of assize,[2] and they took rank after the serjeants at law.[3] They were not members of the Serjeant's Inn, of which all the judges were necessarily members.[4] They were not summoned to Parliament with the other judges.[5] They continued to hold this inferior position till 1579. In that year, on the appointment of Robert Shute to the office of Baron, it was determined to place him on the same footing as the judges of the other two common law courts. His patent declared that, "he shall be reputed and be of the same order, rank, estimation, dignity, and pre-eminence to all intents and purposes as any puisne judge of either of the other two courts."[6]

This change was no doubt due to the growth of the equitable jurisdiction of the Exchequer and of its jurisdiction over common pleas; and it is probable that the growth of these two branches of its jurisdiction was due to the growing predominance of the legal element among the Barons.[7] Thus, in the case of *Stradling* v. *Morgan*,[8] it was argued that if a statute gave a penalty to be recovered in any of the king's courts of record, an action could not be brought in the Exchequer, unless the plaintiff were an officer of the court or a debtor to the king, because it was a common plea. The second and third Barons were of this opinion;[9] but Saunders the Chief Baron, who had held the posts of a judge of the Common Pleas and chief justice of the Queen's Bench, argued from Glanvil that any common plea could be heard in the court, and minimized the effects of the ordinances

---

[1] Foss, Judges iii 348.

[2] Thus when the statute of 14 Edward III. St. 1 c. 16 defined the persons who could try cases at nisi prius (below 279), it provided that, if the justices of the one Bench or the other did not come into the county, they could be tried by "The Chief Baron of the Exchequer if he be a man of the law;" the other Barons were not mentioned.

[3] Foss, Judges iv 15; Fortescue, De Laudibus c. 50 notes that when a serjeant is made a judge the value of the rings he gives to the Barons of the Exchequer is smaller than the value of those given to the Chief Baron and the judges of the other courts.

[4] Above 197; vol. ii 485, 492; Foss, Judges v 11, 95.

[5] Ibid 95.   [6] Ibid 409-410; vi 18-21.

[7] For instances of the appointment of lawyers to be Barons in the Tudor period see Dasent ii 33 (1546-1547); Foss, Judges vi 19, says that under Henry VII. and VIII., "they were advancing in legal education and entering into the Inns of Court. Several instances occur of there being members, and even readers there after they had become Barons."

[8] (1560) Plowden at pp. 207-209.   [9] At p. 208.

and statutes which restricted the Exchequer jurisdiction.[1] This would seem to show that the judges of the court who were lawyers encouraged litigants who wished to sue there.

When the Barons of the Exchequer had come to be chosen from the lawyers it became clear that some official was wanted to supply the technical knowledge of matters of account which the Barons had formerly possessed. The duty of supplying this knowledge was turned over to the cursitor Baron—an official whose duty it was to know the "cursus" or course of the Exchequer. Such an official seems to have been appointed in 1323;[2] but it is probable that the office grew in importance, and became definitely a separate office, as a result of this change in the status of the other Barons.[3] Besides keeping the other Barons informed as to the course of the Exchequer,[4] he examined and audited the accounts of the sheriffs. In 1834 these duties were handed over to the Commissioners for auditing the public accounts;[5] and the office was abolished in 1857.[6]

Thus, from the year 1579, the Barons were appointed from among the serjeants, and they rode the circuits like the other judges. But, long after this date, we can see in the wording of the statute book a reminiscence of the older status. When the Barons were, with the other judges, empowered to do judicial acts, the expression always used is "Barons being of the degree of the coif."[7]

---

[1] " He denied that to be a statute which was called the Statute of Rutland, for he said it was only an ordinance made by the king without the authority of Parliament, touching the order of the court of Exchequer. And as to the other statute that refers to Magna Carta, he said that there is no such restraint in Magna Carta," at p. 209; Coke rightly denied Saunders' view of the Statute of Rutland, Second Instit. 551.

[2] Tout, op. cit. 198.

[3] This probably gave rise to the opinion held by Foss, Judges vi 16, 26 that the title and office were created for the first time in 1610; but it would seem that the puisne Baron had before done the duties of the cursitor Baron, and that the puisne Baron was commonly called by that name, see references cited by Foss, vi 21, 22, 25-26; it became definitely a separate office at the end of the sixteenth century, just as the office of Chief Baron had become definitely a separate office at the beginning of the fourteenth century, above 232.

[4] " He informeth the rest of the Barons of the course of the court in any matter that concerneth the king's Prerogative," Practice of the Exchequer Court, written at the end of the sixteenth century, cited Foss, vi 25; a similar account is given by Vernon in a book which he published on the Exchequer in 1642—he says, " The cursitor Baron being so called because he is chosen most usually out of some of the best experienced clerks of the two Remembrancers', or clerke of the Pipe's office, and is to informe the bench and the king's learned counsel from time to time, both in court and out of court, what the course of the Exchequer is," cited Foss, vi 25-26.

[5] 3, 4 William IV. c. 90.

[6] 19, 20 Victoria c. 86; Foss says, ix 109, that then his sole remaining duty was the notification in the court of Exchequer of the sovereign's sanction to the election of the sheriffs of London, " and witnessing the attendant ceremonies of counting the hobnails and chopping the fagots as rent service to the crown;" these formalities are now performed in the king's remembrancer's office.

[7] That is having attained the degree of serjeant at law, vol. ii 486-492; instances are 31 Charles II. c. 2 § 3; 56 George III. c. 100 § 1.

The jurisdiction of the court of Exchequer can be grouped under three heads. (1) It was a court of revenue. (2) It was a court of common law. (3) It was a court of equity. The revenue jurisdiction was the oldest. The two other branches of its jurisdiction were grafted upon it at a time when each judge grasped at any kind of jurisdiction (and its profits) which he could obtain.

(1) It was a court of revenue held before the Treasurer and the Barons. This court of revenue decided questions between the crown and the taxpayer, and between the crown and the accountants to the crown. As a court of revenue it had certain peculiarities in its procedure which presented analogies both to the courts of common law and to the court of Chancery. These peculiarities are known as the cursus scaccarii.[1] It was by following up the analogies so suggested that the court of Exchequer became a court of common law and a court of equity as well as a court of revenue. We shall see that the jurisdiction of the Exchequer as a court of equity has been taken away by statute ; but this statute did not take away the peculiarities which characterized the jurisdiction of the court of revenue by virtue of the cursus scaccarii, even though these peculiarities gave in substance a kind of equitable jurisdiction.[2] By virtue of the cursus scaccarii, "all kinds of equitable matter raised either on suggestion, petition, or plea were dealt with, and parties furnished with summary means of asserting their rights against the crown, and of having the matter determined at once by the court, in a way wholly dissimilar to the practice of any other court, and presenting a peculiar union of legal and equitable procedure ".[3]   A good instance of this peculiar union of legal and equitable procedure used in the Exchequer, sitting as a court of revenue, is furnished by the power possessed by it of removing matters affecting the revenue or the property of the crown from the cognizance of other courts. Eyre, C.B., described it as a kind of injunction to stay proceedings in another court qualified by the liberty given to sue in the Exchequer. He speaks of it as being of a piece with the anomalous jurisdiction of the court of revenue in the Exchequer, which has here adopted an equitable, rather than a

---

[1] Dialogus (Præfatio), " Sane scaccarium suis legibus . . . subsistit ; " Pollock, C.B., Attorney-General v. Halling (1846) 15 M. and W. at p. 693 said, " It (the court) has been in the constant habit of proceeding both after the forms of other courts of common law and in the manner also of a court of equity. The 'course of the Exchequer,' involving both these modes of procedure, is part of the ancient and general law of the realm."

[2] Attorney-General v. Halling 15 M. and W. 687, dissenting from Attorney-General v. Corporation of London (1845) 14 L.J.N.S. Ch. 305.

[3] Attorney-General v. Halling 15 M. and W. at p. 698.

legal procedure.[1]   The reforms in practice and procedure made by the Common Law Procedure Acts [2] only applied to the Revenue side of the Exchequer in so far as they were expressly made to do so by the Queen's Remembrancer's Act and the Crown Suits Act.[3]   Even at the present day certain parts of the Exchequer practice and procedure present peculiarities which have disappeared from the other courts.

This cursus scaccarii is probably the nearest approach to a body of administrative law that the English legal system has ever known ; and the court of Exchequer, sitting as a court of Revenue, is the nearest approach to an administrative court. The resemblance would have been closer if the court had continued to be staffed by Exchequer clerks to the exclusion of the common lawyers.   But the fact that, from an early date, the lawyers were taking their places beside the officials [4] illustrates the manner in which the technical conceptions of the common law were beginning to pervade all the departments of the state ; and the fact that in 1579 the lawyers finally ousted the officials is a striking proof of the vigorous life and the capacity for expansion which the common law was showing at the end of the sixteenth century.

(2) It was a court of common law held before the Treasurer and the Barons.   The court of Exchequer like the other common law courts had exclusive jurisdiction over the officials of the court.   This jurisdiction existed as early as Henry II.'s reign. The Dialogus mentions several privileges possessed by the Barons and other officers of the Exchequer.[5]   " The records of the subsequent times," says Madox,[6] "speak more distinctly.   They mention the privilege of impleading and being impleaded in the Exchequer only ; freedom from toll for things bought for their own use ; freedom from suit to county courts, hundred courts, etc.; and other privileges.   It is also to be understood, that several of the residents at the Exchequer had privilege not only for themselves, but also for their clerks and their men."   The rights and privileges possessed by the court were thus wider than, though similar in kind to those possessed by the other courts.[7]

---

[1] Cawthone v. Campbell, Lowndes, and others, cited Manning, Exchequer of Pleas i 164 seqq.; cp. 2 Salk. 546, where Walter, C.B., is reported to have said that, " where one entitled to the privilege of the court is sued in C.B., this court sends a supersedeas ; but if it be in B.R. they do not send a supersedeas, for that would be to supersede the king ; but the practice is to send up the writ book by the puisne Baron, and demand privilege."

[2] 16, 17 Victoria c. 113 ; 17, 18 Victoria c. 125.

[3] 22, 23 Victoria c. 21 ; 28, 29 Victoria c. 104 ; Attorney-General v. Sillem (1864) to H.L.C. 704 ; below 246.

[4] Above 232 and n. 4.

[5] I. 8.

[6] ii 12.

[7] Above 203.

It possessed another privilege which was peculiar to it. The crown had peculiar advantages with regard to debts owing to it. Among these advantages was the right of the crown to require payment from the debtor of its debtor, and from the debtor of that debtor to an indefinite extent.[1] When statutes and ordinances were passed to prevent the court from holding common pleas, the court made this right of the crown the foundation of a fiction by means of which they secured a jurisdiction which the legislature had denied to them. The plaintiff[2] who wished to sue for breach of contract or other injury was supposed to be a debtor to, or an accountant of the crown; and it was supposed that unless he could recover his debt or damages he was thereby the less able (quo minus sufficiens existit) to satisfy the crown. As early as 1345-1346 this device for suing in the Exchequer had been resorted to in order to prevent the defendant from waging his law.[3] It appears to have been generally used in the latter part of the sixteenth century, and thus by means of this writ of Quominus the court obtained a general jurisdiction over common pleas.[4] Proceedings in this court began by writ of Quominus, just as proceedings in the court of King's Bench began by bill of Middlesex and Latitat. In 1692-1693[5] an attempt was made to do for this process, what the Act of Charles II. had done for the process of Latitat,[6] and compel the plaintiff to express the true cause of action in his writ; but the bill was dropped after a first reading. The Uniformity of Process Act[7] applied to the Quominus process in the court of Exchequer in the same way as it applied to the Latitat process in the court of King's Bench.[8]

(3) It was a court of equity held before the Treasurer, the Chancellor of the Exchequer, and the Barons. We have seen that the jurisdiction of the court as a court of revenue involved

---

[1] Dialogus ii 16; Britton i 5, above 231 n. 5; Coke, Second Instit. 551; Attorney-General v. Poultney (1665) Hardres 403, 404, Hale, C.B., showed how this principle ought to have been limited; he said suppose A indebted to the king in £100; B to A in £1000; C to B in £10,000—"These several debtors should have the benefit of the king's prerogative against lands and goods for recovering their several debts. There would be no inconvenience if the king's debt were so levied, though in the 10th degree . . . but to make the king's prerogative instrumental . . . to satisfy other men's debts (i.e. in this case to recover the £900 or the £9900 would be unreasonable, inconvenient, and mischievous to the subject; " Coke, Fourth Instit. 115 agrees with Hale that some limitation ought to be imposed; in 1621 a bill which would have had the effect of imposing some limitation passed the Commons, but was dropped in the Lords, Hist. MSS. Com. Fourth Rep. App. Pt. I. 123.

[2] When the plaintiff is privileged the suit is by Quominus (App. XXI.): when the defendant is privileged the suit is, as in other courts, by Bill, 2 Salk. 546.

[3] Y.B. 20 Ed. III. (R.S.) i 116-120; for law wager see below 305-308.

[4] Bl. Comm. iii 286; App. XXI.

[5] Hist. MSS. Comm. Fourteenth Rep. App. Pt. VI. 342 no. 693.

[6] Above 221.   [7] 2 William IV. c. 39.   [8] Above 222.

the possession of certain equitable powers. This fact was recognized as early as Henry II.'s reign—though the term "aequitas" was not then used in quite the same sense as that which it afterwards acquired.[1] We shall see that equitable jurisdiction became the peculiar province of the Lord Chancellor, and that in his court it acquired a very technical meaning. The court of Exchequer had its chancellor; it possessed certain equitable powers by virtue of the cursus scaccarii; and the writ of subpœna—the peculiar process of the court of Chancery—was certainly known in the Exchequer as early as Henry IV.'s reign,[2] and was generally used in 1574.[2] Probably the court, like the courts of the counties Palatine and Wales,[4] silently assumed this equitable jurisdiction in the course of the sixteenth century.[5] The flexible nature of the rules of equity in the fifteenth and sixteenth centuries, and its administration through common law forms,[6] made it the easier for a court which possessed affinities with the common law courts and with the court of Chancery, to assume a jurisdiction of this kind. In the end the court of Exchequer obtained a general equitable jurisdiction on grounds similar to those upon which it obtained a general common law jurisdiction. "Any person," says Blackstone, "may file a bill against another upon a bare suggestion that he is the king's accomptant but whether he is so or not is never controverted."[7] From the equity side of the court an appeal lay to the House of Lords. There is an instance of such an appeal in 1641, in which it was alleged that conflicting decisions had been given by this court, and the court of Chancery.[8] The

---

[1] Dialogus i 4, the duty of the officials is "ut regis utilitati prospiciant; salva tamen æquitate secundum constitutas leges scaccarii;" for the meaning of the term equity at different periods see below 467-469; vol. ii 245-249, 334-347; vol. v 215-218.

[2] Cotton, Records 410; Reeves, H.E.L. ii 495, 496; Coke, Fourth Instit. 119; a petition of 3 Henry V. (4 Rot. Parl. 84) complains of writs of subpœna sued out of the Chancery and the Exchequer for matters determinable at Common Law; for the writ see App. XVII. B.

[3] Manning, Exchequer of Pleas i 38.

[4] Above 111, 116, 125; cf. Spence, Equitable Jurisdiction i 352; Pike, History of the House of Lords 298-299.

[5] Coke, Fourth Instit. 118-119 was ignorant of the origin of this jurisdiction; he based it partly on the possession of a chancellor, partly on the provisions of 33 Henry VIII. c. 39; but that Act is concerned mainly with the court of Surveyors, and the few clauses which concern the Exchequer give no warrant for the assumption by the Exchequer of a general jurisdiction in equity.

[6] Below 450-451.

[7] Comm. iii 45, 46; in Attorney-General v. Halling (1846), 15 M. and W. at p. 693, it is said that, "The course of the Exchequer involving both a form of legal and equitable procedure, the usurped jurisdiction naturally divided itself in this way; and after so dividing itself the branches became gradually entirely separate, and formed two separate sides, the plea side and the equity side of the court—the revenue, however, still remaining as before and involving both."

[8] Hist. MSS. Comm. App. Fourth Rep. Pt. I. 87; a bill of review also lay in the Exchequer itself as was the case with the Chancery, Hardres 174; below 427, 438.

equitable jurisdiction of the court was taken away in 1842,[1] and handed over to the court of Chancery.

The Court of Exchequer Chamber

We have seen that in Edward I. and II.'s reigns the judges and other officials of the Exchequer were accustomed to meet in a chamber in the Exchequer buildings to discuss legal and other questions connected with Exchequer business.[2]   Probably this practice gave rise to the idea that these meetings were the meetings of a court,[3] which was naturally called by the name of the chamber in which it met.[4]   From time to time the legislature found it convenient to confer special powers upon the meetings of judges and others who met in this Exchequer Chamber.   Hence the term "court of Exchequer Chamber" came to be the name for several quite distinct tribunals.

(1) One of these tribunals arose, not from any act of the legislature, but from a practice of the judges, which was fostered by the close relations which had always subsisted between the judges of the two Benches, and, after 1579, between the judges of all the three common law courts;[5] and it probably dates back to the informal meetings in the Exchequer Chamber of which we read in the thirteenth and early fourteenth centuries.[6]   If any difficult case arose in any one of the three common law courts it might, after argument in that court and at the discretion of the court,[7] be adjourned to be argued before all the judges and barons in the Exchequer Chamber.[8]   After a full discussion there, judgment was given by the court in which the proceedings had been begun.   Important cases were so discussed in the fourteenth, fifteenth, and sixteenth centuries.[9]   One of the last was the *Case of Ship Money* in 1637.[10]

---

[1] 5 Victoria c. 5 ; the jurisdiction had been regulated 57 George III. c. 18 ; 1 George IV. c. 35 ; 3, 4 William IV. c. 41 § 25 ; 6, 7 William IV. c. 112.

[2] Above 233.

[3] "From such meetings it is easy to see that there arose gradually that ' Exchequer Chamber ' which the legislation of later periods erected as a formal court of appeal," Tout, op. cit. 57.

[4] See below 496-497 for a similar development in the case of the court of Star Chamber.

[5] Y.B. 3, 4 Ed. II. (S.S.) xxiii.   [6] Above 233 n. 9.

[7] Warrain v. Smith (1614) 2 Bulst. 146—"this ought to proceed ex motione Curiæ, but not of the party concerned ; this ought to be after argument, but not before."

[8] Coke, Fourth Instit. 119 ; Reeves, H.E.L. iii 668 n. a.

[9] E.g. Y.B. 6, 7 Ed. II. (S.S.) 44—note from the Record which states that " never before within the memory of anyone living hath such a case as this ever come before the court of the lord king ; " Y.B. 2 Rich. III. pl. 26 ; Capel's case (1581) 1 Co. Rep. 62 ; Shelley's Case (1586) ibid 106 a ; Chudleigh's Case (1589) ibid 132 a.

[10] 3 S.T. 825.

(2) As soon as the court of Exchequer began to assume the characteristics of a common law court, the question of the manner in which the errors of the court were to be corrected was bound to arise. The court of King's Bench assumed that, as the court of Exchequer was a law court, it had the power to correct, its errors, just as it had the power to correct the errors of the court of Exchequer was a law court, it had the power to correct always denied that the court of King's Bench had power to amend errors from the revenue and plea side of the Exchequer. In 1338 they addressed a memorial to the crown in which they showed from the history of the Exchequer that the court of King's Bench never had this jurisdiction; but that if error was alleged the king issued a special commission to the Barons " associatis sibi aliis fidelibus Regis " to examine and correct the error.[1] We have seen that the position of the court of Exchequer was for a long period very different from the position of the other courts of law. As Mr. Pike[2] says, " the principle which is clearly brought out in all the documents relating to the matter, is that judgments in the Exchequer were not judgments at common law. The natural corollary was that when error was alleged, these judgments could not be either affirmed or reversed in the same manner as judgments at common law. In other words the King's Bench might correct a judgment of various courts of record, including the court of Common Pleas, but could not correct a judgment of the court of Exchequer."

The Barons made good their position.[3] An Act passed in 1357-1358[4] established a court to hear errors in the Exchequer. The constitution of that court followed the lines suggested by the Barons in 1338. It enacted that " where a man complaineth of error made in process in the Exchequer, the Chancellor and Treasurer shall cause to come before them in any Chamber of Council nigh the Exchequer, the record of the process out of the Exchequer, taking to them the justices and other sage persons such as to them seemeth to be taken . . . and if any error be found they shall correct and amend the rolls."

The working of this statute was not found to be wholly satisfactory; and in 1378[5] the commons petitioned that errors in the Exchequer should be redressed in the King's Bench. The reply

---

[1] Y.B. 14 Ed. III. (R.S.) xvii-xxix.   [2] Ibid xxix.
[3] There are several instances of commissions addressed to members of the Council, judges and others, 2 Rot. Parl. 154 no. 41 (18 Ed. III.); Coke, Fourth Instit. 105, 106; in 1348 (2 Rot. Parl. 168 no. 26), the crown was petitioned that errors be redressed in the King's Bench, and not by the same persons who gave the judgment, " Car il n'est mye semblable a verite homme doit avoir bone conceite contre sa opinion demesne; " in this case the Chancellor, Treasurer, and two judges were assigned to hear the case.
[4] 31 Edward III. St. 1 c. 12.   [5] 3 Rot. Parl. 24, no. 105.

to the petition was that a statute had been made which must be observed. The reason for this dissatisfaction with the court was its great delays. If the court was adjourned to a fixed day, and the Chancellor and Treasurer did not appear on that day, the writ of error discontinued, and the plaintiff was obliged to begin the action again. As many as six writs have been found on the record.[1] A statute of 1588-1589[2] attempted to remedy the evil. It recited that "these two (the Chancellor and the Treasurer) being great officers of the realm . . . they be many times upon sudden warning called away," so that they cannot be present at the day of adjournment in the Exchequer; and enacted that, if either one of them, or both of the chief justices be present, there should be no discontinuance. No judgment could, however, be given unless both were present.[3] In 1664[4] a similar provision was made in case of the absence of the Chancellor or Treasurer or either of the chief justices on the days when writs of error were returned; and in 1668[5] the vacancy of the office of Lord Treasurer necessitated an Act to make it possible for the judgment of the court to be given by the Lord Chancellor or Lord Keeper.[6]

The judgment of the court was thus given by the Lord Treasurer and Chancellor, or after 1668, by the Lord Chancellor or Lord Keeper. The majority of the judges decided in the *Bankers' Case*[7] that they were merely assistants; so that in that case Lord Keeper Somers was able to reverse the decision of the court of Exchequer contrary to the opinion of the majority of judges.

(3) Parliament was only occasionally summoned in the sixteenth century; and, as Parliament was the only court which could amend errors of the King's Bench, the want of a court which could hold regular sessions was much felt. To supply this want a new court of Exchequer Chamber was created in 1585[8] for the purpose of amending the errors of the King's Bench. The statute recited that erroneous judgments in the King's Bench could only be reformed in Parliament, and that that court " is not in these days so often holden as in ancient times it hath been." It enacted that where any judgment should be given in

---

[1] Manning, Exchequer of Pleas i 482.
[2] 31 Elizabeth c. 1 § 1.   [3] Ibid.
[4] 16 Charles II. c. 2—apparently under this statute it was sufficient if one of the chief justices was present.
[5] 19, 20 Charles II. c. 9 (Rec. Com. Ed.); in the ordinary editions of the statutes 20 Charles II. c. 4.
[6] The Lord Keeper's powers were the same as those of the Lord Chancellor's below 410.
[7] (1696) 14 S.T. at p. 105.
[8] 27 Elizabeth c. 8; amended by 31 Elizabeth c. 1 §§ 2 and 3.

the King's Bench in any action of debt, detinue, or covenant, account, action upon the case, ejectione firmæ, or trespass (if first begun in the King's Bench), except where the crown is a party, the plaintiff or defendant could sue out a writ of error either to Parliament or to the court of Exchequer Chamber. It provided that the court of Exchequer Chamber should consist of the justices of the Common Pleas, and the Barons of the Exchequer, or any six of them.[1] An appeal to this court was not to preclude a further appeal to Parliament.[2]

After the passing of this Act error still lay from the Common Pleas to the King's Bench, and from thence direct to the House of Lords. Error still lay direct from the King's Bench to the House of Lords in all proceedings other than those mentioned in the Act of Elizabeth. It was only over the proceedings specified in the Act (if originally begun in the King's Bench) that this court of Exchequer Chamber had jurisdiction.[3]

In 1830[4] the King's Bench was deprived of its jurisdiction to amend the errors of the court of Common Pleas; the two courts of Exchequer Chamber created by the Acts of 1357-1358 and 1585 were amalgamated; and the court of Exchequer Chamber was made a court of appeal intermediate between the three common law courts and Parliament. The court consisted of the judges of the two courts which had not given the decision against which the appeal was brought.

The procedure in error of the Exchequer Chamber was lengthy, cumbrous, and expensive. As early as 1602 Manningham had noted that, "the abuse of the statute for reforming errors in the King's Bench, etc., hath frayed the clients from their suits, when they can have noe judgment certaine or speedy."[5] The commissioners who reported on the practice and procedure of the court in 1831 recommended certain reforms;[6] and some improvements were made by the Common Law Procedure Act of 1852.[7] In the first place the Act got rid of the old idea that the procedure in error was a new proceeding,[8] by abolishing the writs of error, and substituting therefor a memorandum in error, which was to be a part of the old proceedings—a step in the cause. After this Act, therefore, the parties proceeded by memorandum in error on the record, or on a Bill of Exceptions. In the second place the Act provided other ways of questioning the decision.

---

[1] 31 Elizabeth c. 1 § 2; it sufficed if three were present at the days of return of the writs or adjournments, the whole six must, however, give judgment.
[2] § 3.   [3] Bl. Comm. iii 411.
[4] 11 George IV., 1 William IV. c. 70 § 8.
[5] Manningham's Diary (C.S.) 98.
[6] Parlt. Papers 1831, x 407-408; cf. ibid 1851 vol. xxii.
[7] 15, 16 Victoria c. 76 §§ 148, 149, 152, 157.   [8] Above 214.

The parties could bring error on a special case stated, or they could move for a new trial; and they could appeal to the Exchequer Chamber from the refusal to grant a new trial, unless the court were unanimous in such refusal. On such an appeal the court had larger powers than on a writ of error or a memorandum in error. It could take all the circumstances into consideration, and, even though it thought that there had been misdirection, it could refuse a new trial if it considered that the misdirection was not in a material point. It could also, if it saw fit, give such judgment as ought to have been given in the court below. The Act did not apply to proceedings on the revenue side of the Exchequer. Certain sections, however, were applied to such proceedings by the Queen's Remembrancer's Act.[1] That Act allowed in revenue proceedings a memorandum in error on the record, or on a Bill of Exceptions, or on a special case stated. It did not allow an appeal from a refusal to grant a new trial.[2]

But though the Act had thus effected certain reforms it had really only tinkered with the problem of providing a satisfactory system of questioning the decision of the lower courts. No satisfactory solution was reached till the Judicature Acts swept away the whole of this primitive system of procedure in error, and substituted for it the rational system of appeal by means of a rehearing of the case, which the Chancery had always employed.[3]

The Official Staffs of the Courts of Common Law

To these courts of common law large staffs of officials were attached. The history of their growth is long and curious; and one peculiar feature of that history is common to all the central courts—to the court of Star Chamber and the court of Chancery as well as to the common law courts. I shall, therefore, by way of introduction, say a few words about this peculiar feature. It will help us to understand much that would otherwise be obscure in the history of the judicial system.

The peculiar feature common to the history of the official staffs of the central courts is the idea that many of these offices were the freeholds or the properties of the officials. I shall in the first place say something of the origin and application of this idea ; and, in the second place, of the reasons for its extraordinarily long life in the English judicial system.

(i) The remote origins of the official staffs of the courts are to be found in that very early period when no clear distinction was drawn between office and property. We have already seen

---

[1] 22, 23 Victoria c. 21.
[2] Attorney-General v. Sillem (1864) 10 H.L.C. 704.
[3] Below 643.

that this was a characteristic feature of the Anglo-Saxon state ;[1] and this confusion, which is natural enough to a very primitive legal system, was perpetuated partly by feudal ideas, and partly by the fact that certain archaic ideas on these matters were retained by and stereotyped in the common law.

We have seen that the feudal system was both a system of land tenure and a system of government. The lord from whom land was held by his tenants had powers of government over those tenants.[2] The conception of tenure was applied not only to the land, but also to many other things connected with the land ; and, among those other things, to the governmental rights which either went with the tenure of land, or were annexed to it by usurpation or royal grant. The creation of these rights was one method of getting governmental functions performed ; and so, when kings or other rulers wished to get these functions, governmental or otherwise, performed, they had recourse to this expedient. They did not make a contract with a person to perform these functions : they granted him a right to perform these functions on certain terms. Thus the office held by such an official was regarded as a piece of property which gave the official certain rights and placed him under certain duties, just as the tenure of a piece of land gave the tenant certain rights and placed him under certain duties. We shall be able the better to understand this conception of the nature of these offices and the position of their holders if we look at a concrete case. Many such cases could be collected from the Year Books ;[3] but I have purposely selected a relatively late case which comes from the middle of the sixteenth century.

In 1556[4] one Vaux brought an assize of novel disseisin against Jefferen and others because, as he alleged, he was entitled to enjoy the office of filazer[5] in the court of Common Pleas as the grantee of Baldwin, the late Chief Justice ; and he showed how he was admitted, and " that he was seised by taking three-pence of A.B. for a *capias* against C.D. in a plea of trespass."[6] The defendant replied that the plaintiff had been dismissed from his office by Mountague, C.J., for various misdemeanours, and

---

[1] Above 19.   [2] Above 17.

[3] See e.g. Y.BB. 5 Ed. II. (S.S.) 229—assize of novel disseisin for the third part of the bailiwick of the marshalcy of the Justices in Eyre; 8 Ed. III. Hil. pl. 47—assize of novel disseisin for the fourth part of the office of serjeant of the Common Pleas with its appurtenances ; an objection that, though the whole office might be a freehold, a fractional part was not, was overruled.

[4] Vaux v. Jefferen and others (1556) Dyer 114 b.

[5] An official who filed writs and issued process thereon, also spelt filacer or philaser ; there were separate filazers for different groups of counties, see App. XXIX.

[6] For the doctrine of seisin in its application to such incorporeal hereditaments as offices see vol. iii 96-101,

that he the defendant had been admitted to it. "And it was moved that the defendant Jefferen was no disseisor, for he came in by the court, and then the court was the disseisor. *Sed hoc non allocatur* by all the judges for the new officer is to look to that at his peril ; and if there was no cause of forfeiture in the old clerk, then the new clerk shall be judged disseisor of the officer." In the end it was held that the old clerk was properly dismissed and the new clerk was properly appointed, so that judgment was given for the defendant.

This conception of the nature of offices, and the position of their holders, came very naturally to the mediæval common law, because that common law had a very rudimentary law of contract and a very highly developed law of property in land and rights connected with land.[1] The expedient of appointing officials by granting them offices to hold as their property on certain terms seemed obviously right ; and it would not be going too far to say that it was universally adopted in the Middle Ages both by government and by other employers of labour.[2] There is nothing strange in this. What is strange is its extraordinary long life and its wide prevalence in the English judicial and political system. There are very many cases similar to that cited above which come from all periods of our legal history ;[3] and these same ideas were introduced into the colonies.[4] Blackstone[5] correctly stated the law of the eighteenth century when he said that, "offices, which are a right to exercise a public or private employment, and the fees and emoluments thereunto belonging, are incorporeal hereditaments." It was not until the beginning of the nineteenth century that legislation, inspired largely by Bentham's teaching, rooted these ideas out of the judicial system.[6]

(ii) What, then, were the reasons for the extraordinary long life of this idea ?

Firstly, one reason was the precocity and the continuity of the development of the English state. We have seen that, by the end of the thirteenth century, the political influence of feudalism had been reduced to very small dimensions.[7] But it had been reduced to small dimensions by powerful kings acting

---

[1] Vol. ii 355-356.

[2] This accounts for a good many of the tenures by Serjeanty in the thirteenth century, see vol. iii 47-48.

[3] For some of these cases see below 259-261.

[4] See Blankard v. Galdy (1694) 4 Mod. 222—a lease of the office of provost marshal in Jamaica; in R. v. Vaughan (1769) 4 Burr. 2494 it was said *arguendo* that, "the office of clerk of the supreme court of the island of Jamaica was sold under a decree in Chancery, upon the cestui que trust of it dying insolvent. Mr. Lawton bought it, and afterwards devised one moiety of it. The representatives of Mr. Paxton sold the other moiety. The sub-divisions of it have since been both devised and sold. The office was consequently very carelessly executed by deputies."

[5] Comm. ii 36.   [6] Below 262.   [7] Above 176-179.

through courts which were still under the influence of feudal ideas. Just as these courts, while destroying the political influence of feudalism, made the English land law more completely and more permanently feudal than the land law of any other state in Europe,[1] so they perpetuated these feudal ideas as to the creation and tenure of proprietary offices. The rapidity of the success of the institutions of English central government caused those institutions to be staffed by officials whose offices had been granted to them to have and to hold in fee, in tail or for life,[2] in return for fees to be collected by them for doing the duties attached to those offices.

Secondly, the government found that this was a very convenient arrangement. Governments are rarely good payers—least of all the governments of mediæval states. We shall see that there was often little enough money for the judges;[3] and there was still less for the other officials of the courts. It was therefore a convenient arrangement for a government, which wanted duties done and had no money to pay for them, to grant an office and the right to get fees from the public for executing the duties of the office. The office thus granted might turn out to be a valuable property. Candidates might even be willing to pay the government a handsome sum to secure it, or it might be used to reward servants or favourites.[4] The growing elaboration of the machinery of government necessarily increased the number of such offices.[5] This meant an increase in that motive power of all governments—patronage. Naturally governments cherished a conception which gave them much patronage.

Thirdly, it was fostered by the fact that the growth of the official staffs which carried out the work of the courts was wholly unregulated by the legislature.[6] The numbers of these officials grew, partly by reason of the increase of the business of the courts, partly by reason of the necessity for a division of labour thereby caused, and partly by reason of the growing elaboration of procedure and pleading. These were, so to speak, natural causes of growth. But the proprietary nature of these offices perverted the natural growth of the official staffs. In the first place the idea that the office was a freehold prevented it from expanding naturally to meet new needs. To appoint a second official to do the work, when it got beyond the powers of the original official, was objected to by the original official, because

---

[1] Vol. ii. 199-200.
[2] " A man may have an estate in them, either to him and his heirs, or for life, or for a term of years, or during pleasure only," Bl. Comm. ii 36; for an instance of a grant in tail see below 258.
[3] Below 252-253.   [4] For instances see below 260-261.
[5] Below 256; cf. Mr. Churchill's Paper, L.Q.R. xlii 212.   [6] Ibid.

it deprived him of fees—it diminished the value of his property.[1] He was entitled to the fees and he must have them. The extra work was therefore done by a deputy appointed by himself who performed his duties for a fraction of the fees. Sometimes these deputies became new and independent officials—we shall see that this was what happened in the case of the officials which did the work of the Clerk of the King's Bench.[2] But, in the second place it is clear that the device made the original office very valuable. If extra work could be done by deputy, why not get a deputy to do all the work? Thus very valuable sinecures were created. Courtiers desired these places ; and, if there were none vacant, kings were easily induced to create new sinecure places about the courts to satisfy their creditors or to please their favourites.[3] The creation of these offices cost them nothing.

Fourthly, the idea that the officer has a freehold in his office, coupled with the fact that many highly placed people both in the fashionable and the judicial world had an interest in these offices, made the system extraordinarily difficult to eliminate. Mediæval statutes in vague terms sometimes attempted to secure honesty in the appointment and conduct of officials.[4] But they did not attempt to touch a system which, to mediæval men, seemed an obvious and necessary system. In the sixteenth and seventeenth centuries, however, modern ideas were beginning to assert themselves. But the legislation passed to give effect to them was quite ineffectual. In 1551-1552 an apparently comprehensive statute was passed forbidding the purchase and sale of judicial offices.[5] But the statute contained two fatal flaws. Both offices which could be held for estates of inheritance,[6] and offices which were in the gift of the chief justices of the King's Bench and Common Pleas,[7] were excluded. We shall see that both these classes of offices covered a wide ground.[8] Attempts in 1690 [9] and 1692-1693 [10] to legislate against the buying and

---

[1] Below 257 n. 1.

[2] Below 257 ; what Roger North says of the Chancery illustrates this : "First the six (clerks) did all the work that originally might be done by a single secretary ; and then their clerks that rose to ten a piece, mere copiers under them, have got to be officers, and thirty more added to them. And still all of them have clerks, who may in time hope to be officers too, and beard their masters, as they do the six clerks," Lives of the Norths i 127.

[3] Below 260 ; cf. S.P. Dom. (1611-1618) 510, xciv 122—a statement of changes in the courts of Chancery, King's Bench, and Common Pleas by grants of special offices for making writs of subpœna, capias, supersedeas, latitat, etc.

[4] See e.g. 20 Edward III. c. 1 ; 12 Richard II. c. 2.

[5] 5, 6 Edward VI. c. 16 § 1.   [6] § 3.   [7] § 6.

[8] Below 257-258 ; App. XXIX., XXX.

[9] Hist. MSS. Com. Thirteenth Rep. Pt. V. 17 no. 244.

[10] Ibid Fourteenth Rep. Pt. VI. 362 no. 710.

selling of offices failed ; and, as the judges and their staffs were some of the chief offenders, it is not strange that such legislation as was passed to check the abuses of the system was practically a dead letter.[1]   Occasionally, indeed, sound sense appears in the reports—if offices in the courts, said Coke,[2] could be sold and transferred for lucre and gain, " good clerks would be deterred from applying themselves to get knowledge and experience," and there would also ensue "corruption in the officers and extortion from the subjects and other great inconveniences." These were true words—but from them the conclusion was drawn, not that these offices could not be transferred at all, but that they could not be transferred for a term of years !   One or two other minor restrictions were laid down as to the sale of judicial offices ;[3] but it was not at all certain how far these were good law, and how far a custom to the contrary might not prevail.[4]   " *Quis custodiet ipsos custodes ?* "   Judges and statesmen alike were too deeply involved in the toils of this vicious system to be able, even if they had wished, to free themselves from it. The path of the reformer was always blocked by a phalanx of vested interests.[5]

The results of this system may be read at large in the Reports published by the Parliamentary Commissioners at the beginning of the nineteenth century.[6]   It is clear that all the central courts of the country suffered from its effects ; and we shall see that the abuses to which it gave rise were more flagrant in the court of Chancery than in the courts of common law.[7]   This was due partly to the vicious system of procedure which had been evolved in the Chancery, partly to the fact that very large sums of money were involved in Chancery suits, and partly to the fact that the Chancellor, being a political officer, the Chancery was more accessible to the corrupting influence of politics.   All this we shall see more clearly in a later chapter.   At this point we must turn to the official staffs of the common law courts, and examine the effects of these mediæval ideas upon their evolution.

---

[1] See Spence, Equitable Jurisdiction of the Court of Chancery i 401 for some wholly disregarded legislation as to the fees of the Masters.

[2] Sir George Reynel's Case (1612) 9 Co. Rep. at f. 97 b.

[3] See e.g. Auditor Curle's Case (1610) 11 Co. Rep. 26—judicial offices cannot be granted in reversion ; and cf. Bl. Comm. ii 36.

[4] See Veale v. Priour (1664) Hardres at p. 357, where Hale, C.B., said, " Judicial offices are not grantable in reversion ; but ministerial offices are; and by usage and custom a judicial office may be granted in reversion."

[5] Thus Hale, in discussing the possibility of reforms in the process of the Common Pleas and King's Bench, mentions as a difficulty the fact that it, " will quite destroy some offices in the King's Bench and very much improve the value of others, especially Henley's Office," Harg. Law Tracts 372 ; Henley held the office of Chief Clerk (as to which see below 257); see Bridgman v. Holt (1693) Shower, P.C. 111.

[6] Below 262 n. 2.   [7] Below 425-428.

To relate the history of all the officials of the courts would be impossible and useless. A glance at Appendix XXV., where the list of the officials of the court of King's Bench at different periods is set out in tabular form, will make this clear.[1] All that can here be attempted is a short explanation of how the survival of the mediæval idea, which has just been described, gave rise to the official organization which existed at the beginning of the nineteenth century, and a short account of the legislation which has eliminated it. The subject will fall under the following three heads : Firstly, the incomes of the judges ; secondly, the officials of the courts ; and thirdly, the reforms of the first half of the nineteenth century.

(i) *The incomes of the judges.*

We have seen that the judges of the common law courts were royal officials who held their office generally at the pleasure of the crown, and sometimes during good behaviour.[2] Their offices never became, as they became in France,[3] saleable freeholds ; and therefore they occupied a position different to that occupied by those of the officials of their courts who had such a freehold. From the first they were paid salaries by the crown which in the course of years were gradually and continuously increased.

In the twelfth century the judges do not appear to have had a regular salary ;[4] but, in 1268, Robert Brus, the first chief justice of the King's Bench, was granted a salary of 100 marks.[5] This salary, or something like it, was usually paid to the chiefs of the courts in Henry III.'s reign, and salaries of from £20 to £40 to the other judges.[6] But in the following reigns the salaries of the chief justices seem generally to have been from £40 to £60, and the salaries of the other judges 40 marks.[7] In addition, the crown provided them with robes till the reign of Henry VI., when this allowance was commuted for a money payment.[8] These salaries were by no means regularly paid ;[9]

---

[1] This list is taken from the Second Report of the Commission appointed to enquire with the Administrative Departments of Courts of Justice, Parlt. Papers (1874) vol. xxiv; similar Tables relating to the other courts will be found in the report, and from them it appears that their condition was very similar; this also appears from the detailed Reports referred to below 262 n. 2.

[2] Above 195 and n. 2.

[3] Esmein, Histoire du Droit Francais (11th Ed.) 451-464.

[4] Foss, Judges ii 26—grants of land and other things were sometimes made to them, and, like other officials of the courts, they were exempt from scutage ; on the whole subject see Dugdale, Orig. Jurid. c. 40.

[5] Above 205 ; Foss, Judges ii 155.   [6] Ibid 155-156.

[7] Ibid iii 44 ; Bolland, The Eyre of Kent (S.S.) iii, xli.

[8] Foss, Judges iii 44 ; ibid iv 228, 389.

[9] " It was no uncommon occurrence for a judge to have to wait two, three or four years for the payment of his salary," Eyre of Kent (S.S.) iii, xli ; see ibid, xlii, xliii for the difficulties experienced by Hervey of Staunton, the presiding judge at the

and both the smallness of the salary and the irregularity of its
receipt had not a little to do with the great judicial scandal of
Edward I.'s reign, as a result of which nearly all the judges lost
their places.[1] Even after Edward I.'s reign large landowners
found it expedient to make grants of pensions, rents, or lands to
the king's judges.[2] Additional fees were granted to the judges
by Edward III.,[3] and these fees were increased by Henry IV.;[4]
but, as a petition to Parliament in 1440 shows,[5] their salaries
were then much in arrear. During the sixteenth century increases in their salaries were several times made.[6] As fixed at
the end of the sixteenth century, they remained in substance
during the earlier half of the seventeenth century,[7] though their

---

Eyre of Kent of 1313-1314; he eventually got an order for a payment of a sum on
account out of the fines and amercements inflicted at the Eyre.

[1] Vol. ii 294-299; cf. Eyre of Kent (S.S.) iii xlii.

[2] For grants made by the Knights Hospitallers in 1338 to the chief justice of the
King's Bench, and to the judges of the Common Pleas and Exchequer see Y.B.
8 Ed. II. (S.S.) xiii, xiv.

[3] Foss, Judges iii 357-358.   [4] Ibid iv 227.

[5] R.P. v 14 cited Foss, Judges iv 227-228; and Dugdale, Orig. Jurid. c. 40; it
appears also from R.P. iv 437 that there were arrears in 1434.

[6] In 1544; Foss, Judges v 99; in 1574, ibid 403—an increase to meet their expenses on circuit which had formerly been borne by the sheriff; and at some time
before 1598, ibid 405.

[7] In 1598 the amounts are stated in Foss, Judges v 405-406 as follows :—

The Lord Cheefe Justice of England :—

Fee, reward, and robes	.	.	.	.	£208	6	8
Wynne, 2 tunnes at £5 the tunne	.	.	.		10	0	0
Allowance for being justice of assize	.	.	.		20	0	0

Lord Cheefe Justice of the Common Pleas:—

Fee, reward, and robes	.	.	.	.	£141	13	4
Wyne, 2 tunnes	.	.	.	.	.	8	0	0
Allowance as justice of assize	.	.	.	.	20	0	0
Fee for keeping the assize in the Augmentation Court	.	12	10	0

Each of the three justices in these two courts :—

Fee, reward, and robes	.	.	.	.	£128	6	8
Allowance as Justice of Assize	.	.	.	.	20	0	0

The Lord Cheefe Baron of the Exchequer :—

Fee	.	.	.	.	.	£100	0	0
Lyvery	.	.	.	.	.	12	17	8
Allowance as Justice of Assize	.	.	.	.	20	0	0

Each of the three Barons :—

Fee	.	.	.	.	.	£46	13	4
Lyvery a peece	.	.	.	.	.	12	17	4
Allowance as Justice of Assize	.	.	.	.	20	0	0

In 1624 Whitelocke, Liber Fam. (C.S.) 100 states the amounts as follows :—

Fees of the Justices to be paid at Michaelmas and Annuntiation—

To the cheife justice	.	.	.	.	.	£258	6	8
To the chief justice of Common Pleas	.	.	.	194	19	9
To the chief barons and justices of either bench	.	.	188	6	8
To the barons of the exchequer	.	.	.	.	113	6	8

This included an allowance of £23 6s. 8d. for circuits, ibid 104; the amounts for
James I.'s reign appear to have been substantially similar, Foss, Judges vi 9;
S.P. Dom 1603-1610, 482, xl 61.

payment was sometimes irregular.[1]   Under the Commonwealth
they were raised to £1000 a year inclusive of all fees and allowances;[2] and, during the latter part of the seventeenth century,
£1000 a year seems to have been the salary of the puisne judges,
in addition to fees and allowances,[3] and a number of customary
presents from officials of their courts and others.[4]   Their salaries
were increased by statute in 1759,[5] 1779,[6] 1799,[7] and 1809;[8] and
the statute of 1799 also provided for retiring allowances.   The
Commissioners appointed in 1815 to examine into the duties,
salaries, and emoluments of the officers, clerks, and ministers of
courts of justice reported that the salary of the chief justice of
the King's Bench was £4000, that the salaries of the chiefs of
the other two courts was £3500, and that the salaries of the
puisne judges of all these courts was £2400.[9]

But, from the earliest times, the salaries of the judges had
not formed their only source of income.   Though they did not
hold their offices as their freeholds, though they could be dismissed by the crown, they nevertheless drew a considerable part
of their income from fees.   Probably in the Middle Ages this
source of income was the most valuable; and the fact that it
was the most valuable explains the eagerness with which the
judges tried to attract business to their courts.   It is, of course,
impossible to state exactly how much the judges got from this
source; but it is clear that it was a considerable sum.   Thus in
1522 the amount at which they were assessed for purposes of
taxation was considerably larger than their official salaries.[10]   In
1627 James Whitelocke reckoned his total income as judge of

[1] "Memorandum, that the Treasurer dallyed out all the vacation, and all Hillary
term (1627), without payment of our wages, whereupon myself and Dodridge and
Jones caused writs of *Liberate* upon the statute of 18 Hen. VI. to be drawn, thereby
to charge the clerk of the petit bag, but the Lord Keeper called us to stay and he
wold interpose," Whitelocke, Liber Fam. (C.S.) 108-109; it appears from S.P. Dom.
1603-1610 482, xl 61 that their salaries were in arrear in 1608.
[2] Foss, Judges vi 218, 401.
[3] Ibid vii 298; the salaries of all the judges were fixed at this figure by a bill of
1691-1692, to which the royal assent was refused Hist. MSS. Com. Fourteenth Rep.
Pt. VI. 76 no. 565.
[4] "The Stationers Company annually supplied them with almanacks, and to the
judges of the Common Pleas the warden of the Fleet sent two, and each of the
prothonotaries three, sugar loaves at the commencement of January," Foss, Judges
vii 298; these customary presents still continued at the beginning of the nineteenth
century; thus the chief justice of the King's Bench got four yards of cloth from
Blackwell hall and thirty-six sugar loaves from the officers of the court on the plea
side, while the puisne judges a silver plate and eighteen sugar loaves from the same
officers, Parlt. Papers 1818 vii 251, 253; it was the same in the other courts, ibid
1819-1820 ii 184-186; ibid 1822 xi 111. Note that the numbers of the pages
in the Parlt. Papers given here and elsewhere are not the printed numbers of the
report, but the MS. numbers of the pages of the bound volume.
[5] 32 George II. c. 35 § 9.   [6] 19 George III. c. 65.
[7] 39 George III. c. 110.   [8] 49 George III. c. 127.
[9] Parlt. Papers referred to in n. 4.   [10] Foss, Judges v 99.

the King's Bench, after all expenses paid, at £974 10s. 10d.[1] At the end of the seventeenth century Thomas Rokeby, a judge first of the Common Pleas and then of the King's Bench, stated his income in the years 1689-1698 ; and it seems that he made sums varying from £378 19s. to £1063 18s. 4d. in addition to his salary of £1000 a year.[2] When the income of the judges from fees was taken away in 1826 their salaries were raised from £2400 a year to £5500.[3]

The income of the chief justices was considerably more than this, not only because their salaries were higher, but also because they had an additional source of income. By the end of the seventeenth century they had asserted both as against the puisne judges[4] and as against the crown[5] the right to appoint to many of the offices in their courts ; and, as these offices had in many cases become valuable freeholds, with either no duties to be performed, or with duties which could be performed by a deputy at a very small charge, this patronage had actually become more lucrative than all the other sources of their income put together. But to explain this we must pass to our second head—the officials of the courts.

(ii) *The officials of the courts.*

The earliest information which we get about the officials of the courts of common law shows that they were paid almost entirely by fees. In fact it would be true to say that the official staff of all the central courts (except the Lord Chancellor and the judges) was almost entirely self-supporting. It would seem that the clerks who served during the Eyre of Kent in 1313-1314 got certain allowances from the damages recovered ;[6] and this share of damages recovered continued under the name of " Damages Cleer "[7] to be the perquisite of the clerks of the King's

---

[1] Liber Fam. (C.S.) 106.   [2] Foss, Judges vii 299.   [3] 6 George IV. c. 84.

[4] Roger North seems to hint, Lives of the Norths i 127-128, that by his day the puisne judges had acquiesced with a bad grace—" The chief justice had the disposing of the officers of the court : but, at the admission, the other judges, not caring to see the pudding creep and have no share, expect to be attended ; the consequence whereof is a small present. I have observed that upon change of some officers there were bickerings against this power of the chief justice . . . as if placing of officers was the act of the court, in which they sat in parity of voice with his lordship ;" it is clear from a return made in 1825 that the patronage enjoyed by the puisne judges was inconsiderable, Parlt. Papers 1825 xix 300-302 ; see App. XXIX.

[5] Below 261.

[6] Eyre of Kent (S.S.) iii, xliii-xlvi ; for other instances see Y.BB. 4 Ed. II. (S.S.) 124 ; 6, 7 Ed. II (S.S.) 65—the record there cited states that the whole of the damages in that case was paid to the clerks.

[7] " The share of damages that was given to the clerks was known, at any rate in later times, as 'damna clericorum,' or, in the vernacular, 'damages cleer,'" Eyre of Kent iii, xlv : the nature of the payment is thus explained by C. G. Cook, English Law (1651) at pp. 46-47—" A man sues and recovers : now by the law

Bench and Common Pleas, till it was abolished by a statute of 1665.[1] But probably the largest part of the remuneration of the official staff of the courts came from fees in connection with the very numerous acts that must be done to set and keep in motion the complicated machinery of the courts, from the issue of the original writ to the execution of final judgment. The names of some of the officials in the list given in Appendix XXV. will show this. No doubt in the earlier part of the mediæval period these clerks and others increased their incomes by illicit means. There are many complaints of this sort of misconduct in the thirteenth century; and many other officials of the courts besides the judges were involved in the great judicial scandal of Edward I.'s reign.[2] But, as the business of the courts increased, the temptation to resort to these means diminished. Their regular fees proved to be enough and more than enough for their ever-growing official staffs.[3] And both the numbers of these staffs and the fees payable to them seem to have been generally settled by the officials with no sort of external supervision or interference.[4] In 1818 the Commissioners reported[5] that "Constant receipt by the present officers and the information as to a similar receipt by their predecessors, derived either verbally or from books of accounts or written memoranda, are for the most part the grounds on which the officers at the present time have acted in regard to the amount of the fees they have severally received."

In order to appreciate the conditions under which these official staffs grew up we must recall those ideas as to the appointment and tenure of office by these officials which have been already explained. Many of these officials owned their offices.

there is a supposal (and but a supposal if that is to be supposed which is well known to the contrary) that the recoveror hath his debt, or his damage, and costs of suit. Now . . . if the suit were for so small a matter that it exceed not £3 6s. 8d. recovered, then it (the law) took nothing: but if it were more, then it took 2s. upon every pound. Now although I suppose at the original this was or ought to have been a sufficiency to have tried the cause, and to be added to the judgment, and paid by the defendant, yet now it comes only to the master of the office who assigns costs upon the judgment, and this paid before execution, which the party haply never lives to see performed."

[1] 17 Charles II. c. 6. [2] Vol. ii 295.

[3] The office of chief clerk of the king in the Common Pleas (the *custos brevium*) was in 1311 sufficiently important to be put among the offices which were only to be filled with the consent of Parliament, Tout, Edward II. 369; below 258 n. 2.

[4] A bill was before Parliament in 1614 to compel a statement of all fees payable in courts of law and equity and the ecclesiastical courts, and to reform such fees as were "excessive or newly encroached within 30 years last past;" but it failed to get further than a first reading, Hist. MSS. Comm. Fourth Rep. App. Pt. I. 120; for an order of 1309 appointing a clerk to the Chief Justice of the Common Pleas, see Y.B. 6 Ed. II. (S.S.) xxiii-xxv.

[5] Parlt. Papers 1818 vii 250; cf. North's account of the way in which the number of Prothonotaries in the Common Pleas rose from one to three, Lives of the Norths i 127.

They were their property which they had bought. They therefore resented any increase in the number of the officials appointed
to do their work—however necessary—because such increase
diminished the value of the office.[1] If any part of the work was
delegated to others it was for them to appoint the delegates, and
to retain a part—often a considerable part—of the fees paid to
them for their work. If new officers were appointed to fulfil
some new duty, they were appointed under the same conditions;
and their appointment was a new piece of patronage to be
scrambled for.[2] When appointed, they likewise resented any
increase in their numbers, and appointed delegates to do the
work they could not do. The result was, that at the beginning
of the nineteenth century, there was a regular hierarchy of
officials—at the top there were the dignified officials who took
large sums for doing nothing, and at the bottom there were the
poorly paid clerks who did the work. I shall in the first place
illustrate the anomalous position of some of these officials by
considering one or two concrete cases; and in the second place
call attention to two curious consequences which ensued.

(a) Some of these officials had absolute sinecures. Two instances will suffice. The most striking instance was the Chief
Clerk of the court of King's Bench.[3] He is described as "The
principal officer of the court in all matters relative to civil suits."[4]
The Chief Justice nominated to the office, so that its emoluments
"may as he chooses, be either applied to his own use or may
furnish the means of providing for his family."[5] No doubt the
chief clerk once had duties to perform; but long before the nineteenth century, these duties had been delegated to other officers
who had acquired separate and independent positions of their
own.[6] The Commissioners could hardly defend the existence

[1] Thus in Cavendish's Case (1587) 1 And. 152 the judges gave as their excuse
for not obeying the queen's wish to admit Cavendish to an office for making certain
writs, that "Auters queux pretendont droit a fair les dits breves poient estre per
ceo disseisies de lour franktenement queux ils claime en fesance de ceux breves et
fees pur ceo;" see below 424-425, 441 for illustrations of this idea in the case of
the Chancery officials.

[2] We can see the kind of way in which offices grew up from a passage in the
report of the Common Law Procedure Commissioners, Parlt. Papers 1831 x 416;
criticizing the chaotic state of the practice in Judges' chambers, and especially the
absence of any provisions for keeping a record of the proceedings, they said that the
judges' clerks used to file office copies of affidavits, and to charge for furnishing
them, which charge the taxing officers had always disallowed; can we doubt but that
in the Middle Ages such a custom would have led to all of the clerks of the judge
becoming officers of the court for this purpose, with power to charge? As each
judge had a clerk there would then have been from twelve to fifteen persons doing
work which, as the Commissioners said, could be well enough done by one.

[3] Parlt. Papers 1818 vii 302-303.   [4] Ibid 302.   [5] Ibid.
[6] Ibid; the duties once belonging to the office are thus described: "It is one
of the duties of the Chief Clerk to inrol the pleadings and judgments on the civil
side of the court, but the ingrossments on the roll are now made by the attornies.

of such an official. All they could say was that the office served a useful purpose in that it helped to remunerate the Chief Justice ; and they pointed out that the existence of this method of remuneration had been indirectly sanctioned by the legislature, when it increased the salaries of the other judges and not that of the Chief Justice.[1] The other instance is the Custos Brevium of the court of Common Pleas. The Commissioners reported in 1819-1820 that this office had been "granted by letters patent in the 29th year of the reign of Charles II. (after the determination of grants for life then subsisting) to certain persons named in the letters patent and their heirs and assigns in trust for the Earl and Countess of Lichfield and the issue of the countess in tail ; " and that "the office was now held under this grant." [2]

Other officials had work to do, but did it by deputies who were paid a fraction of the fees received. Thus, at the beginning of the nineteenth century, the three years' annual income of the official who held the office of filazer exigenter and clerk of the outlawries of the court of King's Bench was £5104 16s. 9d. and he paid his deputy only £567 5s.[3] Others, again, had a good deal of work to do, but they were paid not only for the work they did, but also a proportion of the fees for work which they formerly used to do, but had long since devolved upon others. Thus the Prothonotaries in the court of Common Pleas were officials who did a good deal of work now done by the Masters.[4] In the Middle Ages their duties had also included the entering of pleas on the rolls.[5] They had got rid of this work certainly as early as 1632 ;[6] and in the nineteenth century this work was done by the attornies of the parties to the action ;[7] but the Prothonotaries still collected a fee for this work.[8] In 1805 a bold

The other duties of the Chief Clerk are performed by the Secondary on the Plea side, the Clerk of the Rules on the plea side, the Clerk of the Papers, the Clerk of the Doquets and judgments, the Signer of the Writs, the Clerk of the Declarations, and the Clerk of the Common Bails Estreats and Posteas," Parlt. Papers 1818 vii 303.

[1] " Upon various occasions when the salaries of the other judges have been augmented by the authority of Parliament, the Chief Justice has been left upon his ancient establishment. We conceive this omission arose from the general understanding that the office of Chief Justice had the benefit of the emoluments receivable by the Chief Clerk ; and we consider every one of those acts of Parliament to be an indirect legislative recognition of the right of the Chief Justice to apply to his own use those emoluments," ibid 302.

[2] Ibid 1819-1820 ii 187; cf. Y.B. 6 Ed. II. (S.S.) i xx-xxv for its earlier history.

[3] Ibid 1810 ix 128; see extracts from the Report in App. XXX.

[4] Ibid 1819-1820 ii 202—e.g. they reported to the court on matters referred to them by it, they taxed costs, and they informed the court of its practice and of the state of the causes in it, and they received money paid into court and paid it out again.

[5] See Y.B. 38 Hy. VI. Pasch. pl. 18, cited vol. iii 646-647 ; Lives of the Norths i 127.

[6] Parlt. Papers 1819-1820 ii 214.   [7] Ibid 202.

[8] " He was the proper officer of the court who was to enter up the replications etc.—upon the record in Latin, and not by paper books brought in by attornies with

attorney objected to pay the customary fee to the Prothonotary on the entry of a declaration, on the ground that he, and not the Prothonotary, had done the entèring. It is hardly surprising to find that the court, after taking time to consider its judgment, held that the Prothonotary's fees was ancient and just.[1] Judges who might aspire to hold such offices as the clerkship of the King's Bench, must have felt that it was necessary to suppress the application of logical reasoning to the fees taken by the officials of the courts.

How necessary such suppression was in the pecuniary interest of the judges is made quite clear by some of the figures given by the Commissioners, who reported in 1810 upon the saleable offices existing in courts of law. In the King's Bench there were fifteen saleable offices, some of which were absolute sinecures, while, in the case of others the work was done by deputy.[2] Three of these officers—the chief clerk, the custos brevium, and the filazer exigenter and clerk of the outlawries—had incomes which, on a three years' average amounted to £13,405 2s. 7d., out of which they paid £767 5s. to their deputies. In the Common Pleas matters were not quite so bad ; but there then were twenty-one saleable offices, eleven of which were executed by deputy. The fees of these eleven officers returned an income which, on a three years' average, amounted to £4406 10s. 5d. out of which they paid £739 0s. 1d. to their deputies. The value put upon these offices by the legislature can be seen by comparing the salaries allotted to the chiefs of the courts with those allotted to the puisne judges. The latter, as we have seen, were fixed at £5500,[3] the former were fixed at £10,000 for the Chief Justice of the King's Bench,[4] at £8000 for the Chief Justice of the Common Pleas,[5] and at £7000 for the Chief Baron of the Exchequer.[6]

(b) From this state of things two curious consequences ensued.

In the first place the mediæval idea that these offices were a species of freehold property, recoverable and capable of being settled like freehold property in land, was followed out to all its consequences, not only in the rules relating to their transfer and

---

serjeant's hands, as now the use is. But yet the fees are taken as if the Prothonotary did all, as his office required, by himself," Lives of the Norths i 127.

[1] Parlt. Papers 1819-1820 ii 214.

[2] Report from Commissioners on Saleable Offices in the courts of law, Parlt. Papers 1810 ix 128-131 ; see the extracts from this report printed in App. XXX. ; there does not seem to be much evidence as to the amounts which these offices were actually sold for ; but in 1695 Luttrell notes, Diary iii 535, that a filacer's place worth £1000 had fallen to Treby, C.J. ; and in 1696, Diary iv 81, he mentions a similar official whose place was worth £400.

[3] Above 255.   [4] 6 George IV. c. 82 § 9.

[5] Ibid c. 83 § 8.   [6] Ibid c. 84 § 2.

devolution, but also in the manner in which they were created and held.[1]   They imitated freehold interests in land not only in respect to the estates which could be created in them, but also in the manner in which some of the principles of tenure were in effect applied to them.   The imitation of the principles of tenure arose in the following way : What the Chief Justices or other persons did in relation to the offices to which they appointed, the higher officials of the hierarchy imitated.   They had of course the right to appoint the deputies who did their work ; and when the posts which these deputies filled developed into independent offices, which were both valuable and saleable, they still retained the right to appoint to them.   Thus a glance at the Appendix will show that, in the court of King's Bench, the chief clerk appointed by the Chief Justice could himself appoint to no less than five saleable offices ;[2] while in the court of Common Pleas the three Prothonotaries appointed their Secondaries.[3]   Thus we actually get something which is analogous to subinfeudation. The Chief Justice, the chief clerk and the chief clerk's appointee correspond to chief lord, mesne lord, and tenant.

In the second place the right to this valuable patronage not infrequently gave rise to litigation.   The king, moved by his favourites, tried to get a share.   Sometimes he tried to appoint to some new office which would have cut into the profits of the old office.   Thus in *Cavendish's Case*[4] Elizabeth granted to Cavendish a certain new office in the court of Common Pleas. The judges refused to admit the grantee because to admit him would be to disseise existing officers of their freeholds ;[5] and in the end the queen was obliged to give way.   James I. tried to create the same office in favour of one Murray, groom of the bed chamber ;[6] and, though this time Murray got his office, " the king forbade himself, under penalty of breaking his recorded faith, to exercise his alleged prerogative of ordering the course of the Common Pleas offices."[7]   Sometimes the king tried to usurp the patronage of the Chief Justices.   In the sixteenth century Mary tried to appoint to the office of Exigenter in the Common Pleas during a vacancy in the chief justiceship ; but, as soon as a Chief Justice was appointed, he nominated his nephew, and his nominee

---

[1] A good illustration of this will be found in a case of an assize brought for an office in the court of Chancery reported in Y.B. 9 Ed. IV. Pasch. pl. 20 ; a later illustration is a precedent in the Modern Conveyancer (3rd Ed. 1725) ii 347 of a lease for seven years of the office and place of Deputy Secretary and Clerk in the Barbadoes.

[2] App. XXX.

[3] Parlt. Papers 1819-1820 ii 203 ; ibid 1810 ix 130.

[4] (1587) 1 And. 152.   [5] Above 257 n. 1.

[6] Bacon's Works (Ed. Spedding) vii 683-684.   [7] Ibid vii 686.

was adjudged to have a good title.[1] During the seventeenth century there were numerous dealings in the office of the clerk-ship of the King's Bench. In James I.'s reign it had got into the hands of trustees for Somerset; and, on Somerset's conviction for the murder of Overbury, it got into the hands of trustees for Buckingham.[2] By virtue of royal grants it had devolved at the Revolution upon trustees for the Duke and Duchess of Grafton.[3] It was not till 1693 that the King's Bench finally decided, in the case of *Bridgman* v. *Holt*, that the office was in the gift of the Chief Justice.[4] The House of Lords seemed inclined to interfere on behalf of one of their own order; and, when the judges refused to seal a Bill of Exceptions to their ruling, an attempt was made to bring the judges before the House of Lords to answer for their refusal. The judges very properly replied that the House had no jurisdiction to hear original petitions; and the Lords were obliged to acquiesce.[5]

On questions of this kind the judges, at any rate after the Revolution, were generally able to have the last word. But they sometimes give a touch of unconscious humour to the situation by the high constitutional reasons which they put forward for their decisions in favour of themselves. In *Cavendish's Case* there was talk of it being contrary to Magna Carta to deprive a man of his freehold, and of the dreadful fate of the Despencers, of Empson, and of others who had perverted the law;[6] and in *Bridgman* v. *Holt* Magna Carta and trial by peers made their appearance.[7] And the high constitutional ground thus taken, if it did not deceive their contemporaries, has at any rate succeeded in deceiving an eminent constitutional historian of the last century. Hallam cites *Cavendish's Case* as a striking illustration of the independence of Elizabeth's judges.[8] We may perhaps question whether a good Whig of Hallam's date would have been quite so enthusiastic about this case if he had appreciated the sort of cause in which all these high-sounding constitutional doctrines

---

[1] Skrogges v. Coleshil (1559) Dyer, 175 a.

[2] See Spedding, Letters and Life of Bacon vii 101-102; Liber. Fam. (C.S.) 46, 57-58; it is interesting to note that, when Finch was made Chief Justice by Charles I., he entered into an agreement not to appoint to certain offices in his court without the king's consent, Hist. MSS. Comm. Fourth Rep. App. 22.

[3] See the title set out in Bridgman v. Holt (1693) Shower, P.C. 111; there was also a controversy in 1689 between the Duke of Grafton and Pollexfen, C.J., relative to the office of the Clerk of the Treasury and keeper of the records in the Common Pleas, Hist. MSS. Comm. Twelfth Rep. Pt. VI. 116 no. 94; and between North, C.J., and Lord Berkeley who was the grantee of the crown, as to the clerk-ship of the Treasury of the Common Pleas, Lives of the Norths i 128.

[4] Shower, P.C., at p. 115.   [5] At p. 119; below 367-368.

[6] (1587) 1 And. 155-158.   [7] Shower, P.C., at p. 121.

[8] C.H. i 279 n.; I do not mean to say that Elizabeth's judges were subservient; evidence of their independence in better causes can be produced, see vol. v 347-348.

were produced. At any rate it is quite certain that it was abuses of the kind which the judges in that case defended by all this heavy constitutional artillery, that Hallam's fellow Whigs were helping to demolish. To their work we must now turn.

(iii) *The reforms of the earlier part of the nineteenth century.*

In 1810 a commission had reported upon the saleable offices existing in the courts of law ;[1] but the findings of this commission covered but a small field. The whole ground was covered by a series of reports issued between 1818 and 1822[2] upon the officials of the courts of common law. These commissioners presented a very complete analysis of the existing state of the official staff of the common law courts ; and, as they explained in their reports, in so doing they broke new ground. There had been some enquiries, by means of juries of the officials of these courts, into their duties and fees in the reigns of James I. and Charles I.,[3] and during the Commonwealth.[4] There had also been some enquiries at the Revolution ;[5] and, as we have seen, some abortive attempts to legislate.[6] A Commission had been appointed in 1733 to enquire into the state of the courts of common law, and equity, and the ecclesiastical courts ; but it had confined its enquiries to the court of Chancery.[7] Thus these reports upon the staffs of the common law courts threw a flood of light upon the abuses of what had been hitherto one of the most obscure parts of the judicial system.

The immediate consequence of their publication was a rearrangement of the salaries of some of the judges and the abolition of a large number of sinecure offices.[8] Special Acts were passed in the case of some of these offices ;[9] and, in 1837, a more general Act abolished twenty offices in the court of King's Bench, sixteen in the court of Common Pleas, nine in the court of Exchequer, and one in the court of Exchequer Chamber.[10] It then created the office of Master with a fixed salary. It attached five

---

[1] Parlt. Papers 1810 ix.

[2] Ibid 1818 vii 243 (King's Bench); ibid 1819-1820 ii 175 (Common Pleas); ibid 1822 xi 99 (Exchequer and Exchequer Chamber).

[3] Ibid 1818 vii 248-249; cf. S.P. Dom. 1627-1628, 383, lxxxi 17.

[4] Whitelocke, Mem. iii 358 notes that in 1651 " the committee appointed to consider of the inconveniences and delays in the proceedings of law, met several times, and desired the judges in their several courts to return to them a list of the offices in their courts, and what fees they receive, and what work and employment they do for the same."

[5] Hist. MSS. Com. Twelfth Rep. Pt. VI. 192 no. 104; 313, no. 160.

[6] Above 250-251.

[7] Parlt. Papers 1819-1820 ii 180; for its recommendations on the subject of the court of Chancery see below 436.

[8] 6 George IV. c. 82 (King's Bench); 6 George IV. c. 83 (Common Pleas); 6 George IV. c. 84 (Salaries).

[9] Ibid c. 89; 8, 9 Victoria c. 34.   [10] 7 William IV. and 1 Victoria c. 30.

Masters to each court, and placed upon them the duties of the officials whose offices had been abolished. In 1843[1] the crown office attached to the court of King's Bench was remodelled. In 1852[2] the clerical staff of the judges and the subordinate officers of the courts (ushers, court keepers, etc.) were reformed. The result of these changes was that, at the time of the passing of the Judicature Acts, there were two chief classes of officials attached to the common law courts.[3] They were the Masters and the Associates. Each of them possessed a staff of clerks. All officials were paid by fixed salary.

The duties of the Masters were to attend court in rotation, to hear summonses and make interlocutory orders, to hear matters referred by the consent of parties or by order of the court, to tax bills, to report on matters referred to them by the court. In their offices was done all the business incidental to legal proceedings. The action of the court in all its stages was there initiated and recorded. The titles of their various offices—the writ of summons office, the appearance to the summons office, the rule office, the judgment office, sufficiently illustrate the work done.

There were three Associates attached to each court, who sat in court when the judge was sitting at nisi prius. Their duties were to impanel juries, to call on the causes, to read documents put in, to receive verdicts. At Chambers they made for the judge an abstract of the record of causes to be tried before him, they received the list of suitors, they handed the postea[4] to the successful party.

These were the two chief classes of officials. In addition there were still surviving two other of the older officials. The King's Coroner and Attorney had functions on the crown side of the court of King's Bench similar to those of a Master on the Plea side. The King's Remembrancer was an official of the court of Exchequer who also performed duties similar to those of a Master. He had, in addition, certain ceremonial duties to perform in connection with swearing in the Lord Chancellor, the Barons of the Exchequer, and the Lord Mayor of London. He protected the interests of the crown, if he saw that they were likely to be inadvertently affected in the course of any cases heard in the Exchequer. He could originate proceedings for penalties, debts, and duties due to the crown.

Thus, while some of these courts still kept a few of their older and distinctive officials, the greater part of the staff of each court

---

[1] 6, 7 Victoria c. 20.   [2] 15, 16 Victoria c. 73.

[3] This account is taken from the excellent historical summary contained in the Second Report of the Commission appointed to enquire into the Administrative Departments of Courts of Justice, Parlt. Papers 1874 vol. xxiv.

[4] For the meaning of this term see below 281 and n. 7.

was arranged on a comparatively simple and uniform plan. Some further changes were made by the legislation which followed upon the passing of the Judicature Acts, of which I shall speak in a later chapter.[1]

II. The Itinerant Justices

We have seen that in the twelfth century itinerant justices travelled round the country, and that they were commissioned to perform many various governmental functions, judicial and administrative.[2]   We have seen too, that the character of the commissions under which they acted varied.   Some gave them wide judicial and administrative powers, and others gave them only a limited judicial authority.[3]   During the first half of the thirteenth century there was no great change.   Bracton tells us that the circumstances under which and the forms in which such commissions were given to these justices were infinitely various.[4] But we can see from his book that a distinction was growing up between the justices commissioned to hear all pleas, and those commissioned only to take the assizes or to deliver a gaol.[5]   It is not, however, till the end of the thirteenth and the beginning of the fourteenth century that these commissions were regularly issued at definite dates,[6] or that their forms were definitely fixed.[7] We shall see that some of these commissions became obsolete at an early date, while others continued to be issued right down to modern times ; and that the courts held by the justices under the latter class of commissions gradually came to be integral parts of the judicial system, closely linked up with the common law courts.

In describing the history of these itinerant justices I shall begin by describing the commissions under which they acted ; and I shall deal firstly with those that became obsolete at an early date, and secondly, with those which have had a more permanent importance.   I shall then describe the process by which the courts held by the itinerant justices under the latter class of commissions became integral parts of the system of common law jurisdiction.   Lastly, I shall say a few words as to the modifications in this system of itinerant justices which were made in regard to London and Middlesex.

<hr>

[1] Below 647-648.   [2] Above 49-51.   [3] Ibid.
[4] " Et infiniti sunt casus, et formæ infinitæ quibus constituuntur justitiarii," f. 112.
[5] " Quandoque ad omnia placita, quandoque ad quædam specialia, sicut assisas novæ disseysinæ et mortis antecessoris capiendas et ad gaolas deliberandas, quandoque ad unicam vel duas et non plures," f. 105 b ; see above 204 n. 5.
[6] Below 277.   [7] Below 277, 280.

*The Commissions under which the Itinerant
Justices acted*

1. The Commissions which became obsolete at an early date.

The General Eyre.[1]

Of these commissions the most extensive and the most important was the commission which empowered justices to hear all pleas. These justices were known specifically as the justices in eyre. They were said to hold a general eyre for the county or counties round which they were commissioned to make their perambulation or iter. In the thirteenth and early fourteenth centuries this general eyre took a very important place in the government of the county. It did on a large scale for those parts of the kingdom included in the eyre what the sheriff's tourn did for the hundred;[2] and the methods used by the justices in eyre were essentially the same as those used by the sheriff. The number of records and reports which we have of these eyres,[3] and the accounts which are given of them by the contemporary law books,[4] show that they were important events both in the judicial and in the administrative world of that period. It will therefore be necessary to relate the history of the court held under this commission, and to describe its work, at a somewhat greater length than will be necessary in the case of the other more limited commissions.

"The business of an Eyre," says Mr. Bolland,[5] "fell into three main divisions—Pleas of Juries and Assizes; Pleas of the Crown; Gaol Delivery—and into these three divisions, under these three headings, are the Rolls of an Eyre divided." This division of the records of an eyre tells us something of the nature of the institution. We shall see that other justices with much less extensive commissions were authorized to try cases by means of juries and assizes, and to take out and try prisoners in gaol. It was the authority which the justices in eyre had to try pleas of the crown, and the extensive interpretation put upon this power, which was the characteristic feature of the general

---

[1] The fullest account of the general eyre will be found in the three volumes of the S.S. edition of the Eyre of Kent in 1313-1314, and Mr. Bolland's introductions to those volumes; for the "equity" administered in the eyre by Bill see below 448-449; vol. ii 336-344.

[2] Above 76-81.

[3] See the list of sixteen MSS. used for the S.S. edition of the Eyre of Kent, the Eyre of Kent (S.S.) i xvi; reports of an eyre in Cornwall are printed in Y.B. 30, 31 Ed. I. (R.S.) 74 seqq.

[4] Bracton f. 115 b seqq.; Britton i 18-134; Fleta i 19, 20.

[5] The Eyre of Kent (S.S.) i xvii, xviii; cf. Coke, Fourth Instit. 184, who points out that "The stile of this court was 'Placita de juratis et assisis et coronæ de itinere Johannis de Vallibus et sociorum justiciariorum itinerantium apud Ockham in comitatu Rutland in crastino Epiphaniæ Domini, Anno regni regis Edwardi 14.'"

advantages of securing a due observance of the peace." [1]   Thus at the Eyre of Kent, "Sir H. de Staunton declared the will of our Lord the King, and the reason of their coming, in this wise, the King's will was that all evil doers should be punished after their deserts, and that justice should be ministered indifferently to rich as to poor ; and for the better accomplishing of this, he prayed the community of the county by their attendance there to lend him their aid in the establishing of a happy and certain peace that should be both for the honour of the realm and for their own welfare." [2]   Bracton tells us [3] that it was then the practice of the justices to retire and confer with the " busones " [4] of the county—the influential persons that is, " ad quorum nutum dependent vota aliorum."   In these " busones " we can see the persons whose names appear in the commissions of gaol delivery and oyer and terminer, [5] and who in later days were, as justices of the peace, to rule the county. [6]

On the return of the justices to court the sheriff surrendered his rod of office, and took an oath to do loyally all things appertaining to his office.   His rod was then handed back to him, and the other officials of the county took a similar oath. [7]   The justices then took the rolls of the sheriff and the coroners, and the rolls of any sheriffs or coroners who had held office since the last eyre. [8]   Then all who claimed to enjoy any franchises in the county must put in their claims. [9]   Failure to do so might, as we have seen, have serious results for the franchise owners, if then or at any future period their titles were questioned by a writ of Quo Warranto. [10]

After these and other preliminary matters had been disposed of, the preparations began for the main business of the eyre—the receiving of presentments upon the many matters contained in the Articles of the Eyre.   The first step was to choose the presenting juries.   In the details of the method of choice the practice seems to have varied. [11]   But in all cases the bailiff of the hundred seems

---

[1] " Quæ sit causa adventus eorum, et quæ sit utilitas itinerationis, et quæ commoditas si pax observetur," f. 115 b.

[2] The Eyre of Kent (S.S.) i 2.   [3] f. 115 b.

[4] There has been considerable controversy as to the meaning and derivation of this word, see the Eyre of Kent (S.S.) i xxvii-xxxi where all the suggestions hitherto made are considered ; Mr. Bolland connects it with *boujon* (spelt sometimes *bougern*, or *bozon*, or *boucon*), which means (1) a large arrow, and (2) an iron rule for measuring cloth ; from boujon we get boujonneur—an official measurer, well known in the cloth-making districts of north France and Flanders ; it is suggested that " busones " is the Latinized form of boujouneurs, i.e. the persons who measured up things authoritatively.

[5] Below 274, 280.   [6] Below 285 seqq.
[7] Eyre of Kent (S.S.) i 4, 5, 6.   [8] Ibid 4, 5.
[9] Ibid 14.   [10] Above 89.
[11] See the Eyre of Kent (S.S.) i xxxiv-xxxv.

to have chosen two or four electors, and these electors chose themselves and twelve others from their hundred. This number was reduced to twelve, and these twelve formed the jury. To these juries the Articles of the Eyre were read, and they were required to give a distinct and precise answer by a certain day. They were also ordered to arrest at once any suspected persons, or, if this was not possible, to give secretly a list of such persons to the justices.[1]

The Articles of the Eyre ranged over the whole field of government.[2] We have many sets of these Articles from different periods; and it is clear that, as time went on, they grew rapidly.[3] Thus the Articles of enquiry contained in the hundred rolls[4] were added permanently to the Articles of the Eyre; and to distinguish them from the older Articles they were called the Nova Capitula—the New Articles. Mr. Bolland tells us that the Articles of the London Eyre of 1321 were seven times as long as the Articles of the London Eyre of 1244. The object of these Articles was to extract from the juries "information on every subject where a possible answer might afford ground for extracting an amercement from somebody, or driving someone to make fine with the King."[5] In the Eyre of Kent in 1313-1314 they number 142.[6] They comprised enquiries into the neglect of police and other duties of the counties, hundreds, townships, and boroughs, into the misdoings of all officials, into the usurpation or misuse of franchises, into the proprietary rights of the crown such as escheats, wardships, and other sources of revenue. Upon the answers which the juries made to these Articles the subsequent proceedings of the eyre were founded. These proceedings were taken both against the persons presented by the juries, and against the juries themselves if they made a false presentment.

The justices were not without means of checking the correctness of the presentments made by the juries. They had before

---

[1] Bracton f. 116 a ; Eyre of Kent (S.S.) i 20.

[2] See Vinogradoff, Oxford Studies vol. vi no. xi 10-72, and Eyre of Kent (S.S.) i xxxix-xli for an account of the various sets of extant articles and their history.

[3] "Capitula vero quæ illis duodecim proponenda sunt, quandoque variantur secundum varietatem temporum et locorum, et quandoque augentur quandoque minuuntur," Bracton f. 116 a.

[4] Above 88.

[5] The Eyre of Kent (S.S.) i xxxviii ; Maitland says, "We might classify the articles under the two heads of revenue and crime, but in so doing might overlook the fact that a distinction between the doing of penal justice and the collection of the king's income is only gradually emerging. The itinerant judge of the twelfth century has much of the commissioner of taxes," Pleas of the Crown for the County of Gloucester xxvi.

[6] The Eyre of Kent (S.S.) i 28-46 ; other printed lists of these articles will be found in Hovenden iii 262-267 ; Bracton ff. 116, 117 ; Britton i 24-97 ; Fleta i 20 ; Statutes of Uncertain Date (Rec. Comm.) i 233 ; Bracton (R.S.) ii App. I. and II.

them the sheriff's and the coroner's rolls. " We are reminded," as Maitland has said,[1] " of a schoolmaster before whom stands a class of boys saying their lesson. He knows where they go wrong for he has the book. Every slip is cause for an imposition unless his pupils have purchased a favourable audience." And it must be added, the Justices were sometimes encouraged to find many occasions for these " impositions " by the fact that they were paid out of the money which they were able thus to collect.[2] Two illustrations will show the sort of way in which they went to work. The first is from the Cornish Eyre of 1302.[3] Berewick, J., told the commonalty of Cornwall that they must pay a fine, " for know that we have found several errors in the rolls of this county." The errors, which were very technical, were then pointed out by the judge.[4] The commonalty at once offered a sum of £80, and Berewick ordered persons to be chosen to assess the fine, and that its imposition should be entered on the rolls. The second comes from the Northampton Eyre of 1330, and is noted by Fitzherbert.[5] Hale[6] thus gives the effect of Fitzherbert's summary: " It was presented that A had killed B, and it was demanded of the presenters whether he were *in decenna*, they answered *He was not;* then it was demanded where he abode ; they say with the parson of the town, and thereupon the parson was amerced for his manupast ; then it was demanded who was present when he slew him ; they say C ; it was then demanded of them whether C received him (i.e. arrested him) ; they say *Not*, wherefore C was amerced ; then it was demanded where the felon was ; they say *he is escaped ;* then it was demanded whether it were done in the day or the night ; they answer *in the evening ;* Therefore the whole vill was amerced."

It seems to be clear that the main work of the eyre was this overhauling of the work of the officials and courts of the county since the preceding eyre. No doubt, as the reports show, a

---

[1] P. and M. ii 643 ; " Though they must be quite sure they forget nothing—they will be amerced for any omission when the Justices detect it, and detect it they almost certainly will—they must also be quite sure that every tittle of what they present is the truth, for amercements and fines again await any variation from strict provable historical fact," the Eyre of Kent (S.S.) i 38-39 ; for the difference between a fine and an amercement see above 77 n. 6.

[2] Ibid xxvi ; above 252 n. 9.

[3] Y.B. 30, 31 Ed. I. (R.S.) 240-242.

[4] " One is that four men were outlawed at four county courts in succession, and were allowed to give mainprise, and then the same men came and brought a writ to remove the appeal, and the appeal was removed at their suit : this was an error ; for they ought to have been taken, etc. Another error is, that a married woman sued an appeal without naming her husband ; and this is another error ; and so on of other errors," ibid 240.

[5] Fitzherbert, Ab. *Corone* pl. 293.

[6] P.C. ii 74 ; cf. Pleas of the Crown for the County of Gloucester xxxiii-xxxiv.

certain number of civil cases were heard during the eyre, and a certain number of criminal cases were tried; but the transaction of this sort of business was not its chief function. The trial and hanging of criminals was left to subordinate justices of gaol delivery who worked with the justices in eyre. As Mr. Bolland says the eyre "was little concerned with the administration of justice;" its business was "to see that every fact in connection with every sort of criminal trial, either before themselves or at any previous gaol delivery, that might possibly furnish a reason for somebody being amerced, was brought to their notice. . . . The Crown Pleas division of the eyre existed to fill the king's coffers and not to maintain his peace." [1]

The eyre was thus useful to the king, and was used by him as a means to extort money; but there can be little doubt that, for this very reason, it tended to secure the efficiency of the local government. As Maitland has said, "a just and regular infliction of pecuniary penalties" was a very effective means of "bringing the unprofessional policeman to a sense of his duties." [2] It was a series of very practical applications of Hobbes' aphorism that it is "the constant fear of punishment which maketh men just." At a time when the law-abiding instinct had hardly been formed this constant fear of punishment was the only way of securing a small modicum of justice; and, even when that instinct has been formed, the state which tries to dispense with this expedient will do so at its peril. The emancipation by the legislature in 1906 of unions of workmen and masters from some of the sanctions of the common law has been followed by the growth of a new industrial and commercial feudalism as dangerous to the orderly development of the state, and as selfish and narrow in its outlook, as that mediæval feudalism which the eyre and other institutions of royal justice were struggling to master during this mediæval period.

Naturally the efficiency of the eyre, both as a method of raising revenue and as a method of securing the observance of public duties, made it an exceedingly unpopular institution. The Cornish men in 1233 betook themselves to the woods rather than face the justices. [3] It came to be an established rule that an eyre should not be held more often than once in seven years; [4] and in 1261 the county of Worcester declined to admit the justices because the seven years had not elapsed. [5] In the fourteenth century the rolls of Parliament attest its continued

---

[1] The Eyre of Kent (S.S.) i xlii-xliii.
[2] Pleas of the Crown for the County of Gloucester xxxiii-xxxiv.
[3] P. and M. i 181.　　　　　　[4] This is stated by Britton i 3.
[5] Foss, Judges ii 192.

against the justices in eyre.[1] On the other hand they are
classed by Coke with commissions of oyer and terminer.[2]   In
Coke's time they had long ceased to exist.[3]   Their historical
importance is that indicated by Mr. Pike. They are the connecting link between the justices in eyre and the justices of oyer
and terminer.

2. The Commissions of more permanent importance.

The Commission of Oyer and Terminer.[4]

This was a commission addressed to certain of the king's
justices and others directing them or any two or three of them
to enquire concerning certain crimes committed in certain counties
" eaque omnia audiendum et terminandum."   These commissions
might be either general, to enquire into all crimes committed
within the area of the commission ; or special, to enquire into a
particular case, or in a particular place, or into certain specified
crimes.[5]

The Commission of Gaol Delivery.[6]

This was a much narrower commission than the commission
of oyer and terminer.[7]   It was addressed to certain persons
directing them to deliver the gaol of a certain place and to try
the prisoners therein.   In Edward I.'s reign a royal judge was
often not on the commission ; in fact in 1292 the commissioners
of oyer and terminer were directed to enquire into the misdeeds
of the commissioners of gaol delivery.[8]   But in later times the
differences between this commission and that of oyer and
terminer became very slight ;[9] and there was not as a rule any
reason for distinguishing between them, because as we shall see,[10]
both commissions were in practice executed by the same person.

The Commission of the Peace.

The judges of the court of King's Bench, together with other
dignified officials, and the judges of all the other courts of common
law in their several courts, were also *ex officio* justices of the

---

[1] R.P. ii 305 no. 21, " qu'il ne grante en nulle partie du Roialme Eire ne Trailbaston durante la guerre . . . fors en horrible cas;" R.P. iii 24, no. 101; Y.B.
2 Ed. III. Trin. pl. 15 (quoted Y.B. 14, 15 Ed. III. (R.S.) xxxvi), they were said to
be in a certain case " come Justices in Eire ; " Coke, Second Instit. 540 said, " they
in the end had such authority as justices in Eyre."

[2] Fourth Instit. 186.

[3] Second Instit. 540; their declension is ascribed by Coke to the fact that writs
of error lay from them to the King's Bench.

[4] App. XXIII. C.   [5] Coke, Fourth Instit. 163 ; Hale, P.C. ii 10-31.

[6] App. XXIII. D.   [7] P. and M. i 179 ; ii 642.   [8] R.P. i 86 no. 30.

[9] Stephen, H.C.L. i 106-107.   [10] Below 280.

peace.[1] Thus it happened that, when the work of these commissions of oyer and terminer and gaol delivery came to be
done almost entirely by the judges of the common law courts,
these judges had, in addition to their other powers, the powers
given by this commission.   But, though it thus came to be
technically true to say that these justices had, in addition to
their other powers, the powers given by the commission of the
peace, it is not a fact of much importance ; because the powers
given by the commission of the peace did not materially add to
the powers conferred upon them both by their other commissions
and by statute.[2]

The Commission of Assize.

The foregoing commissions conferred upon the commissioners
a criminal jurisdiction.   The commission of assize conferred
upon them a limited civil jurisdiction.   But, in order to explain
what this jurisdiction was, it is necessary to make a short
digression, and explain the meanings attached to the word
" Assize " in the twelfth century.   The subsequent history of the
word will show us that this commission came to be the most
important of all these commissions, because the commissioners
of assize gradually got all and more than all of the powers conferred by the other commissions.

The word " Assisa "[3] means originally the sitting of a court
or assembly.   It then comes to denote the things done, the
enactments passed, at such a court or assembly.   Thus we speak
of the Assize of Clarendon, or the Assize of Northampton.
Certain of these enactments in Henry II.'s reign introduced a
new procedure for the trial of questions as to the ownership or
possession of lands held by free tenure.[4]   The Grand Assize[5]
introduced this new procedure for the determination of questions
of ownership ; the possessory assizes for the determination of
questions of possession.   These possessory assizes[6] were three
in number.   The assize of novel disseisin provided for the trial
of the question whether A has disseised or dispossessed B of his
freehold ; the assize of mort d'ancestor for the trial of a dispute
as to who is the heir of the person last seised of a given estate

[1] Bacon, Use of the Law, Works (Ed. Spedding) vii 476; Bl. Comm. i 338.

[2] Mr. Turner points out, Encyclopædia of English Law iii 79 that "all justices
of assize and gaol delivery were in the commission of the peace within the precincts
of their courts, just as all judges of the King's Bench were *ex officio* in the commission of the peace for all counties.   At the present time all judges of the Supreme
Court of Judicature are specially named in the commission of the peace for each
county."

[3] Jacob's Law Dictionary, sub. voc. *Assisa;* Maitland, Justice and Police 152-153.

[4] Above 47; below 327-329; vol. ii 179; vol. iii 6-7, 8-11.

[5] Below 327-329.

[6] P. and M. i 124-128 ; for their forms see App. III.

of inheritance; the assize of darrein presentment for the trial of a dispute as to who was last seised of the right to present to a vacant living. In addition there was the Assize Utrum to determine whether land was held by some one of the lay tenures or by a spiritual tenure, i.e. in frankalmoin.[1]

The commission of assize was a commission addressed to certain persons authorizing them to try the possessory assizes in certain counties named in the commission. It thus conferred a very limited civil jurisdiction. But the trial of these cases often involved difficult questions of law—more difficult questions than those which emerged in the trial of ordinary criminal cases. For this reason, one at least of these commissions was usually a royal judge. As the law tended to become more elaborate, the need to employ professional lawyers to do the work not only of the commission of assize, but also of the other commissions, came to be generally recognized. One expedient adopted was to give to these commissioners of assize the powers given by the other commissions,[2] and another was to add to their powers by statute.[3] Thus the judges of assize came to exercise a power very little inferior to that exercised by the courts of common law; and the courts which they held came to be called "the Assizes." We still speak of "the Assizes" in this sense, though the old possessory assizes were falling out of use in the sixteenth century, and have been abolished since 1833.[4]

These developments of the powers of the judges of assize will form the subject of the following section.

The Process by which the Courts held by the Itinerant Justices became Integral Parts of the System of Common Law Jurisdiction

This was a long and somewhat complicated process. I shall discuss it under the following heads (1) The growth of the practice of regularly issuing the commissions at definite times; (2) The nisi prius system; (3) The predominant position assumed by the justices of assize; (4) The relation of the justices of assize to the common law courts; (5) The legal and political results of the circuit system.

(1) The growth of the practice of regularly issuing the commissions at definite times.

The sections in the Charters of 1215 and 1217, which pro-

---

[1] P. and M. i 123-124; for the form see App. II.; for tenure in frankalmoin see vol. iii 34-37.
[2] Below 280.   [3] Below 279.
[4] 3, 4 William IV. c. 27 §§ 36, 37.

vided for the circuits of justices to take the possessory assizes, give us the impression that the commission of assize was then regularly issued at definite times.[1] But this impression is false, as the clauses of the Charter were not in fact observed. Mr. Turner has pointed out that in practice a special commission of assize was issued on the application of each person who wished to proceed in this way. "No justices," he says, "were sent into the counties to take all the assizes which might be brought before them, but special commissions were granted to justices to take particular assizes."[2] Hundreds of these commissions were issued annually in the latter years of Henry III.'s reign;[3] and an ordinance of 1259, which provided that commissions to try assizes and other cases should only be issued to certain named persons, all of whom were professional lawyers, seems to show that these commissions were not always issued to the most competent persons.[4] But towards the end of Henry III.'s reign general commissions began to be issued—though it was still apparently necessary that separate letters patent should be issued to allow the justices to take each assize.[5] In 1272, the first year of Edward I.'s reign, a new ordinance originated the regular circuits of these justices. The country was divided into groups of counties, and to each group two justices were assigned to take the " Assisæ, jurata et certificationes."[6] It was enacted in 1285 that these assizes should be taken three times a year;[7] and in 1330 it was again provided that they should be taken three times a year, or more often if need be.[8]

As it was with the commission of assize, so it was with the commissions of Oyer and Terminer and Gaol Delivery. They were at first very irregularly issued. The king could issue them as he pleased; and he was accustomed to issue them, at the suit of private persons, to commissioners who were acting in concert with the petitioners. Parliament protested against the injustice so caused;[9] and statutes were passed to ensure that the justices

---

[1] For the clause in the Charter of 1215 see above 56 n. 7; the Charter of 1217 § 13 provided for a circuit once a year; it further provided that, " Ea quæ in illo adventu suo in comitatu per justitiarios prædictos ad dictas assisas capiendas missos terminari non possunt, per eosdem terminentur alibi in itinere suo, et ea quæ per eosdem, propter difficultatem aliquorum articulorum, terminari non possunt, referantur ad justitiarios nostros de banco et ibi terminentur," § 14.

[2] Encyclopædia of English Law, sub. voc. Circuits and Assizes iii 76.

[3] Ibid.

[4] Bracton's Note Book i 20; this, as Maitland says, "looks like an attempt of the baronial council to limit the king's power of appointing anyone whom he pleases, to act as justice for this occasion only, an attempt prophetic of future statutes;" for other instances of similar orders see Encyclopædia of English Law iii 76.

[5] Ibid iii 76-77.
[6] Ibid 77.
[7] 13 Edward I. St. 1 c. 30.
[8] 4 Edward III. c. 2.
[9] Stephen, H.C.L. i 107-110.

of assize or the justices of either bench should always be on these commissions.[1] Thus, although the king did not abandon his right to issue these commissions on special occasions,[2] they were generally issued on the occasions upon which the justices of assize travelled round the country, and these justices were always among the commissioners. We shall now see that by this time the civil jurisdiction of the justices of assize had been largely extended by the legislature.

(2) The nisi prius system.

The phrase "nisi prius" is used by Bracton. He explains that the justices in Eyre were accustomed to order that all cases in the court of Common Pleas originating in the county in which they were making their circuit, should be adjourned before themselves; but that, as their coming might be hindered for divers causes, a day in the Common Pleas was always given to the parties by the judges of the court "nisi justitiarii itinerantes prius venerint ad partes illas."[3] But the origin of the modern nisi prius system is a clause of the Statute of Westminster II. (1285),[4] which applied the practice mentioned by Bracton to the circuits of the justices of assize, in such a way that it gave them a general jurisdiction over civil cases begun in the courts of Common Pleas or King's Bench. In substance the statute provided that for holding inquisitions into minor trespasses, and for the trial of pleas begun in either of the Benches, a day and place certain should be appointed in the county; that such cases should not be determined in the Benches unless the judges of assize failed to come into the county to try them; and that these judges of assize should be "two sworn justices," that is, two of the judges of the courts of King's Bench or Common Pleas. In all these cases the sheriff was directed to summon the jurors to Westminster only "nisi prius" the justices of assize first came into the county.[5] This scheme was further enforced

[1] 27 Edward I. St. 1 c. 3; 2 Edward III. c. 2; 4 Edward III c. 2; cf. Reeves, H.E.L. ii 82, 86, 87, 188, 301.

[2] Above 274 n. 5; in fact, as Professor Baldwin points out, Select Cases before the Council (S.S.) xxx, lxxv, during the thirteenth and the greater part of the fourteenth century the Council generally did not hear cases, but referred them to a commission of Oyer and Terminer.

[3] "Bene poterit iter multipliciter impediri, revocari, vel suspendi, et unde semper dabitur dies partibus a justitiariis de banco, sub tali conditione, nisi justitiarii itinerantes prius venerint ad partes illas, et quo casu semper remanebunt placita illa in banco quosque iter inceptum fuerit," f. 110; cf. f. 352 for a similar nisi prius clause in an essoin de malo.

[4] 13 Edward I. St. 1 c. 30; Y.B. 4 Edward II (S.S.) lix-lxi.

[5] For this clause in the statute, and the judicial writ to the sheriff to summon the jury see App. XXIII. B; the procedure for summoning the jury is thus described in the King v. Edmonds (1821) 4 B. and Ald. at p. 479—"There have always . . . been two successive processes to enforce the attendance of the jury. First a venire

in 1299.[1] In 1318 it was extended to all pleas of land;[2] and in 1328 it was provided that such pleas of land should be tried at nisi prius at the suit not only of the demandant but also of the tenant.[3] In 1340[4] it was provided that cases begun in the King's Bench could be tried at nisi prius by a justice of the Common Pleas and vice versa; and that all pleas begun in either of the Benches could be tried at nisi prius by the Chief Baron of the Exchequer "if he be a man of the law," or by the justices of assize, provided they were judges of one Bench or the other, or king's serjeants. The result was that all civil cases begun in the court of King's Bench or Common Pleas could be heard, either by the justices of assize (provided that they were judges of one Bench or the other or king's serjeants), or by the judges of these two courts sitting to hear cases at nisi prius, or by the Chief Baron of the Exchequer if "a man of the law" and specially commissioned to try cases at nisi prius.

Later, this nisi prius system was extended in two directions. In the first place it was extended from actions begun in either of the two Benches to common pleas begun in the court of Exchequer. In this, as in other respects, the court of Exchequer was not originally in quite the same position as the other two common law courts. Though the Barons of the Exchequer, if they were "men of the law" could act as justices of assize and hear cases at nisi prius, common pleas begun in the Exchequer would not be heard by these justices at nisi prius unless a special commission was issued for that purpose. It was not till 1839[5] that the necessity for this special commission was dispensed with. In the second place this nisi prius system was adapted to the trial of criminal cases. If a man was indicted in a county, and the indictment was removed by writ of certiorari into the King's Bench, the case might be sent to be tried before the justices of assize in any other county as a nisi prius record.[6] It was often desirable to remove cases in this way to the court of King's Bench if a fair trial could not be had in the county; but it would have delayed the business of the court of King's Bench if it had been necessary to try all such cases there.

returnable in the court above. . . . To this process the sheriff formerly made an actual return of the names of jurors as summoned, but the jurors themselves did not appear. This therefore was followed by a second process . . . this process is still issued in its primitive and unqualified form for trials at Bar; but, for trials at nisi prius, it contains a clause . . . qualifying the command for their attendance in the court above, in case the Justices of Assize shall before the day appointed, come into the county;" cf. Forsyth, Trial by Jury 169-171.

[1] 27 Edward I. St. 1 c. 4   [2] 12 Edward II. St. 1 c. 3.
[3] 2 Edward III. c. 16.   [4] 14 Edward III. St. 1 c. 16.
[5] 2, 3 Victoria c. 22.
[6] Hale, P.C. ii 39-41; further powers to pursue this course were given by 6 Henry III. c. 6.

That this nisi prius system was an enormous relief to litigants and jurors is obvious. They were saved the expense and trouble of a toilsome journey to Westminster.[1] It was also a relief to the courts of common law. In Edward II.'s reign, before the nisi prius system was fully developed, it had been necessary to create two divisions of the court of Common Pleas, one of which was employed in hearing the trial of issues which in later days would have been tried in the country at nisi prius.[2] In fact, I think it may be said that it was only by the help of this system that the extreme centralization of justice which resulted from the decline of the local courts was made bearable.

(3) The predominant position assumed by the justices of assize.

We have seen that the justices of assize were always on the commissions of Oyer and Terminer and Gaol Delivery;[3] that the justices always included some of the judges of the two Benches and the Exchequer; and that, by virtue of the nisi prius system, they exercised a jurisdiction practically co-extensive with that exercised by the courts of common law. It is obvious that it was only a professional lawyer who was competent to exercise this large jurisdiction. Thus, although certain of these commissions continued to be issued to laymen as well as lawyers, it was the lawyers who did the work, because they alone were competent to do it. This fact was recognized by a clause in the commissions of Oyer and Terminer and Gaol Delivery which rendered their presence necessary at all meetings of the court.[4] The professional lawyers in course of time came to represent the court for all purposes, and entirely ousted the amateurs.[5] We shall see that, in the case of the justices of the peace, a similar clause

[1] As to this see Y.B. 8 Ed. II. (S.S.) xvi-xxi; moreover the character of the service made persons willing to pay sheriffs handsomely to avoid it, and so increased their illicit perquisites, see ibid xi-xiii and the statutes there cited.

[2] Y.B. 3, 4 Ed. II. (S.S.) xxiv-xxviii.

[3] Above 277-278.

[4] The form runs, "Sciatis quod assignavimus vos et tres vestrum, *quorum* aliquem vestrum vos præfatos (then follow the names of the judges) unum esse volumus;" hence the professional judges were said to be of the "quorum;" we shall meet this expression again in dealing with the justices of the peace, below 290.

[5] "For centuries the trials of offences under such commissions (Oyer and Terminer) . . . have been held before a single judge, and the proceedings are nevertheless represented on the record as taking place not before the judge but before the other judges sitting under the commission. Now, this, we apprehend, must have proceeded on the ground that, while the whole body of justices named in the commission constituted the court of Oyer and Terminer, each judge sitting under it represented the court; so that whatever took place before the single judge was considered as done constructively, before the whole court," Leverson v. the Queen (1869) L.R. 4 Q.B. at p. 403 *per* Cockburn, C.J.; see also ibid at p. 405 where he states that it was the invariable practice that no lay member of the court took part in the proceedings; in Edward II.'s reign a knight usually sat with the judge at nisi prius, Y.B. 3, 4 Ed. II. (S.S.) xxviii.

in their commission was evaded, and that, in consequence, precisely the opposite result was reached.[1]

Though these justices of assize were in practice the judges of the common law courts, though they exercised a jurisdiction almost as large as that exercised by these judges, they acted on circuit, not by virtue of their position as judges, but by virtue of their temporary commissions. But, as in fact these commissions were regularly issued, the courts which sat by virtue of them were as permanent as the courts of common law. As the theoretically temporary character of these courts sometimes caused practical inconvenience it was provided in 1547[2] that prisoners found guilty by a justice acting under one commission could be sentenced by a justice acting under another commission; and similarly that actions begun before a justice acting under one commission could be continued by justices acting under another.

(4) The relation of the justices of assize to the common law courts.

Under the nisi prius system the relations of the justices of assize to the common law courts had always been very close. The extent of their powers could be interpreted by the King's Bench or Common Pleas;[3] and cases of difficulty could always be adjourned into the Common Pleas.[4] Moreover, when the judges were sitting at nisi prius to hear cases begun in either of the Benches, they for all purposes represented the court in which the action had been begun. A trial at nisi prius was in all respects equivalent to a trial before the full Bench—hence the saying " the day at nisi prius and the day in banc are in consideration of law the same." [5] As Willes, J., said,[6] the judges at nisi prius " act in all points touching the trial and its incidents as and for the court from which the record comes. . . . The postea,[7] or record of the proceedings before them, stands in the place of the record of the proceedings at bar before the superior court in which

---

[1] Below 290.

[2] 1 Edward VI. c. 7 § 5; Reeves, H.E.L. iii 473-474.

[3] See Y.B. 11, 12 Ed. III. (R.S.) 620 where the court of Common Pleas adjudicated upon the powers of a judge sitting at nisi prius; cf. Y.B. 17 Ed. III. (R.S.) 276.

[4] Above 277 n. 1; 13 Edward I. St. 1 c. 30; cf. Y.B. 3, 4 Ed. II. (S.S.) 35.

[5] " When *Nisi Prius* is granted, a day will be given to the parties in the Common Bench unless the justice comes into the county; therefore, if the justice does come into the county, the defendant has not a day in court. And, moreover, if the defendant makes default in the county, the default there will be adjudged to be a default here, for all is adjudged to be one day," Y.B. 20 Ed. iii. (R.S.) i 340 *per* Willoughby, J.; cf. Y.BB. 4 Ed. II. (S.S.) 128 *per* Staunton, J.; 11, 12 Ed. III. (R.S.) 338; the King v. Joliffe (1791) 4 T.R. at p. 293 *per* Buller, J.; Ex pte. Fernandez (1861) 10 C.B. N.S. at p. 57 *per* Willes, J.

[6] Ex pte. Fernandez (1861) 10 C.B. N.S. at p. 44.

[7] The enrolment of the verdict with the judgment of the court thereon was, from its first word, called the postea, Y.B. 3, 4 Ed. II. (S.S.) xxvii.

the action is instituted.   Such postea is accepted as conclusive and entered upon the record of the court in banc ; and in the great majority of instances the judgment of that court is pronounced as a matter of course according to the result of the trial before the judge of assize."

It follows from this that the rules, firstly as to the procedure in error from the courts held by these justices, and secondly as to obtaining a new trial were essentially similar to the rules which obtained in the two Benches.

(i) In criminal cases, before 1907, a writ of error lay for errors on the record, or the judge might reserve a point for the consideration of the court of Crown Cases Reserved.[1]   Since 1907[2] an appeal lies to the court of Criminal Appeal.   In civil cases, the judgment of the justices of assize, being the judgment of the court from which the nisi prius record came, a writ of error or a Bill of Exceptions lay to the court of error from that court.[3]

(ii) The justices of assize could always adjourn a case into the court from which the nisi prius record came.[4]   Though they could give judgment in the case, they need not do so ; and, if they did not, and the court from which the nisi prius record came thought that there had been irregularity in the proceedings, it could decline to proceed and leave the parties to start proceedings afresh.[5]   In other words, there was a new trial. Normally judgment was entered by the court from which the nisi prius record came on the fourth day of the term following the trial ; but, at the beginning of the seventeenth century, it became customary to allow a motion to be made to the court within these four days to stay the entry of the judgment given according to the findings of the jury at nisi prius.   If the motion was successful a new trial was granted.   The court could not, however, enter a verdict for the other party without a new trial unless there had been a special verdict ; and special verdicts were difficult to frame properly.   To obviate this difficulty, and to avoid the expense of a new trial, it became the practice for

---

[1] Above 217.   [2] 7 Edward VII. c. 23 ; above 217-218.
[3] Y.B. 16 Ed. III. (R.S.) i 234 per Derworthy arg.; "It is familiar learning that upon a Bill of Exceptions tendered at the assizes or at nisi prius in town, judgment is entered as a matter of course in the court from which the record comes, according to the opinion expressed at nisi prius, and the exceptions can only be discussed in the court of error from that court, in like manner as if they were exceptions to the opinion of the court in banc upon a trial at bar," Ex pte. Fernandez (1861) 10 C.B. N.S. at p. 45 per Willes, J.
[4] Above 277 n. 1.
[5] " If the justices appointed to take assizes erred in taking the assize we will not give judgment upon the verdict when it is adjourned before us," Y.B. 16 Ed. III. (R.S.) i 234 per Hillary, C.J.

the judge, with the consent of the parties, to give leave to move the court to enter a verdict for the other side, if they considered that his direction to the jury had been erroneous.[1]

(5) The legal and political results of the circuit system.

We have seen that, but for this system, the extremely centralized judicial system, which was the result of the victory of the common law courts over the older local courts, would hardly have been tolerable either to litigants or to jurors.[2] This system provided some relief without any appreciable decentralization, and without the two great disadvantages which decentralization would have entailed.

The first disadvantage of too extensive a measure of decentralization would have been the danger that local differences in the rules of law substantive and adjective would have sprung up. This would have been a real danger at a time when difficulties in means of communication, and difficulties in the diffusion of knowledge, somewhat easily led to the formation of local customs. It was, as Hale had pointed out,[3] met completely by his circuit system. "For those men are employed as justices, who, as they have had a common education in the study of the law, so they daily, in Term-time, converse and consult with one another ; acquaint one another with their judgments ; sit near one another in Westminster Hall, whereby their judgments and decisions are necessarily communicated to one another, either immediately, or by relations of others. By this means their judgments, and their administrations of common justice, carry a consonancy, congruity, and uniformity, one to another : whereby both the laws and the administrations thereof are preserved from that confusion and disparity that would unavoidably ensue if the administration was by several incommunicating hands, or by provincial establishments."

The second disadvantage of decentralization, which was prevented by circuit system, was one which would have been felt at all times, and acutely felt both in the Middle Ages and right down to the end of the seventeenth century. The circuit system helped, as Hale points out,[4] to prevent " factions and parties in the carriage of business, which would soon appear in every cause of moment, were the trial only before men residing in the counties ; " and its efficacy in this direction was helped by the rule that the judges of assize must not exercise their jurisdiction in the counties in which they had been born, or in which they resided.[5]

---

[1] East Railway Co. v. Smitherman (1883), cited Thayer, Evidence 241 n. 1 ; Dublin Railway Co. v. Slattery (1878) 3 A.C. at pp. 1204-1205.
[2] Above 280.
[3] Hist. Com. Law (6th Ed.) 341.   [4] Ibid 340-341.
[5] 8 Richard II. c. 2 ; 13 Henry IV. c. 2 ; 33 Henry VIII. c. 24.

That it did not entirely prevent factions and parties in the Middle Ages and later we shall see ;[1] but there can be no doubt that it exercised a powerful influence in this direction.

The maintenance, then, both of uniformity and impartiality in the administration of the law were the two great legal advantages which resulted from the circuit system. Its chief political advantage was that it provided the central government with a means of controlling the conduct of the local government, which was exercised by judicial officers and to a large extent under judicial forms. We have seen that the judges of assize inherited some of the old political functions of the justices in eyre ;[2] and these functions were exercised, like those of their predecessors, under the judicial forms of indictment and presentment. Obviously this tended to strengthen the belief, inculcated by many mediæval lawyers and political philosophers, that the maintenance of a supreme law was the great aim of government.[3] It is a belief which is a condition precedent for the stability of any sort of constitutional government ; and the fact that it was very universally held in the seventeenth century was of priceless value to those who fought the battle for constitutional government in that century.[4] That it was then universally held was due in no small degree to the manner in which the working of the circuit system had caused the idea of the supremacy of the law to be no mere technicality of the lawyers or abstraction of the philosophers, but an article in the political creed, and a part of the political instinct of all Englishmen.

London and the Circuit System

The fact that the courts of common law sat at Westminster, the fact that London was a densely populated area, and the fact that the City of London had very extensive franchises, made special arrangements necessary in the application of the circuit system to London and the county of Middlesex. These special arrangements were made for the trial both of civil and criminal cases.

(1) Civil Cases.

The court of King's Bench supersedes all special commissions in any county in which it happens to be sitting. It usually sat in Middlesex. Therefore for a long time after other civil cases were usually tried by a judge at nisi prius, Middlesex cases were tried at the bar of the court of King's Bench. The same rule also held in the case of actions begun in the other common law

[1] Below 483-485; vol. ii 415-416.   [2] Above 272-273.
[3] Vol. ii 196, 253-255, 435, 441-442.   [4] Vol. vi 82-86.

courts. Great delay to the business of the courts was thereby occasioned. It was therefore enacted in 1576[1] that such cases should be tried at nisi prius by any of the judges of the three courts of common law.

(2) Criminal Cases.

London was by charter a county. In 1327 the Lord Mayor, the Recorder, and the Aldermen got the right to be put upon all commissions of Gaol Delivery, and Oyer and Terminer for the City of London. In practice they tried Middlesex prisoners also.[2] In 1834 the central criminal court was established.[3] The judges of the courts of common law, the Lord Mayor, Aldermen, Recorder, and certain other city officials, the Lord Chancellor and certain others, or any two of them were made the judges of the court. It was provided that the crown could issue commissions of Oyer and Terminer and Gaol Delivery to the judges of the court to try criminal cases arising in the City of London, the county of Middlesex, and certain parts of the counties of Essex, Kent, and Surrey.

III. The Justices of the Peace

In the courts of common law and the courts held by the itinerant justices was vested almost all the common law jurisdiction of the country, civil and criminal. Royal justice had won a complete victory over the older local courts, communal, feudal, or franchise. But there was still left to the old courts and the old officials—to the hundred, the tourn, and the sheriff—certain police duties and a criminal jurisdiction over small offences. Even these duties were inadequately fulfilled mainly because the organization and procedure of these courts were antiquated. Royal justice won its final victory when, in the fourteenth and fifteenth centuries, it absorbed almost entirely this last remnant of their jurisdiction.

We have seen that justices specially commissioned by the crown had introduced all over the country the newer remedies and the more effective procedure of the courts of common law. The same device was used to reform the police system and the petty criminal jurisdiction of the older courts. They too were first controlled and then supplanted by persons specially commissioned by the crown who came to be called the Justices of

---

[1] 18 Elizabeth c. 12; Reeves, H.E.L. iii 667, 668.

[2] Thomas, Mayor's Court Rolls xii; Stephen, H.C.L. i 118. At the trial of Elizabeth Canning (1754) 19 S.T. at p. 673 some of the aldermen tried to modify the sentence proposed by Willes, C.J., and his sentence was only carried by a majority.

[3] 4, 5 William IV. c. 36; and see Leverson v. Reg. (1869) 4 Q.B. 394; it is a superior court against which no mandamus will lie, The Queen v. the Justices of the Central Criminal Court (1883) 11 Q.B.D. 479.

the Peace. Successive statutes added to their duties, and made them in time the rulers of the county. They were efficient rulers; for, in the seventeenth century, Coke could say of their rule "it is such a form of subordinate government for the tranquillity and quiet of the realm, as no part of the Christian world hath the like."[1]

To give a full account of the office of the Justice of the Peace would here be out of place. "Long ago," says Maitland, "lawyers abandoned all hope of describing the duties of a justice in any methodic fashion, and the alphabet has become the one possible connecting thread."[2] All that can here be attempted is a brief historical sketch of their rise, and their relation to the judicial system of the country. I shall deal with this subject under the following heads: (1) the rise and general importance of the justice of the peace; (2) the courts held by the justices of the peace; (3) their powers in relation to the apprehension of criminals, and the conduct of the preliminary enquiry in criminal cases; (4) their relation to the courts of common law.

(1) The rise and general importance of the justices of the peace.

We have seen that in Henry II.'s reign the sheriff was the ruler of the county, but that, even then, the crown was beginning to view his power with suspicion.[3] The coroner was placed by his side as a check upon him. But we have seen that the coroner's office became elective.[4] Consequently his efficiency as a guardian of the royal interests declined. It was seen that it was only justices appointed by and acting under commissions from the crown who were capable of controlling effectually the working of the local government. From many experiments made in this direction, from the last years of the twelfth century onwards, there emerged, in the middle of the fourteenth century, the justices of the peace.

In 1195 Hubert Walter the Justiciar issued a proclamation for the preservation of the peace. Knights nominated for the purpose were to take, from all aged fifteen years and upwards, the form of oath contained in the proclamation, to the effect that they would aid the preservation of the peace in certain specified ways.[5] These knights were to receive all prisoners

---

[1] Fourth Instit. 170.   [2] Justice and Police 84.
[3] Above 50, 66.   [4] Above 84.
[5] "Quod omnes homines regni Angliæ pacem domini regis pro posse suo servabunt; et quod nec latrones nec robatores nec eorum receptatores erunt, nec in aliquo eis consentient; et quod cum hujusmodi malefactores scire poterunt, illos pro toto posse suo capient et vicecomiti liberabunt, qui nullo modo deliberentur nisi per dominum regem vel capitalem Justitiam suam; et si illos capere non poterunt, eos ballivis domini regis quicunque fuerint, scire faciunt. Levato autem

arrested, and hand them over to the sheriff. In them we may see the origin of the keepers or conservators of the peace, who are the immediate ancestors of the justices.[1]

During the thirteenth century knights were appointed not only to serve on the commissions of Assize, Oyer and Terminer and Gaol Delivery,[2] but also to perform other specified duties connected with the preservation of the peace. In 1264 Simon de Montfort appointed custodians of the peace; and the institution was continued after the close of the civil wars.[3] In 1285 the Statute of Winchester[4] organized the police system of the country; and, by it, justices were assigned to receive the presentments made by the constables as to infringements of the statute.[5] "Under Edward II. the writs and orders concerning the custodians of the peace are exceedingly numerous and show a slight progression in the function of the office. Indeed, by the close of the reign, the business of the conservator was taking the form which it was to assume in the hands of the justice of the peace under Edward III."[6] In 1327, the first year of Edward III.'s reign, statutory provision was made for the appointment of conservators of the peace in each county.[7] They were given power to punish offenders in 1328;[8] and in 1330[9] their powers were enlarged. They were to receive presentments, and send those presented for trial before the justices of Gaol Delivery; the sheriff and his officers were not to release such persons by writ of mainprize, if not by law mainpernable; and they could punish the sheriff or his officers if they infringed the statute. In 1333,[10] 1337,[11] and 1343[12] there was further legislation confirming or enlarging the powers of the keepers of the peace; and in 1344 persons assigned to keep the peace, together "with other wise and learned in the law" were empowered to hear and determine felonies and trespasses.[13]

clamore insequendi utlagos, robatores, latrones, aut eorum receptatores, omnes sectam illam plene facient pro toto posse suo; et si quem viderint vel manifestum fuerit sectam illam non fecisse, vel sine licentia se ab ea subtraxisse, eos tanquam malefactores ipsos capient et vicecomiti liberabunt, non deliberandos nisi per regem aut ejus capitalem justitiam," Stubbs, Sel. Ch. 264.

[1] For various officials such as coroners, constables, and the like who continued to be ex-officio conservators without being justices of the peace see Bl. Comm. i 338; and cp. Lambard, Eirenarcha Bk. i c. 4; Entick v. Carrington (1765) 19 S.T. at p. 1061 *per* Lord Camden, C.J.; Blackstone includes in his list certain persons, e.g. the judges of the King's Bench, who were ex-officio justices of the peace, above 274-275.

[2] Above 274, 280.
[3] Beard, The Office of Justice of the Peace in England, 20, 21.
[4] 13 Edward I. St. 2.   [5] §6.
[6] Beard, op. cit. 28.   [7] 1 Edward III. St. 2 c. 16.   [8] 2 Edward III c. 6.
[9] 4 Edward III. c. 2; Beard points out, op. cit. 36, that sometimes commissions of Oyer and Terminer were issued to the keepers of the peace, but that this was not usual.
[10] Beard, op. cit. 37-38.   [11] Ibid 39.   [12] Ibid 39-40.
[13] 18 Edward III. St. 2 c. 2.

In 1349 came the Black Death, which swept off a large part of the labouring population of the country.[1] The Ordinance of Labourers (1349), and the ensuing statutes, called into existence a new class of officials—the justices of labourers. From 1349 to 1351 the duty of executing these statutes was entrusted in some cases to the keepers of the peace.[2] From 1351 to 1352 the experiment of joint commissions of the peace and for the execution of these statutes was tried.[3] From 1352 to 1359 the commissions were separated ; and finally in 1359 the commissions were reunited.[4] In 1361 [5] there were assigned in every county in England " one lord and with him three or four of the most worthy in the county with some learned in the law," to keep the peace, to arrest and imprison offenders, to imprison or take surety of suspected persons, and to hear and determine felonies and trespasses done in the county ; and in 1363 they were ordered to hold their sessions four times a year.[6] From about this time they came to be known not as keepers or conservators, but as justices of the peace [7]—a change in their title which denotes an increase in their judicial powers.

Henceforward their duties—police, judicial, and administrative —have been continually added to by the legislature. Lambard, who wrote his classic treatise on the justice of the peace in Elizabeth's reign,[8] remarks [9] that Husey (who was Chief Justice of the King's Bench in 1485) " did thinke that it was enough to loade all the justices of the peace of those days with the execution onely of the statutes of Winchester and Westminster for robberies and felonies ; the statute of forcible entries ; the statutes of labourers, vagabonds, livery, maintenance, embracery, and sheriffs ;" and, he asks, " how many justices thinke you now may suffice (without breaking their backs) to beare so many, not loads but stacks of statutes that have since that time been laid upon them." The "loads and stacks" have been increasing from that time to this.

The number of justices for each county and their qualifications have varied at different periods. A statute of 1388 [10] fixed the number at six for each county, to which number the judges of assize were to be added. Two years later it was raised to eight.[11] But, with the multiplication of their duties, their numbers

---

[1] For the economic effects of the Black Death see vol. ii 459-460; vol. iii 203-206; for an exhaustive account of the legislation produced see Putnam, The Enforcement of the Statutes of Labourers 1349-1359.

[2] Ibid 10-13.   [3] Ibid 13-15.
[4] Ibid 15-17.   [5] 34 Edward III. c. 1.
[6] 36 Edward III. St. 1 c. 12.
[7] They are called Justices in 36 Edward III. St. 1 c. 12.
[8] Vol. iv 117-119.   [9] Bk. i c. 7.
[10] 12 Richard II. c. 10.   [11] 14 Richard II. c. 11.

increased ; and now no certain number is fixed.[1] As to their qualifications, it was enacted in 1389 [2] that they should be the most sufficient knights, esquires and gentlemen of the land ; in 1414 [3] that they should be resident in their counties ; and in 1439 [4] that they should have land to the value of £20 a year—a property qualification which was raised in 1732 [5] to £100 a year. But these qualifications were modified in 1906. It is now sufficient if they reside either in the county or within seven miles thereof, and no property qualification is required.[6]

Both the justices of labourers [7] and the justices of the peace [8] were entitled to wages payable out of the fines inflicted by them. The amount of the wages of the justices of the peace was fixed in 1388 [9] at 4s. a day during the time that the sessions lasted ; but, as their number was restricted to eight by the statute of 1390,[10] it was thought that only eight could claim these wages.[11] Lambard tells us [12] that, when he wrote, the whole allowance was sometimes spent in "defraying their common diet."   In the end these payments became as obsolete as the wages formerly paid to the knights of the shire.

Before entering office they were obliged to "take out their Dedimus Potestatem"—that is take the oath of office and pay certain fees.[13]

Their authority originally depended upon the terms of their commission. But, as succeeding statutes added to their duties, this commission became exceedingly confused, on account, as Lambard says, of "the untoward huddling of things together

---

[1] Bl. Comm. i 340, 341.
[2] 13 Richard II. St. 1 c. 7.
[3] 2 Henry V. c. 4.
[4] 18 Henry VI. c. 11.
[5] 5 George II. c. 18.
[6] 6 Edward VII. c. 16.
[7] Putnam, op. cit. 44-49.
[8] 12 Richard II. c. 10.
[9] Ibid.
[10] 14 Richard II. c. 11 ; exclusive of peers who by this statute were declared not to be entitled to wages.
[11] Webb, Local Government, i 305.
[12] Eirenarcha, Bk. iv. c. 21.
[13] Webb, Local Government i 303 ; in the seventeenth century there were often complaints that justices neglected to perform this duty and were therefore incompetent to act, ibid 321 ; Lambard, Bk. i c. 10 gives the following version of the oath of the justices :—

> " Doe equall right to rich and poor,
>   as wit and law extends :
> Give none advice in any cause,
>   that you before depends :
> Your Sessions hold as statutes bid :
>   the forfeits that befall
> See entered well, and then estreat
>   them to the Chequer all :
> Receive no fee, but that is given
>   by King, good use, or right
> Ne precept send to party self,
>   but to indifferent wight."

and gentlemen incorporated : for abroad in other countries noblemen meddle not with any parcel of justice, but in martial affairs :
matter of justice that belongs to the gownmen ; and this is it that
makes those noblemen the more ignorant and the more op-
pressors ; but here amongst us they are incorporated with those
that execute justice, and so being warriors are likewise made instruments for peace ; and that makes them truly noble." In the
second place the training in the work of government which these
men got as justices made them efficient members of Parliament,
and had no small influence in gaining for Parliament its supremacy in the state. As Gneist truly said,[1] these justices gave the
English constitution " a foundation upon which the conduct of
the highest state business could be left to changing cabinets."

During the last quarter of the nineteenth century great
changes were made in the powers and the personnel of the
justices of the peace. The greater part of their administrative
duties have been placed in the hands of elected councils.[2] They
are no longer drawn exclusively from the class of landed gentry.
Advisory committees assist the Lord-Lieutenant to nominate the
justices,[3] and, in consequence, the persons appointed are more
representative of all classes of the community. But the justices
still retain their judicial powers, and some small remnant of those
administrative powers which gave them, in the sixteenth, seventeenth, and eighteenth centuries, entire control over the local
government of the country.

(2) The courts held by the justices of the peace.

These courts fall into two main classes : (i) The courts of
Quarter or General Sessions; and (ii) The Petty Sessions.

(i) The courts of Quarter or General Sessions.

The courts of quarter sessions for the whole county have
always been held four times a year at times prescribed by statute.[4]
At times other than those fixed by statute courts of general
sessions can be held. The methods and procedure of these
courts followed the pattern usual in the fourteenth century.
Like the sheriffs' tourns, the general Eyre, and, to some extent,
the courts held by the judges of assize, they were more than
mere judicial courts. A jury was summoned, a general charge
as to matters into which the jury must enquire was given by one
of the justices, the jury then made their presentments, and, on

---

[1] History of the English Constitution ii 372.
[2] 51, 52 Victoria c. 41 (County Councils); 56, 57 Victoria c. 73 (Parish and
District Councils).
[3] Halsbury, Laws of England xxi 539.
[4] 36 Edward III. St. 1 c. 12; 12 Richard II. c. 10; 2 Henry VI. St. 1 c. 4;
11 George IV., 1 William IV. c. 70 § 35; 57, 58 Victoria c. 6.

these presentments, indictments were drawn up, and the persons indicted were tried. By means of this process of presentment and indictment the quarter sessions, like the other older courts, not only tried criminal cases, but also supervised the whole administration of local government.[1] It was not till the latter part of the sixteenth, and during the course of the seventeenth centuries, that a procedure more fitted to the conduct of administrative work began to emerge.[2] Of the development of this side of the work of quarter sessions I shall say something in a later volume. Here we are concerned only with the judicial work of the quarter sessions to which these judicial forms continued to be properly applicable.

The jurisdiction of quarter sessions was very wide. It extended nominally to all crimes except treason, subject to the proviso that cases of difficulty must be sent to the assizes. During the eighteenth century the custom sprang up of always sending to the assizes cases which might be capitally punished. Capital cases under the old law were numerous. It was thus, as Stephen points out, an indirect effect of the old law as to capital punishment, that it narrowed the power of the quarter sessions.[3] In 1842 it was enacted that over treason, murder, felony punishable on a first conviction with penal servitude for life, .and certain other specified offences, the quarter sessions should have no jurisdiction.[4] It possesses also an appellate jurisdiction from the petty sessions where such a right has been given by statute.[5]

(ii) The Petty Sessions.

The numerous statutes which conferred jurisdiction upon justices of the peace, often gave to two or more justices the power to inflict penalties for the breach of those statutes. These Acts, however, usually left the form and manner of administering this summary jurisdiction entirely unprovided for. Many difficult questions were thereby caused. Some of them were dealt with by means of writs of certiorari obtained from the court of King's Bench in order to quash convictions before the justices.[6] In 1848[7] an Act was passed which codified the law as to the procedure to be observed by the justices in the exercise of their summary jurisdiction. The name "petty sessions" was given by a statute of 1826 to sessions of the justices held to supervise the lists of persons qualified to serve on juries;[8] but even in 1849

---

[1] Vol. iv 142-144.
[2] Ibid 144-145.
[3] H.C.L. i 114-115.
[4] 5, 6 Victoria c. 38.
[5] Harris, Criminal Law (8th Ed.) 491.
[6] Stephen, H.C.L. i 122, 123; the control of the King's Bench by means of these writs is coeval with the institution of justices, for early illustrations see Putnam, op. cit. 92-97.
[7] 11, 12 Victoria c. 43.
[8] 6 George IV. c. 50 § 10.

it was hardly a technical expression.[1]   It was, however, then becoming the usual name for these courts ; and since that date the powers of the petty sessions to deal with crime either on account of the petty nature of the crime, or on account of the youth of the offender have been considerably enlarged,[2] many reforms are introduced by the Justices of the Peace Act, 1949.[2a]

(3) Their powers in relation to the apprehension of criminals and the conduct of the preliminary enquiry in criminal cases.

The apprehension of criminals.

Under the older statutes which regulated the preservation of the peace—the Assizes of Clarendon (1166) and Northampton (1176) and the Statute of Winchester (1285)—the duty of apprehending criminals devolved upon the inhabitants at large. The Assize of Arms (1181) and the Statute of Winchester contained provisions which defined the arms which all free men must carry.   All were obliged to pursue the criminal when the hue and cry was raised.   Neglect of these duties entailed an amercement of the individual, the township or the hundred.[3]   The sheriffs and the constables were under special obligations, as conservatores pacis, to fulfil these duties.   After the jurisdiction of the justices of the peace was established these duties devolved upon them.   But the statutes which defined their powers gave them no further power to apprehend criminals than that possessed by private persons.   They might arrest persons actually committing, or who had actually committed a felony; or they might arrest a person if *they themselves* suspected, on reasonable grounds, that a felony had been committed.   Lambard states[4] that some justices were accustomed to issue precepts to attach persons suspected *by others* of felony ; but that the whole court, 14 Henry VIII., had condemned the practice.   The reason assigned was, that, if the bailiff who executed the warrant suspected the person, he might arrest without warrant.   If he had no such suspicion the arrest was illegal.   It is true that certain statutes of Philip and Mary's reign gave the justices power to examine prisoners brought before them.[5]   Coke explains that this simply gave the justices power to issue a warrant to a constable to see the peace kept during the apprehension of the person suspected by the accuser.   This warrant is " merely to assist the party that knoweth or hath suspicion of the felony."   It gives no right to break open any man's house in order to apprehend the suspected person,

---

[1] 12, 13 Victoria c. 18 mentions in the preamble "certain meetings of the justices called petty sessions."   [2a] 12, 13, and 14 Geo. 6, c. 101.

[2] Stephen, H.C.L. i 124-126; Maitland, Justice and Police 123-129.

[3] Above 70, 71, 270; Reeves, H.E.L. iii 713-717.   [4] Bk. ii c. 6.

[5] 1, 2 Philip and Mary c. 13; 2, 3 Philip and Mary c. 10; below 296.

"for it is in law the arrest of the party that hath the knowledge or suspicion, who cannot break open any house." In agreement with Lambard he says, " We hold the resolution of the Court, viz. of Brudnel, Pollard, Broke, and Fitzherbert in 14 H. VIII. to be law, that a justice of the peace could not make a warrant to take a man for felony, unless he be indicted thereof, and that must be done in open sessions of the peace." [1]

Nevertheless it is clear both from Coke[2] and Lambard that there was a practice growing up of issuing warrants to arrest suspected persons. Indeed Lambard states some arguments in support of it.[3]

In the seventeenth and eighteenth centuries the convenience of the practice brought it into common use. It was, as Stephen points out, "specially convenient in the case of a hue and cry. If offenders were to be followed from township to township, the different constables of each being required to join, a written authority from a known public officer would be a great convenience." In fact the phrase "to grant a hue and cry" came to signify the issue of a warrant.[4] So common, and indeed necessary, had the practice become that Hale[5] defended its legality. "My lord Coke," he says, " in his jurisdiction of courts hath delivered certain tenets, which, if they should hold to be law, would much abridge the power of justices of peace, and give a loose to felons to escape unpunished in most cases." The language of the older statutes is so vague that Hale makes a very plausible argument upon them. His thesis is that the justices may issue a warrant to apprehend a person suspected of felony, "*though the original suspicion be not in himself but in the party that prays his warrant.*"[6] That, however, is just what the older authorities denied.

Hale's statement of the law for his own day was probably sounder than his history, in this particular point. The power to arrest persons suspected of felony was recognized by several statutes of the eighteenth century.[7] It was put upon a clear statutory basis, and the procedure to be followed was regulated in 1848.[8]

The conduct of the preliminary enquiry in criminal cases.

Early law did not contemplate any preliminary enquiry into the guilt or innocence of an accused person. Criminals were

---

[1] Fourth Instit. 176-178; for a full account of the mediæval law on this topic see vol. iii 598-604.

[2] He says, ibid p. 178, " Though commonly the houses or cottages of poor and base people be by such warrants searched, yet, if it be lawful, the houses of any subject, be he never so great, may be searched by such warrant upon bare surmises."

[3] Bk. ii c. 6.   [4] Stephen, H.C.L. i 190.

[5] P.C. ii 107.   [6] Ibid 109, 110.

[7] Stephen, H.C.L. i 190 n. 2.   [8] 11, 12 Victoria c. 42.

presented for trial either by the jury of presentment, or in consequence of the finding of a coroner's inquest. If they were taken in the act they were generally executed out of hand.[1]

The coroner's inquest must always have partaken somewhat of the character of a preliminary examination ; and we have seen that the powers of the coroner as to taking depositions and binding over witnesses to appear at the trial have been enlarged by statute.[2] Two statutes of Philip and Mary's reign, which conferred similar powers on the justices of the peace, are the origin of this part of their jurisdiction. It was enacted in 1554[3] that prisoners arrested for felony should not be let to bail or mainprize except by two justices in open sessions. These justices, when the prisoner comes before them, " shall take the examination of the said prisoner and information of them that bring him," and shall put into writing the material evidence against the prisoner before they release him on bail. It was enacted in 1555[4] that such examination should take place whether or no the prisoner was actually bailed: and that the justices could bind over to appear at the trial any witnesses against the prisoner whose evidence they deemed to be essential.

These statutes were evidently designed to arm the justices with new powers against prisoners.[5] They do not contemplate a strictly judicial enquiry into the facts of the case.[6] In fact in the seventeenth century the examination conducted by the magistrates was of an inquisitorial nature. The prisoner was closely examined. The witnesses for the prosecution were not examined in his presence. Their evidence was only for the information of the court.[7] Even as late as 1823[8] it was stated to the grand jury that, when a magistrate was conducting this preliminary examination, he was acting inquisitorially and not judicially ; that such proceedings might and ought to be conducted in secret; and that information so ascertained might be communicated to the prosecutor but not to the party accused.

---

[1] P. and M. ii 577, 578.   [2] Above 84-85.

[3] 1, 2 Philip and Mary c. 13.   [4] 2, 3 Philip and Mary c. 10.

[5] For the growth of these ideas in the criminal law of the sixteenth century see vol. v 190-195.

[6] Hale from this point of view compares the provisions of the Act of 1554 which relate to the justice of the peace with the provisions of the same Act which relate to coroners. "The justices of the peace are to put into writing the information . . . *or so much thereof as shall be material to prove the felony ;* but the coroner is to put into writing *the effect of the evidence given to the jury before him being material,* without saying *so much as is material to prove the felony,*" P.C. ii 61. The judges themselves issued the warrants and conducted the preliminary examinations in important cases; thus Coke in Overbury's case (1616) is said to have taken three hundred examinations, Campbell, Lives of the Chief Justices i 279, 280; cp. ibid ii 175-176; Lives of the Norths i 205; S.P. Dom, 1629-1631 38, cxlviii 66.

[7] For instances see Stephen, H.C.L. i 221-228.

[8] Ibid i 227, 228.

In 1836 the Prisoners' Counsel Act [1] allowed accused persons to inspect all depositions taken against them. In 1848 [2] it was enacted that the witnesses for the prosecution should be examined in the presence of the accused. The accused person was allowed to make any statement he pleased, or to call any witnesses he pleased; but he was not to be obliged to do either; and the magistrate must inform him of this. The preliminary examination before the magistrates is thus made an entirely judicial proceeding.

As a matter of fact the establishment of a system of professional police [3] has, in the nineteenth century, more clearly differentiated the functions of the magistrate and the policeman. The magistrate can act as a judge now that he is no longer required to supplement the deficiencies of the police force. It is for the same reason that the apprehension of suspected persons by means of warrants can now no longer be regarded with suspicion. In the seventeenth century the power against which Coke protested, meant the issue of a warrant, and the examination of the prisoner by the detective who was getting up the case. The person so apprehended is now brought before a magistrate who can have no interest in acting otherwise than judicially.

(4) The relation of the justices of the peace to the courts of common law.

The justices of the peace are subjected to the control of the courts of common law by means of the prerogative writs. [4] By means of the writ of certiorari their decisions can always be questioned, unless this right has been taken away by statute. By means of the writ of mandamus they can be ordered to hear a case falling within their jurisdiction.

In former days they were also subject to the control of the Council and the court of Star Chamber. Lambard refers to the court of Star Chamber as the "best guide and direction" [5] a justice can have in dealing with cases of riot. In many cases the Lord Chancellor gave his annual charge to both justices of the peace and justices of assize in the Star Chamber. [6] In many other cases the exercise of their administrative duties was controlled by the Council or the court of Star Chamber. [7] The

[1] 6, 7 William IV. c. 114.
[2] 11, 12 Victoria c. 42; Maitland, Justice and Police, 129.
[3] For an account of this see Stephen, H.C.L. i 194-200, Maitland, Justice and Police, chap. x; above 147.
[4] Above 226 231.   [5] Bk. ii c. 5; cf. 4 Henry VII. c. 12.
[6] Les reportes del cases in Camera Stellata (1593-1609) viii, ix, 19, 56, 101, 186, 326, 367; for some remarks addressed by Bacon to the justices of the peace in 1617 see Spedding, Letters and Life vi 304-306.
[7] Hudson 63, 64, 109; vol. iv 77-79.

abolition of the Star Chamber placed them more directly under the control of the courts of common law. But they were still controlled, in respect of certain of their duties, by departments of the Council, represented in modern times by the Local Government Board and the Board of Trade.[1] As we have seen, modern legislation has transferred most of these administrative duties to elected councils.[2] The result is that, as the judicial duties of the justices are almost their sole duties, their Quarter Sessions are now controlled entirely, or almost entirely, by the courts of common law or their modern representatives — the Supreme Court of Judicature[3] and the Court of Criminal Appeal.[4]

IV. THE JURY

We must now pass from the courts which interpret and apply the rules of the common law to the various methods by which that law has at different periods decided the disputed questions of fact which arise within those courts. This is not the place to attempt to map out minutely the debatable boundary line between law and fact.[5] It is clear that in any legal system the distinction between questions of law and questions of fact is a primary distinction. To apply a fixed rule of law to a given state of facts is one thing. To decide whether one of two alternative states of fact exists, or has existed, is another.

The method almost universally employed by the common law to ascertain the truth about disputed facts is the jury. The jury is, as Blackstone terms it, "The principal criterion of truth in the law of England."[6] Hence we get the well-known maxim, "ad quæstionem facti non respondent judices: ita ad quæstionem juris non respondent juratores."[7] The maxim itself is probably not much older than the seventeenth century.[8] Taken literally it is not true. Incidental questions of fact forming no part of the issue have always been decided by the court. The maxim refers only to questions actually at issue between the parties—not to incidental matters arising before and during the trial. Such questions of fact at issue between the parties the jury "adjudge upon their evidence" and "thereupon give their ver-

---

[1] Maitland, Justice and Police, 87.   [2] Above 292 n. 2.
[3] Below 638.   [4] Above 217-218.
[5] As to this see Thayer, Evidence, chap. v.   [6] Bl. Comm. iii 348.
[7] Altham's case (1611) 8 Co. Rep. at f. 155 a.
[8] Thayer, Evidence, 185 and n. 4; Thayer gives good reasons for the view that Coke is the earliest authority for the maxim, and very likely its author; we shall see that he is also very probably the author of the maxim actio personalis moritur cum persona, vol. iii c. 5; but, because the former maxim neatly expressed the truth, it soon gained currency; thus Vaughan, C.J., in Bushell's case (1670) Vaughan Rep. 149, speaks of it as "that Decantatum in our books."

dict." [1] The jury so employed is the most distinctive, and, in the opinion of those who have had large experience of its working, the most valuable part of the common law system.[2]

In order to understand its origin and history we must go back to a time when a reasonable adjudication upon disputed facts would have been impossible. More primitive methods decided the facts at issue between litigants. Of these we must take some notice, partly because they lingered on as survivals till a late period in the history of English law, but chiefly because we must look for the origin of the jury in a period when these ideas were flourishing. The jury was, so to speak, born into an atmosphere permeated with these ideas; and it naturally long retained many marks of its ancient environment. I shall therefore speak firstly of the Older Methods of Trial, and secondly of Trial by Jury.

The Older Methods of Trial

In modern times we understand by a trial a process of reasoning from evidence by means of which the truth as to the facts in issue is elicited. There were no such trials as this in ancient law. The terms applied to the processes used were probatio, purgatio, or defensio. The term triatio does not become common till the fourteenth century.[3] In fact the parties tried their own cases by processes such as compurgation, ordeal, or battle.[4] The parties themselves, or the court selected the process by which the proof or the defence must be made. This selection by the court has been called the "medial judgment;"[5] and this medial judgment determined "not only what the trial should be, but how it should be conducted and when, and what the consequences should be of this or that result."[6]

The first step was the statement by the plaintiff of his claim;

---

[1] Case of the Chancellor of Oxford (1614) 10 Co. Rep. 56 b; Thayer, Evidence, 189; see Bl. Comm. iii 331-333 for a list of matters determined by the judges by the evidence of their senses.

[2] Below 348.

[3] Thayer, Evidence, 16 n. 1; Maitland, Lectures on the Forms of Action at Common Law 309-310; Bracton saw a clear distinction between the newer processes of assisæ, juratæ, and inquisitiones on the one hand, and, the older processes of purgatio or defensio on the other—"Et sciendum quod sunt assisæ sive juratæ sive inquisitiones de transgressionibus et aliis. Item sunt purgationes, ut si crimen imponatur vel delictum, purgatio erit probatio innocentiæ. Item est defensio contra præsumptionem, quæ nec dicitur jurata sive inquisitio nec purgatio, scilicet ubi quis dicit aliquid esse et inde producit sectam, exinde sequitur probatio contra sectam," f. 290 b.

[4] Thus in the Eyre of Kent (S.S.) ii 54, Spigurnel arg., speaking of a defendant who failed to clear himself by compurgation says, "He put himself on neither jury nor justices, but betook himself to his law, wherein he himself passed judgment on himself, since if he had made his law he would have gone quit of the debt for ever."

[5] Bigelow, History of Procedure chap. viii.   [6] Thayer, Evidence 9.

and, before the proceedings could go any further, there must be more than the plaintiff's mere word. He must produce a secta —a body of witnesses who testified, not to the facts in issue, but to the genuineness of the plaintiff's cause of complaint.[1] They were generally friends and dependents of the plaintiff, and their word was no proof of his case. It merely raised a slight presumption in his favour which the defendant could meet by compurgation.[2] It was only if the assertion of the plaintiff and his secta was backed by strong circumstantial evidence—for instance if a thief had been taken with the stolen goods on him, or if he had other evidence as to the genuineness of his cause of action such as a document—that its production amounted to proof.[3] Magna Carta[4] provided that "no bailiff should for the future put any man to his law on the bare assertion of any person, unless the assertion was backed by trustworthy witnesses produced for this purpose." The meaning of this clause, as the writer of the Year Book of 1304 explains, was not altogether clear; but the opinion which he favoured was that it meant that a defendant could not be compelled to defend himself by wager of law unless the plaintiff produced a sufficient secta.[5] Probably the clause applied both to civil and criminal cases, and meant that no one could be made to prove his innocence by any of the recognized forms of proof unless there was a sufficient prima facie case made out against him, either by the secta of a plaintiff or by the presentment of a jury.[6] But, with the growth of

---

[1] Thayer, Evidence 11.

[2] Bracton, explaining the way in which an exceptio can be proved says, "Item non per sectam, quæ fieri poterit per domesticos et familiares, secta enim probationem non facit, sed levem inducit præsumptionem, et vincitur per probationem in contrarium, et per defensionem per legem," f. 400 b; cp. ibid f. 214 b. "Si autem instrumentum non habuerit, nec se ponere voluerit in juratam, habet tamen sectam unam vel plures forte, sive sint familiares sive non, ex secta sua habet ad minus presumptionem, et standum erit presumptioni, donec probatur in contrarium. Probari poterit contrarium per defensionem et per legem, quia lex vincit sectam."

[3] Thayer, Evidence 13, and cases there cited.

[4] "Nullus ballivus ponat de cetero aliquem ad legem simplici loquela sua, sine testibus fidelibus ad hoc inductis," Charter of 1215 § 38; in 1217 and in subsequent reissues the clause ran, "Nullus ballivus ponat de cetero aliquem ad legem manifestam nec ad juramentum, etc.;" this probably was meant to make it clear that "lex" applied to battle, compurgation, and the jury as well as to ordeal, McKechnie, Magna Carta 375; on the clause as a whole see ibid 370-375.

[5] "Nullus ballivus de cetero ponat aliquem ad legem manifestam. Duplicem habet intellectum; videtur, quod nullus ponatur in juratam nisi fuerit ad hoc summonitus, et per fideles summonitores, et ejus summonitio testificata. Alius intellectus est quod defendens in brevi de debito et aliis brevibus consimilibus non admittatur ad legem suam sine testibus ad hoc inductis. Alius intellectus et melior, quod defendens in brevi de debito et in aliis brevibus consimilibus non ad legem ponatur nisi querens arramaverit sectam versus enim, etc.," Y.B. 32, 33 Ed. I. (R.S.) 516; Fleta ii 63, 10, and Holt, C.J., in City of London v. Wood (1701) 12 Mod. 669 seem to agree.

[6] McKechnie, Magna Carta 372-373; for the recognized forms of proof see below 302-311.

other ideas of a trial, and with the adoption of the jury as the general and usual mode of trying disputed facts, the production of a secta became a mere form. As early as 1314 it was said in argument that it could not be examined.[1] In 1343 the courts decided that this view of the law was correct,[2] and that its existence did not even create a presumption in favour of the plaintiff.[3] But in the twelfth,[4] and perhaps as late as the fourteenth century, it was a necessary form ;[5] and as a purely formal allegation in pleading, it lasted on till 1852. Till that date the plaintiff's declaration always concluded with the words "et inde producit sectam."[6]

When the plaintiff has made his claim and produced his secta, the defendant must make his defence. Both the claim and the defence were made orally ;[7] and, in both, the right form must be used with absolute verbal accuracy—qui cadit a syllaba cadit a tota causa.[8] The issue, thus defined, was then decided by some one of several alternative methods either chosen by the parties, or awarded by the medial judgment of the court. Final judgment followed as of course the result given by the method prescribed. Generally it was the accused or the defendant who must go through the prescribed form to prove that he was not guilty or that he was not liable to the plaintiff.[9] Sometimes, it is true, we see some signs that the court, in deciding as to the sort of proof to be used, or as to which of the parties was to make it, was influenced by rational considerations as to the probabilities of the truth of the contentions of the parties to the

---

[1] Y.B. 7 Ed. II. p. 242.

[2] Y.B. 17, 18 Ed. III. (R.S.) 72.

[3] "*Gaynesford, arg.* In a plea of land, when Suit is tendered, it is only by way of form ; but in a plea which is founded on contracts which requires witnessing, the Suit is to such a degree capable of giving testimony that without Suit, in case exception be taken to the matter, the party is not entitled to an answer. *Shardelow*, J. Certainly it is not so," ibid.

[4] Rot. Cur. Reg. ii 102 (1199) cited Thayer, Evidence 15 n. 5.

[5] Y.B. 18 Ed. II. 582 ; but cf. the Eyre of Kent (S.S.) ii 35—in a case where the plaintiff alleged he had Suit, but did not produce it, and tried to put forward a tally instead, Bereford, C.J., said, " A good pleader would not have tendered Suit in this case, but would have counted in this wise : *And if he will deny it, see here his deed in proof thereof.*"

[6] Stephen, Pleading (Ed. 1827) 370 ; 15, 16 Victoria c. 76 § 49.

[7] For some of these early forms see vol. ii 107, 108, 109, 111

[8] This phrase occurs in the Statute of Wales (1284) § 8—" Neccessarie habet ille qui petit quod narret versus deforciantem et exprimat rationem peticionis suæ, et hoc per verba veritatem continencia sine calumpnia verborum, non observata illa dura consuetudine, qui cadit a sillaba cadit a tota causa."

[9] " The criminal procedure of the barbarians had rested to a great degree on the system of negative proofs. In the absence of positive evidence of guilt, and sometimes in despite of it, the accused was bound to clear himself by compurgation or the ordeal," Lea, Superstition and Force 73 ; so too in civil cases ; thus Fleta ii 63, 11 says, " Semper incumbit probatio neganti ; in paritate autem juris prius admittatur defensor quam pars actrix in probatione."

litigation.[1]   But it was not till the thirteenth century that, under
the influence of the ideas of Roman law, the modern idea began
to emerge that the person who advances a claim or makes a positive assertion should always be put to prove it.[2]   We shall now
see that the nature of some of these older modes of proof was
such that any such general rule would not have been fair to defendants, because, in many cases, proof was not a burden but a
benefit.   It was therefore only right that defendants should be
allowed this benefit of proof.

Such then in outline was the course of the primitive trial.
We must now describe the principal methods [3] known to English
law for deciding the facts in issue.   They were four in number :
Witnesses, Compurgation or Law Wager, Battle, and Ordeal.

(1) *Witnesses.*[4]

Trial by witnesses has a modern sound ; but such a trial
meant in the twelfth century something very different from the
trials of modern law.   These witnesses were analogous, not to
our modern witnesses, but to the secta.   They were persons produced by plaintiff or defendant to swear to a belief in his tale.
"There was no testing by cross examination ; the operative
thing was the oath itself, and not the probative quality of what
was said, or its persuasion on the judge's mind." [5]   The plaintiff
told his tale and produced a secta to support it.   Then the defendant put forward his defence and a body of witnesses to support it.[6]   According as the court considered the one or other
secta to be more credible, so the case was decided.   But, it
would seem, that the credibility of the plaintiff's and defendant's
bands of witnesses was decided in primitive times and much later,
not by the nature of their testimony, but simply by looking to
see if they all told the same tale and by counting their heads.
Thus in 1308-1309 [7] the question at issue was whether a woman's

---

[1] Vol. ii 110, 116 ; and for some tendencies in this direction in the borough courts
see vol. v 107-108.
[2] Lea, op. cit. 74, and references there cited.
[3] For some other subordinate methods of proof see P. and M. ii 637.
[4] P. and M. ii 634-637 ; Thayer, Evidence 17-24.   [5] Ibid 17.
[6] " Si sectam produxerit, hoc est, testimonium hominum legalium qui contractui
inter cos habito interfuerint praesentes, qui a judice examinati, si concordes inveni-
antur, tunc poterit vadiare legem suam contra petentem et contra sectam suam prolatam : ut si duos vel tres testes produxerit ad probandum, oportet quod defensio fiat
per quatuor vel per sex.   Ita quod pro quolibet teste duos producat juratos usque ad
xii," Fleta ii 63, 10 ; it will be observed in this passage that both the secta and the
compurgators are treated as witnesses, so that the two modes of proof shade off into
one another ; the refusal of the courts in the fourteenth century to treat either secta
or compurgators as witnesses made the two modes of trial quite distinct.
[7] Y.B. 1 Ed. II. (S.S.) 111 ; Thayer, Evidence 23 ; cf. Bracton f. 301 b where
apparently the examination of the secta is merely to see " si in omnibus bene con-
veniat."

husband was alive. The woman "came and proved her husband's death by four people who were sworn, and who agreed with each other in all things." At another day the other party "proved that the husband was alive by twelve people who were sworn and who agreed with each other in all things." And because the latter proof "was better and greater than the woman's proof" she lost her action. As late as 1560 in the case of *Thorne* v. *Rolff*[1] an issue as to the life or death of a woman's husband was tried in this way. The plaintiff brought two witnesses, the defendant none; and, though it was admitted that "their testimony tended to no full proof," it was held that the plaintiff must recover because "the better proof"[2] must win the day.

Thus these bands of witnesses were treated as formal tests. Their testimony was not weighed, but, provided they told a consistent tale, their numbers were balanced one against another, and the party whose band of witnesses was the more numerous won. But it is clear that an institution of this kind had in it possibilities of development; and, in the thirteenth century, English lawyers like Bracton, who had learned from the civil and canon law something of a more rational system of procedure, were just the men to encourage these developments. We shall see that it was just this work of rationalizing native customs by ideas drawn from the civil and canon law that they were doing in many branches of English law.[3] And so in the thirteenth century we find several cases in which these bands of witnesses were examined by the judges, and in which a decision was arrived at by considering the credibility of the tales which they told.[4] In a case of the year 1234 conflicting claims to a stray mare were decided by the examination of the two sets of witnesses, and the discovery, as a result of that examination, that the tale of one set was consistent and the other inconsistent.[5] As Maitland says, in the days of Bracton this mode of trial was, under these influences, developing into a serious rival of trial by jury.[6] There were many cases in which such a proof was admissible; and it sometimes almost seems as if a jury is only summoned as a last

---

[1] Dyer 185.

[2] "And their testimony tended to no full proof, but by conjecture and presumptions. . . . And these testimonies were entered *verbatim* upon the record before judgment was given; and no witness of the life of the man was given upon the part of the tenants; therefore it was considered that the demandant should recover seisin, etc. . . . Also it was said that *qui melius probat melius habet*," ibid.

[3] Vol. ii 146, 175-176, 177, 202-206, 269-270.

[4] Bracton thus states the law, "Poterit tamen inculpatus ita excipere et respondere, quod uterque onerabitur ad sectam producendam, et cum hinc inde fuerunt secta diligenter examinata. pro ea judicabitur quæ probabilior et verisimilior esse probabitur," f. 159.

[5] Bracton's Note Book, case 1115; P. and M. ii 635.

[6] Ibid 636; cf. Calendar of Mayor's Court Rolls, xxxvii-xxxix, 102, 118, 182.

resort.[1]   Probably if lawyers of Bracton's school had continued to develop English law, trial by the inquest of a jury would have developed into a procedure something like the inquisitory procedure of the canon law,[2] and jury and witnesses alike would have been governed by the rules as to proof which the canon lawyers were elaborating.[3]

But, fortunately for English law, this was not to be.   As Maitland has pointed out, the jury was being adapted for judicial purposes before the inquisitory machinery of the canon law had been developed.[4]   The lawyers of Edward I.'s reign rarely knew as much canon law as Bracton.[5]   They were much more at home with a jury ; and to submit the facts to a jury was much less trouble than to weigh testimony.[6]   Therefore the trial by jury ousted the trial by witnesses before that trial, in its rationalized form, had had time to become familiar to them.   The modern witness, and the modern law of evidence only gradually began to appear when, in the course of the sixteenth century, the jury were losing their character of witnesses.[7]   In one case, and in one case only, did the old trial by witnesses survive.   The question whether a husband was dead, so that his widow could claim dower, was tried in this way till 1834.[8]   This may possibly have originated in the fact that it was difficult to prove death by a jury in cases where the husband had died beyond the seas.[9]   However that may be, it lingered on as a solitary survival.[10]

---

[1] " Si autem neutra pars sectam habuerit, nec probationem, nec saltem præsumptionem, nec instrumentum, et utraque pars de veritate ponat se super patriam pro defectu sectæ vel alterius probationis quam ad manum non habuerit, tunc fiat inquisitio de veritate," Bracton, f. 304 b ; for some of the cases in which this mode of proof was used in the thirteenth century see Thayer, Evidence 19-24.

[2] Below 315-320.

[3] See Bracton ff. 396, 396 b, where a trial of the validity of a charter by both the witnesses to the charter and an inquest is contemplated—obviously both are treated as witnesses ; for this practice see below 334.

[4] P. and M. ii 636—" The main institute of our new procedure is the inquest of the country.   This has taken possession of England before people have thought of balancing the evidence given by two sets of witnesses."

[5] Vol. ii 287 and n. 4.

[6] P. and M. ii 636 ; thus in 1346 it was ruled by Sharshulle, J., that " in every case in which enquiry is to be made as to the points of the writ by assize or by jury, no proof by witness can be made," Y.B. 20 Ed. III. (R.S.) ii 168-170 ; below 318.

[7] Below 334-336 ; vol. ix 178-185.

[8] P. and M. ii 636 : Y.B. 16 Ed III. (R.S.) ii 86-90 ; Selden, Notes to Fortescue, De Laudibus c. 21 ; Coke, Fourth Instit. 279 ; Faux v. Barnes (1698) 1 Ld. Raym. 174 ; Reeves, H.E.L. ii 401-402 ; it should be noted that in 1313 the question whether a life tenant was dead or alive was also tried in this way, Y.B. 6, 7 Ed. II. (S.S.) 59—from which it would seem that by that date this mode of trial was being restricted to the proof of life or death, but that it was not quite so restricted as it afterwards became.

[9] P. and M. ii 636 ; Reeves, H.E.L. ii 401 ; cp. Y.B. 20 Ed. III. (R.S.) ii 168-170.

[10] Proof of age, which formerly used to be tried by witnesses, was in 1515 tried by jury ; but the jurors in this case still retained a trace of the older mode of proof

But naturally, as a law of evidence arose, it tended to change its character. Though, in the thirteenth century, rationalizing influences drawn from the canon law had failed to make it an effective rival to the jury, in the seventeenth century rationalizing influences drawn from the common law converted this old trial by witnesses into "a trial by the justices upon proofs made before them." [1]

This method of trial disappeared in 1834 when, with the abolition of the real actions, the single case in which it was applicable disappeared. [2]

(2) *Compurgation or law wager.* [3]

If a defendant on oath and in a set form of words [4] will deny the charge against him, and if he can get a certain number of other persons (compurgators) to back his denial by their oaths, he will win his case. If he cannot get the required number, or they do not swear in proper form, "the oath bursts," and he will lose. [5] Though oaths were used in the Roman law of procedure, this institution of compurgation was not known to it. [6] It was, however, common to the laws of many of the barbarian tribes who overran the Roman empire. [7] Because it was so common and so widespread the church adopted it. Churchmen who could command the services of their fellow ecclesiastics as compurgators found it to be a system "admirably suited for their defence in an age of brute force." [8]

According to the older formulas the compurgators took the same oath as their principal. They swore that he did not owe the debt, or that he was not guilty. And therefore they were liable to the penalties for perjury in just the same way as their principal. [9] But, in the course of the twelfth century, it came to be thought that the compurgators should only be required to swear to their belief in the truth of their principal's assertions; and to this opinion legal sanction was given by Innocent III. [10] This was due to a wish to remove the temptation to commit

by a band of witnesses in that each could give a reason for his decision, Keilway 177, cited Thayer, Evidence 20.
[1] Case of the Abbot of Strata Mercella (1592) 9 Co. Rep. at p. 30 b.
[2] Thayer, Evidence 24.
[3] Ibid 24-34; Lea, Superstition and Force, Essay I.; P. and M. ii 631-634; Bl. Comm. iii 341-348.
[4] For these forms see Lea, op. cit. 58; Bl. Comm. iii 343.
[5] P. and M. ii. 599.　　　　　[6] Lea, op. cit. 34.
[7] " The Salians, the Ripuarians, the Alamanni, the Baioarians, the Lombards, the Frisians, the Norsemen, the Saxons, the Angli and Werini, the Anglo-Saxons and the Welsh, races whose common origin must be sought in the prehistoric past all gave to this form of purgation a prominent position in their jurisprudence, and it may be said to have reigned from southern Italy to Scotland," ibid.
[8] Lea, op. cit. 35.　　　　[9] Ibid 64-65.　　　　[10] Ibid 71-72.

perjury; but it destroyed much of the efficacy of this method of proof, because it prevented any effective punishment of a compurgator who swore falsely.[1] Partly for this reason, partly because the revived study of the civil law was teaching men more modern ideas about procedure and evidence, compurgation about this period began to be looked on with disfavour. But it still had many centuries of life before it, and it was in the two succeeding centuries that precise rules were laid down by the common law as to the forms which must be used in carrying out this process. For instance, there does not seem to have been originally any certain rule as to the number of compurgators required. Three to six compurgators were generally thought sufficient in the manorial courts;[2] and Fleta thought that their number should always be double that of the secta.[3] It was not till 1342[4] that it was settled that the number must be twelve. Then, too, in the fourteenth century some very minute rules were laid down as to the manner in which compurgation must be made where a married woman was sued for her ante-nuptial debt;[5] and in 1344-1345 a case is reported to show how a dumb person must wage his law.[6]

Cases of this kind show that compurgation was still a living thing. In fact it was used frequently in the manorial courts;[7] in the courts of boroughs, where it was valued as an alternative to trial by battle;[8] and in the ecclesiastical courts.[9] And, although in the twelfth century it was viewed with disfavour in the royal courts, it was only very gradually that it became an institution of negligible importance. The Assize of Clarendon (1166) enacted that accused persons of bad character should, although they had successfully made their law, depart from the kingdom within eight days.[10] The assizes took its place in real

---

[1] Lea, op. cit. 72.

[2] Select Pleas in Manorial Courts (S.S.) 7, 18, 37—six; 140, 151—three; 173 —five.

[3] II. 63, 10, cited above 302 n. 6.

[4] Y.B. 16 Edward III. (R.S.) ii 16; Co. Litt. 295; Bl. Comm. iii 343.

[5] "The law was made in this form. The wife held her hand over the book, and the husband held his under the book and made the law in his own name and in the name of his wife. And the case was that the loan was made to the wife while she was sole, and therefore she put her hand over the book, etc. But if the loan had been made to the wife while she was covert, in the opinion of some she would not have held her hand over the book, etc ; nor would the husband have made the law in his own name and in that of his wife jointly, but in his own name only," Y.B. 4 Ed. II. (S.S.) 13; cf. Y.B. 2, 3 Ed. II. (S.S.) 67; for the reason of the distinction between ante and post nuptial debts see vol. iii 531-532.

[6] Y.B. 18, 19 Ed. III. (R.S.) 290.   [7] P. and M. ii 632.

[8] Ibid 632-633; cf. Y.B. 20 Ed. III. (R.S.) i 134-136, where a citizen of London, having offered to prove his case by battle, the City objected, and claimed that the court ought not to allow him to wage battle; Mayor's Court Rolls, xxx-xxxvii.

[9] P. and M. ii 634.

[10] "Vult enim dominus rex quod ipsi qui facient legem suam et mundi erunt per legem, si ipsi fuerint de pessimo testimonio et publice et turpiter diffamati testi-

actiohs,[1] except in the case of incidental questions arising in these actions—e.g. as to whether the defendant had been duly summoned.[2] It was not allowed when the crown was a party; and this excluded it from criminal prosecutions, and proceedings in the court of Exchequer.[3] It was never allowed when trespass, deceit or forcible injury was the gist of the action.[4]

But, though its scope was thus narrowed, it could still be sometimes used in certain of the older personal actions—in Debt, Detinue, and Account; and, when it could be used, the right of action did not survive against the executor of a deceased defendant.[5] The executor could not swear that his testator did not owe because he did not know the truth, and therefore it was thought that he could not be made liable at all. Even in these three personal actions this method of proof could not always be used. Thus if Debt was brought on a deed,[6] or if it was brought for a penalty provided by a statute for some wrongful act,[7] there could be no defence by compurgation. Generally it seems to have been confined to cases in which a plaintiff had nothing more than his bare word to support his action.[8] In such cases it was thought (not altogether unreasonably) that the defendant's oath, backed by the oaths of twelve other persons, was a sufficient defence.[9] Even in cases of this kind the law was always ready to find excuses for excluding this defence. Thus if Debt was brought for services rendered by a person who was under a legal obligation to render them—for instance an attorney for his fees—compurgation was excluded;[10] and it was only a defendant's own acts which could be proved in this way.[11] But, though the occasions upon which the defence could be used were limited, as long as the personal actions of Debt, Detinue, and Account were in frequent use, there were opportunities for its use. It declined as they ceased to be used. We shall see that, in the course of the sixteenth and seventeenth centuries, much more efficient substitutes were found for them. Debt was superseded by Assumpsit,[12] Detinue by Trover,[13] and Account

monio multorum et legalium hominum, fores jurent terras regis, ita quod infra VIII. dies mare transibunt nisi aura eos detinuerit," § 14.

[1] Below 327-329; Y.B. 6, 7 Ed. II. (S.S.) 82-83.
[2] Y.B. 16 Ed. III. (R.S.) ii xix, xx; Bl. Comm. iii 345.
[3] Ibid 346, 347.   [4] Ibid 346; cf. Bracton f. 315 b.
[5] Eyre of Kent (S.S.) ii 41; Bl. Comm. ii 347.
[6] Y.B. 3, 4 Ed. II. (S.S.) 200.
[7] City of London v. Wood (1701) 12 Mod. 669.
[8] Y.B. 19 Ed. III. (R.S.) 328.
[9] Y.B. 16 Ed. III. (R.S.) ii xviii, xix.   [10] Bl. Comm. iii 346.
[11] " No one can make his law in respect of the act of another; and since you say that they did not request your services, it is not of an act of your own that you are offering to make your law," Y.B. 5 Ed. II. (S.S.) 2 per Staunton, J.
[12] Vol. iii 429 seqq.   [13] Ibid 350-351; vol. vii 402 seqq.

by the equitable remedies provided by the court of Chancery.[1]
Thus, as Blackstone said,[2] compurgation was " out of use, being
avoided by the mode of bringing the action, but not out of
force."   In 1708,[3] 1799,[4] and 1824 actions were successfully
defended in this way.   The case of *King* v. *Williams*[5] in 1824
was the last instance of its use.   It was finally abolished in
1833.[6]

(3) *Battle.*[7]

Trial by battle is almost universally found among the barbarian tribes from whom the nations of modern Europe trace
their descent.   It was not merely an appeal to physical force
because it was accompanied by a belief that Providence will give
victory to the right.   Christianity merely transferred this appeal
from the heathen deities to the God of Battles.   The trial by
battle is the *judicium Dei* par excellence.

The Anglo-Saxons seem to have been almost the only nation
who did not possess it.   It appeared in England as a Norman
novelty.[8]   But after its appearance it was used, here as abroad,
to settle a large variety of disputed questions.   Witnesses called
by the adverse party, and even one's own witnesses, if they
appeared to be adverse, might be compelled to defend their
veracity by the battle.[9]   A court might be compelled to defend
its judgment in this manner.[10]   A man could in this way prove
his innocence of crime, his right to property, or right to obtain
payment of a debt.[11]   It was used, not merely in the ordinary
litigation of private persons, but also in international controversies.   When the kings of Castile and Navarre referred their
claims to Henry II., each side was accompanied by champions
to settle in the usual way any incidental points which might

---

[1] Below 458-459; in Account it was allowed in 1346 though the plaintiff had
tallies to prove the payment of the money, Y.B. 20 Ed. III. (R.S.) i 448.
[2] Comm. iii 348.   [3] Lea, op. cit. 86.   [4] Ibid.
[5] 2 B. and C. 538.   [6] 3, 4 William IV. c. 42 § 13.
[7] Neilson, Trial by Combat; Lea, Superstition and Force, Essay II.; Thayer,
Evidence, 39-46; P. and M. ii 597, 630, 631.
[8] Lea 115; Thayer, Evidence, at p. 41, points out that it was therefore unpopular, that a large scope was given to the ordeal, and that when that was
abolished there was an " unusually wide gap " to be filled by the new method of
trial by jury.
[9] Bracton f. 151, "cum autem warrantus præsens fuerit, aut statim warrantizat,
aut defendat quod ei warrantizare non debet, et negat.   Et quo casu, si negaverit,
oportet quod appellatus, qui in seysina fuerit, hoc disrationet versus eum per
corpus suum, et sic perveniri poterit inter eos ad duellum; " in some cases a party
might vary some of the facts stated by him in former proceedings, and prove these
variations in this way, ibid f. 157.
[10] Glanvil viii 8; P. and M. ii 663, 664; Lea 123, 124; Reeves, H.E.L. i 206;
above 73 n. 7.
[11] As to debt see Glanvil x 5; P. and M. ii 203; but battle soon ceased to be
available in such cases, ibid 204.

arise. "A duellist in fact seems to have been reckoned a necessary adjunct to diplomacy." [1]

Thus in early law to begin a law suit, or even to be a witness in a law suit when the other side was skilled in warlike weapons, was a perilous process. It was only certain classes, such as infants, women, or those over sixty years of age who could decline the battle. [2] They might employ champions; and soon the power to appoint champions became extended to able-bodied litigants. But it is clear that "the use of a professional gladiator is inconsistent with a pious reference to the judgment of God." [3] In England the champion was a witness; and if it could be proved that he was perjuring himself he was liable to lose a hand or foot. [4] But, in spite of this, champions were freely used; and in 1275 they were recognized by a statute, which enacted that they need not swear as to their own knowledge of the cause which they were hired to maintain. [5] Churches, [6] landowners, [7] and communities permanently retained such champions. [8]

The forms of a trial by battle are described at length by Blackstone, [9] as such a trial was still part of the law of England when he wrote. But we can see that even when Glanvil was writing it was beginning to be looked upon with disfavour. The manner in which he contrasts the trial by battle with the new form of trial by the Grand Assize shows that the best lawyers already distrusted it. [10] It became obsolete for reasons very similar to those which were fatal to compurgation. The church turned against it. [11] It appeared merely barbarous to those learned in the civil law. [12]

In England it lasted till the nineteenth century as a possible alternative in real actions to the Grand Assize, and as a means

---

[1] Lea 129, 130.

[2] See the judgment of Ellenborough, C.J., in Ashford v. Thornton (1818), 1 B. and Ald. 405, 456.

[3] Lea 182. The foreign civilians compared them with the Roman gladiators, ibid 187.

[4] Bracton f. 151 b, citing the case of Elias Pigo; Glanvil ii 3; the champion must assert that he knows the truth of the cause for which he fights, P. and M. ii 604.

[5] 3 Edward I. c. 41 (Statute of Westminster I.).

[6] Lea 197, citing an agreement of 1258 between the abbey of Glastonbury and Henry de Fernbureg.

[7] P. and M. ii 630.   [8] Ibid 664; Lea 196, 197.

[9] Comm. iii 338-341; App. XXVII; cp. Bolland, Year Book Manual, 96-97.

[10] II. 7. "In the midst of the dry details of his treatise we come suddenly upon a passage full of sentiment, which testifies to the powerful contemporaneous impression made by the first introduction of the organized jury into England," Thayer, Evidence, 41, 42.

[11] Lea 208; Innocent III. condemned it at the Lateran council 1215.

[12] Ibid 211, 212; in 1231 Frederic II. in his code for Naples prohibited it when any other proof was possible; but Staunford who wrote in 1557 on the pleas of the crown still professes belief in it, Pleas of the Crown c. 15.

of disproving an appeal of murder.[1] It was practically obsolete
by the end of the thirteenth century.   When it does occur in the
Year Books it is described as though it was a legal curiosity.[2]
Isolated cases, however, still kept it in remembrance.   In 1571
Dyer reports how the judges in their scarlet robes and the
serjeants adjourned to Tothill fields where a crowd of four thousand
persons had gathered to witness the fight.[3]   But the demandant
made default and the fight did not take place.   Another case
occurred in 1638,[4] but, owing to the interposition of Charles I.,
who ordered the judge to find some method of preventing it,[5] no
fight took place.   A bill to abolish it was proposed in the Long
Parliament ; but it was not carried ;[6] and the case of *Ashford* v.
Thornton[7] (1818) showed that battle was still a legal method of
proof in appeals of murder.   In 1819 trial by battle was for all
purposes abolished.[8]

(4) *Ordeal.*[9]

Trial by battle was in a sense a mode of trial by ordeal.   The
trial by ordeal rests upon the belief that God will intervene by a
sign or a miracle to determine a question at issue between two
contending parties.   This belief is almost universally found
among primitive races.   Without taking account of less important
forms of the ordeal,[10] we find that the person who can carry red-
hot iron, who can plunge his hand or his arm into boiling water,
who will sink when thrown into the water, is deemed to have
right on his side.[11]   The belief is so natural that very modern
illustrations of it are not wanting.   Mr. Lea tells us that in 1811
a Neapolitan noble, suspecting the chastity of his daughter, exposed her to the ordeal of fire, from which she barely escaped
with her life.[12]   Like the other methods of proof it decayed ; and
for very similar reasons.   It opened the door to corruption.[13]   It

---

[1] Battles in the military court before the constable and marshal are quite
distinct ; the arms, for instance, are different, Bl. Comm. iii 337, 339 ; Neilson 167,
168 ; cp. " The order of battel in the Court of Chivalry," composed by Thomas of
Woodstock, Duke of Gloucester, Black Book of the Admiralty (R.S.) i 300-329.

[2] Thayer, Evidence, 43, 44 ; see Y.BB. 17 Ed. III. (R.S.) 20 (appeal of murder) :
20 Ed. III. (R.S.) i 482 (writ of right) ; Fitzherbert, Ap. *Corone* pl. 78 (appeal
of robbery) ; it had begun to die out early in the thirteenth century, Select Pleas of
the Crown (S.S.) xxiv.

[3] Lowe v. Paramour, Dyer 301.

[4] Claxton v. Lilburn, cited Lea 244, 245.   [5] Lea, op. cit. 244.

[6] Ibid 245 ; see Hist. MSS. Com. Fourth Rep. App. Pt. I. 48, 59, 95 for some
petitions to Parliament by the parties in the case of Claxton v. Lilburn.

[7] 1 B. and Ald. 457.   [8] 59 George III. c. 46.

[9] Lea, Essay III. ; Thayer, Evidence, 34-39 ; P. and M. ii 596, 597.

[10] See Lea 334-379.

[11] For details as to these see ibid 278, 286, 318.

[12] At p. 317 ; for other modern instances of a similar sort of superstition see
ibid 290, 357, 367, 397.

[13] Lea 404, 405.

was hard to get convictions.   Between 1201 and 1219 Maitland
has only found one case in which it did not acquit the accused.[1]
William Rufus, on an occasion when it had let off fifty persons
whom he wished to see convicted, openly mocked at it.[2]   The
Assize of Clarendon enacted that persons of bad fame who had
successfully passed through the ordeal should abjure the kingdom.[3]
Finally it was condemned by the Lateran Council of 1215.   In
England this decree was promptly observed.   In a writ addressed
by Henry III. to certain of his itinerant justices in 1219 the use
of the ordeal was prohibited.[4]   For this reason it is not mentioned
as a method of proof in Bracton's work.   We shall see that the
gap thus left was one of the causes which helped on the growth
of trial by jury.[5]

Such were the older methods of proof.   The court was interested simply in determining which of the two parties must go
through the forms of the selected proof, and in seeing that the
forms were observed.   The decision followed, as of course.
They seem to us barbarous and unreasonable.   But, for the age
in which they flourished, it is difficult to see that any other
methods would have been possible.   A judicial mind is not one
of the possessions of the impulsive person who feels keenly ; and
such a temperament is the prevailing characteristic of a barbarous
race.   We do not expect, even in modern times, an impartial
account of contemporary political events.   Lawsuits in a
primitive age, when men were bound closely together by ties of
kindred or neighbourhood, were more exciting than politics are
to us.   Many persons regard the submission of international
disputes to arbitration as visionary, and even cowardly.   It must
have appeared to men of that time as absurd to submit their
feuds to the decisions of a court.   Trial by battle was the obvious
solution ; and law obtained a great triumph when it regulated its
conditions.   The age was superstitious, and miracles were plentiful because they were believed.   It did not appear absurd to
hope that God would protect the right.   But it was also an age
of corruption ; and in a really corrupt age it is easier to meet
a perjured claim by more detailed and particular perjury than
to establish the truth.   Battle, ordeal, and compurgation were

[1] Select Pleas of the Crown (S.S.) 75.
[2] Eadmer, Hist. Nov. (R.S.) 102, " Igitur cum principi esset relatum, condem-
natos illos tertio judicii die simul omnes inustis manibus apparuisse, stomachatus,
taliter fertur respondere, Quid est hoc ?   Deus est justus judex ?   Pereat qui deinceps hoc crediderit.   Quare, per hoc et hoc, meo judicio amodo respondebitur, non
Dei, quod pro voto cujusque hinc inde plicatur."
[3] § 14 cited above 306 n. 10.
[4] For the writ see below 323 n. 10 ; Thayer, Evidence 37, 38 ; P. and M. ii 597.
[5] Below 323-324.

suited to the age in which they flourished.   Growing civilization demanded a clearer and a more certain test.

Trial by Jury

I shall deal with the history of trial by jury under the five following heads : (1) The origin and the English development of the jury ; (2) The different varieties of jury ; (3) The development of the judicial functions of the jury ; (4) Methods of controlling the jury ; (5) The legal and political effects of the jury system.

(1) The origin and the English development of the jury.

" Everywhere," says Maine,[1] " in the Teutonic countries we find deputies of the king exercising authority in the ancient courts, insisting that justice be administered in the king's name, and finally administering a simpler justice of their own amid the ruins of the ancient judicial structures fallen everywhere into disrepute and decay." The jury is one of the most famous of the devices by which the king introduced into the law a simpler, a more rational, and a more equitable method of administering justice than any of the methods provided by the archaic formalism of the older customary laws.

The Carlovingian kings, "imitating it may be the procedure of the Roman fiscus, assumed the privilege of determining their rights by means of an inquisitio."[2] They summoned the members of any community they pleased, and made them supply any information which they desired touching the administration of their government. Such information might be required either for the purposes of a pending litigation, or to supply information upon such matters as the detection of crime or the misconduct of officials. This institution survived in the provinces conquered by the Normans. It was made use of by the Norman dukes, and brought by them to England.[3] It is this institution which is the root from which the English jury springs. As Maitland says,[4] the jury, when first it makes its appearance in England, is, in essence, " a body of neighbours summoned by some public officer to give, upon oath, a true answer to some question." It may be that England was not wholly unprepared to receive the jury when it first made its appearance. We shall see that the church had been developing for its own purposes an inquisitory

[1] Early Law and Custom 172.

[2] P. and M. i 120; Thayer, Evidence 47-48; see the references to the Theodosian code cited by Brunner, Schwurgerichte 74 n. 1.

[3] P. and M. i 120; Thayer, Evidence 47-48; for a very full account of the development of the jury in Normandy see Haskins, Norman Institutions chap. vi.

[4] P. and M. i 117.

procedure which it was applying in its own courts;[1] and, "in the days of Dunstan and Oswald the English church was borrowing ideas and institutions from the Frankish."[2] Some of the Scandinavian nations seem to have evolved an institution which was something like a jury.[3] But, if we except the passage about the accusing thegns in Ethelred's law[4] there seems to be nothing in the Anglo-Saxon laws, secular or ecclesiastical, which suggests a jury. This single passage from Ethelred's law does not carry us very far. It may be that such an institution might have developed into a jury ; but, as we have seen,[5] it does not necessarily point to the existence of any similar institution. And so we must conclude with Maitland that though there may be more than one possible origin for the jury, though England may have been prepared for its introduction, it was definitely introduced by the Norman kings.[6]

If this is the origin of the jury it is not surprising to find that its sphere, when it made its appearance in England, was wide. Domesday Book, which was, as we shall see, an enquiry into the extent, value, and tenure of the greater part of the land of England,[7] was compiled from the verdicts of jurors. The enquiry was made "by the oath of the sheriff, and all the Barons and their Frankish men, and of the whole hundred, and of the priest, reeve, and six villeins from each township."[8] In a suit about some land at Ely about 1080 certain English were chosen to say upon oath what they knew of the facts.[9] Henry II. made the most extensive use of it in all departments of government.[10] Thus under the Assize of Clarendon and Northampton very comprehensive questions were to be addressed to juries. They were required to answer, among other things, as to persons suspected of crimes, as to escheats, as to outlaws, as to the misdoings of officials.[11] The Inquest of Sheriffs required them to answer a series of interrogatories as to the doings of the sheriffs.[12] The ordinance of the Saladin Tithe required them to answer questions as to the property of their neighbours, in order that the tax might be fairly assessed.[13] We have already seen how extensively it was used by the justices in Eyre to supervise all the activities of the local courts, whether judicial or administrative.[14]

---

[1] Below 315. [2] P. and M. i 121. [3] Ibid 122.
[4] Above 12 n. 10. [5] Ibid.
[6] P. and M. i 122. [7] Vol. ii 155 seqq.
[8] Inquisitio Eliensis, cited Stubbs, Sel. Ch. 86.
[9] Bigelow, Placita Anglo-Normanica 24 ; see also Haskins, Norman Institutions 234-235.
[10] See Haskins, op. cit. 235-236.
[11] Stubbs, Sel. Ch. 143, 150. [12] Ibid 148.
[13] Ibid 160. [14] Above 268-271.

More especially is Henry II.'s reign remarkable for the use which he made of a jury for the purpose of civil litigation connected with land. The Grand Assize, the possessory assizes, and the assize utrum apply this procedure to settle questions of the ownership and possession of land held by a lay tenure, and to determine whether the land is held by a lay or an ecclesiastical tenure.[1] As Maitland has said, this meant that Henry II. " placed at the disposal of litigants in certain actions that inquest of the country which ever since the Norman Conquest had formed part of the governmental machinery in England." [2]

This system of enquiry by jurors was used not only by the central courts, but also by the local courts. We have seen that it was used in the tourn and leet, by the coroner, and in the quarter sessions of the justices of the peace.[3] And in these local course the jury continued to be used for general administrative purposes long after it had come to be used almost entirely for judicial purposes in the central courts.[4] One reason for this limitation of its functions in the sphere of central government is to be found in the rise and growth of Parliament in the thirteenth and fourteenth centuries. When Parliament became the grand inquest of the nation there was no longer any need to send judges round the country to collect information or to assess taxes by means of the inquests of juries. Another reason is to be found in the fact that the machinery of the general Eyre became a less suitable instrument for the supervision and control of the local government as the work of government grew more complex.[5] So gradually, in the course of the fourteenth century, the use of the jury in connection with the central government came to be chiefly confined to judicial functions. It is this use of the jury, and its development under the exigencies of this use, that is peculiar to England.

Why was it peculiar to England? We have seen that the jury came from abroad; and in France there is plenty of evidence that, down to the thirteenth century and later, juries were used both for administrative purposes and in litigation. French law long knew an "inquisitio per turbam" by means of which an enquiry could be made into the contents of a body of customary law. It goes back to the days of the Carolingian kings; and,

---

[1] Above 47, 275-276; below 327-330.

[2] P. and M. ii 602; Professor Haskins, Norman Institutions 198 seqq. has proved that Geoffrey, the father of Henry II., directed that litigation as to the See of Bayeux should be tried " secundum assisam meam; " but this assize, being made for a particular case, can hardly be said to antedate the general assizes made by Henry II. for England; at the same time this and other cases cited by Professor Haskins shows that trial by sworn inquest was growing more and more frequent.

[3] Above 77, 85, 136, 292-293.

[4] Above 293; vol. iv 135-137, 142-144.   [5] Above 272.

like the jury, its members gave through its foreman a collective verdict from its own knowledge.[1] Then, too, Beaumanoir in the thirteenth century recognizes a procedure by which a person arrested on suspicion might agree to be tried by his country, and could be forced to give that consent—a procedure almost identical with the English trial by petty jury;[2] and both in ecclesiastical law, and in some of the older French customs, a procedure by which a jury can present a person as suspected was known.[3] Why did these institutions decay in France while they flourished and developed in England?

The answer must be sought in the very different course which the legal history of the two countries has pursued.

In France the royal power was obliged to struggle for supremacy against great feudatories. The struggle was long and doubtful; and the crown in creating a centralized government owed much to the doctrines of the civil and canon law that had come with the legal renaissance of the twelfth century.[4] The canon lawyers, at the end of the twelfth and the beginning of the thirteenth century, had invented a new procedure, wholly opposed to the older forms, which was based upon an inquisitio of a kind very different from the old Carolingian inquisitio. It is true that, like the Carolingian inquisitio, it was a procedure based, not on the action of the injured party, but on the action of the state. It was promoted by the judge or by some person who set the judge in motion. But the subsequent procedure differed entirely from the procedure of the old inquisitio. Under the older procedure the person accused might clear himself by one of the older methods of proof. Under this new procedure the accused was arrested; and then followed a searching examination both of the accused himself and of witnesses.[5] On paper this was a fair and rational mode of trial as, to secure a conviction the canon law exacted full proof—that is two witnesses who had seen the crime committed.[6] But, as it was difficult to get this full proof, the lawyers soon began to think it lawful to take all measures to get it. The scales were weighted against the accused

[1] Brissaud, Histoire du Droit Francais i 245-247; Esmein, Histoire du Droit Francais 794-795; Brissaud, op. cit. i 245, says, "La turbe est une sorte de jury. L'un des témoins ou sages coutumiers qui la composent, élu comme notre chef du jury, le rapporteur de la turbe, répond au nom du tous. Ceux-ci ne sont pas interrogés un à un; on les questionne tous ensemble. La reponse—qu'on aurait pu appeller *verdict* au sans étymologique du mot, *vere-dictum*—est collective, tandisque, dans l'enquête ordinaire, elle est individuelle."

[2] Esmein, History of Continental Criminal Procedure (Continental L. Hist. Series) 64-66.

[3] Ibid 83-84; P. and M. i 121.

[4] Vol. ii 122, 253-254; vol. iv 190-196.

[5] Esmein, History of Continental Criminal Procedure 79-83, 85 seqq.

[6] Ibid 259-260; P. and M. ii 656-657.

by means of admissions extracted by torture and witnesses examined in secret.[1]   Naturally the old idea that the accused was in the position of a defendant, as against whom the state must proceed under much the same rules as any other plaintiff, died out.   From the moment of his arrest the state acted on the presumption that the accused was guilty.[2]   This procedure gradually made its way into the law of all continental states. It became part of the common law of Europe, and stands out as the great rival to the system of trial by jury which had been developed in England.

The English state in the eleventh and twelfth centuries had a government which was more highly centralized than that of any state of Europe.   That it had acquired such a government was due to the extent of the power of the crown.   Thus it happened that the delegates of royal power could make their influence felt all over the country, and royal justice everywhere superseded the justice administered by the local courts.   One of the most important instruments of the royal power was the inquisition held under the supervision of a royal judge by means of a jury.   And, wherever the royal justice was introduced, this method of determining facts accompanied it.   Thus the jury system spread as rapidly and as widely as the justice of the royal courts, and as the rules of that common law which those courts were both making and administering.   But the rapidity of the development of the common law caused it to develop a set of fixed principles before the ideas of the civil and canon lawyers had had time to exercise an overwhelming influence upon the substance of its rules.[3]   Thus its rules retained many archaic ideas which these lawyers would probably have banished from it.   The common law was, it is true, influenced by some of these ideas in the twelfth and thirteenth centuries, as the books of Glanvil, and more especially of Bracton show.[4]   But this influence was neither lasting nor complete ; and it was ceasing to operate at the end of the thirteenth century.[5] This rapidity of development, which caused the retention of certain archaic ideas, and the cessation of the influence of the civil and canon lawyers, are the decisive factors in the early history of trial by jury.   They made its unique development in England possible ; and therefore we must examine the manner in which they operated.

(i) The earliest part of a primitive body of law to attain fixity

---

[1] Vol. v 170-176 ; P. and M. ii 654-655.

[2] Vol. v 174-175.

[3] " Henry II.'s reforms were effected just in time.   But for them, we should indeed have known the inquest, but it would in all likelihood have been the inquest of the canon law, the enquête of the new French jurisprudence," P. and M. i 602.

[4] Vol. ii 202-206, 267-286.   [5] Vol. ii 287-288.

is the law of procedure; and the English common law was no exception to this rule. It was beginning to attain some fixed rules of procedure at a time when men's idea of a trial were dominated by the archaic ideas which centred round the old formal methods of proof—battle, compurgation, and ordeal. Naturally there was a tendency to treat the jury, which was taking their place, as a formal proof.[1] It was simply substituted for them, and was adapted with as little change as possible to its new position. We can see this most clearly if we look at the formal record of a trial.[2] The record states the commission of the judges, the presentment of the grand jury, the indictment, the plea, the fact that the accused places himself on his country, the summons of the jury, the verdict, and the judgment. It " takes no notice either of the evidence or of the direction given by the judge to the jury." [3] The jury is regarded as a formal test to which the parties have submitted. The judgment follows, as under the old system, the result of that test. But to ask in what manner one of the old tests worked, to lay down rules for its working, would have been almost impious ; for are not the judgments of God past finding out ? The record tells us that when the jury was first introduced the method by which it arrived at its verdict inherited the inscrutability of the judgments of God.

(ii) The jury was a body of neighbours called in, either by express law, or by the consent of the parties, to decide disputed questions of fact. The decision upon questions of fact was left to them because they were already acquainted with them, or if not already so acquainted with them, because they might easily acquire the necessary knowledge. For this reason it has been said that the primitive jury were witnesses to rather than judges of the facts. They were in a sense witnesses. But they were more than witnesses. They were a method of proof which the parties were either obliged or had agreed to accept.[4] It was the easier so to regard them, because they represented the sense of the community —hundred or shire—from which they were drawn ; and in the days when such communities had each its court, when individuals lived more simple and more similar lives, the sense of the community was a thing more distinctly realized.[5] They were perhaps regarded by some as fulfilling somewhat the old judicial functions of the older suitors or doomsmen who made the judgment of the court.[6]

[1] P. and M. ii 624.
[2] For specimens of the record in civil and criminal cases see Jacob's Law Dictionary, *sub. voc.* Trial ; the same remarks apply to both kinds of record.
[3] Stephen, H.C.L. i 309.   [4] Below 326, 329, 330.   [5] P. and M. ii 621-622.
[6] Vinogradoff, Magna Carta Commem. Essays 92-93 ; and this would account for the survival of the idea that the jury should not be composed of persons who were manifestly the inferiors of the parties to the litigation. below 324 n. 7.

No doubt the judges might have treated them as witnesses ; and, if the judges had been men who had absorbed the principles of the canonist procedure and the canonist rules of evidence, they would have so treated them.[1] In that case the jury would probably have had no history. But, from the end of the thirteenth century, the judges were ceasing to be men who knew anything of the canon or civil law. They were coming to be drawn from the practitioners in the royal courts ;[2] and as yet the law administered in the royal courts had no rules as to parol evidence. Under these circumstances it was, as we have seen, less trouble to the judges to treat this band of witnesses as a formal proof of the facts.[3] But this meant that more stress was laid upon their judicial and less upon their witnessing capacity. And, under these influences, their judicial capacity tended to grow more and more predominant. Thus, although as late as 1346[4] the verdict of a majority was taken, it was finally settled in 1367[5] that their verdict must be unanimous. So too it was a very ancient rule that the jurors could not separate till after they had given their verdict—the quasi-corporate character of this band of judges must be maintained till they had discharged their duty ;[6] and to hasten their deliberations it was the law that they could neither eat nor

---

[1] Bracton knew something of the canon and civil law, vol. ii 271-286, and there are signs in his book of a tendency to treat the jury as witnesses ; thus he says, ff. 143, 143 b, " Justiciarius igitur si discretus sit . . . inprimis debet inquirere, si forte dubitaverit, et jurata suspecta fuerit, a quo vel a quibus illi duodecim didicerunt ea, quæ in veredicto suo proferunt de indictato, et audita super hoc responsione, de facili perpendere poterit, si dolus subfuerit vel iniquitas.   Dicat forte aliquis vel major pars juratorum, quod ea quæ ipsi proferunt in veredicto suo didicerunt ab uno in conjuratoribus suis, et qui interrogatus forte dicet quod illa didicit ab illo tali, et sic descendere poterit interrogatio et responsio de persona in personam usque ad aliquam vilem et abjectam personam cui non erit fides aliquatenus adhibenda ; " and again he says f. 143 b, " possunt justitiarii si viderint expedire, ex causa necessaria, si grave crimen latens sit, et juratores forte amore, odio, vel timore, celare voluerunt veritatem, separare juratores ab invicem, et quemlibet per se, et separatim examinare, ad veritatem sufficienter declarandam."   It is no wonder that, in the days of Bracton, trial by witness " looks like a serious rival of trial by jury," P. and M. ii 636 ; above 303 ; for if the jury had been persistently treated in the way the two modes of trial might well have merged into a trial by an enquête of witnesses, as in France, see P. and M. ii 655.

[2] Vol. ii 318-319.

[3] P. and M. ii 24-25 ; Roper, in his life of More, tells us that More said of the judges, " They see, that they may, by the verdict of the jury, cast off all quarrels from themselves upon them, which they account their chief defence."

[4] " Note that an assize was brought at Northampton, in which eleven recognitors agreed, and the twelfth would not agree, and said that he never would agree with his fellows.   And the verdict of the eleven was accepted, and it was awarded that the twelfth should go to prison," Y.B. 20 Ed. III. (R.S.) ii 534-536 ; for the earlier cases see Thayer, Evidence 86-88 ; Emlyn's notes to Hale, P.C. ii 297-299.

[5] Y.B. 41 Ed. III. Mich. pl. 36.

[6] Y.B. 24 Ed. III. Hil. pl. 10 ; Bl. Comm. iii 376 ; and in the Middle Ages, when the parties or their friends would be only too ready to use all the devices either of corruption or intimidation, it was a very necessary rule.

drink till they had given their verdict.[1] It was only very gradually that these rules were relaxed in civil cases ;[2] and they have
been only very partially relaxed in criminal cases.[3] Thus,
although it was not till the latter part of the seventeenth century
that the jury lost their character as witnesses,[4] their character of
judges was already predominating in the fourteenth century.
It was for this reason that trial by jury was able to be developed
into a method of trial which, by the end of the mediæval period
could from the point of view of its fairness to the accused, be
contrasted very favourably with the continental procedure derived from the canonical inquisitio.[5]

(iii) The earlier codes of customary law left the redress of
wrongs wholly to the party injured. He proceeded by way of
criminal appeal.[6] But, as soon as the state began to increase in
power, the insufficiency of this method of procedure began to
appear.[7] In England, as abroad, "a new was placed by the side
of the old procedure, and the new was in name an inquisitory
procedure. It is 'to inquire of,' as well as to 'hear and determine' criminal causes that the king's justices are sent through
the shires."[8] Presentment by a jury and indictment at the

---

[1] Y.BB. 21, 22 Ed. I. (R.S.) 272 ; 3, 4 Ed. II. (S.S.) 188 ; Co. Litt. 227 b ; Bl.
Comm. iii 375-376 ; in Y.B. 14 Hy. VII. Trin. pl. 4 there is a long discussion on
this topic—Brian, C.J., thought that any eating or drinking after they were sworn
made their verdict void, but Fineux, C.J., thought that this would not avoid the verdict if they had agreed on their verdict first, unless corruption could be proved ; it
seems to have been agreed Y.B. 20 Hy. VII. Mich. pl. 8 that if the jury ate and
drank together at their own expense the verdict would stand.

[2] It was recognized as early as 1401, Y.B. 2 Hy. IV. Trin. pl. 1 (p. 22), that a
jury could give their verdict to the judge after the court had risen ; and that they
could then have meat, drink, and beds, but that they could not separate, and must
give their verdict in court the next day ; this was the common practice in 1561,
Plowden at p. 211 ; and it was recognized by Coke, Co. Litt. 227 b ; a verdict given
in this way was called a " privy verdict ; " and Coke says that when this privy verdict was given in court on the following day it might be either confirmed or altered ;
see 9 S.T. at p. 186 ; at the time of Blackstone the jury could separate after giving
a privy verdict, Comm. iii 377, though Blackstone considered that it was a dangerous
practice, as the jury might be tampered with, and therefore should seldom be used ;
this opinion of Blackstone's has been endorsed by the Court of Appeal in Fanshaw
v. Knowles [1916] 2 K.B. at p. 547, in which case a good historical summary of the
law on this subject will be found.

[3] The jury may separate after being sworn in a trial for felony other than
murder, treason, or treason felony, 60 Victoria c. 18 ; but not after the judge has
summed up, R. v. Ketteridge [1915] 1 K.B. 467 ; possibly a separation of the jury on a
trial for misdemeanour before the judge has summed up does not necessarily invalidate the verdict, R. v. Kinnear (1819) 2 B. and Ald. 462, though it clearly did invalidate the verdict in the seventeenth century, Trial of Lord Delamere (1686) 11 S.T.
at p. 559 ; and cp. Fanshaw v. Knowles [1916] 2 K.B. at pp. 546-547 ; the conditions
under which they are now allowed refreshments and fire are laid down by 33, 34
Victoria c. 77 § 23 ; it would seem that, till then, after retiring to consider their verdict the old rule prevailed, see Halsbury, Laws of England, xviii 256.

[4] Below 332-336.   [5] Fortescue, De Laudibus cc. 21-23.
[6] Vol. ii 108-110, 361-364.   [7] Vol. ii 197-198, 256-257, 360.
[8] P. and M. ii 655.

king's suit rapidly took the place of the old criminal appeal.
We shall see that both the composition of the petty jury which
tried those presented, and the means taken to compel a consent
to trial by a petty jury, show that the king's judges were quite
as ready as the canonists to adopt very ruthless means to secure
convictions.[1]   But, here again, the fact that the new procedure
was introduced at a time when the older ideas of a trial still
prevailed, saved English law from some of the worst features of
the continental system.   The procedure by way of indictment
at the king's suit copied many of the features of the older procedure by way of criminal appeal; and, among other features,
it still retained the idea that the accused was in the position of
a defendant as against whom the plaintiff must establish his
claim—even though that plaintiff was the crown.[2]

We shall see that many times in the history of English constitutional law the survival of archaic ideas has helped forward
the cause of the liberty of the subject.   The survival of the
mediæval conception of the rule of law, as interpreted by Parliament and the courts, helped to determine both the form and
the issue of the constitutional controversies of the seventeenth
century.[3]   But there is no more striking illustration of this truth
than the history of the jury.   Because it was accepted as a
means of determining the facts at a time when the older methods
of proof dominated men's conception of a trial, and because the
English judges came to be very ignorant of any legal system but
their own, it was not dissected into a body of separate witnesses
under the rationalizing influence of the conceptions of the civil
and canon law.   It was consequently developed upon native
lines into a wholly original method of determining the facts at
issue in all manner of legal proceedings.   When, in the latter
half of the fifteenth century, Fortescue wrote in praise of the
laws of England, the jury system had come to be regarded as
the most valuable feature of that common law of which all
Englishmen were proud ; and, because it had attained that
position, it helped very materially to limit the sphere within
which, in the sixteenth century, the Council and the Star
Chamber were able to introduce a criminal procedure analogous
to that in use on the Continent.[4]   In later centuries it has helped
no less materially to ensure that administrative discretion shall
only be exercised in accordance both with the law and the public
opinion of the day.

[1] Below 325, 327.
[2] Vol. iii 621-622 ; "the new procedure becomes as accusatory as the old ; the
Appeal and the Indictment are regarded as institutions of the same order," P. and
M. ii 655.
[3] Vol. ii 441-443 : vol. iv 174, 187-189.   [4] Vol. v Bk. iv Pt. I. c. 4.

The jury would never have won this popularity, it would never have attained these results, if it had not been developed and controlled by the action of the courts, the legislature, and the Council. But before I can relate the history of this development and this control I must first deal with the manner in which juries of different kinds were for different purposes introduced into the English judicial system.

(2) The different varieties of the jury.

We must distinguish, in the first place, the juries used in criminal cases from those used in civil cases; and both these varieties of jury can in their turn be divided into two sub-varieties. In criminal cases there is the grand jury or the jury of presentment, and the petty jury. In civil cases there are the assizes and the jurata.

A. The juries used in criminal cases.

(i) *The grand jury or the jury of presentment.*

We have seen that the earliest recorded juries were employed to discover and present facts in answer to enquiries addressed to them by the king.[1] The function of the jury of presentment shows that it is the lineal descendant of these juries. It is summoned to discover and present to the king's officials persons suspected of serious crime. It is probable that the regular use of the jury for this purpose in the royal courts dates from the Assize of Clarendon. This seems to be clear from the first clause of that assize—the provisions of which have been set out above.[2] It made the use of the presenting jury general, both in the courts held by the king's judges and in the sheriff's tourns. We have seen that both at the Eyre and the tourn presentments were made by representative juries from the hundred.[3] These juries could present either from their own knowledge or from the information of others, just as at the present day the grand jury may present matters which they themselves have observed, or, as is more usual, may endorse the indictments or accusations made by others.

We have seen that in the thirteenth century the jury was

---

[1] Above 313.
[2] Above 77 n. 1; it may be noted that § 6 of the Constitutions of Clarendon (1164) provides that, for the purpose of accusations before the ecclesiastical courts, the sheriff, on the demand of the bishop, "faciet jurare duodecim legales homines de vicineto seu de villa, coram episcopo, quod inde veritatem secundum conscientiam suam manifestabunt;" and a similar ordinance was made for Normandy in 1159, Haskins, Norman Institutions 329-330; both, however, deal only with accusations before the ecclesiastical courts.
[3] Above 77, 268-269.

selected, as directed by the Assize of Clarendon, from the several hundreds.   Juries of this kind were needed to answer the detailed enquiries contained in the articles of the Eyre.   But, when the general Eyre ceased, when criminal justice had come for the most part to be administered by either the itinerant justices acting under more limited commissions, or by the justices of the peace in quarter sessions, the method of the selection of the grand jury changed.[1]   The sheriff was directed to summon for the business either of the assizes or of the quarter sessions twenty-four persons from the body cf the county.   From these, twenty-three are chosen, a majority of whom decides whether to "find a true bill" or "ignore" the accusations preferred.[2]

The presentments made by the grand jury do not and never did amount to an assertion that the person presented is guilty. They are merely an assertion that he is suspected.[3]   Of the steps taken to test that suspicion by means of a petty jury and otherwise I shall speak directly.[4]   We shall see that in the thirteenth and earlier part of the fourteenth century all or some members of the grand jury always formed part of the petty jury; and the judges sometimes considered that when the members of a petty jury who had presented a person as suspected, acquitted him, they had contradicted themselves, and could be punished.[5]   But, as the grand jury came to be separated from the petty jury, the distinctive character of their functions was more clearly realized.   It came to be recognized that the function of the grand jury is merely to say whether from the evidence for the prosecution (at which alone they look) there is probable ground of suspicion.[6]

The grand jury of modern times still retains some traces of antiquity which have been lost to the other varieties of the jury. They consider the evidence in secret,[7] and the court does not

[1] P. and M. ii 646-647; Reeves, H.E.L. ii 425-426; but the detailed history of this change has not yet been worked out.

[2] Hale, P.C. ii 153-155; 6 George IV. c. 50; 33, 34 Victoria c. 77; it may be noted that in Hale's day twenty-four were to be returned from each hundred as well as twenty-four from the body of the county.

[3] "Nunc autem dicendum est de indictatis per famam patriæ, quæ præsumptionem inducit, et cui standum est donec indictatus se a tali suspitione purgaverit. Ex fama quidem oritur suspitio, et ex fama et suspitione gravis præsumptio, tamen probationem admittit in contrarium, sive purgationem," Bracton f. 143; cf. P. and M. ii 645-646.

[4] Below 323-327.   [5] Below 325.

[6] Bl. Comm. IV. 300; cp. Hawles's remarks on the Earl of Shaftesbury's grand jury 8 S.T. at pp. 838-839.

[7] It was only in some of the political cases at the end of Charles II.'s reign that attempts were made to make them consider the evidence in public, see Proceedings against the Earl of Shaftesbury (1681) 8 S.T. 771-772; and for a note of another case in 1683 see ibid 825; see Luttrell's Diary i 101 for a note of a case in 1681 in which a bill was taken away from the grand jury by the clerk of the crown office before they could endorse it; they at once drew a bill against the clerk of the crown office and sent it to another grand jury.

control or advise them as to their findings in the individual cases which come before them. It merely charges them generally as to the nature of the business which they are about to consider. They can always act if they please on their own knowledge ; and Holt tells us that they often so acted at the end of the seventeenth century.[1] They can act at the present day in much the same way as they acted in the thirteenth century.

(ii) *The petty jury.*[2]

At the end of the twelfth century a person appealed, i.e. accused of crime by a private person, could get by payment the right to be tried by a jury.[3] His strict right was to prove his innocence by one of the orthodox ways—by battle, compurgation, or ordeal.[4] Similarly, if a person was presented by a grand jury as suspected he must clear himself either by compurgation or ordeal—not by battle because there could be no battle when the crown was the accuser.[5] It would seem that in the twelfth century the presenting jurors, together with other persons sometimes taken from the four neighbouring townships, decided as to the mode of proof by which the accused must clear himself.[6] Difficulties arose when these older methods of proof began to be discredited. Compurgation was not regarded by the king as a proof of innocence, and the Assize of Clarendon required those who had proved their innocence in this way to objure the realm.[7] The ordeal was abolished by the Lateran Council in 1215.[8] How then was the guilt or innocence of a suspected person to be determined? A writ addressed to the judges in 1219[9] tells them that nothing had as yet been determined. It directs that those accused of great crimes and suspected should be imprisoned—but not so as to endanger life or limb ; that those whose crimes were less heinous should abjure the realm ; and that those accused of small offences should be released if they would find securities to keep the peace. But, it concludes, much must be left to the discretion of the justices.[10] It was the need to find some new means

---

[1] In his argument in the Earl of Macclesfield v. Starkey (1684) 10 S.T. at p. 1356 he says, " It is the constant universal practice of grand juries, after they have dispatched the bills that are brought to them in form, they go and consult amongst themselves what they know of their own knowledge, or are informed of concerning any of the matters relating to the business of the county within their charge and authority, and according as upon enquiry they find matter to present, they do present it to the court. . . . This is done by them every assizes and sessions."

[2] On the whole subject see C. L. Wells, The Origin of the Petty Jury, L.Q.R. xxvii 347; Early Opposition to the Petty Jury in Criminal Cases, L.Q.R. xxx 97.

[3] P. and M. ii 615-616.   [4] L.Q.R. xxvii 347.

[5] " Rex non pugnat, nec alium habet campionem quam patriam," Bracton f. 142 b.

[6] L.Q.R. xxvii 348-349.   [7] Above 306.

[8] Above 311.   [9] Rymer, Foedera i 228.

[10] " Cum igitur nihil certius providerit in hac parte concilium nostrum ad præsens, relinquimus discretioni vestræ hunc ordinem prædictum observandum in hoc itinere

of determining the guilt or innocence of a suspected person that led to the gradual evolution of the petty jury.

At first, it would seem, the grand jury who had presented were asked "præcise dicere" guilty or not guilty.[1] Sometimes, as in the earlier period when the presenting jury determined the mode of proof, others were added to their number in order to make the trial jury more representative;[2] and sometimes part only of the presenting jury were on the jury which determined guilt or innocence.[3] The uncertainty of practice during the thirteenth and early part of the fourteenth centuries left the judges very free to follow what procedure seemed best to them in the circumstances.[4] Gradually the practice shaped itself under the influence of the two opposing considerations of the interest of the prisoner and the interest of the crown.

As early as the days of Bracton it was recognized that upon an enquiry as to the guilt or innocence of the prisoner, the prisoner ought to be allowed to object to members of the jury on the ground that they were his personal enemies;[5] and Britton[6] allowed an accused person to object to the presence on the trial jury of persons who had presented him for trial. In 1302 an accused knight objected to the jury both because they had presented him, and because, not being knights, they were not his peers. The latter cause of objection was deemed to be valid; a jury of knights was impanelled; and he was given a chance to object to individual members of this jury.[7] It was probably for these reasons that the custom grew up of selecting from the several juries of the hundreds a special trial jury of twelve

---

vestro, ut, quo personas hominum, formam delicti, et ipsarum rerum veritatem melius cognoscere poteritis, hoc ordine, secundum discretiones et conscientias vestras in hujusmodi procedatis."

[1] L.Q.R. xxvii 350—Mr. Wells says, " There are many instances of trial by jury in criminal cases to be found in the Assize Rolls, published and unpublished, from the time of Richard I. to the close of the reign of Edward I., all of which I have examined. By far the larger number of these cases, down to the reign of Edward I., show that the jury of the hundred, the presentment jury, does give the verdict of guilty or not guilty."

[2] Ibid 350, 354-356—they were sometimes afforced by adding representatives of the four neighbouring townships, sometimes in other ways; P. and M. ii 645.

[3] L.Q.R. xxvii 357-359.   [4] The Eyre of Kent (S.S.) i xlix.

[5] " Cum igitur procedendum sit de hujusmodi ad inquisitionem, ut ad judicium securius procedatur, et ut periculum et suspitio tollatur, justitiarius dicat indictato quod, si aliquem ex duodecim juratoribus suspectum habeat, illum justa ratione amoveat," f. 143 b.

[6] I. 30.

[7] Y.B. 30, 31 Ed. I. (R.S.) 531—the judge says, " Quia vos estis miles, volumus quod vos sitis judicati per vestros pares—Et nominabantur milites. Et quærebatur si voluerit aliquas calumpnias contra eos proponere;" probably it is due to a reminiscence of the same idea that the rule that knights must be on an assize to which a peer was a party lasted till 24 George II. c. 18; see Newdigate v. Earl of Derby (1554) Plowden 117; below 336 n. 8.

persons.[1] The number twelve was probably fixed upon because
it was necessary to have some limit to the number. The custom
of adding persons to the presenting jury had been found to be
inconvenient in practice, because the number of the jury was too
great ; and twelve was the number at that time of the jury which
presented.[2] On the other hand, the crown, being interested in
securing convictions, was opposed to the total elimination from
the petty or trial jury of all the members of the presenting jury.
As Parning, J., said in 1340[3] "if indictors be not there it is not
well for the king." We can well understand this dictum of
Parning's if we remember that the indictors who acquitted could
be and sometimes were punished for their action by the court.[4]
But the feeling against this practice of including indictors on the
trial jury grew to be so strong that, in 1351-1352, it was enacted
that no indictor should be put on an inquest upon the deliverance of one indicted for trespass or felony, if he were challenged
for this cause by the accused.[5] The petty jury thus disengaged
itself from the grand jury or jury of presentment, and gradually
came to be drawn, like the other varieties of the jury, from the
country at large.

In spite of the statute of 1351-1352 the crown still retained
means of influencing the petty jury which it only gradually re-
linquished.[6] The jury was selected by its officers ; and we shall
see that for a long time the prisoner was not allowed to produce
witnesses.[7] Even when he was allowed to produce them it was
not till the beginning of the eighteenth century that they could
be sworn ;[8] and for a still longer period the accused was not

[1] L.Q.R. xxvii 357.
[2] Ibid 356-357—" These combination juries numbered from twenty-four to
eighty-four jurors, and the number became embarrassingly large and unwieldy ; " a
tendency therefore grows up " to select some special jurors for the case to be added
to the original presentment jury ; " " the number twelve was fixed upon, probably
because that was the number of the presentment jury from the hundred.   Therefore
just as the presentment jury represented the voice of the hundred in making the
accusation, so the jury ' of the country,' with the same number, represented the
whole county in deciding whether the accused was guilty or not."   The process by
which twelve came to be the usual number of the jury was very gradual ; thus
Bracton, f. 255 b, says that, though for the assize of mort d'ancestor there must be
twelve at least, for the assize of novel disseisin there must be seven at least ; and
the grand jury, the grand assize, the attaint jury, and the inquest of office were not
twelve in number.
[3] Y.B. 14, 15 Ed. III. (R.S.) 260.
[4] L.Q.R. xxvii 350 citing a case of 15 Edward I. ; the Eyre of Kent (S.S.) i 153 ; cp.
Select Pleas of the Crown (S.S.) no. 130 ; L.Q.R. xxx 106 ; there was a curious case
in the Eyre of Kent (S.S.) i 112 in which a man, acquitted of homicide at a sessions
of Gaol Delivery, was indicted at the Eyre on the same facts ; five of the acquitting
jury were on the indicting jury, and they were committed to prison as attainted, and
ordered not to serve on another jury during the Eyre.
[5] 25 Edward III. St. 5 c. 3 ; the rule seems also to have been extended to
treason by the seventeenth century, Co. Litt. 157 b.
[6] See generally L.Q.R. xxx 105 seqq.
[7] Below 336.   [8] Ibid.

allowed the help of counsel.[1]   We shall see that the working of
the modes by which the jury were controlled in criminal cases
favoured the crown.   There was probably no remedy for a
wrongful conviction;[2] but for an acquittal the jury were, till
1670, liable to be fined and imprisoned.[3]   We have seen that
the remedy of a new trial was only applied to the verdicts of
juries in criminal trials very partially and gradually.[4]

But the petty jury was a form of the jurata; and we shall
see that to a trial by a jurata the accused must consent.[5]   His
strict right was to be tried by one of the older methods of proof
—by compurgation or ordeal.   But, as those older modes of
proof had become obsolete, if he did not consent to be tried by
a jury he could not be convicted; and if he was not convicted
his property would not be forfeited.   Considering the various
advantages which this mode of trial gave the crown, considering
that if the accused could avoid a conviction he might save his
property for his family, it is not surprising that prisoners often
refused to consent to be tried by a petty jury.   What was to be
done with such persons?   The obvious answer is, impanel a
jury and try them whether they consent or not.   It has taken
more than five hundred years to arrive at this obvious answer.

It is true that Bracton thought that this might be done.[6]   It
is true that at least two precedents can be produced where this
was done.[7]   But Maitland points out that these two precedents
stand alone.[8]   In spite of Bracton's authority, such a change in
the old law, on a matter that touched life and limb, could not
be endured.   The end of the thirteenth century was not a time,
like the middle of the twelfth century, when far-reaching legal
changes could be made by the authority of the crown alone.
Public opinion could now force a hearing ; and public opinion,
as we may see from one or two of the clauses of Magna Carta,[9]
was apt to be retrogressive in its ideas.   The author of the
" Mirror of Justices " was in some ways a fair representative of
the average conservative opinion of the day.   He considered it
"an abuse " that men were driven by the judges to put them-

---

[1] The rule is stated Y.B. 30, 31 Ed. I. (R.S.) 529-530; for the gradual modification of this rule see Stephen, H.C.L. i 424-425; the rule itself was not got rid of till
1836, 6, 7 William IV. c. 114 ; cf. Thayer, Evidence 161 n.

[2] Below 340.   [3] Below 343-344.

[4] Above 216-217.   [5] Below 330.

[6] ff. 142 b, 143 b; at f. 133 b it is suggested that he should be treated as
convicted.

[7] Hale, P.C. ii 322.

[8] P. and M. ii 648 ; Gloucester Pleas xxxix—see cases 111, 161, 213, 316, 330,
414, 435 ; the prisoner is either kept in prison, abjures the country, is bound over to
keep the peace, or the case is adjourned as the writ of 1219 directs.

[9] Above 58-60; see Thayer, Evidence 56, 57.

selves on their country, when they had offered to defend themselves by their bodies.[1]

The result was, not that the older methods of proof were restored, but that on an indictment for felony consent to be tried by a jury was compelled by the peine forte et dure.[2] In 1275[3] statutory force was given to this expedient. It was enacted that notorious felons (not those merely lightly suspected) who declined to put themselves upon their country when indicted at the king's suit should have "strong and hard imprisonment." Britton,[4] among other details, adds that they are to be put in irons. But at the beginning of the thirteenth century nothing is said as to pressing to death; and, as Stephen says, the rule as to eating and drinking on alternate days shows that this is an innovation.[5] In fact, the "peine" was made more "forte" and more "dure" as the obstinacy of accused persons increased.[6] In 1406 a judgment of Gascoigne C. J. expressly mentioned pressing to death.[7] This senseless barbarity was part of the law of England till 1772. In that year it was enacted that standing mute in cases of felony should be equivalent to a conviction.[8] In 1827 it was enacted that if the prisoner stands mute in cases of treason, felony, or misdemeanour, a plea of not guilty shall be entered and that the trial shall proceed as if the prisoner had pleaded.[9]

B. The juries used in civil cases.

(i) *The Assizes.*

(a) The Grand Assize.

The Grand Assize was a special variety of jury introduced by legislative enactment to determine the question which of the two parties to a writ of right had the better right—majus jus—to lands held by free tenure. It was probably enacted by a Council held at Windsor—probably, Round thinks, in 1179; and,

---

[1] V. i §§ 19, 126, 127.

[2] In the case of treasons and misdemeanours refusal to plead or standing mute was equivalent to a conviction, Stephen, H.C.L. i 298.

[3] 3 Edward I. c. 12; Reeves, H.E.L. ii 48-50, 426; he thinks (quoting Fleta I. 34, 33) that it reinacted an old penalty against those who declined to adopt any method of proof.

[4] I. 26, 27; Fleta I. 34, 33 says nothing of irons.

[5] H.C.L. i 300, and see also the words of the writ of 1219; those suspected were to be imprisoned but "ita quod non incurrent periculum vitæ et membrorum;" this would seem to show that the view of Hale (P.C. ii 322) and Coke (Second Instit. 179) that the peine forte et dure existed at common law is erroneous.

[6] See L.Q.R. xxx 104.

[7] Thayer, Evidence 75, quoting Y.B. 8 Hy. IV. Mich. pl. 2; if the prisoner declined to plead a jury was sworn to see if he was mute of malice or by the visitation of God, Stephen H.C.L. i 298.

[8] 12 George III. c. 20. [9] 7, 8 George IV. c. 28.

if this date is correct, " it synchronizes," as he says, " in a very interesting manner with the advent of Glanvil to power." [1] Glanvil himself describes it as a " regale beneficium," [2] by means of which a man may defend the right to his free tenement without the risk of the doubtful issue of the battle. The tenant could choose either the battle or the Grand Assize ; [3] and if the plaintiff objected to his choice of the Grand Assize he must support his objection with valid reasons. [4]   The case being one which can be tried by the Grand Assize, the plaintiff must take the next step by obtaining another writ, " that by four knights from the county and from the neighbourhood there be elected twelve legal knights from the same neighbourhood to say upon oath which of the two parties to the action has the better right in the land which is the subject of the action." [5]   If some or all of the sixteen persons differed or were ignorant of the facts more must be summoned till there were at least twelve who would agree upon their verdict. [6]   Their verdict closed the question between the plaintiff and the tenant once for all. [7]

We can see from Glanvil's account that this was a new procedure.   The tenant could, if he pleased, defend himself by the battle ; [8] and many incidental questions, e.g. questions as to summons, [9] or whether it was a case for the Grand Assize, [10] could be decided by battle or compurgation in the accustomed manner. At the same time we can see that the idea that the " visinetum " should decide these questions was growing ; for this method of decision is sometimes placed by the side of the old methods. [11]

---

[1] E.H.R. xxx 268-269.

[2] ii 7 ; on the question whether the epithet Magna applied to assisa is, or is not an interpolation, see Reeves i 187 n. 2.

[3] Glanvil ii 3 and 6.   [4] Ibid.

[5] " Ut per quatuor legales milites de comitatu, et de visineto eligantur duodecim milites legales de eodem visineto, qui super sacramentum suum dicant uter litigantium majus jus habeat in terra petita," ibid ii 10 ; but the procedure seems to have varied ; in a case reported in the Eyre of Kent (S.S.) ii 83 the four knights were chosen by the assent of the parties, and then they chose sixteen of themselves and others ; then the parties and their attornies chose twelve ; and this seems to have been in substance the procedure in 1406, Y.B. 7 Hy. IV. Trin. pl. 28 ; knights girt with swords were always the recognitors of the Grand Assize ; and in Y.B. 20 Ed. III. (R.S.) ii 374-376 persons who acted without disclosing the fact that they were not knights were imprisoned ; see Thayer, Evidence 45-46.

[6] Glanvil ii 17 ; ii 21, it is said, " Si vero reperiantur nulli milites de visineto nec in comitatu ipso qui rei veritatem inde sciant, quid juris erit " ?   The law is left doubtful ; it was suggested Y.B. 20 Ed. III. (R.S.) ii 374 that the sheriff of the next county should summon four knights.

[7] Ibid ii 18, " Lites enim per magnum assisam domini regis legitime decisæ, nulla occasione rite resuscitantur imposterum."

[8] Ibid ii 5.

[9] Ibid i 9, " Si summonitiones omnes negaverit pro qualibet jurabit duodecima manu."

[10] Ibid ii 6.

[11] E.g. ii. 3, on the question whether a champion after wager of battle has died a natural death, pending the suit ; ii 6, on a question of consanguinity.

The Grand Assize fell into disuse with the growth of more modern and convenient remedies for settling the question of the ownership of real property. But it lived on till the abolition of real actions in 1833.[1] The latest case was that of *Davies* v. *Lowndes* tried in 1835 and again in 1838.[2]

(*b*) The Possessory Assizes.

We have seen that the possessory assizes were three in number—the assize of novel disseisin introduced probably in 1166, the assize of mort d'ancestor introduced by the Assize of Northampton in 1176, and the assize of darrein presentment introduced at some uncertain date in Henry II.'s reign.[3] In the cases to which these assizes applied the parties had no choice. They were obliged to proceed by this method of trial "beneficio constitutionis regni."[4] The proceedings began with a writ to the sheriff to summon twelve free and lawful men of the neighbourhood to answer the questions as to seisin raised by the assize.[5] This procedure lasted till the abolition of real actions in 1833.[6]

(*c*) The Assize Utrum.

The Assize Utrum was introduced originally to determine the question whether land was held in frankalmoin, i.e. by a spiritual tenure, or by some lay tenure.[7] This was an important question in the twelfth century because upon it depended whether the spiritual or lay court had jurisdiction. An assize to decide this question is contemplated by the Constitutions of Clarendon— perhaps it was introduced by them.[8] But the issue whether a given piece of land was held in frankalmoin by the church of A, or was the lay fee of B, was not a simple question to answer; and so it soon happened that this assize was treated as a jurata,[9] which could decide not merely the actual points put in issue by the assize, but also any side issues which the case involved. It

---

[1] 3, 4 William IV. c. 27 § 36.

[2] 1 Bing. N.C. 597; 5 Bing. N.C. 161.

[3] Above 47, 275-276; P. and M. i 124-127; vol. iii 8-11, 23, 24.

[4] Glanvil xiii 1.

[5] "Ab initio elegendi sunt duodecim liberi et legales homines de visineto secundum formam in brevi expressam," ibid xiii 6.

[6] It may, however, be noted that, as the assize of mort d'ancestor did not lie of lands devisable, it followed from 32 Henry VIII. c. 1 and 12 Charles II. c. 24 that, after those Acts had made all lands devisable, no such assize could be brought, Bl. Comm. iii 186-187.

[7] P. and M. i 123-124; vol. iii 25-26; for these tenures see vol. iii 34 seqq.; other assizes utrum are mentioned by Glanvil xiii 2, but these do not develop.

[8] § ix—"Si calumnia emerserit inter clericum et laicum, vel inter laicum et clericum, de ullo tenemento quod clericus eleemosinam velit attrahere, laicus vero ad laicum feudum, recognitione duodecim legalium hominum, per capitalis justitiæ regis considerationem terminabitur, utrum tenementum sit pertinens ad eleemosimam sive ad laicum feudum, coram ipso justitio regis."

[9] Below 330-331.

came therefore to be known as the jurata de utrum, which was later corrupted into the phrase juris utrum;[1] and, till 1571, it was used chiefly by parsons to recover land which belonged to their churches.[2] The history of the development of this assize brings us to what has come to be the most usual form of jury used in civil cases—the jurata.

(ii) *The Jurata.*

The term jurata and assisa are often used convertibly by the earlier writers, such as Glanvil, to mean a body of persons summoned by public authority to answer some disputed question of fact.[3] But the two terms had a distinct meaning as we may see by the expression, used both by Bracton and Fleta, "assisa vertitur in juratam." The broad difference was this : the assisa was a body of jurors summoned to answer certain specific questions, in accordance with a positive law which enacted that such questions should be answered in this particular way. Their sole power was to answer these particular questions. Incidental questions might be answered in Glanvil's day by battle or other ordinary method of proof.[4] But as time went on the ordinary method of proof came to be the jury. The parties would usually agree to submit these preliminary or incidental questions to a jury. The new body of persons so summoned in accordance with the agreement of the parties to decide these questions is the jurata into which the assize is converted ;[5] and this jurata usually decided the case.[6] Booth [7] says "the assize is said to be turned into a jury when they are to enquire of matters put in issue out of the point of the assize, i.e. out of the point of seisin and disseisin, which points must first be determined before the assize can be taken as to the seisin and disseisin, as if the tenant plead in abatement to the writ, as villeinage, etc., or other matters

---

[1] Y.B. 20 Ed. III. (R.S.) ii, xxiii-xxviii.

[2] Bl. Comm. iii 252-253 ; Blackstone points out that, "since the restraining statute of 13 Elizabeth c. 10 whereby the alienation of the predecessor . . . is declared to be absolutely void, the remedy is of very little use, unless the parson himself has been deforced for more than twenty years ; for the successor, at any competent time after his accession to the benefice, may enter, or bring an ejectment."

[3] Y.B. 12, 13 Ed. III. (R.S.) xli ; Co. Litt. 154 b.

[4] Glanvil xiii 11.

[5] Y.B. 12, 13 Ed. III. (R.S.) xlviii, "the actual result is not to change the functions of the twelve men summoned in the first instance, but to substitute other twelve for them ;" but as early as Edward II.'s reign the same twelve acted as a jurata, the Eyre of Kent (S.S.) iii 38; and the same thing seems to have happened in a case reported in Y.B. 3, 4 Ed. II. (S.S.) 50, 51 ; in Y.B. 11, 12 Ed. III. (R.S.) 608 there is a case in which the same inquest acted as a jury as to one defendant and an assize as to the others.

[6] "When a man pleads, and the assize is changed into an inquest, it is not the practice to return and plead to the point of the assize," *per* Bereford, C.J., Y.B. 3, 4 Ed. II (S.S.) 127.

[7] Booth, Real Actions (Ed. 1701) 213, 214; see Reeves, H.E.L. i 354, 355.

triable by a jury, and issue is taken ; or matters in bar, as a release, agreement, etc." There were also other differences as to the method of summons. The assize as we have seen was summoned in the writ by which the action was begun. The jury was summoned by writ of Venire facias, when the parties were at issue on some specific fact raised by the pleadings.[1]

We have seen that even in Glanvil's time incidental questions might be referred to a jurata, the visinetum, or the patria. But in his book they stand side by side with the older methods of proof. The new forms of action invented in the thirteenth century gave to the newer method of trial a great extension.[2] It was the necessary mode of trial in all actions of trespass, and the various offshoots of that action, which were destined in time to take the place of so many of the older forms. In 1304 proof by battle was refused in an action of trespass ;[3] and Britton, for this reason, recommended the procedure by way of action for trespass, rather than the procedure by way of appeal.[4] It was the mode in which the questions raised by writs of entry were answered.[5] It soon became common form for the one party, when he had stated on the pleadings a fact denied by the other, to "put himself upon the country ; " and for the other "to do the like." Fortescue[6] in the fifteenth century can, with substantial truth, state perfectly generally that, "as oft as suitors in the courts of the king of England, are come to the issue of their plea upon the matter of the fact, forthwith the justices by virtue of the king's writ, do write unto the sheriff of the county, wherein the deed is supposed to be done, that he do cause to come before the same justices at a certain day by them limited, xii. good and lawful men, neighbours to the place where the fact is supposed to be done . . . to the end that by their oaths it may certainly be known, whether the deed were done as the one party affirmeth, or else as the other party denieth."

Such then were the different varieties of jury which were used for judicial purposes during the Middle Ages. I must now

---

[1] Y.B. 12, 13 Ed. III. (R.S.) liv, "an action in which the facts were to be ascertained through a body of men summoned by virtue of an original writ, to pronounce upon issues mentioned in that writ, was regarded as belonging to a class different from actions in which the issue of fact to be evolved out of the pleadings was unknown at the time of commencement, and had to be determined by a body of jurors to be brought together at some future time by virtue of a judicial writ of Venire facias."

[2] P. and M. i 128, 129 ; ii 617 ; Thayer, Evidence 66, 67.

[3] Y.B. 32, 33 Ed. I. (R.S.) 318, 320.

[4] I. 123 ; similarly in the sixteenth century assumpsit took the place of debt and trover of detinue to evade compurgation.

[5] P. and M. ii 617 ; vol. iii 11-13.

[6] De Laudibus c. 25 ; the same fact is recognized by the statute 15 Henry VI. c. 5 cited Thayer, Evidence 67, 68.

describe the process by which these juries became juries of the sort known to our modern law.   They acquired their modern characteristics as they gradually lost their character of witnesses, and became merely the judges of the facts in issue; and they owed their efficiency as judges of the facts to the methods by which at different periods in our legal history they were controlled.   These two topics will form the subject of the two following sections.

(3) The development of the judicial functions of the jury.

The development of the judicial functions of the jury was gradual.   The best proof of this fact is the tenacity with which the law clung to the idea that they must come from the immediate neighbourhood of the place in which the facts in issue occurred.   We have seen that at the Eyre the jurors were drawn from the different hundreds ;[1] and Fortescue tells us that four at least of the jury must come from the hundred wherein the fact is alleged.[2]   In civil cases six were required in 1543-1544 ;[3] but in 1584-1585 the number was reduced to two in personal actions.[4] Though Coke said that in such cases a jury should come from the town, parish, or hamlet "within which the matter of fact issuable is alleged,"[5] it is clear that the rule as to the presence of hundredors was then coming to be overlaid with many fine distinctions.[6]   In 1705[7] it was enacted that it was sufficient if the jury came from the body of the county.   It was not, however, till 1826 that the necessity to have hundredors on the jury in criminal cases was formally abolished.[8]

Long before this date, however, the jury had ceased to be witnesses and had become judges of the facts.   This result had been brought about mainly by two sets of causes—firstly by the evolution of the manner in which the jury were accustomed to inform themselves of the facts in issue, and secondly by growth of the law as to the persons whom the parties were able to object to as jurors.

[1] Above 268-269.
[2] De Laudibus c. 25.
[3] 35 Henry VIII. c. 6 § 1.
[4] 27 Elizabeth c. 6 § 5.
[5] Co. Litt. 125.
[6] Ibid 157.
[7] 4 Anne c. 16 § 6; extended by 24 George II. c. 18 to actions on penal statutes, Bl. Comm. iii 359.
[8] 6 George IV. c. 50 § 13 ; when Blackstone wrote there must be " a competent number of hundredors," Comm. iv 346; but it is said in Hargreave's and Butler's notes to Co. Litt. 125 a, that the rule had long been deviated from in practice, " Lord Hale taking notice that, even during his time, he never knew an instance of a challenge for want of hundredors in treason or felony, and the sheriffs, as we are well informed, now always summoning juries from the county at large."   For the rule that if a sufficient number of jurors did not appear the number could be filled up by a panel of " tales de circumstantibus," or even by a jury composed entirely of such persons, provided that one of the jurors summoned had appeared, see Alfrid Denbawd's case (1613) 10 Co. Rep. 102 b; in such cases the parties were said to " pray " and the judges " to award a tales."

(i) How the jury might inform themselves was not in the thirteenth century defined. The answer to that question comprises, indeed, a large part of the law of evidence, the main rules of which are far more recent.[1] Bracton[2] and Britton[3] consider that the jury should take the best means they can to get at the truth, and talk it over among themselves. If they were still ignorant they might be afforced by those who knew better.[4] Juries were summoned from persons likely to know. Thus we have a jury of Florentine merchants living in London summoned to decide as to an act alleged to have taken place at Florence; and a jury of cooks as to the quality of food sold.[5] Such juries are perhaps the ancestors both of the modern special jury and the modern expert witness. They partake of the character of both. That juries could still decide of their own knowledge in the seventeenth century was stated in a proclamation for jurors, drawn by Bacon and issued in 1607;[6] in 1670 it was made use of by Vaughan, C.J., in *Bushell's Case*[7] to prove that jurors could not be fined for finding a verdict contrary to the direction of the court; and Hale,[8] writing a little later could say: "It may so fall out, that the jury upon their own knowledge may know a thing to be false that a witness swore to be true; or may know a witness to be incompetent or incredible, though nothing be objected against him; and may give their verdict accordingly." How a jury came by its knowledge was not originally a matter with which the law concerned itself. Just as the law neglected to define the limits and rationale of judicial notice,[9] so it neglected to examine the methods employed and the material used to form a verdict.

At the same time it was perfectly clear that verdicts were not as a rule founded on first hand knowledge. "Even in the

---

[1] Stephen, Digest of the Law of Evidence 197.   [2] ff. 185 b, 325.

[3] II. 87; the fact that the jury could always demand a view of the premises in an assize illustrates the fact that they were expected to inform themselves.

[4] Bracton f. 185 b.

[5] Cases cited by Thayer, Evidence 94; as to the jury de medietate linguæ, see 27 Edward III. St. 2 c. 8; 28 Edward III. c. 13; Mayor's Court Rolls, xlii.

[6] "The law of this our realm . . . neither ties them to the evidence and proofs produced, neither disableth any witness (except in case of perjury) to be used; but leaveth both supply of testimony and the discerning and credit of testimony, wholly to the juries' consciences and understanding, yea to their private knowledge," Spedding, Letters and Life of Bacon iii 390.

[7] Vaughan's Rep. 147-149.

[8] Common Law 348; so too in 1681 in the proceedings against the Earl of Shaftesbury, 8 S.T. at p. 803, Pemberton, C.J., said to the jury, "Look ye, gentlemen, you are to go according to the evidence of the witnesses; you are to consider of the case according to the things alleged and proved, unless you know anything yourselves: But if any of you know anything of your own knowledge that you ought to take into consideration, no doubt of it."

[9] Thayer says, Evidence 279, that it was not till 1824, when Starkie wrote on the law of Evidence, that any special mention of this subject occurs.

early years of the thirteenth century they were not, and were
hardly supposed to be, eye-witnesses." [1]   Hence we get at
different periods various methods of informing the jury.   (a) In
cases where there was a dispute as to the genuineness of a deed
the jury and the witnesses to the deed were summoned together.
We can see a confusion between the old trial by witnesses and
the modern jury when the parties put themselves upon the
witnesses and a jury. [2]   The growing difference between the jury
and the ordinary witness caused the cessation of this practice in
the course of the sixteenth century. [3]   Coke [4] tells us that if a
witness named in the deed be returned of the jury it is a good
cause of challenge.   (b) The practice of delivering deeds, charters [5]
or fines [6] to the jury is of old standing.   "These things, *par
excellence*, used to be known as 'evidence.'" [7]   It was settled in
1361 that they must be produced in open court and not delivered
privately to the jury. [8]   (c) Counsel took upon themselves responsibility for the truth of the statements which they made, [9]
and stated facts in evidence to the jury. [10]   (d) During the whole
of the mediæval period much evidence was allowed to be pleaded.
It was then on the record, and the jury was more likely to
notice it than if it had merely been stated by the judge or by
counsel. [11]

It is not till the sixteenth century that the practice of relying
upon the sworn testimony of witnesses became general.   One
reason for this was the fact that such evidence was usually of
the most untrustworthy description.   As Mr. Bolland has said, [12]
"the origination and prosecution of suits that were based upon
purely invented facts and supported by evidence that was wholly
deliberate perjury seems to have ranked almost as a recognized
profession."   The result was that the courts, in order to cope
with this evil, so enlarged the definition of the offences of maintenance and conspiracy that it was very dangerous to come

---

[1] P. and M. ii 626.

[2] Fortescue, De Laudibus, c. 32; Thayer, Evidence 97-100, 102, 104; for
cases in which this occurred see Y.BB. 11, 12 Ed. III. (R.S.) 338; 14, 15 Ed. III.
190.

[3] Thayer, Evidence 102.   [4] Co. Litt. 157.

[5] Y.B. 6 Ed. II. (S.S.) 235.   [6] Ibid 199.   [7] Thayer, Evidence 104.

[8] Ibid 110, citing Staffordshire Coll. (Salt. Soc.) xiii 6-7; the rule was also
clearly laid down in 1409 in Y.B. 11 Hy. IV. Mich. pl. 41, there cited.

[9] Vol. iii 638.   [10] Y.B. 6 Ed. II. (S.S.) 198.

[11] "We say nowadays that facts are to be pleaded, and not the evidence of facts.
That was early said, but it was very far indeed from being rigidly enforced.   Often
we find the courts allowing one to set forth his case fully 'for fear of the laymen'
i.e. in order that the jury might not pass upon questions of law, and might not go
wrong through any misapprehension of the facts," Thayer, Evidence 115; for the
demurrer to evidence—an expedient for withdrawing the case from the jury—see ibid
234-239; vol. iii 638-639.

[12] The Eyre of Kent (S.S.) i xxxiii.

forward as a witness.   Such a witness exposed himself not only to the risk of physical violence from the other side, but also to proceedings for these offences.   Thus in 1450 Fortescue, C.J., is reported as saying,[1] "If a man be at the bar and say to the court that he is for the defendant or plaintiff, that he knows the truth of the issue, and prays that he may be examined by the court to tell the truth to the jury, and the court asks him to tell it, and at the request of the court he says what he can in the matter, it is justifiable maintenance.   But if he had come to the bar out of his own head, and spoken for one or the other, it is maintenance and he will be punished for it.   And if the jurors come to a man where he lives, in the country, to have knowledge of the truth of the matter, and he informs them, it is justifiable ; but if he comes to the jurors, or labours to inform them of the truth it is maintenance, and he will be punished for it ; so Fortescue said, and it was admitted by the court."   This shows, both that the jurors were expected to make their own inquiries, and that the law discouraged the volunteer witness.

It is clear, however, that, in the sixteenth century, when Sir Thomas Smith wrote, witnesses held a far more important place than they held in the time of Fortescue.[2]   In fact during the Tudor period the tide had turned in favour of the witness.   He was a person to be encouraged rather than intimidated—at any rate when he was a witness for the crown.   This is illustrated by the statute of 1562-1563 which provided that witnesses could be compelled to attend,[3] by the reluctance of the court of Star Chamber to punish such witnesses for perjury,[4] and by the limitations placed by that court upon proceedings against them for conspiracy.[5]   When once witnesses for the crown had been encouraged to come forward in this way, it is easy to see how the practice of calling them in all classes of cases became general. Coke admits that juries are most commonly led by the depositions of witnesses.[6]   But we may perhaps see, at once a survival

---

[1] Y.B. 28 Hy. VI. Pasch. pl. 1, cited Thayer, Evidence 128, 129.

[2] Republic 147, 148, " Witnesses be sworn and heard before them, not after the fashion of the civil law, but so that not only the twelve, but the judges, the parties, and so many as be present may hear what each witness doth say.   The adverse party or his advocates . . . interrogateth sometimes the witnesses and driveth them out of countenance."

[3] 5 Elizabeth c. 9 § 12.

[4] Hudson, Treatise on the Star Chamber 77, 81 says, " A long debated question hath been whether perjury committed by any witnesses upon indictments for the king shall be examined and punished in the Star Chamber.   And the reason yielded hath been for that it will deter the king's witnesses to yield their testimonies in all cases ; " he notes that it had been at last decided that they could be so punished ; but not " *perjury committed against the life of a man for felony or murder*," when the prisoner has been convicted ; " and one reason is lest it should deter men from giving evidence for the king."

[5] Floyd v. Barker (1608) 12 Co. Rep. 23.   [6] Third Instit. 163.

of the old theories, and a reminiscence of the way in which they had become modified, in the rule, disputed by Coke,[1] that no witnesses could be called for the prisoner in cases of treason or felony ; and in the rule, which lasted to the end of the seventeenth century,[2] that the witnesses for the prisoner in such cases could not be sworn.   Vaughan, C.J., too, could say in 1670 that " the evidence in court is not binding evidence to a jury." [3]   But these were survivals.   By the middle of the seventeenth century the witnesses and the jury were regarded as so distinct that " it was said by the court that if either of the parties to a trial desire that a juror may give evidence of something of his own know-ledge to the rest of the jurors, that the court will examine him openly in court upon his oath, and he ought not to be examined in private by his companions." [4]   In 1816 it seems to have been assumed that if a judge had directed a jury to find a verdict of their own knowledge a new trial might have been granted.[5]

(ii) The process of divesting the jury of their character as witnesses was assisted by the growth of the law as to the persons to whom the parties might object as jurors.

We have seen that the prisoner might object to the presence of the "indictors" on the petty jury.[6]   The fact also that a jury-man was a villein was a cause of challenge.   Both Fortescue [7] and Coke [8] give numerous cases in which persons could challenge jurymen.   It is clear that the challenges "propter defectum," i.e. for some defect in capacity, as villein tenure; "propter affectum," i.e. for partiality ; "propter delictum," i.e. on account of conviction for certain offences ; or on account of the relation-ship of the sheriff who returned the jury or of some of the jurors themselves to one of the parties to the action [9]—are all based upon the judicial character of the jury.   In fact in the fourteenth

---

[1] Third Instit. 79.   The practice of allowing the accused to call witnesses sprang up at the beginning of the seventeenth century, Thayer, Evidence 160, n.

[2] Treason, 7 William III. c. 3 § 1 ; Felony, 1 Anne St. 2 c. 9 § 3.

[3] Bushell's Case, Vaughan's Rep. at p. 152.

[4] Bennet v. Hundred of Hartford (1650) Style 233 ; so Salk. 405 (1702) " If a jury give a verdict of their own knowledge they ought to tell the court so that they may be sworn as witnesses . . . the fair way is to tell the court before they are sworn that they have evidence to give ; " cp. Duncomb, Trials per pais c. 12, cited Halsbury, Laws of England xviii 256 n. (f).

[5] R. v. Sutton, 4 M. and S. 532.

[6] Above 324-325.   [7] De Laudibus c. 27.

[8] Co. Litt. 156-158 ; cp. Bl. Comm. iii 359-364 ; to avoid inconveniences caused by challenges cases were removed into the King's Court as it could summoi. juries from any part of the county, Reeves, H.E.L. i 348 n. a; it was recognized in 1339 that an assize or a jury might, if a peer were a party to the action, be challenged if no knights were on it, Y.B. 12, 13 Ed. III. (R.S.) 290—a rule due perhaps to a con-fusion between judicium parium and trial by jury, above 59, 60, 317 ; in 1343 the rule is laid down that in a criminal case the prisoner cannot challenge more than two juries without cause, Y.B. 17 Ed. III. (R.S.) 280.

[9] See Vernon v. Manners (1573) Dyer 319 a.

century witnesses were distinguished from the jury on these lines. A witness might be under age; and a witness could not be challenged.[1] The manner in which these challenges were tried was by the sworn evidence of the persons challenged. "This," as Thayer says, "may well have been a provocation to the same thing in the regular jury trial."[2] In other cases the law has been developed by giving a wider extension to rules made in the first instance merely to assist the procedure of the court.[3]

(4) Methods of controlling the jury.

When the character of the jury as witnesses was more prominent than their character as judges of the facts, they were obviously guilty of something like perjury if they gave a false verdict. It was to punish jurors who had thus perjured themselves that the writ of attaint was invented. Naturally, both the character of the remedy and the conditions under which it lay were modified with modifications in position and functions of the jury; and, when the jurors lost their character as witnesses, it gradually became obsolete, and other methods arose of controlling the jury. The history of these developments must now be traced.

It is not certain exactly when or how the writ of attaint arose. But it is probable that it arose from the royal legislation which established the possessory assizes. Glanvil tells us that the verdict of the Grand Assize was as final as the verdict of the battle;[4] but that a special punishment had been devised for the members of such an assize who had sworn falsely. They were to lose their chattels, to be imprisoned for a year at least, and to be accounted infamous.[5] Glanvil does not mention the writ of attaint; but it appears in 1202, shortly after he wrote;[6] and, when it first appears, it is confined to the possessory assizes.[7] The successful bringing of this writ entailed not only the punishment

---

[1] Thayer, Evidence 100, 101.

[2] Ibid 123, 124; for a case of 1346 illustrating the way in which challenges were tried see Y.B. 20 Ed. III. (R.S.) i 486-490.

[3] Thus the perjury of a juror was the only perjury known to the law till a statute of Elizabeth extended it to witnesses, Stephen, H.C.L. i 307; so the only form of forgery known till 1 Henry V. c. 3 was "the reliance on a false document in a court of law," P. and M. ii 539.

[4] "Ea enim quæ in curia domini Regis per duellum semel fuerint terminata negotia perpetuam habent firmitatem," Glanvil ii 3.

[5] "Poena autem in hac assisa temere jurantium ordinaria est et ipsi regali institutioni eleganter inserta. Si enim ipsi juratores perjurasse in Curia fuerint legitime convicti, vel in jure confessi, omnibus catallis, et rebus mobilibus spoliabuntur . . . salvis eis tenementis solis liberis, præterea in carcerem detrudentur et ibi per annum ad minus in prisona detinebuntur, insuper de cetero legem terræ amittentes perpetuam infamiæ notam inde merito incurrent," ibid 19.

[6] Select Civil Pleas (S.S.) no. 216.   [7] Below 338.

of the jurors but also the reversal of their verdict.[1] This difference between the effect of the remedies for a false verdict in the Grand Assize and in the petty assizes looks as if it sprang from direct legislation. It might well seem to Henry II. that it would be inexpedient to disturb the long-established rule that a decision upon a writ of right was final; but this consideration would hardly apply to verdicts in the new possessory assizes into which no question of the title to the property entered.

This remedy of attaint is discussed at some length by Bracton. In his days the law relating to it was not quite the same as it afterwards became under the combined influence of legislation and judicial decision. In the first place, it was only available in the case of a false finding in one of the possessory assizes. As we have seen, this limitation was probably due to the express provisions of the ordinance by which the writ was granted; but Bracton rationalizes this rule by explaining that trials both by the Grand Assize and the jurata really depended on the consent of the parties, whereas trials by the possessory assizes did not depend on such consent; and that it was the fault of the parties if they had consented to a perjured jury.[2] Obviously this explanation is specious rather than sound. A punishment was provided for jurors in the Grand Assize who had perjured themselves;[3] and the parties had as much and as little chance of foreseeing the perjury of an assize as they had of foreseeing the perjury of a jurata. In the second place, Bracton had learnt something of the nature of perjury from his study of the canon and civil law; and, as we have seen, he is sometimes inclined to treat the jurors as if they were witnesses.[4] This leads him to draw all sorts of distinctions between various kinds of false verdicts. He distinguishes a false from a fatuous or mistaken verdict.[5] He would mitigate the punishment for a false verdict according to the circumstances of the case. Those newly added to the assize, or those who before conviction have amended

---

[1] " Et considerandum erit quod prædicti xii juratores male juraverint, et quod querens recuperet seisinam suam, et ille tenens in misericordia, et juratores si præsentes fuerint custodiantur, et si absentes capiantur," Bracton, f. 292.

[2] " Et in magna assisa ideo non jacet convictio, quia cum petens offerat se disrationare dictum suum, oportet quod tenens se defendat vel per duellum vel per magnam assisam, per quod istorum duorum elegerit, et cum de voluntate sua capiat ad assisam, illam recusare non poterit, quod si fecerit, videtur quod defensionem suam reprobaverit, sicut in assisis observatur, ubi quis se ponat in juratam aliqua ratione (ut prædictum est) non poterit juratorum dictum postmodum reprobare, quod si faceret, nihil aliud esset quam facere probationem suam nullam, et ideo non admittitur convictio," Bracton, ff. 290, 290 b.

[3] Above 337.   [4] Above 318 n. 1.

[5] " Si autem sacramentum fatuum fuerit licet falsum, tamen non committit perjurium, licet re vera res aliter se habeat quam juraverat, et quia jurat secundum conscientiam, eo quod non vadit contra mentem," Bracton, f. 288 b; cf. f. 181 b.

their finding should be treated more leniently.[1] In the third place, the uncertainty as to the number of the jury led to uncertainty as to the number of the attaint jury. All that can be said is that they must be double the number of the original jury, but that there need not be more than twenty-four.[2] In the fourth place, the fact that the jury need not then be unanimous leads him to distinguish between the minority who have given a true, from the majority who have given a false verdict. The former naturally escape punishment when the verdict of the attaint jury proves that they were right.[3]

A good deal of the law propounded by Bracton became obsolete when the position of the jury came to be more clearly defined. When the number of the jury came to be usually twelve,[4] the number of the attaint jury was fixed at twenty-four. When the rule as to unanimity was fixed[5] all the jury were equally liable. Naturally, also, many incidental matters connected with the issue and effects of the writ were gradually settled by the courts. Thus it was settled that it could be issued by the chief justice at a general Eyre as well as by the Chancellor,[6] that a prima facie case must be made out for its issue,[7] and that there could be no second attaint on the same facts.[8] There were also decisions as to the venue of the attaint jury,[9] and as to the mode of its choice.[10] But these were details. The greatest changes in the law as to attaint were due, firstly, to the extensions of the remedy by the legislature, and, secondly, to the growth of a disinclination to treat the jury merely as witnesses.

(i) As trial by jury came to be the usual method of trying disputed facts the necessity of finding some method of controlling the jury came to be more and more obvious ; and the line of least resistance was to extend the scope of the attaint. Nor did it in those days appear to be anomalous to make this control take the form of a semi-criminal proceeding. As we have seen, complaints

---

[1] Ff. 289, 292 b.
[2] "Si autem convincendi sunt juratores per 24, videndum erit quot juratores fuerunt in assisa, ut quilibet ad minus duos habeat comvictores, et si plures habeat non nocet," Bracton, f. 288 b.
[3] "Si forte duodecim concordes non fuerint in assisa capienda sed discordes, poterunt viginti quatuor quosdam liberare, et quosdam damnare, sicut accidit de Alberto comite Somerset," f. 292.
[4] Above 325.   [5] Above 318.
[6] The Eyre of Kent i 158 ; Y.B. 30, 31 Ed. I. (R.S.) 124.
[7] The Eyre of Kent i lxxix 51.   [8] Ibid i 156.
[9] Y.B. 12 Rich. II. 159, 160.
[10] "These four and twenty jurors were chosen with the assent of the parties and of such of the jury of twelve as were present, for these were allowed equal right of challenge regarding the jury of four and twenty as was allowed to the parties," Eyre of Kent i 166.

against judges sometimes took this penal form [1]—indeed such complaints were treated together with complaints against jurors by Bracton ; [2] and, after all, the jurors were guilty of something very like perjury.   And so the writ of attaint was extended.   In 1275 it was provided that the king might issue the writ upon verdicts in real actions, whether the inquest proceeded as an assize or a jury. [3]   In 1327 [4] it was extended to writs of trespass, and the Chancellor was to issue the writ " without speaking therefor to the king "—in other words it was made a writ of course.   In 1331 [5] and 1354 [6] it was extended to pleas of trespass begun otherwise than by writ ; and in 1360 [7] to all actions real and personal, with the further proviso that it was to be granted to the poor without fine.   It is clear that this line of statutes applied only to civil proceedings.   Attaint did not lie upon the proceedings in a criminal appeal ; [8] and no one ever seems to have thought that it would lie against a jury who had found a verdict of guilty upon an indictment.   But Bracton [9] and Hale [10] seem to think that it might lie against a jury who had acquitted. This, however, was denied by Hudson in his treatise on the Star Chamber, [11] and by Vaughan, C.J., in *Bushell's Case ;* [12] and the absence of any cases in which such attaints were brought would seem to show that they were right.   In point of fact the procedure in criminal cases was so favourable to the king that he had little need to resort to this remedy ; and, as Thayer says, " the doctrine was ancient that one should not be twice put in jeopardy of life or limb for the same offence." [13]   Moreover, as we shall see, the king had other ways of dealing with juries who declined to convict. [14]

---

[1] Above 213-214.

[2] " Item in culpa poterit esse judex sive justitiarius et non jurator, ut si cum jurator veritatem dixerit et rationem dicti sui assignaverit et justitiarius pronunti-averit in contrarium, et hoc facit ex certa scientia.   In hoc casu tenebitur ex male-ficio male pronunciando et pervertendo scienter justum judicum juratorum, et sic non erunt juratores in culpa, sed justitiarius.   Si autem hoc fecerit per ignorantiam vel per imperitiam, tenebitur ex quasi maleficio, sed cum eo propter imperitiam, mitius erit agendum quoad poenam," f. 289.

[3] 3 Edward I. c. 38; cf. Eyre of Kent iii xlvii-xlviii ; Thayer, Evidence 146 n. 4 ; Reeves, H.E.L. ii 33-34.

[4] 1 Edward III. c. 6.   [5] 8 Edward III. c. 7.   [6] 28 Edward III. c. 8.
[7] 34 Edward III. c. 7.   [8] 22 Ass. pl. 82.

[9] " Est tamen quædam jurata, quæ aliquando admittit convictionem, ut si fiat jurata de aliquo quod tangat dominum regem et facit contra dominum regem, convinci poterunt juratores per alios ; ut coram Martino de Pateshul de Henry de Movewedene, qui aliquando fuit in custodia domini regis tempore Huberti de Burgo," f. 290 b ; but cf. Thayer, Evidence 156—as he says the passage may not refer to a criminal case.

[10] P.C. ii 310, citing Fitz. Ab. *Attaint* pl. 60, 64.   [11] At p. 72.

[12] Vaughan at p. 146; it would seem that the law was taken as settled in this sense in 1690, Hist. MSS. Com. Thirteenth Rep. App. Pt. V. p. 21.

[13] Evidence 158-159.   [14] Below 343-344.

(ii) We have seen that, from the end of the thirteenth century onwards, the court treated the jury, not as a collection of witnesses who could be separately examined, but as a mode of proof to which the parties had submitted their case.[1] They did not regard them altogether as witnesses, but rather as a set of arbitrators who were under a legal duty to find the facts correctly. If they did not find the facts correctly, they were liable to be punished by the writ of attaint. It is clear from a case decided in 1337 that this liability was differentiated from the perjured witnesss's liability, in that it was coming to be regarded, not entirely as a liability for swearing falsely, but rather as a liability for a verdict which was in fact false.[2] The court refused to undertake the task of examining whether the jury had or had not believed their verdict. They merely examined by means of an attaint jury whether it was correct—"the thought of man is not triable."[3] The practical result of this was that all the rules as to adjusting the punishment, according as the verdict was deliberately false or only fatuous or mistaken, disappeared. If the original jury was convicted by the attaint jury sentence followed in one stereotyped form.[4] They were imprisoned for a year, forfeited their goods, became infamous, their wives and children were turned out, and their lands laid waste.

These developments of the writ of attaint obviously increased both the sphere of the remedy and the severity of the punishment. But, as at the same time, the judicial character of the jury was developing, the remedy gradually lost its usefulness, and ended by becoming a mere anachronism.

The growth of the practice of summoning witnesses or producing other evidence to inform the jury naturally raised the question whether the attaint jury could look at any evidence other than that which had been before the original jury. It was settled in 1467 that they could not.[5] But, even with this mitigation, the consequences of an attaint were beginning to be felt to be too severe. In 1451 there was a case in which the parties were unwilling to resort to the remedy, because the jury who gave

---

[1] Above 317-318.

[2] "And in this plea Sharshulle, J., said that when witnesses are joined to the Twelve, one should never have the Attaint, because the Twelve can never be convicted until the witnesses are, and they cannot be, because their oath is to tell the truth outright, just as they were sworn to do in a Great Assize, and not to say it on their knowledge," Y.B. 11, 12 Ed. III. (R.S.) 338-340.

[3] See vol. iii 374, 375.

[4] Y.B. 11, 12 Ed. III. (R.S.) 479-480; it would seem, however, the jurors could escape by making fine with the king, Eyre of Kent i 169.

[5] Y.B. 7 Ed. IV. Hil. pl. 14, cited Thayer, Evidence 138; it would seem, however, that this was not the rule at an earlier period, Eyre of Kent i lxxix; though they were not liable if the verdict was reversed owing to the discovery of a fact of which they could have known nothing, Y.B. 2, 3 Ed. II. (S.S.) 157.

the false verdict had been terrorized, and it was not considered fair to expose them to so severe a penalty.[1]   But so long as the jury retained anything of its character as witnesses the attaint held its ground.   Thus Fortescue mentions it with approval as a necessary adjunct to a jury trial ;[2] and in 1495[3] an attempt was made to increase its usefulness by a modification of the penalty imposed on the jury who had given a false verdict.   It was provided that a jury, on conviction, should, if the amount at issue was of the value of £40, forfeit £20, be fined at the discretion of the court, and be accounted infamous ; and that if the amount at issue was under the value of £40 they should forfeit £5.   But, as the injured party had the option of proceeding either under this statute or at common law,[4] it did not effect very much. In 1553 there is a note in Wriothesley's Chronicle of an attaint jury who, after an all-night sitting, convicted a jury ; but the chronicler notes that it was the " first attainte that had passed for many years in London."[5]   This confirms the truth of Sir Thomas Smith's statement[6] that, " Attaints be very seldom put in use, partly because the gentlemen will not meet to slander and deface the honest yeomen their neighbours ; so that of long time they had rather pay a mean fine than to appear and make the inquest. And in the meantime they will entreat, so much as in them lyeth, the parties to come to some composition and agreement among themselves. . . . And if the gentlemen do appear, gladlier they will confirm the first sentence for the causes which I have said, than go against it."   In 1665 Hyde, C.J., declared that it was a " fruitless " remedy.[7]   But, in spite of the fact that it had become a mere anachronism, a bill for the reform of the law, which was brought in in the House of Lords in 1690, proposed to revive it in civil cases, to extend it to criminal cases, and to reform it by a diminution in the penalties imposed on conviction.[8]   But the bill dropped, and in the eighteenth century attaint ceased to be used.   In 1757 Lord Mansfield declared that the writ was then " a mere sound ; "[9] and in 1825 it was abolished.[10]

The disuse of the writ of attaint in the sixteenth century did not mean that all control over the jury was lost.   We have seen that in the Middle Ages the court exercised a very stringent con-

---

Thayer, Evidence 138.   [2] De Laudibus c. 26.

[3] 11 Henry VII. c. 24; reinacted 27 Henry VIII. c. 3, and made perpetual 13 Elizabeth c. 25.

[4] Bl. Comm. iii 404.   [5] Wriothesley's Chronicle (C.S.) ii 84-85.

[6] De Republica, Bk. iii c. 2 ; and Hudson agrees, Star Chamber 14.

[7] 1 Keble 864 ; Blackstone said that he had seen no instance later than the sixteenth century, Comm. iii 404.

[8] Hist. MSS. Comm. Thirteenth Rep. App. Pt. V. No. 244 § 17 p. 21.

[9] Bright v. Eynon, 1 Burr, at p. 393.

[10] 6 George IV. c. 50 § 60.

trol.   Members of a jury of presentment who, as members of the petty jury, found the prisoner not guilty, were fined and imprisoned; [1] and the court always assumed the power to punish such forms of misconduct in jurors as separating, or eating or drinking, before they had returned their verdict. [2]   In Edward III.'s reign a grand juryman who had revealed matters which had come before him in that capacity was indicted for felony, and one of the judges thought that he might have been indicted for treason. [3]   In Richard II.'s reign a jury which had given a verdict of acquittal was so threatened by the judge that they wished to retract it, but were not allowed to do so. [4]   But, in spite of the efforts of the judges, the disordered state of the country during the latter part of the mediæval period made the jury system almost unworkable. [5]   Juries were habitually returned to suit the convenience of the local magnate who possessed the greatest influence; and if a jury seemed likely to show any signs of impartiality it was either bribed or terrorized. [6]

It was the action of the Council and the Star Chamber which reformed these practices. [7]   Their action with respect to the jury had the same effect as it had in many other spheres of government—it restored its proper working. [8]   That the Council and Star Chamber had the right to exercise powers of control, which in the Middle Ages the common law courts had failed to exercise with effect, was admitted on all hands.   The legislature gave this power in wide terms to the Council of Wales in 1534; [9]   Lambard [10] and Coke [11] approved of it; and Sir Thomas Smith, though he disapproved the practices of punishing jurors merely for finding verdicts contrary to the evidence, admitted that corrupt jurors ought to be punished. [12]   But, in the sixteenth century, the Star

---

[1] Above 325.   [2] Above 318-319.

[3] Fitz. Ab. *Corone* pl. 207 = 27 Ass. pl. 63.

[4] Fitz. Ab. *Corone* pl. 108.   [5] Below 483-484, 490-491; vol. ii 415-416.

[6] For an illustration see Plumpton Correspondence (C.S.) 171.

[7] " Preparing, labouring, or soliciting of jurors," is stated by Hudson at pp, 91-92 to be one of the branches of the jurisdiction of the Star Chamber; at p. 123 he relates how, " an extent had gone out against one Harvey; and the jury, being laboured, could find no goods of Harvey's but an old barrel and a turkey cock.   And for this scorn the court ordered his majesty's attorney-general to put in an information against the jury."

[8] Below 507-508; vol. iv 77-80, 84-85.

[9] 26 Henry VIII. c. 4 § 2.   [10] Archeion 105-106.

[11] In Floyd v. Barker (1608) 12 Co. Rep. 23, he said at pp. 23-24, " When a jury hath acquitted a felon or traitor against manifest proof, there they may be charged in the Star Chamber, for their partiality in finding a manifest offender not guilty."

[12] " I have seene in my time (but not in the raigne of the Queene nowe) that an enquest for pronouncing one not guiltie of treason contrairie to such evidence as was brought in, were not onely imprisoned for a space, but an houge fine set upon their heads, which they were faine to pay : An other enquest for acquiting an other, beside paying a fine of money, put to open ignominie and shame.   But those doings were even then of many accounted verie violent, tyrannical, and contrarie to the

Chamber was apt to treat any verdict of acquittal which it considered to be against the weight of evidence as corrupt. In *Throckmorton's Case* the acquittal of the prisoner was followed by the fining and imprisonment of the jury ;[1] and Hudson notes[2] that "in the reigns of Henry VII., VIII., Queen Mary, and the beginning of Elizabeth's reign there was scarce one term prætermitted but some grand inquest or jury was fined for acquitting felons or murderers." It would seem, however, both from Sir Thomas Smith and Hudson that at the end of the sixteenth century the tendency was to use this power only if the verdict was so obviously foolish that corruption might be presumed.[3] But it was quite clear that the powers both of the Star Chamber and of the common law courts were still as indefinite as they had been in the Middle Ages.

It is not therefore surprising that, after the Restoration, the common law courts should suppose that they still possessed these powers. Coke could be cited to prove that they possessed them ; and they were exercised in several cases.[4] But it is clear that public opinion was beginning to come round to the view expressed by Sir Thomas Smith that it was only a corrupt verdict which ought to be thus punished ; and that merely to find a verdict contrary to the direction of the court or contrary to the evidence ought not to expose the jury to penalties. In at least one case effect was given to this view ;[5] it was approved by the House of Commons ;[6] and an unsuccessful attempt was made to give it legislative sanction.[7] It was the argument of Vaughan,

libertie and custome of the realme of England. Wherefor it commeth verie seldome in use, yet so much at a time the enquest may be corrupted, that the Prince may have cause with justice to punish them," De Republica Bk. iii c. 1.

[1] (1554) 1 S.T. 869.

[2] Star Chamber 72 ; cf. Moore 730-731 for several cases in which this course was pursued by the court of wards.

[3] A saying of Bacon's, reported by Hyde, C.J., Star Chamber cases (C.S.) 20, was to the effect that, "if you shall meet with ignorant juries, your duty is to open their eyes, you may not lead them by the nose."

[4] Leach's Case (1664) Th. Raym. 98 ; R. v. Hood (1666) Kelyng 50-51 ; R. v. Windham (1667) 2 Keble 180 ; S.P. Dom. 1664-1665 39, ciii 105 ; cf. ibid 1667-1668 327, where a jury withdrew a verdict of acquittal under pressure from the court.

[5] Hale, P.C. ii 312-313 relates that in 1665, in the case of R. v. Wagstaffe, "it was agreed by all the judges of England that this fine was not legally set upon the jury, for they are the judges of matters of fact, and although it was inserted in the fine, that it was *contra directionem curiæ in materia legis*, this mended not the matter, for it was impossible any matter of law could come in question, till the matters of fact were settled and stated and agreed by the jury, and of such matter of fact they were the only competent judges ;" the fining took place at the gaol delivery at Newgate ; and Hale cautiously concludes that, "Although the long use of fining jurors in the king's bench in criminal cases may possibly give a jurisdiction to fine in these cases, yet it cah by no means be extended to other courts of sessions of gaol delivery, *oyer and terminer*, or of the peace or other inferior jurisdictions," ibid 313.

[6] 6 S.T. 992 seqq.

[7] Hargrave's Preface to Hale's Jurisdiction of the House of Lords xcviii n. y.

C.J., in *Bushell's Case*[1] which finally fixed the law on these lines. In that case the jurors had, in spite of very brutal treatment by the court,[2] persisted in acquitting the Quakers, Penn and Mead. In consequence they had been fined and imprisoned. They were brought up before the court of Common Pleas on a writ of Habeas Corpus and discharged. It is true that the judgment of the court in this case was reversed on the ground that the case, being a criminal case, was not cognizable by the court of Common Pleas; and that this reversal was in accordance with the opinion of Vaughan, C.J.[3] Nevertheless the argument by which Vaughan proved the illegality of punishing jurors for their verdicts was so obviously right, and so obviously in accordance with the views which public opinion approved, that it has ever since been accepted as good law.

Vaughan drew more clearly than it had ever been drawn before the distinction between two very different classes of misconduct of which jurors may be guilty. " Much of the office of jurors in order to their verdict is ministerial, as not withdrawing from their fellows after they are sworn, not withdrawing after challenge . . . not receiving from either side evidence after their oath not given in court, not eating and drinking before their verdict, refusing to give a verdict, and the like; wherein if they transgress they are finable; but the verdict itself, when given, is not an act ministerial but judicial, and according to the best of their judgment, for which they are not finable nor to be punished, but by attaint."[4] He proved conclusively that a jury could not be punished for judicial acts, firstly from the nature of their functions, secondly from the manner in which they were expected to perform their functions, and thirdly from the absurdity of any other conclusion.

Firstly, the jury are the judges of the facts, and not the judge. If the judge can order the jury on pain of punishment to take his view of the facts, what is the use of the jury? They might as well be abolished—"a strange new found conclusion, after a trial so celebrated for many hundreds of years."[5] And, as the jury are judges of the facts, a disagreement with the judge as to the findings of fact deducible from the evidence cannot be penal. " I

[1] (1670) Vaughan's Rep. 135.

[2] Marvel tells us in one of his letters, Works ii 350, that "the jury not finding them guilty, as the Recorder and Mayor would have had them, they were kept without meat and drink some three days, till almost starved, but would not alter their verdict; so fined and imprisoned."

[3] Above 203.

[4] Vaughan's Rep. at p. 152; thus in Welcden v. Elkington (1578), Plowden at p. 519 it is recorded that "because a box of preserved barberies, and sugar candy, and liquorish, were found with John Mucklow, one of the jury, after he was departed from the bar, the said Mucklow was committed to the Fleet, until he had made a fine to the Queen."

[5] At p. 143.

would know whether anything be more common than for two men, students, barristers, or judges to deduce contrary and opposite conclusions out of the same case in law? And is there any difference that two men should infer distinct conclusions from the same testimony?"[1] Secondly, the jury may well know more about the case than the judge, since they may have means of knowledge which the judge has not got. The judge can only know so much of the case as can be gathered from the evidence produced in court. The jury may have private knowledge of the facts, parties, or witnesses, which they are entitled and required to use.[2] Thirdly, if the jury can be punished by the court for not obeying the direction of the judge some very absurd results, at any rate in civil cases, will follow. "If they do follow his direction, they may be attainted, and the judgment reversed for doing that, which if they had not done, they should have been fined and imprisoned by the judge, which is unreasonable. If they do not follow his direction and be therefore fined, yet they may be attainted, and so doubly punished by distinct judicatures for the same offence, which the common law admits not."[3]

Vaughan's reasoning was conclusive, and the practice of fining and imprisoning the jury for judicial acts came to an end. The only way in which the crown could now exert pressure to get a favourable verdict was by exercising care in the choice of the jury—a mode of pressure which Charles II. and James II. freely employed. But such practices were irregular, and they came to the end at the Revolution. They had supplied no method of regular control; and it was obvious that some regular method of controlling the verdicts of juries was essential to the proper working of the jury system. This regular method of control was found in the growth of the practice of granting new trials if the verdict was clearly contrary to the weight of evidence.[4] Some of the arguments of Vaughan's judgment were, as Thayer has pointed out,[5] applicable to this practice. How, for instance, can it be known that the verdict is irrational, seeing that the jury may have other sources of information than the evidence produced in court? The answer is to be found in the fact that the character of the jury as judges of the facts had by this time prevailed over their character as witnesses; and that, in consequence, the court was laying down the modern rule that a juryman should lay before the court as a witness any information which he

---

[1] At p. 141. [2] At p. 147.
[3] At p. 148; this reductio ad absurdum of the practice did not, of course, appl⋅⋅ to criminal cases in which the writ of attaint did not lie; it had formerly been held by the judges that fining was illegal when attaint lay, ibid at pp. 144-145.
[4] Above 225-226. [5] Evidence 169.

possessed.[1] Thus a state of things was produced which Vaughan himself admitted entitled the court to exercise some control. " If," he said,[2] " the jury were to have no other evidence for the fact, but what is deposed in court, the judge might know their evidence, and the facts from it equally as they."[3] Because this condition is now fulfilled there can be no logical objection to this modern method of control.

The power of the court to discharge a jury which cannot agree may perhaps be said to be another indirect means of control. The Doctor and Student asserted,[4] but Coke[5] denied that the court had this power. But Hale[6] and Blackstone[7] recognize its existence. The question was put beyond doubt by the decision of the Court of Queen's Bench and Exchequer Chamber in *Winsor* v. *The Queen*,[8] where Cockburn, C.J., showed that it was a power necessary to the proper working of the jury system.[9]

(5) The legal and political effects of the jury system.

The defects of the jury system are obvious. They are twelve ordinary men—" a group just large enough to destroy even the appearance of individual responsibility."[10] They give no reasons for their verdict, which is perhaps apt, and it is apt, in times of political excitement, to reflect the popular prejudice of the day. Experience shows that they are capable of intimidation.[11] It is said that they are always biased when a pretty woman or a railway company happen to be litigants. Though a good special jury is admitted to be a very competent tribunal, the common jury may be composed of persons who have neither the desire nor the capacity to weigh the evidence, or to arrive at a conclusion

[1] Above 336 ; at the same time the personal knowledge of the jurors may sometimes assist matters ; Chalmers tells us of a jury who came to a speedy decision for the plaintiff in a doubtful case where there had been hard swearing on both sides ; on his asking a juryman how they managed it, he replied, " I don't know the plaintiff but the defendant is a friend of mine, and I know he is a d——d liar," L.Q.R. vii 17.

[2] Vaughan's Rep. at p. 147.

[3] He was careful to add that this would afford no justification for punishing the jury—" even then the judge and the jury might honestly differ in the result from the evidence, as well as two judges may, which often happens," ibid.

[4] Docto r and Student, Pt. II. c. 52—If the jurors cannot agree, " I think that then justices may set such order in the matter as shall seem to them by their discretion to stand with reason and conscience by awarding of a new inquest, and by setting fine upon them that they shall find in default, or otherwise as they shall think best by their discretion, like as they may do if one of the jury die before verdict, or if any other like casualties fall in that behalf."

[5] Third Instit. 110.   [6] Hale, P.C. ii 294, 295.

[7] Bl. Comm. (12th Ed.) iv 360.   [8] (1866) L.R. 1 Q.B. 289, 390.

[9] At p. 306.   [10] Stephen, H.C.L. i 568.

[11] E.g. Ireland of the present day, England under the Plantagenets, at the time of the Popish Plot, and at the end of the eighteenth century.

upon the facts in issue. But in spite of these obvious defects, distinguished judges, who have spent many years working with juries, have combined to praise the jury system. Fortescue, Coke, Hale, Blackstone, and Stephen are witnesses whose evidence should be conclusive. We may add to these names that of Chalmers, whose experience in the new county courts led him to the same conclusions. In fact the jury system works well from the point of view of the litigant, the judge, the jury itself, and the law.

The litigant gets a body of persons who bring average common sense to bear upon the facts of his case. "A jury," says Chalmers, "is a far better tribunal than a judge for dealing with questions of fact. The more I see of juries the higher is the respect I have for their decisions. . . . They have a marvellous faculty for scenting out a fraud."[1] Their findings create no precedent ; and thus they can decide hard cases equitably without making bad law. Litigants are generally contented with the measure of justice which they mete out ; and this is no small gain to a legal system.

Judges have, as we have seen, from the earliest times appreciated the relief from responsibility which the jury system affords to them.[2] Both Hale[3] and Stephen[4] emphasize this fact. And not only does the collaboration of the jury relieve the judge from the responsibility of deciding simply upon his own opinion, it also helps him to take, as the adviser and director of the jury, a more truly judicial attitude. Thus it helps to preserve the dignity of the Bench ; for, if the judge preserves this judicial attitude, no odium can attach to him whatever be the verdict of the jury. And so, as De Tocqueville has said,[5] "the jury which seems to diminish the power of the magistrate really gives it its pre-eminent authority."

The jury itself is educated by the part which it is required to take in the administration of justice. The jury system teaches the members of the jury to cultivate a judicial habit of mind. It helps to create in them a respect for law and order. It makes them feel that they owe duties to society, and that they have a

---

[1] L.Q.R. iii 10-11. [2] Above 318 and n. 3.

[3] "It were the most unhappy case that could be to the judge if he at his peril must take upon him the guilt or innocence of the prisoner," Hale, P.C. ii 313.

[4] "It saves judges from the responsibility—which to many men would appear intolerably heavy and painful—of deciding simply on their own opinion upon the guilt or innocence of the prisoner," H.C.L. i 573.

[5] "Le jury, qui semble diminuer les droits de la magistrature, fonde donc réellement son empire," Démocratie en Amerique ii 192 ; and even if he is called on to act without a jury, "son pouvoir moral est bien plus grand : les souvenirs du jury le suivent encore, et sa voix a presque autant de puissance que celle de la société, dont les jurés etaient organe," ibid.

share in its government. It is this education of the members of
the jury that De Tocqueville regarded as the most valuable consequence of the system. "We should regard it as a school
which gives instruction gratuitously and continuously. Where
each juryman can learn his rights, where he mixes day by day
with the best educated and most enlightened of the upper classes,
where the law is taught to him in the most practical way, and is
explained in á manner which he can understand by the efforts of
the bar, by the direction of the judge, and even by the passions
of the parties." [1]

The effects of the jury system upon the law are no less remarkable and no less beneficial. It tends to make the law
intelligible by keeping it in touch with the common facts of life.
The reasons why and the manner in which it thus affects the law
are somewhat as follows : If a clever man is left to decide by
himself disputed questions of fact he is usually not content
simply to decide each case as it arises. He constructs theories
for the decision of analogous cases. These theories are discussed,
doubted, or developed by other clever men when such cases come
before them. The interest is apt to centre, not in the dry task
of deciding the case before the court, but rather in the construction of new theories, the reconciliation of conflicting cases,
the demolition or criticism of older views. The result is a series
of carefully constructed, and periodically considered rules, which
merely retard the attainment of a conclusion without assisting in
its formation. [2] It is only the philosopher, or possibly the professor of general jurisprudence, who can pursue indefinitely these
interesting processes. Rules of law must struggle for existence
in the strong air of practical life. Rules which are so refined
that they bear but a small relation to the world of sense will
sooner or later be swept away. Sooner if, like the criminal law
or the commercial law, they touch nearly men's habits and conduct ; later if, like the law of real property, they affect a smaller
class, and affect them less nearly. The jury system has for some
hundreds of years been constantly bringing the rules of law to
the touchstone of contemporary common sense. The beneficial

---

[1] "On doit le considérer comme une école gratuite et toujours ouverte, où
chaque juré vient s'instruire de ses droits, où il entre en communication journalière
avec les membres les plus instruits de les plus éclairés des classes élevées, où les lois
lui sont enseignées d'une manière pratique, et sont mis à la portée de son intelligence par les efforts des avocats, les avis du juge, et les passions mêmes des parties,"
Démocratie en Amerique ii 190.

[2] An instance is afforded by § 29, 4 of the Sale of Goods Act 1893, which makes
the question whether demand or tender of delivery has been made at a reasonable
hour a question of fact ; " it was formerly," says Chalmers, " a question of law, and
some highly technical rules for determining it were laid down by Lord Wensleydale."

effects of this process can be best illustrated by a comparison with some of the rules evolved by the court of Chancery which never worked with a jury. " One finds oneself," says Chalmers,[1] " in a rarified atmosphere of morality and respectability in which life is hardly possible. Look at the equitable doctrines of constructive notice and constructive fraud. Look at the impossible standard of duty laid down for trustees."[2] The legislature has done something to remedy these things.[3] Most perhaps was done by Sir George Jessel who was a profound equity lawyer with the mind of an acute juryman. He did much to bring the rules of equity to the touchstone of common sense ; and his influence has been felt by all his successors.

Judges must explain the law to the jury. They must separate the rule of law from the question of fact. This produces both precision in the statement of the rule, and a clear outside judgment on the facts. Bagehot[4] said of the Parliamentary head of a government office, " his function is to bring a representative of outside sense and outside animation in contact with the inside world. No man is a perfect representative of outside sense . . . that many-sided sense finds no microcosm in any single individual." The jury is to the inside technical world of our common law system a representative of that outside sense, and outside animation.

---

[1] L.Q.R. vii 19.

[2] Lindley, M.R., said in Perrins v. Bellamy [1899] 1 Ch. at p. 798, " My old master, the late Lord Justice Selwyn, used to say, the main duty of a trustee is to commit *judicious* breaches of trust."

[3] E.g. Judicial Trustees Act, 59, 60 Victoria c. 35 § 3.

[4] English Constitution 201.

CHAPTER IV

THE HOUSE OF LORDS

IN this chapter we are concerned with the House of Lords, not as a branch of the legislature, but as a law court. This differentiation of functions is not primæval. We have seen that in early days executive legislative and judicial functions shade off into one another ; and it is because the body which developed into the House of Lords had close relations with all these sides of government that it acquired its varied judicial powers. It will therefore be necessary to say a few words as to the origin and development of the House of Lords in order to explain why it has acquired these powers. I shall therefore, by way of introduction, say so much of its origin and development as is necessary to explain the character of the different kinds of jurisdiction which it has exercised at different periods in the history of English law ; and then I shall relate the history of the process by which the boundaries of that jurisdiction have been fixed.

I. The Origins of the Judicial Powers of the House of Lords

We have seen that down to the reign of John the Curia Regis possessed legislative, executive, and judicial powers. We have seen, too, that its size varied according to the nature of the occasion on which it was summoned ; that it generally consisted of a small body of professional advisers, sometimes of a much larger body of tenants in chief.[1] The movement which led to the granting of Magna Carta altered the whole position of the Curia Regis. The victory of the Barons meant that the king was no longer practically absolute. It was clear that the nation had both the desire and the power to exercise some sort of control upon the government. The question of the form of the body which will exercise this national control is the great constitutional question of the reigns of Henry III. and Edward I. From the

[1] Above 35.

various experiments tried during that period there was evolved the Model Parliament of 1295.[1] It was far from being a purely feudal assembly based upon tenure, like the Commune Concilium of Magna Carta.[2] Elective and representative principles—familiar already in local government—found a place beside feudal principles. From the union of the feudal and the elective and representative principles, we get in time our modern Parliament—the House of Lords and the House of Commons.

Bracton, writing in Henry III.'s reign has little to say of this new body. He knows the King's Bench and the Common Bench;[3] he knows also the Commune Concilium, the authority of which is needed for the issue of new original writs;[4] but the King's Bench is still the highest court. Fleta, writing a little later, knows a court higher than the King's Bench—the Parliament. "The king has his court in his council in his Parliament, held in the presence of the prelates, earls, barons, and other learned men, where doubtful points in law are determined, new remedies are devised for new wrongs, and justice is distributed according to every man's deserts."[5] His words are large and vague—larger and more vague that those in which he describes the constitution of older and more settled courts. But if we look at one of our earliest printed Parliament Rolls—the Roll of 1305[6] —we shall see that large and vague words are needed to describe the facts.

This Roll raises many interesting questions as to the constitution of the Parliaments of the thirteenth and fourteenth centuries.

(1) What does the term Parliament mean? A Parliament is rather a discussion or a colloquy than a body of persons. "It is but slowly," says Maitland,[7] "that this word is appropriated to colloquies of a particular kind, namely, those which the king has with the estates of his realm, and still more slowly that it is transferred from the colloquy to the body of men whom the king has summoned. As yet any meeting of the King's Council that has been solemnly summoned for general business seems to be a Parliament." It is, in fact, a large meeting of the King's Council afforced by elected representatives from the counties and boroughs. The petitions are presented "at" the Parliament to

---

[1] Vol. ii 302-304.   [2] Above 55-56; vol. ii 213.
[3] Above 204 n. 5.
[4] "Et sunt quædam brevia formata super certis casibus, de cursu et de communi concilio totius regni concessa et approbata, quæ quidam nullatenus mutari poterint absque consensu et voluntate eorum," f. 413 b.
[5] "Habet enim Rex curiam suam in concilio suo, in Parliamentis suis, præsentibus prelatis, comitibus, haronibus, proceribus et aliis viris peritis, ubi terminatæ sunt dubitationes judiciorum, et novis injuriis emersis nova constituuntur remedia, et unicuique justitia, prout meruit, retribuetur ibidem," Fleta ii 2, 1.
[6] Edited by Maitland for the Rolls Series.   [7] Introd. lxvii.

the king and Council. The Council is the "core and essence" of the Parliament.[1]

(2) What is the nature of the King's Council? This is a difficult question.[2] Probably the working body of the Council consisted of the king's great officers of state and the judges. It is not easy to say how many more persons may have been added to the Council on any particular occasion. In later history we meet with many bodies called by the name of Council to which the epithets "magnum" or "ordinarium" are added;[3] but in the Middle Ages these are merely epithets.[4] In the thirteenth century the Council was sometimes a small body of professional advisers, sometimes it consisted of these advisers and the whole House of Lords. A distinct court like the court of King's Bench has a distinct style. Nothing illustrates better the fluctuating and indistinct character of the Council than the fact that it has no such distinct style. "The styles," says Hale,[5] "of the consilium ordinarium, and of the great court of Parliament consisting of the king, lords, and commons, and of the lords' house, are so variously and promiscuously used, that it causeth great difficulty in determining whether the proceedings be in the one or the other . . . it is necessary in such cases to observe the whole record and the nature of the business so transacted, and the whole circumstances of the case, and the constant interpretation, acceptance and usage of succeeding times, to give a true conclusion whether the things were transacted and assented to by both Houses, or only by the lords' house, or the consilium ordinarium." We have seen that in Edward I.'s reign the courts of law were only just beginning to get an independent existence[6] These large meetings of the Council, at which the king meets the estates, include the courts of law; and so, as Professor Baldwin has said, we seem to get "a survival of the conception of a single governing institution."[7] But this single

[1] For a later instance (1429) of the use of the term Parliament to mean a great council or general assembly of the Lords Spiritual and Temporal, see Nicolas, Privy Council iii, *lxii;* cp. Pollard, Evolution of Parliament 33-34.

[2] Parliament Roll xxxvi-xlvii; below chap. vi.

[3] Hale, Jurisdiction of the House of Lords 23, 70-73.

[4] Professor Baldwin, The King's Council 112-114, has pointed out that the term "ordinary council" does not occur till the reign of Henry VIII., and that it is a mistake " to project the idea " of a division between ordinary and privy councillors into the Middle Ages; he thinks that though the rank of the councillors differed, there was no organic difference between different councils; "the only vital distinction of this kind which the Middle Ages really demanded was that between the Parliament and the Council;" that distinction, as we shall see, grew up in the course of the fourteenth century, below 360, 486-489.

[5] Hale, Jurisdiction of the House of Lords, chap. iii.

[6] Above 195-196, 204-207, 231-233.

[7] "With great comprehensiveness the Parliaments of Edward I. were made to include not only the several estates, but all of the existing courts of law. In the remerging of these branches there seems to have been a survival of the conception

governing institution is now no longer only a body of officials and magnates : it includes representatives from the counties and boroughs. We shall see that this addition will set in motion a train of events which will in time completely differentiate the King's Council in Parliament from any other council or court.[1]

(3) What does the King's Council do at a Parliament? Business of state is transacted, and there will sometimes be taxation and legislation.[2] But it is to two other functions that we must look for some of the origins of the later jurisdiction of the House of Lords. (i) It hears important cases.[3] It is not merely a court of appeal. It exercises original jurisdiction. It is not tied down by the technical rules which are beginning to fetter the two Benches. Like the Curia Regis of Henry II.'s time, it can administer a species of equity because it is a supreme court. Why any particular case should be heard in Parliament rather than elsewhere is not clear. All that can be said is that "the causes heard in Parliament are important causes, important because they concern the king, or because they concern very great men, or because they involve grave questions of public law, or because they are unprecedented."[4] Most of these cases were determined by the Council; some after the estates had been dismissed. All, however, were regarded as being determined by the Council in Parliament. In fact "throughout the Middle Ages cases were likely to be heard at alternate stages in Parliament and before the Council."[5] (ii) It answers petitions. The writ appointing the receivers of petitions stands at the head of the Roll. The Roll itself shows that it is the answering of petitions which is its chief duty. Two earlier ordinances of the eighth[6] and twenty-first[7] years of the reign show that their

of a single governing institution," The King's Council 309 ; Select Cases before the Council (S.S.) xx, xxi.

[1] Below 360.   [2] Parliament Roll, xlviii-liv.

[3] Such cases are those of Nicholas Segrave (no. 449); a suit as to tallage between the citizens of Salisbury and the Bishop (no. 451); proceedings in consequence of riots at Oxford (nos. 452, 453); proceedings against the citizens of Winchester for an escape (no. 456).

[4] Maitland, Parliament Roll, lxxxv; for an instance of a case heard before the Council because it affected great men see Baldwin, Select Cases before the Council (S.S.) 5, l, lii.

[5] Ibid xiii.

[6] Ryley, Placita 442 ; Stubbs, C.H. ii 286 n. 2 ; it is provided that because of the inconvenience caused by the large mass of petitions, "all the petitions which touch the seal come first to the Chancellor, those that touch the Exchequer to the Exchequer, those that touch the justices and the law of the land to the justices, those that touch the Jewry to the justices of the Jewry. If the requests be so great or so much of grace that the chancellor and the others cannot grant them without the king, then they shall carry them with their own hands to the king to know his will. . . . Thus the king and his council without burden of other business can attend to the important business of his realm and of foreign lands ; " cp. Reeves, H.E.L. ii 289, 290.

[7] Ryley 459 ; Stubbs, C.H. ii 286 n. 3 ; similar provisions were made, and receivers of petitions were appointed.

number was so great that it was necessary to make arrangements for their classification. The petitions were of varied kinds. They came chiefly from individuals and communities. Some asked for things which the petitioners could get by an action at law. These were sent to the ordinary courts. Sometimes they asked favours of the king. Sometimes they asked for relief which no known writ could give. Sometimes they asked for new legislation. All these petitions came before the Council who, perhaps, examined the petitioner. It then either endorsed an answer which sent the petition to one of the ordinary courts, or it laid the matter before the king.[1] In the answers we "very rarely find anything in point of decision or judicature;" we usually find only "a recommendation to those proper courts, persons, or places where they (the petitions) were naturally and legally determinable." They are a council of "advice, preparation, and direction," rather than a council of "jurisdiction or decision;"[2] and the Council continued to act thus after it had become definitely separated from the House of Lords.[3] In later days some of these petitions will be addressed directly to the Chancellor; others will, if assented to by the king and both Houses, become statutes; others will be dealt with by the king in Council. But the time has not yet come when the functions of Parliament, the court of Chancery, and the Council, can be clearly distinguished. In the meantime the Council in Parliament is doing just what Fleta describes it as doing. It is providing new remedies for new wrongs. It is distributing justice according to each man's deserts.

During the fourteenth and fifteenth centuries the same process of differentiation in governmental institutions which had given rise to the courts of common law divided Parliament from the Council, and Parliament into two Houses. The origin of the judicial functions exercised by the House of Lords can be traced ultimately to this twofold division; and therefore it is necessary to say something of its causes.

The King's Council in Parliament in Edward I.'s reign can be divided into three fairly distinct groups. Firstly there were the "curiales"—the group of professional councillors who had been, from the time of the Norman Conquest, the backbone of the Curia Regis. They included "a varying number of justices, barons of the exchequer, clerks of the chancery, and other learned men".[4] Secondly there were the magnates, lay and

---

[1] Parliament Roll lx-lxiv; Maitland thinks that "the entries on the roll stand to the endorsed petitions in the relation of copies to original documents."

[2] Hale, Jurisdiction of the House of Lords 25.

[3] Baldwin, Select Cases before the Council (S.S.) xviii.

[4] Baldwin, The King's Council 312-314.

ecclesiastical.　They were the large landowners who were
entitled to a special summons on important occasions because
they were the most important tenants of the crown.[1]　Thirdly
there were the elected representatives from the boroughs and the
counties.　The separation of the curiales from the magnates;
the alliance between the magnates assembled in the House of
Lords and the elected representatives assembled in the House of
Commons, which resulted in the settlement of the constitution of
the two Houses of Parliament; and the settlement of the respective powers of these two Houses in relation to judicature—these
were the three causes which gave rise, in the course of the
fourteenth and fifteenth centuries, to the new grouping both of
institutions and functions, from which the various kinds of jurisdiction exercised by the House of Lords emerged.　The origins
of these varieties of jurisdiction I shall therefore describe under
these three heads.

(1) The separation of the curiales from the magnates.

Hale,[2] writing at the latter part of the seventeenth century,
pointed out that, "In the great court of Parliament at least the
figure and model of the consilium regis and the persons whereof
it consisted is to this day preserved in the Lords' House in
Parliament.　For thither are summoned the great officers,
whether they are peers or not; as the chancellor, treasurer,
privy seal, secretaries of state, judges, barons of the exchequer,
masters of chancery, king's serjeant and attorney, the treasurer
of the household, steward and chamberlain of the household, and
most if not all the king's privy council."　But long before Hale's
day these officials had ceased to be the "core and essence" of
the Parliament.　In fact this separation of the officials from the
magnates, which made the Council and the House of Lords quite
separate institutions, had begun in Henry III.'s reign, and became
permanent in Edward II.'s reign.[3]　"It is noticeable," says
Professor Baldwin,[4] "that in point of numbers, while Edward I.
could summon as many as thirty such officials at a time,
Edward III. rarely invited more than ten, sometimes only seven
or five or less, to come to Parliament."　The cases which came
before Parliament were said in 1327 to be heard, not "coram
rege et concilio suo in Parliamento," but "coram domino rege et
consilio suo in presentia regis procerum et magnatum regni in
Parliamento suo."[5]　Thus the phrase "king in his council in
Parliament," came to mean, not a joint session of the Council

---

[1] Baldwin, The King's Council 311-312, 315.
[2] Jurisdiction of the House of Lords 58-59.
[3] Pollard, Evolution of Parliament 90-91.
[4] The King's Council, 316-317.　　　　　　[5] Ibid 317.

and Parliament, but simply a session of the House of Lords, to which the judges and certain other officials of the crown were summoned merely as assistants.[1]

A powerful cause making for this separation was the growth of the idea that the magnates specially summoned to Parliament, and sitting together in the House of Lords, were peers; and that to be a member of the peerage conferred a special status.[2] The notion was fostered by the clause of Magna Carta which provided for a trial by peers;[3] and, whatever may have been the original meaning of this clause,[4] it was used in the fourteenth century to give to the peers who sat in the House of Lords the right, if accused of treason or felony, to be tried by their peers in that House.[5] It is clear that this privilege made the class of peers a very distinct class, and separated it from the royal officials who were also summoned to the King's Council in Parliament.

Who, then, constituted this class of peers?[6] The Earl was from the first a dignified official, and the title was always a name of dignity.[7] The first Duke was the Black Prince. "His dukedom in fact was only a superior kind of earldom." Marquis and Viscount were foreign terms introduced at a still later period.[8] The Baron was never a dignified official.[9] The title was originally used to designate the tenure of a certain estate rated as a barony; and until the middle of Edward III.'s reign the summonses of barons to Parliament were quite capricious. The first person to be created a Baron by letters patent was John de Beauchamp who was created Baron of Kidderminster in 1387.[10] It was not till about that time that a barony began to be regarded as a dignity, and for a long period it is not quite clear how far a barony represented property, how far it represented dignity. We are reminded of the conflict between property and jurisdiction which existed in the manor. But with the abolition of tenure by military service barony by tenure lost its meaning. The barony became a dignity simply; and the Baron took rank as a peer.[11] The case of the Spiritual Lords is more difficult. That they

---

[1] "As the prelates and lords absorbed all the independent functions of the justices and their associates, 'the council in Parliament' as an expression inevitably shifted from its original meaning. Although it was used less frequently than before, it meant nothing less than the House of Lords, wherein a few of the law officers of the crown remained in a subordinate capacity," Baldwin, The King's Council 318; cp. Pollard, Evolution of Parliament 105-106.

[2] Below 358 n. 5.   [3] § 39 (1215).
[4] Above 59, 60.   [5] Below 386-388.
[6] See Pollard, Evolution of Parliament, chap v.
[7] Pike, House of Lords, chap. v.   [8] Ibid 348.
[9] Ibid chaps. vi, vii.   [10] Ibid 110, 111.
[11] Ibid 129-131; in 1669 barony by tenure was declared obsolete; see the Berkeley Peerage Case (1861), Anson, Parliament (5th Ed.), 215-218.

were held to be barons in the Middle Ages is clear.[1] But they could not take part in a sentence of death.[2] They did not claim to be tried by their peers because they denied their liability to be tried by laymen.[3] Thus they did not share what had come to be the distinctive mark of the peerage. In Henry VIII.'s reign the Abbot of Tavistock was termed a Spiritual Lord of Parliament; and this is the position which they have finally assumed.[4] It is true that they possess all the other privileges of the peerage; and these in former days were numerous.[5] It might perhaps have been more in accord with history to have concluded with Selden that they were peers, though they had no right to be tried by their peers.[6] But it is trial by peers that the law has singled out as the test of peerage; and with this test they cannot comply.

This separation between the classes of magnates and the royal officials, which had made up the King's Council in Parliament in Edward I.'s reign, was no doubt helped by the long standing feud between the great barons and these royal officials.[7] The strong government of Henry II. and Edward I. had crushed the disorderly anarchic feudalism of the sort that had run riot in Stephen's reign. But the great barons eagerly embraced the opportunity to embarrass the royal officials who managed the central government, by declining to admit their equality in an assembly in which the baronial influence was all powerful. This doctrine of the peerage, and the accompanying right to trial by peers in the House of Lords, was an excellent means to this end;[8] and so we get the establishment of the idea of the peerage, and the acquisition by the House of Lords of a criminal jurisdiction over peers.

There was another direction also in which this jealousy between the magnates and the official classes was operative. We have seen that the great business of Edward I.'s Parliaments was

---

[1] Selden, Privileges of the Baronage, Works iii 1537-1539; Pike, House of Lords 160, 161; Phillimore, Eccl. Law (Ed. 1895) 60-62.

[2] In Edward IV.'s time Littleton thought that they could appoint a Procurator, Pike, House of Lords 218; Coke, Third Instit. 31.

[3] They were tried by jury in the ordinary way; Bishop of Coventry (1307); Bishop of Hereford (1324); Bishop of Carlisle (1401); Bishop of Rochester (1574); Archbishop Cranmer (1553).

[4] Pike, House of Lords 163, 164.

[5] Selden, loc. cit. 1533-1586; instances are: If a peer was a party a knight must be on the jury till 1751; freedom from arrest in civil actions; clergy; letters missive were sent them by the chancellor instead of a writ of subpoena; see Marowe, op. cit. 395-396 for special rules in the case of outlawry.

[6] Ibid 1538; cp. Jurisdiction in Parliament, Works iii 1589.

[7] " Until the death of Edward I. the strife was repressed with difficulty, but it came all the more surely during the reign of his successor," Baldwin, The King's Council 315.

[8] Pollard, Evolution of Parliament 94.

the hearing of petitions.   In 1305 clerks to receive and classify
the petitions, and committees to receive only or to receive and
answer them were appointed ; and these committees were composed chiefly of officials and partly of magnates.[1]   As the
fourteenth century proceeded, the magnates tried to keep the
answering of these petitions in the hands of committees appointed
by themselves.   Thus in 1316 groups of receivers were appointed,
who were usually clerks of the Chancery, to receive and classify
the petitions, while the duty of hearing them was turned over to
persons called triers or auditors or examiners who were " bishops
and barons with only a few of the judges and officers to aid them " [2]
In Edward III.'s reign a further step was taken in the elimination of the authority of the officials.   At the request of the
Commons, these auditors were deprived of the power to answer
the petitions if the answer involved the determination of any
matter of law.[3]   All such petitions must be determined by the
House itself.   And so, as Hale says,[4] " as the grandeur of the
Lords prevailed, so by degrees the power of the auditors and consilium decayed."   Their appointment became a mere formality,
but it was not till 1886 that the formality of appointing them
was dropped.[5]

But the House of Lords had other and more important work
to do than the answering of petitions.[6]   They were the advisers
of the king upon matters of state policy domestic and foreign.
Hence, as Professor Baldwin says, "scores of petitions both public
and private, ' from the brevity of time ' went unanswered and were
left over from Parliament to Parliament ".[7]   The Lords tried in
vain to cope with the flood,[8] and at length, in the fifteenth century, they pursued the only possible course, and turned them
over to the Council.[9]   Thus the greater part of the jurisdiction
which the Lords had grasped at, but could not hold, was abandoned to the officials who composed the Council ; and, in the
sixteenth century, it was divided between the Council, the Star
Chamber, and the Chancery.[10]   For all that, the claim to deal
with these petitions, put forward by the House of Lords in the
fourteenth century, left its mark on the jurisdiction of the House.
It enabled it to assert vague powers to hear important cases

[1] Parliament Roll (R.S.) no. 1, and see Introd. lvii-lxi.
[2] Baldwin, The King's Council 323-324 ; Hale, Jurisdiction of the House of
Lords, chap. xii.
[3] Baldwin, op. cit. 325.
[4] Jurisdiction of the House of Lords 77.
[5] Anson, Parliament 344—" The receivers were judges or masters in the courts ;
the triers were chosen from among the temporal peers."
[6] Baldwin, The King's Council 326, citing R.P. ii 316.
[7] The King's Council, 326.   [8] Ibid 326-327.
[9] Ibid 327-328.   [10] Below 405-409.

criminal or civil, which were not precisely defined till the seventeenth century.[1] We shall see, too, that the form in which their jurisdiction in error was exercised was intimately related to their right to receive and adjudicate upon petitions for redress presented to the King and his Council in Parliament.[2]

(2) The alliance between the magnates assembled in the House of Lords and the elected representatives assembled in the House of Commons.

We have seen that in Edward III.'s reign the Commons had requested the Lords not to allow the auditors of petitions to answer petitions which involved the determination of any matter of law.[3] It is this jealousy of any interference with the law which was the bond of union between the Lords and Commons. From the early years of the fourteenth century, both Lords and Commons maintained that it was only in Parliament that there could be any legislation, or any alteration of either the common or statute law.[4] It was indeed admitted that the Council might have powers of legislating an emergency—such as the emergency which called forth the Ordinance of Labourers in 1349; [4a] and that it might, on similar grounds, have a moderate power to suspend statutes; [5] but, from the time when the statute of 1322 [6] which repealed the Ordinances of the Lords Ordainers was enacted, it was steadily maintained that the legislative power was in the whole Parliament, and in it alone. Now it is clear that this alliance of Lords and Commons to maintain, as against the Council, their control over the law, united both the Houses very closely with the common law courts and judges. We shall see that the common lawyers were beginning to be an important group in the House of Commons; [7] and that both they and the judges were unwilling to take their law from the Council.[8] This unwillingness was strengthened by the fact that the Council in the fourteenth and fifteenth centuries was exercising a jurisdiction supplementary to that of the common law courts, and by processes and on principles which were not those of the common law.[9] It was only natural therefore that the common lawyers should, for both these reasons, consider that errors in law were amendable not by the Council but by Parliament.

---

[1] Below 365 seqq.　　　　[2] Below 370-371.
[3] Above 359.　　　　[4] Vol. ii 435-440; Baldwin, op. cit. 318.
[4a] See B. Putnam, Enforcement of the Statute of Labourers, 2.
[5] Vol. ii Bk. iii c. 5; Baldwin, op. cit. 319, 320.
[6] " The matters which are to be established for the estate of our lord the king and of his heirs, and for the estate of the realm and of the people, shall be treated, accorded, and established in parliaments by our lord the king, and by the consent of the prelates, earls, and barons, and the commonalty of the realm, according as hath been heretofore accustomed," 15 Edward II. Statutes (R.C.) i 189; Stubbs, C.H. ii 382-383; vol. ii Bk. iii c. 5.
[7] Vol. ii Bk. iii c. 5.　　　　[8] Below 361.　　　　[9] Below 486.

It is no doubt true that in the days when the Council and the King's Bench and Parliament were hardly distinct, and not yet rivals, precedents could be found for a jurisdiction in error by the Council.[1] But, so soon as these bodies became distinct and rival bodies, there was but little hesitation on the part of the common law judges in asserting the inability of the Council to exercise a jurisdiction in error. In 1366 a judgment of the Common Pleas was reversed by the Council; but, says the Year Book,[2] "the judges paid no attention to this reversal before the Council, because that was not a place where judgment could be reversed." After this decision, the jurisdiction to amend the errors of the common law courts was left to Parliament.[3] Though the Council might advise the judges, or even give directions as to the hearing of a case,[4] its only jurisdiction in error was over courts which exercised a jurisdiction outside the sphere of the common law courts.[5]

The jurisdiction which the House of Lords thus assumed tended to be generally a jurisdiction in error, and not an original jurisdiction. There are many petitions in which the petitioner was told to pursue his remedy at common law.[6] In 1377 all the judges in Parliament stated that error in the Common Bench ought to be amended in the King's Bench, and should not be brought immediately into Parliament.[7] In 1402 the Commons complained that, after judgment given, the parties were often compelled to answer afresh sometimes before the king, sometimes before the Council, and sometimes before Parliament; and they prayed that after judgment the parties should not be thus made

---

[1] Above 209-210; as Baldwin says, op. cit. 335, "there was a conflict of precedents arising from the fact that these two bodies of authority were not clearly distinguished."

[2] Y.B. 39 Ed. III. Pasch. p. 14—"Les justices ne pristerent nul regard al reverser devant le consel pour ce que ne fuit place ou judgment purroit estre reverse."

[3] Baldwin, op. cit. 336.

[4] Professor Baldwin says the reason for this apparent anomaly is that "a judicial opinion or word of advice need not be a matter of record, but a final judgment it was thought should only be made by a court of record;" but we shall see that the technical idea of a court of record was not quite reached at this period, vol. v 157-160; the reason rather is that a judgment made law—at any rate for the parties: advice or directions to the judges did not.

[5] Below 520-522.

[6] In a case before Parliament in 1290 a litigant was told, " Nec est juri consonum vel hactenus in curia ista usitatum, quod aliquis sine lege communi et brevi de cancellaria de libero tenemento suo respondeat, et maxime in casu ubi breve de cancellaria locum habere possit," Ryley, Placita 43; similarly in 1389 the Lords told a petitioner, "que la dite Petition n'estoit pas Petition du Parlement, einz que la matiere en ycelle compris deust estre discus par la Commune Ley. Et pur ce agarde fuist . . . que le dit Adam ne prendroit riens par sa suite," R.P. iii 259, 13 Rich. II. no. 10.

[7] R.P. ii 330, 50 Ed. III. no. 48.

to answer, but that the judgment should be final till reversed by attaint or error.[1]   Thus, although it is nowhere explicitly stated that the jurisdiction of the House of Lords over cases within the jurisdiction of the common law courts was only a jurisdiction in error, it was in fact generally a jurisdiction of this kind.   Obviously the House would have had no time to be constantly hearing cases which could be perfectly well heard by these courts.   In fact it had not time enough even to hear the writs of error brought before it.[2]   Like its jurisdiction over petitions, its jurisdiction in error fell into abeyance in the course of the fifteenth century.   But, unlike its jurisdictions over petitions, this jurisdiction was never appropriated by the Council.   It was always recognized as belonging to the House ; it was revived in the latter half of the sixteenth and the earlier half of the seventeenth centuries ; and its limitations were fixed in the last half of the latter century.[3]

(3) The settlement of the powers of the two Houses in relation to judicature.

As jurisdiction to correct the errors of the King's Bench was said to be in Parliament, the question at once arises, Why did this jurisdiction come to be vested in the Lords to the exclusion of the Commons ?   That it was so vested only in the Lords was definitely stated by all the judges in 1485 ;[4] it had then been generally recognized for at least a century,[5] and it has never been judicially questioned.   Hale, nevertheless, thought that the right of the Commons to share in the judicial powers of the Lords, though "much disused," was still a subsisting right ;[6] and Coke [7] and Holt [8] seem to have been of the same opinion. But, firstly, the cases cited in support of this view are generally either of a political character, or come from a date before the

[1] R.P. iii 510, 4 Hy. IV. no. 110.
[2] Above 359.   [3] Below 370-375.
[4] " Per dominos tantum et non per communitatem assignabitur senescallum qui cum dominis spiritualibus et temporalibus per consilium justiciariorum procedent ad errorem corrigendum," Y.B. 1 Hy. VII. Pasch. pl. 5 (p. 20).
[5] Below 363.
[6] Jurisdiction of the House of Lords, chap. xxii ; cp. Pike, House of Lords 290, 291, 294 n. 2.
[7] Fourth Instit. 23, and instances there cited ; there is a note upon erroneous judgments in Parliament in the House of Lords MSS. of the year 1624, Hist. MSS. Comm. Third Rep. App. Pt. I. 34-35, in which the idea of the need for the consent of the Commons appears—" A judgment was anciently reversed in Parliament by petition to the King, referred by him to Parliament, the Lords then appointed a committee to examine the errors, and afterwards acquainted the Commons with their decision, as it is the judgment of the King and Lords with assent of the Commons."
[8] He said in R. v. Knollys (1694) 1 Ld. Raym. at p. 15, " The judicial power is only in the Lords, but legally and virtually it is the judgment of the King as well as of the Lords, and perhaps of the Commons too."

constitution and powers of Parliament were definitely settled;[1] and, secondly, they are sometimes instances of the exercise of legislative rather than judicial powers.[2] These two powers were, as we shall see, by no means accurately distinguished in the earlier part of the mediæval period and even later.[3] The exercise of both might originate in petitions for relief; and the character of the relief sought often did not fall clearly into one or other category. This confusion has helped to mislead later historians and judges who have read into these cases ideas and distinctions which were unknown when they were decided.

In spite then of these weighty authorities to the contrary, it is probable that the Commons never seriously claimed to share the judicial powers of the Lords; and there are three reasons why this was so. (i) It was not quite forgotten that jurisdiction in error was to the King and his *Council* in Parliament. Though the House of Lords had reduced the official members of the Council—the judges, law officers, and others—to the rank of assistants, they were still attached to the House in that capacity; and the House could therefore consult them in the hearing of appeals. It might therefore be contended that the House of Lords was still a Council of the crown; but the House of Commons had never claimed to possess that status.[4] After Richard II.'s reign it is clear from the way in which petitions of error were addressed that it was generally recognized that this jurisdiction belonged to the Lords only. These petitions were generally addressed "al roy et al nobles," or "al nobles seigneurs en parlement;"[5] and after Henry IV.'s reign the proceedings are said to be "coram nobis prelatis et proceribus in

---

[1] The cases of the Bishop of Hereford and Thomas of Lancaster, in which the judgment was reversed by the whole Parliament at the beginning of Edward III.'s reign, cited by Hale, op. cit. chap. xxii, are clearly of a political character; Segrave's Case, Parliament Roll of 1305 (R.S.) 257, comes from the very early days of Parliament, and was also a political case; Professor Baldwin, op. cit. 330 n. 2, cites two cases in which the Commons were recited to have taken part in a judgment; the first is from the Close Roll of 39 Ed. III. m. 27; the second is clearly political, as it is the reversal of the judgment declaring Roger Mortimer a traitor, R.P. ii 256.

[2] A good instance of this confusion is the case of the Earl of Salisbury, cited by Hale, op. cit. chap. xvi; it appears that he assigned as an error that the judgment against him was, " sauns petition ou assent des communes en le dit parlement queux de droit serront peticioners ou assentours de ceo que serra *ordeine per ley* en parlement," R.P. iv 18, 2 Hy. V. no. 12.

[3] Vol. ii 308, 434 and nn. 4, 5; vol. iv 183-186.

[4] Baldwin, op. cit. 308; as Pike, House of Lords 50, says, " The King in his Council in his Parliament . . . was not necessarily a Parliament including the Commons, but a Parliament of Lords Spiritual and Temporal with the King and his Council sitting therein. In this assembly it seems, too, that we must recognize the ancient Common Council of the Realm which Bracton mentioned as the necessary authority for the form of an original writ."

[5] Hale, Jurisdiction of the House of Lords 138.

Parliamento." [1] (ii) Though the House of Lords could claim to be a Council of the crown, it undoubtedly was a branch of the Parliament. Thus an appeal to a body styled "the King in his Council in Parliament" could only be to the House of Lords.[2] (iii) The Commons did not desire to be burdened with the duty of judicature. As Maitland has said in another connection,[3] we must often, in dealing with the courts of the Middle Ages, "put duty in the first line, right in the second." In answer to a petition by the Commons in 1400 it was declared that judgments in Parliament belonged only to the King and the Lords and not to the Commons, saving that in respect of legislation, taxation, and other such things for the profit of the realm they might be asked for their advice and consent.[4] The petition of the Commons was perhaps intended to apply only to appeals for crime in Parliament,[5] which in Richard II.'s reign had been extensively used for political purposes.[6] But, in later years, it was taken to apply to all the jurisdiction exercised by the Lords.[7] Whether or not such an interpretation was correct, it is pretty clear that the Commons never asserted from that date onwards any claim to share the judicial powers of the Lords.

We can thus see the origins of the judicial powers of the House of Lords partly in its old association with the Council, partly in the separation of the official members of the Council from the magnates, partly in the growth of the idea of the peerage, partly in the settlement of the constitution of Parliament and of the relations between the two Houses of Parliament. All these causes contributed to give the House of Lords the very

[1] Hale, Jurisdiction of the House of Lords 142; Hale's comment is very apposite, "This it seems obtained upon two reasons: 1. Because the lords were intent as much as possible to exclude the commons from a concurrent judicature in such cases, which possibly was not so well obviated by the general words of *parliamentum* or *curia nostri parliamenti*, which by construction might possibly extend to both houses. 2. Because they were intent also to exclude the *consilium ordinarium* from a concurrent voice in these cases, and to bring them to be only assistants."

[2] "The essential part of 'the King in Council in Parliament,' for the purpose of this jurisdiction, was therefore at the time (1377) considered to be the Parliament; and as the Commons formed no necessary part of 'the King in Council in Parliament,' the word Parliament must be interpreted to mean the House of Lords," Pike, House of Lords 289.

[3] Parliament Roll (R.S.) lxxxvi; cp. Baldwin, op. cit. 330.

[4] R.P. iii 427, 1 Hy. IV. no. 79.

[5] The words of the petition are, "que nul record soit fait en Parlement encontre les ditz Communes qu'ils sont ou serront parties as ascunes juggementz donez ou as doner en apres en Parlement."

[6] Below 378-379.

[7] See the Y.B. cited above 362 n. 4; cp. Selden, Judicature in Parliament, Works iii 1637; Professor Pollard, Evolution of Parliament 331 n. 3 doubts whether the renunciation of the Commons was intended to be permanent; but it is clear that the case in the Commons Journals i 45 to which he refers is merely an inquiry without any reference to strictly judicial proceedings.

various kinds of jurisdiction exercised by it from time to time during the fourteenth century. But, during that century, the spheres of its jurisdiction had been by no means accurately defined. The collapse of Parliamentary government, which occurred in the fifteenth century, and the outbreak of the Wars of the Roses, stopped all chance of any settlement of this problem;[1] and in the sixteenth century the powers assumed by the King and Council[2] gave little opportunity to the House of Lords to exercise its judicial powers. Almost the only one of its judicial powers which was actively exercised was its power to try peers accused of treason or felony. However, the fact that it had other judicial powers was recognized; and these powers were naturally revived with the revival of the powers of Parliament in the seventeenth century. It was therefore during that century that the extent of the judicial powers of the House of Lords were at length ascertained and settled upon their modern basis. To the history of this process of definition we must now turn.

II. The Settlement of the Judicial Powers of the House of Lords

If we look at the judicial powers of the House of Lords from the point of view of the settlement ultimately arrived at, we can classify them under the following three heads : Civil Jurisdiction ; Criminal Jurisdiction ; and Jurisdiction in Cases of Privilege. Under these heads therefore I shall relate the history of their settlement upon their modern basis.

(1) Civil Jurisdiction.

The history of the civil jurisdiction of the House of Lords falls under two heads : Original Jurisdiction, and Jurisdiction arising from proceedings pending or decided in the inferior courts.

Original Jurisdiction

We have seen that in Edwards I.'s reign the jurisdiction exercised by Parliament was as often original as not; but that in the fourteenth and fifteenth centuries there was a growing tendency not to exercise such jurisdiction. At the same time there are precedents of cases heard originally by the Lords. If the king's interest was specially concerned he would commission

---

[1] Below 483-485, 490-491 ; vol. ii 413-417.   [2] Below 503-508.

the Lords to hear the case. Thus petitions of right and monstrans de droit, cases of lunacy, cases where, owing to the turbulence and strength of one of the parties, justice could not be got
in the ordinary courts, were heard by the Lords in this way.[1]
During the Tudor period many of these cases were dealt with by
the Council. There are no precedents for the exercise of any
sort of original jurisdiction by the Lords during that period. In
1621 there are three cases in which they assumed such jurisdiction ;[2] and their assumption of this jurisdiction was justified by
Selden,[3] who had, in that year, been commissioned by a committee of the Lords to draw up an account of the privileges of
the peers.[4] His work is based upon old records taken from a
time when the constitution of Parliament was not fixed. The
records could be made to justify any pretension of the Lords.
But, being merely statements of facts occurring at a time when
there were no rules upon the subject, they could equally well
serve the purposes of those who opposed these pretensions. They
were interpreted by the Lords as giving them the widest jurisdiction. In 1626 they entertained the petition of a private person
with reference to riots which had taken place at Banbury. Other
cases were depending before them when the Parliament was dissolved.[5] They entertained many such cases during the Long
Parliament; but, as Hale justly observes, this is hardly a time
from which precedents could be safely drawn. The cases of
Lilburne (1646) and of Maynard (1647) produced a controversy
on the subject.[6] Prynne published a book entitled " A Plea for
the Lords and House of Peers," in which he asserted the jurisdiction in the widest term ; and the influence of the book is
evident from the proceedings of the Lords in the Convention
Parliament. It is significant, however, that the Commons declined to admit their jurisdiction " so largely as they had asserted
it." The Lords in no way receded from their claims. In 1663
they sentenced to fine and imprisonment two persons called
Fitton and Carr for libels upon Lord Gerard of Brandon.[7] Both
petitioned the Commons, and committees were appointed to examine the cases. Fitton's case was, on the report of the committee, argued at the bar of the House of Commons. Mr. Offley,
his counsel, referred to what was undoubtedly one of the main
causes of the increased jurisdiction claimed by the Lords when

---

[1] Hale, Jurisdiction of the House of Lords 104.
[2] Ibid (Hargrave's Preface) xxii; Hist. MSS. Comm. Fourth Rep. App. II.
[3] Judicature in Parliament, Works iii 1590.   [4] Hale, op. cit. xxix-xxxi.
[5] Ibid li-liii; L.Q.R. xvii 167-169.
[6] Spence, Equitable Jurisdiction i 395, 396; L.Q.R. xvii 167, 168.
[7] Hargrave's Preface xcix, c; for another petition in 1663 which involved an
exercise of an original jurisdiction see Hist. MSS. Comm. Seventh Rep. App. 171.

he said that "the jurisdiction of the Star Chamber is now transformed into the House of Lords but somewhat in a nobler way." Nothing further was done in these cases—possibly the Commons thought that they might be justified on the ground of privilege.

The decisive controversy arose in 1666 in the case of *Skinner* v. *The East India Company*.[1] Skinner presented a petition to the king against the East India Company. He complained that they had seized his ship, that they had assaulted him in his warehouse at Jamba in Sumatra, and that they had taken away an island which belonged to him. The king referred the matter to the Archbishop of Canterbury, the Lord Chancellor, the Lord Privy Seal, and Lord Ashley to report. After hearing the Company the referees reported in Skinner's favour. The king then sent a message to the Lords recommending them to do the petitioner justice; and Skinner himself also petitioned them. The Lords ordered the Company to put in an answer. The Company denied the allegations, and pleaded to the Lords jurisdiction, "because the matters of complaint in the petition are such, for which remedy is ordinarily given in the courts of Westminster Hall, wherein these respondents have right to be tried, and ought not to be brought hither per saltum." The plea was, however, overruled, and they were ordered to pay £5000 damages to Skinner. In the meantime the Company had petitioned the Commons. The Commons voted that the proceedings of the Lords were illegal. Two conferences produced no result; and a prorogation till October 1669 was ineffectual to stop the dispute. The king again prorogued the Houses in the December of that year till February 1670. When they met he proposed that both sides should erase all records of the matter from their books. The proposal was accepted, and peace restored.[2] The victory remained with the Commons; and the law was settled in accordance with the views of all the leading lawyers of that day.[3] A slight attempt to revive this jurisdiction was made in 1693,[4] when a petition was presented to the Lords against certain judges for not sealing a Bill of Exceptions. But on hearing the judges the

---

[1] Hargrave's Preface ciii seqq.; 6 S.T. 710; Hist. MSS. Comm. Eighth Rep. App. 165-174; it was apparently thought by some that the jurisdiction assumed by the Lords could be justified on the ground that the cause of action arose out of England, S.P. Dom. 1663-1664, 673, ci 81.

[2] The unfortunate Skinner never got anything, S.P. Dom. 1668-1669, 71; later he took proceedings in the court of Exchequer, which seem to have been fruitless, House of Lords MSS. 1693-1695, xxxvi 56, no. 763.

[3] Their views were not so unanimous in the earlier part of the century; for Selden's view in favour of the Lords see above 366; and Prynne took the same view.

[4] Bridgeman v. Holt, Shower, P.C. 111; Hargrave's Preface clxxxiv-clxxxviii; House of Lords MSS. 1693-1695 no. 755.

petition was withdrawn.[1] The Lords have never again attempted to revive their claim to exercise an original jurisdiction.

Jurisdiction Arising from Proceedings Pending or Decided in the Inferior Courts

In the earlier records of Parliament we find many species of this kind of jurisdiction; but the different species are not clearly distinguished from one another. From the point of view of later history the various species of this kind of jurisdiction claimed or exercised by the House of Lords can be classified as follows: (i) Interference in the course of the proceedings of the lower courts. (ii) Proceedings by way of error from the common law courts. (iii) Proceedings by way of appeal from the equitable jurisdiction of the Chancellor.

(i) Interference in the course of the proceedings of the lower courts.

In the fourteenth century a court might voluntarily adjourn difficult cases to Parliament in order that the opinion of all the judges upon them might be taken.[2] In later times an adjournment into the Exchequer Chamber served the same purpose.

Sometimes, on the complaint of a litigant, Parliament would order the record to be brought before itself, and either settle the case or give directions to the court below as to how it should be settled.[3] This practice was most frequent when the king's interests were affected. But the same causes which led to the cessation of the original jurisdiction of Parliament operated here. It was seen that such interferences with the process of the lower courts tended to delay justice. Thus in Edward II.'s reign Thomas Hobledon prayed that a writ of error depending in the King's Bench might be removed into Parliament. But the answer was "sequatur placitum coram rege quousque revocatum vel affirmatum fuerit".[4] The case of the Stauntons' was a curious case, and perhaps illustrates, as Hale thinks, the fact that the courts below were beginning to set their faces against such inter-

---

[1] Part of the answer of the judges (Shower 117, 118) was as follows: "If the pretended Bill was duly tendered to these respondents, and was such as they were bound to seal, these respondents are answerable only for it by the course of the common law, in an action to be brought on that statute (West. II. c. 31) which ought to be tried by a jury . . . by the course of the common law and not in any other manner. And the respondents further show . . . that the petition is a complaint in the nature of an original suit . . . not being any more triable by your lordships than every information or action for breach of any statute law is."

[2] Hale, Jurisdiction of the House of Lords 114; Reeves, H.E.L. ii 291; for a case when this was done see Y.B. 8 Ed. II. (S.S.) 179.

[3] For instances see Reeves, H.E.L. ii 290, 291.

[4] Hale 116; R.P. ii 75 (8 Ed. III. n. 14); Ryley, Placita 409 (14 Ed. II.).

ferences.[1]   Geoffry de Staunton brought an action against John de Staunton and Amy his wife in the Common Bench.   A question arising on the pleadings as to the admissibility of a certain averment, he got from the king in his Council in Parliament, a writ ordering the justices to proceed.   They did not proceed; and the Chief Justice of the Common Bench asserted that the law of the Parliament was bad.   On this Geoffry presented another petition.   This time the Chief Justice was ordered either to proceed to judgment before the rising of the Bench or to bring the record into Parliament; and it is stated on the roll that this order "assentu est per touz en plein Parlement, et commande per les Prelatz, Countes, Barons et autres du Parlement."[2] The Chief Justice appeared, and Parliament ordered the court to give judgment for Geoffry.   But, after the judgment had been given, the defendants sued out a writ of error in the King's Bench.   There the same delays and adjournments to Parliament were repeated till the plaintiffs in error finally abandoned the case.   Certainly the case looks as if the justices were beginning to dislike the interference of the Parliament, as they were only induced to obey by the order of the full Parliament.   An attempt was made in 1341 to provide a remedy for these difficulties.   A statute passed in that year[3] recites that delays have been caused by the difficulty of the cases and by the divers opinions of the judges, and enacts that at every Parliament a prelate, two earls, and two barons shall be chosen to hear complaints of such delays. They were empowered to cause the record and the judges to come before them, and, by the advice of themselves, the Chancellor, Treasurer, the judges, and other of the King's Council, to order the justices to give judgment in accordance with their opinion.   If the case could not otherwise be determined they must bring it before the next Parliament.   The statute seems shortly afterwards to have dropped out of use.   Coke mentions it in his commentary on Littleton,[4] but he says, in the Fourth Institute,[5] that "the frequent use of the Court of Exchequer Chamber hath been the cause that this court hath been rarely put in use."   He can only cite one commission under the statute which was granted in 1345.   The Lords seem silently to have dropped the claim to exercise this species of jurisdiction; and they did not revive it in the Stuart period.   But an attempt was

---

[1] Hale, Jurisdiction of the House of Lords 117, 118; Pike, House of Lords 50-53; Y.B. 13, 14 Ed. III. (R.S.) xxxvi-xlii.

[2] R.P. ii 123 (14 Ed. III. no. 31).

[3] 14 Edward III. St. 1 c. 5.   [4] Co. Litt. 71 b, 72.

[5] At p. 68; it was reported in 1689 that in the crown office there was "no footstep of any such commission," Hist. MSS. Comm. Twelfth Rep. App. Pt. VI. 87.

made to revive this statute in a bill for the reform of the law which was considered by the House of Lords in 1690.[1] After that date no more has been heard of either this statute or this jurisdiction.

(ii) Proceedings by way of error from the common law courts. We have seen that a jurisdiction in error was recognized as belonging to the Lords in the fourteenth and fifteenth centuries. Like other parts of their jurisdiction it was little used during the Tudor period. But three cases in which writs of error were brought are known in Elizabeth's reign; [2] and the jurisdiction was recognized in the statute which established the new court of Exchequer Chamber to amend the errors of the King's Bench.[3] It was more frequently exercised in the reigns of James I. and Charles I. ; and it has never been seriously disputed.

There were originally two methods by which cases were brought by way of error before the House of Lords. The older method was the petition of error to the king in his Council in Parliament praying that the record might be removed into the full Parliament. The petition endorsed by the king was in the nature of a special commission of the king to Parliament to hear the errors assigned.[4] The later method used generally after Edward IV.'s reign,[5] was the writ of error.[6] The writ was in some respects a writ of course; but up to the time of the Long Parliament there was always a petition to the king for the writ. At the time of the Long Parliament the practice began of issuing the writ on the attorney-general's warrant ; [7] and this practice was continued after the Restoration. Hale disapproved of this practice ; [8] and, in the latter part of the century, the practice of petitioning the crown for the issue of the writ seems to have been revived.[9] The writ of error when issued, operated, like the

---

[1] Hist. MSS. Comm. Thirteenth Rep. App. Pt. V. no. 244; § xix of the bill runs as follows: " And whereas it is provided by a law made in the fourteenth year of King Edward III. that delays of judgment in other courts shall be redressed in Parliament, which has been rarely put in practice. . . . Be it enacted that from henceforth a Committee of Lords shall be chosen at every Parliament in like manner as is appointed by the said Act, in order to execute the said power thereby given."

[2] 23 Elizabeth ; 27 Elizabeth; 31 Elizabeth; Hargrave's Preface vi, vii ; Dyer 375.

[3] Above 244.

[4] Hale, Jurisdiction of the House of Lords 135-143.

[5] Ibid 136; Hale, ibid 136, remarks that the Register of Writs contains only a petition of error to the House of Lords, not a writ of error, because the writ of error was the later method of procedure; as we shall see, the Register of Writs is an essentially mediæval book, vol. ii 512-520.

[6] Ibid chaps. xxv-xxviii ; App. X. B.

[7] Hale, op. cit. 145; for instances of such a petition see Hist. MSS. Comm. Third Rep. App. 19; S.P. Dom. 1625-1626 15, i 110.

[8] Op. cit. 145.

[9] S.P. Dom. 1661-1662 44, xliv 40; 524, lxi 84; 1689-1690 123; 1690-1691 46; 1691-1692 12, 17, 106, 323.

old petition, as a commission from the king to Parliament to hear the errors. Hale points out that, in consequence, the action of the House of Lords in reversing or dismissing a case brought before it by writ of error was strictly speaking the action of the king as well as the House.[1] But just as the once actual presence of the king in the court of King's Bench came to be a fiction, so the presence and actual share of the crown in giving these judgments was merely a form ; and we shall see that the same remark applies to the criminal jurisdiction of the Lords.

The writ was directed to the Chief Justice of the King's Bench or other court which had given the decision in which error was alleged. He brought up the roll and a transcript, and the transcript having been examined with the roll, the roll was returned to the court from which it had come. The plaintiff then assigned his errors, and got a writ of Scire Facias to the defendant to hear the errors assigned. The defendant appeared and pleaded " in nullo erratum," and the case was heard.[2] Cases once begun were not discontinued by a prorogation. They were discontinued by a dissolution.[3] When the case had been heard, it was sent back to the court from which it had come with a command to issue execution accordingly.

Writs of error could be brought from the court of King's Bench in England, from the court of Exchequer Chamber,[4] and from decisions on the common law side of the court of Chancery.[5] After the Act of Union with Scotland [6] error lay from the Scotch courts. In the Middle Ages error lay from the court of King's Bench in Ireland to the English court of King's Bench.[7] Later it lay either to the King's Bench in England or to the Irish Parliament ; [8] and from the Irish Parliament error lay to the English Parliament.[9] In 1719, in the case of *Annesley* v. *Sherlock*,[10] the Irish House of Lords denied that error lay to the British House. The result was an Act which declared that the right of final appeal was in the British House of Lords, and

---

[1] Op. cit. 153-154.

[2] Coke, Fourth Instit. 21 ; Y.B. 1 Hy. VII. Pasch. pl. 5.

[3] Hale, Jurisdiction of the House of Lords, chap. xxix; Lords Journals xii 581-583.

[4] See Hist. MSS. Comm. Thirteenth Rep. 30 for an unsuccessful attempt to appeal straight to the House of Lords without first appealing to the Exchequer Chamber.

[5] Hale, op. cit. 124.

[6] 5 Anne c. 8 ; the Act does not so provide, but, as the Scotch was merged in the English Parliament, appeals were held to lie to the Parliament of the United Kingdoms, L.Q.R. xvii 363.

[7] Y.B. 13, 14 Ed. III. (R.S) lxxii, lxxiii.

[8] Hale, Jurisdiction of the House of Lords 124.

[9] See Luttrell's Diary iv 360, 382, 494, 500 for a case in 1698-1699 in which this jurisdiction was exercised.

[10] Lecky, History of Ireland i 447, 448.

denied that the Irish House of Lords had any sort of appellate jurisdiction.[1] In 1782 this Act was repealed; and in 1783 all rights claimed by the British Parliament over the Irish Parliament were renounced.[2] The position of the Irish courts was thereby assimilated to that which the Scotch courts had held after the accession of James I. and before the Act of Union. The Act of Union with Ireland (1800) gave the right of final appeal to the House of Lords of the United Kingdom.[3]

We shall see that the reforms of the nineteenth century abolished this procedure in error in the House of Lords,[4] just as they abolished it in the lower courts,[5] and substituted for it the system of appeal by means of a rehearing of the case which had always prevailed in the Chancery.

(iii) Proceedings by way of appeal from the equitable jurisdiction of the Chancellor.

The court of Chancery was, as we shall see,[6] of much later origin than the courts of common law. It had two sides, a common law side and an equity side. From the former, as we have seen,[7] error lay to the House of Lords; but it was not till the latter half of the seventeenth century that that House established its right to hear appeals from the latter.

The first discussion of the question whether any appeal lay from the equitable jurisdiction of the Chancellor occurs in a Year Book of 1459.[8] Prisot, C.J., overruled the arguments of Choke and Ashton, and laid it down that, though error lay to Parliament from the common law side of the Chancery, no appeal lay from a decision of the Chancellor upon a matter of equity.[9] The matter again arose in 1534;[10] but, though it seems to have been thought that the Chancellor might review his own decrees,[11] the discussion upon the question whether they could be reviewed in Parliament or any other court was stopped by the king's secretary.[12] The fact that the decisions of the Chancellor were only subject to review by himself naturally caused dissatisfaction;[13] and the judges, being consulted by Elizabeth, certified that she might refer a decision to them to review.[14] In at least one case

---

[1] 6 George I. c. 5.
[2] 22 George III. c. 53; 23 George III. c. 28.
[3] 39, 40 George III. c. 67.
[4] Below 644.
[5] Above 246; below 643.
[6] Below 403-404.
[7] Above 371.
[8] Y.B. 37 Hy. VI. Hil. pl. 3.
[9] At p. 14.
[10] Y.B. 27 Hy. VIII. Trin. pl. 6 pp. 14-20.

[11] Ibid at p. 15 *per* Knightley *arg.*; and this view prevailed, Rolle, Ab. *Chancery* Z, i 382.

[12] Y.B. 27 Hy. VIII. Trin. pl. 6 p. 16—counsel was arguing that a decision of the Chancellor could be reviewed, not by himself, but in a higher court, but "Le Secretary luy enterrupte, et dit ne parlez plus del autorite de cest Court."

[13] Spence, Equitable Jurisdiction i 394.

[14] Ibid citing 1 Rolle Rep. 331.

she acted on this opinion.[1] It would seem, therefore, that at the beginning of the seventeenth century the only way of questioning a decision of the court of Chancery sitting as a court of equity was either by means of a rehearing by the Chancellor, or by a petition to the king to appoint commissioners to rehear the case.[2] The only other way open to a dissatisfied litigant of questioning a decision of the Chancellor was to get an Act of Parliament to reverse it; and this course was sometimes pursued in the earlier half of the seventeenth century.[3] James I. was thus well warranted in declaring in 1616 that the Chancery was independent of any other court and subject to him alone.[4]

The claim of the House of Lords to interfere with the decisions of the Chancellor began in 1621. There was a long discussion in *Bourchier's Case* in that year;[5] but his complaint took the form, rather of a complaint against the Chancellor, than of an appeal against his decree. He was obliged to apologise to the Chancellor;[6] and a committee of the Lords reported that there were no precedents for entertaining such appeals.[7] Presumably this resolution stopped other petitions against decrees of the Chancellor which had been presented to the House.[8] In *Mathew's Case*, in 1624,[9] the Lords were at first inclined to hear the appeal; but eventually, in accordance with the report of their committee, they declined to hear it, and asked the king to appoint commissioners to review the decision. This, as Hale justly says, "is an instance of greater weight against the inherent jurisdiction of the Lords than a cart load of precedents since that time in affirming of their jurisdiction."

Down to the meeting of the Long Parliament in 1640 there are one or two cases in which petitions were presented to the House of Lords asking for a review of a decree in Chancery.[10] But in other cases, as we have seen, litigants seem to have preferred to proceed by private Act.[11] The infrequency of Parliaments in Charles I.'s reign, and their short duration, prevented any discussion on the rights of the House of Lords to exercise

[1] Fourth Instit. 85.
[2] Vawdray's Case (1616) 1 Rolle Rep. 331; S.C. 3 Buls. 116; Pennington v. Holmes (1637) Spence i 395 n. *f.*
[3] S.P. Dom. 1598-1601 520-521, cclxxvi 80; Hist. MSS. Comm. Third Rep. App. 22, 30, 34 (Court of Requests).
[4] Works (Ed. 1616) 558.
[5] Hale, Jurisdiction of the House of Lords 195; Debates in the House of Lords (C.S.) 106-120.
[6] Debates in the House of Lords (C.S.) 119-120.
[7] Hale, op. cit. 195.
[8] Hist. MSS. Comm. Third Rep. App. 21.
[9] Ibid 34-35; Hale, op. cit. 196-197; Lords Journals iii 421.
[10] Hist. MSS. Comm. Fourth Rep. 12 (1626); ibid 14 (1628).
[11] Above n. 3.

this jurisdiction ; and dissatisfied litigants generally petitioned the king.[1] But the claim of the House of Lords to revise the decrees of the Chancellor sitting as a judge in equity, as they revised the judgments of the courts of common law, was revived in 1640. In that year the Lords reversed a decree of the Chancellor.[2] But in 1646 and 1647 the cases of Maynard and Lilburne gave rise to a discussion of the limits of the jurisdiction of the House of Lords ; and most of the noted lawyers of the time, except Prynne, thought that the House had no right to exercise this jurisdiction.[3]

After the Restoration the House asserted its right to hear appeals from the Chancery.[4] Litigants preferred to appeal to it rather than to apply to the king to appoint commissioners. In fact, after 1639, there is no instance of such a commission having been appointed.[5] In 1669 the Commons had proposed a bill to settle the jurisdiction of the House of Lords, which the Lords had rejected ; and the Commons had in like manner rejected an alternative proposal of the Lords.[6] But there was no discussion on the subject of the right of the House to hear these appeals till the case of *Shirley* v. *Fagg* arose in 1675 ;[7] and the discussion was then caused to some extent by the fact that Fagg was a member of the House of Commons,[8] and to a large extent by the desire to impede the business of the House. The House of Commons denied the right of the Lords ; and they had on their side Lord Nottingham the Lord Chancellor, Hale, Vaughan, and practically all the lawyers of any note. A prorogation did not stop the quarrel ; but, after a second prorogation of fifteen months, the question was dropped ; and the Lords have ever since retained this jurisdiction. It was not, however, till 1726 that their right to hear appeals against interlocutory orders was established ;[9] and, till the end of the century, books appeared

---

[1] S.P. Dom. 1633-1634 370-371, cclvii 47, 48 ; ibid 1638-1639 154, cccciv 37 ; 168, cccciv 66.

[2] Hist. MSS. Comm. Fourth Rep. App. 41 ; ibid 47—an order of the Chancellor was reversed ; L.Q.R. xvii 167.

[3] Spence, Equitable Jurisdiction i 396.

[4] Hist. MSS. Comm. Seventh Rep. App. 143 (1661), 170 (1663), 180 (1664-1665) ; Eighth Rep. App. 107 no. 64 (1666-1667), 110 no. 79 (1666-1667), 112-113 no. 98 (1667), 114 no. 107 (1667) ; Ninth Rep. App. Pt. II. 31 no. 114 (1673) ; S.P. Dom. 1670 153.

[5] L.Q.R. xvii 164 ; there was a petition to the king for such a commission in 1675-1676 owing to the dispute on the question of the appellate jurisdiction which was then at its height, S.P. Dom. 1675-1676 419.

[6] Marvel, Works ii 284, 295 ; for further information as to the contents of these bills see Hist. MSS. Comm. Eighth Rep. App. 108 n. (t).

[7] 6 S.T. 1122 ; Hargrave's Preface to Hale's Jurisdiction of the House of Lords cxxxv seqq. ; Hist. MSS. Comm. Ninth Rep. App. Pt. II. 56 no. 227.

[8] Reresby, Memoirs 100 ; cf. Marvel, Works ii 459.

[9] Spence, Equitable Jurisdiction i 396 n. (c).

which denied their right to exercise this jurisdiction.[1] The victory of the Lords was probably due to political causes. The Commons had come to be more jealous of the powers of the Crown than of the Lords, and they did not wish it to have the power to appoint commissioners to review the decisions of the Chancery.[2]

A little later in the century the Lords asserted their right to hear appeals from the court of Chancery in Ireland.[3] This right they exercised till the legislation of 1782 and 1783 put an end to it. The jurisdiction was resumed by the House of Lords of the United Kingdom after the Act of Union in 1800.[4] On the other hand Lord Nottingham succeeded in persuading the Lords that a proposed assumption of jurisdiction to hear appeals from ecclesiastical courts was contrary to the express provisions of the statute of 1533-1534, which had made the court of Delegates the final court of Appeal in those cases.[5]

Thus the House of Lords acquired its appellate jurisdiction from the courts of law and equity. Its judgments are binding upon all lower courts and upon itself. Selden and Hale, indeed, thought that a decision of the House of Lords might be reversed by itself or by the full Parliament.[6] But Selden does not discuss the question, and Hale bases his assertions on precedents of the fourteenth and fifteenth centuries. As we have seen, the limits of the jurisdiction of the House of Lords were not then settled, and the distinction between judicial and legislative acts was not clearly drawn. In accordance with the opinions of many eminent lawyers the House of Lords decided in 1898 that it was bound by its own rulings upon questions of law.[7] "There may," said Lord Halsbury, " be a current of opinion in the profession that such and such a judgment was erroneous; but what is that occasional interference with what is perhaps abstract justice as compared with the inconvenience—the disastrous inconvenience

---

[1] Atkyns, C.B., who as we shall see, below 465, was a great opponent of the jurisdiction of the court of Chancery, wrote a tract, which he addressed as a petition to the House of Commons, against the appellate jurisdiction of the Lords in equity cases; it is printed in his Parliamentary and Political Tracts which were published in 1734.

[2] Spence, op. cit. i 396 ; Hargrave's Preface clxiii.

[3] Hist. MSS. Comm. Eleventh Rep. App. Pt. II. 124 no. 142 (1679) ; ibid 303 no. 443 (1685).

[4] Above 372.

[5] Hist. MSS. Comm. Ninth Rep. App. 113 nos. 560, 561 ; see 2 Swanst. 326-330 for Lord Nottingham's argument ; for the court of Delegates see below 603-605 ; in 1726 the Lords resolved not to assume appellate jurisdiction in matters of Lunacy, C. P. Cooper, Chancery 161 ; for this jurisdiction see below 473-476.

[6] Selden, Judicature in Parliament, Works iii 1590 ; Hale, Jurisdiction of the House of Lords, chap. xxi.

[7] London Streets Tramway Company v. London County Council [1898] A.C. 375.

—of having each question subject to being reargued, and the dealings of mankind rendered doubtful, by reason of different decisions, so that in truth and in fact there would be no real final court of appeal?"

It is quite clear that all the members of the House of Lords are not competent to act as the highest Court of Appeal from the courts of common law and equity—"whatever the extraction of men be, yet they are not born with the knowledge of the municipal laws of a kingdom, nor can be supposed to be inspired with the knowledge of the law by the acquest or descent of a title of honour." [1] We have seen that, in the Middle Ages, cases heard in Parliament were often heard by the Council, in which the Chancellor and the judges took their places; but that, from about the middle of the fourteenth century, such cases were heard by the whole House of Lords. [2] Hale says [3] in defence of this practice, that, "since the time that the whole decision of errors has been practised in the House of Lords by their votes, the judges have been always consulted withal, and their opinions held so sacred, that the Lords have ever conformed their judgments thereunto, unless in cases where all the judges were parties to the former judgment, as in the case of ship money." But it was clearly possible that the Lords might decide on less sufficient grounds; and, as Hale himself admits, advantage was taken of their power so to decide in the reign of Charles II. "It is grown a fashion in the Lords' House," he says, [4] "for lords to patronize petitions, a course, that if it were used by the judges of Westminster Hall, would be looked upon, even by the Parliament itself, as indecent, and carrying a probable imputation or temptation at least to partiality." Even the bishops have been known to use their position as lords of Parliament to pronounce a decision in favour of their order, contrary to the opinion of the judges. [5] As a rule the Chancellor or ex-Chancellor or the Lord Chief Justice, if a peer, supplied the House with some knowledge of law. But Lord Holland in 1827 maintained the right of lay peers to sit and vote on appeals; [6] as late as 1834 the House

---

[1] Hale, Jurisdiction of the House of Lords 155.

[2] Above 353, 361, 363-364.   [3] Op. cit. 159.

[4] Ibid 201; cf. Lord Shaftesbury's speech in 6 S.T. at p. 1176-1177; and the cases of Reeve v. Long (1695) Salk. 227, and Bertie v. Falkland (1697) 3 Ch. Cas. 129, cited L.Q.R. xvii 366-367.

[5] In 1783, in the case of the Bishop of London v. Ffytche, cited L.Q.R. xvii 367, the courts of Common Pleas and King's Bench, and seven out of eight judges consulted by the House, were in favour of the defendant; the House decided for the Bishop by nineteen votes to eighteen, and in the nineteen votes were included the votes of the thirteen bishops; as Mr. Bevan points out, L.Q.R. xvii 367-368, "many years later much litigation and then legislation had to be expended on that day's work".

[6] L.Q.R. xvii 369.

decided a case without the presence of any professional lawyer;[1] and in 1905 Earl Spencer said that he remembered that, when a mere boy, he had been called in to make a quorum, and that he had sat and heard appeals.[2]

It was in the *O'Connell Case* in 1844 that the rule was laid down, which has been since adhered to, that only lords learned in the law should vote upon appeals.   It was justly said that "if noble lords unlearned in the law should interfere to decide such questions by their votes instead of leaving them to the decision of the law lords . . . the authority of this House as a court of justice would be greatly impaired."[3]   In the case of *Bradlaugh* v. *Clarke*, in 1883, a lay peer attempted to vote; but his vote was ignored.[4]   So binding is this modern convention which excludes all lay peers from a session of the House when sitting as a final Court of Appeal, that it was decided by the Committee of Privileges in 1905 that there was no objection to allowing a peer who was a barrister to be heard as counsel on an appeal to the House.[5]   But this resolution only applies to the appellate jurisdiction of the House.   It does not apply "to the appearing of barristers who are peers before Committees of the House, or before the House when sitting under the presidency of the Lord High Steward on a criminal case."[6]

(2) Criminal jurisdiction.

The history of the criminal jurisdiction of the House of Lords falls under two heads: the obsolete jurisdiction, and the jurisdiction now existing.

The Obsolete Jurisdiction

(i) Edward III.'s statute of Treasons[7] provided that "because many other like cases of treason may happen in time to come, which a man cannot think nor declare at this present time, it is accorded, that if any other case, supposed treason, which is not above specified, doth happen before any justices, the justices shall tarry without any going to judgment of the treason till the cause be showed and declared before the king and his Parliament, whether it ought to be judged treason or other felony." This clause gave to Parliament a right to declare whether certain acts were treason.   But it is not clear whether the clause refers to the judicial or to the legislative powers of Parliament, because at that time the line was not clearly drawn between

---

[1] L.Q.R. xvii 369.
[2] In re Lord Kinross [1905] A.C. at p. 476.
[3] L.Q.R. xvii 369.
[4] Ibid 370.
[5] In re Lord Kinross [1905] A.C. 468.
[6] Ibid at p. 480.
[7] 25 Edward III. St. 5 cc. 2, 12.

these distinct powers. Nor was it clear, at the time when the statute was passed, how far the Commons had a right to share in the judicial powers of Parliament. It is therefore perhaps impossible to say definitely whether the clause referred to judicial or to legislative powers.[1] There was an attempt to use the clause at the time of Strafford's impeachment; but his counsel, Sir R. Lane, argued that it had been repealed by Acts of 1399 and 1553.[2] The abandonment of the impeachment shows that the clause was considered to have ceased to be law.

(ii) The crown could originally accuse great offenders in Parliament. In 1305 the king's attorney accused Nicolas de Segrave before the Parliament of that year.[3] The earls, barons, magnates, and others of the Council adjudged him worthy of death. In 1331 Lord Berkeley was accused in Parliament of the murder of Edward II. He put himself upon his country and was acquitted.[4] In 1377 Alice Perrers was similarly accused in Parliament;[5] but in the following year she brought a writ of error. The gist of the error assigned was, that there was no regular trial according to the forms of the common law;[6] and this perhaps shows that, as the jurisdiction and procedure of the ordinary courts were becoming fixed, such extraordinary proceedings before Parliament were beginning to be regarded as irregular. The jurisdiction was, however, revived under the Stuarts, and was regarded by Selden as still existing.[7] In Charles I.'s reign Earl Bristol was accused by the king before the House of Lords;[8] and in 1641 Charles had recourse to a similar procedure in the case of the Five Members.[9] The procedure was on that occasion declared to be illegal, and has never been revived.

(iii) One subject could originally "appeal," i.e. accuse another before Parliament of a crime. This method of proceeding was used for political purposes in Richard II.'s reign. In 1387-1388 the Lords Appellant accused the Archbishop of York, Robert de

---

[1] Hale considers that it refers to the legislative power, P.C. i 263; and this was the opinion of all the judges in the Earl of Clarendon's case (1663) 6 S.T. 316; Stephen, H.C.L. ii 252, 253, thinks it refers to the judicial power, and probably he is right; the lawyers of the seventeenth century were obliged to consider precedents in their constitutional rather than their historical aspect because they were the weapons which they used against the prerogative; we have seen, above 368, that the judges were in the habit of consulting with the Parliament on points of law, and it is probable that the statute had this practice in view, see Reeves, H.E.L. ii 291.

[2] 1 Henry IV. c. 10; 1 Mary, Sess. 1 c. 1 § 3; 3 S.T. 1472.
[3] Parliament Roll 1305 (R.S.) no. 449.
[4] Stephen, H.C.L. i 147, 148; R.P. ii 57.
[5] R.P. iii 12; Reeves, H.E.L. ii 463.
[6] R.P. iii 40.
[7] Judicature in Parliament, Works iii 1599-1607.
[8] (1626) 2 S.T. 1267.
[9] 4 S.T. 83.

Vere, Duke of Ireland, the Earl of Suffolk, Tressilian, Chief Justice of the King's Bench, and Sir Nicholas Brember, Lord Mayor of London, of treason. In 1397 the king's party in their turn accused the Duke of Gloucester and the Earls of Arundel and Warwick of treason, in "accroaching the royal power."[1] In consequence of these cases a statute was passed in 1399,[2] which provided that all appeals for things done within the realm should be tried and determined according to law; and that from henceforth no appeals should be made or in anywise pursued in Parliament. Notwithstanding this statute the Earl of Bristol was allowed to bring various charges against Earl Conway and the Duke of Buckingham in 1626.[3] It was probably considered that the statute applied only to proceedings begun by way of appeal, and not to proceedings begun in any other way. Selden, at any rate, seems to have been of opinion that the House might deal with accusations made by private persons.[4] But in 1663, when Earl Bristol accused Lord Clarendon of treason, the Lords resolved, in accordance with the opinion of the judges, that "a charge of high treason cannot by the laws and statutes of this realm be originally exhibited by one peer against another unto the House of Peers."[5] No attempt has since been made to revive this jurisdiction.

The Jurisdiction now Existing

(i) Impeachment.[6]

An impeachment is a criminal proceeding initiated by the House of Commons against any person. The person impeached is tried before the whole House of Lords presided over by the Lord High Steward if a peer is impeached for treason or felony, or by the Lord Chancellor or Lord Keeper in all other cases.[7] The judgment is given in accordance with the vote of the majority of the House, and, on the demand of the House of

---

[1] Stephen, H.C.L. i 152-154; Reeves, H.E.L. ii 463-466.

[2] 1 Henry IV. c. 14.   [3] 2 S.T. 1267.

[4] "I doubt not but such complaints have been, and may be received, and the parties proceeded against in Parliament, or else that high court should not have so much authority to receive information *pro domino rege* from private persons as the inferior courts have," Judicature in Parliament, Works iii 1612.

[5] 6 S.T. 317.

[6] Stephen, H.C.L. i 156-160; Anson Parliament 337-341; Erskine May, Parliamentary Practice (12th Ed.) chap. xxv.

[7] The law was so stated in 1678 by the Attorney-General, Hist. MSS. Eleventh Rep. App. Pt. II. 25; but Bl. Comm. iv 257, and Erskine May, op. cit. 590 seems to limit the occasions on which the Lord High Steward presides to impeachments for treason; it would seem, however, that he would preside if the peer were impeached for felony, just as in the case when a peer is tried by his peers for felony, below 388; and Foster seems to take that view stated in the text, Crown Law 143.

Commons made through its Speaker, the House passes sentence. The last instance of an impeachment was the case of Lord Melville in 1805; and, as it is improbable that this procedure will ever be revived, it might almost be regarded as another case of the obsolete jurisdiction of the House of Lords. On the other hand it is still legally possible, so that, whatever may be the political probabilities, it is impossible to treat it as wholly obsolete. I do not propose to treat of this procedure in detail, as it is fully described in many books of constitutional history and law. I shall only call attention to one or two points in the history of impeachments under the following heads : the origin of impeachments; the constitutional importance of impeachments; the disuse of impeachments.

The Origin of Impeachments.—Impeachment means accusation; and the word gradually acquired the narrower technical meaning of an accusation made by the House of Commons to the House of Lords.[1] The first impeachment comes from the year 1376; and the practice of impeachment originated in the prevalent political ideas and conditions of that period. Firstly, at that period, and indeed all through the Middle Ages, political thinkers and writers throughout Western Europe taught that the ideal to be aimed at by all rulers and princes and their officials was government in accordance with law.[2] Secondly, the House of Commons and the House of Lords were united in desiring to limit the activities of the royal officials or favourites and to prevent them from breaking the law.[3] Thirdly, the limits of the jurisdiction of the House of Lords were ill defined. It was open to receive petitions and complaints from all and sundry; and it could deal with them judicially or otherwise as it saw fit.[4] It was essentially a court for great men and great causes; and it occasionally seems to have been thought that it could apply to such causes a *lex Parliamenti*—a law which could do justice even when the ordinary law failed.[5] Probably some such thought as this was at the back of the minds of those who in Edward III.'s

---

[1] Pike, House of Lords 205-206. [2] Vol. ii 121-122, 196, 253-255, 435.
[3] Above 360. [4] Above 359.
[5] Thus in the criminal appeals of treason brought in Parliament in 1387-1388, "the Lords of Parliament considered the matter, and with the assent of the king and by their common assent it was declared that in so high a crime as is alleged in this appeal . . . the cause must not be decided elsewhere than in Parliament, nor by any other law than the law and course of Parliament, and that it appertains to the Lords of Parliament . . . to be judges in such cases. . . . Moreover, they do not mean to rule or govern so great a case as this appeal, which, as aforesaid, is not to be tried or determined out of Parliament, by the course process and order used in any inferior court or place in the realm, which courts and places are only to execute the ancient laws and customs of the realm, and the ordinances and establishments of Parliament," R.P. iii 236, cited Stephen, H.C.L. i 152-153; and this idea was long-lived, below 384 and n. 2.

Statute of Treason gave the king and Parliament a power to declare certain acts to be treasonable.[1]

It was thus only natural that the Commons, when they discovered that royal officials or others had broken the law, and that the government of the state was therefore badly conducted, should make a complaint to the House of Lords, which took the form of an accusation against the delinquents; and that the Lords should entertain and deal with it. Probably therefore the practice of impeachment arose partly from the prevalent political ideal—government according to law, partly from the alliance of the two Houses to secure the sanctity of the law as against royal officials or favourites, and partly from the wide and indefinite jurisdiction which the House of Lords exercised at that time.

The impeachment has two points in common with the criminal appeal. Firstly it is an accusation of crime not initiated by the crown. Secondly, a criminal appeal, if it was brought by or against great men, and affected the state, could before the statute of 1399[2] be brought before the House of Lords. But here the resemblance ceases. Hale points out that an impeachment is essentially different from the criminal appeals affected by the statute of 1399, because "it is a presentment by the most solemn grand inquest of the whole kingdom." In reality the two procedures are historically very far apart. We shall see that the criminal appeal is a very primitive procedure which goes back to the days of blood-feud, and wergild.[4] We have seen that the impeachment originates partly in political ideas prevalent in western Europe in the later Middle Ages, and partly in the political conditions prevailing in England in the fourteenth and fifteenth centuries.

The Constitutional Importance of Impeachments.—The last mediæval impeachment was in 1459. During the Wars of the Roses the place of impeachments was taken by Acts of Attainder, which were used by the rival factions much as criminal appeals had been used in Richard II.'s reign. During the Tudor period these Acts of Attainder were used to get rid of the ministers whom the king had ceased to trust, or of persons considered to be dangerous to the state. But, in the later period, the accused was often heard in his defence;[5] and, at a time when the legislative and judicial functions of Parliament were not clearly distinguished, it was possible to regard them, as Coke regarded

---

[1] Above 377.   [2] 1 Henry IV. c. 14; above 379.
[3] P.C. ii 150.   [4] Vol. ii 44-46, 197-198, 361-364.
[5] Henry VIII. thought it necessary to get a judicial opinion that an Act of Attainder would not be invalid though the person attainted was not heard in his defence, Coke, Fourth Instit. 37-38.

them,[1] as judgments of the full Parliament—a point of view which is still maintained by modern writers.[2] The practice of impeachment was revived in 1620-1621 with the impeachment of Sir Giles Mompesson. Between that date and 1715 there were fifty cases of impeachments brought to trial. Since that date there have only been four.[3] Thus the great period of impeachments was the seventeenth and the early years of the eighteenth centuries. It is therefore in the impeachments of this period, and more especially in the impeachments of the period before the Revolution of 1688, that we must seek the reasons for their constitutional importance.

The Parliamentary opposition in the reigns of the two first Stuart kings was, as we shall see, essentially a legal opposition, based on precedents drawn from the records of the mediæval Parliaments, and aiming at the attainment of the mediæval ideal—the maintenance of the common law.[4] Under these circumstances the impeachment was its natural weapon. By means of it the greatest ministers of state could be made responsible, like humbler officials, to the law. Thus the greatest services rendered by this procedure to the cause of constitutional government have been, firstly the establishment of the doctrine of ministerial responsibility to the law, secondly its application to all ministers of the crown, and, thirdly and consequently the maintenance of the supremacy of the law over all. The two impeachments which have contributed most to the attainment of these results are Buckingham's impeachment in Charles I.'s and Danby's impeachment in Charles II.'s reign; and of the two the latter is the most important. It was Buckingham's impeachment which decisively negatived Charles I.'s contention that not only was he personally above the law, but also his ministers acting under his orders. It was Danby's impeachment

---

[1] " If a nobleman had been erroneously attainted of treason, etc., he might have had his writ of error in Parliament. . . . But if the attainder be established by authority of Parliament then he must exhibit his petition in Parliament to be restored of grace," Fourth Instit. 21; clearly Coke, whose extensive study of mediæval records often leads him to adopt a very mediæval point of view, is blurring the distinction between a legislative and a judicial act, though the distinction was well enough known in his day, vol. iv 185-187; but the procedure on an Act of Attainder, being like that upon a modern private bill—quasi-judicial, helped to perpetuate the confusion.

[2] " Whenever a fitting occasion arises for its exercise, a bill of attainder is undoubtedly the highest form of parliamentary judicature. In impeachments the Commons are but accusers and advocates; while the Lords alone are judges of the crime. On the other hand, in passing bills of attainder the Commons commit themselves by no accusation, nor are their powers directed against the offender; but they are judges of equal jurisdiction, and with the same responsibility as the Lords; and the accused can only be condemned by the united judgment of the crown, the Lords, and the Commons," Erskine May op. cit. 594.

[3] For the list see Stephen, H.C.L. i 159.   [4] Vol. vi 103.

which decided that the king could not by use of his power to pardon stop an impeachment. A pardon could be pleaded to an indictment; but an indictment was a proceeding taken in the king's name. An impeachment was a proceeding taken in the name of the Commons; and he could no more stop it by granting a pardon than he could stop a criminal appeal brought by a private person.[1] It was also resolved in *Danby's Case* that, though the House, if a peer is impeached for treason, sits under the presidency of the Lord High Steward, it has " power enough to proceed to trial though the king should not name a High Steward;" [2] and this fact was emphasized by a change in the form of the High Steward's commission.[3] Thus although the trial nominally takes place before the king in Parliament, the king plays no active part. As we have seen, this elimination of the crown from all active share in the judicial functions of Parliament was taking place concurrently in the case of Parliament's civil jurisdiction.[4] The influence of the crown being thus eliminated, impeachments became as the Commons said in 1679, " the chief institution for the preservation of the government ".[5]

Thus the practice of impeachment has had a large share in establishing English constitutional law upon its modern basis. But its efficacy was or should have been strictly limited to prosecuting offenders against the law. It is because its efficacy was thus limited that, during the eighteenth century, it has fallen into disuse.

The Disuse of Impeachments.—So soon as the aim of the Commons came to be, not only to secure the observance of the law by the king's ministers, but also to secure their adhesion to the line of policy which they approved, the weakness of impeachments as a constitutional weapon began to appear. This further aim of the House of Commons was clearly manifested in the Long Parliament; and the weakness of this weapon appeared in the case of the Earl of Strafford. The success of his policy would

---

[1] 11 S.T. 783, 787 ; cf. Burnet, History of My Own Time (Airy's Ed.) ii 206-207.

[2] Foster, Crown Law 145 ; 11 S.T. 809

[3] " The committee of this House (the House of Commons) took exception to these words in the commission, viz. ' Ac pro eo quod Officium Seneschalli Angliæ (cujus presentia in hac parte requiritur) ut accepimus jam vacat ; ' and desired that they might be left out ; as implying that the constituting of a Lord High Steward was necessary ; and therefore proposed these words to be inserted in their stead, viz. ' Ac pro eo quod Proceres et Magnates in Parliamento nostro assemblati nobis humiliter supplicaverunt, et Seneschallum Angliæ hac vice constituere digneremus ; ' to which amendments the lords of the committee did agree," 11 S.T. 809-810 ; similar resolutions were come to in 1678, Hist. MSS. Com. Eleventh Rep. App. Pt. II. 31.

[4] Above 371.   [5] 11 S.T. 828.

have been fatal to constitutional government, but it was impossible to prove that its pursuit was treasonable. That the House saw this weakness in their favourite remedy is clear from the clause of the Grand Remonstrance, in which it was pointed out to the king, " that it may often fall out that the Commons may have just cause to take exception at some men for being councillors and yet not charge these men with crimes, for there be grounds of diffidence which lie not in proof." [1] But, until the growth of the system of Cabinet government, impeachment was the only remedy open to them. The king chose his ministers ; and, unless they could be convicted of crimes, there was no way of getting rid of them. It is for this reason that the charges made against unpopular ministers in the latter half of the seventeenth century were often supported by very little evidence. It is for this reason that claims were sometimes made to put ministers on their trial for offences created for that purpose by Parliament. [2] Mediæval precedents might no doubt have been invoked for taking such a course, [3] but they were obviously inapplicable in an age which had learnt to draw the modern distinction between judicial and legislative acts. Clearly the weapon of impeachment was breaking down ; and it ceased to be necessary to use it for political purposes when it became possible to get rid of ministers by an adverse vote of the House of Commons. The four last impeachments—those of Lord Macclesfield (1724), Lord Lovat (1746), Warren Hastings (1787), and Lord Melville (1805)—were not occasioned by the political conduct of the accused, who were all charged with serious breaches of the criminal law.

[1] § 198 ; as Finch, S.G., said in one of the debates on Clarendon's impeachment, " Your impeachment is in the nature of an indictment, and must contain so much of certainty as to put him to plead, that so he may not demur," 6 S.T. 354.

[2] Thus in the proceedings against Scroggs in 1680 Maynard is reported to have held the monstrous doctrine that " enormous offences may be impeached by the name of treason notwithstanding the statutes," 8 S.T. 202 ; to which Finch very justly replied that " no crime can be declared treason but by king, lords, and commons . . . what is said by Maynard is a doctrine so mischievous that this age or the next may rue it," ibid 205 ; in 1667, on Clarendon's impeachment Sir R. Howard said, " Though common law has its proper sphere, 'tis not in this place ; we are in a higher sphere," 6 S.T. 336 ; and on another occasion a committee of the House of Commons claimed to " do for preservation of itself whatsoever is not repugnant to natural justice ; " but the House of Lords, when pressed to commit Clarendon on a general charge of treason, properly reminded the Commons that, " the practice of all judges and justices in favour of liberty . . . is to examine on oath the particular crimes before commitment, that the ground may appear to them for commitment, or else they are of duty to bail where the offence is bailable though the accusation may be laid to be treason ; much more should the Parliament be careful herein, who gives examples and precedents of justice to all other courts. If the king and his council are not to imprison without special crime . . . whence comes this power of the House of Commons by vote to enforce a commitment ? " 6 S.T. 366 ; and in 1788 it rejected the view that it was not bound by the ordinary rules of evidence, Trial of Hastings (1796) Pt. ii 49-54.

[3] Above 380 and n. 5.

The case of Warren Hastings showed that the remedy of impeachment was far too clumsy and dilatory a remedy in a case of any complication; and therefore it is improbable that it will ever be used again, even in a case where it is desired to put a minister on his trial for a criminal offence. But, if the procedure upon it could be altered to suit modern needs, it might still be a useful weapon in the armoury of the constitution. It does embody the sound principle that ministers and officials should be made criminally liable for corruption, gross negligence, or other misfeasances in the conduct of the affairs of the nation. And this principle requires to be emphasized at a time when the development of the system of party government pledges the party to defend the policy of its leaders, however mistaken it may be, and however incompetently it may have been carried out; at a time when party leaders are apt to look indulgently on the most disastrous mistakes, because they hope that the same indulgence will be extended to their own mistakes when they take office; at a time when the principle of the security of the tenure of higher permanent officials is held to be more important than the need to punish their negligences and ignorances. If ministers were sometimes made criminally responsible for gross negligence or rashness, ill considered activities might be discouraged, real statesmanship might be encouraged, and party violence might be moderated. Ministers preparing a legislative programme or advocating a policy would be forced to look beyond the immediate election or the transient notoriety which they hope to win by this means, because they would be forced to remember that they might be called to account for neglecting to consider the probable consequences of their policy. If officials were sometimes made similarly responsible for their errors, it might do something to freshen up that stagnant atmosphere of complacent routine, which is and always has been the most marked characteristic of government departments.

(ii) Trial by Peers.

I have already said something of the origin of trial by peers. We have seen that in the eleventh and twelfth centuries the expression was used, in quite an untechnical sense, to mean trial by a court of the old type, in which all the suitors were judges, and in which the inferiors of the person to be judged could not be among the suitors.[1] At this point I must say something, firstly of the development of the principle of trial by peers, and the limitations upon the sphere of its application; and secondly of the modes in which such a trial is conducted.

---

[1] Above 59-60.

The development of and the limitations upon the principle of trial by peers.

The history of the development of this principle in England is curious.   It came to have two entirely different meanings according as it was applied to commoners or to peers.

As applied to commoners it very soon came to be confused with trial by jury.   In Edward I.'s reign, as we have seen,[1] it was considered that the principle was complied with if, on the trial of a knight, the petty jury was composed of knights ; and even this condition was soon lost sight of.   Later lawyers had no hesitation in identifying trial by any jury with trial by peers ; and no doubt they were the more willing to do so because, in this way, trial by jury could be connected with Magna Carta.[2] Even Hale could deny that the most striking instance of the survival of the principle—the trial of a peer accused of treason or felony by the whole House of Lords—was a judicum parium, and could lament that in such a case "the party has lost that trial that the law of the land and Magna Carta so much assert, the legale judicium parium suorum."[3]

As applied to peers[4] the principle has had a more variegated history.   It was only gradually reduced to precision as, firstly the cases in which, and secondly the persons to which, it was applicable, were ascertained.

(*a*) It is probable that, when the king's court was chiefly a court for great men and great causes, there was no very pressing need to define or even to emphasize the principle, as some of the magnates would generally form a part of the court.[5]   But, when the common law courts presided over by professional lawyers began to absorb the judicial business of the state, and when the professional judges came to be regarded as the court,[6] the need for emphasis and definition began ; and it came to be the more pressing as, both the proceedings against John in the court of the king of France,[7] and the thirty-ninth clause of Magna Carta,[8] had, so to speak, advertised the principle.   The reason for and the definition of the scope of the principle suggested by Bracton are the beginnings of its limitation within its modern limits.   He justified the principle on the ground that no man can be judge in his own case.   If therefore the king is taking legal proceedings against his vassal he cannot judge, nor can his judges, because they

---

[1] Above 324, 336 n. 8.   [2] Vol. ii 215.

[3] Jurisdiction of the House of Lords 88.

[4] On this subject the best authority is now L. W. Vernon Harcourt's book on His Grace the Steward and Trial by Peers.

[5] Harcourt, op. cit. 211.

[6] Magna Carta Commemoration Essays 88-89.

[7] Harcourt, op. cit. chap. viii.   [8] Above 59.

represent him. But, in order that serious misdeeds may not go unpunished, "curia et pares judicabunt."[1] And this reason for allowing the "curia et pares" to judge, namely that serious misdeeds may not go unpunished, is made to limit the application of the maxim. It should be applied only to those greater wrongs which involve forfeiture and capital punishment.[2] This suggestion, tentatively put forward by Bracton, is stated as settled law by Fleta[3] and Britton.[4] But this limitation of the principle was not altogether to the taste of the magnates. In 1341 they procured the passing of a statute which enacted in substance that no peer or official, by reason of matters touching his office or for any other reason, should be made to answer anywhere but before the peers in Parliament, except at the suit of private persons or in proceedings taken against peers who were accountants to the crown.[5] The judges protested against this statute,[6] and it was repealed in the next Parliament.[7] A statute of 1441 recognized that the principle of trial by peers was confined to accusations of treason and felony ;[8] and in 1471 Littleton ruled that it applied only to proceedings begun by indictment, and not to criminal appeals.[9]

(b) When it was the custom to bring great men and serious offences against the state to trial in Parliament,[10] no definition was possible of the classes of persons to whom the principle was applicable. The growing distinction of the status of the peerage made this definition possible.[11] This is brought out by the case of Simon de Bereford in 1331. He was accused of being implicated in the treasons of Mortimer, and, at Edward III.'s request, was brought up for trial before the House of Lords. The House

[1] " Et tunc videndum quis possit et debeat judicare, et sciendum quod non ipse rex, quia sic esset in querela propria actor et judex, in judicio vitæ membrorum et exhæredationis, quod quidem non esset, si querela esset aliorum. Item justitiarii ? non, cum in judiciis personam domini regis, cujus vices gerit, representet. Quis ergo judicabit ? videtur, sine præjudicio melioris sententiæ, quod curia et pares judicabunt, ne maleficia remaneant impunita, et maxime ubi periculum vitæ fuerit, et membrorum vel exhæredationis, cum ipse rex pars actrix esse debeat in judicio," f. 119, 119 b.

[2] " Si autem levis fuerit transgressio quæ pœnam infligat pecuniariam tantum et levem bene possunt justitiarii sine paribus judicare," f. 119 b ; then he goes on to say that if the transgressio is " gravis et proxima exhæredationi," " ibi debent pares justitiariis associari "—a suggestion which may, as Harcourt points out op. cit. 287 n. 2, have given rise to the practice of inserting the names of peers in the commissions of Oyer and Terminer, above 274, 280.

[3] I. 21, 11.   [4] i 102.

[5] 15 Edward III. St. 1 ; Harcourt, op. cit. 343-344 ; Pike, House of Lords 194-197.

[6] R.P. ii 131, 15 Ed. III. no. 42.

[7] 15 Edward III. St. 2 ; Harcourt op. cit. 344 ; R.P. ii 139, 17 Ed. III. no. 23 ; cf. Rymer, Foedera v 282.

[8] 20 Henry VI. c. 9.   [9] Y.B. 10 Ed. IV. Pasch. pl. 17.

[10] Above 354, 378.   [11] Above 357-358.

consented to try him on account of the enormity of his crimes ; but it protested that, " although the peers, as judges of Parliament, have taken upon them . . . to make and render the said judgment yet the peers that now are or shall be in time to come, are not bound or charged to give judgment upon others than peers." [1]   But the practice was still uncertain ; and nothing contributed more to prevent it becoming certain than the political use which was made in Richard II.'s reign of criminal appeals in Parliament.[2]   Each party in turn accused the leaders of the party opposed to them of treason, whether they were peers or not. The Act of 1399 [3] eliminated this cause of confusion, and helped to establish the principles, firstly that such appeals were not to be tried by the House, and secondly that the only persons who were entitled to be so tried were peers.   The statute of 1441,[4] probably enacted because of the trial of the Duchess of Gloucester for witchcraft before an ecclesiastical tribunal,[5] extended the privilege of trial by peers as thus defined to peeresses.

The modes in which a trial by peers is conducted.

The president of the court by which a peer is tried by his peers for treason or felony is the Lord High Steward.   He was one of those great officers of the household in the courts of the feudal potentates of the tenth and eleventh centuries, who became hereditary dignitaries in the thirteenth and fourteenth centuries.[6]   In that capacity he was, together with such officials as the Constable and the Marshal, a leader of the feudal nobility ; and, as the feudal nobility in the fourteenth century led the Parliamentary opposition to the crown, these great officials naturally play a great part in tracts like the Modus Tenendi Parliamentum, which magnify the importance of Parliament in the state.[7]   Probably the connection between the Lord High Steward and trial by peers will be best explained by the analogy of the ordinary manor.   Just as the Lord's Steward kept the courts to which his tenants owed suit, so the Steward of England kept the court to which the peers of England owed suit, and in which they were tried by their peers.   Whether this explanation is correct or not, it is certain that, in the fifteenth century, the Lord High Steward is the official who presides at the trial of a peer accused of treason or

[1] Pike, House of Lords 186 ; R.P. ii 53-54, 4 Ed. III. no. 26 ; this case was in 1681 made a precedent for refusing to try a commoner impeached of treason, Case of Fitzharris 8 S.T. 223 ; Bl. Comm. iv 256-257 ; but this was contrary to the opinion of Selden, Judicature in Parliament, Works iii 1589, and is not now regarded as good law, Erskine May, op. cit. 588 n. 3.

[2] Above 378-379.   [3] Above 379.

[4] 20 Henry VI. c. 9.   [5] Harcourt, op. cit. 380-381.   [6] Ibid Pt. I.

[7] Ibid 147 ; for another tract which magnifies the office see ibid 148-151.

felony; and, as we have seen, he presides whether he is indicted or impeached.[1]

But the mode in which the trial is conducted, and the position of the Lord High Steward, are very different according as Parliament is or is not in session.

If Parliament is in session all the peers are the judges, and the question of guilty or not guilty is decided by a majority of votes.[2] It would seem that in the eighteenth century, if not earlier, the House could act, even though no Lord High Steward had been appointed [3]—again we see the tendency to eliminate the crown from any participation in the judgments of the House.[4] Thus a trial before the whole House is the nearest modern approach to the old judicium parium. It is not quite the same thing as the old judicium parium because, in earlier days, this judicium was merely a sentence as to how the proof should be made, whereas in the modern trial by peers each peer decides on the evidence as to the guilt or innocence of the accused.[5] But it would be true to say that it is the old judicium parium modified by the modern conception of a trial.

If Parliament is not in session the Lord High Steward tries the accused by a jury of peers. His position in relation to this jury is exactly the same as the position of any other judge in relation to a jury. He directs them as to the law, and they must find the accused guilty or not guilty in accordance with the facts and with his direction as to the law. Like any other jury they must give a unanimous verdict.[6] Exactly when or why this procedure was devised is a matter of controversy. There is a case in which it was used in 1415,[7] and it emerged again in 1499.[8] A Year Book report of 1400 puts it back still earlier;[9] but, as the House of Lords reported in 1690,[10] there are many difficulties in accepting the tale told by this Year Book. Harcourt thought that the Year Book report was forged to supply a precedent for

---

[1] Above 379 n. 7.   [2] Foster, Crown Law 143.

[3] Ibid 143, 148, 149; Case of Ferrers (1760) 19 S.T. 586; it is true that in the commission the old form is followed and the presence of the Steward is stated to be required—"cujus presentia in hac parte requiritur;" but Foster treats this as proving " no more than that the Great Seal having no authority to vary in point of form, hath from time to time very prudently followed ancient precedents," op. cit. 148.

[4] Above 371, 383.   [5] Pike, House of Lords 174.

[6] Coke, Third Instit. 28-31; but each peer gives his verdict individually, ibid 30.

[7] Harcourt, op. cit. 379.   [8] Ibid 429-432.

[9] Y.B. 1 Hy. IV. Mich. pl. 1

[10] Hist. MSS. Com. Twelfth Rep. App. Pt. VI. 407-418 no. 204; the committee reported that peers should only be judged in full Parliament—" There is a Year Book in the time of Hen. IV. which gives circumstances to the trial of peers out of Parliament, but the records of that time falsify the book;" and to this the House agreed.

the trial of the Earl of Warwick in this way in 1499.[1] But there are difficulties in the way of this suggestion which he by no means meets.[2] Possibly this procedure grew up so to speak naturally. The Lord High Steward was obviously the official to preside at the trial of a peer. A trial by a jury of peers was certainly a trial by peers. There is some reason to think that, when the practice on these matters was still unfixed, such a trial would have been accepted as regular.[3] So soon as Parliaments became infrequent, it became obvious that some provision for the trial of peers must be made ; and a trial by a procedure of this sort was the obvious expedient. Whatever may have been its origin, the custom to try peers in the court of the Lord High Steward by a jury of peers was finally established by the precedent of 1499.[4]

A trial in this court, as compared with a trial before the whole House of Lords, gave the crown the obvious advantage that it could select the jury. Full advantage was taken of this in the state trials of the sixteenth and seventeenth centuries. On that account the House of Lords seemed inclined to question the legality of such trials in 1690 ;[5] but nothing came of this suggestion ; and, instead, the constitution of the court was reformed. It was enacted in 1695-1696[6] that, on a trial for treason or misprision of treason, all peers who had a right to vote should be summoned at least twenty days before the trial.

Whether the trial is before the whole House or in the court of the Lord High Steward, a true bill is found by the grand jury, and the indictment is removed to the appropriate court by writ of certiorari.[7]

(iii) The Criminal Appeal Act 1907.[8]

We have seen that under this Act the House can hear appeals from the court of Criminal Appeal if the certificate of the attorney-general is obtained that the case "involves a point of law of exceptional public importance, and that it is desirable in the public

---

[1] Op. cit. chap. xii.

[2] See Pike's review of Harcourt's book L.Q.R. xxiii 442 ; and Harcourt's reply, L.Q.R. xxiv 43.

[3] The petition praying for the reversal of the judgment against Harcla, Earl of Carlisle, complained that he was not " atteint par *enquest* de ses piers," Harcourt, op. cit. 334 ; and see ibid p. 302.

[4] For the use sometimes made at the end of the fifteenth century of the court of the Constable and Marshal see Harcourt, op. cit. chap. xi ; below 575.

[5] Hist. MSS. Com. Twelfth Rep. App. Pt. VI. 417-418, no. 204.

[6] 7, 8 William III. c. 3.

[7] Stephen, H.C.L. i 165. The last instance of the trial of a peer by the House of Lords is that of Earl Russell for bigamy [1901] A.C. 446; the last instance of a trial in the court of the Lord High Steward is that of Lord Delamere for treason in 1686, 11 S.T. 510.

[8] 7 Edward VII. c. 23 § 1 (6).

interest that a further appeal should be brought." [1]   If the House allows an appeal against an order of the court of Criminal Appeal quashing a conviction, the effect is to restore the original conviction.[2]   In this respect the allowing of an appeal by the House against an order of the court of Criminal Appeal resembles the reversal of a judgment on a writ of error.

(3) Jurisdiction in Cases of Privilege.

We must consider in the first place the extent of the jurisdiction which the House possesses by virtue of its privileges, and in the second place the relation of this jurisdiction to that exercised by the ordinary courts of law.

The extent of this jurisdiction.

The Lords have by their privileges jurisdiction in three classes of cases.   (i) They can fine and imprison for a definite term for contempt.[3]   What the House will adjudge to be a contempt is within its own discretion.   In the seventeenth and eighteenth centuries the Lords pushed this jurisdiction to its most extreme limits.[4]   They punished " libels and slander, not only against the House of Lords collectively, but against every Lord individually ; and not only when the libel and slander related to the actual exercise of their legislative, judicial, or consultative functions, but when it was foreign to such exercise." [5]   The distinction drawn by Hargrave in this passage is now the distinction observed.[6]   (ii) The House of Lords can decide on the effect or the validity of the creation of a new peerage by the crown.   Thus in 1711 it decided that the acquisition of an

---

[1] Above 218.

[2] R. v. Ball [1911] A.C. at pp. 74-76 ; and see ibid at p. 70 n. 1.

[3] If the prisoner is not committed for a definite term he will probably be released by a prorogation, 6 S.T. 1296 ; cf. Stockdale v. Hansard (1839) 9 A. and E. 127 ; the Commons cannot commit for a definite term, and have not fined since 1666.

[4] See Floyd's Case (1621), Hargrave's Preface xvi-xix ; Blunt's Case (1621), and Morley's Case (1623), Hargrave, Jurisconsult Exercitations, i 284 ; Cases of Fitton and Carr (1667), Hargrave's Preface xcix, c ; Hist. MSS. Com. Eighth Rep. App. 101 no. 14, 102 no. 29 ; it was settled in 1690 that privilege could not be claimed against the jurisdiction exercised under the Articles of War, ibid Thirteenth Rep. App. Pt. V. 93 no. 285.

[5] Hargrave, Jurisconsult Exercitations i 289 ; see the list of cases printed in Stockdale v. Hansard (1839) 9 A. and E. at p. 12 ; a good illustration will be found in a case of 1698 noted in Luttrell's Diary iv 369—" Yesterday the Lords heard a case about a breach of privilege committed against the Earl of Northampton by breaking into his fishery, which the Earl of Peterborough's son claimed a right to."

[6] For a similar rule as to contempts of other courts see M'Leod v. St. Aubyn, [1899] A.C. at p. 561, where Lord Morris pointed out that this power " is not to be used for the vindication of the judge as a person. . , . Committal for contempt of court is a weapon to be used sparingly, and always with reference to the interests of the administration of justice ; " as late as 1799 (R. v. Flower 8 T.R. 314) a person was committed for publishing a libel on a member of the House.

English peerage did not entitle a Scotch peer to a seat. In 1782 it reversed that decision. In 1856 it decided that a life peer could not sit in the House.[1] (iii) If there is a disputed claim to an old peerage the Lords can decide as between the claimants if, and only if, the matter is referred to them by the crown. Holt, C.J., in the case of *R.* v. *Knollys*,[2] declined to pay any attention to an adjudication of the Lords upon a question of this kind, because the matter had not been referred to them by the crown. The decision was questioned by the Lords at the time ; but in the debate on the Wensleydale Peerage Case in 1856 Lord Campbell admitted its justice.[3] Such cases are now usually referred by the crown to the House of Lords ; but this was not necessarily the case at earlier periods in our history. They were referred sometimes to the Council,[4] sometimes to the Council and judges,[5] sometimes to the Marshal[6] because, as we shall see, the court of the Constable and Marshal was concerned among other things with pedigrees and the right to bear arms.[7] The House of Lords in deciding these cases is not bound by its own decisions.[8] It must try each case on its merits according to the best historical evidence available to it. Some modern historians, forgetting that the state of historical knowledge varies with each succeeding age, and that historical theory is subject to infinitely wider variations, have subjected many of the past decisions of the Lords to a good deal of unmerited ridicule.

The relation of privilege to the law.

Privileges of Parliament confer upon each House of Parliament the rights and powers essential to its efficiency ; and it is for this reason that, in the seventeenth century, each House found it necessary to guard them jealously, and to assert them boldly. But, after 1688, when the battle for the constitution had been won, Parliament showed a tendency to extend and to use its privileges in a fashion almost as arbitrary as the king had used his prerogative. This arbitrary conduct soon brought to the front the question of relation of privilege to the law. And, in dealing with this question, the courts had very few precedents

---

[1] Anson, Parliament 219.

[2] (1694) 1 Ld. Raym. 10 ; Holt declined to give to a committee of the Lords the reasons for his decision ; there was talk of a committal, "which vanished in smoke," ibid at p. 18.

[3] Hansard cxl 329.

[4] Pike, House of Lords 130—the FitzWalter Case (1669).

[5] Dasent xix 357-358 (1590)—claim to the barony of Powys ; cf. Nicolas iii 324-326 (1428)—earldom of Salisbury.

[6] S.P. Dom. 1666-1667, 477, clxxxix 106—claim to the barony of Dudley.

[7] Below 578-580.

[8] St. John Peerage Claim [1915] A.C. at pp. 308-309, 314.

on which they could rely. In the Middle Ages the judges had declined to give opinions on questions of privilege;[1] and the decisions given by the Stuart judges, even when they could be defended, were for obvious reasons suspected after the Revolution. The problem was therefore a new one; and that it was boldly faced was due mainly to Holt, C.J. We have seen that in 1694, in the case of *R.* v. *Knollys*,[2] he set his face against the claim of the House of Lords to extend its own privileges at its will and pleasure; and in *Ashby* v. *White*[3] and the subsequent proceedings arising out of that case,[4] he opposed a similar claim by the House of Commons. Of these cases I shall speak more at length in a later volume.[5] Here it will be sufficient to indicate the manner in which these decisions, and other decisions of the eighteenth and nineteenth centuries, have defined the relation of privilege to the law. It is a subject not altogether free from obscurity; for, as Erskine May says,[6] "the precedents of Parliament are contradictory, the opinions and decisions of judges have differed, and the most learned and experienced men of the present day are not agreed." Nevertheless I think that the cases, when properly understood, lay down a fairly clear rule.

There are two maxims or principles which govern this subject. The first tells us that "Privilege of Parliament is part of the law of the land;" the second that "Each House is the judge of its own privileges." Now at first sight it may seem that these maxims are contradictory. If privilege of Parliament is part of the law of the land its meaning and extent must be interpreted by the courts, just like any other part of the law; and therefore neither House can add to its privileges by its own resolution, any more than it can add to any other part of the law by such a resolution. On the other hand if it is true that each House is the sole judge of its own privileges, it might seem that each House was the sole judge as to whether or no it had got a privilege, and so could add to its privileges by its own resolution. This apparent contradiction is solved if the proper application of these two maxims is attended to. The first maxim applies to cases like *Ashby* v. *White*[7] and *Stockdale* v. *Hansard*[8] in which the question at issue was the existence of a privilege claimed by the House. This is a matter of law which the courts must decide, without paying any attention to a resolution of the House on the subject. The second maxim applies to cases like

---

[1] Vol. ii 561.
[2] 1 Ld. Raym. 10.
[3] (1704) 2 Ld. Raym. 938.
[4] R. v. Paty (1705) 2 Ld. Raym. 1105.
[5] Vol. vi 268-272.
[6] Parliamentary Practice 126.
[7] (1704) 2 Ld. Raym. 938.
[8] (1839) 9 A. and E. 1.

that of the *Sheriff of Middlesex*[1] and *Bradlaugh* v. *Gosset*[2] in which an attempt was made to question, not the existence, but the mode of user of an undoubted privilege. On this matter the courts will not interfere because each House is the sole judge of the question whether, when, or how it will use one of its undoubted privileges.

[1] (1840) 11 A. and E. 273.   [2] (1884) 12 Q.B.D. 271.

CHAPTER V

THE COURT OF CHANCERY

IN this chapter I shall deal firstly with the history of the court of Chancery, and secondly with the jurisdiction exercised both by the court of Chancery and by the Chancellor.

I. THE HISTORY OF THE COURT

I shall deal with the history of the court of Chancery under the following heads: the growth ·of the court; the organization of the court; the defects in the organization of the court, and its reorganization in the nineteenth century.

The Growth of the Court

We have seen that under the Norman and Angevin kings the Chancery was a secretarial bureau, and that the Chancellor was the secretary of state for all departments.[1]   Naturally the connection of the Chancellor and the Chancery with the Curia Regis —the governing body of the kingdom—was close.   The Chancellor, as Professor Tout has said, was "the king's natural prime minister."[2]   The beginnings of the separation of the Chancery from the Curia Regis, and its organization as a department of state as distinct as the department of the Exchequer, must be dated from the year 1238.   In that year Henry III. dispensed with baronial chancellors holding the office for life, and took the office into his own hands.   For some years after that date there was a rapid succession of officials who held the seal, but whose claim to the title of Chancellor is doubtful.[3]   The barons sometimes protested, but, even after they had got the upper hand in 1258, no attempt was made to create a Chancellor of the old

---

[1] Above 37.

[2] " The Chancery was of course the great secretarial department, the office of state, and its head, the chancellor, was not merely a supreme judge, like the modern lord chancellor, but the king's natural prime minister," Place of Edward II. in English History 58.

[3] Ibid 58, 59; Dibben, Chancellor and Keeper of the Seal under Henry III. E.H.R. xxvii 39.

type for life. The system by which the king took the profits of
the seal, and paid the Chancellor a fixed fee for the maintenance
of a body of clerks was continued ;[1] and though the terms upon
which Edward I.'s great Chancellor, Robert Burnell, held his
office show a reversion to the old type of Chancellor, the experiment was not again repeated. His successor—Langton—was a
Chancery clerk who did not take the profits of the seal, and was
paid his fixed fee. Except for a very few years in Edward II.'s
reign, this arrangement was afterwards adhered to,[2] and by the
end of that reign the profits of the seal were accounted for at the
Exchequer.[3] The result was that "the Chancellor, though still
a court official following the king, had a staff of his own entirely
separate from the chaplains and clerks of the household. The
clerks of the Chancery, living with their chief a self-contained
and semi-independent collegiate life . . . soon developed a departmental tradition and esprit de corps that began to rival the
strong corporate feeling of the Exchequer officials."[4]

But the Chancellor was destined to become something very
much more than a mere departmental chief. Though a "salaried
officer of limited powers and tenure of office" had been substituted for "the old type of irresponsible magnate," yet this officer
was bound to become an important official in the state because
he kept the Great Seal.[5] It is, in fact, the Chancellor's position
as Keeper of the Great Seal which puts him at the head of the
English legal system, and makes him the legal centre of the constitution.

We have seen that the English legal system had become a
system of royal justice. This royal justice must be called into
action by original writs which must be sealed by the Chancellor ;
and so, as Lambard says, the Chancery is "the forge or shop of
all originalls."[6] In the same way all important government acts
—treaties with foreign states, the assembly of Parliament, royal
grants—must pass the seal, and must therefore come under his
review. Applicants for justice in the courts of common law,
petitioners to the king, to the Council, or to Parliament, will
sooner or later come to the Chancery either for an original writ,
or to obtain the execution of the answer endorsed upon their

---

[1] E.H.R. xxvii 51.   [2] Tout, op. cit. 60, 181-183.
[3] "When the profits of the seal were accounted for in the Exchequer, the
Chancery sheds the last vestiges of its original position as a dependent office of the
court, and stands forth in its later character as a self-sufficing office of state," ibid
186.
[4] Ibid 59-60.   [5] E.H.R. xxvii 51.
[6] Archeion (Ed. 1635) 58. Writs which began a legal proceeding were called
"original." Those which were issued in the course of a legal proceeding were
called "judicial."

petition. The Chancellor and the Chancery are thus in direct connexion with all parts of the constitution.[1] This accounts for the extraordinary range and variety of the Chancellor's duties. Of their range and variety Bentham's critical summary will give us the best idea.[2] He is "(1) a single judge controlling in civil matters the several jurisdictions of the twelve great judges. (2) A necessary member of the Cabinet, the chief and most constant advisor of the king in all matters of law. (3) The perpetual president of the highest of the two houses of legislature. (4) The absolute proprietor of a prodigious mass of ecclesiastical patronage. (5) The competitor of the Minister for almost the whole patronage of the law. (6) The Keeper of the Great Seal; a transcendent, multifarious, and indefinable office. (7) The possessor of a multitude of heterogeneous scraps of power, too various to be enumerated." It is no wonder that lawyers and statesmen regard the Great Seal—the clavis regni—with an almost superstitious reverence. It is treason to counterfeit it;[3] and they come to think that if it is used—it may be contrary to the will, or during the madness of the sovereign—the Act is as authentic as if the sovereign had really sanctioned it.[4]

It is the relation of the Chancellor and the Chancery to the judicial system of the country with which I must here deal. In two respects that relation was close; and it is from that close relation that much of the jurisdiction of the Chancellor and the court of Chancery arises.

(i) The Chancellor had control over the issue of original writs.

---

[1] The intimate relation of the Chancery with all departments of government is well described in a Treatise on the Masters written when Ellesmere was Chancellor: "Both the Parliament is summoned by writs out of the Chancery; the acts made and enrolled are kept in the Chancery; all commandments of that court are expedited either by writs out of the Chancery, or by the Chancellor's serjeants at arms; the Lord Chancellor is ever speaker of that House without further choice or appointment . . . and the clerk of the Parliament has his fee out of the hanaper as an office of the Chancery. The reason of their attendance there I take to be, not only for the receiving of petitions; but as the judges are there, that, by observing the minds and the reasons of the Lords that make the laws, they may the more agreeably to their reason expound and interpret the said laws; so the masters of Chancery are there also, that they may likewise frame the writs that are to be made upon those laws in like correspondence; and as the judges furthermore may inform the lords how former laws of this realm presently stand touching any matter there debated; so may they also be informed by the masters of the Chancery (of whom the greatest number have always been chosen men skilful in the canon and civil law) in laws that they shall make touching foreign matters, how the same shall accord with equity, jus gentium, and the laws of other nations," Hargrave, Law Tracts, 308, 309.

[2] Cited Parkes, Chancery 437; cp. C. P. Cooper, Chancery 381, 382 n.

[3] 25 Edward III. St. 5 c. 2 § 5.

[4] As to the making of a new Great Seal during the Great Rebellion see Foss, Judges vi 211-212; as to the use of the Great Seal during the madnesses of George III. see Erskine May, Constitutional History i 181-182, 186-187, 188, 208-214.

The power to issue original writs gave to the Chancellors of the twelfth and early thirteenth centuries a large control over the rights which the royal courts recognized. Writ, remedy, and right are correlative terms. "A comparison of a collection of formulas which Henry III. sent to the Irish Chancery in 1227, with Glanvil's treatise shows us that the number of writs which were to be had as of course, had grown within the intervening forty years."[1] But the growth of baronial power tended to fetter the control of the Chancellor. The Provisions of Oxford (1258) show that the barons did not wish to leave the Chancellor an uncontrolled power to issue original writs[2]—a power which was equivalent to a power to make new law. The Statute of Westminster II. (1285) shows that the practice was then in a transition state. A certain discretion was allowed ; but cases of real difficulty and importance must be referred to Parliament.[3]

The growth of the powers of Parliament in the thirteenth and fourteenth centuries made it clear that it is in Parliament that the legislative power is vested. For this reason the register of original writs became practically closed except in so far as it was added to or altered by new legislation. At the same time the Statute of Westminster II. gave to the Chancellor the power to vary slightly the forms of writs in order that justice might be done in similar cases ; and, as we shall see, much use was made of this power.[4] The fact that it is the Chancellor who is given authority to supply such deficiences, may help to explain why he comes to be thought of as an official who can do justice even when there is no remedy at common law. It is one of those ideas which helps to connect the Chancellor and the Chancery with the royal right to temper justice with equity. But this connexion of the Chancellor with the issue of writs tended to become merely ministerial as the control of Parliament and the common law courts became more complete. Such judicial work as he still retained in this connexion was chiefly in connexion with writs directly affecting the king's interest. This jurisdiction eventually came to be known as his common law jurisdiction,[5]

---

[1] P. and M. i 149; for the history of the Register of Writs see vol. ii Bk. iii c. 5.

[2] Stubbs (Sel. Ch.) 389, " Ke il ne enselera nul bref fors bref de curs sanz le commandement le rei, e de sun cunseil ke serra present."

[3] 13 Edward I. St. 1 c. 24, " Et quotienscunque decetero evenerit in Cancellaria quod in uno casu reperitur breve, et in consimili casu cadente sub eodem jure et simili indigente remedio, concordent clerici de Cancellaria in brevi faciendo, vel atterminent querentes in proximo parliamento, et scribant casus in quibus concordare non possunt et referant eos ad proximum parliamentum, et de consensu jurisperitorum fiat breve, ne contingat de cetero quod curia diu deficiat querentibus in justitia perquirenda ; " for an example of this procedure see R.P. iv 153 9 Hy. V. n. 12.

[4] For instance by writs of trespass or deceit on the case.

[5] Baldwin, The King's Council 239-240.

and, as we shall see, gradually came to be quite distinct from his equitable jurisdiction.[1] That equitable jurisdiction is, as we shall now see, much more closely connected with the intimate relations of the Chancellor and the Chancery with the King's Council.

(ii) The Chancellor and the Chancery had from the first been closely connected with the King's Council.[2]

Of the Council and its history I shall speak in the next chapter. Here it will be sufficient to say that it was in the direct line of descent from the Curia Regis of the twelfth century. The detachment from it of the courts of common law deprived it of much of its jurisdiction; and the rise and growth of the powers of Parliament deprived it both of other branches of jurisdiction and of legislative authority. But it still continued to be the executive government of the country, and it still continued to exercise the wide judicial powers which, owing to its close connexion with the king, it had always exercised. By reason of its close connexion with the king, these judicial powers had always been extraordinary—that is, they had always been something above and beyond the ordinary law. In the twelfth century the ordinary law had been that archaic customary law which was administered in the local courts; but in the fourteenth century the ordinary law had come to be the law administered in the common law courts. It had become apparent, however, in the course of the fourteenth and fifteenth centuries that the need for a court exercising this extraordinary jurisdiction was as necessary to temper the rigidity and the technicality of this common law, as, in former days, it had been necessary to override the archaic formalism of the old customary law.[3] But the Chancellor and the Chancery had, throughout their history, been closely connected with the king and his Council; and, although the Chancery was tending to become a distinct department of state,[4] this close connexion was, during the Middle Ages, hardly weakened, far less severed. As Professor Baldwin very truly says,[5] " It was the singular success of the Chancellors that, while both the Exchequer and the King's Bench were being drawn

---

[1] Below 449-452.
[2] Baldwin, The King's Council 237-238.
[3] "And considering that the Prince of this Realme is the immediate minister of justice under God, and is sworn at his coronation to deliver to his subjects *æquam et rectam justitiam*, I cannot see how it may otherwise be, but that besides his court of meere Law, he must either reserve to himselfe or referre to others a certaine soveraigne and preeminent power, by which he may both supply the want, and correct the Rigour of that positive or written Law, which of itself neither is, nor can be made such a perfect Rule, as that a man may thereby truely square out justice in all cases that may happen," Lambard, Archeion 76-77.
[4] Above 396.   [5] The King's Council 240-241.

into the current of the common law, their own court remained comparatively free from this system. For this reason it was possible, in the course of time, to make the Chancery the principal organ of a jurisdiction outside the realm of the common law."

The Chancery was able to become "the principal organ" of this extraordinary jurisdiction for three reasons : firstly, its head the Chancellor was, as Keeper of the Great Seal, closely related to the administration of the law ; secondly the Chancellor was a leading member of the Council ; and thirdly the Chancery itself was a well organized and efficient department of state.

(i) We have seen that the Chancellor's duties in relation to the issue of original writs brought him into close connexion with the administration of the common law.[1] We have seen too that the Council exercised a general supervision and control over the courts of common law.[2] Naturally the Chancellor as an important member of the Council, and closely connected with the administration of the law, acquired a large share of that control. The chiefs of the common law courts were appointed by the crown ; but, in the fifteenth century, he admitted the puisne judges to their offices, and probably had some share in their nomination.[3] Moreover the duties of the Chancellor in connexion with the law, and the intimate relations between the Council and the judges, caused the relations between the Chancellor and the Chancery and the common law courts to be close all through the mediæval period. The judges sometimes took part in the decisions of the Council,[4] or of the Chancellor if he was sitting alone ;[5] and in the fourteenth century three common law judges became Chancellors.[6] In fact it was made a matter of complaint by the Commons in 1400 that the business of the common law courts was delayed because the judges were called from their courts to assist in discussing cases in the Chancery.[7] We shall see that the common law and the equitable jurisdictions of the Chancellor were not sharply differentiated till the sixteenth century.[8] It was not till they were thus differentiated that these

---

[1] Above 397-398.   [2] Above 209-210.

[3] It is clear from Fortescue's account of the manner of making new judges, De Laudibus c. 51, that in the middle of the fifteenth century the Chancellor admitted them to their offices ; cp. Spence, Equitable Jurisdiction i 356.

[4] Baldwin op. cit. 245.

[5] Thus in 1397 a decree was made " by the advice of justices and other skilled persons of the Chancery," Baldwin, op. cit. 246 n. 4 ; Select Cases in Chancery (S.S.) xix, xx 89, 90 (1408) ; for their assistance in various kinds of cases see vol. iv 432 ; v 220-222.

[6] Parning (1341) ; Thorpe (1371) ; Knyvet (1372).

[7] R.P. iii 474, 2 Hy. VI. no. 95.

[8] Below 449-452.

intimate relations between the Chancery and the common law judges ceased.[1]

(ii) The Chancellor's close relations with the courts of common law, and his position as a leading member of the Council naturally led to his taking a large share in dealing with certain classes of petitions which were constantly being addressed to the Council.   If the petitioner alleged that, through some defect in the law, he could get no remedy by bringing an ordinary action, his petition could naturally be best dealt with by the Chancellor, because of his close relation to the administration of the law.   Moreover, as he was a high official, closely connected with the king, and often an ecclesiastic, it was very fitting that petitions which asked that justice should be done on moral grounds by an exercise of the king's extraordinary power should be dealt with by him.[2]   From the latter part of the thirteenth century we can see a tendency thus to delegate matters to the Chancellor.   The Ordinances of 1280, and 1293 provided, as we have seen, that all petitions which involved the issue of a document under the Great Seal should go first to the Chancellor.[3] Both in Edward I.[4] and II.'s[5] reigns there are many cases in which petitions were referred to the Chancellor both by the king and by Parliament.   In Edward III.'s reign the position which he was beginning to acquire in relation to these petitions is illustrated by a writ issued in 1349 to the Sheriff of London.   The writ directed that petitions relating to the common law should be brought before the Chancellor, that petitions relating to the grant of the king's grace should be brought before the Chancellor or the Keeper of the Privy Seal, and that only petitions of which these officials could not dispose should be brought before the king in person.[6]   This order is no doubt only of a temporary

---

[1] See a case in 1342, Y.B. 16 Ed. III. (R.S.) ii 113 n. 11 in which the King's Bench, after consultation with the clerks of the Chancery as to the form of a writ, reversed a decision of the Common Pleas ; cf. Y.B. 47 Ed. III. Mich. pl. 14—a case in which the judges referred a matter to the Chancellor.

[2] Baldwin, The King's Council 241-242.   [3] Above 354 nn. 6 and 7.

[4] See Campbell, Chancellors i 189-190 for some records of these cases.

[5] Ibid i 209-212 for some cases of this reign ; Baldwin, op. cit. 242, says that in this reign " a large portion of the petitions considered in Parliament were endorsed with words like the following : ' Soit ceste petitioun maunde en chancellerie . . . et le chaunceller . . . appellez devant lui ceux qui sont appeller face outre droit et reson.'"

[6] " Volumus quod quilibet negocia tam communem legem regni nostri Anglia quam graciam nostram specialem concernencia penes nosmetipsos habens exnunc prosequenda, eadem negocia, videlicet, negocia ad communem legem penes. . . . Cancellarium nostrum per ipsum expedienda, et alia negocia de gracia nostra concernenda penes eundem Cancellarium seu dilectum clericum nostrum Custodem sigilli nostri privati prosequantur (sic) ; ita quod ipsi vel unus eorum peticiones negotiorum que per eos, nobis inconsultis, expediri non poterunt, una cum avisamentis suis inde, ad nos transmittant vel transmittat, absque alia prosecucione penes nos inde facienda, ut hiis inspectis, ulterius prefato Cancellario seu Custodi inde significemus velle nostrum," Select Cases in Chancery (S.S.) xvii, xviii.

nature;[1] but it is significant of the position which the Chancellor was acquiring. It shows that he is becoming associated with petitions which ask something of the king's grace, and that, in relation to petitions dealing with such matters and with questions of law, he has a position of decisive importance in the Council. And this conclusion is corroborated by the evidence both of the petitions themselves and of the statutes. As early as Edward I.'s reign petitions had been addressed to the Chancellor and Council;[2] and this form of address become frequent in Edward III.'s reign.[3] After that reign they were habitually addressed sometimes to the Chancellor and Council, sometimes to the Chancellor or Council, sometimes to the Chancellor alone.[4] Several statutes of Edward III.'s reign gave jurisdiction over specified matters, sometimes to the Chancellor, sometimes to the Chancery, sometimes to the Council or the Chancery.[5]

(iii) This predominance of the Chancellor in relation to petitions addressed to the Council was due not only to his personal position. It was due, as these statutes of Edward III.'s reign show, quite as much to the fact that he was the head of an organized department of state—the Chancery, which had by this time become stationary at Westminster.[6] It is the Chancery which is named in some of these statutes; and the fact that the Chancellor was at its head enabled him the more easily to set in motion its machinery to give the relief which was sought. Because this department was, through the Chancellor, closely connected both with the common law courts and with the Council, it was able to give any relief ordered, either by the issue of ordinary writs, or by carrying into effect the orders given by the Council by virtue of its extraordinary jurisdiction.[7] It was natural, therefore, that petitions which asked for the redress of wrongs legal or moral should be referred to the

<hr>

[1] Kerly, Equity 31, 32.   [2] Baldwin, op. cit. 248.   [3] Ibid 248-249.
[4] Ibid 249-252, 254-255; Close Rolls (Rec. Com.) xxix; Select Cases in Chancery (S.S.) 21 (after 1396).
[5] 20 Edward III. c. 6; 27 Edward III. St. 1 c. 1; 36 Edward III. St. 1 c. 9; 37 Edward III. c. 18; all cited Baldwin, op. cit. 243-244; as Professor Baldwin says, "The Acts show us that at that time the attitude of Parliament towards the Chancery was in the main one of confidence."
[6] The Chancery was showing signs of becoming thus stationary in Edward I.'s reign, Tout, op. cit. 61; but it was often itinerant; in a petition of 1281 it is said that the Chancery is "multotiens in remotis partibus," Mun. Gild. (R.S.) ii Pt. I. 170; it was ordered to follow the king in 1300, 28 Edward I. St. 3 c. 5; and in Edward II.'s reign there are entries of payments for horses to carry the Chancery Rolls, Palgrave, Council n. F; Foss, Judges iii 336; that it was not always with the king appears from Y.B. 6 Ed. II. (S.S.) 231.
[7] "The extension of the power of the Chancery at this time was without doubt based upon its general efficiency and popularity. This is shown by the expressions of many individual petitioners, who particularly asked to have their cases referred to the Chancellor," Baldwin, op. cit. 244.

Chancellor, because with the help of his department, the Chancery, he had an adequate machinery for determining the kind of relief which was needed, and the means of making it effective. Moreover, the Council, being overburdened with work, was glad to delegate the hearing of petitions to the Chancery; and so, as Professor Baldwin says, "out of the business that Parliament and the Council had not the time or the energy to perform, the jurisdiction of the Chancery was being built up."[1] But under these circumstances it was inevitable that the Chancery should assume some of the characteristics of a court. It is clear that the facts stated in these petitions must be sifted,[2] and that the persons against whom allegations were made in them must be given an opportunity to make a defence.[3] It is not surprising, therefore, to find that, in the course of the fourteenth and fifteenth centuries, its new position as a court was becoming well marked. Thus in 1340[4] it is mentioned as a court along with the courts of common law. In 1345[5] the clerks of the Chancery petitioned that they might have the same privilege as the clerks of the courts of common law possessed[6]—the privilege that their trespasses should be cognizable only by their chief the Chancellor. In 1394 the Chancellor was empowered to give damages if the suggestions in the bill were found to be untrue;[7] and in 1436 this power was confirmed, and a power to take security for costs was added.[8]

Thus it is clear that the position of the Chancellor in relation both to the courts of common law and to the Council, his position as the head of the Chancery, and the organization of the Chancery itself, were all combining during the latter half of the fourteenth century to give to the Chancellor and the Chancery very important judicial functions. It is clear, too, that there was a tendency for these functions to be exercised by the Chancellor

---

[1] Select Cases before the Council (S.S.) xix.

[2] For the method of delegating committees of the Council to examine the facts see Baldwin, ibid xliv.

[3] Select Cases in Chancery (S.S.) 89-90 (1408), when there was a full hearing with counsel.

[4] 14 Edward III. St. 1 c. 5.

[5] R.P. ii 154 nos. 41, 42; it is significant that in Y.B. 8 Hy. IV. Mich. pl. 13 Gascoigne, C.J., should find it necessary to point out that for certain purposes the Chancery could not be regarded as a judicial court.

[6] Above 203.

[7] 17 Richard II. c. 6; Coke, Fourth Instit. 82-83, points out that this power only arose after the untruth of the allegations in the bill had been established, so that it only arose after the final hearing of the cause, and not at all stages of the suit.

[8] 15 Henry VI. c. 4; Coke, Fourth Instit. 83-84; in later days the court considered that, apart from any statutory authority, it had an inherent power to give costs, see Corporation of Burford v. Lenthall (1743) 2 Atk. 551 per Lord Hardwicke, C.; and cp. Andrews v. Barnes (1888) 39 C.D. at pp. 138-141.

in the Chancery on his own initiative. If matters were referred to him by the Council or Parliament he could clearly thus act;[1] and, even if they were not so referred, the fact that he often presided at the sessions of the Council at which they were heard, emphasized the importance of his position. Thus, " he summons the parties ; assigns a day for the case ; addresses a question to the litigants ; answers an objection ; admits an attorney in spite of the opposition of other councillors ; discusses a case on his own responsibility ; and announces the decision of the court."[2]   But, though the part played by the Chancellor in the decision of cases specially referred to him, or in the hearing and decision of cases by the Council, indicates that there is a tendency towards the assumption by the Chancellor of an independent jurisdiction as the head of an independent court of Chancery, he did not attain this position till the end of the fifteenth century.   During the greater part of that century the jurisdiction which he exercised as the head of the Chancery was closely connected both with the Council and with the courts of the common law.   In very many of these cases it is quite clear that the decision was regarded as the act of the Council[3]—we are sometimes told the names of the councillors who were present.[4]   In other cases, if the question at issue involved an interference with, or an application of, common law rules, he acted with the advice of the serjeants and the judges.[5]   It was not till 1474[6] that we get a case in which the Chancellor made a decree by his own authority.   After that date such decrees soon began to be frequent,[7] because, by that time, the jurisdiction of the Chancellor and the court of Chancery was fast coming to be a jurisdiction exercised independently of the Council.[8]

The causes of this last development, which made the Chancery a separate court with the Chancellor at its head, were three

[1] " The other members of the Council are represented as assessors or advisers, when in the reign of Richard II. the Chancellor was instructed to act ' by his discretion with the advice of the Council ; ' and again he is to ' take such of the Council as he shall see fit,' " Baldwin, op. cit. 246.

[2] Ibid 245.

[3] " It is important to observe that throughout the fourteenth and most of the fifteenth century the Chancellor was unable to act in these matters without the Council, and that the rendering of decrees was thus far always on the authority not of the Chancellor but of the Council—*ordinatum* or *decretum est per consilium* being still the proper form," Baldwin, op. cit. 246 ; Select Cases in Chancery (S.S.) xix, xx ; Select Cases before the Council (S.S.) xxiii-xxiv ; and for this reason purely equitable cases come before the Council all through the mediæval period, ibid xxxiii-xxxiv.

[4] Select Cases in Chancery (S.S.) 38.

[5] Above 400 n. 5.

[6] Select Cases in Chancery (S.S.) xx.   [7] Ibid.

[8] " Towards the end of the fifteenth century purely equity matters generally came before the Chancellor alone, though this rule is not without exceptions," ibid xx.

in number. In the first place well marked lines of cleavage were becoming apparent in the kinds of jurisdiction exercised by the Council and the Chancery. In the second place new institutions or new machinery were being formed to deal with these separate branches of jurisdiction. In the third place the new political settlement involved in the establishment of the New Monarchy by the Tudors gave a large impetus to the establishment of separate courts on these lines. Thus we may say that jurisdictional, institutional, and political causes combined to establish upon its modern basis an independent court of Chancery with the Chancellor at its head. Let us see how these three causes operated.

(i) During the fifteenth century it is becoming possible to classify the various classes of cases which came before the Chancellor and the Council as follows :—

(a) There was a jurisdiction over cases which fell altogether outside the common law, such as cases which concerned alien merchants, maritime or ecclesiastical law. The common law courts had no jurisdiction over such cases. Thus the question whether the king should have certain goods arrested in an alien ship, supposed to belong to the enemy, was debated in the Chancery ;[1] certain cases involving ecclesiastical law were there debated in Edward III.'s reign ;[2] and in Edward IV.'s reign, in the well-known case of the carrier who broke bulk,[3] the Chancellor thought that the matter was properly determinable before the Council because the plaintiff was an alien merchant, and the case therefore depended on the law of nature and not upon municipal law.

(b) There was a jurisdiction in cases where the common law gave a remedy, but where, owing to the disturbed state of the country, or to the power of the defendant, the ordinary courts could not act; and (c) closely allied to this jurisdiction there was a jurisdiction to deal with cases which could not be dealt with by the ordinary courts because the law itself was at fault.

All through the Middle Ages the turbulence of the country and the power of the defendant was quite as often the ground for the interference of the Chancellor as the strictness of the law.[4] It was not till the Tudor period that the "overmighty

---

[1] Hargrave, Law Tracts 311; 31 Henry VI. c. 4; 14 Edward IV. c. 4; Select Cases in Admiralty (S.S.) i liv, lv; as to a similar jurisdiction delegated to the Court of Requests, see ibid lxv; the King v. Carew (1682) 1 Vern. 54, 55.

[2] Hargrave, Law Tracts 312.

[3] Y.B. 13 Ed. IV. Pasch. pl. 5; cp. Observations concerning the office of Chancellor, 110, 111; Select Cases in Chancery (S.S.) cases 3, 9, 96.

[4] Select Cases in Chancery (S.S.) xxii; for the disorderly state of the country at this period see below 483-485, 490-491; vol. ii 414-416.

subject" was effectually curbed by the enlargement of the powers of the Council. This change contributed largely towards the formation of a distinct court of equity. The nature and scope of the equitable jurisdiction became more definite when the Chancellor was relieved of cases which called for equity, not because the law was at fault, but because its enforcement was impossible. But it was only gradually that the equitable jurisdiction lost all traces of its early connexion with the incompetence of the criminal law. A case which called for equity upon the latter ground was heard by the Chancellor as late as the reign of Elizabeth; [1] and as late as 1686 the court of Chancery entertained applications for changing the venue in actions at law in cases where, owing to the power of one of the parties, a fair trial could not be had.[2] But the court gradually confined itself to giving compensation in such cases, leaving the culprits to be punished by the court of Star Chamber or by the common law courts.[3] In more modern times the court has declined to exercise any jurisdiction for the repression of crime, unless the exercise of such jurisdiction is incidental and necessary to the due exercise of the equitable jurisdiction of the court.[4] But to the end the old connexion survived in the forms of the court. Until the nineteenth century bills in Chancery usually charged the defendant with combination and confederacy; [5] and in the last resort a commission of rebellion might issue to enforce appearance.[6] But these were survivals. As early as the second half of the fifteenth century the purely equitable jurisdiction was showing signs of becoming quite distinct from the criminal or quasi-criminal jurisdiction of the Council. It was coming to be concerned mainly with such matters as uses, contracts, and matters of account. This fact is illustrated by an entry on the Close Roll of 1468, on the occasion of the handing over the seal to Kirkham, M.R. It is there recorded that "the king willed and commanded . . . that all manner of matters to be examined and discussed in the court of Chancery, should be directed and determined according to *equity and conscience, and to the old course and laudable custom of the same court*, so that if in any such matters any difficulty or question of law happen to rise, that he

---

[1] Spence i 687—the defendant under colour of a distress for rent due by the plaintiff violently took from him, among other things, the hand loom by which he earned his living; Puckering, L.K., ordered restoration of the loom and the payment of five marks damages for the outrage.

[2] 1 Vern. 439; Spence i 699. [3] Ibid 351, 689, 691.

[4] Gee v. Pritchard (1818) 2 Swanst. 413.

[5] Warren, Law Studies i 479.

[6] Spence i 371; North, Lives of the Norths i 258, says that if the defendant did not appear upon subpœna and proclamations, "then he was a rebel, and commissioners, that is a petit army, was raised to fetch him in as standing out in rebellion."

therein take the advice and counsel of some of the king's justices, that right and justice may be duly ministered to every man." [1]

(*d*) The jurisdiction, chiefly of a quasi-ministerial character, which was exercised in the case of writs or claims affecting the king's interests, was, as we shall see, already showing signs of becoming quite separate from the equitable jurisdiction. [2]

(ii) This separation of these distinct fields of jurisdiction was giving rise to the growth of new institutions or new machinery.

We shall see that a court of Admiralty was constituted in the middle of the fourteenth century ; [3] and that it naturally absorbed a large part of the mercantile and maritime business which had formerly been dealt with by the Council. It is true that the Council never wholly lost touch with these cases, because then as now, they were often closely connected with questions of foreign policy. [4] But we shall see that, during the sixteenth century, the court of Admiralty absorbed most of this jurisdiction, and that in many cases the Council acted by means of directions given to this court. [5]

The separation of cases which were brought to the Council because, owing to the disturbed state of the country, the ordinary courts could not act, from cases which were brought there because the law itself was at fault, was accentuated by a tendency to a separation in the machinery by which redress was given. The department of the Chancery was responsible for giving redress in cases where that redress required an instrument under the great seal. But the great seal was not the only seal which the king possessed. When the Chancery had become a department of state separate from the royal household, the king devised a private or privy seal for his own personal use. [6] But, by the beginning of the fourteenth century, it was used for business of state, and its keeper had become an official at the head of an office. [7] Its keeper and his office remained independent of the Chancellor and his office ; [8] and, during the course of the fourteenth century, the process of the privy seal was often used by the Council instead of the Chancery process of the great seal, because it was less cumbrous and more secret. [9] Petitioners too preferred it because it was less expensive. [10] Thus the keeper of the privy seal tended to assume a position analogous to that of the Chancellor.

---

[1] Close Rolls 7 Ed. IV. (Rec. Com.) xxxi.
[2] Below 452.
[3] Below 546.
[4] Below 504.
[5] Below 503-504.
[6] Tout, The Place of Edward II. in English History 60-61.
[7] Ibid 162-164.
[8] Ibid 167-168.
[9] Baldwin, op. cit. 256-257.
[10] Ibid 261.

We have seen that in the writ of 1349 the keeper of the privy seal was associated with the Chancellor in answering petitions of grace ;[1] he sometimes presided over the Council when judicial business was transacted ;[2] and petitions were sometimes addressed to him.[3]   The use of this process was made the subject of protest in Parliament at the end of the fourteenth century ; but it still continued to be used.   Thus, as Professor Baldwin has pointed out,[4] " we may speak of the Council and the Chancery, not as two distinct bodies of authority, but as the same body in two diverging methods of operation."   It could act, that is, either through the Chancery by the process of the great seal, or through the office of the privy seal by the process of that seal.   " With the government there was the alternative between the greater secrecy and dispatch of the privy seal procedure and the greater formality and security afforded by the Chancery procedure.   The method of the privy seal therefore was adopted by the Council in all its political activities and for such judicature as most affected interests of state.   To the suitor, on the other hand, there was offered a measure of choice whether he would have his case determined more expeditiously and at less cost by the summary procedure of the privy seal, or at greater expense but with more security in the Chancery.   To some such considerations as these was it due that the Council in time became the great tribunal for criminal trials, while the Chancery was mainly a court for cases concerning property."[5]   It should be noted also that the private suitor was naturally inclined to prefer the Chancery because it was always open, while the Council, in its judicial work, generally observed the legal terms.   Obviously this made both for the usefulness and popularity of the Chancery.[6]

It is clear that this differentiation in machinery and practice tended to give the Chancellor and the Chancery a more independent position.   This tendency was further emphasized by the breakdown of the Council during the Wars of the Roses.   This led to the practice of addressing all sorts and kinds of petitions to the Chancellor [7]—a practice which obviously tended to consolidate the independent position which the Chancellor and the Chancery were already gaining.   When, in the latter years of Edward IV.'s reign, the jurisdiction of the Council began to revive, it began to resume the hearing of criminal cases which

---

[1] Above 401 n. 6.
[2] " There was a marked inclination in judicial proceedings to assemble the Council under the keeper of the privy seal in the absence of the chancellor," Baldwin, op. cit. 258-259.
[3] Ibid 259-260.   [4] Ibid 260-261.   [5] Ibid 261.
[6] Baldwin, Select Cases before the Council xxiv.
[7] Baldwin, op. cit. 428-429.

affected the peace of the state,[1] leaving to the Chancellor and the Chancery jurisdiction over civil cases.   But it was inevitable that the independent position thus assumed by the Chancellor to administer extraordinary justice in such cases should bring into clear relief the contrast between the extraordinary jurisdiction of the court, and its ordinary jurisdiction exercised in relation to writs and other matters in which the king's interests were concerned.   Consequently it is just about this time that the contrast between his equitable or extraordinary, and his legal or ordinary jurisdiction begins to be clearly drawn.[2]

(iii) All these tendencies towards division both in fields of jurisdiction and in institutions were finally clinched by the policy pursued by the Tudors.   They recreated a strong executive government, and made it the predominant partner in the constitution.[3]   They accomplished this work by a reorganization of the Council, by a new classification of its powers,[4] and by the creation of a number of new courts.[5]   We shall see that the judicial powers of the Council came to be exercised in the court of Star Chamber, and that that court tended to become a court of criminal equity, which was to a large extent separate from the Council acting as an executive body.[6]   We shall see also that the commercial and maritime jurisdiction of the court of Admiralty was much extended.[7]   But here we are concerned with the Chancellor and the court of Chancery.   From the early years of the sixteenth century it is clear that it has become a separate court, possessed of both a common law and an equitable jurisdiction, and that the latter jurisdiction is by far the most important.

The beginning of the regular series of decrees and order books in 1545 shows that the equitable jurisdiction of the court was then becoming settled,[8] and the constantly increasing number of cases which it heard during the sixteenth and seventeenth centuries shows that it satisfied a real want.   " Sir Thomas More was Chancellor about three years and seven months, and there remain nearly 500 of the suits commenced during this period.   Of the suits brought in the reign of James 1. there exist about 32,220, making an average of about 1464 suits in each year of the reign. . . . The suits instituted during the nine

[1] Baldwin, op. cit. 431-435 ; below 492-493.   [2] Below 451-452.
[3] Vol. iv 54-107.   [4] Below 495-496.
[5] Thus we get the court of Commissioners of Sewers, 23 Henry VIII. c. 5 ; the court of Augmentations, 27 Henry VIII. c. 27 ; the court of Wards and Liveries 32 Henry VIII. c. 46 ; the court of Surveyors, 33 Henry VIII. c. 39 ; see Coke, Fourth Instit. 121, 122, 188, 276 ; we shall see vol. ix 34-35 that the new powers given to the last three of these courts had some influence on the development of the subject's remedies against the crown.
[6] Below 497-502.   [7] Below 546-547.
[8] Vol. v 264.

years (1673-1682) that Lord Nottingham held the great seal have been estimated at not less than 15,000 which calculation yields a yearly average of about 1650."[1] This increase in the number of cases heard took place in spite of the fact that the political often interfered with the judicial duties of the Chancellor, and in spite of the fact that Chancellors, whose knowledge of law and equity was of the slightest, were sometimes appointed for political reasons.

This growing importance of the judicial work of the Chancellor and the court of Chancery was the cause of a gradual change in the character of the persons appointed to hold the office of Chancellor.[2] In the Middle Ages the Chancellors were for the most part ecclesiastics and statesmen. It was only very rarely that they were lawyers.[3] Wolsey (1515-1529) was the last of the great ecclesiastical Chancellors of the mediæval type. His successor, Sir Thomas More (1529-1532), was the first of the lawyer Chancellors of the modern type; and both his immediate successors—Audley (1532-1544) and Rich (1547-1551)—were trained lawyers. But statesmen and ecclesiastics still continued to be appointed. Wriothesley (1544-1547) was a politician; Goodrich (1552-1553) was a bishop; and Mary's Chancellors, Gardiner (1553-1555), and Heath (1556-1558), were ecclesiastical Chancellors who approximated to the mediæval type. Elizabeth's first Lord Keeper, Nicholas Bacon (1558-1579), was, after More, the first really distinguished lawyer to preside over the Court of Chancery. It was while he held office that it was declared, first by royal warrant,[4] and then by statute[5] that the office of Lord Keeper conferred the same powers and jurisdiction as the office of Lord Chancellor. He was succeeded by Sir Thomas Bromley (1579-1587)—a lawyer who had held the post of solicitor-general. But after him came another lay Chancellor—Sir Christoper Hatton (1587-1591). The three succeeding holders of the office—Puckering (1592-1596), Egerton who was created Lord Ellesmere by James I. (1596-1617), and Francis Bacon (1617-1621) — were lawyers; and the two last very eminent lawyers. Egerton did much to establish on its modern lines the procedure of the court; and to his efforts the final settlement of its relations to the courts of common law was largely due. This settlement was perhaps his most important

---

[1] C. P. Cooper, Public Records i 356 n.; ibid Chancery, 104-105 n.

[2] For a more detailed account of the Chancellors of this period see vol. v 218-257.

[3] For these exceptional cases see above 400; their appointment was probably due to special causes, vol. ii 557-558.

[4] Egerton Papers (C.S.) 29.   [5] 5 Elizabeth c. 18.

achievement because, as we shall see,[1] it gave the court a position of equal and in some respects of superior authority to that of the courts of common law; and it thus assured the free and continuous development of equity. Francis Bacon continued his work. The speech which he made when he took his seat in the court,[2] and the comprehensive orders which he issued,[3] are the best proof of the large effects which his predecessor's work had had upon the procedure and the jurisdiction of the court.

Bacon's successor, Bishop Williams (1621-1625) was not a lawyer; but all his successors down to the execution of Charles I. were lawyers. They were Coventry (1625-1640), Finch (1640), Lyttleton (1641-1645), and Lane (1645-1649). Shaftesbury (1672-1673) was the last of the lay Chancellors. He had been educated as a lawyer, but had never practised; and his appointment was due to political reasons of a not very reputable kind.[4] Roger North tells us that on the Bench his dress and appearance were "more like a university nobleman than an High Chancellor of England;"[5] that he slighted the bar and trampled on the forms of the court; but that the bar finally compelled him to respect both.[6] But North was his political opponent, and his statements are not corroborated by any other authority.[7] Another political opponent—Dryden—praised his judicial purity and his speedy justice. In fact, Shaftesbury was well aware of some of the defects of the court. He had been on the commission for legal reform which had been appointed in 1652, and was a member of the Parliament which in 1653 had, after a two days' debate on the corruptions of the court, resolved that it should be abolished.[8] As Chancellor he issued a comprehensive set of Orders as to the practice of the court, which apparently never came into force.[9] It was no doubt a scandal that a non-lawyer should be made a Chancellor at that date, for the rules of Equity were fast developing into a settled system.[10] But they were hardly yet very clearly or finally settled—it is not till the

---

[1] Below 463-465.
[2] Spedding, Life and Letters of Bacon vi 182-193; vol. v 252.
[3] Bacon, Works (Ed. Spedding) vii 755; vol. v 253.
[4] Vol. vi 525-526.   [5] Examen 60.
[6] "He slighted the bar; declared their reign at an end. He would make all his own orders his own way, and in his discourse trampled on all the forms of the court. . . . They soon found his humour and let him have his caprice; and after, upon notice, moved him to discharge his orders; and thereupon, having the advantage, upon the opening, to be heard at large, they shewed him his face, and that what he did was against common justice and sense. And this *Speculum* of his own ignorance and presumption, coming to be laid before him every motion day, did so intricate and embarrass his understanding, that, in a short time, like any haggard hawk that is not let sleep, he was entirely reclaimed," ibid 58.
[7] Vol. vi 526-527.
[8] Below 431-432.   [9] Vol. vi 527.
[10] Below 468.

Chancellorship of his successor Lord Nottingham (1673-1682) that they began to assume their modern form and fixity.[1]   This fact, coupled with the growing organization of the court combined, as we shall now see, to render the task of the lay Chancellors of the sixteenth and seventeenth centuries less difficult than it might at first sight appear.

Even in the Middle Ages the ecclesiastical Chancellors, by consulting the judges, often recognized their inability to deal with the business of the court without assistance.[2]   And, in the sixteenth and early seventeenth centuries, the lay Chancellors generally took care to get the assistance of the judges or masters of the court or both.   In 1529, just before Wolsey's fall, a commission was issued to judges, masters of the court, and others, authorizing them to hear and determine all causes committed to them by the Chancellor.[3]   While Wriothesley, Rich, and Goodrich were Chancellors, similar commissions were issued to certain of the masters, or to certain of the masters and of the judges.[4] Hatton took care always to get the assistance of the masters of the court,[5] and Williams was frequently assisted by the judges and the masters.[6]   Thus the growth of an organized official staff helped to minimize the hindrance which the ignorance of some of the Chancellors might have caused to the development of the rules of equity.   But before I describe this staff I must first notice the COURT OF REQUESTS,[7] a minor court of equity which flourished during the Tudor and early Stuart period.

The establishment of the court of Requests was due to the large increase in the judicial business of the Council and the Chancery under the Tudors.[8]   It was related both to the judicial side of the Council, which, as we shall see, came, in the course of the Tudor period, to be known as the court of Star Chamber, and to the court of Chancery ; but in its origin it was more closely related to the court of Star Chamber.   We have seen that the Council and the court of Star Chamber used the privy seal and the process of the privy seal, while the Chancery used the great seal and the process of the great seal ;[9] and that this helped to separate the jurisdiction exercised by the Council from that exercised by the Chancellor and the Chancery. The court of Requests was always closely connected with the privy seal.   The Lord Privy Seal was its president,[10] and it

---

[1] Vol. vi 539-548.   [2] Above 400.
[3] Foss, Judges v 262.   [4] Ibid 278-279.
[5] Ibid 505, citing Egerton Papers (C.S.) 125.
[6] Ibid vi 383.
[7] For this court see Leadam, Select Cases in the Court of Requests (S.S.).
[8] Baldwin, op. cit. 442.   [9] Above 407-408.
[10] Select Cases in the Court of Requests (S.S.) xi.

naturally used the process of the privy seal.[1] Therefore, as Lambard pointed out, it was closely connected with the Star Chamber.[2] But in respect of the nature of the jurisdiction which it exercised it was more closely connected with the court of Chancery.[3] Though it occasionally exercised a quasi-criminal jurisdiction in cases of riots, forgery, and such like offences, resembling that of the Star Chamber,[4] it usually exercised an equitable jurisdiction in civil cases similar to that exercised by the court of Chancery.

Originally the court exercised jurisdiction at the suit either of poor men or of the king's servants;[5] and possibly both its name and the nature of its jurisdiction were suggested by a court called by a similar name which had long been established in France.[6] With the suits of poor men the office of the privy seal had a traditional connexion.[7] But it is clear that the later court of Requests did not come into being till 1493.[8] Henry VII. created a sort of standing committee of the Council primarily to deal with suits of poor men and of the king's servants.[9] At first it travelled about the country with the king;[10] but it gradually became a stationary court. Wolsey fixed it in the White Hall of Westminster Palace;[11] and, from the end of Henry VIII.'s reign onwards, the legal assessors of the court assumed entire control,[12] with the result that it became a court which was quite separate from the court of Star Chamber.[13] These legal assessors were styled Masters of Requests, and from their title the court got its name.[14] They were at first two in number; but in Elizabeth's reign there were two masters ordinary, and two masters extraordinary. The first followed the queen in her numerous progresses, while the second remained at Whitehall.[15] Four

[1] Select Cases in the Court of Requests (S.S.) xxi.

[2] " In that it hath continually been served with a clerk that was ever therwithal one of the clerks of the king's privy seal: it seemeth to communicate with the Star Chamber itself, and to derive the authority immediately from the royal person, as that doth," Lambard, Archeion 225.

[3] " In that the Court of Requests handleth causes that desireth moderation of the rigour which the common law denounceth, it doth plainly participate with the nature of the Chancery," ibid 224.

[4] Select Cases in the Court of Requests (S.S.) lxxxix.

[5] Ibid; " I do well remember that within these 40 years the bills of complaints presented there, did ordinarily carry the one, or the other of these two suggestions, namely that the plaintiff was a very poor man, not able to sue at the common law, or the king's servant ordinarily attendant upon his person or in his household," Lambard, Archeion 229.

[6] Esmein, Histoire du droit Francais (11th Ed.) 428-431, 432-434; Select Cases (S.S.) xi, xii; Coke, Fourth Instit. 97.

[7] See an order of 13 Richard II. Nicolas i 18 b, cited Spence, op. cit. 351; Baldwin, op. cit. 259.

[8] Select Cases (S.S.) x.

[9] Ibid.

[10] Ibid xii, xiii; cp. Baldwin, op. cit. 447.

[11] Select Cases (S.S.) xi.

[12] Ibid xix.

[13] Ibid xli.

[14] Ibid xiv, xv.

[15] Ibid xix.

masters ordinary were appointed in James I.'s reign, but royal progresses still continued; and the masters were sometimes called upon to sit in the court of Star Chamber.[1] It was made a matter of complaint that the proceedings of the court were thereby hindered, " for that there is not one person certeyne that doe alwayes sit judge there, but they sitt by turnes and by starts."[2]

In spite of this defect the social and economic changes which were taking place all through the Tudor period made a court of this kind very useful. It supplemented and assisted both the Star Chamber and the Chancery; and there is no doubt that it was popular. Like other courts it tended to extend its jurisdiction; and both the expense of the proceedings in the court, and delays in its procedure tended to increase.[3] But to the end it always remained, at least in theory, a court for poor suitors.[4]

Towards the end of Elizabeth's reign the court was attacked by the courts of common law.[5] We shall see that the courts of common law showed at this period a jealousy of all jurisdiction other than their own. They had, as we have seen, won a complete victory over the older local courts.[6] They now attacked courts which had greater powers of resistance because they had sprung, like themselves, from the crown. Their theory was that a court could not be a legal court unless its jurisdiction was based either upon an Act of Parliament or upon prescription. Upon this theory the court of Chancery and the Council were by prescription legal courts. But more recent committees of the Council, and the court of Requests, could show neither a statutory nor a prescriptive title. The courts of common law, therefore, denied that the court of Requests was a legal court.[7] Sir Julius Cæsar urged in its defence that it was substantially the same court as the King's Council. It is true that it had sprung from the King's Council. But it is clear that in James I.'s reign it was a court quite separate from the King's Council, because no place was assigned to the judges of the court among the Privy Councillors.[8] He urged also that the legality of its jurisdiction had been recognized by the judges. This was to

---

[1] Select Cases (S.S.) xx.   [2] Ibid xcvii.
[3] Ibid xcvi-xcix; Lambard, Archeion 229, 230.
[4] Select Cases (S.S.) xv.
[5] Ibid xxii-xlvi; Sir Julius Cæsar, one of the Masters of Requests, wrote an elaborate vindication of the court in 1596, of which Mr. Leadam gives an account in his introduction to the Select Cases xxii-xxxv.
[6] Above, chap. ii.   [7] Below 415; Select Cases xl.
[8] See the petition of the Masters of Requests to be allowed such a place, ibid xcix, c.

some extent true.[1] The answer of the common lawyers was given by Coke. " As gold or silver may as current money pass even with the proper artificer, though it hath too much alloy, until he hath tried it with the touchstone : even so this nominative court may pass with the learned as justifiable in respect of the outside by vulgar allowance, until he advisedly looketh into the roots of it, and try it by rule of law ; as (to say the truth) I myself did."[2] But it is clear that the " touchstone " was not so much the rule of law as the changed outlook and the growing independence of the common law courts.

In 1590 we find the earliest record of a writ of Prohibition issued against the court by the court of Common Pleas.[3] In 1598 occurred the case of *Stepney* v. *Flood*, which, in Coke's opinion, finally decided the illegality of the court.[4] But in spite of these decisions, and of others to the same effect in James I. and Charles I.'s reigns,[5] the court continued to thrive. Its cause list was full, because it met a want which was felt. In 1627, when Lord Manchester was Lord Privy Seal, Fuller says that the court was in such repute that " what was formerly called the Almes Basket of the Court of Chancery, had . . . as much *meat* in, and *guests* about it (I means suits and clients) as the Chancery itself."[6] Even Coke was obliged to admit that it might be well if its jurisdiction were established by Parliament.[7]

Blackstone considers that the court of Requests was "virtually abolished " by the Act of 1641 which abolished the jurisdiction of the Council in England.[8] It is true that this Act does not mention the court of Requests. It is true also that the decisions of the preceding reigns directed against the court had been based on the principle that the court of Requests was a separate

---

[1] Select Cases xxxii-xxxv ; but there were only four instances, the earliest of which was a century after the establishment of the court.

[2] Fourth Instit. 98.

[3] Select Cases xxxvi, xxxvii, followed by other cases in the Common Pleas and King's Bench.

[4] Fourth Instit. 97 ; Cro. Eliza. 646 (sub nomine Stepney v. Lloyd), Anderson, C.J., and Glanvil, J., said, " This court hath not any power by commission, by statute or by common law ; " and they contrasted it with courts like the court of Wards which had such power by statute ; in Paine's case (1608), Yelv. 111, it was ruled that perjury was not there punishable, as the court had no jurisdiction.

[5] Earl of Derby's case (1614) 12 Co. Rep. 114 ; Penson v. Cartwright (1615) Cro. Jac. 345 ; Calmadie's case (1640) Cro. Car. 595.

[6] Campbell, Lives of the Chief Justices i 360, citing Fuller ii 169.

[7] Fourth Instit. 98, " And although the law be such as we have set down ; yet in respect of the continuance that it hath had by permission, and of the number of decisions therein had, it were worthy of the wisdom of a Parliament, both for the establishment of things for the time past, and for some certain provision with reasonable limitations . . . for the time to come."

[8] Bl. Comm. iii 50 ; so Hale, Jurisdiction of the House of Lords 57, says, " This court he (the keeper of the privy seal) held for a while, but being under a discontinuance, it hath now for many years been asleep."

court, and not the Council;[1] and that no attempt was made to put the Act in force against the court, which continued to sit till 1642.[2] But, after the Restoration, though Masters of Request were appointed, they performed no judicial duties. They merely examined personal petitions for royal favours.[3] As Leadam says, " Charles II. was too well advised to imperil a yet unsettled throne by an exercise of prerogative which would have excited lively apprehension throughout the country. If, it would have been asked, the king, despite the decisions of the judges of Elizabeth, and in the face of the Act of 1641, could re-establish the court of Requests, then, why not the Star Chamber?"[4] This is probably the gist of the matter; and this justifies Blackstone's view of the effect of the Act of 1641.

The court of Chancery was therefore left the sole court of equity We must now consider the way in which it was organized.

The Organization of the Court

The two most important sets of officials of the court were the Masters and the Clerks. There were many other officials,[5] but these are the most important, and therefore I shall speak only of them in this section.

The Masters.

Writers of the seventeenth century state that the Chancellor was the sole judge of the court.[6] But, being much occupied with political duties, he often needed assistance. From the reign of Henry VIII. onwards he was generally assisted by the Master of the Rolls, who was the chief of the Masters in Chancery. I shall first describe the position of the Masters, and then trace the history of their chief.

Fleta, in his chapter on the Chancery, says that there were associated with the Chancellor " honest and prudent clerks who were sworn to be faithful to the king, and who had a full knowledge of the laws and customs of England ; whose duty it was to hear and examine the prayers and complaints of petitioners, and, by royal writs, to give the fitting remedies for the injuries which they had brought to light."[7] Elsewhere he calls these clerks

---

[1] Select Cases xlix.

[2] Between 28th of April and 17th of May 1642, 556 orders were made, ibid l.

[3] Ibid c, ci. [4] Ibid lii.

[5] Fleta II. 36 ; Observations Concerning the Office of Lord Chancellor 36-39 ; App. XXVI.

[6] Coke, Fourth Instit. 84 ; Observations Concerning the Office of Chancellor 31 ; Spence, op. cit. i 357 and note.

[7] " Clerici honesti et circumspecti Domino Regi jurati, qui in legibus et consuetudinibus Anglicanis notitiam habeant pleniorem ; quorum officium sit supplicationes et querelas conquerentium audire et examinare et eis super qualitatibus injuriarum ostensarum debitum remedium exhibere per brevia regis," II. 13, 1.

"collaterales," "socii," and "præceptores" of the Chancellor.[1]
In fact during the Middle Ages we find them called by very
various titles, all implying that they are assistants to the Chancellor.[2] Their number seems from an early date to have been
fixed at twelve;[3] and it continued to be twelve. But in the
time of Hatton and Egerton we meet with Masters Extraordinary who did certain ministerial acts in the country.[4] They
were paid in early times partly by fees, but chiefly in kind.
They lived together in the king's house, and later in a special
dwelling set apart for them;[5] and they had certain allowances
of clothes, food, and drink. They were all in Orders before
Henry VIII.'s reign; and the Chancellor seems to have acquired
the patronage of all livings under 20 marks in order that he
might be able to reward the Masters, and other officials of the
Chancery.[6] In the treatise on the Masters there is a complaint
that other officials of the Chancery had usurped their duties, and
had diminished the value of their offices by intercepting their
fees.[7] But, that they gained considerable profit from the increased business of the Chancery, is clear from the fact that
in 1621 it could be asserted that eight of their number had given
£150 a piece for their offices.[8]

They were in early times occasionally appointed by the
crown. In the reign of Edward IV. the Chancellor acquired the
right, which he exercised till 1833, of appointing eleven of them.[9]
The appointment of their chief, the Master of the Rolls, remained
with the crown. The Chancellor admitted them to office by
placing a cap upon their head in court.[10]

The duties of the Masters were in earlier times very various.
Their large range made it necessary that they should be acquainted not only with the common law, but also with the canon
and civil law.[11] They can be summarized as follows: (1) Fleta
describes them as superintending the issue of all original writs.[12]
By the end of Elizabeth's reign their duties in this respect seem

---

[1] II. 13, 12.
[2] In the Treatise on the Masters (written while Egerton was Lord Keeper,
1596-1603), Hargrave's Law Tracts 294, they are styled "Magistri cancellarii, concilium regis in cancellaria, socii, collaterales, clerici de prima forma, clerici primi
gradus, clerici de majore gradu, clerici magni, clerici ad robas"—the reason for the
last name is that they wore robes or gowns of the king's gift.
[3] Ibid 297. [4] Ibid; Spence i 365. [5] Below 419.
[6] Treatise on the Masters 315-317; Y.B. 3, 4 Ed. II. (S.S.) xix.
[7] Treatise on the Masters 315-317.
[8] Spence i 361 n. a, citing a speech of Sir E. Coke in the House of Commons.
[9] Treatise on the Masters 293; 3, 4 William IV. c. 94 § 16.
[10] Treatise on the Masters, 294; they are there compared to Doctors in a
University.
[11] Ibid 301, 309, 310; in Mary's reign there was a complaint that they neglected
the common law for the civil law, and that in consequence writs were carelessly
issued, History of the Chancery 36 seqq. [12] II. 13, 1.

to have been confined to the issue of writs of grace such as subpoena, supplicavit, certiorari, or ne exeat regno ; and even these
often issued as of course.[1]　(2) They acted occasionally as the
king's secretaries.[2]　(3) They attended the House of Lords
without writ, and were often nominated triers of petitions.[3]
Originally they took rank above the Attorney- and Solicitor-
General, the King's Counsel, and the serjeants, till one Dr.
Barkley in 1576 ventured to address the House without leave.
Since that time they took rank below the serjeants.[4]　(4) They
assisted the Council and the Chancery in the various branches of
their jurisdiction.[5]

Their duties became specialized with the growing jurisdiction
of the court of Chancery.　At an early period they examined
witnesses in causes depending in the Chancery.[6]　But this duty
had, by the end of Elizabeth's reign, devolved on special
examiners and Masters Extraordinary.[7]　Their chief duty was to
assist the Chancellor in the hearing of cases, and also on seal
days, i.e. on days when he heard motions on interlocutory
matters.[8]　They were sometimes compared to the pedanei
judices of the later Roman law, because the Chancellor could
delegate to them the duty of hearing and reporting upon certain
parts of a case.[9]　This system of delegation seems to have been
carried to an excess ; and Bacon's Orders [10] defined and restricted
the matters which could be so delegated.　The effect of his
Orders was to fix the position of the Masters as assistants to the
court, whose duty it was to report upon matters referred to them.
Their position became more definite with the development of the
jurisdiction of their chief, the Master of the Rolls.

The Dialogus de Scaccario mentions a clerk of the Chancery
whose duty it was to oversee the scribe who composed the
Chancellor's Roll.[11]　Possibly this official is the Clerk or Curator
of the Rolls, and the Master of the Rolls of later law.[12]　In

---

[1] Treatise on the Masters 301, 302 ; cp. Bacon's Orders no. 85.

[2] Treatise on the Masters 303.　　　　　　　　[3] Ibid 308, 309.

[4] Ibid 298, 299 ; cp. S.P. Dom. 1603-1610 346, xxvi 29, 30.

[5] Treatise on the Masters 309-313.

[6] Ibid 303.　　　　　　　　　　　　　　　[7] Spence i 365.

[8] Treatise on the Masters 307 ; Observations, etc., 36, 37.　The term " inter-
locutory " seems to have originated with Lord Ellesmere ; Norburie, Abuses of
Chancery (Hargrave, Law Tracts at p. 443), talks of " those orders which the last
Lord Chancellor not unaptly termed *interlocutory*, being before hearing."

[9] E.g. taking of accounts, the hearing of applications relating to procedure, the
examination of interrogatories, or the sufficiency of answers, and, till Bacon's time,
demurrers, Spence i 361.

[10] Orders 45-53.　　　　　　　　　　[11] Stubbs, Sel. Ch. 178.

[12] The title of the Master of the Rolls in the Middle Ages is Clerk or Curator of
the Rolls, Spence i 100, 357 ; History of the Chancery 21, 22.　He is not called
Master of the Rolls in any statute till 11 Henry VII. c. 18 ; till Henry VIII.'s reign
he was a cleric, Spence i 357 n. *d*.

Edward II.'s reign William Airmyn was the principal clerk in the Chancery—he was sometimes even spoken of unofficially as vice-chancellor ; and " he was the first Chancery clerk to combine the offices of keeper of the rolls of Chancery and keeper of the *domus conversorum* in which these rolls ultimately found their home." [1] This would seem to show that the office was growing in distinctness and assuming its modern shape. In 1378 Parliament confirmed a grant of this House made by Edward III. to the Keeper of the Rolls ; [2] and in 1388 he was assigned a place above the judges. [3] The Chancellor admitted him to office by putting him into the possession of this domus conversorum, [4] which thus became " the College of the Chancery men." [5]

We have seen that, with the development of the jurisdiction of the Chancery, the judicial duties of the Masters began to increase. From the first a large share of these judicial duties fell to the Master of the Rolls who was sometimes assisted by the judges. [6] Thus in 1433 he was commissioned, during the absence of the Chancellor in France, to exercise the jurisdiction belonging to the court of Chancery. [7] In the reign of Henry VIII., as at an earlier period, he is sometimes called vice-chancellor. [8] But up to this reign his jurisdiction differed from that of the other Masters in degree rather than in kind. The practice, which dates from the time of Wolsey, of delegating to him a certain jurisdiction by special commission, gave him in time a jurisdiction which is quite different from that of the other Masters. [9] These commissions were at first addressed not only to the Master of the Rolls, but also to the judges and the other Masters. They empowered the persons named to hear the kind of cases specified in the commission. Later they were addressed to the Master of the Rolls only, and empowered him to hear cases generally. [10] The practice had become so usual that Coke states generally that

---

[1] Tout, Edward II. 184 ; the domus conversorum had since Henry III.'s days been a home for converted Jews, Lambard, Archeion 67-68.

[2] History of the Chancery 20-21.

[3] Discourse, etc., 18, 19. In James I.'s reign his place was between the two chief justices.

[4] Spence i 357.   [5] Lambard, Archeion 67.

[6] Spence i 358 and notes ; Discourse, etc., 90-109. There are the following references to the judicial capacity of the Master of the Rolls in the Year Books of the fifteenth century : 1 Hy. VII. Pasch. pl. 1 ; 1 Hy. VII. Trin. pl. 5 ; 4 Ed. IV. Mich. pl. 5 ; 11 Ed. IV. Trin. pl. 14 ; 12 Ed. IV. Mich. pl. 11 ; cp. 11 Henry VII. c. 25.

[7] Nicolas iv 158.

[8] Discourse, etc., 20 ; from Henry VI.'s reign we find bills addressed to him ; but this was usual only when the office of Master of the Rolls was associated with that of Lord Keeper.

[9] Campbell, Chancellors i 506.

[10] Spence i 365, 366 ; see S.P. Dom. 1611-1618 335, lxxxiv 3 for a commission to Sir Julius Cæsar, M.R., to hear and examine causes in the Chancery.

in the absence of the Lord Chancellor he hears causes and makes Orders.[1] From 1623 he appears to have had some share in regulating the practice of the court, as, after that date, many of the general Orders were issued by the Chancellor and the Master of the Rolls.[2] He comes to be in fact the general deputy of the Lord Chancellor.

It was not certain, however, whether the Master of the Rolls exercised these powers by virtue of his position as Master, or by virtue of the special commission addressed to him. In the eighteenth century the jealousy of the other Masters raised the question of his authority to act as general deputy of the Chancellor.[3]

The controversy illustrates the gradual way in which the jurisdiction of the Chancery had developed. It was clear that originally the Master of the Rolls had been simply one of the Masters. Like them he acted for the Chancellor. His grant of office contained no explicit reference to judicial duties;[4] and it was not clear whether he could be authorized to act alone by royal commission,[5] or whether proceedings before him were not invalid in the absence of two of the other Masters.[6] But it was clear that another judge was needed for the Chancery. It was possible, owing to the uncertainty of the older practice, and the certainty of the more recent practice, to contend that there had always been a subordinate judge in the Chancery. The controversy concerned but a small point of legal history. But the arguments used on either side remind us of the larger political controversies of the seventeenth century. Both were argued as questions of legal history. In both each side tried to elicit, from the uncertain precedents and forms of an earlier age, the answer to a question of which the makers of those precedents and forms had never dreamed.

[1] Fourth Instit. 97; but as late as the beginning of the seventeenth century the office was treated as a sinecure; when Egerton, who had held the office for seven years together with the office of Lord Keeper, became Chancellor it was conferred by James I. on a Scotch favourite who knew nothing of the duties of the office; but this experiment was not repeated.

[2] Spence i 359 n. a.

[3] A Mr. Burroughs wrote " a history of the Chancery relating to the judicial power of that court and the rights of the Masters," maintaining that the Master of the Rolls had only judicial authority *qua* master. This was answered in the " Discourse of the Judicial Authority of the Master of the Rolls," attributed to Lord Hardwicke and Sir J. Jekyll. Burroughs replied with his " Legal Judicature in Chancery; " see C. P. Cooper, Chancery 349, 350 n.

[4] Legal Judicature in Chancery 97-100.

[5] Discourse, etc., 137-144; Legal Judicature 177.

[6] Ibid 182-185, 268; Discourse, etc., 162, 163; in Smith v. Turner (1684) 1 Vern. 273, 274, it is stated that the Master of the Rolls had no jurisdiction in the absence of two of the other masters; and cp. Merreitt v. Eastwicke, ibid 264-266; but it is stated in the report of Smith v. Turner that the record does not bear out the reports of these cases.

The question was settled by statute in 1729.[1] It was enacted that all Orders made by the Master of the Rolls (except such Orders as the Lord Chancellor alone could make) should be valid, subject to an appeal to the Lord Chancellor. But the Master of the Rolls was still regarded merely as deputy of the Lord Chancellor. C. P. Cooper,[2] writing in 1828, said, "the sittings of the Master of the Rolls still continue to be regulated upon the old notion of his having no authority to hear causes, except in the Chancellor's absence and as his deputy, and this, extraordinary as it may appear, is the only reason that can be assigned for the Master of the Rolls not sitting on Wednesday and Friday evenings during term, and at other times when the Chancellor was anciently in the habit of holding his sittings."

The Clerks.

In addition to the Masters the Chancery possessed an extensive staff of clerks. The most important of these are known as the Six Clerks.[3] Their duty was to write and examine the writs before they were sealed. If a wrong writ was issued they were liable.[4] They were under the superintendence of the Master of the Rolls, and assisted him in keeping the Rolls.[5] They acted also, in earlier times, as the solicitors of the parties. With the increase in the jurisdiction of the court their duties became at once less burdensome and more profitable. The duty of drawing up the writs fell on the cursitors.[6] The appointment of a registrar of the court, as early as Henry V.'s reign, relieved them of the duty of recording the orders and decrees of the court.[7] At a later date the creation of offices for filing affidavits [8] and for filing bills and answers [9] relieved them of the custody of these documents. The growing business of the court made it impossible for them to act as solicitors to the parties. They are declared, it is true, in Lord Clarendon's Orders, to be the proper

---

[1] 3 George II. c. 30. [2] Chancery 350, 351.

[3] Fleta II 13, 15 says, " Habet etiam sex clericos suos prænotarios in officio illo, qui cum clericis memoratis familiares regis esse consueverunt, et præcipue ad victum et vestitum, quia ad brevia scribenda secundum diversitates querelarum sunt intiulati (sic) ; et qui omnes pro victu et vestitu de proficuo sigilli, in cujuscumque usus provenerint, debent honeste inveniri ; " they were in Orders till 14, 15 Henry VIII. c. 8 ; Reeves H.E.L. iii 250.

[4] Spence i 366.

[5] History of the Chancery 32 ; for other regulations made for keeping the Rolls in 1592 see Egerton Papers (C.S.) 194.

[6] Fleta II 36 ; Bacon's Works vii 699, 700.

[7] Some information as to this office will be found in a petition of the Registrar to Archbishop Laud in 1637, S.P. Dom. 1637, 561 cccclxxii 26 ; it is there stated that his duties had formerly been discharged by the Six Clerks ; but the author seems to have thought erroneously that the office only dated from Henry VIII.'s reign, as to this see Spence i 366 n. e.

[8] Ibid i 366 ; Bacon, loc. cit. [9] Egerton Papers (C.S.) 198-200.

and only officers of the court to inform themselves, and to report to the court on the state of their client's causes.   But the clients often employed their under clerks,[1] and finally their own solicitors.[2] The Six Clerks, however, still continued to keep the records, and to make for their supposed clients copies of the proceedings for which they took large fees.   From the time of Charles I. they divided the cases among them by an alphabetical arrangement.[3]

Although they had ceased to superintend the business of the suitors, their remuneration increased with the increase in the amount and value of the business of the court.   The suitors were obliged to take copies of the proceedings, which they did not need, because the Six Clerks had nominally the conduct of the suits.   They still further lightened their duties, without diminishing their salary, by an agreement which they came to in 1785.[4] It was arranged that their business should be conducted in one room, and that they should take it in turns to be present; that the one present should do all the business arising in any suit, whether or not it was appropriated to himself, and should credit the clerk, to whom the suit was appropriated, with the fees. Thus each clerk drew his salary for two months' work in the year.   Seeing that their under clerks attended court, and that the parties' own solicitors conducted the causes, their sole work consisted in keeping certain records, in signing certain documents connected with the cause, and in taking large fees for badly-executed and needless copies of such documents.[5]

The Six Clerks were assisted by a body of persons known in later law as the Sixty Clerks.[6]   They were at first merely the employees of the Six Clerks.   In 1596 they were regularly estab-

[1] Ex parte the Six Clerks (1798) 3 Ves. 589, 601; Pepys, Diary ii 133 relates how, in 1661, he went to the Six Clerks' Office to find a clerk to advise him in a Chancery suit.

[2] It is clear from Hudson's treatise on the Star Chamber that the class of professional solicitors was new at the beginning of James I.'s reign, as he says at pp. 94, 95, "in our age there are stepped up a new sort of people called solicitors, unknown to the records of the law, who, like the grasshoppers of Egypt, devour the whole land;" for the history of solicitors see vol. vi 448-457.

[3] Ex parte the Six Clerks 3 Ves. 590.   [4] 3 Ves. 595-596.

[5] See the evidence given before the Chancery Commission of 1826, cited Parkes, Chancery, 576; below 440-441; it is not surprising that in the seventeenth century the king claimed a share in the appointment to such valuable sinecures, S.P. Dom. 1635 251, ccxcii 36; 1661-1662 580, lxiv 13; 1676-1677 193, 248; see above 260-261 for similar claims by the king in the case of the officials of the courts of common law; but as was the case with the officials of the common law courts the Chancellor or Master of the Rolls seem to have asserted their rights to this patronage after the Revolution; thus in 1696 Luttrell notes in his Diary (iv 159) that a Six Clerk's place has fallen vacant which will be worth 6000 guineas to Trevor the Master of the Rolls.

[6] Fleta II 13, 15 mentions, "clerici juvenes et pedites, quibus de gratia Cancellarii concessum est pro expeditione populi brevia facere cursoria; dum tamen sul advocatione clericorum superiorum fuerint, qui eorum facta in eorum receperin pericula."

lished as officers of the court. They took an oath on entering the office and were called the sworn clerks. Egerton fixed their numbers at eight to each Six Clerks. This number was afterwards raised to ten.[1] After many disputes, owing to attempted changes in the Commonwealth period, their status was fixed in 1668. Their number was fixed at sixty ; they were to be chosen from those who had served seven years as clerks to the Six Clerks ; and they were paid by a fixed percentage of the fees paid by suitors to the Six Clerks.

Defects in the Organization of the Court, and its Reorganization in the Nineteenth Century

As soon as the business of the court of Chancery began to increase complaints begin to be heard of its defective organization. There is much evidence as to the nature of these defects in the sixteenth and early seventeenth centuries ; and the defects then pointed out were substantially the same as those which existed in an aggravated form at the beginning of the nineteenth century. During the period of the Commonwealth an attempt was made to remove them. But all the schemes of reform which were put forward during that period perished at the Restoration ; and the attempts made to revive them at the Revolution failed. It was therefore not till the nineteenth century that these long standing defects were removed. From this summary it will be seen that the subject can best be treated chronologically, and divided into the following four periods : (1) The period before the Great Rebellion ; (2) the period of the Commonwealth ; (3) the period after the Restoration ; and (4) the reorganization of the court in the nineteenth century.

(1) The period before the Great Rebellion.

Parliamentary debates and pamphlets of this period supply abundant evidence of the discontent which was felt with the court.[2] The causes of this discontent were two-fold—the judicial staff was inadequate, and abuses of many kinds were rampant amongst the official staff of the court.

(i) *The inadequacy of the judicial staff.*

It was said in a debate in Parliament in 1623 that 35,000 subpoenas had been issued in one year.[3] This may have been an

[1] Ex parte the Six Clerks 3 Ves. 589, 599.
[2] Thus Chamberlain wrote to Nethersole in 1624, " Chancery has lately become a protection for cozening rather than a relief for the honest," S.P. Dom. 1623-1625 278, clxviii 8.
[3] Commons Journals i 573-574.

exaggeration; but it is probable that over 20,000 were issued.[1] It was thus obvious that the work was too much for the Chancellor and the Master of the Rolls. In fact in 1621 a bill had been brought forward in the House of Lords to create two assistant judges of the court; but it had never got beyond a first reading.[2] The result was a constantly increasing arrear of causes, and long delays in the administration of justice. This evil was aggravated by the suspicions entertained, not without reason, that the justice when administered was not always pure.[3] Bacon's confession of corruption showed that the Lord Chancellor himself could not always be trusted; and, as we shall now see, matters were much worse in the offices of the court.

(ii) *The abuses rampant amongst the official staff.*

The official staff of the court of Chancery was recruited and paid upon exactly the same plan as the official staffs of the courts of common law; and the same results ensued.[4] The officials were appointed for life, and paid by fees upon the business done. Thus, when the business of the court began to increase, the value of these offices rose. The officials contrived to pass on the work to deputies; and thus valuable sinecure places came into being.[5] Their holders were naturally the most determined opponents to effective reform. They formed a close body who resented any increase in their numbers because it would diminish their fees. To the end there continued to be twelve masters and six clerks of the court.[6] The deputies of these officials who did their work were generally underpaid;[7] and so they naturally tried to recoup themselves by questionable practices. Sometimes they concealed business from their superiors and kept the fees. Sometimes they paid the fees over and relied upon bribes for expedition.[8] Thus,

---

[1] Sir F. Fane, patentee of the subpoena office, put the number at 16,000; some intermediate figure is probably correct.

[2] Hist. MSS. Com. Third Rep. App. 22; Coke in a debate in the House of Commons in 1621 agreed that the work of the court was too much for the Chancellor and the Master of the Rolls, Commons Journals i 594.

[3] Abuses of the High Court of Chancery, Harg. Law Tracts 433; this tract was written soon after the fall of Bacon while Bishop Williams was Chancellor.

[4] Above 246-262.   [5] Above 257-258.

[6] Observations concerning the Chancery, cited Parkes, Chancery 149-153, " The several Masters of the Rolls for the time being . . . having the nomination of the Six Clerks, Examiners, and Registrars found it more profitable to continue them at that small number, and sell their offices for great sums of money to men altogether ignorant of the practice of the court, than to admit deserving men gratis, and, as business increased, to have increased able and honest working attornies, as the judges of the other courts of justice did."

[7] Exact relation of the Proceedings of the late Parliament (1653), cited Parkes 129; D'Ewes, Autobiography i 210, notes in the Six Clerks " Their extreme tenacity and love of the world, daily plotting how to keep short the gains of their under-clerks and to advance their own."

[8] Lives of the Norths i 263.

while the actual work was badly done by underpaid deputies, the suitor paid enormous fees to sinecure officials. These officials naturally regarded their offices merely as property. They were sold or given away by the king or the Chancellor;[1] and sometimes sold by the holders of the office.[2] An attack upon one of these officials always appeared to those interested in the patronage, not as the act of dismissing a useless servant, but as the act of depriving a man of his freehold. It was on this ground that the Six Clerks escaped abolition in the time of the Commonwealth.[3] It followed that all those who, from their experience of the court, were most competent to reform it, were the most interested in maintaining it in its existing condition. Commissions of enquiry revealed abuses, but they could do little to remedy them.[4] From the Lord Chancellor who sold the higher offices, to the under clerk who did the work of the higher official, all had an interest in maintaining the system. The court, it was said with some truth, was a "mere monopolie to cozen the subjects of their monies."

These abuses were similar to the abuses which, as we have seen, prevailed in the offices of the courts of common law. But there is no doubt that we hear considerably more of the abuses of the court of Chancery. This was to some extent due to political causes. The common lawyers were powerful enough in the House of Commons to prevent a direct attack upon their own courts. On the other hand they had, as we shall see,[5] a long standing grudge against the court of Chancery, which they were not sorry to gratify by voicing the prevailing discontent with its organization.[6] But it was not wholly due to political causes. There were several reasons why this system of appointing and

---

[1] See above 422 n. 5 for the manner in which during this period the king profited by this patronage, and for the manner in which after the Revolution it was appropriated by the Chancellor and the Master of the Rolls; there are many other allusions to the value of these places; thus in 1621 it was said that the Masters had paid £150 each for their places, Commons Journals i 594; D'Ewes's father paid for his Office of Six Clerk £5000, and between 1622 and 1630 his income varied from £1216 15s. 4d. to £1981 10s. 8d. per annum, Autobiography i 177; cf. S.P. Dom. 1636-1637 269, cccxl 5.

[2] Luttrell, Diary iv 669 notes that "Roger Meredith Eyre has sold his place of one of the Masters in Chancery to Thomas Geery, Esq., barrister at law;" cf. Hist. MSS. Com. Fourteenth Rep. App. Pt. VI. p. 315 no. 670—an appeal to the House of Lords in 1693 turning on the sale by a sworn clerk of his place.

[3] Ex parte the Six Clerks (1798) 3 Ves. 599, 600; a letter from North, C.J., to the Secretary of State in 1676 illustrates the difficulty of getting rid of even the most incompetent clerk, S.P. Dom. 1676-1677 127-128.

[4] In 1598 a commission had enquired into the fees taken by the officials of the court, see Egerton Papers (C.S.) 208, 214.

[5] Below 459-463.

[6] Thus in 1620 and 1623 the grand committee of Justice had considered the abuses of the court, and a bill to regulate its proceedings had been introduced in 1621, Parkes, Chancery 92; Harl. Miscell. iii 552; Spence, Equity i 400-401.

paying officials produced much worse effects in the case of the court of Chancery than in the case of the courts of common law.

Firstly a suit in equity very often lasted very many years. This no doubt is true of some common law actions; but it is clear that the fact that many equitable cases involved the taking of accounts and enquiries, necessarily made the proceedings more lengthy than the general run of common law actions, which turned on a clear cut issue of fact or law. Obviously this gave the officials a great chance of increasing their revenues. As early as 1382 it had been said of the Masters that they were "over fatt both in bodie and purse and over well furred in their benefices, and put the king to verry great cost more than needed."[1] The dilatory nature of the proceedings in their offices, the high fees which they exacted, the manner in which they made use of their position to exact their fees and even additional gratuities, are clearly proved by contemporary evidence. Suits, it was said had lasted for twenty years.[2] In consequence money was paid for expedition. A regular trade in the placing of causes upon the lists, which was termed "heraldry," was carried on in the registrar's offices.[3] It was in vain that the statutes fixed the fees to be taken by the Masters. It was in vain that the Chancellor ordered them to hear causes with speed and regularity.[4] Suitors naturally gave presents to those who were in possession of uncontrolled power. It is well to remember that it was the fact that a suitor was obliged to pay for three attendances at a Master's office when only one was given which first called Bentham's attention to the condition of English law.[5]

Secondly, the fact that the procedure of the court was wholly written afforded another chance to the official of making money. The suitor was not in a position to object to being compelled to pay for unnecessary copies of unduly lengthened documents;[6] and these practices of the masters and the six

---

[1] Treatise of the Masters, Harg. Law Tracts 314; the writer at pp. 314-317 complains that their profits had been curtailed by the appointment of additional officers; in 1625-1626 the Masters petitioned for regular salaries, S.P. Dom. 1625-1626 515, xli 33; but it is clear that with the increasing jurisdiction of the court they had found additional sources of revenue.

[2] Commons Journals i 574; one of the speakers (Mr. Alford) said that his suit had lasted thirty years.

[3] Lives of the Norths i 266; Parkes, Chancery 325-328.

[4] 1 James I. c. 10; 13 Charles II.; Spence (Equity i 401, 402) says that the latter statute was printed as a private Act and so escaped attention—"the late Mr. Agar, K.C., brought it to light in Lord Eldon's time, but it was totally disregarded."

[5] Mill, Dissertations and Discussions i 336.

[6] Harg. Law Tracts 429, 447; it appears from Lord Keeper Coventry's Orders, issued in 1635, that the masters unduly lengthened the proceedings by making special certificates and needless recitals, see Spence i 403-405.

clerks were imitated by their underlings.   A writer of 1627[1]
tells us that, "the under clerks with their large margins, with
their great distance between their lines, with protraction of words,
and with their many dashes and slashes put in place of words,
lay their greediness open to the whole world ; and I have heard
many say, that they are as men void of all conscience not caring
how they get money so they have it ; and that with as good a
conscience they may take a purse by the highway, but not with
so little danger ; . . . I did see an answer to a bill of forty of
their sheets, which, copied out, was brought to six sheets."

Thirdly the practice of the court was unsettled, and many of
the Chancellors were not competent to settle it.   No trouble
was taken to distinguish suits which were merely frivolous from
those which were real.   "Of ten bills," said Norburie, "hardly
three have any colour or shadow of just complaint."[2]   Every-
thing was referred to the Masters.[3]   Counsel made needless
interlocutory motions which entailed new references, commissions
to take evidence, or Orders to interrogate the parties.   " It hath
ever been noted that none will be so ready to move as he that
hath the worst cause ; for he hath nothing else to trust to.   If
he cannot get his adversary on the hip by some trick or other in
order or reference, and so bring him to some hard composition,
actum est with him."[4]   Even if a decree were made the Chancellor would reopen the whole matter on bare surmise ; and that
might mean new orders, references, and examinations.[5]   "A
cause in Chancery, though never so plaine, after a reference or
two, and a generation or pedigree of orders, the controversie will
become so intricate, that, the merits of the cause being lost, all
the labour lies in the managing of reports and orders."[6]   When
a decree was made it was often couched in terms so vague that

---

[1] Carey, The Present State of England, Harl. Miscell. iii 552, 557 ; for similar
abuses in Lord Hardwicke's time see Campbell, Chancellors v 63-64.

[2] Harg. Law Tracts 434.

[3] " For what a miserable thing it is, that the plaintiff should bring the defendant
from the furthest part in England to answer an idle bill ; which done, he will perhaps quarrel at some part of the answer, get it referred to some Master of the
Chancery, and consequently overruled for insufficient ; and so having vexed and put
him to great expenses, leave him in the end to wipe his sleeve for any recompense he
shall get, be the cause ever so ridiculous," ibid 434, 435.

[4] Ibid 443.

[5] " I dealt with a client not long since that had an injunction for the possession
of lands.   His adversary moved by a great councillor to dissolve the same.   It was
granted, unless we should show good cause to the contrary by a day, albeit the
motion was grounded, only on a mere suggestion, not verifiable by any affidavit,
certificate or other evidence in the world. . . . We attended six days at least to
show cause, which cost us £10 at the least.   We were heard at last and showed
cause, *which was easy to do*, and kept our possession," ibid 440, 441.

[6] Vindication of the Professors and Profession of the law, by William Cooke
(1642), cited Parkes 126 ; Roger North, Lives of the Norths i 262 refers to the
" superfetation of orders."

the Registrars could draw what Orders they pleased ; and this obviously led to rehearings and further Orders.[1] During this period the rules of equity were so vague that enormous scope was left to those who desired to persuade a weak or a corrupt Chancellor.[2]

Fourthly the Chancellor exercised no detailed supervision over his officials. It is true that Chancellors like Bacon or Coventry issued Orders to regulate practice ; but they were of little avail. Bacon's Orders of 1618 had specially prohibited general references to the Masters ; [3] but Coke in 1621 said that the Chancellor practically made the Masters his deputies by the general character of his references to them.[4] Coventry issued a series of Orders relating to the Masters ; but Spence, writing in 1846, said that some of the evils against which these Orders were directed, were felt in his day.[5] In many cases the Bar was more able than the Bench.[6] Partly from want of capacity, partly from want of time, the Chancellor was unable to prevent abuses which were concealed from him by the plausibility of counsel or the interest of officials.

A tale related by Sir John Bramston in his Autobiography is perhaps the best illustration of the effects of these abuses upon the ordinary litigant. He tells us that during the civil war his grandmother had begun a suit in Chancery to recover some tithes to which she was entitled. She died, and he continued the action. The amount in dispute was £4. " It cost, to recover that £4, £200 at least. I have the bills for so much by me and yet most of the council would not take fees of me." [8]

(2) The period of the Commonwealth.

This was a period in which all existing institutions, and the whole body of English law were put upon their trial. The execution of the king involved a revolution in public law ; and the successive written constitutions under which the government was carried on represent the various attempts made by Cromwell and the victorious army,

> " To cast the kingdoms old
> Into another mould."

[1] Lives of the Norths i 263, 264.　　[2] Harg. Law Tracts, 430.
[3] Order 47 (Works vii 766).　　[4] Commons Journals i 594.
[5] Op. cit. i 403.
[6] Proposals for regulating or taking away of Chancery, cited Parkes 153-156; and the same evil was felt in the eighteenth century ; thus it was said that in the time of Lord Chancellor King (1725-1727) the cases were equitably arranged by the then leaders of the Chancery Bar, Sir P. Yorke and Mr. Talbot, Campbell, Chancellors, iv 643, 644.
[7] Bramston, Autobiography (C.S.) 16.
[8] No doubt because Sir John Bramston was the son of Sir John Bramston Chief Justice of the King's Bench 1634-1642.

With the changes made or projected in public and private law I shall deal in later volumes.[1] At this point I shall make a short digression, and give a brief account of the changes made or projected in the judicial system. The nature of these changes will help us to understand the very radical changes adopted or proposed to be adopted to reform the court of Chancery.

The common lawyers had generally been favourable to the cause of the Parliament;[2] and, although comparatively few approved of the execution of the king and the revolutionary measures which accompanied it, though drastic changes were proposed in the judicial system of the common law,[3] very little change was actually made.[4] The King's Bench became the Upper Bench;[5] the Common Pleas remained as before; and it was not till 1657 that the jurisdiction of the court of Exchequer was in any way affected;[6] some of the Palatine jurisdictions were included in the judges circuits;[7] the reform made by the Act of Settlement[8] in the tenure of the judges offices was anticipated when they were appointed during good behaviour.[9] But otherwise the machinery of justice worked much as usual. The justices of the peace continued to perform their functions, and the judges rode their circuits.

Many other reforms were proposed. There were some who allowed their distrust of the legal profession so to obscure their judgment that they proposed measures which were obviously absurd. A good instance is the extraordinary proposal that the court of Appeal from the Upper Bench and the Common Pleas should be staffed by a panel of seven persons, to be chosen from a body of twenty, none of whom were to be, "pleading or practising lawyers, judges, or officers of these two courts."[10] And there are other instances of proposals almost equally absurd.

---

[1] Vol. vi 149-163, 412-430. [2] Below 514. [3] Below 429-430.

[4] Robinson, Anticipations under the Commonwealth of Changes in the Law, Essays A.A.L.H. i 469.

[5] Acts and Ordinances of the Commonwealth (Ed. Firth and Rait) i 1262-1263.

[6] Ibid ii 1127—the Commissioners of Customs were given power to determine certain disputes relating to the payment of Customs.

[7] A sheriff was appointed for Durham 1645-1646, ibid i 831 ; and the judges of the northern circuit were ordered to hold the assizes there in 1651, ibid ii 517, in 1652, ibid ii 907, and in 1659, ibid ii 1305 ; in 1653 all the privileges of the county Palatine of Lancaster were continued, ibid ii 722, 844, 845, 1137 ; but the judges of the northern circuit held the assizes there, ibid ii 921 ; an ordinance was made for Chester in 1644 while it was in hostile occupation, ibid i 503 ; but otherwise, neither its franchises, nor those of Ely seem to have been affected by the Commonwealth legislation; for these franchise jurisdictions see above 92, 109, 114, 117.

[8] Above 195.

[9] Robinson, op. cit. 478; Charles II. at first appointed his judges to hold office by this tenure, 1 Sid. 2; but he soon reverted to the practice of appointing them during pleasure, above 195.

[10] Somers' Tracts vi 240-241; the twenty were to be chosen by Parliament, or, if Parliament was not sitting, by the Council of State.

Thus in 1650, one, John Jones, wrote a tract which he called the
" New Returna Brevium," [1] in which he advocated the abolition of
the central courts of common law and the court of Chancery, and
the vesting of all jurisdiction in local courts. [2]   But this was too
much even for the Nominated Parliament of 1653.   It was prepared to abolish the court of Exchequer and to vest its jurisdiction
in the Upper Bench ; [3] it was prepared to abolish the Palatine
jurisdictions of Durham, Lancaster, Chester, and the franchise of
Ely ; [4] but it was not prepared to abolish either the Upper Bench
or the Common Pleas.   It was prepared to make the sale of offices
illegal, [5] to credit the nation with all fees paid by suitors, and to
pay the judges by a fixed salary [6]—reforms which would have
gone far to render effective its proposed legislation against
extortion, bribery, and the solicitation of judges. [7]   It was also
prepared to establish a system of county courts to hear all cases
civil and criminal arising in the county ; [8] but it was not prepared to free these courts from dependence on the courts of
common law.   The judges of these county courts were to be five
persons chosen for three years by the Council of State from a list
of ten chosen by the general sessions of the peace, and they were
to be assisted by a judge either of the Upper Bench or Common
Pleas. [9]   The establishment of efficient county courts was in fact
a reform for which there was a crying need.   It had been proposed before ; [10] and it always occurs in the various proposed reforms of this period. [11]   Thus in 1656 William Shepherd, [12] who
had been asked to advise the Council of State upon questions of
law reform, published a book entitled " England's Balme," [13] which
advocated the establishment all over the country of local courts
of record, staffed by competent judges. [14]

[1] The " New Returna Brevium," or the law returned from Westminster, and restored in brief to its native, ancient and proper habitation, language, power, purity,
integrity, cheapness, briefness, plainness.   Rescued out of the sacrilegious hands, barbarous disguises, œnigmatical intricacies, lucrative constructions, extorted verdicts,
false judgments, and bribeful executions of her perjured impostors, false interpreters,
jailers, catchpols, attorneys, etc.

[2] Pp. 21-33.   [3] Somers' Tracts vi 231, Sect. lxxxvi.
[4] Ibid 231-232, Sect. lxxxvii.   [5] Ibid 186.
[6] Ibid 240; Robinson, op. cit. 478.   [7] Somers' Tracts vi 189.
[8] Ibid 212-213 ; there was also a proposal to have a permanent court at York
for the five northern counties, Whitelock, Memorials iv 161.
[9] Somers' Tracts vi 212-213.   [10] Above 188-189.
[11] See Robinson, op. cit. 475-476.
[12] For some account of Shepherd, see Bk. iv. Pt. I. c. 8.
[13] " England's Balme, or Proposals by way of Grievance and Remedy humbly
presented to His Highness and the Parliament, towards the regulation of Law, and
better administration of Justice; " the author states, in the address to the Parliament prefixed to the book, that he was called " by His Highness from my country
to wait upon him, to the end he might advise with me and some others, about some
things tending to the regulation of the law."
[14] Pp. 20, 63, 64.

But none of these proposed changes took effect, so that, as I have already pointed out, the machinery of common law jurisdiction, central and local, was less affected by the constitutional changes than any other institution in the English state.

Far more drastic changes were made in the courts which administered a jurisdiction either supplementary to or rivalling that of the common law courts.   The Council's jurisdiction in England, the court of Star Chamber, the Councils of Wales and the North,[1] the criminal and corrective jurisdiction of the ecclesiastical courts,[2] and the court of Wards and Liveries[3] had been abolished.   It is true that the Commonwealth government found it necessary to establish High Courts of Justice to deal, as the Star Chamber had dealt, with political offences ;[4] and that it gave them powers to try and sentence to death those convicted of treason—a jurisdiction more extensive than any that the Star Chamber had ever possessed.[5]   It is true that it had been found necessary to provide special courts to exercise the jurisdiction over grants of probate and administration, and cases of disputed marriages, which was formerly exercised by the ecclesiastical courts.[6]   But, apart from these courts, the only courts which still exercised a jurisdiction outside the common law courts were the courts of Admiralty and the court of Chancery.   The jurisdiction of the former court over prize,[7] and, in spite of the professional jealousy of the common lawyers,[8] over commercial and maritime cases was several times recognized.[9]   But it was generally admitted that something must be done to reform the latter court.   Both the professional rivalry of the common lawyers,[10] and the many abuses existing in the court made it inevitable that such an attempt should be made.

The attack began in the Parliament of 1653.   In a two days'

---

[1] Below 515.

[2] Below 620; Robinson, op. cit. 472-473.

[3] Acts and Ordinances of the Interregnum i 833, ii 1043 ; it was a court established in 1540, above 409 n. 5, to look after the king's rights to the incidents of tenure ; it was formally abolished in 1660 by the Act of 12 Charles II. c. 24 which abolished the military tenures.

[4] Ibid ii 492 (1650)—for the Eastern Counties ; 780 (1653) ; 917 (1654) ; cf. Robinson, op. cit. 468-469 ; Whitelock, Memorials iv 332 says that in 1658 commissioners were nominated to try "the present conspirators against the Protector and Government," but he says, "I never sat with them, it being against my judgment."

[5] Below 488, 503.

[6] Acts and Ordinances of the Interregnum i 564 (1644)—the Prerogative Court of Canterbury ; ibid ii 496 (1650-1651)—marriages ; ibid ii 702 (1653)—Probate and Administration ; cf. Robinson, op. cit. 474 ; jurisdiction over legacies was transferred to the common law courts, Acts and Ordinances of the Interregnum ii 959 (1654).

[7] Ibid i 35 (1642) ; ii 66 (1649) ; below 561.

[8] Below 556.

[9] Acts and Ordinances i 1120 (1648); ii 78 (1649) ; 712 (1653) ; below 556.

[10] Below 459-462.

debate the abuses of the court were fully exposed.[1]   We are
told that, "in the course of the debate the court of Chancery
was called by some members the greatest grievance in the
nation.   Others said, that for dilatoriness, chargeableness, and
a faculty for bleeding the people in the purse vein, even to their
utter perishing and undoing, that court might compare with it
not surpass any court in the world.   That it was confidently
affirmed by knowing gentlemen of worth, that there were depending in that court 23,000 cases, some of which had been
there depending five, some ten, some twenty, some thirty years and
more ; that there had been spent therein many thousand pounds
to the ruin, nay utter undoing, of many families. . . . That what
was ordered one day was contradicted the next, so, as in some
causes there had been 500 orders and more . . . so that some
members did not stick to term the Chancery a mystery of
wickedness, and a standing cheat, and that in short so many
horrible things were affirmed of it, that those who were or had
a mind to be advocates for it, had little to say on the behalf of
it, so . . . it was voted down."[2]

The committee to which questions of law reform were entrusted was instructed to bring in a bill to abolish the court, and
to make provision by another for causes then depending in
equity, and for the justice and ministration of equity.[3]   A bill
to effect these two latter objects was subsequently brought in
and committed.[4]   It proposed to effect a few changes in the
rules of equity, and many more in the machinery of its administration.[5]   It is with the latter proposals that we are here
concerned.   Some of them were undoubtedly improvements.
Thus the time within which pleas and demurrers were to be
heard was fixed ;[6] six masters sitting in public were to hear all
references ;[7] penalties were inflicted if any cause was heard out
of its turn ;[8] no official was to execute his office by deputy ;[9]
a table of fees, much lower than those formerly in use, was drawn
up.[10]   The common lawyers also secured the insertion of clauses
limiting the power of the court to grant injunctions against
proceedings at common law [11]—the advantage of which was, to
say the least, very dubious.[12]   And still more comprehensive
schemes were in the air.   For instance, William Shepherd pro-

---

[1] Two papers upon the court were circulated among members, called "Observations on the Court of Chancery," and "Proposals for regulating or taking
away of Chancery;" they are printed by Parkes, Chancery 149-156.
[2] Cited, C. P. Cooper, Chancery 7, 8; cf. Harl. Miscell. iii 558; v 156.
[3] Whitelock, Memorials iv 29.   [4] Ibid iv 47.
[5] Somers' Tracts vi 202-211.   [6] § 13.
[7] § 15.   [8] § 17.   [9] § 28.   [10] § 40.
[11] §§ 25, 26.   [12] Above 411; below 463, 464-465.

posed a scheme for the uniformity of the procedure in all the courts at Westminster, and for the fusion of the jurisdiction of the courts of law and equity,[1] very much like that actually carried out in the nineteenth century by the Judicature Acts.[2] But the Nominated Parliament was dissolved before its bill for the reform of the Chancery could become law; and matters went on very much as before.   But one change had been made. In 1649 the judicial strength of the court had been increased— the great seal having been entrusted to three commissioners, Whitelock, Keble, and Major Lisle, assisted by Lenthall, the Master of the Rolls.[3]   Whitelock, however, complained that the whole burden of the work fell on him;[4] and he admitted that the manner in which the administration of equity was conducted gave no satisfaction to the public.[5]

In 1654 Cromwell embodied many of the provisions of the bill introduced into the Nominated Parliament in an Ordinance which he ordered the commissioners to enforce.[6]   As Mr. Kerly remarks, "the principle upon which the Ordinance is framed is a thorough distrust of the persons who would have to enforce it."   Nothing was left to their discretion.   So far was this carried that the administration of any jurisdiction in equity was rendered almost impossible.   Whitelock, Widdrington (who had succeeded Keble), and Lenthall, M.R., protested against it. Some of their objections were captious.   They objected, for instance, to the rule requiring the commissioners to sit at the same time as the Master of the Rolls.   But others were reasonable.   It was clearly impossible to obey the rule that all causes

[1] England's Balme pp. 21, 64-65, 83, 145-146; he says at pp. 64-65, "That all suits be commenced in their proper courts, as now they are; but that where a cause is begun in one of them, that is a court of law, if matter of equity arise in it, that that court shall determine it, and not send it to another court.   And so on the other side, if it be a court of equity, and matter of law arise, that the same court determine it; but that they call two of the judges of the law to the hearing of the cause which shall have voyces in the judgment.   The matters of law to be tried by rules of law, and matters of equity in a court of law to be tried by petition, witnesses, or bill and answer; as the judges of the court shall direct.   That one and the same method of proceeding, of matters of law and equity be used in all the courts at Westminster, Great Sessions, Provincial Courts, and the rest of the courts of the Nation."

[2] Below 638, 640.

[3] Foss, Judges vi 401; Lisle was the only one who was not a practising lawyer; he is said to have been a student at one of the Temples, but it is uncertain whether he was ever called to the bar, ibid vi 453.

[4] Memorials ii 532—" The burthen of the business (hancery lay upon me, being ancient in commission, and my brother Keeble of little experience in practice, my brother Lisle of less, but very opinionative."

[5] "The business of the Chancery was full of trouble this Michaelmas term (1652) and no man's cause came to determination, how just soever, without the clamour of the party against whom judgment was given; they being stark blind in their own causes, and resolved not to be conv nced by reason or law," ibid iii 468.

[6] Acts and Ordinances of the Commonwealth ii o49-967.

should be heard and determined on the day on which they were set down, because, as the commissioners pointed out, "Equity causes depend upon so many circumstances in cases of fraud, that ofttimes three or four days are not sufficient for the orderly hearing of a single cause."[1]   Cromwell, however, insisted upon obedience to the Ordinance as it stood.   Lenthall, M.R., yielded; but Whitelock and Widdrington declined to obey; and they were replaced by Colonel Fiennes.   The seals were thus in the hands of two military officers, Colonel Fiennes and Major Lisle. In 1657 Parliament limited the duration of the Ordinance to the duration of the present Parliament and no longer.[2]   It then appointed a committee to consider the whole question of the court of Chancery, and to bring in a bill to regulate it, if the committee saw fit to do so.[3]   No such bill was introduced; and, as Cromwell's Ordinance had lapsed with the dissolution of Parliament, matters were further complicated by the claims of the old officials to return to their places.[4]   In 1659 Parliament passed a resolution that the court should be reformed and regulated;[5] but no attempt was made to give effect to it.   In the following year the Restoration of the king was peacefully effected.

The Restoration brought back the old unreformed judicial system.   Many of the reforms which the Commonwealth statesmen had proposed deserved to be carried out, and have in fact been carried out in the course of the succeeding centuries.   They could not be carried out during this period because they were opposed by almost all those who had had a technical training in the system which it was proposed to reform.   Without such a training it is possible to abolish a few abuses; it is possible to make suggestions for reform; but it is not possible to carry out any great work of constructive reform.   The attempt to effect the impossible only created confusion with the result that the desire for any kind of permanent settlement replaced the desire for reform, and extinguished for many a year all thoughts of removing from the English legal system the many anomalies which disfigured it.   In the history of the failure of these projected law reforms of the Commonwealth statesmen we can see some of the causes and some of the consequences of the failure of the Commonwealth itself.

---

[1] Whitelock, Memorials iv 191-201;   Robinson, op. cit. 470-472.

[2] Commons Journals vii 527.

[3] Ibid vii 528.

[4] Parkes, Chancery 172; cf. Ex Parte the Six Clerks (1798) 3 Ves. at pp. 599-601.

[5] Commons Journals vii 678; a bill to regulate proceedings at law and in equity had already been discussed and rejected, ibid vii 627.

(3) The period after the Restoration.

During the reigns of the two last Stuart kings no attempts were made by the legislature to reform the defects in the organization of the court of Chancery. The first part of Charles II.'s reign was a period of reaction in favour of all things established: the latter part a period of fierce political and religious controversy. Neither period therefore was favourable to legislative reforms of this kind. Nor did the Chancellors do anything to adapt the organization of the court to modern needs.[1] Clarendon and North issued some general Orders. North attempted some reforms in the procedure of the court;[2] and perhaps if he had been longer in office he would gradually have effected more. But he was too timid ever to have effected very much. He was frightened of the outcry which the officials of the court, the bar, and the solicitors would certainly have raised;[3] and for the same reason he "showed no disposition to retrench officers of the just profit of their places."[4]

It might reasonably have been expected that some instalment of reform would have come with the Revolution both from the Chancellors themselves and from the legislature. But nothing was done by the Chancellors. Some attempts at reform were, however, made by the legislature. We have seen that enquiries were made in 1689 into the number and fees of the officials of the courts of law and equity,[5] and that in 1690 a bill was introduced into the House of Lords to regulate these fees, and to abolish the sale and purchase of these offices.[6] This bill also proposed to effect some salutary reforms in the procedure of the court of Chancery. For instance, it proposed to forbid the filling of bills "with impertinent matter to increase the charge of defendants who are to pay for copies of the same,"[7] and to diminish the fees payable by litigants on other occasions.[8] Other salutary

---

[1] The report of the Chancery commission of 1826 at p. 10 refers to Bacon's Orders (1619), Coventry's Orders (1635), the Orders of Whitelock, Lenthall, and Keble (1656), and Clarendon's Orders (1661); and says, "There are many other detailed Orders upon insulated parts of the practice, and upon the fees of the offices of the court; but these Orders have not introduced any alteration in the general system, nor essentially in the practice of the court."

[2] Lives of the Norths i 259-268.

[3] "Another thing that made him decline falling so early upon a book of orders, was, that it would give so great alarm to the bar and officers, with the solicitors, as would make them confederate and demur, and, by making a tumult and disturbance, endeavour to hinder the doing anything of that kind which they would apprehend to be very prejudicial to their interests," ibid 260.

[4] Ibid i 264.

[5] Above 262; Hist. MSS. Com. Twelfth Rep. App. Pt. VI. 313 seqq. no. 160.

[6] Above 250; Hist. MSS. Com. Thirteenth Rep. App. Pt. V. 17 seqq. no. 244.

[7] Ibid 18, 19.   [8] Ibid 19, 20.

reforms [1] were suggested in the same year during the discussion of another abortive bill to restrict the jurisdiction of the court.[2] In 1691 and 1692 bills were introduced into the House of Lords to regulate the abuses of the Six Clerks' office,[3] and to prevent the hearing of bills of Review by the same persons who had given the decision to be reviewed : [4] but neither of them became law.   The reform of the officials of the courts was again taken up by the legislature in the earlier part of the eighteenth century, probably because the revelations made on the occasion of the impeachment of Lord Macclesfield [5] had called public attention to the subject.   From 1729 to 1733 a committee of the House of Commons enquired into the fees of the officials of all the courts. It appeared that many new offices had sprung up since a committee had enquired into the subject in 1598 ; but it was found very difficult to say what officials were attached to the courts or what were their fees.[6]   As the result of these enquiries the House of Commons asked the king to appoint a commission of enquiry into the officials of the courts and the fees charged by them.   The commission was appointed, and in 1740 it issued a report, which apparently dealt only with the court of Chancery.[7]   The commissioners recommended that a table of fees should be prepared, that easy remedies should be given against extortionate officials, that offices should not be bought and sold or executed by deputy, and that there should be no expedition of money.[8]   Hardwicke signed the report ; but he introduced no measure of reform. During the remainder of the eighteenth century all projects of reform seem to have been abandoned.   Nothing was done by the legislature, and no general Orders were made by any Chancellor from Hardwicke (1737-1757) to Loughborough (1793-1801).[9]

The failure of all these attempts at legislative reform, and the inaction of the Chancellors is the more to be regretted as the defects of the court were, throughout this period, being constantly aggravated by the increase in its business.   This increase was due partly to the abolition of the court of Requests and Star

---

[1] Hist. MSS. Com. Thirteenth Rep. App. Pt. V. 139, 140; it was proposed to legislate against unnecessary delays, to regulate fees, and to provide that bills of Review should not be heard by the same persons as had given the decision to be reviewed; a tract of 1654 written by a defender of the court, cited Parkes, Chancery 183-184, had advocated some of these reforms.

[2] Hist. MSS. Com. Thirteenth Rep. App. Pt. V. 128 seqq. no. 304; below 464.

[3] Parkes, Chancery 255-258.

[4] Hist. MSS. Com. Thirteenth Rep. App. Pt. V. 308-313, no. 438; another bill to effect this object failed to pass in 1692, ibid Fourteenth Rep. App. Pt. VI. 117-118, no. 601.

[5] Below 440.   [6] Parkes, Chancery 305-311.

[7] Parlt. Papers 1819-1820 ii 180; above 262.

[8] Ibid 313-317.   [9] Campbell, Chancellors v 455.

Chamber,[1] partly to the fact that bankruptcy business was beginning to be brought within the jurisdiction of the Lord Chancellor,[2] and partly to the increase in the wealth and commerce of the country. It naturally followed that the evils arising from the inadequacy of the judicial staff, and the abuses rampant amongst the official staff, continued to increase.

(i) *The inadequacy of the judicial staff.*

There had been no increase in the judicial strength of the court. In 1688 the scheme of putting the seal permanently in commission was seriously considered. But the experiment was not found to work satisfactorily. The immense pressure of work is said to have ruined the health of several Lord Chancellors and Lord Keepers; and it proved fatal to Lord Talbot.[3] The development of the system of equity caused the more distinguished lawyers to take such pains with cases, which were likely to be leading, that both the duration of the causes which were being heard, and the arrears of causes waiting to be heard continued to increase. Lord Hardwicke (1736-1756) was, next to Lord Eldon, the most eminent judge who has ever presided in the court of Chancery. But it is said that "his decrees were very few in comparison to the many causes that came under discussion in that court in his time. The hearings, rehearings, references to masters, reports and exceptions to those reports, exorbitant fees to counsel, and the length of time to which every cause was protracted, made the suitors weary, and glad to submit to any decree suggested and agreed upon by their counsel."[4]

The delays under Lord Eldon were notorious.[4a] They arose partly from the desire to consider so carefully each case that permanent and final justice should be done; and for this reason it must be admitted that to some extent the delays which troubled the suitor were a permanent gain to the system of equity. They partly also arose from a dilatory habit of mind which tended to grow upon him, at a time when the expanding population and commerce of the country were bringing into still stronger relief the defects of the court.[5] A judge should, it is true, take time to consider a doubtful case. But Lord Eldon would often express a clear opinion after hearing the argument,

---

[1] A book had been published in 1653 by John March showing that the abolition of the courts of Wards and Requests had occasioned such an increase in the business of the Chancery that it was necessary to increase its judicial staff, Parkes, Chancery 195.

[2] Below 470-471.   [3] C. P. Cooper, Chancery 14-16.

[4] Cooksey, Sketches of an essay on the life of Hardwicke, cited C. P. Cooper, Chancery, 16, 17; for a different view see addenda et corrigenda. [4a] See vol. xiii 624.

[5] In 1745 the money in court was £1,723,957, 10s. 1d.; in 1825 it was £39,174,722, 8s. 7d., C. P. Cooper, Chancery, 104 n.

and then, as Campbell says,[1] "he expressed doubts—reserved to himself the opportunity for further consideration—took home the papers—never read them—promised judgment again and again—and for years never gave it—all the facts and law connected with it having escaped his memory." Yet Romilly, from large personal experience, said that however long he took to consider a cause, he had rarely known him differ from his first impression.

The existing delays were aggravated by the system of rehearings and appeals which a determined litigant could demand upon the most trivial points. Any point arising in the course of a suit might be discussed—(1) Before the Master of the Rolls; (2) Before the same person by way of rehearing; (3) Before the Lord Chancellor; (4) Before the same person by way of rehearing; (5) Before the House of Lords. Upon these appeals and rehearings, other than appeals to the House of Lords, new evidence could be adduced.[2] This was clearly a practice which tended still further to lengthen the proceedings. As Beames, the secretary to the Chancery commission of 1826, said justly, "a right of litigation which is limited alone by the means of gratifying it, places the poor suitor at the mercy of his rich antagonist; and at the same time operates this hardship upon the other suitors of the court, that their causes are necessarily postponed to make way for the discussion and rediscussion of the same question between the same parties."[3]

At the latter part of Lord Eldon's tenure of office the arrears of business grew so great that the business of the court declined.[4]

[1] Chancellors vii 625; ibid 626 it is said that a solicitor's bill contained the following item, " To attendance on the Lord High Chancellor of Great Britain in his private room, when his Lordship begged for further indulgence from me till tomorrow—16s. 4d." Some verses (cited ibid 640) give a good picture of an ordinary day in court:—

> Mr. Leach
> Made a speech,
>   Angry, neat, but wrong:
> Mr. Hart,
> On the other part,
>   Was heavy, dull, and long:
> Mr. Parker
> Made the case darker,
>   Which was dark enough without:
> Mr. Cook
> Cited his book,
>   And the Chancellor said—I doubt.

[2] Maddock, Chancery (Ed. 1815) ii 439-440.
[3] Report of the Chancery Commission (1826), 113.
[4] C. P. Cooper, Chancery, chap. vii; Mr. Shadwell, K.C., in his evidence before the Chancery commission, said, " The load of business now in court is so great that three angels could not get through it;" Mr. Bickersteth said that the delay between setting the cause down, and the hearing, exceeded all the other unnecessary delays put together. For a full account of Chancery Procedure see vol. ix 335-408.

In fact the time consumed in merely waiting to be heard amounted to a denial of justice. The appointment of a Vice-Chancellor in 1813 did not, for causes which will be dealt with later, afford any material relief. C. P. Cooper writing in 1828 said,[1] "two briefs in causes on Further Directions set down before the Vice-Chancellor are at this moment on my table. The real and personal estates in both cases are considerable, and neither the legatees nor residuary legatees have yet received any part of their bequests. In one suit the bill was filed rather more, and in the other rather less than twenty years since, and, during more than half that time, the causes have, in different stages, been waiting their turn to be heard."

(ii) *The abuses rampant amongst the official staff.*

The sale of the office of Master was carried on with greater eagerness as the value of the office rose.[2] The barefaced way in which these transactions were carried out is illustrated by some of the evidence given upon Lord Macclesfield's impeachment for corruption. The following is a typical instance. Master Elde deposed that he had offered the Chancellor £5000 for the post. Cottingham (the Chancellor's agent) stood out for guineas. "I immediately went to my Lord's being willing to get into the office as soon as I could. I did carry with me 5000 guineas in gold and bank notes. I had the money in my chambers, but did not know how to convey it; . . . but recollecting I had a basket in my chambers, I put the guineas into the basket and the notes with them. I went in a chair and took the basket with me in my chair. When I came to my Lord's house I saw Mr. Cottingham there, and gave him the basket, and desired him to carry it up to my Lord. I saw him go upstairs with the basket, and when he came down he intimated to me that he had delivered it. When I was admitted, my Lord invited me to dinner and some of my friends with me, and he was pleased to treat me and some members of the House of Commons in a very handsome manner. I was, after dinner, sworn in before them. Some months after I spoke to my Lord's gentleman, and desired him if he saw such a basket he would give it me back. He did so, but no money was returned in it."[3]

The value of the office at the Revolution was £1000. At the beginning of the eighteenth century it was £6000. The

---

[1] Chancery 92. For an account of Cooper's career and writings see vol. xiii 289, 290, 498.

[2] See Lives of the Norths i 297-298 for Lord North's hesitation whether he should sell or give these offices—in the end "he gave way to follow the steps of his predecessors."

[3] 16 S.T. 871-873.

reason was that the money in court was under the absolute control of the Master, who was not bound to account for any interest received.[1] As the money in court was constantly increasing, the interest formed a handsome addition to the Master's income. But they were not content with this. They tried to increase their incomes still further by speculation.

Shortly after the bursting of the South Sea Bubble (1725) rumours were heard that all was not right with the money in court.[2] An enquiry was ordered. In consequence of that enquiry the Lord Chancellor, Lord Macclesfield, was impeached; and a deficit which was finally found to amount to £100,871 6s. 8d. was discovered in the accounts of four of the Masters.[3] In consequence two Acts were passed which deprived the Masters of the control of the suitors' money, and placed it in the Bank of England under the control of a new official called the Accountant-General of the court of Chancery.[4] After this episode it was impossible to sell again the office of Master. But it was still regarded as a piece of patronage belonging to the Lord Chancellor. It was stated in 1826 that the Lord Chancellor had appointed an officer in the militia who had not been engaged in ten cases of importance in his life.[5]

The Six Clerks still continued to draw salaries ranging from £885 to £2000 a year for their two months' work in the year.[6] From the evidence given before Lord Eldon's commission in 1826 it would appear that their sole duties were to file and preserve the records, to certify the court respecting them, and to sign copies. Even these duties were not, and need not, be adequately performed. At the beginning of the nineteenth century a considerable quantity of the records had been stolen and sold for waste paper; and the court had held that they were not responsible for the correctness of the copies which they signed and for which they took fees.[7] Their witness (Mr. Vesey) when examined before the commission of 1826, stated that questions

[1] Parkes, Chancery 283 ; a similar system prevailed in the court of Admiralty, where the interest on the money in court in Prize Cases made a handsome addition to the Registrar's salary, Report of Commissioners appointed to enquire into the Duties, Salaries, etc., of the offices of courts of Justice, Parlt. Papers (1824) ix 12 ; this system was modified by 53 George III. c. 151.

[2] Campbell, Chancellors, iv 535-538; Parkes 293, 299.

[3] See the Order of the Lord Chancellor of Jan. 19 1749, printed in Parlt. Papers 1860 vol. xxxi 137 App. no. 4 ; and for a detailed account of the whole matter see ibid xii-xiv.

[4] 12 George I. c. 32; 12 George I. c. 33; 54 George III. c. 14; the office of Accountant-General was abolished in 1872, 35, 36 Victoria c. 44, and his duties were handed over to the Paymaster-General, see the judgment of Swinfen Eady, J., in re Williams Scottish Estates [1910] 2 Ch. at pp. 492-493.

[5] Letter to the *Times*, cited Parkes, App. 584.

[6] Ibid 575.   [7] Ibid 575, 576.

of difficulty might arise, the determination of which might necessitate the presence of the whole six; but he was wholly unable
to give any specific instance of the occurrence of any such case,
or to imagine any question more important than the propriety of
an engrossment.[1]

Throughout the offices of the Masters, the Six Clerks, the
Examiners and the Registrars, the abuses arising from the existence of sinecure officials, and from their payment by fees for
office copies which were not required, continued to exist in an
aggravated form. "There was hardly an office in Chancery,"
said the commissioners in 1740, "which was not a patent office,
and whereof the duties were not systematically discharged by
deputy. In the case of the subpœna office . . . it seems that
there were three patentees, one of them a clergyman appointed
under the great seal at the nomination of Anne Charlotte, Lady
Dowager Freschville. But neither nominatrix nor nominees
attended to the office. Deputies were appointed to do the work,
and to earn for themselves and their patrons the fees taken from
the public."[2] The extent of these abuses is very clearly explained in a tract of 1707.[3] "It seems," says the writer, "very
ridiculous that anyone should be obliged to take and pay for
copies of what he before had, or has no occasion for at all, and
yet this is the case here; for everyone must take copies of interrogatories (which are of themselves of no use) if he will have
copies of the depositions for which he has occasion; nay every
person is now obliged to take copies of the interrogatories
exhibited by himself (and often twice over, both from the
Examiners' and Six Clerks' office) although he had the original
before, if he will have a copy of the depositions taken thereon."
Similarly suitors were obliged to pay for copies of reports and
certificates for which they had no occasion. The registrar's
deputies expanded the Orders (sometimes inserting the whole of
the counsel's brief) to increase the fees. " And as the length of
the Orders increase the charge, so it does the delay, which gives
birth to the new perquisite of expedition money." The insertion

---

[1] Parkes, App. 576, 577.   [2] Cited Parlt. Papers 1874 xxiv 590.
[3] Reasons for passing a bill for preventing delays and expenses in suits in Law
and Equity, Harleian Misc. xi 49, 53-55; the party paid, for bills and answers, 8d.
a sheet to the Six Clerks' office; 3s. a side for recitals from the registrar's office; and
about 2s. a side for like recitals from the Six Clerks' office if the decree were enrolled
—so that he paid three times for the same thing; it was stated by the House of
Lords in 1705, Lords Journals xviii 146, that a copy abstract of the bill was made for
the commissioners to take evidence, which was as often as not "an impertinent
scribble" or merely a blank piece of parchment; and the same thing went on throughout the Chancery offices; the affidavit office, formerly sold for £250, was in 1707
reckoned to bring in £1000 a year. This state of things tempted solicitors to charge
for copies they never got, Lives of the Norths i 32, 33.

of such matters merely misled the parties and led to further rehearings and appeals.[1] The evidence given before the commission of 1826 showed that the same abuses still existed. The following evidence was given by Mr. Lowe, a solicitor: "What do you mean by being on good terms with the registrar? Taking office copies. Do you ever take them when they are not wanted? They are never wanted. It is quite idle to think that an office copy is ever wanted. Are not the copies now taken for the purpose of conferring a benefit on the registrar? Entirely so—nothing else. Do the registrars expect the parties to take copies? They do not take money; but the office copy is the registrar's hood."[2]

We are not surprised to get a consensus of evidence throughout the eighteenth century that it was better to sacrifice just claims rather than embark upon a suit in equity.[3]

(4) The reorganization of the court in the nineteenth century.

In 1813 the increasing arrear of causes caused the creation of a Vice-Chancellor to assist the Chancellor in the exercise of his equitable jurisdiction.[4] This measure did not give any material assistance in reducing the arrears, as he could only decide cases specially delegated to him by the Chancellor, and the parties could appeal to the Chancellor. More cases were decided; but there were so many appeals that the cause lists were as full as ever.[5] In consequence of repeated motions in Parliament a commission was appointed in 1824 to enquire into the state of the court. At the head of the commission was Lord Eldon. Though the inadequacy of the court to deal with the equity business of the country, and the defects in its organization were notorious, the commissioners stated that they were satisfied, "that much misconception has arisen relative to the causes of that delay which so frequently occurs in the progress of a Chancery suit; and that much of it is imputable, neither to the court, nor to its established rules of practice; but to the carelessness of some parties, the obstinacy or knavery of others, or the inattention or ignorance of agents. Under these impressions we pro-

---

[1] Reasons, etc., 55, "Most of the suggestions of the bill are fictitious, and the answer frequently falsified by depositions (which are the real foundation of the decree, but are never recited therein) so that the recitals of a fictitious bill and untrue answer, rather give the decree an aspect of injustice . . . and often-times drew the parties into rehearings and appeals, upon a mistaken notion of the hardship of their case."

[2] Cited Parkes, Chancery, App. 571.

[3] Reasons, etc., 50 (1707); Parkes, Chancery 326, citing a work of 1750; C. P. Cooper, Chancery (1828) 112.

[4] 53 George III. c. 24.

[5] C. P. Cooper, Chancery 117; Report of the Chancery Commission of 1826, 37.

ceed to consider by what alterations in the practice of the court of Chancery, the time expended, and the cost incurred, may be reduced beneficially for the suitors." [1]   A commission acting "under these impressions" was hardly likely to effect much. Even the practice of making the parties take office copies was not entirely condemned.[2]   The Six Clerks, it is true, were considered to be useless; and it was recommended that they should be used to tax costs.[3]   Certain small amendments in practice were also recommended.   The *Times* spoke truly when it said that the report of the commission was an apology for all the abuses of the court.[4]   The root of the evil—the want of an adequate judicial staff—was not touched.   Certain parts of the practice were improved by Orders founded upon the proposals of the commissioners.   That merely meant that the cause was ready for hearing the sooner, and so waited longer on the list for a hearing.[5]

It was not till after the Whig victory in 1830 that the reform of the court was seriously taken in hand.   The changes made in the twenty years following placed the organization of the court upon an altogether new basis.

(i) Changes in the judicial organization of the court.

In 1831 the Bankruptcy jurisdiction was removed from the Lord Chancellor and given to a Chief Judge in Bankruptcy, assisted by three other judges and six commissioners.   Appeals were taken to a court of Review and from thence to the Chancellor.[6]

In 1833 it was enacted that the Master of the Rolls should sit continuously, and his jurisdiction was extended to the hearing of motions, pleas and demurrers.[7]

In 1842 the equity jurisdiction of the court of Exchequer was transferred to the court of Chancery, and two additional Vice-Chancellors were appointed.[8]

In 1851 a court of Appeal intermediate between the courts of the Vice-Chancellors and the Master of the Rolls, and the House of Lords, was established.   It consisted of two Lords Justices in Chancery and the Lord Chancellor if he liked to sit there.   They could be assisted, on the request of the Lord

[1] Report 9.   [2] Ibid 23.   [3] Ibid 33.
[4] Cited Parkes, Chancery, App. 530.
[5] C. P. Cooper, Chancery 65-67.
[6] 1, 2 William IV. c. 56 § 1; 10, 11 Victoria c. 102 § 2, the court of Review was abolished and its jurisdiction was handed over to a Vice-Chancellor.
[7] 3, 4 William IV. c. 94.
[8] 5 Victoria c. 5.   It was thought that only one of these Vice-Chancellors would be permanently needed; but it was found later that two were permanently needed, and provisions were made accordingly, 14, 15 Victoria c. 4 § 1; 15, 16 Victoria c. 80 § 52.

Chancellor, by the Master of the Rolls, the Vice-Chancellors, or any of the judges. They heard appeals from the Vice-Chancellor and the Master of the Rolls; and to them was given the jurisdiction of the Lord Chancellor to hear Bankruptcy appeals.[1]

In 1869[2] the London Court of Bankruptcy was established. The judge of it was called the Chief Judge in Bankruptcy. He was assisted by such other judges of the superior courts of law and equity as the Chancellor might appoint. The court was a court of law and equity, and the judge was given all the powers possessed by the superior courts of law and equity. Appeals from it were heard by the Lords Justices in Chancery.

Thus the courts of equity consisted (1) of the three Vice-Chancellors and the Master of the Rolls sitting separately as judges of first instance. The court of first instance in Bankruptcy was the London Court of Bankruptcy; (2) of the Lords Justices in Chancery, who were usually assisted by the Master of the Rolls, sitting together as a court of appeal in equity and bankruptcy; and (3) of the House of Lords.

(ii) The reform of the official staff of the court.

In 1833 the appointment of the Masters was transferred to the crown; their jurisdiction was defined; they were to be paid by a fixed salary; and the taking of any fee or gratuity was made an indictable offence. The court fees were fixed and lowered; and no suitor was to be compelled to take office copies. It was provided that the Six Clerks should be gradually reduced to two.[3]

In 1842 the Six Clerks and other useless officers were abolished. It was provided that costs should be taxed by a new official styled a Taxing-master, to be appointed from among solicitors of twelve years' standing.[4]

In 1852 came a more complete measure of reform.[5] The Masters were abolished.[6] "That," says Mr. Kerly,[7] "was the commencement of efficient reform. Delay and expense were the necessary concomitants of the administration of parlour justice, in which the Master and the opposing solicitors were all anxious to accommodate each other, and there was neither publicity nor any definite rule as to time to urge them to activity." It was provided that the Master of the Rolls and the Vice-Chancellors should sit at Chambers to despatch such part of the business of

---

[1] 14, 15 Victoria c. 83. [2] 32, 33 Victoria c. 71.

[3] 3, 4 William IV. c. 94 §§ 13, 16, 19, 28, 41.

[4] 5, 6 Victoria c. 103. For an account of the manner in which the taxation of costs was conducted before the Act see Silkstone and Haigh Moor Coal Co. v. Edey [1901] 2 Ch. at pp. 655, 656.

[5] 15, 16 Victoria cc. 80, 86, 87.

[6] Ibid c. 80 § 1. [7] Equity 280.

the court as "without detriment to the public advantage arising from the discussion of questions in open court" could be best there heard.[1] Matters heard in court could be adjourned to Chambers;[2] and it was directed that the Chamber business should be carried on concurrently with that of the court.[3] The judge sitting in Chambers was given the same powers as the judge sitting in court.[4] The Master of the Rolls and the Vice-Chancellors were each directed to appoint two Chief Clerks to be attached to their Chambers, from among the Chief Clerks to the old Masters, or solicitors of ten years' standing.[5] They were empowered to direct what cases or parts of a case should be heard by their Chief Clerks. It was provided that any suitor could bring before the judge any matter heard before a Chief Clerk. The procedure in Chambers, whether before the judge or the Chief Clerk, was to be modelled upon the procedure of the court, not upon that of the Masters.[6] The court was empowered to appoint conveyancing counsel to whom conveyancing matters could be referred.[7] It was provided that all allowances for office copies should cease; that all the new officials should be paid by salary; and, with a reminiscence of now past abuses, a severe penalty was imposed, "if any officer of the court of Chancery or any of the judges thereof shall for anything done or pretended to be done relating to his office situation or employment wilfully take . . . any fee, gift, gratuity, or emolument."[8]

The changes effected by the Judicature Acts and the legislation consequent upon them,[9] having completely got rid of the old traditions which hung around the Masters offices, the Chief Clerks in 1897 were allowed to take the title of Masters of the Supreme Court.[10]

In 1853 the Masters Extraordinary were abolished. In their place were established the commissioners to administer oaths, to be appointed by the Lord Chancellor from among solicitors practising within ten miles of Lincoln's Inn Hall.[11] This Act is now repealed, and the appointments, duties, and liabilities of these commissioners are now regulated by the Commissioners for Oaths Act 1889.[12]

II. THE JURISDICTION OF THE COURT OF CHANCERY AND THE CHANCELLOR

The jurisdiction exercised by the court of Chancery and the Chancellor falls into three clearly marked divisions. There is

---

[1] 15, 16 Victoria c. 80 § 11.
[2] § 27.
[3] § 12.   [4] § 13.
[5] § 16.
[6] §§ 29, 32, 33, 39.
[7] §§ 40, 41.
[8] 15, 16 Victoria c. 87 §§ 1, 3, 4.
[9] Below 647-648.
[10] Halsbury, Laws of England ix 67 n. (h).
[11] 16, 17 Victoria c. 78.
[12] 52, 53 Victoria c. 10.

the common law jurisdiction, the equitable jurisdiction, and other miscellaneous branches of jurisdiction. Of these the equitable jurisdiction is by far the most important. But it was only gradually that the first two of these three species of jurisdiction acquired their distinctive characteristics. Therefore in relating their history I must begin by saying a few words by way of introduction as to the origins of the common law and equitable jurisdictions. I shall then sketch the history of these three branches of jurisdiction exercised either by the court of Chancery or the Chancellor.

Origins

We can see the germs of all these three kinds of jurisdiction in the Middle Ages;[1] and though the jurisdiction conferred by special statutes could always be clearly distinguished from the common law and equitable jurisdictions, the line between these two last mentioned kinds of jurisdiction was by no means clearly drawn.

The distinction between the strict rule of law and modifications of that law on equitable or moral grounds is a distinction well known to many systems of law;[2] and it was familiar to English lawyers from the twelfth century onwards.[3] It is not therefore the distinction between law and equity which is peculiar to English law. What is peculiar is the vesting of the administration of law and equity in two quite separate tribunals. The result has been that the distinction between law and equity has in England been given a sharpness and a permanence which it possesses in no other legal system.[4] The questions then which we must here consider are, firstly, why did this separation of tribunals occur? And, secondly, why did it originate the distinction between the common law and the equitable jurisdiction of the Chancellor?

(1) Why did law and equity come to be administered by separate courts?

It is quite clear that the jurisdiction exercised by the undifferentiated Curia Regis of the twelfth century was marked by two of the chief characteristics which we associate with a court of equity. Proceedings were begun by a petition to the king for his interference;[5] and that interference might result in remedies which, by reason both of their character and their methods of enforcement, were, as Professor Adams has said, "as much out-

---

[1] Above 405-407.
[2] Pollock, The Transformation of Equity, Essays in Legal History (1913) 287-290.
[3] Vol. ii 245-249, 334-347.   [4] Below 449.
[5] G. B. Adams, Col. Law Rev. xvi 89-90.

side of, and in violation of, the ordinary system of justice which prevailed throughout the Anglo-Norman state, as ever Equity was at any later time in relation to the Common Law system." [1] But, in the course of the thirteenth and fourteenth centuries, these remedies, the rules to which they gave rise, and the machinery by which they were enforced, rapidly developed and hardened into a regular system of law. As that system reduced the remedies and rules and machinery of the older courts to insignificance, the rules of the Curia Regis became the ordinary common law of the country, and ceased to possess that characteristic of being something outside the ordinary law, which had once given to them an equitable character. At the same time the other equitable characteristic which they had once possessed—their immediate dependence upon the royal power—weakened. In the first place the Curia Regis acquired a number of writs de cursu which any litigant could purchase. In the second place the Barons, and later the Parliament, perceiving that the power to make new writs was in substance a power to make new law, limited the king's discretion to invent new remedies.[2] Thus the system of the common law tended to become rigid and technical; and this tendency was strengthened, when, at the close of the thirteenth century, its development began to be controlled almost entirely by men who had been trained as practitioners in the royal courts.[3] But, naturally, the equitable characteristics which had marked the jurisdiction of the Curia Regis did not at once vanish from those separate courts which had sprung from it. We can see traces of them, certainly as late as the first quarter of the fourteenth century, both in the three common law courts, and in the courts held by the itinerant justices.

In the days of Bracton the court of King's Bench and the King's Council were to a large extent staffed by the same men.[4] The two institutions which became in later days the court of King's Bench and the Council were not as yet distinct; and, even when they became distinct, the connexion between the two was close. Cases occur as late as Edward III.'s reign in which the proceedings seem to be heard by a tribunal which is both court and Council.[5] Naturally this tended to preserve the tradition that the court of King's Bench ought to administer both law and equity; and the fact that the tradition was thus preserved in the court of King's Bench helped to preserve it also in the court of Common Pleas. The King's Bench was the court in which

[1] G. B. Adams, Col. Law Rev. xvi 93. [2] Above 39S.
[3] Vol. ii 318, 556-559.
[4] Above 204-205; Baldwin, The King's Council, 61-62.
[5] Above 209-210.

the errors of the Common Pleas were corrected ; both courts were staffed by men who had had a similar training ; and judges were sometimes moved from one Bench to the other.[1] In fact, as I shall show in a later volume,[2] both the court of Common Pleas and the court of King's Bench did apply to cases which came before them ideas and doctrines which we have come to associate with equity rather than with law. But early in the fourteenth century these cases were becoming rare. As Professor Baldwin has pointed out, quite early in the thirteenth century the King's Bench was tending to hear cases in accordance with " The formulaic procedure" of the common law.[3] That tendency was more pronounced in the case of the court of Common Pleas. The King's Bench continued in some cases to employ " the free and unrestricted procedure of the old Curia Regis."[4] But, by the middle of the fourteenth century, in both courts, the common law procedure was generally followed ;[5] and, as that procedure had now hardened into a very technical system, this is a sure sign that the capacity of these courts to administer equity had disappeared.

The court of Exchequer was a court of a character different from that of the King's Bench and Common Pleas.[6] Its connexion with the Council was intimate; and, in the thirteenth and early part of the fourteenth century, cases which demanded the application of equitable principles frequently came before it. But we have seen that early in the fourteenth century it had come to concern itself mainly with its proper function—the consideration of cases connected with the king's revenue.[7]

That the justices in Eyre administered a large equitable jurisdiction in proceedings begun by bill has been discovered by Mr. Bolland. Of the origin and nature of these bills I shall speak later.[8] Here it will be sufficient to say that they are, so far as we know, peculiar to the General Eyre.[9] The reason for this is perhaps to be found partly in the fact that the justices in Eyre represented the person, and were on that account specially commissioned to exercise these powers, of the king ;[10] and partly in the fact that their court gave to dwellers in the country a unique opportunity to ap-

---

[1] See Foss's Tables of the Judges of the Courts of King's Bench and Common Pleas, Lives of the Judges, iii 25-26, 201-202, 353-355.

[2] Vol. ii 334-336, 343-345. [3] The King's Council 62.

[4] Ibid 62. [5] Ibid 64. [6] Above 231-237.

[7] Above 235. [8] Vol. ii 336-343.

[9] The Eyre of Kent (S.S.) ii, xxiii—Mr. Bolland says, " The vagueness of the address and the frequent absence of any date make it impossible to say with any certainty that all these bills were presented in Eyre, though when we get any trustworthy indication of time in connexion with venue it usually seems to point to such a presentation."

[10] Above 267 n. 4.

peal to those powers of administering equity which the king still possessed.[1] This would explain why bills, like the bills in Eyre, were not presented to the King's Bench or Common Pleas. Litigants who approached the courts at Westminster with cases of this kind would be more likely to petition the Council. However that may be, they are a striking and a late example of the equity which the Curia Regis and the King's Bench in its early days were accustomed to administer. But we have seen that in the course of the fourteenth century the General Eyre ceased ;[2] and that its place was taken by itinerant judges who acted under limited commissions, and tried cases according to the strict procedure of the common law.[3]

Thus all these common law tribunals ceased to administer equity. Litigants, if they wanted equity, were driven to a tribunal the procedure of which had remained free from the technical rules which governed the procedure of the common law courts ; and so cases which called for equity went to the Council, and later to the Chancery.[4] The precocious fixity attained by the rules of the common law had caused the administration of equity to be handed over to a tribunal which had come to be perfectly distinct from any of the common law courts. And this is the origin of the most unique feature of English as contrasted with, for instance, Roman equity. The Roman prætor urbanus administered both law and equity ; and therefore it was easier to fuse the two systems : the Chancellor and the common law judges were distinct and often rival authorities. Thus Justinian could effect what the English Judicature Acts could not effect. He fused law and equity : they, for the most part, only fused the courts which administered law and equity.

(2) Why did this separation of tribunals originate the distinction between the common law and the equitable jurisdiction of the Chancellor ?

We have seen that the Chancery had always possessed some common law jurisdiction ; and that that jurisdiction continued to exist after the common law courts had become distinct tribunals,

---

[1] Mr. Bolland says, Eyre of Kent (S.S.) ii, xxiii, " All these bills appear to be country bills, and I feel no doubt that if any of them were not presented in Eyre—in a General Eyre, to be quite accurate—they were at any rate presented in those less comprehensive Eyres of ' Justices erranz ' commissioned to hold common pleas, to whom the king gave also authority ' to hear . . . any complaints whatsoever and to make fitting amends therefor ; ' " possibly also the Eyre, being held at a distance from London, and cases pending before the other courts being adjourned there, above 266-267, it was less easy to sue out an original writ during the Eyre ; thus in the Eyre of Kent (S.S.) iii 74 it is said that a plaintiff " must seek a remedy by a bill of trespass or felony during the Eyre, or, if the Eyre be not sitting, by a writ of trespass."

[2] Above 272.   [3] Above 274-283.   [4] Above 399-400.

largely, though not exclusively, because of the close connexion which the Chancery had with the issue of original writs, and with the subsequent proceedings on some of these writs.[1]   It was inevitable that, as the common law became a fixed and rigid system, powers exercised in accordance with its rules should come to be distinguished from powers not so exercised; that ordinary jurisdiction exercised in accordance with common law rules should fall apart from extraordinary jurisdiction exercised on equitable or moral grounds.   In the first case only the legal rule could be considered; in the second considerations of fairness and the claims of conscience could also be weighed.   And this difference was emphasized and given a technical significance by a necessary difference in the procedure employed.   It is quite obvious that the ideally fair decision could not be arrived at by the verdict of a jury.   It could only be arrived at by a patient examination of the parties and the witnesses, and all other relevant circumstances.

Thus in later days the distinction between the procedure upon the ordinary or common law or Latin side of the Chancery, and the procedure upon the extraordinary or equitable or English side was clearly marked.[2]   The usual common law process was begun by original writ.   The plantiff then put in his declaration or statement of claim.   The defendant pleaded to it; and there might sometimes be a reply and a rejoinder.   The pleadings ended either in a demurrer, i.e. admitting the facts the parties were at issue as to the law; or, in a conclusion to the country on a question of fact.   In equity the proceedings began by bill asking for relief and for the summons by subpœna of the defendant.   The defendant answered; and there might sometimes be further pleadings.   At some stage in the case the defendant was examined.   The court gave judgment both on the facts and the law.   It is clear from the case of *Hals* v. *Hynchley* (1420)[3] that the line between these two methods of procedure was not then clearly drawn.   The case was begun by a bill of Hals and other plaintiffs praying for a remedy for a disseisin for which they had no remedy at law.   A subpœna was issued.   The defendant appeared and pleaded; and, after further pleadings, there was a conclusion to the country in the usual form.   A commission was issued to take the inquisition; and a judgment was given in form very similar to a judgment at common law.   It follows, that

---

[1] Above 398-399.   [2] Kerly, History of Equity 50-52.
[3] L.Q.R. i 445-453; Y.B. 12, 13 Ed. III. (R.S.) cv-cviii; cp. the petition of the Hansards (1389) Select Cases before the Council (S.S.) 77 where the common law form "consideratum est," and the equitable form "decretum est," are combined in an order of the Council.

as there was no distinct line drawn between the two forms of procedure used in the Chancery, so there was as yet no distinct line drawn between the cases which fell under either procedure. Proceedings were begun by bill which would in later times have fallen under the common law jurisdiction of the court.

As a matter of fact in the fourteenth and early fifteenth centuries the relations between the Chancellor and the common law judges were very close. They sat together and discussed together the cases in which applications were made to the Chancellor.[1] And it was natural that these intimate relations should exist. If the Chancellor was to modify the law on equitable grounds it was essential that he should know what the law was.[2] Indeed till 1852[3] he could always require the judges to assist him in the hearing of a case, or to give him their opinions on a point of law.[4] But we shall see that towards the end of the fifteenth century the court of Chancery was awakening the jealousy of the courts of common law.[5] Therefore the relations between the Chancellor and the common law judges were ceasing to be so intimate as they had formerly been ; and, consequently, the distinction between common law jurisdiction and equitable jurisdiction was tending to come into clearer relief.

Its growing distinctness is illustrated by a case reported in 1469.[6] The Chancellor, putting the case of an official privileged to be sued only in the Chancery, said that he might use either his legal or his equitable jurisdiction ; "for if it appear upon the matter showed in the suit that there is conscience, he may judge thereof according to conscience." But all the judges denied that he could admit considerations of conscience in a case which ought to be ruled according to the common law. Staunford, writing in 1590, states that there were two opinions upon this point in Edward IV.'s day ;[7] but he inclines to the opinion that merely equitable defences did not avail in matters falling within the common law jurisdiction of the court. When Coke wrote his Fourth Institute the distinction was clearly settled in its modern form.[8] " In the Chancery," he says, " are two courts, one ordinary, wherein the Lord Chancellor . . . proceeds according

---

[1] Vol. v 220-222. [2] Ibid.

[3] 15, 16 Victoria c. 86 § 61.

[4] Spence, op. cit. i 383-384 ; in Gore v. Gore (1722) 10 Mod. at p. 501, Lord Macclesfield said that he considered himself bound by the opinions of the judges when he had referred a case to them, and had not heard the arguments by which they had been guided, *secus* where the judges had assisted at the hearing and he had heard the arguments ; for then the decree was his own, and he must be satisfied.

[5] Below 459.

[6] Y.B. 8 Ed. IV. Trin. pl. 1 ; Office of the Chancellor, 45, 64.

[7] L.Q.R. i 454. [8] Fourth Instit. 79, 80.

to the right line of the laws and statutes of the realm . . .
another extraordinary, according to the rule of equity." After
describing the extent of the common law jurisdiction he points
out its relation to the jurisdiction of the common law courts.
" If the parties descend to issue, this court (the Chancery) cannot
try it by jury, but the Lord Chancellor . . . delivereth the record
by his proper hands into the King's Bench to be tried there . . .
and after trial had, to be remanded into the Chancery, and there
judgment to be given. But if there be a demurrer in law it
shall be argued and adjudged in this court (the Chancery). . . .
Upon a judgment given in this court a writ of error doth lie returnable into the King's Bench." [1]

The Common Law Jurisdiction

The common law jurisdiction of the court was never a very
important part of its jurisdiction. It consisted of a few scattered
and somewhat unrelated pieces of jurisdiction which can be
grouped under the following heads : (a) Jurisdiction connected
with the issue of and the procedure upon certain writs. Under
this head fell pleas on the writ of scire facias to repeal letters
patent or recognizances, or arising out of executions upon
recognizances or statutes merchant or staple.[2] Palgrave thinks
that some part of this jurisdiction arose from the practice of
enrolling covenants, grants, releases, etc., on the close rolls, and
securing their performance by deeds of recognizance acknowledged
in Chancery. "The power of issuing writs of execution belonged
to the court and thus it was authorized to judge of the default
by which the recognizance was forfeited." [3] (b) Cases in which
the king or a grantee of the king was concerned. Thus proceedings by way of petition of right or monstrans de droit to recover
property from the crown ; or traverses of office found for the
crown,[4] fell within this branch of the jurisdiction of the court.

[1] Dyer 315 a ; Coke, Fourth Instit. 80 ; Office of the Chancellor 76 ; Y.B. 27
Hy. VIII. Trin. pl. 6, the question whether error lay arose in the Chancery, but
was not decided ; whether error lay to Parliament was questioned by Plowden
393 (marginal note), and that it lay to the King's Bench was denied in Rex v. Carey
(1682), 1 Vern. 131 ; Blackstone, Comm. iii 48, says he has seen no traces of such
a writ since 1572 ; but there is a note of a petition for and a warrant authorizing
the issue of such a writ in 1667-1668, S.P. Dom. 1666-1667 182-183, clxxiv 59 ;
ibid 1667-1668 308.
[2] Fourth Instit. 79-80 ; Sir George Reynel's Case (1612) 9 Co. Rep. 95 a ; Bl.
Comm. iii 47-48 ; Spence i 336 ; for the writ of Scire Facias see App. XI. ; a recognizance is defined to be " a writing acknowledged by the party to it before a judge
or officer having authority for the purpose and enrolled in a court of record," Anson,
Contracts (8th Ed.) 59 ; for statutes merchant and staple see vol. iii 131-132.
[3] The Council 95.
[4] For these proceedings see vol. ix 24-29 ; a case of this kind is Sir George
Reynel's Case (1612) 9 Co. Rep. 95 a.

This was accounted for either on the ground that the king can always sue in what court he pleases;[1] or on the ground that it was more fitting that these proceedings should be brought in the Chancery, because there they were begun by petition or bill and depended on the king's grace, and not by a writ which asserted a legal right to redress and did not lie against the king.[2] (c) Personal actions brought by or against officers of the court. This was a form of jurisdiction which, as we have seen,[3] all the superior courts of law possessed, and therefore belonged to the court of Chancery.

Many of these cases were connected with the king's rights to the incidents of military tenure, and therefore disappeared with the creation of the court of Wards.[4]

The Equitable Jurisdiction

Lord Ellesmere in the *Earl of Oxford's Case*[5] well expressed the principle upon which this jurisdiction rested when he said that the Chancellor interfered " for that men's actions are so divers and infinite, that it is impossible to make any general law which may aptly meet with every particular act, and not fail in some circumstances." The fact that the " general law " laid down by the common law courts was often peculiarly narrow and technical made the interference of the Chancellor peculiarly necessary. It is clear that a jurisdiction resting upon such a foundation will be at first very vague ; but it tended to become more fixed with time. The question of its relation to the jurisdiction of the common law courts then arose. This question was settled by James I. ; and, having been settled, the principles of equity, though modified by changes in manners and modes of thought, and by changes in the common law itself, attained a large part of the fixity and technicality of the law which they had started by attempting to modify.

To write fully of the equitable jurisdiction of the Chancellor would be to write the history of equity itself.[6] The briefest

---

[1] " It is a great prerogative in opening of justice that the king may enter by what gate he will . . . as if the king will bring a writ of escheat, which is merely a common plea, he may bring it in his court of the king's bench . . . and if the king shall have choice of his courts upon his demand, much more shall he have it upon his defence," Bacon's argument in the case De Rege Inconsulto, Works (Ed. Spedding) vii 701.

[2] Ibid 694.

[3] Above 203 ; for cases of this kind see Select Cases in Chancery (S.S.) nos. 1, 48.

[4] Eq. Cases Ab. i 128 (2); for this court see 32 Henry VIII. c. 46 ; Coke, Fourth Instit. c. 35 ; above 409 n. 5.

[5] (1615) 1 Ch. Rep. at p. 6.

[6] For an account of this see vol. v 278-336 ; vol. vi 640-671.

sketch only can be here attempted. The subject falls naturally and chronologically into three periods: (1) Equitable jurisdiction up to the middle of the seventeenth century; (2) the conflict between the court of Chancery and the courts of common law; and (3) The modern development of the equitable jurisdiction.

(1) Equitable jurisdiction up to the middle of the seventeenth century.

Blackstone accurately sums up the condition of the equitable jurisdiction at the end of the fifteenth century, when he says [1] that "no regular judicial system at that time prevailed in the court; but the suitor when he thought himself aggrieved found a desultory and uncertain remedy, according to the private opinion of the Chancellor, who was generally an ecclesiastic, or sometimes (though rarely) a statesman." But, in the course of the sixteenth and earlier half of the seventeenth centuries, we can distinguish certain principles upon which the Chancellor based his interference, the development of which was assisted by the growing organization of the court.

These principles can be grouped under the five following heads :—

Firstly, the recognition, protection and development of uses and trusts. Of the history of this branch of the jurisdiction of the court I shall speak at length in later volumes.[2] Here it will be sufficient to say that the Chancellor so developed the duties of the feoffees to uses, that is the persons to whom property had been conveyed on trust, that the interest of the cestui-que use, that is the person for whose benefit the property was conveyed, became a form of equitable ownership of a sort which has no parallel in any other system of law. This branch of equitable jurisdiction was from the first, and has always continued to be, its most important branch. As Maitland has said, in the early days of the court it made its fortune. It imparted a much needed element of elasticity into the mediæval land law, and gave to landowners far wider powers over their property than they possessed at common law. But there is no doubt that the possession of these powers facilitated frauds on purchasers, frauds on creditors, evasions of the mortmain laws, and evasion of the rights of king and lords to the incidents of military tenure. Hence, from the latter part of the fourteenth century onwards, these uses were controlled and regulated by the legislature.[3] These attempts at legislative control culminated in 1535 in the

---

[1] Comm. iii 53. [2] Vol. iv 407-480; vol. v 304-309; vol. vi 641-644.
[3] Vol. iv 443-449.

Statute of Uses. That statute adopted the plan of abolishing in certain cases the dual ownership of the feoffees to uses and the cestui-que use, by taking from the feoffees to uses so much of their legal estate as was sufficient to give to the cestui-que use a legal estate corresponding to his equitable interest.[1] One result of the statute, therefore, was to give jurisdiction over the uses which had been thus turned into legal estates to the courts of common law. We shall see that for some time before 1535 the rivalry between the courts of common law and the court of Chancery had been growing acute;[2] and, on that account, the common lawyers assisted the passage of a statute which gave them jurisdiction at the expense of the court of Chancery.[3] But the statute did not apply to all uses. It did not, for instance, apply to cases where the feoffees were possessed of chattels real or personal to the use of others; nor did it apply to cases where they had active duties to perform, for instance if they were given land to the use that they should collect and pay the rents to a beneficiary.[4] Thus the court of Chancery still retained some of its jurisdiction; and it regained much of the jurisdiction of which the statute had deprived it in the latter half of the seventeenth century. The court of Wards and the courts of common law had decided in *Tyrrel's Case*[5] that if land was conveyed to A to the use of B to the use of C, the statute gave B the legal estate, and that the second use in favour of C was void; but after the Restoration the court of Chancery decided to enforce this second use as a trust.[6] Thus the old distinction between legal and equitable estates in conveyances of property to which the Statute of Uses applied was restored; and so, in another form, the court of Chancery recovered its old jurisdiction.

Secondly, the court of Chancery interfered to enforce contracts on principles very different from any known to the common lawyers. We shall see that in the earlier part of the mediæval period the courts of law had no adequate remedy for the enforcement of simple contracts. The action of covenant was only available if the contract was in writing and under seal; and the action of debt applied only to certain kinds of executed contract, and was for other reasons an unsatisfactory action.[7] Having no adequate remedy for the enforcement of contracts, the courts of common law developed no adequate theory of contract. They had not yet grasped the idea that the essence of contract is consent, and that consent ought, under certain circumstances, to give

[1] Vol. iv 461-463.   [2] Below 459-460.
[3] Vol. iv 453-455.   [4] Ibid.
[5] (1557) Dyer 155 a.   [6] Vol. iv 469-473; vol. vi 307-309; vol. vi 641-642.
[7] Vol. ii 366-368; vol. iii 417-424.

rise to an actionable obligation. But the Chancellors had from the first approached the subject of contract from this point of view;[1] for the majority of the Chancellors were ecclesiastics; and breach of faith was a sin punishable by the ecclesiastical law.[2] It is true that the lay courts issued writs of prohibition if they caught the ecclesiastical courts attempting under this pretext to enforce contracts.[3] But the Chancellors carried with them into the court of Chancery the idea that faith should be kept; and enforced agreements, just as they enforced trusts, whenever they thought that in the interests of good faith and honest dealing, they ought to be enforced.[4] This might well have brought the whole of the law of contract under the jurisdiction of the court of Chancery, had not the common law courts awakened in time to the necessity of providing a remedy for the breach of simple contracts. Fortunately for the common law the rivalry between the common law courts and the court of Chancery roused the judges of those courts to action before it was too late. From the middle of the fourteenth century onwards, they so developed a form of the action of trespass on the case, called the action of assumpsit,[5] that it became an adequate remedy for the breach of simple contracts;[6] and, in and through this action, the common law theory that simple contract is an agreement based upon consideration was developed.[7] This theory of contract proved to be so adequate that it was accepted by the court of Chancery, which, by the end of the sixteenth or the beginning of the seventeenth centuries, refused to enforce simple contracts made without consideration.[8] In consequence of this development the interference of equity was rendered less necessary; but it was not rendered wholly unnecessary. The only remedy which the common law courts could give was damages. If a plaintiff wanted specific relief he was obliged to come to the court of Chancery.[9] The equitable jurisdiction was therefore needed, not because of the inadequacy of the common law conception of contract, but because of the inadequacy of the common law remedy for breach of contract.

---

[1] Vol. v 295-296.

[2] L.Q.R. v 236; below 621.

[3] "Placita de debitis, quæ fide interposita debentur, vel absque interpositione fidei, sint in justitia regis," Constitutions of Clarendon § 15; vol. ii 305.

[4] Vol. v 294-298; cf. Diversite des Courtes cited Kerly, Equity 88; Y.B. 8 Ed. IV. Pasch. pl. 11.

[5] "Assumpsit" means literally "he has promised."

[6] Vol. iii 429 seqq.

[7] Ibid 453; vol. viii 2-42.

[8] Vol. v 321-322; older cases to the contrary were overruled.

[9] In Y.B. 21 Hy. VII. Mich. pl. 66 Fineux, C.J., said that if one bargain that I shall have his land to me and my heirs for £20, and I pay, I may have action on the case, and need not sue out a subpœna; but to this Brook in his Abridgment adds the remark that "by this he will get nothing but damages, but by subpœna the Chancery can compel the defendant to convey the estate or imprison him, *ut dicitur.*"

But in this period it was not settled what cases did, and what did not entitle a plaintiff to specific relief. Specific performance of contracts to convey chattels or to do positive acts was sometimes decreed, if the court thought that such a decree was, in the circumstances, just.[1] It was not till the eighteenth century that it was settled that equity would only grant specific relief if damages were not an adequate remedy[2]—a restriction which has led to the application of this relief chiefly in the case of contracts for the sale of interests in land.

Thirdly, the Chancellor interfered in a class of cases where, owing to the rigidity of the law, the enforcement of the strict legal right was clearly contrary to equity. Fraud, forgery and duress were some of the chief grounds of his interference.[3] Even after judgment at law he would issue an injunction against the enforcement of the judgment;[4] and this, as we shall see, gave rise to the contest between the court of Chancery and the courts of common law. Such interference was very necessary. The courts of common law allowed fraud to be set up as a defence; but they were unable to order the cancellation and delivery up of documents obtained by fraud.[5] Thus if a bond had been wholly or partially satisfied, but not given up, the obligor might sue at law for the whole amount.[6] "The question at law is whether it were sealed and delivered or the like, and that being found by verdict, judgment followeth that the whole sum shall be paid; whereas the Chancery examineth, not the sealing and delivery of the bond, but what was at first due, what hath been paid since, what doth remain unpaid; and accordingly doth order the party to take but what is justly due unto him, with his damages and costs, and will not suffer him to take £800 because he had a judgment for so much, where it was proved that all was paid but £20, as the case was lately in Chancery."[7] On similar principles the Chancellor would relieve against mistake, where an instrument had been drawn up which did not express the true intent of the parties;[8] or against accident, where, for instance, a money bond had imposed a penalty in case of non-payment by a day, and accident had prevented payment by

---

[1] Kymburley v. Goldsmith (Hy. VI.) Cal. (R.C.) i *xx* (a ton of woad); Tyngelden v. Warham (Ed. IV.) ibid ii *liv* (contract to build a house); for later cases see vol. v 322-323; vol. vi 658 659.
[2] Cuddee v. Rutter (1719) 1 P. Wms. 570; cf. McManus v. Cooke (1887) 35 C.D. 682.
[3] Select Cases in Chancery (S.S.) cases 8 and 9 (duress); 2 and 99 (fraud); Bief v. Dyer (Rich. II.), Cal. i *xi* (forgery).
[4] Spence i 674.   [5] Ibid 622-624.
[6] In Edward IV.'s reign there had been conflicting decisions as to whether equity would relieve in that case; it was ultimately settled that it would, Kerly, Equity 90.
[7] Report of Cases in Chancery i App. 35.   [8] Spence i 633.

that day.[1] After some conflict of opinion it was decided that
the latter relief would always be given against penalties, if incurred by slight negligence;[2] but it was not till later that relief
was given against all penalties merely because they were penalties.[3]
It is upon this species of equitable interference that the equitable
conception of a mortgage is founded. It was settled in James
I.'s reign that the mortgagor always had an equity of redemption
although the mortgagee's estate was absolute at law.[4] In 1640
it was said that the court would relieve a mortgagor "to the tenth
generation." [5]

Fourthly, the procedure of the court enabled the Chancellor
to give remedies in cases in which the common law either could
not act at all, or could not act with effect.[6] The Chancellor by
means of the writ of subpœna and his power to commit for
contempt exercised strict control over the persons of all parties
to a suit. He could order them to act in any way he saw fit in
order to secure justice. Thus he could examine them; and, in
aid of proceedings either in his own court or in the courts of
common law, could enforce the discovery of documents in their
possession.[7] It was because he was able to exercise this control
that he was able to give remedies which the common law courts
could not give. The decree for specific performance is one
instance of this. Another is the issue of an injunction. The
courts of common law might give a remedy when the wrong
had been done; they could not interfere to prevent it.[8] Such
interference was an early subject of the Chancellor's jurisdiction.[9]
Bills to prevent waste were common in Elizabeth's reign.[10]
Others were filed to secure parties in the legal possession of
their estates; and it was injunctions of this kind that helped to
make the action of ejectment an efficient means of finally determining questions of ownership of land.[11]

Fifthly, the organization of the court of Chancery made it a
tribunal much more efficient than the courts of common law for
the investigation of matters of account. There was, it is true,
an action of account at common law; but it was of very limited

[1] Select Cases in Chancery (S.S.) no. 39; Atkinson v. Harman (Philip and
Mary) Cal. i *cxlii.*
[2] Spence i 602, 603.   [3] Kerly, Equity 145, 146.   [4] Ibid 143.
[5] Bacon v. Bacon, Toth. 133.   [6] Spence i 704-707.
[7] Select Cases in Chancery (S.S.) case 112; Hungerford v. Mayor of Wilton
(Hy. VI.) Cal. i *xxxix;* cf. Spence i 678; Fourth Instit. 85; similarly the court
entertained suits to record evidence if there was ground to suppose that it might
otherwise be lost, Earl of Oxford v. Tyrell (Hy. VII.) Cal. i *cxx.*
[8] Spence i 669.
[9] Select Cases in Chancery (S.S.) case 70; Wakeryng v. Baille (Ed. IV.) Cal.
i *lxii.*
[10] Spence i 671-672.
[11] Ibid 658; for the history of this action see vol. vii 4-23.

application;[1] and, even in the cases in which it could be used, the superior machinery and remedies of the court of Chancery caused that court to gain a practically exclusive jurisdiction.[2] The enforcement of trusts very often involved the taking of accounts.[3] Partnership, the administration of the estates of deceased persons, and suretyship, all became for this reason important heads of equitable jurisdiction.[4]

(2) The conflict between the court of Chancery and the courts of common law.

When two separate and partially competing jurisdictions exist in one state, a conflict between them is sooner or later inevitable. In Henry II.'s reign there had been such a conflict between the temporal and ecclesiastical jurisdictions.[5] A similar conflict arose at the beginning of the sixteenth century between the courts of law and equity.

The nature and occasion of the conflict had been fore-shadowed at the end of the fifteenth century. It had become clear that the law could not be modified upon equitable principles, unless the Chancellor possessed the power of restraining the parties from proceeding at law, or, if they had already done so, from enforcing judgment. From the time of Henry VI. there are instances of injunctions issued not only against the parties, but also against their counsel.[6] The judges were naturally hostile to a claim to treat them, by means of an injunction, as they were accustomed to treat other courts by means of a prohibition.[7] In Edward IV.'s reign Fairfax asserted that the King's Bench might forbid the parties from resorting to any other jurisdiction, if the case fell within the jurisdiction of the common law courts.[8] In another case of the same reign, Huse and Fairfax declared that if the Chancellor committed the parties for disobedience to an injunction, they would release them by Habeas Corpus.[9]

---

[1] For the history of this action see vol. iii 426-428; it applied only to the guardians in socage, bailiffs, receivers, or merchants.

[2] Vol. v 288, 315; vol. vi 650-652; see Malynes, Lex Mercatoria Pt. III. c. xvii; Spence i 649-650; Select Cases in Chancery (S.S.) case 1.

[3] "When a trust is confessed by a defendant's answer, there needeth no further hearing of the cause, but a reference presently to be made upon the account, and so to go on to a hearing of the accounts," Bacon's Orders no. 53.

[4] Vol. v 297-298, 315-321; vol. vi 650-657; for the way in which the court of Chancery absorbed the jurisdiction formerly exercised by the ecclesiastical courts see below 629-630.

[5] Below 615.   [6] Spence i 674.

[7] There is a petition in 1422 that two judges should certify that the common law gives no remedy before a party can sue in Chancery; this would clearly have put the Chancery under the control of the law courts; but the answer is that the statute 17 Richard II. c. 6 (damages and costs) shall be observed, R.P. iv 189 (1 Hy. VI. n. 41).

[8] Y.B. 21 Ed. IV. Pasch. pl. 6 (p. 23).   [9] Y.B. 22 Ed. IV. Mich. pl. 21.

We have seen that in the sixteenth century the jurisdiction of the court was extended and consolidated. Louder complaints, therefore, were heard from the common lawyers ; and the question became so burning that it occasioned a literary controversy. The Doctor and Student [1] discussed the relations between law and equity with a bias in favour of the equitable jurisdiction. It was answered by a serjeant who took the strict common law line.[2] " I marvail much," he says, "what authority the Chancellor has to make such a writ (injunction) in the king's name, and how he dare presume to make such a writ to let the king's subjects to sue his laws ; the which the king himself cannot do right wisely; for he is sworn the contrary, and it is said *hoc possumus quod de jure possumus*." [3]   He argued that the equity of the Chancellor was wholly uncertain and arbitrary ; and that the Chancellors thought the common law needed amendment, only because they were ecclesiastics, and knew not its goodness. " I perceive, by your practice, that you leave the common law of the realm, and you presume much upon your own mind, and think that your conceit is far better than the common law ; and therefore you make a bill of your conceit, and put it into the Chancery saying that it is grounded upon conscience." [4]   This pamphlet was answered by the " Little Treatise concerning Writs of Subpœna." [5]   It was argued that the Chancellor's jurisdiction was sanctioned by statute, by judicial decision, and by practice.   The cases in which a subpœna lay were detailed, and the reasonableness of granting a subpœna in each case was shown.   The frequency with which Wolsey issued injunctions was made one of the articles of his impeachment.[6]   His successor, Sir Thomas More, was a common lawyer.   He had a conference on the subject with the common law judges ; [7] and better relations between these courts and the court of Chancery were established.[8]   But the cause of dispute was still present ; and in Edward VI.'s reign the students of the common law complained to the Council of the encroachments of the Chancery.[9]

---

[1] For an account of this book see vol. v 266-269.

[2] Reply of a serjeant to the Doctor and Student, Harg. Law Tracts 323.   It was written about 1523.

[3] At p. 325.   [4] At p. 328.

[5] Harg. Law Tracts 332 ; for these pamphlets see vol. v 269-271 ; Reeves, H.E.L. iii 396-400; Kerly, Equity 90-93.

[6] Articles 20 and 21, Fourth Instit. 91, 92.

[7] More, Life of More 166.   [8] Vol. v 223-224.

[9] Dasent ii 48-50, "So it is . . . that now of late this Comen Lawes of this realme partely by injunctions, as well before verdictes jugementes, and execucions as after, and parteley by writts of Subpena issuing owte of the Kinges Courte of Chancery, hath nat been only stayed of their direct course, but also many times altrid and violated by reason of decrees made in the saide Courte of Chauncery, moste grounded upon the Lawe Civile, and apon matter depending in the conscience

At the end of Elizabeth's reign the differences became acute. A barrister was indicted under the statute of Præmunire for applying for an injunction after a judgment at common law.[1] We have seen that in that reign the common law courts had attacked the legality of the court of Requests. They could not, and did not, deny the legality of the court of Chancery; but they claimed to confine its jurisdiction within what they considered to be its legal bounds.

The matter came to a head in the reign of James I.[2] Coke decided in several cases that imprisonment for disobedience to injunctions issued by Chancery was unlawful. In one case, "it was delivered for a general maxim in law that if any court of equity doth intermeddle with any matters properly triable at the common law, or which concern freehold, they are to be prohibited."[3] So far did Coke carry his opposition that he even contended that a decree for specific performance was always unjust to the defendant because "it deprived him of his election either to pay damages or to fulfil his promise."[4] The courts of common law saw well enough that their supremacy was at stake. "If the party against whom judgment was given, might after judgment given against him at the common law, draw the matter into the Chancery, it would tend to the subversion of the common law, for that no man would sue at the common law, but originally begin in Chancery, seeing at the last he might be brought thither."[5]

On behalf of the court of Chancery it was contended that these injunctions did not interfere with the common law. The judgment stood. All that the Chancellor was concerned with was the conduct of the parties to the case in which the judgment had been given. The conduct of the parties, it was contended with some force, had never been in issue in the court of common law.[6] This view is justified by cases of the type of *Courtney* v. *Glanvil*.[7] Glanvil had sold to Courtney for £360 a jewel worth £20, and three other jewels for £100. He took a bond for the payment in the name of one Hampton, and then procured an

---

and discrecion of the hearers thereof; who being Civilians and nat lerned in the Comen Lawes, determyne the waighty causes of this realme according either to the said Lawe Civile or to their owne conscience."

[1] Spence i 675; Reeves, H.E.L. iii 735-737.
[2] Campbell, Chancellors, ii 241-245.
[3] Heath v. Rydley (1614) Cro. Jac. 335.
[4] Bromage v. Gennings (1617) 1 Rolle 368.
[5] Throckmorton v. Finch (1598) Third Instit. 124, 125.
[6] Earl of Oxford's Case (1615) 1 Ch. Rep. 1.
[7] (1615) Cro. Jac. 343; it is said in the Reports of Cases in Chancery i App. 43, "that not one judgment of a hundred is pronounced in court, nor the case so much as heard or understood by the judges, but entered by attornies."

action to be brought on the bond in Hampton's name. Judgment was by consent entered for Hampton, out of court, in the vacation, Glanvil paying all the costs. On appeal this judgment had been upheld by the courts of common law. Against its enforcement an injunction had been issued. Not, as Lord Ellesmere explained in the *Earl of Oxford's Case*, " for any error or defect in the judgment, but for the hard conscience of the party." He pointed out, in the same case, that by writs of *audita querela* the judges did in some cases " play the chancellors " by reversing a judgment given.[1]

Coke treated such reasoning as a quibble ; and he maintained that the jurisdiction claimed by the Chancellor was contrary to two statutes, the Statute of Præmunire of 1354,[2] and a statute of 1403.[3] Lord Ellesmere had little difficulty in showing, from the wording of the Statute of Præmunire, and from its connexion with preceding legislation, that it referred to those who sued in ecclesiastical courts, not to those who sued in the king's courts. It applied to the court of Rome, and to those courts which, though locally within the realm, were, in the exercise of their jurisdiction, subordinate to foreign courts.[4] The statute of 1403 caused more difficulty. It recited that after a judgment in the king's courts, parties were summoned anew sometimes before the king himself, sometimes before the King's Council, and sometimes before the Parliament. It then enacted that after such judgment the parties and their heirs should be in peace, unless the judgment were reversed by attaint or error. There was authority tending to show that the statute applied to proceedings in the court of Chancery.[5] Both in the Doctor and Student[6] and in the Treatise on the Subpœna[7] this view seems to be taken. But Lord Ellesmere argued that it applied only to matters determinable at common law by way of legal proceeding, and not to proceedings in the Chancery as a court of equity. He relied upon the fact that the Chancery was not specifically mentioned in the statute ; and he said that, if it were, it is not the judgment which is examined, but the conduct of the parties and the equity of the case.[8]

---

[1] It was urged in the Earl of Oxford's Case, 1 Ch. Rep. at p. 11, that, the judgment in that case being based on a statute, no injunction could issue. Ellesmere retorted with much effect that Coke himself in Bonham's case had said (8 Co. Rep. 118) " that the common law can control Acts of Parliament if they are against right and reason, repugnant, or impossible to be performed."

[2] 27 Edward III. St. 1 c. 1.   [3] 4 Henry IV. c. 23.

[4] Selden also took this view, see his Table Talk (Ed. Reynolds) 153.

[5] Beck v. Hesill (Hy. VI.) Cal. ii *xii.*

[6] Bk. i c. 18.   [7] Harg. Law Tracts 348.

[8] Earl of Oxford's Case 1 Ch. Rep. at pp. 10, 15. But the tract on the Office of the Chancellor 49, 50, and another tract, called a Treatise on the Privileges and Prerogatives of the High Court of Chancery (vol. v 271), take the other view.

James I. referred the matter to Bacon, then Attorney-General, and other counsel, to advise. They advised that there was a strong current of authority since the reign of Henry VII. in favour of the issue of injunctions after judgment, and even after execution; that there were cases in which the judges themselves had advised the parties to seek relief in Chancery;[1] and that the practice was not contrary to the statute[2] of 1403. In accordance with their opinion, James issued, on 26 July, 1616, an order in favour of the Chancery.[3] It may be that the decision was slightly tinged by political considerations. The common law judges, especially Coke, were already tending to manifest an independence opposed to James's absolutist claims. The Chancellor, as a minister of state, was more favourable to these claims.[4] But, considering the rigidity of the practice of the courts of common law at that period, it cannot be said that the views for which the Chancellor contended were unreasonable.

Though the controversy was in fact settled by James's order it lingered on during the rest of the seventeenth century. Parliament and the common lawyers were old allies, so that it was only natural that, when Parliament triumphed, the common lawyers should seek to reopen it. It was said in 1655 that, in the Long Parliament, the House of Lords had decided that the statute of 1403 applied to proceedings in Chancery;[5] and in 1658 the court of Exchequer heard a two days' argument, on the subject.[6] After the Restoration the controversy was again heard of both in the courts and in Parliament. In 1670 proceedings were taken upon the statute of Præmunire, and the case was adjourned to the Exchequer Chamber; but Hale thought that the statute did not apply, and the matter was dropped.[7] In 1673

---

[1] Reports of Cases in Chancery i App. 11, 12; cp. Smith v. Crokew, Star Chamber Cases (C.S.) 38.

[2] Reports of Cases in Chancery 14-25.

[3] Ibid 26, " We do will and command that our Chancellor or Keeper of the Great Seal for the time being, shall not hereafter desist to give unto our subjects, upon their several complaints now or hereafter to be made, such relief in equity (notwithstanding any proceedings at the common law against them) as shall stand with the merit and justice of their cause, and with the former ancient and continued practice and presidency of our Chancery; " there is no doubt that James I. was only too glad of the chance to assert his prerogative. In 1609 he referred with much complacency to his action in this matter, " As God contains the sea within his bounds and marches so is it my office to make every court contain himself within his own limits. And therefore I gave admonition to both sides; to the other courts that they should be careful hereafter to contain themselves within the bounds of their own jurisdiction; and to the courts of common law that they should not be so forward and prodigal in granting their prohibitions," Speech at Whitehall, Works 534-535.

[4] Ellesmere's bias in favour of high prerogative views comes out strongly in his treatment of James Whitelock, Liber Famelicus (C.S.) 33-41; vol. v. 231-232.

[5] Morel v. Duglas, Hardres 23.

[6] Harris v. Colliton, Hardres 120-125.

[7] King v. Standish, 1 Mod. 59.

an application was made for a writ of Prohibition to the court of
Chancery based on the statute of 1403, and Hale directed that
the case should be set down for further argument.[1]   In 1676-
1677 the House of Commons took a hand in the controversy.
It passed a resolution against the extraordinary jurisdiction exercised by the Chancery in matters determinable by the common
law, and directed that a bill should be brought in to restrain it.[2]
Naturally at the Revolution a determined effort was made to
legislate on the lines approved of by the common lawyers.   In
1690 a bill was introduced into the House of Lords with this object.[3]   The bill recited Magna Carta and the statute of 1403, and
declared that, by the action of the Chancery in drawing before
them causes determinable at common law, "the common laws
were subverted and in danger of being totally destroyed, and all
men's estates and property brought to arbitrary determination."
It then proceeded to enact that no court of equity should entertain any suit for which the proper remedy was at common law ; [4]
that no injunction should be issued unless sufficient security was
given for satisfying all damages sustained by reason of its issue ; [5]
and that the common law courts should have power to issue
writs of Prohibition to restrain the court of Chancery if it exceeded its jurisdiction "and encroached upon the laws." [6]   Both
the judges and the commissioners of the great seal were heard
by the House of Lords upon the bill.   All the judges supported
it ; [7] but the commissioners succeeded in showing that, if carried,
it would render the administration of equity wholly unworkable ;
and that, if the administration of equity was thus stopped, very
great hardships and injustices would arise, which the law would
be powerless to prevent.[8]   Consequently the bill was dropped ; and,
though other bills were a little later introduced into the House
of Lords to reform other abuses existing in the court of Chancery,[9] no further proposals were made to reverse by statute
James I.'s order in favour of Chancery.   The last protest made

[1] King v. Welby, T. Raym. 227.
[2] Comm. Journals ix 388 ; cf. Marvel's Letters, Works ii 513.
[3] Hist. MSS. Com. Thirteenth Rep. App. Pt. V. 128 no. 304.
[4] § 1.   [5] § 2.   [6] § 3.   [7] See pp. 134-135, 136.
[8] Thus, Sir A. Keck one of the commissioners of the great seal said that he
looked upon the bill as "a perfect shutting up of Chancery," p. 137 ; and he gave
the following illustrations of the consequences which might ensue if it became law :
" If you have a bailee, and he received £1000 and the bailiff dies, it is lost unless
the Chancery relieve you ; the judges cannot unless they forfeit their oaths.   A man
has bonds ; his house is burnt and the bonds are lost.   He sues in Chancery.   No ;
say the judges, this the king's bench has prohibited to other inferior courts.   They
have granted a prohibition in this case. . . . There are frauds of several sorts.
Barney of Norfolk ; £70,000 bargains drawn into in one year.   These frauds cannot
be examined at common law," at p. 138.
[9] Above 435-436 ; see Luttrell's Diary ii 620 (1692) ; iv 183 (1696-1697).

by a common lawyer was contained in a pamphlet by Sir Robert Atkyns, late Chief Baron of the Exchequer, in which it was maintained that the common law courts could and ought to restrain equitable interference with their jurisdiction by the issue of writs of Prohibition.[1]

From that time the jurisdiction of the court of Chancery to issue injunctions was not contested. Bacon's Orders had laid down certain conditions as to their issue.[2] With the improvement in the procedure and practice of the common law courts they came to be productive of much inconvenience. The court of Chancery liberally issued them with an eye, as Roger North hints, to the profits accruing,[3] and in the seventeenth century[4] and later[5] they were used by litigants to delay justice. Lord Cottenham in 1837[6] stated that, though necessary in some cases, they gave rise to as much injustice as they promoted justice.

(3) The modern development of the equitable jurisdiction.

It was during the latter part of the seventeenth, and during the eighteenth, and beginning of the nineteenth centuries that the principles of the equitable jurisdiction became fixed. To this period we must look for the modern principles of equity. This has been clearly pointed out by Jessel, M.R.[7] "It must not be forgotten," he said, "that the rules of equity are not, like the rules of the common law, supposed to have been established from time immemorial. It is perfectly well known that they have been established from time to time—altered, improved, and refined from time to time. In many cases we know the name of the Chancellor who invented them. . . . Take such things as these: the separate use of a married woman, the restraint on alienation, the modern rule against perpetuities, and the rules of equitable waste. We can name the Chancellors who first invented them, and state the date when they were first introduced into equity jurisprudence; and, therefore, in cases of this kind, the older precedents in equity are of very little value. The doctrines are progressive, refined, and improved; and if we want

---

[1] An enquiry into the jurisdiction of the court of Chancery in causes of equity; for Atkyns see vol. vi 515-516, 671.
[2] Orders 20-28.   [3] Lives of the Norths i 261, 262.
[4] North, ibid iii 55, tells us a curious tale in this connexion of Nicolas Barbon, a speculative builder; he could not afford to borrow at 10 per cent. so he bought goods on credit, and put off paying for them as long as possible; if sued he drew out the proceedings as long as possible and among other expedients he brought a bill in Chancery for an injunction; the amount he ultimately paid in costs was "seldom more than half the charge of borrowing."
[5] Below 635.
[6] Brown v. Newell, 2 My. and Cr. at p. 570.
[7] In re Hallett's estate (1879) 13 C.D. at p. 710.

to know what the rules of equity are, we must look, of course, rather to the more modern than the more ancient cases."

Those doctrines were gradually created and elaborated, as they are at the present day being elaborated, by decided cases. If we look at White and Tudor's leading cases and the notes attached to them, we can see how a leading case lays down a general principle, and how that principle has been modified or extended in its application to varied states of fact. It is in this way, for instance, that the various incidents of the equity of redemption, together with the doctrines of tacking and consolidation have been elaborated. It is in this way that the greater part of the law of partnership, the law as to the administration of the estates of deceased persons, the law as to the separate estate of married women have grown up. Roughly we can classify as follows the various subjects with which equity deals :—[1]

(1) Jurisdiction connected with forms of property recognized in equity.

Under this head fall trusts and powers ; the married woman's separate estate, the restraint on anticipation, and equity to a settlement ; the mortgagor's equity of redemption including the doctrines of tacking and consolidation ; equitable mortgages ; the vendor's lien ; equitable waste.

(2) Jurisdiction over contract or wrongful acts.

Under this head fall specific performance and injunction.

(3) Relief against the rigidity of the law.

Under this head fall relief against penalties ; fraud and undue influence ; accident and mistake.

(4) Jurisdiction acquired by reason of the convenience of procedure of the court.

Under this head fall the administration of the estates of deceased persons, and subjects connected therewith, such as legacies, marshalling of assets, election and conversion ; sureties ; account ; partnership ; set off ; discovery.

(5) Guardianship of infants.

The growth of the equitable jurisdiction was during this period influenced by two sets of causes.

(i) It was modified by external circumstances.

In the first place it was modified by the changes incidental to all progress. " New discoveries and inventions in commerce," wrote Lord Hardwicke,[2] "have given birth to new species of contracts, and these have been followed by new contrivances to break and elude them, for which the ancient simplicity of the

---

[1] See Kerly, Equity 191-263.
[2] Hardwicke's letter to Lord Kames, cited Parkes, App. 501-510.

common law had adopted no remedies; and from this cause courts of equity, which admit of a greater latitude, have, under the head adjuvandi vel supplendi juris civilis, been obliged to accommodate the wants of mankind. . . . Another source of the increase of business in courts of equity has been the multiplication and extension of trusts. New methods of settling and encumbering landed property have been suggested by the necessities, extravagance, or real occasions of mankind. But what is more than this, new species of property have been introduced, particularly by the establishment of the public funds, and various transferable stocks, that required to be modified and settled to answer the exigencies of families, to which the rules and methods of conveying provided by the common law would not ply or bend."

In the second place, it was modified by the changes which these same influences were making in the common law. The common law had lost much of its rigidity by the introduction, chiefly under the influence of Lord Mansfield, of principles which, as Blackstone has pointed out,[1] were similar to those which had prevailed in courts of equity since the time of Lord Nottingham (1673-1682).[2] Lord Mansfield may in some cases have gone further in this direction than the law warranted;[3] but he gave to the common law a bias in favour of what Blackstone calls "liberality of sentiment," which made unnecessary much of that equitable interference with common law rules, which had in former days led to the conflict between the two jurisdictions.

(ii) It was modified by a change in the character of the equitable jurisdiction itself.[4]

In early days there were no fixed principles upon which the Chancellors exercised their equitable jurisdiction. The rule applied depended very much upon the ideas as to right and wrong possessed by each Chancellor. Hence there is a considerable amount of truth in Selden's well-known aphorism. " Equity is a roguish thing. For law we have a measure . . . equity is according to the conscience of him that is Chancellor,

[1] Comm. iv 442.

[2] See Moses v. Macfarlan (1760), 2 Burr. 1005; in Eaton v. Jaques (1780), Dougl. 438, Lord Mansfield recognized the existence of an equity of redemption—a decision promptly overruled by his successor, Lord Kenyon.

[3] Eaton v. Jaques; Phillips v. Hunter (1795) 2 H. Bl. 402, 414; Marriot v. Hampton (1797) 7 T.R. 269; Atkins v. Hill (1775) Cowper 284; Hawkes v. Saunders (1782) ibid 289. " The Court of King's Bench," wrote Junius (Letter xli), " becomes a court of equity, and the judge instead of consulting strictly the law of the land, refers only to the wisdom of the court, and to the purity of his own conscience." There was just enough truth in this description to make it an effective caricature of Lord Mansfield's work, see vol. vii 19-20, 43-46.

[4] For a full account of the gradual modification of equity see vol. v 336-338; vol. vi 668-671.

and as that is larger or narrower, so is equity. 'Tis all one as if they should make the standard for the measure a Chancellor's foot." But in the latter half of the seventeenth century it is clear that the principles of equity were beginning to gain in fixity. Cases decided in the court of Chancery were beginning to be reported,[1] and those cases were cited as authorities and followed. This tendency increased in strength throughout the eighteenth century. The Chancellors themselves admitted that, though they had a discretion, this discretion ought to be exercised in accordance with precedent.[2] Lord Hardwicke, though he claimed for the Chancellor a discretion to judge according to the circumstances—otherwise there might arise a claim for equitable relief even against decrees in equity—distinctly stated that general rules were absolutely necessary to guide the judge's discretion.[3] Blackstone, looking at the older authorities, could say that as equity depended "essentially upon the particular circumstances of each individual case, there could be no established rules and fixed precepts laid down, without destroying its very essence."[4] On the other hand, looking at the administration of equity in his own day, he was forced to admit that it was "a laboured connected system, governed by established rules, and bound down by precedents, from which they do not depart, although the reason for some of them may perhaps be liable to objection."[5]

This change in the character of equity was completed by Lord Eldon. The peculiar characteristics of his mind, which led to so many delays in his court,[6] made him peculiarly fit to settle the principles of equity. He had a thorough grasp of existing rules and principles; but he looked as anxiously into all the facts and circumstances of each case that came before him as if there were no such rules, and as if, therefore, he was under the necessity of determining each case as one of first impression. This being the case, it is not surprising that his decisions have permanently defined the course of the development of many principles of equity. "The doctrines of this court," he said,[7] "ought to be as well settled, and made as uniform, *almost*, as those of the common law, laying down fixed principles, but taking care that they are to be applied according to the circumstances of each case. I cannot agree that the doctrines of this court are to be changed by every succeeding judge. Nothing

---

[1] See vol. v 274-278; vol. vi 616-619 for some account of the history of the equity reports.
[2] See e.g. Cowper v. Cowper (1734) 2 P. Wms. at p. 686 *per* Jekyll, M.R.
[3] Letter to Lord Kames, cited Parkes, Chancery App. 501-510.
[4] Comm. i 61-62.   [5] Ibid iii 432.   [6] Above 437-438.
[7] Gee v. Pritchard (1818) 2 Swanst. at p. 414.

would inflict on me greater pain in quitting this place, than the recollection that I had done anything to justify the reproach that the equity of this court varies like the Chancellor's foot." Lord Eldon realized this ideal—no one could cast this reproach at him. On the contrary, as Mr. Kerly has said,[1] "Equity, when Lord Eldon retired was no longer a system corrective of the common law: it could be described only as that part of remedial justice which is administered in Chancery, while, taken generally, its work was administrative and protective, in contrast with that of the common law, which was remedial and retributive." Hence in the nineteenth century many of the doctrines of equity, like many of the doctrines of the common law, have been restated in codifying Acts.[2] Both alike have attained the certainty of statute law.

Other Branches of Jurisdiction

From a very early date the practice has prevailed of conferring upon the Chancellor special jurisdiction under special statutes. We find instances of this at all periods in the history of the court. In the Middle Ages he was given a special jurisdiction to punish the misdemeanours of sheriffs and other officers,[3] and of purveyors,[4] and to enforce the statutes against those who sued at Rome in respect of matters cognizable in the king's courts;[5] to punish those who received children under fourteen into any of the Orders of Friars without their parents' consent;[6] to grant a special assize to try cases of forcible entries;[7] to issue process for the arrest of felons who had fled into unknown places;[8] to try cases of robbery committed by subjects upon alien friends, on the sea, or in any port within the realm.[9] At a later period various and heterogeneous powers still continued to be conferred upon him. We may take as instances, an Act for settling tithes to be paid in the City of London after the fire,[10] the Habeas Corpus Amendment Act,[11] arbitrations,[12] Jews,[13] Friendly Societies;[14] and canal, navigation, enclosure and tramway acts often added further special powers.[15]

The two most permanent and important branches of this

---

[1] Equity 167.

[2] Instances are the Partnership Act of 1890, and the Trustee Acts of 1888 and 1893.

[3] 20 Edward III. c. 6.

[4] 36 Edward III. c. 9.

[5] 27 Edward III. St. 1 c. 1; 38 Edward III. c. 1.

[6] 4 Henry IV. c. 17.

[7] Ibid c. 8; 13 Henry IV. c. 7.

[8] 2 Henry V. St. 1 c. 9.

[9] 31 Henry VI. c. 4.

[10] 22, 23 Charles II. c. 15 § 12.

[11] 31 Charles II. c. 2.

[12] 9, 10 William III. c. 15 § 2.

[13] 1 Anne St. 1 c. 30.

[14] 33 George III. c. 54.

[15] Parkes, Chancery 424-427.

miscellaneous jurisdiction are the jurisdiction in Bankruptcy, and the jurisdiction in Lunacy.

(1) Bankruptcy.[1]

It is sometimes said that the law of bankruptcy dates from an Act of 1542.[2]   But the object of this Act was rather the prevention of frauds upon creditors than the establishment of a law of bankruptcy.   It was an Act of Elizabeth's reign which introduced a law of bankruptcy, and drew the main lines of that law as it existed for some centuries.[3]   It applied the law only to traders ; it defined what should be regarded as acts of bankruptcy ; and it gave to the Chancellor power to appoint, by commission under the great seal, certain persons to exercise the powers of the Chancellor over the person and property of the bankrupt. The Act gave no jurisdiction in bankruptcy to the court of Chancery.   It gave the Chancellor no control over the commissioners.   If they were in any legal difficulty they usually applied in the seventeenth century to the common law courts. There is no instance of an application to the Chancellor before 1676 ; but after that date the practice of so applying became frequent.[4]   Certain statutory alterations in practice made in Anne's reign united the Chancellor more closely to the bankruptcy jurisdiction.   A statute of 1705[5] introduced the bankrupt's certificate of discharge, and provided that when granted, it should be allowed by the Chancellor, or by any two judges to whom he might refer it.   Till Lord Hardwicke's time (1737-1757) he usually did refer it to the judges.[6]   A statute of 1707[7] introduced assignees chosen by the creditor, to whom the commissioners were required to assign all the bankrupt's effects.   They were subject to the Chancellor's equitable jurisdiction as trustees on a bill being filed against them in the ordinary way.   A statute of 1732[8] at length gave the Chancellor a direct control over bankruptcy matters.   The assignees were made officials of the great seal ; and the Chancellor was, in certain cases, empowered upon the application of the creditor to remove them, or to suspend the commission.[9]

From the date of this statute the Chancellor proceeded to enlarge his jurisdiction.   Lord Hardwicke adjudicated upon

---

[1] For the early history of the law of Bankruptcy see vol. viii 229-245.
[2] 34, 35 Henry VIII. c. 4 ; cf. Coke, Fourth Instit. 277.
[3] 13 Elizabeth c. 7.   [4] C. P. Cooper, Chancery 246, 247.
[5] 4 Anne c. 17.   [6] C. P. Cooper, Chancery 248.
[7] 5 Anne c. 22.   [8] 5 George II. c. 30 § 24.
[9] The duty of the assignees was to collect the property of the bankrupt, to pay dividends, and to account for their receipts and expenditure to the commissioners, Tarleton v. Hornby (1835) 1 Yo. and Coll. 172, 191.

almost every question which a jurisdiction in bankruptcy involved.[1] The immense patronage and large fees which thereby accrued to the Chancellor, sufficiently explain the eagerness with which the jurisdiction was assumed, and the tenacity with which it was retained.[2] Though many questions arising in bankruptcy were capable of being tried, and often were sent by the Chancellor to be tried, by a court of law, it came to be thought that it would be impossible for any but the Chancellor to administer the jurisdiction.[3] The absurdity of burdening an overworked court with this mass of business is obvious ; and the evil results were increased by the method in which original jurisdiction in bankruptcy was exercised.

Original jurisdiction was exercised by commissioners. Their appointment was in the absolute control of the Chancellor ; but when appointed he had no direct control over them.[4] Their charges were high ; they fared sumptuously at the expense of the estate ; and till 1719 they did not act under the sanction of an oath.[5] In London in 1828 there were fourteen lists of commissioners.[6] Each list comprised five names and commissions were issued in rotation to each list. Out of each list three could attend and take fees. The fees which they could take for each meeting were limited by statute.[7] But the statute was evaded by the practice of short meetings and successive adjournments under each commission.[8] It is said that a skilful commissioner could manage thirty meetings in one morning. The result of this state of things was almost inconceivable. "Each of the fourteen lists was unconnected with and independent of the rest . . . one law and one practice prevailed in one list, and another in another. . . . Precedent had no binding force, and was very seldom listened to. As any three out of the five commissioners in each list might attend, the suitor was exposed, even in the same court, to a perpetual change of judge, and this not from one meeting to another, but even in the course of the same meeting. The three commissioners assembled under a number, sometimes a great number of different commissions at once. Their attention was solicited at one and the same moment by many suitors, all equally pressing, and entitled to despatch upon their respective cases ; and these often involving many nice questions

---

[1] C. P. Cooper, Chancery 250.
[2] In 1826 the fees paid to the Lord Chancellor were £12,601 6s. 4d. ; Lord Eldon at first doubted his moral right to touch these fees ; but after consideration he overcame his scruples, Campbell, Chancellors vii 675 n.
[3] Report of the Chancery Commission of 1826 35.
[4] C. P. Cooper, Chancery 245, 260.   [5] Ibid 265-270.
[6] The lists were established about 1714, ibid 261-265.
[7] 5 George II. c. 30 § 42.   [8] C. P. Cooper, Chancery 267, 268.

wit;" their lands and tenements are to be kept without waste, and " they and their household shall live and be maintained completely with the profits of the same; and the residue . . . shall be kept to their use to be delivered unto them when they come to right mind; so that such lands and tenements shall in no wise be claimed within the time aforesaid; and the king shall take nothing to his own use; and if the party die in such estate, then the residue shall be distributed for his soul by the advice of the Ordinary." [1]

It appears from these two clauses that the law divided those of unsound mind into two classes—the idiot and the lunatic. [2] In the former case the right of guardianship was a profitable right analogous to the right of wardship: in the latter case it was in the nature of a duty, and no profit could be made from it. This distinction is recognized by the cases. [3] Blackstone mentions the income of idiots' estates as a source of revenue; but the " clemency of the crown and the pity of the juries " gradually assimilated the condition of idiots to that of lunatics. [4]

The statute mentions only the " the lands and tenements " of the persons of unsound mind. It was doubtful when Staunford wrote whether the prerogative extended to chattels real or personal. [5] At the beginning of the seventeenth century it had been extended to chattels real and personal, [6] but not to copyholds. [7] But it was extended to all classes of property, including copyholds, when the guardianship began to partake of the nature of a duty rather than a right. [8]

Jurisdiction over those of unsound mind, being regarded in early times as a valuable right, was vested originally in the Exchequer. [9] As it came to be regarded in the light of a duty it passed to the Chancellor. His jurisdiction rests upon two bases. (i) It rests upon the share which he took in issuing the

---

[1] Prærogativa Regis § 10.

[2] Bl. Comm. i 292, 294—" The idiot is one that hath had no understanding from his nativity ; " the lunatic " is one who hath had understanding, but . . . hath lost the use of his reason." For the different terms applied by the older writers to express these conceptions, see Pope, Lunacy (Ed. 1877) 10-15. Difficulties sometimes arose in the case of those whom the commission could not find of unsound mind, but who were obviously incapable of managing their own affairs, Sherwood v. Sanderson (1815) 19 Ves. 280; Ex parte Cranmer (1806) 12 Ves. 445 ; cp. the definition contained in 16, 17 Victoria c. 70 § 2.

[3] Frances' Case (1545) Moore 4; Prodgers v. Frazier (1684) 3 Mod. 43; Corporation of Burford v. Lenthall (1743) 2 Atk. 553; Lysaght v. Royse (1804) 2 Sch. and Lef. 153 ; for specimens of the crown grants of the custody of lunatics and idiots see West, Symboleography (Ed. 1615) §§ 365, 368, 369, 370.

[4] Pope, Lunacy 24.   [5] Prerogative 36

[6] Beverley's Case (1603) 4 Co. Rep. at f. 126 a.

[7] (1571) Dyer 302 b; Beverley's Case at f. 126 b.

[8] Scriven Copyholds (Ed. 1846) 52.

[9] Mem. Scacc. Trin. 19 Ed. I. (cited Pope, Lunacy 25).

writs necessary to enquire into the alleged insanity. All proceedings connected with the issue of this writ, and the conduct
of the enquiry under it, formed part of the common law jurisdiction of the court of Chancery; and an appeal lay to the
House of Lords.[1] (ii) The more important part of his jurisdiction rests upon an express delegation by the crown of the
crown's powers and duties over those of unsound mind to the
Chancellor personally.[2] This delegation might equally well
have been made to any other great officer of state; and, while
the court of Wards (1539-1660) was in existence, the jurisdiction
was generally exercised by it.[3] The fact that after 1660 the
delegation was almost always[4] made to the Chancellor, is due,
partly to his position as a great officer of state, responsible for
the issue of the commission, partly to his position as the leading
legal member of the Council. It was to the Council that a
person of unsound mind so found by inquisition could originally
appeal; and from the Chancellor it was to the Council and not
to the House of Lords that lunacy appeals originally lay.[5]

By virtue of this express delegation the Chancellor appoints
the committee for the lunatic, and is under the duty of seeing
that the committee duly administers the lunatic's property. This
jurisdiction has nothing whatever to do with the jurisdiction
exercised by him as the judge of the court of Chancery. "Unsoundness of mind gives the court of Chancery no jurisdiction
whatever. It is not like infancy in that respect. The court of
Chancery is by law the guardian of infants whom it makes its
wards. The court of Chancery is not the curator either of the
person or the estate of a person *non compos mentis*, whom it does
not, and cannot make its ward. . . . It can no more take upon
itself the management and disposition of a lunatic's property,
than it can the management and disposition of the property of a

---

[1] Y.B. 17 Ed. III. (R.S.) 186; F.N.B. 233; Bl. Comm. iii 427; Re Fitz-Gerald
(1805) 2 Sch. and Lef. 436, 437.

[2] "The law has given the custody of him and all that he has to the king, who
is bound of right by his laws to defend his subjects, and their goods and chattels,
lands and tenements; and because every subject is in the king's protection; an
idiot who cannot defend nor govern himself, nor order his lands and tenements, goods
and chattels, the king by right ought to have him, and to order him, his lands, goods
and chattels," Beverley's Case (1603) 4 Co. Rep. at f. 126 a; Tourson's Case (1611)
8 Co. Rep. 170 a.

[3] In some of the earlier warrants to the Chancellor it is stated that the reason
for giving him this jurisdiction is that the court of Wards is abolished, and that he
is the person who issues the writs to enquire into the insanity, S.P. Dom. 1660-1661
328-329, xix 89; ibid 1667 456, ccxvi 141; 1689-1690 19.

[4] In Wigg v. Tiler (1779) 2 Dick 552 several instances are cited in which the
warrant was addressed to the Lord High Treasurer; for the warrant see Campbell,
Chancellors i 15.

[5] 3 P. Wms. 108 n., citing a resolution of the House of Lords in 1726; for the
provisions of the Judicature Act see below 643.

person abroad, or confined to his bed by illness. The court can only exercise such equitable jurisdiction as it could under the same circumstances have exercised at the suit of the person himself if of sound mind." [1]

It was through the control exercised by the Chancellor, as the delegate of the crown, over the lunatic's committee, that the rules as to the management of the property of lunatics have grown up.[2] The underlying principle of these rules is the interest of the lunatic. "Therefore the Chancellor is to administer the estate *tanquam bonus paterfamilias*, taking every advantage fairly to increase and improve it without engaging in risks and hazardous adventures. . . . Whatever tends towards ordinary improvement it is strictly the duty of the administrator to do, considering only the immediate interest of the proprietor of the estate." [3]

The jurisdiction in lunacy was remodelled by a series of statutes consolidated by the Lunacy Act, 1890, under which the jurisdiction is exercised by the Chancellor and the Lords Justices in Chancery assisted by Masters and visitors.

[1] Beall v. Smith (1873) 9 Ch. Ap. at p. 92 *per* James, L.J.
[2] For some early cases illustrating the Chancellor's control over the committee, see S.P. Dom. 1668-1669 202-203 ; Eq. Cases Ab. i 277 (4).
[3] Oxenden v. Lord Compton (1793) 2 Ves. 73.
[4] 53, 54 Victoria c. 5 ; below 643.

CHAPTER VI

THE COUNCIL

THE Council is in the direct line of descent from the Curia Regis of the Norman and Angevin kings. We have seen that the Curia Regis was a large undifferentiated court, composed both of the leading nobility lay and spiritual and of royal officials, by means of which the king carried on all the business of the central government—judicial, legislative, and executive.[1] But we have seen that, during the Middle Ages, there was a tendency to vest these different functions of government in different bodies. The courts of Common Pleas and King's Bench had become distinct tribunals with distinct staffs and distinct rolls on which their proceedings were recorded, administering the common law by means of a limited number of original writs and a formal procedure;[2] and the court of Exchequer had split off from the Exchequer, and had become in like manner a distinct tribunal which determined litigious proceedings connected with the royal revenue.[3] To these three central courts had been entrusted the management of a large part of the judicial business of the state. A similar process had been going on with respect to legislative business. The large Councils of the nobility which, at the end of the thirteenth century, met the king and the representatives of the shires and boroughs at a Parliament, had developed into the House of Lords; and, together with the king and the House of Commons, had become the king in Parliament—the highest governmental authority in the kingdom.[4] That body had acquired by the end of the mediæval period large powers over legislation and finance;[5] and through its control over finance, large powers to criticize and control the conduct of the executive government, and, by means of an impeachment, to try and punish royal officials who broke the law.[6] Moreover it had not ceased to exercise a number of judicial powers, which had belonged to it in the days when the king in his Council in Parliament was regarded as an enlarged meeting of the old undifferentiated

---

[1] Above 35, 39.
[2] Above 195-196, 204-211.
[3] Above 231-237.
[4] Above 352-353, 355-362.
[5] Vol. ii 435-440.
[6] Above 379-385.

Curia Regis. But, as the House of Lords was more immediately connected with this aspect of the Parliament, these powers had come to be exercised by that House ; and, conversely, as it was now part of the Parliament—the body which exercised the legislative power in the state—it had come to be regarded as the court which ought to hear complaints of errors committed by those courts of common law to which the duty of declaring the law had been entrusted.[1] Such a power of finally declaring the law should, it was thought, be entrusted to the body which as a part of the Parliament made law, and not to an executive Council which was concerned mainly with the application and enforcement of the law.[2]

Thus, by the end of the mediæval period, the Council was coming to be thought of mainly as an executive body. But as yet the boundaries between executive functions on the one hand, and judicial and legislative functions on the other, were very indistinct. We shall see in later volumes, that it was not till the seventeenth century that the legislative and fiscal powers of the king and Council were precisely defined.[3] Here we are concerned with the judicial powers which the Council still retained. These were both large and vague. That they were so large and so vague is due mainly to the fact that there were a large number of cases with which the common law could not deal effectively. We have seen[4] that cases which turned upon questions outside the jurisdiction of the common law courts, cases in which the king's interests were affected, cases in which the process of the common law courts could not act effectively, and cases in which the law itself was at fault, were all brought before the Council. They were brought before the Council because it was now the body in immediate contact with the king—the body through which he carried on the work of government. It could for that reason safeguard the interests of king and state ; and it was naturally employed by the king to exercise his prerogative of doing justice to all his subjects in cases in which the ordinary law or the ordinary courts were not able to do it. It is for this reason that the cases which came before the Council sometimes suggested reforms in the law which were carried out by subsequent statutes.[5]

We have seen that at the end of the fifteenth and during the

---

[1] Above 360-361.   [2] Above 361.
[3] Vol. iv 99-105 ; vol. vi 31, 41-49, 112, 251-254.   [4] Above 405-407.
[5] Baldwin, Select Cases before the Council (S.S.) xiv, xv—it is there pointed out that " the case of *Sabina* v. *Bedewynde* (p. 18), in connexion with others of the same kind, led directly to the statute of provisors. *Rex* v. *Middleton* (p. 35) has little value as a question of law, but it was connected with an extensive reform in the appointment of sheriffs and escheators. *Ughtred* v. *Musgrave* (p. 54) was a step in the gradual diminution of the judicial powers of the sheriffs."

course of the sixteenth centuries one branch of this wide jurisdiction was beginning to detach itself, and to become vested in a separate court of Chancery.[1] That court was becoming separate from the Council, and was taking over the jurisdiction to administer justice in cases when the law itself was at fault. But a wide jurisdiction was still left to the Council. It is true that that jurisdiction had aroused the hostility both of the common law courts and of Parliament in the Middle Ages. But we shall see[2] that, though that hostility had done something to limit its jurisdiction in one or two important particulars, it had not succeeded in accurately defining its limits. Hence, when the Tudors began their work of restoring peace to the country, and of making England a territorial state of the modern type, they were able to use the wide jurisdiction still possessed by the Council to effect these objects. Gradually, under pressure of the large amount of judicial work which was thus placed upon the Council, it began to split into two—a judicial court, and an administrative Council. When acting as judicial court it usually sat in the building in the palace of Westminster called the Starred Chamber ; and hence it got the name of the court of Star Chamber.[3] Under the Tudors that court was largely instrumental in restoring good government to the country.[4] But, under the Stuarts, when the nation was divided into two political parties—the party which supported the king and the party which supported the Parliament—the court of Star Chamber naturally came to be used as the most efficient engine of prerogative government. The Parliamentary party tried in vain to dispute the legality of the court ;[5] but, when their hour of triumph came in 1641, they abolished the jurisdiction of the Council in England.[6] The Council was thus deprived of the greater part of its jurisdiction—but not of all. It could still exercise jurisdiction over the dominions of the crown outside England ;[7] and, in the eighteenth century, this jurisdiction so expanded with the expansion of these dominions, that, in the nineteenth century, it became necessary to vest it in a statutory Judicial Committee.[8] To this Committee other pieces of jurisdiction have been assigned by later statutes ;[9] and it exists to-day as the direct lineal descendant of that Curia Regis from which, as from a parent stem, the other institutions of the English central government have sprung.

---

[1] Above 408-409.
[2] Below 486-488.
[3] Below 496.
[4] Below 507-508.
[5] Below 512-513.
[6] Below 515.
[7] Below 516, 520-522.
[8] Below 518.
[9] Below 524.

This summary shows that the history of the Council falls into four well defined chronological periods: the Middle Ages; the Tudor period; the early Stuart period; and the later history.

I. THE MIDDLE AGES [1]

(1) The composition of the Council.

We have seen that in the twelfth century the meetings of the Curia Regis consisted, sometimes of a few officials with perhaps one or two of the greater nobility lay or spiritual; sometimes of a larger body of officials and magnates.[2]   In the earlier years of the reign of Henry III. much the same conditions prevailed. The Council " was anything but an organized or even a stable body.   It consisted rather of a shifting group of bishops, barons, and officers, as many as happened to be present or as could be induced at the time to come." [3]   But, later in the reign, the disputes which arose between the king and his barons set in motion causes which tended to make the Council a more defined body.[4] Henry wished for a Council composed of officials and foreigners devoted to his interests.[5]   The great barons, on the other hand, regarded themselves as having an inherent right to hold the high offices of state, and to be summoned to the Council.   Reforms in the Council therefore figured prominently in their demands;[6] and the idea of a sworn Council consisting of certain definite persons began to take shape.[7]   Such a Council was provided for by the Provisions of Oxford,[8] and after the victory of the barons at Lewes.[9]   After the defeat of Simon de Montfort in 1265 the Council seems to have reverted to the somewhat formless condition which had characterized it at the beginning of the reign;[10] but, before the end of the reign, there is again a definite body of sworn counsellors.[11]

During the first three-quarters of the fourteenth century the

---

[1] On this subject the best authority is now Professor J. F. Baldwin's able and exhaustive treatise on The King's Council in England during the Middle Ages; the last chapter of that book deals with the beginnings of the revival of the Council in the earlier years of the Tudor period.

[2] Above 35.   [3] Baldwin, op. cit. 20.

[4] See Baldwin, Select Cases before the Council (S.S.) xvi, xvii.

[5] Baldwin, op. cit. 24; it is there pointed out that Henry was not wholly capricious, but that he wished "to secure a class of office-holders and counsellors who should be detached from the interests of the barons;" that among the foreigners there were many able administrators, and that he promoted Englishmen who had gained experience in the Curia Regis, and who were dependent on himself.

[6] Ibid 25-27.

[7] See ibid 28-29 for such a scheme outlined in 1244.

[8] Sel. Ch. 388.   [9] Ibid 412-414.   [10] Baldwin, op. cit. 35.

[11] Ibid 35-36—as Professor Baldwin points out, " on previous occasions, so far as we can be sure, the Council had been sworn under pressure of the barons, but now the oath appears as a normal part of the king's government."

Council gradually became a distinct body, separate from the common law courts on the one side, and from Parliament on the other. But its membership was as yet somewhat heterogeneous.[1] It included the great officers of state, such as the Chancellor and the Treasurer; officers of the household, such as the chamberlain and the keeper of the wardrobe; a number of professional lawyers or members of the civil service, such as the judges, certain of the serjeants-at-law, barons of the Exchequer, clerks of the Chancery, escheators, and civil and canon lawyers; occasionally foreigners who were made members for special reasons;[2] a certain number of knights; and a varying number of the nobility lay and ecclesiastical. The last named was a very shifting group. They were not as a rule sworn and retained of the Council like the members of the other groups.[3] But, on account of their material power, they played a very important part in shaping the history of the Council. Their interests now, as in former times, were opposed to the official classes, and to the new men raised to power by royal favour; and they constantly endeavoured to remove them.[4] They got their way in 1310, when the Lords Ordainers were commissioned to remove the king's evil councillors; and in 1316, when it was proposed that the king's Council should consist of a number of prelates, earls, and barons. But government by royal favourites continued. The Dispencers were driven from power by the barons; and finally the king himself was deposed.[5] There were similar struggles throughout the reign of Edward III.;[6] but, in fact, the main work of the Council continued to be done, in this as in the preceding reign, by the official classes.[7] The magnates sometimes protested, and asserted their right to attend; but they often declined to be sworn, and in fact they attended very irregularly,[8] "so that any Council made up mainly of lords and depending upon their support fell to pieces almost as soon as it was formed."[9]

From the close of Edward III.'s reign several circumstances combined to make membership of the Council less heterogeneous. In the first place Parliamentary control became closer. The first

---

[1] Baldwin, op. cit. 69-92; it was not till Richard II.'s reign that the professional members became merely assistants, ibid 77, 83; and that aliens were eliminated, ibid 87.

[2] Ibid 83-87; cp. for an instance of a miscellaneous gathering in 1383, Select Cases before the Council (S.S.) 72.

[3] Baldwin, op. cit. 91.   [4] Ibid 93-94.   [5] Ibid 94-98.   [6] Ibid 98-101.

[7] "Among them (the councillors) there is always to be found a faithful working group with strongly marked official tendencies," ibid 102; as Tout says, Place of Edward II. in English History 29, "The king's court was not a mere fortuitous aggregation of disconnected incompetent courtiers, but a solidly organized institution with traditions of government and influence."

[8] Baldwin, op. cit. 100, 101.   [9] Ibid 100.

impeachment dates from the Good Parliament of 1376, and henceforward Parliament endeavoured in various ways—by legislation and petition—to control the composition and the powers of the Council.[1] In the second place the minority of Richard II. necessitated a closer definition of the Council. In 1377, the day after Richard's coronation, "the entire Council was for the first time given a commission by letters patent," and later all were sworn in the king's presence.[2] In the third place, when Richard attained his majority, the old struggle between the royal favourites and officials on the one side, and the barons on the other began again, and only ended with the deposition of the king.[3] All these influences made for a clearer definition of the Council.[4] Its members began to be marked off from the general body of the nobility on the one side, and from officials like the judges, who became merely assistants, on the other. The councillors were all sworn, and, under Richard II. and the first two Lancastrians, some or all of them were sometimes paid.[5] Moreover, the first two Lancastrian kings accepted the principle that the Council must consist partly of the nobility, partly of influential commoners, and partly of officials.[6] We shall see that this settlement is marked and illustrated by the beginnings of attempts to keep a separate record of the Council's proceedings.[7] It is thus clear that by the end of the reign of Henry V. a definite Council had emerged very different in character from the more vaguely constituted bodies of an earlier period.[8]

[1] Baldwin, op. cit. 116; for some of these legislative Ordinances see ibid 131—Ordinance of 1390; ibid 158—Ordinance of 1406; ibid 174—Ordinances of 1424, 1426, 1430.

[2] Ibid 120.   [3] Ibid 126-144.

[4] "The general result thus far, both of the parliamentary and the royalist influences, was to make the Council a body more narrowly circumscribed and exclusive than it had been before. The lords were accustomed to be sworn and to take up their duties as councillors with seriousness, while the relations of the justices, serjeants, and doctors of law were satisfactorily defined. The Council also in its personnel and methods was made a political question, and so was drawn into the light of publicity and criticism," ibid 146.

[5] Earlier some of the professional members and some of the knights had been paid, ibid 72, 88-89; in 1378 a system of daily wages for all councillors was instituted, ibid 123; the payment of salaries was suggested by the Commons in 1404, ibid 157; but they were not generally paid in Henry V.'s reign, ibid 165.

[6] See ibid 156 for the list of councillors in 1406; but later in Henry IV. and Henry V.'s reign the nobility predominated, ibid 162, 165-166.

[7] Below 490; and see vol. v 161-162 for an account of the history of these records.

[8] We read in the authorities of what apparently were different kinds of councils existing in the fourteenth century. Thus we have a "privatum," a "secretum," a "magnum," and an "ordinarium" consilium; and many authors have tried to distinguish them. But, as Professor Baldwin points out, we have mention also of a "bonum" consilium, a "sapiens" consilium, a "totum" consilium, a "plenum" consilium, a "commune" consilium, "and the list could be extended indefinitely if the French language also were taken into account." He concludes that in the Middle Ages all these terms were merely epithets—"the main fact, which takes away

The minority of Henry VI. led to an increase in the Parliamentary control over the powers and composition of the Council, and made it, during the whole period of that minority, a very strictly defined body.[1] It usually consisted of the five great officers of state—the Chancellor, the Lord Treasurer, the Keeper of the Privy Seal, the Chamberlain, and the Steward of the Household—the Archbishops of Canterbury and York, and from ten to fifteen other members.[2] Besides these regular members of the Council, others distinguished for their knowledge of the law, or other special branches of knowledge, were occasionally summoned.[3] It was only those who had taken a special oath who were the regular members of the Council. We have seen that these regular members had sometimes received salaries. This became the rule during Henry VI.'s minority; and the councillors were fined if they did not regularly attend.[4] Their position, as contrasted with that of the members occasionally summoned, is illustrated by an Ordinance of 1426.[5] That Ordinance alludes to the fact that matters discussed in the Council had been published, and provides that "no person, of what condition or degree that he be, be suffered to abide in the Council, while matters of the said Council be treated therein, save only those that be sworn unto the said Council, but if they be specially called thereto by authority of the said Council."

The Council, as thus constituted, governed the country. But its government was not a success. The continuance of the war with France was ruining the country; and the members of the Council used their position to profit themselves or their friends at the expense of the state.[6] The nobility procured for themselves the great offices of state,[7] to which they considered they had a natural right,[8] and carried all before them at the Council Board. Moreover the nobility and the leading commoners were split up into factions which had no scruples in using their influence on the Council, or in appealing to force to

all reason for subdivision, is that the *consilium regis* unqualified by any adjective was inclusive and flexible enough to answer all the purposes required of the great council, the secret council, and the ordinary council. The only vital distinction of this kind which the Middle Ages really demanded was that between the parliament and the council," Baldwin, op. cit. chap. v.

[1] Ibid 170-174. [2] Nicolas i *ii, iii.* [3] Dicey, Privy Council 44.
[4] Nicolas iii *xx* and 156; above 482; Baldwin, op. cit. 174-176.
[5] Nicolas iii 215; for other Ordinances regulating the Council's procedure, see ibid i 18 a; iii 149-152; R.P. iv 201 (2 Hy. VI. n. 17).
[6] Baldwin, op. cit. 178-179; vol. ii 414-416.
[7] Dicey, Privy Council 27.
[8] This idea comes out very clearly in a piece of advice which the Council gave to Henry VI. in 1436—"To advise the king that he gives offices to such persons as the offices were convenient to, not to high estate a small office, neither to low estate a great office," Nicolas v 3.

gain their ends.[1]   They ran the government simply in their own interests.   Fortescue, Henry VI.'s chief justice and faithful adherent,[2] has analysed the causes of their failure; and the truth of his analysis is abundantly borne out by all the contemporary authorities for the history of this period.   He tells us [3] that the councillors always had business of their own to be treated of in the Council, as well as the business of the king.   " Wherethrough when they come together, they were so occupied with their own matters, and with the matters of their kin, servants, and tenants, that they attended but little . . . to the king's matters.   And also there were but few matters of the king's, but the same matters touched also the said counsellors, their cousins, their servants, tenants, or such other as they owed favour unto.   And what lower man was there sitting in that council, that durst say against the opinion of any of the great lords ?   And why might not these men make by means of corruption some of the servants and councillors of some of the lords to move the lords to partiality, and to make them also favourable and partial as were the same servants or the parties that so moved them ?   Then could no matter treated in the council be kept privy.   For the lords often times told their own councillors and servants, that had sued to them for those matters, how they had sped in them and who was against them."   Fortescue recommended a Council of twelve spiritual and twelve temporal men " of the wisest and best disposed that can be found in all parts of this land."   They were to take an oath like that of the judges; they were to have a president to be chosen by the king ; and they were to meet at certain hours and deliberate upon all matters of state and suggest legislative changes to Parliament.[4]   The Chancellor, Treasurer and Privy Seal should be ex-officio members ; the judges should be summoned as occasion demanded; and the Council should keep a book of rules for its own procedure.

Henry VI.'s reign was not a period in which reforms of this kind could be carried out.   When Henry attained his majority in 1437 a new Council, constituted in a manner similar to the Councils which had governed England during his minority, was appointed ; and it carried on the government in a manner very similar to that in which these Councils had carried it on.[5]   A

[1] Vol. ii 414-416 ; Baldwin, op. cit. 180-181.

[2] For some account of him see vol. ii 566-571.

[3] Governance of England, chap. xv.

[4] " Wherethrough the parliaments shall do more good in a month to the mending of the law, than they shall now do in a year, if the amending thereof be not debated, and by such council riped to their hands."

[5] Baldwin, op. cit. 184-189—" The council that had ruled during the king's minority did not cease to rule him now, and the same aristocratic junto, which had formerly controlled and exploited the government, still retained its actual supremacy."

change came after the peace with France, and the marriage of Henry with Margaret of Anjou. The king and queen began to rely on the Earl of Suffolk rather than on the Council.[1] The salaries of the councillors ceased to be paid, and they ceased to attend.[2] Complaints began to be heard of evil councillors; and Parliament, which was controlled by the great nobility, impeached Suffolk, and he fell.[3] Then came various movements for the reform of the Council led by the Duke of York. He was the leader of the nobility; and they desired, as in Edward II. and Richard II.'s reigns, to take the control of the government out of the hands of the king and queen and their favourites.[4] Moreover the Duke of York could make out a clearer hereditary right to the throne than the House of Lancaster; and thus, to the existing feuds which harassed the country, a new dynastic feud was added. When that feud broke out it split the country into two parties, and civil war ensued. The Council was gradually disintegrated; and, as it disintegrated, "it tended to resume its earlier and more primitive aspect"—a shifting body composed of the nobility and a few officials.[5] The Council did not revive as a definite body till the Tudor kings reformed the Council somewhat on the lines suggested by Fortescue.

(2) The jurisdiction of the Council.

The Council, as Professor Baldwin has said, "was a court of general and undefined authority long before the courts of special character came into existence."[6] Thus its jurisdiction and procedure did not, in the Middle Ages, become so strictly defined and so formal as the jurisdiction and procedure of the common law courts. We have seen that both the Council and the Chancery exercised concurrently a jurisdiction over a large and miscellaneous mass of business with which the common law courts could not, for one reason or another, deal.[7] We have seen too that they exercised it by means of a procedure by bill or petition, accompanied by the examination of the parties and witnesses, which was then simple, speedy, and informal, as compared with the cumbrous procedure of the common law courts.[8] Moreover they could secure the presence of the defendant by writs of *subpœna* or *quibusdam de certis causis*,[9] which,

---

[1] Baldwin, op. cit. 189-191   [2] Ibid 191.   [3] Ibid 193.
[4] Ibid 194 seqq.   [5] Ibid 204.   [6] Ibid 262.
[7] Above 405-407.   [8] Above 450-451.

[9] For specimens see App. XVII.; Professor Baldwin points out that the *subpœna* appears as early as 1363 and the *quibusdam certis de causis* as early as 1346, Select Cases before the Council xxxviii; it appears they "were not derived from any example set by the ecclesiastical courts, but were evolved out of the formulæ at ready in use for administrative rather than judicial purposes," ibid; there seems to be no

because they did not specify the particular wrong complained of, were available for any cause of complaint, and did not compel the plaintiff to choose the right remedy at his peril.[1] Moreover if the defendant did not appear there were very much more efficient means for securing his appearance than the lengthy processes of the common law.[2] We have seen, too, that in initiating these processes the Council often used the machinery of the office of the privy seal, which was more speedy and less formal than the machinery of the Chancery.[3] As Parliament was unable to deal with the masses of petitions presented to it, as these petitions were often left over from Parliament to Parliament, it is not surprising that petitioners "sought the Council as an alternative."[4]

During the fourteenth century Parliament viewed the vague and indefinite jurisdiction of the Council with much suspicion. This arose chiefly from two causes. (i) The Council, as an executive body, was identified with the crown and the prerogative. It was the actions of the crown and the prerogative which Parliament criticized and controlled. (ii) It exercised a rival jurisdiction outside the common law, and used a procedure very different from that of the common law. The parties to the action could be examined;[5] the writs of *subpœna* or *quibusdam de certis causis* by which defendants were summoned to appear gave them no warning of the nature of the plaintiff's cause of complaint;[6] and it sometimes executed its own orders by the summary method of despatching a serjeant at arms.[7] It was more efficient, because it was more powerful than the common law courts. The layman feared and suspected it; and the lawyer hated it because it encroached upon his province. We have seen that in Edward III.'s reign the judges denied that their decisions could be questioned in the Council.[8] They would have liked to confine its jurisdiction to matters falling outside the common law, such as cases concerning aliens, and maritime and ecclesiastical cases.

Both these causes of distrust united against the claim of the

ground for the tradition that John de Waltham invented the *subpœna* in Richard II.'s reign; what he appears to have done is to have translated it into French and issued it under the privy seal, and it was against this that the Commons protested (R.P. iv 84), ibid xxxix.

[1] For this difference between the common law procedure on the one side, and that of the Council or the Chancery on the other, see vol. v 279-287.

[2] Above 406; vol. iii 623-627 ; Baldwin, op. cit. 292.

[3] Above 407-408; Baldwin, op. cit. 255-261.

[4] Baldwin, Select Cases before the Council (S.S.) xviii.

[5] Baldwin, op. cit. 297-298; R.P. iv 84 (4 Hy. V. no. 46).

[6] Baldwin, op. cit. 290-291; R.P. iv 84 (4 Hy. V. no. 46).

[7] Select Cases in the Star Chamber (S.S.) i xxv-xxvii.

[8] Above 361.

Council to deal with a class of criminal cases, which would clearly have fallen within the jurisdiction of the common law courts, if they had been strong enough to deal with them.[1] That there were many such cases all through this period is clear. That a tribunal which could deal with them effectually was needed is equally clear. But the great powers of the Council were often used, not so much with the object of impartially enforcing the law, as with the object of perverting its provisions out of favour to powerful individuals.[2] It is for this reason that the general feeling against the exercise of arbitrary power, and the professional feeling of the common lawyers united against the Council. These feelings are abundantly illustrated by statutes and petitions.

Among the statutes which were thought to guard the supremacy of the common law the lawyers of the fourteenth century placed first the clause of Magna Carta which ordained that no man should be condemned save by the lawful judgment of his peers or by the law of the land. And, though there is no historical justification for their identification of trial by jury with "lawful judgment of peers," they had, as we have seen, some justification in appealing to this clause against the encroachments of administrative discretion.[3] In 1328[4] it was enacted "that it shall not be commanded by the great seal nor the little seal to disturb or delay common right; and though such commandements do come, the justices shall not therefore leave to do right in any point." In 1331[5] there is an enactment against proceedings contrary to "the form of the Great Charter and the law of the land." In 1350[6] it was enacted that "none shall be taken by petition or suggestion made to our Lord the King or to his Council unless it be by indictment or presentment of good and lawful people of the same neighbourhood where such deeds be done in due manner or by process made by writ original at the common law; nor that none be out of his franchises nor of his freeholds, unless he be duly brought in to answer and forejudged of the same by the course of the law." In 1354 and 1368 statutes were passed to the same effect.[7]

---

[1] Nicolas i 107-108 (1400)—where it is stated that the justices of the peace have no power over great offenders.

[2] Above 484; below 491; cp. Baldwin, Select Cases before the Council (S.S.) xxvi.

[3] Above 59-63.

[4] 2 Edward III. c. 8; cp. 14 Edward III. St. 1 c. 14, and 11 Richard II. c. 10.

[5] 5 Edward III. c. 9.   [6] 25 Edward III. St. 5 c. 4.

[7] 28 Edward III. c. 3; 42 Edward III. c. 3; the latter statute recites that people are accused before the Council "more for revenge and singular benefit, than for the profit of the king or of his people."

These statutes did not succeed in making any essential alterations in the procedure of the Council ; [1] but they had one very important result. They prevented the Council from dealing with questions of freehold which were properly determinable by the common law courts by the machinery of the real actions ; [2] and they prevented it from dealing with questions of treason or felony, a conviction for which involved the death penalty and the escheat or forfeiture [3] of freehold. Consequently it came to be thought that the Council could never give sentence of death, but could award only minor corporal punishments and pecuniary penalties.[4] These limitations the Council never transgressed, even in the Tudor period, when, as we shall see,[5] its wide jurisdiction was exercised in the court of Star Chamber. It is clear that this limitation of its jurisdiction over criminal cases had important effects upon the growth of English criminal law. It ensured that the most serious crimes should be tried by the ordinary procedure of the common law courts, and not by the extraordinary procedure of the Council and Star Chamber.[6] We shall see that, consequently, the prisoner got a fairer trial than was possible under a procedure which, in the sixteenth century, was prepared to borrow ideas from the continental forms of inquisitorial procedure in which torture played an important part.[7]

It is clear from the Parliamentary petitions that the House of Commons was anxious to secure, not only the enforcement of these statutes, but also further limitations upon the activities of the Council. Thus in 1351 [8] it petitioned that no man should be put to answer for his free tenement, nor for anything that touches life or member before the King's Council except by process of law before used. The reply is, " Il plest a notre Seigneur le Roi que les Leies de son Roialme soient tenuz et gardez en

---

[1] But it is possible that the requirement that in a civil suit the parties should submit to the jurisdiction was due to the feeling, underlying these statutes, that the jurisdiction was extraordinary, see Baldwin, Select Cases before the Council (S.S.) xli.

[2] For these actions see vol. iii 3-29. In the case of Attewode v. Clifford (1402-1403), Select Cases before the Council (S.S.) 86, a petition concerning freehold addressed to Parliament was sent for hearing to the Council ; the Council in giving judgment, at p. 89, recite both the authority of the Parliament and the assent of the parties.

[3] For escheat and forfeiture see vol. iii 67-72.

[4] Even minor corporal penalties were rarely inflicted in the Middle Ages, Baldwin, Select Cases before the Council (S.S.) xlv.

[5] Below 503 ; cp. Baldwin, op. cit. 298.

[6] Vol. v 188-189.

[7] Ibid ; for the history of torture in England see vol. v 185-187, 194-195.

[8] R.P. ii 228 (25 Ed. III. n. 16) ; cp. R.P. iii 21 (1 Rich. II. n. 87)—the king grants that petitions be not terminated before lords or officers of the Council, " s'il ne soit tiele querele et encontre si graunde persone que homme ne suppose aillours d'avoir droit."

lour force, et que nul homme soit tenu a respondre de son fraunk tenement, sinoun par processe de Ley ; Mes de chose que touche vie ou membre contemptuz ou excesse, soit fait come ad este use cea en arere." In 1378 [1] there is a long reply to a petition of a similar character, to the effect that it is not reasonable to restrain the king from sending for those of his subjects whom he requires. A promise is however given that they shall not be required to answer for their freehold ; but if the king or his Council be credibly informed that for maintenance and oppression the common law cannot be enforced, in that case the persons accused can be lawfully summoned. In 1389 [2] there is a petition against the practice of sending for persons by writs of *quibusdam de certis causis* and *subpœna*. The answer is "Le Roy voet sauver sa Regalie, come ses progenitours ont faitz devant luy." In 1399 [3] there is a complaint that personal actions are removed before the Council by letters of privy seal and are there tried before enemies of the plaintiff or defendant ; the prayer of the petition is that such actions be not tried before the Council. The petition is granted, unless one party is rich and the other poor, so that justice cannot otherwise be done. It is clear that the jurisdiction of the Council is still extremely ill-defined. Parliament has not succeeded in placing any further limitations upon it ; [4] and we have already seen that it had no more success in its efforts to make changes in the Council's procedure. [5]

We have seen that after the deposition of Richard II. the powers of Parliament increased ; and that it exercised constant control over both the composition of the Council, and its conduct of the government. [6] In fact during the latter part of Henry VI.'s reign the king's ministers seem almost more dependent on Parliament than upon the crown. [7] It is this phenomenon which has led some historians to compare this period with the modern relations between Parliament and the ministers of the crown, and to talk of the "constitutional experiment". The result of this increased control over the Council obtained by Parliament was

---

[1] R.P. iii 44 (2 Rich. II. n. 49) ; cp. R.P. iii 506, 507 (4 Hy. IV. n. 78), a petition of a similar nature reciting Edward III.'s statutes ; a similar answer is returned.

[2] R.P. iii 267 (13 Rich. II. n. 33) ; cp. R.P. iii 323 (17 Rich. II. n. 52) ; ibid 471 (2 Hy. IV. n. 69) ; ibid iv 84 (3 Hy. V. n. 46) ; ibid 156 (9 Hy. V. n. 25).

[3] R.P. iii 446 (1 Hy. IV. n. 162).

[4] Lambard, Archeion 130-165 gives a very clear account of these Parliamentary activities, and concludes that they still left the king and Council free to redress hardships which were not redressible by the common law ; at the same time he concludes that they show that " the course of the common law should be commonly holden," " that men should not be causelessly convented before the king and his Council," and that the Council could not " determine finally concerning freehold or inheritance," op. cit. 155 ; cp. Select Cases in the Star Chamber (S.S.) i lix, lx.

[5] Above 487-488.   [6] Above 482, 483.

[7] Nicolas i *lxii, lxiii,* and 297 ; vi *lii-liv.*

not so much the limitation as the recognition of its jurisdiction. Petitions addressed to Parliament were sent to the Council to be answered.[2] So usual a proceeding was this, that in 1420 we find a petition directed against those who endorse bills to the Council with the words "by authority of Parliament," without having such authority.[3] Statutes strengthened and recognized its authority. In 1411[4] it was given a jurisdiction in cases of riot. In 1452[5] penalties were enacted against those who did not appear before the King's Council when warned to do so. In fact the aims of Parliament, or rather of the "over mighty subjects" who dominated it, were rather personal than constitutional. Feudalism of the older type had been crushed in the thirteenth century; but men's political ideas were cast in a feudal mould,[6] The victory of the Parliament meant, not the victory of law but the victory of the great nobles. They gained the power to use the Council, and all the other organs of government for their personal ends—to divert the state organization to feudal uses.[7] The failure of Parliamentary government conducted on these lines was demonstrated by the Wars of the Roses.

We have seen that as the result of this failure the whole machinery of government was paralysed. It is significant that the Book of the Council, which begins to run continuously in 1421, stops in 1435, and is not resumed till 1540.[8] This, Professor Baldwin thinks, is due mainly to the entire breakdown of the Council[9]—a breakdown which, as we have seen, had something to do with an increase in the business of the Chancery, because it helped it to develop into a tribunal distinct from the Council.[10] During the latter years of Henry VI.'s and the earlier years of Edward IV.'s reign, "suitors generally ceased to ad-

---

[1] See the case of John Roger (1428), Nicolas iii 313; he had shipped wool contrary to the statute; the Council consulted the judges whether they should fine him or send him to be tried by a jury; the judges advised a fine as he might corrupt the jury; he was fined 200 marks or more if he can pay; cp. Palgrave, Council 70.

[2] R.P. iv 99, 100 (4 Hy. V. n. 15); ibid 321, 322 (6 Hy. VI. n. 17).

[3] R.P. iv 127 (8 Hy. V. n. 23); but Mr. Leadam, Select Cases in the Star Chamber (S.S.) i xxiii-xxiv, thinks that the object of this petition was to make "the suit and request of the Commons indispensable to any bill preferred by a litigant."

[4] 13 Henry IV. c. 7 § 2.

[5] 31 Henry VI. c. 2; Reeves, H.E.L. ii 535, 536; Select Cases in the Star Chamber (S.S.) i lx-lxi.

[6] "A parliament of Richard II. threatens to dissolve itself, but no mediæval parliament threatens to sit in permanence," Stubbs, C.H. iii 520. We have in this sentence the whole contrast between the mediæval and the seventeenth century ideas as to the manner in which pressure could best be brought to bear upon the crown.

[7] Fortescue, The Governance of England, chap. xv cited above 484.

[8] Baldwin, op. cit. 420; for an earlier journal of 15 and 16 Richard II. see ibid App. II.; for the records generally see vol. iv 61-63; vol. v 161-162; Nicolas in his first six volumes has printed the Acts of the Council down to 1460.

[9] Op. cit. 420-421.   [10] Above 408-409.

dress their complaints to the Parliament or the Council, where they were not likely to be heard, but made address either to the king or to the Chancellor."[1]   The Council had, as we have seen, a procedure which made it well fitted to suppress the disorders which were paralysing the government.[2]   As Professor Baldwin says, "all the methods which ultimately made the Star Chamber a terrible power were well developed under the House of Lancaster."[3]   But the members of the Council were themselves implicated in the riots, the forcible entries, the maintenance, and oppression which they were asked to suppress.[4]   They were therefore incapable of acting with impartiality,[5] or of using honestly and faithfully their powers to punish offences of which they themselves were guilty.   On the contrary they treated these offences with leniency,[6] and even protected the offenders by the lavish issue of pardons which covered all imaginable offences.[7]

Fortescue saw all this very clearly when he recommended an able, well-paid, and impartial Council as the remedy for the want of governance from which the country was suffering.[8]   He was not a man to exalt unduly the powers of king and Council at the expense of Parliament;[9] but it is clear that he did not consider that the mediæval legislation had impaired the powers of the Council to exercise a wide jurisdiction to deal with the prevalent disorder.   In fact, as we shall now see, the Tudors proved the correctness of his diagnosis of the causes of the evils from which the country was suffering, and the efficacy of his

---

[1] Baldwin, op. cit. 428.   [2] Above 486.

[3] Op. cit. 306; he points out in Select Cases before the Council (S.S.) ci, that the case of Esturmy v. Courtenay (1392), which was given a full hearing before the Council (pp. 77-81), was, "as a case of violence and oppression the first of a series of trials such as afterwards pertained to the court of Star Chamber. It was a trial on criminal charges of one of the peers of the realm, for which the Council, apart from the House of Lords, demonstrated its competence."

[4] Vol. ii 415-416; cf. the tale told by Huse, C.J., in Y.B. 1 Hy. VII. Mich. pl. 3; he said that when he was Edward IV.'s attorney, "il veist touts les seigneurs jures a garder les statuts queux ils ove auters avoient alonques compile ensemblement per commandement de mesne le roy, et eux diligentment executer; et il veiast deins un heure tanques ils furent en le Star Chamber, divers de les Seigniors faire retainements per oath et serment, et autres choses, que furent directment contrairies a lour dits suretes et oaths."

[5] See Select Cases before the Council (S.S.) cx.

[6] Baldwin, op. cit. 304-305, cp. Select Cases in the Star Chamber (S.S.) i lxii; Select Cases before the Council (S.S.) cii.

[7] " After Jack Cade's rebellion the government, as an act of amnesty, promised pardons to all who should ask for them, and the number granted with the specification of every conceivable crime amounted to a veritable suspension of justice. Again in 1459-1460 there was another season of the most lavish grants of such pardons," Baldwin, op. cit. 305; see the case of the Bedford Riot (1439), Select Cases before the Council (S.S.) 104-107, and Professor Baldwin's comment at p. cxiv.

[8] Above 484; Governance of England, chaps. xv, xvi.

[9] De Laudibus, chaps. 9 and 13; cp. the Case of Ship Money (1637) 3 S.T. at p. 1136 per Crooke, J.; for this book of Fortescue's see vol. ii 569-571.

suggested remedy. It was not till the beginning of the seventeenth century that men began seriously to contend that the mediæval legislation had done more than exclude the jurisdiction of the Council in cases of treason, felony, and freehold. With these two epochs in the history of the Council—its revival under the Tudors, and the constitutional conflict which raged round it in the early Stuart period—I shall deal in the two following sections.

II. THE TUDOR PERIOD

During the latter part of Edward IV.'s reign there are signs of a revival of the Council's jurisdiction;[1] and this revival was well maintained in Richard III.'s reign.[2] But it was not till Henry VII.'s reign that the Council regained all and more than all its old authority. It was through the Council, acting both as an executive and a judicial body, that England at last got a government which was both stronger and more efficient than she had had since the reign of Henry II. Henry VII. set the example, followed by his successors, of keeping the initiative in his hands, but of working with a Council[3] composed partly of peers and partly of commoners.[4] These councillors, chosen and trusted by the crown, and promoted for their efficiency, were, as Professor Baldwin has said,[5] a new "aristocracy of service." The success of this policy gave to the Council during the Tudor period an influence over the government of the country which it had never possessed before and has never possessed since. Helped by the Council, the Tudor kings mastered the lawlessness of the preceding period, successfully piloted the English state through the difficult transition from mediæval to modern, and reformed the church on lines which harmonized admirably with the form which the modern English state was assuming.[6]

The first task which the Tudor kings set before themselves was the task of mastering the prevailing lawlessness. In order to cope with this they made the fullest use of the judicial powers

[1] Baldwin, op. cit. 433-434.   [2] Ibid 434-435.

[3] Bacon, History of Henry VII. (cited Baldwin, op. cit. 436), says, "To his Council he did refer much, and sat oft in person; knowing it to be the way to assist his power and inform his judgment;" Professor Baldwin says that during the first years of the reign the king's presence is indicated in nearly half the records which we have.

[4] See Professor Baldwin's analysis, op. cit. 436.

[5] Op. cit. 452; as Lambard said, Archeion 122, "Whether they be nobles or no it is not material, seeing that the calling cometh not by birth, but groweth by election;" the fact that the Council consisted largely of new men of humble birth chosen for their administrative capacity was made matter of complaint by the Northern rebels in 1536, Nicolas vii iii, iv; cp. Baldwin, op. cit. 453-454; vol. iv 39.

[6] Below 589-591, 597-598.

of the Council. A new register of the Council's proceedings called the " Book of Entries," which was begun at the beginning of Henry VII.'s reign, consists for the most part of judicial business.[1] But in order to give the Council larger powers to deal quickly with the mass of judicial work which the disturbed state of the country brought before it, and in order to reconcile public opinion to the exercise of these powers, the government wisely followed older precedents,[2] and, in certain cases, put the jurisdiction of the Council on a statutory basis.

The first of these statutes is the Act of 1487,[3] Pro Camera Stellata. It recites that by unlawful maintenances, by giving of liveries and "retainders by indentures,"[4] by untrue demeanings of sheriffs in making of panels and other false returns, by bribery of jurors, by great riots and unlawful assemblies, the policy and good rule of this realm is almost subdued. It therefore enacted "that the Chancellor and Treasurer of England for the time being, and Keeper of the king's Privy Seal ;[5] or two of them, calling to them a bishop and a temporal lord of the king's most honourable Council, and the two Chief Justices of the King's Bench and Common Pleas, for the time being, or other two justices in their absence, upon bill or information put to the said Chancellor for the king, or any other, against any person for any misbehaviour before rehearsed, have authority to call before them by writ or by privy seal the said misdoers, and them and other by their discretion, by whom the truth may be known, to examine, and such as they find therein defective, to punish them after their demerits, after the form and effect of statutes thereof made, in like manner and form as they should and ought to be punished, as if they were thereof convict after the due order of the law." The object of the Act was clearly to constitute a strong committee to deal with the offences which had imperilled and were still imperilling the authority of the state. Other Acts of this period pursued the same policy. Thus in 1495 the Chancellor, the Treasurer, the Chief Justices, and the Master of the Rolls were given power to examine complaints as to perjuries committed by jurors, and to punish the offenders.[6] In 1539 Henry VIII.'s famous Statute of Proclamations established a tribunal consisting of most of the important officers of state to

---

[1] Baldwin, op. cit. 437.   [2] Above 490.   [3] 3 Henry VII. c. 1.

[4] I.e. contracting to supply small bodies of soldiers. For a specimen of one of these contracts see Oman, Warwick 36, 37.

[5] 21 Henry VIII. c. 20 provided that the President of the Council should also be one of the judges ; Lambard, Archeion 202-205, thought that this Act made it plain that these four officials were the judges and the rest only necessary assistants, and that it enabled the bill or information to be addressed either to the king or to the Chancellor ; cp. Select Cases in the Star Chamber (S.S.) ii, xii, xiii.

[6] 11 Henry VII. c. 25 ; 12 Henry VII. c. 2.

deal with offences against proclamations published in accordance with the provisions of the Act.[1]

The most famous of these Acts is the Act Pro Camera Stelleta of 1487.[2] It is famous not so much on account of the results actually effected by the court which it established—in fact, there are very few records of trials before a court constituted in accordance with its provisions[3]—as on account of the use made of the Act by those who in later days disputed the legality of the jurisdiction exercised by the court of Star Chamber.[4] We shall see that, in the seventeenth century, the Parliamentary party when it abolished the court,[5] took a view as to the effect of this Act which is opposed both to the best legal opinion of the sixteenth and seventeenth centuries, and to the best opinion of the present day. But the fact that the Parliamentary party in the seventeenth century adopted this view as to the effect of this Act long exercised a disturbing influence upon the minds of later constitutional historians, because these historians were too apt to assume that the legal views expressed by the Parliamentary party were correct.[6] It is therefore necessary at this point to explain what this Act really did and what it did not effect.

Firstly, it gave statutory sanction to the practices of summoning by writs of subpœna or privy seal persons accused of committing the offences specified in the statute, and of examining them. It thus obviated the constitutional objection to those practices which had figured so prominently in the mediæval Parliaments.[7] Secondly, it did not in any way affect the wide and still undefined jurisdiction exercised by the Council. As Coke said, it was affirmative—that is it gave jurisdiction to this statutory committee ; it was not negative—that is it did not deprive the Council of any jurisdiction it previously possessed.[8]

---

[1] 31 Henry VIII. c. 8 § 4. [2] 3 Henry VII. c. 1.
[3] L.Q.R. xviii 254; cp. Hudson, Star Chamber 23.
[4] Below 512. [5] Below 515.
[6] The confusion of which later constitutional historians are guilty can be explained by their consciousness of the error of the view, taken by the Parliament in 1641, that the Star Chamber was created by the Act of 1487, and by their desire to prove that the Star Chamber was an illegal court; thus Hallam, C.H., i 55 n. contends that the Star Chamber could not base any claims on the Act of 1487, as the court established by the Act was not the Star Chamber, and he concludes that therefore the Star Chamber was an illegal court; but if the Star Chamber is the Council (as he admits), and if the Act merely confirmed its jurisdiction in certain points, as Coke and Bacon both contend, his deduction is clearly erroneous; cp. Prothero, Constitutional Documents ciii, civ.
[7] Select Cases in the Star Chamber (S.S.) i lxiv, lxv.
[8] "The Act of 3 H. 7, being in the affirmative is not in some things pursued. . . . And it is a good rule that when the Act of 3 H. 7 is not pursued, there (if there be many judicial precedents in another sort) they must have warrant from the ancient court," Coke, Fourth Instit. 62; cp. Lambard, Archeion 197-200, who takes the same view.

But, thirdly, the court set up by the Act was probably regarded as a committee of the Council. It followed that both the powers given by the Act and the mode of their exercise therein prescribed could be used by the whole Council. Hence the Council could by virtue of the authority given by the Act examine upon interrogatories defendants brought before it.[1]

All of these Acts had merely a temporary importance. To a large extent their enactment was due to the political conditions prevailing at the beginning of the Tudor period; and therefore, when these political conditions altered, they became obsolete. As the Tudor scheme of government through the Council developed, a different organization of the Council and its business came into being. This new organization was grounded upon two lines of cleavage which, as the sixteenth century proceeded, gradually grew up within the Council. The first of these lines of cleavage was a distinction between the Council with the king and the Council at Westminster. The second was a distinction between the full members of the Privy Council and the ordinary members of the Council. Both these lines of cleavage had something to do with the separation of the Council acting as an executive body from the Council acting as a judicial body—between, that is, the Privy Council and the court of Star Chamber. When this separation became well marked the Council sitting in the Star Chamber—that is the court of Star Chamber—did all and more than all of the work of these statutory committees, and so rendered them unnecessary.

Firstly, in certain Ordinances of 1526, which Henry VIII. devised for the establishment of the Council, a distinction is drawn between the Council with the king and the Council at Westminster.[2] This was a distinction which had appeared from time to time during the Middle Ages;[3] but during this period it tended to become sharper and more permanent. "Henceforth," as Professor Baldwin says, "the monarchy was generally successful in maintaining two co-ordinate boards working simultaneously. The one following the king was commonly known as the 'Council at court;' while the other continued to be called 'the king's Council in the Star Chamber.'"[4] The former body became the

---

[1] "This Act in one point is introductory of a new law, which the former court had not, viz. to examine the defendant, which being understood after his answer made, to be upon oath upon interrogatories, which this ancient court proceeding in criminal causes had not, nor could have but by Act of Parliament, or prescription, the want thereof especially in matter of frauds and deceits . . . was a mean that truth could not be found out," Coke, Fourth Instit. 63.

[2] Baldwin, op. cit. 446-447.

[3] Baldwin, Select Cases before the Council (S.S.) xvi.

[4] Ibid 448.

Privy Council,[1] and, being more immediately connected with the king, naturally became the body which considered all questions of policy domestic and foreign. The latter transacted the routine business both administrative and judicial. Secondly, we find in Henry VIII.'s reign a group of persons employed to perform some of these routine duties, but not full privy councillors.[2] Thus there are councillors employed to do the work afterwards done by the Masters of Requests. There are persons employed to assist in judicial business; and some of these persons were employed specially, others, like the judges,[3] were regarded as being ex officio obliged to assist if and when required. It is obvious that these supernumerary or ordinary councillors would be wanted, not so much for the political questions which were discussed by the Council with the king, as for the administrative and judicial business which came before the Council at Westminster.

It is this branch of the Council which sat at Westminster which developed into the court of Star Chamber. The name has been variously and fancifully[4] derived. Blackstone derives it from the word "Starra"—the term used for the contracts and obligations of the Jews. These were deposited in certain places, the chief of which was the Exchequer at Westminster.[5] The room so used came to be appropriated to the Council; and hence the Council took the name, Star Chamber. Coke,[6] Sir Thomas Smith,[7] Camden,[8] and Lambard,[9] derived the name from the fact that the roof of the room, where the Council sometimes sat, was ornamented with stars. Additional probability is lent to this theory by the fact that the "Sterred Chambre" is first referred to in 1348. Only the year before Edward III. had made extensive additions to the palace of Westminster, which comprised among other things a new council chamber.[10] On either view the name is the name of a place where the Council sometimes sat.

That the Council at Westminster developed its judicial at the expense of its administrative side is probably due to the fact that the amount and importance of its judicial business was greater than the amount and importance of its administrative

[1] For an account of the very important part played by the Privy Council in the sphere of administration during this period, see vol. iv 70-105.

[2] Baldwin, op. cit. 450-452; cp. Lambard, Archeion 123-124.

[3] Below 497 n. 3.

[4] Hudson 8; cp. Lambard, Archeion 183-184; James I. Works 559.

[5] Comm. iv 263 n.; above 45-46.

[6] Fourth Instit. 66.   [7] Commonwealth, Bk. iii c. 4.

[8] Britannia (Ed. 1607) 130.   [9] Archeion 184-185.

[10] Baildon, Les Reportes in Camera Stellata, xlii-xlv. As he points out, the word "starra" could hardly become "sterred" or "stellata."

business. In fact the need of a special branch of the Council to deal with judicial work had long been felt.[1] But the severance between the two sides of its activity was never complete.[2] However, it gradually became more complete as the sixteenth century advanced, until, at the end of that century, the court of Star Chamber had begun to present the appearance of a court intimately related to, but yet distinct from the Privy Council. Persons like the chief justices, who were not full privy councillors, habitually sat there and took part in its decisions, in order that it might have professional help in the performance of those judicial activities which were the chief part of its business.[3] It developed a distinct style,[4] a distinct procedure,[5] a distinct official staff,[6] and always sat in a distinct place.[7] It is not surprising therefore that it began to be regarded as a distinct tribunal; and that, as it consisted of all the privy councillors and of others besides, it gradually absorbed those smaller statutory committees with limited judicial functions which had been established at the end of the fifteenth century.

The process by which this result attained was gradual, and we have few definite data; but we can see the lines upon which the separation proceeded in the Acts of the Privy Council; and we can trace both the existence of and the causes for this separation in the books of contemporary writers upon the Star Chamber.

(i) The Acts and Proceedings of the Privy Council contain indications that the Council sitting in the Star Chamber for the purpose of judicial work was becoming a distinct court. In 1564 a person was ordered to appear every day the Lords sat in the Star Chamber.[8] In 1578 a person was ordered to appear the first day of the next Star Chamber.[9] Dasent notes [10] in 1580-1581 that entries on the Council records relating to business

[1] Baldwin, Select Cases before the Council (S.S.) xix, xx; the same phenomenon appears in the Council of the North, Reid, King's Council in the North 247-249.
[2] Below 502.
[3] Below 500. The question whether the judges were full members had been a matter of controversy; Coke, Fourth Instit. 62, said that the two chief justices took part in the decisions of the court "as it hath been resolved and daily experience teacheth;" but Mr. Leadam says that Y.B. 8 Hy. VII. Pasch. pl. 7 contradicts him, Select Cases in the Star Chamber (S.S.) i xxxiv-xxxv; but this decision only applies to the statutory Court created by the Act of 1487, in which they were clearly only assessors, ibid i xxxviii, lix; ii xii; Lambard, Archeion 199; Coke could testify from personal experience that it was never taken to apply to the court of his day, see Select Cases in the Star Chamber (S.S.) i xliv.
[4] Below 499. [5] Below 501. [6] Below 500.
[7] "The Lords sitting in the Sterre Chambre became a phrase; and when we consider the influence of names in human affairs, and how comparatively weak any body of men remain until they have found an incorporate appellation . . . we can hardly doubt but that this circumstance contributed to assist the Council in maintaining their authority," Palgrave, Council, 38, 39.
[8] Dasent vii 189. [9] Ibid x 383; cp. xii 277.
[10] Ibid xii *vii*; xiii *vii*.

in the Star Chamber are written on different sized paper, and are interleaved in the MS. It is clear that the Star Chamber generally sat only in term time,[1] and that matters which came before the Star Chamber did not necessarily come before the Council. Certainly as early as 1570 the Council declined to accept a plea that the matter was coming before the Star Chamber, though in the end the plaintiff was directed to prosecute his suit there.[2] As early as 1553 a commission was issued by Edward VI. to the Earl of Bedford and nine others to hear suits in order to relieve the Council of this work;[3] and from 1582 onwards it is clear that the Council was desirous of getting rid of the mass of private litigation which was brought before it. In the April of that year there is the following entry[4]: "The Lordes and others of her Majesties Privie Councell considering what multitude of matters concerning private causes and actions betwene partie and partie were daylie brought unto the Councell Bourde, wherewith their Lordships were greatlie troubled and her Majesties speciall services oftentymes interrupted, for remedye whereof it was agreed among them that from henceforthe no private causes arrising betwene parties for any action whatsoever which maye receyve order and redresse in any of her Majesties ordinary Courtes shal be receaved and preferred to the Bourde, onlesse they shall concerne the preservacion of her Majesties peace or shalbe of some publicke consequence to touche the government of the Realme." This resolution does not seem to have been followed by much result. It was repeated in 1589;[5] and in the same year there occurs an entry which shows that the court of Star Chamber is regarded almost as an ordinary court distinct from the Council. The entry is dated Oct. 22nd[6] and runs as follows: "Whereas in a cause depending betwene Johne Love of Ellawe in the county of Suffolk, yeoman, plaintiff,

---

[1] Coke, Fourth Instit. 65; Select Cases in the Star Chamber (S.S.) i lxviii.
[2] Dasent vii 405; viii 12.   [3] Egerton Papers (C.S.) 24-25.
[4] Dasent xiii 394, 395.
[5] Ibid xviii 181-183; it is there recorded that their Lordships had promised that they will not for private favour evade the order; and they reserve to themselves the right to hear any cases in which a denial of justice in the ordinary courts is alleged, or any cases where there is an information for treason or conspiracy; thus ibid xix 195 (1590) the Council requested Clynch, J., and Serjeant Walmsley to look into a case then depending in the Star Chamber.
[6] Ibid xvii 195; the separation of the Council from the Star Chamber is also brought out by the entry cited above n. 2, ibid vii 404-405, of the year 1570; in that case a complaint had been made to the Council and an order in the case had been given; but the order had been disobeyed, and the plaintiff had begun another suit in the Star Chamber; thereupon the Council wrote to him as follows: "They meane not to suffer Thauctorite of their Table to be so much prejudiced as to indure that any matter of complaint brought and delt by them shuld by the complainant himself be removed *to any other Coourte* before the same be heard by their Lordships and ordered."

and Thomas Love and Cyprian Hullocke, defendants, the parties being called before their lordships yt appeared unto them that the said cause was depending in the Starre Chamber, where the same is to receave tryall, and in that case by their Lordships late order not to be determined at the Counsell Borde; the parties, therefore, together with the said cause, were this daye dismissed and left to their triall *in the Starre Chamber, or in suche other court of Justice or Conscience* where the same is properly to be determined." The Council did not however abandon all its jurisdiction. In fact an order similar to that of 1589 is made in 1591.[1] It is clear, however, that the Council sitting in the Star Chamber is coming to be regarded as a separate court, and that this court is taking much of the judicial work which formerly came before the Privy Council.

(ii) The evidence of contemporary writers upon the court of Star Chamber points in the same direction. Camden,[2] Sir Thomas Smith,[3] Lambard,[4] and Crompton[5] regard the Star Chamber as a separate court, but as a court which has a close connexion with the Privy Council. We may gather the same thing from Coke and Bacon; and their evidence is entitled to great weight because they were both distinguished members of the court. Coke in his Fourth Institute treats of the Council and the court of Star Chamber in separate chapters.[6] Bacon treats it as a separate court which exercises "the high and pre-eminent power" reserved to the King's Council "in causes that might in example or consequence concern the state of the commonwealth."[7] The best evidence, however, of the nature of the process which was separating the court of Star Chamber from the Privy Council is Hudson's treatise on the Star Chamber.[8] We can see from that work that the court, its official staff, and its procedure were being gradually shaped by the cases decided there, and by the eminent men who sat as judges. We see a process at work similar in its nature to the process which in earlier days separated the courts of common law from the Curia Regis.

The court had the official style of "The Lords of the Council sitting in the Star Chamber;" and persons were cited to appear "coram Domino Rege in Camera Stellata coram Consilio

---

[1] Dasent xxi 240.
[2] Britannia 130 (Ed. 1607) cited Prothero 175.
[3] Commonwealth, Bk. iii c. 4.   [4] Archeion 116-218 (Ed. 1635).
[5] Courts 29, " Le Court de Starre Chambre est Hault Court, tenus auant le Roy et son Counsell et auters."
[6] Caps. 2 and 5.   [7] History of Henry VII.
[8] Printed in the 2nd vol. of Collectanea Juridica; for an account of Hudson and his treatise see vol. v 164-166.

ibidem." [1]　The style of the court illustrates its connexion with the Council; and it is clear that the actual presence of the king was not yet entirely a fiction.[2]　During the last quarter of the sixteenth century its membership had become definitely fixed. It included all privy councillors, other persons sworn of the Council but not privy councillors, among whom were always some of the judges, and such peers and bishops as were summoned by the crown.[3]　In earlier days it would seem that some thought that all peers had a right to attend.[4]　But it is clear that, when Hudson wrote, they were definitely excluded unless specially summoned.[5]

The court had also its proper officials—a clerk of the court examiners, an usher, attorneys of the court and a serjeant.[6]　As the business of the court increased the officials tended to increase in number, and the fees to grow in amount.　Hudson notes as new officers, a clerk to make warrant for processes, to record appearances, and to deliver certificates; another to keep the record of bills, pleadings, examinations and commissions; another to enter affidavits and orders; a registrar to draw decrees.[7] He says that formerly there were only two attorneys to the court who acted for the parties, but that their number had risen to four.[8]　As in the court of Chancery, these officials were paid by fees and copy money, with the usual result that the process became costly and lengthy.[9]　Thus we read that the power of examining the parties "was used like a Spanish inquisition to rack men's consciences, nay to perplex them by intricate questions, thereby to make contrarieties which may easily happen to simple men; and men were examined upon 100 interrogatories,

---

[1] Baildon, Les Reportes, etc., lii lv; Coke, Fourth Instit. 65; Select Cases in the Star Chamber (S.S.) i xvii.

[2] A seat was always reserved for the sovereign before which the purse and mace were laid, Manningham's diary (C.S.) 53; Bacon said in 1610, "that Concilium non habet potestatem delegatam sed inhærentem," and it is but Rex in Cathedra," Spedding, Letters and Life iv 178-179; and in 1619-1620 he mentioned two cases in which the king had sat in the Star Chamber, ibid vii 70-71.

[3] See James I.'s speech in the Star Chamber in 1616, Works 559; above 497 n. 3.

[4] Hudson, 24-25.

[5] Ibid; cf. Dudley's Case (1604) Les Reportes, etc., 171; Camden, Britannia (Ed. 1607) 130; Coke, Fourth Instit. 65, appears to contradict himself, as he seems to say firstly that "all the lords spiritual and temporal are members," and secondly that "such other lords of Parliament as the king shall name are members."

[6] Hudson 37-48. He notes at p. 29 that, "the causes of equity in Chancery growing many, and other employments of special service pressing the principal officers, the clerk of the court hath of latter times been trusted with the direction of things of course;" and that the serjeant "made great profit by preparing convenient places for young noblemen and men of quality, which flock thither in great abundance, when causes of weight are there heard and determined," at p. 48.

[7] Ibid 40, 41.　　　　　　　　　　[8] Ibid 45.

[9] It seems that Egerton had at one time begun to make enquiries with a view to remedy these abuses, Egerton Papers (C.S.) 271-272, 429-432.

nay, and examined of the whole course of their lives."[1] When the interrogatories in one case could only be contained on a parchment roll four yards long, we are not surprised that a rule was made confining them to sixteen sheets with fifteen lines on a sheet.[2] The question of costs, and the question what privileges officials and suitors of the court possessed, are discussed by Hudson.[3]

The procedure in use in the court was becoming fixed. In civil cases the plaintiff filed a bill and the procedure thereon was similar to that of the court of Chancery.[4] In criminal cases there was either a written information by the Attorney-General, as in the court of King's Bench,[5] or a complaint by the Attorney-General *ore tenus*.[6] The ordinary rules of procedure were enforced upon all parties, even, as Hudson specially notes, upon the Attorney-General.[7] He has much to say upon the form of the bill, upon answers, examinations, interrogatories, pleas, and demurrers.

It is clear, therefore, that the Star Chamber was becoming a settled court; and it is probable from Hudson's account that this result was largely due to Lord Ellesmere's reforms in its practice and procedure.[8] He was doing for the court of Star Chamber what he was doing for the court of Chancery.

We may conclude, therefore, that the court of Star Chamber, as it became a settled court, was separating from the Council; or, to put the same thing in a different way, that the judicial work of the division of the Council which sat at Westminster in the Star Chamber had become so important, that this division of the Council was beginning to exhibit the characteristics of a judicial court. Thus it heard cases publicly,[9] some of the judges were generally present,[10] and it usually sat only in term time.[11] But though the Council sitting in the Star Chamber was thus coming to be a judicial court distinct from the Privy Council, it

---

[1] Hudson 169.
[2] Baildon, Les Reportes, etc., 10, 11; Hudson 151.
[3] Ibid 46, 135, 142-168.   [4] Ibid 150-157, 161-168.
[5] Coke, Fourth Instit. 63.
[6] Hudson 126-128. Coke notes that this procedure is rare; it must proceed "upon the confession of the party in writing under his hand, which he again must freely confess in open court, upon which confession in open court, the court doth proceed. But if his confession be set down too short, or otherwise than he meant, he may deny it, and then they cannot proceed against him but by Bill or Information, which is the fairest way." For a full account of the procedure of the court see vol. v 178-188.
[7] At p. 137.   [8] Ibid 27, 238, 239.
[9] Select Cases in the Star Chamber (S.S.) i lvi.
[10] Above 500.
[11] Select Cases in the Star Chamber (S.S.) i lxviii; some of these features are anticipated by precedents in the mediæval period, Select Cases before the Council (S.S.) 97.

was, after all, a division of the Council.[1] "The clerk of the Council was the clerk of the Star Chamber, and the proceedings of the Star Chamber ran in the name of the Council."[2] In Hawarde's collection of Star Chamber reports (1593-1603) much miscellaneous business is recorded;[3] and conversely the Privy Council, whether sitting at Westminster or elsewhere, still did some judicial work.[4] In fact, neither in the sixteenth century nor at the present day is it possible to draw the line quite precisely between judicial and administrative work—we shall see that at the present day the Judicial Committee of the Privy Council performs functions which are not strictly judicial.[5] In 1641 the Act which abolished the court of Star Chamber was entitled "an Act for the regulating of the Privy Council and the taking away the court commonly called the court of Star Chamber."[6] This title shows that the two bodies were separate, and yet so closely connected that it was impossible to distinguish accurately between them.

The increase of business which had led to this new organization of the Council led also to the creation of a number of provincial Councils in different parts of the country. The most important of these were the Councils of Wales and the Marches, and of the North.[7]

The Council of Wales and the Marches probably originated in the Council of the Prince of Wales which, from Edward I.'s reign onwards, had exercised authority in the Principality. The jurisdiction of this Council was extended in Henry VII.'s reign to the Marches, and it developed into the Council of Wales and the Marches.[8] It did its appointed work efficiently;[9] and its existence and legality were recognized by the statute of 1543.[10] The Council of the North was reorganized[11] on the model of the

---

[1] As Bacon said in a letter to James I., "The Star Chamber in the institution thereof hath two uses; the one as a supreme Court of Judicature; the other as an open Council," Spedding, Letters and Life vii 70; thus in 1590, Dasent xix 222, the Council ordered that a person should attend "on us at the Star Chamber."

[2] Select Cases in the Star Chamber (S.S.) i, xii.

[3] Thus at pp. 19, 56, 101, 186, 326, 367 we get proclamations of Orders in Council, and the Lord Chancellor's annual charge to the judges of assize and the justices of the peace.

[4] Thus in the Orders 3 and 9 made by the Council in 1627, cited in the App. to Selbourne's Judicial Procedure in the Privy Council, Wednesday and Friday afternoons were set apart, "for despatch of suitors, if the greater occasions of state do not hinder."

[5] Below 524-525.　　　　　　　　[6] 16 Charles I. c. 10.

[7] A Council had also been set up in the West in 1540, 32 Henry VIII. c. 50; but owing to local opposition it had soon ceased to exist, Coke Fourth Instit. 246.

[8] Above 126-128; Skeel, The Council in the Marches of Wales 28, 29, 269, 270.

[9] In 1538 Lee could write to Henry VIII., "Your subjects in Wales be in such order that, since Christmas, I hear of neither stealing, riots, murders, nor manslaughter," L. and P. xiii, i no. 222.

[10] 34, 35 Henry VIII. c. 26. It was popular at first because it brought justice to the doors of the people; there was great indignation when, contrary to expectation, persons were still summoned to Westminster, L. and P. iv no. 2201.

[11] Reid, op. cit. 147-149; for the earlier history see ibid Pt. I.

Council of Wales and the Marches after the Pilgrimage of Grace; but with a somewhat less extensive authority.[1] Both Councils exercised, within the area of their respective jurisdiction, judicial and administrative powers similar in kind to those which the Privy Council and the court of Star Chamber exercised over the whole of England.[2] They controlled the local government— according to the Act of 1543 justices of the peace in Wales and the Marches were to be appointed by the advice of the Council.[3] Their relation to the Council and Star Chamber was that of assistants and subordinates;[4] and, that being so, the fact that a case fell within their jurisdiction, did not impede the concurrent jurisdiction of the Council and Star Chamber.[5]

We must now turn to the nature of the judicial work done by the Council, the Star Chamber, and these provincial Councils.

The jurisdiction of the Council, civil and criminal, continued to be almost as wide as it had been in the Middle Ages; and the limitations upon its power were still somewhat indefinite. The growth of the court of Chancery and of the court of Requests was taking away much of the Council's purely equitable jurisdiction. The court of Admiralty took cognizance of many maritime and mercantile cases which formerly were brought before it. It was coming to be recognized that cases with which the ordinary courts could adequately deal should be left to them.[6] It was certain that it could not deal with freehold, treason, or felony.[7] Within these limits it acted freely.

[1] Skeel, op. cit. 80, 276, 277—"The Council of the Marches was the older and more important body. . . . The Presidents of the Northern Council were, with the great exception of Wentworth, men of no special note. . . . The powers of the Council of the North were also less extensive . . . e.g. it could not punish treason." The Council of the North regularly heard civil cases, L. and P. xx, ii no. 109; ibid xxi, ii no. 596—a session of twenty days for this purpose; Reid, op. cit. 149-150.

[2] The Council of Wales was, by the instructions issued in the latter part of the sixteenth century, empowered to hear all complaints and petitions concerning all civil and criminal causes put up to them by persons unable to sue at common law, to hear all complaints as to the misdeeds of officials, to issue proclamations, to compound for all forfeitures arising from the breach of penal statutes, to punish perjury of jurors, to repress all manner of crimes, to use torture in case of suspicion of treason, murder or felony, to punish seditious rumours, to see that the laws as to enclosures were obeyed, to enquire into cases of bribery in connexion with assessments for the subsidy or taking of musters or providing armour, to see that the ecclesiastical courts did their duty, Skeel, op. cit. 89-93; cf. Prothero, Documents 363-388 for the seventeenth century instructions to these Councils.

[3] 34, 35 Henry VIII. c. 26 § 21.

[4] Dasent v 299; vi 101; vii 141, 177, 309, 336; viii 204, 207, 231; x 116, 117, 206; xiii 131, 246; xix 57; cf. for communications between the Privy Council and the Council of the North, Letters and Papers xiii, i no. 1269 (1538); ibid xx, ii no. 109; and for some instructions to that Council, S.P. Dom. Add. (1547-1565) 399; ibid (1566-1579) 463; Reid, op. cit. 158-160.

[5] Hudson 117.

[6] Dasent xx 251, an appeal is dismissed as fit for the justices.

[7] Above 488; cp. Hudson 118. It would appear that the court could only act, as the court of Chancery acted, by restraint of the person; thus the Council

We can roughly divide the cases which came before the Council into two classes : (i) cases which in some way concerned the state ; (ii) private cases.[1]

(i) The first class comprises many different kinds of cases. We have seen that matters concerning foreign trade and foreign merchants were regarded as peculiarly within the jurisdiction of the Council. Though many of these cases came before the court of Admiralty, the Council never ceased to be able to take cognizance of them. Sometimes they determined them, sometimes they sent them to the court of Admiralty, to the cinque ports, or to arbitration. Thus we get before the Council cases of piracy, prize, salvage, insurance, and miscellaneous disputes arising in the course of trade.[2] It intervened to arrange compositions with creditors in cases where the trader through no fault of his own had become insolvent. It sometimes even went so far as to imprison the creditor who would not assent to a reasonable composition.[3]

The court was deemed to be especially bound to look into matters which might concern the safety of the state. It acted, says Hudson,[4] as "the curious eye of the State and the King's Council prying into the inconveniences and mischiefs which abound in the Commonwealth." It was not strictly bound by the straight rules of the common law in dealing with such matters. "By the arm of sovereignty it punisheth errors creeping into the Commonwealth, which otherwise might prove dangerous and infectious diseases, or it giveth life to the execution of laws, or the performance of such things as are necessary in the Commonwealth, yea, although no positive law or continued custom of common law giveth warrant to it."[5] But such powers could only be used for weighty causes. If used for common cases it would destroy "order and course."[6]

On these principles the court acted in punishing libellous and scandalous words, conspiracy and false accusations, riots, fraud, maintenance, forgery,[7] and, above all, it saw to the due execution of the laws against recusants.[8] In fact, the line was

wrote in 1590 to Scotland (Dasent xix 380-382), "Theire Lordships had not onie aucthorytie orderlie by anie lawe (as Counsailors onlie of State) to sease anie lands and goods of anie subject which proceedings belonged onlie to Judyciall Courts, . . . but yet theire Lordships had don what they might doe in lyke cases, which was to commytt him the partie to pryson, there to remaine untill he performed theire order ;" this view is borne out by the case of Saxy, below 505.

[1] This is in substance the division which Lambard makes, Archeion 93.

[2] They occur in all the volumes of the Acts of the Privy Council, see especially Dasent xiv, *xxviii ;* for details see vol. v 136-137.

[3] See e.g. Dasent xvii 56.

[4] Op. cit. 126.

[5] Hudson 107.

[6] Ibid 214, 215.

[7] Ibid 62-123 ; vol. v 197-214.

[8] Acts of the Privy Council passim.

sometimes difficult to draw between a Star Chamber case and a case for the court of High Commission.[1] It could act more effectually than the ordinary courts, because it could examine the parties,[2] and where occasion required, it habitually employed torture.[3] In so acting the court made permanent and valuable additions to our criminal law ; and it is clear that both the law itself and its administration needed improvement. Hudson supplies a striking illustration of the defects of the law.[4] One Saxy had by a forgery got judgment for £800 against his factor Hudson. Hudson was in prison, having been taken in execution upon the judgment so obtained against him. After the judgment had been got, Saxy was convicted of the forgery ; and yet the judge decided that this was no ground for relieving Hudson, " holding the judgment given so sacred that they would not deliver the innocent without the consent of the forger, who maliciously remained in prison himself, rather than he would deliver his wronged factor." The administration of the law was liable to be overborne by force, and its purity was not always above suspicion. Sometimes even the warrants of the Star Chamber itself could not be executed.[5] Officers sometimes raised riots to further their own ends under the pretence of justice.[6] Juries were habitually influenced. Hudson tells us that, during the hearing of a case of this kind, the Earl of Leicester said that he did not know that writing a letter to influence a juror was an offence.[7] No less a person than Sir R. Manwood, Chief Baron of the Exchequer, procured at the assizes a corrupt verdict in favour of one of his servants, and made use of his position to force one Roger Underwood, a very poor man, to give him a valuable chain.[8]

It is clear that these powers, when honestly exercised, were valuable and useful. It is true that the punishments inflicted often appear excessive and brutal ; but we must remember, in the first place, that the enormous fines which it imposed were

[1] Allen v. Jemmat and others, Star Chamber Cases (C.S.) 72, 73.

[2] Coke, Fourth Instit. 63.

[3] Dasent iii 230, 407 ; iv 171, 201, 284.   [4] Op. cit. 65, 66.

[5] Dasent xiii 106 ; xx, *xxii ;* the warrants of the court were sometimes forged, ibid xx 242 ; xxiv 486, 487.

[6] Hudson 83.   [7] Ibid 92.

[8] Dasent xix 424 ; xx 95, 219 ; xxii 449, 450 (1592), we have his submission and confession, " this day also the Lord Chief Baron having made and subscribed the above said submission before their Lordships touching his great offences and indignities committed to the dishonour of their Lordships in general, and to som of them in particular, and further promised to their Lordships that a chein formerly taken by the said Chief Baron from one Roger Underwood, a very poor man, pretending yt to be his own, should be forthwith delivered into the hands of the Lord Cobham, and likewize to be ordered by his Lordship for the matter in question touching the said chain, as in equity and conscience his lordship shal think meet and reasonable ; " for another notice of this case see Manningham's Diary (C.S.) 91.

habitually reduced, for as Hudson says, they were imposed not
" secundum qualitatem delicti," but " in terrorem populi ; " [1] and,
in the second place, that, apart from political cases, the cruelty
of the Star Chamber was the cruelty of the times rather than
cruelty of the court.[2]   The punishments awarded by statute law
were quite as severe.

(ii) The Council continually interfered in private disputes.

We have seen that the number of these cases was so great
that it seriously interfered with the administrative work of the
Council.   Some of these cases were brought before the court
because for various reasons it was impossible to get justice elsewhere.[3]   Others were cases concerning corporate bodies with
which the crown deemed itself to have especial concern,[4] whether
they were trading corporations, Oxford or Cambridge colleges,
or corporate towns.[5]   But, when all deductions have been made,
it is clear that the Council heard a large number of cases which
were purely private.   This is no doubt partly due to the fact
that a stronger and purer justice could there be had.   Partly
also it is due to the fact that the age was litigious.   When recourse to open force is prevented feuds will be prosecuted by
litigation.[6]   The court was open to all—" from king to beggar." [7]
The pertinacious litigant—even the personal litigant of the
female variety [8]—made good use of their opportunities.   A

---

[1] Hudson 224 ; Baildon, Les Reportes, etc., lxii, and App. VII. ; Gardiner,
History of England i 284.

[2] Baildon lxii, lxiii.

[3] Thus Hudson said at p. 57, the court used to direct a trial and to order that
the parties should abide by the result ; as he says, if this course were now pursued,
" great titles would not have five verdicts on the one side and six on the other, and
the land spent before the suit ended ; " cp. Lambard, Archeion 102-107 for instances
of cases of wrong-doing which the ordinary law was powerless to punish.

[4] Hudson 56.

[5] Dasent i 137 (City and Town of Oxford) ; ii 296 (Bailiffs of Oxford and Oriel
College) ; vii 119 (City and Town of Oxford) ; xix 318-321 (St. John's College,
Oxford) ; xiv 44, 78 (Trade of soap boilers at Gloucester) ; xix 277 (Corporation of
Waterford) ; xxii 444 (the towns of Colchester and Halstead, piracy of trade marks).

[6] This is a feature common to all ages.   Roger North noticed, in the latter
part of the seventeenth century, that " The Cornish men are very fierce and contentious, and strangely given to indict one another. . . . This, as they say, prevents
bloodshed ; which would follow if revenge had not that vent," Lives of the Norths
i 155-156.   A similar use was made of the Spanish Inquisition, Ranke, Turkish and
Spanish Monarchies, 62, 63 (Kelly's Tr.).   When a province is newly settled in
India there is an immediate rush of litigation to the courts, Maine, Early History
of Institutions, 289 ; he says, " If the transition from one state of society to another
in modern India was not sudden, but gradual and slow, as it universally was in the
old Ayran world, we should see the battle with technicalities going on in Court at
the same time that the battle was waged out of Court with sword and matchlock ; "
and this is just the picture presented to us by the Acts of the Privy Council ; see
e.g. Dasent xxii 226 ; and cp. Y.B. 12, 13 Ed. III. (R.S.) cxi, cxii ; Reid, op. cit. 178.

[7] Hudson 129.

[8] Baildon, Les Reportes, etc., lx ; in Rilie v. Sheldon (1603) 161, a woman who
appeared before the court after two verdicts against her, and sundry petitions to the
queen, was called " a clamorous and impudent woman," and ordered to be whipped,

tailor's bill,[1] matrimonial squabbles,[2] testamentary suits,[3] the ownership of a horse,[4] disputes between landlord and tenant,[5] poaching,[6] sharp practice of all kinds were brought before the board.[7] "Nothing," says Dasent, "is more remarkable than the constant devotion with which this comparatively trivial daily work was carried on by those whose whole energies might well have been absorbed in the anxious consideration of the dangers which were so closely besetting the country and the Queen. To Burghley and Walsingham, engaged in laboriously unravelling the tangled threads of a skein of conspiracy and murder, the details of the settlement of a quarrel between two Norfolk neighbours must have been supremely uninteresting : but they seldom missed a meeting of the Council." [8]

The jurisdiction of the provincial councils was substantially similar to that of the Star Chamber. In addition these Councils had power to determine personal actions and an equitable jurisdiction ; but they could not issue injunctions to stop proceedings before the common law courts.[9] Their common law and equitable jurisdiction was not rendered illegal by the Act of 1641,[10] which put an end to the jurisdiction of the Council and Star Chamber and of any courts exercising a like jurisdiction ; and we have seen that, after the Restoration, the Council of Wales was reconstituted, and continued to exercise this jurisdiction till it was abolished by statute in 1689.[11]

The testimony of contemporary writers and of modern historians proves that both Council and Star Chamber were, during the whole of the Tudor period, necessary and efficient institutions. Lambard calls the Star Chamber a " most noble and praisworthy court," and notes that by " the influence of its supereminent authority all other courts of law and justice that we have, are both the most surely supported, and the more evenly kept and managed." [12] " It is," says Coke, "the most honourable court

---

and her husband was fined £20 for not better governing his wife ; Lady Russel (1604, 1605), however, had her say—" all the Courte and presence murmuring and makynge greate noyse, gyving no care to anythinge she saide, her owne Counselle goinge from the barre allso ; yet shee wente one w^thoute any change or any waye abashed at all, in a very boulde and stoute manner . . . whose revenge of her tongue seemed to be the summe of her desire," Rilie v. Sheldon (1603) 276 ; in 1602 the lords had made an order that no woman was to appear in person ; but it does not appear to have been observed.

[1] Dasent viii 144. [2] Ibid vii 197 ; ix, *xxiii*. [3] Ibid xiv 49.
[4] Ibid i 29. [5] Ibid x 78 ; xi, *xxvii, xxviii ;* xii 18 ; xiv, *xxxi.*
[6] Ibid xi, *xxvii.* [7] Ibid xx, *xx,* 126, 127, 133, 134.
[8] Ibid xiv, *x.*
[9] Instructions for the Council of Wales (1617) xvii, xxi, Prothero, Documents 384-385 ; Reid, op. cit. 349, 362-363.
[10] Above 127 ; below 515.
[11] Above 127-128. [12] Archeion 217.

(our Parliament excepted) that is in the Christian world. . . . And it is truly said, Curia Cameræ Stellatæ, si vestustatem spectemus est antiquissima, si dignitatem, honoratissima. This court, the right institution and ancient orders thereof being observed, doth keep all England quiet." [1]   Bacon [2] called it "one of the sagest and noblest institutions of this kingdom". Palgrave, whose descriptive summary is as just as it is eloquent, [3] truly says that "the judicial character of the 'Lords and others of the Council' was so marked and prominent that they appeared to form the ruling aristocracy of the kingdom. Their vigilant equity was the safeguard of the weak and feeble. The poor looked to them for aid. Rich and powerful men feared their state, gravity, and discretion. The highest powers of justice seemed to be vested in them. The kingdom was under their magistracy and rule." In fact, the powers wielded by the Council and Star Chamber guided England through the great changes of this century of Renaissance and Reformation, enforced a high standard of duty on all other courts and persons entrusted with governmental functions, and thus not only gave internal peace to the country, but fitted Englishmen to use wisely that large measure of liberty which they acquired in the following century.

We shall now see that, during the closing years of the Tudor period, the jurisdiction thus wielded by the Council and Star Chamber had begun to excite the professional jealousy of some of the common lawyers. But this professional jealousy was quite ineffectual to limit the jurisdiction wielded by these bodies, until, by reason of the use made of the court of Star Chamber by the Stuarts, it was reinforced by a national opposition to the Stuart scheme of government in state and church.

III. The Early Stuart Period

The growing organization and jurisdiction of the court of Star Chamber, the creation of the various subordinate Councils throughout the country, the rapid development of the court of Chancery and the Court of Requests, and the growth of the jurisdiction of the court of Admiralty, threatened the supremacy of the common law system. All these courts acted upon principles and by means of a procedure unknown to the common law. It was natural, therefore, that the common lawyers should take alarm. I have already described the attack made by the common law courts upon the courts of Chancery and Requests; and we shall see that in the latter half of the sixteenth century they made a similar attack upon the court of Admiralty. But during the

---

[1] Fourth Instit. 65.   [2] History of Henry VII.   [3] Council 104-108.

greater part of the Tudor period there are very few signs of any conflict between the common law courts on the one side and the Council and Court of Star Chamber on the other. A decision in a case of 1493 that, according to the true construction of the Act Pro Camera Stellata, only the Chancellor, Treasurer and Privy Seal were the judges, and that the others were only assistants,[1] looks, Mr. Leadam thinks,[2] "like an attempt prompted by the jealousy entertained by the common law judges against the prerogative to impair the activity of the Star Chamber." Whether it was so or not, it failed;[3] and Coke considered that it rightly failed.[4] In 1550 there is a case in which the common law judges refused to obey the orders of the Council, because they considered that such obedience would be a breach of their oaths to obey the law and to stay no process of the common law.[5] In 1566 the judges put a restrictive interpretation upon the statutes which gave the Star Chamber power to punish for perjury.[6] But such cases are very rare ; and, in fact, during the earlier part of Elizabeth's reign, they do not seem to have been quick to resist the Council's interference with their jurisdiction.[7] But in the latter part of the reign the judges began to criticize the proceedings of the Council ; we can trace divergencies of opinion between the common lawyers and other members of the Council in the Star Chamber itself; and the legality of the Star Chamber and of certain other branches of the Council began to be questioned.

In 1591 the judges addressed to the Lord Chancellor and the Lord Treasurer an opinion as to imprisonments by the Council, "against the laws of the realm."[8] They complained that many had been imprisoned merely for prosecuting ordinary actions at the common law ; that persons discharged by the courts of common law had been again committed to prison ; and that persons had been imprisoned " till they would release the lawful benefit of their suits, judgments, or executions." They then gave it as their opinion that a committal by the Queen's special command, by order from the Council, or for treason, was good ; " but if any person shall be committed for any other cause, then the same ought specially to be returned."

---

[1] Y.B. 8 Hy. VII. Pasch. pl. 7—they reasoned on the analogy of Edward III.'s statute relating to the Exchequer Chamber, above 244.

[2] Select Cases in the Star Chamber (S.S.) i lix.

[3] Ibid i lviii, lix ; cf. Hudson, op. cit. 50.

[4] Fourth Instit. 62, cited below 513.

[5] Dasent, iii 159-160.   [6] Onslowe's Case, Dyer 342 b.

[7] Select Pleas of the Admiralty (S.S.) ii 22-23, 113 n. 2.

[8] Printed in vol. v App. I ; for the constitutional significance of this protest see vol. vi 32-34.

In a case reported in 1602[1] we find the professional feeling of the common lawyers strongly marked. Yelverton, judge of assize, had taken precedence of Burghley, the Lord President of the Council of the North, on the strength of a statute of Richard II.'s reign.[2] For this he was summoned before the court of Star Chamber. "The Lord Admiral was bitter against the judges, and said that he thought that the professors of the law would press their honours, and titles, and dignities from them." The Secretary said that the Council of State could alter or order the placing of persons of honour or office. On the other hand, the Lord Keeper and both the Chief Justices supported the judge— saying that the Council of State could not alter the course of the common law. One of them added that "he woulde be sorrye if yt coulde." On this occasion the court differed in opinion. But at another sitting, in the absence of the Chief Justice, it was ordered that Yelverton confess his fault at the assizes. In the end the Queen interfered and changed his circuit. An order had already been issued that the Vice-President of the Council of the North should also have precedence of the judge of assize.[3]

In this state of professional feeling we are not surprised that the legality of the jurisdiction of the Council was attacked, when-ever it was possible to do so. We have seen that certain branches of the Council were founded upon statutory authority.[4] It was impossible to go behind this, unless it could be shown that such authority had been exceeded. An attempt to do this was made, but without success, in the cases of the Council of Wales and the Council of the North.

The Council of Wales and the Marches had been, as we have seen, created by the prerogative; but it had been recognized by statute. In 1604 one Fairley had been imprisoned for dis-obedience to an order of the Council. He sued out his writ of Habeas Corpus. The writ was disobeyed by the Council. This ultimately brought on the question as to the territorial limits of the jurisdiction of the Council.[5] The judges resolved that it had no jurisdiction over the English counties of Worcester, Hereford, Gloucester and Shropshire.[6] But though the authority of the Council within the four shires was in consequence much dimin-

---

[1] Les Reportes, etc., 150; see Reid, op. cit. 351-354. It may be noted that in the case of Falkland v. Mountmorris and others 1631 (Cases in the Star Chamber (C.S.) 19, 20) Hyde, C.J., laid far more stress on undue means taken to influence a jury than the rest of the court.

[2] 20 Richard II. c. 3.   [3] Dasent xxxii 488.   [4] Above 502.

[5] For this controversy see Bacon's Works vii 569-611; Bacon argued in 1605 for the jurisdiction; see also S.P. Dom. (1603-1610) 398, xxxi 14; ibid 404-405, xxxi 30, 32; ibid 423, xxxii 13, for the views of Lord Eure, the Lord President of the Council; and cp. Egerton Papers (C.S.) 417.

[6] Coke, Fourth Instit. 242, 243.

ished, the crown did not intend entirely to relinquish it. It was seen that to do so would admit the illegality of all branches of the Council's jurisdiction founded on the prerogative alone.[1] As it was clear that the prerogative had usage, more or less recognized by the legislature, to support it, the royal advisers did not consider it expedient to submit to the views of the common lawyers. In 1605 an attempt was made to deal with the matter by statute. But this failed; and in 1607, when Bacon was Solicitor-General, a series of reformed instructions were issued for the guidance of the Council. The royal claims were maintained; but the extraordinary criminal jurisdiction of the Council was practically confined to Wales. But, after the Parliamentary proceedings of 1605, the maintenance of even a civil jurisdiction aroused a strong opposition. In Herefordshire the bishop and twenty-six of the leading gentry protested; and in Worcestershire the sheriff declined to obey the orders of the Council.[2] In 1608 the Privy Council decided to ask the judges whether the maintenance of the civil jurisdiction was legal; and, as there had long been a similar agitation against the Council of the North,[3] it was decided to argue at the same time the question of its legal position. The two cases were parallel as this Council had also been recognized by statute.[4] It was clear that a constitutional question of some importance had been raised. The case was argued for six days before the judges; and the opinion of the judges was given by Coke. As it was never published it was probably not favourable to the crown. This is the more probable, as Coke tells us, that in 1609 the judges resolved that the criminal jurisdiction given to the Council of the North to hear and determine certain criminal offences at their discretion, and to decide real actions and other civil suits was illegal.[5]

The crown did not, however, abandon its claims to exercise jurisdiction through the Council either in Wales and the Marches or in the North. In 1610 the grievances of the English counties were brought before Parliament. The king promised inquiry; but he did little more than promise. Though the agitation continued nothing was done; and in 1617 new instructions were issued, which gave to the Council of Wales and the Marches an extensive civil jurisdiction, an equitable jurisdiction, and a

---

[1] This danger was pointed out in 1610, S.P. Dom. (1603-1610) 649, lviii 56; and had been already experienced, ibid 531, xlviii 47.

[2] For other cases of agitation against the jurisdiction see S.P. Dom. (1603-1610) 398, xxxi 14; ibid 637, lvii 96; cp. ibid (1611-1618) 229, lxxvii 53; see ibid 262, lxxviii 74, 75, 76, for the efforts of Sir Herbert Crofts, the member for Hereford, on behalf of the four shires in the Parliament of 1610.

[3] Reid, op. cit. 221-222, 346-350, 355-358.

[4] 32 Henry VIII. c. 50; 13 Elizabeth c. 13; Fourth Instit. 246.

[5] Fourth Instit. 245, 246; Reid, op. cit. 358-359.

jurisdiction similar to that of the Star Chamber.[1] Similarly, the decision against the Council of the North was evaded, by omitting the clauses objected to in the commission, and inserting them in the secret instructions to the Council.[2] James I., on the protest of the judges of the court of Common Pleas, gave orders that the instructions should be enrolled.[3] But in 1632 the King's Bench was still issuing prohibitions against it.[4] Their effect upon the Council was small, as Charles I. in 1629 had directed it to keep within its jurisdiction, but if it kept within it to disregard Prohibitions.[5] Coke could only recommend some sort of statutory settlement of its jurisdiction.[6]

The attack upon these branches of the Council's jurisdiction, though backed by the common law courts, had failed. The opponents of the jurisdiction of the Council had a much weaker case against the Star Chamber itself. The more recently established branches of the Council—the Council of Wales and the Marches, and the Council of the North—were in a position like that held by the Court of Requests. They could not pray in aid a prescriptive title. In the Star Chamber the jurisdiction of the Council itself was exercised; and for the exercise of some kind of jurisdiction there were abundant precedents. Its position was more analogous to that of the court of Chancery. The common lawyers might dislike it, but they could not deny that for some purposes it was a legal court. Their attack upon it, therefore, took the form of an attempt to limit its jurisdiction. In order to do this, they contended that, as a distinct court, it owed its origin to the statute of 1487. That statute had in reality only defined, as certain earlier statutes had defined, some of the branches of the Council's jurisdiction which the circumstances of the time had rendered especially important; and, with a view to their more efficient exercise, it had entrusted them to a special committee.[7] But it was clear that at the beginning of the Tudor period the court of Star Chamber had begun to present the appearance of a court more or less separate from the Council

[1] Prothero, Documents 378-387; for an instance of the Prohibitions issued against the Council of Wales see Fox v. Blackwood (1615) Cro. Jac. 347—a Prohibition against meddling with freehold because it was a matter determinable by the common law.

[2] Fourth Instit. 246.

[3] They had granted prohibitions against the President and Council, ibid 246.

[4] Gardiner, History of England vii 238, 239.

[5] S.P. Dom. (1628-1629) 585, cxlv 23; cp. Rymer, Foedera xix 421; for Wentworth's manner of dealing with recalcitrants see Rushworth ii 88, 215-222; Wentworth's life in D.N.B. 273; S.P. Dom. (1631-1633) 450-451, cc xxvi 1.

[6] The existing statutory recognitions of this branch of the Council Coke treats as a recognition merely of its existence; "but what jurisdiction they have is the question," Fourth Instit. 246.

[7] Above 494-495.

acting as an executive body; and the power which the Star Chamber exercised of examining the defendant upon interrogatories was based on this Act.[1] It was therefore plausible to contend that these phenomena were due to the statute of Henry VII. It followed that the jurisdiction of the Star Chamber was limited by its provisions.

This theory was not in accord with historical fact; and it was condemned by the leading lawyers of the day irrespective of political party and professional bias. Hudson says:[2] "I well remember that the Lord Chancellor Egerton would often tell, that in his time, when he was a student, Mr. Serjeant Lovelace put his hand to a demurrer in this court, for that the matter of the bill contained other matters than were mentioned in the statute of 3 Henry VII., and Mr. Plowden, that great lawyer, put his hand thereto first, whereupon Mr. Lovelace easily followed. But the cause being moved in court, Mr. Lovelace, being a young man, was called to answer the error of his ancient Mr. Plowden, who very discreetly made his excuse at the bar that Mr. Plowden's hand was first unto it, and that he supposed that he might in anything follow St. Augustine. And although it were then overruled, yet Mr. Serjeant Richardson, thirty years after, fell again upon the same rock, and was sharply rebuked for the same." Coke in his Fourth Institute [3] argues strongly in the same sense. " This act of 3 Henry VII. did not raise a new court; for there was a court of Star Chamber, and all the King's Privy Council judges of the same . . . and therefore the sudden opinion in 8 Henry VII., and of others not observing the distinction between Acts declaratory of proceedings in an ancient court, and Acts introductory of a new law in raising of a new court, is both contrary to law and continual experience." It follows that the court had jurisdiction over offences other than those mentioned in the act, "and this must of necessity be in respect of the former jurisdiction." Bacon, as we have seen, upheld the legality of the court.[4] There is a strong case in favour of a view in which Coke and Bacon agreed.

But it is clear that the common lawyers were viewing with increasing suspicion any exercise of jurisdiction outside their own. Hudson probably well represents the views of the profession at the beginning of James I.'s reign when he says[5] that, "being in the second part of this treatise to handle the

---

[1] Above 495.   [2] Op. cit. at p. 51.

[3] At pp. 62, 63; the argument also appears in 1630, see Chambers' Case, Cro. Car. 168.

[4] Above 508; of the same opinion was Sir Th. Smith, Commonwealth, Bk. iii c. 4; and Lambard, Archeion 185-186, 197-200.

[5] Op. cit. at p. 49; cp. Lambard, Archeion 125-129.

jurisdiction of this high court [the Star Chamber], I must steer a course full of peril betwixt Scylla and Charybdis; for if on the one side I shall diminish the force, or shorten the stretching arm of this seat of monarchy, I should incur . . . much danger of reprehension; and if on the other side I should extend the power thereof beyond the due limits, my lords the judges, and my masters the professors of the common law, will easily tax me for encroaching upon the liberty of the subject, and account me not only unworthy of the name of my profession, but of the name of an Englishman."

As the controversy between the king and Parliament grew more bitter, it became more and more apparent that it could not be settled by merely legal reasoning. That controversy absorbed all existing differences of opinion upon many varied matters, and ranged the disputants in one of the two opposing camps. The upholder of the rights and privileges of Parliament, the common lawyer, the low churchman, and the Puritan opposed the upholder of the absolute prerogative, the upholder of the Council, and the high churchman. Both sides sought to prove their views by their interpretation of precedents drawn from history; and in both cases the interpretation was one-sided. But we have taken our law from the Parliamentary statesman, and we are apt, therefore, to forget that the historical basis upon which it purports to rest is often questionable. The legal views of their opponents have been ruled to be erroneous; and we are too ready, perhaps, to think that they are erroneous because their historical basis is false.

The tyrannical proceedings of the Star Chamber aroused popular feeling against it.[1] It was, it is true, an efficient court where the case before it was not political. But the political cases, though they were the smallest part of its daily business,[2] made the most noise at the time, and have given to it its reputation in history. The Parliamentary statesman saw the expediency of abolishing the most efficient means of prerogative government.[3] The common lawyer saw a means of at length triumphing over a rival judicature. The Puritan saw the fall of a court by which he had been persecuted.[4] The jurisdiction of the Council, there-

[1] See the cases of Prynne, Burton, and Bastwick, Gardiner, History of England viii 228-233.

[2] Les Reportes, etc., lii; Reports of Cases in the Star Chamber (C.S.); Gardiner, op. cit. vii 85.

[3] Clarendon, History of the Rebellion (Ed. 1843) 28.

[4] The limit was not clearly drawn between the jurisdiction of the Star Chamber and the High Commission, Cases in the Court of Star Chamber (C.S.) 72; we shall see, below 608-609, that the reason is to be found in the fact that the High Commission occupied, in relation to the ecclesiastical department of the state, a position fundamentally similar to that occupied by the Council and the Star Chamber in relation to the secular departments.

fore, fell with the victory of the Parliament in 1641.[1] The preamble to the Act is a good illustration of the historical method
of the Parliamentary statesman. It is hardly less one-sided
than the reading of history to be found in Finch or Berkeley's
judgments in the *Case of Ship Money*. It adopted a legal theory
which had been decisively condemned by the best lawyers of the
day.

The preamble recites Magna Carta, and the statutes of
Edward III.'s reign passed against the jurisdiction of the Council.[2] It recites the fact that it has no proper Latin plea roll,
as by statute it ought to have. It recites the statute 3 Henry
VII. c. 1 and its amendment by the statute 21 Henry VIII. c.
20, and states that the "judges have not kept themselves to the
points limited by the said statute." These historical facts are
evidently intended to show that the court is illegal. We have
seen that they show nothing of the kind. But though we cannot
take our history from preambles to statutes passed in times of
political excitement, we still take our law as to the jurisdiction
of the Council from this particular statute. I must therefore
state its provisions in some detail.

The Star Chamber, the Council of Wales, the Council of the
North, the jurisdiction of the Star Chamber exercised by the
court of the Duchy of Lancaster, and the court of Exchequer
of the county Palatine of Chester were abolished; and "from
henceforth no court, council, or place of judicature shall be
erected . . . within this realm of England or dominion of Wales,
which shall . . . exercise the same or the like jurisdiction as is
or hath been . . . exercised in the said Court of Star Chamber."[3]
It was further enacted[4] "that neither His Majesty nor his Privy
Council have, or ought to have, any jurisdiction . . . by English
bill, petition, articles, libel, or any other arbitrary way whatsoever, to examine or draw into question, determine or dispose of
the lands, tenements, hereditaments, goods or chattels of any of
the subjects of this kingdom, but that the same ought to be
tried and determined in the ordinary courts of justice, and by the
ordinary course of the law." Penalties were imposed upon any
official who infringed the provisions of the Act;[5] and the
procedure upon the writ of Habeas Corpus was applied with

[1] 16 Charles I. c. 10; it is said that the king at first delayed his assent to the bill,
but that on the Commons threatening to adjourn he thought better of it and gave
his assent, S.P. Dom. (1641-1643) 44 cccclxxxii 34.

[2] Above 487.

[3] 16 Charles I. c. 10 §§ 1, 4; as we have seen, when the Council of Wales was
restored in 1660 "the same or the like jurisdiction" was not restored to it, above
126-127.

[4] § 5.   [5] 16 Charles I. c. 10 §§ 6 and 7.

improvements to the case of persons imprisoned by the Council.[1]

Thus a number of courts, and a body of law, which threatened to be a serious rival to the common law, came to an end. With the effect of this Act upon English law as a whole, and upon the jurisdiction of the common law courts I cannot now deal fully. At this point it will be sufficient to say that it is largely due to this Act that English law knows a theory of ministerial responsibility and not a system of administrative law; and that the common law courts permanently enlarged their jurisdiction criminal and civil.

IV. THE LATER HISTORY

When the Act of the Long Parliament deprived the Council of all jurisdiction over English bills or petitions, it deprived it of the greater part of the jurisdiction which it then exercised. But it did not deprive it of all its jurisdiction, because it still left it able to deal with appeals initiated by bill or petition from places outside the jurisdiction of the ordinary courts of law and equity. The expansion of England during the eighteenth century caused this jurisdiction to become of increasing importance. From the first it was dealt with by a committee of the Council, the constitution and jurisdiction of which are now regulated by numerous statutes. I shall therefore describe in the first place the history of this committee, and in the second place its jurisdiction.

(1) The appeal committee of the Privy Council.

In 1667 we hear of a committee of the Council for trade, the foreign plantations, and to hear appeals from the islands of Jersey and Guernsey.[2] The attorney-general and the king's advocate were directed to assist the committee in the hearing of these appeals. In 1696 it was ordered that, "all appeals from any of the plantations be heard *as formerly* by a committee who are to report the matters so heard by them to His Majesty in Council"; and "that all the lords of the Council or any three of them be appointed a committee for that purpose."[3] This committee, when it sat to hear appeals, was generally a small committee, consisting of "the chief legal authorities, the Bishop

---

[1] § 8. It may be noted that the Commonwealth governments found themselves obliged to set up similar courts to deal with disaffected persons which had considerably larger powers than the court of Star Chamber had ever possessed, see Acts and Ordinances of the Commonwealth ii 492 (1650), 780 (1653), 917 (1654).

[2] Cited Safford and Wheeler, The Practice of the Privy Council (Ed. 1901) 134; cf. Acts of the Privy Council (Colonial Series) i Introd.

[3] Ibid ii 310.

of London, one or other of the two Secretaries of State, and such other members of the Council as were interested in the matters in hand."[1] But each of these smaller committees was regarded as the committee for appeals from the Plantations,[2] which was in substance a committee of the whole Council.[3] It was only natural therefore that many miscellaneous matters relating to colonial government shall be referred to it by the Council. The most famous of these references was that of the petition of the House of Representatives of Massachusetts, presented by their agent Benjamin Franklin in 1774, praying for the removal of the Governor and the Lieutenant-Governor. Wedderburn, the Solicitor-General, made a personal attack upon Franklin, and the petition was contemptuously rejected[4]—an action which as much as any other single event helped to cause the American Civil War.

As the eighteenth century advanced, the colonies increased in number and importance, and our Indian Empire was founded.[5] This naturally led to an increase in the number of appeals heard,[6] and to the gradual formation of rules of procedure. Thus rules were laid down as to the conditions under which appeals lay,[7] as to the manner in which the cases of the parties must be presented,[8] and as to costs.[9] The committee were aware of the importance of laying down uniform rules throughout the British Dominions. For instance, in 1765, in a case which involved the construction of a will relating to land, "their Lordships thought it highly fit for the sake of uniformity and certainty in a matter upon which titles to land may depend, that a case should be made for the opinion of the court of King's Bench."[10] The fact that so many appeals came to the committee would seem to show that its jurisdiction was both needed,[11] and commanded approval. But occasionally the colonial authorities were recalcitrant. Orders were sometimes disobeyed,[12] and proceedings were sometimes continued in the colonial courts in spite of the pendency of an appeal.[13] Occasionally the proceedings of the

---

[1] Acts of the Privy Council (Colonial) ii *ix.*

[2] Ibid ii *ix x.*   [3] Ibid ii *vii viii;* ibid iii *viii ix.*

[4] Ibid v 385-388; and cf. introd. *xiv xv.*

[5] 13 George III. c. 63 provided for the establishment of a supreme court at Fort William, and enacted (§ 18) that appeals should lie to the Privy Council.

[6] "Taking the fifty years from 1720-1770, a comparison between the number of appeals in the first decade of the period and the last show a change from 87-134, and in the last year of the said half century the number reached 23, whereas the average of the ascertained yield of previous years was no higher than 11; in 1755 and in 1765 it reached 18," ibid v *xxxi.*

[7] Ibid ii *xiii xiv.*   [8] Ibid iii 228.

[9] Ibid ii *xv.*   [10] Ibid iv 694.

[11] Ibid ii *xii* for illustrative cases.   [12] Ibid ii 743 (1727).

[13] Ibid iv 309-311 (1755).

committee were spoken of in the colonial courts with great disrespect, even by the colonial judges.[1]

It is clear, however, that the mass of judicial business which came before the committee was giving it some of the characteristics of a law court. Thus the hearing was usually public; and in 1829 reports of its decisions began to be published.[2] In 1832 its jurisdiction was still further increased. A statute passed in that year abolished the court of Delegates,[3] and handed over its jurisdiction to hear appeals from the ecclesiastical courts and the court of Admiralty to this committee of the Privy Council.[4] It was obvious that both the constitution and the powers of a committee of the Council entrusted with these important judicial functions needed to be more clearly defined. For these reasons an Act was passed in 1833 "for the better administration of justice in His Majesty's Privy Council." [5]

The Act constituted the following persons members of the Judicial Committee: The President of the Council, the Lord Chancellor, and such members of the Privy Council who hold or shall have held the offices of Lord Keeper or First Commissioner of the Great Seal, Chief Justice of any of the three common law courts, Master of the Rolls, Vice-Chancellor, Judge of the Prerogative Court of the Archbishop of Canterbury, Judge of the Court of Admiralty, Chief Judge in Bankruptcy, and in ecclesiastical cases, every archbishop or bishop being a privy councillor. The crown was empowered to appoint two other persons to be members, to summon other members, or to direct the attendance of the judges.[6] By the Judicial Committee Act of 1871 the crown was empowered to appoint four paid members of the Judicial Committee from among the judges of the superior courts, or the Chief Justices of the High Courts in Bengal, Madras, or Bombay;[7] and Acts of 1895[8] and 1913[9] have added to the committee certain Canadian, Australian, and South African judges who are members of the Privy Council. By the Appellate Jurisdiction Act of 1876 the archbishops and bishops have ceased

---

[1] Thus the Attorney-General of the Barbadoes told the Council that, in 1772, when, " Mr. Keeling's counsel objected to the impropriety of suffering His Majesty's Order, which was mandatory to the court, to be impeached by the parties, they were surprised into silence by this very remarkable reply of the judges, *that His Majesty in Council was as likely to err as the judges of that Court*," Acts of the Privy Council (Colonial) vi 536; cf. ibid vi 505-506 for some uncomplimentary remarks made by counsel in Rhode Island.

[2] Selborne, Judicial Procedure in the Privy Council 23.

[3] Below 605. [4] 2, 3 William IV. c. 92.

[5] 3, 4 William IV. c. 41. [6] Ibid §§ 1, 6, 16, 30.

[7] 34, 35 Victoria c. 91. [8] 58, 59 Victoria c. 44.

[9] 3, 4 George V. c. 21.

to be members of the committee, but in certain cases they may be called in as assessors.[1]

Any four of these persons formed a quorum.[2] This number was subsequently reduced to three.[3] Provisions were made as to the procedure of the committee upon certain points and upon costs.[4] It was directed that the report of the committee should be read in open court.[5] In other respects the practice and procedure of the Council was unchanged.[6] But it was provided in 1915[7] that the Judicial Committee might sit in more than one division. The limits on the numbers in the Judicial Committee were removed by the administration of Justice Act, 1928.[7a]

In two important respects the practice and procedure of the Judicial Committee differs from that of the House of Lords.

(i) The Judicial Committee is not always bound by its own decisions;[8] its decisions do not bind the English common-law courts.

(ii) It had always been the practice of the Privy Council, dating certainly from the Orders of the seventeenth century, never to notice in their report to the crown any dissentient opinion.[9] It was resolved to adhere to that practice in 1833; and it was further enforced by an Order of 1878.[10] In fact, there have only been three cases in which there has been any publication of dissentient opinions.[11] This rule is supported mainly on the ground that it adds moral weight to a tribunal which must give the law to many different races in different stages of civilization.[12] This consideration is no doubt decisive. At the same time it is obvious that the student or the historian of law, and perhaps even the legislature, derive considerable benefit from the opposite practice followed in the House of Lords.

The practice in both these matters springs from the fact that the Judicial Committee is a committee of an executive Council. As we shall see, when we come to deal with the jurisdiction of

[1] 39, 40 Victoria c. 59 §§ 14, 24; for the provisions of that Act which amalgamate the paid staff of the Judicial Committee with that of the House of Lords see below 645.

[2] 3, 4 William IV. c. 41 § 5.　　　　[3] 6, 7 Victoria c. 38.
[4] 3, 4 William IV. c. 41 §§ 7-15.　　[5] Ibid § 3.
[6] Selborne, Judicial Procedure, etc., 26, 27.
[7] §, 6 George V. c. 92.
[8] It is clear that it is not bound by its own decision if the decision was given ex parte, Tooth v. Power [1891] A.C. at p. 292; or in certain ecclesiastical cases Ridsdale v. Clifton (1877) 2 P.D. at pp. 306-307; Read v. Bishop of Lincoln [1892] A.C. at pp. 654-655; whether this applies to any other cases quære; for the practice followed by the House of Lords see above 375-376.
[9] Selborne, Judicial Procedure, etc., 27-30.
[10] It was ordered that the ancient rule be strictly adhered to, "that no disclosure be made touching the matters treated of in Council, and no publication made by any man how the particular voices went."
[11] Two cases of Mr. Gorham in 1853, and the case connected with Essays and Reviews in 1864; see Phillimore, Eccl. Law (Ed. 1895) 975-977.
[12] Selborne, Judicial Procedure, etc., 54-63.

the Judicial Committee, it is not easy, even at the present day, to divide quite clearly judicial from executive functions. The Act of 1833 no doubt gives to the Judicial Committee many of the essential characteristics of a court. But Lord Selborne pointed out, that "when the Judicial Committee is spoken of as a court or a tribunal, having jurisdiction, and delivering judgments, those who use that phraseology do not mean, that it has, like the other courts, a delegated, but self-contained and independent judicial function ; the whole legal operation, which receives its final consummation and sole efficacy from the direct official action of the Sovereign in Council is always implied. This may be called form ; and so may all other acts of the royal authority when exercised according, not to arbitrary rule, but to constitutional usage. But such forms are facts ; and their influence has determined the whole course of procedure in this jurisdiction. including its procedure in judgment." [1] Historically, however, it is the oldest of our royal courts. The act of the crown in allowing or dismissing an appeal, according to the advice contained in the report of the Judicial Committee, is the direct lineal descendant of the judgment given by the king in person in the Curia Regis.

(2) The jurisdiction of the appeal committee of the Privy Council.

(i) Appellate jurisdiction over the foreign dominions of the crown.

Appeals from the Channel Islands were the earliest instances of this branch of the Council's jurisdiction ; and this jurisdiction was extended by analogy to the Isle of Man, and to all the foreign plantations of the crown. With the growth of the colonies it has become by far the most important part of the jurisdiction of the Judicial Committee.

The Channel Islands were anciently part of the Duchy of Normandy, and therefore their law is founded upon the laws and customs of Normandy.[2] As early as the reign of Edward III. the court of King's Bench decided that it had no jurisdiction over these islands ; "ideo recordum retro traditur cancellario ut inde fiat commissio domini regis ad negotia prædicta in insula prædicta audienda et terminanda secundum consuetudines insulæ prædictæ." [3] An Order in Council of Henry VII.'s reign (1495) directed that all appeals from these islands should go, not to any

---

[1] Judicial Procedure, etc., 44-45. A valuable analysis of the basis of appeals to the Judicial Committee was given by Lord Maugham in Renouf v. A.-G. for Jersey (1936) A. C. 445.

[2] Hale, Common Law, 266, 267 ; Coke, Fourth Instit. 286 ; 8 S.T. N.S. App. C.

[3] Cited Hale, Common Law 267, 268.

English court, but to the king and Council ·[1] and another Order to a similar effect was made in 1565.[2] The courts at Westminster, and especially the court of Chancery and the court of Requests, were prohibited from hearing causes there arising. In 1572 an Order was issued regulating appeals from Jersey;[3] and this is probably the earliest Order in Council passed with this object. A similar Order relating to Guernsey was made in 1580.[4] Hudson treats the jurisdiction as well settled.[5] We have seen that these appeals are specially alluded to in the Order of 1667.[6] The jurisdiction of the Judicial Committee in relation to these appeals contains one archaic trait. We have seen that an appeal in early law often takes the form of a personal complaint against the judge.[7] The Channel Islands possess a peculiar appeal termed a "doléance." It has been defined to be "a personal charge against a judicial officer—a personal charge either of misconduct or of negligence."[8] It still exists in a modified form as a convenient form of procedure, which can be used without implying any disrespect to the judge whose conduct is the subject of complaint.[9]

The Isle of Man[10] was originally part of the kingdom of Norway. In the reign of Edward III. the Earl of Salisbury conquered the island from the Scotch, and received a grant of it from the king. He sold it to William le Scroope. Henry IV. seized it after Scroope's rebellion, and granted it to the Earl of Northumberland. After his rebellion it was granted in 1405 to the House of Stanley; and it remained in that family until it was sold in 1765 to the crown.[11] The question of the right of the Council to hear appeals from the Isle of Man does not appear to have been raised till the case of *Christian* v. *Corren* in 1716.[12] The Council asserted its right to hear appeals on the ground

---

[1] Cited Safford and Wheeler 228; see 8 S.T. N.S. App. C. for an account of various Orders in Council relating to the Channel Islands.

[2] Safford and Wheeler 229.

[3] Ibid 229, 233. [4] Ibid 224-247.

[5] Star Chamber 62; but he evidently thinks it strange that ordinary cases should be tried there as a matter of course, "How it is drawn to the council table from a public court of justice I know not; sure I am, it is more proper the subject should appeal for justice to a public court of justice rather than to a private board, although the most honourable in the world;" cp. Dasent viii 61, 75, 76; xv. 286, 335.

[6] Above 516. [7] Above 213-214.

[8] Crédit Foncier of England v. Amy (1874) 6 P.C. at p. 155. It was termed "odious" by the code of 1771.

[9] Ex parte Nicolle (1879) 5 A.C. at p. 348.

[10] For its earlier history see Coke, Fourth Instit. 283; Hale, Common Law 255; Attorney-General for Isle of Man v. Mylchreest (1879) 4 A.C. 294, 301.

[11] For some doubts as to the title of the Stanley family see Egerton Papers (C.S.) 281; for an instance of a pardon granted by the Earl of Derby see ibid 132-134.

[12] 1 P. Wms. 329; the Christian family and the Derby family seem to have been old antagonists, see S.P. Dom. 1663-1664 274, lxxx 75.

that a right to apply to the crown for redress for wrongs done by any court existed in all cases where there was a tenure from the crown. Parker, C.J., expressly compared it with the copyholders right to apply to the court of Chancery; and "Lord Derby also, at length, rather than that some things in the grant made by the crown to his ancestors should be looked into, chose to submit and express his consent."

In fact it was becoming recognized that the crown in Council was the proper tribunal to hear appeals from English dominions outside England, or outside the jurisdiction of the English courts. In 1683 it had been decided that an appeal lay to the king in Council from the county Palatine of Chester;[1] and in 1724 it was laid down generally that all appeals from the Plantations ought to be heard by the king in Council.[2] Appeals will also lie from places outside the British Empire over which the crown has jurisdiction if so provided by Order in Council issued under the provisions of the Foreign Jurisdiction Act, 1890.[3]

The appellate jurisdiction of the Council is founded upon the principle that it is the prerogative of the crown to entertain applications for redress from its subjects. The subject has as a rule no *right* to appeal unless that right has been specially conferred upon him.[4] Such grant may be contained in a statute, ordinance, letters patent, charter, order in council, or in the instructions to the governor.[5] But the subject can always petition the crown for leave to appeal; and the crown can grant such leave in civil or criminal cases, unless that right has been expressly taken away by the legislature. To take away the prerogative of the crown to grant such leave express words must be used. The mere statement that the decision of the court of any colony shall be final will not suffice.[6] The only instance in which this right has been thus expressly taken away, is the clause in the Act establishing the Australian Constitution, which provides that the crown shall not be able to grant leave to appeal upon any question, "as to the limits inter se of the Constitutional powers of the Commonwealth and those of any

---

[1] Jennet v. Bishop, 1 Vern. 184.

[2] Fryer v. Bernard, 2 P. Wms. 262. [3] 53, 54 Victoria c. 37.

[4] Mayor of Montreal v. Brown and Springle (1876) 2 A.C. 168, 184; the case turned on French Canadian law; and it was said that, "It must be borne in mind that the rule of law in this country that an appeal does not lie unless given by express legislative enactment, does not prevail in French or Canadian law, when the presumption is in favour of the existence of what one of the judges of the Queen's Bench in Canada terms 'the sacred right of appeal.'"

[5] Safford and Wheeler 710.

[6] Johnston v. the Minister and Trustees of St. Andrew's Church (1877) 3 A.C. 159. In so far as Cuvillier v. Aylwin, 2 Knapp P.C. 72, lays down a contrary rule it has been overruled, re Louis Marois (1862) 15 Moo. 189, 193; Cushing v. Dupuy (1880) 5 A.C. at pp. 417, 418.

State or States, or as to the limits inter se of the Constitutional powers of any two or more States," unless the High Court of Australia certifies that the question is one which ought to be determined by the Council.[1]

The conditions under which leave to appeal will be granted differ according as the case is civil or criminal.

In civil cases it has been laid down that leave to appeal from the Supreme Court of Canada or the High Court of Australia should not be granted, " save when the case is of gravity involving matter of public interest or some important question of law, or affecting property of considerable amount, or where the question is otherwise of some public importance or of a very substantial character."[2] But even if a case does comply with the requisites of public importance, and substantial character, the judgment appealed from may appear to the Council to be so clearly right that they will refuse leave.[3]

The Council is much slower to grant leave to appeal in criminal cases. To make a practice of granting leave in such cases would offer a serious obstruction to the administration of justice. "The rule has been repeatedly laid down, and has been invariably followed, that Her Majesty will not review or interfere with the course of criminal proceedings, unless it is shown that, by a disregard of the forms of legal process, or by some violation of the principles of natural justice, or otherwise, substantial and grave injustice has been done."[4]

This appellate jurisdiction is by far the most important branch of the jurisdiction of the Privy Council both in bulk and also by reason of its political importance. In fact, just as the act of the crown in allowing or dismissing an appeal according to the advice contained in the report of the Judicial Committee is the direct lineal descendant of the judgment given by the king in person in the Curia Regis,[5] so the Judicial Committee itself is now doing for the Empire somewhat the same service as the Curia Regis formerly did for England. Like the Curia Regis it

---

[1] 63, 64 Victoria c. 12 § 74; the section goes on to provide that, "except as provided in this section this Constitution shall not impair any right which the Queen may be pleased to exercise by virtue of Her Royal Prerogative to grant special leave of appeal from the High Court to Her Majesty in Council;" for a case illustrating the application of this section see Jones v. Commonwealth Court of Conciliation, etc. [1917] A.C. 528.

[2] Prince v. Gagnon (1882) 8 A.C. at p. 105; *Daily Telegraph* v. McLaughlin [1904] A.C. 776.

[3] La Cité de Montreal v. Les Ecclesiastiques, etc. (1889) 14 A.C. at p. 662.

[4] In re Abraham Mallory Dillett (1887) 12 A.C. at p. 467; cf. Falkland Islands Co. v. the Queen, 1 Moo. P.C. N.S. 312; Reg. v. Bertrand (1867) 1 P.C. at p. 530; Ex parte Deeming [1892] A.C. 422; Lanier v. the King [1914] A.C. 221; Ibrahim v. Rex ibid at p. 615; Arnold v. the King Emperor ibid 644.

[5] Above 34, 520.

is, as Professor Pollard has pointed out,[1] creating a common law for the disparate parts of the Empire, and so paving the way for "common politics and a common Parliament."

(ii) We have seen that an Act of 1832 constituted the Privy Council the final court of appeal in ecclesiastical causes.[2] Later statutes dealing with ecclesiastical matters have in some cases added to its jurisdiction.[3] But the Acts of 1857,[4] which transferred the ecclesiastical jurisdiction over Probate and Divorce to the newly-constituted Probate and Divorce court, provided that appeals in such matters should go to the House of Lords.

(iii) The same Act of 1832 provided that the Privy Council should be the court of final appeal from the court of Admiralty, and from the Vice-Admiralty courts in the colonies;[5] and the Act of 1833 transferred both this jurisdiction and the jurisdiction to hear appeals in cases of Prize to the Judicial Committee created by that Act.[6]

(iv) Statutes have given the Judicial Committee cognizance of certain matters of a quasi-judicial character. Thus, till 1907, applications for the extensions of patents[7] came before it; and applications for a licence to print a book when the proprietor of the copyright refuses to publish after the author's death,[8] still come before it. Applications in connexion with the alteration of the statutes of the Universities and Colleges of Oxford and Cambridge come before a committee of the Council, now called the Universities Committee, two of the members of which must be the Lord Chancellor and a member of the Judicial Committee.[9] It is provided generally by the Act of 1833 that the crown may, as under the older practice, specially refer any matter it sees fit to the Judicial Committee.[10] Under the statutory power many miscellaneous questions have been so referred—a dispute between the legislative Council and the legislative assembly of Queens-

---

[1] " It is, in fact, in almost precisely the position of the *curia regis* under Henry II. and his successors, which, borrowing from various sources of jurisprudence, welded these elements together, and applying them in judicial eyres to the local customs of English shires, created a common law, and prepared the way for common politics and a common Parliament," The Commonwealth at War 225-226.

[2] 2, 3 William IV. c. 92.

[3] 3, 4 Victoria c. 86 ; 55, 56 Victoria c. 32.

[4] 20, 21 Victoria cc. 77, 85 ; below 624, 630.

[5] For the alterations made by the Judicature Acts see below 643.

[6] 3, 4 William IV. c. 41 § 2 ; for the earlier history of this jurisdiction see below 561-565 ; it had also a certain jurisdiction connected with ships under the Foreign Enlistment Act 1870, 33, 34 Victoria c. 90 §§ 14, 27.

[7] 5, 6 William IV. c. 83 ; 46, 47 Victoria c. 57 § 25 ; 7 Edward VII. c. 29 § 18.

[8] 5, 6 Victoria c. 45 § 5.

[9] 25, 26 Victoria c. 26 § 1 (Oxford); 19, 20 Victoria c. 88 (Cambridge); 40, 41 Victoria c. 48 § 44.

[10] 3, 4 William IV. c. 41 § 4 ; see above 517 for the older practice.

land;[1] a question as to the validity of certain Orders in Council relating to Jersey;[2] disputes between two prelates;[3] a dispute between the Legislative Council of Southern Rhodesia and the British South Africa Company.[4] When matters are thus referred to the Judicial Committee the question is discussed merely judicially. If it is desired to discuss them from a political point of view the matter is referred to a mixed committee.[5]

These quasi-judicial functions exercised by the Judicial Committee at the present day may help us, by the way of analogy, to understand some of the difficulties which meet us in the earlier history of the Council. There is no doubt that the Judicial Committee is a perfectly distinct committee of the Council possessing most of the characteristics of a law court. But we can see that it hears cases quite different in kind from those which come before an ordinary law court ; and that in some cases its members sit upon other committees of the Council. We can hardly expect to find that the relations between the Council and the Star Chamber were precisely defined in the seventeenth century, when in the present century, we see the members of the Judicial Committee taking cognizance of matters not strictly judicial, and assisting other committees of the Council in the work of administration.

The Statute of Westminster, 1931, has made it possible for the Dominions to abolish the appeal to the Judicial Committee, and this has for the most part been done. The only appeals now coming from those parts of the Commonwealth then known as Dominions are those from New Zealand, Ceylon, and from Australia in other than " inter se " matters.

[1] Safford and Wheeler 775.
[2] In the matter of the States of Jersey (1853) 8 S.T. N.S. 285.
[3] In re the Bishop of Natal (1864) 3 Moo. P.C. N.S. 116, 156, 157.
[4] In re Southern Rhodesia [1919] A.C. 211.   [5] Safford and Wheeler 770.

CHAPTER VII

COURTS OF A SPECIAL JURISDICTION

I N this chapter I shall consider certain courts which administered bodies of law which fell outside the jurisdiction of the ordinary courts of law and equity. These courts fell into three groups: The courts which administered the Law Merchant; the court of the Constable and the Marshall; and the Ecclesiastical courts.

I. THE COURTS WHICH ADMINISTERED THE LAW MERCHANT

I shall deal with the history of the Law Merchant in subsequent volumes.[1] But, in order to understand the history of the courts which administered it, it is necessary at this point to give a short and summary account of its leading characteristics.

The Law Merchant of primitive times comprised both the maritime and the commercial law of modern codes. From the earliest period in their history an intimate relationship has subsisted between them. Both applied peculiarly to the merchants, who, whether alien or subject, formed in the Middle Ages a class very distinct from the rest of the community. Both laws grew up in a similar manner from the customary observances of a distinct class. Both laws were administered in either the same or in similar courts, which were distinct from the ordinary courts. Both laws differed from the common law. Both had in the Middle Ages an international character; and both continued to possess this international character right down to modern times.[2]

(i) Maritime Law.

The maritime laws of the Middle Ages were contained in certain bodies of local customs, which, like all such customs, showed a tendency to expand as they grew older. Each of these bodies of custom took its name from some one port. Each was

---

[1] Vol. v 60-154; vol. viii 99-300.

[2] " The maritime law is not the law of a particular country, but the general law of nations," *per* Lord Mansfield, Luke v. Lyde (1759) 2 Burr. 887; " The law of merchants is jus gentium and the judges are bound to take notice of it," Mogadara v. Holt (1691), Shower 318.

adopted by other ports, and one or other of them ruled the coasting trade of the whole of mediæval Europe.[1] The body of customs adopted by England, and inserted at a later date into the Black Book of the Admiralty,[2] were the judgments of Oleron. They originated in the laws of the commune of Oleron ; they were adopted by the seaport towns of Normandy and Brittany ; and they were transplanted to Damme, Bruges, and to England.[3] A copy of Edward II.'s reign, representing an early version, is to be found in the archives of the City of London,[4] and in the Red Book of Bristol.[5] Such was the repute of these laws of Oleron that mariners of other countries came there to obtain the judgment of its court.[6] The body of customary sea laws in force in the Mediterranean was known as the Consolato del Mare, and is probably of Catalan origin.[7] It was probably drawn up in the fifteenth century for the use of the consuls of the sea at Barcelona, from older collections of the customs of seaport towns within the kingdom of Aragon,[8] just as the Black Book was drawn up from the laws of Oleron for the use of the court of Admiralty in England. Before they had thus been reduced to writing they had been introduced into the Mediterranean ports, as the laws of Oleron had been introduced into the ports of the Atlantic and the North Sea. "They were introduced from Barcelona first of all into Valencia, then into the island of Majorca, then into Sicily, then into Roussillon, all of which countries were under the sceptre of the kings of Aragon before any version of them was printed at Barcelona. Within half a century after they were printed in the Book of the Consulate of the Sea at Barcelona, they were translated into the languages of Castile and of Italy. They were translated into French before the conclusion of the sixteenth century, into Latin some time in the seventeenth century, into Dutch at the beginning of the eighteenth century, and into German in the course of the same century."[9] From the Baltic come two codes of sea laws. One comes from Lubeck ;[10] and the other and the more important from Wisby.[11] The latter is the more important, because, while the Lubeck code influenced mainly trade within the Baltic, the Wisby code influenced the trade of the Baltic with foreign ports.[12]

---

[1] Black Book of the Admiralty (R.S.) ii xxxix seqq.
[2] For an account of this work see vol. v 125-127.
[3] Black Book of the Admiralty i lxiii ; cp. R.P. iii 498 (4 Hy. IV. n. 47).
[4] Black Book of the Admiralty i lxvii.   [5] L.Q.R. xvii 234.
[6] Black Book of the Admiralty ii xxxvii.
[7] Ibid iii xxxiv ; vol. v 70-71.
[8] Black Book of the Admiralty iii xxxv.   [9] Ibid lxxiii.
[10] Ibid iv xxi, xxii.   [11] Ibid iv xxiii.
[12] This code had, as we might expect, a cosmopolitan character ; it comes in fact from three sources—the first is a Baltic source, and the earliest laws attributable

Other towns possessed bodies of sea laws of their own.   Thus we possess the laws of Amalphi[1] and of Trani;[2] and it is clear from the Domesday of Ipswich that that town possessed a court in which pleas relating to maritime matters were pleaded from tide to tide.[3]   But these three codes—the laws of Oleron, the Consolato del Mare, and the maritime laws of Wisby, became the leading maritime codes of Europe.   In fact these codes, " form as it were a continuous chain of maritime law, extending from the easternmost parts of the Baltic Sea through the North Sea, and along the coast of the Atlantic to the Straits of Gibraltar, and thence to the furthest eastern shores of the Mediterranean."[4]

(ii) Commercial Law.

It is probable that in Europe, in the troubled times of the ninth and tenth centuries, the merchants had always known a special market law.   With the increase of commerce in the eleventh and twelfth centuries, and the rise of great commercial cities, the law of the merchants received a great impetus.[5]   Many of the commercial cities of Italy codified its rules;[6] and so it became at once more definite and more elaborate.   " As original authorities for the early history of the law merchant," says Mr. Mitchell, " the Italian commercial statutes are invaluable; they throw a flood of light on the origin and development of commercial rules and customs that then or afterwards found their way into the commercial laws of Europe."[7]   We shall see that the Italian jurists had produced in their Libri Feudorum something in the nature of a model code of feudal law.[8]   In the same way their collections of mercantile custom were the model to which the usages of the merchants of other states tended more or less to approximate.   Usages differed from place to place. But it was generally recognized that the laws of markets and fairs and the law administered by the specially mercantile courts within the boroughs was a special law merchant, differing from the ordinary law.

Thus for mercantile as for maritime affairs various towns had their codes of customs by which mercantile transactions were governed.   As we might expect, the towns which possessed laws dealing with maritime matters were the towns to which some sort of mercantile laws were a necessity.   Oleron,[9] Barcelona,[10]

---

to this source come from Lubeck; the second is a Flemish source and represents the Flemish version of the laws of Oleron; and the third is a Dutch source and represents the laws observed at Amsterdam, ibid iv xxvii seqq.

[1] Black Book of the Admiralty iv vii-xv.   [2] Ibid iv xv, xvi.
[3] Ibid ii 23.   [4] Ibid iv xxvi, xxvii.
[5] Vol. v 66, 67-71 ; cf. Mitchell, The Law Merchant, 22-26.
[6] Vol. v 75.   [7] Mitchell, op. cit. 30.   [8] Vol. ii 142.
[9] Black Book of the Admiralty ii 254 seqq.   [10] Ibid iii lxix-lxxii.

and Wisby [1] all possessed such bodies of law. In England
similar bodies of law are contained in the White Book of London, [2]
the Red Book of Bristol, [3] and the Domesday of Ipswich ; [4] and
the Carta Mercatoria and the Statute of the Staple contain
special codes of rules adapted to foreign merchants. [5] Just as the
various seaport towns imitated the customs of some one port, so
the various towns modelled their charters and their laws upon
certain of the more famous towns in England, such as London,
Bristol, Oxford, or Winchester. [6]

Both the maritime and the commercial law of the Middle
Ages thus grew up amid similar surroundings, governed the relations of persons engaged in similar pursuits, and was enforced
in similar tribunals. It is for this reason that the relations between them have always been of the closest. [7] Even in England,
where they have come to be applied in different courts, it has
been impossible to ignore their close connexion. Both, as we
have seen, have appeared to English judges to be rather a
species of jus gentium than the law of a particular state. The
separation between them effected by the jealousy of the courts
of common law has produced much inconvenience ; [8] and it was
never complete.   " It was," says Sir Travers Twiss, " the practice
of the consuls of the sea, before pronouncing their decision to
consult the Prudhomes of the sea and the Prudhomes of the
merchants. . . .   In the High Court of Admiralty of England

[1] Black Book of the Admiralty iv 265, 386.
[2] Munimenta Gildhallæ, R.S. vol iii.
[3] Edited by Bickley.
[4] Black Book of the Admiralty ii 16-207.
[5] Below 542.
[6] For a table illustrating this affiliation of mediæval boroughs see Gross, The
Gild Merchant, i App. E ; for a similar affiliation in Germany see Schulte, Histoire
du droit d'Allemagne (Trad. par Fourniere) 163, 365.
[7] In the Middle Ages they are usually classed together ; thus in 1313 justices to
settle piracy claims were told to proceed "secundum legem et consuetudinem dicti
regni et similiter legem mercatoriam," Select Pleas of the Admiralty (S.S.) i xix;
in 1320 a similar direction was given to arbitrators between England and Flanders
in a case of spoil, ibid xxii ; a complaint that a ship of Placentia had been spoiled
by one of Bristol was heard by a jury of mariners and merchants " prout de jure et
secundum legem mercatoriam foret faciendum," ibid xxiv ; in the seventeenth
century Malynes, when he wrote his Lex Mercatoria, found it necessary to devote
a large part of his treatise to the sea laws ; thus he says in the preface " And even
as the roundness of the globe of the world is composed of the earth and waters ; so
the body of the Lex Mercatoria is made and framed of the Merchants Customs and
the Sea Laws, which are involved together as the seas and the earth ; " and ibid 87,
" For without navigation commerce is of small account ; " at p. 303, when considering the courts peculiar to merchants, he deals first with the Admiralty court ; for
Malynes and his book see vol. v 131-134.
[8] In 1833 a select committee recommended an extension of the jurisdiction of
the Admiralty so as to enable it to " exercise concurrent jurisdiction in questions of
title to ships generally, and of freight, and possibly of some other mercantile matters,
with a power of impanelling a jury of merchants, if the judge thinks fit or either of
the parties require it," Williams and Bruce, Admiralty Practice (Ed. 1886) 13 n. k.

it is the practice for the judge to be assisted by two of the Elder Brethren of the Trinity House of Deptford-le-Stroud, whilst the registrar of the court, at a subsequent stage of the proceedings, has the assistance of two merchants." [1]

Such then was the Law Merchant. In the earlier part of the Middle Ages it was administered in local courts; but, in the middle of the fourteenth century, the rise of the court of Admiralty caused a cleavage between the maritime and the commercial branches of this law. In the sixteenth century the court of Admiralty showed signs of absorbing both these branches; but, in the latter part of the sixteenth and in the earlier part of the seventeenth centuries, this extension of Admiralty jurisdiction was prevented, and the cleavage between these two branches was widened, by the action of the common law courts. Their jealousy confined the court of Admiralty to maritime causes, and led them to appropriate to themselves jurisdiction over commercial causes. In the end they assimilated what they had succeeded in appropriating and constructed our modern system of commercial law. In consequence of their action our commercial law does not, like the systems of most continental states, form together with maritime law, a separate "code de commerce." It has become a branch of the common law, distinct from the maritime law administered in the court of Admiralty.

The peculiar history of the Law Merchant in England is thus due to the peculiar history of the courts which have administered it at different periods. It is clear from this summary that that history falls into three well defined periods: the period when the Law Merchant, maritime and commercial, was administered in local courts; the rise and development of the court of Admiralty and the settlement of its jurisdiction; the absorption of the commercial side of the Law Merchant into the common law.

The Period when the Law Merchant, Maritime and Commercial was Administered in Local Courts

Maritime Courts.

The courts which had jurisdiction in maritime matters were for the most part the courts of seaport towns. The Admiral was not an official who held a court with a fixed jurisdiction. He was an official who ruled a fleet, having incidentally certain disciplinary powers over those under his command. These powers "probably enabled the Admiral to deal with depredations committed by the ships immediately under his command;

---

[1] Black Book of the Admiralty iii lxxx.

but it does not appear to have included a power to hold a court administering justice generally in maritime cases." [1]

In the earlier part of the Middle Ages many seaport towns had jurisdiction in maritime cases. The Domesday of Ipswich tells us that, " the pleas yoven to the lawe maryne, that is to wite, for straunge marynerys passaunt and for hem that abydene not but her tyde, shuldene be npleted from tyde to tyde." [2] Padstow and Lostwithiel possessed similar courts which sat at tide time on the seashore. Yarmouth possessed a court of like nature. [3] The court at Newcastle dates from Henry I.'s reign. [4] It would appear from the Red Book of Bristol that a court sitting at a seaport was one of the recognized tribunals of the Law Merchant; [5] and the Book itself contains rules upon maritime matters. [6] When the court of Admiralty was established, many towns, jealous of their ancient rights, got by royal charter exemption from its jurisdiction; [7] and the statutes of Richard II.'s reign which, as we shall see, limited the competence of this court, tended to preserve them. [8] In fact, throughout the fifteenth and sixteenth centuries their jurisdiction was recognized and safeguarded by the legislature. [9] But the court of Admiralty was naturally hostile to them; and, when, in the latter half of the sixteenth century, that court, supported by the growing strength of the crown, began to assert itself, [10] their privileges began to be questioned. At different periods in the fifteenth and sixteenth centuries the jurisdiction of Tynemouth, Scarborough, Chester, King's Lynn, Harwich, and Dartmouth were either called in question by, or successfully asserted against, the court of Admiralty. [11] In 1570 Elizabeth found it necessary to

---

[1] Select Pleas of the Admiralty (S.S.) i xli; it was a court " for military action not for civil jurisdiction," Spelman (Works Ed. 1727), Admiralty Jurisdiction, 221; the sheriff also had some authority by royal writ at this period, see Selden, Mare Clausum ii c. 14.

[2] Black Book of the Admiralty ii 23.

[3] Select Pleas of the Admiralty i xiii, xiv.

[4] Stubbs, Sel. Ch. 112, " Inter burgensem et mercatorem si placitum oriatur finiatur ante tertiam refluxionem maris."

[5] In cap. i of the Red Book it is said that the lex mercatoria attaches to markets, and that markets are held in five places " in civitatibus, nundinis, portubus super mare, villis mercatoriis, et burgis."

[6] Cap. viii.

[7] Select Pleas of the Admiralty (S.S.) i xiv; 15 Richard II. c. 3 recites that the jurisdiction of the Admiral prejudices " many Lords, Cities and Boroughs through the realm;" in the fifteenth century the claims of local lords sometimes made it difficult for the crown to fulfil its treaty obligations, Select Cases before the Council (S.S.) cvii-cviii.

[8] Below 548; Marsden, Law and Custom of the Sea (Navy Records Soc.) i xiii, xiv.

[9] 2 Henry V. St. 1 c. 6; 32 Henry VIII. c. 14; 5 Elizabeth c. 5 § 42; 27 Elizabeth c. 11.

[10] Below 546-547.

[11] Select Pleas of the Admiralty (S.S.) ii xix-xxi; cf. Hist. MSS. Com. Ninth Rep. xi for the Admiralty jurisdiction over the Medway possessed by Rochester.

complain of the encroachments made by the Mayor's court of the City of London upon the Admiral's jurisdiction;[1] and, in the earlier half of the seventeenth century the crown waged war against them.[2] Many succumbed to these attacks; but some survived till the nineteenth century. These survivals were swept away by the Municipal Corporations Act of 1835.[3] The only local jurisdiction left was that of the Cinque Ports. It is the oldest of all the courts which have ever exercised Admiralty jurisdiction in England, and "it presents the type and original of all our Admiralty and maritime courts."[4]

The franchises possessed by the Cinque Ports were very extensive. They were extensive because the Cinque Ports were indispensable to the crown; and so could insist upon getting almost what privileges they pleased.[5] It was admitted in the Eyre of Kent in 1313-1314 they could even exclude the justices in Eyre;[6] and it was held in 1581 that their decisions could only be reversed in the court of the Lord Warden.[7] Like other large franchises, the jurisdiction exercised by the Cinque Ports tended to imitate the developments of royal justice. Thus, like some of the Palatinates,[8] they developed an equitable jurisdiction in the sixteenth and seventeenth centuries.[9] But obviously their Admiralty jurisdiction must always have been the most important branch of their jurisdiction; and it has certainly had the longest life. From the earliest times they were exempt from the jurisdiction of the Admiralty. Owing probably to the antiquity and extent of their jurisdiction, this exception is not expressly given in their charters. But its existence is undoubted, and

---

[1] Select Pleas of the Admiralty (S.S.) ii xii, xiii; cf. Legge v. More (1539) ibid i 83.

[2] S.P. Dom. 1619-1623 97, cxi 38; ibid 1633-1634 70, 109, 290; ibid 1634-1635 343; and the same policy was pursued in Ireland, ibid 1639 75.

[3] 5, 6 William IV. c. 76; see Webb, Local Government ii 359 n. 1 for a list of places which possessed an Admiralty jurisdiction.

[4] Select Pleas of the Admiralty (S.S.) ii xxi; cf. Lord Warden of the Cinque Ports v. the King (1831) 2 Hagg. Admir. 438, 443·444.

[5] This is illustrated by a claim made by the barons of the Cinque Ports in 1299 in which they tell the king that, "Your barons of the Cinque Ports have sworn to give their lives in fighting all (your enemies), and they pray that it may please you to remember how you have sworn to your people to maintain their rights in accordance with the laws, customs, and franchises which your ancestors, the kings of England have given, and you have yourself granted and confirmed. And let the King's Council be well assured that if wrong or grievance be done to them in any way against justice, they will forthwith forsake their wives and children and all they possess, and go to make their profit upon the sea wheresoever they think they will be able to acquire it," Marsden, Law and Customs of the Sea (Navy Records Soc.) i 54-55; it appears from Y.B. 5 Ed. II. (S.S.) 17 that the charters of the Ports and those of the Abbots of Battle were so inconsistent that the judges referred the matter to the king, who told them to proceed without regard to the charters.

[6] The Eyre of Kent (S.S.) i lix.

[7] Dyer 376 a—though Dyer apparently doubted the correctness of the decision.

[8] Above 111, 116, 125.   [9] Monro, Acta Cancellaria 24, 730.

their Admiralty jurisdiction included even a jurisdiction in Prize till the Lord High Admiral in 1702 prevented them from exercising it.[1] When in 1856 the general civil jurisdiction of the Lord Warden of the Cinque Ports was abolished, his Admiralty jurisdiction was saved;[2] and in 1869, when Admiralty jurisdiction was given to the new county courts, it was provided that appeals in Admiralty cases from the county courts within the jurisdiction of the Lord Warden should lie to him.[3] His jurisdiction is not touched by the Judicature Act of 1873, and it still survives.[4]

The jurisdiction over maritime cases, thus exercised by the local courts, was supervised and controlled by the crown. The crown was for many reasons specially interested in these maritime cases, because foreign affairs were peculiarly within its province. The courts of common law had no adequate machinery for supervising the actions or the transgressions of foreigners ; and such matters frequently gave rise to diplomatic questions [5] in the shape of expensive claims for compensation. In fact we shall see that it was largely owing to the necessity the crown was under of protecting itself against such claims that the creation of the court of Admiralty was due.

In this period the crown supervised the doings of the local courts in the following ways.

Writs were sometimes sent to the mayors and bailiffs of the seaport towns directing them to proceed.[6] If they did not obey the writ they were attached for contempt. Sometimes special commissions were issued to the king's justices or others to try cases of spoil or piracy.[7] As it was very often impossible for

---

[1] Marsden Law and Custom of the Sea (Navy Records Soc.) ii xv, 191-192.

[2] 18, 19 Victoria c. 48 § 10.   [3] 31, 32 Victoria c. 71 § 33.

[4] 46, 47 Victoria. c. 18 § 13 (Municipal Corporations Act 1883) ; 57, 58 Victoria c. 60 § 571 (Merchant Shipping Act 1894). The regular place for the sitting of the court was the aisle of St. James's Church, Dover, but the judge now usually sits at the Royal Courts of Justice.

[5] See e.g. Cosfeld v. Leveys (1322) Select Cases before the Council (S.S.) 32 ; R. v. Rouceby (1354) ibid lxxii.

[6] In 1315 a writ was sent to mayor and bailiffs of Rye to enquire into a ship spoiled by pirates in Orwell haven, the goods of which had been taken to Rye ; the writ was not obeyed, and a writ was sent to the constable of Dover Castle to arrest the mayor and bailiffs, Select Pleas of the Admiralty (S.S.) i xx; in 1323 a writ was sent to sheriff of Gloucester to arrest a ship with the help of the mayor of Bristol, and to try the case in the mayor of Bristol's court, ibid xxiv ; in 1328 a writ was sent to the sheriff of Southampton to arrest French goods, ibid xxvi ; in 1352 a writ was sent to the mayor of Southampton to arrest certain pirates and bring them before the Council, ibid xxxix ; in 1349 in the case of Pilk v. Venore a case was removed from the Bristol court into the Chancery ; the Bristol court applied the law of Oleron, ibid ii xliii.

[7] In 1308 Edward II. issued a commission to certain "auditores" to enquire of spoils alleged to have been committed by Frenchmen upon Englishmen, Select Pleas of the Admiralty (S.S.) i xviii; in 1338 a commission was issued to certain persons to enquire as to ships of the Count of Gueldres which had been spoiled,

foreigners, who had been spoiled of their goods, to get justice from an English jury,[1] they often petitioned the Council. The petition in such cases was often referred to the Chancellor;[2] but it was sometimes heard by the Council, and writs were issued according to the result of the trial.[3] In 1353 such a case was tried by the Admiral and the Council;[4] and this is, as we shall see, just before the first mention of the Admiral's court.

The courts of common law sometimes, but rarely interfered in such matters.[5] They had in fact no jurisdiction over contracts made or torts committed abroad.[6]

With respect to crimes committed out of the bodies of counties the question how far the common law courts had jurisdiction is perhaps more doubtful. Hale asserts that they did possess such a jurisdiction before 1365; and in support of his opinion he cites eight cases of the reigns of Edward I., II., and III.[7] But these cases do not completely prove Hale's position, as Cockburn, C.J., points out in *Reg.* v. *Keyn;*[8] and in the Eyre

Select Pleas of the Admiralty (S.S.) i xxvii; in 1339 a commission was issued to Stonore, C.J., and two others to try a case of piracy committed by English upon Spanish, Portuguese, and Catalan merchants in Southampton water, ibid xxix.

[1] Ibid xxiii.

[2] Ibid xxv; in 1325 a petition by one whose ship had been robbed at sea by the men of Yarmouth; in 1327 a case of piracy of English upon Frenchmen.

[3] Ibid xxxviii, a case of 1343; xxxix a case of 1352; in 1347 the Council ordered restitution of goods taken by pirates, and, in default, the arrest of those to whom the goods had come.

[4] Ibid xl; and see Baldwin, Select Cases before the Council (S.S.) xxvii-xxviii.

[5] It would appear that in 1296 (case cited by Selden, Works iii 1895) the Common Pleas declined to recognize the jurisdiction of the Admiral and asserted that it had general jurisdiction. The court said it could try a murder committed at sea as well as on the land when the murderer came to land. The MS. from which Selden cites has disappeared, Select Pleas of the Admiralty i xvii, xviii. The following are instances in which the courts of common law seem to have exercised what in later law would have been called an Admiralty jurisdiction: 1276 an action in the King's Bench relating to a claim by the king to goods captured from the enemy, Marsden, Law and Custom of the Sea (Navy Records Soc.) i 8; 1322 an action to recover damages for spoil at sea was heard in the King's Bench, Select Pleas of the Admiralty i xxiii; 1323 a case before the Bristol court was moved by certiorari into the King's Bench ibid i xxiv; 1341 an action by the king in the court of Exchequer as to enemy goods detained by the captors, Law and Custom of the Sea i 69.

[6] Y.BB. 1, 2 Ed. II. (S.S.) 110, 111; 12, 13 Ed. III. (R.S.) 364, 366; 21 Ed. IV. Pasch. pl. 23 p. 10 *per* Brian; at the end of the fourteenth century it would appear that there was no remedy for breach of charter party made abroad, Copyn v. Snoke, Select Pleas of the Admiralty ii lix; in 1280 it was decided that the common law courts had no jurisdiction over torts committed abroad, ibid ii xliii, xliv, lix; on this account applications were sometimes made to the Chancellor; above 405; below 554; and cf. Select Cases in Chancery (S.S.) 58; and see generally vol. v 117-119, 140-142.

[7] Hale, P.C. ii 12-15.

[8] (1876) 2 Ex. Div. 163-167, "It appears that of these eight cases four were in the nature of a civil remedy, and, as it would seem were properly within the jurisdiction of the court of King's Bench; four were cases of piracy, which may have been dealt with on the principle that piracy is triable anywhere and everywhere. Moreover, as to two of the latter cases, it is doubtful whether the offence was not committed within the body of a county, and therefore triable at common law."

of Kent, Staunton, J., seems to have thought that on the high seas the ordinary criminal courts had no jurisdiction.[1] It is not, however, improbable that, at a period when the court of Admiralty did not exist, the ordinary courts did sometimes exercise such jurisdiction. Criminal cases were at first tried in the court of Admiralty by a jury;[2] and in cases of piracy the commissioners were sometimes directed to proceed " secundum legem et consuetudinem regni nostri ". Generally, however, they were directed to proceed "secundum legem mercatoriam," or, " maritimam ;"[3] and from this fact we can infer that even criminal cases were decided according to a maritime law which was a law apart from the common law, and closely related to the law of the merchants.

Commercial Courts.

The courts which administered the commercial law of the period necessarily presented features very similar to the courts which administered the maritime law. The Law Merchant applied both to the domestic trader and to the foreign merchant.[4] Both formed in a sense a separate class. But, as we might expect, the separation is far more clearly marked in the latter than in the former case. These courts were either (i) the courts of Fairs and Boroughs, or (ii) the courts of the Staple.

(i) In the Anglo-Saxon period commerce had been practically confined to fairs held in " burhs "—strong places specially protected by the king's peace.[5] In return for this protection the king took a toll. This right to take a toll was, like other governmental rights, granted out to his subjects. Thus the right to hold a fair and take its tolls became a franchise;[6] and therefore, to allow another fair to be set up so near to an already existing fair that it abstracted its custom, was a nuisance to the franchise for which an action lay.[7] As in the case of the other franchises,

---

[1] " That is not an arm of the sea across which a man can distinguish what another is doing on the other side of the water, and across which he can see from shore to shore; and in such case the coroner shall come and perform his office," The Eyre of Kent (S.S.) i 133 ; S.C. Fitz. Ab. *Corone* pl. 399.

[2] Select Pleas of the Admiralty (S.S.) i xxi, xxii-xxiv ; Black Book of the Admiralty i 45, 49, 83.

[3] Select Pleas of the Admiralty (S.S.) i xvi ; in 1377 a case of piracy was tried at common law "secundum legem et consuetudinem regni ac legem maritimam ;" but there was a proviso that this was not to be an encroachment on the Admiral's rights, ibid i xlviii ; for a similar commission issued in 1374 see Marsden, Law and Custom of the Sea (Navy Records Soc.) i 99-101.

[4] The term merchant at this period was not confined to large traders ; it embraced all who traded ; the distinction between the craftsman and the merchant is later, Gross, Gild Merchant i 107 and n. 2.

[5] Vol. v 103-104.

[6] Above 93 ; Gross, Select Cases on the Law Merchant (S.S.) i xvi, xvii.

[7] Y.B. 4 Ed. II. (S.S.) 93 ; Morpeth Corporation v. Northumberland Farmers' Auction Mart [1921] 2 Ch. 154 ; for a discussion of the same principle as applied to the franchise of Ferry see Hammerton v. Earl of Dysart [1916] 1 A.C. 57.

the right to hold a court was incident to it.[1] This court comes
to be known as the court of "piepowder." "The term 'piepowder' (*piepoudres, pede pulverosi*)," says Gross,[2] "was not
applied to this tribunal, as Sir Edward Coke and various other
writers believed, because justice was administered as speedily as
the dust could fall or be removed from the feet of the litigants,
but because the court was frequented by chapmen with dusty feet,
who wandered from mart to mart." The name was perhaps
originally a nickname; but it became general, and was adopted
in the official style of the court.[3]

It is clear from the records of the courts of these fairs that
they were of the same type as the courts of similar fairs which
existed all over Europe.[4] The court, if it belonged to a borough,
was held by the mayor or bailiffs of the borough, if it belonged
to a lord, by his steward;[5] and the borough or other lord was
responsible for the maintenance of order during the period of the
fair.[6] But though the court was held by the mayor, bailiffs, or
steward, the judges of the court, in the thirteenth and fourteenth
centuries, were the merchants who attended the fair.[7] The
court's jurisdiction extended to all cases except those concerning
land, and except pleas of the crown.[8] Thus it heard actions for
breach of contract, and actions of trespass; and it dealt with
various minor offences committed in the fair.[9] It could exercise
this jurisdiction irrespective of the amount at issue in the case,[10]
and it could hear cases which had arisen outside the limits of the
fair.[11] The procedure of the court was summary, and its session

---

[1] Select Cases on the Law Merchant (S.S.) i xvii.

[2] Ibid i xiii, xiv; see ibid n. 2 for various early examples of the use of the term;
the lawyers from the days of the Y.BB. recognized that the right to hold this court
was incident to the grant of a fair, see the authorities cited ibid xviii n. 1; cf. Coke,
Fourth Instit. 272.

[3] The style of the court was, "Curia Domini Regis pedis pulverisati tenta apud
civitatem X., coram majore et duobus concivibus secundum consuetudines civitatis a
tempore cujus, etc., ac secundum privilegia et libertates concessa et confirmata;" or
if not held in a borough "coram X senescallo feriæ."

[4] See vol. v 91-93, 106-112.

[5] Gross, op. cit. i xxii, xxiii.

[6] At St. Ives, for instance, "a constabulary force was provided by St. Ives and
twelve neighbouring townships or manors of the Abbot (of Ramsey). Each of these
vills were expected to provide one or two constables and from two to eight men for
the night watch," ibid xxxiv.

[7] Red Book of Bristol i 70—" In omni curia mercati singula judicia reddi debent
per mercatores ejusdem Curiæ, et non per majorem nec per senescallum mercati;"
cf. Select Pleas in Manorial Courts (S.S.) 153; Select Cases on the Law Merchant
(S.S.) i 25, 30, 91; ibid at p. 90, it is stated that, by the Law Merchant, judgments
must be given by all the merchants native and foreign; the principle was also admitted by the king's courts, Plac. Abbrev. 321 (1315); Mayor's Court Rolls 131.

[9] Ibid; cf. vol. v 108-109.

[8] Select Cases on the Law Merchant (S.S.) i xxiv.

[10] Select Cases on the Law Merchant (S.S.) i xxiv and authorities there cited.

[11] Ibid n. 7; Red Book of Bristol i 70—" Cum placitum moveatur in Curia seu foro
mercati de re facta extra limites mercati, non propter hoc demittatur."

was continuous.[1] These two characteristics are common to all the fair courts of Europe;[2] and in England both the borough custumals,[3] and Bracton[4] emphasize the need for this summary procedure in cases which concern merchants and mariners. We shall see that this summary procedure both in England and abroad took practical shape in many relaxations of the ordinary rules of procedure which would have hampered the development of commercial law.[5]

The lords of these fairs were, as we have seen, sometimes individuals, sometimes corporate boroughs.

In cases where the lords of the fair were individuals the fairs were sometimes held by these lords in a borough; and in that case the jurisdiction of the ordinary courts was sometimes superseded during the time of the fair.[6] Sometimes the fairs were held at a place which, except during the fair, was not an important centre of commerce. A good illustration is afforded by the fair of the Abbot of Ramsey held at St. Ives in Huntingdonshire.[7] From the records of this court it is clear that it was attended by merchants from all over England and even from abroad. " In the thirteenth century," says Gross, " it was regarded by Englishmen and foreigners as one of the most important in England, ranking with those of Boston, Winchester, and Stamford. . . . It was frequented by many merchants from the Continent especially from the Netherlands and France."[8] In the various cases which came before the court there are mentioned the communitates of Stamford, Nottingham, Leicester, Huntingdon, Godmanchester, Bury St. Edmunds, Wiggenhall, and Ypres.[9]

In cases where the borough had the franchise of fair its piepowder court was often regarded merely " as a phase or special

---

[1] " Lex ipsa consequitur se ipsam continue . . . et ita est attachiamentum sive adjornacio harum legum de hora in horam. . . . In portubus attachiamenta sive adjornaciones sunt similiter ordinatum . . . scilicet de tyda in daytydam, nec computari debet tidæ noctuales," Red Book of Bristol i 57; Borough Customs (S.S.) ii 183-185.

[2] Vol. v 106-107.

[3] Above n. 1.

[4] He speaks of persons, " qui celerem habere debet justitiam, sicut sunt mercatores quibus exhibatur justitia pepoudrous," f. 334.

[5] Vol. v 81-83, 96, 107.

[6] " The principal fair of a borough or city might be under the control of a bishop or abbot, and during its continuance supreme judicial authority over the town might be placed in his hands, ordinary jurisdiction being vested in his piepowder court to the exclusion of the civic court," Select Cases on the Law Merchant (S.S.) i xxi; instances are there cited from Hereford, York, Winchester, and Westminster; cf. also ibid xxii n. 3.

[7] Select Pleas in Manorial Courts (S.S.) 130-160; Select Cases on the Law Merchant (S.S.) i xxviii-xxxv.

[8] Ibid xxxiii ; see also ibid 91.

[9] Select Pleas in Manorial Courts (S.S.) 134.

session " of the ordinary borough court.[1] But sometimes the two courts were kept quite distinct.[2] In other cases the pie-powder court was kept separately during the time of the fair, and during the remainder of the year, the law merchant was administered in the ordinary borough court.[3] It is obvious that whether or not a borough had the franchise of a fair it was in most cases a centre of trade. The law took account of this fact, and allowed that by custom a borough might have the right to hold a court of piepowder, just as if it possessed this franchise.[4] And, whether or not it held such a court, the fact that it was a centre of trade often caused the customary law administered in its court to be better suited to the needs of commerce than the common law. At Winchelsea, Rye, and Fordwich, in the fifteenth century, the judges were directed to " have recourse to the laws of nature on which are founded and whence proceed all written laws." [5] Such a direction clearly made for the reception and recognition of reasonable mercantile customs, and enabled such courts, when necessary, to administer the Law Merchant.[6]

On the Continent the large towns enjoyed a great measure of independence ; and this caused the mercantile courts and the law which they administered to play a very important part in the development of the Law Merchant.[7] In England, on the other

---

[1] Select Cases on the Law Merchant (S.S.) i xx—" Sometimes the proceedings of this tribunal are entered in the ordinary plea rolls of the borough court, as though the former tribunal were regarded as a mere phase or special session of the latter without any separate organization of its own. When this was the case the pie-powder court sat from time to time, as need required, for the benefit of visiting traders or strangers, and tried only suits in which they were concerned ; pleas between burghers were excluded from its jurisdiction ; " see Mayor's Court Rolls xvi, xxvi.

[2] Ibid xx, xxi.

[3] " At Bristol a piepowder court was held during the fair of fourteen days, and during the remainder of the year the Tolsey court, which is first mentioned in 1373, administered justice according to the Law Merchant. In this tribunal, which was suspended while the fair lasted, actions begun in the piepowder court might be continued," ibid xxi.

[4] Y.B. 13 Ed. IV. Pasch. pl. 2 ; Pendred v. Chambers (1591) Cro. Eliza. 256 ; Goodson v. Duffill (1612) 2 Bulstr. 23 per Williams, J. ; and cf. S.C. reported Cro. Jac. 313 ; Coke, Fourth Instit. 272.

[5] Borough Customs (S.S.) ii 59.

[6] The Bristol treatise on the Law Merchant, Red Book of Bristol i 57 recognizes this ; the Law Merchant, it says, holds place in boroughs as well as fairs, " quia in civitatibus et nundinis sive feriis *quod idem est* fiunt emptiones et venditiones mercandisarum continue ; " we find that at Bristol (about 1240) it was the rule that, " burgenses inter se invicem, et burgenses versus extraneos, et extranei versus burgenses, et extranei versus extraneos possunt placitare de debitis majoribus sive minoribus de die in diem, sine breve, secundum consuetudinem villæ," Borough Customs (S.S.) ii 183 ; for similar rules see Leges Quatuor Burgorum (1270), and Waterford (1300), ibid ii 184 ; in London a court was held daily for foreign merchants, Liber Albus (R.S.) 295-296 ; at Ipswich we read of, " the plees be twixe straunge folk that man clepyth pypoudrous," " the pleas in tyme of fayre be twixe straunge and passant," " the please yoven to the law maryne," Black Book of the Admiralty (R.S.) ii 23.

[7] Vol. v 151.

hand, there was already a common law, recourse to which was easy, and there was a legislature which had already begun to interfere with purely mercantile matters.[1]   And though in England the custom of the merchants was recognized as a law apart from the common law,[2] the relation between these two laws was close.[3]   At an early period the Law Merchant, so far as it applied to domestic transactions, showed signs of becoming absorbed in a common law which had adopted certain of its rules.[4]   The Bristol treatise on the Law Merchant, which comes from the fourteenth century, testifies to this tendency.   The writer regards the Law Merchant as a mere off-shoot of the common law,[5] and he can only point to three specific differences.[6]   Parties, he says, may always sue at common law, and this is the usual course [7] —a fact borne out by the absence of similar treatises in the custumals of other boroughs dealing specially with the Law Merchant.

It is not therefore surprising to find that, in the latter half of the fifteenth century, the court of piepowder was declining in importance.   In 1466 and 1467 the court of Common Pleas considered that the steward or other person who held the court, and not the suitors, was its judge [8]—a view which tended to diminish its usefulness, as it deprived the merchants who attended it of much of their power to shape directly the law there administered. In 1477 [9] a statute still further diminished the usefulness of the court, by restricting its jurisdiction to matters arising within the limits of the fair, and occurring during the time that the fair was

[1] 3 Edward I. c. 23 (liability for debts of a fellow burgess); 11 Edward I. and 13 Edward I. St. 3 (Statutes Merchant and Staple); Cunningham, op. cit. i 259-264 gives a list of such statutes and ordinances; as he says, at p. 265, " In Germany trade was not freed till the eighteenth century from disadvantages of the same sort as those which the first Edward did much to remove in our own land."

[2] Y.BB. 20, 21 Ed. I. (R.S.) 68; 21, 22 Ed. I. (R.S.) 74, 458; Fleta II. 58. 5; 61. 2.

[3] In 1343 Parning the Chancellor drew a writ of trespass against a bailiff who had failed to do justice in the court of a market, Register f. 99 b—" Nota breve diligenter " is the marginal note.

[4] Thus in Edward I.'s reign some of the judges seem to wish to give effect to the merchant custom of proving debts by tally, Y.B. 21, 22 Ed. I. (R.S.) 456, 458; below 569.

[5] Red Book of Bristol i 68, " Lex communis quæ est mater legis mercatoriæ et quæ suam filiam in certis privilegiis et in certis locis dotavit."

[6] Ibid 57, 58, " Primo quod celerius deliberat se ipsum ; " secondly, the pledge ad respondendum answers for the whole debt and costs : thirdly, " in eo quod non admittat ad legem in parte negativa sed semper in ista lege querentis est probare."

[7] Ibid 57, " Sed si domini et partes placitantes magis voluerit deducere et prosequi placita de appellis in dictis locis coram eis inchoata in aliis curiis ad communem legem, et recusare legem mercatoriam, bene possunt, et ita faciunt communius quam aliter per totum regnum ; " cp. Borough Customs (S.S.) ii lxxxv.

[8] Y.BB. 6 Ed. IV. Mich. pl. 9 per Littleton ; 7 Ed. IV. Hil. pl. 27 (p. 23) per Littleton.

[9] 17 Edward IV. c. 2.

held.[1]   We shall see that this statute, and the interpretation put upon it by the courts, combined with economic and social changes to bring about the total decay of the court in the sixteenth and seventeenth centuries.[2]

(ii) These courts of fairs and boroughs dealt mainly with domestic trade: the courts of the Staple dealt mainly with foreign trade.   In order to understand the reason for the creation of these special courts it is necessary to say something of the manner in which the merchants were organized in the Middle Ages.

In the borough charters there is frequent mention of the Gild Merchant.   This was an association of traders within the town, and, in some cases, of traders living outside its precincts, for the better management of trade.[3]   It sometimes arbitrated upon mercantile disputes.[4]   But as a rule it did not exercise a regular jurisdiction, its chief function being that of a trade combination of a rigidly protective character.[5]   It was only those who belonged to the Gild Merchant who could trade freely within the town ; and its conduct was sometimes so oppressive that trade was driven from the town.[6]   In fact all the various privileges, jurisdictional and administrative, which the towns possessed could be, and often were used in a manner adverse to the commercial interests of the country.   The foreign merchant was hampered at every turn by the privileges of the chartered towns.   They were averse to allowing him any privileges except those which they had specially bargained to give to him.[7]   " The Great Charter provides that merchants may freely enter and dwell in and leave the realm : but the same Great Charter con-

---

[1] The plaintiff or his attorneys must swear that " the contract or other deed contained in the declaration was made in or committed within the fair and within the time of the said fair, where he taketh his action, and within the bounds and jurisdiction of the same fair."

[2] Below 569.

[3] Gross, Gild Merchant i chap. iii.   " The words, 'so that no one who is not of the Gild may trade in the said town except with the consent of the burgesses,' which frequently accompanied the grant of a Gild Merchant, express the essence of this institution," p. 43.

[4] L.Q.R. xvii 238.

[5] Gross, Gild Merchant i 43-50; as to the distinction between Gild and Borough see ibid chap. v.   This distinction tended to become obliterated in the fourteenth century, ibid p. 76; with other privileges that of having a Gild Merchant helped on the idea of municipal incorporation, ibid p. 105 ; but " the judicial authority of the Gild Merchant was at first very limited, its officers forming a tribunal of arbitration, at which the brethren were expected to appear before carrying their quarrels into the ordinary courts.   The functions of these officers were inquisitorial rather than judicial.   But in some places their powers appear to have been gradually enlarged during the thirteenth century so as to embrace jurisdiction in pleas relating to trade," ibid p. 65.

[6] Ibid 52, and Statutes there cited.

[7] For specimens of such bargains by London with the merchants of Amiens, Corbeil, and Nesle see Munimenta Gildhallæ (R.S.) iii 164-175.

firms all the ancient liberties and customs of London and the other boroughs, and thus takes away with one hand what it gives with the other. The burghers have a very strong opinion that their liberties and customs are infringed if a foreign merchant dwells within their walls for more than forty days, if he hires a house, if he fails to take up his abode with some responsible burgher, if he sells in secret, if he sells to foreigners, if he sells in detail."[1] And it should be noted that all these restrictive rules were held to be valid by the common law.[2]

The crown, on the other hand, was for many reasons interested in supporting the foreign merchant. It was able to take a broader view of the commercial interests of the country than any set of burghers ; and its intelligence was quickened by the fact that it was easier to negotiate a supply from the alien merchant in return for protection, than to deal with a Parliament.[3] For these reasons the needs of the crown gave to the alien merchant a defined position—in some respects superior to that of the native merchant —and the protection of a separate set of courts.

In 1303 the Carta Mercatoria[4] gave to certain foreign merchants, in return for certain customs duties, exemption from certain municipal dues, freedom to deal wholesale in all cities and towns, power to export their merchandise, and liberty to dwell where they pleased. They were promised speedy justice "secundum legem mercatoriam" from the officials "feriarum, civitatum, burgorum, et villarum mercatoriarum ; " and any misdoings of these officials were to be punished. If the mayor and sheriffs of London did not hold their court from day to day another judge was to be substituted for them. In all pleas, except those of a capital nature, half the jury was to consist of foreign merchants. No future grant of liberties to any town was to derogate from the rights conferred upon the foreign merchants.

The growth of the powers of Parliament in Edward III.'s reign gradually prevented the crown from obtaining supplies by

---

[1] P. and M. i 447, 448 ; cp. Lombards v. Mercers (1359) Select Cases before the Council (S.S.) 42 ; Mayor's Court Rolls 49.

[2] " In this case it was resolved that the said custom of London, ' that no person whatsoever, not being free of the City of London, shall by any colour, way, or mean whatsoever, directly or indirectly, by himself or any other, keep any shop or any other place whatsoever, inward or outward, for show or putting to sale of any wares or merchandises whatsoever by way of retail, or use any trade, occupation, mystery, or handicraft, for his gain or sale, within the City of London,' is upon the whole matter disclosed in the return a good custom," City of London's Case (1610) 8 Co. Rep. at pp. 124 b, 125 a.

[3] Stubbs, C.H. ii 170, 208-210, 572 ; see Select Cases before the Council (S.S.) lxxvi-lxxvii.

[4] Munimenta Gildhallæ (R.S.) ii Pt. I. 205-211.

separate negotiations with the alien merchants.[1]   But in 1353[2] similar privileges and a larger measure of protection was secured to them by the statute of the Staple.

With a view to the better organization of foreign trade and the more convenient collection of the customs, certain towns, known as the Staple towns, were set apart.[3]   It was only in those towns that dealings could take place in the more important articles of commerce, such as wool, woolfells, leather, lead, and tin.   Eleven such towns were named for England, one for Wales, and four for Ireland.[4]   In each of these towns special courts were provided for the merchants who resorted thither.   A mayor and two constables were to be chosen annually to hold the court of the Staple; and the authorities of the town in which the Staple was held were ordered to be attendant upon them.[5]   They were to apply the Law Merchant, and not the common law.   All manner of pleas concerning debt, covenant, and trespass fell within their jurisdiction.   The jurisdiction of the king's courts was excluded except in cases touching freehold or felony;[6] but the doings of the court were subject to the supervision of the Council.[7]   The mayor and constables had the assistance of two alien merchants, one of whom was chosen from the merchants who came from the north, the other from the merchants who came from the south.[8]   Provision was made for the trial of cases in which aliens were concerned by a mixed jury, and for an appeal in cases of difficulty to the Chancellor and the Council.[9] A speedy means was provided for the recovery of goods of which merchants had been robbed at sea, or which had been cast away and thrown up on the shore.[10]   Merchants going and returning to the Staple towns were protected against purveyance.[11]   They were promised lodgings in the towns at a reasonable rent,[12] and they were taken into the king's special protection.[13]   These privileges were specially stated to be granted notwithstanding

---

[1] Stubbs, C.H. ii 576; in 1362 and 1371 it was enacted that the merchants should not set any subsidy on wool without the consent of Parliament; for some further account of these grants by the merchants see E.H.R. xxxiii 311-313.

[2] 27 Edward III. St. 2.

[3] The Staple system dates from Edward I.'s reign; for its organization in Edward II.'s reign see Tout, Edward II. 241-266; and cp. E.H.R. xxxi 596-606; xxxiii 297-319; the system was consolidated by this statute, Stubbs, C.H. ii 447, 448; after the statute changes were made in the places where the Staple was held. Gross, Gild Merchant i 141-143. To be a Staple town was a privilege highly prized; for as Coke says (Fourth Instit. 238) "riches followed the Staple."

[4] 27 Edward III. St. 2 c. i.

[5] Caps. viii and xxi.

[6] 27 Edward III. St. 2 c. v, vi, viii, and xxi.

[7] Heyron v. Proute (1463), Select Cases before the Council (S.S.) 110 seqq.; native merchants were not allowed to sue in other courts, ibid, and App. l.

[8] 27 Edward III. St. 2 c. xxiv.   [9] c. viii and xxiv.

[10] c. xiii.   [11] c. iv.   [12] c. xvi.   [13] c. xx.

any privilege, franchise, or exemption granted to any towns or individuals.[1]

All these courts—maritime and commercial—administered, and, by administering, helped to create the Law Merchant. It was a law which necessarily differed at many points from the ordinary law, for "no technical jurisprudence peculiar to any country would have been satisfactory to traders coming from many different countries."[2] For the most part it was law laid down by the merchants in their courts; and, though particular rules may have differed slightly in different places,[3] its character was essentially cosmopolitan. Of the contents of this customary law the common law courts as yet knew very little. It was admitted to be a law quite distinct from the common law.[4] If a case occurred before them which turned upon a rule of this law merchants were summoned to inform the court.[5] In fact, except in the cases in which English statutes made rules for merchants,[6] or regulated mercantile customs,[7] the common law courts had little chance of becoming acquainted with its important principles. We have seen that, during the fourteenth and fifteenth centuries, they were beginning to absorb jurisdiction over the smaller commercial transactions of internal trade;[8] but the important principles of commercial law were applicable mainly to the larger transactions of foreign trade; and, as we have seen, the common law courts had at this period no jurisdiction over contracts made or torts committed abroad.[9] One illustration of the ignorance of the common law courts of the commercial usages of the period, and of the rules of law which governed those usages, will sufficiently explain why the courts and law of the merchants were at this period wholly distinct from the common law courts and the common law. We know from the records of the fair courts that a writing obligatory payable to bearer was known among the merchants as early as the thirteenth century.[10] We shall see that these writings are one of the germs from which sprang the

---

[1] c. xxviii. [2] Smith, Mercantile Law (Ed. 1890) Introd. lxx.
[3] The Carta Mercatoria (Munimenta Gildhallæ (R.S.) ii Pt. I. 206-207) implies this, "Et si forsan supra contractu hujusmodi contentio oriatur, fiat inde probatio vel inquisitio, secundum usus et consuetudines feriarum et villarum mercatoriarum ubi dictum contractum fieri contigerit et iniri."
[4] Above 528.
[5] In Edward II.'s reign a dispute on a question of law arising in the fair of St. Ives was brought into the King's Bench; twelve merchants from London, Winchester, Lincoln, and Northampton were summoned to give evidence as to the law, Plac. Abbrev. 321, cited Select Pleas in Manorial Courts (S.S.) 132.
[6] Above 537 n. 7.
[7] See 3 Edward I. c. 23, and Second Instit. 204, for the abrogation of the rule that one burgess was liable as a kind of surety for the debt of his fellow burgess.
[8] Above 537-538. [9] Above 534 n. 6.
[10] Select Pleas in Manorial Courts (S.S.) 152; Mayor's Court Rolls 94, 172, 200-201.

negotiable instruments of our modern law.[1] But the first reported
case upon a negotiable instrument in the common law courts
comes from the year 1603.[2]

The Rise and Development of the Court of Admiralty and the Settlement of its Jurisdiction

(1) The rise and development of the Court of Admiralty.

The earliest mention of the term Admiral is in a Gascon
Roll of 1295, in which Berardo de Sestars was appointed Admiral
of the Baion fleet.[3] There are similar mentions of Admirals in
these Rolls in 1296 and 1297. In 1300 Gervase Alard was
appointed Admiral of the Cinque Ports ; and this appears to be
the earliest use of the title in England. " It would appear that
the title of Admiral, originating probably in the East, and afterwards adopted by the Genoese and other navies of the Mediterranean, came by way of Gascony to England, and was there
adopted about the beginning of the fourteenth century." [4] We
have seen that in the earlier part of the fourteenth century the
Admiral did not possess any jurisdiction except a disciplinary
jurisdiction over the fleet under his command.[5] He does get
such jurisdiction about the middle of that century, owing to the
diplomatic difficulties in which the king found himself involved,
from the want of some efficient authority to coerce the marauding
and piratical propensities of his subjects.

It appears from the documents contained in the record known
as the " Fasciculus de Superioritate Maris " that the kings of
England had been constantly negotiating with foreign countries—
more especially with France and Flanders—as to claims in respect
of piracies committed by English subjects.[6] From 1293 to 1337

---

[1] Vol. v 114 ; vol. viii 115-126.

[2] Martin v. Boure, Cro. Jac. 6-8 ; there may have been one or two slightly
earlier cases which did not get into the reports, vol. viii 159.

[3] Select Pleas of the Admiralty (S.S.) i xii. The Black Book of the Admiralty
(i 56, 72) contains references to an Admiralty court in the reigns of Henry I. and
John, but these are apocryphal tales of the fourteenth century, Select Pleas of the
Admiralty i xi.

[4] Ibid xii.

[5] Above 530; Lambard, Archeion (Ed. 1635) 49, 50. The court of Admiralty
for some time exercised a jurisdiction over the navy, and merchant ships in time of
war ; the last remnant of it was suits against merchantmen for carrying naval flags,
Encyclopædia Britannica (10th Ed.) *Tit.* Admiralty.

[6] The documents contained in the Fasciculus are described in Select Pleas of
the Admiralty i xxx-xxxiv. It contains (1) the case of certain English merchants in
respect of depredations committed between 1297 and 1304, and in it the sovereignty
of the sea is claimed for England; this case is printed by Coke, Fourth Instit. 142-
144 ; (2) the appointment of commissioners to advise as to French Piracy claims,
partly printed by Coke, Fourth Instit. 144 ; (3) a treaty made by Edward I. with
Count Guy of Flanders 1297 ; (4) a document addressed to commissioners appointed
to deal with piracy claims by Flanders, partly printed Coke, Fourth Instit. 144.

attempts had been made at arbitration. In 1337 Edward made payments out of his own pocket to the Flemings, the Genoese, and the Venetians; and the claims of the French were put an end to by war. In 1339 a commission was appointed to consider the piracy claims made by Flanders. It may be that the resolution to erect a court of Admiralty was the result of recommendations made by that commission. We have seen that the older methods of administering justice in such cases had been found to be very unsatisfactory; and in the following year the battle of Sluys gave to England that command of the sea, which had been already claimed in the thirteenth century, and so rendered the erection of such a court the more possible. " Thus it is not unreasonable to suppose that after the battle of Sluys Edward III., acting upon the advice of the commissioners of 1339, extended the jurisdiction of the Admiral, which had up to that date been mainly disciplinary and administrative, so as to enable him to hold an independent court and administer complete justice in piracy and other maritime cases." [1] In 1353 a case was heard before the Admiral and the Council; [2] and in 1357 there is the earliest distinct reference to a court of Admiralty.[3] In 1360 John Paveley was appointed "capitaneus et ductor" of the fleet, with powers, not only disciplinary, but also judicial; [4] and in 1361 the commission to Sir Robert Herle conferred upon him similar powers, and gave him power to exercise them by a deputy.[5] This power was probably inserted in order to provide a judge for the new court. There were at first several Admirals and several courts; but from the early fifteenth century there is one Lord High Admiral and one court of Admiralty. In 1482 we have a patent of the judge of the court.[6]

The earliest parts of the Black Book of the Admiralty, which refer to the office and the court of the Admiral, probably date from the period between 1332 and 1357.[7] It is clear from them that the jurisdiction of the court was as yet new. There is an

---

[1] Select Pleas of the Admiralty i xxxv, xxxvi.   [2] Ibid xl.

[3] Ibid xli, xlii—The King of Portugal had made a claim on behalf of a Portuguese subject in respect of goods taken by an Englishman from a French vessel, and Edward III. says that the Admiral had adjudged them to belong to the English captor.

[4] "Querelas omnium et singulorum armatæ prædictæ audiendi et delinquentes incarcerandi, castigandi, et puniendi, et plenam justitiam, ac omnia alia et singula quæ ad hujusmodi capitaneum et ductorem pertinent, et pro bono regimine hominum prædictorum necessaria fuerint faciendi, prout de jure et secundum legem maritimam fuerit faciendum," ibid xlii.

[5] Ibid xlii, xliii.

[6] Ibid lv; it empowers him, " ad cognoscendum procedendum et statuendum de et super querelis causis et negotiis omnium et singulorum de hiis quæ ad curiam principalem Admirallitatis nostræ pertinent."

[7] Parts A, B, and C; for an account of the Black Book see vol. v 125-127.

article expressly directed against the withdrawal of cases from the court ;[1] in 1361 a commission of Oyer and Terminer, directing that a case of robbery and murder at sea should be tried by the common law, was recalled on the ground that the matter fell within the jurisdiction of the Admiral's court and ought to be tried by the Admiral according to maritime law ;[2] and in 1364 a writ of supersedeas issued to the judges on the ground that the Admiral had already tried the case.[3] The part of the Black Book dealing with the procedure and practice of the court[4] (which dates from the fifteenth century) shows that it was being settled on the model of the civil law. But the jealousy shown by Parliament of the jurisdiction of all courts exercising an Admiralty jurisdiction,[5] the frequent interferences of the Council,[6] and the breakdown of the executive government in the latter half of the fifteenth century,[7] were fatal to the efficiency of the new court of Admiralty. A statute of 1414 which appointed Conservators of Truces and gave them jurisdiction in cases where truces were broken ;[8] a statute of 1450 which gave this jurisdiction to the Chancellor and the Chief Justices ;[9] and a statute of 1453 which empowered the Chancellor to make restitution of ships or goods spoiled at sea[10]—all illustrate the fact that the court could not accomplish the main object for which it was created. In fact it did not become an efficient court till the second half of the sixteenth century. This is proved by the fact that "no records of its proceedings exist of earlier date than 1520, and no prize records of any importance before the end of Elizabeth's reign."[11]

The restoration of efficient government by the Tudors removed the causes which had retarded the development of the court in the Middle Ages.

Under the Tudors the court of Admiralty assumed a position of very much greater importance in the state. Both in Henry VIII.'s and Elizabeth's reigns much attention was paid to naval matters—Trinity House was incorporated in 1516 ; Deptford dockyard was constructed at about the same period ; and it was also a period for expanding foreign trade. The regular series of the records of the court begin in 1524.[12] It was settled in 1585 that

---

[1] Select Pleas of the Admiralty i 69.
[2] Ibid xlv ; Law and Custom of the Sea (Navy Records Soc.) i 84-88.
[3] Select Pleas of the Admiralty i xlv.
[4] i 178-220 ; 246-280 ; 345-394.
[5] Above 531 ; below 548.
[6] Select Cases before the Council (S.S.) xxix.
[7] Above 485, 490-491.   [8] 2 Henry V. St. 1 c. 6 ; vol. ii 473
[9] 29 Henry VI. c. 2 ; vol. ii 473-474.
[10] 31 Henry VI. c. 4 ; vol. ii 474.
[11] Marsden, Law and Custom of the Sea (Navy Records Soc.) i 118.
[12] Select Pleas of the Admiralty i lvii,

the judge of the court of Admiralty, though a deputy of the Admiral, did not cease to be judge during a vacancy of the office of Admiral.[1] The criminal jurisdiction of the court was extended ; and, just as the crown asserted its right to exercise a larger jurisdiction in ecclesiastical matters, so it asserted its right to exercise a larger jurisdiction, through the court of Admiralty and the Council, in maritime and commercial causes. The Council records show how close was the connexion between the Council and the Admiralty.[2]

During this period the court sat at Orton Key near London Bridge.[3] Later it sat, like the ecclesiastical courts, at Doctors' Commons.[4] We shall see that the determined attack of the common law courts in the seventeenth century left the court with but a small part of the jurisdiction which it had exercised under the Tudors, and denied it the status, which it had formerly possessed, of a court of record.[5] But we shall see that statutes of the nineteenth century restored to it some parts of the jurisdiction of which the common law courts had deprived it. They restored also its status of a court of record, and gave to its judge many of the powers possessed by the judges of the superior courts of common law.[6]

That appeals from the court of Admiralty lay originally to the king in Chancery is clear from a statute of 1533.[7] The king on each occasion appointed *Judices Delegati* to hear the appeal. In the Tudor period these Delegates were civilians, but in later times a judge of one of the common law courts was associated with them. In 1563 it was enacted that their decision should be final.[8] The records of this court begin early in the seventeenth century. We have seen that in 1832 the jurisdiction of the Delegates was transferred to the Council, and that in 1833 the constitution of the Judicial Committee of the Council which heard such appeals was regulated by statute.[9]

---

[1] Select Pleas of the Admiralty ii xii.

[2] Dasent i 154, 155; iii 149, 467, 469; vii *xviii;* xiv *xxviii*, xx *xiv-xvi;* xxiv 196, 356, 385-393, 403-405.

[3] Select Pleas of the Admiralty i lxxix; Bl. Comm. iii 69.

[4] In fact the judge of the court of Admiralty and the Dean of the Arches were often the same person, Anson, The Crown (3rd Ed.) ii 259-260; 3, 4 Victoria c. 65 § 1 provided that the Dean might sit for the judge of the Admiralty court.

[5] Below 553; Select Pleas of the Admiralty i xlv. A writ of supersedeas, issued in 1364, implies that it is a court of record; but the contrary was stated by Coke, Fourth Instit. 135; cp. Sparks v. Martyn (1668) 1 Ventris 1.

[6] 24 Victoria c. 10 §§ 14, 17, 23, 24; below 558-559.

[7] 25 Henry VIII. c. 19 § 4; for earlier commissions to hear appeals see Select Pleas of the Admiralty ii lix-lxii.

[8] 8 Elizabeth c. 5; this was not necessarily so before, Select Pleas of the Admiralty i 18-20; and in 1712 conflicting opinions were given on the question whether their decision was final in Prize Cases, Marsden, Law and Custom of the Sea (Navy Records Soc.) ii 227-230.

[9] Above 518.

(2) The Jurisdiction of the Court of Admiralty.

We have seen that in the fourteenth century there were several Admirals and several courts. Their jurisdiction was wide and vague. It comprised the ordinary criminal and civil jurisdiction of later days,[1] the prize jurisdiction,[2] and the jurisdiction over wreck and other droits of the crown or the Admiral.[3] These Admiralty courts were beginning to encroach upon the rights of those seaport towns which possessed Admiralty jurisdiction;[4] and, since their jurisdiction was undefined, great irregularities were committed.[5] For these reasons they aroused a Parliamentary opposition similar in kind to that aroused by the jurisdiction of the Council. The result of this opposition was seen in two statutes of Richard II.'s reign which defined their jurisdiction. A statute of 1389[6] recites that "a great and common clamour and complaint hath been often times made before this time, and yet is, for that the Admirals and their deputies hold their sessions within divers places of this realm, as well within franchise as without, accroaching to them greater authority than belongeth to their office." It enacts that, "the admirals and their deputies shall not meddle from henceforth with anything done within the realm, but only of a thing done upon the sea, as it hath been used in the time of King Edward, grandfather of our Lord the King that now is." A statute of 1391[7] enacts more specifically, "that of all manner of contracts, pleas, and quarrels, and all other things rising within the bodies of the counties, as well by land as by water, and also of wreck of the sea, the Admiral's court shall have no manner of cognizance, power nor jurisdiction." But, "nevertheless, of the death of a man, and of a mayhem done in great ships, being and hovering in the main stream of great rivers, only beneath the bridges of the same rivers nigh to the sea, and in none other places of the same rivers, the Admiral shall have cognizance."[8] In view of further petitions as to the encroachments of the Admiral's courts it was enacted in 1400 that those sued wrongfully in these courts

---

[1] Select Pleas of the Admiralty i xlvi-liv.
[2] Ibid xli, xlii; Rymer, Foedera vi 14, 15.
[3] Select Pleas of the Admiralty xliv, xlv; ibid ii xxv, xxvi.
[4] R.P. iii 322 (17 Rich. II. n. 49) the towns of Bristol, Bridgewater, Exeter, Barnstaple, and Wells complained of the encroachments, errors, and delays of the court held by the Admiral in the south-west of England; appeals, they say, have been pending three years and more, "pur diverse delaies de la ley de Civil, et subtill ymagination de les parties pleintiffs;" cf. Sampson v. Curteys, Select Pleas of the Admiralty i 1; Gernsey v. Henton ibid 17, which bear out the statements in the petition.
[5] Marsden, Law and Custom of the Sea (Navy Records Soc.) i xiii.
[6] 13 Richard II. St. 1 c. 5.   [7] 15 Richard II. c. 3.
[8] The statute also (§ 4) recognizes the disciplinary powers of the Admiral.

should have a right of action for double damages.[1] Though petitions were still directed against them and their procedure,[2] these statutes effected some settlement of their jurisdiction ; and the courts of common law maintained their observance by the issue of writs of supersedeas, certiorari or prohibition.[3]

When, in the fifteenth century, these local Admiralty courts were superseded by the high court of Admiralty, its jurisdiction was limited by these statutes ; and, till the Tudor period, it does not seem to have been an active court.[4] But we have seen that the reign of Henry VIII. witnessed a revival of interest in the navy, and an increased activity in the high court of Admiralty. We shall see that its criminal jurisdiction was reformed by a statute of 1536 ;[5] and a statute of 1540[6] gave to the Admiral a jurisdiction in matters of freight and damage to cargo. The patents of Henry VIII.'s admirals not only omit the proviso to be found in earlier patents, confining their jurisdiction within the limits marked out by the statutes of Richard II.'s reign, they also insert a non obstante clause dispensing with those statutes.[7] It therefore becomes possible to see in outline the main heads of the modern jurisdiction of the court.

In modern times the main division is between the Ordinary or " Instance " Jurisdiction, and the Prize Jurisdiction. Though this division was not so clearly defined in the Tudor period as in later days, I shall adopt it as the most convenient in tracing the history of this topic.

(i) The Ordinary or Instance Jurisdiction.

This jurisdiction falls under three heads : (*a*) Criminal Jurisdiction ; (*b*) Civil Jurisdiction ; and (*c*) Admiralty Droits.

---

[1] 2 Henry IV. c. 11.
[2] R.P. iii 498 (4 Hy. IV. n. 47), the prayer is for the enforcement of remedies against the admirals and their deputies, " et auxi que les ditz Admiralles usent lour Leies tant soulement par la Ley de Oleron et anxiens Leyes de la Meer, et par la Leye d'Engleterre,et nemye par Custume, ne par nulle autre manere ; " R.P. iii 642 (11 Hy. IV. n. 61), the prayer is that the justices of the peace may have power to enquire into the doings of the Admirals and their agents.
[3] Coke, Fourth Instit. 137, 138; Select Pleas of the Admiralty ii xli.
[4] Above 546.
[5] Below 550-551.
[6] 32 Henry VIII. c. 14.
[7] The patent of Henry Duke of Richmond (1525) gives him power " audiendi et terminandi querelas omnium contractuum inter dominos proprietarios navium ac mercatores seu alios quoscunque cum eisdem dominis ac navium ceterorumque vasorum proprietariis pro aliquo per mare vel ultra mare expediendo contractuum omnium et singulorum contractuum ultra mare proficiendorum vel ultra mare contractuum et in Anglia et ceterorum omnium quæ ad officium Admiralli tangunt. . . . Aliquibus statutis, actubus, ordinationibus, sive restrictionibus in contrarium actis editis ordinatis sive provisis, non obstantibus," Select Pleas of the Admiralty i lviii ; the later commissions are very similar ; but they omit the non obstante clause.

(a) Criminal Jurisdiction.

We have seen that after 1363 the Admiral's criminal jurisdiction was recognized as exclusive on the high seas.   This exclusive jurisdiction could be exercised over British subjects, over the crew of a British ship whether subjects or not, and over any one in cases of piracy at common law.[2]   It could be exercised over no other persons.[3]   The act of Richard II. recognized also a jurisdiction in cases of homicide and mayhem committed on rivers below the bridges.[4]   This jurisdiction was, above low water mark, concurrent with that possessed by the courts of common law.[5]

We have seen that the procedure in the Admiral's court had come to be modelled on the procedure of the civil law.   The early precedents for trial by jury were not followed,[6] and trial by witnesses took its place.   In 1536 dissatisfaction with this method of trial produced a statute, the ultimate effect of which was to transfer to the judges of the courts of common law the criminal jurisdiction of the Admiralty.[7]

The statute recites that those who have committed crimes upon the sea, " many times escaped unpunished because the trial of their offences hath heretofore been ordered . . . before the Admiral . . . after the course of the civil laws ; the nature whereof is, that before any judgment of death can be given against the offenders, either they must plainly confess their offences (which they will never do without torture or pains) or else their offences be so plainly and directly proved by witness indifferent, such as saw their offences committed, which cannot be gotten but by chance at few times, because such offenders commit their offences upon the sea, and at many times murder and kill such persons being in the ship or boat where they commit their

---

[1] 13 Richard II. St. 1 c. 5 ; 15 Richard II. c. 3.

[2] Stephen, H.C.L. ii 27-29 ; in cases of piracy by statute, jurisdiction only exists over British subjects ; 11 William III. c. 7 gave the crown power to appoint commissioners to try piracy cases in the colonies or at sea ; for an instance of a commission issued under this Act in 1725 see Law and Custom of the Sea (Navy Records Soc.) ii 262-263 ; for an opinion on the interpretation of the Act see ibid ii 252-255.

[3] R. v. Keyn (1877) 2 Ex. Div. 63 ; the effect of the decision was overruled by the Territorial Waters Jurisdiction Act 41, 42 Victoria c. 73 ; the Act declares that offences committed by anyone within the territorial waters of the crown, i.e. on the sea to such a distance as is necessary for the defence of the dominions of the crown, are within the jurisdiction of the Admiral.

[4] 15 Richard II. c. 3.

[5] Sir Henry Constable's Case (1601) 5 Co. Rep. 107, " Below the low water mark the Admiral has the sole and absolute jurisdiction.   Between the high water mark and low water mark the common law and the Admiral have *divisum imperium* interchangeably."

[6] Select Pleas of the Admiralty (S.S.) i liv.

[7] 28 Henry VIII. c. 15.

offences, which should witness against them in that behalf; and also such as should bear witness be commonly mariners and ship men, which, because of their often voyages and passages in the seas, depart without long tarrying." It provides that treasons, felonies, robberies, murders and confederacies, committed in any place where the Admiral has jurisdiction, shall be enquired into and tried by commissioners appointed by the crown as if the offences had been committed on land. The commissions could be issued to the Admiral, his deputy, or three or four other substantial persons to be appointed by the Lord Chancellor. " It seems," says Marsden, "to have been more efficient than the old common law courts or the Admiralty court; no record has been found of a pirate being hanged by the latter, and only three by the former, whereas twenty-two were hanged in the years 1549-1551, and 113 in 1561-1583."[1] In 1799 this Act was extended to the trial of all offences committed on the high seas.[2] As the three or four substantial persons to be appointed under the act of Henry VIII. came to be invariably the judges of the common law courts, the indirect result of the Act was to transfer the criminal jurisdiction of the Admiralty to the judges of the courts of common law.[3]

Special commissions under this Act have been rendered obsolete by later legislation. In 1834 the Central Criminal Court Act gave to that court the jurisdiction of these special commissioners,[4] and in 1844 a similar jurisdiction was given to the ordinary justices of Oyer and Terminer and Gaol Delivery.[5] Provisions to the same effect are contained in the Criminal Law Consolidation Acts[6] and the Merchant Shipping Acts.[7]

The criminal jurisdiction of the Admiralty has thus for almost four centuries been exercised by the judges of the courts of common law. It has, for this reason, almost wholly lost the international character which marked all branches of the maritime law in the Middles Ages. Piracy "at common law" is perhaps the only

---

[1] Law and Custom of the Sea (Navy Records Soc.) i 149.
[2] 39 George III. c. 37. It was asserted in a bill introduced into the House of Lords in 1683, Hist. MSS. Com. Eleventh Rep. App. Pt. II. 295 no. 434, that if a man was wounded on the high seas and died in England of the wound neither the courts of common law nor the court of Admiralty could try him for murder—which is not improbable see 2, 3 Edward VI. c. 24; the bill provided that in such cases the justices of Oyer and Terminer and Gaol Delivery should have jurisdiction; but evidence was given to show that if the party died abroad the court of the Constable and Marshal had jurisdiction, and that if he died in England the Admiralty had jurisdiction, and the bill was dropped.
[3] Stephen, H.C.L. ii 19.
[4] 4, 5 William IV. c. 36 § 22.   [5] 7, 8 Victoria c. 2
[6] 24, 25 Victoria c. 96 § 115 ; c. 97 § 72 ; c. 98 § 50 ; c. 99 § 36 ; c. 100 § 68.
[7] They deal with crimes committed on British ships or by British seamen. 17, 18 Victoria c. 104 § 267 ; 18, 19 Victoria c. 91 § 21 ; 57, 58 Victoria c. 60 §§ 686, 687.

crime, which still retains some trace of an international character, in the rule, that it can be tried by the court of any country wherever and by whomsoever committed.[1]   The criminal jurisdiction of the Admiralty, having been administered by the common law judges, has become part and parcel of the common law, to be spelt out of English statutes, to be changed only as that law is changed.   This fact was strikingly illustrated by the case of *Reg. v. Keyn*.[2]   No consensus of opinion amongst international jurists was held sufficient to give to the English courts a criminal jurisdiction over foreigners not recognized by English law.   Cockburn, C.J., denied that a consensus of jurists could effect, in maritime law, what, in another branch of the old Law Merchant, he allowed might be effected by a consensus of merchants.[3]   The case was decided by a bare majority.   We may, perhaps, conjecture that it would have been decided the other way, if the criminal jurisdiction of the Admiralty had been developed in the court of Admiralty, and not by the judges of the courts of common law.

(b) Civil Jurisdiction.

We have seen that under the Tudors the crown seemed inclined to disregard altogether the limitations which statutes had imposed upon the jurisdiction of the court of Admiralty.   The extent of the jurisdiction which it claimed will appear from a list of the cases which, during this period, were brought before the court.[4]   It practically comprised all mercantile and shipping cases.   " All contracts made abroad, bills of exchange (which at this period were for the most part drawn or payable abroad) commercial agencies abroad, charter parties, insurance, average, freight, non-delivery of, or damage to, cargo, negligent navigation by masters, mariners, or pilots, breach of warranty of seaworthiness, and other provisions contained in charter parties ; in short, every kind of shipping business was dealt with by the Admiralty court." [5]   The Admiralty court was, in fact, regarded as one of the recognized tribunals of the Law Merchant.[6]   In addition, the court exercised jurisdiction over various torts committed on the sea, and in public rivers, over cases of collision, salvage, fishermen, harbours and rivers, and occasionally over matters transacted abroad, but otherwise outside the scope of Admiralty jurisdiction.[7]

---

[1] For this offence see vol. vi 400-401.   [2] (1877) 2 Ex. Div. 63, 202.
[3] Goodwin v. Robarts (1875) L.R. 10 Ex. 337 ; below 573.
[4] Select Pleas of the Admiralty (S.S.) i lxv-lxxi ; cp. Malynes, Lex Mercatoria, 303, 304 (Pt. III. c. xiv).
[5] Select Pleas of the Admiralty (S.S.) i lxvii.   [6] Malynes, Pt. III. c. xiv.
[7] Select Pleas of the Admiralty (S.S.) i lxx ; in the sixteenth century " even marriage contracts and wills made abroad are occasionally met with as the subject of suits in Admiralty."

We have seen that during Elizabeth's reign the common law courts began their attack upon the Chancery and the Council. It was not to be expected that they would tamely acquiesce in this growth of the jurisdiction of the Admiralty. Moreover, as we have seen, they were able to base their attack upon a statutory foundation.

The common law courts had issued writs of prohibition, based upon these statutes, from an early period. It is probable, however, that during the earlier part of the Tudor period the statutes had been disregarded; and, as we have seen, the aid of the legislature had even been invoked on behalf of the Admiralty.[1] The Admiralty, also, had sometimes assumed the offensive, by means of a process of contempt, taken against those who brought proceedings upon maritime causes in another court.[2] It would appear that when the common law courts resumed their efforts against the Admiralty, they at first had recourse to writs of supersedeas and certiorari issuing from the Chancery. But such applications to the Chancellor often left the Admiralty with the disputed jurisdiction. It was seen that writs of prohibition were the most effective instrument of attack or defence which the common law courts possessed.[3]

In 1575 a provisional agreement was arrived at; but, after 1606, when Coke was raised to the Bench, the agreement was repudiated.[4] Coke, as Buller, J., once said, "seems to have entertained not only a jealousy of, but an enmity against, that jurisdiction."[5] He denied that the court was a court of record. He denied it the necessary power to take stipulations for appearance, and performance of the acts and judgments of the court. He denied that it had any jurisdiction over contracts made on land, either in this country, or abroad, whether or no they were to be performed upon the sea; and similarly he denied its jurisdiction over offences committed on land, either in this country, or abroad.[6] In support of his positions he did not hesitate to cite precedents which were far from deciding what he stated that

---

[1] 32 Henry VIII. c. 14 gave the court a certain jurisdiction in cases concerning charter parties and freight.

[2] Select Pleas of the Admiralty (S.S.) i lxviii 78; on proof of the facts the party in contempt was arrested.

[3] Ibid ii xli; for a list of Prohibitions, see ibid i lxxiii-lxxviii; ii xli-lvii; Fourth Instit. 137-142; Prynne, Animadversions, 75-77; for a specimen of the writ, see App. XII. A 2.

[4] Select Pleas of the Admiralty (S.S.) ii xiv; Coke, Fourth Instit. 136; Zouch, Jurisdiction of the Admiralty Asserted, Assertion v.

[5] Smart v. Wolff (1789) 3 T.R. 348; Holt also said, 1 Ld. Raym. 398 that, "heretofore the common law was too severe against the Admiral;" cp. Prynne 103.

[6] Fourth Instit. 136-138; Thomlinson's Case (1605) 12 Co. Rep. 104; 2 Brownlow 16, 17 (1611).

they did decide.[1]   It is fairly certain that the earlier prohibitions were all founded upon the exercise by the Admiralty of jurisdiction within the bodies of counties.   The common law had not in the past claimed jurisdiction over contracts made or offences committed abroad, and probably not over contracts made and offences committed in ports intra fluxum et refluxum maris.[2] Such jurisdiction was now coveted.   By supposing these contracts or offences to have been made or committed in England the common law courts assumed jurisdiction; [3] and thus by a "new strange poetical fiction," and by the help of " imaginary sign-posts in Cheapside "[4] they endeavoured to capture jurisdiction over the growing commercial business of the country.   The other common law judges followed Coke's lead.   It is not, of course, to be expected, that all the cases, decided at a time when the common law courts were engaged upon a systematic series of encroachments, should be consistent.[5]   But it is clear that they were all tending in one direction, regardless of the fact that the procedure of the common law courts, and the law which they applied, were far less fitted than that of the Admiralty, to deal with the cases over which they claimed jurisdiction.   Whitelock tells us that in 1630 "Sir Henry Martyn, doctor of laws, and judge of the Admiralty, made a great complaint to the king against the judges of the King's Bench, for granting prohibitions against that court; and all the judges were before the king about it, and they mannerly and stoutly justified their proceedings in those cases to be according to law, and as their oaths bound them."[6]

The merchants keenly felt the ill effects of these attacks made by the common law courts; and the delays in the administration of justice thereby occasioned sometimes gave rise to diplomatic

---

[1] Prynne, Animadversions, 75-77; De Lovio v. Boit (1815) 2 Gall 407-418 *per* Story, J.

[2] Above 534-535; De Lovio v. Boit, at pp. 400-405; Y.B. 13 Hy. IV. Mich. pl. 10; see Bk. iv Pt. I. c. 3 for an account of the evolution of the law on this topic.

[3] Bl. Comm. iii 107; vol. v 140-142.

[4] Prynne, Animadversions, 95, 97.

[5] In Sir R. Buckley's Case (1590) 2 Leo. 182, which was a case of an agreement made in England for assistance at sea in taking a prize, the Admiralty jurisdiction seems to be recognized; in Tucker v. Cappes and Jones (1625) 2 Rolle 497, which was a suit on a contract made in Virginia, a Prohibition was refused; it was said that the Admiralty had jurisdiction over things done in foreign parts, that foreign contracts were governed by the civil law, and that it was not reasonable that the common law should judge of them; but Coke said (1611) 2 Brownlow 17, that if a question of civil law arose the judges could consult with the civilians; it was said in Ambassador of King of Spain v. Joliff and others, Hob. 78, 79, that "the Admiralty of England can hold no plea of any contract but such as ariseth upon the sea: no, though it arise upon any continent, port, or haven in the world out of the king's dominions. . . . The courts of common law have unlimited power in causes transitory."

[6] Memorials i 40; cp. S.P. Dom. 1629-1631 124, 164.

difficulties.[1]   A conflict of jurisdiction must always give advantages to the unscrupulous litigant.   It was clear that the Admiralty
process was more speedy, and therefore more fit to deal with the
cases of merchants and mariners.   "Not one cause in ten comes
before that court but some of the parties or witnesses in it are
pressing to go to sea with the next tide."[2]   The Admiralty could
issue commissions to examine witnesses abroad, and it could examine the parties themselves.   "The merchant if he can avoid
the Admiralty, where he must answer upon oath, and proof may
be made by commission, thinks himself secure from any danger
at the common law."[3]   The Admiralty could arrest the ship, and
thus give far more effective security to those who had been employed upon it.   The Admiralty could allow all the mariners to
sue together for their wages, whereas the common law courts
insisted upon separate actions.   The judges of the court of Admiralty, being civilians, were far more likely to be able to understand contracts made abroad with reference to the civil law.[4]
Two cases, put by Sir Leoline Jenkins in his argument before
the House of Lords in 1669-1670, illustrate the incompetence of
the common law courts to deal with the jurisdiction which they
claimed.   In the first case put, a Spanish merchant resident in
Spain owes money to A.   The Spanish merchant has a ship in
an English port, which the Admiralty process alone can reach.
An action is brought by A in the court of Admiralty.   The ship
is arrested; but in consequence of a prohibition it is released.
What is the use of suing a debtor in Spain with no available
property in this country?   In the second case A owes money to
a Spanish merchant.   The Spaniard sues in the Admiralty, and
is prohibited.   He then sues at common law, and, to prove his
case, produces a copy of his contract.   A pleads "non est
factum."   The original is in Spain deposited with a notary who
will not part with it.   The Spaniard looses his case for want of
evidence.[5]

Another compromise was attempted in 1632.   Charles I.
issued a commission to the Privy Council, empowering it to reconcile the differences between the common law courts and the
Admiralty.[6]   Sir Leoline Jenkins said that the agreement arrived
at was "the result of many solemn debates, and not of artifice

---

[1] S.P. Dom. 1611-1618 146, lxx 61—complaint by the Spanish Ambassador of
the delays of the Admiralty caused by Prohibitions.
[2] Wynne, Life of Sir Leoline Jenkins i lxxxii.
[3] Zouch, Jurisdiction, etc., 130.
[4] Life of Jenkins i lxxvii, lxxxiii; Zouch, 129, 130.
[5] Life of Jenkins i lxxxi, lxxxii.
[6] See S.P. Dom. 1631-1633 427, 516, 519; see ibid 243-246 for a collection of
arguments and tracts on this topic.

or surprise."[1]   We can well believe this, if we consider the ill results which followed from the assumption of jurisdiction by the courts of common law.   The agreement conceded to the Admiralty a jurisdiction in the following cases : (1) In the case of contracts made, or wrongs committed, beyond the sea, or upon the sea.   (2) In suits for freight or mariners' wages, or for the breach of charter parties for voyages to be made beyond the sea, though the charter parties were made within the realm, and the money was payable within the realm.   But if the proceeding was for a penalty, or the question was whether the charter party was made or not, or, if made, had been released, the common law courts were to have jurisdiction.   (3) In suits for building, amending, saving or necessary victualling of a ship, brought against the ship itself, though the cause of action arose within the realm.   (4) The court was allowed a jurisdiction to inquire of, and to redress, all annoyances and obstructions in all navigable rivers beneath the first bridges, and also to try personal contracts and injuries done there which concerned navigation upon the sea.   (5) It was provided that if any person was imprisoned, and, upon a writ of Habeas Corpus being obtained, the exercise of jurisdiction by the Admiralty in any of these points was certified as the cause of the imprisonment, the parties should be remanded.

It is probable that this agreement was acted upon for a few years.[2]   Prynne cites a case in which the House of Lords upheld the jurisdiction of the Admiralty in 1645 ;[3] and during the interregnum Ordinances of 1648, 1649, and 1653[4] conceded to the court a jurisdiction similar to that which was conceded to it by the agreement of 1632.[5]   In fact some of these Ordinances ordered the judges of the Admiralty to proceed in spite of prohibitions ; and in 1656 orders were issued to the judges of the common law courts to be sparing in granting prohibitions, and to the judges of the Admiralty not to encroach upon the jurisdiction of the common law courts.[6]

But, as we have seen, the Great Rebellion ensured the victory of the common law over jurisdictions which threatened to

[1] Life of Jenkins i lxxxi ; it is printed by Prynne 101, and in the first edition of Croke's reports ; but in the later editions of these reports it is stated not to be law ; it is only mentioned in two cases, Rolle, Abridgement 533, and T. Raym. 3.
[2] See e.g. S.P. Dom. 1639-1640 173-174, ccccxxxvi 21—the king interposed to secure the observance of the fifth clause of this agreement.
[3] Animadversions 123-125.
[4] Acts and Ordinances i 1120 ; ii 78, 712.
[5] Williams and Bruce, Admiralty Practice, 12.
[6] Whitelock, Memorials iv 233 ; " I was against these letters," says Whitelock, " and advised rather to confer with the judges about it, who being upon their oaths must observe them ; and justice ought to run in free and legal course."

be its rivals. A bill to declare and settle the jurisdiction of the Admiralty failed to pass in 1641;[1] and in 1661 a similar bill met with no better success.[2] In 1669-1670 a more determined effort was made. A bill introduced into the House of Lords in that year proposed that the jurisdiction of the court should extend to all suits respecting contracts made or other matters done beyond or upon the sea concerning shipping or goods shipped, freight, mariners' wages, and breach of charter parties; to suits for building, mending, saving or victualling ships if brought against the ship; and to suits connected with the navigation of navigable rivers below bridges.[3] But in spite of the fact that the merchants of London petitioned Parliament to pass the bill, and in spite of Sir Leoline Jenkins' convincing argument in its favour,[4] it failed to pass. The civil jurisdiction of the court was consequently reduced to a very low ebb. "The common law," said Holt, "is the overruling jurisdiction in this realm; and you ought to entitle yourselves well, to draw a thing out of the jurisdiction of it."[5] Torts committed on the high seas; contracts made on the high seas to be there executed; proceedings in rem on bottomry bonds executed in foreign parts; the enforcement of the judgments of foreign Admiralty courts; suits for the wages of mariners[6]—were almost the only pieces of jurisdiction which it was allowed to exercise. Pepys[7] tells us that he went to St. Margaret's Hill in Southwark, "where the judges of the Admiralty come, and the rest of the Doctors of Civil law." He remarks, "I perceive that this court is yet but in its infancy (as to its rising again); and their design and consultation was, I could overhear them, how to proceed with the most solemnity, and spend time, there being only two

---

[1] Hist. MSS. Com. Fourth Rep. 73.
[2] Ibid Seventh Rep. 155. [3] Ibid Eighth Rep. 141 no. 271.
[4] Printed by Wynne, Life of Jenkins i lxxvi-lxxxv.
[5] Shermoulin v. Sands (1698) 1 Ld. Raym. at p. 272.
[6] Contracts made at sea, not maritime in their nature, were claimed by the common law courts as not proper for the Admiral; contracts, maritime in their nature, but made on land, were claimed by reason of their locality; convenience of process gave the Admiralty jurisdiction over seamen's wages after a struggle, cf. Winch 8 (1622); T. Raym. 3 (1660); 1 Keb. 712 (1664); 2 Ld. Raym. 1247 (1707); the courts were very puzzled to find some principle on which they could justify this exception, cf. 4 Burr. 1944; 2 Ld. Raym. 1452; in Clay v. Sudgrave (1700) 1 Salk. 33, it was stated that, though against the statute, it was allowed for the sake of convenience, and, "communis error facit jus;" the exception was narrowly construed; though the mariners could sue in the Admiralty the master could not; the Admiralty was also allowed to have jurisdiction in cases of ransom contracts till 22 George III. c. 25 made these contracts illegal, Wilson v. Bird (1695) 1 Ld. Raym. 22; and in cases where the master hypothecated his ship for necessaries, Benzen v. Jefferies (1697) 1 Ld. Raym. 152.
[7] Pepys' Diary, March 17, 1662-1663; as Jenkins truly said in his argument before the House of Lords, "Every place in Europe intrusts the Admiral with more ample jurisdiction than England does."

businesses to do, which of themselves could not spend much time."

It is clear that the court of Admiralty had on its side not only historical truth, but also substantial convenience. Prynne, Zouch, and Jenkins prove clearly both these facts. It is clear, too, that the opposition of Coke and the common lawyers was unscrupulous. But the common law had, after the Great Rebellion, gained the upper hand. And, from the point of view of the common law, the attack had been skilfully directed upon a position which it was worth much to secure; for the prize was nothing less than the commercial jurisdiction of a country the commerce of which was then rapidly expanding. Its commerce was in the future destined to expand beyond the most sanguine dreams of the seventeenth century. Coke could not foresee this. But he worshipped the common law; and he rendered it by no means the least of his many valuable services when he directed, and sometimes misdirected, his stores of technical learning to secure for it this new field. To the litigant his action meant much inconvenience. To the commercial law of this country it meant a slower development.[1] But to the common law it meant a capacity for expansion, and a continued supremacy over the law of the future, which consolidated the victories won in the political contests of the seventeenth century. If Lord Mansfield is to be credited with the title of the founder of the commercial law of this country, it must be allowed that Coke gave to the founder of that law his opportunity.[2]

Modern legislation has restored to the court of Admiralty many of the powers, and much of the jurisdiction of which it had been deprived in the seventeenth century.[3] It has been restored, as we have seen, to its ancient position of a court of

---

[1] Select Pleas of the Admiralty (S.S.) ii lxxx, " Many points of maritime law that were afterwards painfully elaborated by the common lawyers had for at least a century been familiar to the civilians; " e.g. the liability of a carrier for loss by thieves was discussed at Westminster in 1671 ; but it had been settled in the Admiralty as early as 1640; the same thing is true as to many questions relating to Bills of Exchange, Bills of Lading, General Average, and Insurance; the common law followed the Admiralty "with tardy steps, perhaps unconsciously, certainly without acknowledgment;" for the history of the development of the law on these matters see vol. viii c. 4.

[2] The use made by the Government of the powers of the court caused a similar jealousy of the Admiralty in the United States; the Massachusetts House of Representatives, just before the Revolution, resolved that, " the extension of the powers of the court of Admiralty within this province is a most violent infraction of the right of trial by juries," Williams and Bruce 5 n. k; cp. Ramsay v. Allegre (1827) 12 Wheaton 611 ; but, as Roger North says, " it is the foible of all judicatures to value their own justice and pretend that there is none so exquisite as theirs; while, at the bottom, it is the profits accruing that sanctify any court's authority ; " we have seen that the judges had at this period a direct pecuniary interest in increasing the business of their courts, above 254-255.

[3] 3, 4 Victoria c. 65; 13, 14 Victoria c. 26; 24 Victoria c. 10.

record; and its judge has been given the powers possessed by the judges of the superior courts of common law. It has been given jurisdiction in cases of salvage, bottomry, damage, towage, goods supplied to foreign ships, building, equipping, and repairing ships, disputes between co-owners. In addition, it has been given a new jurisdiction in the case of booty of war, if the crown sees fit to refer any such question to it, and a new jurisdiction under the Foreign Enlistment Act.[1] But the contests of the seventeenth century have left their mark upon the law administered by the court. The common law courts often came to decisions, similar to those which the Admiralty had already given upon the principles of the civil law. But the decisions, though the same in substance, were the decisions of English courts and enunciated rules of English law. The law administered by the court of Admiralty possesses, it is true, affinities with the maritime law of foreign countries. The law of Oleron, and other maritime codes, may still be usefully cited in English courts. But Admiralty law has lost the international character which it once possessed. It is essentially English law. "The law which is administered in the Admiralty court of England is the English maritime law. It is not the ordinary municipal law of the country, but it is the law which the English court of Admiralty, either by Act of Parliament or by reiterated decisions and traditions and principles, has adopted as the English maritime law."[2] "Neither the laws of the Rhodians, nor of Oleron, nor of Wisby, nor of the Hanse towns, are of themselves any part of the Admiralty law of England. . . . But they contain many principles and statements of marine practice, which, together with principles found in the Digest, and in the French, and other Ordinances, were used by the judges of the English court of Admiralty, when they were moulding and reducing to form the principles and practice of their court."[3] These statements could not have been made by the judges of the court in the sixteenth, or even in the seventeenth centuries. The contact with, and the control exercised by the courts of common law, have affected in a similar way both the civil and the criminal jurisdiction of the court.

(c) Admiralty Droits.

The crown had originally certain rights to property found upon the sea, or stranded upon the shore.[4] The chief kinds of property to which the crown was thus entitled were, great fish

---

[1] 3, 4 Victoria c. 65 § 22; 33, 34 Victoria c. 90 § 19.
[2] The Gaetano and Maria (1882) 7 P.D. at p. 143.
[3] The Gas Float Whitton, No. 2 [1896] P. at pp. 47, 48.
[4] Stat. Prærogativa Regis (17 Ed. II. St. 1 c. xi); on the whole subject see L.Q.R. xv 353.

(such as whales or porpoises),[1] deodands,[2] wreck of the sea, flotsam, jetsam, and lagan,[3] ships or goods of the enemy found in English ports or captured by uncommissioned vessels, and goods taken or retaken from pirates.[4]

In early days, before the rise of the court of Admiralty, many of these droits were granted to the lords of manors, or to the towns which possessed Admiralty jurisdiction. Yarmouth had such rights;[5] and in 1829 Dunwich and Southwold spent £1000 to determine the question whether a puncheon of whisky, taken up in the sea, was within the jurisdiction of one town or the other.[6] The Lord Warden of the Cinque Ports and the ports themselves shared these droits between them.[7] In 1836 there was litigation between the crown and the owner of the manor and castle of Corfe and the Isle of Purbeck, as to the right to 49 casks of brandy.[8] If not so granted out, they were dealt with by the common law courts or by special commissioners.[9]

After the rise of the court of Admiralty the Lord High Admiral became entitled to these droits by royal grant. At the end of the fourteenth and the beginning of the fifteenth century it would appear that he shared them with the crown;[10] from the reign of Henry VI. they were generally granted to him. "The Admiral's Patents of the sixteenth and following centuries contain express grants of royal fish, wrecks, waifs, flotsam, jetsam, and lagan, as well as many other perquisites connected with the sea and the seashore."[11] In Anne's reign, George, Duke of Denmark, the Lord High Admiral, surrendered his

---

[1] Lord Warden of Cinque Ports v. the King (1831) 2 Hagg. Adm. 438.

[2] I.e. a thing causing the death of a man, Stephen, H.C.L. iii 77, 78; Holmes, Common Law 24-26; Select Pleas of the Admiralty ii xxvi, xxvii; they were abolished 9, 10 Victoria c. 62.

[3] "That nothing shall be said to be wreccum maris but such goods only which are cast or left on the land by the sea. . . . Flotsam is when a ship is sunk or otherwise perished and the goods float on the sea. Jetsam is when the ship is in danger of being sunk, and to lighten the ship the goods are cast into the sea, and afterwards, notwithstanding, the ship perish. Lagan (vel potius Ligan) is where the goods which are so cast into the sea, and afterwards the ship perishes, and such goods are so heavy that they sink to the bottom, and the mariners, to the intent to have them again, tie to them a buoy or cork . . . and none of these goods are called wrecks so long as they remain in or upon the sea," Sir Henry Constable's Case (1601) 5 Co. Rep. 106; for an early proclamation of Henry I. relating to wreck see E.H.R. xxix 434.

[4] Select Pleas of the Admiralty ii xxxix; The Germania [1916] P. 5.

[5] Ibid xxii.   [6] Ibid.   [7] Ibid xxiii.

[8] The King v. 49 Casks of Brandy 3 Hagg. Adm. 257; 5 Co. Rep. 107 b it is said that "those of the west country prescribe to have wreck in the sea so far as the   may see a Humber Barrel."

[9] Select Pleas of the Admiralty (S.S.) i xli.

[10] Black Book of the Admiralty (R.S.) 1 150; Select Pleas of the Admiralty ii xxiv.

[11] Ibid xxv.

droits during the war for a fixed annual sum. The office was in commission after his death, except for a short time, when it was held by George, Duke of Clarence, afterwards William IV. The droits during this period were always reserved to the crown, but in terms which showed that they had been previously annexed to the office of Admiral.[1]

The right to droits carried with it a certain jurisdiction. Inquisitions were held into these droits at the ports,[2] or the Vice-Admirals or droit gatherers reported them to the Admiral.[3] The large terms of the Admiral's Patents incited them, or their grantees, to frequent litigation with private persons or other grantees of the crown.[4] If the property was unclaimed, it belonged to the Admiral or other person entitled, who might or might not reward the finder.[5] If a claimant appeared, he was entitled to restoration on proof of his claim, and the payment of a reasonable salvage. Such salvage was often allowed to the Vice-Admirals of the coast as a reward for taking possession of, and looking after, the property.[6]

The Admiralty droits, where the right has not been granted to other persons, are now transferred to the consolidated fund.[7] But it is provided that the crown may reward the finder. In 1854 they were put under the control of the Board of Trade;[8] and in 1894 the method of dealing with wreck, flotsam, jetsam, and lagan found within British jurisdiction, was regulated by the Merchant Shipping Act.[9]

(ii) Prize Jurisdiction.[10]

The term Prize is applied to the property of a belligerent captured at sea. Prizes can as a rule only be made by some vessel acting under the authority of the government.[11] It is clear that many complicated questions must arise as to the

---

[1] The King v. 49 Casks of Brandy 3 Hagg. Adm. at pp. 280, 281; "During the last French war the sums raised by droits was very large. Sums of £100,000, £190,000, and £58,360 are mentioned as having been paid to members of the royal family; the last sum is stated to have been paid out on account of the building, etc., of the Pavilion at Brighton," Select Pleas of the Admiralty ii xxxix.

[2] Ibid xxvii-xxxii. [3] Ibid xxxvii.

[4] Ibid xviii, xix, xxii; in 1619 there was a dispute between the Lord Warden and the Admiral as to wrecks on the Goodwins; in 1632 there is a report to the Admiral on the encroachments of lords of manors.

[5] Ibid xxxviii.

[6] Ibid xxxvii; as to wreck see ibid xxxix-xli; Hamilton v. Davis (1771) 5 Burr. 2732.

[7] 1 William IV. c. 25; 1, 2 Victoria c. 2.

[8] 17, 18 Victoria c. 120 § 10. [9] 57, 58 Victoria c. 60 §§ 510-529.

[10] Roscoe, History of the Prize Court.

[11] Pitt-Cobbett, Leading Cases in International Law (Ed. 1892) 205; prizes can only be made by private vessels if they have been attacked in the first instance, ibid 211.

ownership of the ships or goods so captured. Such questions
tended to become more complicated with the growth, during the
eighteenth century, of that part of international law which relates
to the rights and duties of neutrals. Many sentences of the
court sitting in prize from the seventeenth century onwards are
preserved, but, unfortunately, they shed little light upon the law
applied.[1] It was Lord Stowell who, by his decisions in the
many cases arising out of the wars at the end of the eighteenth
and the beginning of the nineteenth century, settled the principles
of prize jurisdiction of the Admiralty, as he settled many of the
principles of the instance jurisdiction of the court.

" The prize jurisdiction," says Mr. Marsden, " originated in
the disciplinary powers conferred upon the Admirals of the early
fourteenth century by their patents." [2] They adjudicated upon
the rights of the captors to their prizes, because the king, being
entitled to these prizes, naturally claimed to decide what was and
what was not prize.[3] The king often made over a share of the
prize to the captors.[4] Somtimes he granted a certain proportion of
it to the Admiral ; [5] but somtimes, to encourage privateers, even
this proportion was made over to the captors.[6] We have seen
that in earlier days cases of this kind had been heard sometimes
by the Council, and sometimes by the common law courts ; but
that their inability to cope with the difficulties caused by the
piratical propensities of Englishmen had led to the establishment
of a court of Admiralty.[7] Therefore it would probably be true
to say that the prize jurisdiction of the court was one of the
oldest branches of its jurisdiction. There is a case as early as
1357 in which the Admiral decided upon the validity of a capture
at sea.[8]

In the course of the fifteenth century it was becoming obvious that a regular tribunal was needed to deal with such cases ;

---

[1] Marsden, Law and Custom of the Sea (Navy Records Soc.) i 408; with regard to these records Mr. Marsden says, ibid ii viii, " The prize records are in a fair
state of preservation, and the prize sentences, in particular, appear to have been
carefully filed and preserved. They exist in vast numbers, and were at an early
date bound in volumes and indexed. They are, however, disappointing as regards
the light which it might have been expected they would throw upon the growth of
prize law. Framed, as they are, in the same bald and technical terms, they contain little more than a bald statement of the condemnation or order for restitution
of the ship or goods in dispute. The sentences of the court of Delegates . . . unfortunately have not been nearly so well preserved. Many of them are in a state
of decay and many are missing."

[2] E.H.R. xxiv 675.   [3] Ibid 675, 677.   [4] Ibid 675-676.

[5] " The patents of the Lord High Admiral of the fifteenth and sixteenth centuries
contain grants of shares and perquisites which are probably the origin of the Lord
Admiral's tenths of prizes which he enjoyed by virtue of his office throughout the
sixteenth century," ibid 676.

[6] Ibid 677.   [7] Above 544-545.

[8] E.H.R. xxiv 680; cf. Rymer, Foedera vi 14, 15 ; Roscoe, op. cit. 4-5.

and the court of Admiralty had by the end of the century come to be regarded as the proper tribunal.[1] Thus in 1498 a treaty between Henry VII. and Louis XII. stipulated that mariners should give notice to the Admiral of any spoil which they had taken, and that they were not to dispose of it till the Admiral had adjudged it to be lawful prize.[2] But it is not till the end of the sixteenth century, that the prize jurisdiction of the Admiralty began to take definite shape. "Unless complaint was made to the king of a capture being unlawful, captors were probably seldom disturbed in their prizes."[3] If complaint was made the question was generally dealt with as a matter of state policy by the king and Council.[4]

In the latter part of the sixteenth century the distinctive prize jurisdiction began gradually to emerge;[5] and in 1589 we get the first formal sentence of condemnation.[6] The prize jurisdiction was distinguished from the criminal jurisdiction of the Admiralty over piracy for which, as we have seen, special provision was made;[7] and it gradually became distinct from the instance jurisdiction. We have seen that there was a great development of the instance jurisdiction in the sixteenth century.[8] The principles upon which the court proceeded in dealing with cases falling within that jurisdiction were mainly those principles of the Law Merchant, maritime, and commercial, which had been developed by the Italian and Dutch lawyers. On the other hand the prize jurisdiction was necessarily governed by political considerations, and depended largely on the proclamations issued from time to time by the crown.[9] These proclamations and the decisions of the court gradually gave rise

---

[1] E.H.R. xxiv 683-684.

[2] Rymer, Foedera xii 690-694; cf. ibid xiv 147-151.

[3] E.H R. xxiv 681.

[4] " For the two centuries after this date (1357) there are few indications in the records of its dealing with prize cases; they usually came before the Council or the chancellor or commissioners appointed *ad hoc*," ibid 680; for an instance of such a commission in 1413 see Marsden, Law and Custom of the Sea (Navy Records Soc.) i 124; 2 Henry V. St. 1 c. 6 required notice of the capture of prizes to be given to the Conservators of Truces created by that Act; they were clearly intended by the Act to exercise some sort of prize jurisdiction—a fact which testifies to the inefficiency of the Admiralty, above 546; cf. Marsden, Law and Custom of the Sea i 116-117.

[5] Select Pleas of the Admiralty (S.S.) ii xvii, xviii.

[6] Marsden, Law and Custom of the Sea (Navy Records Soc.) i xxi, 254.

[7] Above 550-551; cf. E.H.R. xxiv 683-684.

[8] Above 552.

[9] Mr. Marsden's article E.H.R. xxiv 684-690, 691-696 shows that the exercise of the jurisdiction was governed mainly by these proclamations; cf. S.P. Dom. 1664-1665 369, where it appears that the judges of the prize court were expected to be governed by the king's declaration of what was and what was not contraband in coming to a conclusion whether to condemn or release a prize; for the relation of prize law to the prerogative see below 566-568.

to a body of prize law. There were many such decisions, as captors sailing under commissions granted by the allies of England, as well as captors sailing under English commissions, resorted to the court of Admiralty; and the international character of the law thus evolved tended to be emphasized by the fact that "these cases frequently resolved themselves into suits between the respective ambassadors of the powers to which the captor and the prize belonged."[1] The fact that this jurisdiction in prize was regarded as something different from the instance jurisdiction is illustrated by the fact that writs of prohibition were not so frequently issued in prize cases, as in other cases,[2] and ceased to be issued after Coke's fall in 1616.[3]

Throughout the sixteenth and early seventeenth centuries no formal distinction was made between the instance and the prize jurisdiction. But the two jurisdictions were obviously coming to be regarded as distinct during the period of the Commonwealth.[4] After the Restoration the court held distinct sittings for prize business; special rules were issued for the regulation of the exercise of this jurisdiction;[5] and the records of such business were kept distinct. From the middle of the century onwards this business increased.[6] It became the custom to issue special commissions to the Admiral at the beginning of a war, requiring the judge of his court to hear prize cases,[7] as the ordinary commission did not mention this jurisdiction.[8] The prize court thus became a court almost entirely distinct from the instance court. Lord Mansfield could say in 1781 that, "the whole system of litigation and jurisprudence in the Prize Court is peculiar to itself: it is no more like the court of Admiralty than it is to any court

---

[1] Select Pleas of the Admiralty (S.S.) ii xvii, 170.

[2] Lindo v. Rodney (1783) 2 Dougl. 613, 618, 619; cf. Select Pleas of the Admiralty (S.S.) ii lxxix; but even in prize cases they were sometimes issued, E.H.R. xxiv 690; Law and Custom of the Sea (Navy Records Soc.) i 359.

[3] Law and Custom of the Sea i 359.

[4] A distinct prize jurisdiction was given to the court of Admiralty in 1642, Acts and Ordinances of the Interregnum i 35; and Ordinances of 1643, 1644, 1645, 1648, and 1649, ibid ii 66-78, also recognized it; a comparison of these Ordinances with those relating to the instance jurisdiction make it clear that by that time the two jurisdictions were distinct; Roscoe, op. cit. 28-29, 32.

[5] See Marsden, Law and Custom of the Sea (Navy Records Soc.) ii 53-57 for the rules of 1665; Roscoe, op. cit. 35-38.

[6] Marsden, Law and Custom of the Sea (Navy Records Soc.) ii viii.

[7] Lindo v. Rodney 614; re Banda and Kirwee Booty (1866) 1 Ad. and Eccl. 129; 13 Charles II. c. 9; 22, 23 Charles II. c. 11; 6 Anne c. 13; for a specimen of such a commission see Marsden, Law and Custom of the Sea (Navy Records Soc.) ii 287.

[8] An opinion that this jurisdiction was originally regarded as inherent in the court was given by W. Murray (the future Lord Mansfield) and G. Lee, Marsden, Law and Custom of the Sea (Navy Records Soc.) ii 330-331; in 1793 a claim to this effect was put forward by the Admiralty Court of Ireland; and it is said to have been the opinion of Sir W. Wynne that the Admiralty of Scotland had a similar jurisdiction, and this was also the opinion of Murray and Lee, Marsden op. cit.

in Westminster Hall." [1]   The Naval Prize Act of 1864, passed
to enact permanently the provisions formerly made at the beginning of a war, gives to the court of Admiralty the jurisdiction of
a Prize Court throughout His Majesty's dominions; [2] and this
jurisdiction is now exercised by the Probate, Divorce, and
Admiralty division of the High Court. [3]   The appeal from the
Prize Court was to a special commission issued at least once in
every reign to all Privy Councillors, the Vice-Chancellor, and all
the judges of the courts of common law, empowering them or
any three of them to hear appeals, and to call to their assistance
Doctors of the Civil Law, and a surrogate or surrogates. [4]
After 1833 this jurisdiction was, as we have seen, handed over
to the Judicial Committee of the Council. [5]   We shall see that
though appeals from the Instance Court now go to the House of
Lords, appeals from the Prize Court still go to the Council. [6]

It was in fact inevitable that the distinction between the
prize and the instance business of the Admiralty should grow
more definite with the growing definiteness of the principles of
International law on the one side, and the principles of Admiralty
law as administered in English courts on the other.   The court
of Admiralty administers, as we have seen, English Admiralty
law.   Though for historical reasons it resembles in general outline the maritime law of Europe, it is essentially English law. [7]
On the other hand, it has been laid down by the two greatest
judges who have ever sat in a Prize Court that that court administers
International law.   Lord Mansfield said, [8] " By the law of nations
and treaties every nation is answerable to the other for all
injuries done by sea or land, or in fresh waters, or in port.
Mutual convenience, eternal principles of justice, the wisest regulations of policy, and the consent of nations, have established a
system of procedure, a code of law, and a court for the trial of
prize.   Every country sues in these courts of the others, which
are all governed by the same law equally known to each."
Lord Stowell said in the case of *The Recovery*, [9] "It is to be
recollected that this is a court of the law of nations, though

---

[1] Lindo v. Rodney at p. 614.

[2] 27, 28 Victoria c. 25.   [3] 54, 55 Victoria c. 53 § 4.

[4] Report of the Commissioners appointed to enquire into the Duties, Salaries,
etc., of courts of justice, Parlt. Papers (1824) ix 90, 91 ; but before 1629 a separate
commission was issued to hear each appeal, and it was not till 1762 that judges of the
common law courts were added, Marsden, Law and Custom of the Sea (Navy
Records Soc.) ii 267 n. 2.

[5] Above 518 ; Bl. Comm. iii 69, 70 ; 3, 4 William IV. c. 41 § 2.

[6] 54, 55 Victoria c. 53 § 4. 3,   [7] Above 559.,

[8] Lindo v. Rodney at p. 616.

[9] (1807) 6 C. Rob. 348, 349 ; and this is recognized by the statutes which deal
with the prize jurisdiction, see e.g. 27, 28 Victoria c. 25 §§ 35 and 37.   See vol.
xiii 680.

sitting here under the authority of the king of Great Britain. It belongs to other nations as well as to our own; and, what foreigners have a right to demand from it, is the administration of the *Law of Nations* simply, and exclusively of the introduction of principles borrowed from our own municipal jurisprudence."

It is clear that an English statute can compel a judge to depart from these principles; but it has been held by the Privy Council in the case of *The Zamora*[1] that nothing short of a statute can have this effect. That case in effect decides that an Order in Council can no more alter an established rule of international law, than a similar Order could alter an established rule of English law; and that therefore such an Order must be disregarded by a Prize Court.[2]

This decision settles a controversy which has a long history, and settles it in a manner which is not wholly consonant to the current of previous authority. It is clear that in the sixteenth and seventeenth centuries the judges of the court of Admiralty, exercising this jurisdiction, were very much under the thumb of the crown, which was accustomed to issue its Orders to them;[3] and that this was also the case with the Vice-Admiralty courts of the eighteenth century.[4] It is true that the judges sometimes protested against these Orders; and in 1672 Sir Leoline Jenkins hinted at resignation if the Order was persisted in.[5] But it seems to have been agreed that if an Order could be justified by a treaty, the court could not go behind it;[6] and it was probably the better opinion in the eighteenth century that, even if it could not be so justified, the court must obey it, even though

---

[1] [1916] 2 A.C. 77.   [2] Ibid at pp. 90-94.

[3] A letter of 1593 from Howard to Cæsar directing him to condemn a Spanish prize to the captor, though she was not captured under letters of marque, Marsden, Law and Custom of the Sea (Navy Records Soc.) i 281; in 1610 Nottingham wrote to Trevor, one of the judges of the Admiralty, directing him to set free Spanish goods, but to detain Hamburg goods according to the Order of the Lord Treasurer, ibid i 380-381; Roscoe, op. cit. 40-43.

[4] See a letter of the judge of the Minorca Vice-Admiralty Court to the Lords of the Admiralty in 1746 stating that he will follow their Orders in condemning ships, ibid ii 323; and see ibid n. 1; for a similar letter of Byng to the same court see ibid ii 345-346.

[5] In a letter he wrote, probably to Williamson, remonstrating against the Prize rules of 1672, he says, "Could I find upon my own search, or the King's Councell show me any law or precedents for this case of subjects and friends, I should with as little difficulty as any man, proceed to that sentence. However I shall not onely with perfect submission, but with unfeigned satisfaction too, lay down my charge at his Majestie's feet, if his Majestie shall please to believe, or my Lords his commissioners to determine, that my so doing will be better for his Majestie's present service," ibid ii 78-80.

[6] See a letter of 1689 from Hedges, judge of the Admiralty, to Nottingham as to an Order in Council directing the condemnation of Hamburg ships, ibid ii 133; and cf. ibid ii 59 n. 1, from which it is clear that Jenkins admitted that a treaty might alter the established law, and that, in his opinion, the interpretation of such treaties belonged, not to the court, but to the Privy Council.

obedience might, in the event of an obviously illegal Order, expose the country to reprisals.[1]

The question therefore arises, which of these views is correct? The judgment in the case of *The Zamora* is, it seems to me, correct in so far as it decides that an Order in Council which contravenes a statute or a principle of international law which has been accepted as a part of the common law, must be disregarded by a Prize Court. But I doubt very much whether it is correct in deciding that such an Order can be disregarded if it contravenes a rule of international law which has not been incorporated into the common law. That there are many such rules the case of *Reg.* v. *Keyn*[2] shows; and it is because the judgment in the case of *The Zamora* neglects this distinction that I doubt whether it is historically sound.

As a matter of history it is certainly the fact that from the earliest times royal proclamations, Orders in Council, and treaties have played at least as great a part in shaping prize law as the decisions of the courts or statutes.[3] As a matter of law it is obvious that the ascertainment of the contents of those rules of international law which have not been incorporated with the common law is intimately bound up with the prerogative of the crown in relation to foreign affairs; and in this department the prerogative of the crown is absolute, except in so far as it is restricted by statute or the rules of the common law.[4] The principles laid down in the case of *The Zamora* would lead to the conclusion that no act of the prerogative, such as the conclusion of a treaty, could change a rule of international law; so that, unless a distinction be drawn (for which there is very little authority)[5] between the exercise of the prerogative to make a

---

[1] Thus, in the report of the law offices in 1753 on the Silesian loan, the following passage seems to imply that the crown might order the judges to give a sentence which was not in accordance with the rules of international law: "*Where the judges are left free*, and give sentence according to their conscience, though it should be erroneous, that would be no ground for reprisals," Marsden, Law and Custom of the Sea ii 355; thus there was good authority for Lord Stowell's dictum in the case of *The Fox* (1811) 1 Edw. 312-314 (overruled by *The Zamora* [1916] 2 A.C. at pp. 95-96) that an Order in Council, though contrary to international law, bound the court. It should be noted that Lord Stowell's ruling in the case of *The Maria*, cited [1916] 2 A.C. at p. 95, to the effect that the court must be guided by international law is not inconsistent with this dictum, as he would have agreed that this was always the case if no Order in Council had intervened, and in the case of *The Maria* he was thinking of such a case; similarly in the case of *The Lucy* (1809) 1 Edw. 122, he did not refuse to be bound by an Order in Council, but merely decided that it did not in the circumstances apply to the case before the court. See vol. xiii 689.

[4] Thus, for instance, the crown has absolute power to make war or peace, or to make a treaty which does not alter English law or impose a charge on the subject; and if its officers, by its orders, injure a foreigner outside the jurisdiction of the English courts, this is an act of state for which no legal redress can be got, Buron v. Denman (1848) 2 Exch. 167.

[5] See above 566 n. 5 and 6.

treaty, and the exercise of the prerogative to issue an Order in Council to carry out the treaty, new rules of international law laid down by a treaty, e.g. the rules laid down in the Declaration of Paris, would be invalid unless sanctioned by the legislature. As a matter of political expediency the wisdom of the decision is more than doubtful. The prize jurisdiction can only be exercised in time of war ; and in time of war the discretion of the executive should be as little fettered as possible.[1]

However this may be, it is on all hands admitted that it is the principles of international law which form the basis of the law administered by the Prize Court. Thus, by reason of its international character, the prize jurisdiction of the Admiralty resembles more closely than the ordinary jurisdiction of the court the maritime law of the Middle Ages and the sixteenth century.

The Absorption of the Commercial Side of the Law Merchant into the Common Law

With the increase of commerce in the fourteenth and fifteenth centuries, a division and specialization of trades and industries began to take place. The large trader or the merchant became entirely distinct from the small trader or the craftsman. The old Gild Merchant, which embraced all the traders in a town, gave place to separate companies of merchants on the one side, and to separate craft gilds on the other.[2]

The internal trade of the country continued to be regulated by the companies of merchants, or the craft gilds, which usually possessed large powers over trade, and sometimes a monopoly of trade in their own town.[3] It was strongly felt that "a general liberty of trade without a regulation doth more hurt than good ; "[4] and throughout the eighteenth century there are cases in which the courts upheld these powers.[5] They were finally abolished by the Municipal Corporations Act of 1835.[6]

[1] This view seems to have been taken by the Commonwealth judges, when they referred a case to Cromwell's decision, on the ground that the matter was " of so high a nature, and so consequential to this nation, that what evil might arise from a public judgment in these cases may by your judgment be rectified," S.P. Dom Suppl. Interreg. 84, Feb. 16 1623/4, cited Marsden, Law and Custom of the Sea ii 124 n. 1.

[2] In Edward II.'s reign the crafts in London were divided into the two classes of officia mercatoria and officia manuoperalia, Munimenta Gildhallæ i 495 ; but the trade of London was so extensive that it was in advance of other towns, Gross, Gild Merchant i 129.

[3] Ibid chaps. vii and viii; Newcastle Merchant Adventurers (Surtees Soc.) i xxxiii, xxxiv, xxxiv-xl.

[4] Mayor and Commonalty of Colchester v. Goodwin (1666) Carter's Rep. 114, 120.

[5] Mayor of Winton v. Wilks (1705) 2 Ld. Raym. 1129, Holt considered that a power to restrain persons from exercising their trade was bad; but such powers were upheld in Bodwic v. Fennell (1748) 1 Wils 233 ; Wooley v. Idle (1766) 4 Burr. 1951.

[6] 5, 6 William IV. c. 76 § 14, " Whereas in divers cities, towns, and boroughs a certain custom has prevailed, and certain bye-laws have been made, that no person

Though the old organization of trade lingered on till the nineteenth century, the internal trade of the country had in the sixteenth century practically ceased to be ruled by a special law and by special courts. The companies of merchants and the craft gilds possessed no jurisdiction of their own. Some few courts of fairs survived. But the fairs and their courts were decadent by the end of the sixteenth century.[1] There are few entries on their plea rolls;[2] and the courts of common law rigidly confined their jurisdiction to what they considered to be its proper sphere.[3] Thus, except in so far as statutes drew a distinction between traders and others,[4] the traders' or the merchants' dealings were not treated differently from those of any other class in the community. They were governed by the common law and generally by the common law courts. The common law had borrowed certain rules from the Law Merchant. The rules that there is no warranty of title in a sale of goods,[5] and that, under some circumstances, a sale in market overt by a non-owner will pass the property,[6] probably come from this source. The merchant's view of the efficacy of the earnest money to bind the bargain was recognized by the Statute of Frauds.[7] By the end of the sixteenth century the internal trade of the country was regulated by a common law thus modified and not by a separate Law Merchant.

The foreign trade of the country continued for a longer period to be governed by a separate Law Merchant. In France, Italy, and Germany juristic literature and mercantile practice had created a body of mercantile law.[8] During the sixteenth

not being free of a city, town, or borough, or of certain gilds, mysteries or trading companies within the same . . . shall keep any shop or place for putting to show or sale any or certain wares or merchandise by way of retail or otherwise, or use any or certain trades, occupations, mysteries, or handicrafts for hire, gain, or sale within the same; be it enacted that notwithstanding any such custom or bye-law, every person in any borough may keep any shop for the sale of all lawful wares and merchandises by wholesale or retail, and use every lawful trade . . . within any borough."

[1] " The increase of wealth, bringing a permanent and continuous local demand for commodities together with the improvement of transport facilities and means of communications, due largely to the creation or repair of roads in the eighteenth century, diminished the importance of fairs and periodical markets and tended to sap the vitality of the old tribunals of justice or rendered many of them wholly obsolete," Select Cases on the Law Merchant (S.S.) i xix.

[2] Ibid.

[3] Howel v. Johns (1600) 1 Cro. 773; Goodson v. Duffield (1612) Cro. Jac. 313; cf. Hall v. Pyndar (1536), Dyer 132 b, pl. 80, and the cases cited in the margin.

[4] Instances are the earlier bankruptcy Acts, and the earlier Acts rendering the real estate of deceased persons liable to their debts.

[5] 3 Co. Rep. 22; Morley v. Attenborough (1849) 3 Ex. at p. 511, *per* Parke, B.

[6] Coke, Second Instit. 713, 714.

[7] Carta Mercatoria (Munimenta Gildhallæ ii Pt. I. 205); 29 Charles II. c. 3 § 17: P. and M. ii 206, 207.

[8] Vol. v 60-102.

and seventeenth centuries this mercantile law was being adapted to the use of Englishmen by writers like Malynes, Marius, Molloy, and Beawes. They all considered the merchant as a class apart and subject to a separate law.[1] "It is a customary law," says Malynes,[2] "approved by the authority of all kingdoms and commonwealths, and not a law established by the sovereignty of any prince;" and, "the said customary law of merchants hath a peculiar prerogative above all other customs, for that the same is observed in all places."[3] "That commonwealth of merchants," says Davies,[4] "hath always had a peculiar and proper law to rule and govern it; this law is called the Law Merchant whereof the laws of all nations do take special knowledge." Davies, however, recognized that it was only the foreign trade of the country that was now ruled by this special law. "Merchandises that cross the seas are goods of another nature, quality, and consideration than other goods and chattels, which are possessed within the realm, and do not cross the seas."[5]

It is clear from these writers that specific differences between the Law Merchant and the common law could still be pointed out. There was no survivorship in the case of merchants who were joint tenants. Wager of law was unknown among them. Bills of exchange, policies of assurance, assignments of debts were all unknown to the common law.[6]

But, by the end of the seventeenth century, this Law Merchant was being gradually absorbed into the general legal system of the country. As in the case of the internal trade, so in the case of the foreign trade, the older mercantile courts had ceased to exist. Jurisdiction was therefore assumed by the ordinary courts of law and equity.

We have seen that in the Middle Ages the courts of the Staple were the chief courts which regulated the dealings of foreign merchants. Malynes says, "our staple of wools is now out of use, and staple towns are all, as it were, incorporated into London."[7] It is clear from his account of the courts which

[1] Smith, Merc. Law (Ed. 1890) lxxx, lxxxi; in the East India Company v. Sandys (1684) 10 S.T. at pp. 523-525, Jeffries, C.J., drew a clear distinction between inland and foreign trade.

[2] Lex Mercatoria Preface. [3] Lex Mercatoria 3.

[4] The Question concerning Impositions (Ed. 1656) 10; Davies was Attorney-General for Ireland to James I.

[5] Ibid 11, 12, citing Y.B. 13 Ed. IV. pl. 9; he said that he had wondered why there were so few cases in the books concerning merchants—"But now the reason thereof is apparent, for the common law of the land doth leave these cases to be ruled by another law, namely, the Law Merchant, which is a branch of the law of nations," ibid 16, 17.

[6] Ibid 12-15; Malynes 73-76; East India Company v. Sandys (1684) 10 S.T. at p. 524.

[7] Lex Mercatoria 155.

then administered the Law Merchant that there was in England, in the latter part of the seventeenth century, no effective court specially set apart for the merchants.[1] In the sixteenth and earlier seventeenth centuries the Council and the court of Admiralty had supplied the place of such a court. But the jurisdiction of the Council in England had come to an end in 1641 ; and we have seen that the courts of common law had deprived the Admiralty of the greater part of its jurisdiction over mercantile causes. In 1601[2] a court had been established in London consisting of the recorder, two doctors of the civil law, two common lawyers, and eight "grave and discreet" merchants, to hear insurance cases, "in a brief and summary course, as to their discretion shall seem meet, without formalities of pleadings or proceedings." But it had been held, in 1658, that proceedings before this court were no bar to an action at law ;[3] and it was constantly hampered by prohibitions.[4] Merchants were therefore driven, either to arbitration,[5] or to the courts of law, or, in matters which involved the taking of accounts, to the court of Chancery.[6] Reported cases of the seventeenth century illustrate the effect of this upon the Law Merchant. They show that mercantile law was ceasing to be the law of a class, and that it was becoming part of the general law of the land. The earlier cases upon Bills of Exchange treated them as ruled by special customs, applicable only to merchants, which it was necessary to prove.[7] In 1699 Treby, C.J., said that Bills of Exchange at first extended only to merchant strangers trading with English merchants ; afterwards to inland Bills between merchants trading with one another in England ; and

---

[1] Lex Mercatoria Pt. III. chaps. xiv-xx ; see vol. v 148-154 for some further reasons why no such courts were developed in England.

[2] 43 Elizabeth c. 12 ; reinacted and amended 13, 14 Charles II. c. 23.

[3] Came v. Moye 2 Sid. 121.

[4] It was said in 1787 that, from the reign of Elizabeth to 1765, when Lord Mansfield became Chief Justice, it had not heard sixty cases on marine insurance, Smith, Merc. Law, lxix.

[5] Malynes, Pt. III. c. xv ; cp. Dasent xxii *xxxiv ;* xxiii *xlvi ;* 9 William III. c. 15 was passed to facilitate these arbitrations ; cp. House of Lords MSS. 1699-1702 454.

[6] "Merchants' causes are properly to be determined by the Chancery, and ought to be done with great expedition ; but it falleth out otherwise, because they are by commission commonly referred to merchants to make report of the state thereof unto the Lord Chancellor," Malynes 319 ; there was an affinity between the jus gentium of the merchants and English equity, as there was between the Roman jus gentium and jus naturale, *per* Buller, J., Lickbarrow v. Mason (1793) 2 T.R. 63 ; in 6 East 21 *note* it is said that "the right of stopping in transitu is founded wholly upon equitable principles which have been adopted in courts of law."

[7] In Oaste v. Taylor (1613) Cro. Jac. 306, the custom of the merchants is fully set out ; similarly in Woodward v. Rowe (1669) 2 Keb. 105 , in Witherley v. Sarsfield (1689) Shower 127, Holt said that the act of drawing a bill made a man a trader for this purpose ; for the history of Bills of Exchange see vol. viii 126-145, 151-170.

lastly to all persons whether traders or not; and that there was now no need to allege and prove the custom.[1]

The process was assisted, after the Revolution, by the greater freedom allowed to foreign trade. In the sixteenth and seventeenth centuries foreign trade was in the hands of companies incorporated by the crown with exclusive rights to trade.[2] The validity of such grants was upheld, in 1684, in the *East India Company* v. *Sandys*.[3] It is clear that such an organization of trade will tend to the settlement of disputes by the arbitration of the governing body of the company. But, in 1693, trade had been to a large extent freed by a resolution of Parliament, "that it is the right of all Englishmen to trade to the East Indies, or any part of the world, unless prohibited by Act of Parliament."[4] It was a natural, though perhaps an indirect result, of the Great Rebellion and the Revolution that the ordinary courts should thus absorb jurisdiction over mercantile cases. The fact that the Law Merchant was not English law, but jus gentium, had been used to prove that the crown had such large powers over trade, that it could impose impositions, or create a monopoly.[5] It was clear that the Law Merchant must be administered in the ordinary courts of law or equity if it was to be made to harmonize with the now established principles of English public law.

The complete incorporation of the Law Merchant with the common law was not effected till the time of Lord Mansfield. Up to his time mercantile business had been divided between the courts of law and equity. Little progress had been made in the task of creating a body of systematic principles. Lord Mansfield created such a body of principles;[6] and this entitles him to the fame of being " the founder of the commercial law of

---

[1] Bromwich v. Lloyd 2 Lut. 1582, 1585; cp. Chalmers, Bills of Exchange, xlv-xlvii, as to the result of this upon the English law of Bills of Exchange.

[2] Gross, Gild Merchant i 140-156; Hall, Customs Revenue i 50-54; vol. viii 199-202, 208-211.

[3] 10 S.T. 371; cp. Company of Merchant Adventurers v. Rebow (1687) 3 Mod. 126, 128.

[4] Newcastle Merchant Adventurers (Surtees Soc.) i xli-xliv.

[5] This is the argument of Davies' work upon impositions, chap. vi; " Forasmuch as the general law of nations which is and ought to be law in all Kingdoms, and the Law Merchant which is also a branch of that law, and likewise the Imperial or Roman law, have ever been admitted by the kings and people of England in causes concerning Merchants and Merchandise. . . . Why should not this question of Impositions be examined and decided by the rules of those laws, so far forth as the same doth concern Merchants or Merchandises, as well as by the rules of our Common Law of England ? " cp. Bate's Case (1606) 2 S.T. at p. 389.

[6] " We find in *Snee* v. *Prescott* that Lord Hardwicke himself was proceeding with great caution, not establishing any general principle, but decreeing on all the circumstances of the case put together. Before that period we find that in courts of law all the evidence in mercantile cases was thrown together ; they were left

this country." The Law Merchant has thus ceased to be a separate body of law administered by separate courts : "it is neither more nor less than the usages of merchants and traders . . . ratified by the decisions of courts of law, which, upon such usages being proved before them, have adopted them as settled law."[1]

II. The Court of the Constable and the Marshal

The court of the Constable and the Marshal was concerned primarily with the discipline of the army, and matters related thereto. It was concerned also with two matters which were closely connected with an army commanded by the nobility and their relations—heraldry, and slanders upon men of noble blood. The first of these two branches of its jurisdiction is by far the most important; but the second has had a longer life, and a somewhat different history.

(1) The discipline of the army.

At all periods armies need to be governed by laws other than those which govern the rest of the community. These laws were administered in the Middle Ages by the Constable and Marshal's court.

"Always," says Hale,[2] "preparatory to an actual war, the kings of the realm, by advice of the Constable and Marshal, were used to compose a book of rules and orders for the due order and discipline of their officers and soldiers, together with certain penalties on the offenders; and this was called martial law. We have extant in the Black Book of the Admiralty and elsewhere several examples of such military laws." The maintenance, then, of the rules to be observed in the army was the main part of the jurisdiction of the court; and it possessed also certain other allied branches of jurisdiction. It took cognizance of all contracts relating to " deeds of arms," and all things " that touch war within

---

generally to a jury, and they produced no established principle. From that time we all know the great study has been to find some certain general principles, which shall be known to all mankind, not only to rule the particular case then under consideration, but to serve as a guide for the future. . . . I should be very sorry to find myself under a necessity of differing from any case on this subject which has been decided by Lord Mansfield, who may be truly said to be the founder of the commercial law of this country," *per* Buller, J., Lickbarrow v. Mason (1787) 2 T.R. at p. 73. See Fifoot, Lord Mansfield, ch. 4.

[1] Goodwin v. Robarts (1875) L.R. 10 Ex. 337, 346; cp. Brandao v. Barnett (1846) 12 Cl. and Fin. 787; Bechuanaland Exploration Company v. London Trading Bank [1898] 2 Q.B. 658; Edelstein v. Schuler and Co. [1902] 2 K.B. 144, 154.

[2] History of the Common Law 42; for an account of these rules see Cockburn's charge to the Grand Jury in Reg. v. Nelson and Brand, Special Report 89-91; Black Book of the Admiralty (R.S.) i 282-299, 453-472; for some later specimens of these commissions see Egerton Papers (C.S.) 243, 246.

the realm." [1]   Instances of such matters were agreements to hire soldiers, or questions of prisoners or prize.[2]   It would seem from the case of *The Parson of Langar* v. *Conyngsby* in 1361 that error lay from this court to the Council.[3]

It is clear from statutes of Richard II. and Henry IV.'s reign that the legislature desired to prevent the court from encroaching upon the province of the common law.   A statute of 1384 [4] enacted that pleas concerning the common law should not for the future be " drawn before " the Constable and Marshal.   But this enactment left it uncertain what suits properly concerned the common law, and what concerned Constable and Marshal.   To solve this question it was declared in 1389-1390 [5] that, "to the Constable it pertaineth to have cognizance of contracts touching deeds of arms and of war out of the realm, and also of things that touch war within the realm, which cannot be determined nor discussed by the common law, with other usages and customs to the same matters pertaining."   It was further provided that every plaintiff in the Constable and Marshal's court should declare his cause of action ; and that, if any complained that the cause of action was not there cognizable, he should be able to get a writ of Privy Seal to stop the proceedings of the court till the question of jurisdiction had been determined.   In 1399 [6] it was declared that criminal appeals for matters done out of the realm should be determined in the Constable and Marshal's court, but that appeals for matters done within the realm should be tried at common law.   These statutes limited the jurisdiction of the court in much the same way as contemporary statutes limited the jurisdiction of the court of Admiralty.[7]   In effect their result was to declare that over matters relating to war done outside the realm the court had an unlimited jurisdiction, civil and criminal ; [8] but that within the realm it only had jurisdiction over alien enemies,[9] in matters arising out of some past war, such as

---

[1] 13 Richard II. St. 1 c. 2 ; Black Book of the Admiralty i 281, " the office of the Conestable and Mareschalle in the time of werre is to punysh all manner of men that breken the statutes . . . by the king made to be keped in the oost." . . . They also have " knowleche upon all maner crymes, contracts, pleets, querelle, trespas, injuries, and offenses don beyonde the see in tyme of werre betwene souldeour and souldeour, bytwene merchaunts . . . and artificers necessary to the oost."

[2] Knapp 149-152 and note, citing Hale's MS. treatise on the prerogative.

[3] Select Cases before the Council (S.S.) 47.

[4] 8 Richard II. c. 5.   [5] 13 Richard II. St. 1 c. 2.

[6] 1 Henry IV. c. 14 ; cf. R.P. IV. 349-350 (8 Hy. VI. no. vii)—a petition praying for the enforcement of this statute ; for appeals to the Council under this statute and the statutes of Richard II.'s reign see Select Cases before the Council (S.S.) lxxxii-lxxxiii.

[7] Above 548.

[8] See Y.BB. 13 Hy. IV. Mich. pl. 10; 37 Hy. VI. Pasch. pl. 8; Hearne, Curious Discourses (Ed. 1720) 259, 260 ; Hale, Common Law 41 n. d.

[9] Perkin Warbeck's Case, cited 7 Co. Rep. 6 b.

prisoners or prize, or in cases where a war was actually proceeding.[1] Probably these limitations were more or less strictly observed until the reign of Edward IV. Thus in 1394 the court held that it had no jurisdiction to try an action for breach of contract made outside the realm, but unconnected with any military operations.[2] Edward IV. extended the powers of the court without any regard for these statutory limitations. In 1462 and 1467 the court was empowered to try all cases of treason " summarily and plainly without noise and show of judgment on simple inspection of fact." [3]

The Tudors did not attempt to use the court in this fragrantly illegal manner; but just as they extended the jurisdiction of the court of Admiralty without much regard for earlier statutes or precedents, so they extended the jurisdiction of the court of the Constable and Marshal. In both cases they made use of the obscurity of the law to assume the powers which they considered to be necessary for the welfare of the state. We have seen that the jurisdiction of the court within the realm was limited ; but it was within the realm that the Tudors required its assistance. At a time when there was no standing army a jurisdiction over soldiers was capable of being confused with a jurisdiction over all citizens liable to serve as soldiers. On the principle that prevention is better than cure it was plausible to say that the jurisdiction of the court was legal, not only when war was actually proceeding, but also at a time of merely apprehended disturbance.[4]

That these extensions of the court's jurisdiction were regarded as illegal we can see from a case of Elizabeth's reign cited by Camden. The queen desired to proceed by martial law against a fanatic who had attacked Sir J. Hawkins ; but she was told that it was illegal to proceed " ex jure militari sive castrensi " unless it was a time of real disturbance ; [5] and Sir Thomas Smith

---

[1] Black Book of the Admiralty i 281, " Yf any of the personnes be oone [our own subject], and the other personne be a straunger, the connestable and mareschalle shall have knowlech in the said matere done in the werre beyonde the see, and of all manere dedes of armies here within the londe doone he hath congnoissaunce, and of the offenses doon beyonde the see he hath knowleche of here in the londe ; " Knapp 149-152.

[2] Copyn v. Snoke, Select Pleas of the Admiralty (S.S.) ii lix.

[3] Maitland, C.H. 266 ; cp. Harcourt, Court of the Lord High Steward 390-393.

[4] For an account of the commissions issued to the Constable in accordance with these ideas see Forsyth, Leading Cases, 553-555, and Hallam, C.H. i 240-243 ; for another earlier instance in 1549 see Wriothesley's Chronicle (C.S.) ii 15-16, 18-19. It may be noted also that the Lord-Lieutenants were given power in case of emergency to use martial law, Prothero, Documents 154 ; for the Lord-Lieutenants see vol. iv 76-77.

[5] Camden, Annales s.a. 1573 (cited Prothero, Documents, etc., 176).

was of the same opinion.[1] But, though illegal, these extensions of the court's jurisdiction did not excite much public feeling during the Tudor period.

Under the Stuarts the question of the extent and limitations of the jurisdiction of the court was raised. The Petition of Right declared that these extensions of the court's jurisdiction were illegal.[2] It therefore condemned the view that the court had under any circumstances jurisdiction over any one within the realm in time of peace. It should be noted also that the question what was a time of peace was clearly settled. It was a time of peace if the central courts were open, and the sheriff could execute the king's writ.[3] The Petition of Right did not however deny that the Constable and Marshal's court had jurisdiction over soldiers in time of war. It was a declaratory Act;[4] and it is clear from the exposition of contemporary lawyers that it was not intended to abolish its legitimate jurisdiction.[5] No doubt the crown lawyers were guilty of putting a very strained construction upon the Petition of Right when they laid it down that, as the Petition was merely declaratory, it did not condemn the recent extensions of the court's jurisdiction.[6] The reasonable construction of the Petition was that it was exactly these extensions which it did condemn; but that it did not intend to condemn the jurisdiction admitted to belong to it by the mediæval statutes.

The Great Rebellion soon showed that a court with a jurisdiction limited in this way was quite useless to preserve discipline in a modern army. The Parliament found it necessary to take

[1] Commonwealth, Bk. ii c. iv; cp. 12 Co. Rep. 12, 13.

[2] The Petition, after setting out these illegal extensions of martial law, declares that "such commissions as aforesaid . . . and all other of a like nature, are wholly and directly contrary to the said laws and statutes of this your realm."

[3] "The time of peace is when the courts of Westminster are open." "If the Chancery and courts of Westminster be shut up . . . it is time of war, but if the courts be open it is otherwise; yet if war be in any part of the kingdom, that the sheriff cannot execute the king's writ there is *tempus belli*," Rushworth, Pt. II. vol. ii App. 79, 81, citing the opinions of Coke and Rolle; see also Hale, P.C. i 344; Common Law 42-43; but the case of Marais [1902] A.C. 109 shows that the courts must be sitting in their own right and not merely as licensees of the military authorities; this is a necessary development of the common law doctrine due to the change in the character of modern warfare. See Keir and Lawson, Cases in Constitutional Law, 4th Ed.

[5] Thus, Lord Conway in a letter to Laud, says, "My lord of Northumberland did write to me, that having had occasion to look into the power he hath to give commissions, the lawyers and judges are all of opinion that martial law cannot be executed here in England, *but where an enemy is really near to an army of the king's*," Rushworth, Pt. II. vol. ii 1199; similarly Lenthall, the Speaker of the Long Parliament, writing in the name of the Parliament, assumes that martial law is legal if the courts are not open, S.P. Dom. 1641-1643, 13 ccclxxxi 36; cf. L.Q.R. xviii 120 n. 7; for a tract dealing with this topic see S.P. Dom. 1631-1633, 244, ccviii, xiv.

[6] The Case of Ship Money (1637) 3 S.T. at p. 1234.

further powers for the discipline of their troops.[1]   Codes of rules were drawn up for the government of these troops;[2] and after the Restoration similar codes were issued by Charles II. and James II.[3]   Thus the code of 1666 was modelled on that of 1642 ; and similar codes were drawn up in 1672 and 1686.   The crown, it is true, endeavoured to maintain an appearance of keeping within the letter of the law.   In 1672 it was stated that the provisions of the codes drawn up in that year were only to be enforced abroad ; and in 1685, after the suppression of Monmouth's rebellion, Kirke was directed to send soldiers guilty of serious crimes to the ordinary courts for trial, as the military code was only in force during the actual rebellion.[4]   Though some attempt was thus made to maintain the limitations which the law placed upon the martial law exercised by the Constable and Marshal's court, it is clear that the military jurisdiction of that court was obsolete.   This jurisdiction had come to be exercised by the officers of the army ; and this was recognized in an Order issued by James II. in 1687.[5]

But though these codes of rules and the courts of officers who administered them were obviously necessary, their legality was more than doubtful.[6]   It was not till the passing of the first Mutiny Act in 1689[7] that the military law and the courts which administered it were legalized.   Since 1689 jurisdiction over the army has passed to these courts martial which have been legalized and extended by the successive Mutiny Acts of the eighteenth and nineteenth centuries.[8]   Thus the military jurisdiction of the court of the Constable and Marshal ceased to exist because it was not needed ; and, together with its military jurisdiction, all memory of its jurisdiction over such connected matters as prisoners of war and prize disappeared so completely that even Lord Mansfield was ignorant of it.   In the case of *Lindo* v. *Rodney* [9] he said,

---

[1] See Acts and Ordinances of the Interregnum i 37 (1642) ; 486 (1644) ; 675 (1645) ; 715 (1645) ; 842 (1646).

[2] Clode, Military and Martial Law 10-12.   [3] Ibid 12-19.

[4] Clode, Military Forces of the Crown i 478.

[5] " His Majesty has been pleased, for the better preventing of disorders, and redressing the same, to appoint a Council or General Court Martial, consisting of the General Officers, and other Officers of the army, who are appointed to meet at the Horse Guards every Friday morning, for hearing and examining all complaints that shall be brought before them upon any difference between any persons in his Majesty's pay, and the punishing all misdemeanours of officers and soldiers ; as also to hear and determine all petitions or complaints that shall be brought before them by any other person, not being in his Majesty's pay, against any officer or soldier," Bramston, Autobiography (C.S.) 306.

[6] Vol. vi 226-230.   [7] 1 William and Mary c. 5.

[8] See L.Q.R. xviii 121-122.

[9] (1782) 2 Dougl. at p. 614 ; it may be noted that the court of Admiralty in the sixteenth century assumed jurisdiction over booty captured on shore in foreign lands, E.H.R. xxiv 696.

"As to plunder or booty in a mere continental land war . . . it has never been important enough to give rise to any question about it. There is no instance in history or law, ancient or modern, of any question before any legal judicature ever having existed about it in this kingdom." But we have seen that in the Middle Ages this was one of the branches of the military jurisdiction of the court of the Constable and Marshal.[1]

But, though the military jurisdiction of the court has ceased to exist, the limitations placed upon it by the Petition of Right, and the subsequent development of courts martial exercising jurisdiction over the soldiers of the crown, have had a very permanent constitutional result. Their joint effect has been to vest jurisdiction over civilians in times of riot and rebellion in the ordinary courts of common law, and not in military courts. Civilians are even then governed by the rules and processes of the common law, and not by the rules and processes applicable to the soldier. At such times the common law lays it down that the right and the duty of the ordinary citizen is to protect life and prevent crime "by the immediate application of any amount of force which, under the circumstances, may be necessary";[2] and, till in 1906 the Trade Disputes Act weakened the supremacy of the common law over some of the disputes most likely to lead to disorder, its rules had generally been found to be sufficient.[3] Just as the victory of the common law courts over the Admiralty left them free to develop mercantile law upon their own lines, just as their victory over the Council stopped the growth of any system of administrative law, so their victory over the Constable and Marshal's court has left the case of riot or rebellion to the common law, and has caused the "state of siege"[4] to be practically unknown in England.

(2) Heraldry and slanders upon men of noble blood.

Heraldic cases formed a very ancient branch of the jurisdiction of the court;[5] and so necessary did this heraldic jurisdiction appear that, when the court ceased to sit after the summoning of the Long Parliament, provision was made in 1645-1646 for the exercise of this branch of its jurisdiction.[6] After the Restora-

---

[1] Above 574.

[2] The charge of Cockburn, C.J., to the Grand Jury, Reg. v. Nelson and Brand 85.

[3] For a summary of the later history of Military and Martial Law see L.Q.R. xviii 119-132; obviously they are not sufficient in a national crisis such as the Great War of 1914-1918 and require to be supplemented by Defence of the Realm Acts.

[4] Dicey, Law of the Constitution (9th Ed.) 291-294.

[5] Rushworth, Pt. II. vol. ii 1054-1055; cf. Oldis v. Donmille (1695) Shower P.C. 58; as other courts assumed jurisdiction over their own officials, so it assumed jurisdiction over the heralds, see S.P. Dom. 1619-1623, 321 cxxiv 27.

[6] Acts and Ordinances of the Interregnum i 838.

tion and even after the Revolution, it still continued to exercise it. In 1668 it seems to have been thought that this branch of the jurisdiction of the court might be used to provide an alternative to the prevalent habit of duelling. A bill introduced into the House of Lords in that year [1] recited that, among other things, "the contending about place and precedency, and usurpations of arms and other ensigns of honour," often occasion duels ; and proceeded to give the Earl Marshal and other commissioners power to determine such questions, and to penalize persons who sent accepted or carried challenges, or who took part in duels. The bill, though supported by the king and the Duke of York, was dropped ; and thus a chance of giving to the Marshal a really useful jurisdiction disappeared. But the Marshal still continued to exercise his jurisdiction in matters of heraldry. In 1699 [2] and 1700 [3] Luttrell reports proceedings of this kind in the Marshal's court. But the decision in the case of *Oldis* v. *Donmille* in 1695 [4] that a writ of prohibition could be issued against the court, left it at the mercy of the common law courts and when, in the case of *Chambers* v. *Jennings* in 1702,[5] the court of Queen's Bench held, contrary to an opinion expressed by the Council in 1622,[6] that the court was not properly constituted in the absence of the Constable, it is clear that the end had come.[7] *Sir H. Blount's Case* in 1737 [8] is the last reported case in which it exercised jurisdiction ; and in Blackstone's time its jurisdiction had fallen into "contempt and disuse." [9] The powers formerly exercised by the court were left to the heralds "who consider it only as a matter of lucre and not of justice ; whereby such falsity and confusion have crept into their records . . . that, though formerly some credit has been paid to their testimony, now even their common seal will not be received in evidence in any court of

---

[1] Hist. MSS. Com. Eighth Rep. App. Pt. I. 122 no. 168.

[2] "*Saturday* 16 *Sept.*—Yesterday in the afternoon the court of honour sat, the Duke of Norfolk being present, assisted by Dr. Oxenden, etc., where Sir John Sweetapple paid for his coat of arms ; Sir Jonathan Jennings obtained leave to prosecute a gentleman that took his coat of arms ; Mr. Whitrow of Devonshire was ordered to put in bail to try the taking of a coat of arms that did not belong to him, and several motions were made," Diary iv 560-561.

[3] Ibid 687.

[4] Shower, P.C. 58 ; cf. Hist. MSS. Com. Thirteenth Rep. App. Pt. V. 347 no. 46 ; House of Lords MSS. (1695-1697), 154 no. 995.

[5] 7 Mod. 125.

[6] S.P. Dom. 1619-1623, 436, cxxxii 83 ; for Charles I.'s reference of this question to the Council see ibid 412, cxxxi 72.

[7] It may be noted that the court thought that there might be more ground for saying that the Marshal alone could hold a court for the trial of heraldry cases, though it was clear that it could not try cases of words spoken against men of honour, 7 Mod. at p. 128 ; but Holt's reasoning, ibid 127-128, applied to all branches of the jurisdiction of the court.

[8] 1 Atk. 296.   [9] Comm. iii 105.

justice in the kingdom." [1] Modern historians have abundantly justified the perspicacity of the courts in refusing this evidence.

It is probable that the downfall of the court was very largely caused by the way in which it used its jurisdiction to redress slanders upon men of honour. It was a recognized [2] and unpopular [3] branch of its jurisdiction in the Middle Ages and later; it is clear that it was exercised very oppressively in the earlier part of the seventeenth century; [4] and it was this kind of oppression which was the gravamen of Clarendon's attack upon the court in the Long Parliament. [5] It was largely for this reason that the Long Parliament voted that the court was a grievance. [6] But it apparently continued to exercise this jurisdiction after the Restoration; and it is worthy of note that the case of *Chambers* v. *Jennings* [7] which, as we have seen, [8] was fatal to the existence of the court, was a case of slander upon a knight.

III. The Ecclesiastical Courts

These courts have had a longer history than the courts of common law or equity ; and at all periods in their history the prevailing views held as to the relations betweenChurch and State have influenced both their relations to the English judicial system, and the character of the law which they have administered. Therefore to understand the history of these courts it is necessary to say something by way of introduction as to the relations between Church and State in England at different periods. It will then be possible to treat of the courts themselves, and of their jurisdiction.

The Relations between Church and State

This subject falls naturally and chronologically into two divisions—the Pre-reformation, and the Post-reformation periods.

(1) The Pre-reformation period.

During the whole of the mediæval period the relations be-

---

[1] Comm. iii 105 ; Blackstone lamented the disuse of the heralds' visitations which supplied evidence of marriages and descents which was useful in litigation as to the titles to estates ; it may be noted that in 1678 a bill to register these events in the heralds' office failed to pass, Hist. MSS. Com. Ninth Rep. 118, no. 595.

[2] See Y.B. 36 Hy. VI. Pasch. pl. 8-(p. 20) *per* Prisot, C.J.

[3] R.P. iii 420 (1 Hy. IV. no. 44).

[4] For an instance see S.P. Dom. 1637, 569-570, ccclxxi 61.

[5] Life of Clarendon (Ed. 1842) 934 ; he told the House of Commons of the extravagant proceedings of the court since the last Parliament, "and that more damages had been given there for contumelious and reproachful words of which the law took no notice, in two days, than had been given by all the juries in all the courts in Westminster Hall, in the whole term," ibid 935.

[6] Rushworth, Pt. II. vol. ii 1056.

[7] (1702) 7 Mod. 125.   [8] Above 579.

tween Church and State were dominated by the theory of the survival of the Roman Empire. Of this theory and its effects upon English legal history I shall have something more to say in later books of this history.[1] Here it will be sufficient to say that, from the date of the establishment of the Holy Roman Empire by the coronation of Charles the Great by Leo III. in 800, Western Europe believed that there was still a Roman emperor who ruled the world in matters temporal, just as there was a Pope who ruled the world in matters spiritual. In the dark days of the ninth century, which followed upon the death of Charles the Great, it almost seemed that this theory was on the point of extinction.[2] But it was never forgotten; and it was revived by the great German emperors of the tenth century. They restored the papacy; and, in the eleventh century, the revival of the study of the civil law and the growth of the canon law made it a living political and religious force, which dominated the political and religious ideas of Western Europe till the Renaissance and the Reformation of the sixteenth century.[3]

On its temporal side this theory had never been much more than a theory; and it tended to become less and less in accord with the political facts of Western Europe, as the modern territorial state grew to maturity. At the same time the claim made from time to time by some of the kings of these states that they were emperors within their realms, testifies to the long life of the theory that the emperor was the highest of temporal potentates.[4] But on its spiritual side it did correspond with the political and ecclesiastical facts of the Middle Ages. The claim of the Pope to be the head of a universal church was, in the Middle Ages, far less a mere theory than the parallel claim of the emperor to be head of a universal state. In fact, during the eleventh and twelfth centuries, the dominion of the papacy had been consolidated by a series of able Popes—pre-eminent amongst whom were Gregory VII. (1073-1080), and Innocent III. (1198-1216). That dominion was maintained and enforced by the rules of the

---

[1] Vol. ii 121, 127.

[2] Vol. ii 10-11, 121-123.

[3] Ibid 127-133; vol. iv 11-23.

[4] Thus in the preamble to the statute of appeals, 24 Henry VIII. c. 12, Henry VIII. asserts that, " by divers sundrie olde autentike histories and cronicles it is manifestly declared and expressed that this realme of England is an impire." So in an Arrêt of the Parlement of Paris in 1417 (cited in the report of the Ecclesiastical Commission 1883, 171) it is said, " Le Roi notre Sire est Empereur en son Royaume, non tenant d'aucun que de Dieu, et non resortissant à quelque personne ou Seigneur que ce soit : et comme Roi et Empereur peut faire Loix en son Royaume, contre lesquels nul de son Royaume peut venir, *directe nec indirecte*, et mêmement par voye d'appel sur peine de Leze-Majestie; " cf. Figgis, Divine Right of Kings (1st Ed.) 42-43.

canon law which was accepted as the "jus commune" of the church throughout Western Europe.[1]

In England, as in other countries in Western Europe, the supremacy of the Pope and the binding force of the canon law were fully recognized.[2] It is not therefore surprising to find that there are no great English writers upon the ecclesiastical law. The larger litigation went to Rome, and foreign canonists were usually employed.[3] If Englishmen were employed they were obliged to spend a large part of their time at Rome;[4] and foreign books were the best authorities upon a foreign system of law. From 1239 when William of Drogheda wrote his book about the procedure of the ecclesiastical courts,[5] to John of Ayton,[6] who wrote on the legatine constitutions between 1333 and 1348, we hear of no books written by English canonists. William of Lyndwood,[7] who finished his commentaries upon the provincial constitutions of the Archbishops of Canterbury in 1430, is still one of the leading English authorities on the canon law; and, as Maitland points out, the provincial constitutions on which he commented contain little that is new," and "are only a brief appendix to the common law of the universal church."[8] Lyndwood himself regards them as a supplement merely to that law which was founded upon the decretals of the Pope—a

[1] For some account of the canon law see vol. ii 137-142; and cf. vol. iv 228-232; here it will be sufficient to say that the Corpus Juris Canonici is made up of the following parts: (1) The Decretum Gratiani, which comprehended the papal legislation down to 1139; (2) The five books of the Decretals of Gregory IX. (1234); (3) The Liber Sextus of Boniface VIII. (1298); (4) The Clementines (1313); (5) The Extravagantes, i.e. the more important of the later decretals; the professors of the canon law added many explanatory glosses upon all parts of the canon law; generally one gloss was accepted as the most important and was known as the Glossa Ordinaria.

[2] This may be said to have been proved by Maitland in his book on the Canon Law in the Church of England, as against the views of Stubbs, contained in the report of the Ecclesiastical Courts Commission 1883 App. 21-51, and in his Lectures on Mediæval and Modern History; there has been some criticism of Maitland's views; but Mr. H. W. C. Davis, in a valuable paper read before the Historical Congress 1913, and printed in Sonderabdruck aus der Zeitschrift der Savigny-Stiftung für Rechtsgeschichte 346, says very truly that "it is improbable that future research will invalidate the positive conclusions of Maitland."

[3] P. and M. i 193; below 583.

[4] The life of Adam of Murimuth (see his Chronicles (R.S.) x, xi) illustrates this. In 1311 he was at Rome, appearing for the University of Oxford against the Black Friars; in 1312 he went to Avignon as counsel for Archbishop Winchelsey; in 1314 he was one of the king's envoys to the papal court on behalf of John de Sandale, the king's nominee to the deanery of St. Paul's; in 1316 and 1317 he was still there, acting for the king; in 1319 he was at Avignon to get the Popes consent to a grant made by the clergy to the king; in 1323 he was again at Avignon.

[5] Vol. ii 227.

[6] Dict. Nat. Biog. sub. voc. Acton; Maitland, Canon Law 6-8. His treatise is printed with that of Lyndwood in the edition of Lyndwood's Provinciale published at Oxford in 1679. His name is spelt variously—Athon, Acton, Eaton, Ayton.

[7] For Lyndwood see Maitland, Canon Law 4-6.

[8] Canon Law 37.

sovereign legislator whose authority it was heresy to question.[1] It follows that they were valid only in so far as they interpreted or enforced this papal legislation.[2] As we might expect, the tone of these commentaries upon the provincial constitutions "implies the existence of a circle of English readers who are always looking to the mainland for new commentaries on the Decretals, the Sext, and the Clementines, and who would be ashamed if they fell behind their foreign colleagues in the conventional art of citation." [3]

The canon law recognized the Pope not only as the supreme legislator, but also as supreme judge of the church ; and, as judge, he possessed not merely appellate, but also original jurisdiction. He could be called in by a litigant at any stage in the suit ; and not merely the judgments he pronounced, but also any dicta he might be inclined to express, had the force of law.[4] He could delegate his powers to legates *a latere*, who, by virtue of their commission, superseded all the ordinary courts. "The metropolitan must plead as plaintiff before the suffragan, the superior before the inferior, if the *princeps* will have it so." [5] In fact the Pope could, and did to a large extent, make himself the "Universal Ordinary." He has, says Bracton,[6] ordinary jurisdiction over all in things spiritual, as the king has ordinary jurisdiction over all in his realm in things temporal. It is clear from books of practice on the canon law that, whenever any considerable sum was at stake in an action, the usual course was to "impetrate" an original writ from Rome nominating papal delegates to hear the case.[7] In the thirteenth century the number of English cases which came before the Pope was larger than that from any other country in Europe.[8] The methods by which, as we shall see, the Archbishop of Canterbury attracted much of the business of the ordinary courts to his provincial courts, were probably suggested by the practice of the Roman Curia.[9]

Such, then, was the system of the canon law, in force in England and in all the other countries of Western Europe. But the church and its law must necessarily exercise its activity within

---

[1] The test exacted of persons suspected of Lollardy was subscription to the Decretum, the Decretals, the Sext, and the Clementines, Maitland, Canon Law 46.

[2] Ibid 16-42.   [3] Ibid 8.   [4] Ibid 103-105, 130.   [5] Ibid 129.

[6] "Imprimis sicut dominus papa in spiritualibus super omnibus habeat ordinariam jurisdictionem, ita habet rex in regno suo ordinariam in temporalibus, et pares non habet neque superiores; et sunt qui sub eis ordinariam habent in multis, sed non ita meram sicut papa vel rex," f. 412, cited ibid 106 n. 1.

[7] Maitland, Canon Law 108-115; this is clear from William of Drogheda's Summa (1239) dealing with procedure in ecclesiastical cases, vol. ii 283.

[8] Ibid 122, 123 ; for the way in which the canon law was studied in England, and the chances of preferment which a knowledge of it offered, see vol. iv 230-232.

[9] Maitland, Canon Law 116-120.

a state; and, whatever extreme churchmen might contend for, it was impossible that all ecclesiastical persons should live exempt from all temporal jurisdiction.   Moreover, the canon law attempted to exercise a wide control over the laymen *pro salute animæ*.   As the state grew into conscious life it was inevitable that occasions for disputes between the temporal and spiritual powers should arise.   Two systems of courts exercising two systems of law cannot long co-exist in a rapidly progressive state without disputes as to the limits of their respective authority. Within a certain sphere each was supreme.   But there was always a debatable land over which neither party was completely sovereign.

The precocious growth of the state in England brought this necessary antagonism between the claims of Church and State into prominence at a comparatively early period.   The controversy about investitures was settled in England in 1106; but it was not till 1122 that a similar controversy in Germany was ended by a similar compromise.   In the royal writ of prohibition the royal courts had a weapon of precision which in the end secured for them the jurisdiction which they claimed.   All questions touching lay fee, all questions concerning advowsons, all criminal cases, save cases of felony where a clerk was the culprit, all cases of contract and tort, were gradually drawn into the royal courts; and they were drawn into the royal courts in spite of the protests of churchmen.   It is true that churchmen sitting as royal justices helped to secure the victory of the common law; but it is clear that the canon law and the churchmen *qua* churchmen must have regarded this assumption of jurisdiction by the state as an encroachment.[1]   Even this link between the courts of the state and those of the church was broken, when, from the end of the thirteenth century onwards, the benches of the common law courts gradually ceased to be staffed by ecclesiastics, and began to be staffed by common lawyers who had made their career at the bar.[2]   We shall see that, from that time onwards, the professional jealousy of the common lawyers led them to restrict the jurisdiction of the ecclesiastical courts whenever it was possible to restrict it.[3]

---

[1] Maitland, Canon Law 74, "Some of these prelates were in all likelihood far more at home when they were hearing assizes as *justiciarii domini regis* than when they were sitting as *judices ordinarii*, and they were already leaving the canon law to their schooled officials. . . . Many a mediæval bishop must have wished that, besides having two capacities, he had been furnished with two souls, unless indeed, the soul of one of his subordinates would serve as a *anima damnanda*." In Normandy also the bishops took an active part in the business of the Duke's Curia Haskins, Norman Institution 57-58.

[2] Vol. ii 318.   [3] Ibid 304-306.

The efforts of the judges were seconded by the Council [1] and the legislature. In Edward I.'s reign the statute or writ "Circumspecte Agatis" had attempted to settle a few of these controversies as to jurisdiction; [2] but it was not till the following reign that the subject was fully dealt with by the "Articuli Cleri" of 1315. [3] These articles were an attempt to delimit accurately the spheres of the lay and spiritual jurisdictions, and they were the basis of all the subsequent legislation upon this subject during the remainder of the mediæval period. Later statutes were passed to secure the church in such privileges as it possessed, to settle later controversies, and to repress new modes of evading the law. [4] As a rule they neither add to nor diminish the immunities of the church. [5]

The Articuli Cleri make it clear that the king intends to be the predominant partner in the state. [6] The rolls of Parliament make it clear that the king was backed by the nation. They are full of complaints about the extortions [7] and encroachments [8] of the ecclesiastical courts, and about such matters as the abuses of sanctuary [9] and compurgation. [10] National feeling was fostered by the successes of England in the Hundred Years' War; and, with the growth of national feeling, indignation at the anti-national position sometimes taken up by the church under papal pressure, gave rise to the series of statutes which attempted both to regulate such abuses, and to secure against the claims of Rome the supremacy of English law and the English state. The Statute of Carlisle (1306-1307), [11] which forbade religious houses to send money out of the kingdom to pay taxes imposed by their foreign superiors, began this series. It was followed by the statutes of Provisors and the two statutes of Præmunire which attempted to check, in the interests of patrons and of the state, the abuses of

[1] Valence v. Bishop of Worcester (1294) Select Cases before the Council (S.S.) 5-8.
[2] 13 Edward I. St. 4.   [3] 9 Edward II. St. 1.
[4] The chief statutes are 14 Edward III. St. 4; 18 Edward III. St. 3; 25 Edward III. St. 4; 50 Edward III. c. 5; 1 Richard II. c. 13; 4 Henry IV. c. 2; below 586.
[5] Perhaps clerical immunities were added to by 50 Edward III. c. 5, which exempted priests from liability to arrest while performing divine service; and their powers were added to by the statutes passed by Henry IV. as to heresy, 2 Henry IV. c. 15, 2 Henry V. St. 1 c. 7; below 617.
[6] See c. 7 (dealing with directions to absolve an excommunicate), "The king decreeth that hereafter no such letters shall be suffered to go forth, *but in case where it is found that the king's liberty is prejudiced by the excommunication.*"
[7] See e.g. R.P. ii 230 (25 Ed. III. no. 35); ibid 305 (45 Ed. III. no. 24); ibid 335 (50 Ed. III. no. 84); ibid iii 43 (2 Rich. II. no. 46).
[8] R.P. i 219-220 (35 Ed. I.); ibid ii 319 (17 Ed. III. no. 32).
[9] R.P. iii 37 (2 Rich. II. no. 28); ibid 50 (2 Rich. II. no. 4); for sanctuary see vol. iii 303-307.
[10] Ibid iii 23 (1 Rich. II. no. 93); for compurgation see above 305-308.
[11] 35 Edward I. c. 2; confirmed by 4 Edward III. c. 6; 5 Edward III. c. 3.

papal patronage. The aim of the statute of Provisors [1] was to protect spiritual patrons against the Pope. It was enacted that if the Pope attempted to appoint, the right of presentation should lapse to the crown. The bishops, it should be noted, took no public part in the enactment of this statute. The first statute of Præmunire [2] punished those who drew "any out of the Realm in Plea *whereof the cognizance pertaineth to the king's court*, or of things whereof judgments be given in the king's court, or which do sue in any other court to defeat or impeach the judgment given in the king's court". It did not intend to affect cases over which the king's court never claimed jurisdiction. The second statute of Præmunire [3] was aimed at those who "purchased or pursued, in the court of Rome or elsewhere," any "Translations, processes, and sentences of Excommunications, Bulls, Instruments, or any other things whatsoever which touch the king, against him, his crown, and his regality," [4] whereby the king's court was hindered in its jurisdiction over pleas of presentment. The guarded answer returned by the bishops, in reply to the question addressed to them as to the papal power in this respect, shows an obvious desire to conciliate the Parliament without committing themselves to any statement contrary to canon law. [5] It is clear that such legislation is as "anti-ecclesiastical" as the issue of writs of prohibition. To argue from such legislation, or from the issue of such writs, that the ecclesiastical courts imagined that they were independent of the Pope or the canon law, would be about as reasonable, as to argue from the Grand Assize and the possessory assizes that the feudal courts admitted the royal claim

---

[1] 25 Edward III. St. 6; Maitland, Canon Law 69; for a good general account of this matter see Baldwin, Select Cases before the Council (S.S.) lvi seqq.

[2] 27 Edward III. St. 1 c. 1.

[3] 16 Richard II. c. 5; for an account of the circumstances leading up to this legislation see Select Cases before the Council (S.S.) lxiv-lxvii.

[4] § 6.

[5] The spiritual peers, being asked their advice as to papal claims, protested "quil n'est pas lour entention de dire ne affirmer que nostre Saint Piere le Pape ne poet excommenger Evesques ne qu'il poet faire translations des Prelatz solonc la ley de Seinte Eglise;" but they said that if bishops were excommunicated for obedience to the Pope's commands; or such translations were made whereby the king was deprived of them against his will; "que ce est encountre le Roi et sa corone sicome est contenuz en la petition avant nome," § 4; as Mr. Davis well says, op. cit. 355, "The English clergy repeatedly protested against the statutes of Præmunire . . . they were bound to do so. Whatever anomalies they might be compelled to endure for the sake of peace, they could not accept the principle that the laity may legislate for the church. The laity can neither make nor abrogate canon law. Laymen sometimes claimed the right to commit both these enormities and could not be restrained. But to yield before superior force is one thing : to condone it is another. The Pope himself, we are told, may be obliged to put up with laws or customs which he is powerless to sweep away;" as to clerical protests against both this and the Reformation legislation, see Pollard, Royal Hist. Soc. Tr. 3rd Series viii 18.

to jurisdiction over all cases of ownership or possession of free-hold.[1]

The state successfully asserted its rights to the jurisdiction which it claimed. But we can see from the benefit of clergy,[2] from the statute of Circumspecte Agatis,[3] and the Articuli Cleri[4] that it was willing to allow a large sphere to the ecclesiastical courts and the canon law. In one respect, indeed, it allowed to the rival jurisdiction a larger authority than it possessed in any other country in Europe. It abandoned to it absolute jurisdiction over testamentary and intestate succession to personal property.[5] Where the jurisdiction of the ecclesiastical courts was admitted, the state automatically enforced their sentences of excommunication by the imprisonment of the excommunicate.[6]

Thus matters stood before the Reformation. The jus commune of the Western church was administered in the ecclesiastical courts. The common law was administered in the royal courts. The royal courts claimed exclusive jurisdiction in certain matters. Other matters they were content to leave to the ecclesiastical courts. Certain rights allowed to the Pope by the canon law had been curtailed by English statutes, which the royal courts would enforce if called upon to do so. Within their respective limits the canon law enforced by the ecclesiastical courts, and the common law enforced by the royal courts were separate systems of law, differing in many of their rules, deriving their binding force from different sovereigns.

The claims made by these rival systems produced much friction. But the prevailing theories as to the relations between Church and State made it impossible for either of these rival powers to do without the other. Papal dispensations from the rules of the canon law acknowledged the power of the Pope; but they enabled the crown to use the revenues of ecclesiastical benefices for the maintenance of his civil service. Diplomatic reasons thus demanded some kind of arrangement; and throughout the Middle Ages such arrangements were made on a profit-sharing basis.[7] These arrangements produced peace; but it was a peace which made reform impossible. Abuses were allowed to

[1] Cp. Select Cases before the Council (S.S.) lx.
[2] Below 615-616; vol. iii c. 2 § 3. [3] 13 Edward I. St. 4.
[4] 9 Edward II. St. 1. [5] Below 625-630.
[6] Maitland, Canon Law 58, 59; below 630-631; App. XVIII.
[7] "In the thirteenth century it was recognized that the Chancellor might confer all benefices in the king's gift of less value than twenty marks by virtue of his office. In 4 Edward II. the Council recommended the king to give orders that this patronage should be exercised in favour of the clerks of the Chancery, the Exchequer, and the two Benches. In spite, too, of the strict ecclesiastical laws against pluralities, the Pope allowed the king's clerks to hold several benefices in plurality," Y.B. 3, 4 Ed. II. (S.S.) xix; cp. Tout, Edward II. 230-235.

spring up unchecked, until an entirely new theory as to the relations between Church and State materially altered both the law administered in the ecclesiastical courts, and their relation to the English judicial system.

(2) The Post-reformation period.

At the beginning of the sixteenth century many circumstances combined to show that the old theories as to the relations between Church and State were breaking down. All over Europe centralized territorial states were taking the place of the loosely knit feudal monarchies of the Middle Ages. The wealth and corruption of the church, and more particularly the abuses of the ecclesiastical courts, were exciting extreme unpopularity. The doctrines of the church, also, were beginning to be assailed with the more effective weapons which the New Learning had provided.[1]   England, like the rest of Europe, felt these influences. Cases like that of Hun[2] bore witness to the unpopularity of ecclesiastics, their courts, and officials; the case of Standish[3] shows that Henry VIII., backed by popular opinion, was minded to assert a larger control over ecclesiastics; and Wolsey, who was perhaps the most far-seeing statesman of the day, was already taking measures to reform the corruption of the church. But neither Henry nor England had any desire to separate from the general system of the Western church. There were but few adherents to Protestant doctrine. If the Pope would have consented to Henry's demands for an increased control over the clergy, if the church had been reformed as Wolsey desired, there appeared to be no necessity for a break with Rome. The Anglican church might have had a history very similar to that of the Gallican church.[4]

The divorce question made this solution impossible. The Pope, coerced by Charles V., could not grant the divorce; and therefore a break with Rome became necessary. Although the break was accomplished with as little external change as possible, it necessarily involved an altogether new view as to the relations between Church and State. In the preambles to Henry's statutes we can see the gradual elaboration of the main characteristic of these changed relations of Church and State—the theory of the Royal Supremacy. The dual control over things temporal and things spiritual is to end. The crown is to be supreme over all persons and causes. The canon law of the Western church is

---

[1] See vol. iv 14-16, 29-30.
[2] Hallam, C.H. i 59; Stephen, H.C.L. ii 452, 453.
[3] Maitland, Canon Law, 87-89.
[4] Ibid 85-87; Ecclesiastical Commission 1883, 170-176.

to give place to the " King's Ecclesiastical Law of the Church of England."[1] These great results were achieved by the Reformation Parliament which sat from 1529-1536.

The first Acts of this Parliament, carried in spite of the opposition of the clergy, were directed against certain abuses in the church and its courts;[2] and the clergy were compelled in 1531 to recognize the Royal Supremacy " so far as the law of Christ allows."[3] In 1532 it was so clear, from the unsatisfactory progress of the divorce, that there would be legislation aimed more directly at Rome, that Warham, the Archbishop of Canterbury, drew up a formal protest against all statutes to be passed in the ensuing session, which should prejudice the ecclesiastical or papal power.[4] Parliament passed an Act against the payment of Annates; but the Act was respectful to "our Holy Father the Pope," who was still allowed to charge certain fees for the consecration of bishops; and the king was given a discretion as to its enforcement.[5] In 1533 the Statute of Appeals was the necessary consequence of the king's marriage, and of the divorce proceedings taken before Cranmer.[6] In the preamble to that statute the relations between the new Anglican church and the state were sketched by the king himself with his own hand.

The preamble runs as follows: " By divers sundry old authentic histories and chronicles it is manifestly declared . . . that this realm of England is an Empire . . . governed by one supreme head and king . . . unto whom a body politic, compact of all sorts and degrees of people, divided in terms and by names of spirituality and temporality be bounden and owe to bear next to God a natural and humble obedience ; he being also institute . . . with plenary whole and entire power, pre-eminence, authority, prerogative and jurisdiction to render and yield justice and final determination to all manner of folk, residents, or subjects within this his realm in all causes . . . happening to occur . . . within the limits thereof without restraint or provocation to any foreign princes or potentates of the world. The body spiritual whereof having power when any cause of the law divine happened to

---

[1] The first mention of this term is in 27 Henry VIII. c. 20 § 1.

[2] 21 Henry VIII. c. 5 (Probate); 21 Henry VIII. c. 6 (Mortuaries); 21 Henry VIII. c. 13 (Pluralities).

[3] See the recognition printed at pp. 70, 71 of the report of the Ecclesiastical Commission of 1883.

[4] Ecclesiastical Commission 1883, 33.

[5] 23 Henry VIII. c. 20.

[6] 24 Henry VIII. c. 12; see the reprint of the statute with the alterations made by the king himself in the preamble at pp. 213, 214 of the Ecclesiastical Commission report of 1883; in the text I have modernized the spelling.

come in question or of spiritual learning, it was declared . . . by that part of the said body politic called the spirituality (now being usually called the English Church) which . . . is sufficient and meet of itself, without the intermeddling of any exterior person . . . to declare and determine all such doubts and to administer all such offices and duties as to their rooms spiritual doth appertain . . . : and the laws temporal for trial of property of lands and goods for the conservation of the people of this realm in unity and peace . . . was and yet is administered . . . by sundry judges and administers of the other part of the said body politic called the temporality, and both their authorities and jurisdictions do conjoin together in the due administration of justice the one to help the other : and . . . the king his most noble progenitors and the nobility and commons of this said realm at divers and sundry Parliaments as well in the time of King Edward I., Edward III., Richard II., Henry IV., and other noble kings of this realm made sundry . . . laws . . . for the entire and sure conservation of the prerogatives, liberties, and preeminences of the said imperial crown of this realm, and of the jurisdictions Spiritual and Temporal of the same, to keep it from the annoyance as well of the See of Rome as from the authority of other foreign potentates."

Let us contrast this new Anglican theory with the mediæval theory as stated by Bracton. "Among men," says Bracton, "there are differences in status, because some men are pre-eminent and preferred and rule over others. Our lord the Pope, for instance, is pre-eminent in matters spiritual which relate to the priesthood, and under him are archbishops, bishops, and other inferior prelates. Also in matters temporal there are emperors, kings, and rulers in matters relating to the kingdom, and under them dukes, courts, barons, magnates or vavassors, and knights." [1] Whatever Henry might assert it is clear that there is very little in common between his view of the relation of Church and State as sketched in the preamble to the Statute of Appeals, and the view upon this matter which was generally held in the Middle Ages.

Henry VIII. often inserted in the preambles to his statutes reasoned arguments designed to prove the wisdom of the particular statute.[2] And, in drawing up these arguments he never hesitated

---

[1] "Apud homines vero est differentia personarum, quia hominum quidam sunt præcellentes et prelati, et aliis principantur. Dominus Papa videlicet in rebus spiritualibus, quæ pertinent ad sacerdotium, et sub eo archiepiscopi, episcopi, et alii prælati inferiores. Item in temporalibus sunt imperatores, reges, et principes in hiis quæ pertinent ad regnum, et sub eis duces, comites barones, magnates sive vavasores, et milites," f. 5 b; cp. above 583 n. 6.

[2] E.g. The Statute of Uses, see vol. iv. 460.

to colour facts and events to suit his purpose. But the preamble to this Statute of Appeals is remarkable, partly because it manufactures history upon an unprecedented scale, but chiefly because it has operated from that day to this as a powerful incentive to its manufacture by others upon similar lines. Nor is the reason for this phenomenon difficult to discover. The Tudor settlement of the relations of Church and State was a characteristically skilful instance of the Tudor genius for creating a modern institution with a mediæval form. But, in order to create the illusion that the new Anglican church was indeed the same institution as the mediæval church, it was necessary to prove the historical continuity of these two very different institutions; and obviously this could only be done by an historical argument. When this argument had been put forward in a statutory form it became a good statutory root of title for the continuity and catholicity of this essentially modern institution. But a merely statutory title gave an obvious handle to its opponents, and could hardly be expected to satisfy its supporters. It is not therefore surprising that lawyers, theologians, and ecclesiastical historians soon began, from their different points of view, to amplify and illustrate this historical argument, in order to prove that it rested upon a solid basis of historic truth. Two great professions thus have had and still have a direct professional interest in maintaining this thesis. The lawyers are tied to it by their statutes and cases: the ecclesiastics by the tradition and the authoritative declarations of their church.[1] Naturally, therefore, its truth is still believed and maintained by a long array of imposing names. It was not till an historian arose who, besides being the greatest historian of this century, was both a consummate lawyer and a dissenter from the Anglican as well as from other churches,[2] that the historical worthlessness of Henry's theory was finally demonstrated.

Later statutes of Henry's reign further amplified and defined the supremacy which he claimed. The Act of Supremacy recognized the king as "the only Supreme Head in earth of the Church of England,"[3] having full power to correct all "errors,

---

[1] Mr. Davis, op. cit. 351, accounts for Stubbs' attitude by saying that he was "uncritical in his attitude towards legal tradition;" but surely the most obvious explanation is that he was always first and foremost a cleric, and therefore bound by his profession to receive the clerical tradition; for this tradition see below 596; that the legal tradition was similar no doubt tended to confirm him in his belief; Mr. Davis op. cit. 351-353 has given a very good account of the legal tradition as it appears in Phillimore, Hale, and Coke; for this tradition see below 596.

[2] Maitland says in his book on the Canon Law Preface, "It may be expedient for me to say that I am a dissenter from both (the English and the Roman) and from other churches."

[3] 26 Henry VIII. c. 1.

heresies, abuses, offences, contempts, and enormities" which by any manner of spiritual authority ought to be reformed ; and the form of oath taken under the provisions of this Act denied to the Pope any other authority than that of Bishop of Rome.[1]   It was by the authority of this Act that Henry gave an extensive commission to Cromwell to act as his Vicar-General, from which it is clear that Henry was beginning to regard himself as possessing all that "usurped" authority which once belonged to the Pope.   This fact is further illustrated by the Act of 1545 [2] which declares that the king has power to exercise all ecclesiastical jurisdiction, " and that the archbishops, bishops, archdeacons, etc., have no manner of jurisdiction ecclesiastical but by, under, and from the king."   In accordance with this theory the bishops and archbishops took out commissions to exercise their ordinary powers and authorities.[3]

Most of the other statutes of Henry's reign are the logical consequence of these changed relations between Church and State. Annates and all other payments to Rome were definitely cut off.[4]   In the Act for the submission of the clergy [5] it was provided that no new canons should be enacted, except in convocations summoned by the king's writ, with licence to assemble and make canons.   The existing canons were to be revised by a committee of thirty-two, of whom sixteen were chosen from laymen and sixteen from ecclesiastics.   Further provision for this revision of the canon law was made by other statutes of this reign ; and it was enacted that, in the meantime, those which did not conflict with God's law and the king's should be still in force.[6]   No such revision was in fact made in Henry VIII.'s reign ; but the teaching of the canon law was in every way discouraged at the universities.   In place of lectures on canon law lectures on civil law were established ; and degrees soon ceased to be taken in canon law as a separate faculty.[7]   The Act of 1545 allowed the doctors of the civil law, though laymen and married, to exercise ecclesiastical jurisdiction.   This discouragement of the canon law was a necessary consequence of Henry's settlement.   It is clear that the canon law as taught in the Middle Ages would have been in entire conflict with the new order.[8]

---

[1] Report of Ecclesiastical Commission 1883, 72.

[2] 37 Henry VIII. c. 17.

[3] Report of Ecclesiastical Commission 1883, 37, 38.

[4] 25 Henry VIII. c. 20.   [5] Ibid c. 19.

[6] 27 Henry VIII. c. 15; 35 Henry VIII. c. 16; for further provisions on this subject in Edward VI.'s reign see Dasent iii 382, 410, 471.

[7] Strype, Memorials i c. 29; Anthony Wood, Fasti s.a. 1536 ; Hale, Precedents, etc., xxxiv, xxxv; vol. iv 232.

[8] Maitland, Canon Law, 92-99; as to the persons competent to be judges under the older law see Ecclesiastical Commission 1883, 26; vol iv 232.

Thus it may be said that the great work of Henry's reign was to effect an entire change in the relations between Church and State. The church ceased to form part of the Western church in communion with Rome; and the law of the church ceased to be the canon law of Rome. But beyond that there was little change. The Act of the Six Articles reaffirmed most of the leading doctrines of the Roman Catholic Church;[1] and the existing organization of the ecclesiastical courts was maintained. The king had put himself in place of the Pope. The king's ecclesiastical law administered by civilians was put in place of the canon law of Rome. "The Reformation," says Archdeacon Hale,[2] "if under that general term we may include the whole series of events by which this country was freed from the authority of the Bishop of Rome, was in its commencement nothing more than a legal and political Reformation; a renunciation of the intrusive power of the Pope over the king's subjects, and an assertion of the competency of the Anglican church to decide by her own tribunals all questions relative to Divine Law and to spiritual learning. A Reformation in religion soon followed; but it was a providential and not a necessary consequence."

Little need be said of the reigns of Edward VI. and Mary.[3] They are episodes which added little of permanent importance to Henry's settlement. Edward VI. applied the doctrine of the royal supremacy in its extreme form. Henry had left the authority of the bishops unimpaired. Edward in many cases excluded their authority. He directly appointed them; process in the ecclesiastical courts ran in his name; only those who had special authority from him could exercise jurisdiction;[4] and frequent commissions issued by him, in virtue of his supremacy, in many cases superseded the authority of these courts. As we might expect, their jurisdiction fell into contempt.[5] At the same time reforms in doctrine, and the reform of the canon law were hastily pressed forward. Mary on the other hand went to the opposite extreme. The old state things as 'it existed in 1529 was as far as possible restored.

Elizabeth's reign is marked by a recurrence to Henry VIII.'s

---

[1] 31 Henry VIII. c. 14; as Gairdner says, Lollardy and the Reformation ii 221, this Act was "a great effort to steady matters upon the old lines."

[2] xxxvi, xxxvii; at p. 39 he points out that there was no change in the ordinary routine of the courts; the officials made no change except that of adding to their names the words "regia auctoritate suffultus."

[3] Ecclesiastical Commission 1883, 41-43; Hale xliv-xlvii.

[4] Dasent ii 13-14, 114-115, 148.

[5] The Consistory Court of London has no Act books between the years 1546 and 1554, Hale xliv.

principles, both as regards the relations between Church and State, and as regards the position and jurisdiction of the ecclesiastical courts. "The policy of Elizabeth and her ecclesiastical settlement is historically linked on directly to that of her father."[1] The church was given a more definitely Protestant character, but with as little change of the older order as was possible. In the Acts of Supremacy and Uniformity the relations between Church and State were permanently and definitely ascertained.

The Act of Supremacy[2] annexed to the "imperial crown of this realm" all "such jurisdictions, privileges, superiorities and pre-eminences spiritual and ecclesiastical, as by any spiritual or ecclesiastical power or authority hath heretofore been or may lawfully be exercised or used for the visitation of the ecclesiastical state, and persons, and for reformation, order and correction of the same and of all manner of errors, heresies and schisms, abuses, offences, contempts and enormities." This supremacy was of wide and somewhat indefinite extent. But it did not go the whole length of Henry VIII.'s later statutes or of Edward VI.'s statutes. The crown made no claim to "the ministering either of God's Word or of the Sacraments."[3] It simply claimed to be the Supreme Governor over all causes and persons to the exclusion of any foreign power.[4] The existing organization of the ecclesiastical courts was maintained; but, with a view to the better maintenance of the authority of the crown and the new ecclesiastical settlement, the crown was empowered to entrust its powers to commissioners appointed under the great seal.[5] This power was exercised when the court of High Commission was created in 1559. Some attempts were made to pursue the plan of revising the canon law. But, though the revision had been completed by Cranmer and Peter Martyr, it never obtained legislative sanction.[6] The mediæval canon law, so far as it was in harmony with the new settlement, still continued to be administered by the civilians, who combined their practice in the ecclesiastical courts with their practice in the court of Admiralty.[7] Just as the exercise of the jurisdiction of the court of Admiralty

---

[1] Ecclesiastical Commission 1883, 41.   [2] 1 Elizabeth c. 1 § 8.
[3] Article 37; cp. Ecclesiastical Commission 1883, 73.
[4] 1 Elizabeth c. 1 § 9; the difference between the supremacy claimed by Henry VIII. and that claimed by Elizabeth is well brought out by Selden in his Table Talk; he said, " There's a great deal of difference between Head of the church and Supreme Governor as our canons call the king. Conceive it thus. There is in the kingdom of England a College of Physicians, the king is Supreme Governor of those, but not Head of them, nor President of the College, nor the best physician." I owe this reference to Dr. Hutton, the Dean of Winchester.
[5] 1 Elizabeth c. 1 § 8; below 606.   [6] Ecclesiastical Commission 1883, 45.
[7] For the history of the development of the profession of the civilians in England see vol. iv·232-238.

was controlled by the writ of prohibition, so (in spite of all protests)[1] was the exercise of the jurisdiction of the ecclesiastical courts.

Administered in this way, the law of the church, like the maritime law, has ceased to possess an international character.[2] It has become national like the church itself. "The ecclesiastical law of England," said Lord Blackburn,[3] "is not a foreign law. It is a part of the general law of England—of the common law —in that wider sense which embraces all the ancient and approved customs of England which form law, including not only that law administered in the courts of Queen's Bench, Common Pleas, and Exchequer, to which the term common law is in a narrower sense confined, but also that law administered in Chancery and commonly called Equity, and also that law administered in the courts Ecclesiastical, that last law consisting of such canons and constitutions ecclesiastical as have been allowed by general consent and custom within the realm, and form . . . the king's ecclesiastical law."[4]

But though Henry's settlement as to the courts, and as to the ecclesiastical law was followed in its main lines, though his views as to the supremacy of the crown over the church were retained in a modified form, the doctrines of the church were given a more definitely Protestant character. The matters which the court of High Commission could declare to be heresy were

[1] Coke, Second Instit. 601-609 gives the objections of Archbishop Bancroft and the answers of the judges; in his anxiety to escape from these prohibitions the archbishop comes near to hinting that there has been a breach of continuity— "As both the Ecclesiastical and Temporal jurisdictions be now united in his Majesty, which were heretofore *de facto* though not *de jure* derived from several heads, we desire to be satisfied by the judges, whether . . . the former manner of Prohibitions . . . importing an Ecclesiastical Court to be *aliud forum a foro regis*, and the Ecclesiastical law not to be *legem terræ*, and the proceedings in those courts to be *contra Coronam et Dignitatem Regiam* may now without offence to the King's Ecclesiastical prerogative be continued, as though either the said jurisdictions remained now so distinguished and several as they were before, or that the laws Ecclesiastical, were not the King's and the Realm's Ecclesiastical Laws;" to which the orthodox answer was given "that both jurisdictions were ever *de jure* in the Crown, though the one sometimes usurped by the See of Rome; but neither in the one time nor in the other hath ever the form of Prohibitions been altered, nor can be but by Parliament," pp. 601, 602.

[2] Above 559.

[3] Mackonochie v. Lord Penzance (1881) 6 A.C. at p. 446.

[4] The logical result of this view is that Christianity is part of the law of England; but this particular consequence has been, if not denied, at least deprived of all practical effect by the decision in Bowman v. Secular Society [1917] A.C. 406, in which it was held that a trust to pay money to a society, the objects of which were inimical to Christianity, was valid; there can be no doubt that the propagation of such views is contrary to ecclesiastical law, below 618; but the House of Lords has held in this case that it is not contrary to 'the law as administered in the secular courts; this is a departure from the old views as to the relation between the ecclesiastical and the secular law; and for this reason there is, on historical grounds, much to be said for the dissenting judgment of Lord Finlay, L.C.; for an account of the history of the law on this topic see vol. viii 402-420.

defined.[1]   Statutory force was given by the Act of Uniformity, to the second book of common prayer of Edward VI.'s reign, with certain alterations and additions;[2] and not only the ecclesiastical courts, but also the justices of Oyer and Terminer and of Assize, were empowered to see to the observance of the Act.[3]

This settlement has been fully accepted both by the judges and the bishops.   In *Caudrey's Case*,[4] " It was resolved that the said Act (the Act of Supremacy) . . . concerning ecclesiastical jurisdiction was not a statute introductory of a new law, but declaratory of the old."[5]   The relations between Church and State were explained almost in the words of the preamble of Henry VIII.'s Statute of Appeals ; and the historical argument, as to the continuous independence of the church, hinted at in that preamble, was expanded and improved.   Though the canon law had been laid under contribution it never was the law of the Church of England.   " As the Romans fetching divers laws from Athens, yet being approved and allowed by the state there, called them notwithstanding jus civile Romanorum : and as the Normans, borrowing all or most of their laws from England, yet baptized them by the name of the laws and customs of Normandy : so, albeit the kings of England derived their ecclesiastical laws from others, yet so many as were proved, approved, and allowed here by and with a general consent, are aptly and rightly called the King's Ecclesiastical Laws of England."[6]   In 1851 the two archbishops and the twenty bishops of England declared the " undoubted identity of the church before and after the Reformation ; " and that though severed from Rome the church had in no respect severed her connexion " with the ancient Catholic Church."[7]

---

[1] 1 Elizabeth c. 1 § 20 ; below 618.
[2] 1 Elizabeth c. 2 § 2.   [3] §§ 4 and 5.
[4] (1591) 5 Co. Rep. 1.   [5] At p. 8 a.
[6] At p. 9 b ; at p. 32 b it is laid down that, " If it be demanded what canons, constitutions, ordinances and synodals provincial are still in force within this realm, I answer that it is resolved and enacted by authority of Parliament, that such as have been allowed by general consent and custom within the realm, and are not contrariant or repugnant to the laws, statutes and customs of the realm, nor to the damage or hurt of the king's prerogative royal, are still in force within this realm, as the king's ecclesiastical laws of the same;" cp. the Queen v. Millis (1844) 10 Cl. and Fin. at p. 678 *per* Tindal, C.J., " The law by which the Spiritual Courts of this kingdom have from the earliest times been governed and regulated is not the general canon law of Europe, imported as a body of law into this kingdom, and governing those courts *proprio vigore*, but, instead thereof, an ecclesiastical law, of which the general canon law is no doubt the basis, but which has been modified and altered from time to time by the ecclesiastical constitutions of our Archbishops and Bishops, and by the legislature of the realm, and which has been known from early times by the distinguishing title of the King's Ecclesiastical Law ; " and this is substantially the modern view, see Halsbury's Laws of England xi 359 n. (*d*).

[7] Phillimore, Ecclesiastical Law (1895) 3 ; cp. Martin v. Mackonochie (1868) L.R. 2 Ad. and Eccl. 116 for a full statement of the orthodox legal and ecclesiastical view.

Both the legal and the doctrinal theory obscure the very fundamental change which had taken place at the Reformation.[1] The relations between Church and State, and the position of the ecclesiastical courts had been fundamentally altered. The church had been brought within the state; and subjected to the power of the crown. That has involved in the course of time other consequential changes. Having been brought within the state, its position has been modified with changed ideas as to the balance of powers within the state, and as to the limits of state control. The court of High Commission wielded the royal supremacy, when the royal supremacy over the church conferred powers as large and indefinite as the royal prerogative in the state. That court disappeared, with the court of Star Chamber, when so large a prerogative was found incompatible with liberty.[2] Similarly the royal supremacy conferred a wide dispensing power. That too was limited at the Revolution when it was found to put too large a discretionary power in the hands of the crown.[3] Since the Revolution the growth of the power of Parliament, and the development of the system of Cabinet government, has in effect vested the powers conferred by the royal supremacy in the ministry of the day. Hence the relation of the church to the state has been altered to suit the views of the majority in the House of Commons which that ministry represents. Membership of the church has ceased to be considered a necessary qualification for full rights in the state; and the jurisdiction of the ecclesiastical courts has necessarily been weakened by the disappearance of the idea that it is the duty of the state church to use coercive measures to secure, *pro salute animæ*, the morality of all the members of the state. On the other hand new statutes have provided new courts or new machinery for the more effective discipline of the clergy in communion with the church.[4]

In this manner the Tudor settlement, without sacrificing what was valuable in the institutions and the doctrines of the past, has founded a church well fitted to be an English state church, because, like the constitution of the English state, it is capable of adaptation to altered circumstances without a palpable breach of continuity. In no respect did the Tudors

---

[1] Above 590-591.

[2] 16 Charles I. c. 11; 13 Charles II. St. 1 c. 12.

[3] Powell, J., in the Seven Bishops Case (1688) 12 S.T. at p. 427, said to the jury, " I can see no difference, nor know of none in law, between the king's power to dispense with laws ecclesiastical, and his power to dispense with any other laws whatsoever. If this be once allowed of there will need no Parliament ; " cp. Stillingfleet, Eccl. Cases, Discourse ii chap. iii.

[4] Below 611-614.

more clearly show their capacity to understand and to represent their people. In the age of Elizabeth, when religious feeling ran high, it often appeared to the more enthusiastic that her establishment was neither Protestant nor Catholic. But however illogical it appeared to the fanatic, it appealed to the more moderate. Being successful it did not long want defenders; and it has secured defenders so skilful that they have made love for the church an important factor in English political life.

The lawyer has deduced from the uncertain utterances of Anglo-Saxon history, and from the anti-ecclesiastical legislation of the Middle Ages, the existence, from the earliest times, of an independent national church; and the theologian has conferred upon it an unique catholicity. The benches of judges and bishops have enunciated the same doctrines in language only technically different. Thus it may be said that the Reformation has done in a similar manner for the church, what the Revolution did for the state. Macaulay's well-known summary of the effects of the Revolution [1] is, if applied to the Reformation, both good law and sound Anglican doctrine. But if we look a little beyond the immediate consequences of either the Reformation or the Revolution we can see that the changes involved have been very far reaching. The result of the Revolution was the transference of control over the executive from the prerogative to Parliament through the growth of the Cabinet system. The result of the Reformation was the abolition of the dual control of Church and State, the transference to the state of complete control over the church, and the substitution for the canon law of the King's Ecclesiastical Law. The crown's prerogative still retains traces of its origin in a feudal society; and it could be described by Blackstone in terms which might have commanded the approval of a Stuart king, and the censure of a Stuart Parliament. The church still retains her courts with some remnants of their ancient jurisdiction, and in her formularies some traces of a Catholicism older than that of Rome.

The Ecclesiastical Courts

The courts which have administered the ecclesiastical law at different periods can be divided into the following groups :—

[1] " The change seems small. Not a single flower of the crown was touched. Not a single new right was given to the people. The whole English law, substantive and adjective, was in the judgment of all the greatest lawyers, of Holt and Treby, of Maynard and Somers, almost exactly the same after the Revolution as before it. Some controverted points had been decided according to the sense of the best jurists; and there had been a slight deviation from the ordinary course of succession. This was all; and this was enough."

(1) The ordinary courts of the Diocese, the Peculiar and the Province; (2) The High Court of Delegates; (3) The Court of High Commission; and (4) the Statutory courts of the nineteenth century.

(1) The ordinary courts of the Diocese, the Peculiar and the Province.

(i) *The Diocese.*

The bishop of each diocese held a Consistory court for the diocese. From about the middle of the twelfth century the Chancellor or "Official" of the bishop usually presided over this court. He was the ordinary judge competent, like the judge of the court of Admiralty, to exercise all the jurisdiction inherent in his principal, except in such cases as the bishop might expressly reserve for his own hearing. In time he came to be the permanent judge of the court, and he retains office after the death, removal, or beyond the pleasure of the bishop by whom he was appointed.[1] But the bishop has never lost the right of withdrawing cases from his cognizance, if he wishes to hear them himself.[2] Similarly, the bishop sometimes delegated jurisdiction over certain parts of his diocese to his " commissary." [3] There was an appeal from the Consistory court to the Provincial court of the archbishop.

Each archdeacon in the diocese held a court for his archdeaconry.[4] The ordinance of William I., removing ecclesiastical pleas from the hundred court, mentions both the archdeacon and the bishop as persons who held pleas in the hundred court.[5] In its origin the office of archdeacon was ministerial. He held a court as a deputy of the bishop, just as the steward held the manorial court as a deputy of his lord. "But the tendency of all such institutions is to create new jurisdictions, and, early in the twelfth century, the English archdeacons possessed themselves of a customary jurisdiction." [6] It was possibly with a view to stop the encroachments of the archdeacon that the bishops adopted the plan of exercising their jurisdiction through

[1] Ecclesiastical Commission 1832, 11, 12; ibid 1883, 25, 26.
[2] Rex v. Tristram [1902] 1 K.B. 816.
[3] He is the official of the bishop in outlying portions of the diocese, Phillimore Eccl. Law, 933.
[4] Ecclesiastical Commission 1883, 25, 26.
[5] Stubbs, Sel. Ch. 85, " Nullus episcopus vel archidiaconus de legibus episcopalibus amplius in hundret placita teneant nec causam quæ ad regimen animarum pertinet ad judicium secularium hominum adducant; " offenders were to be tried " non secundum hundret sed secundum canones et episcopales leges."
[6] Ecclesiastical Commission 1883, 25, 26.

officials.   An appeal lay from the archdeacon's court to the Consistory court.[1]

(ii) *The Peculiar.*

The tendency in all feudal states was to vest jurisdiction in any considerable landowner.   This tendency was felt in the church as well as in the state.   Just as in the state the jurisdiction of the ordinary communal courts was displaced by the franchise jurisdictions, so in the church the jurisdiction of the ordinary Diocesan courts was displaced by the jurisdiction of the Peculiar courts.   One cause for the growth of these Peculiar courts was the conflict between the bishops and their chapters, which resulted in the apportionment of the land, and jurisdiction over the land, between the bishop and the chapter.   Thus both the bishops and the deans of the chapters possessed Peculiar courts.   A second cause was the exemption of the greater abbeys from episcopal jurisdiction.   A third cause was a similar exemption of the king's chapels royal.[2]   The variety of the origins of these Peculiar courts can be seen from the statement of the ecclesiastical commissioners of 1832,[3] that "there are Peculiars of various descriptions in most Dioceses, and in some they are very numerous: Royal, Archiepiscopal, Episcopal, Decanal, Subdecanal, Prebendal, Rectorial, and Vicarial; and there are also some Manorial courts."   Some of these Peculiars were wholly exempt from Episcopal, and even from Archiepiscopal control.   But there was an appeal from them in earlier days to the Pope; and in later days to the High Court of Delegates. Most of the peculiars have been abolished by legislation.[4]

(iii) *The Province.*

The Archbishops of Canterbury and York possessed various

---

[1] It was the duty of Rural Deans to report on the manners of the clergy and laity; this rendered them necessary attendants at the episcopal visitation, and gave them at one time a small jurisdiction; sometimes this was specially delegated to them; but this had ceased to be the case before the Reformation; the jurisdiction was absorbed by the archdeacon, Phillimore, Eccl. Law 211-213.

[2] Ecclesiastical Commission 1883, 26.

[3] Report at p. 11; it was said that " There were some of so anomalous a nature as scarcely to admit of accurate description.   In some instances these jurisdictions extend over large tracts of country, embracing many towns and parishes, as the Peculiar of the Dean of Salisbury.   In others several places may be comprehended, lying at a great distance, apart from each other.   Again some include only one or two parishes; " ibid at p. 21 their number is estimated at 300; cp. Hale, Precedents, etc., xxix-xxxi; one Peculiar of the abbey of St. Albans extended over 26 parishes, and in 1505-1536 700 wills were there proved; in the Commissary's court for the City of London from 1496-1500, 1854 persons were cited, ibid liii.

[4] 1, 2 Victoria c. 106; 3, 4 Victoria c. 86; 10, 11 Victoria c. 98; Phillimore, Eccl. Law 927.

Provincial courts.[1] The Provincial courts of the Archbishop of Canterbury were the following :—

(*a*) The court of the "Official Principal" of the archbishop (usually known as the court of the Arches[2]) was at once the court of Appeal from all the Diocesan courts, and a court of first instance in all ecclesiastical causes. The latter jurisdiction was acquired by a series of encroachments (not without protest on the part of the bishops) analogous to the encroachments of the papal jurisdiction.[3] This jurisdiction was restrained by the statute of Citations,[4] which put an end to the practice of citing persons outside their dioceses, except on appeals, on request of the bishop, or in case of the bishop's negligence to hear the case. "As official principal the judge was held to possess all the judicial power of the archbishop . . . he issued process in his own name, and seems in all respects to represent the archbishop in his judicial character as completely as the chief justice represented the king."[5] Whether or no this deprived the archbishop of the right to sit and act personally in his court is not quite clear.[6]

(*b*) The court of Audience. Just as the bishop did not deprive himself of all jurisdiction by delegation to an official or commissary, so the archbishop did not originally deprive himself of all jurisdiction by delegation to the official principal. He possessed a jurisdiction concurrent with that of the court of the Arches, which was exercised in the court of Audience. In later times this jurisdiction was exercised by the judge of the court of Audience.[7] At one time the archbishop may have exercised a considerable part of this jurisdiction in this court. It is mentioned in a seventeenth century account of the ecclesiastical courts ; and in 1638-1639 there is a mention of appeals from this court to the High Court of Delegates.[8] But it does not appear to have been revived as a separate court after the Restoration ; [9]

---

[1] The Archbishop of Canterbury had also a Diocesan court for the Diocese of Canterbury which was held by a Commissary, Ecclesiastical Commission 1883, 31 ; as to these courts see ibid 31, 32, 44-46.

[2] The offices of Dean of the Arches and Official Principal became merged, Fourth Instit. 337. The courts of both the Official Principal and the Dean sat at St. Mary-le-Bow which was built on arches ; and hence the court of the Official Principal became known as the court of the Arches.

[3] Maitland, Canon Law 117-120. [4] 23 Henry VIII. c. 9.

[5] Ecclesiastical Commission 1883, 31 ; cp. Boyd v. Phillpotts (1874) L.R. 4 Ad. and Eccl. at pp. 320, 321.

[6] Ecclesiastical Commission 1883, 46.

[7] Ibid 31 ; Phillimore, Eccl. Law, 922, 923 ; Coke, Fourth Instit. 337, said that it possessed no contentious jurisdiction, but dealt merely with matters pro forma, e.g. the admission to benefices, etc.

[8] S.P. Dom. 1638-1639, 217, ccccvi 96.

[9] Ecclesiastical Commission 1883, 190 ; it would seem from the patent set out in Boyd v. Phillpotts (1874) L.R. 4 Ad. and Eccl. at p. 321 that the Official Principal has absorbed the jurisdiction of this court.

and it has now fallen into disuse.   It must not be confused with the personal jurisdiction which the archbishop has over his suffragan bishops.[1]

(c) The Prerogative court.[2]   This court was sometimes presided over by the official principal, sometimes by a special commissary.   It took cognizance of the testamentary jurisdiction belonging to the archbishop.   It originally sat in the archbishop's palace; but it was moved, about the time of the Reformation, to Doctors' Commons.   The archbishops attracted to this court most of the testamentary business of the country.   Whenever a man left *bona notabilia* in more than one diocese they claimed to oust the jurisdiction of the bishop.[3]   In spite of much opposition they made good this claim, which was recognized by the canons of 1604.[4]

(d) The court of Peculiars.[5]   This court was held by the Dean of the Arches at Bow Church for the thirteen London parishes, which were exempt from the diocesan jurisdiction of the Bishop of London.

(e) The court of the Vicar-General in which the bishops of the province are confirmed.[6]

The provincial courts of the Archbishop of York were the Chancery court, the Prerogative court, and the court of Audience. These courts corresponded to the court of the Arches, the Prerogative court, and the court of Audience of the Archbishop of Canterbury.[7]

The Public Worship Regulation Act [8] provides for the appointment by the Archbishops of Canterbury and York of a single judge for their provincial courts.   Such person is to hold the posts of the official principal of the Arches court and the Chancery court, and Master of the Faculties [9] to the Archbishop of Canterbury.   The person appointed must be either a practising barrister of ten years' standing, or a judge of one of the superior courts.   He must also be a member of the Church of England. He holds office during good behaviour.

---

[1] Read v. Bishop of Lincoln (1888) 13 P.D. 221; (1889) 14 P.D. 88; but the exact nature of the jurisdiction then exercised is by no means clear, Phillimore, Eccl. Law, 73, 74.

[2] Ecclesiastical Commission 1883, 31.

[3] Lyndwood 174 sub. voc. *Laicis;* Bl. Comm. ii 509; the value of *bona notabilia* was ultimately fixed at £5.

[4] Goffin, The Testamentary Executor, 69, 70.

[5] Ecclesiastical Commission 1883, 31.

[6] Phillimore, Eccl. Law, 922; Rex v. Archbishop of Canterbury [1902] 2 K.B. 503.

[7] Ecclesiastical Commission 1883, 31.

[8] 37, 38 Victoria c. 85 § 7.

[9] I.e. the official who granted dispensations, 25 Henry VIII. c. 21; Fourth Instit. 337.

There is a question whether at any time Convocation ever acted as a court.[1] There is some evidence to show that in the fourteenth and fifteenth centuries persons accused of heresy were brought before Convocation by the bishop who had cognizance of the case. But the members of Convocation did not vote on such trials. It was probably rather in the nature of a body of assessors to the archbishop than a court possessing jurisdiction. Coke, it is true, treats it as having once possessed jurisdiction in cases of heresy;[2] and a majority of the judges in *Whiston's Case*[3] seemed to think that it might still possess such jurisdiction. In 1532[4] the upper house was made a final court of Appeal in ecclesiastical causes which concerned the king—possibly the idea was to follow up the analogy between the temporal and spiritual jurisdictions, suggested in the preamble to the statute, by giving to it the position of the House of Lords. But this jurisdiction was, as we shall see, taken away in the following year.[5] It is clear that Convocation exercises no jurisdiction at the present day.

(2) The High Court of Delegates.

In the pre-Reformation period there was an almost unlimited right of appeal to the Pope in all cases which fell within the jurisdiction of the ecclesiastical courts. This right was fettered to a slight degree by the rules made by the Pope himself,[6] and by the statutes of Præmunire, in those cases in which the civil tribunals claimed exclusive jurisdiction. But where it existed the system of appeals and rehearings was, or might be, never ending. " Not only might a matter in dispute be treated over and over again, delegacy superseding delegacy, and appeal being interposed on every detail of proceeding one after another, but even after a definitive decision a question might be reopened and the most solemn decision be reversed on fresh examination. On this system of rehearing there was practically no limit, for, however solemn the sanction by which one Pope bound himsel^r and his successors, it was always possible for a new Pope to permit the introduction of new evidence or a plea of exceptions. In this way the Roman court remained a resource for ever open to litigants who were able to pay for its services, and the apostolic See avoided the imputation of claiming finality and infallibility for decisions which were not indisputable."[7]

---

[1] Ecclesiastical Commission 1883, 45, 46, 52-69 ; Read v. Bishop of Lincoln (1889) 14 P.D. 114-117.
[2] Fourth Instit. 322 ; cp. Hale, 1 P.C. 390 ; Gibson, Codex 353 n. g.
[3] (1712) Brod. and Free. 325.
[4] 24 Henry VIII c. 12.   [5] 25 Henry VIII. c. 19.
[6] Ecclesiastical Commission 1883, 30 ; E.H.R. xvi 40, 41.
[7] Ecclesiastical Commission 1883, 30.

The statute for the restraint of appeals[1] prohibited all appeals to Rome, and provided that certain[2] appeals should go from the archdeacon to the bishop, and (within fifteen days) from the bishop to the courts of Arches or Audience, and from those courts to the archbishop himself.   His decision was to be final except in cases touching the king.   In that case there was to be an appeal from any of the ecclesiastical courts to the upper house of Convocation.   This statute was superseded by one passed in the following year which provided a new court of appeal for all ecclesiastical causes.[3]   The court created by this Act came to be known as the High Court of Delegates.   The Act provided as follows : " For lack of justice at or in any of the courts of the archbishops of this realm, or in any of the king's dominions, it shall be lawful for the parties grieved to appeal to the King's Majesty in the king's court of Chancery ; and that upon every such appeal a commission shall be directed under the Great Seal to such persons as shall be named by the King's Highness his heirs and successors, like as in case of appeal from the Admiral's court, to hear and definitely determine every such appeal, and the causes concerning the same.   And that such judgment as the said commissioners shall make and decree . . . shall be good and effectual, and also definitive." [4]   An appeal to the same body was provided from such peculiar jurisdictions as were exempt from episcopal or archiepiscopal control.[5]   A person desiring to appeal addressed a petition to the crown in Chancery, on which a commission of appeal issued appointing certain commissioners. If any of these commissioners died pending the appeal, if they were equally divided, or if, for any reason, it was desired to increase the strength of the court, a " commission of adjuncts " issued, adding certain persons to the court.   It followed that the court was differently constituted for the hearing of each appeal.[6] Henry VIII.'s statute declared the judgment of the Delegates to be final ; and in 1678 this clause of the statute was successfully appealed to to refute the contention that the House of Lords could hear appeals from them.[7]   But it was decided by the Elizabethan lawyers that the crown could, like the Pope, issue a Commission of Review, to hear the whole case over again.[8]

[1] 24 Henry VIII. c. 12.

[2] Causes testamentary, causes of matrimony and divorce, rights of tithes, oblations and obventions; this did not apparently include heresy.

[3] 25 Henry VIII. c. 19 ; repealed 1, 2 Philip and Mary c. 8 ; revived 1 Elizabeth c. 1 with a saving for certain pending appeals to the Pope.

[4] § 4.   [5] § 6.

[6] Rothery's Return, Parliamentary Papers 1867 lvii 75, x-xii.

[7] 2 Swanst. 326-330 ; Hist. MSS. Com. Ninth Rep. App. Pt. II. 113 ; cf. ibid Eleventh Rep. App. Pt. II. 216 no. 310 for an attempt to appeal from a decision of the Delegates as to the genuineness of a will.

[8] Ibid.

The court was not a court of first instance. It did not control the court of High Commission, the abolition of which necessarily added to the number of cases heard before it.[1]

The crown had an absolute discretion as to the persons to be appointed. But, as the lawyers of Doctors' Commons were the only lawyers aquainted with canon or civil law, certain of them were usually included in the commission. In some of the earlier cases bishops and judges were included. In the eighteenth century the bishops were rarely included, and were at length entirely excluded [2]—a tendency which was apparently beginning to make itself felt in the earlier half of the seventeenth century.[3]   It was stated in 1832 that in ordinary cases the delegates were three puisne judges and three civilians, though in special cases, temporal peers, and other judges might be added.[4] It is not surprising to find that the court was unsatisfactory. It was a shifting body, so that no general rules of procedure could be established. It did not as a rule give reasons for its decisions. Its members were only paid a guinea a day ; and consequently it was usually composed of the junior civilians. On them, the judges of the common law courts, appointed as delegates, were obliged to rely for their law.[5]   In consequence of the dissatisfaction felt at its working the Ecclesiastical Commission of 1832, in a special report, recommended the transfer of its jurisdiction to the Privy Council ; and this recommendation was carried out in the same year.[6]   The jurisdiction is now exercised by the Judicial Committee of the Privy Council created in 1833.[7]

(3) The Court of High Commission.[8]

When Henry VIII. made himself supreme head of the church he was naturally obliged to exercise some of his powers by

[1] Ecclesiastical Commission 1883, 47 ; below 609.

[2] Rothery's Return xx-xxii.

[3] In 1639-1640 Sir J. Lambe wrote to Laud advising him not to put common law judges on these commissions as such a practice would " by little and little ruin our profession and deduce and turn all ecclesiastical jurisdiction into the common law," S.P. Dom. 1639-1640, 350 ccccxlii.

[4] Ecclesiastical Commission (1832) Special Report 6 ; in 1699, at the hearing of the appeal made by the Bishop of St. David's from the decree of suspension made by the Archbishop of Canterbury, four peers, several judges, and doctors of the civil law were appointed, Lutterell's Diary iv 506 ; for further notes of the course of this appeal see ibid 514, 525.

[5] Ecclesiastical Commission 1832, 6 ; see ibid 159, 160 (Evidence of Joseph Phillimore).

[6] 2, 3 William IV. c. 92 ; but a recourse to the Delegates by the special provision in the patent of a Colonial Bishop was still possible, Rothery's Return 100.

[7] Above 518.   The hearing of ecclesiastical cases was not actually mentioned in this Act ; but it was assumed that this jurisdiction passed, and this was recognized by the Church Discipline Act, 3, 4 Victoria c. 86 § 16.

[8] On the whole subject see R. G. Usher, The Rise and Fall of the High Commission.

delegating them to commissioners. Thomas Cromwell was given a general commission to exercise the powers conferred by the royal supremacy, and to delegate such parts of it as he saw fit to others.[1] Under this power limited commissions were issued;[2] but the first general commission issued to a number of persons dates from a commission issued by Edward VI. in 1549. It was "in substance and in form the first of the long succession of Letters Patent issued by the crown up to the moment of the abolition of the court of High Commission in 1641."[3] Several other general commissions of this kind, and also commissions of a more limited nature, were issued both by Edward VI. and Mary.[4] Another general commission was issued by Elizabeth in 1559;[5] but this commission possessed statutory authority, since Elizabeth's Act of Supremacy had specially authorized its issue.[6] It was not, however, materially different from the former commissions;[7] and, though it had statutory authority, the judges held that, even without statutory authority, the crown had power to issue it by virtue of its supremacy over the church.[8] It was not till the latter part of the sixteenth and the beginning of the seventeenth centuries, when the legality of the powers exercised by the court of High Commission began to be contested, that the question whether or not it rested only upon statutory authority began to assume importance.[9]

The earlier commissions were rather a series of instruments employed by the state to enforce its ecclesiastical policy than the definite creation of an institution exercising judicial functions.[10] On that account the powers of the commissioners were wide. They were entrusted with the duty of enforcing the Acts of Supremacy and Uniformity, of dealing generally with ecclesiastical offences, and of suppressing any movements dangerous to the church.[11] They could conduct their enquiries very much as they pleased,[12] and with or without a jury.[13] They could summon persons on suspicion, and they could examine the

---

[1] Usher 20.   [2] Ibid 21.   [3] Ibid.

[4] Ibid 22-25; Ecclesiastical Commission 1883, 49.

[5] Usher, op. cit. 26-27.

[6] 1 Elizabeth c. 1 § 8; cf. the report of the Ecclesiastical Commissioners 1883, 49-50.

[7] Usher, op. cit. 27.

[8] Caudrey's Case (1591) 5 Co. Rep. 1; cf. the resolutions of the judges in 1605 as reported in Cro. Jac. 37, and Moore, K.B., 755; Usher, op. cit. 33-34; James II.'s lawyers would probably have justified the king's creation of a new court of High Commission in the face of 13 Charles II. St. 1 c. 12 § 3 on some such ground, see Stillingfleet Eccl. Cases ii 200, 201.

[9] Below, 610-611.

[10] Usher, op. cit. 46-47, 50.   [11] Ibid 50-53.

[12] Ibid 56 seqq.

[13] Commission of 1559, Prothero, Documents xli, 228; this clause was omitted in 1611, ibid xliv.

accused on oath.[1]   All these powers they exercised according
to the instructions and under the supervision of the Council;[2]
and, as ecclesiastics and civil and canon lawyers predominated,[3]
naturally their procedure tended to follow the model of the civil
rather than the common law.[4]   Concurrently with this general
commission, special diocesan commissions were issued from time
to time in order to strengthen the bishops' powers, judicial and
otherwise.[5]   These commissions helped to secure the maintenance of the Elizabethan settlement and the episcopal authority
in the dioceses, just as the general commission helped to secure
their maintenance in the kingdom.[6]

As these general commissions came to be regularly issued to
the same persons, they tended to become less a merely executive
instrument of the state, and more one of the regular institutions
of the church.[7]   This process was helped forward by the fact
that the Council began to refer to the ecclesiastical commission
many petitions on ecclesiastical matters which prayed for relief
which could not be got in the ordinary ecclesiastical courts.[8]   In
consequence it began to act, not only as a body entrusted with
the maintenance of the policy of the state in ecclesiastical matters,
but also as a judicial court.   It began to develop forms and
rules of procedure; and as early as 1570 it was referred to by
the Council in terms which showed that it was already regarded as
a court.[9]   The number of the commissioners showed a tendency
to increase,[10] and the extent of the jurisdiction conferred on them
by the commission tended to become more definite.[11]

Under the Stuarts the powers conferred by the commission
were elaborately specified.   The Patent of 1611 recognized the
existing constitution and procedure of the court; and it was the
model followed by all the later commissions of James I.'s reign.[12]
In 1625 there was a short lived provision that, during the session

---

[1] See the Commission of 1611, Prothero, Documents 429; for the ex officio
oath see below 609 and n. 8.
[2] Usher, op. cit. 50.
[3] Ibid 84, 149; Prothero, Documents xlvi.
[4] Usher, op. cit. chap. v.
[5] Ibid chap. xiii; Prothero, Documents xlv, xlvi.
[6] The main commission—the court of High Commission—was the Canterbury
commission; "The Canterbury Commissioners were not expected to perform regular
ecclesiastical routine business in the dioceses, even though their patent vested in
them the requisite authority; if the crown deemed expedient the regular exercise of
such authority in any part of England, a special patent was issued for a single case
or for a certain district. . . . But the court of High Commission itself . . . was
clearly expected to supervise these commissions and to supplement at discretion by
its own broad authority their very limited powers," Usher, op. cit. 285.
[7] Ibid 64.   [8] Ibid 70.
[9] Ibid 71-72, citing Dasent vii 361.
[10] See the Table compiled by Usher, op. cit. 90.
[11] Ibid 104-105, 236-238.   [12] Ibid 241.

of Convocation, the powers of the court should be exercised only by the bishops in Convocation;[1] and in 1611, 1613, 1620, and 1625 provision was made for the creation of a commission to review its decisions.[2]   But the Patents of Charles I.'s reign reverted to the form used in 1601.[3]   The result was that these clauses as to Convocation, and as to the provision of a commission of review disappeared. "Thus the commission became once more absolute, unlimited, and without appeal;"[4] and in 1634-1635 Laud revived its visitatorial powers which had been in abeyance since 1584.[5]

We have seen that in the sixteenth century the commission was being gradually increased in size; and the increase became rapid in James I.'s reign.   In 1611 its numbers were increased from 60 to 92; and in 1625 from 92 to 108.[6]   The reason for this last increase was the discontinuance of the diocesan commissions.   Instead of these commissions, members of the court of High Commission sat in any place where their presence was required.[7]   By this means the court was able to make its power felt all over the country.   Thus a uniform discipline and a uniform administration of the ecclesiastical law could be secured, and so the policy of Charles and Laud could be more effectually enforced all over the country.

The court of High Commission stood to the church and to the ordinary ecclesiastical courts somewhat in the same relation as the Council and Star Chamber stood to the state and the ordinary courts of the state, central and local.[8]   It is no wonder therefore that, throughout its history, its relations to the Council and Star Chamber were close.[9]   Both were semi-political, semi-judicial courts engaged in carrying out in their several spheres a common policy.   Both therefore exercised a jurisdiction which was to a large extent concurrent with that of the ordinary courts[10] —supplementing their deficiences, supporting their authority, and sometimes correcting their miscarriages of justice.[11]   And just as its power and efficiency made the Star Chamber a popular court, so the same qualities draw much business from the ordinary

---

[1] Prothero, Documents xliv, xlv.   [2] Ibid.
[3] Usher, op. cit. 242; Ecclesiastical Commission 1883, 50.
[4] Usher, op. cit. 242-243.   [5] Ibid 243.
[6] Ibid 250.   [7] Ibid 331-332.
[8] For the relation of the High Commission to the other courts see Usher, chap. xiv; for the position of the Council and Star Chamber see above 504-506.
[9] See Usher, op. cit. 312-313.
[10] Ecclesiastical Commission 1883, 50.
[11] See e.g. S.P. Dom. 1637, 520, ccclxxi 43, where Laud contemplates remedying an injustice done by the court of the Arches by means of the High Commission cf. Usher, op. cit. 96-97.

ecclesiastical courts to the High Commission.[1] When it was at
the height of its power there was very little business done by the
court of Delegates.[2] Besides its work of supervising the doings
of the ordinary ecclesiastical courts, its original jurisdiction was
almost co-extensive with that of those ordinary courts. Thus it
comprised many various matrimonial matters—alimony, divorce,
and so forth; immorality and simony, plurality, and other
clerical irregularities.[3] It comprised also heresy, schism and
non-conformity; and, as Professor Usher has noted,[4] these
offences then had a larger meaning than they have now. " The
quarrelling of two old women in church was schism, witchcraft
was heresy, and the failure of the parson to read prayers on a
Wednesday because he was reaping his harvest, was non-
conformity. Neither heresy nor schism was necessarily connected
with Puritanism or Roman Catholicism. Non-conformity applied
equally to those who broke the rules of the church through in-
difference or negligence, and to those who refused to perform
them for conscience sake." Finally, from 1613 onwards, it was
empowered to enforce the Star Chamber rules as to the censorship of the press.[5]

A strong court of this kind was necessary to support the
Established Church against both its Roman Catholic and its
Puritan enemies. Like the court of Star Chamber,[6] it did not
at first arouse much opposition. Its cause lists were full, and,
indeed, continued to be full to the end.[7] But in the last two
decades of the sixteenth century the growing strength of the
High Commission on the one hand, and of the Puritan opposition
to the ecclesiastical policy of the Government on the other, gave
rise to attacks both upon its procedure and jurisdiction. The
feature in its procedure which was the main object of attack was
the *ex officio* oath, because that oath was the most efficient means
of extracting information as to the policy of the opponents of
the Established Church.[8] Those who attacked its jurisdiction

---

[1] Professor Usher quite rightly points out that " It would be difficult to exaggerate
the fundamental importance of the share played by the English people themselves in
the evolution of the court. Without their ready acceptance of its legality, without
their belief in the useful function it performed, neither royal fiat nor statute could
have created such a court and compelled people to resort to it," op. cit. 70-71; for
its popularity even under Laud's regime see ibid 323-324.

[2] Ecclesiastical Commission 1883, 50; Usher, op. cit. 311-312.

[3] Ibid 256-257.   [4] Ibid 257.

[5] Ibid 54, 313; for the history of this censorship see vol. vi 367 seqq.

[6] Above 509, 512-513.   [7] Above n. 1.

[8] Usher, op. cit. 125-126; Hallam. C.H. i 202 says, " This procedure which was
founded wholly on the canon law, consisted in a series of interrogations, so comprehensive as to embrace the whole scope of clerical uniformity, yet so precise and
minute as to leave no room for evasion, to which the suspected party was bound to
answer on oath;" as to its origins, which must be sought in the procedure of the
canon law, see Usher, op. cit. 77 n. 1; according to the law it was clearly not

asserted that it depended upon the Act of Supremacy and that, according to the true interpretation of that statute, its jurisdiction was unduly extended.[1] But the Puritans, though they were a considerable power in the House of Commons, were not yet a majority in that House, and their views found as yet no countenance in the courts.[2]

These conditions were entirely changed under the Stuarts. The claim made by the first two Stuart kings that their prerogative made them the sovereign power in the state united against them both the lawyers and the majority of the House of Commons. And, as at the same time, the Stuart kings allied themselves with the party in the church which was most opposed to the Puritans, the legal and constitutional opposition to the crown found itself allied to the religious opposition to the ecclesiastical policy of the government. That alliance was cemented as the church came to be more and more dominated by churchmen of Laud's school ; and thus a religious element was imported into the legal and political controversy which was destined, for an interval, to prove fatal to the constitution.

The first effect of this alliance was seen in the changed attitude of the common lawyers. Though Coke had, in *Caudrey's Case*,[3] magnified the royal supremacy, he now employed his ingenuity to find reasons for crippling the court of High Commission. He seems to have been a convert to the view that its powers depended upon the Act of Supremacy ;[4] and to have given a most restrictive interpretation to the words of that statute. Thus, though the court was clearly empowered to deal with all ecclesiastical offences, he maintained that it was only " enormous " offences which fell within its cognizance ; and that others must be left to the ordinary ecclesiastical courts.[5] He denied it the right to fine and imprison,[6] and to interpret the limits of its own jurisdiction.[7] He denied the validity of the *ex officio* oath.[8] He commented upon the lengthy provisions of the more recent commissions, and the denial of all right to appeal.[9] His brethren followed his lead. The action of the court was fettered by writs of prohibition ; and persons imprisoned by it were released by writs of habeas corpus.[10] This legal opposition

illegal, see Usher, op. cit. 144-146 ; for the Puritan attacks upon its legality see ibid 129-130, 135.

[1] See two pamphlets of 1591, cited by Usher, 140-141.
[2] Above 596 n. 5.
[3] (1591) 5 Co. Rep. 1.   [4] Roper's Case, 12 Co. Rep. 45.
[5] Usher, op. cit. 185 ; 12 Co. Rep. at p. 48 ; cp. Fourth Instit. 331.
[6] Fourth Instit. 326.   [7] Fuller's Case, 12 Co. Rep. at p. 42.
[8] 12 Co. Rep. 26.   [9] Fourth Instit. 326, 328.
[10] Usher, op. cit. 180-181 ; Fuller, after being imprisoned by the High Commission; got a habeas corpus from the King's Bench, ibid 177 ; Coke, Fourth Instit. 332-334.

died down after Coke's dismissal in 1616 ;[1] but, from the latter part of Elizabeth's reign, the House of Commons had always contained a strong Puritan party ; and attempts had been made to pass legislation hostile to the commission.[2] It had been attacked in 1610 ;[3] and in all succeeding Parliaments Laud's religious policy was a grievance of as much importance as any of the constitutional questions of the day.[4] The strengthening of the High Commission to enforce this policy, and its activity during the eleven years of prerogative rule (1629-1640), ensured its downfall when the Long Parliament met.

In 1641 [5] the clause of the Act of Supremacy which gave the crown power to exercise its supremacy through commissioners was repealed ; the court was abolished ; and it was provided that no similar court should be again set up. The Act then went on to abolish the criminal and corrective jurisdiction of all the other ecclesiastical courts. It did not, however, abolish their civil jurisdiction ; and during the Interregnum provision was made for the exercise of their jurisdiction over grants of probate and administration,[6] and for some part of their matrimonial jurisdiction.[7] At the Restoration the criminal and corrective jurisdiction of the other ecclesiastical courts was revived ;[8] but the court of High Commission was explicitly exempted from the Act ; and the repeal of the clause of Elizabeth's Act of Supremacy, upon which, as it was now agreed, its legality depended, was confirmed.[9]

(4) The Statutory Courts of the nineteenth century.

Certain statutes of the last century have provided a new and a more convenient procedure, and, in some cases, new courts, for the exercise both of criminal and civil jurisdiction.

The procedure of the ecclesiastical courts had become so dilatory and expensive that much difficulty had been found in bringing to justice clergy guilty of immoral conduct. The ecclesiastical commissioners reported in 1832 that " some cases of a flagrant nature, which have occurred of late years, have attracted the attention of the public to the corrective discipline of the church, as administered by the ecclesiastical courts, and

---

[1] Some prohibitions continued to be granted, Usher, op. cit. 317-319; as Professor Usher says, "The common law judges gave up any direct attack, and acquiesced, albeit in a somewhat jealous and disapproving spirit, in the commission's continued existence and activity."

[2] Ibid 130, 132, 146-147.　　　[3] Prothero, Documents 302-305.
[4] Vol. vi 128-133.　　　[5] 16 Charles I. c. 11.
[6] Acts and Ordinances i 564 (1644); ii 702 (1653).
[7] Ibid ii 496 (1650-1651)—cases of forcible and pretended marriages.
[8] 13 Charles II. St. 1 c. 12.　　　[9] § 3.

have at the same time exhibited in a strong light the inconveniences which have attended the application of the ordinary process of the courts to such suits ; namely, an injurious delay in effecting the desired object of removing ministers of immoral and scandalous lives from the administration of the sacred offices of the church ; and the large expense incurred in such suits." [1]

The Church Discipline Act of 1840 [2] was passed to deal with the cases of clerks " who may be charged with any offence against the laws ecclesiastical, or concerning whom there may exist scandal or evil report as having offended against the said laws." [3] It enacted that no criminal suits should be instituted otherwise than according to procedure provided by the Act. [4]

In cases where a clerk is charged with an offence the bishop, may, on the application of a complainant, or of his own motion, issue a commission to five persons to enquire. They must report to the bishop whether there are prima facie grounds for instituting proceedings. [5] With the consent of the party accused, the bishop may pronounce sentence without further proceedings. [6] If he does not consent, articles are drawn up against the party accused. [7] If he admits the truth of the articles the bishop (or his commissary specially appointed for that purpose) may pronounce sentence. [8] If not, either the bishop assisted by three assessors may hear the case, or the bishop may send the case to be tried by the court of the Province. [9] But the letters of request for this purpose must have been sent before the filing of the articles. [10] An appeal is provided to the court of the Province and to the Privy Council. [11] In order to avoid the double appeal, most cases were sent by the bishop to the court of the Province in the first instance. [12]

The provisions of the Act did not apply to persons instituting suits to establish a civil right. [13] They did apply to all exempt and peculiar places, except those belonging to bishoprics or archbishoprics. [14] Pending the enquiry or trial, the bishop was empowered to inhibit the party accused from continuing to perform the services of the church. [15] This Act has for most purposes been repealed, in respect of those classes of offences which come within the provisions of the Clergy Discipline Act of 1892. [16]

---

[1] At p. 56. [2] 3, 4 Victoria c. 86. [3] § 3. [4] § 23.
[5] §§ 3, 4, 5. [6] § 6. [7] § 7. [8] § 9.
[9] §§ 11, 13. [10] § 13. [11] § 15.
[12] Ecclesiastical Commission 1883, xlvi.
[13] 3, 4 Victoria c. 86 § 19. [14] § 22. [15] § 14.
[16] 55, 56 Victoria c. 32 § 14, 3 ; see Bowman v. Lax [1910] P. 300 ; and cp. Beneficed Clerk v. Lee [1897] A.C. 226 where it was held that the offence of simony was not an immoral act within the meaning of the Act of 1892, and so

That Act provides that a clergyman convicted of treason, certain felonies and misdemeanours, or adultery, or against whom a bastardy order, or a decree for judicial separation has been made, shall ipso facto forfeit his preferment within twenty-one days.[1] It provides that a clergyman may be prosecuted, in the Consistory court of his diocese, by any of his parishioners, if he is convicted by a temporal court of an act (other than those named above) constituting an ecclesiastical offence, or, if he " is alleged to have been guilty of any immoral act, immoral conduct, or immoral habit, or of any offence against the laws ecclesiastical, being an offence against morality, and not being a question of doctrine or ritual."[2] The bishop may in all cases disallow the prosecution if he sees fit. The trial is before the bishop's chancellor; but, if either party so requires, questions of fact must be decided by five assessors.[3] There is an appeal on any question of law, and, with the leave of the appellate court, on any question of fact, either to the court of the Province or to the Privy Council.[4]

In 1874 the Public Worship Regulation Act[5] gave to the existing ecclesiastical courts a new machinery for the trial of offences against the ceremonial law of the church. An archdeacon, a churchwarden, or any three parishioners of the archdeaconry or parish within which a church or burial ground is situate, may represent to the bishop that unlawful additions have been made in the fabric or ornaments of the church, or that there has been use of unlawful ornaments, or neglect to use prescribed ornaments, or that there has been failure to comply with the rules of the book of Common Prayer, as to the conduct of services.[6] The bishop may, if he pleases, refuse to institute proceedings.[7] If he thinks that proceedings should be taken, he may himself, with the consent of both parties, deal finally with the case.[8] If they do not consent, the case is heard by the judge of the court of the Province.[9] From his decision an appeal lies to the Privy Council.[10] The working of this Act has not been found to be altogether satisfactory. The ecclesiastical commissioners of 1883 reported that it added little to the powers conferred on the court of the Arches by the Church Discipline

came within the Act of 1840. The sections of the Church Discipline Act, which are saved, are contained in the schedule; they relate to the definition of terms; the power of the bishop to pronounce sentence at once with the consent of the parties; the power of the bishop to inhibit the accused party pending enquiry; the requirement that witnesses be examined on oath; powers as to exempt or peculiar places.

[1] § 1. [2] § 2; cp. Sweet v. Young [1902] P. 37.
[3] § 2, a, c, e. [4] § 4.
[5] 37, 38 Victoria c. 85. Cp. Ecclesiastical Commission 1883, xlvii-xlix; and Green v. Lord Penzance (1881) 6 A.C. 657
[6] § 8. [7] § 9. [8] § 9.
[9] § 9. [10] § 9.

Act; and that, in practice, proceedings taken under it were no more convenient than proceedings taken under the earlier Act.[1]

The Benefices Act of 1898[2] gave to the bishop in certain cases[3] the power to refuse to institute a person presented to a benefice. An appeal from such refusal lies to the archbishop of the Province, and to a judge of the supreme court, nominated pro hac vice by the Lord Chancellor.[4] The judge decides any question of law, and finds the facts. The archbishop gives judgment as to whether the facts so found render the presentee unfit for the duties of the benefice.[5] From this decision there is no appeal.[6] The same tribunal is given a jurisdiction in cases where a bishop has superseded and inhibited an incumbent, by reason of negligent performance of his duties. The incumbent can in such cases appeal to this tribunal. The judge decides whether there has been negligence. The archbishop, if negligence is found, decides whether it is good ground for the inhibition.[7]

The Jurisdiction of the Ecclesiastical Courts

In the twelfth century the ecclesiastical courts claimed to exercise a wide jurisdiction. (1) They claimed criminal jurisdiction in all cases in which a clerk was the accused, a jurisdiction over offences against religion, and a wide corrective jurisdiction over clergy and laity alike " pro salute animæ ". A branch of the latter jurisdiction was the claim to enforce all promises made with oath or pledge of faith. (2) They claimed a jurisdiction over matrimonial and testamentary causes. Under the former head came all questions of marriage, divorce, and legitimacy ; under the latter came grants of probate and administration, and the supervision of the executor and administrator. (3) They claimed exclusive cognizance of all matters which were in their nature ecclesiastical, such as ordination, consecration, celebration of service, the status of ecclesiastical persons, ecclesiastical property such as advowsons, land held in frankalmoign, and spiritual dues.

These claims were at no time admitted by the state in their entirety ; and in course of time most of these branches of jurisdiction have been appropriated by the state. All that is left at the present day is a certain criminal or corrective jurisdiction over the clergy, and a certain jurisdiction in respect of some of

---

[1] At p. xlix.   [2] 61, 62 Victoria c. 48.   [3] §§ 2, 3, 1.
[4] § 3, 1.   [5] § 3, 2.   [6] Ibid.
[7] § 9; for a case of this kind see Rice v. the Bishop of Oxford [1917] P. 181; see the judgment of Lord Coleridge, J., at p. 186.

the matters contained under the third head. The history of this jurisdiction I must now sketch.

(1) Criminal and corrective jurisdiction.

(i) *Criminal jurisdiction.*

In the twelfth century the church claimed that all clerks should be exempt from any kind of secular jurisdiction, and, in particular, that " criminous clerks " should be subject to the exclusive jurisdiction of the ecclesiastical courts.[1] In answer to this claim Henry II., in 1164, propounded the scheme contained in the third clause of the Constitutions of Clarendon,[2] which he contended represented the laws in force in the time of Henry I. According to this clause the clerk must be accused before the temporal court, and he must there plead his clergy. He must then be sent to the ecclesiastical court for trial, and a royal officer will attend the trial. If he is found guilty and degraded the royal officer will bring him back, as a layman, to the temporal court to suffer the layman's punishment. Becket objected to this scheme on three grounds: firstly, a clerk ought not to be accused before the temporal court; secondly, a royal officer ought not to be present in the ecclesiastical court; and thirdly, further punishment by the lay court involved an infringement of the rule that no man ought to be punished twice for the same offence. The first two of these objections were good according to the canon law. As to the third, the canon law was not at that date clear; but the principle for which Becket contended was shortly afterwards condemned by Innocent III.[3] The results of Becket's murder were curious. The temporal courts maintained their claim to bring the criminous clerk before them; but they abandoned their claim to punish the degraded clerk. This abandonment gave rise to the Privilege or Benefit of Clergy. Originally, Benefit of Clergy meant that an ordained clerk charged with felony could be tried only in the ecclesiastical courts. But in course of time it entirely changed its nature. It became a complicated set of rules, exempting from capital punishment certain persons found guilty of certain felonies, which

---

[1] P. and M. i 430-440; Maitland, Canon Law 132-147.

[2] Sel. Ch. 138, " Clerici rettati et accusati de quacunque re, summoniti a justicia regis venient in curiam ipsius, responsuri ibidem de hoc unde videbitur curiæ regis quod ibidem sit respondendum; et in curia ecclesiastica, unde videbitur quod ibidem sit respondendum; ita quod justicia regis mittat in curiam sanctæ ecclesiæ ad videndum qua ratione res ibi tractabitur. Et si clericus convictus vel confessus fuerit, non debet de cetero eum ecclesia tueri; " for previous legislation in Normandy on some of the matters covered by the constitutions of Clarendon see Haskins, Norman Institutions 170-174, 329-333.

[3] P. and M. i 437, 438 and notes.

were not abolished till 1827. Of the history of this development I shall speak when I come to deal with the criminal law of the Middle Ages.[1]

(ii) *Corrective jurisdiction.*

The ecclesiastical courts exercised a wide and vague control over the religious beliefs and the morals of clergy and laity alike. The state regarded itself as under a duty to enforce obedience to the laws of God; and the ecclesiastical courts were the instruments through which the state acted. The result was "a system of moral government emanating from the episcopal order, and forming that part of the pastoral care, which is fully expressed in the Consecration Service, when the bishop promises that such as be unquiet, disobedient, and criminous within his diocese, he will correct and punish, according to such authority as he has by God's word, and as to him shall be committed by the ordinance of this realm."[2]

I shall divide the extensive jurisdiction thus exercised by the ecclesiastical courts into two heads : (*a*) offences against religion, and (*b*) offences against morals.

(*a*) Offences against religion.

Of such offences the most important is heresy. It was regarded as a species of high treason against the church. "A man who did not begin by admitting the king's right to obedience and loyalty, put himself out of the pale of the law. A man who did not believe in Christ or God put himself out of the pale of human society; and a man who on important subjects thought differently from the church, was on the high road to disbelief in Christ and in God, for belief in each depended ultimately upon belief in the testimony of the church."[3] The infrequency of heresy, down to the time of Wicklif and the Lollards, makes it somewhat uncertain in what manner the ecclesiastical courts could deal with it. The case of the deacon, who was burnt at Oxford because he apostatized for the love of a Jewess, is the only undoubted case mentioned in the older books.[4] But heresy was known on the Continent, and there is no doubt that the canon law distinctly laid it down that the penalty was death by burning.[5] It is to this rule of the canon law that Lyndwood

---

[1] Vol. iii 294-302.   [2] Hale, Precedents lvii.   [3] Stephen, H.C.L. ii 438.

[4] Maitland, Canon Law, 158-175; Bracton ff. 123 b, 124; Bracton explains that, as a rule, degradation is a sufficient punishment for the clerk; but if convicted of apostacy he must be burnt, "secundum quod accidit in concilio Oxoniensi celebrato a bonæ memoriæ S. Cantuariensi archiepiscopo, de quodam diacono qui se apostatavit pro quadam Judæa, qui cum esset per episcopum degradatus, statim fuit igni traditus per manum laicalem." Cp. Hale, P.C. i 394 for two other doubtful cases.

[5] Lyndwood 293 refers to a decree of Frederic II., which had been approved by the Pope, and incorporated into the Canon Law as c. 18 in Sexto, 5, 2.

refers as authority for the proposition that heretics must be burnt.[1] The accounts we have of the story of the deacon and the Jewess are too obscure to make it an authority for any distinct legal proposition.   But the case of Sawtre (1400) is a clear case in which the rule of the canon law was applied.   He was convicted of heresy before the Bishop of Norwich and recanted his heresy. He fell again into heresy, and was condemned by the archbishop and his provincial Council, as a relapsed heretic.   On this conviction the king issued a writ de hæretico comburendo.[2]

This case clearly shows that the common law recognized the rule of the canon law, and that therefore such a writ lay at common law.   It was not till a fortnight after this writ was issued that the statute of 1400[3] was passed with a view to strengthen the hands of the law in dealing with heresy.   That statute provided that persons "defamed or evidently suspected" of heresy should be detained in the bishop's prison till they abjured; and that if they declined to abjure, or relapsed, they should be burnt. By a later Act of 1414[4] all officials "having governance of people" were directed to take an oath to use their best endeavours to repress heresy.   They were to assist the ecclesiastical courts whenever required; and the justices of assize and the justices in quarter sessions were to receive indictments of heresy, and to deliver over the persons indicted to be tried by the ecclesiastical courts.   These statutes thus gave the clergy power to arrest and imprison by their own authority, and to requisition the aid of the civil power in so doing.[5]

Henry VIII.'s legislation necessitated some changes in the law relating to heresy.   By an Act of 1533[6] it was declared that speaking against the authority of the Pope, or against spiritual laws repugnant to the laws of the realm, should not be heresy. The Act of 1400 was repealed, and the bishops were thereby deprived of the power to arrest and imprison on suspicion.   The tourn and the leet, as well as the justices of assize and the quarter sessions, were given power to receive indictments of heresy.   Thus an accusation for heresy must, as a rule, begin by an indictment before some recognized temporal court.   The result was a great cessation in prosecutions for heresy.[7]   The

---

[1] At p. 293 sub voc. *pœnas in jure expressas*, "Sed hodie indistincte illi qui per judicem ecclesiasticum sunt damnati de Heresi, quales sunt pertinaces et relapsi, qui non petunt misericordiam ante sententiam, sunt damnandi ad mortem per sæculares potestates, et per eos debent comburi seu igne cremari, ut patet in constitutione Frederici quæ incipit *ut commissi* § *item mortis* . . . quæ sunt servandæ ut patet e. ti. *ut inquisitionis*."

[2] Stephen, H.C.L. ii 445-447; Maitland, Canon Law 176, 177.
[3] 2 Henry IV. c. 15.   [4] 2 Henry V. St. 1 c. 7.
[5] Stephen, H.C.L. ii 450.   [6] 25 Henry VIII. c. 14.
[7] Stephen, H.C.L. ii 455.

Act of the Six Articles[1] (1539) made the holding of certain opinions felony ; and it was provided that commissions should issue to the bishop and other persons to enquire into these offences four times a year.

In Edward VI.'s reign all the previous legislation touching heresy was repealed.[2] The common law was thus restored ; but the common law was the law settled by Sawtre's case. The result was curious. Persons might be and were in fact[3] burnt for heresy in a Protestant country by virtue of a rule of the common law which was derived directly from the papal canon law.

We have seen that Elizabeth's Act of Supremacy authorized the establishment of the court of High Commission for the trial of ecclesiastical offences.[4] But it considerably limited the powers of this court to declare opinions heretical.[5] If, however, a man was convicted of heresy by the court he might be burned according to the rule of the common law ; and heretics were burned in 1575 and 1612. In the latter case Coke's opinion was against the legality of the issue of the writ de hæretico comburendo, but four judges were against him.[6] In 1677[7] "all punishment of death in pursuance of any ecclesiastical censures " was abolished. But the Act contained a proviso that nothing in it shall " take away or abridge the jurisdiction of Protestant archbishops or bishops, or any other judges of any ecclesiastical courts, in cases of atheism, blasphemy, heresy, or schism, and other damnable doctrines and opinions, but that they may proceed to punish the same according to His Majesty's ecclesiastical laws, by excommunication, deprivation, degradation, and other ecclesiastical censures not extending to death." Many of these offences can now be punished in the temporal courts : but by virtue of this saving it is probably theoretically possible that persons guilty of such offences may be excommunicated, and imprisoned for six months by an ecclesiastical court. But the jurisdiction of these courts over these matters has fallen into disuse ; and reasoned arguments in support of heretical or even atheistical opinions is

---

[1] 31 Henry VIII. c. 14.　　　　　[2] 1 Edward VI. c. 12.

[3] In 1550, Joan Boucher was burnt as a heretic.

[4] 1 Elizabeth c. 1 § 8.

[5] § 20. They could adjudge nothing heresy but such as had been adjudged to be heresy " by the authority of the canonical scriptures, or by the first four general councils, or any of them, or by any other general council wherein the same was declared heresy by the express or plain words of the said canonical scriptures, or such as hereafter shall be . . . determined to be heresy by the High Court of Parliament of this realm with the assent of the Clergy in their Convocation ; " as Stephen says, H.C.L. ii 461, this meant that no one could be declared heretic, because of his views as to the Catholic and Protestant controversy, unless he was an anabaptist.

[6] 12 Co. Rep. 93 ; cp. Egerton Papers (C.S.) 446-447.

[7] 29 Charles II. c. 9.

now not only not a criminal offence, but is not even regarded as contrary to public policy.[1]

(*b*) Offences against morals.

The ecclesiastical courts exercised a wide disciplinary control over the moral life of the members of the church. The extracts published by Archdeacon Hale from the Act Books of six ecclesiastical courts between the years 1475 and 1640 illustrate the nature of this jurisdiction. The offences dealt with are varied and numerous. They comprise adultery, procuration, incontinency, incest, defamation, sorcery, witchcraft, misbehaviour in church, neglect to attend church, swearing, profaning the Sabbath, blasphemy, drunkenness, haunting taverns, heretical opinions, profaning the church, usury, ploughing up the church path.[2] The methods by which the ecclesiastical courts proceeded were well calculated to produce evidence of the commission of such offences. They might proceed: (1) By inquisition. In this case the judge was the accuser. He might proceed upon his own personal knowledge or on common fame. As a rule the apparitors or other officers supplied the information; and they used their powers in many cases in the most corrupt manner.

---

[1] Bowman v. Secular Society [1917] A.C. 406; above 595 n. 4; see vol. viii 402-420 for the history of the law on this topic.

[2] Cp. Chaucer's summary in the Friar's Tale :—

    " Whilom there was dwellyng in my countré
      An érchedeken, a man of gret degré,
      That boldely did execucioun,
      In punyschyng of fornicacioun,
      Of wicchecraft, and eek of bauderye,
      Of diffamacioun, and avoutrie,
      Of chirche-reves, and of testamentes,
      Of contractes, and of lak of sacramentes,
      And eek of many another maner crime,
      Which needith not to reherse at this tyme ;
      Of usur, and of symony also ;
      But certes lecchours did he grettest woo ;
      They schulde synge, if that they were hent ;
      And small tythers they were fouly schent,
      If eny persoun wold upon hem pleyne,
      Ther might astert him no pecunial péyne.
      For smale tythes and for smal offrynge,
      He made the people pitously to synge.
      For er the bisschop caught hem in his hook,
      They weren in the archedeknes book :
      And hadde thurgh his jurediccioun
      Power to have of hem correccioun.

In vol. xxv (11-56) of the Archælogia Cantiana there is an account of various presentments made between the reigns of Elizabeth and Anne in certain parishes in the Deanery of Westbere ; they are of the same general character as those collected by Hale; but the extracts after the Restoration deal as a rule simply with ecclesiastical matters ; see also R.H.S. Tr. 1907, 263 for some further illustrations from the diocese of Ely.

Chaucer probably represented the popular view when he makes the Friar say of the "sompnour"—

> " A sompnour is a renner up and doun
> With maundementz for fornicacioun,
> And is y-bete at every tounes ende."

Or (2) they might proceed on the accusation of some individual who was said to " promote the office of judge ". Or (3) they might proceed by Denunciation. In that case the person who gave the information was not the accuser, nor subject to the conditions attaching to this position.[1] This system was, as Stephen says, " in name as well as in fact an inquisition, differing from the Spanish Inquisition in the circumstances that it did not . . . employ torture, and that the bulk of the business of the courts was a comparatively unimportant kind ".[2] The number of cases tried show that up to 1640 the system was in full vigour. In the Archdeacon of London's court, between November 27, 1638, and November 28, 1640, there were thirty sittings and 2500 causes entered. If each person attended on two or three court days the number of persons prosecuted would be less than this. But the records show that 1800 people were before the court in that time, "three-fourths of whom, it may be calculated, were prosecuted for tippling during Divine Service, breaking the Sabbath, and non-observance of Saints' days." [3] It is not difficult to see why the Parliament in 1641 abolished the criminal jurisdiction of the ecclesiastical courts. A system which enabled ecclesiastical officials to enquire into the most private affairs of life upon any information was already out of date.

This jurisdiction was restored to the ecclesiastical courts in 1661 ; [4] and there is no legal reason why at the present day they should not try cases of adultery or fornication. But between the Restoration and the present day their jurisdiction has been much curtailed, and has finally altered its shape, not only because men's ideas upon methods of moral government have changed, but also because the state has interfered to punish offences which were once left to the ecclesiastical courts. In 1533 unnatural offences, and in 1541 witchcraft were made felonies.[5] In 1603 bigamy was made felony.[6] In 1823 jurisdiction in cases of perjury was taken away from the ecclesiastical courts.[7] In 1855 [8] suits for defamation, and in 1860 [9] suits against laymen for brawling in church were similarly removed. In 1908 certain forms of incest

---

[1] Hale, Precedents lvii, lviii ; see vol. v 170-176 for further information as to the criminal procedure of the canon law.

[2] H.C.L. ii 402.   [3] Hale, Precedents liv.   [4] 13 Charles II. St. 1 c. 12.
[5] 25 Henry VIII. c. 6; 33 Henry VIII. c. 8.
[6] 1 James I. c. 11.   [7] 4 George IV. c. 76.
[8] 18, 19 Victoria c. 41.   [9] 23, 24 Victoria c. 32.

were made misdemeanours.[1]   It was a principle laid down by
Coke, as an established maxim in law, "that where the common
or statute law giveth remedy in foro seculari (whether the matter
be temporal or spiritual), the conusance of that cause belongeth
to the king's temporal courts only ; unless the jurisdiction of the
spiritual courts be saved, or allowed by the same statute, to proceed according to the ecclesiastical laws."[2]   The result is that
while the jurisdiction of the ecclesiastical courts over certain kinds
of immorality still in theory remains, in practice these courts are
only called upon to act in the case of the clergy.   In this respect,
as we have seen, their jurisdiction has been improved.[3]   They
are no longer " courts of law having authority over the sins of
all the subjects of the realm."   They are " courts for enforcing
propriety of conduct upon the members of a particular profession."[4]

The ecclesiastical courts at one time claimed a species of corrective jurisdiction in all cases in which there had been *fidei læsio*.
This, if conceded, would have given them an extensive jurisdiction over contract.   But from Henry II.'s reign onwards the
temporal courts prohibited the ecclesiastical courts if they attempted to exercise this species of jurisdiction ; and after a
struggle the temporal courts prevailed.[5]

(2) Matrimonial and Testamentary causes.

(i) Matrimonial.

The ecclesiastical courts had, certainly from the twelfth
century, undisputed jurisdiction in matrimonial causes.   Questions
as to the celebration of marriage, as to the capacity of the parties
to marry, as to the legitimacy of the issue, as to the dissolution
of marriage, were decided by the ecclesiastical courts administering the canon law.[6]   The common form of the writ of prohibition
always alleged that the matter over which jurisdiction had been
assumed was neither matrimonial nor testamentary.[7]

[1] 8 Edward VII. c. 45.
[2] Co. Litt. 96 b ; cp. Phillimore v. Machon (1876) 1 P.D. 481.
[3] Above 611-614.   [4] Stephen, H.C.L. ii 437.
[5] Constitutions of Clarendon c. 15 ; Circumspecte Agatis 13 Edward I.; vol. ii
305 ; vol. iii 424.
[6] Glanvil vii 13, 14 ; P. and M. ii 365, 366 ; cp. Y.B. 12 Rich. II. 75 *per* Thirning,
J. ; but it should be noted that it was said in that case that a question of legitimacy
could be tried either by a jury or the bishop ; Charlton, C.J., said, ibid at p. 74,
" there is a great diversity in the case of bastardy, when one is party or where he
is not a party, and the reason is that where he is not party it will be tried by the inquest, because this is not peremptory, but in a case where he is a party, it will be
sent to the bishop, because this is peremptory, as well between privies of the blood
as strangers and all others."
[7] Bracton, f. 407 b.

The temporal courts had no doctrine of marriage. But questions as to the validity of marriage might come incidentally before them. Was a woman entitled to dower? Was the child of a marriage entitled to inherit English land? What if the parties, ignorant of any impediment, marry in good faith and have issue? What if the jurors in an assize find facts from which a marriage can be presumed? In answering some of these questions the temporal courts sometimes laid down rules about marriage which were at variance with the the rules of the canon law. The canon law laid it down clearly that mere consent—without any further ceremony, and without co-habitation—sufficed. The temporal courts laid more stress upon some ceremony, or some notorious act. The death-bed marriage was not regarded as sufficient to establish a claim to dower. A child, according to the rules of the canon law, could be legitimated per subsequens matrimonium; but it was not legitimate for the purpose of inheriting English land.[1] If the parties were ignorant of an impediment to the marriage, and later whether or not they were ignorant, the children were legitimate, if born before divorce,[2] or, later, if their parents were not divorced. For the purposes of an assize a de facto marriage would be recognized.[3] It was probably a consideration of some of these rules of the temporal courts, adjudicating on marriage, or rather on the reputation of marriage, for very special purposes, which led the House of Lords in 1843[4] to assert, in defiance of the canon law of the Middle Ages, that the presence of an ordained clergyman was necessary to constitute a valid marriage.

Over the law of divorce the ecclesiastical courts had complete control till 1857. This jurisdiction comprised suits for the restitution of conjugal rights, suits for nullity, either when the marriage was ab initio void, or when it was voidable, and suits for a divorce a mensa et thoro by reason of adultery or cruelty.

---

[1] Bracton, f. 417 b; Maitland, Canon Law 53-56. In Edward III.'s reign, " it appears that after the Statute of Merton (vol. ii 218 n. 1, 221) the question of bastardy was not referred to an ecclesiastical court, when it was admitted that the parents of the alleged bastard had been legally married, but it was denied that the child had been born in wedlock," Y.B. 11, 12 Ed. III. (R.S.) xxiii. The plea of special bastardy, i.e. the plea that the child was born before wedlock, was tried by the jury; but it was only available in a possessory action and not in a writ of right. In the latter writ only a plea of general bastardy, which was tried by the bishop was, as a rule, available, see Y.BB. 5 Ed. II. (S.S.) xxi-xxiv; 6, 7 Ed. II. (S.S.) xl-xliii; naturally the efforts of the common law courts both to uphold their doctrines as to who was legitimate for the purpose of inheritance, and to uphold this procedural rule, gave rise to some intricate law.

[2] For the evolution of the law on this topic see Y.B. 11, 12 Ed. II. (R.S.) xxxii.

[3] P. and M. ii 372-383.

[4] The Queen v. Millis, 10 Cl. and Fin. 534; Beamish v. Beamish, 9 H.L.C. 274; P. and M. ii 369, 370-372.

The ecclesiastical courts could pronounce a marriage void ab initio ; and in that case the parties were said to be divorced a vinculo matrimonii. But they had no power to pronounce a divorce a vinculo if there had been a valid marriage.[1]

For a short time after the Reformation the ecclesiastical courts seemed to have considered that they had this power.[2] But this opinion was overruled in 1602.[3] A valid marriage was therefore indissoluble, except with the aid of the legislature. At the end of the seventeenth century a practice sprang up of procuring divorces by private act of Parliament.[4] The bill was introduced into the House of Lords, who strictly examined the circumstances of the case. As conditions precedent it was necessary to have obtained a divorce a mensa et thoro from the ecclesiastical court, and to have recovered damages against the adulterer in an action at common law for criminal conversation.

This anomalous state of the law made divorce the privilege of the very rich, as Maule, J., forcibly pointed out in his address to a prisoner who had been convicted of bigamy, after his wife had committed adultery, and deserted him. " Prisoner at the bar," he said, " you have been convicted of the offence of bigamy, that is to say, of marrying a woman while you have a wife still alive, though it is true she has deserted you, and is still living in adultery with another man. You have, therefore, committed a crime against the laws of your country, and you have also acted under a very serious misapprehension of the course which you ought to have pursued. You should have gone to the ecclesiastical court and there obtained against your wife a decree a mensa et thoro. You should then have brought an action in the courts of common law and recovered, as no doubt you would have recovered, damages against your wife's paramour. Armed with these decrees you should have approached the legislature, and obtained an Act of Parliament, which would have rendered you free, and legally competent to marry the person whom you have taken on yourself to marry with no such sanction. It is

---

[1] Ecclesiastical Commission 1832, 43.

[2] Encyclopædia Britannica (10th Ed.) Tit. Divorce. In the Marquis of Northampton's Case (Ed. VI.) the delegates pronounced in favour of a second marriage after a decree of divorce a mensa et thoro ; and in the Reformatio Legum the power to grant a complete divorce was recommended ; some very loose ideas as to marriage and divorce were prevalent at this period—thus the Marquis of Northampton considered that the fact that his wife had committed adultery entitled him to marry again, Dasent ii 164.

[3] Foljambe's Case ; Porter's Case, 3 Cro. 461.

[4] 1669 Lord de Ross ; 1692 Duke of Norfolk ; see House of Lords MSS. 1699-1702 xli, xlii ; before 1715 only 5 such bills were known, between 1715 and 1775 there were 60, between 1775 and 1800 there were 74, between 1800 and 1850 there were 90 ; in 1690 a bill was passed to annul a marriage celebrated under duress, Hist. MSS. Com. Thirteenth Rep. App. Pt. V. 217 no. 361.

quite true that these proceedings would have cost you many hundreds of pounds, whereas you probably have not as many pence. But the law knows no distinction between rich and poor. The sentence of the court upon you therefore is that you be imprisoned for one day, which period has already been exceeded, as you have been in custody since the commencement of the assizes."

In 1857 all jurisdiction over divorce and over "all causes and suits and matters matrimonial" was taken from the ecclesiastical courts and vested in a court called the Divorce court.[1] The Lord Chancellor, the chief justices, and the senior puisne judges of the courts of common law, and the judge of the court of Probate were made the judges of the court; and the judge of the court of Probate was made the judge ordinary of the court.[2] In some cases he could sit alone, in others he must sit with one of the other judges of the court. When he sat alone there was an appeal to the full court.[3] An appeal to the House of Lords from decisions upon petitions for dissolution or nullity of marriage was provided in 1868.[4]

In this court was vested the jurisdiction and powers of the ecclesiastical courts, the powers of the legislature to grant an absolute divorce, and the powers of the common law courts to award damages in an action for criminal conversation.[5] The latter action was abolished.[6] In addition a wife deserted by her husband was enabled to apply to the magistrate for a protection order.[7]

The Act has been in the opinion of the person most qualified to judge a complete success. Sir Francis Jeune wrote,[8] "Probably few measures have been conceived with such consummate skill and knowledge, and few conducted through Parliament with such dexterity and determination. The leading opponent of the measure was Mr. Gladstone, backed by the zeal of the High Church party, and inspired by his own matchless subtlety and resource. But the contest proved to be unequal. After many debates, in which every line, almost every word, of the measure was hotly contested . . . it emerged substantially as it had been introduced. Not the least part of the merit and success of the Act of 1857 is due to the skill which, while effecting a great social change, did so with the smallest possible amount of innovation."

---

[1] 20, 21 Victoria c. 85.
[2] §§ 8 and 9.
[3] § 55.
[4] 31, 32 Victoria c. 77.
[5] 20, 21 Victoria c. 85 §§ 6, 7, 27, 31, 33.
[6] § 59.
[7] § 21.
[8] Encyclopædia Britannica (10th Ed.) loc. cit.

(ii) Testamentary.

The ecclesiastical courts obtained jurisdiction over grants of Probate and Administration, and, to a certain degree, over the conduct of the executor and the administrator. All these branches of their jurisdiction could be exercised only over personal estate. This abandonment of jurisdiction to the ecclesiastical courts has tended, more than any other single cause, to accentuate the difference between real and personal property; for even when the ecclesiastical courts had ceased to exercise some parts of this jurisdiction, the law which they had created was exercised by their successors.

(a) *Jurisdiction over grants of Probate.*

The origin of this jurisdiction is difficult to discover. Neither the civil nor the canon law sanctioned it ;[1] and we hear nothing of it in England in the twelfth century. Selden says "I could never see an express probate in any particular case older than about Henry III." [2] Testators rather sought the protection of the king or of some powerful individual ; and the effect might be somewhat similar to that of a grant of probate in later law.[3] But as early as the reign of Henry II. it is probable that jurisdiction in cases of disputed wills belonged to the ecclesiastical courts. Glanvil says definitely that this was the law in his day ;[4] and amid all the disputes of Henry II.'s reign, as to the limits of the jurisdiction of the ecclesiastical courts, no claim to exercise this species of jurisdiction was put forward by the king's courts.[5] Once admit that the ecclesiastical courts have jurisdiction to decide cases of disputed wills, and a jurisdiction to grant probate will soon follow. At the same time old ideas died hard. Some lords of manors successfully asserted the right to have all the wills of their tenants proved in their courts. Possibly in some cases this is a survival from the days when, probate in the technical sense being unknown, the protection of a lord was sought for a will ;[6] though in other cases it may, as Maitland suggests, have originated in later grants from the Pope.[7]

---

[1] Selden, Original of the Ecclesiastical Jurisdiction of Testaments, chap. i.
[2] Ibid, chap. vi ; cp. P. and M. ii 339.
[3] Selden, ibid, chap. v, cites a case in Saxon times in which a testator made three copies of his will ; one he kept ; another he handed to the Abbot of Ely, the chief beneficiary ; the third he gave to the alderman " et petiit ab illo ut suum testamentum stare concederet ; " ibid, chap. vii, there is a case of King John assenting to or licencing the will of a certain Oliver de Rocheford.
[4] " Placitum de testamentis coram judice ecclesiastico fieri debet," vii 8.
[5] Selden, Original, etc., chap. v.
[6] Britton i 75 does not mention this among the royal franchises.
[7] P. and M. ii 340. Alexander II. granted to the Cistercians in England the right to grant probate of the wills of their tenants and farmers, and in other cases

In a constitution made by Archbishop Stratford in 1380, the jurisdiction is said to belong to the church, "consensu regis et magnatum regis."[1] Lyndwood says, "de consuetudine tamen hæc approbatio in Anglia pertinent ad judices ecclesiasticos;"[2] and Selden considers that it rests upon immemorial custom—though he conjectures that it may have been handed over to the church by a Parliament of John's reign.[3] We shall see that this is more probably true of the jurisdiction over grants of administration to one who has died intestate. But the fact that about this time the ecclesiastical courts got jurisdiction over grants of administration, over legacies, and, in some cases, over debts due by or to a deceased testator, may have been decisive in favour of this closely allied branch of the same jurisdiction.

(b) Jurisdiction over distribution of intestates' goods and grants of Administration.

Probably jurisdiction over the distribution of intestates' goods belonged originally to the temporal courts.[4]

In Saxon times the kindred who inherit would seem to have been the persons who superintended the distribution of intestates' goods.[5] This is the arrangement which we find in Glanvil; and neither Walter de Mapes nor John of Salisbury mention this branch of the jurisdiction of the ecclesiastical courts, though they have much to say respecting them.[6]

A canon made at a Council held at St. Paul's before Othobon[7] (1268) speaks of "a provision made as to the goods of intestates which is said to have emanated from the prelates of the realm with the consent of the king and barons." In the opinion of Selden[8] and of Maitland[9] this refers to § 27 of Magna Carta, which provides that the goods of an intestate shall be distributed by the hands of his near relations and friends "per visum ecclesiæ salvis unicuique debitis."[10] This was the rule known to Bracton. "Ad ecclesiam et ad amicos pertinet executio bonorum."[11] A claim to superintend the distribution made by the kinsfolk will without much difficulty become a claim to administer; and the claim was here peculiarly strong. The man who dies intestate

this jurisdiction may be the result of mere usurpation; in 1342 Archp. Stratford complained of this; and this was not a single instance, Lyndwood 260, 263.

[1] Hensloe's Case (1600) 9 Co. Rep. 36; Lyndwood 176 sub voc. *ecclesiasticarum libertatum.*

[2] Ibid 174 sub voc. *approbatis.*

[3] Original, etc., chap. vi; cp. P. and M. ii 339 n. 4.

[4] Selden, Disposition of Intestates' Goods, chap. i; Dyke v. Walford (1846) 5 Moo. P.C. 434, 487.

[5] Charter of Henry I. § 7 (Sel. Ch. 101).

[6] Selden, Disposition, etc., chap. ii.

[7] John of Athona 122.

[8] Disposition, etc., chap. iii.

[9] P. and M. ii 358 n. 2.

[10] Magna Carta 1215.

[11] F. 60 b.

will probably have died unconfessed ;[1] and, unless the death was sudden,[2] there could be no sure and certain hope as to the state of such a person. The church should obviously see that the property, of which he might have disposed by will, is distributed for the good of his soul. Distribution by the kinsfolk "pro anima ejus" of Henry I.'s Charter ; distribution "per visum ecclesiæ" of Magna Carta ; actual administration by the Ordinary, perhaps mark the stages by which the ecclesiastical courts acquired jurisdiction. Up till Edward III.'s reign the court actually administered and made the distribution among those relatives of the deceased who were entitled. But its conduct was so negligent and even fraudulent that the legislature interfered.[3] The court was obliged to delegate its powers to administrators, whom it was obliged to appoint from among the relatives of the deceased.[4] Instead of distributing the estate the ecclesiastical courts merely granted administration. These administrators were by the statute assimilated in all respects to executors ; and so, like executors, they became the personal representatives of the deceased.

(c) Jurisdiction over the conduct of the executor and administrator.

In the thirteenth century the ecclesiastical courts obtained jurisdiction over legacies, and in certain cases over debts due to or by a testator.

According to the civil law the bishop had a concurrent jurisdiction with the lay courts over legacies left in pios usus ;[5] and there is a vague provision made by some Council of Mentz which seems to give the bishop an indefinite right of interference.[6] But in other countries this does not appear to have given to the ecclesiastical courts any jurisdiction beyond that over legacies left in pios usus. In Glanvil's time legacies could be recovered in the king's court ;[7] and Selden gives specimens of writs of the time of Henry III. ordering executors to fulfil the wills of their testators.[8] But it is possible that the royal courts assumed

---

[1] Bracton, f. 60 b ; P. and M. ii 355, 356.

[2] As to this see vol. iii 535.

[3] A constitution of Archp. Stratford in 1342 recites that the clergy as executors and administrators have converted goods to their own use, " in ecclesiarum fraudem seu damnum suorum creditorum liberorum et suarum uxorum qui et quæ quam de jure tam de consuetudine certum quotam dictorum bonorum habere deberet ; " cp. 13 Edward I. c. 19 ; Bl. Comm. ii 495.

[4] 31 Edward III. St. 1 c. 11 ; 21 Henry VIII. c. 5 ; vol. iii 566-571.

[5] Selden, Original, etc., chaps. iii and iv.

[6] Cited ibid, chap. iv, " Si heredes jussa testatoris non impleverint, ab episcopo loci illius omnis res quæ eis relicta est canonice interdicatur cum fructibus et cæteris emolumentis ut vota defuncti impleantur."

[7] vii 6, 7 ; xii 17.   [8] Original, etc., chap. vii.

jurisdiction in some of these cases for special reasons; and it is probable that, even in Henry II.'s reign, the ecclesiastical courts had a jurisdiction concurrent with that of the temporal courts. No writ of prohibition issued if a suit for legacies was begun in the ecclesiastical courts.   Selden said that he had seen none on the plea rolls of either Richard I., John, or Henry III.; [1] and both Bracton and Fleta state definitely that no prohibition lies in such a case.[2]   In 1230 it was decided that a legatee could not recover in the king's court, but must sue in the ecclesiastical court.   When the Ordinary was obliged by law to delegate its power over the goods of an intestate to an administrator, the ecclesiastical courts naturally assumed jurisdiction over the due distribution of the estate by the administrator.

These courts never possessed more than a limited jurisdiction over debts due to or by a testator; and that jurisdiction was effectively exercised only for a short time.   In the twelfth and thirteenth centuries the heir might sue and be sued on the debts of the deceased in the king's courts.[4]   But in the latter part of the thirteenth and in the fourteenth centuries the heir ceased to be able to sue for the debts of the deceased, and became liable to be sued only if the deceased had bound himself and his heirs to pay by instrument under seal.[5]   It was the executor or administrator who was allowed to sue or made liable to be sued upon debts due to or by the deceased; and, as the king's courts gave him rights of action, and in some cases made him liable to be sued, the ecclesiastical courts lost their jurisdiction in these cases.[6]   But, as the result of this development, the executor or administrator took the position of the personal representative of the deceased; and, in the Middle Ages, the ecclesiastical courts, by the control which they exercised over these personal representatives, assumed a general jurisdiction over the administration of the estate.[7]

This jurisdiction of the ecclesiastical courts was clearly the consequence of the jurisdiction over probate, legacies, and the administration of intestates' effects which they had been allowed to assume in the thirteenth century.   That they should have gained this jurisdiction about this time is not perhaps strange. As Selden points out,[8] the clergy played a part—perhaps the most important part—in the events which led to the passing of Magna Carta.   There were English precedents for the jurisdiction

---

[1] Original, etc., chap. viii.
[2] Bracton f. 407, " Item non locum habet prohibitio in causa testamentaria si catella legentur et inde agatur in foro ecclesiastico;" Fleta ii 57. 13.
[3] Bracton's Note Book, case 381.
[4] Vol. iii 5 574-576.   [5] Ibid.   [6] Ibid 576-583, 584-585.
[7] Ibid 591-595.   [8] Disposition, etc., chap. iv.

of the ecclesiastical courts—though not for their exclusive jurisdiction.   The only serious rival to these courts was the king's
court.   The judges of that court were generally clerics ; and they
acted loyally as temporal judges ;[1] but they cannot have been
altogether opposed to "arranging a concordat" with the ecclesiastical courts, which eventually gave those courts in England a
jurisdiction over matters testamentary larger than that possessed
by any other ecclesiastical courts in Europe.   For, as Lyndwood
says, this jurisdiction "de consuetudine Angliæ pertinet ad judices
ecclesiasticos . . . secus tamen est de jure communi."[2]

At the end of the mediæval period this extensive jurisdiction
of the ecclesiastical courts was beginning to decay ; and the decay
became rapid in the sixteenth and seventeenth centuries, because
their jurisdiction was attacked on two sides.   On the one hand
the jealousy of the common law courts so crippled their jurisdiction that they were unable to act effectively.[3]   On the other hand
the court of Chancery was able to supply their place.[4]   The
courts of common law, though they could cripple the jurisdiction
of the ecclesiastical courts, could not take their place, because
their procedure was not well fitted for the exercise of an administrative jurisdiction.[5]   On the other hand the procedure of the
court of Chancery was, as we have seen, well fitted to exercise
this jurisdiction.[6]   It was its procedure which made it possible
to conceive distinctly the complicated equities which arise in the
administration of an estate ; and so it is the rules evolved by that
court which have made our modern law on this subject.

The Statute of Distribution, it is true, attempted to strengthen
the jurisdiction of the ecclesiastical courts with a view to secure
the proper distribution of the effects of an intestate.   It enabled
the ecclesiastical courts to call administrators to account, and
gave the judge power to take bonds for this purpose.[7]   But the
superior procedure of the court of Chancery prevailed.[8]   The ecclesiastical courts in practice retained jurisdiction only over grants
of probate and administration.   When, in 1857, their jurisdiction
in matters testamentary was taken away, it was provided that the

---

[1] P. and M. i 111-113, 139.

[2] P. 170 sub voc. *insinuationem ;* by "de jure communi," Lyndwood means the
canon law—the common law of the church.

[3] Vol. iii 556-559.   [4] Vol. v 316-321.

[5] Vol. iii 591.   [6] Above 458-459.

[7] 22, 23 Charles II. c 10 §§ 1, 2, 3 ; see vol. iii 560-561.

[8] In Matthews v. Newby (1682) 1 Vern. 133 Lord North said that the ecclesiastical court had "but a lame jurisdiction."   Its jurisdiction was sometimes simply
disregarded ; thus in Bissell v. Axtell (1688) 2 Vern. 47, the Chancellor ordered a
fresh account to be taken of the intestate's personal estate, though one had already
been taken by the ecclesiastical court ; for the earlier history of the growth of this
jurisdiction see vol. v 316-321 ; vol. vi 652-657.

court of Probate then established should have no jurisdiction over legacies, or over suits for the distribution of residues.[1]

The Act of 1857 established a court of Probate, presided over by a single judge, to whom was given the rank and precedence of the puisne judges of the superior courts;[2] and it was provided that he should be the same person as the judge of the court of Admiralty.[3] He was given the jurisdiction to make grants of probate and administration formerly exercised by the ecclesiastical courts.[4] An appeal from his decision lay to the House of Lords.[5]

(3) Jurisdiction over matters of exclusively ecclesiastical cognizance.

The ecclesiastical courts still have jurisdiction over many matters of exclusively ecclesiastical cognizance, such as questions of doctrine and ritual, ordination, consecration, celebration of divine service, disputed applications for faculties.[6] They formerly had jurisdiction over many questions concerning ecclesiastical property such as tithes, church dues, and dilapidations; but recent statutes have much curtailed their jurisdiction over these matters.[7] Over one species of ecclesiastical property the temporal courts have always kept a firm hand. From Henry II.'s day the advowson has been regarded as real property, and subject to the jurisdiction of the temporal courts.[8] It would, however, appear from the Constitutions of Clarendon that Henry was at that time prepared to allow the ecclesiastical courts jurisdiction over property held in frankalmoin.[9] But in the thirteenth century this jurisdiction was denied to them. All questions relating to land, other than consecrated soil, became the subject of temporal jurisdiction, and subject to rules of temporal law.[10]

The process by which the ecclesiastical courts enforced obedience to their decrees was excommunication. It was to the spiritual courts what outlawry was to the temporal courts.[11] If the excommunicate did not submit within forty days, the ecclesiastical court signified this to the crown, and thereon a writ

---

[1] 20, 21 Victoria c. 77 § 23.　　　[2] Ibid §§ 4, 5, 8.
[3] § 10.　　　[4] § 4.　　　[5] § 39.
[6] Ecclesiastical Commission 1883, li.
[7] 6, 7 William IV. c. 71 (tithes); 31, 32 Victoria c. 109 (church-rates); 34, 35 Victoria c. 43 (dilapidations).
[8] Constitutions of Clarendon c. 1; vol. iii 138-143.
[9] c. 9; the assize utrum (App. II.) was provided to try the question whether or no the property was held by this tenure.
[10] P. and M. i 224-230.
[11] Thus an outlaw, like an excommunicate, could not be plaintiff; it was sufficient to plead his outlawry, Y.B. 20 Ed. III. i (R.S.) 430, or his excommunication, ibid 120.

de excommunicato capiendo[1] issued to the sheriff. He took
the offender and kept him in prison till he submitted. When he
submitted the bishop signified this, and a writ de excommunicato
deliberando issued.[2]

The temporal consequences of excommunication were serious.
The excommunicate could not do any act which was required to
be done by a probus et legalis homo. "An excommunicated
person," says Bracton,[3] "cannot do any legal act, so that he cannot act, or sue anyone, though he himself may be sued. . . .
And if he has obtained a writ it is not valid. For, except in
certain cases, it is not lawful either to pray or speak or eat with
an excommunicate either openly or secretly." He is a man
who has "a leprosy of the soul." The law was substantially
the same when Blackstone wrote. "He cannot," he says,
"serve upon juries, cannot be a witness in any court, and, which
is worst of all, cannot bring an action either real or personal, to
recover lands or money due to him."[4] It was, however, open to
the excommunicate to plead that he was only excommunicated
because he had refused to submit to the jurisdiction of the
ecclesiastical court in a case in which it had no jurisdiction, and
in which a writ of prohibition had been issued. In that case the
king's court would disregard the excommunication.[5] An Act of
Elizabeth's reign[6] required the cause of the excommunication
to be signified by the ecclesiastical court as well as the fact of
excommunication; and, if the king's court considered the cause
to be insufficient, it could quash the writ de excommunicato
capiendo and release the prisoner.[7]

The use of excommunication as part of the ordinary process
of the ecclesiastical courts was somewhat anomalous. "Excommunication," as Bacon said,[8] "is the greatest judgment upon the

---

[1] App. XVIII.; it was only the bishop's certificate which could be received as
evidence of an excommunication, The Eyre of Kent (S.S.) iii xxxii.

[2] It was apparently thought in 1313-1314 that if the bishop died the excommunication lapsed, The Eyre of Kent (S.S.) ii 185.

[3] "Excommunicato enim interdicitur omnis actus legitimus, ita quod agere non
potest, nec aliquem conveniri, licet ipsa ab aliis convenire. . . . Cum excommunicato autem nec orare, nec loqui, nec palam nec abscondite, nec vesci licet,
exceptis quibusdam personis." "Separatus est a communione gentium propter
lepram quæ est in anima," f. 426 b.

[4] Bl. Comm. iii 102.

[5] Bracton f. 426 b; cf. Y.B. 20 Ed. III. ii (R.S.) 214, seqq.

[6] 5 Elizabeth c. 23.

[7] "Before the 5 El. c. 23, this court could not discharge a man taken upon an
excommunicato capiendo, unless he was excommunicated pending a prohibition,"
per Gould, J., Rex v. Fowler (1701) 1 Ld. Raym. at p. 619; the proper remedy was
motion to quash the writ and not Habeas Corpus, ibid per Holt, C.J., differing from
the King v. Sneller (1681) 1 Eq. Cases Ab. 415. Note that in 1313-1314 Staunton,
J., thought that the cause of excommunication should be stated, The Eyre of Kent
(S.S.) iii 163, 164.

[8] Spedding, Letters and Life iii 121.

earth . . . ; and therefore for this to be used unreverently, and to be made an ordinary process to lackey up and down for fees, how can it be without derogation to God's honour, and making the power of the Keys contemptible." This view had been expressed by the House of Commons as early as 1584[1]; and an attempt was made in 1695-1696[2] to give effect to these suggestions, and substitute for it "some ordinary process;" but nothing was done till 1813. In 1812 the case of Mary Ann Dix —a woman not of age, who was imprisoned for two years on a writ de excommunicato capiendo for not paying costs in a suit for defamation—aroused the Legislature.[3] In the following year it was enacted that excommunication should cease to exist as part of the process of the ecclesiastical courts to enforce appearance, and as a punishment for contempt. The suggestion made in 1584 was adopted;[4] for the writ de excommunicato capiendo was substituted the writ de contumace capiendo;[5] and the rules applying to the older writ were made applicable to the new. Excommunication is still a punishment for offences of ecclesiastical cognizance; and, on a definitive sentence for such an offence, the writ de excommunicato capiendo can still issue; but it is provided that a person pronounced excommunicate shall not incur any civil penalty or incapacity, except such imprisonment (not exceeding six months) as the court pronouncing the excommunication may direct.[6]

---

[1] Strype, Whitgift, p. 70, cited Tanner, Tudor Constitutional Documents, 194.
[2] House of Lords MSS. 1695-1697 226, no. 1043.
[3] Memoirs of Sir Samuel Romilly, ii 233.
[4] Tanner, op. cit. 194. [5] 53 George III. c. 127 § 1. [6] § 3.

CHAPTER VIII

THE RECONSTRUCTION OF THE JUDICIAL SYSTEM

BAGEHOT[1] writing of the period of the Reform Act of 1832 said, "I am afraid the moral of those times is that these English qualities as a whole—merits and defects together—are better suited to an early age of politics than to a later. As long as materials are deficient, these qualities are most successful in hitting off simple expedients, in adapting old things to new uses, and in extending ancient customs; they are fit for instantaneous little creations, and admirable at bit by bit growth. But when, by the incessant application of centuries, these qualities have created an accumulated mass of complex institutions, they are apt to fail unless aided by others very different. The instantaneous origination of obvious expedients is of no use when the field is already covered with the heterogeneous growth of complex past expedients; bit by bit development is out of place unless you are sure which bit should, which bit should not, be developed; the extension of customs may easily mislead when there are so many customs; no immense and involved subject can be set right except by faculties which can grasp what is immense and scrutinize what is involved." These words might have been written of the judicial system of the country as it existed at the beginning of the nineteenth century. It was the result of "bit by bit growth." It was compounded in all its parts of a "heterogeneous growth of complex past expedients." Even before 1832 Bentham's teaching had begun to influence the legislature. After 1832 its influence was much increased; and law reform became the order of the day. Of the effects of his teaching upon the substantive rules of English law I shall speak in a later volume. Here I shall speak only of its effects upon the judicial system. Its effect, during the last sixty years of the nineteenth century, was at first a gradual reform and then an entire reconstruction of that system. It is with this process of reform and reconstruction that I shall deal briefly in this chapter under the following heads: the amalgamation of the

[1] Biographical Studies 284.

courts and their respective jurisdictions; the creation of a uniform code of procedure; the creation of a uniform official staff; and, the housing of the courts.

The Amalgamation of the Courts and their Respective Jurisdictions

One of the most inconvenient of all the anomalies which disfigured the English judicial system was the ill-defined and clashing jurisdictions of the various courts which administered the law.   Courts of common law and equity, the court of Admiralty, and the ecclesiastical courts administered separate bodies of law, with a separate procedure, and a separate vocabulary of technical terms.[1]   The limits of their jurisdiction were uncertain; and the suitor might in some cases pursue his way through the courts, to find, perhaps in the House of Lords, that he had from the first mistaken his court.[2]   In other cases concurrent proceedings on the same facts were possible.   Thus the limits of the jurisdictions of the courts of common law and the court of Admiralty were ill defined;[3] and the Judicature Commissioners stated that it happened "not infrequently" that simultaneous proceedings upon the same transaction were taken in these two courts.[4]   As they pointed out, this conflict was rendered the more perplexing by the fact that the final courts of appeal from these two sets of courts were different.[5]   But the most striking illustration of this anomaly was the almost complete separation existing between the courts of common law and equity.   It is the most striking illustration because the two sets of courts administered systems

---

[1] The Judicature Commission, Parlt. Papers, 1868-1869 vol. xxv, reported at p. 10, that "the present modes of procedure in the court of Chancery, the courts of Common Law, the court of Admiralty, and the courts of Probate and Divorce are in many respects different; the forms of pleading are different, the modes of trial and of taking evidence are different, the nomenclature is different, the same instrument being called by a different name in different courts; almost every step in the cause is different . . . nor is the difference due entirely to the different nature of the cases which the courts are called upon to try; for often the same question has to be tried, and the same remedy sought, by a totally different method, according as the proceeding is in the court of Chancery, the courts of Common Law, or the court of Admiralty."

[2] In Knight v. Marquis of Waterford (1844) 11 Cl. and Fin. 653, fourteen years of litigation merely resulted in the discovery by the House of Lords that the plaintiff had mistaken his remedy; see a similar case cited in A Century of Law Reform 208; and cp. Preface to 11 Hare's Reports xiv.

[3] "The court of Admiralty has jurisdiction over a claim for damage to cargo, when the owner is not domiciled in England, but it has no jurisdiction over the claim of the shipowner for freight due in respect of the same cargo. . . . In the same way the jurisdiction of the court of Admiralty over claims for necessaries supplied to a ship is restricted to the case of a foreign ship. . . . But if it happens that for some other cause the ship is under arrest . . . then the court can exercise jurisdiction over claims for building, equipping, or repairing the ship.   All these claims may at the same time be litigated by a different procedure in a court of common law," Parlt. Papers 1868-1869, vol. xxv 8.

[4] Ibid.   [5] Above 370-372, 524.

of law, which were not merely rival, but even directly contradictory. In 1768 Blackstone had noted this fact, and called it an extraordinary "solecism;"[1] and in 1834 Palgrave[2] had emphasized it. "It must," he said, " appear a singular anomaly to a foreigner, when he is informed that our English tribunals are marshalled into opposite, and even, hostile ranks : guided by maxims so discrepant, that the title which enables the suitor to obtain a decree without the slightest doubt or hesitation if he files a bill in equity, ensures a judgment against him should he appear as plaintiff in a declaration at common law. And exercising their respective jurisdictions by means of forms and pleadings, which have as little similarity as if they existed among nations whose laws and customs were wholly strange to each other." A cause set down for trial at common law might be stopped for two or three years by the issue of an injunction. It might well happen, that if the injunction were dissolved at the end of the period, the plaintiff's most important witnesses were dead or out of the kingdom. An action nearly completed might be stopped by the issue of an injunction, obtained for an insufficient answer to an intricate and voluminous bill, filed for the sole purpose of delay, and without merits either in law or equity.[3] As Bentham said, " A man who owes a sum of money which it is not agreeable to him to pay, fights a battle so long as he can on the ground of common law, and when he has no more ground to stand upon, he applies to a court of equity to stop the proceedings in the common law court, and the equity court stops them of course." [4]

During the first quarter of the nineteenth century the first steps towards reform were taken by the appointment of numerous commissions to enquire into the condition of the courts. The commission appointed to enquire into the work of the court of Chancery presented two reports in 1826[5] and 1828.[6] Between 1829 and 1834 a commission appointed to enquire into the practice and procedure of the courts of common law presented six reports.[7] In 1823 there was a report on the courts of the Archbishop of Canterbury,[8] in 1824 on the courts of the Bishop of

---

[1] "Sure there cannot be a greater solecism, than that in two sovereign independent courts, established in the same country, exercising concurrent jurisdiction, and over the same subject matter, there should exist in a single instance two different rules of property clashing with or contradicting each other," Comm. iii 441.

[2] The Council 1 : cp. Warren, Law Studies i 485, 486. See vol. xiii 132 seqq.

[3] Third Report of Commission appointed to enquire into the Courts of Common Law, Parlt. Papers 1831, vol. x p. 20.

[4] Rationale of Judicial Evidence, Works (Ed. Bowring) vii 493.

[5] Parlt. Papers 1826, vol. viii.   [6] Ibid 1828, vol. vii.

[7] Referred to above 131.   [8] Parlt. Papers 1823, vol. vii.

London,[1] and in 1832 on the ecclesiastical courts generally.[2] In 1824 there was a report on the court of Admiralty, of Delegates, and the Prize Jurisdiction of the Admiralty.[3] Legislation founded upon some of these reports effected something. But much remained to be done. In particular this legislation did nothing to remove the evils resulting from the entire separation of the courts which administered law from those which administered equity.

Though this anomaly had been pointed out by the common law commis ioners in 1831, it was not till some twenty years late: that any serious attempt was made to remove it. Another body of common law procedure commissioners reported in 1852-1853[4] that the powers and machinery of the courts of common law were insufficient to deal fully with matters falling within the scope of their own jurisdiction. For instance, parties were obliged to resort to a court of equity to compel the discovery of facts within the knowledge of the other party, or of documents, when they were ignorant in whose custody they were. Following the recommendations of the common law commissioners of 1831, they gave it as their opinion that, "every court ought to possess within itself the means of administering complete justice within the scope of its jurisdiction." To attain this object, it was proposed to give to the courts of common law a power to grant the specific performance of contracts by an extension of the writ of mandamus, and to give them the power to restrain threatened breaches of contract by an extension of the writ of prohibition. It was proposed that the right to a peremptory injunction should operate as a legal defence, and, generally, that the courts of common law should have the right to repel inequitable defences. On the other hand, it was proposed to give to the court of Chancery certain powers belonging to the courts of common law, and, in particular, to require it to decide all legal questions arising in the course of a case, without sending them to a court of common law for decision.[5]

Certain of these recommendations were carried out by the Common Law Procedure Act of 1854.[6] The effect of that Act is well summarized in the report of the Judicature Commission. "The Court of Chancery," said the commissioners, "is now not

---

[1] Parlt. Papers 1824, vol. ix.   [2] Referred to above 605, 611-612.
[3] Parlt. Papers 1824, vol. ix.

[4] Second Report of the Commissioners for enquiring into the practice and procedure of the Superior Courts of Common Law, Parlt. Papers 1852-1853, vol. xl pp. 34, 35, 38, 39; their first report was issued in 1851, Parlt. Papers 1851 xxii, and their third and final report in 1860, Parlt. Papers xxxi.

[5] Second Report, etc., 40-42; cp. Third Report of the Common Law Commissioners of 1831, Parlt. Papers x 74, 75.

[6] 17, 18 Victoria c. 125 §§ 68, 79, 83.

only empowered, but bound to decide for itself all questions of common law without having recourse as formerly to the aid of a Common Law Court. . . . The Court is further empowered to take evidence orally in open Court, and in certain cases to award damages for breaches of contract, or wrongs, as at common law; and trial by jury—the great distinguishing feature of the common law—has recently for the first time been introduced into the Court of Chancery. On the other hand, the Courts of Common Law are now authorized to compel discovery in all cases in which a court of Equity would have enforced it in a suit instituted for that purpose. A limited power has been conferred on Courts of Common Law to grant injunctions, and to allow equitable defences to be pleaded, and in certain cases to grant relief from forfeitures." [1]

The extent, however, to which the Common Law Procedure Acts had fused law and equity was slight. Practically the Acts only applied where a court of equity would have granted an absolute and perpetual injunction. In such a case the court of common law could give effect to the equitable defence without departing from the usual form of a common law judgment— "that the plaintiff take nothing by his writ, and that the defendant go thereof without day." But the common law courts could not give any effect to equitable defences in cases in which a court of equity would have granted only a temporary or conditional injunction. "We cannot," said Lord Campbell, "enter into equities and cross equities; we should often be without means to determine what are the fit conditions on which relief should be given; no power is conferred upon us to pronounce a conditional judgment; no process is provided by which we could enforce performance of the condition. There are no writs of execution against person or goods adapted to such a judgment." [2] It cannot therefore be said that the Acts in any way accomplished the ideal of the commissioners of 1831 or 1851. The courts of common law and equity did not possess within themselves the means of administering complete justice within the scope of their jurisdiction. Injunctions were still needed; and, in any case where a court of equity had concurrent jurisdiction, it might still use injunctions, as before, to stay proceedings at law. [3] It was said at the time that "the fusion of the several

---

[1] First Report of the Judicature Commission, Parlt. Papers 1868-1869, vol. xxv p. 6.

[2] Wodehouse v. Farebrother (1855) 5 E. and B. 277; see Mines Royal Societies v. Magnay (1854) 10 Exch. 495; Gorely v. Górely (1856) 1 H. and N. 144. Cp. Gee v. Smart (1857) 8 E. and B. 313; De Pothonier v. De Mattos (1858) 27 L.J. N.S. Q.B. 260, for cases in which an equitable plea was admitted.

[3] Brenan v. Preston (1853) 10 Hare 331.

jurisdictions had gone little further than to add to that which was artificial in the court of Chancery, the not less obscure technicalities which are peculiar to the courts of law ".[1]

The commissioners appointed in 1851 had proposed to go further in the direction of fusion. But the Chancery judges had opposed this proposal, unless it were made part of a larger scheme for remodelling the judicial system as a whole.[2] It was becoming more and more clear that this was the true solution. The passing of the Companies Acts, and the consequent rise of the limited company, enforced this truth. Directors of companies are both agents and trustees Simultaneous proceedings arising upon the same facts were, in fact, brought against them in the courts of common law and the courts of equity. If the scandal of conflicting decisions was to be avoided it was clear that there must be one supreme court administering both law and equity.[3] It was this expedient alone which could get rid of the separate modes of procedure and pleading which still prevailed in the courts of equity and common law, in the courts of Admiralty, Probate, and Divorce. These considerations induced the Judicature Commission to report in 1868 in favour of a complete fusion of jurisdiction and procedure. The result was the passing of the Judicature Acts, and the Appellate Jurisdiction Act, which have completely remodelled the form, the jurisdiction, and the procedure of the courts.

(1) The Judicature Acts.

The first Judicature Act was passed in 1873, and came into operation in 1875. By virtue of its provisions (as modified by later Acts) the court of Chancery, the courts of King's Bench, Common Pleas, and Exchequer, the court of Admiralty, the court of Probate, the Divorce court, and the London court of Bankruptcy were consolidated, and formed into one Supreme Court of Judicature in England.[4]

The Supreme Court of Judicature was then divided into two parts, (i) the High Court of Justice, (ii) the Court of Appeal.[5] Both these branches of the Supreme Court were constituted superior courts of record.[6] The clause of the Act of Settlement relating to the judges' tenure of office was re-enacted, and they

---

[1] 11 Hare's Reports, Preface xxix.
[2] Warren, Law Studies i 550-557.
[3] First Report of the Judicature Commission, Parlt. Papers 1868, vol. xxv 7.
[4] 36, 37 Victoria c. 66 § 3; by 38, 39 Victoria c. 77 § 9 the London Court of Bankruptcy was not to be merged in the Supreme Court; but it was again merged by 46, 47 Victoria c. 52 § 93.
[5] 36, 37 Victoria c. 66 § 4.　　　　　　　[6] §§ 16 and 18.

were incapacitated from sitting in the House of Commons.[1] It was provided that the judges of the High Court and the court of Appeal respectively should, without prejudice to existing rights, have similar privileges, and be subject to similar duties.[2]

(i) *The High Court of Justice.*

The existing judges of the court of Chancery, the courts of common law, the Probate and Divorce court, and the court of Admiralty were constituted judges of the High Court.[3] But it was provided that the Chancellor of the Exchequer and the Lord High Treasurer should no longer have the judicial powers which they might formerly have exercised in the court of Exchequer.[4] For the future any barrister of ten years' standing was qualified to be appointed a judge of the court.[5] The style of the judges is " Justices of the High Court."[6]

To the High Court was assigned the jurisdiction exercised by the following courts :—[7]

(1) The high court of Chancery as a common law court as well as a court of equity, including the jurisdiction of the Master of the Rolls as a judge or master of the court of Chancery, and any jurisdiction exercised by him in relation to the court of Chancery as a common law court ;

(2) The court of King's Bench ;

(3) The court of Common Pleas at Westminster ;

(4) The court of Exchequer as a court of Revenue as well as a common law court ;

(5) The High Court of Admiralty ;

(6) The court of Probate ;

(7) The court for Divorce and Matrimonial Causes ;

(8) The London court of Bankruptcy ;

(9) The court of Common Pleas at Lancaster ;

(10) The court of Pleas at Durham ;

(11) The courts created by Commissions of Assize, of Oyer and Terminer, and of Gaol Delivery, or any of such Commissions.

It was provided that the High Court should also hear appeals from petty and quarter sessions, and from the county courts.[8] The jurisdiction exercised by the court of Crown Cases

---

[1] 36, 37 Victoria c. 66 § 9 ; 38, 39 Victoria c. 77 § 5.
[2] 36, 37 Victoria c. 66 §§ 5 and 6.
[3] §§ 5 and 8.   [4] §§ 66 and 97.
[5] To be appointed President of the Probate, Divorce, and Admiralty Division the barrister must be of fifteen years' standing, 54, 55 Victoria c. 53 § 2.
[6] 40 Victoria c. 9 § 4 ; 44, 45 Victoria c. 68 § 8.
[7] 36, 37 Victoria c. 66 §§ 16 and 17.
[8] 36, 37 Victoria c. 66 § 45.

Reserved was vested in the judges of the High Court, or any five of them at least, of whom the Lord Chief Justice of England must be one.[1]

It was provided that in the High Court rules of law and equity should be administered concurrently;[2] and certain rules were laid down according to which this legal and equitable jurisdiction was to be administered.[3] Subject thereto it was provided generally that "in all matters, not hereinbefore particularly mentioned, in which there is any conflict or variance between the Rules of Equity, and the rules of the Common Law, with reference to the same matter, the Rules of Equity shall prevail."[4]

For the convenience of business (but not so as to prevent any judge of the court from sitting wherever required) the High Court was divided into the following divisions :[5] The Chancery Division ; the King's Bench Division ; the Common Pleas Division ; the Exchequer Division ; the Probate, Divorce, and Admiralty Division. It was provided generally that all causes and matters should be distributed among the several Divisions and judges of the High Court in such manner as might be determined by Rules of Court to be made under the authority of the Act.[6] Subject thereto there was assigned to the Chancery Division (1) all causes and matters which by any Act of Parliament were assigned to the court of Chancery ; (2) the administration of the estates of deceased persons ; (3) the dissolution of partnerships or the taking of partnership or other accounts ; (4) the redemption or foreclosure of mortgages ; (5) the raising of portions or other charges on land ; (6) the sale and distribution of the proceeds of property subject to any lien or charge ; (7) the execution of trusts charitable or private ; (8) the rectification or setting aside, or cancellation of deeds or other written instruments ; (9) the specific performance of contracts between vendors and purchasers of real estates, including contracts for leases ; (10) the petition for sale of real estates ; (11) the wardship of infants, and the care of infants' estates.[7] To the four other Divisions there was assigned the jurisdiction which belonged to the courts of King's Bench, Common Pleas, Exchequer, Probate, Divorce, and Admiralty before the passing of the Act.[8]

In pursuance of a statutory power[9] given to the crown, the

---

[1] § 47 ; 44, 45 Victoria c. 68 § 15 ; see above 217-218 for the court of Criminal Appeal which has superseded the court for Crown Cases Reserved.

[2] 36, 37 Victoria c. 66 § 24.

[3] § 25. [4] § 25, 11

[5] § 31 ; 47, 48 Victoria c. 61 §§ 5 and 6.

[6] 36, 37 Victoria c. 66 § 33. [7] Ibid § 34. [8] Ibid.

[9] 36, 37 Victoria c. 66 § 32 ; the Order in Council was made Dec. 16, 1880, and came into force Feb. 26, 1881.

King's Bench, Common Pleas and Exchequer Divisions were in 1881 merged in the King's Bench Division. The powers which belonged to the respective presidents of these Divisions were vested in the Lord Chief Justice of the King's Bench, who had, by a previous Act, been given the title of the Lord Chief Justice of England.[1]

As a general rule the jurisdiction of the High Court can be exercised by a single judge of the court.[2] Certain matters, however, must come before a Divisional Court. That is a court which is, as a general rule, composed of two of the judges of the High Court.[3] Instances of cases which must come before a Divisional Court are matters formerly heard by any of the common law courts in banc, appeals from quarter and petty sessions, and from other inferior courts of record.[4] Some difficulty has arisen in the case of appeals to the High Court from these inferior courts of record. The older method of appeal from these courts was the same as the method of appeal from any of the common law courts, i.e. by writ of error on the record, or on a bill of exceptions. We shall see that the Judicature Acts, and the orders and rules made thereunder have abolished proceedings in error in the case of appeals to the court of Appeal.[5] These Acts and Orders did not touch directly appeals to the King's Bench Division from inferior courts of record. But the Judicature Act of 1884 § 23 gave the court power to make rules for regulating appeals from courts inferior to the High Court. Under that Act an Order has been made which provides for an appeal by way of notice of motion. It has been held that this in effect substitutes an appeal by way of notice of motion for the old proceedings in error. But the Order changes only the procedure, not the substantive law. " All which was matter of substance in the old form is still a condition precedent to the new appeal. The misdirection must be of a character which could be the subject of a bill of exceptions, and the old authorities on that subject would apply." [6] As we shall see,[7] this is the only class of case in which this old learning has now any practical importance.

---

[1] 44, 45 Victoria c. 68 § 25 ; 36, 37 Victoria c. 66 § 5.
[2] Ibid § 39.
[3] § 40 ; 39, 40 Victoria c. 59 § 17 ; 47, 48 Victoria c. 61 § 4.
[4] 36, 37 Victoria c. 66 §§ 41 and 45.
[5] Below 643 ; thus the difficulty did not arise in the case of the Mayor's Court in London, because error lay originally to the Exchequer Chamber, and therefore the appeal now lies to the court of Appeal, Le Blanch v. Reuter's Telegram Co. (1876), 1 Ex. Div. 408.
[6] Darlow v. Shuttleworth [1902] 1 K.B. 724-734, 732.
[7] Below 643.

To supply the place of the courts held before the Justices of Assize it was provided that the crown by commission of Assize, or by any other commission, general, or special, might assign to any judge of the High Court, or to any of the other persons usually named in such commissions, the duty of trying cases within the places named in the commission.[1] Similarly it was provided that continuous sittings should be held throughout the year to try cases arising in Middlesex and London, by as many judges as the business to be disposed of might render necessary.[2] Persons acting under these commissions, or judges sitting to try cases arising in Middlesex and London, have all the powers of the High Court. They are to be "deemed to constitute a court of the said High Court of Justice."

(ii) *The Court of Appeal.*

The following persons were declared to be ex officio members of the court : The Lord Chancellor, the Master of the Rolls, the Lord Chief Justice of England, the President of the Probate, Divorce, and Admiralty Division, and any person who has held the office of Lord Chancellor, if, on the request of the Lord Chancellor, he consents to act.[3] The Appellate Jurisdiction Act of 1913 adds the Lords of Appeal in Ordinary as ex officio judges of the court.[4] The crown was empowered to create not more than five ordinary judges of the court of Appeal.[5] Persons qualified to be so appointed are barristers of not less than ten years' standing, persons qualified to be appointed Lords Justices of Appeal in Chancery, or persons who have held the office of Judge of the High Court for not less than one year. They are to be styled Lords Justices of Appeal.[6]

The following jurisdiction was given to the court of Appeal :—[7]

(1) The jurisdiction and powers of the Lord Chancellor and court of Appeal in Chancery, both as a court of Equity and as a court of Appeal in Bankruptcy.

(2) The jurisdiction and powers of the court of Exchequer Chamber ; together with jurisdiction to hear applications for a new trial or to set aside a verdict or judgment in the High Court.

---

[1] 36, 37 Victoria c. 66 § 29. [2] Ibid § 30.
[3] Ibid § 6 ; 44, 45 Victoria c. 68 §§ 2 and 4 ; 54, 55 Victoria c 53 § 1.
[4] 3, 4 George V. c. 21 § 2 ; for the Lords of Appeal in Ordinary see below 644.
[5] 36, 37 Victoria c. 66 § 6 ; 39, 40 Victoria c. 59 § 15 ; 44, 45 Victoria c. 68 § 3.
[6] 36, 37 Victoria c. 66 § 8 ; 40 Victoria c. 9 § 4 ; it is provided by 8 Edward VII. c. 51 § 6 that the Lord Chancellor may require any judge of the High Court to sit as an additional judge in the court of Appeal.
[7] 36, 37 Victoria c. 66 § 18 ; 53, 54 Victoria c. 44 § 1.

(3) The jurisdiction of the Privy Council in respect of Lunacy appeals, and appeals from the Instance jurisdiction of the Admiralty.

(4) The jurisdiction and powers of the court of Appeal in Chancery of the county Palatine of Lancaster, and the jurisdiction and powers of the Chancellor of the Duchy and county Palatine of Lancaster.

(5) The jurisdiction and powers of the court of the Lord Warden of the Stannaries.

We have seen that under the old practice at common law a suitor, if dissatisfied, might either (1) proceed by way of writ of error for errors on the record, or by writ of error on a bill of exceptions. If the court of error thought that there had been any misdirection, however trifling, it was bound to order a new trial. Or (2) he might move the court in banc for a new trial. From a refusal to grant a new trial there was no appeal.[1] We have seen that some small reforms were made by the Common Law Procedure Act.[2] But the old system was really incapable of reform. The only possible course was taken when the Judicature Acts swept away the whole of the common law procedure in error, and substituted for it the Chancery system of appeal by means of a rehearing of the case.[3] The Acts provide that all appeals from any final order, decree, or judgment shall be heard by not less than three judges of the court, unless the parties consent to a hearing before two judges. If the parties consent to such a hearing, and the two judges differ in opinion, the case must, on the application of either party, be reargued before three judges of the court before appeal to the House of Lords. Appeals upon any interlocutory order, decree, or judgment must be heard by not less than two judges.[4] Subject to these rules, the court may sit in two divisions at the same time.[5]

The Acts also provide that the jurisdiction in Lunacy, formerly vested in the Lords Justices of Appeal in Chancery, may be vested by the crown in any of the judges of the High Court or court of Appeal.[6] Such jurisdiction is now vested in the Lords Justices of the court of Appeal.

(2) The Appellate Jurisdiction Acts.

It was intended in 1873 to abolish the jurisdiction of the House of Lords as a final court of Appeal. If the Judicature

---

[1] Above 222-224, 225-226.   [2] Above 245-246.

[3] R.S.C. O. 58; First Report of the Judicature Commission, Parlt. Papers 1868-1869 vol. xxv 20-22; this applies to revenue cases, but only so far as is expressly provided by the rules, R.S.C. O. 68, rules 1 and 2.

[4] 38, 39 Victoria c. 77 § 12; 62, 63 Victoria c. 6.

[5] 38, 39 Victoria c. 77 § 12; now three divisions, 2 Edward VII. c. 31 § 1.

[6] 38, 39 Victoria c. 77 § 7.

Act of 1873 had been carried into effect as it was drawn and passed, the appellate jurisdiction of the House of Lords would have disappeared.[1] But the operation of the Act was suspended till 1875 ;[2] and it was then allowed to become operative without the clauses affecting the jurisdiction of the House of Lords. The Appellate Jurisdiction Act was passed in 1876.[3] It recognized and reformed the Appellate jurisdiction of the House of Lords ; and it provided a scheme by which the House of Lords and the Judicial Committee of the Privy Council—the two highest courts of Appeal in the British dominions—will eventually be, for the most part, composed of the same official members.

In order to increase the judicial strength of the House of Lords it was provided that the crown might appoint two persons to act as Lords of Appeal in Ordinary. They take rank and sit and vote as Barons during their life,[4] and they hold their offices on the same terms as the other judges. Any barrister in England or Ireland, or any advocate in Scotland of fifteen years' standing, or any person who has held high judicial office for two years, may be appointed.[5] In the hearing of Admiralty appeals the House may require the assistance of nautical assessors.[6] The House cannot hear any appeal unless not less than three of the following persons are present : The Lord Chancellor, the Lords of Appeal in Ordinary, or such peers of Parliament as are holding or have held high judicial office.[7] The House may sit to hear appeals during a prorogation ; and, if the crown by sign manual warrant so direct, during a dissolution of Parliament.[8]

Appeals lie to the House of Lords from the court of Appeal in England, and from any court in Scotland or Ireland from which error or appeal lay to the House of Lords immediately before the passing of the Appellate Jurisdiction Act.[9] The Act requires that, "every appeal shall be brought by way of petition to the House of Lords, praying that the matter of the order or judgment appealed against may be reviewed before His Majesty the King in his court in Parliament, in order that the said court may determine what of right, and according to the law and custom of this realm, ought to be done in the subject matter of such appeal."[10]

[1] 36, 37 Victoria c. 66 § 20.   [2] 38, 39 Victoria c. 77 § 2.
[3] 39, 40 Victoria c. 59.   [4] Ibid § 6 ; 50, 51 Victoria c. 70 § 2.
[5] Ibid § 25, and 50, 51 Victoria c. 70 § 5. High Judicial Office is defined to be one of the following offices : Lord Chancellor of Great Britain or Ireland, or member of the Judicial Committee of the Privy Council, or Lord of Appeal in Ordinary, or Judge of one of the superior courts of Great Britain or Ireland.
[6] 54, 55 Victoria c. 53 § 3.   [7] 39, 40 Victoria c. 59 § 5.
[8] Ibid §§ 8 and 9; 50, 51 Victoria c. 70 § 1, allows a Lord of Appeal to take his seat during a prorogation.
[9] 39, 40 Victoria c. 59 § 3.   [10] § 4.

In order to assimilate the official staff of the Judicial Committee with that of the House of Lords the Act provides that, "whenever any two of the paid judges of the Judicial Committee of the Privy Council have died or resigned, His Majesty may appoint a third Lord of Appeal in Ordinary . . . and on the death or resignation of the remaining two paid judges of the Judicial Committee of the Privy Council, His Majesty may appoint a fourth Lord of Appeal in Ordinary."[1] Inasmuch as the Lords Justices of Appeal and certain Colonial and Indian judges[2] who are members of the Privy Council, are members of the Judicial Committee,[3] the official staff of the two courts is not identical. But the most important members of the staff of the two courts are now identical.

The Creation of a Uniform Code of Procedure

At the beginning of the nineteenth century the procedure of the courts bore upon it the traces of all the varied epochs through which the law had passed in the course of its long history. Such mediæval processes as real actions, appeals of murder, deodands, trial by battle, and compurgation, though practically dead, were still legally possible. The devices of a later period in the history of the law had peopled the courts with legal fictions. The most famous of them—the casual ejector and John Doe and Richard Roe—still led an active and busy life. At common law the system of pleading too often effectually obscured the real merits of the case. "At a moment," said Bowen, L.J.,[4] "when the pecuniary enterprises of the kingdom were covering the world, when railways at home and steam upon the seas were creating everywhere new centres of industrial and commercial life, the common law courts of the realm seemed constantly occupied in the discussion of the merest legal conundrums which bore no relation to the merits of any controversies except those of pedants, and in the direction of a machinery that belonged already to the past." The procedure in the courts of equity suffered from different but no less fatal defects. Even Lord Eldon's commission could not deny the defects, though it attempted to assign

[1] 39, 40 Victoria c. 59 § 14; 3, 4 George V. c. 21 § 1 provides for the appointment of two more Lords of Appeal.

[2] 58, 59 Victoria c. 44; 8 Edward VII. c. 51 § 2; Colonial Judges of courts from which an appeal lies mediately or immediately to the Privy Council can be asked to attend the Judicial Committee as assessors, 8 Edward VII. c. 51 § 1.

[3] 44, 45 Victoria c. 3 ; above 518.

[4] Paper on the Administration of the law in the reign of Queen Victoria in " The Reign of Queen Victoria," edited by T. H. Ward, i 285, printed in Essays A.A.L.H. i 516; cp. A Century of Law Reform 209-221. The history of common law pleading and procedure will be given in vol. iii 597-656, and vol. ix 222-235 ; and the history of the equitable procedure in vol. ix 335-408.

them rather to the law than to the procedure of the court.[1] "A Bill in Chancery," said Bowen, L.J.,[2] "was a marvellous document which stated the plaintiff's case at full length and three times over. There was the first part in which the story was circumstantially set forth. Then came the part which 'charged' its truth against the defendant—or, in other words, which set it forth all over again in an aggrieved tone. Lastly came the interrogating part, which converted the original allegations into a chain of subtly framed enquiries addressed to the defendant, minutely dove-tailed, and circuitously arranged, so as to surround a slippery conscience and to stop up every earth.[3] No layman, however intelligent, could compose the 'answer' without professional aid. It was inevitably so elaborate and so long that the responsibility for the accuracy of the story shifted during its telling from the conscience of the defendant to that of his solicitor and counsel, and truth found no difficulty in disappearing during the operation." The system of equitable procedure might be well devised to secure complete justice in a world where considerations of time and cost could be disregarded—but in no other place. It is admitted that Dickens's pictures of Jarndyce v. Jarndyce and Bardell v. Pickwick, of Doctors' Commons and the Ecclesiastical Courts, of the beadle, the local justice, and the constable contain much real history.

Some attempts at reform were made in consequence of the reports of the various commissions which were issued during the first half of the nineteenth century. But it was not till the complete reconstruction effected by the Judicature Acts had been accomplished that complete reform was possible. As a necessary consequence of the changes made by the Judicature Acts, a simplified code of procedure adapted to all branches of the Supreme Court has been provided ; and the judges of that court have been given power to make such new rules as may from time to time be required.[4] So far as possible the strong points of the various systems of procedure in force in the various courts merged in the Supreme Court have been adopted.[5] The aim of the new code of procedure is to preserve so far as possible the advantages

---

[1] At p. 34 of the Report of 1826 it was said that "many suits owe their origin to, and many others are greatly protracted by questions arising from the niceties and subtleties of the law and practice of conveyancing."

[2] Administration of the Law, etc., 290, 291 ; cp. A Century of Law Reform 177-202, 221-227.

[3] If the questions were evaded the Bill might be amended till a plain answer was got ; this process was known as "scraping the defendant's conscience," ibid 186.

[4] 36, 37 Victoria c. 65 § 23 and Schedule of Rules ; 39, 40 Victoria c. 59 § 17 ; 44, 45 Victoria c. 68 § 19 ; 56, 57 Victoria c. 66 ; 57, 58 Victoria c. 16 § 4.

[5] See Phillimore, Eccl. Law, 956, 957, as to the contributions made by the procedure of the ecclesiastical courts.

of the old system of pleading without its rigidity. To ensure a clear statement of the issues of fact and law before the court, and yet to make it impossible that a suitor with a good case should lose his case merely by a fault in its statement. This aim has been in a great measure fulfilled. The distinguishing character- istic of older systems of procedure, and of procedure in England until the reforms of the nineteenth century, was that " one could say next to nothing about actions in general, while one could discourse at great length about the mode in which an action of this or that sort was to be pursued and defended." [1] Now we have a law about actions in general; and it can be said that "it is not possible for an honest litigant to be defeated by any mere technicality, any slip, any mistaken step in his litigation. . . . Law has ceased to be a scientific game, that may be won or lost by playing some particular move." [2] "I think," said Collins, M.R., in 1906, " that the relation of rules of practice to the work of justice is intended to be that of handmaid rather than mistress, and the court ought not to be so far bound and tied by rules, which are after all only intended as general rules of procedure, as to be compelled to do what will cause injustice in the particular case." [3] This sentence admirably expresses the new manner of regarding rules of procedure which has come with the reforms of the nineteenth century.

The Creation of a Uniform Official Staff

We have seen that the offices attached to the courts were nests of abuses and anomalies, because the courts, both of common law and of equity, had been staffed by a body of officials which had been gradually and silently evolved either by real necessity or by the desire to create patronage. [4] Payment by fees, saleable offices, and sinecure places were the predominant characteristics of a bureaucracy which could not be defended even upon historical grounds.

We have seen that extensive reforms had been made during the first half of the nineteenth century; and that the most crying abuses had been remedied. [5] But something more remained to be done to fit the offices of the courts to the reconstructed system inaugurated by the Judicature Acts. Thus just as the courts, and their jurisdiction, and procedure have been remodelled, so has the official staff attached to them. A commission appointed

---

[1] P. and M. ii 560.
[2] Bowen, L.J., Administration of the Law, etc., 310.
[3] In re Coles and Ravenshear [1907] 1 K.B. at p. 4.
[4] Above 246-262.   [5] Above 262-264.

to enquire into the administrative departments of the courts of Justice issued two reports in 1874, the second of which contains an elaborate history of these departments.[1] The commission recommended that one general department should be formed, in place of the separate departments formerly attached to the different courts. This recommendation was followed. An Act passed in 1879[2] established the Central Office of the Supreme Court, in which were merged the existing official staffs. This Act now regulates the duties and the tenure of these officials.

The Housing of the Courts

The housing and the position of the courts during the first half of the nineteenth century would have afforded a very fair index to the law which they administered, and the procedure which they employed. The English judicial system was perhaps the most completely centralized of any existing system. Yet, as late as 1860, the courts and the offices attached to the courts were scattered all over London.[3] The Rolls court was in Chancery Lane, and the other courts of equity were in Lincoln's Inn. The offices and chambers attached to these courts were scattered about among the adjoining lanes and inns. The courts of common law sat at Westminster Hall; but the judges' chambers were in the Rolls gardens. The Masters' offices of the Kings' Bench were in the Temple; those of the Common Pleas were in Serjeants' Inn and Chancery Lane; those of the Exchequer were in Stone Buildings, Lincoln's Inn. The judge of the Probate and Divorce court, having no court of his own, borrowed the Lord Chancellor's court in Westminster Hall; but his registrar's office and the depository of wills were at Doctors' Commons. The judge of the court of Admiralty was in the same destitute condition. He borrowed sometimes the Hall of the College of Advocates, sometimes the court of the Master of the Rolls at Westminster. The offices attached to his court were also at Doctors' Commons. The Lord Chancellor and the Lords Justices in Chancery sat in Lincoln's Inn Hall. In fact the head of the legal profession was really a tenant at will of the Benchers of Lincoln's Inn.

The law reforms of the century were fitly symbolized by the opening in 1884 of the new Royal Courts of Justice. All

---

[1] Parlt. Papers 1874, vol. xxiv.

[2] 42, 43 Victoria c. 78; cp. Covington v. Metropolitan Rly. [1903] 1 K.B. at p. 235.

[3] Report as to bringing the courts together into one place, Parlt. Papers 1860, vol. xxxi 89.

branches of the Supreme Court, and the offices connected with it, are now housed under one roof.

The nineteenth century has seen many acts which have codified branches of English law. A good codifying Act sifts the mass of material accumulated in the course of a long historical development, and restates, in clear propositions, the essence of the principles and rules concealed therein. The legislation described in this chapter may be said to have codified the English judicial system. Taking as its basis the courts which had for centuries administered, and by administering had created, the various branches of English law, it has rearranged them on a simpler plan. It has provided them with a uniform code of procedure, and an adequate official staff. Without sacrificing what was valuable in the forms and machinery of the past, it has provided a system suited to the needs of the present.

The history of the rise and growth and decay of the many various courts which have administered English law at various stages of its development, of their relations to one another, and of their several supplementary or competing spheres of jurisdiction, explains the form which the rules of English law have assumed. But many other influences have from time to time determined the contents of those rules. The contents of legal rules express, through the various agencies by which the law is made, the manner in which the community wishes that certain of the activities of its members shall be regulated ; they express its approbation or disapprobation of certain kinds of conduct ; and therefore they are affected by all those various elements which go to make up the public opinion of the community at any given epoch. It is true that these rules sometimes lag behind public opinion, and are occasionally in advance of it. But they are always tending sometimes more and sometimes less rapidly to reflect it. Thus a history of these rules cannot be made intelligible unless they are viewed in relation to the history of the views of the community upon all the topics which are touched upon by them ; for they are simply the technical reflection of those views, and give technical expression to them. Therefore in relating the history of these rules it will not be sufficient to look merely at the purely legal authorities for them—at the statutes, the cases, and the authoritative text-books. It will be necessary to look also at all the influences—political, religious, intellectual, social, and economic—which have at different periods determined the contents of the technical rules contained in the purely legal authorities. Told in this way the history of the development of legal rules is profitable not only to the lawyer, but also to all who are concerned with the many sides of the national life which are affected by them. An attempt to tell the story of the gradual and continuous evolution of the rules of English law on these lines is made in the ensuing Books of this History.

APPENDIX

I

The Grand Assize

Rex vicecomiti salutem. Prohibe N. ne teneat placitum in curia sua quod est inter M. et R. de una hida terræ in illa villa, quam idem R. clamat versus præfatum M. per breve meum nisi duellum inde vadiatum fuerit, quia M. qui tenens est, posuit se inde in assisam meam, et petit recognitionem fieri, quis eorum majus jus habeat in terra illa. Teste etc.

GLANVIL II. 8.

Rex vicecomiti salutem. Summone per bonos summonitores, quatuor legales milites de viseneto de Stoke quod sint ad clausum Paschæ, coram me vel Justitiis meis apud Westmonasterium ad eligendum super sacramentum suum xii legales milites de eodem viseneto, qui melius veritatem sciant, ad recognoscendum super sacramentum suum, utrum M. an R. majus jus habeat in una hida terræ in Stoke quam R. clamat versus M. per breve meum, et unde M., qui tenens est, posuit se in assisam meam et petit recognitionem fieri, quis eorum majus jus habeat in terra illa, et nomina eorum imbreviari facias. Et summone per bonos summonitores M. qui terram illam tenet, quod tunc sit ibi auditurus illam electionem, et habeas ibi summonitores etc. Teste etc.

GLANVIL II. 11.

II

The Assize Utrum

Rex vicecomiti salutem. Summone per bonos summonitores duodecim liberos et legales homines de visineto de illa villa quod sint coram me vel Justitiis meis eo die parati sacramento recognoscere, utrum una hida terræ quam N. persona ecclesiæ de illa villa clamat ad liberam Elemosinam ipsius ecclesiæ suæ versus R. in illa villa sit laicum fœdum ipsius R. an fœdum ecclesiasticum. Et interim terram illam videant et nomina eorum imbreviari facias. Et summone per bonos summonitores predictum R. qui terram illam tenet quod tunc sit ibi auditurus illam recognitionem. Et habeas ibi etc. Teste etc.

GLANVIL XIII. 24.

III

The Possessory Assizes

A. Novel Disseisin.

Rex vicecomiti salutem. Questus est mihi N. quod R. injuste et sine judicio disseisivit eum de libero tenemento suo in illa villa, post ultimam transfretationem meam in Normaniam. Et ideo tibi precipio quod si prefatus

651

N. fecerit te securum de clamore suo prosequendo tunc facias tenementum illud reseisiri de catallis quæ in eo capta fuerunt, et ipsum tenementum cum catallis esse facias in pace usque ad clausum Paschæ, et interim facias duodecim liberos et legales homines de visineto videre terram illam et nomina eorum imbreviari facias et summone illos per bonos summonitores quod tunc sint coram me vel Justitiis meis parati inde facere recognitionem. Et pone per vadium et salvos pledgios predictum R. vel ballivum suum si ipse non fuerit inventus, quod tunc sit ibi auditurus illam recognitionem. Et habeas ibi etc. Teste etc. GLANVIL XIII. 33.

B. Morte D'Ancestor.

Rex vicecomiti salutem. Si G. filius T. fecerit te securum de clamore suo prosequendo tunc summone per bonos summonitores duodecim liberos et legales homines de visineto de illa villa quod sint coram me vel Justitiis meis eo die parati sacramento recognoscere si T. pater predicti G. fuit seisitus in dominico suo sicut de fœdo suo de una virgata terræ in illa villa die qua obiit, si obiit post primam coronationem meam, et si ille G. propinquior heres ejus est, et interim terram illam videant, et nomina eorum imbreviari facias, etc. Summone per bonos summonitores R. qui terram illam tenet, quod tunc sit ibi auditurus illam recognitionem. Et habeas ibi summonitores etc. Teste etc. GLANVIL XIII. 3.

C. Darrein Presentment.

Rex vicecomiti salutem. Summone per bonos summonitores duodecim liberos et legales homines de visineto de villa illa quod sint coram me vel Justitiis meis. eo die parati sacramento recognoscere quis advocatus presentavit ultimam personam, qui obiit, ad ecclesiam de illa villa quæ vacans est, ut dicitur ; et unde N. clamat advocationem, et nomina eorum imbreviari facias. Et summone per bonos summonitores R. qui presentationem ipsam deforciat, quod tunc sit ibi auditurus illam recognitionem, et habeas etc. Teste etc. GLANVIL XIII. 19

IV

WRIT OF DEBT

Rex vicecomiti salutem. Præcipe N. quod juste et sine dilatione reddet R. centum marcas quas ei debet ut dicit ; et unde queritur quod ipse ei injuste deforciat, et nisi fecerit summone eum per bonos summonitores quod sit coram me vel Justitiis meis apud Westmonasterium a clauso Paschæ in quindecim dies, ostensurus quare non fecerit. Et habeas ibi summonitores et hoc breve. Teste etc. GLANVIL X. 2.

V

WRITS OF RIGHT

A. To the Sheriff.

Rex vicecomiti salutem. Præcipe A. quod juste et sine dilatione reddet B. unam hidam terræ in villa illa unde idem B. queritur quod prædictus A. ei deforciat, et nisi fecerit summone eum per bonos summonitores quod sit ibi coram me vel Justitiis meis in crastino post octabis clausi Paschæ apud locum illum, ostensurus quare non fecerit. Et habeas ibi summonitores et hoc breve. Teste etc. GLANVIL I. 6

APPENDIX

 653

B. To the Lord of the Land.

George II. by the grace of God of Great Britain, France, and Ireland, king, etc., to Willoughby earl of Abingdon greeting. We command you that without delay you hold full right to William Kent esquire, of one messuage and twenty acres of land with the appurtenances in Dorchester, which he claims to hold of you by the free service of one penny yearly in lieu of all services, of which Richard Allan deforces him. And unless you so do let the sheriff of Oxfordshire do it, that we no longer hear complaint thereof for defect of right. Witness etc.   BL. COMM. III. App. no. 1 § 1.

C. To the Sheriff Quia Dominus Remisit Curiam.

George II. by the grace of God etc. to the sheriff of Oxfordshire greeting. Command William Allan that he justly and without delay render unto William Kent one messuage and twenty acres of land with the appurtenances in Dorchester, which he claims to be his right and inheritance, and whereupon he complains that the aforesaid Richard unjustly deforces him. And unless he shall so do, and if the said William shall give you security of prosecuting his claim, then summon by good summoners the said Richard that he appear before our Justices at Westminster on the morrow of All Souls to show wherefore he hath not done it. Witness ourself etc. Because Willoughby earl of Abingdon, the chief lord of that fee, hath thereupon remised unto us his court.   BL. COMM. III. App. no. 1 § 4.

VI

JUSTICIES

Rex vicecomiti salutem. Præcipio tibi quod Justicies N. quod juste et sine dilatione faciat R. consuetudines et recta servitia quæ ei facere debet de tenemento suo quod de eo tenet in illa villa sicut rationabiliter monstrare poterit eum sibi deberi, ne oporteat eum amplius inde conqueri pro defectu recti. Teste etc.   GLANVIL IX. 9.

VII

PONE

Rex vicecomiti salutem. Pone coram me vel Justitiis meis die illo loquelam quæ est in comitatu tuo inter A. et N. de una hida terræ in illa villa quam ipsa A. clamat versus predictum N. ad rationabilem dotem suam. Et summone per bonos summonitores predictum N., qui terram illam tenet, quod tunc sit ibi cum loquela sua. Et habeas ibi etc. Teste etc.   GLANVIL VI. 7.

VIII

TOLT

Charles Morton Esquire sheriff of Oxfordshire to John Long bailiff errant of our lord the king and of myself greeting. Because by the complaint of William Kent Esquire personally present at my county court, to wit, on Monday the 6th day of September in the thirtieth year of the reign of our lord George the second by the grace of God etc., at Oxford in the shire house there holden, I am informed, that although he himself by the writ of our said Lord the King of right patent directed to Willoughby earl of Abingdon, for this that he should hold full right to the said William Kent of one messuage and twenty acres of land with the appurtenances in Dorchester within my said county, of which Richard Allan deforces him, hath been brought to the said Willoughby earl of Abingdon; yet for that the said Willoughby earl of Abingdon favoureth the said Richard Allan in this part, and hath hitherto delayed to do full right according to the exigence of the said writ, I command you on the part of our said lord the king, firmly enjoining, that in your proper person you go to the court baron of the said Willoughby earl of Abingdon at Dorchester aforesaid, and take away the plaint, which there is between the said William Kent and Richard Allan by the said writ, into my county court to be next holden, and summon by good summoners the said Richard Allan, that he be at my county court on Monday the fourth day of October next coming at Oxford in the shire house there to be holden, to answer to the said William Kent therof. And have you there then the said plaint, the summoners, and this precept. Given in my county court at Oxford in the shire-house, the sixth day of September, in the year aforesaid.

BL COMM. III. App no. 1 § 2.

IX

FALSE JUDGMENT

A. From the County Court.

Henricus etc. vicecomiti salutem. Si A. te fecerit securum de clamore suo prosequendo tunc in pleno Comitatu tuo recordum facias loquelam quæ est in eodem Comitatu per breve nostrum de recto inter A. petentem et B. tenentem de uno mesuagio et centum acris terræ cum pertinentiis in C. unde idem A. queritur falsum sibi factum fuisse judicium in eodem Comitatu; et recordum illud habeas coram Justitiis nostris apud Westmonasterium tali die sub sigillo tuo, et per quatuor legales milites ejusdem Comitatus ex illis qui Recordo illi interfuerunt; et summone per bonos summonitores prœdictum B. quod tunc sit ibi auditurus Recordum illud; et habeas ibi summonitores, nomina quatuor militum, et hoc breve.   F.N.B. 18 B.

B. From the Court Baron—Accedas ad curiam.

Rex vicecomiti salutem. Si A. fecerit te securum de clamore suo prose-quendo, tunc assumptis tecum quatuor discretis et legalibus Militibus de Comitatu tuo, in propria persona tua accedas ad curiam B. de C. et in plena curia illa recordum facias loquelam quæ fuit in eadem curia per breve nostrum de recto inter A. petentem et B. tenentem de uno mesuagio etc. Unde A. queritur falsum sibi factum fuisse judicium in eadem curia; et recordum illud habeas coram Justitiis nostris apud Westmonasterium tali die sub sigillo tuo, per quatuor legales homines ejusdem curiæ ex illis qui Recordo illi inter-fuerunt; et summone etc. [as in A.] et habeas ibi nomina prædictorum quatuor hominum et hoc breve.   F.N.B. 18 D.

X

WRIT OF ERROR

A. To remove a case into the King's Bench.

George II. by the Grace of God etc. To our trusty and beloved Sir John Willes knight greeting. Because in the record and process, and also in the giving of judgment, of the plaint which was in our court before you and your fellows our Justices of the bench, by our writ between William Burton gentleman and Charles Long late of Burford in the county of Oxford gentle-man, of a certain debt of Two hundred pounds, which the said William de-

mands of the said Charles, manifest error hath intervened, to the great damage
of him the said William, as we from his complaint are informed : we, being
willing that the error if any there be, should be corrected in due manner, and
that full and speedy justice should be done to the parties aforesaid in this
behalf, do command you, that, if judgment thereof be given, then under your
seal you do distinctly and openly send the record and process of the plaint
aforesaid, with all things concerning them, and this writ ; so that we may
have them from the day of Easter in fifteen days, wheresoever we shall then
be in England : that the record and process aforesaid being inspected, we
may cause to be done thereupon, for correcting that error, what of right and
according to the law and custom of our realm of England ought to be done.
Witness etc.   BL. COMM. III. App. no. 3 § 6.

B. To remove a case from the King's Bench into Parliament.

Rex etc. dilecto et fideli nostro W. S. Militi, Capitali Justitio nostro ad
placita coram nobis tenenda assignato, salutem. Quia in Recordo et Processu, ac etiam in reversatione et revocatione judicii in Curia nostra coram
nobis de querela et judicio in Curia nostra de Banco coram F.N milite et
sociis suis Justitiis nostris de Banco, per breve nostrum inter J. S. et E. B.
de placito Transgressionis et Ejectionis firmæ eidem J. per præfatum E. fieri
suppositi, unde in eadem Curia nostra de Banco consideratum fuit quod
prædictus J. nihil caperet per breve suum prædictum, sed esset in misericordia pro falso clamore suo inde, et quod idem E. iret sinè die. Necnon in
redditione Judicii pro eodem J. in Curia nostra coram vobis versus eundem
E super revocationem judicii prædicti ut dicitur error intervenit manifestus
ad grave damnum ipsius E. sicut ex querela sua accepimus. Nos errorem
si quis fuit modo debito corrigi et partibus prædictis plenam et celerem
Justitiam fieri volentes in hac parte, vobis mandamus, quod si Judicium prædictum in Curia nostra de Banco prædicto, ut præfertur, redditum, in Curia
nostra coram nobis revocatum et adnullatum existit, tunc Recordum et Processus judicii prædicti in revocationem ejusdem cum omnibus ea tangentibus
in præsens Parliamentum nostrum distincte et aperte sine dilatione mittatis,
et hoc breve, ut, inspectis recordo et processu prædictis ulterius inde de
assensu Dominorum Spiritualium et temporalium in eodem Parliamento ex-
istentium pro errore illo corrigendo fieri faciamus quod de Jure et secundum
legem et consuetudinem Regni nostri Angliæ fuerit faciendum. Teste etc.
                         REGISTER (4th Ed. 1687) App. 38.

XI

SCIRE FACIAS

A. Rex vicecomiti salutem. Cum I. filius C. primo die Julii anno regni
domini E. nuper regis avi nostri decimo in cancellaria sua recognoverit se
debere B. et D. £20 unde eis solvisse debuit in festo Natalis domini tunc
proximo futuro 100/- et in festo tali 100/- et in festo tali tunc proxime sequenti
£10, sicut per inspectionem rotulorum cancellariæ dicti avi nostri nobis con-
stat, et eas ei nondum solvit, ut dicitur, ac iidem B. et D. juxta statutum inde
editum elegerint sibi liberari pro prædictis viginti libris omnia catalla et
medietatem terræ ipsius I. filii C. tenendam juxta formam statuti prædicti :
Tibi præcipimus quod scire facias præfato I. filio C. quod sit in cancellaria
nostra tali die ubicumque fuerimus in Anglia, ad ostendendum si quid pro se
habeat vel dicere sciat quare omnia catalla sua et medietas terræ suæ præfatis
B. et D., vel eorum alteri, pro prædictis viginti libris liberari non debeant,
juxta formam statuti prædicti. Et habeas ibi nomina illorum per quos ei scire
feceris et hoc breve. Teste etc. REGISTER (4th Ed. 1687) 298 b, 299.

B. Rex vicecomiti salutem. Cum P. in curia domini Edwardi nuper regis Angliæ patris nostri coram justiticariis nostris apud Westmonasterium, per considerationem ejusdem curiæ nostræ recuperasset versus T. £20 et etiam 20/- pro damnis suis quæ habuit occasione detentionis debiti prædicti : Prædictus T. prædictas viginti libras eidem P. nondum reddidit, prout ex gravi querela ipsius P. accepimus. Et quia volumus ea quæ in curia prædicti patris nostri rite acta sunt debitæ executioni demandari : Tibi præcipimus quod per probos etc. scire facias prædicto T. quod sit coram nobis ubicumque fuerimus in Anglia ostensurus, si quid pro se habeat vel dicere sciat, quare prædictæ viginti libræ et etiam prædicti viginti solidi de terris et catallis suis in balliva tua fieri, et prædicto P. reddi, non debeant, si sibi viderit expedire. Et habeas etc. [as in A.]. Teste etc.

REGISTRUM JUDICIALE 12.

XII

A. PROHIBITION

(1) *To the Ecclesiastical Court.*

Rex judicibus illis ecclesiasticis salutem. Indicavit nobis R. quod cum I. clericus suus teneat ecclesiam illam in illa villa per suam presentationem, quæ de sua advocatione est, ut dicitur, N. clericus eandem petens ex advocatione M. militis, ipsum I. coram vobis in curia Christianitatis inde trahit in placitum. Si vero prefatus N. ecclesiam illam diracionaret ex advocatione predicti M., palam est quod jam dictus R. jacturam inde incurreret de advocatione sua. Et quoniam lites de advocationibus ecclesiarum ad coronam et dignitatem meam pertinent, vobis prohibeo ne in causam illam procedatis donec diracionatum fuerit in curia mea ad quem illorum advocatio illius ecclesiæ pertineat. Teste etc. GLANVIL IV. 13.

Writ to the sheriff if the foregoing be disobeyed.

Rex vicecomiti salutem. Prohibe judicibus illis ne teneant placitum in curia Christianitatis de advocatione illius ecclesiæ, unde R. advocatus illius ecclesiæ queritur quod N. inde eum trahit in placitum in curia Christianitatis quia placita de advocationibus ecclesiarum ad coronam et dignitatem meam pertinent. Et summone per bonos summonitores ipsos Judices quod sint coram me vel Justitiis meis eo die ostensuri quare placitum id tenuerunt contra dignitatem meam in curia Christianitatis. Summone etiam per bonos summonitores prefatum N. quod tunc sit ibi ostensurus quare prefatum R. inde traxerit in placitum in curia Christianitatis. Et habeas ibi etc. Teste etc.

GLANVIL IV. 14.

(2) *To the Court of Admiralty.*

Edwardus sextus dei gracia Anglie Francie et Hibernie Rex fidei defensor et in terra Ecclesie Anglicane et Hibernice supremum caput, Griffino Leson legum doctori commissario curie admirallitatis et deputato nobilis et prepotentis viri domini Thome Seymer preclari ordinis garterii militis domini Seymour de Sudley magni Admiralli Anglie Hibernie Wallie Calicie et Bolonie et marchiarum eorundem Normanie Gasconie Acquitanie alio-ve judici in hac parte competenti cuicumque, Salutem. Ostensum est nobis nuper in curia nostra coram nobis ex gravi querela Thome Spycer Thome Mannyng Johannis Edmonds Roberti Edmonds Johannis Marrett Walteri Edde Johannis Johnson Johannis Hynd Johannis Buckytt et Willielmi Baynard quod cum in statuto in parliamento domini Ricardi nuper Regis Anglie secundi post conquestum apud Westmonasterium anno regni sui tertio-

decimo edito inter cetera contineatur quod Admiralli et eorum deputati se de
aliqua re infra regnum Anglie facta nisi solummodo de re super mare facta
prout tempore domini Edwardi nuper regis Anglie progenitoris nostri debite
usum fuerat nullatenus intromitterent; Cumque eciam in parliamento dicti
domini Ricardi apud Westmonasterium anno regni sui quintodecimo tento
inter cetera declaratum ordinatum et stabilitum existit quod de omnibus contractibus placitis et querelis ac de omnibus aliis rebus factis sive emergentibus
infra corpus comitatus tam per terram quam per aquam ac eciam de wrecco
maris curia Admiralli nullam habeat cognicionem potestatem nec jurisdiccionem sed sint omnia hujusmodi contractus placita et querele ac omnia alia
emergentia infra corpora comitatuum tam per terram quam per aquam (ut
predictum est) ac eciam wreccum maris triata terminata discussa et remediata
per leges terre et non coram Admirallo nec per Admirallum nec ejus locum
tenentem quovismodo; Quidam tamen Edwardus Cleyton firmarius serenis-
sime domine Anne de Cleva domine et (ut asserit) proprietarie tam dominii de
Boyton in comitatu Suffolcie ac cujusdam rivuli fluvialis fluminis-ve et aque
sive crece maris juxta Boyton predictam existentis, statuta et leges predicta
minime ponderans nec verens, sed contra eadem machinans, dictos Thomam
Thomam Johannem Robertum Johannem Walterum Johannem Johannem
Johannem et Willielmum contra debitam legis regni nostri Anglie formam, et
contra vim formam tenorem et effectum statutorum illorum indebite pergravare
opprimere et fatigare ipsos Thomam Thomam Johannem Robertum Johannem
Walterum Johannem Johannem Johannem et Willielmum in curia admirallitatis coram vobis apud Suthwerck in comitatu Surreie, asserendo et libellando
de et pro eo quod predicti Thomas Thomas Johannes Robertus Johannes
Walterus Johannes Johannes Johannes et Willielmus mensibus Marcii Aprilis
Maii Junii Julii Augustii Septembris Octobris Novembris Decembris
Januarii Februarii et Marcii anno domini millesimo quingentesimo quadra-
gesimo sexto eorum-ve mensium, quolibet pluribus sive aliquo, cum eorum
cimbis rethibusque et aliis piscium capiendorum instrumentis suis in dicto
rivulo flumine aqua sive creca (supponendo ut supradictum est dictam
dominam Annam esse proprietariam rivuli sive aque illius) absque licentia
dicte domine Anne, aut firmarii sui, antedicti piscati fuerant ac pisces inde
ad valenciam sexaginta librarum ceperant et habuerant, caute et subdole
libellando quod rivulus flumen aqua sive creca predicta infra fluxum et refluxum maris ac infra jurisdiccionem marittimam curie Admirallitatis pre-
dicte fore, ubi revera rivulus flumen aqua sive creca illa infra corpus comitatus
Suffolcie et extra jurisdiccionem Admirallitatis existit, traxit in placitum Ac
ipsos Thomam Thomam Johannem Robertum Johannem Walterum Johannem
Johannem Johannem et Willielmum in curia Admirallitatis antedicte com-
parere ad inde eidem Edwardo respondendum astrinxit, ac eos eo pretextu
per diffinitivam dicte Curie Admiralittatis sentenciam condempnari totis suis
viribus conatur, et indies machinatur, in nostri contemptum et ipsorum
Thome Thome Johannis Roberti Johannis Walteri Johannis Johannis Johannis
et Willielmi dampnum prejudicium depaupertacionem et gravamen mani-
festa ac contra formam statutorum predictorum. Unde nobis supplicaverunt
iidem Thomas Thomas Johannes Robertus Johannes Walterus Johannes
Johannes Johannes et Willielmus eis remedium in hac parte provideri festinum;
Et Nos jura corone nostre regie prout vinculo juramenti astringimur manu-
tenere volentes, et contra eadem nolentes ligeos nostros suspencionibus violari
illicitis, vobis prohibimus et precipimus ne placitum predictum premissa
aliqualiter tangens coram vobis ulterius teneatis, nec quicquam inde at-
temptetis seu attemptari permittatis aut procuretis quod in nostri contemptum
aut ipsorum Thome Thome Johannis Roberti Johannis Walteri Johannis
Johannis Johannis et Willielmi dampnum prejudicium seu gravamen quoquo

modo cedere valeat, sub violatoris legis nostre penam periculo incurrendi sentenciam seu decretum, si que in ipsos Thomam Thomam Johannem Robertum Johannem Walterum Johannem Johannem Johannem et Willielmum fulminaveritas seu fulminari fecistis quovismodo, eis et eorum cuilibet relaxantes et ipsos penitus absolventes de eisdem periculo incumbente Teste Ricardo Lyster apud Westmonasterium XXV die Januarii anno regni nostri primo.

Per curiam

ROOPER.

SELECT PLEAS OF THE ADMIRALTY (S.S.) ii 3.

(3) *Modern form.*

Edward VII. by the grace of God etc. to the [judge of the County Court holden at   ] and to [*name of plaintiff*] of   , greeting : Whereas we have been given to understand that you the said   have [entered a plaint against] C.D. in the said court, and that the said court has no jurisdiction in the said [cause] or to hear and determine the said [plaint] by reason that [*state facts showing want of jurisdiction*].

We therefore hereby prohibit you from further proceeding in the said [action] in the said court.   Witness etc.

B. CONSULTATION.

Rex officiali curiæ Cantuariensis et ejus commissariis salutem. Monstravit nobis A. quod cum ipsa petat coram vobis in curia Christianitatis executionem cujusdam sententiæ in causa testamentaria, pro ipsa A. et contra T. executorem testamenti B. matris predictæ A. super quadraginta libris in testamento predictæ B. eidem A. legatis, per officialem episcopi Londoniensis latæ, et post modum per vos confirmatæ : dictus T. executionem sententiæ predictæ satagens impedire, breve nostrum de prohibitione, ne placitum de catallis et debitis quæ non sunt de testamento vel matrimonio in curia Christianitatis teneretis, vobis dirigi procuravit : cujus brevis pretextu vos executioni sententiæ memoratæ supersedistis hucusque ; ad grave damnum ipsius A. et præjudicium manifestum. Et quia per dictum breve nostrum non prohibetur, quin de catallis in testamento legatis agi possit in curia Christianitatis, nolentes jurisdictionem quæ ad forum ecclesiasticum pertinet taliter impediri : vobis significamus, quod in causa, ubi petitur ab executore legatum sub nomine legati in testamento relictum, procedere poteritis, et ea facere quæ ad forum ecclesiasticum noveritis pertinere, prohibitione nostra predicta non obstante. Teste etc.   REGISTER (4th Ed. 1687) 45 A.

XIII

CERTIORARI

A. Old Forms.

Rex vicecomiti salutem. Quia quibus libet certis de causis certiorari velimus super Recordo et Processu cujusdam inquisitionis factæ coram te et custodibus Placitorum Coronæ nostræ in Comitatu tuo apud N. per breve nostrum super quadam rediseisina I. per R. facta, ut dicitur, de uno Messuagio cum pertinenciis in N., Tibi præcipimus, quod si judicium inde redditum sit, tunc Recordum et Processum prædicta cum omnibus ea tangentibus nobis sub sigillo tuo distincte et aperte mittas, et hoc breve, ita quod ea habeamus tali die ubicunque tunc fuerimus in Anglia, ut inspectis Recordo et Processu prædictis ulterius inde fieri faciamus quod de jure et secundum legem et consuetudinem regni nostri Angliæ fuerit faciendum. Teste etc. F.N.B. 242 B.

Rex etc. Quia quibusdam certis de causis Certiorari volumus super Recordo et Processu cujusdam inquisitionis captæ coram dilectis et fidelibus nostris W. et P. Justitiis nostris ad Gaolam nostram de N. assignatis deliberandam, pro morte E. unde C. pro morte predicto rectatus fuit, ut dicitur, quæ quidem Recordum et Processus coram vobis certis de causis venire fecimus, quæ penes vos resident, ut dicitur ; vobis mandamus quod Recordum et Processus prædicta cum omnibus eo tangentibus nobis sub sigillis vestris distincte etc. F.N.B. 245 F.

B. Modern Form.

Edward VII. by the grace of God etc. To the   greeting : We, willing for certain causes to be certified of   , command you that you send to us in our High Court of Justice on the   day of   , the aforesaid, with all things touching the same, as fully and entirely as they remain in   , together with this writ, that we may further cause to be done thereupon what of right we shall see fit to be done. Witness etc.

XIV

Quo Warranto

Rex Vicecomiti salutem. Summone per bonos summonitores A. quod sit coram justitiariis nostris apud Westmonasterium tali die, ostensurum quo warranto tenet visum francpledgii in villa de R. in prejudicium hundredi nostri de B. sine licencia et voluntate nostra vel predecessorum nostrorum quondam regum Angliæ, et emendas pro transgressione assisa panis et cerevisciæ in eadem cepit, in predjudicium nostrum non modicum et gravamen, ut dicitur. Et habeas ibi summonitores et hoc breve. Teste etc.

La vieux Natura brevium (Tottell 1584) 160 b.

XV

Mandamus

A. Old Form.

Carolus II. Dei gratia etc. C. L. Majori Burgi de E. in comitatu G. salutem. Cum A. in locum et officium Majoris Burgi prædicti debite electus fuerit, secundum consuetudinem villæ prædictæ hactenus usitatam, in quod quidam locum et officium Majoris Burgi prædicti prædictus A., secundum consuetudinem villæ prædictæ, admitti debet ; Tu tamen C. L. Major Burgi prædicti præmissa non ignarus, prædictum A. in locum et officium Majoris Burgi prædicti non ad huc admisisti, nec juramentum eidem A. in eo casu semper usitatum administrari non administrasti, sed prædictum A. admittere et jurare omnino recusasti, in ipsius A. damnum non modicum, et gravamen et status sui lesionem manifestam, sicut ex querela sua accepimus ; Nos igitur præfato A. debitam et festinam justiciam in hac parte fieri volentes, ut est justum, tibi Mandamus firmiter injungentes quod, immediate post receptionem hujus brevis, præfatum A. in locum et officium Majoris Burgi prædicti, in quo sic ut prefertur debite electus fuit, cum omnibus libertatibus privilegiis preheminenciis et commoditatibus ad locum et officium illius pertinentibus et spectantibus sine dilatione admittas, et juramentum eidem A. secundum consuetudinem in eo casu hactenus usitatam, administras seu administrari facias, vel causam nobis significes in contrarium, ne tuo defectu querela ad nos perveniat ; Et qualiter hoc preceptum nostrum fueris executorem nobis constari facias in Octabas Sancti Hillarii ubicunque tunc fuerimus in Anglia, hoc breve nostrum tunc remittens. Teste etc. THESAURUS BREVIUM (Ed. 1687) 159.

B. Modern Form.

Edward VII. by the grace of God etc. To   , of   , greeting. Whereas by [*here recite Act of Parliament or Charter if the act required to be done is founded on one or the other*]. And whereas we have been given to understand and be informed in the King's Bench Division of our High Court of Justice before us that [*insert necessary inducement and averments*]. And that you the said   were then and there required by [*insert demand*] but that you the said   well knowing the premises, but not regarding your duty in that behalf, then and there wholly neglected and refused to [*insert refusal*] nor have you or any of you at any time since   , in contempt of Us and to the great damage and grievance of   , as we have been informed, from their complaint made to Us. Whereupon we being willing that due and speedy justice should be done in the premises as it is reasonable, do command you the said   and every of you, firmly enjoining you, that you [*insert command*], or that you show us cause to the contrary thereof, lest by your default the same complaint should be repeated to Us, and how you shall have executed this Our Writ make known to us in Our said Court forthwith, then returning to Us this Our said writ, and this you are not to omit.

Witness [   ] the   day of   in the   year of our reign.   By the Court.
                                     (Signed.)

XVI

HABEAS CORPUS AD SUBJICIENDUM

A. Old Form.

Carolus Dei gratia etc.   Johanni Liloe militi Guardiano prisonæ nostræ de le Fleet salutem.   Præcipimus tibi quod corpus Walteri Earl militis in prisona nostra sub custodia tua detentum, ut dicitur, una cum causa detentionis suæ, quocunque nomine prædictus Walterus censeatur in eadem, Habeas Corpus ad subjiciendum et recipiendum ea quæ curia nostra de eo ad tunc et ibidem ordinare contingant in hac parte, et hæc nullatenus omittas periculo incumbendo ; et habeas ibi hoc breve.   Teste Hyde apud Westmonasterium quarto die Nov. anno 8.

B. Modern Form.

Victoria by the grace of God etc.   To J. K. Keeper of our gaol of Jersey, in the Island of Jersey, and to J. C. Viscount of the said Island, greeting. We command you that you have the body of C. C. W. detained in our prison under your custody, as it is said, together with the day and cause of his being taken and detained, by whatsoever name he may be called or known, in our Court before us at Westminster, on the 18th day of January next, to undergo and receive all and singular such matters and things which our said Court shall then and there consider of him in this behalf ; and have there then this writ.   Witness Thomas Lord Denman at Westminster, the 23rd day of December in the 8th year of our reign.   By the Court

ROBINSON.

XVII

A. The Writ of *Quibusdam certis de causis.*

Rex, Ricardo Capellano uxoris Johannis de Grymmestede chivalier, salutem. Quibusdam certis de causis coram consilio nostro propositis, tibi præcipimus firmiter injungentes, quod omnibus aliis prætermissis, sis in propria persona tua coram dicto consilio nostro in cancellaria nostra, die Mercurii proxima post festum Epiphaniæ Domini proximo futurum, ad respondendum ibidem super hiis quæ tunc tibi objicientur ex parte nostra, et ad faciendum ulterius et recipiendum quod curia nostra consideraverit in hac parte. Et habeas ibi hoc breve. Teste custode etc. apud Eltham xxvi die Decembris. Per consilium. (PALGRAVE COUNCIL 132.)

B. The Writ of *Subpœna.*

Edwardus etc. dilecto sibi Ricardo Spynk des Norwyco, salutem. Quibusdam certis de causis, tibi præcipimus firmiter injungentes, quod sis coram consilio nostro apud Westmonasterium, die Mercurii proximo post quindenam nativitatis Sancti Johannis Baptistæ proximo futurum : ad respondendum super hiis quæ tibi objicientur ex parte nostra, et ad faciendum et recipiendum quod curia nostra consideraverit in hac parte. *Et hoc subpœna centum librarum nullatenus omittas.* Teste meipso apud Westmonasterium, tercio die Julii, anno regni nostri tricesimo septimo. (PALGRAVE COUNCIL 41.)

XVIII

WRIT DE EXCOMMUNICATO CAPIENDO

Rex vicecomiti Lincolnensi salutem. Significavit nobis venerabilis pater Henricus Lincolniæ episcopus per literas suas patentes, quod B. suus parochianus vel suæ diocesæ, propter suam manifestam contumaciam auctoritate ipsius episcopi ordinaria excommunicatus est, nec se vult per censuram ecclesiasticam justitiari. Quia vero potestas regia sacrosanctæ ecclesiæ in querelis suis deesse non debet : tibi præcipimus quod prædictum B. per corpus suum secundum consuetudinem Angliæ justities, donec sanctæ ecclesiæ, tam de contemptu quam de injuria ei illata ab eo fuerit satisfactum. Teste etc.

XIX

THE QUO WARRANTO ENQUIRIES

A. The Commission to enquire and Articles of enquiry.

The Commission.

Rex dilectis et fidelibus suis Ricardo de Fukeram et Osberto de Bereford salutem. Sciatis quod assignavimus vos ad inquirendum per sacramentum proborum et legalium hominum de Comitatibus Salop. Stafford et Cestr. per quos rei veritas melius sciri poterit et inquiri, de quibusdam juribus libertatibus, et rebus aliis nos et statum nostrum necnon et statum communitatis Comitatuum prædictorum contingentibus, et insuper de factis et gestibus Vicecomitum et Ballivorum quorumcumque in Comitatibus prædictis, prout in articulis quos vobis inde tradiderimus pleniter continetur. Et ideo vobis mandamus quod ad certos dies et loca quos ad hoc provideritis inquisitiones illas faciatis juxta continentia articulorum prædictorum. Et eas distincte et apte scriptas nobis sub sigillis vestris et sigillis eorum per quos factæ fuerint sine dilatione mittatis. Mandavimus enim Vicecomitibus nostris Comitatuum

prædictorum quod ad certos dies et loca quos eis scire faciatis tot et tales probos etlegales homines de ballivis suis coram vobis venire facient per quos
rei veritas in præmissis melius sciri poterit et inquiri. In cujus rei testa-
monium etc. Teste etc.

 Similar commissions were issued appointing two commissioners for
  each of the following groups of counties :—
    (1) Kent, Surrey, Sussex, Middlesex and the City of
     London.
    (2) Wilts, Southampton, Berkshire and Oxfordshire.
    (3) Somerset, Dorset, Devon and Cornwall.
    (4) Northampton, Rutland and Lincoln.
    (5) York.

The Articles of Enquiry.

(1) Quot et quæ dominica maneria Rex habet in manu sua in singulis
 Comitatibus tam scilicet de antiquis dominicis Coronæ quam de
 esceactis et perquisitis.

(2) Quæ etiam maneria esse solent in manibus Regum predecessorum
 Regis, et qui ea tenent nunc, et quo waranto, et a quo tempore,
 et per quam, et quomodo fuerint alienata.

(3) De fœdis etiam domini Regis et tenentibus ejus qui ea modo teneant
 de ipso in capite, et quot fœda singuli ipsorum teneant, et quæ
 fœda teneri solent de Rege in capite et nunc tenentur per medium,
 et per quem medium, et a quo tempore alienata fuerint, et qualiter,
 et per quos.

(4) De terris etiam tenentium de antiquo dominico coronæ tam liberorum
 sokemannorum quam bondorum, utrum per ballivos aut per eosdem tenentes, et per quos ballivos, et per quos tenentes, et a quibus alienatæ fuerint, qualiter, et quo tempore.

(5) Simili modo inquiratur de firmis Hundredorum, Wappentake, et
 Trythyng, Civitatum, Burgorum, et aliorum reddituum quorumcunque, et a quo tempore.

(6) Quot etiam Hundreda, Wappentake, et Trythynga sint nunc in manum
 domini Regis, et quot, et quæ in manibus aliorum, et a quo tempore, et quo waranto, et quantum valeat quod libet Hundredum
 per annum.

(7) De sectis antiquis, consuetudinibus, serviciis, et aliis rebus domino
 Regi et antecessoribus suis subtractis, qui ea subtraxerint, et a
 quo tempore, et qui hujusmodi sectis (sc secta) consuetudines
 servicia et alia ad dominum Regem pertinentia et consueta sibi
 ipsis appropriaverint, et a quo tempore, et quo waranto.

(8) Qui etiam alii a Rege clamant habere retornam vel extractas brevium,
 et qui tenent placita de vetito namii, et qui clamant habere Wreccum maris, quo waranto et alias libertates regias, ut furcas, assisas
 panis et cerevisiæ, et alia quæ ad coronam pertinent, et a quo
 tempore.

(9) De hiis etiam qui habent libertates per Reges Angliæ sibi concessas,
 et eas aliter usi fuerint quam facere debuissent, qualiter, a quo
 tempore, et quo modo.

(10) Item de libertatibus concessis quæ impediunt communem justitiam
 et regiam potestatem subvertunt, et a quo concessæ fuerint, et a
 quo tempore.

(11) Qui insuper de novo appropriaverint sibi chacias liberas vel warennas
 sine waranto, et similiter qui ab antiquo hujusmodi chacias et
 warennas ex concessione Regia habuerint, et fines et metas earum
 excesserint, et a quo tempore.

(12) Qui etiam domini aut eorum senescalli seu ballivi quicunque seu etiam domini Regis ministri non sustinuerint executionem mandatorum domini Regis fieri, aut etiam facere contempserint, vel aliquo modo ea fieri impedierint, a tempore constitutionum factarum apud Marleberne anno regni domini Regis Henrici patris Regis nunc Quinquagesimo secundo.

(13) Item de omnibus purpresturis quibuscunque factis super Rege ve regale dignitate, per quos factæ fuerint, qualiter, et a quo tempore.

(14) De fœdis militaribus cujuscunque fœdi, et terris aut tenementis datis vel venditis religiosis, vel aliis in prejudicium Regis, et per quos, et a quo tempore.

(15) De Vicecomitibus capientibus munera ut consentiant ad concelandas felonias factas in ballivis suis, vel qui negligentes extiterint ad felones hujusmodi attachiandos quocunque favore tam infra libertates quam extra, simili modo de clericis et aliis ballivis vicecomitum, de coronatoribus et eorum clericis et ballivis quibuscunque qui ita fecerint tempore domini Henrici Regis post bellum de Evesham, et qui tempore domini Regis nunc.

(16) De Vicecomitibus et Ballivis quibuscunque capientibus munera pro recognitoribus removendis de assisis et juratis, et quo tempore.

(17) Item de Vicecomitibus et aliis Ballivis quibuscunque qui amerciaverint illos qui summoniti fuerint ad inquisitiones factas per preceptum domini Regis pro defalta cum per eandem summonitionem personæ venierint sufficientes ad inquisitiones hujusmodi faciendas, et quantum, et a quibus ceperint occasione prædicta, et quo tempore.

(18) Item de Vicecomitibus qui tradiderint Ballivis extorsoribus, populum gravantibus supra modum, Hundreda, Wapentaka, vel Trithingga ad altas fermas ut sic suas fermas levarent, et qui fuerint illi Ballivi, et quibus fuerint hujusmodi damna illata, et quo tempore.

(19) Item cum Vicecomites non debeant facere turnum suum nisi bis in anno qui pluries fecerint in anno turnum suum, et a quo tempore.

(20) Item cum fines pro redisseisinis aut prepresturis factis per terram vel aquam, pro occultatione thesauri et aliis hujusmodi ad dominum Regem pertineant, et ad Vicecomites hujusmodi attachiare, qui ceperint hujusmodi, et a quibus, et quantum.

(21) Item qui potestate officii sui aliquos malitiose occasionaverint et per hoc extorserint terras, redditus, ante alias prestationes, et a quo tempore.

(22) Qui receperint mandatum domini Regis ut ejus debita solverent, et a creditoribus receperint aliquam portionem ut eis residuum solverent, et nichilominus totum sibi allocari fecerint in Scaccario vel alibi, et a quo tempore.

(23) Qui receperint debita Regis vel partem debitorum, et debitores illos non acquietaverint, tam tempore domini Regis Henrici quam tempore domini Regis nunc.

(24) Item qui summonierint aliquo ut fierent milites, et pro respectu habendo ab eis lucra receperint, et quantum et quo tempore : Et si aliqui magnates vel alii sine precepto Regis aliquos distrinxerint ad arma suscipienda, et quo tempore.

(25) Item si Vicecomites aut Ballivi aliqui cujuscunque libertatis non fecerint summonitiones debito modo secundum formam brevis domini Regis, ut aliter fraudulenter seu minus sufficienter executi fuerint precepta regia prece pretio vel favore, et quo tempore.

(26) Item de hiis qui habuerint probatores imprisonatos, et fecerint eos appellare fideles et innocentes causa lucri, et quandoque eos impedierint ne culpabiles appellarent, et a quo tempore.

(27) Item qui habuerint felones imprisonatos, et eo pro pecunia abire et a prisona evadere promiserint liberos et impune, et qui pecuniam extorserint pro prisona dimittenda per plevinam cum sint repleggiati, et a quo tempore.

(28) Item qui dona vel lucra aliqua receperint pro officiis suis exercendis vel non exercendis, vel exequendis vel aliter executi fuerint seu excesserint fines mandati Regis, aliter quam ad officium suum pertinuit, et quo tempore.

(29) Et omnia ista inquirantur tam de Vicecomitibus Coronatoribus eorum clericis et ballivis quibuscunque quam de dominis et ballivis libertatum quarumcunque.

(30) Item qui Vicecomites vel custodes castrorum vel maneriorum domini Regis quorumcunque, vel etiam qui visores hujusmodi operationum ubicunque factarum per preceptum Regis, magis computaverint in eisdem quam rationabiliter apposuerint, et super hoc soldatas allocari sibi fieri procuraverint. Et similiter qui petram, mæremium (i.e. materiam), vel alia ad hæc operationes empta seu provisa, ad opus suum retinuerint, seu amoverint, et quod, et quantum damnum dominus Rex inde habuit, et quo tempore.

(31) D Esceacto ibus et Subesceactoribus, in seisina domini Regis facientibus vastum vel destructionem in boscis piscariis vivariis warennis infra custodias sibi commissas per dominum Regem, quare, si, et de quibus, et quo modo, et quo tempore.

(32) Item de eisdem si occasione hujusmodi seisinæ ceperunt bona defunctorum vel heredum in manum domini Regis injuste, donec redimentur ab eisdem, et quod, et quantum ita ceperint pro hujusmodi redemptione, et quid ad opus suum proprium inde retinuerint, et quo tempore.

(33) Item de eisdem qui ceperint munera a quibuscunque pro officio suo exequendo vel non exequendo, quantum, et a quibus, et quo tempore.

(34) Item de eisdem qui nimis sufficienter extenderint terras alicujus in favorem ejusdem, vel alterius in custodia illarum terrarum, dari vendi vel concedi debuerat, in deceptionem domini Regis, et ubi, et quomodo, et si, qui pro inde ceperint, et quantum, et quo tempore. HUNDRED ROLLS (Rec. Comm.) I. 13, 14.

B. Rotuli Hundredorum.
Veredictum Burgi de Tavistock,
Factum per sacramentum (of twelve jurors whose names follow).

Qui dicunt quod locus ubi villata de Tavistock nunc sita est, et abbatia, aliquando fuit Adelredi Regis Angliæ ante conquestum, qui illum dedit Ordulpho comiti fratri suo, et idem Ordulphus de licentia prædicti Regis ibidem fieri fecit abbatiam, quæ nunc est, in puram et perpetuam eleemosinam, et quidam abbas ejusdem loci prædictam villam fecit levari, quæ nunc valet per annum octo libras, quam idem abbas nunc de domino Rege tenet in capite per baroniam, simul cum aliis terris pertinentibus ad baroniam, per quindecim fœda militum et dimidiam.

Item idem abbas habet assisam panis et cervisiæ, pilloriam et tomberellum in prædicto burgo, a tempore quod non extat memoria, et habet mercatum in eodem burgo et nundinas semel in anno ; sed nesciunt quo warranto . . .   I. 80 no. 25.

Veredictum duodecim juratorum forinseci Hundredi de Tavistock, scilicet.

(Here follow the names of the twelve jurors.)

Qui dicunt quod locus de Tavistock cum forinseco hundredo ibidem, aliquando fuit domini Adelredi tunc Regis Angliæ ante conquestum, ut intelligunt, et idem Adelredus dedit eundem locum cum forinseco hundredo Ordulpho comiti fratri suo, qui ex licencia fratris sui quandam Abbatiam nigrorum monachorum Sancti Bendicti, in pura et perpetua eleemosina, pro animabus predecessorum suorum et successorum Regum Angliæ, et tenent abbas ejusdem loci et conventum quindecim fœda et dimidiam en fief de Haubergh de domino Rege in capite, et habent in manerio de Hurdewick ejusdem hundredi furcas a tempore quod non extat memoria, ignorant tamen per quod servicium dicti religiosi fœda teneant et quantum valent per annum, proficium tamen dicti hundredi valet unam marcam per annum, et de redditu assisæ per annum novem libras, ut intelligant.

Item dicunt quod Roger de Prideaus, aliquando Vicecomes Devoniæ, per Robertum Pollard, tunc clericum suum, et Johanem Collan et ceteros forestarios de Dertamor, injuste intravit in liberum manerium de Hurdewick dictorum religiosorum, qui ibidem ostia fregerunt et fugabant ad Lideford comitis Cornubiæ quadraginta averia, et ibidem detinuerunt donec iidem religiosi quinque marcas eidem vicecomiti dederant.

Item dicunt quod Ricardus de Seton, tunc senescallus Cornubiæ, per potestam officii injuste intravit in prædictam abbatiam, volens Robertum abbatem loci ejusdem ejicere, et extorsit ab eodem centum solidos ut ipsum dimitteret.

Item dicunt quod Johannes de Wykiæ et Robertus Chapman, tunc ballivi Johannis Beaupre senescalli Cornubiæ, eo tempore injuste per potestatem officii sui, ceperunt in burgo de Tavistock dictorum religiosorum Johannem vicarium de Middleton, et eum duxerunt de dicta villa ad castellum de Lansacon in Cornubia, ipsum ibidemimprisonantes, et antequam eum dimiserunt extorserunt ab eo quatuor marcas.

Item dicunt quod. iidem Johannes et Robertus eodem modo ceperunt Johannem de Kerdewille, et ipsum apud Lam'ton imprisonaverunt, et ita extorserunt ab eo quatuor solidos antequam eum dimittebant.

Item dicunt quod comes Cornubiæ, per Wilecoccum Rossel et Petrum Whiffing ballivos suos, apud Esse novam levaverunt consuetudinem ; capiunt enim de singulis bargis et batellis cum sablone, in aquam de Tamar transeuntibus, duodecim denarios ubi nihil solitum est exigi.   I. 80 no. 36.

C. Placita de Quo Warranto 170 (Com. Devon. Ed. I.).

Abbas de Tavistock summonitus fuit ad respondendum domino Regi quo warranto tenet hundredum de Tavistock, quod pertinet ad Coronam domini Regis, et quo warranto clamat habere visum franci pledgii, furcas, tumberellum, pilloriam, et emendationem assisæ panis et cerevisciæ fractæ, mercatum, nundinas, in Tavistock, sine licencia domini Regis vel predecessorum suorum Regum Angliæ.

Et Abbas venit, et quo ad hundredum dicit quod hundredum illud est annexum baroniæ suæ quam tenet de domino Rege et de pertinenciis ejusdem baroniæ.   Et eo waranto illud tenet.

Et Willelmus de Gyselham, qui sequitur pro domino Rege, dicit quod hundredum est quoddam speciale annexum Coronæ et dignitati domini Regis, quod nullus habere potest nisi ex speciali dono domini Regis et petit judicium desicut prædictus Abbas nullum speciale warantum ostendit.   Dies datus est coram domino Rege a die Paschæ in unum mensem ubicumque etc. de audiendo judicio suo etc.

Et quo ad visum francipledgii, furcas, tumberellum, pilloriam, et emendationem assisæ panis et cerevisciæ, dicit quod hujusmodi libertates pertinent ad
hundredum, et desicut ipsemet tenet prædictum hundredum petit judicium.
Dies data est ei de audiendo judicio suo ut supra. Et quo ad mercatum et
nundinas dicit quod ipse et omnes predecessores sui, Abbatas ejusdem loci,
habuerunt prædictum mercatum et nundinas in manerio de Tavistock, a tempore quo non extat memoria. Et hoc petit quod inquiratur per patriam. Et
Willelmus de Gyselham similiter. Ideo inquiritur. Et juratores dicunt supra
sacramentum suum quod prædictus Abbas, et omnes predecessores sui, a quo
non extat memoria, semper usi sunt prædictis mercato et nundinis apud
Tavistock. Dies datus est a die Paschæ in unum mensem coram domino
Rege ubicumque etc. de audiendo judicio etc.

[For a full account of these Rolls see Miss Cam's Essay, Vinogradoff,
Oxford Studies vi, xi chap. ii.]

XX

The Bill of Middlesex and Latitat

Middlesex, to Wit.[1]

The Sheriff is commanded that he take Charles Long, late of Burford in
the county of Oxford, if he may be found in his bailiwick, and him safely keep,
so that he may have his body before the lord the king at Westminster, on
Wednesday next after fifteen days of Easter, to answer William Bornton,
gentleman, of a plea of trespass ; *and also* to a bill of the said William against
the aforesaid Charles, for two hundred pounds of debt,[2] according to the custom of the court of the said lord the king, before the king himself to be exhibited ; and that he have there then this precept.

The within named Charles Long is not found in my bailiwick.[3]

George II.[4] by the grace of God etc. to the sheriff of Berkshire greeting.
Whereas we lately commanded our sheriff of Middlesex that he should take
Charles Long, late of Burford in the County of Oxford, if he might be found
in his bailiwick and him safely keep, so that he might be before us at Westminster at a certain day now past, to answer unto William Burton gentleman
of a plea of trespass ; *and also* to a bill of the said William against the aforesaid Charles, for two hundred pounds of debt, according to the custom of our
court, before us to be exhibited ; and our said sheriff of Middlesex at that day
returned to us that the aforesaid Charles was not found in his bailiwick ;
whereupon on the behalf of the aforesaid William in our court before us it is
sufficiently attested, that the aforesaid Charles lurks and runs about (*latitat
et discurrit*) in your county : therefore we command you that you take him,
if he may be found in your bailiwick, and him safely keep, so that you may
have his body before us at Westminster on Tuesday next after five weeks of
Easter, to answer to the aforesaid William of the plea and bill aforesaid : and
have you there then this writ. Witness sir Dudley Ryder knight, at Westminster, the eighteenth day of April, in the twenty-eighth year of our reign.

By virtue of this writ[5] to me directed I have taken the body of the within
named Charles Long ; which I have ready at the day and place within contained, according as by this writ it is commanded me.

BL. COMM. III. App. no. 3 § 4.

---

[1] Bill of Middlesex for trespass.   [2] *Ac etiam* in debt.
[3] Sheriff's return, *non est inventus.*   [4] *Latitat.*
[5] Sheriff's return, *Cepi corpus.*

XXI

Writ of Quominus in the Exchequer

George II. by the grace of God etc. to the sheriff of Berkshire greeting. We command you, that you omit not by reason of any liberty of your county, but that you enter the same, and take Charles Long, late of Burford in the county of Oxford, gentleman, wheresoever he shall be found in your bailiwick, and him safely keep, so that you may have his body before the barons of our exchequer at Westminster, on the morrow of the holy Trinity, to answer William Burton our debtor of a plea, that he render to him two hundred pounds which he owes him and unjustly detains, whereby he is less able (*quo minus*) to satisfy us the debts which he owes us at our said exchequer, as he saith he can reasonably show that the same he ought to render : and have you there this writ. Witness sir Thomas Parker knight, at Westminster, the sixth day of May, in the twenty-eighth year of our reign.

BL. COMM. III. App. no. 3 § 4.

XXII

The Eyre

A. Breve omnibus justitiariis simul, quod erit eorum warrantus, et publice legetur in comitatu patens.

Rex dilectis et fidelibus suis A. B. C. D. salutem.   Sciatis quod constituimus vos justitiarios nostros ad itinerandum in comitatu tali, de omnibus placitis et assisis tam coronæ nostræ quam aliis, quæ emerserint, postquam justitiarii nostri ultimo itineraverunt in comitatu illo, et etiam de illis, quæ summonita fuerunt et atterminata fuerunt, et non finita coram justitiariis nostris de banco apud Westmonasterium, vel coram justitiariis nostris itinerantibus qui ultimo itineraverunt in eodem comitatu, de omnibus placitis, vel tantum de assisis novæ disseysinæ, mortis antecessoris capiendis, vel gaolis deliberandis, ita quod omnes assisæ illæ et omnia placita illa sint coram vobis in eodem statu quo remanserunt per preceptum nostrum, vel per præfatos justitiarios nostros itinerantes, vel per præfatos justitiarios nostros de banco. Mandavimus enim vicecomiti nostro A. quod ad diem et locum quam ei scire facietis, faciet coram vobis summonitiones fieri, et attachinmenta venire, cum brevibus assisarum et placitorum prædictorum.   Et ideo vobis mandamus, rogantes quod in fide, qua nobis tenemini, ad hæc exequenda fideliter et diligenter intendatis, ut tam fidem vestram quam diligentiam ad hoc appositam debeamus merito commendare.   Teste etc.   BRACTON, f. 109.

B. Breve de generali summonitione clausum.

Rex vicecomiti salutem.   Summoneas per bonos summonitores omnes archiepiscopos, episcopos, abbates, priores, comites, barones, milites et libere tenentes de tota balliva tua, et de qualibet villa quatuor legales homines et præpositum et de quolibet burgo duodecim legales burgenses per totam ballivam tuam, et omnes illos qui coram justitiariis itinerantibus venire solent et debent, quod sint apud talem locum, tali die, anno regni nostri tali, coram dilectis et fidelibus notris A. B. C. D. quos justitiarios nostros constituimus, audituri et facturi præceptum nostrum.   Facias etiam venire tunc coram eisdem justitiariis nostris omnia placita coronæ nostræ quæ, placitata non sunt, et quæ emerserunt, post quam justitiarii nostri ultimo itineraverunt in partibus illis, et omnia placita, et omnia attachiamenta ad placita illa pertinentia, et omnes assisas, et omnia placita quæ posita fuerunt ad primum assisam coram justitiariis cum brevibus assisarum, ita quod assisæ illæ et placita pro defecto tui vel summonitionis tuæ non remaneant. Facias etiam clamari et sciri per totam ballivam tuam quod omnes assisæ et omnia placita quæ fuerunt attachiata et atterminata et non finita coram justitiariis nostris de banco, vel coram justitiariis nostris qui ultimo itineraverunt in comitatu tuo de omnibus placitis, vel coram justitiariis notris illuc missis ad assisas novæ disseysinæ capiendas, et gaolas deliberandas, tunc sint coram præfatis justitiariis nostris, apud talem locum, in eodem statu in quo remanserunt per præceptum nostrum vel per præceptum justitiariorum nostrorum prædictorum itinerantium, vel per justitiarios nostros de banco. Summoneas etiam per bonos summonitores, omnes illos qui vicecomites fuerunt post ultimam itinerationem prædictorum justitiariorum nostrorum in partibus illis, quod tunc sint ibidem coram prædictis justitiariis nostris itinerantibus cum brevibus assisarum et placitorum, quæ tempore suo receperunt, et ad respondendum de tempore suo, sicut respondere debent coram justitiariis itinerantibus, et habeas ibi summonitores et hoc breve. Teste etc.

BRACTON, f. 109 b.

C. Writ of resummons at the close of the eyre.
Rex vicecomiti salutem. Præcipimus tibi quod sine dilatione clamare facias in comitatu tuo et per comitatum tuum in diversis hundredis, et mercatis, et per omnes partes de comitatu tuo, quod omnia placita quæ per brevia nostra vel per præceptum justitiariorum nostrorum de banco atterminata fuerunt apud Westmonasterium infra octabas S. Hilarii ultimo præteritas et Paschæ proxime sequentes, et quæ per præceptum nostrum posita fuerunt sine die occasione itinerationis talis, sint coram justitiariis nostris de banco apud Westmonasterium ad talem terminum in eodem statu in quo fuerunt quando remanserunt sine die per præceptum nostrum occasione prædicta, tam de essoniis faciendis et non faciendis, quam de omnibus aliis circumstantiis eorundem placitorum. Alia vero placita, quæ per præceptum nostrum vel per præceptum prædictorum justitiariorum nostrorum itinerantium posita fuerunt post certum diem ad talem terminum, apud talem locum, ad talem terminum et talem, ibi deducantur et teneantur, sicut ibi posita fuerunt, et habeas ibi hoc breve, et alia brevia omnia quæ penes te habes pertinentia ad prædicta placita. Teste etc.

BRACTON f. 426.

XXIII

COMMISSIONS OF THE JUSTICES OF ASSIZE

A. Assize.
Rex etc. dilectis et fidelibus suis R. M. uni Justiciorum suorum de Banco, et J. L. uni Justiciorum suorum ad placita coram nobis tenenda assignato Salutem. Sciatis quod constituimus vos Justitiarios nostros, una cum hiis quos vobis associaverimus, ad omnes assisas, jurata, certificationes coram quibuscunque Justitiis tam per diversa brevia domini Johannis nuper regis Angliæ patris nostri, quam per diversa brevia nostra in Comitatibus nostris South., Wiltes., Dors., Somerset, Devon, et cornub, ac in civitate Exon. arreniatas capiendas. Et ideo vobis mandamus, quod ad certos dies et loca quos vos ad hoc provideritis, Assisas, Jurata, et certificationes illas capiatis; Facturi inde quod ad justitiam pertinet secundum legem et consuetudinem regni nostri Angliæ. Salvis nobis amerciamentis inde provenientibus. Mandavimus enim Vicecomitibus nostris comitatuum et civitatum prædictorum, quod ad certos dies et loca quos eis scire faciatis assisas, jurata, et certificationes illas una cum brevibus originalibus et omnibus alias ea tangentibus coram vobis venire faciant. In cujus rei testimonium etc.

COKE, 4th Institute 158.

B. Nisi Prius.

Rex vicecomiti salutem. Præcipimus tibi quod venire facias coram Justitiariis nostris apud Westmonasterium in Octabas Sancti Michælis, vel coram Justitiariis nostris ad Assisas in comitatu tuo, per formam Statuti nostri inde provisam, capiendas assignatis, *si prius* die lunæ proximo ante festum etc. Apud etc. venierint, duodecim tam milites quam alios etc.

STAT. WEST II. (13 Ed. I. St. 1) c. 30.   COKE, 4th Institute 159.

C. Oyer and Terminer.

Elizabeth Dei gratia etc.   Carissimis consanguineis suis Willielmo Marchioni Winton, Henrico Comiti South etc. ac dilectis et fidelibus suis Rogero Manwood, uni Justitiorum suorum de Banco, Johanni Jeffray, uni Justitiorum ad placita coram nobis temenda assignato, Johanni Arundell militi etc.   Johanni St John, Humfredo Walrond, Willielmo Pool, Petro Edgcombe, Thomæ Morton etc.   Salutem. Sciatis assignavimus vos et tres vestrum, quorum aliquem vestrum vos prefatos Rogerum Manwood et Johannem Jeffray unum esse volumus, Justitiarios nostros ad inquirendum per sacramentum proborum et legalium homintm de comitatibus nostris South., Wiltes., Doreset, Somerset, Devon, et Cornub. et eorum quolibet, ac aliis viis, modis, et mediis quibus melius sciveritis, aut poteritis, tam infra libertates quam extra, per quos rei veritatem melius sciri poterit, de quibuscunque proditionibus, misprisionibus proditionum, insurrectionibus, rebellionibus, murdris, feloniis, homicidiis, interfectionibus, burglariis, raptibus mulierum, congregationibus, et conventiculis illicitis, verborum prolationibus, coadjutationibus, misprisonibus, confæderationibus, falsis allegantiis, transgressionibus, riotis, routis, retentionibus, escapiis, contemptibus, falsitatibus, negligentiis, concelamentis, manutenentiis, oppressionibus, cambipartiis, deceptionibus, et aliis malefactis, offensis, et injuriis, quibuscunque, nec non accessariis eorundem infra comitatum prædictum et eorum quamlibet, tam infra libertates quam extra, per quoscunque et qualitercunque habita, facta, perpetrata, sive commissa. Et per quos, vel per quam, cui, vel quibus, quando, qualiter, et quo modo, ac de aliis articulis et circumstantiisprænmissis, et eorum aliquid vel aliqua qualitercunque concernentia. Et ad easdem proditiones, et alia præmissa (hac vice) audienda et terminanda secundum legem et consuetudinem regni nostri Angliæ. Et ideo vobis mandamus quod ad certos dies et loca quos vos vel tres vestrum, quorum aliquem vestrum ex vobis præfatos Rogerum Manwood et Johannem Jeffray unum esse volumus, ad hoc provideritis diligenter, super præmissis faciatis inquisitiones, et præmissa omnia et singula audiatis et terminetis, ac ea faciatis et expleatis in formam prædicta, facturi inde quod ad Justitiam pertinet secundum legem et consuetudinem regni nostri Angliæ. Salvis nobis amerciamentis et aliis ad nos inde spectantibus. Mandavimus enim Vicecomitibus nostris comitatuum prædictorum quod ad certos dies et loca, quos vos vel tres vestrum, quorum aliquem vestrum ex vobis præfatos Rogerum Manwood et Johannem Jeffray unum esse volumus, eis sciri feceritis, venire facere coram vobis, vel tribus vestrum, quorum aliquem vestrum vobis præfatos Rogerum Manwood et Johannem Jeffray unum esse volumus, tot et tales probos et legales homines de ballivis suis, tam infra libertates quam extra, per quos rei veritas melius sciri poterint et inquiriri. In cujus rei testimonium has literas nostras fieri fecimus patentes. Teste me ipse apud Westmonasterium 27 die Junii Anno Regni nostri decimo octavo.

COKE, 4th Institute 162, 163.

D. Gaol Delivery.

Elizabeth etc. Dilectis et fidelibus suis A. B. C. D. etc. Salutem. Sciatis quod constituimus vos, tres, et duos vestrum, quorum aliquem vestrum vos præfatos A. B. etc. unum esse volumus, Justitiarios nostros ad Gaolam nostram castri nostri de C. de prisona in ea existente hac vice deliberandos. Et ideo vobis mandamus quod ad certum diem quam vos, tres vel duo vestrum (quorum vos præfatos A. B. etc. unum esse volumus) ad hoc provideritis, conveniatis apud castrum prædictum ad gaolam illam deliberandam, facturi inde quod ad justitiam pertinet secundum legem et consuetudinem regni nostri Angliæ. Salvis nobis amerciamentis et aliis ad nos inde spectantibus. Mandavimus enim Vicecomiti nostro Comitatus nostri M. quod ad certum diem quam vos, tres, vel duo vestrum (quorum vos præfatos A. B. etc. unum esse volumus) ei sciri feceritis, omnes prisones ejusdem gaolæ, et eorum attachiamenta coram vobis, tribus, vel duobus vestrum (quorum aliquem vestrum ex vobis præfatos A. B. etc. unum esse volumus) ibidem venire facere. In cujus rei testimonium has literas nostras fieri fecimus patentes. Teste etc.

COKE, 4th Institute 168.

XXIV

COMMISSION OF JUSTICES OF THE PEACE

George II. by the grace of God, etc. to A, B, C, D etc. greeting.

Know that we have assigned you, jointly and severally, and every one of you, our justices to keep our peace in our county of W. And to keep and to cause to be kept all ordinances and statutes for the good of the peace, and for preservation of the same, and for the quiet rule and government of our people made, in all and singular their articles in our said county (as well within liberties as without) according to the force, form, and effect of the same ; and to chastise and punish all persons that offend against the form of those ordinances or statutes, or any one of them, in the aforesaid county, as it ought to be done according to the form of those ordinances and statutes ; And to cause to come before you, or any of you, all those who to any one or more of our people concerning their bodies or the firing of their houses have used threats, to find sufficient security for the peace, or their good behaviour, towards us and our people ; and if they shall refuse to find such security, then them in our prisons until they shall find such security to cause to be safely kept.

We have also assigned you, and every two or more of you (of whom any one of you [*quorum*] the aforesaid A, B, C, D etc. we will shall be one) our justices to enquire the truth more fully, by the oath of good and lawful men of the aforesaid county, by whom the truth of the matter shall be the better known, of all and all manner of felonies, poisonings, inchantments, soceries, art magic, trespasses, forestallings, regratings, ingrossings, and extortions whatsoever ; and of all and singular other crimes and offences, of which the justices of our peace may or ought lawfully to enquire, by whomsoever and after what manner soever in the said county done or perpetrated, or which shall happen to be there done or attempted ; And also of all those who in the aforesaid county in companies against our peace, in disturbance of our people, with armed force have gone or rode, or hereafter shall presume to go or ride ; And also of all those who have there lain in wait, or hereafter shall presume to lay in wait, to maim or cut or kill our people ; And also of all victuallers, and all and singular other persons, who in the abuse of weights or measures, or in selling victuals, against the form of the ordinances and statutes, or any one of them therefore made for the common benefit of England and our people thereof, have offended or attempted, or hereafter shall presume in the said county to offend or attempt ; And also of all sheriffs, bailiffs, stewards, constables, keepers of gaols, and other officers, who in the execution of their offices about the premises, or any of them, have unduly behaved themselves, or hereafter shall presume to behave themselves unduly, or have been, or shall happen hereafter to be careless, remiss, or negligent in our aforesaid county ; And of all and singular articles, and circumstances, and all other things whatsoever, that concern the premises of any of them, by whomsoever, and after what manner soever, in our aforesaid county done or perpetrated, or which hereafter shall there happen to be done or attempted in what manner soever ; And to inspect all indictments whatsoever so before you or any of you taken or to be taken, or before others late our justices of the peace in the aforesaid county made or taken, and not yet determined ; and to make and continue processes thereupon, against all and singular the persons so indicted, or who before you hereafter shall happen to be indicted ; until they can be taken, surrender themselves, or be outlawed : And to hear and determine all and singular the felonies, poisonings, inchantments, soceries, arts magick, trespasses, forestallings, regratings, ingrossings, extortions, unlawful assemblies, indictments aforesaid, and all and singular other the premises, according to the laws and statutes of England, as in the like case it hath been accustomed, or ought to be done ; And the same offenders, and every of them for their offences by fines, ransoms, amerciaments, forfeitures, and other means as according to the law and custom of England, or form of the ordinances and statutes aforesaid, it has been accustomed, or ougl t to be done, to chastise and punish.

Provided always, that if a case of difficulty, upon the determination of any the premises, before you, or any two or more of you, shall happen to arise ; then let judgment in no wise be given thereon, before you, or any two or more of you, unless in the presence of one of our justices of the one or other bench, or of one of our justices appointed to hold the assizes in the aforesaid county.

And therefore we command you and every of you, that to keeping the peace, ordinances, statutes, and all and singular other the premises, you diligently apply yourselves ; and that at certain days and places, which you, or any such two or more of you as is aforesaid shall appoint for these purposes, into the premises ye make inquiries ; and all and singular the premises here and determine, and perform and fulfil them in the aforesaid form, doing therein what to justice appertains, according to the law and custom of England : Saving to us the amercements, and other things to us therefrom belonging.

And we command by the tenor of these presents our sheriff of W. that at certain days and places, which you, or any such two or more of you as is aforesaid, shall make known to him, he cause to come before you, or such two or more of you as aforesaid, so many and such good and lawful men of his bailiwick (as well within liberties as without) by whom the truth of the matter in the premises shall be the better known and inquired into.

Lastly, we have assigned you the a oresaid A. B. keeper of the rolls of our peace in our said county. And therefore you shall cause to be brought before you and your said fellows, at the days and places aforesaid, the writs, precepts, processes, and indictments aforesaid, that they may be inspected, and by a due course determined as is aforesaid.

In witness whereof we have caused these our letters to be made patent. Witness ourself at Westminster etc.

BURN, JUSTICE OF THE PEACE (Ed. 1755) II. 69-71.

XXV

TABLE OF OFFICIALS OF THE COURT OF KING'S BENCH AT DIFFERENT PERIODS

1740 and 1815.		1874.
(1) King's Coroner and Attorney		Queen's Coroner and Attorney
(2) Secondary on the Crown Side		
(3) Clerk of the Rules on the Crown Side		
(4) Clerk of the Affidavits on the Crown Side	Abolished 1843 (6, 7 Vict. c. 20)	Master in Crown Office
(5) Examiner, Calendar Keeper, and Clerk of the Grand Juries. [Held by one person]		4 Clerks 1 Messenger (6, 7 Vict. c. 20)
(6) Clerks in Court in the Crown Office		
(7) Clerk in Court for the Crown		
(8) Chief Clerk in the Court of King's Bench		
(9) Secondary on Plea Side or Master		
(10) Clerk of the Rules Plea Side		
(11) Clerk of the Papers		
(12) Clerk of the Docquets and Judgments		
(13) Signer of the Writs		
(14) Clerk of the Declarations		
(15) Clerk of the Common Bails, Estreats and Posteas		5 Masters
(16) Custos Brevium et Recordorum	Abolished 1837 (1 Vict. c. 30)	23 Clerks 1 Messenger
(17) Clerk of the Inner and Upper Treasuries		(1 Vict. c. 30)
(18) Clerk of the Outer Treasury		
(19) Clerk of Nisi Prius for London and the Circuits		
(20) Bag bearer to Custos Brevium		
(21) Clerk of Nisi Prius in Middlesex		
(22) Signer of the Bills of Middlesex		
(23) Clerk of the Errors		
(24) Filacer, Exigentor, and Clerk of the Outlawries for all counties but Monmouth and Essex		
(25) Filacer, etc., for Monmouth and Essex		
(26) Receiver-General and Comptroller of the Seal	6 Geo. IV. c. 89 Authorized Purchase. 8, 9 Vict. c. 34 purchased and abolished	
(27) Crier aud Usher of the Court		4 Ushers
(28) Under Ushers, Criers and Court-keepers		Housekeeper
(29) Keeper of Westminster Hall		3 Clerks allowed (15, 16 Vict. c. 73)

(30) Clerk to the Lord Chief Justice		2 Clerks each allowed (15, 16 Vict. c. 73)
(31) Clerks to Puisne Judges		Merged in Associate (15, 16 Vict. c. 73)
(32) Associate and Marshal at Nisi Prius in London and Middlesex		
(33) Clerk at the Sittings in London and Middlesex	Abolished 1837 (1 Vict. c. 30)	
(34) Crier at the Sittings in London and Middlesex		
(35) Train-bearer to the Lord Chief Justice		Train-bearer to the Lord Chief Justice
(36) Hall-keeper and Bar-keepers in London		
(37) Marshal of the King's Bench Prison		
(38) Clerk of the Papers in the King's Bench Prison		
(39) Deputy Marshal of the King's Bench Prison		
(40) Chaplain of the King's Bench Prison	Abolished 1842 (5 Vict. c. 22)	
(41) Clerk of the Day Rules in the King's Bench Prison		
(42) Turnkeys in the King's Bench Prison		
(43) Tipstaves		
		3 Tipstaves
		Associate, cp. 15, 16 Vict. c. 73
		3 Clerks
		Marshals to Judges, cp. 15, 16 Vict. c. 73
		(Parliamentary Papers xxiv, 1874. 2nd Report of Commission appointed to enquire into the administrative departments of Courts of Justice)

XXVI

TABLE OF OFFICIALS OF THE CHANCERY AT DIFFERENT PERIODS

Lord Chancellor's Officers—

1740	1815		1874
(1) Principal Secretary	The same offices except nos. 9 and 39		Principal Secretary 2 Clerks Office-keeper
(2) Secretary of Presentations			Secretary of Presentations
(3) Clerk of the Presentations		Abolished 2, 3 Will. IV. c. 111, work done by Secretary of Presentations and Principal Secretary	
(4) Secretary of Commissions			Secretary of Commissions
(5) Secretary of Decrees and Injunctions		Abolished 15, 16 Vict. c. 87	
(6) Secretary of Lunatics			Registrar in Lunacy 4 Clerks 15, 16 Vict. c. 87 16, 17 Vict. c. 70 25, 26 Vict. c. 86
(7) Secretary of the Briefs			
(8) Clerk of the Briefs			
(9) Secretary of Appeals	Not extant		
(10) Clerk of the Appeals			
(11) Clerks of the Letters Patent		Abolished 2, 3 Will. IV. c. 111	Clerk of the Patents (3, 4 Will. IV. c. 84)
(12) Examiner of Letters Patent			
(13) Clerk of the Dispensations and Faculties (14) Clerk of the Crown		Abolished 2, 3 Will. IV. c. 111	Clerk of the Crown 3 Clerks 1 Messenger 3, 4 Will. IV. c. 84
(15) Purse-bearer			Purse-bearer (does duty as Chaff Wax and Sealer)
(16) Chaff-Wax (17) Sealer		Abolished 15, 16 Vict. c. 87	
(18) Gentlemen of the Chamber		One abolished 15, 16 Vict. c. 87	Gentlemen of the Chamber
(19) Serjeant-at-Arms			Serjeant-at-Arms Train-bearer
(20) Pursuivant to the Great Seal			Messenger to Great Seal
(21) Usher of the Hall at the Lord Chancellor's			Usher of the Hall at Lincoln's Inn Messenger during absence from Town
(22) Usher of the Court (23) Crier of the Court		Abolished 15, 16 Vict. c. 87	Attendant on Furnaces, Lincoln's Inn

(24) Tipstaff, being deputy of Warden of the Fleet		Tipstaff
(25) Doorkeeper of the Court	Abolished 15, 16 Vict. c. 87	Caretaker of Courts Lincoln's Inn
		Porter to the Great Seal
(26) Keeper of the Court		Keeper of Court at Westminster
		3 Persons to keep order in Court
Master of the Rolls Officers—		
(27) Chief Secretary		Secretary
		2 Clerks
		1 Office Cleaner
(28) Under Secretary		
(29) Secretary of Causes		Secretary of Causes
(30) Secretary of Decrees and Injunctions		
(31) Clerk of the Chapel		Preacher at the Rolls Chapel
(32) Gentlemen of the Chamber (2)		2 Gentlemen of the Chamber
(33) Usher of the Hall at the Rolls		Usher of the Court
(34) Tipstaff		Tipstaff
		2 Court Cleaners
(35) Keeper of the Records in the Tower		
(36) Porter at the Rolls		Porter to the Court
(37) Masters in Chancery Extraordinary	Abolished 16, 17 Vict. c. 78	Commissioners to administer oath 16, 17 Vict. c. 78
(38) Clerk of the Custodies of Idiots and Lunatics	Abolished 2, 3 Will. IV. c. 111; 5, 6 Vict. c. 84.	
(39) Clerk of the Leases	Not extant	
(40) Masters in Chancery	Abolished 15, 16 Vict. c. 80	Chief Clerks :—
		3 at the Rolls
		9 at the Vice-Chancellors
		46 Clerks
		4 Porters
		4 Caretakers of Courts
		(15, 16 Vict. c. 80; 23, 24 Vict. c. 149; 30, 31 Vict. c. 87)
(41) Accountant General		Assistant Paymaster General for Chancery
		43 Clerks
		1 Office Cleaner
		(35, 36 Vict. c. 44)
(42) Register and Deputy Registers		Registrars (12)
		15 Clerks
		12 Assistant Clerks
		(3, 4 Will. IV. c. 94; Vict. c. 5)

(43) Clerks of Entries		2 Clerks of Entries; 2 Bag-bearers; 4 Office Cleaners. (14, 15 Vict. c. 83; 30, 31 Vict. c. 87)
(44) Register of Affidavits	Duties given to Clerks of Records and Writs (15, 16 Vict. c. 87)	
(45) Examiner's Office		2 Examiners 2 Clerks 1 Office Cleaner (16 Vict. c. 22)
(46) Six Clerks' Officer	Abolished 5, 6 Vict. c. 103	7 Taxing Masters 14 Clerks 1 Office-keeper (5, 6 Vict. c. 103)
(47) Sworn Clerks	Abolished 5, 6 Vict. c. 103	
(48) Waiting Clerks	Abolished 5, 6 Vict. c. 103	
(49) Clerk of Enrolments	Abolished 5, 6 Vict. c. 103	Clerk of Enrolments 3 Clerks (5, 6 Vict. c. 103)
(50) Clerk or Master of Report Office	Abolished 3, 4 Will. IV. c. 94	Clerk of Records and Writs 21 Clerks 1 Messenger, 1 Office-keeper, 1 Porter (5, 6 Vict. c. 103)
(51) Clerk of the Hanaper	Abolished 15, 16 Vict. c. 87	Report Office added 18, 19 Vict. c. 134
(52) Petty Bag Office		Clerk of the Petty Bag 2 Clerks 1 Office Cleaner (12, 13 Vict. c. 109)
(53) Prothonotary	To be abolished 2, 3 Will. IV. c. 111	
(54) Cursitors	Abolisheld 5, 6 Will. V, c. 82. Duties transferred to Petty Bag Office	
(55) Subpœna Office	Abolished 15, 16 Vict. c. 87. Duties transferred to Clerks of Records and Writs	
(56) Sixpenny Writ Office	Abolished 15, 16 Vict. c. 86	
Offices connected with Bankruptcy Jurisdiction—		
(57) Secretary of Commissions of Bankrupts	Abolished 15, 16 Vict. c. 77	

(58) Clerk of Enrolments in Bankruptcy		Abolished 5, 6 Vict. c. 122 and 15, 16 Vict. c. 77	
(59) Office for execution of laws concerning Bankruptcy		Abolished 2, 3 Will. IV. c. 111	
(60) Receiver of the Fines			
Vice-Chancellor's (53 *Geo III. c.* 24) *Officers*—			
	Secretary to the Vice-Chancellor Train-bearer to the Vice-Chancellor Usher to the Vice-Chancellor	Appointed 53 Geo. III. c. 24	3 Secretaries to the Vice-Chancellors 3 Clerks of the Chamber 3 Train-bearers 1 Usher 6 Order-Keepers 2 Caretakers of Court (5 Vict. c. 5)
Lord's Justices Officers—			
	5 Commissioners of Lunatics		2 Secretaries 2 Clerks of the Chamber 2 Train-bearers 2 Order-Keepers 1 Caretaker of Court (14, 15 Vict. c. 83) 2 Masters in Lunacy 12 Clerks 1 Office keeper (5, 6 Vict. c. 84; 8, 9 Vict. c. 100) 3 Visitors of Lunatics 1 Secretary 4 Clerks (16, 17 Vict. c. 70; 25, 26 Vict. c. 86) Surveyor Stockbroker (15, 16 Vict. c. 87 § 21) Official Solicitor to the High Court of Chancery (Appointed 1836) 6 Conveyancing Counsel to the Court of Chancery (15, 16 Vict. c. 80)

XXVII

TRIAL BY BATTLE

This picture is the reproduction of an engraving to be found in Madox's "History of the Exchequer" (i 551). It is taken from an Assize Roll of Henry III 's reign, the date of which is uncertain (Select Pleas of the Crown, S.S. i xxix). It represents a trial by battle in a criminal case, fought between Walter Bloweberme and Hamon le Starre. Walter Bloweberme had appealed Hamon le Starre of robbery. Hamon elected to defend himself by battle. He was defeated and hanged.

Trial by Battle upon issue joined in a writ of right.

When the tenant in writ of right pleads the general issue, viz. that he hath more right to hold than the demandant hath to recover, and offers to prove it by the body of his champion, which tender is accepted by the demandant ; the tenant in the first place must produce his champion, who, by throwing down his glove as a gage or pledge, thus *wages* or stipulates battle with the champion of the demandant, who by taking up the gage or glove, stipulates on his part to accept the challenge. The reason why it is waged by champions, and not by the parties themselves, in civil actions, is because, if any party to the suit dies, the suit must abate and be at an end for the present ; and therefore no judgment could be given for the lands in question, if either of the parties were slain in battle, and also that no parties might claim an exemption from this trial, as was allowed in criminal cases where the battle was waged in person.

A piece of ground is then in due time set out, of sixty feet square, enclosed with lists, and on one side a court erected for the judges of the court of common pleas, who attend there in their scarlet robes ; and also a bar is prepared for the learned serjeants at law. When the court sits, which ought to be by sunrising, proclamation is made for the parties, and their champions, who are introduced by two knights, and are dressed in a suit of armour, with red sandals, bare legged from the knees downwards, bare headed, and with bare arms to the elbows. The weapons allowed them are only batons, or staves, of an ell long, and a four cornered leather target, so that death very seldom ensued in this civil combat. . . . When the champions, thus armed with batons, arrive within the lists or place of combat, the champion of the tenant then takes his adversary by the hand, and makes oath that the tenements in dispute are not the right of the demandant, and the champion of the demandant, then taking the other by the hand, swears in the same manner that they are ; so that each champion is, or ought to be, thoroughly persuaded of the truth of the cause he fights for. Next an oath against sorcery and enchantment is to be taken by both the champions, in this or similar form : "Hear this, ye justices, that I have this day neither eat, drank, nor have upon me, neither bone, stone nor grass ; nor any enchantment, sorcery or witchcraft, whereby the law of God may be abased, or the law of the devil exalted. So help me God and His saints."

The battle is thus begun, and the combatants are bound to fight till the stars appear in the evening, and, if the champion of the tenant can defend himself till the stars appear, the tenant shall prevail in his cause; for it is sufficient for him to maintain his ground, and make it a drawn battle, he being already in possession; but, if the victory declares itself for either party, for him is judgment finally given. This victory may arise from the death of either of the champions, which indeed hath rarely happened, the whole ceremony, to say the truth, bearing a near resemblance to certain rural athletic diversions, which are probably derived from this original. Or victory is obtained if either champion proves *recreant*, that is, yields, and pronounces the horrible word of *craven*, a word of disgrace and obloquy, rather than of any determinate meaning. But a horrible word it is indeed to the vanquished champion, since, as a punishment to him for forfeiting the land of his principal by pronouncing that shameful word, he is condemned, as a recreant, *amittere liberam legem*, that is, to become infamous and not be accounted *liber et legalis homo;* being supposed by the event to be proved forsworn, and therefore never to be put upon a jury, or admitted as a witness in any cause.

BL. COMM. III. 338-341.

Trial by Battle upon an appeal of felony.

The form and manner of waging battle upon appeals are much the same as upon a writ of right, only the oaths of the two combatants are vastly more striking and solemn. The appellee, when appealed of felony, pleads *not guilty*, and throws down his glove, and declares he will defend the same by his body. The appellant takes up the glove, and replies that he is ready to make good the appeal, body for body. And thereupon the appellee, taking the book in his right hand, and in his left the right hand of his antagonist, swears to this effect: "Hear this, O man whom I hold by the hand, who callest thyself John by the name of baptism, that I, who call myself Thomas by the name of baptism, did not feloniously murder thy father, William by name, nor are any way guilty of the said felony. So help me God and the saints, and this I will defend against thee by my body, as this court shall award." To which the appellant replies, holding the Bible and his antagonist's hand in the same manner as the other: "Hear this, O man whom I hold by the hand, who callest thyself Thomas by the name of baptism, that thou art perjured; and therefore perjured, because that thou feloniously did murder my father, William by name. So help me God and the saints; and this I will prove against thee by my body, as this court shall award." The battle is then to be fought with the same weapons, viz. batons, the same solemnity, and the same oath against amulets and sorcery, that are used in the civil combat; and if the appellee be so far vanquished, that he cannot or will not fight any longer, he shall be adjudged to be hanged immediately; and then, as well as if he be killed in battle, providence is deemed to have determined in favour of the truth, and his blood shall be attainted. But if he kills the appellant, or can maintain the fight from sunrising till the stars appear in the evening, he shall be acquitted. So also if the appellant becomes recreant, and pronounces the horrible word of *craven*, he shall loose his *liberam legem*, and become infamous, and the appellee shall recover his damages, and also be forever quit, not only of the appeal, but of all indictments likewise for the same offence.

BL. COMM. IV. 341, 342.

XXVIII

A list of the courts of Request, courts of conscience, and all other local courts in England and Wales having jurisdiction in personal actions, except the superior courts at Westminster and in the Counties Palatine.

PARLT. PAPERS (1840) xli 556-557.

ENGLAND

BEDFORDSHIRE County Court.
  Ampthill Honor Court.
  Bedford Court of Pleas.

BERKSHIRE County Court.
  Abingdon Court of Record.
  Newbury Court of Record.
  Reading Court of Record.
  Wokingham Court of Record.

BUCKINGHAMSHIRE County Court.
  Buckingham Court of Record.

CAMBRIDGESHIRE County Court.
  Cambridge Court of Record.
  Ely Court of Requests.
  Whittlesea and Thorney Court of Requests.
  Wisbeach Court of Requests.

CHESHIRE County Court
  Bucklow Court of Record.
  Macclesfield (Hundred) Court of Record.
  Macclesfield (Manor and Forest) Court of Record.
  Wirrall Hundred Court.
  Chester Portmote and Pentice Courts.
  Congleton Court of Pleas.
  Hyde, etc., Court of Requests.
  Macclesfield Court of Requests.
  Stockport, etc., Court of Requests.

CORNWALL County Court.
  Penryn Forryn Manor Court.
  Penwith Hundred Court.
  Stannaries Court.
  Falmouth Court of Record.
  East Looe Court of Record.
  West Looe Court of Record.
  Saltash Court of Record.

CUMBERLAND County Court.
  Carlisle Court of Record.

DERBYSHIRE County Court.
  High Peak Small Debt Court.
  Castleton Small Debt Court.
  Scarsdale Court of Record.
  Chesterfield Court of Record.
  Derby Court of Record.
  Derby Court of Requests.

DEVONSHIRE County Court.
  Bideford Court of Record.
  Bradninch Court of Record.
  Dartmouth Court of Record.
  Devonport Court of Record.
  Exeter Provost Court.
  Exeter Court of Requests.
  Plymouth Court of Record.
  Plymouth Court of Requests.
  Plymton Earle Court of Record.
  Tiverton Court of Record.

DORSETSHIRE County Court.
  Dorchester Court of Record.
  Lyme Regis Court of Record.
  Wareham Court of Record.
  Weymouth and Malcombe Regis Court of Record.

DURHAM County Court.
  Barnard Castle Manor Court.
  Chester Deanery Manor Court.
  Craike Manor Court.
  Frosterley Manor Court.
  Gateshead Manor Court.
  Gilligate Borough and Manor Court.
  Halmote Courts of the Lord Bishop of Durham.
  Holy Island Manor Court.
  Norham Castle Manor Court.
  Norham Town Manor Court.
  Raby, etc., Manor Court.
  Bishop Auckland Borough Court.
  Durham Manor Court Leet and Court Baron.
  Gateshead Borough Court.
  South Shields Court Baron.
  South Shields Court Leet.
  Whickham Manor Court.
  Darlington Borough Court.
  Stockton Court Leet and Court Baron.
  Sunderland Borough Court.
  Bishop Wearmouth Court of the Manor of the Rectory.
  Houghton Manor Court.
  St. Andrew Houghton Manor Court.

ESSEX County Court.
  Havering - atte - Bower Ancient Court.
  Colchester Hundred Court and Foreign Court.
  Harwich Court of Record.
  Maldon Court of Record.
  Saffron Walden Court of Record.

GLOUCESTERSHIRE County Court.
  Berkeley Hundred Court.
  St. Briavel's Manor Court.
  Grumbald's Ash Hundred Court.
  Henbury Hundred Court.
  Thornbury Hundred Court.
  Gloucester Court of Requests.
  Cirencester Court of Requests.
  Tewkesbury Court of Record.

HAMPSHIRE County Court.
  Knighton or Knight's Court, Isle of Wight.
  Isle of Wight Court of Requests.
  Newport Court of Record.
  Portsmouth Court of Record.
  Romsey Court of Record.
  Southampton Common Court.
  Winchester Court of Record.

HEREFORDSHIRE County Court.
  Hereford Mayor's Court.
  Leominster Court of Record.

HERTFORDSHIRE County Court.
  Hertford Court of Record.
  St. Alban's Court of Requests.
  Watford Court of Requests.

HUNTINGDONSHIRE County Court.
  Huntingstone Hundred Court.
  Ramsey Court of Pleas.
  Godmanchester Court of Pleas.
  Huntingdon Court of Pleas.

KENT County Court.
  Canterbury Court of Pleas.
  Canterbury Court of Requests.
  Deal Court of Requests.
  Dover Court of Requests.
  Dover Court of Record.
  Faversham Court of Portmote.
  Faversham Court of Requests.
  Folkestone Court of Requests.
  Gravesend Court of Record.
  Gravesend Court of Requests.
  Greenwich Court of Requests.
  Hythe Court of Record.
  Ramsgate Court of Requests.
  Rochester Court of Record.

Rochester Court of Requests.
Sandwich Court of Record.
Sandwich Court of Requests.
Sevenoaks Court of Requests.
Tenterden Court of Record.

LANCASHIRE County Court.
  Amounderness Wapentake Court.
  Blackburn Wapentake Court.
  West Derby Wapentake Court.
  Lonsdale Wapentake Court.
  Salford Wapentake Court.
  Ashton-under-Lyne Court of Requests.
  Bury Court of Requests.
  Clitheroe Court of Record.
  Lancaster Court of Record.
  Liverpool Court of Record.
  Liverpool Court of Requests.
  Manchester Court of Requests.
  Oldham Court of Requests.
  Poulton Court of Requests.
  Preston Court of Pleas.
  Rochdale Court of Requests.
  Warrington Court of Requests.
  Wigan Court of Pleas.

LEICESTERSHIRE County Court.
  Leicester Court of Pleas.
  East and West Goscote Court of Pleas.
  Ashby-de-la-Zouche Court of Requests.
  Leicester Court of Record.
  Leicester Court of Requests.
  Hinchley Court of Requests.
  Loughborough Court of Requests

LINCOLNSHIRE County Court.
  Epworth Manor Court.
  Kirton in Lindsey Manor Court.
  Alford Court of Requests.
  Barton upon Humber Court of Requests.
  Boston Court of Pleas.
  Boston Court of Requests.
  Brigg Court of Requests.
  Caistor Court of Requests.
  Grantham Court of Record.
  Great Grimsby Court of Record.
  Great Grimsby Court of Requests.
  Holbeach Court of Requests.
  Horncastle Court of Requests.
  Lincoln Court of Requests.
  Louth Court of Requests.
  Market Rasen Court of Requests.

LINCOLNSHIRE—*Continued*.
Spalding Court of Requests.
Spilsby Court of Requests.
Stamford Court of Record.
Tattershall Court of Requests.
Wragby Court of Requests.

MIDDLESEX County Court, Kingsgate Street.
Sheriff's Court, Red Lion Square.
City of London Court of Requests.
Tower of London Court of Record
Tower Hamlets Court of Requests.
Westminster Palace Court.
Westminster Court of Requests.

MONMOUTHSHIRE County Court.
Monmouth Court of Record.
Newport Court of Record.

NORFOLK County Court.
King's Lynn Court of Conscience.
King's Lynn Guildhall Court.
Norwich Guildhall Court.
Norwich Court of Requests.
Thetford Court of Record.
Yarmouth Court of Record.
Yarmouth Court of Requests.

NORTHAMPTONSHIRE County Court.
Northampton Court of Record.
Peterborough Court of Common Pleas.

NORTHUMBERLAND County Court.
Alnwick Court Baron.
Chatton Court Baron.
Denwick Court Baron.
Longhoughton Court Baron.
Lesbury Court Baron.
Lucker Court Baron.
Thirston Court Baron.
Alnwick Manor and Borough Court
Canongate Court Baron.
Alnmouth Court Baron.
Warkworth Court Baron.
Rothbury Court Baron.
Ridsdale Court Baron.
Prudhoe Court Baron.
Corbridge Court Baron.
Newburn Court Baron.
Bamburgh Borough Court Baron
Bamburgh Castle Court Baron.
Belford Court Baron.
Long Benton, Beliston, and East Coanwood Court Baron.

Bewick Court Baron.
Blenkinsop Court Baron.
Bulbeck Court Baron.
Ford Court Baron.
Etal Court Baron.
Halton Court Baron.
Henshaw Court Baron.
Hexham Court Baron.
Hexham Court of Record.
Melkridge Court Baron.
Morpeth Court Baron.
Ridley and Thorngrafton Court Baron.
Newcastle - on - Tyne Borough County Court.
Newcastle-on-Tyne Court of Conscience.
Newcastle - on - Tyne Burgess Court.
Newcastle-on-Tyne Non-burgess Court.
Tynemouth Court Baron.
Wark Court Baron.
Nether Witton Court Baron.
Wooler, Wark and Stamford Courts Baron.
Tweedmouth and Spittle Court Baron.
Berwick-upon-Tweed Court of Pleas.
Morpeth Court Baron.

NOTTINGHAMSHIRE County Court.
Nottinghamshire Peverel Court.
Newark Court of Record.
Nottingham Court of Record.
East Retford Court of Record.

OXFORDSHIRE County Court.
Banbury Court of Record.
Oxford Court of Record.
Woodstock Court of Record.

RUTLAND County Court.
Oakham and Uppingham Court of Requests.

SHROPSHIRE County Court.
Bradford at Wellington Court of Record.
Bishop's Castle Court of Record.
Bridgnorth Court of Record.
Broseley Court of Requests.
Ludlow Court of Record.
Oswestry Court of Record.
Shrewsbury Court of Record.
Shrewsbury Court of Requests.
Wenlock Court of Record.

SOMERSETSHIRE County Court.
Chew-Magna Hundred Court.
Keynsham Hundred Court.
Portbury Hundred Court.
Taunton-Dean Hundred Court.
Whitstone Hundred Court.
Bath Court of Requests.
Bridgwater Court of Record.
Bristol Court of Conscience.
Bristol Court of Requests.
Bristol Tolzey Court.
Wells Court of Record.

STAFFORDSHIRE County Court.
Offlow Hundred Court at Walsall.
Tutbury Honor Court.
Lichfield Court of Record.
Lichfield Sheriff's Court.
Walsall Court of Record.
Wolverhampton Court of Requests.
Newcastle-under-Lyme.

SUFFOLK County Court.
Aldeburgh Court of Record.
Bury St. Edmunds Court of Record.
Eye Court of Record.
Ipswich Court of Record.
Ipswich Court of Requests.
Oreford Court of Record.
Southwold Court of Record.

SURREY County Court.
Brixton Court of Requests.
Guildford Court of Record.
Kingston-on-Thames Court of Record.
Southwark Court of Requests.

SUSSEX County Court.
Durnford Hundred Court.
Arundel Borough Court.
Chichester Court of Record.
Hastings Court of Record.

WARWICKSHIRE County Court.
Birmingham Court of Requests.
Coventry Court of Record.
Coventry (County of City) County Court.
Stratford-on-Avon Court of Record.
Sutton Coldfield Court of Record.
Warwick Court of Record.

WESTMORLAND County Court.
Kendal Court of Requests.

WILTSHIRE County Court, Northern Division.

WILTSHIRE County Court, Southern Division.
Bradford Court of Requests.
Chippenham, etc., Court of Requests.
Devizes Court of Record.
Marlborough Court of Record.
Melksham Court of Requests.
Salisbury Court of Record.
Trowbridge Court of Requests.
Warminster Court of Requests.
Westbury Court of Requests.

WORCESTERSHIRE County Court.
Droitwich Court of Record.
Evesham Court of Record.
Kidderminster Court of Requests.
Old Swinford Court of Requests.
Worcester Court of Pleas.

YORKSHIRE County Court.
Allertonshire Liberty Court.
Ewcross Wapentake Court.
Keighley Manor Court.
Kimberworth Court Baron.
Knaresborough Borough, Forest, and Liberty Courts.
Langborough Court Baron.
Pickering Manor Court.
Pontefract Honor Court.
Richmond and Richmondshire Baron Court.
Ripon Court Military
Rotherham Court Baron.
Skipton Honor Court.
Staincliffe Wapentake Court.
Wakefield Court Baron.
Whitby Strand Liberty Court.
Barnsley Court of Requests.
Beverley Court of Record.
Beverley Court of Requests.
Doncaster Court of Pleas.
Doncaster Court of Requests.
Ecclesall Court of Requests.
Halifax Court of Requests.
Hedon Court of Record.
Kingston-upon-Hull Court of Record.
Kingston-upon-Hull Court of Requests.
Pontefract Burgess and Foreign Court.
Richmond Court of Record.
Ripon Canon Fee Court.
Rotherham Court of Requests.
Scarborough Court of Record.
Sheffield Court of Requests.
York Court of Record.

WALES

ANGLESEY County Court.

BRECONSHIRE County Court.
  Duke of Beaufort Court Baron.
  Brecon Court of Record.

CARDIGANSHIRE County Court.

CARMARTHENSHIRE County Court.
  Kidwelly Honor or Lordship and
    Liberty Court.
  Perfeth Court Baron.
  Carmarthen Court of Record.
  Kidwelly Hundred and Mayor's
    Court.

CARNARVONSHIRE County Court.

DENBIGHSHIRE County Court.
  Bromfield and Yale Lordship
    Court.
  Chirk Lordship Court.
  Cynlleth-yn-Jail Manor Court.
  Denbigh Court of Pleas.
  Ruthin Lordship Court.

FLINTSHIRE County Court.

GLAMORGANSHIRE County Court.
  Cardiff Court of Record.
  Neath Borough Court.

MERIONETH County Court.

MONTGOMERYSHIRE County Court.
  Arnstley, Isgoed, and Ywchgood
    Court Baron.
  Montgomery Court of Record.
  Welchpool Borough Court.

PEMBROKESHIRE County Court.
  Haverfordwest Monthly and Fif-
    teen Days' Courts.
  Pembroke Borough Court.

RADNORSHIRE County Court.
  Painscastle Court Baron.
  Rhyader Court Baron.
  Knighton Court Baron.
  New Radnor Borough Court.

XXIX

A LIST OF THE OFFICES IN THE GIFT OF THE LORD CHANCELLOR, THE
MASTER OF THE ROLLS, THE CHIEF JUSTICES, AND THE CHIEF BARON
OF THE EXCHEQUER.   PARLT. PAPERS (1825) xix 294.

The Lord High Chancellor of England

Accountant-General.
11 Masters in Chancery.
4 Sub or Deputy Registers.
Clerk of the Reports.
2 Entering Clerks.
24 Cursitors.
Register of Proceedings under Commissions of Bankrupts.
5 Commissioners of Lunatics.
Clerk of the Letters Patent.
Examiner of Letters Patent.
Purse Bearer.
Principal Secretary.
Receiver of Fines in the Cursitors Office.
Secretary of Decrees, Injunctions, and Appeals.
Secretary of Commissions of Peace, and of Commissions of Bankrupts.
Secretary of Commissions of Lunacy.
Secretary of Presentations.
Secretary of Briefs.
Gentleman of the Chamber.
Usher of the Hall.
4 Persons for keeping order in the Court.

The Master of the Rolls

2 Examiners.
6 Clerks.
Keeper of the Records in the Tower.[1]
Keeper of the Records in the Rolls Chapel.
3 Clerks of the Petty Bag.
Usher of the Court.
Preacher at the Rolls Chapel.
Reader at the Rolls Chapel.
Chief Secretary.
Under Secretary.
Secretary of Causes.
Secretary of Decrees and Injunctions.
2 Gentlemen of the Chamber.
Usher of the Hall.
Porter at the Rolls.

The Lord Chief Justice of the Court of King's Bench

The Chief Clerk.
2 Clerks of the Treasury and Custos Brevium.
2 Filazers, Exigenters, and Clerks of the Outlawries for all the Cities and Counties of England, except Essex and Monmouth.
Filazer, Exigenter, and Clerk of the Outlawries for the Counties of Essex and Monmouth.
Clerk of Nisi Prius in Middlesex.
Clerk of the Errors.
Associate and Marshal at the Sittings of Nisi Prius in London and Middlesex.
Clerk at the Sittings of Nisi Prius in London and Middlesex.
Clerk to the Lord Chief Justice.
Crier at the Sittings of Nisi Prius in London and Middlesex.
Trainbearer to the Lord Chief Justice.
Housekeeper at the Treasury Chamber.

Lord Chief Justice of the Court of Common Pleas

First Prothonotary.
Third Prothonotary.
Clerk of the Essoigns.
Clerk of the Warrants, Inrolments and Estreats.
Clerk of the Supersedeas.
Exigenter.
Clerk of Errors in the Exchequer Chamber.
Clerk of the King's Silver.
Filacer for London, Middlesex, Bedford, Berks, Bucks, Oxford, Cornwall, Gloucester, Hereford, and Worcester.
Filacer for Hants, Wilts, Sussex, Surrey and Kent.
Filacer for Norfolk, Stafford, Northampton, Salop, Rutland, Monmouth, Bristol, Dorset, Poole, Somerset, Lancaster, Chester and Durham.
Filacer for Derby, Leicester, Nottingham and Warwick.
Filacer for Essex and Herts.

---

[1] The appointment of this Officer is made with the approbation of His Majesty under his Sign Manual.

Filacer for Cambridge, Huntingdon, Lincoln and City, and Suffolk.
Filacer for Cumberland, Northumberland, Westmorland, Newcastle,
  Devon, Exeter, Kingston-upon-Hull, York and Yorkshire.
Clerk of the Jurata.
The Associate.
The Marshal.
Crier.
2 Clerks to the Chief Justice.
Treasury Keeper.
Clerk of the Treasury.
Clerk of the Errors in Common Pleas.

The Lord Chief Baron of His Majesty's Court of Exchequer

Master and Accountant-General.
Master.
Clerk to the Masters.
Clerk of Reports.
Marshal and Associate.
2 Clerks to the Lord Chief Baron.
Examiner.

XXX

EXTRACTS FROM THE REPORT OF THE COMMISSIONERS UPON SALEABLE OFFICES IN THE COURTS OF LAW

PARLT. PAPERS (1810) IX 128-131.

The King's Bench.

In the Court of King's Bench the following persons hold Offices or Appointments which are saleable, and the right of nomination to such Offices or Appointments is as follows, viz. :—

	Appointed by
The Chief Clerk	
The Clerk of the Treasury and Custos Brevium	} The Lord Chief Justice.
The Filacer Exigenter and Clerk of the Outlawries	
The Clerk of the Rules on the Plea side	
The Clerk of the Papers on the same side	
The Clerk of the Declarations	
The Clerk of the Common Bails Estreats and Posteas	} The Chief Clerk.
The Clerk of the Dockets	
The Clerks of the Inner and Outer Treasury	
The Clerks of Nisi Prius	} The Custos Brevium
The Bagbearer on the Plea side	

The net annual receipts of the several Officers above mentioned, upon an average of three years ending at the period when the accounts were last made up respectively were as follows : subject to the deduction of the Property Tax, and to the allowances made to the several Deputies by whom the Duties of some of the Offices were discharged, viz. :—

Offices Executed by Deputy

The Chief Clerk . . .	£6,280 18 6	Paid the Deputy £200 0 0
The Custos Brevium . . .	2,019 7 4	The Deputies are paid by fees assigned to them.
The Filacer Exigenter and Clerk of the Outlawries . . }	5,104 16 9	Paid Deputies 567 5 0
The Clerk of the Declarations .	194 0 0	Paid Deputy 120 0 0
The Clerk of the Common Bails, Estreats and Posteas . }	229 3 10	„ „ 100 0 0
The Clerk of the Dockets .	851 1 6	„ „ 290 7 2
The Clerk of Nisi Prius for the Western and Oxford Circuits }	343 11 4	„ „ 79 0 10
	£15,022 19 3	£1356 13 0

Offices Executed in Person

	£15,022 19 3
The Clerk of the Rules on the Pleas side	3,383 11 7
The Clerk of the Papers on the Pleas side . . .	1,580 0 11
The Clerk of the Inner Treasury	325 15 5
The Clerk of the Outer Treasury	158 19 6
The Clerk of Nisi Prius for London and other Cities .	689 1 1
The Clerk of Nisi Prius for Northern and Norfolk Circuits	517 10 8
The Clerk of Nisi Prius for Home and Midland Circuits .	200 12 8
The Bag bearer	85 10 0
	£21,964 1 1

The Common Pleas.

The following Persons hold Offices or Appointments which have been considered as saleable, and the right of nomination to such Offices or Appointments is as follows :—

Appointed by

The first and third Prothonotaries
The Clerk of the King's Silver
The Clerk of the Jurata
The Clerk of the Essoigns
The Clerk of the Warrants, Inrolments and Estreats } The Lord Chief Justice.
The Exigenter
The Clerk of the Supersedeas
The Filacers
The Clerk of the Errors in the Exchequer Chamber

The second Prothonotary
The Clerk of the Juries } The Lord Chief Justice on the nomination of the Custos Brevium.

The three Secondaries   The respective Prothonotaries.

The net annual receipts of the several Officers of the Court of Common Pleas above mentioned, upon an average of three years ending at the periods when the accounts were last made up respectively were as follow : subject to the deduction of the Property Tax, and to the allowances made to the several Deputies by whom the duties of some of the Offices were discharged, viz. :—

Offices Executed by Deputy

	£	s.	d.			£	s.	d.
The Clerk of the King's Silver .	538	9	4	Paid Deputy		216	12	10
The Clerk of the Jurata, on an aver-age of two years . .	206	10	7	„	„	12	12	0
The Clerk of the Essoigns . .	140	0	0	„	„	70	0	0
The Clerk of the Warrants, Inrol-ments, and Estreats . .	683	16	0	„	„	221	19	3
The Clerk of the Juries . .	72	13	11	„	„	12	12	0
The Clerk of the Errors in the Ex-chequer Chamber . .	2,333	16	7	„	„	125	0	0
The Filacer for Surrey, Sussex and Kent, Hants and Wilts .	271	4	0	„	„	45	4	0
The Filacer for Norfolk and Norwich, Stafford, Northampton, Salop, Rutland and Monmouth, Lan-caster, Chester and Durham .	56	5	0	„	„	11	5	0
The Filacer for Derby, Leicester, Notts. and Warwick . .	30	0	0	„	„	6	0	0
The Filacer for Cambridge and Huntingdon, Suffolk and Lincoln	31	5	0	„	„	6	5	0
The Filacer for Essex and Herts	42	10	0	„	„	11	10	0
	£4,406	10	5			£739	0	1

Offices Executed in Person

	£	s.	d.
	4,406	10	5
Three Prothonotaries each £1,627 13s. 4d. including £225 each deducted in their Return for Premiums on Life Insurance	4,883	0	0
The Register and Clerk of the Supersedeas . . .	7	3	4
The Filacer for London and Middlesex, Bedford, Berks, Bucks, Oxford, Cornwall, Gloucester, Hereford, and Worcester including £429 5s. deducted in his Return for Premium on Insurance and Interest of Purchase Money	1,299	5	0
The Filacer for Somersetshire, Bristol, Dorset, and Poole	31	14	11
The Filacer for Devon and Exeter, Cumberland, Westmorland, Northumberland, and Newcastle-upon-Tyne, Yorkshire, City of York, and Kingston-upon-Hull . . .	64	10	6
Three Secondaries, including £120 each deducted in their Return for Interest of Purchase Money and Premiums of Insurance	1,410	0	0
	£12,102	4	2

XXXI

WRIT DE CORONATORE ELIGENDO

Rex etc. Vicecomiti W. Salutem. Quia J. D. unus Coronatorum nostrorum in comitatu tuo minus sufficiens vel idoneus est ad ea quæ ad officium Coronatoris in eodem Comitatu pertinent excipienda ut ex testimonio fide

digno accepimus. Tibi præcipimus quod in pleno Comitatu tuo ex assensu
ejusdem Comitatus loco ipsius J. eligi facias unum alium Coronatorem qui
præstito sacramento prout moris est extunc ea faciet et conservet quæ ad
officium Coronatoris pertinent in Comitatu prædicto et talem eum eligi facias
qui melius sciat et possit officio illi intendere. Et nomen ejus sciri facias.
Teste etc.

REGISTRUM BREVIUM, Appendix 19-20.

INDEX

A

B